Twentieth-Century Literary Criticism

Guide to Gale Literary Criticism Series

When you need to review criticism of literary works, these are the Gale series to use:

If the author's death date is:	You should turn to:
After Dec. 31, 1959 (or author is still living)	***CONTEMPORARY LITERARY CRITICISM*** for example: Jorge Luis Borges, William Faulkner, Ernest Hemingway, Iris Murdoch
1900 through 1959	***TWENTIETH-CENTURY LITERARY CRITICISM*** for example: Willa Cather, F. Scott Fitzgerald, Henry James, Mark Twain, Virginia Woolf
1800 through 1899	***NINETEENTH-CENTURY LITERATURE CRITICISM*** for example: Fyodor Dostoevsky, Nathaniel Hawthorne, George Sand, William Wordsworth
1400 through 1799	***LITERATURE CRITICISM FROM 1400 TO 1800*** (excluding Shakespeare) for example: Anne Bradstreet, Daniel Defoe, Alexander Pope, François Rabelais, Jonathan Swift, Phillis Wheatley ***SHAKESPEAREAN CRITICISM*** Shakespeare's plays and poetry
Antiquity through 1399	***CLASSICAL AND MEDIEVAL LITERATURE CRITICISM*** for example: Dante, Homer, Plato, Sophocles, Vergil

Gale also publishes related criticism series:

BLACK LITERATURE CRITICISM
Covers the most significant black authors of the past 200 years

CHILDREN'S LITERATURE REVIEW
Covers authors of all eras who have written for the preschool through high school audience

DRAMA CRITICISM
Covers dramatists of all nationalities and periods of literary history

POETRY CRITICISM
Covers poets of all nationalities and periods of literary history

SHORT STORY CRITICISM
Covers the major short fiction writers of all nationalities and periods of literary history

WORLD LITERATURE CRITICISM, 1500 TO THE PRESENT
Covers 225 authors of all nationalities from the Renaissance to the present

ISSN 0276-8178

Volume 48

Twentieth-Century Literary Criticism

Excerpts from Criticism of the
Works of Novelists, Poets, Playwrights,
Short Story Writers, and Other Creative Writers
Who Lived between 1900 and 1960,
from the First Published Critical
Appraisals to Current Evaluations

Laurie DiMauro
Editor

Drew Kalasky
Marie Lazzari
Thomas Ligotti
Sean René Pollock
David Segal
Janet M. Witalec
Associate Editors

LIBRARY
FORSYTH TECHNICAL COMMUNITY COLLEGE
2100 SILAS CREEK PARKWAY
WINSTON-SALEM, NC 27103-5197

STAFF

Laurie DiMauro, *Editor*

Marie Lazzari, Thomas Ligotti, Sean René Pollock, David Segal, Janet M. Witalec, *Associate Editors*

Jeffery Chapman, Jennifer Gariepy, Ian A. Goodhall, Michael Magoulias, Dale Miller, Brigham Narins, Lynn M. Zott, *Assistant Editors*

Jeanne A. Gough, *Permissions & Production Manager*

Linda M. Pugliese, *Production Supervisor*

Paul Lewon, Maureen Puhl, Camille Robinson, Jennifer VanSickle, *Editorial Associates*

Donna Craft, Rosita D'Souza, Sheila Walencewicz, *Editorial Assistants*

Sandra C. Davis, *Permissions Supervisor (Text)*

Maria L. Franklin, Josephine M. Keene, Michele Lonoconus, Denise M. Singleton, Kimberly F. Smilay, *Permissions Associates*

Jennifer A. Arnold, Brandy C. Merritt, Shalice Shah, *Permissions Assistants*

Margaret A. Chamberlain, *Permissions Supervisor (Pictures)*

Pamela A. Hayes, Keith Reed, *Permissions Associate*

Arlene Johnson, *Permissions Assistant*

Victoria B. Cariappa, *Research Manager*

Maureen Richards, *Research Supervisor*

Robert S. Lazich, Mary Beth McElmeel, Tamara C. Nott, *Editorial Associates*

Kelly Hill, Daniel J. Jankowski, Donna Melnychenko, *Editorial Assistants*

Mary Beth Trimper, *Production Director*

Catherine Kemp, *Production Assistant*

Cynthia Baldwin, *Art Director*

Nicholas Jakubiak, C. J. Jonik, *Keyliners*

Since this page cannot legibly accommodate all copyright notices, the acknowledgments constitute an extension of the copyright notice.

While every effort has been made to ensure the reliability of the information presented in this publication, Gale Research Inc. neither guarantees the accuracy of the data contained herein nor assumes any responsibility for errors, omissions, or discrepancies. Gale accepts no payment for listing; and inclusion in the publication of any organization, agency, institution, publication, service, or individual does not imply endorsement of the editors or publisher. Errors brought to the attention of the publisher and verified to the satisfaction of the publisher will be corrected in future editions.

The paper used in this publication meets the minimum requirements of American National Standard for Information Sciences—Permanence Paper for Printed Library Materials, ANSI Z39.48-1984. ∞™

This publication is a creative work fully protected by all applicable copyright laws, as well as by misappropriation, trade secret, unfair competition, and other applicable laws. The authors and editors of this work have added value to the underlying factual material herein through one or more of the following: unique and original selection, coordination, expression, arrangement, and classification of the information.

All rights to this publication will be vigorously defended.

Copyright © 1993
Gale Research Inc.
835 Penobscot Building
Detroit, MI 48226-4094

All rights reserved including the right of reproduction in whole or in part in any form.

Library of Congress Catalog Card Number 76-46132
ISSN 0276-8178
ISBN 0-8103-7973-2

Printed in the United States of America

Published simultaneously in the United Kingdom
by Gale Research International Limited
(An affiliated company of Gale Research Inc.)
10 9 8 7 6 5 4 3 2 1

The trademark **ITP** is used under license.

Contents

Preface vii

Acknowledgments xi

Frans Bengtsson (1894-1954) 1
  Swedish biographer

Hans Carossa (1878-1956) 14
  German autobiographer

Thomas Hardy (1840-1928) 36
  English novelist; entry devoted to The Return of the Native

D. H. Lawrence (1885-1930) 90
  English novelist; entry devoted to Lady Chatterley's Lover

Bolesław Prus (1845-1912) 154
  Polish novelist

William Thomas Stead (1849-1912) 185
  English journalist

Gertrude Stein (1874-1946) 206
  American novelist

Preston Sturges (1898-1959) 266
  American film director

Mark Twain (1835-1910) 326
  American novelist; entry devoted to The Prince and the Pauper

Charlotte Yonge (1823-1901) 363
  English novelist

Literary Criticism Series Cumulative Author Index   393

Literary Criticism Series Cumulative Topic Index   461

TCLC Cumulative Nationality Index   467

Title Index to *TCLC*, Vol. 48   471

Preface

Since its inception more than ten years ago, *Twentieth-Century Literary Criticism* has been purchased and used by nearly 10,000 school, public, and college or university libraries. *TCLC* has covered more than 500 authors, representing 58 nationalities, and over 25,000 titles. No other reference source has surveyed the critical response to twentieth-century authors and literature as thoroughly as *TCLC*. In the words of one reviewer, "there is nothing comparable available." *TCLC* "is a gold mine of information—dates, pseudonyms, biographical information, and criticism from books and periodicals—which many libraries would have difficulty assembling on their own."

Scope of the Series

TCLC is designed to serve as an introduction to authors who died between 1900 and 1960 and to the most significant interpretations of these authors' works. The great poets, novelists, short story writers, playwrights, and philosophers of this period are frequently studied in high school and college literature courses. In organizing and excerpting the vast amount of critical material written on these authors, *TCLC* helps students develop valuable insight into literary history, promotes a better understanding of the texts, and sparks ideas for papers and assignments. Each entry in *TCLC* presents a comprehensive survey of an author's career or an individual work of literature and provides the user with a multiplicity of interpretations and assessments. Such variety allows students to pursue their own interests; furthermore, it fosters an awareness that literature is dynamic and responsive to many different opinions.

Every fourth volume of *TCLC* is devoted to literary topics that cannot be covered under the author approach used in the rest of the series. Such topics include literary movements, prominent themes in twentieth-century literature, literary reaction to political and historical events, significant eras in literary history, prominent literary anniversaries, and the literatures of cultures that are often overlooked by English-speaking readers.

TCLC is designed as a companion series to Gale's *Contemporary Literary Criticism,* which reprints commentary on authors now living or who have died since 1960. Because of the different periods under consideration, there is no duplication of material between *CLC* and *TCLC*. For additional information about *CLC* and Gale's other criticism titles, users should consult the Guide to Gale Literary Criticism Series preceding the title page in this volume.

Coverage

Each volume of *TCLC* is carefully compiled to present:

- criticism of authors, or literary topics, representing a variety of genres and nationalities
- both major and lesser-known writers and literary works of the period
- 10-15 authors or 4-6 topics per volume
- individual entries that survey critical response to each author's work or each topic in literary history, including early criticism to reflect initial reactions; later criticism to represent any rise or decline in reputation; and current retrospective analyses.

Organization of This Book

An author entry consists of the following elements: author heading, biographical and critical introduction, list of principal works, excerpts of criticism (each preceded by an annotation and followed by a bibliographic citation), and a bibliography of further reading.

- The **author heading** consists of the name under which the author most commonly wrote, followed by birth and death dates. If an author wrote consistently under a pseudonym, the pseudonym will be listed in the author heading and the real name given in parentheses on the first line of the biographical and critical introduction. Also located at the beginning of the introduction to the author entry are any name variations under which an author wrote, including transliterated forms for authors whose languages use nonroman alphabets.

- The **biographical and critical introduction** outlines the author's life and career, as well as the critical issues surrounding his or her work. References to past volumes of *TCLC* are provided at the beginning of the introduction. Additional sources of information in other biographical and critical reference series published by Gale, including *Children's Literature Review, Contemporary Authors, Dictionary of Literary Biography, Short Story Criticism,* and *Something about the Author,* are listed in a box at the end of the entry.

- Most *TCLC* entries include **portraits** of the author. Many entries also contain reproductions of materials pertinent to an author's career, including manuscript pages, title pages, dust jackets, letters, and drawings, as well as photographs of important people, places, and events in an author's life.

- The **list of principal works** is chronological by date of first book publication and identifies the genre of each work. In the case of foreign authors with both foreign-language publications and English translations, the title and date of the first English-language edition are given in brackets. Unless otherwise indicated, dramas are dated by first performance, not first publication.

- **Criticism** is arranged chronologically in each author entry to provide a perspective on changes in critical evaluation over the years. All titles of works by the author featured in the entry are printed in boldface type to enable the user to easily locate discussion of particular works. Also for purposes of easier identification, the critic's name and the publication date of the essay are given at the beginning of each piece of criticism. Unsigned criticism is preceded by the title of the journal in which it appeared. Publication information (such as publisher names and book prices) and parenthetical numerical references (such as footnotes or page and line references to specific editions of works) have been deleted at the editors' discretion to provide smoother reading of the text.

- Critical excerpts are prefaced by **annotations** providing the reader with information about both the critic and the criticism that follows. Included are the critic's reputation, individual approach to literary criticism, and particular expertise in an author's works. Also noted are the relative importance of a work of criticism, the scope of the excerpt, and the growth of critical controversy or changes in critical trends regarding an author. In some cases, these annotations cross-reference excerpts by critics who discuss each other's commentary.

- A complete **bibliographic citation** designed to facilitate location of the original essay or book follows each piece of criticism.

- An annotated list of **further reading** appearing at the end of each author entry suggests secondary sources on the author. In some cases it includes essays for which the editors could not obtain reprint rights.

Cumulative Indexes

- Each volume of *TCLC* contains a cumulative **author index** listing all authors who have appeared in Gale's Literary Criticism Series, along with cross-references to such biographical series as *Contemporary Authors* and *Dictionary of Literary Biography.* For readers' convenience, a complete list of Gale titles included appears on the first page of the author index. Useful for locating authors within the various series, this index is particularly valuable for those authors who are identified by a certain period but who, because of their death dates, are placed in another, or for those authors whose careers span two periods. For example, F. Scott Fitzgerald is found in *TCLC,* yet a writer often associated with him, Ernest Hemingway, is found in *CLC.*

- Each *TCLC* volume includes a cumulative **nationality index** which lists all authors who have appeared in *TCLC,* arranged alphabetically under their respective nationalities, as well as Topics volume entries devoted to particular national literatures.

- Each new volume in Gale's Literary Criticism Series includes a cumulative **topic index,** which lists all literary topics treated in *Nineteenth-Century Literature Criticism, TCLC, Literature Criticism from 1400-1800,* and the *CLC* Yearbook.

- Each new volume of *TCLC,* with the exception of the Topics volumes, contains a **title index** listing the titles of all literary works discussed in the volume. In response to numerous suggestions from librarians, Gale has also produced a **special paperbound edition** of the *TCLC* title index. This annual cumulation lists all titles discussed in the series since its inception and is issued with the first volume of *TCLC* published each year. Additional copies of the index are available on request. Librarians and patrons have welcomed this separate index: it saves shelf space, is easy to use, and is recyclable upon receipt of the following year's cumulation. Titles discussed in the Topics volume entries are not included in the *TCLC* cumulative index.

A Note to the Reader

When writing papers, students who quote directly from any volume in Gale's Literary Criticism Series may use the following general forms to footnote reprinted criticism. The first example pertains to material drawn from periodicals, the second to material reprinted from books.

[1] T. S. Eliot, "John Donne," *The Nation and the Athenaeum,* 33 (9 June 1923), 321-32; excerpted and reprinted in *Literature Criticism from 1400 to 1800,* Vol. 10, ed. James E. Person, Jr. (Detroit: Gale Research, 1989), pp. 28-9.

[2] Clara G. Stillman, *Samuel Butler: A Mid-Victorian Modern* (Viking Press, 1932); excerpted and reprinted in *Twentieth-Century Literary Criticism,* Vol. 33, ed. Paula Kepos (Detroit: Gale Research, 1989), pp. 43-5.

Suggestions Are Welcome

In response to suggestions, several features have been added to *TCLC* since the series began, including annotations to excerpted criticism, a cumulative index to authors in all Gale literary criticism series, entries devoted to criticism on a single work by a major author, more extensive illustrations, and a title index listing all literary works discussed in the series since its inception.

Readers who wish to suggest authors or topics to appear in future volumes, or who have other suggestions, are cordially invited to write the editors.

ACKNOWLEDGMENTS

The editors wish to thank the copyright holders of the excerpted criticism included in this volume, the permissions managers of many book and magazine publishing companies for assisting us in securing reprint rights, and Anthony Bogucki for assistance with copyright research. We are also grateful to the staffs of the Detroit Public Library, Wayne State University Purdy/Kresge Library Complex, and the University of Michigan Libraries for making their resources available to us. Following is a list of the copyright holders who have granted us permission to reprint material in the volume of *TCLC*. Every effort has been made to trace copyright, but if omissions have been made, please let us know.

COPYRIGHTED EXCERPTS IN *TCLC*, VOLUME 48, WERE REPRINTED FROM THE FOLLOWING PERIODICALS:

American Literature, v. XXVIII, January, 1957. Copyright © 1957, renewed 1985 Duke University Press, Durham, NC. Reprinted with permission of the publisher.—*Ariel: A Review of International English Literature,* v. 8, April, 1977. Copyright © 1977 The Board of Governors, The University of Calgary. Reprinted by permission of the publisher.—*Ball State University Forum,* Spring, 1984. © 1984 Ball State University. Reprinted by permission of the publisher.—*The Centennial Review,* v. XXIX, Fall, 1985 for "Gertrude Stein: American Librettist" by Paul Cohen. © 1985 by *The Centennial Review*. Reprinted by permission of the publisher and the author.—*The Durham University Journal,* v. LXV, March, 1973. Reprinted by permission of the publisher.—*English Studies,* Netherlands, v. 53, February, 1972. © 1972 by Swets & Zeitlinger B.V. Reprinted by permission of the publisher.—*English Studies in Canada,* v. XIII, December, 1987 for "Explaining Composition: Gertrude Stein and the Problem of Representation," by Alan R. Knight. © Association of Canadian University Teachers of English 1987. Reprinted by permission of the publisher and the author.—*Film Comment,* v. 6, Winter, 1970-71. Copyright © 1970 by Film Comment Publishing Corporation. All rights reserved. Reprinted by permission of the Film Society of Lincoln Center.—*Films in Review,* v. I, February, 1950. Copyright 1950, renewed 1977 by the National Board of Review of Motion Pictures, Inc. Reprinted by permission of the publisher.—*The Georgia Review,* v. XXXIII, Winter, 1979. Copyright, 1979, by the University of Georgia. Reprinted by permission of the publisher.—*New German Studies,* v. VII, Summer, 1979; v. VII, Autumn, 1979. Copyright © 1979 by The Editors, *New German Studies*. Both reprinted by permission of the publisher.—*New York Herald Tribune Books,* January 31, 1926; April 10, 1932. Copyright 1926, renewed 1954; copyright 1932, renewed 1960, New York Herald Tribune Inc. All rights reserved. Both reprinted by permission.—*The New York Times Book Review,* June 4, 1933; April 25, 1943. Copyright 1933, renewed 1961; copyright 1943, renewed 1971 by The New York Times Company. Both reprinted by permission of the publisher.—*Nineteenth-Century Fiction,* v. 26, June, 1971 for " 'The Return of the Native' as a Tragedy in Six Books" by Richard Benvenuto. © 1971 by The Regents of the University of California. Reprinted by permission of The Regents and the Literary Estate of Richard Benvenuto.—*The Paris Review,* v. 32, Fall, 1990, © 1990 The Paris Review, Inc. Reprinted by permission of the publisher—*PMLA,* v. 98, January, 1983. Copyright © 1983 by the Modern Language Association of America. Reprinted by permission of the Modern Language Association of America.—*The Polish Review,* v. XXVIII, 1983. © copyright 1983 by the Polish Institute of Arts and Sciences in America, Inc. Reprinted by permission of the publisher.—*Quarterly Review of Film Studies,* v. 7, Spring, 1982. Copyright © 1982 by Harwood Academic Publishers GmbH for Redgrave Publishing. Reprinted by permission of the publisher.—*Sight and Sound,* v. 47, Winter, 1977-78. Copyright © 1978 by The British Film Institute. Reprinted by permission of the publisher.

COPYRIGHTED EXCERPTS IN *TCLC*, VOLUME 48, WERE REPRINTED FROM THE FOLLOWING BOOKS:

Baetzhold, Howard G. From *Mark Twain and John Bull: The British Connection.* Indiana University Press, 1970. Copyright © 1970 by Indiana University Press. All rights reserved. Reprinted by permission of the publisher.—Baylen, Joseph O. From *The Tsar's "Lecturer-General": W. T. Stead and the Russian Revolution of 1905.* Georgia State University College of Arts and Sciences, 1969, Reprinted by permission of the publisher.—Bazin, André. From *The Cinema of Cruelty: From Bunuel to Hitchcock.* Edited by François Truffaut, translated by Sabine d'Estrée with Tiffany Fliss. Seaver Books, 1982. Copyright © 1975 by Editions Flammarion, Paris, France. English language translation copyright © 1982 by Seaver Books. All rights reserved. Reprinted by permission of the publisher.—Bengtsson, Frans G. From *The Long Ships: A Saga of the Viking Age.* Translated by Michael Meyer. Copyright

1954 by Frans G. Bengtsson. All rights reserved.—Carossa, Hans. From "The Practice of Medicine," in **400 Years of a Doctor's Life.** Edited by George Rosen and Beate Caspari-Rosen. Henry Schuman, 1947. Copyright 1947 by Henry Schuman, Inc.—Chessman, Harriet Scott. From **The Public Is Invited to Dance: Representation, the Body, and Dialogue in Gertrude Stein.** Stanford University Press, 1989. Copyright © 1989 by the Board of Trustees of Leland Stanford Junior University. Reprinted with the permission of the publishers, Stanford University Press.— Colby, Vineta. From **Yesterday's Woman: Domestic Realism in the English Novel.** Princeton University Press, 1974. Copyright © 1974 by Princeton University Press. All rights reserved. Reprinted by permission of the publisher.— Corliss, Richard. From **Talking Pictures: Screenwriters in the American Cinema.** The Overlook Press, Inc., 1974. Copyright © Richard Corliss, 1974. Reprinted by permission of the publisher.—Cowan, James C. From "Lawrence, Joyce, and the Epiphanies of 'Lady Chatterley's Lover'," in **D. H. Lawrence's "Lady:" A New Look at Lady Chatterley's Lover.** Edited by Michael Squires and Dennis Jackson. University of Georgia Press, 1985. © 1985 by the University of Georgia Press. All rights reserved. Reprinted by permission of the publisher.—Daleski, H. M. From **The Forked Flame: A Study of D. H. Lawrence.** The University of Wisconsin Press, 1987. © H. M. Daleski 1965. All rights reserved. Reprinted by permission of the publisher.—DeKoven, Marianne. From "Gertrude Stein and the Modernist Canon," in **Gertrude Stein and the Making of Literature.** Edited by Shirley Neuman and Ira B. Nadel. Northeastern University Press, 1988. © Marianne DeKoven 1988. All rights reserved. Reprinted by permission of the publisher.—Emerson, Everett. From **The Authentic Mark Twain: A Literary Biography of Samuel L. Clemens.** University of Pennsylvania Press, 1984. Copyright © 1984 by the University of Pennsylvania Press. All rights reserved. Reprinted by permission of the publisher.—Fleishman, Avrom. From **Fiction and the Ways of Knowing: Essays on British Novels.** University of Texas Press, 1978. Copyright © 1978 by the University of Texas Press. All rights reserved. Reprinted by permission of the publisher and the author.—Gerber, John C. From **Mark Twain.** Twayne, 1988. Copyright © 1988 by G. K. Hall & Co. All rights reserved. Reprinted with the permission of Twayne Publishers, an imprint of Macmillan Publishing Company.—Guerard, Albert J. From an introduction to **The Return of the Native.** By Thomas Hardy. Holt, 1950. Introduction copyright, 1950, renewed 1978 by Albert J. Guerard. Reprinted by permission of the author.—Gustafson, Alrik. From **A History of Swedish Literature.** University of Minnesota Press, 1961. © copyright 1961 by the American-Scandinavian Foundation. Renewed 1989 by Cleyonne Gustafson. All rights reserved. Reprinted by permission of the American Scandinavian Foundation.— Heilman, Robert B. From "'The Return': Centennial Observations," in **The Novels of Thomas Hardy.** Edited by Anne Smith. London: Vision Press, 1979. © 1979 Vision Press. All rights reserved. Reprinted by permission of the publisher.—Henderson, Brian. From an introduction to **Five Screenplays.** By Preston Sturges, edited by Brian Henderson. University of California Press, 1985. Copyright © by University City Studios, Inc. All rights reserved. Courtesy of MCA Publishing Rights, a Division of MCA Inc.—Hofrichter, Ruth J. From **Three Poets and Reality: Study of a German, an Austrian, and a Swiss Contemporary Lyricist.** Yale University Press, 1942. Copyright, 1942, by Yale University Press. Renewed 1970 by Ruth J. Hofrichter. All rights reserved. Reprinted by permission of the publisher.—Horsman, Alan. From **The Victorian Novel.** Oxford at the Clarendon Press, 1990. © Oxford University Press, 1990. All rights reserved. Reprinted by permission of the publisher.—Howells, William D. From a letter in **Mark Twain—Howells Letters: The Correspondence of Samuel L. Clemens and William D. Howells, 1872-1910.** Edited by Henry Nash Smith and William M. Gibson with Frederick Anderson. Cambridge, Mass.: The Belknap Press of Harvard University Press, 1960. Copyright © 1960 by the Mark Twain Company. Copyright © 1960 by Mildred Howells and John Mead Howells. Copyright © 1960 by the President and Fellows of Harvard College. Renewed 1988 by Mark Twain Foundation, William W. Howells and Elinor Lucas Smith. Excerpted by permission of the publishers and the Literary Estate of William D. Howells.—Jackson, Dennis. From "Literary Allusions in 'Lady Chatterley's Lover'," in **D. H. Lawrence's "Lady:" A New Look at "Lady Chatterley's Lover."** Edited by Michael Squires and Dennis Jackson. University of Georgia Press, 1985. © 1985 by the University of Georgia Press. All rights reserved. Reprinted by permission of the publisher.—Knapp, Bettina L. From **Gertrude Stein.** Continuum, 1990. Copyright © 1990 by Bettina L. Knapp. All rights reserved. Reprinted by permission of the publisher.—Krzyzanowski, Jerzy R. From "B. Prus' 'The Doll': An Ironic Novel," in **Russian and Slavic Literature.** Edited by Charles A. Ward. Slavica, 1976. Copyright © 1976 by Slavica Publishers, Inc. All rights reserved. Reprinted by permission of the author.—Lawrence. D. H. From **Lady Chatterley's Lover.** N.p., 1928.— Mast, Gerald. From **The Comic Mind: Comedy and the Movies.** Bobbs-Merrill, 1973. © 1973, 1979 by Gerald Mast. All rights reserved. Reprinted by permission of the author.—Meyers, Jeffrey. From **D. H. Lawrence and the Experience of Italy.** University of Pennsylvania Press, 1982. Copyright © 1982 by the University of Pennsylvania Press. All rights reserved. Reprinted by permission of the publisher.—Miłosz, Czesław. From **The History of Polish Literature.** Second edition. University of California Press, 1983. Copyright © 1969, 1983 by Czesław Mołosz. Reprinted by permission of the publisher.—Morgan, Rosemarie. From **Women and Sexuality in the Novels of Thomas Hardy.** Routledge, 1988. © Rosemarie Morgan 1988. Reprinted by permission of the publisher and the author.—Moynahan, Julian. From **The Deed of Life: The Novels and Tales of D. H. Lawrence.** Princeton University Press, 1963. Copyright © 1963 by Princeton University Press. Renewed 1991 by Julian Moynahan. All rights reserved. Reprinted by permission of the author.—Perloff, Marjorie. From "Six Stein Styles in Search of Reader," in **A Gertrude Stein Companion: Content with the Example.** Edited by Bruce Kellner. Greenwood Press, 1988. Copyright © 1988 by Bruce Kellner. All rights reserved. Reprinted by permission of Greenwood Publishing Group, Inc. Westport, CT.—Regan, Robert. From **Unpromising Heroes: Mark Twain and His Characters.** University of California Press, 1966. © 1966 by The Regents of the University of California. Reprinted by permission of the publisher.—Sanders, Scott R. From "Lady Chatterley's Loving and the Annihilation Impulse," in *D. H. Lawrence's "Lady:" A New Look at Lady Chatterley's Lover.* Edited by Michael Squires and Dennis Jackson. University of Georgia Press, 1985. © 1985 by the University of Georgia Press. All rights reserved. Reprinted by permission of the publisher.—Schatz, Thomas. From *Hollywood Genres: Formulas, Filmmaking, and the Studio System.* Random House, 1981. Copyright © 1981 by Random House, Inc. All rights reserved. Reproduced with permission of McGraw-Hill, Inc.—Schickel, Richard. From *Schickel on Film: Encounters—Critical and Personal—with Movie Immortals.* Morrow, 1989. Copyright © 1989 by Lorac Productions, Inc. All rights reserved. Reprinted by permission of William Morrow and Company, Inc.—Smith, Warren Sylvester. From *The London Heretics, 1870-1914.* Dodd, Mead & Company, 1968. Reprinted by permission of the Literary Estate of Warren Sylvester Smith.—Squires, Michael. From *The Creation of Lady Chatterley's Lover.* Johns Hopkins University Press, 1983. Copyright © 1983 by The Johns Hopkins University Press. All rights reserved. Reprinted by permission of the publisher.—Stimpson, Catharine R. From "Gertrude Stein and the Transposition of Gender," in *The Poetics of Gender.* Edited by Nancy K. Miller. Columbia University Press, 1986. Copyright © 1986 Columbia University Press. All rights reserved. Used by permission of the publisher.—Sturges, Preston. From *Five Screenplays.* Edited by Brian Henderson. University of California Press, 1985. Scripts copyright 1941 by Universal Pictures, a Division of Universal City Studios, Inc. All rights reserved.—Sturges, Preston. From *Preston Sturges.* Edited by Sandy Sturges. Simon and Schuster, 1990. Copyright © 1990 by Anne Sturges. All rights reserved.—Sumner, Rosemary. From *Thomas Hardy: Psychological Novelist.* St. Martin's Press, 1981, Macmillan, London, 1981. © Rosemary Sumner 1981. All rights reserved. Used with permission of St. Martin's Press, Inc. In Canada by Macmillan, London and Basingstoke—Twain, Mark. From a letter in *Mark Twain—Howells Letters: The Correspondence of Samuel L. Clemens and William D. Howells, 1872-1910.* Edited by Henry Nash Smith and William M. Gibson with Frederick Anderson. Cambridge, Mass.: The Belknap Press of Harvard University Press, 1960. Copyright © 1960 by the Mark Twain Company. Copyright © 1960 by Mildred Howells and John Mead Howells. Copyright © 1960 by the President and Fellows of Harvard College. Renewed 1988 by Mark Twain Foundation, William W. Howells and Elinor Lucas Smith. Excerpted by permission of the publishers and the Literary Estate of Mark Twain.—Wagenknecht, Edward. From an introduction to *The Prince and the Pauper.* By Mark Twain. The Heritage Press, 1964. Copyright © 1964 by The George Macy Companies, Inc. Reprinted by permission of the author.—Walker, Jayne L. From *The Making of a Modernist: Gertrude Stein from "Three Lives" to "Tender Buttons."* Amherst: The University of Massachusetts Press, 1984. Copyright © 1976, 1984 by Jayne L. Walker. All rights reserved. Reprinted by permission of the publisher.—Wiggins, Robert A. From *Mark Twain: Jackleg Novelist.* University of Washington Press, 1964. Copyright © 1964 by the University of Washington Press. Reprinted by permission of the publisher.

PHOTOGRAPHS AND ILLUSTRATIONS APPEARING IN *TCLC*, VOLUME 48, WERE RECEIVED FROM THE FOLLOWING SOURCES:

Drawing by John Woodcock: **p. 8;** Herbert Römer, Braubach: **p. 14;** The Henry E. Huntington Library and Art Gallery: **p. 51;** Cartoon by Will Dyson: **p. 66;** Photograph by Wheeler of Weymouth: **p. 81;** Culver Pictures, New York: **pp. 90, 206;** Estate of Mrs. Frieda Lawrence Ravagli, courtesy of the Humanities Research Center, University of Texas at Austin: **p. 111;** Photograph by Maria Huxley: **p. 142;** Beinecke Rare Book and Manuscript Library, Yale University: **pp. 213, 235;** The Metropolitan Museum of Art, Bequest of Gertrude Stein, 1946. (47.106): **p. 224;** Man Ray © 1993 Man Ray Trust/ARS-N.Y.: **p. 259;** Department of Special Collections, Research Library, UCLA: **p. 319.**

Frans Bengtsson
1894-1954

(Full name Frans Gunnar Bengtsson) Swedish biographer, novelist, essayist, and poet.

INTRODUCTION

Bengtsson is considered one of the most distinguished figures in twentieth-century Swedish literature. He is known principally for his imaginative and witty treatment of historical subjects in such works as *Karl den XII:s levnad* (*The Sword Does Not Jest: The Heroic Life of King Charles XII of Sweden*) and *Röde Orm* (*The Long Ships: A Saga of the Viking Age*). Adamantly opposed to the spirit of modernity, Bengtsson greatly admired medieval literature as well as the English tradition of contemplative and critical prose exemplified by Edward Gibbon, Charles Lamb, and William Hazlitt. In both his fiction and nonfiction, Bengtsson eschewed detailed renderings of character psychology, concentrating rather on portraying heroic figures and accurately depicting the times in which they lived.

Bengtsson was born and raised in the southern province of Skåne, a region traditionally devoted to farming and shipping and imbued with the lore of seafaring that features strongly in *The Long Ships*. While studying at Lund University, Bengtsson completed a doctoral thesis on Geoffrey Chaucer and published two collections of verse, *Tärningkast* and *Legendem om Babel*. These volumes, which include evocations of heroic themes as well as revivals of medieval verse forms, prefigure the concerns of Bengtsson's major works. Bengtsson later published accomplished Swedish translations of the *Chanson de Roland*, John Milton's *Paradise Lost,* and Henry David Thoreau's *Walden*. During his lifetime his work received both scholarly recognition and popular acclaim; his epic biography of Charles XII won the Swedish Academy's annual prize in 1938, and *The Long Ships* became a best-seller. Bengtsson died in 1954.

Bengtsson's studies of historical figures focus on men of action, including François Villon, Oliver Cromwell, and Stonewall Jackson. In these works he sought to integrate scholarly precision and artistic gracefulness, qualities that are most evident in *The Sword Does Not Jest*. The quasi-legendary stature of the ascetic monarch Charles XII was considered by critics to be the ideal vehicle for Bengtsson's talents. The energetic and compelling narrative of the biography avoids interpretation of his psychological motivation, while nevertheless providing a rich portrayal of his life. Moreover, Bengtsson's deft and lucid handling of military matters received universal praise, prompting one critic to call the biography the greatest interpretation of military matters since Julius Caesar's *Commentaries*.

Considered by some critics to be his masterpiece, *The Long Ships* reflects Bengtsson's fascination with medieval civilization. Spanning the tenth and eleventh centuries, this novel traces the life of Orm, a Viking from Skåne living in the reign of Harald Bluetooth. Orm's adventures provide an elaborate depiction of Dark Age Europe, featuring Ireland, the Black Sea kingdom of the Bulgars, and the opulent caliphate of Córdoba. Critics have noted that *The Long Ships* is suffused with satire. For example, Orm converts to both Islam and Christianity while maintaining a resolutely pagan outlook. Commenting on *The Long Ships* and *The Sword Does Not Jest,* the Swedish critic Alrik Gustafson stated: "In both of these works [Bengtsson] shoulders his learning effortlessly, with the skill of a scholar who defies the dust of learning and recaptures those vital realities of life in the past which have too often been written about in heavy, measured, lifeless periods."

PRINCIPAL WORKS

Tärningkast (poetry) 1923
Legenden om Babel (poetry) 1925
Litteratörer och militärer (essays) 1929
Silversködarna (essays) 1931
De långhåriga merovingerna och andra essayer (essays) 1933
Karl den XII:s levnad (biography) 1935-36
  [*The Life of Charles XII, King of Sweden 1697-1718,* 1960; also published as *The Sword Does Not Jest: The Heroic Life of King Charles XII of Sweden,* 1960]
Sällskap för en eremit (essays) 1938
Röde Orm, sjöfarare i västerled (novel) 1941
  [*Red Orm,* 1942]
Röde Orm, hemma i österled (novel) 1945
  [Translated together with *Röde Orm, sjöfarare i västerled* as *The Long Ships: A Saga of the Viking Age,* 1954]
A Walk to an Ant Hill, and Other Essays (essays) 1950
Dikter (poetry) 1950
Den lustgård som jag minns (memoirs) 1953
Tankar i gröngräset (essays and lectures) 1953
Folk som sjöng och andra essayer (essays) 1955
Breven till Tristan (letters) 1986

CRITICISM

Gurli Hertzman-Ericson (essay date 1937)

[*In the following review of* The Life of Charles XII, King of Sweden 1697-1718 *Hertzman-Ericson praises Bengtsson's synthesis of scholarship, language, and moral concerns in his portrayal of Sweden's former monarch.*]

In the flood of new books each year, there are always a few that stand out. These few are not the ones which merely present a faithful picture of a milieu, a family, or a period. They are those books which by reason of the author's grasp of his subject and his ability to take a long view acquire something of that timeless quality without which no work can long endure.

Frans G. Bengtsson's two-volume life of Charles XII with its nine hundred pages stands alone. To be sure, it is not the length of a book that determines its destiny. But *Charles XII* is a noble work. One reads it from the first page to the last with unflagging interest. There are certain passages, especially in the second part, which perhaps only an officer can fully appreciate. But these expert accounts of battles and strategic marches are the necessary accompaniment of that line of march which led from the barren Swedish countryside across Europe and into those semi-Asiatic tracts where a mighty army and an empire whirled away and disappeared like a wind over the steppes. What one admires in Frans G. Bengtsson is not merely his erudition, his skill in hammering out the metal of speech in sounding rhythms, and his capacity to assimilate the historical material, but rather his power to paint a vivid and harmonious portrait of an almost legendary figure who has stood closer to the heart of the Swedish people than any other. In an age of compromise, shoddiness, and utilitarianism, he turns to a man who in his tragic greatness approaches the heroic, a man who never haggled or made terms with justice, and who always remained the strong man however ill his lot. Statecraft seldom coexists with morality, and consequently the life of Charles XII became the tragic drama of a man of honor amongst a band of crowned brigands who spoke another language from his.

The author shows us how the soul of the young prince is formed from his earliest childhood years, how it takes on impressions from the environment and yet retains its inalienable stamp of loftiness and integrity, traits of character which grow stronger rather than weaker during the two war years when it became the dismal fate of Charles XII to lead his people and his country toward their ruin. For a brief period this little country far up in the north shone like a flaming meteor, which describes its curve across the vault of heaven and is just as quickly extinguished—a country which a fifteen-year-old boy received as his kingdom, a country which little by little and century by century had broadened out and grown in greatness, not through marriage or inheritance, but by long and honest travail with plough and axe and sword. This country which he loved and which he desired to protect from predatory neighbors, he left at the age of eighteen and did not see again for fifteen long years, years in which a chapter of world history was written.

Charles XII was a boy whose chief pleasure was in hunting bears in the forest at Kungsör when word came that the Saxon forces had crossed the boundary of Lifland. Shortly after this the King of Denmark invaded Holstein and a few months later came Czar Peter's declaration of war. The tocsins rang and the bitter times ripened the youth to manhood.

Faithfully the author follows him in battle and in camp, all the long way through Germany, Poland, the Baltic provinces, and into Russia where the ominous twilight thickens. He may criticize him and wonder about his motive, but what he has constantly before his eyes is the hero, the morally invincible, the strong, lonely man whose destiny was fulfilled beneath relentless stars—a man who demanded much of others, but still more of himself, a man who never stooped to the luxury and fastidiousness of contemporary princes, but remained a soldier among soldiers, the comrade who shared the hardships of camp life with his men and ate their simple fare. And yet he does not become in Frans G. Bengtsson's picture a remote or hazy ideal; he stands out as a human being with a sense of humor and of reality and with a rare fidelity not only to ideas but also to his fellow men.

Charles XII has been accused of having led his people to their ruin, but was he not perhaps a tool in the service of higher powers? With irrefutable logic the author points out how after Narva his stars were on the wane and how events and accidents conspired together in a manner approaching the tragedies of fate in ancient literature. If the weather had been different, if a trifling misunderstanding had been removed, the outcome might have been quite another. Even at the siege of Poltava the situation which Charles was patiently trying to create was ultimately realized, "but an ironical fate had permitted the realization to take place only as a consequence of the King's inability to profit from the great chance for which he had striven." When his strategical skill was most needed, the King was sick unto death and his field marshals were at loggerheads.

So the brave little Swedish people wandered on to destruction, but even in their ruin a kind of legendary glamour and an indomitable courage shone from their pale faces.

The Swedish Empire fell asunder, finally destroyed by a bullet at Fredrikshall, and a new age began forthwith. "But," says Frans G. Bengtsson, "the mighty hero of the war slept, unmoved by all that came after, sublimely tranquil in the bronze of his sarcophagus, as though he had been immortalized in a state of lofty indifference and irrevocable peace. He had entered, as one of the last and greatest, into the kingdom where dwell the masters by the grace of God." (pp. 354-55)

Gurli Hertzman-Ericson, "A New Biography of Charles XII," in The American Scandinavian Review, *Vol. XXV, No. 4, December, 1937, pp. 354-55.*

Hal Borland (essay date 1943)

[*In the following excerpt, Borland lauds Bengtsson's reworking of Norse history and literature.*]

Old Eric of the beard and flaming temper had been banished from Iceland and had gone west to the rocks and ice of what he, with grim Viking humor, called Greenland. Leif, identified later as The Lucky, was exploring the waters of Greenland and listening to tales of land still farther west. In Ireland the Danes who had ruled by force still laughed, though a little less loudly, at tales of Brian Boru and his growing band of followers. And England was still a prime source of income for any resolute band of sword wielders from the north; Ethelred was king in Essex, and Ethelred was known as the Unready. The time was the late tenth century.

It is against this background that Frans Bengtsson, the Swedish historical novelist, has laid the story of Orm, the red-haired Dane, [in his novel ***Red Orm***]. Orm, left at home when his father and brothers went raiding, was captured, in turn, by rival raiders, sailed south first as a prisoner, then as a warrior, then as a galley slave of the Mohammedans. He was freed from the slave's oar by Almansur, the vizier of the caliph, became a warrior once more and in due time escaped with his own men to return to the northern seas, to Denmark and to the court of wrothy old King Harald Blue-Tooth.

Orm's prowess as a swordsman won him a place among King Harald's favorites, won the attentions of Ylva, the king's daughter, and set him on the sea road to conquest again, this time to England. The climax of Orm's saga came at Maldon, where the Danes won the first of their painful series of battles with Ethelred's Englishmen and forced the payment of a stiff ransom for peace. There, too, Orm found Ylva, married her, turned Christian and decided to return to his homeland for what may be the next canto of his saga.

There are the rough outlines of an excellent tale which comes as near the spirit of the old sagas and eddas as you will find in recent print. Bengtsson is peculiarly able in carrying his reader into the midst of the ancient days. His story has the drive, the action, the violence, at times the severely simple poetry of the old tales. And for all the economy of characterization—which was equally true of the contemporary sagas—his people live. They fight simply as a way of life. Their business is plunder. They are seamen and warriors, living and dying by the sword. Their lives are governed by luck, and as long as their luck holds they are prosperous and victorious. When it ends life is no longer worth living. If they turn from Odin to Allah, from Allah to Christ, it is only for better luck. The priest, of whatever faith, is judged by his luck and his gifts. The king, the chieftain or the lesses leader, holds his position by power and power alone.

Neither Eric nor Leif enters the story. Brian Boru is only a cloud on the horizon, for Clontarf is still some years away. There is little international complication for the simple reason that there is no real nationalism. Those refinements, as well as complicated reasons for warfare, were yet to be achieved. This was a day when rival chieftains fought out their differences face to face, even as Orm fought Sihtric at King Harald's great hall at the yule feast—fought to the death.

Red Orm is a Viking story from the first line, swift-paced, true to its times, excellently done. It is escape fiction only in conveying to perfection the whole flavor of a vanished period and people.

Hal Borland, "Viking Sea Road," in The New York Times Book Review, *April 25, 1943, p. 6.*

Giles Romilly (essay date 1954)

[*In the following excerpt, Romilly praises the narrative exuberance of* The Long Ships, *while faulting the emotional detachment evident in the work.*]

The Long Ships comprises a number of excellent and exciting stories strung loosely together on the adventures of a hero, Orm, son of a Viking thane. Never dull, nor even long-winded, though it fills five hundred pages of exactingly close type, it is perfectly suited to the tastes of, for instance, readers of Mr. C. S. Forester. It can be taken straight; to extract full enjoyment, however, the following procedure may be recommended. First, skip or otherwise surmount the historical information somewhat solemnly purveyed by Mr. Michael Meyer, whose palatable and lucid translation is no such hardship. Next, laugh off the quaint, fatherly tone of Mr. Bengtsson's Prologue. Lastly, taking a deep breath, decide to endure the company, at close quarters almost physically oppressive, of such monstrous figures as King Harold Bluetooth, King Sven Forkbeard, King Ragnar Hairy-Breeks, of their slave-trading thanes and jarls, and of the "shaven men" bringing Christian baptism to "shores of night and violence" where Thor and Odin prevailed. This need not take long; already on page 24 the graduated reader, comfortably involved in a competent description of a thane's nagging wife, will know at once that there is going to be no profound psychology to hold him back, nor anything profound of any sort. Settled into a banquet of adventure by sea and land, with man-size helpings of battle and murder, robbery and rape, he will find it a treat to go vicariously "a-viking."

The character of ***The Long Ships*** being untragic and unromantic, it is a relief, if only for propriety's sake, that its hero lives happily-ever-after. Glad of this, I suffered nevertheless a churlish, if not exactly "jarlish" disappointment, in that no feeling stronger than relief seemed to have been kindled. This saga, for all its masterful and erudite control, has no touch of the imaginative genius of, for instance, Sigrid Undset's *Kristin Lavransdatter*. The material is organised with affection rather than with love; at times, inevitably in so big a work, affection seems unorganised, merely polymathic, and a lack of creative fusion is felt. Mr. Bengtsson does a very clever sketch of Ethelred the Unready absorbedly swatting flies as he receives Viking chieftains who have come for their Danegeld. But he might be a tenth-century journalist doing it as a feature. He is always the amused outsider. He will have his chuckle, and in themselves his chuckles are unexceptional; artistically, some of them are misplaced. Artistically, the gift that Mr. Bengtsson lacks is innocence. His style suggests the decorative associations—impeccable, unoriginal, bland—of the label "Swedish modern."

> Giles Romilly, in a review of "The Long Ships," in The New Statesman & Nation, Vol. XLVII, No. 1200, March 6, 1954, p. 294.

Robert A. Hunter (essay date 1955)

[*In the following excerpt, Hunter maintains that* The Long Ships *is a successful parody of the historical novel because of its satirical portrayal of both Christian and Viking values.*]

The newspaper book reviewers, who invariably go with the glamour and successfully avoid the perils of criticism by simply recounting juicy morsels of plot, thickly interlarded with the more salient adjectives in the monstrous vocabulary of indiscriminate praise, have done it again. Certainly *The Long Ships* is worth its weight in adjectives, though in plugging the book, the yea-sayers have, as usual, neglected to evaluate the author's achievements.

For the late Frans G. Bengtsson, a gentle Swede who realized that the final step to be taken in the development of the historical novel is its parody, has written that anomaly of American publishing—a *good* Best Seller. The saga of Orm Tostesson of the Mound in Skania is a cunning dissertation on the Viking world at the close of the tenth century, told in a narrative style adapted in part from saga literature and therefore suited to Bengtsson's use of exaggeration and understatement, often for comic effects. The book is fun because Bengtsson's enjoyment is infectious and his humor has the authority of sound scholarship and an historical imagination that can render a sullen age articulate. A complete bibliography of his source material, including original texts in a number of languages, would reveal the lengths to which serious scholarship can go before it can be borne lightly. Thus, the real adventure of the novel is Bengtsson's artful reconstruction of fragments in a vast mosaic—the period of roughly 980-1010 A.D.—in the form of a little world of intimate and realistic dimensions.

It is pleasant to watch the Battle of Maldon develop from a chance encounter and near-engagement of Danish and Swedish fleets in the *Sund* and to realize that such determinants as gold and women, luck and revenge, strong ale and the ennui of strong men could at one time in history initiate or decide the course of great events. Bengtsson's characters are alive with the appetites and illusions of a free-roving age, and he is a master of the terse, epigrammatic sally on the human comedy in old Scandinavia:

"The Bishop read grace, King Harald having commanded him to be brief about it, and then they drank three toasts: to the honor of Christ, to the luck of King Harald, and to the return of the sun."

In his broad satire on the coming of Christianity to the heathen north, Bengtsson can convince us of the essential sanity of a world in which the Seven Deadly Sins are the cardinal virtues of a healthy, happy warrior. Indeed, the unsung hero of *The Long Ships* is no less than medieval man's omniverous appetite for life and awesome capacity for enjoyment. Despite the long catalogue of grunts and groans from Maldon to Constantinople, of galley whips and clipped ears and rolling heads, one is disconcertingly aware of Bengtsson's approval—and our own. Read his delightful essay, **"The Long-haired Merovingians,"** in *A Walk to an Ant Hill,* published by the Foundation in 1950. Then you will appreciate what he is about when you take up *The Long Ships.* The nearest approach to Bengtsson's humor in the United States can be found in the cartoons of Charles Addams.

Frans Bengtsson was a remarkable writer, linguist and historian, a man of great learning and insatiable curiosity. In *A Walk to an Ant Hill* his interests range from medieval *grotesquerie* to Stonewall Jackson. He has translated Icelandic prose and verse, the *Chanson de Roland,* François Villon, *Paradise Lost* and (of all people) Thomas Hardy. Before his recent death he had secured for himself a permanent place in Swedish letters. (pp. 89-90)

> Robert A. Hunter, in a review of "The Long Ships," in The American-Scandinavian Review, Vol. XLIII, No. 1, Spring, 1955, pp. 89-90.

Walter W. Gustafson (essay date 1955)

[*In the following excerpt, Gustafson praises the historical accuracy and popular appeal of* The Long Ships.]

[*The Long Ships*] has already proved to be the most popular book translated from Swedish in recent years both in England and the United States and has been widely acclaimed by many reviewers of various newspapers and periodicals. Tragically enough in the midst of all this success, the author passed away on December, 19, 1954, at the age of sixty.

It is not difficult to account for the popular success of this novel at home and abroad. The sagas are well told from beginning to end, a mordant humor often adds spice to the narrative; there is considerable romance as well as sex interest, and no dearth of large glamorous historical canvases. In short, the book has all the appeal calculated to catch and hold the interests of many and to produce an interesting historical novel. But transcending and including all these factors, is the gift of style and writing characteristic of an accomplished and versatile man of letters.

After the author had earned various academic degrees from Lund University, he served a long and arduous apprenticeship to the literary Muse. Like so many Scandinavians, he made his debut as a poet; later he became an essayist of grace and charm; he wrote a brilliant life of Charles XII of Sweden [*Karl den XII:s levnad*]; and in 1941 he offered the first volume of his Viking stories, *Red Orm on the Western Way,* to be followed in 1945 by a volume *Red Orm at Home and on the Eastern Way.* These two volumes have now been translated by Michael Meyer to form the new volume, *The Long Ships,* a superb collection of Viking exploits and experiences.

It is a book that is eminently readable from beginning to end, full of verve and gusto almost in the Chaucerian manner. Many of the tales suggest medieval fabliaux with their vitality and humor—this is especially true of the stories about priests and their fatal fascination for women where a kind of wry, tongue-in-cheek humor is evident. One is continually reminded of the Icelandic sagas by the simple style, the zest for combat and danger, poetic improvisations and mordant irony.

Red Orm, when still a young man, is abducted by Vikings from his home in Northern Scania, carried along the Southern Baltic coast and through the North Sea southward along the French coast. In Spain the Vikings are captured by Moors, and Orm becomes a galley slave for several years and later a member of the guard of Almansur, the great Moorish chieftain. He runs away on a ship carrying a large church bell, to reach the coast of Ireland. From there he makes his way to celebrate Christmas at the court of King Harold Blue Tooth of Denmark, and then home to Scania. But he is soon irked by peace and his mother's fond attentions and makes his way to England with a Viking fleet, to fight in the battle of Maldon (the battle so vividly set forth in the late Anglo-Saxon lay, "The Battle of Maldon"). Later on he becomes a Christian and wins as his fair bride the daughter of King Harold Blue Tooth. The second volume first tells of his adventures at home in the northern wilderness district of Scania, to which he fled in order to escape the vengeance of King Sven, and later describes his Odyssey over Russian rivers to win a treasure hoard buried under rocks in the Dnieper River. As is indicated by this rapid survey, most of the Viking countries form the background for Viking exploits and adventures.

The author in this welter of adventures is not merely a captivating and skillful storyteller, as might be assumed from the account, but also a scholarly historian well grounded in the life and manners of the Vikings. Many episodes show the superficial character of the conversion to Christianity of the heathen Scandinavians (which modern research confirms). In the accounts of Athelred the Unready, the battle of Maldon, the battle of the Stone Tower which followed, and the collection of the Danegeld there is much of interest to the student of English history. The descriptions of the Thing, the battles, the journeys, the christening party, and the fertility dance of the women illustrate vividly and authentically various phases of old Scandinavian life. Even in the details of Viking life and folklore the author seems well informed, as, for instance, when he mentions the Viking practice when approaching land, of removing the dragon's head on the prow of a ship in order to conciliate the land spirits (*land vetter*).

There are many large glamorous historical scenes the visual representation of which might test the resources of even our modern cinemascopic screens. Such scenes of special grandeur and vividness are the Yule festival at the court of King Harold Blue Tooth at Gellinge, Denmark, and the contest man to man which follows (*envig*). Every person at all interested in Germanic life and origins will be thrilled by these magnificent pictures.

The translation is competently done by Michael Meyer, as a rather careful checking with the original has brought out, even though here and there one might find fault with certain renderings and especially with the weakening and softening of the idiomatic vigor of the original. The book is attractively composed, printed and bound, and a new type has been designed to give a feeling of fluidity, power, and speed. The maps supplied at the front of the book are very helpful in following the Europe-embracing journeys. The Kipling poem, "Harp Song of the Dane Women," adds something to the tone of the book, though it is more from the women's viewpoint.

In general, one can say that it is a thrilling book of Viking tales to be read for sheer pleasure and also for profit as an authentic reconstruction of Viking folkways and manner of life. (pp. 115-17)

Walter W. Gustafson, in a review of "The Long Ships," in Scandinavian Studies, *Vol. 27, No. 2, May, 1955, pp. 115-17.*

An excerpt from *The Long Ships*

In the church at Maldon, which was of stone, some of the English were still holding out. They had fled up into the tower when the Vikings had stormed the city, priests and women being among them; and they had drawn the steps up with them as they ascended, that they might not be pursued into their retreat. The Vikings suspected that they had taken much treasure with them, and strove their utmost to persuade them to descend from their tower and bring their treasure with them. But neither by fire nor by force of arms could they achieve anything; and the people had plenty of food and drink with them in the tower, and sang psalms and appeared to be in good heart. When the Vikings approached the tower to try to induce them by words to act sensibly and come down and part with their treasure, they cast down stones, curses, and filth upon their heads, yelling with triumph when any of their missiles met their mark. All the Vikings agreed that stone churches and their towers were among the most vexatious obstacles that a man could find himself confronted with.

Frans Bengtsson The Long Ships *Knopf, 1954.*

Lawrence S. Thompson (essay date 1955)

[*In the following essay, Thompson explores the poetic nature of Bengtsson's essays and fiction.*]

With the death of Frans Gunnar Bengtsson on 19 December 1954, at the age of sixty, modern Swedish literature lost one of its most original personalities. Bengtsson is known to English-speaking readers only for ***The Long Ships*** (1954; translation by Michael Meyer from ***Röde Orm, sjöfarare i västerled,*** [*1941*], and ***Röde Orm, hemma i österled,*** [*1945*]; translation of first volume only by Barrows Mussey in 1943 as ***Red Orm***). However, Bengtsson's literary production is much more extensive, and he has distinguished himself not only as a novelist but also as a poet, and essayist, and a biographer.

Between the time when he took his baccalaureate ("fil. kand.") at Lund in 1920 and his licentiate there in 1930, he published two volumes of poetry and one collection of essays. The poetry, ***Tärningkast*** (1923) and ***Legenden om Babel*** (1925), used historical themes and was distinguished for stylistic virtuosity and formal perfection. The first collection of essays, ***Litteratörer och militärer*** (1929) immediately attracted attention for profound insights and an attitude of complete indifference to moral prejudices in the search for the historical truth. Characteristic of the whole tone of Bengtsson's creative work is a sentence on one of the first pages of ***Litteratörer och militärer***: "At that time he was twenty-five years old and had just committed his first murder and his first longer poem, both of them quite innocuous debuts."

Two other collections of essays, ***Silversköldarna*** (1931) and ***De långhåriga merovingerna*** (1933), were written with the same effort to enliven history with the color of a spectacle staged for the gods of the future with a script by one of the most competent masters of descriptive prose in our century. Bengtsson sought for the potentially colorful in tedious old chronicles and memoirs and transformed it into ballads in prose. It is quite natural, therefore, that he should select Charles XII as the subject of his first longer work [***Karl den XII:s levnad***]. Voltaire and Dr. Johnson had already recognized the incomparable hero of Narva as an almost inexhaustible source of inspiration for the creative writer. In *The Vanity of Human Wishes* (1749), published exactly four decades after Poltava, Johnson wrote somewhat pompously:

> He left a name at which the world grew pale,
> To point a moral or adorn a tale.

Bengtsson, fascinated like all other Swedes by the great warrior king, published his two volumes of ***Karl XII:s levnad*** in 1935 and 1936. Awarded the Swedish Academy's annual prize in 1938, this great biography translates the dry facts of history into a moving drama, replete with details and imagery that only a poet could envision. If the essays are, in a sense, prose ballads, the biography of Charles XII meets every qualification of the epic except the quality of metrical composition.

One more collection of essays, ***Sällskap för en eremit***, appeared in 1938. One other significant aspect of Bengtsson's literary production prior to ***The Long Ships*** should be noted. During the 1920's he earned a high reputation as a skilled and sympathetic translator. His Swedish versions of *Walden* (1924), *Paradise Lost* (1926), and the *Song of Roland* (1929) have almost made these works Swedish classics, much like the Tieck-Schlegel Shakespeare or the Florio Montaigne.

The Long Ships is Bengtsson's crowning achievement as a creative writer. Bengtsson had been fascinated by the Middle Ages from the beginning of his literary career, and he had already touched on the Viking period in his essays. It is natural that he should choose the age of Harald Bluetooth for his second major work, for this era holds the same relative position in the Scandinavian Middle Ages as that of Charles XII does in modern times. For the hero of his tale Bengtsson selected Röde Orm, a fictitious chieftan from his native Scania. Orm's saga was written a full millennium after men began to spin yarns about Egil Skallagrimsson and Grettir the Strong, but Bengtsson's skill as a story-teller is no whit inferior to the Icelanders.

Bengtsson takes Orm a-viking when he is hardly a man. Orm survives years of Moorish captivity and escapes back to Scania with a treasure. Smitten by Ylva, daughter of Harald Bluetooth, he trails her to England where he is converted and wins her for his bride. After years of comparative peace, Orm embarks on his last great foray, this time far to the south of Kiev, to the weirs of the Dniepr where the Bulgar's gold is hidden. After one more adventure against a renegade priest, Orm and his brother-in-arms, Toke Gray-Gullson settle down to age contentedly and tell their grandchildren how they rowed the Caliph's galley for my lord Almansur.

Here is the world of the year 1000 and thereabouts as seen by the untutored but by no means stupid Northmen. At the same time Bengtsson is able to present naive, plain-spoken humanity, stripped of convention and prejudice. Orm allows himself to be converted, but he sees much of the sham of the new religion and clings steadfastly to many things that are good in the old. He had already accepted Allah in Spain, for he had a thoroughly practical view of religion: "We men of the north do not worship our gods except in time of necessity, for we think it foolish to weary them with babbling." Orm travelled widely and took the world at its face value. He was unimpressed by Ethelred's London, barely a village compared with glorious Córdoba. He never sailed his long ship into the Bosphorus, but he heard all of the stories of the glitter and wickedness of Miklagard from his unfortunate brother Are.

Bengtsson is a master of the shrewd Scandinavian peasant wisdom, much of which he absorbed as a child in Scania where his father superintended a large estate. In ***The Long Ships*** he expresses this wisdom in few words and has it reinforced with a battle-axe. He has a marvelous sense of legend and history. He writes as the ancient story teller might have spoken, but, without offense to the reader, he cautiously suggests the insight that only a modern can have. He maintains a sense for the archaic in the dialogue and the narrative, but it is never strained or artificial.

As a poet Bengtsson reaches his greatest heights in ***The Long Ships.*** Toke, the poet of the tale, outdoes any southern *improvisatore* with his extemporaneous verse, wholly in the eddic vein but with all the strength and originality of the ancient singers. A single example, felicitously rendered into English by Meyer with clever adaptation of the alliteration in the Swedish, must suffice. Toke sees Bluetooth's fleet fade into the distance and he goes to release Mirah, the Moorish lass he kidnapped in a box from the court of the Danish king. There had been a narrow escape, for the Harald had sat on the box to quaff a farewell cup of ale. Toke sings with sly humor:

> Dread the hour
> When Denmark's despot
> Bulbous sat
> On brittle box-lid.
> Faintly yet I
> Fear my freight be
> Broken-boned
> By Bluetooth's burden.

Frans G. Bengtsson is essentially a poet in all his work.

In the spirit of Carlyle he said: "History is the noblest of all subjects." Even though he is a meticulous antiquarian, a scholar with an enormous background of reading in all the subjects of which he writes, Bengtsson seeks and exploits everywhere the theatrical and the spectacular. He takes his readers to the highest heavens of the Olympian chronicler and surveys objectively the stage of world history. His essays and biographical studies bring history to life no less than does the tale of Orm's adventures.

For us there is a particularly effective example in his treatment of the blood and gore of our Civil War. With perfect logic he portrays the transformation of the rebel general Stonewall Jackson from a profoundly religious professor into the fabled warrior of the Second Bull Run and Antietam. Again there is the brilliant portrait of melancholy U. S. Grant, the man who was a failure in everything but war. He takes the reader on the terrible retreat of the grand Army from Moscow, the fateful expedition of Alexander's elite troops into the depths of Asia, the adventures of a Scottish mercenary in the banditry of the Thirty Years War in Germany.

It is characteristic of Bengtsson to seek the romantic elements in war and ages of unrest. He is fascinated by the similarity of war to chess, a favorite pastime as he once indicated in an essay. Above all our Great Rebellion found in Bengtsson an enthusiast who would have been welcome at any Civil War Roundtable from Chicago to Atlanta. He contrasted the romance of the Thirty Years War or the Civil War with the meaningless stupidity of modern wars, and he had a special distaste for the depressing realism of many authors who wrote about World War I. He felt that the great leaders who emerged in the wars of the past could never find a proper rôle in a modern war simply because the armed conflicts of our day offer no possibility of action for a distinguished leader or a military genius. Had Röde Orm lived in our time he could never have slipped through the net of Bluetooth's Gestapo, and he would have been subjected to an effective brain-washing by the Caliph's thought-police.

Bengtsson has grave misgivings about the democratization of modern culture, the transformation of the human spirit into uninspired, uniform mediocrity. This position has much to support it if we try to imagine a Stonewall Jackson or a Röde Orm as the products of our American public schools of the twentieth century. Bengtsson admired many second-rate historical novelists such as Hervey Allen and Kenneth Roberts simply for their ability to ignore psychological analysis (which he detested) and to portray men of action in vivid colors. However, Bengtsson was under no illusions about literary quality. Among modern writers he singled out Joseph Conrad as a special favorite, a creative artist who was free from any taint of "western European provincialism" and could review mankind with the justifiable aloofness of the artist but with the breadth of the man to whom nothing human was alien.

Frans G. Bengtsson developed no new style, but he does represent a strong reaction to the weak and colorless language of many historical essayists and even novelists of our time. He seeks the full flavor of the times of which he writes, and if his poetic instincts overwhelm academic conventions, he has no compunctions about junking the latter. In language as well as form and thought Bengtsson is an *Einzelgänger*. His genius elevates him above the hacks who flood the literary market place with historical biography and fiction, and his sense of the essential poetry of history never lets him drop to the melodramatic. He may have cherished a profound pessimism about the destiny of modern man, but poetry was no *triste métier* for him. Rather it was *la gaie science*. Like Villon, whose ballade of the dames of yesteryear he admired intensely, Bengtsson brings an "insubstantial pageant" to his readers.

Frans G. Bengtsson belongs to no school of creative writers or historians. He would have been promptly rusticated from any into which an overzealous critic might have matriculated him. He may not endure through the centuries that have laughed and wept with Villon, but for those of us who can revel in a pure display of genius, a rousing story, and a mastery of prose and poetic style, Bengtsson has a firm position in twentieth century literature. (pp. 75-9)

> Lawrence S. Thompson, "Frans G. Bengtsson, 1894-1954," in Kentucky Foreign Language Quarterly, Vol. II, No. 2, 1955, pp. 75-9.

The Times Literary Supplement (review date 1960)

[*In the following excerpt,* The Life of Charles XII *is acclaimed as an impeccable work of scholarship, despite Bengtsson's inadequate interpretation of his subject's eventual defeat and demise.*]

In the modern world the great exception among the heroes seen as neurotic extroverts is Charles XII of Sweden: a man who applied the bronze-age criteria he happened to be born with to the surrounding world without ever noticing their incongruity. But then Charles is possibly the only European conqueror who seems to have had no imagination. The wars of the eighteenth century, carefully controlled struggles that were only a predictable pattern in the complex reallocation of the balance of interests, meant little to him. Instead of offering Swedish support to the highest bidder in the wars of the Spanish succession, he frittered away the toughest nation in Europe in the valueless steppes beyond the Baltic; a policy of marginal relevance even in the time of his predecessor Gustavus Adolphus.

Policy meant little more to Charles than to some early Vandal chieftain who would have considered it disgraceful to die in bed: he was a brilliant campaigner, he liked fighting, he disliked the pretensions of Augustus the Strong, and the siren road to Moscow shimmered alluringly before his invincible Drabants. For a brief period between Narva and Pultava he did indeed "regale a sober century with a belated piece of folklore"; then it was all over, and with it the role of Scandinavia as the arbiter and civilizer of eastern Europe.

Sweden was the only country that could still have produced such a figure; a realm where no king had lived into decent middle age for the previous century and a half; where the nobility today bear names predominantly Scottish or German, the indigenous houses wiped out by the

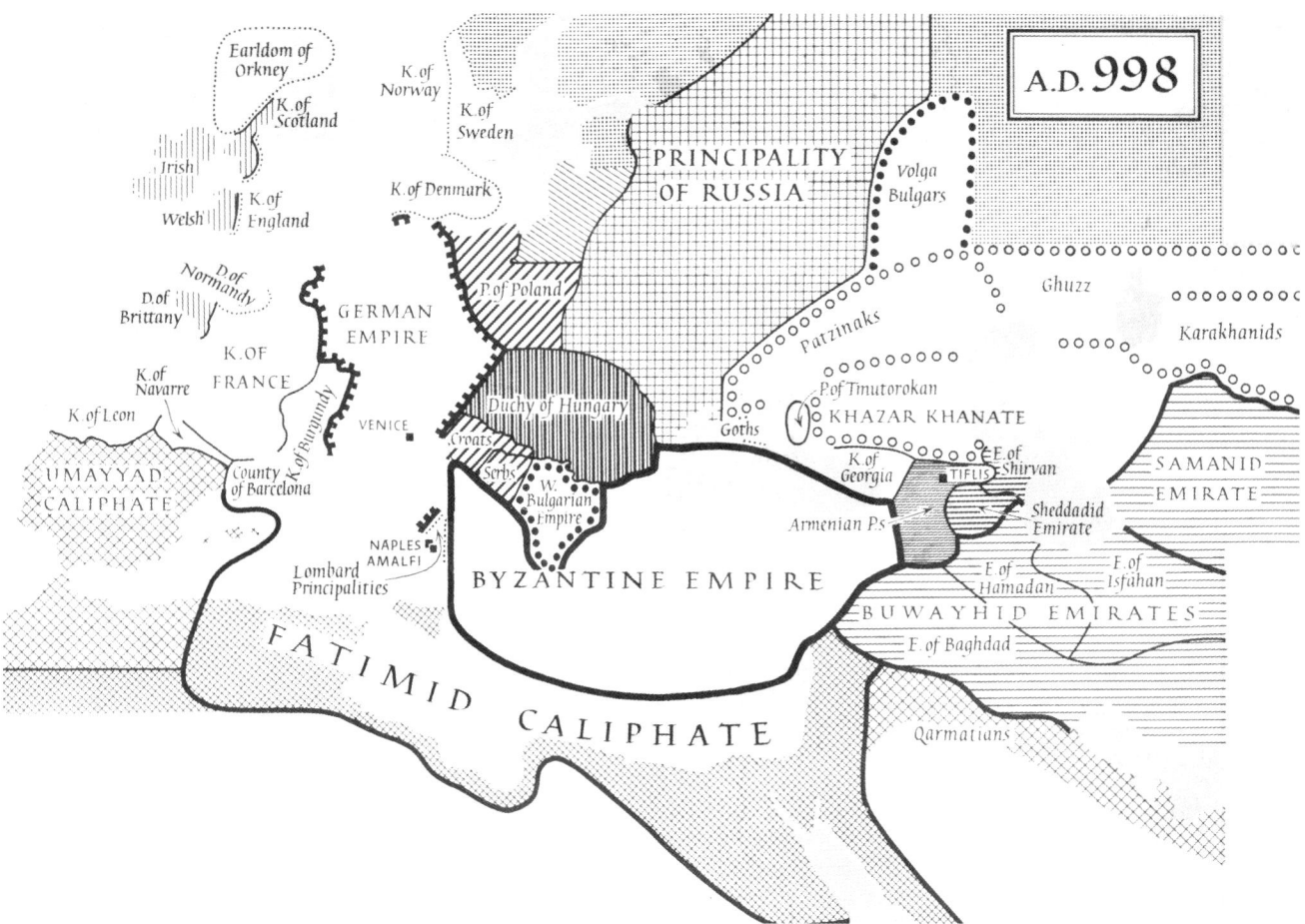

Political divisions at the time of Orm's adventures in The Long Ships.

attrition of continuous soldiering, their only interest; and behind both a tough yeoman peasantry not yet transformed into a middle class, and the mines of Dalacarlia.

None of this of course has anything to do with the eighteenth century; but because of his very alienness Charles lodged himself, like the Lisbon earthquake, in the iconology of the period, a mythopoeic force, fertile for analogy or speculation, but inassimilable to the world picture of the time.

How then is a modern historian to approach him? Internationally his significance was small: a certain uneasiness that he might intervene which precipitated a visit from Marlborough; a few extra balks for Peter the Great, and the precipitation, by a few years, of Sweden's withdrawal from the European complex. Psychologically he has none of the fascination of the Napoleonic monsters that have stalked Europe since his time. He was the ultimate viking, but a Swede and little pervious to romance. Some twenty-five years ago the late Frans G. Bengtsson attempted to present Charles to the modern reader [in his ***The Life of Charles XII***]. One of the few major Scandinavian writers to emerge in the present century, he approached history as did Schiller and Gibbon, as a combination of literature and scholarship. Deeply erudite and an exquisite stylist, he suffered all the melancholy romanticism of the Gothic North, tempered and repressed by the pervasive Swedish distrust of all that is not tangible to organized common sense.

Charles also seems to have carried an epic quality for Bengtsson, for though his wit plays around the others, Peter the Great, Augustus, Lewenhaupt, the Polish magnates, the King himself is always treated with complete seriousness. But somehow he fails to be Arthurian; just a man remarkably good at his job, capable of inspiring tremendous achievements, but with little consciousness of his own significance and faintly dull to read about.

The scholarship is impeccable (though it would surely not have been too pedantic to add some sort of bibliography?). Fresh sources, particularly journals of the period, have been used. The battles are perspicuously demonstrated and the vast and frequently obscure material is always under complete control. Unquestionably this is the best work on Charles XII in English—but it is not Bengtsson's masterwork. Partly this is the fault of the translation, though not of the translator. The tensions existing between the formal written language and colloquial Swedish, which Bengtsson uses with such art, are absent in modern English so that his rhetoric occasionally seems to verge on the purple and the subtle distinctions of his irony appear portentous. Partly it derives from Bengtsson's deliberate reluctance to interpret: the cause of Charles's failure is dismissed in a few lines, divided between the Russian weather and the waning enthusiasm of his troops after seven years' campaigning.

> "The Ultimate Viking?" in The Times Literary Supplement, No. 3049, August 5, 1960, p. 491.

Mac Lindahl (essay date 1960)

[*In the following review of* The Sword Does Not Jest: The Heroic Life of King Charles XII of Sweden, *Lindahl discusses Bengtsson's portrayal of the history and culture of the Swedish province of Scania.*]

The late Frans G. Bengtsson was born and grew up in the northwestern part of Sweden's southernmost province, Scania. There you will find two kinds of native inhabitants, those who are as taciturn as the Vermonters, and those who talk as big as the Texans. The latter kind, when properly educated through academic studies in the university town of Lund, may sometimes develop into poets, dramatists, chroniclers for periodicals, or authors of such rare stature as Frans G. Bengtsson.

Their environment has made the Scanians unique. Because of their closeness to the sea, they have had salt in their veins since time immemorial. So while the farmers—and this is the granary of Sweden—cultivate their kale and plow their fields, they think often of faraway shores and distant ports. The next thing they do is to rig their schooners and set sail for Bombay or Hong Kong. Bengtsson wrote one eminently successful novel in two parts about this kind of people—his people—which in its English-language version was called ***The Long Ships.*** A better tale of the life of the early Vikings has yet to be told.

The talkative Scanian is more creative in a realistic way than any other Swede. He may, therefore, one night, when helping a cow give birth to a calf, compose a poem and sell it the next day to a literary magazine in Stockholm. A critic states that "the author of this poem was indeed very far from the realities of life when he put his words down on paper." To which Frans Bengtsson could, of course, only comment that he wondered if the critic had ever been as close to the realities of life as he, the poet, had been on the night when both the calf and the poem were born.

In telling about how he came to write ***The Long Ships*** Bengtsson has in a brief essay confessed that the Icelandic Saga influenced his language and style. He recalled in particular one sentence in which it was said: "When Atle walked homewards, he came to think of the people he would slay. Their deaths moved him so that he broke into laughter and tears of joy rolled down his cheeks." Frans Bengtsson may have used this anecdote about himself merely because he wanted an excuse for writing an essay. Certainly, he did not need the Icelandic Saga as an inspiration; his language in its full literary bloom was with him from his earliest days of writing. That he could apply this instrument also to other forms of expression is clear through the rest of his production. One outstanding example has now been translated beautifully and flawlessly by Naomi Walford and is available under the title ***The Sword Does Not Jest.*** It is the biography of Sweden's King Charles XII.

The volume has a foreword by Eric Linklater (many of whose books Bengtsson has transposed into his rich and harmonious Swedish), illustrations, a complete index, and an end map, which shows the young king's incredible ability to move around on horseback or by foot in a Europe and Near East where there was then not much comfort to a traveler, much less to a warrior and conqueror.

Here is the story of competence amidst incompetence, for while Charles did not lack brave soldiers, he certainly had an equally ample supply of lieutenants-general and admirals-in-chief under his command who did as much harm to their lord and master as only men of their rank can. Over the years the fabulous exploits of this king of Sweden have acquired a heavy layer of miracle and myth. The king's grave has been opened, his remains autopsied and X-rayed, and an endless flow of papers has been delivered concerning his death and the bullet that finally felled him in a Norwegian trench at Frederiskhald.

Bengtsson, whose words do not jest, has at long last drawn a portrait of the man as he must have been. The picture is as rich in detail as a Brueghel, and we are thus given not only the tragic story of a great man surrounded by mental midgets and clever foes but the story of his times as well.

> Mac Lindahl, "Autopsy of a Viking Hero," in Saturday Review, Vol. XLIII, No. 51, December 17, 1960, p. 25.

Eric Linklater (essay 1960)

[*In the following excerpt, taken from the introduction to the English translation of* The Sword Does Not Jest: The Heroic Life of King Charles XII of Sweden, *Linklater asserts that Bengtsson's objective scholarship, together with his aesthetic rather than moral judgement of historical figures, make the biography his masterpiece.*]

At a critical period in the War of the Spanish Succession the Duke of Marlborough delivered a personal letter from Queen Anne to Charles XII of Sweden, and in conversation gravely informed the King that had his tasks permitted he would have been happy to serve under His Majesty 'to acquire the knowledge he yet lacked of the arts of war'. The victor of Blenheim and Ramillies knew how to use flattery, and his flattery was nicely weighed, not only against a political danger, but contemporary opinion; in which, with evidence to give it substance, the young King was regarded as a military genius.

He was indeed a remarkable man, with all the attributes of a hero, some of the qualities of a saint, and the limitations of a madman. Voltaire said he was 'the only person in history who was free from all weakness', and certainly it was a most uncommon strength, of mind and body, that put so much of his short life into the long campaign that began with a brilliant victory at Narva, in 1700, and came to its finish and defeat at Poltava in 1709. At Narva, in a November snowstorm, he fought as audaciously and successfully as Nelson at Aboukir Bay; but the annihilation of a Russian army did not bring about the collapse of Russia, and nine years later, in the heat of June and the wheatfields of the Ukraine, Peter the Great took revenge for the battle he had so bleakly lost on the wintry Baltic shore. The long campaign was over, but for Charles there remained a chapter of adventure that might have been filched from a Norse saga.

His probity was absolute. So far from double-dealing, he hardly dealt at all: he had no sense of diplomacy, nor respect for it. His courage was legendary, and his mastery of tactics was irreverently relieved by episodes, or escapades, in which he behaved like some resurrected hero from a folk-tale of the Volsungs; but a Polish girl, in whose father's house he lodged, thought him 'as gentle as a lamb and as shy as a nun', and while three of his Generals talked loudly and praised their host's wine, she watched with wonder the King who sat quietly, drinking milk and eating bread and salt. 'The sword does not jest', he wrote; and neither did Charles. It would have been better, for Sweden and much of Europe, if he had; but the world would have been poorer by the loss of a tragical, horrifying, and stupendous tale in which a virtue as narrow and implacable as the edge of a sword evoked from a multitude of men a stark and awful courage, a strength of will and physical endurance that seem more than human, and buried itself to no purpose under ruin as lurid as a viking's pyre.

Frans G. Bengtsson, who wrote [*The Sword Does Not Jest: The Heroic Life of King Charles XII of Sweden*], was by study, temperament, and talent well suited to essay, in a long and detailed narrative, the explication of so strange and potent a man; for Bengtsson, who lived a quiet and sedentary life, was full of a passionate admiration for all that was strenuous and heroical, but curbed and disciplined his passion by an exacting scholarship, and held it in proportion by a robust and curious sense of humour. His judgment of men and their actions was aesthetic rather than moral. He was attracted to large simplicities, and with exquisite urbanity recorded their whims and differences. He wrote an essay on the long-haired Merovingians—that blood-boltered, incestuous, and maniacal dynasty which, in the darkest of ages, founded the Kingdom of the Franks—and discussed their bestial improprieties and the extravagance of their tyranny in a mood of sustained and luminous admiration for their sheer improbability. He wrote a novel, called in its English translation *The Long Ships,* about vikings, and without abating his natural wonder at their strength and audacities created vikings who were real and credible people; where it seemed advisable, he quietly and seriously made fun of them. In Sweden he was not only a very popular writer, but scholars respected him for his sedulously pursued and scrupulous knowledge of history.

In person he was large and slow of movement. A massive figure, a thirsty, witty, and loud-laughing man whose laughter was silenced before the end. In comparison with Charles his chosen hero—that slim, coltish, dedicated and innocent figure—it would not be wholly false or absurdly fanciful to see him as Falstaff (a Falstaff turned bookish and donnish) sitting down to write with love and percipience of a Prince Hal who had never kept bad company and sat late in taverns. Frans Bengtsson sat late in many, but kept good company. At the University of Lund, in the fatly living province of Scania, he spent a somewhat longer time than was strictly necessary for the taking of a degree, and there his chosen friends were Otto Berch, son of a landed proprietor whose farms marched with an estate that had been managed by Bengtsson's father; and Karl Ragnar Gierow, poet and dramatist, who is now Director of the Royal Theatre in Stockholm. It was my good fortune to meet Frans Bengtsson, for the first time, in the company of Otto Berch and Karl Ragnar Gierow—their friendship continued after they had left the university—and my conjoint, inseparable memory is of hearty and generous men who, with analytical noses and discriminating palates, would solemnly discuss their claret and turn, from that grave matter, to loud and lively, but always tolerant, argument about the literature and history of France and England and the hinterlands of Scandinavian culture. They had been educated to a generous knowledge of their world. They were serious in their chosen tasks, but solemn only about their wine—or so it seemed to the visitor they so richly entertained.

But a good many years later I discovered, I think, a closer truth about Frans Bengtsson. I was staying with Otto Berch, in the house he had inherited, and Frans and Karl Ragnar Gierow were also there. We drove one day to the estate where Frans had lived as a boy, and Frans, by that time ponderous in movement (he was older than the other two) and a little pontifical in manner, assumed the authority for telling me, the stranger, how things had been managed, when such-and-such improvements had been made, where So-and-so had lived in his nonage and what he had said and done. He spoke in much the same sort of tone as, in Kipling's poem *The Land,* old Hobden used to the titular proprietor of the fields on which, through unremembered centuries, his ancestors had lived and worked, and asserted his better knowledge of them:

> "Hob, what about that River-bit?" I turn to him again,
> With Fabricius and Ogier and William of Warenne.
> "Hev it jest as you've a mind to, *but*"—and here he takes command.
> For whoever pays the taxes old Mus' Hobden owns the land.

Certainly, that afternoon, Frans Bengtsson sounded as if he held a senior title to the fields on which his father's employer had paid taxes—and through blood or study, or both together, he had, I think, inherited and acquired a true sense of identification with his native soil. He knew its history, and realized his part in it. But because, by sympathy and education and the working of an alertly sensitive mind, he was also a European (and markedly an Anglophile), he had no room in him for either the excesses or the narrownesses of nationalism. Born and bred in Sweden, as much a part and parcel of it as Kipling's Hobden was a Briton of the Clay, his strong aesthetic judgment knew no boundaries but would settle with enthusiasm wherever a native bloom grew tall and straight—and, for preference, a little out of line with its neighbours.

He inspired great affection, and was famous for a gentle eccentricity: he practised the art of playing chess against himself, with perfect impartiality. At the last, he succumbed to melancholy. But melancholy has been the fate of many remarkable men and great minds, from Grettir the Strong to Dean Swift; and Frans, when his humour and geniality had been spent, made their choice of loneliness. The modern world was not entirely to his liking, and who shall complain that his taste was faulty? All that can be said in dispraise of the failure of his will to live is that his sense of humour was less persistent, or less sturdy, than his aesthetic judgment of what he saw and heard.

But his life of Charles XII is the justification of his life. It is a truly noble work in which the passion of a native inspiration is overlaid, calmed, and civilized—but never subdued—by the dispassion of an intelligence which had become as much European as Swedish: a dispassion that lies about the fervour of his admiration for Charles like a smooth, a rather cold, a perfectly lucent pool in which a Moby Dick may swim with small and quainter fishes. There are many strange characters in the pool—it is, of course, an ocean rather than a pool, but clear as a chalkstream—and always it is Charles, it is Moby Dick, who lashes it to storm.

I have likened Frans Bengtsson to a bookish Falstaff in love with an immaculate Prince Hal; I have suggested, as description of his quality, a burly and sometimes jocular aestheticism. But perhaps it would be as close to the truth to see him as an Ahab in pursuit of a great white incommunicable whale—with this difference, that Ahab Bengtsson caught and anatomized his whale. Whether he was still defeated by it must be a matter for opinion. I do not think he was. I think a mind of heroic tincture was successful in its dissection of an heroic capacity—that intelligence and sympathy have analysed a splendid anachronism—and that a literary genius has constructed, from a multitude of characters caught in an enormous web, a magnificent story. (pp. ix-xiii)

Eric Linklater, in an introduction to The Sword Does Not Jest: The Heroic Life of King Charles XII of Sweden *by Frans G. Bengtsson, translated by Naomi Walford, St. Martin's Press, Inc., 1960, pp. ix-xiii.*

Henry G. Leach (essay date 1961)

[*In the following review, Leach praises Bengtsson's accurate depictions of military campaigns in* The Sword Does Not Jest: The Heroic Life of Charles XII of Sweden.]

In some respects [**The Sword Does Not Jest: The Heroic Life of King Charles XII of Sweden**] is the best history of military campaigns since Caesar's *Commentaries*. All facts and contemporary opinions now available more than two centuries after the events are marshalled by Bengtsson, even the exact number of troops and machines in every battle, and the historian records his own interpretation both of the wisdom of the king's planned strategy and the psychology of Peter the Great and of Charles and his men. The account is enhanced by Bengtsson's ironic and imaginative style.

Bengtsson is one of the classic Swedish authors of our century. He may be called a traditionalist, for his poetry is more akin to Longfellow than to Martinson, his essays remind one of the whimsicality of Charles Lamb, his fiction is cousin to Defoe, his histories more like Trevelyan than Toynbee. Merrily he characterizes the obstinate Swedish Admiral Wachtmeister: "The King sent order after order, but Wachtmeister sat on his fleet like a hen on her chickens, anxious and immovable. He would hazard anything else—his blood, his life—but not his lovely ships!"

Frans Bengtsson wrote an essay also about Charles XII, published by The American-Scandinavian Foundation in 1950, in which he explains the King's popularity. Yes, the very name of Charles still evokes adulation in Sweden, and in his lifetime he won the admiration of Western Europe.

In **The Sword Does Not Jest** Bengtsson pays tribute also to his hero's saintly qualities. Charles was ascetic to a degree. He abstained also from alcohol, preferring milk. Nor did he indulge in those outbursts of rhetoric which sometimes win battles for other generals without firing a shot.

May I observe that King Charles was not only a soldier but a mathematician who could have built up a Sweden in the economics of peace, a man whom an Einstein would have enjoyed conversing with. He collaborated with Swedenborg on his dry dock, his salt factory, and his canal, and developed a simpler system of numbers built not on our Arabic decimal system of ten, which requires fractions sometimes incommensurable, but on a number whose cube root is exact. Charles preferred 64 but Swedenborg argued for 8!

Had Charles not been very ill in June, 1709 and obliged to delegate the supreme command to Field-Marshal Rehnsköld, whose military experience had been limited to directing divisions of army, cavalry, or artillery by the King's command, the disaster at Poltava might have been averted. But God—or was it Fortune, or Luck, or Health, or just old Fate, as the King finally thought?—that at last had forsaken the unconquerable Charles before he was able to advance upon Moscow.

Henry G. Leach, in a review of "The Sword Does Not Jest," in The American-Scandinavian Review, *Vol. XLIX, No. 1, Spring, 1961, p. 86.*

Alrik Gustafson (essay date 1961)

[*In the following excerpt from his* A History of Swedish Literature, *Gustafson places Bengtsson in the intellectual milieu of Lund University during the 1930s and describes his prose as a combination of erudition and whimsy.*]

The university community at Lund out of which came one of the major poets of the 1930's, Hjalmar Gullberg, and the poet-dramatist Karl Ragnar Gierow, has also contributed to contemporary Swedish letters three of the most original masters of prose, Frans G. Bengtsson

(1894-1954), Fritiof Nilsson Piraten (b. 1895), and Sigfrid Lindström (1892-1950). Of these three Bengtsson is by far the most versatile, a poet, essayist, and biographer as well as a novelist, while nearly all the work of Nilsson Piraten and Lindström falls into the genres of prose fiction and is basically rather limited and traditional. But each of these authors places the inimitable stamp of his own temperament on conventional literary forms, lending to these forms fresh (if not new) perspectives and turns of thought. Their having been strenuously exposed in formative academic years to the rather special intellectual atmosphere of Lund during and after the First World War has had more than a little to do with their ways of reacting toward life and has influenced sharply the form which their work has taken. The Lund of the 1920's, and for some years earlier, was learned and skeptical and given to a kind of intellectual horseplay which delighted in waggish irony and the spinning of tall tales of whatsoever provenance and variety. Dialectical subtleties, learned discursiveness, challenging irreverences, poetic digressions, burlesque humor, a not exactly modest use of the bottle—these were the motley ingredients of the through-the-night bouts of camaraderie indulged in by some of the more gifted Lund students of the day. Regular attendance at lectures and the systematic pursuit of academic studies were apparently cardinal sins to such students. Bengtsson is perhaps not unduly exaggerating when, in an autobiographical essay entitled **"How I Became an Author,"** he tells us that during "four years at the University . . . I heard ten lectures, wrote a great deal of bad verse, and played three or four games of chess which were good enough to be published." But this offhand attitude toward formal studies led in later years neither to nonscholarly habits of mind nor to professional ineptitude nor to literary sterility on the part of those who, like Bengtsson, may seem to have idled away their university years. Bengtsson himself became with time an amazingly learned man, Nilsson Piraten a highly regarded lawyer, Lindström a competent journalist whose literary production was worlds removed from the superficialities of the daily pursuits of journalism.

Frans G. Bengtsson's learning became, in fact, legendary, and is reflected everywhere in his poetry and prose. But this learning never weighs down his literary work, rather gives to it a rare, venturesome flavor, in part because he handles it with such vigorous zest and in part because his intellectual bent is always on the lookout for strange and exotic phenomena, for unusual and colorful characters and episodes, often out of the distant past and far-flung climes. Bengtsson has been called "the last troubadour," and the label fits him in almost every respect. In a period when Swedish poets sang by preference in restrained, unadorned phrases or experimented with advanced modernistic forms, Bengtsson in his two volumes of verse—*Tärningskast* **(Throw of the Dice,** 1923) and *Legenden om Babel* **(The Legend of Babel,** 1925)—deliberately cultivated ornately overwrought effects and sweeping sonorous cadences. In a sense he was just as traditional in his choice of subject matter, ransacking the corridors of legend and history for colorful and finely toothsome motifs and themes, motifs and themes worthy of a learned modern troubadour's lute. When he turned to prose (which he did early) he was just as belligerently traditional in taste, his essays resembling in form the informal essays of such English Romantics as Lamb and Hazlitt, and his two arresting ventures in extended prose forms—the two-volume biography of Charles XII (tr. *The Life of Charles XII, King of Sweden 1697-1718,* 1935, 1936) and the novel *Röde Orm* (tr. *The Long Ships,* 1941, 1945)—being conceived and executed in respectively heroic-romantic and burlesque-romantic veins.

Bengtsson's poetry is competent but somewhat strained in its effects, and on the whole it has not worn well. It was as an essayist that he first attracted a host of admirers, a host which increased rapidly in numbers with each successive volume. His first collection of essays bore the title *Litterörer och militärer* **(Literary and Military Figures,** 1929), followed in Bengtsson's lifetime by *Silversköldarna* **(The Silver Shields,** 1931), *De långhåriga merovingerna* **(The Longhaired Merovingians,** 1933), and *Sällskap för en eremit* **(Company for a Hermit,** 1938). A posthumous collection, *Folk som sjöng och andra essayer* **(People Who Sang and Other Essays),** appeared in 1955. One of the reasons for Bengtsson's smashing success as an essayist was that the informal essay as a respectable literary genre was before his appearance practically nonexistent in Swedish literature. His success in the genre was partly the success of novelty. Swedish poets and novelists of distinction could be numbered in the dozens if not scores, but no essayists of real distinction had appeared before Bengtsson in 1929. But Bengtsson's success as an essayist derives even more from the fact that he was really a master of the genre, a natural purveyor of informal prose which need not fear comparison with some of the greatest French and English essayists.

He invariably writes about what he likes, as all great informal essayists have done. Many of his essays are on literary or historical subjects, but he tosses off with equal facility and comprehension delightful and often pungent observations on such diverse subjects as ghost stories and the difficulty of maintaining an optimistic view of human existence; popular ditties and man's relation to nature; the mysteries of the ant world and the fine art of lying. Adventurers from all times and climes and military heroes from the earliest ages down to the American Civil War especially attract him, as do great literary individualists such as Byron, Carlyle, and Henry David Thoreau, whose *Walden* he has rendered into Swedish. Among his other notable translations have been those of *The Song of Roland* and *Paradise Lost.* Fabulous erudition vies with offhand whimsicalities in nearly all of Bengtsson's essays, as in the famous one on Villon in which he notes in passing, without batting an eyelash: "He was at this time twenty-five years old and had just committed his first murder and written his first longer poem, fairly innocuous things both." At times whimsicality takes over completely, as when he writes about his curious vagaries in matters of literary taste (**"Before a Bookshelf"**) or provides the reader with an inventory of the physical and mental habits of semi-domesticated cats, rats, and bats (**"My Closest Companions"**). A reasonably representative selection of Bengtsson's essays is available in English under the title *A Walk to an Ant Hill and Other Essays.* All in all Bengtsson may be said to combine in his essays the whimsicalities of Charles Lamb, the vigor and independence of spirit of William Hazlitt, and the heroic-romantic idealism of Robert Louis Stevenson. The only flaw which mars his essays is an occasional bit of stylistic coquetry.

Bengtsson's frequent preoccupation in his essays with past heroic ages and their representative personalities carries over into his two larger works, on Charles XII and on the Viking period. In his biography of Charles XII he is at his brilliant best in the serious reconstruction of history; in *The Long Ships* he is at his zestful best in a burlesque treatment of the Viking age. In both of these works he shoulders his learning effortlessly, with the skill of a scholar who defies the dust of learning and recaptures those vital realities of life in the past which have too often been written about in heavy, measured, lifeless periods. Which of these two works is his best is a matter of taste. Each of them is in its kind a masterpiece, the Charles XII biography majestic and monumental in line, *The Long Ships* gutty and sly in its human portraiture, madly comic in its handling of episode and narrative movement. Perhaps the Charles XII work will weigh heavier in the judgment of future generations, especially because in the presence of the final fate of Sweden's hero king Bengtsson dispenses with his usual freewheeling style and faces the tragic dilemma of human life on a level of utterance worthy of his elevated subject. Bengtsson's motto as an artist was, "I paint thus, donna Bianca, because it amuses me to paint this way," but in the Charles XII book he painted for this and *other* reasons. (pp. 529-32)

Alrik Gustafson, "The Modernistic Ground Swell and Attendant Social Criticism," in his A History of Swedish Literature, *University of Minnesota Press, 1961, 438-540.*

FURTHER READING

Bullock, Florence Haxton. Review of *Red Orm*, by Frans Bengtsson. *The New York Herald Tribune Weekly Books* 19, No. 34 (18 April 1943): 10.
    Favorable assessment of *Red Orm*.

Strode, Hudson. "A Fine, Brave Tale of the Viking Days." *The New York Herald Tribune Book Review* (19 September 1954): 5.
    Praises *The Long Ships* as "the finest evocation of the Viking age that this reviewer has ever read."

Hans Carossa
1878-1956

German autobiographer, novelist, and poet.

INTRODUCTION

Carossa is best known for novels and works of autobiography that express his search for self-realization and his attempts to reconcile his conflicting ambitions as both a doctor and a writer. These works reflect Carossa's admiration for Johann Wolfgang von Goethe, particularly Goethe's advocacy of individualism and the contemplative life. Critics have praised Carossa for his precise and lucid prose style, for his revival of Goethean thought, and for the humane and highly spiritual qualities that characterize his life and works.

Carossa was born in 1878 in Bad-Tölz, Bavaria. Both his father and grandfather were physicians, the profession which Carossa himself later chose. On his fifteenth birthday, Carossa's parents presented him with a fifteen-volume edition of Goethe's works. Between 1898 and 1903, Carossa studied medicine in Munich, Nuremburg, and Leipzig, receiving his M.D. from the University of Leipzig in 1903. Carossa inherited his father's medical practice in 1906 and worked as a doctor in Bavaria for the rest of his life.

In 1907 Carossa published his first work, the poetry collection *Stella Mystica*. That year also marked the beginning of his correspondence with the Austrian writer Hugo von Hofmannsthal, who became his mentor. Carossa published his second volume of poetry, *Gedichte*, in 1910 and for the remainder of his life continued to publish poetry on a regular basis. *Doktor Bürgers Ende,* his first novel, was published in 1913. During World War I, Carossa served as a medical officer on the eastern and western fronts, and his wartime experiences were recorded in *Rumänisches Tagebuch* (*A Roumanian Diary*). During the 1920s and early 1930s, Carossa produced three more works of autobiography and the novel *Der Arzt Gion* (*Doctor Gion*). The Nazi party's rise to power in Germany and its claim that nazism was a pure expression of Goethean thought prompted Carossa to write two works, a novel and a volume of autobiography, that condemned the party's policies and tenets. In the novel *Geheimnisse des reifen Lebens,* Carossa described an unnamed country in which young men dressed in black uniforms conduct mass arrests. Although the autobiographical *Das Jahr der schönen Täuschungen* concerns the German people's delusions of grandeur in 1900, critics believe that Carossa intended the work to be a thinly disguised critique of the nazis' delusions of 1940. Carossa refused to give public sanction to the party's programs and institutions despite the nazis' persistent demands for such support. However, he occasionally made concessions in return for the release

of prisoners, such as the Jewish writer Alfred Mombert, from concentration camps. In *Ungleiche Welten,* Carossa recounted his life in nazi Germany. Carossa completed *Der Tag des jungen Arztes,* the final book in his autobiographical sequence, in 1955, one year before his death.

Carossa's novels and autobiographies focus on moral and spiritual issues. In these works the overarching theme is the importance of achieving a synthesis of one's artistic aspirations and one's responsibilities to society. The autobiographical works *Eine Kindheit* (*A Childhood*) and *Verwandlungen einer Jugend* (*Boyhood and Youth*) trace the development of Carossa's imaginative traits which eventually culminates in his desire to become an artist. Parallel to his artistic development is the growing awareness of his responsibility to society and the importance of self-sacrifice. Carossa's final volume of autobiography, *Der Tag des jungen Arztes,* concerns the conflict between his life as a doctor and his life as a writer. In his fiction Carossa most clearly articulated this theme in *Doktor Bürgers Ende,* a novel about a young doctor whose inability to reconcile his longings for a life devoted to art with the ethical demands of a medical career leads to suicide. Nevertheless, Carossa's prose works convey a strong sense of optimism, a quality especially evident in the novel *Doctor Gion,* in which the protagonist succeeds in healing his patients both physically and spiritually. Dr. Gion guides his patients, whom critics contend are symbols of post–World War I Germany, to an understanding of the principles, such as composure and detachment in the face of turmoil, on which he believes life should be based.

In his novels and autobiographies, Carossa focused on incidents of everyday life, avoiding the depiction of dramatic events or intense emotion. For example, *Doktor Bürgers Ende* presents a first person account of a doctor's daily routine, revealing the mental suffering of the troubled main character only indirectly. While some critics have argued that the anecdotes that comprise much of Carossa's work are occasionally superfluous to his larger themes, others find his meticulous attention to mundane incidents praiseworthy because in them, they argue, he observes significance in details that many writers overlook. In a review of *A Childhood* and *Boyhood and Youth,* Edwin Muir has written that out of seemingly trifling events Carossa "constructed . . . a more complete and proportioned image of the world than any other writer of his time."

PRINCIPAL WORKS

Stella mystica (poetry) 1907
Gedichte (poetry) 1910; also published as *Gesammelte Gedichte* [enlarged edition], 1948
Doktor Bürgers Ende (novel) 1913; also published as *Die Schicksale Doktor Bürgers,* 1930
Eine Kindheit (autobiography) 1922
  [*A Childhood,* 1930]
Rumänisches Tagebuch (autobiography) 1924; also published as *Tagebuch im Kriege,* 1934
  [*A Roumanian Diary,* 1930]
Verwandlungen einer Jugend (autobiography) 1928
  [*Boyhood and Youth,* 1930]
Der Arzt Gion (novel) 1931
  [*Doctor Gion,* 1933]
Führung und Geleit (autobiography) 1933
Geheimnisse des reifen Lebens (novel) 1936
Das Jahr der schönen Täuschungen (autobiography) 1941
  [*Year of Sweet Illusions,* 1950]
Gesammelte Werke. 2 vols. (novels, autobiography, and poetry) 1949-50
Ungleiche Welten (autobiography) 1951
Der Tag des jungen Arztes (autobiography) 1953; also published as *Der Tag des jungen Arztes* [enlarged edition], 1955

---

*These works were published in 1957 as *Geschichte einer Jugend* and are collectively referred to as "Jugendgeschichte."

CRITICISM

Edwin Muir (essay date 1930)

[*Muir was a distinguished Scottish novelist, poet, critic, and translator. With his wife, Willa, he translated works by various German authors unfamiliar to the English-speaking world, including Gerhart Hauptmann, Hermann Broch, and, most notably, Franz Kafka. Throughout his career, Muir was intrigued by psychoanalytic theory, particularly Sigmund Freud's analyses of dreams and Carl Gustav Jung's theories of archetypal imagery, both of which he often utilized in his work. In the following excerpt, he comments on the themes and style of* A Roumanian Diary, A Childhood, *and* Boyhood and Youth.]

In December 1928 there appeared in Germany under the imprint of the Insel Verlag a beautifully produced little volume in honor of the fiftieth birthday of Hans Carossa. Among the twenty-five writers who collaborated in rendering him homage were Austria's two greatest poets, Hugo von Hofmannsthal and Rainer Maria Rilke, and several of Germany's most gifted young writers, among them Paul Alverdes, whose small but exquisite masterpiece, *The Whistlers' Room,* has since been translated into English. At that time Carossa's name, I think it is safe to say, was virtually unknown either in England or America; and even now only the few who have happened to come across that strange book, ***A Roumanian Diary,*** published some time ago, will recognize it. That little volume had itself an ironical fate. It was caught in the spate of war books, and seems to have been allotted for review to experts who wished to see how Roumanian atrocities compared with Russian, or to generals who were resolved to uphold their own ideas on strategy against the author's. It was, however, a book bound to puzzle or exasperate the ordinary war reviewer; for, although the diary of a busy medical officer during the German campaign against Roumania, the most moving incident in it was the death of a cat. Besides, there was no glorification or impeachment of warfare, no noticeable symptom of patriotism or of pacifism: none of the usual and natural responses to the War.

There is indeed something enigmatical in all Carossa's books. He has a trick of unexpected emphasis, of passing over things which other writers would seize upon, and concentrating, yet never disproportionately, on some point which, but for his vigilance, would have been overlooked. These points are chosen with an unfathomable skill, by a faculty not so much of selection as of subconscious divination; and the light in which he sets them irradiates all the stretches of experience, whether terrible or merely dull, lying between, so that these never need to be described. Carossa's uniform method as a writer is to make some great alteration in our imaginative conception of life while ostensibly making only a minute one; and his art is an art almost entirely of implication. It is this, probably, that makes one feel in all his writings a sort of natural magic; a natural magic not fugitive and indefinable as in poetry, but constant and almost reasonable. Everything he touches is transmuted, yet never robbed of its diurnal reality; it becomes—one can only put it in this way—at once more ordinary and more strange.

Occupation with trifles, submission of experience to mysterious lights: these are often ways of escaping from problems too disagreeable for the writer to face; and a hasty reader might find Carossa evasive. But one has only to turn to a passage here and there in *A Roumanian Diary* to see how great is one's mistake. The following, for example:

> Like a swarm of hornets the shells dashed against the rocks, tearing the flesh from the limbs of the living and the dead. Sometimes German wounded called to us, sometimes Roumanian, who were now being mutilated for a second time by the fire of their comrades. Some of them suffered in silence; others twisted like wounded snakes. Through the zone of death we saw Germans lightly wounded descending the mountain, a few white and shaken, but others walking jauntily, dressed up as if for a fancy-dress ball in the gay-colored belts, jackets, and military decorations of their dead enemies. One had brought back a gramophone with him from the Roumanian lines; now an idea suddenly struck him, he placed it on a stone and set it going, the page in *Figaro* began to sing, and like the voice of a mad soul Mozart's music rose in a world of ruin.

Or again:

> Turning round I looked down in the face of a dying man of about thirty; his eyes were closed, his mouth terribly twisted with pain. His fingers still clutched fast the hem of my cloak. Through a gray cape which covered his breast a slight vapor was rising; R. threw it back; under his torn ribs his lungs and heart lay exposed, the heart beating sluggishly.

(pp. 404-05)

How can one describe the spirit which breathes through these two scenes? It is a soft light that beats upon them; yet how definite is the detail, macabre in the gramophone-playing, horrible in the "slight vapor" rising from the dying man's breast. There is a sentence in the same book which suggests better than any formula could Carossa's implicit attitude to his themes: "The world, rough, raw and monstrous as it is—I live in it as in a thin and gaudily iridescent soap-bubble, holding my breath to keep it from bursting". In his books every object is touched with the solicitous skill of a physician who knows the pressure which will maintain its true shape, or restore it, if it is lost, and who "holds his breath" lest any too violent movement should injure or destroy it, whether it be "raw and monstrous" or delicate. Every object is to him like a thing infinitely fragile and infinitely valuable, which must not even be handled too much, but rather placed in a not too urgent light. His style is a pure illuminating medium. It is clear as water; but it has an inner lustre like the limpid stream he found near the Roumanian front, which gave the common brown pebbles a gleam as of gold. He dips an object or an experience into that stream, and immediately it glows with all the hues which the customary light has dulled or worn away. His books paint a perpetual morning world where all things seem newly awakened, and have their first bloom upon them.

This quiet radiance plays with a particular magic round the scenes in his two little masterpieces, *Eine Kindheit* and *Verwandlungen einer Jugend.* There has probably been no books on childhood such as these since mystics like Traherne. By an inflection here and there, by the rhythm of the prose, sweet, tranquil and pure, they do indeed faintly but persistently recall Traherne. But the radiance which lies over them is less bright, and more diffused; it does not come directly from heaven, like Traherne's, but circuitously, through the hidden forces of the earth, which to the child are secretly bound with the heavenly ones. It is imminent in such things as a favorite splinter of granite, or a glass bead which the boy loves to swing against the window-pane; in all animals, in stones and trees, in houses, and especially in the house which is his home. To this world can be applied the words which Hofmannsthal applied to Carossa's work itself. "Of Carossa's books," he says, "nay, of any chapter in them, one can speak as of some mysteriously operative substance such as radium from which a life-giving power goes out, only some of whose effects we know, and through which we feel that we are brought in contact with quite obscure realms; yet those powers work in silence, and are more akin to the powers in the growing seed or in the tree which heals itself than to those which come to being in the tempest." Sometimes those forces appear in some dreadful guise, but then the child feels protective powers spontaneously arising to restore the balance, and heal the wound in the world which enfolds him. Take this curious passage, for example, from *Eine Kindheit:*

> All things, even the most terrible, when we encounter them, must take on a form consonant with our own nature; everyone has a profound knowledge of this, and because of it good men live in the world without fear. I had never been a nervous child, and though I had no desire to look on death, neither did I ever try to avoid it. With a feeling of solemn exaltation, while a shudder which brought tears to my eyes ran over me, I had seen in the mortuary the robed dead lying between their burning candles, and I had not thought of corruption. The feeling that the invisible God Who chose to manifest Himself in shadowy hints had here for once operated solemnly and immediately: this childish feeling with its grave terrors mastered me and allowed no trace of animal panic to rise. Strangely comforted I went my way, and everyone I met afterwards seemed to me very beautiful and good.

Here we see clearly the powers which make the bark of the tree heal itself, and the reciprocal working of the forms of the child's world.

To these forces the child resigns himself with an astonishing faith, which may be due simply to the fact that being three-parts potentiality, he has a deeper knowledge of all potential things than a grown man can have. Accordingly his affection goes out to all sorts of objects, making us feel that the life of children is indeed a kind of fabulous life. (pp. 405-06)

Carossa's world of childhood has another main quality which all but the greatest writers on childhood have overlooked: it has an order far more immutable than that of the adult's world, an order in which all things seem to have rested on their stations forever. There like eternal patterns exist the figures, simple as an abstraction, immutable as the tables of a law, of father and mother, servant and teacher; figures which indeed seem all the more intensely real because they are incarnate symbols, because father and mother and teacher and servant are more than the general idea of a human being, and because through them the child guesses at the order of the world and resigns himself to it with greater security. That order is to him almost absolutely permanent; for the child has a sense of duration which not only runs back, like ours, into the past, but—as it has not still been undermined by doubt—forward into the future as well. In that world everything seems to have an additional dimension, and to exist in some space at right angles to Time; and it is here, and not in isolated passages, that Carossa reminds us of Traherne. As one watches the little boy in *Eine Kindheit* moving with such mysterious confidence and certainty in his world filled with beings greater than himself, one is reminded of the famous passage in which Traherne tells how, on "a lowering and sad evening, being alone in the field, when all things were dead and quiet, a certain want and horror" fell upon him. He goes on to tell of the thoughts which came to comfort him, and some of these seem to take us into the very heart of Carossa's work. Among them were that he was "concerned in all the world", that "in the remotest borders the causes of peace" delighted him, that "a remembrance of all the joys" he had from his birth ought always to be with him, and that "the presence of Cities, Temples, and Kingdoms" ought to sustain him.

This is an almost complete key to Carossa's work. His intention, never explicit, is essentially to show that we are concerned in all the world and that distant and invisible things, "the presence of Cities, Temples, and Kingdoms", sustain us, and, more particularly in his books on childhood, to remind us of all the joys we have had from our birth. There is, it can almost be said, no pain in his books, for pain has been transmuted in memory, or understood anew in relation to all that world in which we are concerned. In reading even his most trifling incidents we are conscious of the unshakable order of that world; and the movements of his figures there have something of the serenity of the motions of the stars. Trifling or erratic at first sight, we presently feel in them the thrill of an ethereal harmony, which comes from our divination that here all the things that have been torn from their stations have been set back upon them again. This is Carossa's rare distinction as a writer: that he not merely describes things, but quietly, as if by an act of mystical legerdemain, restores them to their places—where alone they are truly what they ought to be. This is why there is serenity in his descriptions even of pain. He does not soften it; he sees it as a mysterious and terrible force; but in the powers which rise to combat it he discerns the order of the world, and remembers that we all rest upon it. He has a constant sense that at every moment, no matter how terrible, the reconciling powers which hold the universe together are near us. His apprehension of those powers is in the last resort a mystical one; and like all mystics he finds significance in incidents and modes of experience which by the normal mind are accepted either as mysteries or commonplaces. But he differs from most mystics in always trying to provide a practical and everyday justification for his intuitions; for his perpetual object is completeness. It is therefore only in some of his rare dreams that we get a pure mystical vision, which he sets down without comment, and simply as part of the reality which he is trying to understand.

> I was a child again, and walking over stony mountains through a thunderstorm. I had a white scroll of paper in my hand, and did not lift my eyes from it. If I ask myself now what was on that white scroll, I must confess that it was blank, not a letter nor a sign on it; and yet I was enraptured by what I read there. Low rolling clouds rained upon it, lightning flashes flickered over it, the sky and the crags thundered, and from the distance the uncanny spirits of the dead called to me; but I read ineffably blissful words upon that blank paper, and was unmoved by the storm and the cries of the dead.

Even when he is describing the cries of the dying, Carossa seems to be reading on this scroll which is invisible to us of things which have lent to his utterance that peculiar purity, sweetness and serenity which are without a rival in modern German prose.

There has been a sort of literary agitation recently against books on childhood, an agitation justified partly, no doubt, by the mawkishness or irresponsibility of so much of that class of literature. It is assumed, and nine times out of ten perhaps rightly, that the writer is indirectly attempting to reassume the privileges of the child, and to be found charming by being found appealing. Yet it is obvious that there are as many ways of writing about the preoccupations of childhood as about those of adulthood; about sex, for example, to take the most salient of all, for its advent marks the end of the one stage and the beginning of the other. The saving virtue in any description of childhood and love, both so difficult to describe without excess of sentiment, is a sense of proportion, a just evaluation of the most subtle and yet insistent realities; and this virtue Carossa has in a high degree. For a writer who tries to set every object in its place in relation to the whole cannot overlook the fact that his main theme, childhood, has its right relation too; and it is impossible that he should treat it in the style, for example, of Mr. A. A. Milne or Sir James Barrie. With Carossa the choice of childhood is indeed, one almost feels, a just incident of his method as a writer, which is, as I have said, to emphasize an overlooked factor, and to make a great alteration in our imaginative conception of life while ostensibly making only a small one. In describing the child growing up within its unit of the family, he insensibly evokes for us an image of humanity growing up within a unity far larger and more complex, yet still human. And, as he describes them, the virtues of this smaller economy are the same essentially as those of the greater. Childhood is not to him, as it is to Sir James Barrie, the period of irresponsibility; he is free from that almost universal illusion of the adult mind looking back on its first protected years. On the contrary he shows the child reasoning on cause and effect, guessing at and taking on responsibility almost as naturally as it plays and day-dreams, and recognizing gradually that it is part of an economy.

This is one of the qualities which distinguish Carossa's descriptions of childhood from those of more conventional writers; another is his strong sense of continuity and tradition. Real integrity in a people consists in its truth to the deepest things in its experience from the time of its emergence; real integrity in an individual consists in the same thing. This is no doubt the true sense in which the child is father to the man; and this also is probably what makes us feel that the man who has quite erased his childhood is distorted from the pre-ordained human norm. In reading Carossa we divine that the truths which he expresses reach back through all his life; that they have the same continuously creative force as the traditions of a people. So although his subject matter is limited, he is more naturally and universally human than any other writer of his age. Nor is his humanity merely quietistic; the virtues he unobtrusively fortifies in us are active ones, and he fortifies them in the most natural way, by means of those "life-giving powers" of which Hofmannsthal spoke, "only some of whose effects we know", but all of which are salutary. He himself was for many years a busy doctor in the poor quarter of Munich, and an overworked medical officer during the War. And this fact may perhaps best explain his gnomic sentence, already quoted, about the "rough, raw and monstrous" world which one must live in as in a soap-bubble, holding one's breath to keep it from bursting. In his daily life he saw no doubt enough of the rawness of the world; yet his vocation taught him that its health or sickness, its harmony or disharmony, depended upon an almost infinitesimal delicacy of balance, which a single erroneous movement could derange. Every sentence he wrote holds this double implication: of a world "rough, raw and monstrous", and yet depending upon a balance of forces so sensitive that the mind can only guess at it. His two most characteristic books describe a few trifling incidents in the life of a boy; yet out of these he has constructed probably a more complete and proportioned image of the world than any other writer of his time. (pp. 406-08)

Edwin Muir, "A Note on Hans Carossa," in The Bookman, *New York, Vol. LXXII, No. 4, December, 1930, pp. 404-08.*

William Maxwell (essay date 1932)

[*An American novelist, short story writer, editor, and critic, Maxwell worked as a fiction editor for the* New Yorker *for nearly forty years. In the following excerpt, he commends Carossa for his realistic re-creations of a child's experience in* A Childhood.]

Ever since Richard Hughes's little fiends took over the pirate ship on that hilarious but far from innocent voyage, it is the fashion to look at all children through the heavy bi-focals of the modern psychologist, and to find them as chockfull of potential criminality as their poor but inhibited fathers and mothers. The attitude of the traditional author recreating his own childhood is different. He assumes nearly always that when he was a child, the world, too, was somewhat younger, and brightness fell rather more frequently from the air. The older method at its best, as it is in the opening pages of Goethe's *Dichtung und Wahrheit* and as it is in [*A Childhood*] by Hans Carossa, illuminates certain moments of childhood with such an intense light that forever after, thinking of them, one has to stop and remember, uncertain whether they actually occurred or one read about them in a book.

The child with whom this book is concerned is in no apparent way different from other children. He is no less inquisitive, no less relentlessly logical. All things he accepts at their face value, and his credulity strains neither at gnat nor at camel. Because of his literal-mindedness he frequently is taken in, thereby seeing the world as much from the inside as from the out.

His universe is the quiet, ageless, picture-book world of a Bavarian village; more particularly it is the house, the garden, the market place and the school. It is no ordinary world. And there is little of the commonplace about the people he knows best—the freckle-faced, much abused daughter of the ranger, who is wont to retire periodically for cakes and comfort to those "wise and lovely" beasts, the stags that live under the hill; or the cruel, strangely twisted coffin-maker's son; or the charming and devoted Eva, whose parents had once owned a circus, and who first longs to be a white horse, and later to ride one; or most fascinating of all, the old and broken magician who holds his small grand-nephew speechless and enchanted for half of one night, with the help of his old red robe, his tall, gold-embroidered scarlet cap, his magic wand, and a large quantity of colored paper, silken flowers, candles and conjuror's clap-trap.

So actual is this childhood that one must attribute to the author a power as potent as animates certain moments of childhood. But Uncle Georg's magic was not infallible. When the child shattered his glass against the floor, laid the fragments at his great-uncle's feet and, clasping his knees, begged him to make it whole again, the old man only gazed long at him and said, "Perhaps some other time. I'm too tired tonight." Hans Carossa's interpretation of the child mind likewise has its limitations. The incidents of the book are thoroughly real, and the illusion complete, but the final meaning, the inner portion of childhood, is not here.

The significance, at times bordering upon the mystical, which he attaches to these sharply remembered happenings, and the profounder implication which he occasionally makes are clearly the attempt of a mature mind to reconstruct, with certain memories as symbols, the intricate order of ideas, impressions and fancies in this child's mind. But a child's mind works through symbols that are either unintelligible or unknown, nearly always, to the adult. To reconstruct the metaphysics of a seven-year-old requires a more genuine magic than Uncle Georg's, and a more direct intuition than the author of *A Childhood* possesses. Perhaps it is impossible.

William Maxwell, "The Clues in the House,"

in New York Herald Tribune Books, *April 10, 1932, p. 2.*

Graham Greene (essay date 1933)

[*A prominent English novelist, Greene is noted for his best-selling suspense novels and for more serious works of fiction, particularly* The Power and the Glory *(1940). In his major works, he explored the problems of spiritually and socially alienated individuals living in the corrupt and corrupting societies of the twentieth century. Considered a shrewd literary critic, Greene exhibited a taste for the works of neglected authors. In the following excerpt from a review of* Doctor Gion, *he finds the novel is flawed by poorly depicted characters and overwrought symbolism.*]

Doctor Gion is a puzzling and disappointing book. Herr Carossa has won a very high reputation by his autobiographical studies, but faced in his novel for the first time with the need of inventing relationships which have no existence outside his brain, he fails. These characters—the young doctor, the sculptress who in her nervous fear of life is meant to symbolize post-War Germany where men and women under the shock of death and disaster hesitate to bring children into the world, the young pregnant peasant woman, symbol of reviving hope—are emotionally real to the author, but he cannot find the descriptions, the dialogue, the intonations which will make them real to others. . . .

It is interesting to try to find the point at which **Doctor Gion** loses interest. The conception is a good one: a doctor with a clinical imagination a little obsessed by symptoms studies from his surgery "the prison of this age."

> Daily he had been assailed by disheartened spirits, inimical to all new life; he saw the joy of existence gradually diminishing in all classes of the population; the numbers of those who turned away from it yearly increasing, and at times, in hours of gloomy foreboding, he would remember that oceanic tribe who, having come under the rulership of white men, no longer regarded life as worth the living, refused to propagate themselves and quickly died out.

Cynthia, the sculptress, is an example of this new attitude:

> He could not but honour the ruthlessness with which she wished to conquer the demon of the age by repudiating her inmost femininity and sending into the world, instead of small children dooned to death, a series of perfected shapes in clay, wood or marble.

If only Herr Carossa had stopped there, had contented himself with noting and had not, like Doctor Gion, tried to cure. For with the introduction of the peasant girl who consciously surrenders her life in order that her child may be born, the symbolism of the story begins to weigh it down. Symbolism should be insinuated; it should appeal to the reader unconsciously. This maternal peasant, the star-gazing child whom Doctor Gion adopts, the war-shocked ex-serviceman who is cured of his mistrust by the child's gift of his telescope, are like marble moralities on the plinth of a memorial. And as the story slips towards the bathos of emblematic sculptuary, the tenderness of its tone becomes an insult to the despairing world it criticizes.

Graham Greene, in a review of "Doctor Gion," in The Spectator, *Vol. 150, No. 5469, April 21, 1933, p. 579.*

Harold Strauss (essay date 1933)

[*Strauss was an American critic. In the following excerpt from a review of* Doctor Gion, *he praises Carossa's style.*]

There is a special quality which suffuses Hans Carossa's writing and somehow obliterates such ordinary factors as characterization and structure. Carossa is a physician; during the war he was a medical officer. In all his books, **Childhood, A Rumanian Diary,** and now in **Dr. Gion,** a physician plays an important role and memories of the war loom large. This indicates how much of himself Carossa puts into his books, and at the same time provides the key to his style.

He seems to open a relaxed mind to the small trickles of memory which are passed unnoticed by novelists more grimly and rigidly addicted to plot. He catches up an association and, by the mere pondering of its presence, makes a book. A quiet book, it is true; a book in which nothing very much happens and which arrives at no very definite end; but somehow a restful and satisfying book. **Dr. Gion** is the word-graph of the mind of a poet as it dwells on an episode, a mood, a face, on nothing. . . .

Carossa is not a dramatist. He never tries to crystallize relationships that are fluent, never strains after form and suspense. He is a doctor who preserves a bedside manner toward his characters, and he has the poet's boldness and license to generalize. What he says would be brash for another; but so infectious is his mood of quiet revery that one has no choice but to surrender. This is a special sort of book which commands a special audience; but that audience will not be faint in its praise.

Harold Strauss, "Hans Carossa's 'Dr. Gion' and Other Recent Works of Fiction," in The New York Times Book Review, *June 4, 1933, p. 6.*

Ronald Peacock (essay date 1938)

[*Peacock is an English critic and educator. In the following essay, he provides an overview of Carossa's themes and techniques.*]

At a time when one set of literary adventurers is giving place to another it is very comforting to come across a figure of unquestioned integrity, one who is clearly rooted in life and a profession, and is obviously much more anxious about philosophical salvation than literary fame. This is not to say there are no writers living eminent by virtue of their art alone. There *are,* and some of them are greater writers than Carossa. But in the circumstances in which we are involved at the present day—and this applies, I sug-

> **An excerpt from *Führung und Geleit* (*Guidance and Companionship*)**
>
> When at the age of twenty-four I settled in the magnificently situated peninsular city of Passau to treat patients, I did so with reservations. I intended to carry on my medical practice only as a secondary occupation, while devoting most of the time to being a poet. I had no clear idea how this was to be accomplished, but regarding one thing I was certain: everyone should know the work, but no one the author. But how much had I misjudged my own nature, and how completely the magical attractive powers of suffering! At first I met the fate of all physicians who begin to practice; it was particularly the serious cases, those that had been abandoned by others, which filled my waiting room. Many assumed that I came from the university equipped with new infallible methods and expected the impossible. Others had known my father as a capable physician and regarded the son as having inherited his experience. The patients in this second group made it least difficult for me; they were already satisfied when I prescribed for them the white pilocarpin tablets, of which the wrapper carried my father's signature.
>
> It happened that one of my first charges was a very beautiful girl, who did gold embroidery and who with her deaf, almost blind mother occupied three rooms along the Lower Sand. When I say "a very beautiful girl" I am thinking only of her face which to the very last day resisted decay, while the rest of her body irresistibly wasted away. . . . In the countenance and nature of the girl I saw a harmonious mingling of Romanic and Old Bavarian ancestral spirits, while the chill of the imminent end which enveloped her figure gave to her trust an irreplaceable value. Actually, she was already beyond all medical treatment, and her godfather acted against her wish when he brought me to her. Yet she showed no irritation because of the surprise visit, and behaved in a very friendly manner. Nevertheless, she first subjected me to a small test. When I examined her heart I heard no beat; the rhythmic pulsations of the left chest wall were likewise absent. Only after listening very attentively could faint distant sounds be heard. "Where have you hidden your heart?" I said; whereupon she laughed: "Now I know at least that when you listen you also hear something. It took some time before your predecessor discovered that my heart is not in the right place."—The cunning one had suppressed the fact that she had been born with a *Situs inversus,* an abnormal location of the organs, where the heart is situated on the right side and the liver on the left. This slight evidence of alertness was enough for her to place her entire confidence in me. Subsequently, she also appeared to give me considerable credit for not showing any fear of infection. Calmly and serenely this uncomplainingly dying girl introduced me to the dark realm of patient suffering and death, so that for a long time I did not recognize it. Unnoticed I became deeply rooted in it and labored in it with all my energy.
>
> Hans Carossa, in his Führung und Geleit, in 400 Years of a Doctor's Life, edited by George Rosen and Beate Caspari-Rosen, New York: Henry Schuman, Inc., 1947.

we know to be practising what he preaches, and to be preaching a wisdom patiently extracted from his daily experience, and honestly believed in. This is Carossa's unique distinction amongst writers of the day. He is by no means the only one whose personality is laid bare in his work; but in his case we have no misgivings at the spectacle. *Ein Mensch!*

Hans Carossa might be called a moralist in the sense in which Thomas Mann uses the word of himself; of one interested in human life and human behaviour, observing men and their ways and commenting on them. There is a clearer tradition of such writing in France than anywhere else, perhaps; the writings of Montaigne, La Bruyère and La Rochefoucauld form a kind to themselves. The English essayists of the eighteenth century are very closely related. There is no tradition of this sort in Germany; the moralist temperament with an itch to write has in consequence tended to use the medium of the novel. But instead of fiction on a big inventive scale, as in Balzac or Dickens or Keller, we have thinly disguised autobiography, reminiscence.

Carossa's work is of this kind. His **Tagebuch im Kriege** is a record of a few months' service mainly on the eastern front in 1916. **Führung und Geleit** is a book of reminiscences. **Eine Kindheit** and **Verwandlungen einer Jugend** are autobiographical. **Die Schicksale Dr. Bürgers, Der Arzt Gion** and **Geheimnisse des reifen Lebens** are tales; but in character they are like the other works. Everywhere there is the record of personal experience, of life and things approached in a philosophical way, first with the aim of discovering the truth about them, and secondly of arriving at fundamental principles of living. In relation to his books we do not ask the question: what is his vision of life?—as we might with Hardy or Mrs. Woolf; nor is it (in the fashion of recent years): what is the 'experience' which urged itself into expression?—as in Mann or perhaps Wiechert; but we are above all interested in the way the man makes contact with experience and how from that contact he learns something about life and the mastering of it. Whilst he approaches life, and all it has to show him, in an open way, that is to say, whilst he is intent and curious about almost all things, the impulse that is most characteristic of him is seen clearest when he is dealing with moments or events or situations from which he crystallizes his philosophy; at least his work is certainly most satisfactory then. For the usual means which the novelist relies on to keep the interest of the reader are for the greater part entirely lacking. There is no vivid portrayal of character, no plot worth speaking of even in his tales, no suspense, no excitement, no sustained interest in a set of people agitated by events or destiny. The important thing the whole time is an attitude. He is a quiet man, contemplating life; aware of the mystery, not without a shy metaphysical strain, but determined to have control of himself and his own business, and thus control life within his own sphere as far as human limits, of which he is humbly conscious, allow; and never to give way even under the greatest stress.

> Im Grunde fühlt wohl jeder einen Sinn in sich,
> der mit und über allen Planeten weiss und wirkt.
> Bleiben wir im engsten Kreise wachsam! Wenn

gest, to more countries than Germany—there is something peculiarly reassuring and attractive in a man whom

> einer vom eigenen Mittelpunkt aus das Nächste, Notwendige erkennt und löst, wie kann ein wandelnder Stern gegen ihn sein? Er hat sich dem Geist aller Sonnen verbunden, immer dient er den Gängen des ewigen Spiels.

Hence his admiration for a surgeon who amidst the chaos of war accomplishes the most difficult work with ease and certainty:

> Diesen Arzt scheint nichts zu drängen und zu hetzen, und ob er blutende Schlagadern unterbindet oder zerbrochene Glieder in Schienen schmiegt, seinen Händen legt sich alles wie von selber zurecht. Das innig-nüchterne Handeln, zu dem auch wir hinstreben, hier geschah es inmitten ungeheurer Zerstörungen still und klar.

'Innig-nüchtern', clear-headed, and yet affectionate—this expression sums up Carossa's approach to the problems of active life.

The two examples and the last remark must have betrayed how much Goethe has influenced him. He was obviously prepared to be influenced by him; in this point there is a temperamental relationship between them. He was sensitive to what Goethe had to say and capable of assimilating it. When comparing points of similarity between the two writers, of course, we should not overlook the difference in the scale of their respective personalities; a mistake which seems impossible but which is often made, and not only in relation to Carossa. Goethe started the method of making literature out of intimate personal experience in a fairly direct way and he has been imitated by writers who placed their faith in the peculiar sanction Goethe gave to the procedure, overlooking both the poverty of their own personal experience in comparison with his, and also of their artistic talent. How dominating Goethe's position in this as in other respects is, appears strikingly when a writer of the front rank, Thomas Mann, excuses his lack of pure invention by reference to Goethe's practice. It is amusing to observe how much honour is done to the writers concerned, and how little to Goethe. After all, he was not altogether without invention.

With these reservations in mind, then, we can say that Carossa's work is undoubtedly in lineal descent from *Werther* and *Dichtung und Wahrheit*. But unlike others he is near to Goethe not only in procedure but in aim and attitude. And this is the really valuable link with Goethe. There is no question of making his method the excuse for self-exhibition; on the contrary, Carossa protests against that class of writers. But there is a sure grasp of some of the enduring values in Goethe's life and philosophy; sure because like sees like and because his own experience is leading him all the time to similar perceptions. Thus there are reciprocal influences at work. We find in Carossa—in a humbler degree, but no less genuine—qualities which characterized Goethe's activity: an eager curiosity in the natural world as well as the human; patience and humility in the approach to them; a sense of reverence and wonder which never flags; and the will to see the parts of the world in relation to the whole and to win a positive creed. In the will to Bildung, we might say briefly. There are parts of his latest book, **Geheimnisse des reifen Lebens,** which, I think, have even too marked a resemblance to the *Wilhelm Meister* manner.

The influence, or relationship, extends to the lyric poetry. There are some who rank Carossa high as a lyric poet; at least they go so far as to speak of him in the same breath with Rilke and George. This is a mistake. Carossa is essentially a prose writer, who at the same time has produced a few good poems. His poetry is 'Gedankenlyrik', we are told; a word which often covers a multitude of sins and dull stuff. Carossa is the same in his poems as in his other work; that is, they spring most frequently from an emotion associated with his philosophical attitude, and his moral perceptions. But the emotion is mostly outweighed by the philosophy and morals. Where this is so, his poems just fail to move as they might. Where he relies entirely on an emotional experience pure and simple, as in **"Und wie manche Nacht"** or **"Wald im Winter,"** or on a scene or single event, as in *Flucht,* he is successful beyond all doubt. It requires a very great lyrical talent to achieve the perfect union between lyric inspiration and philosophical thought, or practical wisdom, or even political; Vogelweide, Wordsworth, Goethe, George have done it. But though Carossa cannot compete with these, and though Goethe's voice is sometimes too audible there are some fine poems in which emotion and thought are fused in forceful poetic symbols: **"Gesang zur Sonne," "Geheimnisse," "Heimliche Landschaft," "Der alte Brunnen."**

We have hinted already that Carossa is not a moral philosopher building up a system of morals, but a man concerned about the practical disposition of life. A medical man, with the supreme object of healing, activity and service are essential values for him. But mere activity and service can never be sufficient without spirit. Unfortunately, the rift between doers and thinkers in the world is probably all too pronounced. But it is founded in temperament, and, since the complication of civilization, in practical necessity. Carossa is painfully aware of this:

> . . . und wieder einmal erhebt sich die schon oft gestellte Frage, wie wohl das unruhige, in hundert kleine Verantwortlichkeiten zerfallende Dasein eines dienenden Menschen von heute mit den hohen Forderungen der Seele in Einklang zu bringen wäre. Wer ist so gross, dass er ein irdisches Geschäft betreiben und zugleich mit Geistes-Augen darauf niederschauen kann?

It is a distinctive merit of Carossa as a *man* that he has done what he here aspires to do; and the distinctive merit of Carossa as a *writer* that he has discovered the intimate connection between those demands of the soul and the life he serves. But it is only for the sake of analysis that we thus separate *man* and *writer;* for what we have said goes to show precisely how the two are locked together. Carossa tells in **Führung und Geleit** how at one time he hesitated whether to give up doctoring and take up writing as a profession. Had he done so he would probably have been lost as a writer; for he would have cut himself from the foundation on which his life, and his writing rests. One half of him follows the urge to lead an active life, and lead it better than most people, according to an ideal; letting events and experience, moreover, continually confirm him in his course. And the other half of him will always be contemplating and trying to put his perceptions into some sort of form. These two sides are complementary; and that is why it is true to say that to deprive himself of an activity in which his natural impulses found their form of expression would have been to cut himself adrift.

All these things, and their togetherness, determine the form of his work. The unit he works with is really the anecdote; the diary form of *Dr. Bürger,* the *Tagebuch im Kriege,* and *Geheimnisse des reifen Lebens* (with its subtitle: *Aus den Aufzeichnungen Angermanns*) show this best of all. We can take it that the method is an accurate reflection of the way Carossa works. He chooses from everyday life small incidents or particular circumstances, mostly of a restricted kind, to describe and represent, and from which some kernel of wisdom can be extracted. On such description or in the telling of the incident he lavishes great care and concern for form. He brings an astonishing skill to bear on the working out and rounding off of these incidents or scenes—with brevity, precision and lucidity—which have, in some way or another, significance, which touch heart or head, or, sometimes, assail the region of fears and apprehension. But there is rarely anything violent in his work; the storm of life has no attraction for him except as a sphere into which calm must be introduced. The war book is a monument to his will to the patient mastery of evil, his will to philosophy. 'Raube das Licht aus dem Rachen der Schlange' is the motto he sets at the head of it; the calm and detachment he shows are impressive to a degree. Even in *Die Schicksale Dr. Bürgers,* a revelation of mental trial and conflict by means of a diary record, the suffering and the turmoil are sidetracked; Dr. Bürger writes about his patients, about Hannah, about Hannah's past life, and it is only indirectly, by hints and remarks here and there that we get to know what is going on inside his mind. In this story Carossa is exposing the dangers of morbid preoccupation with disease and death; the demons that lie in wait for an unstable young man practising as a doctor especially amongst tubercular cases. And more than once the parallel has been drawn between Carossa and Goethe: Werther committed suicide, and Goethe lived, as the literary legend has it; and so, too, Bürger commits suicide, and Carossa lives. But it is a mischievous comparison. The two works cannot be compared for the force of the experience and the power of its presentation. Goethe *was* capable of violent emotional experience; and I doubt whether Carossa is. *Werther* is the expression of emotional turmoil through which Goethe actually lived. *Dr. Bürger* expresses what *might* have happened to Carossa; it is as though he thinks out certain consequences of certain factors in his position. If Carossa were subject to violent spiritual or emotional disorders, he would probably not be what he is; mild, wise, forgiving, healing; unless, of course, he were another Goethe, who was well-nigh everything. It is not the storms of life, then, that attract him; on the contrary, the sphere of everyday life, even its smallest incidents, are what engage his attention, in the belief that they might lead to some insight, some revelation of the way to nobler and wiser living. For these moments of revelation, or the moments when he can seize the opportunity of serving man, or God, or life, he is constantly on the watch, devout, humble, and inspired by a never-failing kindness.

The respect he has for the world as it faces him leads to another of his chief aims in writing: to grasp phenomena in such a way that vision penetrates appearance and reaches the reality; for this, too, belongs to wisdom. This striving in the artist he places higher than the free play of the imagination creating a world of its own:

> Ein Künstler mag aber noch so tief im Unheimlich-Phantastischen wohnen; einmal wird es ihm doch nicht mehr genügen, die Träume seiner Nächte festzuhalten. Früher oder später muss ihm die Einsicht zureifen, dass es eine höhere Stufe gibt, ein reineres Verfahren, wo sich die Traumkraft aufsparen will für die Wachheit des Tages. Ist ein Künstler dahin gelangt, so wird er wohl ruhigere Schlafstunden haben; dafür aber werden sich ihm die schlichten Erscheinungen des alltäglichen Lebens visionär entgegendrängen.

In this urge to *see* things, to detach and grasp them in the revealing light of day, he is again near to Goethe. There are times when he despairs of achieving his wish; doubt suggests the impossibility of it. The very despair, however, shows up the striving:

> Habe wirklich auch ich mir die Lehre vom geduldvollen Schauen gepredigt? Ich glaube, sie gehört nicht mehr zu mir. Wäre mir geholfen, würde ich ein anderer, wenn mir auf einmal im Seelenfinstern die hellen Urbilder der Wesen begegneten? Vielleicht ist uns überhaupt nicht bestimmt, unmittelbar die Dinge zu erkennen, und wir sollten den Gläubigen folgen, die nur durch das kristallene Herz eines Erlösers hindurch den Blick auf sie richten.

But again we judge him less by his results than by his striving. The main value is a moral one and lies in his attitude. It is comparable to Lessing's judgment that the search for truth or God conferred more honour than the possession itself.

It follows that there is much description in his work which is clearly caused by this urge to see appearances in a magic aspect. I cannot help but think that there are many passages where this magic significance that is being sought obstinately refuses to present itself. But Carossa has developed a virtuosity of writing which is always a great delight in itself and helps one over such passages. There is not a single page where we are not aware of an exquisite feeling for the rhythm and architecture of sentence and paragraph; a sensitive ear; chasteness and simplicity. And directing everything is a sure and cultivated taste. These are the most important factors in a style of great distinction.

One probably comes nearest to Carossa's inmost self in the *Tagebuch im Kriege.* But in *Der Arzt Gion* certain features of his moral code appear perhaps more clearly because they are set forth in a compact scheme and receive thereby a certain blunt emphasis. Gion is a doctor who seeks to serve life by means of wisdom and love, at a time of difficulty and distress, moreover (the post-war epoch); and to this purpose draws round him a group of persons in whom he sees healthy life or the possibility of it. Thus he forms a small community guided by him and living according to the principles he conceives to be good. Of these persons the first is Emerenz, a young countrywoman who in contrast to the women of the time prefers to bear the child that will cost her her life, than live herself, to die sterile. Cynthia is a young townswoman of refined intellect and artistic sensibility, of over-nervous constitution and subject to the disintegrating influences of urban civilization. She is groping her way out of sickness and youthful uncertainty and extravagance, and Gion, caring both for her bodily and mental health, guides her to a sane grasp of the roots of life, the conditions under which alone life flourishes, and makes this fruitful for a saner kind of artistic production than the one she had before indulged in. Emerenz is an important example to her. Alruna is a nun who devotes herself to serving the sick as a preparation for the higher life. Toni is a boy untouched by evil and in whom lies all the promise of life. And finally, Johanna, the baby girl, is the symbol of a future springing from the will, the love and the discipline of this group. Cynthia and Emerenz are related to Gion, the central figure, as patients, each with a different problem for him. Alruna is his assistant, incarnating certain virtues which have a higher sanction.

The characters of the book are not remarkably clear or living, with the exception of Gion himself; and that is because they are not there for their own sakes, each with the spark of life in him or her and claiming the world each for themselves. They are only there for Gion's sake; to make up his compact and sane little community. The odd thing, of course, is that he wants them to have the vital spark; but as they are *represented* in Carossa's tale, they are dominated by Gion's scheme. The author constructs very deliberately this little world within the world. It is bound up by unnumerable threads with the outer world, but these are kept fairly hidden, and so it forms a detached sphere shot through with an ideal and pedagogic intention. The impression of deliberate construction outweighs that of the flow of life and events. And the careful choice of a few symbols, such as Cynthia's fantastic sculptures, the loaves of bread (the staff of life) that Emerenz brings with her as a gift from country to town, the memorial to the fallen, with the likeness between the sculptured features of the soldier and those of Emerenz—this careful and pointed choice heightens the impression. It is a reconstruction of a fragment of the world according to a better plan. Hence the unreality of it as it is represented; although it springs from the impulse to come to grips with life and reality, with imperfection, decay and evil. So that even in this work, which is more a piece of fiction than any other of its author, we again find a moral attitude and the impulse to teach it as the ultimate value.

As a moral figure Carossa stands as a protest against the age in which his work has been done; an age of appalling disintegration. Much of the literature of this time, it is true, pretends to be inspired by human, humane, or humanitarian sentiment or ideals; many writers have claimed to be attacking selfishness and vice in all their forms. But to make literary copy of these things, or, at the best, to *talk* merely about them, is different from *being* an example of conscientious and high living. Few radiate such a power of human kindness as Carossa; and few are so devout and anxious, that they could find such simple and utterly true words to express their feeling, as the following, about men who apprehend 'eine neue Verantwortlichkeit, als wären sie die letzten Menschen und müssten das Leben, gleich einer beschadigten Leihgabe, in möglichst wiederhergestellter Form dem Schöpfer zurückliefern.'

When he formulates or indicates certain wise rules of life, he is, of course, often repeating what has been said before, drawing on an ancient store of wisdom. But these things have constantly to be repeated because of the slippery memory of men. It is not the least distinction of Carossa to have drawn on this wisdom in a manner which is in no way commonplace, but makes it valid again, renewing it by virtue of his own vivid experience and urgent need. (pp. 217-25)

> R. Peacock, "Carossa: a Moralist," in German Life & Letters, *Vol. II, No. 3, April, 1938, pp. 217-25.*

Ruth J. Hofrichter (essay date 1942)

[*In the following excerpt, Hofrichter addresses the philosophical and spiritual themes in Carossa's poetry.*]

In *Geheimnisse des reifen Lebens* Angermann says of Sibylle: "Her goal is similar to that which was mine for many years: the vanquishing of death by despising life, complete freedom of the soul, a water-clear existence untouched by fate." Here is some hint of the Catholic influences brought to bear on Carossa's childhood by his mother and through his school environment. And in his autobiography he tells of his own attempts in this direction.

When he was sixteen years old he suddenly realized that he was, after all, destined to become a saint. He had read in a book on contemplation that there is no better means of sharpening the faculties of the spirit than hunger and silence. " . . . yea, even as a bitter almond-tree may be changed into a sweet one by drawing out part of its sap, so to the fasting one would come visions and ecstasies of which a well-fed person could not even dream." Attracted by the prospect, the young neophyte embarked on his voyage toward holiness, turning down second helpings at table and doing without in-between snacks, while maintaining a dignified silence when questioned by his contemporaries. They soon found him out, however, and temptation beset the path of the budding saint. He was offered the choicest morsels at table, and presently invited for a special treat: beer and hazelnut cake. The sight of these ill-assorted dainties was too much for his asceticism; he succumbed to gluttony, and that was the end of his youthful attempt to reach "a water-clear existence untouched by fate."

Later, in more mature vein, Carossa turned from mysticism by an act of will. We see his reasoning reflected in the words of Angermann:

> Did I ever preach the doctrine of patient contemplation? I do not think that I approve of it any more. Would it be of any help to me, would I become a different person, if suddenly in the darkness of my soul the bright images of all crea-

tures were to confront me? Perhaps it is not our lot at all to gain immediate knowledge of things now hidden, and perhaps we should follow the faithful who only contemplate these things through the medium of a redeemer's crystal heart. Or is there another way for us who do not follow the common path—are there exaltations of the soul, unsought, which grant in a flash that which the patient labor of years does not attain?

This thought comes to Carossa time and again, and he offers it under many images. He will see, for instance, small blue butterflies quenching their thirst in the faint moisture of the soil near a broad stream; if they were to drink from the stream itself they would be destroyed.

> Many people feel a danger of this kind when confronted with the great spiritual elements. They keep away from them and make every effort to cover them all their lives with a layer of forgetfulness, just as we preserve phosphorus under water to save us from a conflagration.

A possible way to reach knowledge of these "great spiritual elements," constituting perhaps the ineffable reality behind phenomena, is suggested to him by his contact with Rainer Maria Rilke.

> He [Rilke] said that he had learned from Rodin to look so often and so searchingly at a tree, an animal, a statue, a human being, or a traditional figure of history, that finally an essential vision of the contemplated form emerged in himself. This procedure was not quite unknown to me; a short anthroposophical essay which I happened to read told me the same thing. But I considered such spiritual exercises much too difficult and too time-consuming to attempt them for myself.

He never ceases to hope that such an essential experience of reality will some day be his, even without conscious effort, and especially believes that this may come to pass when he is very old. Then, perhaps, he may reach a state akin to the rare minutes of the evening, when a star already rises in the east while the sun has not quite disappeared—then a higher vision may be attained, surpassing human understanding.

His attitude toward spiritual realization is again parallel to that of Goethe, who also overcame a leaning toward the occult, turning from it by conscious effort during the time of his maturity but admitting that in our old age we all become mystics.

In spite of his emphatic denial of the desirability of reaching knowledge of higher spheres while still in this life, Carossa's poetic work shows instances in which an awareness of a transcending life breaks through his carefully preserved earthly realism. A preoccupation with spiritual spheres of being seems to crowd into his consciousness. A striking example is offered in **"Der alte Taschenspieler,"** a dramatized poem of some length. Here an old magician is talking to his beloved little granddaughter after a successful performance. She often assists him, and now as always she is enraptured by his parlor tricks—the plant that grows before the eyes of the audience, white pigeons flying up to the stars. Though she knows how it is done, her wonder and surprise are ever new. She reminds her grandfather that many years earlier he had done gruesome things, hypnotizing members of the audience and transmitting to them unpleasant experiences. He confesses that in his youth he was given to practices even more dangerous: he was able to fathom the dark subconscious depth of human nature and to use its forces in forbidden ways. India taught him that black magic, and he knows that demons have their part in it. Now, for the sake of his grandchild, he has become a harmless parlor magician.

In another poem, **"Das Mädchen von Dobrowlany"** (1925), Carossa's preoccupation with occult practices takes the form of a letter to a friend who has "left the clear daylight to which we are born" in order to reach the universe of the spirit (*das Geister-All*) by strict and silent discipline. Carossa says that he does not hope to dissuade his friend from his quest nor does he doubt the validity of his aims. He reminds him, however, of a strange and touching episode they witnessed together during the war: In the fields near a sacked Rumanian village many dead were lying. The friends were surveying this scene of desolation when they saw a girl approach from the flaming village, her hair the color of wheat under a scarlet kerchief. She carried a load of linen and with incredible swiftness undressed one corpse after the other, friends and enemies alike, and shrouded them gently in her linen sheets. Then she sat down, facing them, and seemed to wait quietly for more dead. The friends understood that she was insane, totally oblivious to the danger around her.

Carossa suggests that if we were strong enough to approach the living with the self-forgetting love that this transfigured child gave to the dead, we would be rich enough in our own world and have no need to spy into "the sphere of pale spirits."

Carossa's lyrics show his deliberate love of the earth, to which he turns with fervor:

> Und nur lieber wird uns die Erde
> Wenn sich der Himmel vor ihr verhüllt—
>
> And the earth will be the dearer
> If the sky has veiled its face.
>
> Wären wir nicht reich genug
> In unsrer Welt?
> Was hilft's, in andere zu spähn?
>
> Would we not be rich enough in our world?
> What use to spy into another world?

To the eternal values of earth he gives symbolic form in several poems. In **"Heimliche Landschaft"** (**"Secret Landscape"**) a silvery gray snake lies dead and broken in the dust. Children, kneeling down, cover the body with walnut leaves. Hard black beetles come up from the ground to carry back the dead body into the "warm circle of living things."

In **"Die Nebel"** fog and clouds change to rain and bless the fields below. Another *perpetuum mobile* is shown in **"Die Ahnfrau."**

> Wage dich wieder hervor
> Silbernes Mittagsgesicht!

Alle sind aussen im Korn
Alles ist, wie es war.

. . . . .

Husch in dein Sterbegemach
Denk nicht vermoderter Pein!
Sieh, wo du seufzend vergingst,
Atmet das blühende Kind.

. . . . .

Umfliess es mit Geisterglück!
Nun öffnet es Augen voll Traum.
Es blinzelt durch dich in den Tag;
Es lächelt und schläft wieder ein.

Grüsse die Natter im Flur!
Noch reicht man den Milchnapf ihr fromm.
Dort schleicht sie gesättigt hinaus;
Sie fühlt und fürchtet dich.

Klug folgt sie verborgener Spur
Hinab in ihr dunkles Gebiet.
Da liegt unter höhligem Stein
Der Schatz, den du vergrubst.

Du sahst in die ferne Zeit.
Du wahrsagtest Krieg und Verfall.
Treu hast du gedarbt und bewahrt.
Die Schlange weiss darum.

Sie hegt auf dem Hort ihre Brut.
Sie biegt sich um ihn jede Nacht
Zum zauberverstärkenden Ring.
Oft klirrt unbändig das Gold.

Venture again to approach,
Silvery vision of noon!
They are all out in the corn;
Everything is as it was.

. . . . .

Quick to the room where you died!
Think not of pain that is dead!
Lo! Where you sighing expired
Breathes now a rosy child.

. . . . .

Let your bliss flow around him!
Now he opens his eyes, full of dreams.
He gazes through you at the day;
Sinks again into sleep with a smile.

Greet now the snake by the door!
They pour her milk as of old.
She drinks it and now she glides out;
She knows you and fears you still.

She follows the secret path
Down to her gloomy den,
Where lies in the hollow stone
The treasure you buried there.

You looked into distant time,
You saw the war and decay.
Faithful, you starved and saved.
The serpent is aware.

She keeps her brood on the hoard.
She coils herself every night
Around it, a magical ring.
The restless gold resounds.

The poet shows us three aspects of an eternal cycle of life: the body of the dead snake is converted to new animal life, the waters connect the elements with the growth of plant life and, on a different plane, the stream of life flows mysteriously through the generations. All these cycles stay within the boundaries of material being to which he clings. They appear to establish for him a certain balance between material and spiritual values, with which he is resolved to be satisfied.

Nevertheless, he does see another possibility: that of, let us say, metamorphosis—an experience repeating itself as it were in a different sphere and with an altered significance. This "metamorphosis" may well be called the deepest experience of Goethe, and one that permeates all his works. It is also a deep and spontaneous part of Carossa's philosophy. Even in his early poems we see traces of it. **"Die Flucht,"** which belongs to the period of ***Doktor Bürger,*** describes a young physician harassed by the terrible confidence of his dying patients and suddenly seized by the vision of a child in agony. From the depth of this horror he gleans the hope that the cry of pain caused by mortal anguish may be a shout of joy in the universe of the spirit. If this realization is rather naïve, even crude, in its expression, we will find subtler forms for similar experiences later. In **"Von Lust zu Lust"** (1918) we see the transfiguration of earthly passion into essential creative forces. **"Mysterium der Liebe"** (1919) has the same basic theme: the deadly danger of human passion and the courage of human beings who brave these dangers and by overcoming the sheer power of sex make it possible for Eros to be incarnated and resurrected in their purified love. These poems show the persistent idea of sublimation. A recurrence of the cyclic development, coupled with the motif of sublimation, appears in the mystic poem, **"Geheimnisse"** (1918): A star must consume itself so that life may flower on earth—and the human being must reach a stage where he will sacrifice himself and be consumed in burning service.

In the eternal cycles of life on earth, in the deliberate effort of the old magician to keep his feet on the ground, and in the idea of earthly sublimation rather than spiritual realization, we see Carossa's conscious pursuit of a normal reality: he would keep away from everything that distracts his attention from the visible, tangible world, forgetting the cosmic visions which haunt him.

But let us look more closely at the things of earth to which this poet clings with such fervor. Nine of the seventy poems that fill his single slender volume, ***Gesammelte Gedichte,*** treat of morning, noon, and sun, of a warm joyous existence; but twenty-three poems have a background of night, fog, or dusk. Often he cannot face the direct aspect of the sun or the moon; their reflection in the water has an immediate actualness which satisfies him.

This shifting of the stimulus of his experience has a parallel in his novels. We see it in one of the most charming episodes of his autobiography, in Part II, ***Verwandlungen einer Jugend.*** By way of punishment for a number of increasingly grave youthful pranks, the boy was locked into an empty classroom to do some extra work. The shock of this solitary confinement proved a turning point—his behavior improved afterwards. During his stay in this classroom he gazed admiringly at a blue map of the constellations which adorned the wall. "Strange; often he had looked up to the sky, by day and by night, but never had the immeasurable quality taken hold of his feelings as it did now when he looked at the artificial planes dotted with stars and foreign signs." It seems to the boy that his soul is so filled with wonder that it expands beyond its capacity and makes room for new experiences. Here again, as in the poetic instances of reflected sunlight, we see the tendency to get from a small concrete thing the impetus of feeling which others might derive from what is in reality vast or brilliant.

Thus in one of the poems on reflections we see him flee the strength of the sun and turn to its pallid image in the water, which he can scatter at will. It is interesting to compare this attitude with that of Faust in the second part of Goethe's drama. Faust faces the rising sun and, unable to bear its overwhelming light, turns from it to contemplate a rainbow forming in a waterfall:

> Dem sinne nach, und du erkennst genauer:
> Am farbigen Abglanz haben wir das
> Leben. . . .
>
> Let your thought dwell upon this, and you will become convinced that in the colored reflection we have life itself. Goethe, *Faust II,* Act 1.

he says. This idea is closely connected with that of revulsion from the supernatural. All through the first part of the drama he has sought immediate knowledge of a spiritual world, invoking to that end the help of the devil. Now he realizes that only the loving contemplation of physical reality on earth will yield the experiences of spiritual truth. We have seen that Carossa, like Faust, is drawn toward direct spiritual experience in his youth, only to turn from it later in favor of what he feels to be a natural and wholesome spiritual development through the validating experiences of earth. The parallel is oddly complete in the quality of Carossa's own reactions to the concrete world: his love—precisely—of reflected things.

And yet by this very element his poems show that he does not feel altogether at home on earth. In spite of the consciously optimistic philosophy, we have seen that a background of dusk prevails in his lyrics. In turning from the "image" to earthly reality, the brightness of the world is softened for him. Reflections attract him. Also clouds—that changing, floating world—are a frequent component of his landscapes. He shows us

> a pale cloud, its rim dissolved in green; clouds, heavy as sponges saturated with light; great marble clouds; cloudbanks pressing down heavily; clouds reflected in water—grey with deep incisions like oak leaves, having a lining of blue light; the narrow moon cuts with pale incisiveness through grey clouds shot with yellow; clouds beginning to glow, dissolving in a purple haze to let the sun break through, like a trembling drop of clearest light; a black storm cloud is shattered into white fragments by a rock—the landscape is mottled by quick shadows of clouds.

This floating world is in keeping with his love for images reflected in the water. The feeling of unreality created here becomes even stronger when we examine the human beings he describes. There are not many of them, and when they do appear the poet is more concerned with their inner experience than with their appearance. We see:

> —a pale girl; a pale barefoot girl in a grey dress; a grey wanderer; a wife, pale in the pallid lamplight, her hair loosened with dreams as with dew; a child flitting like a ghost; an expectant mother looking out into the misty evening where fallen leaves whirl in black waters, her small tired hands resting in her lap; a motherly face pale as a young girl's; the apparition of a dying child; the imagination of a sick boy sees the women who bring the fever:
>
> Sie scheinen zu lächeln von fern.
> Doch wenn sie näher schleichen,
> Dann sehen sie ganz wie die Toten aus.
> Ihre Augen sind ohne Blick.
>
> They seem to smile from afar.
> But as they creep nearer and nearer,
> They look just as dead people look;
> Their eyes are without sight.
>
> The dream of a dying child: black men scurry around him, the walls float like fog, King and Queen come out of it with crowns—outside snow-white riders with fiery whips wait on dark horses.

This is surely an eerie crowd! The only people permitted to wear brighter colors are certain figures of the poet's memory: a red-cheeked chubby young man and a white-faced tall girl in a green dress—but both reveal to the practiced eye of the doctor that they are marked by death. A girl with hair as light as wheat wears a red kerchief. She is, however, sweetly insane (lest the reader be misled into untimely gaiety by her cheerful appearance). Four of his poems are devoted to unborn children—a sign that the unknown future is full of suggestion for him.

The world of Carossa's lyrics is like a landscape in a luminous mist. Sometimes a slanting ray of light reveals the tantalizing outline of a mountain range, or in the valley the dim course of a great river. In the milky silence, shapeless gray figures approach and recede; we do not know whether their gestures are friendly or threatening, whether this floating scene is one of creation or of dissolution.

There are other minor themes and descriptions, many of them of great charm. Carossa is attracted by the world of plants and of animals, though these themes are not more prevalent than with other lyric poets. His choice is interesting: seeds have a peculiar fascination for him; he shows us darting, airy creatures like butterflies and dragonflies; then again, animals which might play a part in fairy tales or myths: doves, an eagle, a hawk, cats, snakes—these are not dangerous but rather wise or sacred; they live their lives uninfluenced by the world of men.

The metaphors which the poet uses, sparingly and with sensitiveness, make for atmosphere rather than symbolic value. There are however some instances of recurring symbols and they are significant: the world of the stars, the sun, the moon, crystals, ice flowers—all serenely following their own laws and throwing into relief the turbulence and uncertainty of our life. They seem to accentuate the poet's longing for a world without strife and tearing emotions, and their serenity contrasts with the constantly fluctuating impressions of surrounding reality. But brief description cannot do justice to the delicate, delightful quality, the spirit of gentleness and love that pervades these poems. (pp. 21-34)

Reading [Carossa's] verses and his lyric prose, we feel in them an element of natural growth, not one of conscious mastery as we see for instance in Stefan George. On the whole, Carossa is curiously untouched by the heritage of the nineteenth and twentieth centuries; his ancestor is Goethe, though his relation to the great master is one of kinship, not of imitation. It is appropriate that the Goethepreis of 1938 was given to Carossa.

In his own right, and in a high sense, Carossa is a poet, and it is as a poet that he seeks to resolve the problems set up by the impact of the total world on the individual. In the ideas of metamorphosis, of sublimation, of sacrifice and responsibility, his poems combine the demands of life on earth with the selfish instincts of man, and assimilate to a certain degree the great spiritual forces from whose immediate experience Carossa shrinks. Thus elements which by themselves would war against each other are blended and made fruitful. Here the poet fulfills the promise he gave himself: to heal with words as the doctor heals. His poignant and moving verses with their deep sympathetic feeling for nature and human life give moments of comfort and glimpses of better possibilities to his harassed contemporaries; although the reader may sometimes feel that his art, with all its gentle radiance, resembles the butterflies who drink from the faint moisture at the river bank lest the great stream should kill them.

It may well be that Carossa's deepest impulses, dimly seen in his past work, will crystallize in the future and reflect more clearly the reality he seeks. In an enigmatic and tantalizing sentence prefacing his war diary, he compresses the essence of his search: *Raube das Licht aus dem Rachen der Schlange*—"Snatch the light from the jaws of the serpent!" (pp. 40-1)

> Ruth J. Hofrichter, "Hans Carossa," in her Three Poets and Reality: Study of a German, an Austrian, and a Swiss Contemporary Lyricist, Yale University Press, 1942, pp. 9-41.

E. W. Herd (essay date 1951)

[*In the following essay, Herd discusses Carossa's use of dreams in his autobiographies and fiction.*]

Not least amongst the many interesting aspects of the work of Hans Carossa are the frequent use of the dream motif, and the peculiar quality of the dreams recounted. Dreams are to be observed in all Carossa's works except *Eine Kindheit,* and are especially numerous in early works, such as *Tagebuch im Kriege* and *Die Schicksal Doktor Bürgers.* The dreams described are remarkable for their general atmosphere and for their function in Carossa's work. The normal use of the dream-motif in literature before Carossa had been the symbolic, in which the dream presented an image of future developments: this was a device especially favoured by the Romantics, a good example being the dream at the opening of *Heinrich von Ofterdingen.* The dream has often been used to further the action, to reveal information essential to the further development of the action, as for example many of the dreams in the Old Testament or the quasi-biblical dreams in *Emmanuel Quint.* Thirdly, the dream has been used as a vehicle for satire, a realm in which Heine is paramount, *Harzreise* offering several illustrations. The dreams in the work of Carossa however—save one or two exceptions from the earlier works—do not fall into any of these categories. They are not symbolic, they do nothing to further the action—even where there is action to be furthered, and they are not used as vehicles for satire. Not only do Carossa's dreams differ in function from previous examples in literature, but also in their general atmosphere. In spite of their inevitable irrationality they have a dominant tone of healthy normality and of genuineness, which contrasts strongly both with the supernormal dream bearing a definite message, and with the hysterical nightmare, characteristic of Hoffmann's *Elixir des Teufels* or, to quote more recent examples, Ernst Wiechert's *Andreas Nyland,* or Hesse's *Demian.*

Carossa seems to achieve the vraisemblance of the dreams by incorporating into them all the known features of dreams as generally observed. There is complete irrationality—mice change into billiard-balls, grenades into fish; natural laws are in abeyance—'Mein Leib hatte nahezu völlig sein Gewicht verloren; ich fühlte mich wie eine Flaumfeder leicht und musste gewärtigen, das der zunehmende Wind mich alsbald emporheben und zu den Franzosen hinübertragen werde'; grotesque elements are numerous: but all these phenomena are readily accepted by the reader's imagination because they are all normal dream-phenomena. The speed of the action in the dreams is in telling contrast to the leisurely rhythm of the main body of Carossa's work. In the content of the dream Carossa mingles thought and experience as basic ingredients, as for example in a dream from the *Tagebuch im Kriege* which is based on the past experience of family life but in which a present anxiety is expressed by one of the characters when she says 'Die Männer sind schlecht. Sie fürchten sich vor mir und laufen nach Frankreich zum bösen Feind'. Similarly the recent past is mingled with the remote past, as exemplified in the dream of the dead Russian in *Führung und Geleit* who was at the same time Carossa's father. All these features are accepted as common to most dreams and therefore help to produce an air of genuineness. Moreover Carossa nearly always recounts only his own dreams; he only describes the dreams of some other character on three occasions, twice in *Doktor Bürger* and once in *Arzt Gion.* Thus if we accept an autobiographical element in the central male characters of works like *Doktor Bürger, Der Arzt Gion* and *Geheimnisse des reifen Lebens* the great majority of the dreams in Carossa's work are personally experienced, a further factor contributing to their vraisemblance.

As a doctor and an acute observer, Carossa is fully aware

of the physiological basis of the dreams and visions he describes. There are examples in his work of both 'representative' or centrally initiated dreams, and of 'presentative' dreams, which are due to the stimulation of the sense-organs. A typical 'representative' dream in ***Das Jahr der schönen Täuschungen*** Carossa describes as 'einer von jenen Träumen, die uns gerne heimsuchen, wenn wir unserer eigenen Seele nicht mehr völlig sicher sind'. Closely allied to 'presentative' dreams are those in which sense-perceptions are assimilated into the dream; for instance hail on the bedroom windows in ***Das Jahr der schönen Täuschungen*** is taken over into the dream as ravens attacking a box of young starlings; in ***Doktor Bürger*** the noise of grains of corn falling becomes the sound of heartbeats heard in a stethoscope; and in ***Tagebuch im Kriege*** the flaming horizon at the end of a dream is the fire just lit in the stove, or the fall of a body seems to produce the noise of a shell which bursts outside and wakes the dreamer. Apart from the dreams proper there are several examples of visions, hallucinations, etc., the experiences to which Maury in his book *Le Rêve et le Sommeil* gave the name of 'illusions hypnagogiques'. Such is the apparition to Doktor Bürger of his father's ghost, and there are other related experiences which Carossa describes as 'traumartige Empfindungen'. The physical background of the dreams is obviously of importance for Carossa. In ***Tagebuch im Kriege*** he says: 'Bei klarem Wetter vergisst man die nächtlichen Träume schnell; im Trüben haften sie lang'; or again: 'Kein Wunder, dass man viel schläft und viel träumt in diesem Winterwaldzwielicht.' It is remarkable too that his book of war-memoirs should contain the greatest number of dreams, more even than the history of the hypersensitive Doktor Bürger. There is great variation in the length of the dreams and in the amount of detail recorded; some dreams extend over several pages, others are dismissed in a few lines.

We may now consider the function of the dream in Carossa's work. We have already seen that the dream as a consciously-created symbol appears very rarely in Carossa's work. There are in fact three examples of this type of dream, in which Carossa is plainly out to achieve some definite dramatic effect. Hanna's dreams in ***Die Schicksal Doktor Bürgers*** are obviously commentaries on her fate and her relationship to Bürger, whilst Cynthia's dream in ***Der Arzt Gion*** clearly represents her ambivalent attitude towards childbearing. In ***Geheimnisse des reifen Lebens*** occurs a dream which expresses all the elements of the complicated relationship of Angermann to the three women, Barbara, Sibylle and Cordula. It is introduced by the significant words: 'Im Halbschlaf naht ein Traum; er zieht alle Gefahren herbei, die ich so lange ferngehalten; ich weiss es, aber eine Stimme rät mir, ihn gewähren zu lassen'; and of the end of the dream Angermann says: 'Da weiss ich, dass dies die Worte sind, die ich immer von ihr erhofft habe; der Traum verlässt mich, er fliegt wie ein Gewölk mit allen meinen bösen Geistern von mir fort.' The effect aimed at here is clear and simple, and has a direct bearing on the story. On another occasion in ***Geheimnisse des reifen Lebens*** Carossa uses the dream to express his attitude towards the new Hitler Youth movement—a somewhat pathetic comment on the helplessness of the older generation of the 1930s confronted by the new dynamic forces which they did not really understand. But these dreams which admit of a definite interpretation and perform a symbolic or dramatic function are the exceptions. Carossa's normal dreams have no apparent meaning, and do not produce any direct results, either in the course of the action, or in the development of character. Their real function seems to be to help to complete the moralist's picture. Professor Peacock has pointed out that Carossa is a moralist in Thomas Mann's sense of the word: 'one interested in human life and human behaviour, observing men and their ways, and commenting on them'. The dream to Carossa is a normal and integral part of human life, in which character is revealed as surely as in waking existence. Thus the dreams in the purely autobiographical ***Das Jahr der schönen Täuschungen*** are of equal importance and identical in structure with the other anecdotes—the basic unit of Carossa's work—in the illustration of character. A very good example is the long dream in ***Der Arzt Gion*** in which Gion dreams that he has mislaid his stethoscope, and in which his search takes him into the Sirius-Bar. The events of the dream are only of importance in relation to Gion: they have no value in themselves, but the whole episode helps to portray Gion's character, exactly as it is gradually portrayed in the episodes from his waking life. For Carossa the dream is essentially a reflection of personality and is therefore of prime importance in his task of illustrating human characters.

One must not forget that there is nevertheless an element of artificiality, of conscious creation in these apparently so natural dreams. Our recollection of dreams is at best fragmentary, and therefore the artist must create and select in order to produce a dream which has artistic unity. Even were he to be most scrupulous in merely recounting dreams experienced and remembered, the resultant picture and illustration of character would not be complete owing to his inevitably faulty recollection of his dreams. That selection is practised in the accounts of Carossa's dreams is witnessed by the objectivity of the account, by interpellations such as 'wie es in Träumen geht', 'wie es in Traumstädten geht', or 'aber wie sonst im Traum das Unmögliche leicht gelingt . . .' which show the hand of the consciously creative artist.

Carossa's own attitude towards dreams seems undefined. He is uncertain whether he ought to try to interpret his dreams or not. In ***Doktor Bürger*** he is emphatically opposed to interpretation: 'Was wissen deine Träume von dir . . . ! Nie, nie lass uns pochen an ein Reich, worin der Mensch mit seiner Güte und seinen Schmerzen nichts gilt!' This is an early opinion and later, in ***Der Arzt Gion,*** he confirms it by commenting: 'Er schrieb die Träumerei dem Trinken und dem Lesen zu, und nahm sich vor, ihr keinerlei Bedeutung zu geben.' In spite of his disinclination to attempt to interpret his dreams however, it is obvious that Carossa considers them as normal and healthy phenomena. In ***Doktor Bürger*** he relates: 'Ich habe so gut geschlafen wie jemals nach einer Woche voll Arbeit, und kurz vor dem Erwachen noch etwas geträumt'; and as in the above-quoted example from ***Geheimnisse des reifen Lebens*** he seems to attribute a salutary cathartic power to his dreams. He frequently hints at the possibility of significance of his dreams but the meaning remains elusive, and always just beyond his grasp. In *Das Jahr der schönen Täuschungen* he says of one dream: 'Aufwachend fragte ich mich, ob der Traum nicht einen bestimmten Sinn habe . . . '; and in the same work he has a dream the meaning of which is half-apparent, but frightens him and so 'ich erwachte . . . entschlossen, über diesen Traum nicht nachzudenken'. In *Tagebuch im Kriege* he speaks of a dream as having been 'so klar, so voll Hindeutung' but admits that he no longer enjoys recalling his dreams. He distinguishes between the light, empty dreaming he experienced in France, 'da war aller Traum nur Träumerei; locker und sinnlos', and the more oppressive, enigmatic dreams in the Carpathians: 'es ist auch, als versteckten sie vor mir ein geheimes Ziel, dem sie mich auf Umwegen zuführen wollen'. Thus Carossa seems never quite sure whether there is a dream-symbolism, nor whether it is desirable to attempt to interpret dreams: his attitude is never rigidly determined.

It is clear that Carossa considers dreams to be important, not as supernormal revelations, but rather as normal aspects of human existence, and for the artist, as a necessary additional means to portray character and personality. What Werner Mahrholz has said of the whole of Carossa's work: 'das höhere Gesetz der Natur waltet in diesen scheinbar locker und leicht wie zufällig und vorübergehend wiedergegebenen Eindrücken'—this applies in no less degree to the dreams. (pp. 171-75)

> E. W. Herd, "The Dream-Motif in the Work of Hans Carossa," in German Life & Letters, Vol. IV, No. 3, April, 1951, pp. 171-75.

A. V. Subiotto (essay date 1957)

[*In the following excerpt, Subiotto compares Carossa's autobiographies to his novels and suggests why Carossa chose to write autobiography.*]

The most interesting figure in modern German autobiography is undoubtedly Hans Carossa, whose work has a literary value far outstripping the modesty of its presentation. He is not the type of writer who wishes to provide a straightforward, biographically factual account of personal experiences in chronological order. Nor does he see in childhood an escape from present reality into an idealized world of the past enveloped in a mist of nostalgia. The urge that impelled Carossa to autobiography over so many years of his life sprang from a desire to form life into a whole, to reveal a pattern in which individual experiences acquire significance in relation to other experiences. The pattern becomes the more evident as the experiences become distanced in time, for this distancing allows the artist to select and juxtapose, and therefore to ascribe value to particular experiences which in reality are on an equal footing with all other experiences. Carossa has a finely-sharpened consciousness of the processes which determine the spiritual development of an individual, an awareness of childhood, youth and manhood as stages within one all-embracing unity and continuity in which the significance of each stage cannot be fully appreciated independently of its preceding and succeeding stages. Though the majority of important autobiographies are written by established people, whose previous life and work have already aroused interest, they are not confined to this type: the most common and uneventful life-story can become art if regarded imaginatively. This is the way Carossa looked at his early development; he was not a famous man when he began to set down his life on paper. Nothing eventful (except to him) occurred in it, but it was Carossa's early autobiographical writing that first attracted considerable attention to him as an artist. It is not difficult to follow the dominant mode of thought that urged Carossa to seek beneath the levelling and indiscriminate flux of experience for a pattern capable of organizing the whole of his past life and giving it a certain kind of meaning.

A certain predisposition to autobiographical writing may be found in Carossa's only prose work before *Eine Kindheit:* this is *Dr. Bürger,* the story, in outer form modelled on *Die Leiden des jungen Werthers,* of a young doctor who is unable to keep distinct the professional and human approaches to his patients, and who commits suicide in his despair at being the cause through negligence of the death of a patient with whom he has fallen in love. Carossa may have directly experienced everything that his hero experiences (for his own lifelong career was that of a doctor), but this is not autobiographical writing, and to call it veiled autobiography does not contribute to an appreciation of the book's merit as literature. The almost casual and quite fortuitous way in which Carossa started to write *Eine Kindheit* indicates the innate prompting and absence of deliberation that awakened his autobiographical sense. He himself tells in detail of the initial impulse and subsequent process that engendered an interest that has continued unabated throughout his life. In a letter published in *Die Literatur* in 1926 he describes an occurrence in the third night after the outbreak of war in 1914. A motor car was travelling towards Passau and did not stop when challenged by a member of the local 'Heimatwehr', composed mainly of old men from the village in the vicinity. The armed guard then shot in the direction of the car with subsequent fatal results for the driver. Carossa witnessed this incident and helped carry the dying man into a farm house. Then, as he made his way home through the early morning mist by the Danube, reminiscences of a girl playmate in his childhood came without any reason into his head. Once at home, not being able to sleep, in order not to forget them he wrote them down. Then he continues:

> Eine Erinnerung weckte die andere; immer wieder gab es etwas aufzuzeichnen und dieses heimliche Treiben kam auch später, während ich als Infanteriearzt an manchen Fronten diente, nicht zur Ruhe. Ja gerade in Stunden der Arbeit und Gefahr pflegten sich die längst vergessenen Erlebnisse der ersten Jahre unabweisbar aufzudrängen. Doch wurde mir dies im Dienste nie zur Störung, eher zur Forderung. Die zarten Geister, die lange geschlafen hatten, waren sehr frisch und beweglich geworden; sie brachten Wachsamkeit und machten alle Mühe leichter, ja es gab Augenblicke, da sie sich in Schutzgeister zu verwandeln schienen.

In this fashion Carossa began his autobiography. In the same letter he lays bare certain reasons by which he justifies a return in memory to childhood:

> Das Kind lebt jeden Augenblick seines Daseins ganz; es blickt mit einem Ernst, einer Geradheit, einem hellsichtigen Vertraun dem Leben entgegen, die wir später fast nur noch im Traum erfahren. Es weiss nichts von der Schwere, nichts von den dunklen Wegen des Erwachsenen, der das Ewige nicht mehr sehen will und immer wieder von sich selbst abfällt, bis ihm plötzlich ein Ereignis in den Kern hinein erschüttert. Da gedenkt er wieder seines Beginns und des ungebrochenen Lichtes das ihn damals umleuchtete. Wo sonst als in jenen ersten Handlungen und Leiden kann die Grundfigur seines Wesens eingezeichnet sein? Er sehnt sich, den Schutt vieler halbgelebter Jahre wegzuräumen, die geheimnisvolle Inschrift freizulegen und zu lesen, sich an ihr zu prüfen und zu erforschen, ob es nicht etwa doch möglich wäre, nach ihrer Weisung sich neu aufzubauen.

The first of the above quotations gives an explanation of what has impelled many writers of the present century to turn to autobiography or to themes of childhood: in times of uncertainty, anxiety, war and destruction an intense awareness of the past as a living part of the present, organically one with it, serves as a bulwark against disintegration; autobiography becomes a personal symbol of continuity and indestructibility. Operative in the second quotation is the phrase 'die Grundfigur seines Wesens', on the pattern of which a man can reorganize and rebuild his life. The pattern underlies all phases of life, each of which is continually being modified in the light of the general pattern and of subsequent growth.

Although Carossa finds reasons for writing autobiography and a general purpose underlying this activity, he is in no sense didactic. The three books of his childhood and youth—*Eine Kindheit, Verwandlungen einer Jugend* and *Das Jahr der schönen Täuschungen* are simply the considered and urbane presentation of an individual, quite free from any heavy-handed pompousness. Carossa seems to say: 'Here is an individual, no different from a thousand others. Do not attach any particular importance to him.' It is the very simplicity, the unwitting insistence on the *generality* of the picture that makes of it far finer autobiography than many by more famous men. The reason for this lies perhaps in the fact that Carossa was not a famous man, hence was not describing anything exceptional, being simply concerned with presenting an individual life which, thanks to its very ordinariness, becomes at the same time an image of everybody's life. In the different sections of his autobiography, which is incomplete and where writing about his youth follows that about his maturity, Carossa nevertheless succeeds in presenting his development into manhood in a most natural and spontaneous way. He never forces his memory to yield experiences it has long discarded, but allows one episode to evoke another, each being a link in a chain, the power of which lies in the vividness with which each episode inhabits the mind and memory of the author. In this completely unforced recollection of childhood and youth Carossa captures the magic, sometimes the dream-like quality of early life, and his delicate sensibility gently guides these episodes into an organic and continuous whole where both the intrinsic shape and the impeccable language satisfy the reader's sense of form.

With the two symbolic novels ***Der Arzt Gion*** and ***Geheimnisse des reifen Lebens*** Carossa reverts to the traditions of the 'Entwicklungsroman'. In these two books there is patently a strong element of autobiography, seen most immediately in the occupations and predilections of the chief character in each. At the same time a note of didacticism, absent from Carossa's purely autobiographical writing, makes itself evident here: Carossa describes his groups of characters much as if they were under medical observation, and takes the disruptive effects of the First World War as the starting-point for making an objective judgment on the problems of life. He leads on to ethical and mystic conclusions, always with reference to norms of individual behaviour and personal relationships, and the ways in which these can be clarified or strengthened. In these ventures of Carossa's into the novel it can be seen most clearly how the 'Entwicklungsroman' owes so much to the autobiography and how markedly it differs from the romantic or psychological novel, with its 'Fiktion, Intrige und Flausen', where the telling of a story or exposition of character plays such a large part.

In 1955 appeared ***Der Tag des jungen Arztes,*** describing Carossa's first steps in practice in the wake of his doctor father. His death a few months later unfortunately robbed us of an account of the solution to the conflict in himself, adumbrated in this last book, between conscientious devotion to the ideals of medicine and the urge to desert his profession in favour of a freer literary life. Hans Carossa went *towards* life, unlike many artists, and avowedly found his literary through his professional self; in this he gave our times a Goethean picture of the cross-fertilization of literature and life. (pp. 37-40)

> A. V. Subiotto, "Hans Carossa and Modern German Autobiography," in German Life & Letters, Vol. XI, No. 1, October, 1957, pp. 34-40.

Lin Harrison (essay date 1979)

[*In the following excerpt, Harrison remarks on the relationship between theme and structure in Carossa's autobiographies. For a critique of Harrison's arguments, see the essay by Clair Baier (1979).*]

Why do people write their autobiographies? The fundamental urge would seem to be the desire to know what one is. Edwin Muir describes as a general human attribute what must be highly developed in the successful autobiographer:

> there is a necessity in us, however blind and ineffectual, to discover what we are.

In this quest to discover the true self the autobiographer must delve back into his past and try to reconstruct the pattern of his growth. He may feel in need of reassurance that he is on the right path and wishes to establish contact again with his earlier life, where his essential self may reveal itself more clearly, less encumbered with later accretions. Such a motive comes out clearly in H. G. Wells' *Experiment in Autobiography:*

> **Baier on visiting Carossa at his villa in Rittsteig:**
>
> Outside the study, which was itself lined with books, there is a long room, known as the library. In addition to actual books, there hangs, almost as sole picture and certainly as sole portrait in this tastefully decorated room, a not very usual engraving of Goethe. At the far end stands a piano and on this, at the time of my recent visit, a refugee from the East came regularly to play. Carossa explained to me that he can work better when he hears musical strains in the distance. It does not have to be well-played; and, indeed, it needed no great musical skill to detect many mistakes in this strumming—but for Carossa that seemed completely unimportant!
>
> The simple nature of the country life led in the Carossa household, its entire lack of ceremony, and the fact that the presence of an outsider did not seem to have disturbed its normal routine, cannot be stressed too much. In this cellar-kitchen, with every member partaking of the same simple—but very nourishing—repast, one could not help thinking of the down-to-earth life of a local peasant-farmer. True, these people were cultured and well-to-do, but that had not altered their general acceptance of the countryside in which they live. Because Carossa's mastery over German prose is so great, and the problems that he deals with are so universally human, one tends to forget how very much he is a representative son of his Lower Bavarian homeland; no 'Heimatkünstler', but one, nevertheless, whose whole work reflects the manner of life of the country round Passau.
>
> Clair Baier, "A Visit to Hans Carossa," *German Life and Letters* VI, No. 3 (April 1953).

> I began this autobiography primarily to reassure myself during a phase of fatigue, restlessness and vexation, and it has achieved its purpose of reassurance.

By reliving the past, tracing the steps by which he came to hold certain views about man and society, he clears the ground for future work. Other writers, like Rousseau, have felt the need to justify themselves in a hostile world, to lay bare the soul, to pass judgement on the self and leave others to form their own conclusions from the evidence given. In some autobiographies there is a clear didactic intention, in the case of K. P. Moritz's *Anton Reiser* it is the author's desire to present his own childhood as material for educationists. However, these aims of reassurance and self-justification, or the desire to further the understanding of children's inner life, are pursued in the same way, by an attempt to retell and understand the past and to grasp the true nature of the self. After memory has done its work in selecting elements of the past, there still remains to the autobiographer a mass of memories on which to draw. If he is really serious about his task he must have some principles of selection if his autobiography is not to become a rag-bag of diverse experiences. At a particular point in his life a man looks back and sees his past falling into a certain pattern or, more probably, he recognizes a vague shape which becomes a pattern as he writes, in which case the effort of writing is a constant clarification of his self-awareness. This latter element is there to some degree at least in all good autobiography, for the discipline involved in evoking and understanding the past and establishing a relationship with it enters into the style and shaping of the work and assures us of the author's serious intention and involvement.

In Hans Carossa's 'Jugendgeschichte' two themes are of supreme importance: an education in responsibility and the unfolding of a temperament. Of the latter I need only say here that we are aware in the hero's childhood of traits which reappear in a heightened form throughout this autobiography, of imaginative impulses taking firmer shape until they emerge into a desire to become an artist. The author is eager also to point out that a disciplining of his personality was desirable. Time and again other people cure him of aberrations, show him that he is living in an illusion, redirect his energies away from imaginative obsessions. The hero is made aware of the demands of 'real life' in the sense of responsibility to others and the need for self-discipline and sacrifice. These two themes are crucial because they are persistent and because they are at the root of the dilemma which dominates the final volume, ***Der Tag des jungen Arztes,*** that of the conflict between medicine and the literary life. In addition to the working out of these themes, however, there is a great deal of artistic shaping of the past in the 'Jugendgeschichte,' shaping which interprets past experience and relates it to the man writing, and it is to this shaping spirit which pervades the work that I wish to draw attention.

Carossa writes of ***Der Tag des jungen Arztes*** as 'dieses Bilderbuch meiner Jugend' and this phrase may well be applied to the construction of the complete work. The basic unit is the chapter, often dealing with one particular incident: a race, a detention, a poetry-reading, a walk with his mother and sister. Sometimes a chapter draws together experiences which have a common element, as for example a report on his university studies and teachers, experiences at a clinic, a group of encounters with patients. It seems right that the memories of early childhood should appear in chapters under general headings for we know how difficult it is to sort out a chronological order for these experiences. Thus Carossa groups them as they are recalled by an activity, as in 'Der Garten'; by a place, as in 'Der Marktplatz'; or a person, as in 'Die Forelle.' As memories take on a firmer shape we find that an incident comes to fill out a whole chapter. This closed chapter form goes particularly well with the childhood experiences since it corresponds to the way children live from one highlight to the next, in bouts of intensity ('magic', the race, the nativity scene, the sword). At a later stage in the autobiography we can see that incidents are obviously carefully selected from many similar ones and moulded together. It is, for example, extremely unlikely that he would remember all the medical cases ascribed to the one visit to the university clinic. Clearly they are chosen to serve a particular purpose; the story of the 'dumb' girl, for instance, because it illustrates a kind of spiritual healing. In two ways Carossa carefully stresses the importance he attaches to the girl's cure. He inserts another incident, the visit to the Socialist meeting, between the initial discussion of the case and the successful healing, so that we share the hero's suspense as to what will happen, and then he draws a general significance from the event:

> hier war eine regenbogenleichte Brücke geschlagen zu dem schöneren, freieren, bedeutenderen Dasein, dem sich jedes Herz, oft ohne es zu wissen, entgegensehnt.

In the chapter 'Patienten', Carossa tells us about several of his patients, after which he makes a brief reference to his desire as a young man to escape from his life as a doctor and then once again shows the hero involved in his duties. In this way we feel directly that he had little time for his spiritual life, just moments imprisoned in long stretches of routine work. We see too the diverse nature of the patients and their illnesses and how this necessitated the utmost concentration. Here Carossa has selected and arranged medical cases to get nearer the truth of his situation in the past than the exact record of the activity of any one day could achieve.

Carossa's chapters often end with scenes or statements which sum up an experience, a situation, a state of mind in a succinct and poetic manner. Thus, when the hero has caused his childhood adversary, Reisinger, to have a fit his mood is indicated in the following manner:

> Fremd und bedrohlich schimmerten mir die Fenster der Elternwohnung entgegen, und wie nun der erste Schnee zu fallen anfing, war mir, als fiele er auf alle Menschen, nur nicht auf mich.

Coming as it does at the end of a chapter, this striking evocation of the child's feeling of guilty isolation has the slightly dramatic quality which leaves the reader wondering how the situation was resolved. In 'Familienforschung' the hero meets Aldine after having made up his mind to spend an evening without seeing her. The chapter ends with a remark by Aldine which she perhaps never made but which is symbolic of the hold she exercises over the hero's imagination, for it stresses both her 'Frenchness' and the fragile impermanence of their relationship:

> Hast du heute keine Zeit für mich, so sehen wir uns vielleicht nie wieder. Jede Stunde kann eine Nachricht aus Frankreich kommen, die mich abruft.

In its context and brought into prominence at the end of the chapter, this bare statement makes us feel that the hero is trapped.

The hero's relationships with parents and friends are, for the most part, related in episodic form throughout the autobiography and this seems natural and desirable in a chronological account of a life. Occasionally, however, Carossa uses an episodic technique for other purposes. When the obsession with 'magic' loses its power during the child's preparation for his first confession but then reappears in a later chapter this helps to stress its tenacious hold on the boy's imagination. In the final volume the story of the boy patient who has inhaled a watch-key is told in snatches within a long chapter. This gives us the impression of the young doctor carrying a case around with him in his mind, working it over until finally he has an insight into the nature of the sickness.

Whilst there are many such instances of Carossa using the chapter form to order the past meaningfully, there are others where we feel that the past is seriously distorted by this shaping process. At the beginning of **Der Tag des jungen Arztes,** when Carossa is writing about his experience as a medical student in Leipzig, he remarks:

> Von einer Unzahl trauriger Fälle soll dieses Bilderbuch meiner Jugend nicht überschattet werden.

This suggests that he is more concerned to avoid distressing incidents than to uncover the truth of his past experience, and indeed the shape of the first two chapters strongly supports this. The first chapter ends with the death from tetanus of a beautiful boy, but the horror of this is deliberately softened by Carossa's description of the way death restores the distorted body to peace and beauty and by the news that the anti-toxin had just been discovered that would banish the disease. In a similar way, although the second chapter also contains an account of a terrible affliction, there is a deliberate lightening of the atmosphere at the end where Carossa concludes by informing us of the progress of medical science in treating this ailment. In short, the shape of these two chapters does not so much assist in evoking and interpreting the past as in revealing the author's intention not to describe the destructive force of disease without showing the positive aspect in the form of medical advance. The shaping process here has shifted the focus from the author considering his past experience as part of a chain of development to using incidents from the past to reveal his present and positive attitude to the grim experiences a medical student has to face. In the process we tend to lose sight of the young hero having to face the apparently senseless cruelty of disease without the adult author's resources of experience and maturity to combat the horror of it.

It is always harmful to the structure (and thus the truthfulness) of autobiography when we feel that the writer is straying from his main theme. Even if, as in the work under discussion, one can only speak of 'growth' or 'development' in a very general sense as the principal theme, it is nevertheless fairly easy to pick out those elements and incidents which do not impinge meaningfully on the hero's life. Having committed himself to a form of construction which relies on the careful shaping of a limited number of incidents, Carossa has to be extremely careful not to include superfluous material. We find in fact that the embedding of such irrelevant material varies between quite short passages and whole incidents. The final volume in particular reveals a tendency to reminisce, which weakens the impact of the 'Jugendgeschichte.' Carossa tells us, for instance, of how he went to the lectures of an old professor, found himself the only participant, and decided to please the old man by appearing regularly. A charming story, of course, but no more and Carossa openly reveals his motive for including it:

> unter den vielen unnützen Wegen, die ich im Leben gegangen bin, sind wenige, an die ich so gerne zurückdenke.

He is perfectly aware that he is indulging in a pleasant memory, not recording an experience which is a step in his development. There is no cause to weary the reader with detailed analysis of material of this sort, a brief list will suffice to make the point. When Carossa writes about Wilhelm His, who wrote a learned paper on the disinterred bones of Johann Sebastian Bach, or about the Salvation Army and William Booth inviting Cecil Rhodes to pray with him he is indulging in anecdotes. The description, too, of statues and a drawing by Max Klinger, interesting though they are, ought to be connected to some central thread in the final volume; as it is, they are more like diary jottings, isolated in the story. Apart from their account of the brief reunion with Hugo, his boyhood friend, the two chapters dealing with the 'Landshuter Hochzeit' bear a greater resemblance to pages from a travel book than to autobiography. In *Ungleiche Welten* Carossa tells us that the composing of this final volume of the 'Jugendgeschichte' was slow work; there is indeed plenty of indication that he was hard pressed for material.

If the tendency towards anecdote represents a momentary weakening of the shaping spirit in this work, Carossa's use of symbolic gesture, incident and scene reveals it at its strongest. It is clear that there is a sense in which we want all the events in autobiography to be symbolic, for we are less interested in events themselves than in their significance for the writer's personality and development. Thus we could point, for instance, to the hero's experience with the beautiful boy, Trimming, and call it symbolic of a stage of development; Carossa calls it the growth of 'ein neues Organ der Seele'. Similarly, the awakening of sexual curiosity is symbolized in the hero's desire to see Line's breasts. We know that there must have been many experiences which would reveal such steps in growth but Carossa chooses these, perhaps because they have an unusual intensity, to represent that stage of development. This would also apply to a rather different kind of experience, let us say, the incident in which the hero in his early years in medical practice gives an overdose of morphia; it is used as a painful example of the responsibilities and dangers inherent in the doctor's life.

Whilst, then, we can use the term 'symbolic' in this general way, there are scenes in the autobiography where we are especially conscious of symbolic shaping, where we see through the outward appearance to the spiritual significance of events. Let us take a very simple illustration to begin with. When the hero in his childhood has been cured of his obsession with 'magic' the physical actions described convey a psychological change:

> Als sie (Eva) fortgegangen war, lief ich in die Stube, schmiß die ganzen Zaubersachen ungeordnet in die Lade zurück, stieß diese mit dem Fuß hinein, so weit ich konnte . . .

The violence of the verbs 'schmeißen' and 'stoßen' and the indifference conveyed by 'mit dem Fuß' and 'ungeordnet' convince us of the hero's change of heart, the actions are symbolic of his determination to have done with 'magic'. There are many such instances of symbolic actions in the childhood and boyhood sections of the 'Jugendgeschichte.' Thus, drawing the curtain between himself and those who would interfere with his project of creating the nativity scene, the passionate kiss he bestows on the mysterious maps at the end of the detention which brings about the waning of his homesickness, and 'sacrificing' his little treasures to the snake-like tree before leaving home for Landshut express in a symbolic gesture the hero's state of mind at a particular moment. Such symbolic scenes occur throughout the work, drawing together in autobiography what no doubt in life was less clear-cut and thus shaping and interpreting the past, without however losing the 'feel' of evoked experience. Almost at the conclusion of the 'Jugendgeschichte' Carossa relates the illness and death of his father. For a considerable time relations between father and son had been strained, largely due to rumours that the hero intended to forsake medicine and join an artistic cabaret-group as a reader of poetry. In the chapter 'In Vertretung des Vaters,' worried by a postcard he has received, the young man visits his father in Munich. Finding his father too unwell to take his surgery the hero offers to stand in for him and, with his father able to listen to what goes on from a curtained-off part of the room, he sees the patients one by one. In the past the young man has felt resentment against his father for having encouraged him to take up the medical profession but now he surrenders himself to the spirit against which he has struggled:

> Ermutigt fand ich mich in meine Rolle, spielte den Erfahrenen, bat einen um den anderen einzutreten, und ließ mich vom Geiste des hinter dem Vorhang Verborgenen erfüllen.

Once he has done this he feels guided by his father:

> Mein Gedächtnis bediente mich treu mit väterlichen Regeln; es war als lenkte er von seinem Lager aus durch Tür und Vorhang hindurch den Gang der Stunde.

This scene in his father's consulting room is like an examination which the young man successfully passes, and the symbolic overtones are even more pronounced since father and son are soon to be separated by the former's death; yet the father's influence will remain a dominant one. By careful shaping of the past Carossa symbolizes a crucial step in his progress towards acceptance of his profession. Such examples seem to represent truly autobiographical procedure, where the spiritual significance of events appears out of the remembered past in its concrete reality so that the reader experiences something of the past as it actually was and, through the conscious shaping of incidents, interpreted as to its meaning for the author writing.

Nowhere are we more conscious of the shaping hand of the author than in those chapters, significantly at the end of volumes, where there is cause, both in life and art, to take stock of where he stands. They are symbolic scenes in which the past and the writer's interpretation of it are brought together more obtrusively than is the case with any of the scenes discussed above. For example, in 'Turmbesteigung,' he allows himself the device of introducing two old men to discuss the kind of education he has just completed at the Gymnasium in Landshut. At the end of the third volume a long chapter relates a visit to a poet which is also a journey into himself which allows the author to sum up the hero's situation at the end of his first year of university studies. However, and not surprisingly, it is the closing chapter of the 'Jugendgeschichte' which exhibits this kind of symbolic shaping most clearly. The scene is the churchyard where his father is buried and where the hero and a friend sit talking about him. As they do so an old woman walks up to the grave and lays a few simple flowers upon it. Significantly she is the patient who paid the hero's fee in gold and gave him the idea of saving up enough money to become independent. The scene thus serves to remind the hero of the close relationship between doctor and patient, as exemplified by the old lady's devotion to his father, and to bring to mind his previous intention to turn his back on medicine in favour of literature. As he lies in bed the same evening he takes stock of his life and realizes for the first time that the acquisition of money as a means to escape his profession is not the right way for him. Whereas he had formerly wondered whether he loved or hated the community he serves, he now feels 'tief befreundet' with both the living and the dead. In the episode in his father's consulting room the hero had felt his father's spirit guiding him and now he feels this relationship becoming ever deeper despite the intervention of death. Only now do we understand the full relevance of the sentences from Maeterlinck which are quoted at his father's graveside:

> All unsere Toten, die wir auf dem Friedhof wähnen, sind noch in uns. Sie haben keine andere Zuflucht, keinen andered Aufenthaltsort. Solange ein Mensch lebt, weiß man nicht, wer er ist, noch was er tun wird, Vertrauen fassen wir nur zu den Toten.

This new understanding of his father which had begun in the days of his last illness continues to develop after his death, and this is not on the plane of personal relationships alone, for any deeper understanding of his father necessarily leads to a fuller comprehension of the doctor's role in life.

In *Ungleiche Welten* Carossa describes the way in which he constructed *Der Tag des jungen Arztes:*

> Ich blieb dabei auf lauter unscheinbare Einfälle angewiesen, mußte wie die alten Meister der Wandmosaiken Steinchen zu Steinchen setzen und wußte nicht immer voraus, was für ein Bild entstehen würde.

Clearly the single incident rather than an overall theme was his starting point and, as I have indicated, the 'Jugendgeschichte' in general reveals the shaping spirit most strongly in the careful treatment of the single episode. It is true, of course, that these single episodes are bound together in various ways, for example by the pattern imposed on all our lives by typical childhood experiences or by the rhythms of our schooling. Thus each of the four volumes has an overall shape which corresponds to an important theme in the life, for instance, entering a boarding school, becoming accustomed to its ways and leaving; or setting out in medical practice, meeting difficulties and coming to terms with a profession. Never absent for too long are persistent themes in the whole work: the difficulties of a certain kind of temperament, the growth of a love of literature and the desire to write, the relationship with his father. All these are evidence of the autobiographer's wish to understand his past and through artistic shaping to communicate that understanding to his readers.

It is perhaps useful in conclusion to remind ourselves how important in autobiography is the shaping which comes from the relating of everything evoked to some central theme which interprets the overriding interest of the author in his past, his discovery of an underlying pattern which he reconstructs. As I have indicated, there is in Carossa's 'Jugendgeschichte' both a strong sense of episodic shaping and a discernible, though weaker, sense of overall pattern. This might best be finally illustrated by a brief comparison of the third volume, *Das Jahr der schönen Täuschungen,* with *Der Tag des jungen Arztes.* In the former we can best speak of the hero's development in terms of a number of isolated insights: into the use of corpses for study purposes, into the possibility of healing the body through the mind, into the individual's need for occasional periods of spiritual solitude. In the final volume the insights are much less disparate because they are all related to his profession: insights into its responsibilities and rewards, into modes of dealing with patients, into the difficulties inherent in the poet-doctor experience. In so far as it concentrates on his central problem and thus deals with his whole destiny, this final volume most resembles true autobiography. (pp. 92-104)

Lin Harrison, "The Shaping Spirit in Hans Carossa's 'Jugendgeschichte'," in New German Studies, Vol. VII, No. 2, Summer, 1979, pp. 91-104.

Clair Baier (essay date 1979)

[*In the following essay, Baier argues that Lin Harrison (see essay dated 1979) has misinterpreted Carossa's motivation for writing his autobiographies.*]

In welcoming Lin Harrison's 'The Shaping Spirit in Hans Carossa's "Jugendgeschichte",' may I suggest that the essence of Carossa's intention in producing his *Geschichte einer Jugend* would seem to have been forgotten, or at least not to have been rendered fully explicit. Much is made by Mr Harrison at the beginning of his article of the problem as to what constitutes an autobiography. He appears to assume that the author is trying to discover his own self, but it seems to me that Carossa is trying to get others to understand what *they* are. In other words, by describing his own development he believes he is showing us all how the individual human being develops. This is something which intrigues him both as a poet and as a medical man.

It is not without significance that Ronald Peacock's article 'Carossa a Moralist' chooses, by its very title, to look at his prose work from this angle. It should be remembered, too, that the first book of this 'Jugendgeschichte' is not entitled *'meine'* but ***'Eine' Kindheit.*** Indeed, the recently published *Briefe* show that Carossa originally called this 'Knabengeschichte' quite simply 'Vorspiele' and that it was Katharina Kippenberg who suggested that the title be altered.

It is also worth remembering that when it was originally

published in 1922, and indeed for its first five editions—the fifth appeared in 1932—, Carossa included a preface which purported to show that the work was not really his. It consisted, he said, of 'Blätter' handed to him by a wartime comrade in the autumn of 1915. He read them for a second time two years later. 'Diesen ganz ungebrochenen Zustand der ersten zehn Jahre sah ich wie die wichtigste Angelegenheit behandelt, und doch blieb alles nur ein Beginn, ein Versprechen'. Later he met the writer of these 'Blätter' again. There is thus not, as might perhaps have been expected, any suggestion that the fictitious author was a war-casualty. The whole fiction—which was sustained, as we have seen, for some years—served to allow Carossa to distance himself from the individual anecdotes and from the story as a whole, and in so doing give it universal human meaning. (pp. 205-06)

Clair Baier, "Carossa's 'Jugendgeschichte': A Postscript," in New German Studies, *Vol. VII, No. 3, Autumn, 1979, pp. 205-06.*

FURTHER READING

Baier, Clair. "A Visit to Hans Carossa." *German Life and Letters* VI, No. 3 (April 1953): 192-95.
 Describes a visit to Carossa's home.

———. "Hans Carossa's 'Stella Mystica'." *The Modern Language Review* LX, No. 2 (April 1965): 229-32.
 Remarks on the changes Carossa made to his poem "Stella Mystica" as published in 1907 and 1935.

———. " 'Mild Like Mashed Potatoes': A Brief Note on Hans Carossa and D. H. Lawrence." *German Life and Letters* XXXII, No. 4 (July 1979): 327-31.
 Discussion of D. H. Lawrence's appraisal of Hans Carossa.

Golffing, Francis. "A Note on Hans Carossa." *The Hudson Review* XII, No. 2 (Summer 1959): 252-53.
 Comments on the style and themes of Carossa's poetry.

Harrison, Lin. "The Treatment of the Hero in Hans Carossa's 'Jugendgeschichte.' " *Modern Languages* LVI, No. 1 (March 1975): 17-21.
 Thematic analysis of the "Jugendgeschichte," Carossa's autobiographical sequence. Harrison argues that two major themes pervade his autobiographies: his relationship with his father and his conflicting personality traits.

Additional coverage of Carossa's life and career is contained in the following source published by Gale Research: *Dictionary of Literary Biography,* **Vol. 66.**

Thomas Hardy

The Return of the Native

English novelist, poet, short story writer, dramatist, and essayist.

The following entry presents criticism of Hardy's novel *The Return of the Native* (1878). For further information on Hardy's complete career, see *TCLC,* Volumes 4 and 10; for discussion of *Tess of the d'Urbervilles,* see *TCLC,* Volume 18; for discussion of *The Mayor of Casterbridge,* see *TCLC,* Volume 32.

INTRODUCTION

The Return of the Native is regarded as Hardy's first mature novel and his most representative. The story of failed relationships in an isolated and bleak area of Wessex (a fictional location in southwestern England based on Hardy's native region of Dorset), the novel reveals many of Hardy's later concerns, including the alienation of the individual and the role of chance in human affairs. *The Return of the Native* has been particularly praised for its description of Egdon Heath, which is considered one of the finest representations of place in fiction and has been compared with Charles Dickens's London and Mark Twain's Mississippi River. Moreover, Hardy's depiction of the heath as the microcosm of an indifferent universe forms the philosophical underpinning of his later novels.

Hardy wrote *The Return of the Native,* his sixth published novel, between the years 1876 and 1878, while he was living in the village of Sturminster Newton in Dorset. He sent an early version of the novel to Leslie Stephen, the editor of the *Cornhill Magazine,* who rejected it, advising Hardy to make the novel more acceptable to Victorian readers. This revision appeared in the magazine *Belgravia* in serial form in 1878 and was slightly altered for book publication in November of that year. Hardy made later revisions in 1895 and 1912 that placed the previously undefined location of Edgon Heath within the specific geography of the other Wessex novels, including *Tess of the d'Urbervilles* and *Jude the Obscure.* Hardy's notebooks reveal that at the time *The Return of the Native* was written, his poetry took precedence over his fiction, and critics have noted that the novel's themes and atmosphere are reflected in such poems as "By the Barrows," "The Moth-Signal," and "On a Heath."

The Return of the Native spans a single year in the middle of the nineteenth century. In the much-analyzed first chapter Hardy described Egdon Heath, and in the chapters immediately following revealed the interrelationships of the major and minor characters. Eustacia Vye is introduced as a passionate young woman with romantic notions who is dissatisfied with life on the heath. To alleviate her boredom, she has been having an affair with Damon Wildeve, the local innkeeper. When the title character, Clym Yeobright, returns from Paris to found a school for the heathfolk, Eustacia transfers her affections to Clym. In retaliation, Wildeve marries Clym's cousin, Thomasin; shortly thereafter, Clym marries Eustacia against his mother's will. Eustacia, who hates the heath and is obsessed with the glamor of Paris, becomes depressed by Clym's adamant refusal to return to France. The subsequent events of the narrative dramatize Hardy's theme of the malevolence of chance. In pursuing his preparation for educating the community, Clym becomes partially blind from excessive reading and turns to manual labor as an alternative livelihood. Eustacia is mortified by this social decline and renews her liaison with Wildeve as her marriage deteriorates. Clym's mother, wishing for a reconciliation with her son, walks across the heath to his house. A misunderstanding prevents Mrs. Yeobright's entrance to Clym's cottage, and she retraces her steps, dejected and bitter at what she perceives to be the ingratitude and hostility of her son. On her way home she is bitten by an adder and dies, leaving Clym obsessed with grief and guilt. The heath plays a parallel role in the destruction of Eustacia and Wildeve, who both drown in a weir during a tempestuous storm. Whether Wildeve intended to elope with Eustacia, and whether Eustacia committed suicide or drowned accidentally are questions which have greatly occupied critics. At the end of the novel Clym becomes an itinerant preacher discoursing on "morally unimpeachable subjects."

Criticism of *The Return of the Native* has traditionally focused on the image of Egdon Heath. Often treating the heath as a character in its own right, critics have utilized Hardy's conception of "visible essences" to elucidate the heath's complexity. For Hardy, "visible essences" signified the embodiment of abstract themes in fictional characters, in this case the heath itself. Commentators have noted that the heath's characteristics of timelessness and hostility toward civilization are set against humanity's temporality and ethic of progress. Throughout *The Return of the Native* Hardy employs references to past events and classical texts in order to create a sense of humanity's primeval conflict with the natural order, as represented by Egdon Heath, and to assert the superiority of paganism to Christianity. The fate of the main characters depends on their relation to the heath: those who are accepting of their environment survive; those who reject Egdon Heath are destroyed.

The theory of "visible essences" has also been used to clarify the ideological tension represented in the characters of Clym and Eustacia. Critics have considered Clym as the "visible essence" of modern consciousness and Eustacia as the embodiment of pre-Christian paganism. Influenced by nineteenth-century science and philosophy, especially the pessimist writings of Arthur Schopenhauer, Clym views life "as a thing to be put up with." Eustacia, however, is described by Hardy in terms that convey her alienation from the nineteenth century, and is viewed by critics as the "visible essence" of the Hellenic, or pre-Christian, zest for life—the antithesis of Clym's somber sermonizing at the end of the novel.

While *The Return of the Native* initially received hostile criticism from most reviewers and was judged inferior to Hardy's previous book, *Far from the Madding Crowd,* the novel has, nevertheless, proved to be one of Hardy's most widely read and enduring works. Many later critics, such as F. R. Leavis and T. S. Eliot, criticized *The Return of the Native* and Hardy's novels in general for their conventional plots and melodramatic overtones. More recent criticism, however, has sought to explain the power and appeal that *The Return of the Native* exerts on readers despite such perceived flaws as overliterary description, weakly drawn secondary characters, and heavy-handed plotting. For many critics the memorable creations of Egdon Heath, Clym Yeobright, and Eustacia Vye make *The Return of the Native* one of the most remarkable of Victorian novels.

CRITICISM

The Athenaeum (essay date 1878)

[*In the following excerpt,* The Return of the Native *is given an unfavorable review.*]

Mr. Hardy, who at one time seemed as promising as any of the younger generation of story-tellers, has published a book [**The Return of the Native**] distinctly inferior to anything of his which we have yet read. It is not that the story is ill-conceived—on the contrary, there are the elements of a good novel in it; but there is just that fault which would appear in the pictures of a person who has a keen eye for the picturesque without having learnt to draw. One sees what he means, and is all the more disappointed at the clumsy way in which the meaning is expressed. People talk as no people ever talked before, or perhaps we should rather say as no people ever talk now. The language of his peasants may be Elizabethan, but it can hardly be Victorian. Such phrases as "being a man of the mournfullest make, I was scared a little," or "he always had his great indignation ready against anything underhand," are surprising in the mouth of the modern rustic. Indeed, the talk seems pitched throughout in too high a key to suit the talkers. A curious feature in the book is the low social position of the characters. The upper rank is represented by a young man who is assistant to a Paris jeweller, an innkeeper who has served his apprenticeship to a civil engineer, the daughter of a bandsman, and two or three of the small farmer class. These people all speak in a manner suggestive of high cultivation, and some of them intrigue almost like dwellers in Mayfair, while they live on nearly equal terms with the furze-cutting rustics who form a chorus reminding one of "On ne badine pas avec l'amour." All this is mingled with a great deal of description, showing a keen observation of natural things, though disfigured at times by forced allusions and images. The sound of reeds in a wind is likened to "sounds as of a congregation praying humbly." A girl's recollections "stand like gilded uncials upon the dark tablet of her present surroundings." The general plot of the story turns on the old theme of a man who is in love with two women, and a woman who is in love with two men; the man and the woman being both selfish and sensual. We see the last word in its more extended sense; for there is nothing in the book to provoke a comparison with the vagaries of some recent novelists, mostly of the gentler sex. But one cannot help seeing that the two persons in question know no other law than the gratification of their own passion, although this is not carried to a point which would place the book on the "Index" of respectable households. At the same time it is clear that Eustacia Vye belongs essentially to the class of which Madame Bovary is the type; and it is impossible not to regret, since this is a type which English opinion will not allow a novelist to depict in its completeness, that Mr. Hardy should have wasted his powers in giving what after all is an imperfect and to some extent misleading view of it.

A review of "The Return of the Native," in The Athenaeum, *No. 2665, November 23, 1878, p. 654.*

W. E. Henley (essay date 1878)

[*Henley was an English critic and poet who played an important role in the Counter-Decadent movement of the 1890s. A prolific and energetic critic, he was editor of the* National Observer *and the* New Review, *where he was an early defender of works by such writers as H. G. Wells, Thomas Hardy, and George Bernard Shaw. In the following excerpt, Henley discusses the strong points and shortcomings of* The Return of the Native.]

In Mr. Hardy's work there is a certain Hugoesque quality of insincerity; but there is withal so much to admire and be grateful for that it takes high rank among the good romantic work of the generation, and perhaps this quality of insincerity itself is rather apparent than real. Mr. Hardy is so much in earnest in all he does that, even when he is most artificial, he is not without his motive, and has in his own consciousness of well-doing and well-meaning a complete answer to any such charge that may be brought against him. For this reason one feels a great deal of deference in rendering account of him. His work may be, to an outsider, neither wholly satisfactory nor wholly right; but it has so much in it of intention and of execution that the outsider, compelled to strike a balance of opinion, finds that balance immensely in his author's favour. Mr. Hardy has such a right and masterful faculty of analysis; he perceives and apprehends his characters so completely; he has such a strong poetic and dramatic feeling for scenery; such a clear and vivid habit of description; he phrases so adequately and so lucidly, that, carried away by the consideration of these qualities, one fails to remember that his dialogue is only here and there dramatic in the highest sense; that there is much of what looks like affectation in his work; that his sympathy with his personages is rather intellectual than emotional; that he rarely makes you laugh and never makes you cry, and that his books are valuable and interesting rather as the outcome of a certain mind than as pictures of society or studies in human nature; that his tragedy is arbitrary and accidental rather than heroic and inevitable; and that, rare artist as he is, there is something wanting in his personality, and he is not quite a great man. In *The Return of the Native*—which, it may be said in passing, is not by any means so good a book as *A Pair of Blue Eyes*—these defects and these merits are exampled pretty strongly, and the general impression it produces is the one I have tried to set down. The story is a sad one; but the sadness is unnecessary and uncalled for. A chapter of accidents makes the hero seem to cast off his mother, who thereupon dies; a second chapter of accidents sends the heroine to death by drowning. And the hero, burdened with a double remorse, is left to live on, and to take what is substantially the place in the world that he had desired ere destruction came upon him. It is all very mournful, and very cruel, and very French; and to those who have the weakness of liking to be pleasantly interested in a book it is also very disagreeable. Perhaps, too, it is false art; but of that, believing Mr. Hardy to have a very complete theory about his books, I will not speak. To me, however, nearly all that is best in the novel is analytic and descriptive. I know of nothing in later English so striking and on the whole so sound as the several pictures of Egdon Heath, or the introductory analysis of the character of Eustacia Vye. In these Mr. Hardy is seen at his best and strongest. Acute, prescient, imaginative, insatiably observant, and at the same time so rigidly and so finely artistic that there is scarce a point in the whole that can be fairly questioned, he seems to me to paint the woman and the place as no other living writer could have done. Whether he makes the best use of them afterwards need not be here discussed. Nearly all the characters are, it should be added, of value and of interest; Mrs. Yeobright, I think, being particularly to be commended. But so far as its dramatics are concerned *The Return of the Native* appears to be rather well meant than happily done. Such a speech as this, for instance, is admirable: " 'Well, then I spoke to her in my well-known merry way, and she said, "O that what's shaped so venerable should talk like a fool!"—that's what she said to me. I don't care for her, be jowned if I do, and so I told her. "Be jowned if I care for 'ee," I said. I had her there—hey?' " So, too, is this other, a page or two further on:—" ' I han't been [to church] these three years,' said Humphrey, 'for I'm so dead sleepy of a Sunday; and 'tis so terrible fur to get there; and when you do get there 'tis such a mortal poor chance that you'll be chose for up above, when so many baint, that I bide at home and don't go at all.' " And there are things as good as these of frequent occurrence; but they do not constitute the body of what may be called the comic dialogue, and the impression that it produces is, as a consequence, unsatisfactory. To turn to the tragic part is, I think, to have yet more room for sorrow; in one scene—the scene where Clym is informed of the way of his mother's death—Mr. Hardy rises to the situation, and does nobly; but elsewhere he is only excessively clever, and earnest, and disappointing. But, in spite of these shortcomings, the novel is so clever and so strong that it excites both interest and admiration, and takes a first place among the novels of the season. Mr. Hardy has, I ought to note, been at the pains of making a map of his locality, which should be consulted attentively, as it is of considerable use.

> W. E. Henley, in a review of "The Return of the Native," in The Academy, n.s. Vol. XIV, No. 343, November 30, 1878, p. 517.

Albert J. Guerard (essay date 1950)

[*Guerard is an American novelist and critic who has written extensively on the works of Thomas Hardy and Joseph Conrad. In the following excerpt, he discusses* The Return of the Native *as an entertainment, a problem novel, a Wessex romance, and a tragedy.*]

The Return of the Native (1878), though not Hardy's greatest novel, is in some ways his most representative book. . . . It is at once an entertainment, a problem novel, a Wessex romance, and (in part at least) a tragedy. It is neither such a plot boiler as *A Laodicean* nor such a coherent masterpiece as *The Mayor of Casterbridge.* And these are some of the reasons why it repays study and debate. It offers the reader an unusual opportunity to assess both Hardy's weaknesses and his strengths.

There is first of all, the consideration of the novel as an "entertainment," the good or evil demon of melodramatic plot—the dependence on misunderstanding and mischance, on letters and messages that miscarry, on Diggory Venn's ability to overhear crucial conversations, on the holocaust in Shadwater Weir, from which Diggory "came up with an armful of wet drapery enclosing a woman's cold form." Hardy was impelled not only to tell exciting stories, but also to make bitter commentaries on the wasteful disorder of life. He satisfied both impulses in the climax of *The Return of the Native.* The entertainer is seen too in the original conception of Diggory Venn, who was to have been a weird, mysterious agent intervening in human affairs as the preternatural agents of the old ballads intervened. With the characteristic nostalgia of the nineteenth-century man who had lost his religious faith, Hardy longed to spiritualize the natural world; longed, in the depression of his skepticism, to see witches, demons, and ghosts. He could half believe in them. Susan Nunsuch, for example, may be a naïve follower of rural superstition. And yet—the enemy does die a few hours after Susan roasted her wax image. Diggory himself is not one of Hardy's most successful attempts to enrich through mysterious overtone. He does have more than natural luck gambling with Wildeve in that wonderful game played to the light of thirteen glowworms—the occult mystery of the dice staged against the natural mystery of the eternal and staring heath croppers. As a rule, however, Diggory has nothing more other-worldly than the occupational redness of his skin. If we look at him as an ordinary human being, he raises an interesting problem which disturbed the psychologist Havelock Ellis in Hardy's own time. Why are so many of Hardy's men shy, reticent, and unaggressive after Diggory's fashion? Why do they so often withdraw their claims on the women they love? Why do they take pleasure not in living but in seeing others live? One suspects that Diggory would have enjoyed Thomasin's glove even more than Thomasin herself. Here, of course, the older reader's judgment may be different from that of the youthful idealist; this older reader is likely to see Diggory's self-sacrificing withdrawal as a psychic defect. Many of Hardy's men—Henry Knight, Stephen Smith, Gabriel Oak, Giles Winterborne, Christopher Julian, John Loveday, even Clym Yeobright—show this same passivity and peculiar sexlessness. It would be a mistake to suppose that Hardy idealized in these men his own ideal of conduct. He knew that the abnormally unaggressive man can at times cause as much mischief as the sensual egoist, and he referred nostalgically to the "passionate lover of the old-fashioned sort." Perhaps Hardy unconsciously dramatized, in these timid men, his own reticence. The biography signed by the second Mrs. Hardy, but largely written by Hardy himself, remarks that he had developed very late in "virility," though mentally precocious.

The Return of the Native is also a problem novel. The problem involves the eternal conflict of conventionality and freedom, conformity and revolt. Hardy—if we consider all his books—clearly envied the passionate and unrestrained rebels, but identified with the quiet conformists; he believed in spontaneity, but was drawn to restraint. This conflict between sympathy and belief produces one of the valuable contradictions of Hardy's temperament—valuable, since great art often comes from contradiction and conflict. The novel has its calculated jostling of temperaments—Eustacia's longing to escape the heath for a brighter world, if only the world of Budmouth, an hour away, and Clym's longing to settle down. "Take all the varying hates felt by Eustacia Vye towards the heath, and translate them into loves, and you have the heart of Clym." Tired of the fashionable world, Clym preaches an ideal of simplicity; he has turned his back on ambition, and finds culture more important than luxury. Conceivably the attempt to put his ideals into practice could have produced an interesting theme. But Hardy sees the problem too abstractly. Moreover, Clym's commitment to culture is scarcely evident in the action of the novel.

> In consequence of this relatively advanced position, Yeobright might have been called unfortunate. The rural world was not ripe for him. A man should be only partially before his time: to be completely to the vanward in aspiration is fatal to fame . . . To argue upon the possibility of culture before luxury to the bucolic world may be to argue truly, but it is an attempt to disturb a sequence to which humanity has been long accustomed.

Whenever Hardy writes in this manner, we know that his true talents as a novelist are asleep. This is the prose of the lecture platform, not the prose of great fiction. This is the Hardy who, out of a pedantic respect for exactness, kept a map of his characters' movements and paced off the number of their steps across the heath. It is the Hardy who, reducing the complexity of life to abstract simplicities, could conceive such a chapter heading as "A New Force Disturbs the Current."

The Return of the Native is perhaps most of all a Wessex romance, a love story of minute and transient humans played against the background of immemorial country customs (such as the Mummers' play and the Fifth of November fires) and of the eternal and unchanging heath. The rustics also are eternal; they exist to provide comic relief, and to comment pungently on the loves and trials of the protagonists. By 1878 Hardy no longer felt impelled to write a guidebook and treatise on Wessex; he no longer felt obliged to record the tedious processes of agricultural life. Therefore, in his treatment of the Wessex background, in *The Return of the Native,* Hardy is something more than a realist. If the early pages on Egdon Heath are not as good as earlier critics thought, they are not as bad as various modern novelists and critics have claimed. They do offer the extreme amount of mystery and overtone to be extracted from the merely natural—from the "nightly roll into darkness," from the suggestion of immense periods of time, from the metaphorical connection with the mind's "wild regions of obscurity." On this bleak heath all but the most vigilant are lost; it is a fitting background for a story of misplaced longings and rudely unfilled loves.

Many readers, noting so much unhappiness, would classify *The Return of the Native* with the three late tragedies. For this is anything but a cheerful novel, and the happiest creatures we encounter are certain maggoty shapes seen in shallow ponds, "heaving and wallowing with enjoyment." The only persons who escape the general apathy drown in Shadwater Weir; the longings of all the characters are aroused only to be frustrated; and the melancholy descriptions of the heath are scarcely relieved by vague references to life "as a thing to put up with" and to a "long line of disillusive centuries." We should, however, guard against confusing mere gloominess with tragic power. True tragedy requires more than the expression of a melancholy temperament brooding over bad luck. It requires, for one thing, at least one character of a certain magnitude—the magnitude of a Tess Durbeyfield and her animal strength; the magnitude of a Michael Henchard, whose fate is *not* more than he can bear; the magnitude of a Jude Fawley, capable of rejecting the entire human condition and accursed state of man. True tragedy further requires intense psychic conflict and a finally increased understanding of human nature and of our lot on earth. *The Return of the Native* lacks such magnitudes. Eustacia's unregenerate longing for happiness and her personal war against the heath and against a pallidly conformist society are universal enough, and she is one of Hardy's most brilliant creations, but she is not involved in the kind of inward conflict we associate with tragedy. The conflicts of Clym Yeobright are theoretical, schematized, and overstated. Hardy did not understand Clym dramatically, as he did understand the bitter and more complex Jude; he did not, that is, get inside his character in a dynamic way. Did he even understand Clym rationally? What lay behind his turning his back on ambition and a Paris life? Why would such a man take pleasure in humiliating himself by furze cutting? (His own explanations are very incomplete.)

Why would he at last become an itinerant preacher? Hardy himself seems to give inadequate reasons for many of Clym's acts. The picture of negative personality and withdrawal is plausible enough so far as it goes, but it does not go very far. No fascinated curiousity concerning human nature holds us as we read *The Return of the Native.* We read on rather to find out whether these poor sufferers will ever realize their desires.

There nevertheless remains the impression and overtone of tragedy; we do feel, as in the three tragedies, Hardy's own pessimistic reading of life. The heath (though by no means worthy of all the ponderous philosophical nonsense that critics have written about it) is truly a microcosm of the world as Hardy saw it in his fiction—an unfriendly or indifferent environment which cares nothing for our complex human needs and longings, and on which small creatures wander for a few days or a few years before they die. We are no more than the meaningless "never-ending and heavy-laden throng" of ants which Mrs. Yeobright saw a few hours before her death. The mere play of coincidence and circumstance, of brute chance and absurd mischance, contribute to the impression of human defeat. Our human capacity for misunderstanding ourselves and others is enormous, and we often create our own "bad luck." But there is also bad luck that is merely gratuitous. The entire plot hinges on Clym muttering "Mother" in his sleep at just the moment (after all these months) that his mother is actually at the door. It is futile to deplore Hardy's use of chance and coincidence; nearly all great art stylizes and foreshortens reality in one way or another. We may rather deplore his failure, in this particular novel, to give chance and coincidence a more visionary cast and symbolic significance. In *Tess of the d'Urbervilles* and *Jude the Obscure* the unreasonable bad luck of the sufferers adds up to a coherent picture of injustice. However we doubt the fortuitous details, we accept the final interpretation of life. In *The Mayor of Casterbridge* chance and coincidence are symbolic of an inward fate, virtually instruments of a self-punishing compulsion. In *The Return of the Native* coincidence is more coldly manipulated. No doubt Hardy intended the chance events of November the sixth to symbolize or reflect the confused destinies of his characters. But the characters themselves are not sufficiently important to turn melodrama into symbolism and tragedy; their inward sufferings are not sufficiently complex to support and justify the macabre events. The bad luck therefore remains meaningless bad luck, or has no meaning beyond the common Victorian one that sinners must be hounded to their graves. *The Return of the Native* is not a tragedy; it is, rather, the most sombre of the Wessex romances. (pp. xiv-xx)

> *Albert J. Guerard, in an introduction to* The Return of the Native *by Thomas Hardy, Holt, Rinehart and Winston, 1969, pp. v-xx.*

John Paterson (essay date 1959)

[*Paterson is an American educator who has written extensively on* The Return of the Native. *In the following essay, he examines the novel's anti-Christian outlook.*]

In such spots as Egdon, Hardy was to report, where festive Maypole-days could still be faithfully observed, "homage to nature, self-adoration, frantic gaieties, fragments of Teutonic rites to divinities whose names are forgotten, seem in some way or other to have survived mediaeval doctrine." An examination of the manuscript [of *The Return of the Native*] reveals that this handsome celebration of the natural life originally was placed in opposition not to "mediaeval *doctrine*" but, more explicitly and more dramatically, to "mediaeval *Christianity*." In the final terms of the novel, again, the highly charged dancing at East Egdon was to be defined as a recrudescence of paganism: "For the time Paganism was revived in their hearts, the pride of life was all in all, and they adored none other than themselves." In the original terms of the manuscript, the dancing was defined not only as a reaffirmation of the pagan but also, and more specifically, as a rejection of the Christian: "*Christianity was eclipsed in their hearts,* Paganism was revived, the pride of life was all in all, they adored themselves & [sic] *their own natural instincts.*"

In the novel in its present form, Eustacia Vye stands of course outside the conventional categories of good and evil: her "high gods" are William the Conqueror, Strafford, and Napoleon; she prefers Saul or Sisera to Jacob or David; she sides with the Philistines and admires Pontius Pilate. In the text of the manuscript, however, the implications of her perverse and impious loyalties were fully articulated: "*Her chief priest was Byron: her antichrist a well-meaning preacher at Budmouth, of the name of Slatters.*" Indeed, where she now aspires to look "with indifference upon the cruel satires that *Fate* loves to indulge in," she earlier aspired to look "with indifference upon the cruel satires that *God* loves to indulge in."

Of course, not all traces of antichristian sentiment were stricken from the record. At the conclusion of the novel, Hardy could still permit himself the nearly bitter reflection that "human beings, in their generous endeavour to construct a hypothesis that shall not degrade a First Cause, have always hesitated to conceive a dominant power of lower moral quality than their own . . ." As the revisions would testify, however, the virulent censorship current in 1878 more generally had the effect of driving underground what evidently threatened to materialize as

---

Florence Emily Hardy on Wessex:

A peculiarity in the local descriptions running through all Hardy's writings may be instanced here—that he never uses the word "Dorset", never names the county at all (except possibly in an explanatory footnote), but obliterates the names of the six counties, whose area he traverses in his scenes, under the general appellation of "Wessex"—an old word that became quite popular after the date of *Far from the Madding Crowd,* where he first introduced it. So far did he carry this idea of the unity of Wessex that he used to say he had grown to forget the crossing of county boundaries within the ancient kingdom. . . .

Florence Emily Hardy in her The Early Life of Thomas Hardy: 1840-1891, *1928.*

an open denigration of Christianity. It compelled Hardy to suppress the repudiation of the Christian implicit in the novel's celebration of the pagan. The revisions draw attention, then, to a subversive content no longer visible to the naked eye. Indeed, they positively invite a reexamination of *The Return of the Native* as an anticlerical tract.

The antichristian bias of the novel is first of all apparent in its celebration of Eustacia Vye. For as a symbolic character, Eustacia belongs to a world that has not yet been touched by the spectral hand of Christianity: she reincarnates on the withered parish of Egdon Heath the larger and braver vision of the ancient Greeks. Her dignity is described, for example, as "Tartarean"; she strikes with ease "the note of Artemis, Athena, or Hera"; she is said to descend from Homeric kings, "from Alcinous' line, her father hailing from Phaeacia's isle." Elsewhere, she can be chastised by Clym as a rebel in the Promethean tradition: " 'Now don't you suppose . . . that I cannot rebel, in high Promethean fashion, against the gods and fate as well as you.' " And persistently associated with fire as she is—the color of her soul is fancied, for example, as "flame-like," and the pool in which she dies is defined as a "boiling caldron"—she everywhere evokes the image of the Promethean heroine. In its central action in the suffering and death of Eustacia Vye, in other words, *The Return of the Native* dramatizes the tragic humiliation, in the diminished world of the modern consciousness, of an heroic, prechristian understanding of life.

Up to a certain point, of course, the diminished landscape of modern times, the Egdon Heath against which she struggles in vain, is ascribed not to the Christian but to the scientific dispensation. Hardy philosophizes at one point:

> The truth seems to be that a long line of disillusive centuries has permanently displaced the Hellenic idea of life . . . That old-fashioned revelling in the general situation grows less and less possible as we uncover the defects of natural laws, and see the quandary that man is in by their operation.

In this perspective Eustacia Vye, as the anachronistic survival of "the Hellenic idea of life," stands opposed to Clym Yeobright, who, having read aright the grim Darwinian message of the heath and having assimilated at Paris the "ethical systems popular at the time," is prepared to abjure Prometheanism and to accept the modern, or antiheroic, idea of life. Beyond this point, however, it becomes increasingly clear that the deterioration of the heroic Greek consciousness is ascribed less to the scientific revelation, less to the discovery of "the defects of natural laws," than to the establishment of a Christian order and belief.

In the first place, as the interchangeability in Hardy's mind of "God" and "Fate" and as the heroine's contempt for Slatters, "the well-meaning preacher at Budmouth," would intimate, Eustacia's quarrel is ultimately more with the Christian way of life than with the objective structure of the universe. If she is not longer free to despise poor Slatters, she can still, after all, hum Saturday night ballads on the Sabbath and openly declare her aversion for English Sundays. And it is surely significant that of all the parts in the mummers' play, she should draw precisely that of the antichrist, the Turkish Knight, who must, with ritual inexorability, suffer defeat and death at the hands of the Christian champion. In the last analysis, however, nothing more sharply defines Eustacia's antichristian implications than her persistent identification as a black witch, that immemorial antagonist of the Christian faith. Early defined by the peasant chorus as " 'the lonesome dark-eyed creature up there that some say is a witch,' " she is persecuted by Susan Nunsuch for allegedly "bewitching" her children and denounced by Clym for having, "like a devil," destroyed his happiness: " 'Don't look at me with those eyes,' " he declaims, " 'as if you would bewitch me again!' "

That this identification is fundamental to her conception would be verified by the fact that whole scenes are conditioned and even dominated by the formidable image it evokes. The crooked sixpence with which she bribes Johnny Nunsuch to tend her bonfire—" 'Stay a little longer and I will give you a crooked sixpense' "—is represented in folk-tradition as a charm against witchcraft and in the particular context of the novel identifies her as a member of that dark sorority. Still more convincingly, when she summons to her bonfire the dim, half-realized figure of Damon Wildeve, she recreates the presence of the wicked enchantress presiding over unholy fires and evoking out of darkness or out of nothingness shapes and images that are the stuff of no human reality. Thus when her lover does materialize—and the term is used carefully—it is as a form which, if it does not quite suggest the monstrous, does not quite suggest the human either: "Thereupon the contour of a man became dimly visible against the low-reaching sky over the valley, beyond the outer margin of the pool. He came round it and leapt upon the bank beside her." And the scene that follows is rendered in terms that unmistakably suggest a sinister supernatural: Eustacia gazes upon Wildeve as Milton's Satan must have gazed upon the horrid crew called up from the baleful lake, "as upon some wondrous thing she had created out of chaos." Moreover, in exulting over him, she employs a heightened language that leaves no doubt as to the demoniacal nature of her summons: I " 'thought,' " she tells him, " 'I would get a little excitement by calling you up and triumphing over you as the Witch of Endor called up Samuel. I determined you should come; and you have come! I have shown my power . . . .' " Even at the very close of the novel, in fact, when the episode is repeated and a fire is once again seen on Mistover Knap, Hardy evokes the same imagery of magic: "there flashed upon [Eustacia's] imagination some other form which that fire might call up."

Eustacia's status as witch or demon would be supported by the fact that Damon Wildeve, the slave and image of her own invention, is composed of exactly the same stuff. Frequently seen and satirized as "the Rousseau of Egdon," as the type of the decrepit and disreputable romantic, he is just as frequently seen and celebrated as the dreamer of a purely human and, to that extent, unchristian consummation, and hence, like Eustacia herself, he justifies comparison with the darker powers. Suddenly accosted by the reddleman, for example, he starts "like Satan at the touch of Ithuriel's spear." And in the tradition of the revolted angel, he is said to have known better days, to have fallen from high places. " 'He was brought up to better things than keeping the Quiet Woman,' " the peasant chorus observes, in a homely recapitulation of the Satan-story. " 'An engineer—that's what the man was, as we know; but he threw away his chance, and so 'a took a public-house to live. His learning was no use to him at all.' " At one point, indeed, Wildeve, beholding innocence and wounded by a remorse for which there is no cure, evokes the pathos of Satan at the gates of Eden: " 'God, how I envy him that sweet sleep!' " he mourns, observing Clym Yeobright at rest. " 'I have not slept like that since I was a boy—years and years ago.' "

However, as the name "Damon Wildeve," with its evocation of "daimons" and nocturnal orgies would imply, Hardy evidently conceived him as—with Eustacia's "witch"—the agent of powers and energies older even than Satan, as the agent of mysterious powers and energies that once haunted the primeval landscape in the shapes of ogres and goblins and demons until the blight of Christianity drove them to the darkness of cave and fen and forest and at last, except on barbaric Egdon, out of the human imagination altogether. In our first glimpse of him, when he is approached by an indignant Mrs. Yeobright, he assumes, as in his materialization before Eustacia's bonfire, nothing more distinct than a shadowy shape or form: "a vast shadow, in which could be dimly traced portions of a masculine contour, blotted half the ceiling." He assumes, in fact, something of the laborious formlessness of a Caliban: "the back and shoulders of a man came between Mrs. Yeobright's eyes and the fire. Wildeve, whose form it was, immediately turned, arose, and advanced to meet his visitors." The demonism inherent in the character-image of Damon Wildeve would confirm, then, the demonism inherent in the character-image of Eustacia Vye. As the virtual author of a subhuman, if not superhuman, lover, as the practitioner of a black witchcraft, and, above all, as the avatar of the heroic Greek sense of life, Eustacia suggests nothing so much as a pagan exile in a Christian province.

The antichristian sentiment implicit in her pre-Christianity is dramatized, finally, by her opposition to Clym Yeobright, who is actuated in the last analysis less by scientific consciousness than by Christian conscience. Hardy preferred of course to see his hero as the very emanation of the pagan heath: "He was permeated with its scenes, with its substance, and with its odours." He preferred, too, to see him, in his role of meliorist, in his role of schoolmaster to the proletariat of Egdon, as, with Eustacia Vye, a Promethean figure: "As is usual with bright natures, the deity that lies ignominiously chained within an ephermeral human carcase shone out of him like a ray." At the very last, however, Clym has as little in common with the barbaric heath as any character in the novel, and although he does occasionally appear in the image of Prometheus, it is more generally, as his chastisement of Eustacia should indicate, as the reformed Promethean: " 'I have felt more steam and smoke of that sort than you have ever heard of '." His characteristic note is everywhere, in fact, the note of Christian self-renunciation. The scientific humanism he is alleged to have imbibed in the schools of Paris only thinly disguises the Christian martyr.

For if Clym consistently deceives himself and even the author, who will later regard him as quite the nicest of all his heroes, he does not succeed in deceiving his women, whose instinct in this case turns out to be nearly infallible. Thus the skeptical Mrs. Yeobright very correctly understands him as a missionary in disguise: " 'It is right,' " she concedes at one point, " 'that there should be schoolmasters, and missionaries, and all such men. . . . ' " And Eustacia, not far behind in insight, associates him half-satirically with the Apostle Paul: " ' . . . but the worst of it is that though Paul was excellent as a man in the Bible he would hardly have done in real life.' " It becomes a question, in fact, whether Clym even deceives the author who can interpret him, both before and after his tragedy, in terms of Christian metaphors and images or, put otherwise, as an inverted Christian. He is, Hardy remarks, "a John the Baptist who took ennoblement rather than repentance for his text." In his mission to the unwashed denizens of the heath, he is seen as "preaching to the Egdon eremites." And in defending his mission against the more secular intelligence of his mother, he is moved to invoke the aid of St. Paul himself: " 'I get up every morning,' " he tells her, " 'and see the whole creation groaning and travailing in pain, as St. Paul says, and yet there am I, trafficking in glittering splendours with wealthy women and titled libertines. . . . ' "

Certainly, if Clym has earlier flirted, as the humanitarian reformer, with a dangerous Prometheanism, he is, following the deaths of his wife and mother, the very much chastened, the very much frightened, Christian. Like the Sue Bridehead of a later novel, he is converted by tragedy, by his encounter with evil, back to the faith of his fathers. " 'If there is any justice in God,' " he declaims out of a new sense of Christian guilt and remorse, " 'let Him kill me now. . . . If He would only strike me with more pain I would believe in Him for ever!' " And having, at the close of the book, "found his vocation in the career of an itinerant open-air preacher and lecturer on morally unimpeachable subjects," the pseudo-Promethean stands revealed in his true colours as the scripture-quoting Christian: "But his heart was heavy; that mother had *not* crowned him in the day of his espousals and in the day of the gladness of his heart." Indeed, preaching a series of what are called Sermons on the Mount to a captive audience of supernaturally quiescent heath-folk, Clym emerges at the end in the guise of a Christ-figure.

Where Clym was concerned, of course, Hardy's critical faculties would appear to have been temporarily suspended. There are distinct occasions, however, when perhaps unconsciously and certainly in spite of himself, Hardy exposed his hero to the cruelest and most damaging ironies. These occasions are nowhere more in evidence than when Clym's theoretical intelligence is juxtaposed with the practical and instinctive intelligence of the still-unchristened peasant community from which he has, to his considerable sorrow, been separated. There is an irony, retroactive in effect, in the comment evoked by the first news of his coming: " 'Wonderful clever, 'a believe,' " Grandfer Cantle

The house in Sturminster Newton where Hardy wrote The Return of the Native.

crows ecstatically," '—ah, I should like to have all that's under that young man's hair.' " There is an even more specific and more trenchant irony, however—and one more clearly at Clym's expense—in the peasants' response to his program for their intellectual, if not moral, improvement. " 'He'll never carry it out in the world,' " says Timothy Fairway prophetically from the vantage-point of a superior wisdom, a wisdom as old as the heath. " 'In a few weeks he'll learn to see things otherwise.' " " 'Tis goodhearted of the young man,' " says another member of the peasant family with a condescension that events will justify. " 'But, for my part,' " and with this the chapter is brought to an ironic period, " 'I think he had better mind his business.' "

Clym nowhere suffers more from the exposures of irony than in the terminal chapters of the novel where his repudiation of life in a spirit of Christian self-renunciation contrasts dramatically not only with the life-renewing rites of Maypole-day but also with the life-renewing rites of Thomasin's marriage to the reddleman. Whether Hardy intended it or not—and it is hard to believe that he did not—Clym's theatrical conversion is reduced by the "savage" rites of spring and marriage, to ludicrous terms. Thus at the same time that he is distressed by the inconvenience of Thomasin's loving him, she has already set her cap for the less ethereal person of Diggory Venn and just when he is at the point, "with a pleasant sense of doing his duty" of offering his hand in marriage, she asks him, as the head of the family, to bless her union with another. The irony at Clym's expense becomes positively unmistakable in the penultimate scene of the novel when Charley describes for the benefit of the hero (significantly still blind) the joyous wedding-festivities of which they have chosen to be the unobserved and pathetic spectators:

> "Do any of them seem to care about my not being there?" Clym asked.
>
> "No, not a bit in the world. Now they are all holding up their glasses and drinking somebody's health."
>
> "I wonder if it is mine?"

"No, 'tis Mr. and Mrs. Venn's, because he is making a hearty sort of speech. . . ."

In the context of *The Return of the Native,* then, Clym Yeobright not only functions as a figure of Christian piety but becomes, as such, the victim of a number of highly damaging ironies. Moreover, insofar as he serves as Eustacia's foil and antagonist, this Christian hero underlines the antichristian sentiment explicit in her denigrations of Christian mediocrity but more generally implicit in her metaphorical identifications as witch and as Greek heroine. In the death of Eustacia Vye, in other words, and in the Christian apotheosis of Clym Yeobright, *The Return of the Native* commemorates, in an elegiac if not tragic mood, the defeat of pagan consciousness and the triumph of Christian conscience.

The completeness with which the novel exploits the pagan-Christian antithesis only becomes fully apparent with an examination of the subsidiary figures of the reddleman and the peasant chorus. Diggory Venn in his role of reddleman, for example, suggests nothing so much as a creature—goblin, elf, or demon—out of Celtic mythology. Like so many sprites of popular superstition, he makes his habitation, temporarily at least, in "a pit under the hill." He appears and disappears throughout the novel, as Wildeve for one has good reason to know, with an uncanny rapidity that suggests the possession of magical powers: "On [Wildeve's] reaching the top a shape grew up from the earth immediately behind him." Apparently beyond good and evil, he intervenes in, and disrupts, the normal course of human affairs with results that cannot clearly be established as either for better or for worse. And, in the best tradition of folk romance, his psychology is frequently enigmatical. It is, of course, perfectly accordant with this essential conception of the reddleman as a nature-spirit that he should be seen as standing, with Eustacia Vye the black witch and Damon Wildeve her succubus, outside the pale of Christian salvation. The whole race of reddlemen are imagined as "criminals for whose misdeeds other men had wrongfully suffered," as criminals who had escaped the law but who "had not escaped their own consciences, and had taken to the trade as a lifelong penance." They persistently evoke, certainly, an image calculated to horrify the pious imagination, the image of the outcast from the Christian community: they are of the race of "Mephistophelian visitants", they are stamped by reddle "as with the mark of Cain"; and like the heath itself, they are designated, in the figure of Diggory Venn, as "Ishmaelitish."

The antichristian implications of Diggory's reddlemanship are perhaps most clearly dramatized, however, by the specifically Christian implications of the transformation which Hardy reluctantly permitted him at the close of the novel. For his generally middle-class rehabilitation turns out to be, in part at least, a Christian rehabilitation, a species of Christian conversion. Certainly, it is more than adventitious that Diggory should give up the reddle trade and, presumably, the illegitimate powers and privileges that go along with it, at—of all times of the year—*Christmas:* " 'I gave up dealing in reddle,' " he declares to Thomasin's comic astonishment, " 'last Christmas.' " And it is surely more than adventitious that when the red dye does fade from his complexion, it is to disclose not only the lineaments of the respectable dairy farmer but also "the strangely altered hues of an ordinary *Christian* countenance." As the unreconstructed reddleman, that is to say, Diggory is evidently designed to honor the stoic and realistic values of a pre-Christian way of life and, tacitly at least, to criticize the nicer, less permissive values that come in with Christianity. Indeed, insofar as he was, according to Hardy's original prospectus, not to have joined Thomasin in Christian marriage, but "to have retained his isolated and weird character to the last, and to have disappeared mysteriously from the heath, nobody knowing whither," he may very well have been intended to symbolize at the very end the humiliating and tragic defeat, with the institution of Christian discipline, of that elusive and nearly demoniacal spirit of fen and forest that has found its last resting place in savage Egdon.

For the antichristian tendency of the novel, however, the peasant community with its hearty celebration of the natural life and its instinctive distrust of the church is in the last analysis mainly responsible. For where Eustacia and Wildeve and Diggory Venn are identified in symbolic terms with prechristian beliefs and values, the humble members of the peasant society are so identified in relatively realistic terms. Their performances derive, that is to say, from levels of thinking and feeling older than, and happily oblivious to, the innovations of Christianity. In their first appearance in the novel, for example, they are seen as the builders of bonfires that have their antecedents in a barbaric past: "such blazes as this the heathmen were now enjoying are rather the lineal descendants from jumbled Druidical rites and Saxon ceremonies than the invention of popular feeling about Gunpowder Plot." The lighting of the fires represents, in fact, something more, even, than the reincarnated spirit of pagan idolatry. It is positively a gesture of impious defiance in the teeth of whatever powers there be: "to light a fire," Hardy observes,

> is the instinctive and resistant act of man when, at the winter ingress, the curfew is sounded throughout Nature. It indicates a spontaneous, Promethean rebelliousness against the fiat that this recurrent season shall bring foul times, cold darkness, misery and death. . . .

Not surprisingly under these profane circumstances, the citizens of the heath tend in the presence of the bonfire to lose all distinctive moral identity:

> the permanent moral expression of each face it was impossible to discover, for as the nimble flames towered, nodded, and swooped through the surrounding air, the blots of shade and flakes of light upon the countenance of the group changed shape and position endlessly.

Throughout the novel, however, the members of this natural community participate without knowing it in ritual acts of a pagan or pre-Christian origin. In their next major appearance on the occasion of Mrs. Yeobright's Christmas party, they reenact the ancient folkplay, the St. George play, whose Christian veneer scarcely conceals its pre-Christian character as fertility rite celebrating the death of the year and its resurrection in the spring. Hardy is in fact at pains to verify the authenticity of the performance: "Like Balaam and other unwilling prophets," he reports,

> the agents seem moved by an inner compulsion to say and do their allotted parts whether they will or no. This unweeting manner of performance is the true ring by which, in this refurbishing age, a fossilized survival may be known from a spurious reproduction.

At the conclusion of the novel, furthermore, the renewal of life following the deaths of Eustacia and Wildeve is symbolized in the ancient rite of Maypole-day with its celebration of a vitality older and stronger than all that Christianity could bring to bear against it: "The instincts of merry England," Hardy notes with approval,

> lingered on here with exceptional vitality, and the symbolic customs which tradition has attached to each season of the year were yet a reality on Egdon. Indeed, the impulses of all such outlandish hamlets are pagan still: in these spots homage to nature, self-adoration, frantic gaieties, fragments of Teutonic rites to divinities whose names are forgotten, seem in some way or other to have survived mediaeval doctrine.

Even on occasions less ceremonial than the mumming and the Maypoling, however, the denizens of the heath are actuated by emotions that antedate, and comment ironically upon, the sober authority of the Christian tradition. From the beginning of the novel to the end, they are ready at the slightest provocation to break into song and dance whose fervor and violence bodes ill for the cause of Christian piety. Thus they conclude their commemoration of November 5 by whirling about their Promethean bonfire in a mad measure, a species of witches' dance, that is, in fact, specifically described as demoniacal:

> . . . in half a minute all that could be seen on Rainbarrow was a whirling of dark shapes amid a boiling confusion of sparks, which leapt around the dancers as high as their waists. The chief noises were women's shrill cries, men's laughter, Susan's stays and patterns, Olly Dowden's "heu-heu-heu!" and the strumming of the wind upon the furze-bushes, which formed a kind of tune to the *demoniac* measure they trod.

And it is surely more than apt coincidence that the physically-abandoned dance which delays the appearance of the mummers at the Christmas party should be called the "Devil's Dream":

> The air was now that one without any particular beginning, middle, or end, which perhaps . . . best conveys the idea of the interminable—the celebrated "Devil's Dream." The fury of personal movement that was kindled by the fury of the notes could be approximately imagined . . . from the occasional kicks of toes and heels against the door, whenever the whirl round had been of more than customary velocity.

Indeed, it becomes clear that in its sheer physicality, in its unabashed celebration of the human body and its dangerous sexual energies, dancing as it is practiced on Egdon constitutes a clear and present danger to Christian law and order. "A whole village-full of sensuous emotion, scattered abroad all the year long," it is said of the revels at East Egdon, "surged here in a focus for an hour. . . . For the time Paganism was revived in their hearts, the pride of life was all in all, and they adored none other than themselves."

The fact that by "mediaeval doctrine" Hardy had meant "mediaeval Christianity" and that against "Paganism was revived" he had set "Christianity was eclipsed" bears witness that Egdon's celebration of pagan vitality was specifically opposed in his imagination to the prohibitions and restrictions authorized by the Christian tradition. That this was indeed the case would be verified by his comic exploitation of the peasants' informal, not to say tenuous, relations with the local church. To begin with, their attendance at the Christian service would seem at best to be casual and intermittent. "In name they were parishioners," Hardy notes with evident satisfaction,

> but virtually they belonged to no parish at all. . . . Rain, snow, ice, mud everywhere around, they did not care to trudge two or three miles to sit wet-footed and splashed to the nape of their necks among those who . . . lived close to the church, and entered it clean and dry.

Quite as pagan as the great heath whose stubbornly skeptical and pragmatic values they would appear to have inherited, they are utterly unresponsive to such consolations as the church has to offer. " 'I ha'n't been there to-year,' " Grandfer Cantle boasts; " 'and now the winter is a-coming on I won't say I shall.' " " 'I ha'n't been these three years,' " Humphrey reflects, " 'for I'm so dead sleepy of a Sunday; and 'tis so terrible far to get there; and when you do get there 'tis such a mortal poor chance that you'll be chose for up above, when so many bain't, that I bide at home and don't go at all.' "

Certainly, when they do go to church, it is in no spirit of Christian piety. It is rather to witness an unscheduled dramatic exhibition, Mrs. Yeobright rising to forbid Thomasin's banns and Susan Nunsuch plunging the knitting needle into the arm of a "witch." Or to listen to a musical performance more likely to arouse the spirit of the Devil than the spirit of the Lord: " 'Twas the Hundred-and-thirty-third to "Lydia," ' " says Timothy Fairway in his lusty account of the musical prowess of Thomasin's father;

> "and when they'd come to 'Ran down his beard and o'er his robes its costly moisture shed,' neighbour Yeobright, who had just warmed to his work, drove his bow into them strings that glorious grand that he e'en a'most sawed the bass-viol into two pieces. Every winder in church rattled as if 'twere a thunderstorm."

It becomes apparent, in fact, that their response to the service is not far removed from a primitive fetishism. When Mrs. Yeobright forbids the banns, for example, no aspect of the episode surprises Timothy Fairway more than that the parson should have exposed himself as a human being of flesh and blood: " 'I'll speak to you after the service,' said the parson, in quite a homely way—yes, turning all at once into a common man no holier than you or I.' " On the occasion of Yeobright's memorable performance on the bass-viol, he registers the same astonished response: " 'Old Pa'son Williams lifted his hands in his great holy surplice as natural as if he'd been in common clothes. . . .' " And Christian Cantle can pause in his account of Eustacia's pricking-in-church to report the same stirring phenomenon: " 'O, and what d'ye think I found out, Mrs. Yeobright? The pa'son wears a suit of clothes under his surplice!—I could see his black sleeve when he held up his arm.' "

Nothing in the novel, of course, is more significant of the low ebb of Christian worship on Egdon Heath, of its powerlessness in the face of the primitive and unconscious impulses of its citizens, than the machinations of Susan Nunsuch. At the conclusion of the novel, burning Eustacia Vye in effigy, she repeats the Lord's Prayer backwards and repudiates, in effect, two thousand years of Christian piety. Even more dramatically, she has earlier plunged a knitting needle into the arm of the local "witch" and has reduced at once to a comic shambles the conventional rites of the Christian service. It should not be difficult after this to assess the function in the novel of the peasant chorus. It is not only to celebrate a pagan health and sanity but, less directly, to expose Christianity to a comic, and even satirical, light. Certainly, there is more than a trace of irony in Humphrey's bland comment, following the news of Eustacia's pricking-in-church, " 'Tis a very strange thing that whenever one of Egdon folk goes to church some rum job or other is sure to be doing.' "

Nowhere in the novel, however, is Hardy's denigration of Christianity more open than in the ludicrous figure of Christian Candle. For Christian constitutes, as his name would suggest, the caricature of the Christian man. This is first of all apparent in his being placed in opposition to the secular figure of the reddleman, who incarnates, as a nature-spirit, the subdued and skeptical paganism of Egdon Heath itself. Thus when Diggory hails from the darkness the group gathered about the bonfire, the terrified Christian recites a scriptural counterspell and therewith not only emphasizes the secular heresy for which the reddleman stands but also parodies the pietistic response to that heresy: " 'Matthew, Mark, Luke, and John, bless the bed that I lie on; four angels guard—.' " Furthermore, when the reddleman does appear, Christian further defines himself and his subject with, " 'If he had a handkerchief over his head he'd look for all the world like the Devil in the picture of the Temptation.' "

Christian functions most clearly as a satire on Christianity, however, in his relationship to the pagan community of peasants and, specifically, in his separation from that community. Up to a certain point, of course, his Christianity is, like that of his country brethren, rooted in primitive superstition: it exists for him as a source of counterspells with which to deal with the aboriginal ghosts and ogres and demons which constantly possess his fearful imagination. And to this extent, he tends to join the inhabitants of the heath in exposing Christianity to ridicule. In his characteristic role, however, Christian is dissociated altogether from the peasant community with its profane celebration of the joys and virtues of the natural life, and in this role he becomes preeminently the caricature of conventional piety. His dissociation as Christian from their paganism is, in fact, specifically dramatized on the occasion of their "demoniac" demonstration about the reckless flames. For Christian alone stands apart and establishes thereby, as the pious terms of his reproaches should indicate, not only the submerged antichristianity of the infamous dance but also the comic demoralization of the God-fearing man in the presence of so much pagan energy: "Christian alone stood aloof, uneasily rocking himself as he murmured, 'They ought not to do it—how the vlankers do fly! 'tis tempting the Wicked one, 'tis.' " This opposition is indeed explored elsewhere to reveal still further the disadvantages of a Christian education. Thus Christian's physical decrepitude and sexual impotence—he is the man no woman will marry—are in dramatic contrast to the life-worshipping vitality of Grandfer and Timothy and the rest of that lusty crew. And where he lives in constant terror of the sights and sounds of the savage heath, they, complete pagans that they are, feel perfectly at home in this grimmest of all possible worlds. The comic Christian Cantle-pagan chorus antithesis joins, then, with the "tragic" Clym-Eustacia antithesis to compose a critical and sometimes satirical examination of the Christian idea of life.

"A hymn rolls from a church-window," Hardy was to note in 1883, "and the uncompromising No-God-ist or Unconscious God-ist takes up the refrain." Caught in the conflict between reason and emotion, this imaginary figure might just as well have been Thomas Hardy himself. As a young man intended for the clergy, he had lost his faith in the decade of Darwin, Colenso, and the *Essays and Reviews*. But, long after he could no longer avail himself of the consolations of religion, he remained, perhaps inevitably, a man of strong religious needs and feelings. To consider *The Return of the Native* as purely and simply a diatribe against Christianity may very well be, then, to dishonor the complexity of the novel as a dramatic representation of Hardy's mixed feelings. In his portrait of Christian Cantle there is pathos, after all, as well as satire. And if Clym Yeobright is exposed to the irreverent ironies of a skeptical author, so, too, for that matter, are Wildeve and Eustacia, his pagan antagonists. There is in fact a singular appropriateness in the novel's ending, in the Christian and middle-class marriage of Thomasin and Diggory, that far transcends motives of editorial necessity or convenience. Interpreted as it is in a spirit of high comedy, this domestic anticlimax passes an ironical comment on, and in effect reconciles us to, the splendid but wasteful deaths of Wildeve and Eustacia. In the end, then, the novel is as much a dramatic exploration and exposition of the pagan-Christian polarity as an unqualified denunciation of the Christian outlook.

Once this is granted, however, one has still to contend with the bitterness of the unfrocked priest who can love and loathe at once the thing of which he has been deprived. Certainly, if the dramatic balance of the novel is tipped at all, there is little doubt that it is, as this study may have shown, to the disadvantage of the Christian point of view and to the substantial advantage of the pagan. Hardy would be able in the novels of the 1890's, in *Tess* and in *Jude,* to record in more specific terms his quarrel with the Christian order of things. But it is doubtful that, with all his later opportunities for open denunciation, he ever directed a more forceful and more effective attack upon the lost faith of his youth than in this earlier novel. The textual alterations that substituted "doctrine" for "Christianity" and "Fate" for "God" are the very real symptoms, then, of a motive every bit as diabolical as that which governed Eustacia, the reddleman and the deceptively-innocent association of peasants: they disguise the subversive, anti-christian argument which would seem to have been a main motive and organizing force of *The Return of the Native* and which, although it could not openly be asserted, was, and is still, everywhere active beneath its unassuming surface. (pp. 111-27)

John Paterson, " 'The Return of the Native' as Antichristian Document," in Nineteenth-Century Fiction, *Vol. 14, No. 2, September, 1959, pp. 111-27.*

Louis Crompton (essay date 1960)

[*In the following essay, Crompton analyzes* The Return of the Native *as an amalgam of prose romance, epic, and social theory.*]

The writer of prose fiction has, in general, three courses open to him. He may write prose romance, in which case the setting of his story is usually fabulous and its imaginary world either pleasanter than real life or more sinisterly mysterious. Alternatively he may, as in the case of Fielding or Jane Austen, imitate epic or dramatic forms of the tightly plotted sort that Aristotle analyzes in the *Poetics*. Or, again, he may regard himself as a social scientist, and base his novel not on romantic myth or rationalized plot but on some psychological or social theory.

Criticism has, in its turn, tended to align itself with these three modes in placing its emphasis on one or the other: on the analysis of archetypes, on characterization and dramatic probability, or on the novelist's social vision. Partisanship, one notes, has not been unknown. Social realists—Zola, for instance—have usually seen the three modes as an entelechy, romance being a kind of embryo, and dramatic form (now decried as "theatrical") merely a further stage on the way to modern realism. At the moment the social realists are somewhat in retreat, and archetypal critics have gained ground. But have we not formulated the critical problem too crudely in assuming that these readings of fiction are mutually exclusive? There may, rather, be some advantage in aiming at increased breadth of response in the reader quite apart from what we may call the "party lines" of literary criticism.

Take, for instance, *The Return of the Native,* a novel often relegated, with the rest of its author's writings, to the category of "transitional fiction" with the implication that we are here faced with a monstrous mixture of Victorian theatricalism and scientific modernism. Since Hardy is a novelist with a manifestly superb sense of formal unity, such a judgment ought to leave us uneasy. Perhaps the solution lies not in dismissing the book as, formally, a weird hybrid but rather in seeing it as a work of fiction in which the writer is using all three modes simultaneously as part of a carefully wrought whole. Since the first, or romantic, aspect of Hardy's art has up to now received least attention, the aim of what follows is to illuminate this level of meaning and intention, but the reader who has always read the book realistically will do well to keep his "realistic" interpretation firmly in mind. The purpose of this essay is not to replace a story of "real events" by "pure" mythology but to show how the two interpenetrate each other.

The Return of the Native is unusual among the run of Victorian novels in that it contains, on however small a scale, a messianic hero. Such a type is a natural link between romance and tragedy. It is rare in Renaissance tragedy, with its cult of king and courtier, and is probably best represented in English literature by such martyr-plays as *Samson Agonistes* and *Saint Joan*. Since the English novel developed in a period largely hostile both to romance and to religious enthusiasm, its central male characters are usually the heroes who are no heroes, *hommes moyens sensuels* like Tom Jones or the young men in Dickens and Thackeray. The religious figures, on the other hand, are most often the hypocrites and fools appropriate to comic art.

The Return of the Native is, of course, a double tragedy with two main characters, Clym Yeobright and Eustacia Vye. But we may perhaps best understand the structure of the book by looking first at Hardy's male protagonist. The first thing we notice is that he has something of the sense of mission shared by both Joan and Samson. He is both a hero with tragic stature and (more surprisingly, in view of Hardy's agnosticism) a figure in a religious ritual. His character contains the fatal imbalance of the tragic hero at the same time that it raises him above the mob of mediocrities. "Was Yeobright's mind well-proportioned?" Hardy asks:

> No. A well-proportioned mind is one which shows no particular bias; one of which we may safely say that it will never cause its owner to be confined as a madman, tortured as a heretic, or crucified as a blasphemer. Also, on the other hand, that it will never cause him to be applauded as a prophet, revered as a priest, or exalted as a king.

Clym is a sanguine idealist who plans a revolutionary educational scheme. His youthful naïveté is so much insisted upon that it comes as a shock to learn (in the epilogue) that he is past thirty. There is a touch of the young Milton about him, and like Milton he chooses a ridiculously inappropriate mate for his scholarly undertaking. The natural symbols for such a character would suggest altruism, youth, enlightenment (ironically qualified by hints of blindness), pride, and soaring aspiration. His name conveys the first three of these, "Clym" being short for "Clement," and the *yeo*-in "Yeobright" an archaic form of "young." When Hardy tells us that, "As is usual with bright natures, the deity that lies ignominiously chained within an ephemeral human carcase shone out of him like a ray," he evidently wishes us to associate Clym with suffering heroes like Prometheus and disguised gods like Apollo. The peasant bonfires that precede his arrival celebrate the death and rebirth of the Teutonic sun-god, Balder:

> Moreover to light a fire is the instinctive and resistant act of man when, at the winter ingress, the curfew is sounded throughout Nature. It indicates a spontaneous, Promethean rebelliousness against the fiat that this recurrent season shall bring forth foul times, cold darkness, misery and death. Black chaos comes, and the fettered gods of the earth say, Let there be light.

Hardy several times describes Clym's hair as a golden halo, lit by the sinking rays of the winter sun. In view of these facts we should not be surprised that after one of the most elaborate preparations in English literature, Hardy has Clym make his appearance exactly at the moment of the winter solstice. Or rather, that this is the first of two "first" appearances, since Eustacia only hears his voice on this occasion. She does not actually see him till Christmas Day. The year's time in which the action of the novel takes place thus serves a triple purpose. Hardy seems to have considered it an equivalent to the twenty-four hours of classical tragedy. Ruth Firor, in her fascinating study of Hardy's folklore [*Folkways in Thomas Hardy*], has pointed out that it corresponds to the Celtic year, which is based on a vegetation cycle, and has its chief festivals in November and May. But we have also a parallel with the Christian church year, since the book begins with an "advent" leading to the Christmas epiphany and ends with a tragic crisis which occurs on a night "as dark as Gethsemane."

The account of any effort to realize a romantic or messianic ideal of heroism in real life is likely to be hedged with more than a little irony. The would-be hero may be shown up as a likeable but misguided idiot, as in *Don Quixote,* or the whole force of the association may lie in the contrast, as in T. S. Eliot's use of heroic myth to expose a debased and vulgarized present. Hardy's use of heroic archetypes is partly serious and partly ironic, his characters appearing at one moment comparable to their heroic models, at other times ludicrously smaller and weaker. Clym is at the same time the shining hero of romance, the flawed hero of classical tragedy whose *hubris* leads to his downfall, and the diminished hero of modern realism.

Full-fledged heroic romance begins with the hero's birth, as in the Siegmund-Sieglinde portion of the *Ring*. Hardy has preferred to concentrate on what Frye in the *Anatomy of Criticism* has called the secondary, or initiatory, stage of romance. This part of the cycle generally describes the hero's induction into some cult, religious or secular (as in the case of knighthood) and his temporary withdrawal from the world. The eligibility of Egdon as a place of retreat is obvious. It is in real fact the desert against whose ignorance and isolation Clym must struggle. In the famous set-piece with which the novel opens, Hardy compares the heath successively to the classical Tartarus, to Dante's Limbo, and to the wilderness of Genesis 21. Such a cluster of analogues may seem to load the symbolism rather heavily, but each makes its point: Tartarus is the prison of the exiled Titans (and of that bored Olympian, Eustacia), Limbo is the abode of spiritual darkness from which Christ rescues men on Easter Saturday, and Ishmael's desert brings to mind both Venn and Yeobright in their rôles as social outcasts.

In the archetypal romance, the hero's withdrawal is traditionally a period of probation in which he gains knowledge for his coming mission. Hitherto untried, he now undergoes a series of ordeals of which the commonest are temptations to wealth or sexual pleasure. Examples would be the testing of Guyon in Book II of the *Faerie Queene* or of Parsifal in the Grail legends. (Milton is sufficiently aware of the parallels between the tests facing the romantic hero and the temptations of Christ that he pauses, in *Paradise Regained,* to explain the difference.) Failure at this point is felt to be particularly ignominious and usually results in the hero's regression to a state of servitude, called "effeminacy" in Spenser and symbolized in *Samson Agonistes* by physical blindness.

Unlike the hero, whose messianic pretensions we are likely to regard quizzically, the witch is a romance figure that has survived into modern fiction relatively unchanged, her most dangerous powers having always been largely sexual anyway. Within the tradition of nineteenth-century realism, Eustacia Vye is a spoiled neurotic whose imagination, fed on popular novels and romanticized history, has bred dreams doomed to frustration by the fact of her marriage to an unambitious husband. Anyone who attempts to read the book only on this level, however, will probably be baffled by a number of points, particularly her frequent disguises. These can be understood only if one realizes that part of Hardy's purpose is to gather around her the sinister suggestions which surround the witch of romance: hence her reputation for necromancy, the "crooked sixpence" (a witch's charm) with which she plays Johnny for watching the bonfires, and her comparison of herself on another occasion to the witch of Endor.

Perhaps the most curious scene in **The Return of the Native** is Eustacia's appearance in the mummers' play. Her transvestitism sounds like an echo of Shakespeare or Gautier; the meaning of the episode, however, most likely lies in its ritual significance. The mummers' play in which she takes part originally consisted of a combat between Winter and Summer, in which Winter is killed and then revived by the Leech. The engrafting of the St. George legend upon this rite is a late development. Eustacia's part, the "Turkish Knight" who is St. George's antagonist, is a descendant of the original Night-Winter figure. (Hardy elsewhere remarks of Eustacia's hair that "a whole winter did not contain darkness enough to form its shadow: it closed over her forehead like nightfall extinguishing the western glow.") The dénouement, in which St. George is magically restored to life, is an interesting adumbration of the novel's action. Hardy points up the analogy by excerpting from the text the lines that tell of the Saint's marriage to a mysterious dark southerner, "the King of Egypt's daughter." This last detail reminds us that Hardy has already explicitly compared Eustacia to one eastern temptress, Cleopatra, and indirectly to another, Nausicaa, when he makes her father a Corfiote, from "Alcinous' isle."

The great fictional studies of the pathology of the romantic imagination are, of course, *Don Quixote* and *Madame Bovary,* and Hardy, by pairing a starry-eyed idealist with a dissatisfied neurotic, is attempting variations on the themes of Cervantes and Flaubert. But the use of realism to satirize romanticism generates an irony that is double-edged. Commentators not infrequently turns satires on romance upside down and exalt the Don Quixotes over their humdrum neighbors. If realism makes romance look absurd, romance has a way of making real life look absurd, too, when it protests against its dullness and compromises. Consequently we should not be puzzled if both Clym and Eustacia appear to us as simultaneously sympathetic and perverse.

There is a difference, however, between Clym and Eustacia as romantic dreamers. The difference is, indeed, crucial, and lies in the fact that Clym's imagination is essentially pure while Eustacia's is corrupted. Both are at odds with their environment, both are blinded by hopeful illusions, but where Clym suffers from nothing worse than naïve ignorance of the world and women, Eustacia is disastrously egotistical. Diggory Venn's selfless devotion to Tamsin is incomprehensible to her, and she is equally baffled by Clym's disgust with the business of diamond-selling. With superb irony Hardy makes the climax of Clym's courtship the scene in which Eustacia wrests from her unwilling lover a description of the play of lights on the jewels in the Apollo Gallery of the Louvre.

She dreams of herself as a Sultana at the side of a strong-willed emperor, indulging her desire for "music, poetry, passion, war." When Hardy says that Eustacia was "not entirely unlovable" he can hardly mean more than that she inspires the pity we feel for selfish people, weak rather than tyrannous or cruel, whose schemes come to nothing. Moreover, though she dreams of inspiring a grand passion, she is peculiarly cold herself. Despite the hints of banked erotic fires, Hardy, in the celebrated passage in which he calls her a goddess in Cimmerian exile, compares her to Artemis, Hera, and Athena, not to Aphrodite, who would seem to be the obvious choice. Eustacia is able to persuade herself, temporarily, that she is in love with Clym but only so long as she thinks he can realize her dream of a knight in silver armor who will rescue her from the heath.

Eustacia's natural affinities, Hardy tells us, are for "dark" kings like Saul or for worldly sophisticates like Pontius Pilate, both of whom are chiefly notable as antagonists of messianic heroes. Wildeve, however, falls as far short of her ideal as Clym; his lack of aggressive strength so diminishes him in Eustacia's eyes that she comes to prefer suicide to escape with him. As the opposite of an Apollonian figure he is identified with darkness, confusion, and night, and Hardy fixes him in the world of romance by giving him a face shaped like a Gothic shield. "Wildeve" suggests a sabbath of warlocks and witches and Eustacia, appropriately enough, conjures him up on three successive Fifth of Novembers. Wildeve's archetype is the lonely knight of Keats' ballad, wandering on the barren heath under the enchantress' spell. Alternatively, in a realistic sense, he is to Mrs. Yeobright the awful example of a professional man gone wrong through some woman's influence. Hardy describes him as petulant, gloomy, and masochistic, and compares him, fittingly enough, to Rousseau, whose description of himself as just this kind of nympholept has been shocking moralists for two hundred years.

Diggory Venn is a rather more difficult character to place. "Diggory" is a name of Cornish origin. It appears most notably in the medieval tale of *Sir Degarre*, but by the nineteenth century it was used chiefly for rustics and servants. Venn seems to belong with a special group of fictional archetypes, the Ishmaels or outsiders, young men out of luck in fortune or love who stand aside from the main action but occasionally start it off in some new direction. His rôle is like Edgar's in *King Lear*: both are "pseudo-bogeymen" and both show considerable eligibility as heroes, the mixture of stoicism and chivalry they represent being pretty irresistible. The problem for the author is to keep such characters in their secondary billing, since there is always a lively popular demand that he forget about the tragedy and find this man a nice sympathetic girl to settle down with, as Tate did in his revision of *Lear* and Hardy had to in his "Aftercourses."

Everyone has noted that the characters in romance are either all white or all black. Hardy varies this scheme by making his characters black or red, a less radical departure from convention than would at first appear. The dark characters, Wildeve and Eustacia, both suffer from depression of spirits, or as Hardy somewhat grandiloquently calls it, "hypochondriasis." Eustacia's odd accoutrements of watch, hourglass, and telescope recall the paraphernalia of the brooding housewife in Dürer's "Melencholia I," an important icon for nineteenth-century representations of despair. The complement of black in the spectrum of humors is red. Tamsin's red hair symbolizes her sanguine temperament, but the chief connotations of red in the novel seem to be humility and rusticity, the heath-cutters reddish colored leggings being a sign of their social rank. ("Russet," for this reason, means both "red" and "clownish" in Shakespeare and Milton.) Eustacia, who is chagrined at Clym's loss of his "golden halo," is particularly enraged that he should look like a laborer after his eyesight fails:

> Ah! you don't know how differently he appeared when I first met him, though it is such a little while ago. His hands were as white and soft as mine; and look at them now, how rough and brown they are! His complexion is by nature fair, and that rusty look he has now, all of a colour with his leather clothes, is caused by the burning of the sun.

Diggory Venn's redness is also a social stigma.

Romance deals with legendary heroes, high tragedy with kings and rulers, modern realism with people who often give the impression of being smaller and dingier than the average. Hardy relates his characters to myth through his romantic archetypes, and solves the problem of the tragic hero's social elevation by underscoring the Vyes' and Yeobrights' sense of superiority to the general ruck of peasants and small farmers who make up the closed society of the heath. As a naturalist we should also expect him to turn the telescope around and show the characters in reduced scale as insignificant figures in a landscape. He does this in the furze-cutting scenes where Clym is compared to "a mere parasite of the heath, fretting its surface in his daily labor as a moth frets a garment."

The entomological details of the book remind us that the imagery of naturalist fiction is remarkably fixed, as conventional in its own way as the dragons and steeds of chivalry. Steinbeck's turtle, Hemingway's ants, and the rabbits and wounded pheasants of *Tess* are all related symbols of human impotence. In the grim scene of Mrs. Yeobright's death in the August heat, Hardy draws the reader's attention to the plight of the "obscene creatures" wallowing under the half-baked mud and the helplessness of the wasps drunk on the fermented fruit in the orchard.

In romance the hero is free, his story an extended exercise in wish-fulfillment; in tragedy he is subject to fate and moral judgments and in modern realism to biological and economic laws which seriously limit any sense of human responsibility. Certainly, **The Return of the Native** is nearer to the tragic norm than the economic and psychological determinism of *Tess.* When Hardy, in the love scenes, describes the heath as overlaid with a purple mask that hides its harshness, he is indulging in the kind of irony that Schopenhauer would have appreciated, but in general the characters seem to be less the victims of some inexorable natural law than of the play of chance and the operation of a free, and even perverse, human will.

The large number of disastrous accidents have led critics to complain, somewhat irrelevantly, of Hardy's "pessimism." Pessimism is, indeed, less a matter of chance than of a belief in inexorable laws that make for human misery. True, there is a hint of some such fatalism in Clym's marriage. Clym and Eustacia have exactly opposite aspirations, but their characters and situations make it all but inevitable that they should misjudge each other. Eustacia's melancholy and her persecution appeal to Clym's chivalry at the same time that his infatuation makes him blind to the "idle voluptuary" Mrs. Yeobright sees. Nevertheless, there is an element of hubristic wilfulness (Hardy's phrase for this is "pride of life") and even something paradoxically perverse in the steely reserve which underlies his sympathetic and self-sacrificing nature.

This combination of pride and idealism is an instinctive bond between Clym and his mother at the same time that it separates him from her. Mrs. Yeobright is thus reduced to the pathetic rôle of a Cassandra who foresees tragedy but is helpless to prevent it. Nevertheless it is possible to argue that her relationship with her son is the emotional center of the book. Certainly, her journey across the heath as a suppliant for his love is one of the most poignant scenes in English fiction. It is connected with another study of parent-child estrangement, *King Lear*, through several details: the setting, the serpent sting which causes her death, and the boy. But the boy who accompanies her is not an ironic commentator on the action like Lear's fool. Hardy emphasizes his childish self-absorption as a subtle way of underlining Mrs. Yeobright's sense of alienation from her son. His rhythmical questions ("Dó you álways dráw your bréath like thát?") imitate the tragic ballad, which also often takes the form of a dialogue between a sufferer and a coolly detached interlocutor.

Clym's reaction to his mother's death is violent in the extreme. Reaction from a siren is likely to produce a flight to a protective mother-figure; Clym is about to seek out his mother when he finds her prostrate on the heath. The result is a tremendous accession of guilt feelings. Hardy makes him re-enact Oedipus' story when he has him search out the "riddle" of his mother's death in spite of the warnings of the heath-dwellers, and his face, he tells us, resembles the mask of Oedipus when he finds out the truth from Johnny. But his intensely felt remorse is neither Greek nor heroic. There is something childishly histrionic in his outbursts: "I sinned against her, and on that account there is no light for me"; "If there is any justice in God let Him kill me now. He has nearly blinded me, but that is not enough." The desire to return to a world of darkness is clear enough. In the last section Clym lives shut up in the back rooms of his mother's house. Hardy was, indeed, very astute in choosing the Oedipus myth as the counterpoint to the dénouement of his romance. The mood of "Aftercourses" is that of *Oedipus at Colonus*. The tragic hero who has caused the death of the two women he loved most has become the half-blind prophet. Clym is a crippled Christ whose ministry comes after his passion. His Prometheanism past, he preaches on what Hardy ironically calls "morally unimpeachable subjects," his favorite text being the passage in I Kings 2 in which Solomon defers to his mother Bathsheba.

Faced with the problem of marrying Tamsin to Diggory in the epilogue, Hardy handles his task with remarkable tact. Clym has become the puppet-like projection of his dead mother's will, at first planning to marry Tamsin himself in accordance with her wishes, then repeating her objections to Diggory. By introducing the Maypole revels (which he calls "homage to nature, self-adoration, frantic gaities, fragments of Teutonic rites to divinities whose names are forgotten") Hardy completes another ritual pattern. These are the "comic" counterparts of the November bonfires, their polar opposites in the ritual year, just as the "pride of life" which finds expression in these festivals is the comic analogue of tragic *hubris*. Grandfer Cantle and Christian now assume their natural rôles as rustics in a kind of "As You Like It," providing a comic frame for the serious male characters, Grandfer's excess of wilfulness and Christian's humorous will-lessness making them humorous counterparts of Clym and Wildeve.

Frye remarks that in many tragedies the hero makes his first appearance as a "semi-divine figure, at least in his own eyes, and then an inexorable dialectic sets to work which separates the divine pretence from the human actuality." In Eustacia's case, as in Clym's, the movement of the novel is from mythological romance to tragic suffering. She, too, appears first as a glamorous demi-god and ends as a struggling human, bound upon the wheel of fate. With her death we have moved from the world of ritual and romance to the psychological realism of Flaubert and Ibsen.

But if Eustacia's story touches myth at one point and case-history at the other, she has also some of the fascination of a queen of high tragedy. Perhaps we can best understand her if we take a cue from Hardy and compare her to Cleopatra. Like her, she is pleasure-loving, self-indulgent, quick to shift with the winds of fortune, and expert at varying her moods to captivate the men she wants.

She, of course, is candid enough to warn Clym that her love for him may not outlast their marriage, but this candor has its roots in a fatalism that robs her of all moral scrupulosity. She lays the blame for each unfortunate turn of events on "some indistinct, colossal Prince of the World, who had framed her situation and ruled her lot." In this view of life she resembles Merimée's Carmen.

Behind all this, however, we feel a powerful romantic malaise and self-destructiveness. In the MS version of the novel, Hardy described her features as a blend of those of Byron and Marie Antoinette. She is a Rousseauist in her disdain for convention and in her eternal dissatisfaction: she wants only what she does not have. She is saved from the vulgarity of Emma Bovary's excesses only by her unfailing dignity.

A natural queen without realms to rule, she can only look as if she had lost them. If this air of having accidentally mislaid a kingdom strikes the reader as slightly absurd, and makes us think of the actress who is always a little too good for her part, no one needs to be reminded that the sense of discrepancy between the ideal image of one's self and actuality is not only one of the most common of human emotions, but also one of the most painful. Her

Sarah Siddons as "The Tragic Muse" *by Sir Joshua Reynolds—one of Hardy's visual models for Eustacia Vye.*

death is, consequently, a kind of Byronic protest against the very nature of things, against the fact that the world does not offer her any of the images of glory of which she has dreamed. She is, like Kafka's circus performer, a "hunger artist," who refuses to come to terms with reality. In her death she both acknowledges her defeat and asserts her freedom.

Hardy has written a double classical tragedy and a double case-history; in so doing he helps us to realize that literature is intensely conservative in its forms at the same time that it is capable of making radical conquests of new material. This is what Hardy meant in his essay, "**The Profitable Reading of Fiction**," when he urges that we should read novels with the widest range of imaginative reference and in terms of our total literary experience:

> Good fiction can be defined here as that kind of imaginative writing which lies nearest to the epic, dramatic, or narrative masterpieces of the past.... New methods and plans may arise and come into fashion, as we see them do; but the general theme can never be changed, nor (what is less obvious) can the relative importance of the various particulars be greatly interfered with.

Such a statement ought to stand as a warning to readers who think that Hardy's value, for better or for worse, lies all in his iconoclasm. In endorsing or decrying the message, they fail to realize how deeply rooted in tradition Hardy's art is, and consequently fail to bring to the reading of his novels the same imaginative effort one brings, say, to the reading of Joyce or Eliot. But this is exactly what *The Return of the Native* asks of us: any lesser response fails to do justice to its depth and complexity. (pp. 229-40)

> Louis Crompton, "The Sunburnt God: Ritual and Tragic Myth in 'The Return of the Native'," in Boston University Studies in English, *Vol. IV, No. 4, Winter, 1960, pp. 229-40.*

Richard Benvenuto (essay date 1971)

[*In the following essay, Benvenuto examines the tragic elements of* The Return of the Native.]

Most critics have agreed with Hardy that "an austere artistic code" was violated when "circumstances of serial publication" forced him to abandon his "original conception" of *The Return of the Native* and attach a moderately happy ending. Unity of time, preserved in the first five books, is the most obvious fatality of the sixth. If it had been the only or the most important concession, we could prove our fidelity to "an austere artistic code" by closing the covers of the novel after we had finished book five. But the sixth book reshapes the drama of the first five in a way that changes, qualitatively, our total experience of the novel. Up to the end of book five, the novel's direction—its accumulated meaning and range of expectancies—is toward bitter despair and tragedy, the sum of its hard landscape, its primitive fires, and the failure of its people to communicate and forgive. The sixth book celebrates the return of spring and joins Thomasin and Venn; it tells of Maypoles and of grass-plats soft as carpet. Though it would appear that heterogeneous ideas have been yoked together, there is little point in wishing the sixth book away or in pretending it does not exist. Instead, to have full sight of Hardy's original conception of the novel, it is necessary to examine the sixth book and trace the course Hardy's conception took when his publishers stood in its way.

We can start by conceding that *The Return of the Native* reads like a five-act tragedy with a comic epilogue, though that does not define the specific conception of the novel. It tempts us, moreover, to go no further in explaining the apparent failure of the epilogue to cohere with the main narrative. Inconsistency between the two modes or genres is not axiomatic. *Far from the Madding Crowd* fused comedy and tragedy into Hardy's first masterpiece and public success. Bathsheba Everdene undergoes a harrowing personal trauma when she discovers the extent of Troy's intimacy with Fanny Robin. Her marriage collapses, and she is stalked by an increasingly neurotic and aggressive Boldwood. Fanny dies wretchedly, and Troy dies violently. Bathsheba suffers a painful seizure and then endures the suspense of Boldwood's impending execution. The end of it all is her visit to Oak's cottage and their happy, rejuvenating marriage. To make *The Return of the Native* acceptable to public taste, Hardy transplanted the formula that had worked in *Far from the Madding Crowd.* Clym takes on the pitifulness of Boldwood. Thomasin learns to recognize Diggory Venn's hidden virtues; and the two repeat the actions of Bathsheba and Oak, when as widow and country swain they consummate their original courtship.

But *Far from the Madding Crowd* was meant to be a comedic novel. In tragedies like *The Return of the Native,* people do not live happily ever after. That is true, but it is not all there is to say. The sixth book obtrudes not because it shifts the novel out of its proper course and toward comedy, but because it attempts to give resolution and synthesis to the events of the first five—to stop the novel and wrap it up. It would be just as inconsistent, I think, for this novel to resolve its action in the way proper to tragedy. *The Return of the Native* conceives of even the denouements of life as swept up in life's ongoing flux, to which they give no shape or meaning. The difference between Hardy's original conceptions for the two novels is essentially not generic but metaphysical. Absent from *The Return of the Native* is the operative mythology or inherent natural order of *Far from the Madding Crowd.* The Weatherbury farmers and field hands live in a designed universe, where the sequences of events and expectations that make up the world of nature and the world of historical time fall into a pattern which one can harmonize with and prepare for. Oak survives and prospers because he lives close to the bosom of "the Great Mother." Clym Yeobright lives in "the vast tract of unenclosed wild known as Egdon Heath." His world of nature and time remains systemless, and it is in essence unintelligible. The world views of the two novels are poles apart. The one affirms and the other denies that the forces affecting human life operate within a discernible system or order.

Clym is just as close to nature and just as responsive to it as Oak was, but his heath differs from Weatherbury Farm in the way a blank stone differs from a tablet of hieroglyphs. Oak's preparations for the storm interpret nature's intentions revealed to him through a series of signs or legible natural characters. Seeing the large toad, Oak "knew what this direct message from the Great Mother meant." A brown garden-slug "was Nature's second way of hinting to him that he was to prepare for foul weather." Two black spiders reinforce his suspicions, and the position and attitude of the sheep confirm them. "Every voice in nature was unanimous in bespeaking change." A skillful interpreter of nature—he can tell time from the position of the stars—Oak reads between the lines of nature's message: "Apparently there was to be a thunder-storm, and afterwards a cold continuous rain. The creeping things seemed to know all about the later rain, but little of the interpolated thunderstorm; whilst the sheep knew all about the thunder-storm and nothing of the later rain." Tremendous as the storm is, its violence makes sense because it is part of a discernible sequence of operations that fall into an accustomed pattern. Oak puts two and two together because he understands the logic of what is happening. A meaning accessible to rational interpretation exists within nature.

In *The Return of the Native,* nature is illegible. Its signs do not change, but they no longer reveal systematic operations or intentions. Egdon Heath is a mystery, irreducible to formula or logic. It manifests no inherent structure of things and is of no help to men who seek the laws governing the universe. Clym is "fully alive" to its beauty, but he feels also "its oppressive horizontality" which gives him "a sense of bare equality with, and no superiority to, a single living thing under the sun." For all its conditioning influence on human life, moreover, the heath is passive and unstable in its identity. It becomes what different people make it—a hostile prison for Eustacia, liberation for Clym. To Thomasin, "there were not, as to Eustacia, demons in the air, and malice in every bush and bough. The drops which lashed her face were not scorpions, but prosy rain; Egdon in the mass was no monster whatever, but impersonal open ground." Troy was clearly wrong not to detect the coming storm in *Far from the Madding Crowd.* But there is no basis by which to compare the rightness of Thomasin's vision with Eustacia's or that of either with Clym's. Their different views coexist and are as independent as the personalities they reveal.

As though to underscore the absence of any direct message from nature in *The Return of the Native* Hardy turns his characters into sign makers. Eustacia tells Johnny Nunsuch to listen for the sound of a frog jumping with a flounce into the pond at Mistover, which she says is "a sign of rain." The sound is made by Wildeve's throwing a stone to signify his presence. Later, at the window of Clym's and Eustacia's cottage, Wildeve releases a moth which flies towards the candle in the room and burns. "This had been a well-known signal in old times when Wildeve had used to come secretly wooing to Mistover." Both signs are deceptive; they are not what they appear to be. And they replace, even while they exploit, the trustworthy signs nature sends to Oak. In *Far from the Madding Crowd,* a peculiarity in a toad signifies rain; in *The Return of the Native,* the sound of a frog is made a subterfuge. At the sound of the wind on Norcombe Hill, "the instinctive act of humankind was to stand and listen, and learn how the trees on the right and the trees on the left wailed or chaunted to each other in the regular antiphonies of a cathedral choir" (*Far from the Madding Crowd*). The sound is organized music, a blending of the natural and the human, the instinctive and the religious, into one expressive pattern. The "linguistic peculiarity" of Egdon Heath under its November winds "bore a great resemblance to the ruins of human song which remain to the throat of fourscore and ten" (*The Return of the Native*). The union of man with his world has become a specter of itself, and the choir has shrunk to a guttural solo.

The difference between an organized and a chaotic nature extends to the different notions of time which went into the original conceptions of the two novels. Eustacia lives in the present only: "the only 'real-time' for her is Now." She resents and yet accepts the fact that "any love she might win would sink simultaneously with the sand in the glass"; and her actions are "framed to snatch a year's, a week's, even an hour's passion from anywhere while it could be won." For Eustacia, a "blaze of love, and extinction, was better than a lantern glimmer of the same which should last long years." Critical as he is of Eustacia elsewhere, Hardy does not condemn her attitude towards time. It reveals her deeply aroused consciousness, which makes her want all the intensity of life in what we have come to call the existential moment. In *Far from the Madding Crowd,* Hardy was openly scornful of Troy's very similar attitude. Whereas his language conveys a splendor in Eustacia's rejection of past and future, it is sardonic and cursory when describing Troy: "He was a man to whom memories were an incumbrance, and anticipations a superfluity. Simply feeling, considering, and caring for what was before his eyes, he was vulnerable only in the present." Troy's indifference to time, which in itself contrasts with Eustacia's passion for time present, marks him as deficient in consciousness, a purely sensual being, and perhaps even lower in life's scale than that: "Troy was full of activity, but his activities were less of a locomotive than a vegetative nature."

Far from the Madding Crowd stresses the continuity of past and present in human affairs, and Hardy expressed deep approval when a sense of history made itself felt in a place, an occupation, or a man's character. Troy's sense of time is refuted by the world he lives in, where "three or four score years were included in the mere present, and nothing less than a century set a mark on its face or tone." More than his flashy actions or dress, Troy's scorn for history makes him an alien in Weatherbury, whose people, like their "Great Mother," organize their actions into a design that survives for centuries. In the sheep-shearing barn, "the spirit of the ancient builders was at one with the spirit of the modern beholder." Standing before it, one thought of "its past history, with a satisfied sense of functional continuity throughout—a feeling almost of gratitude, and quite of pride, at the permanence of the idea which had heaped it up." It is the "spirit" of its builders which has survived in a "functional continuity" to make an "idea" permanent. Since the human and the natural orders converge in the barn, Hardy's description of it puts human thought in closer conformity to nature than Troy's sensuality is. Taking its cue from the order of nature, the mind gives "medievalism and modernism . . . a common standpoint." The past exists in the present, and the meaning of both is comprehensible.

The contrast in *The Return of the Native* is extreme. Egdon unites past and present, but it is incomprehensible, and its past is prehuman, outside history and the historical consciousness. Instead of the logically structured order of time by which Hardy judges Troy, he creates Eustacia's world out of the structureless forces of man's unconscious origins. During storms, Egdon became "the hitherto unrecognized original of those wild regions of obscurity which are vaguely felt to be compassing us about in midnight dreams of flight and disaster, and are never thought of after the dream till revived by scenes like this." Egdon suggests the permanence of whatever precedes idea, and its resistance to civilization keeps it untouched by the kind of functional continuity Hardy celebrated in the barn. Surviving the vicissitudes of change, the barn successfully accommodates man's life to the system of nature. It is the center of traditional and time-tested ways and patterns of behavior—the sheep-shearing. With a face on which history has impressed no record, Egdon isolates men from a recognizable order or adoptable time scheme. It is the center of superstition and primitivism—wax dolls and druidical fires.

It follows that the native returning to Egdon bears little resemblance to the shepherd at Weatherbury. Oak represents the harmonious integration of the different elements of man's being. Clym suffers the destructive warfare of those elements, and a breakdown in his moral and psychological life accompanies the loss of design in nature and history. Both men are on the threshold of maturity, in between youth and age. But the future of each is forecast by the theoretical construct of human nature of which he is made the image. Oak's "intellect and emotions were clearly separated: he had passed the time during which the influence of youth indiscriminately mingles them in the character of impulse, and he had not yet arrived at the stage wherein they become united again in the character of prejudice." It is impossible to think of Oak hardening in that way. His thoughts and emotions have just the right relation to each other. He thinks compassionately, and his emotions are sane. In Clym, the human organism comes apart; the elements Oak integrated conflict. Clym's face "showed that thought is a disease of the flesh" and that "mental luminousness" competes against "physical need" for the "oil of life." As opposed to the psychological harmony of a man like Oak, Clym experiences "the mutually destructive interdependence of spirit and flesh." Even the native is alien to the heath, for on his face time makes a profound impression.

Until book six, Clym survives—and this is a major source of his strength as a character—the moral ambiguity of human action in a world without ethical design. Clym accepts the position Keats described when he wrote of the loss of innocence and the expansion of the mind's thinking power until "we see not the balance of good and evil."

Clym asks, "Mother, what is doing well?" His question covers more than the commercial world, in which he is barely interested. He wants his vocation to have an intrinsic necessity and value, and there is no guarantee that it will. His moral world is an unfathomable as the heath. Oak never thinks to ask a question like Clym's. He does not have to. He knows instinctively or he learns from nature the right thing to do, and he does it. Always innocent, Oak is less challenging than Clym, but he is not thereby a simplified version of Clym. He is cut from an entirely different cloth. Oak is fortunate enough to live in a world where he need not doubt the rightness of actions which he can align to the established order of his universe.

The original conception of *The Return of the Native* was of a systemless, morally chaotic world, successfully evoked in the novel's first five books. The "consistent conclusion," which "an austere artistic code can assume . . . to be the true one," would necessarily retain this view of the world and continue to record its effect on human action and thought. Austere consistency would forbid any rounding off of the action or any suggestion of a pattern or operative rational system in events that lead to the confusion, wandering, and violent deaths of the dark episode concluding book five. But book six, as we know, was written under the pressure of a public, not an artistic interdict, and it delivers an ordered world of regulated expectancies, the world of *Far from the Madding Crowd.* Action that had directed itself forward powerfully in the absence of design comes to a full circle.

Hardy's editors forced him to impose design upon a world that had stimulated his imagination because of its systemlessness. The "untameable" Egdon Heath loses its near relationship to night for a brighter, almost civilized aspect. The place where fugitives gathered and destroyed each other becomes a stage for bucolic courtship and marriage. Primitive as the Maypole may be, it connotes more of pastoral tradition than of pagan ritual, and it conveys none of the "Promethean rebelliousness" of the fires built on ashes that had once burnt to Thor and Woden. Like Oak, Diggory Venn regains his original respectability as a dairy farmer. Like their counterparts at Warren's Malthouse, the heath dwellers celebrate the restitution of social order in the union of leading man and lady. Clym, the tragic survivor, is more a stranger than a native son now. He is separated from the life of book six by a wood partition or by a dim, green-tinted window. No wonder Hardy complained of interference; he had to change heroes well beyond midstream.

He at least had to make his editors think that he had. But if we keep our attention on Clym, we learn that Hardy retained his original conception while appearing to conform to the demands of serial publication; and that he used the transplanted ending to add to the portrait of his original hero a tragic edge and power it would not otherwise have had. The point of the novel is not simply the native's return, but his destruction. Yet Clym does not fall, does not tragically lose one level of spiritual attainment for another, until book six. At the end of book five, he is stunned and guiltstricken, but not radically altered from what he had been—a fiercely independent and conscientious man.

He never gave in to the pressure of his wife and mother to return to Paris. He was flexible enough to modify his plan of education to satisfy his mother's wishes and keep his original goal in sight. In one of the more powerful scenes of the novel, Eustacia comes upon Clym, a half-blind furze cutter, and finds him singing. She, who has suffered nothing, would have cursed her lot. Clym, who has suffered much, turns his life into song and comforts her. "Yeobright loved his kind" and was ready to sacrifice himself to raise the lower class of heath workers to wisdom. Indeed, Clym loved to excess people who were not worthy of his love. Neither his mother nor Eustacia was as good as he thought her, and neither deserved the sacrifices he made for her.

These qualities give Clym his essential nobility, and they are intensified at the end of book five when Clym magnifies his guilt and his powers of self-denial and stoic endurance. He deteriorates internally and falls from nobility, in book six, by losing the independence and love that had characterized him even when he grieved deliriously for his dead mother. His actions had been those of a man too good for his world. In book six they become those of a man for whom no one is good enough. Though he could once sing in his hardship, he withdraws from the festivities at the Maypole, because "he could not bear to remain in the presence of enjoyment." Though he had typified the future races of men, he becomes enslaved to his memories of the dead, a punctual, ritualistic visitor to his mother's and Eustacia's graves. Violating the ideals that brought him back to the heath from Paris, he objects to Venn as Thomasin's proposed husband because Venn is too countrified and not enough of a gentleman. He feels ashamed for his opinion, and well he might. He has adopted his mother's prejudices and lost the vision by which he would raise men above material ambition. Isolated from Thomasin by her wedding, he finds a congenial companion in the listless Charley, to whom he gives a lock of Eustacia's hair. The two venerate it like a relic.

Clym's actions indicate to me that Hardy kept his original conception with a vengeance. Book six is a harrowing picture of high aspirations corrupting themselves, and Clym's fall is denied the relief or emotional refuge of traditional tragedy, in which a destructive passion is allowed to spend itself. We witness, as though this were all he had left, Clym's diminishing. As Clym and Charley look through the window at Thomasin's wedding reception, Clym asks if anyone seems to care about his not being there. "No, not a bit in the world," Charley answers. When the guests drink someone's health, Clym wonders if it is his, and Charley tells him it is Mr. and Mrs. Venn's. "Well, they haven't concerned themselves about me," Clym rationalizes, "and it is quite right they should not." He feels sorry for himself and has little other feeling besides. Perhaps Hardy's original ending would have worked just as well, but I suspect that it would have left Clym what he was at the end of book five, a pathetic victim of others. His isolation from a world that he wants to return to and the guilt and self-pity that isolate him make Clym tragic—his own tragic victimizer. Hardy satisfied more than the demands of his serial readers by giving them the joy of the makeshift wedding. The estrangement of the beaten man outside the window is more pronounced because of the contrast between what he feels and what he sees. Clym is left precisely where Hardy's original conception required him to be: in an indifferent and ambiguous world, searching to no apparent avail for what it is to do well. (pp. 83-93)

> Richard Benvenuto, " 'The Return of the Native' as a Tragedy in Six Books," in Nineteenth-Century Fiction, Vol. 26, No. 1, June, 1971, pp. 83-93.

Lennart A. Björk (essay date 1972)

[*In the following essay, Björk discusses Hardy's use of Eustacia Vye, Clym Yeobright, and Egdon Heath as "visible essences" illuminating the themes of* The Return of the Native.]

> Novel-writing as an art cannot go backwards. Having reached the analytic stage it must transcend it by going still further in the same direction: why not by rendering as visible essences, spectres, etc., the abstract thoughts of the analytic school?
> *The Early Life of Thomas Hardy,* March 4, 1886.

In Eustacia Vye and Clym Yeobright Hardy created 'visible essences' to convey the abstract theme of ***The Return of the Native.*** As their personal tragedy stages the ideological drama of conflicting views of life, Eustacia and Clym emerge as the thematic polarities of the novel. In their human relationship Hardy visualizes the clash between Hellenism—as he saw it—and nineteenth century thought in all its complexity of Christian, scientific, and philosophical ideas. With the same symbolic technique Hardy puts the two characters into a thematic frame of reference established by an emblematic physical setting, that of Egdon Heath, which far from being a neutral stage provides criteria which elucidate both the theme and the major characters. Thus, the main 'visible essences' of the novel, Egdon Heath, Eustacia, and Clym reciprocally define one another and offer a visual representation of the main ideological concern in ***The Return of the Native.***

In attempting to validate the above hypotheses I shall consider in turn (I) the creation of the thematic framework in chapter one, (II) the pantomime visualization, in chapter two, of the central action of the novel, (III) Eustacia as the 'visible essence' of Hellenism, and (IV) Clym as a projection of nineteenth century thought.

The much quoted description of Egdon Heath at the beginning of ***The Return of the Native*** serves not only to establish a physical background; but in its fusion of aesthetics and philosophy it also outlines the thematic structure of the novel:

> It was a spot which returned upon the memory of those who loved it with an aspect of peculiar and kindly congruity. Smiling champaigns of flowers and fruit hardly do this, for they are permanently harmonious only with an existence of better reputation as to its issues than the present. Twilight combined with the scenery of Egdon

Heath to evolve a thing majestic without severity, impressive without showiness, emphatic in its admonitions, grand in its simplicity. The qualifications which frequently invest the façade of a prison with far more dignity than is found in the façade of a palace double its size lent to this heath a sublimity in which spots renowned for beauty of the accepted kind are utterly wanting. Fair prospects wed happily with fair times; but alas, if times be not fair! Men have oftener suffered from the mockery of a place too smiling for their reason than from the oppression of surroundings oversadly tinged. Haggard Egdon appealed to a subtler and scarcer instinct, to a more recently learnt emotion, than that which responds to the sort of beauty called charming and fair.

Indeed, it is a question if the exclusive reign of this orthodox beauty is not approaching its last quarter. The new Vale of Tempe may be a gaunt waste in Thule: human souls may find themselves in closer and closer harmony with external things wearing a sombreness distasteful to our race when it was young. The time seems near, if it has not actually arrived, when the chastened sublimity of a moor, a sea, or a mountain will be all of nature that is absolutely in keeping with the moods of the more thinking among mankind.

The passage distinguishes between two contrasting sets of ideas and attitudes. On the aesthetic level the difference is between the sort of beauty of the Vale of Tempe in Ancient Thessaly and the sombre sublimity of 'Haggard Egdon'. The Vale of Tempe, or, 'the sort of beauty called charming and fair' appealed to the ancient world, 'to our race when it was young'. Egdon is attractive to the nineteenth century, to 'a more recently learnt emotion'. Hardy does not here directly explain the reasons for this remarkable shift in aesthetics. He implies, however, that it is linked to an overall change in views of life, and here the distinction on the philosophical level appears: 'Fair prospects wed happily with fair times; but alas, if times be not fair'! Hardy does not at once reveal the full meaning of the exclamation which so abruptly changes the character of the passage from descriptive to philosophical. Its significance emerges gradually as the novel progresses but gains complete clarity only when complemented with Hardy's definition, later in the novel, of the intellectual atmosphere of the age in which the tragedy of Eustacia and Clym is enacted. It is a time when 'a long line of disillusive centuries has permanently displaced the Hellenic idea of life', a time characterized by 'the view of life as a thing to be put up with, replacing the zest for existence which was so intense in early civilizations'. In view of this definition of the nineteenth century the implied conclusion in the description of Egdon Heath seems to be that its grim beauty can only be appreciated by modern man who is—as Hardy's characterization of Clym later in the novel makes clear—conditioned by the asceticism of Christianity and the prevailing pessimism of contemporary philosophical thought. In contrast, the passage implies that the spiritual milieu of the Ancients, pre-Christian and non-philosophical, was optimistic, harmonious and partial to a softer kind of beauty—an implication dramatized by the novel as a whole. The proposition is clear: there is a close connection between austerity and joylessness in aesthetics and the same qualities as defining views of life.

The description of Egdon Heath, then, establishes the thematic frame of reference: the antithesis between life in Ancient Greece and that in nineteenth century England. The juxtaposition forms the basic thematic structure of *The Return of the Native* and serves as the main criterion for an understanding of the two major characters, or 'visible essences', Eustacia Vye and Clym Yeobright.

Having thus briefly sketched the physical as well as ideological topography in Chapter One, Hardy proceeds by presenting, in Chapter two,—and, it is to be noted, *before* he introduces the main characters—an outline of the overall thematic development of the novel. The method is still somewhat oblique as Hardy chooses the symbolic form of a pantomime seen through the eyes of Diggory Venn. As the reddleman watches the lonely figure in the dark on top of Rainbarrow, Hardy analyses the symbolic implications of Diggory's vision: 'The first instinct of an imaginative stranger might have been to suppose it the person of one of the Celts who built the barrow, so far had all of modern date withdrawn from the scene. It seemed a sort of last man among them, musing for a moment before dropping into eternal night with the rest of his race'. The person is Eustacia. She is not a Celt but, as she is throughout the novel associated with the pagan world, she is appropriately introduced in a pre-Christian surrounding. As long as she remains on the Barrow, the scene seems 'strangely homogeneous' and the lonely figure 'an organic part of the entire motionless structure'. The harmony is broken, however, by the appearance of the heath-people who are, in spite of their pagan bon-fires, representatives of Christianity in general and the nineteenth century in particular. Diggory's reaction carries interesting emotional overtones: 'the imagination of the observer clung by preference to that vanished, solitary figure, as to something more interesting, more important, more likely to have a history worth knowing than these newcomers, and unconsciously regarded them as intruders'. The positive attitude towards the lonely figure and the opposite towards the heath-people are an early reflection in the novel of Hardy's view of his fictional material—a topic to be discussed below. Of more immediate interest is Hardy's explanation of the purport of the dumb show: 'the only intelligible meaning of this sky-backed pantomime of silhouettes was that the woman had no relation to the forms who had taken her place . . .'. The scene contains, then, the same basic antithesis of paganism and nineteenth century thought as did the description of Egdon Heath. The silent pageant assumes the purpose of a play within a play; like the novel as a whole the pantomime illustrates that Eustacia will not and can not co-exist with agents of the nineteenth century, here in the shapes of the heath-people, later in the form of Clym Yeobright. Eustacia vanishing out of sight into the darkness may be considered a symbolic representation of Hellenism fading away as the nineteenth century advances.

Given that Eustacia is the visible essence of the past culture of Hellenism in the novel, it is with chronological and thematic pertinency that she is the first major character to come into focus. Her personality, and Hardy's attitude towards her, have been subjected to various interpretations; many critics have registered an unfavourable impression of Eustacia and deduce, consequently, that Hardy intended her to be a female antagonist who is justifiably defeated by the male protagonist, Clym. Thus, in the very first reviews Eustacia was regarded as a character 'who only wished to gratify her sensual passions'. And, more recently, she has been described [by Robert C. Schweik in his essay "Theme, Character and Perspective in Hardy's *The Return of the Native*"] as 'a young girl whose dreamy and imaginative yearning has so distorted her views that she understands neither the heath nor the world beyond it'. In this context, Hardy's own opinion of her is very important for it is, of course, his attitude towards Eustacia—in combination with her Hellenic attributes—which explains Eustacia's symbolic function in the novel.

In my opinion, Hardy's view of Eustacia is very charitable, an impression that I find supported by material both external and internal to the novel. Outside **The Return of the Native** Eustacia may profitably be compared to another Hardy heroine, Tess in **Tess of the d'Urbervilles.** These two novels are, indeed, strikingly similar as regards Hardy's conception of the characters and themes in general and the female protagonists in particular. Like Eustacia Tess is firmly linked to a pre-Christian world. Not only does Angel Clare imagine her 'a fresh and virginal daughter of Nature' but he also puts Tess in a pagan environment by calling her 'Artemis, Demeter and other fanciful names' and by discussing with her 'pastoral life in Ancient Greece'. And, in the end of the novel Tess identifies the setting of the final scene, Stonehenge, as 'the heathen temple'. Then, as she realizes how appropriate the place is for the staging of the closing scene of the drama, she tells Angel: '. . . you used to say at Talbothays that I was a heathen. So now I am at home'. Hardy's sympathy for Tess has not been seriously questioned and it seems reasonable to assume that Eustacia is an early version of the child of nature image that was to be projected in Tess; that when Eustacia yields to her emotions she simply listens to the same voice of Nature. Certainly Hardy displays the same compassion for Eustacia as for Tess when, towards the end of **The Return of the Native,** he comments on her hopeless situation. It is to be noted that he blames not Eustacia's passionate and rebellious character but her environment: 'Any one who had stood by now would have pitied her . . . The wings of her soul were broken by the cruel obstructiveness of all about her'. Of additional intrinsic material which points to Hardy's positive attitude towards Eustacia there is first of all the juxtaposition, briefly discussed above, of Eustacia and the heath-people which establishes a favourable attitude towards her even before we know anything about her mental situation. The softness of tone in her portrait is quite different from that of the drawing of the 'intruders' marching in trail 'like a travelling flock of sheep'. Hardy displays, to be sure, good-humour in staging the pranks of the crowd. Strong irony, however, is sensed in the characterization of the person whom, with pointed wit, he has named Christian. This personification of fears and superstitions may seem harmless enough; yet, his frantic and pitiful conduct on the Barrow is markedly and discreditably contrasted to Eustacia's calm and fearless behaviour on the same spot: 'Her extraordinary fixity, her conspicuous loneliness, her heedlessness of night, betokened among other things an utter absence of fear'. In the same way the atmosphere of her pagan platform is in conspicuous terms compared to that of the heath of the nineteenth century Christians below: 'There she stood still, around her stretching the vast night atmosphere, whose incomplete darkness in comparison with the total darkness of the heath below it might have represented a venial beside a mortal sin. It is to be noted in this context that the Barrow is the scene of Eustacia's secret and—from the viewpoint of Egdon society—immoral meetings with Wildeve, whereas, at that very moment, the heath is profoundly disturbed by the social and moral mortification of the postponement of the Christian marriage ceremony of Thomasin and Wildeve. Eustacia, then, is closely linked to the pagan Barrow, which is favourably juxtaposed to nineteenth century Egdon society.

Hardy's admiration for his heroine, however, becomes even more clearly manifested in the close-up presentation of Eustacia in the famous 'Queen of Night' chapter, which also brings the Hellenic theme to the foreground: Eustacia Vye was the raw material of a divinity. On Olympus she would have done well enough with a little preparation'. As she stands on the Barrow, the Olympus of Egdon Heath, 'a new moon behind her head, an old helmet upon it, a diadem of accidental dewdrops round her head, would have been adjuncts sufficient to strike the note of Artemis, Athena, or Hera respectively'. Eustacia's ancestry is traced with equal care to its Greek origin. Her father was 'a Corfiote by birth', 'a romantic wanderer—a sort of Greek Ulysses'; her dignity may derive from a 'latent vein of Aicinous' line, her father hailing from Phæacia's isle'.

Eustacia's looks and origin do not alone, of course, make her a personification of Parnassus. Her 'epicurean heart', taste, behaviour, character, and view of life all contribute to the image of a Hellenic anachronism on Egdon Heath. As Eustacia senses this isolation most of her actions become expressions of rebellion, from the comparatively innocent mumming expedition in men's clothes to the open defiance of the social and religious norms of Egdon Heath when she takes steps to elope with another woman's husband.

The theme of rebellion coincides with the Hellenic motif, and, as such, it is introduced early in the novel: 'to light a fire . . . indicates a spontaneous, Promethean rebelliousness'. The reference, in this context, to the archetypal rebel is not haphazard. As his commonplace books reveal, Hardy had *Prometheus* in mind at the time he was writing **The Return of the Native.** Not surprisingly then, the Promethean rebelliousness of Eustacia's character is throughout the novel conveyed and defined through fire imagery: 'Assuming that the souls of men and women were visible essences, you could fancy the colour of Eustacia's soul to be flamelike'. Such inner warmth, however, is wasted on Egdon Heath since 'celestial imperiousness, love, wrath, and fervour had proved to be somewhat thrown away on netherward Egdon'. Realizing this Eustacia kindles a 'smouldering rebelliousness' and though she cannot help having 'imbibed much of what was dark in its [Egdon's] tone', she remains 'eternally unreconciled thereto'. Her resistance finds expression in a momentary rebellion as she goes, alone, to the village festival which significantly is described as an occasion when 'Paganism was revived in their [the crowd's] hearts'. The warm world of emotions that Eustacia there enters is sharply contrasted to the frozen climate of Egdon Heath: 'her beginning to dance had been steeped in arctic frigidity by comparison with the tropical sensations here'. The contrast between her fiery nature and the coldness and indifference of the natural setting is a repeated theme in the novel: Eustacia returning home from her first meeting with Clym, for instance, is in a state of high elation 'warmed with an inner fire' while the air without is 'charged with silence and frost'.

Thus, Eustacia is alienated from nineteenth century Egdon Heath philosophically and emotionally. In her pagan beauty, of course, she is also aesthetically an anachronism in her modern environment. As a 'visible essence' of Hellenism she shares quite naturally the taste of 'our race when it was young' and finds Egdon Heath distasteful. Not surprisingly she is astounded when, on the evening of Clym's arrival, she overhears his praise of the heath: 'What could the tastes of that man be who saw friendliness and geniality in these shaggy hills'? Eustacia is soon to find out, as the rest of the novel is devoted to Clym's aesthetics and philosophy and to the contrast and ensuing conflict between her and Clym as personifications of different and apparently irreconcilable views of life.

The essential difference between Eustacia and Clym is manifested in the very first presentation of Clym. As in the Egdon Heath passage, Hardy again chooses to convey the major antithesis of the novel in terms of mixture of aesthetics and philosophy:

> The face was well shaped, even excellently. But the mind within was beginning to use it as a mere waste tablet whereon to trace its idiosyncrasies as they developed themselves. The beauty here visible would in no long time be ruthlessly overrun by its parasite, thought, which might just as well have fed upon a plainer exterior where there was nothing it could harm. Had Heaven preserved Yeobright from wearing habit of meditation, people would have said, 'A handsome man'. Had his brain unfolded under sharper contours they would have said, 'A thoughtful man'. But an inner strenuousness was preying upon an outer symmetry, and they rated his look as singular.
>
> Hence people who began by beholding him ended by perusing him. His countenance was overlaid with legible meanings. Without being thought-worn he yet had certain marks derived from a perception of his surroundings, such as are not unfrequently found on men at the end of four or five years of endeavour which follow the close of placid pupilage. He already showed that thought is a disease of flesh, and indirectly bore evidence that ideal physical beauty is incompatible with emotional development and a full recognition of the coil of things.

Like Eustacia, Clym is endowed with physical beauty. Unlike her, however, he is physically deteriorating because of a parasite within—thought, which has revealed to him the true nature of man's existence, 'a full recognition of the coil of things'. His face bears evidence, Hardy deploringly notes, of the 'destructive interdependence of spirit and flesh'. Metaphysical speculation, then, the novel postulates, creates not only new aesthetic standards—as modern man prefers grim Egdon Heath to the Vale of Tempe—it also jeopardizes the very existence of beauty in human beings.

The synthesis of all aesthetic and ideological propositions in the novel is finally stated in the chapter which with bitter irony Hardy has called 'My Mind to Me a Kingdom Is'. He here explains how the various discussions of beauty and attitudes towards life are meant to help define the view of the Nineteenth Century versus Antiquity which the novel dramatizes. The chapter opens with a detailed examination of the male protagonist's facial features:

> In Clym Yeobright's face could be dimly seen the typical countenance of the future. Should there be a classic period to art hereafter, its Pheidias may produce such faces. The view of life as a thing to be put up with, replacing that zest for existence which was so intense in early civilizations, must ultimately enter so thoroughly into the constitution of the advanced races that its facial expression will become accepted as a new artistic departure. People already feel that a man who lives without disturbing a curve of feature, or setting a mark of mental concern anywhere upon himself, is too far removed from modern perceptiveness to be a modern type. Physically beautiful men—the glory of the race when it was young—are almost an anachronism now; and we may wonder whether, at some time or other, physically beautiful women may not be an anachronism likewise.
>
> The truth seems to be that a long line of disillusive centuries has permanently displaced the Hellenic idea of life, or whatever it may be called. What the Greeks only suspected we know well; what their Æschylus imagined our nursery children feel. That old-fashioned revelling in the general situation grows less and less possible as we uncover the defects of natural laws, and see the quandary that man is in by their operation.

Hardy thus resumes the technique of fusing concepts of beauty and life from the description of Egdon and the first scrutiny of Clym's face. The theme is identical, only now Hardy is less implicit; he openly defines the Hellenic-nineteenth century conflict: 'the Hellenic idea of life', 'the zest for existence', he regretfully notes, has had to yield to the resigned 'view of life as a thing to be put up with', embodied in the characters who, like Clym, are the end-product of 'a long line of disillusive centuries'.

Both as regards physical appearance, aesthetics, and view of life, Clym emerges as a personification of modern man in the nineteenth century, the Christian whose faith is harassed by the prevailing scientific and philosophical movements. As such it seems quite proper that he and Egdon

Heath should mutually define one another. In delineating Clym as a projection of his time Hardy implicitly makes Egdon a microcosm of the century: 'he was permeated with its scenes, with its substance, and with its odours. He might be said to be its product . . . ; his estimate of life had been coloured by it'. In the same context, as might be expected, Hardy also defines Clym's nature by contrasting his view of Egdon with that of Eustacia's: 'take all the varying hates felt by Eustacia Vye towards the heath and translate them into loves, and you have the heart of Clym'.

As a product of Egdon Heath and the nineteenth century, Clym does not explicitly reveal much influence from any particular contemporary philosophical creed. But, as has been earlier proposed by Eleanor McCann [in her essay, "Blind Will or Blind Hero: Philosophy and Myth in Hardy's *The Return of the Native,*" *Criticism* (1961)], much of his character may be explained in terms of Schopenhauer's philosophy. As stated above, I see Clym as a 'visible essence' of modern man in general and not as a Schopenhauerian hero. However, Schopenhauer was the leading pessimistic philosopher of the day, and Hardy showed a marked interest in him. McCann's proposition, therefore, seems valuable and is of interest in this context as her analysis of certain aspects of Clym's character explains his ready acceptance of Egdon society and emphasizes and supports the fundamental difference between him and Eustacia in terms of the hypotheses of this study.

According to Schopenhauer there are three possible kinds of adjustment open to the man who has come to realize the painful aspects of human existence: philosophical understanding, aesthetic appreciation, and disinterested morality. Clym avails himself of them all. The first is implied in the discussion with Eustacia when she comments on his complacent way of looking at their future life: 'Ah,—your mind runs off to the philosophical side of it. Well, these sad and hopeless obstacles are welcome in one sense, for they enable us to look with indifference upon the cruel satires that Fate loves to indulge in'. Eustacia's statement is hardly in character. Her passionate and rebellious nature does not allow her to look with indifference upon life; nor is she so given to philosophical speculation as to possess the insight here implied. Her answer is rather meant to stress and illuminate the reconciliation open to Clym through his philosophy. Eustacia's lack of philosophical understanding, as a contrast, is one of the reasons for her break with Clym and, ultimately, for her death.

Clym also attains adjustment by aesthetic appreciation. He possesses that 'subtler and scarcer instinct', that 'recently learnt emotion' which enables him to enjoy the more rugged and sombre kinds of beauty. Egdon Heath, Clym tells Eustacia, 'is most exhilarating, and strengthening, and soothing'. Eustacia, whose Hellenic sense of beauty is paralyzed in this environment, answers resignedly: 'It is well enough for artists; but I never would learn to draw'.

Finally, Clym's nature also opens the way to moral adjustment. His disinterested morality is accentuated throughout the novel, theoretically and practically: 'Yeobright loved his kind . . . He wished to raise the class at the expense of individuals rather than individuals at the expense of the class. What was more, he was ready at once to be the first unit sacrificed'. Living up to his principles, Clym leaves his financially rewarding occupation in Paris in order to educate the masses. Again, Eustacia is quite different. She refuses to accept or partake of Clym's self-denial and the unselfish ethics of Diggory Venn are almost incomprehensible to her.

Thus, certain traits in Clym—particularly when contrasted to Eustacia's character—may be understood in terms of Schopenhauer's philosophy. To what extent Hardy relied on the German pessimistic philosopher in creating Clym cannot, of course, be definitely ascertained, especially as Hardy refused to explicitly endow him with any particular creed or dogma and referred to. Clym's outside influence only vaguely as 'ethical systems popular at the time. However, given the possible specific Schopenhauerian traits in addition to Clym's ideas, looks, tastes, and behaviour in general, it is clear that Hardy in Clym Yeobright created what he considered a prototype of modern man in the nineteenth century.

Finally, then, as is clear in their relation to Egdon Heath, the microcosm of the nineteenth century, and to one another, Eustacia and Clym are irreconcilable. In her Hardy has created with defiant sympathy a 'visible essence' of Hellenism and the concept of pagan self-assertion so heavily marked in his copy of John Stuart Mill's *On Liberty,* and in Clym—with sad compassion—a projection of nineteenth century thought. In their personal human conflict ending with Eustacia's death and Clym's joyless survival, Hardy dramatizes the theme and ideological essence of ***The Return of the Native:*** the painful realization, and admission, that the light, optimism, and luxuriance of the Hellenic view of life have had to yield to the philosophical resignation and emotional restraint of the nineteenth century. (pp. 52-63)

Lennart A. Björk, " 'Visible Essences' as Thematic Structure in Hardy's 'The Return of the Native'," in English Studies, *Netherlands, Vol. 53, No. 1, February, 1972, pp. 52-63.*

Thomas Hardy on aesthetics:

The method of Boldini, the painter of *The Morning Walk* in the French Gallery two or three years ago (a young lady beside an ugly blank wall on an ugly highway)—of Hobbema, in his view of a road with formal lopped trees and flat tame scenery—is of that infusing emotion into the baldest external objects either by the presence of a human figure among them, or by mark of some human connection with them.

This accords with my feeling about, say, Heidelberg and Baden *versus* Scheveningen—as I wrote at the beginning of **The Return of the Native**—that the beauty of association is entirely superior to the beauty of aspect, and a beloved relative's old battered tankard to the finest Greek vase. Paradoxically put, it is to see the beauty in ugliness.

Thomas Hardy in The Early Life of Thomas Hardy: 1840-1891, *1928.*

Avrom Fleishman (essay date 1978)

[*Fleishman is an American educator who has written extensively on the English novel. In the following excerpt, he analyzes the nature of Egdon Heath.*]

One would search long for a commentator on ***The Return of the Native*** who has failed to locate the story of Clym Yeobright and Eustacia Vye in the elaborated space of its landscape. Still it may be said that Egdon Heath has not been recognized as a figure in its own right—in both narrative senses of "figure," as person and as trope. One of the closest observers of the novel, John Paterson, has listed [in his essay "The 'Poetics' of *The Return of the Native*"] some of the heath's associations: ". . . it is a stage grand enough to bear the weight of gods and heroes; more specifically still, it is the prison-house of Prometheus, the fire-bearing benefactor of mankind." Paterson and others have supported such identifications by quoting the novel's repeated attribution of Promethean characteristics to the major characters. Hardy is never one to make his classical allusions evasively; the demonic rebelliousness of Eustacia and the bonded martyrdom of Clym are steadily projected upon the heath in the mode of scenic amplification. Yet the felt connection between the human actors and their inanimate setting exceeds the scope of metonymic associations like the scene-act ratio of Kenneth Burke. The ruling passions of the protagonists in ***The Return*** and the awesome powers of the heath need to be treated as forces of a like nature—the heath manifesting the same impulses as do the fictional characters.

To return to the setting of Hardy's first major novel is to seize his imagination at an originative position, where his sense of the past and his complex feelings about modern life intersected at a place with which he identified himself. Throughout his career, Hardy was inclined to express his strong response to the history-laden landscape of his shire in images of a special kind—special, that is, when compared with those of other Victorian novelists but commonplace in the tradition of local observers with a bent for narrative explanation. He was born, it will be recalled, in a cottage on the edge of the fourteen miles or so of high ground that has come to be identified with Egdon Heath, and he built his home, Max Gate, near its southwest flank five years after writing ***The Return.*** In 1878, the year the novel was published, the Folk-Lore Society was founded in London, and at about this date Hardy joined the Dorset Natural History and Antiquarian Field Club. To the latter he also delivered a paper on "Some Romano-British Relics Found at Max Gate, Dorchester"—found, that is, during the digging of foundations for his house. These delvings in the earth encouraged Hardy in a long series of reflections on the presence underfoot of a many-layered past: beginning as early as the passage in ***The Return*** on Clym's attendance at the opening of a barrow (book III, chapter iii); continuing with the account of unearthed Roman skeletons in ***The Mayor of Casterbridge*** (chapter xi); and developing a fine blend of fascination and detachment in poems like **"The Roman Gravemounds"** and **"The Clasped Skeletons."**

The sense of the past, it has been abundantly demonstrated, touches Hardy's work at innumerable points, but one may be isolated for the present discussion: his adumbration of an animate (or once-animate) being dormant in the earth, whether in the form of a buried skeleton incarnating the ghosts of the past, or of a quasi-human figure underlying or constituting certain topographical features (usually hills), or of a *genius loci* residing not in an aerial or other evanescent medium but in the soil of the place itself. It will be seen that some such preternatural beliefs are at work amid the rationalist skepticism which Hardy tried to maintain and that, while his own beliefs are not to be equated with those of the peasants in his tales, his absorption in them resembles the intellectual sympathy which modern anthropologists and folklorists have been recommending.

The prime instances of buried figures in the Hardy country are, quite naturally, those associated with a number of massive formations which surpass anything comparable in the southwest—the region of England perhaps most densely populated by ancient remains. Foremost is Maiden Castle, a Celtic hillfort a few miles south of Dorchester, which Hardy described as "an enormous many-limbed organism of an antediluvian time . . . lying lifeless, and covered with a thin green cloth, which hides its substance, while revealing its contour." Comparable in fame and grandeur is the Cerne Abbas giant, with his club and explicit phallus, on a hill seven miles north of Dorchester in a region Hardy favored for his rambles; it is mentioned in ***Tess of the d'Urbervilles*** and other writings, most saliently when described by the local peasantry in ***The Dynasts*** as a malevolent ogre, comparable to Napoleon.

Besides those and other gigantic erections in the vicinity, like Stonehenge, additional outcroppings of the land contour Hardy's writings. In a poem titled **"The Moth-Signal,"** specifically set on Egdon Heath and reminiscent of an incident in ***The Return,*** the waywardness of modern domestic life is seen from the perspective of a dweller in the earth:

> Then grinned the Ancient Briton
> From the tumulus treed with pine:
> "So, hearts are thwartly smitten
> In these days as in mine!"

Hardy takes up the point of view of an inhabitant of the heath in a more personal way in another poem, **"A Meeting with Despair"** (noted in the manuscript as set on Egdon Heath):

> As evening shaped I found me on a moor
> Sight shunned to entertain:
> The black lean land, of featureless contour,
> Was like a tract in pain.
>
> "This scene, like my own life," I said, "is one
> Where many glooms abide;
> Toned by its fortune to a deadly dun—
> Lightless on every side."
>
> . . . . .
>
> Against the horizon's dim-discerned wheel
> A form rose, strange of mould:
> That he was hideous, hopeless, I could feel
> Rather than could behold.

Although Hardy metaphorically identifies the pattern and tone of his life with the heath's, he resists the insinuations of the apparition—named "Despair" in the title but referred to only as "the Thing" in the poem itself—so as to argue that the glowing sunset portends better prospects for the future. In a voice we recognize as that of the stupid giant of fairy tales, his interlocutor replies, "Yea—but await awhile! . . . Ho-ho!— / Now look aloft and see!" More striking, perhaps, than either the poem's finale (with the loss of light and portent of defeat) or the similarities between its treatment of Egdon Heath and the novel's is the encounter with an abiding presence there—the black lean land, featureless, in pain, from which a hideous, hopeless form arises.

These poems call to mind others in which one of the most familiar features of Hardy's style, personification, is employed in its mode of gigantism. The best-known instance of this trope is found in **"The Darkling Thrush"**: "The land's sharp features seemed to be / The Century's corpse outleant. . . . " In the periodical publication of the poem, its original title emphasized this figure rather than the thrush: **"By the Century's Deathbed"** enforces the idea not simply of a localized spirit but of the entire earth as a body suffering a secular decline. A more sharply focused version of this image occurs in the poem **"By the Earth's Corpse"** (from the same volume as **"The Darkling Thrush"**), in which Time and "the Lord" conduct a dialogue on the themes of guilt and repetition, while placed like mourners near "this globe, now cold / As lunar land and sea," at some future time "when flesh / And herb but fossils be, / And, all extinct, their piteous dust / Revolves obliviously. . . . "

The most highly developed vision of the earth as an organic, vaguely human being is, however, that of **The Dynasts**. A stage direction of the "Fore Scene" is justly famous for its panoramic sweep, anticipating (but still surpassing) the movement of the camera eye in epically scaled movies:

> The nether sky opens, and Europe is disclosed as a prone and emaciated figure, the Alps shaping like a backbone, and the branching mountain-chains like ribs, the peninsular plateau of Spain forming a head. . . . The point of view then sinks downwards through space, and draws near to the surface of the perturbed countries, where the peoples, distressed by events which they did not cause, are seen writhing, crawling, heaving, and vibrating in their various cities and nationalities.

With the return to this vision in the "After Scene," Europe is "beheld again as a prone and emaciated figure. . . . The lowlands look like a grey-green garment half-thrown off, and the sea around like a disturbed bed on which the figure lies." In this instance, human forms in the mass join with geographical features to create the image of a total organism: the earth itself (or its European portion) as a giant, going through the stages of awakening, struggle, and exhaustion—a composite being living out the disturbances and sufferings of humankind.

Is it this (or a related) giant who confronts the reader from the title of the opening chapter of **The Return:** "A Face on which Time makes but Little Impression"? The rhetoric of the so-called pathetic fallacy suggests that it is a creature on the scale of the earth: it "wore the appearance of an instalment of night" and, reciprocally, "the face of the heath by its mere complexion added half an hour to evening." Not only are vital reflexes, human apparel, and personal physiognomy suggested, but the sustained comparison of Egdon Heath and mankind is raised from mere analogy to essential identity:

> It was at present a place perfectly accordant with man's nature—neither ghastly, hateful, nor ugly: neither commonplace, unmeaning, nor tame; but, like man, slighted and enduring; and withal singularly colossal and mysterious in its swarthy monotony. As with some persons who have long lived apart, solitude seemed to look out of its countenance. It had a lonely face, suggesting tragical possibilities.

It is on the basis of this profound identity that the epithets used for the heath come to resonate like personal designations: "Haggard Egdon," "the untameable, Ishmaelitish thing that Egdon now was," "the people changed, yet Egdon remained." In the most pathetic of these characterizations, the place is defined in relation to other natural forces in a style usually reserved for romantic fiction: "Then Egdon was aroused to reciprocity; for the storm was its lover, and the wind its friend." But the role hardly suits a figure that has emerged as not merely humanized but on a larger-than-individual scale: "singularly colossal and mysterious in its swarthy monotony." Such a colossus can be a hero only of a special sort.

In inventing the name itself, Hardy seems to have had in mind not a place-name but a personal one. Its closest analogue is a forename: *Egbert,* from Old English *ecg* ("sword") and *bryght* ("bright")—the latter term also appearing in the chief surname used in the novel. *Egdon* would be its derivable opposite: the second syllable is equivalent to *dun,* the word used since Anglo-Saxon times to describe the natural shades of landscape, animals, and atmosphere in a dull, brown grey range. (But compare the Celtic name of Maiden Castle: *mai dun* ["strong hill"].) Etymology resolves nothing, but this name goes beyond the expansive suggestiveness of well-wrought place-names in fiction, encouraging instead the identification of a personal presence by a favored technique of characterization.

If these two processes are indeed comparable—if a somewhat amorphous terrain is presented here in the manner in which fictional characters are conventionally introduced—we shall have to revise our expectations of the role of landscape in this novel more radically than we may be prepared to do. Landscape is not satisfied to act in **The Return of the Native** as a background, with human subjects in the foreground (although some positioning of people against a background of natural elements is at work, e.g., in the chapter entitled "The Figure against the Sky"). Instead, Egdon Heath becomes one of the principal agents of the action, a protagonist in the classical sense of the dramatic actor, and probably the most memorable figure to emerge from the events. The title of the novel has been given some new turns in recent criticism, so as to widen its reference beyond the donnée of Clym's return to Wessex. If its individual implications are taken seriously, the title refers somewhat sardonically to Clym's return to the native state in the course of the action; it also suggests more broadly the heath's renewed prominence in the life of the characters and of the modern age generally. "The Return of the Native" would name, then, a story about Egdon Heath.

The operation of these narrative traits makes the term "personification" no longer adequate to describe the process by which Egdon Heath is generated by the text. When natural categories are fixed, one may speak about the ascription of human characteristics to inanimate beings or about the representation of an abstract or other impersonal entity in human terms. But Egdon is not so clear-cut: it is never given as entirely on one side of the animate/inanimate polarity before being assimilated to the other. Even in the opening chapter, the metaphoric expressions by which it is rendered human are immediately posited as literal (or as leading to literal statements about the heath's role in human psychology): "Then [in storms, etc.] it became the home of strange phantoms; and it was found to be the hitherto unrecognized original of those wild regions of obscurity which are vaguely felt to be compassing us about in midnight dreams of flight and disaster, and are never thought of after the dream till revived by scenes like this." Without drawing conclusions about Hardy's version of the unconscious, we find his prose moving from the metaphoric level (movement of storms/movement of phantoms), to statements that posit the heath as the original model of dream landscapes, to a final suggestion of its function as a permanent index of the unconscious "regions" of the mind itself. So steadily cumulative is this assimilation of the heath to the animate level that toward the close of the novel, as intensity of style mounts in tempo with intensity of action, we are prepared to take in stride such passages as this: "Skirting the pool [Eustacia] followed the path towards Rainbarrow, occasionally stumbling over twisted furze-roots, tufts of rushes, or oozing lumps of fleshy fungi, which at this season lay scattered about the heath like the rotten liver and lungs of some colossal animal." While it is Eustacia who is stumbling toward her death, it is the heath that is seen here as a dismembered giant—neither clearly human nor, as Lawrence thought, merely bestial but a "colossal animal" who is martyred and distributed in a spectacular way.

While the interconnections of the animate and the inanimate must be deduced from the rhetorical modes of the opening chapter, later passages state their inherent identity in the heath with some urgency. The chief of these occurs in the first description of Eustacia Vye:

> There the form stood, motionless as the hill beneath. Above the plain rose the hill, above the hill rose the barrow, and above the barrow rose the figure. Above the figure was nothing that could be mapped elsewhere than on a celestial globe.
>
> Such a perfect, delicate, and necessary finish did the figure give to the dark pile of hills that it seemed to be the only obvious justification of their outline. Without it, there was the dome without the lantern; with it the architectural demands of the mass were satisfied. The scene was stangely homogeneous, in that the value, the upland, the barrow, and the figure above it amounted only to unity. Looking at this or that member of the group was not observing a complete thing, but a fraction of a thing.

Hardy employs the term "organic" in the next sentence to describe the internal relations of the "entire motionless structure"; we may apply it equally to the tenor of his thinking in this passage. Although the human figure is to be regarded esthetically as a "necessary finish" and a satisfaction of an "architectural" demand, it is more fundamentally a "fraction" of a larger "unity." Nor is the heath complete without the person: it needs it as its "obvious justification," to become a "homogeneous" being in its own right. The text speaks of this organic unity of the human and the nonhuman "members" of Egdon Heath as "a thing" and elsewhere adds, "a thing majestic without severity, impressive without showiness, emphatic in its admonitions, grand in its simplicity."

Although Eustacia is most striking in her unwilling assimilation into Egdon Heath, other characters exhibit a spectrum of possible relations to it, ranging from identification to detachment. Although the gigantic "thing" takes in both human beings and the heath, there are a number of possible modes of integration, which various characters explore. The peasants live in wary observance of the land and its seasons, but their limited mentalities are none too gently satirized in Hardy's folkish chapters. The reddleman, Diggory Venn, shows himself adroit not only in the world of commercial and (eventually) erotic competition but is especially competent among the highways and byways of the heath. (It is noteworthy that he gets no particular credit for this intimacy with the heath, as measured by the conventions of heroic stature; given Hardy's view of him as an "isolated and weird character"—in the "Author's Note" of 1912—he is scarcely ennobled by his numerous displays of omnicompetence.) It is Clym who displays the most complex relation to the heath, being the one who exercises a series of considered choices in the matter. In his first characterization, his constitution or generation by the place is stressed: "If any one knew the heath well it was Clym. He was permeated with its scenes, with its substance, and with its odours. He might be said to be its product." At the end of his series of ideological shifts and personal misfortunes, he stands before the heath in an alien position, as of one face impervious to another: ". . . there was only the imperturbable countenance of the heath, which, having defied the cataclysmal onsets of centuries, reduced to insignificance by its seamed and antique features the wildest turmoil of a single man." But the most extreme separation from the heath—indistinguishable from a kind of rationalistic stupidity—is represented by the pragmatic objectivity of Thomasin Yeobright: ". . . Egdon in the mass was no monster whatever, but impersonal open ground. Her fears of the place were rational, her dislikes of its worst moods reasonable."

Despite their differences, the characters have a common connection with the heath, a unity of fate that is consistently figured in allusions to Prometheus: "Every night [the heath's] Titanic form seemed to await something; but it had waited thus, unmoved, during so many centuries, through the crises of so many things, that it could only be imagined to await one last crisis—the final overthrow." The iconography of Prometheus chained to a mountain in the Caucasus is strikingly transmuted in this and similar passages: the *scene* of suffering becomes the sufferer (Egdon is not Caucasian but Titanic), while at least part of the demigod's character is ascribed to the land itself in its "unmoved" martyrdom. Yet the myth's primary orientation toward apocalypse (the final overthrow of Zeus) is, as we shall see, fully employed in ***The Return.***

The heath's Promethean, long-suffering form of resistance is picked up in the characterization of the human actors but is resourcefully applied as a differentiating factor. The peasants' lighting of fires to celebrate Guy Fawkes Day, although localized as a modern British survival of the ritual death and rebirth of the year, is seen as the expression of a universal need: "Moreover to light a fire is the instinctive and resistant act of man when, at the winter ingress, the curfew is sounded throughout Nature. It indicates a spontaneous, Promethean rebelliousness against the fiat that this recurrent season shall bring foul times, cold darkness, misery and death. Black chaos comes, and the fettered gods of the earth say, Let there be light." Here humans, heath, and Titans are seen on the same side, resisting—or at least protesting—an imposition from without, the fiat of a being or realm representing black chaos, winter, and death. Humanity joins with the land itself in "Promethean rebelliousness," and it is with one voice that they register their counterfiat; theirs is the voice of the "fettered gods" or Titans, which proclaims light—a biblical equivalent for the Promethean fire that is the subject of this passage.

The chief characters are, however, subtly distinguished in their articulations of this rebellion and thus in their associations with the band of "fettered gods." Eustacia is described from the first in terms derived from the preceding passage: "Egdon was her Hades, and since coming there she had imbibed much of what was dark in its tone, though inwardly and eternally unreconciled thereto. Her appearance accorded well with this smouldering rebelliousness. . . . A true Tartarean dignity sat upon her brow . . . ". The term found in both passages, "rebelliousness," is linked to its consequences of banishment or living burial, whether of humans in Hades or of Titans in Tartarus (the variability of mythological traditions is exploited here to make these roughly equivalent terms for confinement in the earth). It is notable that this passage begins by emphasizing Eustacia's unwilling bondage in Egdon, the setting of her unsatisfactory station in life, but it gradually identifies her with the heath insofar as the latter, too, is unreconciled to its bound condition under the fiat of the ruling gods.

Precisely the opposite shift occurs in the course of Clym's characterization: beginning as one fully at home on the heath—"its product"—he becomes so thoroughly acclimated in his return to the soil that he renounces rebelliousness: "Now, don't you suppose, my inexperienced girl, that I cannot rebel, in high Promethean fashion, against the gods and fate as well as you. I have felt more steam and smoke of that sort than you have ever heard of. But the more I see of life the more do I perceive that there is nothing particularly great in its greatest walks, and therefore nothing particularly small in mine of furze-cutting." Clym's liberal renunciation of the Promethean stance is part of an explicit cultural theme in the novel, concerned with the vulnerability of the modern mind by virtue of its skeptical intelligence, its loss of traditional, organizing mythologies (a loss and a vulnerability in which Hardy felt himself implicated). But Clym's career also involves a break with the creaturely tendency to rebellion against earthbound suffering, a separation from the Titanic "fettered gods" with whom Eustacia, involuntarily, associates herself. And it is this loss of Promethean vision that is his true undoing, for he sees "nothing particularly great in [life's] greatest walks" or, by the same token, in the heath's. (pp. 110-18)

> *Avrom Fleishman, "The Buried Giant of Egdon Heath: An Archeology of Folklore in 'The Return of the Native'," in his* Fiction and the Ways of Knowing: Essays on British Novels, *University of Texas Press, 1978, pp. 110-22.*

Robert B. Heilman (essay date 1979)

[*Heilman is an American educator who has written on the works of William Shakespeare and Thomas Hardy. In the following essay, entitled "The Return: Centennial Observations," he assesses Hardy's plot development, imagery, characterization, and use of language.*]

To return to ***The Return of the Native*** after a long absence, and after some transactions with the later 'major' works, is to find much that is familiar and much that is, well, for lack of a better word, surprising. By 'the familiar' I do not mean matters remembered from a distant reading, but the recurrent practices that one thinks of as Hardyisms—sometimes excellent, sometimes mingling the more and the less effective, sometimes stirring the reader, willy-nilly, to the ho-hum response. Technical tours de force, sometimes brilliant, co-exist with methods that are careless or heavy-handed. What is 'surprising' is that the excellences make one think of the older novelist rather than the relatively young one that Hardy still was in 1878—thirty-eight. Although ***The Return*** is only the third of the seven 'Novels of Character and Environment', as Hardy called them, its ties are mainly with the final four that begin with ***The Mayor of Casterbridge*** (1886) and end with ***Jude the Obscure*** (1895). To say that is to declare ***The Return*** worthy at least of the usual centennial rites. As ritualist I want to observe some aspects of Hardy's fictional art rather than focus on influences (Schopenhauer, Mill, Arnold, Greek drama, modern science, folklore, anthropology, etc.) and on ideas (Hellenism, Hebraism, paganism, Christianity, 'natural energy', harmony with nature, rural decline, fate, destiny, magic, Prometheanism) that have received much attention.

The style is like that of the later novels: it has the ups that gratify and the downs that disappoint. The talk of the rustics rarely lacks vitality. Grandfer Cantle describes his wife as a girl: 'a long-legged slittering maid, hardly husband-high'; Timothy Fairway says he is 'stiff as a ram's horn stooping so long'. Hardy can approach this vein himself: the fifth of November fires 'dwindling weak', like Buonaparte, the reddleman belongs to 'the land of worn-out bogeys'. Hardy draws good images from ordinary life: a road on the heath is like the 'parting line on a head of black hair'; 'the oblique band of sunlight which followed her through the door became the young wife well'; in 'upland hamlets . . . no dense partition of yawns and toilets divided humanity by night from humanity by day'. Now and then there is that revision of the observed reality which almost excites the thrill of the surreal: the Vyes' pool 'lay on the outside of the bank like the white of an eye without its pupil'. On the one hand Hardy can climax a physical description with an allusion to Keats—in the carboniferous period, 'nothing but a monotonous extent of leafage, amid which no bird sang'; on the other he can remind us of Austen—as he often does, surprisingly—with a neat antithesis (Wildeve was a man 'in whom no man would have seen anything to admire, and in whom no woman would have seen anything to dislike'), or an almost epigrammatic generalisation: 'In the heath's barrenness to the farmer lay its fertility to the historian'. He may use Austen balance, of course, to render a perception that goes beyond the limits of Austen comedy: 'He was not so young as to be absolutely without a sense that sympathy was demanded, he was not old enough to be free from the terror felt in childhood at beholding misery in adult quarters hitherto deemed impregnable . . .'. There is often the very apt phrase—the heath as an 'instalment of night . . . before its astronomical hour was come', or a tract of land that 'made itself felt as a vague stretch of remoteness'; and at times the paradoxical phrase—Fairway's 'passionless severity of face'; Eustacia's 'drowsy fervour of manner' and her '[growing] generous in the greediness of a new passion'. Then there is the flashing near-paradoxical distinction between states that one could readily think allied: 'Sometimes his condition had been one of utter remorse, unsoftened by a single tear of pure sorrow . . .'. There is a poetic sureness in this opposition of remorse as hard in turning and sorrow as generous outgoing.

Hardy's range extends from the striking image to the disciplined syntax. Beside the compactness, precision, and imaginative freshness of which he is capable there is often the flaccid, the vague, the verbose, the bumbling, and even the opaque. If he can be brisk and tonic, he can also go soft, as in the sentimental diminutive ('a finch was trying to sing' but the wind 'twisted round his little tail, and made him give up his song'; Eustacia's 'little hands quivered', big girl though she has been said to be), and in the idea that the face of the heath, since it was 'lonely', suggested 'tragical possibilities'. The tendency to pump up feeling artificially leads him into the pathetic fallacy. He all but makes an Iago out of an adder, which 'regarded the assembled group with a sinister look in its small black eyes, and the . . . pattern on its back seemed to intensify with indignation', and a villain out of a storm which 'snapped at the windowpanes'. But 'how ineffectively gnashed the storm!' is his triumphant note on another occasion, even though in the gale 'convulsive sounds came from the branches, as if pain were felt'. The as-if clause contains the lame, awkward passive that Hardy often commits. Observers could locate each fifth of November fire 'by its angle and direction, though nothing of the scenery could be viewed'. Another amateurism of Hardy's is the painful participle: Venn was 'singular in colour, this being a lurid red'. Again, he could hardly find a more uncomfortable way of saying that a door opened directly on a room where people were dancing: 'It became evident at once that the dance was proceeding immediately within the surface of the door, no apartment intervening'. One could make a longish catalogue of Hardy's dangling verbals, but I will stick to one example: 'On reaching the hill the sun had quite disappeared . . .'; one must work through the context to be sure that it was not the sun but Eustacia who reached the hill. Hardy's usual concreteness softens up at times, and he falls into a mushy 'type' or 'sort'. Mrs. Yeobright had 'features of the type usually found where perspicacity is the chief quality enthroned within'. What are those features, one wonders. A fire dies down because 'the fuel had not been of that substantial sort which can support a blaze long'. Dry stream-beds 'had undergone a species of incineration since the drought had set in'; the dead Eustacia 'eclipsed all her living phases'. These limp abstractions, often conjoined with a Latinate vocabulary, give the style a periodic taint of the academic or the bureaucratic. Hardy can be heavy, awkward, and vague all at once: the reddleman 'was an instance of the pleasing being wasted to form the groundwork of the singular, when an ugly foundation would have done just as well for that purpose'. Finally, three brief quotations. In a tense confrontation between Clym and Eustacia, Eustacia says she thinks Clym will kill her, since 'No less degree of rage against me will match your previous grief for her'. This non-colloquial antithesis, in the midst of passionate recriminations, approaches the laughable stiltedness of a ringing melodramatic statement on an outworn stage. There is a different effect when Hardy says, of the corpses pulled from the water at Shadwater Weir, that there was 'not a whiff of life left in either of the bodies'. In 'whiff' the donnish in Hardy is replaced by an off-handedness that is trivialising. Finally 'the good shape of his figure' is singularly tautological.

Such distracting ineptitudes remained with Hardy to the end. Still, they are like a scattering of potholes in an otherwise wellpaved road: they cause discomfort but do not long impede the journey. They are far fewer than the stylistic adequacies and excellences. He can give a fine concreteness to his descriptions; his color sense is almost as active as George Eliot's. He often mixes colors, and he sees many hues, shades, and tints—whites (whitish, silver, burnished silver, pale, pallor of death, Parian marble), yellows and browns (amber, brass, copper-coloured, ensaffroned, bright yellow, gilt, gold, embrowned, neutral brown, russet, rusty, mud-coloured, tawny), reds (blood-coloured, crimson, ruby, scarlet, scarlet-red, metallic violet, lilac, purple), blues (pale blue, deep blue, brilliant blue, blue of the sea, sapphirine), greens (bottle-green, emerald green, olive-green, soft pale green), blacks (dark, frigid grey, crape, jet, sable, shade, shadowy, sooty). He sees light in different ways: 'sparkling starlight', 'shining facets of frost', 'lively luminousness', 'like a streak of phosphorus', 'eyes lit by a hot light'.

In describing Egdon Heath, perhaps the best known topographic personality in English fiction, Hardy perceives not only colors but shapes and textures and tones, the types and ways of flora and fauna, the changes that go with time of day and season, the interplay of person and scene (in heat and cold, fair weather and storm), the distortions of faces in flickering firelight. He records smells less often than sounds—the sounds made by insects and birds, by movements on the ground and against bushes, by different weathers, by winds blowing through different growths and foliages. With an air of ease, inevitability, and passion he gives the heath remarkable life. But for it he also feels a not quite controlled love and reverence, and he sometimes moves from audivisual virtuosity across the border to purple-passage excess; he tends to overpictorialise the scene, especially with associational chromatics, and even more to give the picture an over-heavy frame of significance. Still the heath survives, if less as a bearer of communicated meaning than as a provider of a not quite definable spaciousness—something like the spaciousness that wide grounds confer upon a dwelling even when essential life is centered within it.

Hardy sees the Heath as sombre, solemn, sublime, antique, durable; as 'untameable, Ishmaelitish', a home for a 'thoroughgoing ascetic'. It serves his mood when he is the doom-laden itinerant preacher. It is a 'Titanic form' that 'could only be imagined to await one last crisis—the final overthrow'; a little later the Titan is somewhat reduced, for the Heath is 'like man, slighted and enduring'; again, its 'sombreness' is 'absolutely in keeping with the moods of the more thinking among mankind'. Here Hardy speaks as village pessimist, ready to blame reality for hostility to man (it is his good fortune, and ours, that he antedated the tedious vogue of the 'absurd'). Happily this is only a part of Hardy—less than half, one might say. Though Egdon is at times a savage place, and as such a symbol of cosmic unfriendliness to man, it is also the scene of ongoing life: virtually all the characters in *The Return* adapt well to it and are even devoted to it. Only Eustacia hates it (though Wildeve routinely agrees with her, 'I abhor it too', his emotions are not place-oriented), and the disasters that occur on it—far fewer than the working adjustments to it—are rooted in hearts, though the immediate instruments may be environmental. They always have to be: if one grows desperate in the Sahara, and plunges into some ultimate recklessness, drowning is not what happens to one.

When he makes Egdon symbolise an unfriendly reality, Hardy registers an almost sentimental conception of man as victim that also appears in sidemouth *obiter dicta* (though here less pervasive, I believe, than in the *Mayor* and less intrusive than in *Jude*). He comes up with the strange notion that handsome people are anachronistic because faces are bound to reflect the 'view of life as a thing to be put up with, replacing that zest for existence which was so intense in early civilisations'—a view, he appears to think, made obligatory by 'modern perceptiveness'. Clym loses ambition, Hardy says, because he is at the 'stage in a young man's life when the grimness of the human situation first becomes clear', a stage in which, in France, 'it is not uncustomary to commit suicide'. (That 'not uncustomary' charmingly reduces suicide to a vogue dictated by the makers of fashion.) Now and then Hardy borrows the voices of Clym and Eustacia for such plaints. Eustacia refers dourly to 'the cruel satires that Fate loves to indulge in', and Clym thinks at times that 'he had been ill-used by fortune, so far as to say that to be born is a palpable dilemma, and that instead of men aiming to advance in life with glory they should calculate how to retreat out of it without shame'. Hardy does save Clym for good sense by making that view temporary. But he immediately turns around and chastises Clym and mankind generally for hesitancy to 'degrade a First Cause', and to 'conceive a dominant power of lower moral quality than their own; and, even while they sit down and weep by the waters of Babylon, invent excuses for the oppression which prompts their tears'. Happily this sentimentalising of man as a victim of divine oppression is a thing of the moment; at least it does not undermine the sense of reality which makes Hardy as artist present man's fate as congruent with his nature.

In narrative technique Hardy wavers between an effortlessly progressive and formed narrative and, on the other hand, additions, extemporisations, and manipulations that elicit minor restlessness and the involuntary retention, rather than the willing suspension, of disbelief. The rustics are lively, granted, but their talk-fests go on and on, as if Hardy could not arrest the flux of reportage. On the other hand, he can neglect the dramatic documentation that could give a needed body or verisimilitude. Wildeve an engineer? Clym a 'manager to a diamond merchant'? Hardy seems to have hastily picked the roles out of a hat to serve a purpose: Wildeve's to define a comedown, and Clym's to make possible a rejection, which Clym elaborates at various times, even to an unlikely audience of rustics at a barbering, with the somewhat windy rhetoric of scorn attractive to 'born-again' souls. The indefatigable study which nearly blinds Clym is a misty affair, for Hardy cannot identify a single work that Clym reads (in contrast with the copious reading lists in *Jude*). The seven weeks' delay after the aborted Wildeve-Thomasin wedding is circumstantially vague; we know Wildeve's motives, but it is difficult to imagine, in this conventional community, a long social stasis when a crisis makes action seem inevitable. Then at the time of the marriage Hardy so amply reports the to-do which Clym and his mother make about it that it becomes important, and we expect to see more of the couple. Hardy, however, drops them cold until he can utilise them in the Clym-mother-Eustacia conflict. What he does is shift from documentation to design, from reportage to narrative form that has other necessities. It is a characteristic jump from one way of doing things to another.

Or Hardy may move into effective dramatic documentation from rhetorical generalisation. In the ultimately excellent portrayals of both Clym and Eustacia there is a marked departure from outsized intentions in the introductory accounts making claims that are not sustained. These set-piece descriptions are much noticed, but the key parts of them do not hold up under inspection. The famous notion that 'thought is a disease of flesh' is of such beguiling novelty that its inapplicability to Clym may escape detection. Though Hardy prophesies that Clym's 'beauty . . . would in no long time be overrun by its parasite thought' and asserts that he has 'a wearing habit of meditation', the character presented dramatically reveals neither a philosophic bent nor a suffering from 'a full recognition of the coil of things'. Hardy goes from inapplicable theory (and surely erroneous theory: who has not seen deeply lined faces that go with conventional well-being, and recognised truly philosophic minds behind bland faces?) to half-truth when he declares that Clym's 'look . . . was a natural cheerfulness striving against depression from without, and not quite succeeding.' There is no sign of depression in newly arrived Clym, but much of 'natural cheerfulness'. Indeed the Comtian positivism on which Clym was presumably nourished tends to beget optimism about the human scene, and the religion of humanity leads to such hopeful reformism as motivates Clym's educational fantasy.

Hardy's extended formal picture of Eustacia, which used to be cited as an example of great description, conforms a little better to the Eustacia developed in the later action. A beautiful woman, alluring in a limited environment where she seems exotic, she is intense, romantic, wilful, yearning, and resentful; Hardy says this, and he makes it good in the story (one wonders only why she is so unresisting to the hated heath-bound life imposed on her by her grandfather, who seems less a man of iron than a Smollett-Dickens nautical humour susceptible to management by an energetic woman whom Hardy calls an 'absolute queen' at home). What she cannot sustain—as who could?—are the implied comparisons with Clotho, Lachesis, and Atropos, with Artemis, Athena, and Hera, with Heloise and Cleopatra; the assertion that her style resembled 'the comprehensive strategy of a general' and that she 'could utter oracles of Delphic ambiguity'. All this is much too grand. Partly Hardy has fallen in love with her, partly he uses her to express his annoyance at the heavenly mismanagement that accounts for the 'inequality of lot' and 'captious alternation of caresses and blows that we endure now'. Eustacia is not really 'the raw material of a divinity'; rather than a goddess manquée she is, as various readers have noticed, a full achiever in a human mode identified just two decades before *The Return* appeared—bovarysm. Eustacia is more intelligent and discriminating than Emma, but the basic kinship is there.

Hardy's sense of the inner realities of advancing relationships and developing situations is generally very fine, but his external ways of bringing on change and crisis can stir resistance in even a submissive reader. When a character needs information that will determine what he does, Hardy may have recourse to the most fantastic overhearing since Richardson's Pamela picked up whole paragraphs of praise from anywhere nearby. I will cite just one example: to plot his course as secret protector of Thomasin, Diggory must know what Wildeve and Eustacia are up to, so in the open heath he pulls off a remarkable feat of eavesdropping, creeping up unheard, and unseen under a couple of 'turves' (an Egdon Heath 'Birnam Wood'), to monitor a long conversation. The coincidences which fill up so much space in Hardy's technical arsenal we must basically accept—few critics fail to reiterate this—as symbolisations of the untowardness of things that, in Hardy's *ex cathedra* pronouncements, afflicts humanity. But still his 'life's little ironies' and 'satires of circumstance' are of greatly varying artistic quality: they range from the heavy-handed and contrived to the convincing and the revealing. Diggory's 'van' is the Grand Hotel of Egdon Heath: everybody happens in there when a hiding place or a shelter or a meeting with Diggory will be of use. A very effective irony results from Diggory's schemes to keep Wildeve at home with Thomasin: he so bedevils Wildeve, on his nocturnal expeditions to see Eustacia that Wildeve resolves on a day-time trip, and at the same time Diggory encourages Mrs. Yeobright's growing desire for a reconciliation with Clym and Eustacia. Thus it is quite plausible that Wildeve and Mrs. Yeobright embark on visits at the same time and set up new troubles. But in working out the details Hardy starts manipulating: Wildeve and Mrs. Yeobright not only pick the same day for their visits but the same time of day (Mrs. Yeobright can even see Wildeve, whom she does not recognise, enter the cottage). After such a coincidence has set the stage, the crucial slip into disaster is entirely unforced: we understand Eustacia's not answering her mother-in-law's knock at the door, and her readiness to believe that Clym is waking up from a nap and will open the door. Then Hardy returns to coincidence: Clym does not wake up but has a dream which is a remarkable mirror-image of present events, and Mrs. Yeobright, on her return trip, runs into Johnny Nunsuch, who can hear and report her bitter statements and thus contribute to the remorse of her son. And on her walk, finally, comes an ultimate turn of the screw such as Hardy wilfully applies to guarantee disaster: as if fearful that Mrs. Yeobright may survive exhaustion and disillusion, he inflicts on her, of all things, the bite of a poisonous adder. The Lear allusion includes several parallels: the thankless child, the closed door, the parent on the dangerous heath, and now an excessively literal serpent's tooth.

Mrs. Yeobright has picked an inordinately hot August 31 for her six-mile walk. We are split between protesting that a woman of such practical sense as she has been shown to have would surely postpone the expedition, and acquiescing on the ground that once she has resolved on the initiative, she is so eager to get on with it that she is immune

"But Mr. Hardy, Mr. Hardy, if you only knew all the circumstances" *by Will Dyson.*

to the likely protests of good sense. Be that as it may, this disastrous expedition must also be seen in its quiet, unforced relationship to two others in which good intentions lead to a bad end (though at times Hardy can bark his wares very audibly, he can manage effective structural repetitions so unobtrusively that we may be slow to notice them; critics say much about the over-all structure of *The Return,* but little about these subtler contributions to structural cohesiveness). One expedition takes place later, one earlier. The later depends on one of the best ironies in the book: to please Eustacia, her young admirer Charlie lights another evening fire and thus summons Wildeve and prepares for Eustacia's final journey, which like Mrs. Yeobright's ends in a death assisted by the elements. The earlier one, on the contrary, reveals Hardy in one of his most mechanical devisings. On Clym's wedding day Mrs. Yeobright despatches inheritances of fifty guineas each to Thomasin and Clym. We can see, in retrospect, that Hardy wanted a major break between Mrs. Yeobright and Eustacia, and a quicker action than the slow heat of the inevitable friction between two women different in nature and aspiration. So he suborned disaster by a virtually preposterous series of events.

Whom does Mrs. Yeobright, a shrewed observer of the human scene, pick to carry the hundred guineas (a large sum in the 1840s)? None other than Christian Cantle, who, if not quite the village idiot, has been shown to be much too foolish, fearful, and fragile for such a mission. Only such an incompetent bearer could be deflected into gambling and, of all things, losing the entire hundred to Wildeve. But good news: ever-present Diggory Venn spies on the whole thing, dashes out, forces Wildeve into an unwilling resumption of the game, and wins back the whole hundred (the last twenty-one by the light of thirteen glow-worms drafted by Venn to replace a lantern extinguished by a reckless moth). Surely never has chance reversed itself with such insatiable consistency. Returning home, the miserable Wildeve has to pass and see the happy newlyweds (a heavy irony reversed when, at the lowest stage of her marital fortunes, Eustacia learns that Wildeve has inherited £11,000 and has to be badgered about her choice of men by her grandfather). But the deserving are by no means safe out of it, for Venn delivers the whole hundred guineas to Thomasin. Hardy is in there causing trouble again. For though Venn, spying on the Wildeve-Christian game of chance, has overheard so much that, when he is defeating Wildeve, he can crow over him by repeating to him the exact words that Wildeve had used to Christian, Hardy does not let him hear the key fact: that half the guineas belonged to Clym. Thomasin innocently keeps all the guineas. Mrs. Yeobright, dismayed that she receives no thanks from Clym, goes out to investigate, and Hardy forces her into two steps bound to work out badly. Does she first check out the matter with friendly Thomasin, as would be probable? No, she goes to Eustacia, and then sensible Mrs. Yeobright, of all people, puts her question in the one way bound to be irreparably offensive: 'Have you received a gift from Thomasin's husband?' What is more, she never explains what she means, even as Eustacia naturally falls into angry outbursts which it seems must elicit a clarification. Thus has Hardy made the breach immitigable. Next, Mrs. Yeobright tardily visits Thomasin and learns what happened; Thomasin conveys guineas and facts to Clym; but Clym does not pass the word on to Eustacia. Nor does Eustacia explain to Clym the grudge which she now nurtures. Rarely has disaster been led up to by such machinations, in which Hardy rather resembles the unkind divinities upon whom he likes to cast aspersions. When he is determined to prevent a human muddling through, his darker sensibilities can produce an eminently resistible art.

Yet happily that is less than half the story, for the true artist in Hardy has the larger voice. For one thing, there is the unstrained continuity of events on the evening of 5 November; in an easy-flowing eight and a half chapters Hardy so traces the events of a few hours that he introduces all the main and supporting characters (even the absent Clym by talk of his expected visit) and all the principal situations (Diggory's rejection by Thomasin, the aborted Thomasin-Wildeve wedding, Mrs. Yeobright's hand in these relationships, the Thomasin-Wildeve-Eustacia triangle). Hardy manages a very fluent movement from hour to hour, from scene to scene. In fact, long before films he hits upon a cinematic flow of episodes, and at times he uses a panning technique or a transition by contiguity: we move effortlessly under the guidance, as it were, of a camera following people's steps and their eyes. It is a truism that Hardy likes to open a novel with out-of-doors movement: *The Return* employs a virtuosity of functional motion. Hiking a heath road, Captain Vye catches up with Diggory Venn and his pony-drawn van; inside is the woman who we later learn is Thomasin. Vye moves on, Venn stops for a rest, and we follow his eyes as he looks up and sees a woman's figure atop the highest elevation (Rainbarrow). She leaves, and many people replace her, carrying faggots for fires. We pan to such fires all over the heath, and then settle into a long close-up on the major community fire on Rainbarrow. While they talk, the rustics several times look down to a light which comes from the Quiet Woman Inn, Wildeve's place to which he is supposedly returning with his new bride. Later, when their fire and others are dying, the rustics see one fire which remarkably maintains a steady brightness: they locate it at Captain Vye's place and decide that it is his granddaughter's work. Diggory Venn comes up, looking for the road to Mrs. Yeobright's. She herself stops by to check on the festivities. We follow her when she leaves, walks down off the hill, comes to Diggory's van, meets Thomasin, gets the story of the failed wedding, and goes to the inn to accost Wildeve. We are there when the rustics come down from Rainbarrow for the shivaree which they have been planning. Among other activities they all look up at the Vye fire; Wildeve does too, and he starts to move in that direction. The camera now takes us back to deserted Rainbarrow: Eustacia, whom Venn had seen there earlier, returns, and we have a long close-up on her. As the others had done, she looks down at the Wildeve Inn, and then she walks cross-heath to the bright fire we have seen several times—her own fire, of course. A wait, and then Wildeve, whom we have seen start, arrives. We get a sense of their relationship and then follow the homeward walk of Eustacia's fire-builder, the boy Johnny Nunsuch; he runs into Diggory, whom we have already seen twice, tells him about the Eustacia-Wildeve meeting, and thus inadvertently provides the information which determines Diggory's actions from now on. The sequence of actions which I have sketched should reveal Hardy's extraordinary skill in designing an easy flux of perspectives and scenes in which, without our ever having a sense of hiatus or of arbitrary placement of us by the author, or even of his steering presence, we glide among the many elements, animate and inanimate, that we must know.

This long night of 5 November, brilliant as an introduction, has structural importance: it is balanced by the long night of the next year's 6 November. The symmetry does not mean a too mechanical balance, for the account of the second long night is briefer and more intense; on one, hope sets in, on the other it dies out. The ties are elemental too: on the first, the actions revolve about fires, symbols of cheer and well-being; on the second, the same scenes are swept by wind and rain, indeed a flood that destroys not a race but the self-chosen seeking escape (with a boat to France as ark). The compactness of the two long nights is matched by the compression of the over-all story; taking place in just a year, it is tighter than ***The Mayor*** and ***Jude***, which are life-histories. The year has its own cycle of seasons: a November day of community pleasures and lovers' problems, a new love ready to be born at Christmas (with its twentieth-century secularity), spring courting, June wedding, dog-days crises, November disaster. These seasons enfold a cycle of experience from old love to new, from new love to disillusion, from dreams to despair, from birth (Thomasin's baby, ironically named Eustacia) to death.

Narrative skills and structural felicity are the external manifestations of the fictional essence in which lies the strength of ***The Return*** to hold us and gain assent. The essence is the human reality that Hardy gets hold of in his major characters. In part he uses an unostentatious contrast; it is voiced by Eustacia when Diggory tells her that if he cannot have Thomasin he will do his 'duty in helping her to get [Wildeve], as a man ought'. Eustacia is incredulous. 'What a strange sort of love, to be entirely free from that quality of selfishness which is frequently the chief constituent of the passion, and sometimes its only one!' She hardly understands this, 'and she almost thought it absurd'. Hardy can imagine the love that serves as well as the love that grasps; it is a skilful hedge against sentimentality to see the former through the latter. Eustacia's 'absurd' has another value too: in thus calling Diggory irrational, she establishes a subtle link with the loves of Wildeve, Clym, and herself. For the two men and she are, above all, irrational, and driven. And so is Mrs. Yeobright in her own way. Hardy sees in them a compulsiveness that would take all but very lucky people into disaster. (We need not fall back upon the psychological cliché 'self-destructive'; destructiveness is secondary to, rather than inherent in, compulsive action.)

In Mrs. Yeobright Hardy gets hold of interesting ambiguities. As an influence on Thomasin she reveals conventionality of values, some perceptiveness, and some power of accommodation. She encourages Thomasin to think Diggory lacking in the status her suitors should have: she is right in seeing that Wildeve is not good marital material; and then, having given in, she is as insistent on Wildeve's following through as she was once set against him, even though she feels an intelligent skepticism about his motives. *Vis-à-vis* Clym and Eustacia, she is shrewd in perception but weak in accommodation. If it is snobbery or a superficial notion of 'success' that makes her want Clym to stay on in Paris, she is accurate in treating his educational evangelism as one of his 'new crotchets', as 'wasting your life here', as 'the folly of such self-sacrifice', as 'a castle in the air'. We are convinced in advance of what Hardy calls her 'singular insight into life' and of the limitations which he ascribes to her. He sees clearly her mixed emotions. While she was jealous for Thomasin, she is jealous of Clym and Eustacia—the possessive mother. So she errs in making Eustacia the cause of Clym's conversion, and she condemns Eustacia too harshly. She is sound in insisting that Eustacia is not the right girl for Clym, but the shrill derogatory style that comes out of her defensive motherhood and sense of defeat contributes ironically to the outcome that her insight leads her to oppose—Clym's marriage. All this Hardy perceives brilliantly. He skillfully uses Mrs. Yeobright's point of view on the wedding day, and compresses the ambiguities of her feeling into a single sad comment: 'O, it is a mistake! . . . And he will rue it some day, and think of me!'

The heart of the matter is the Clym-Eustacia relationship, and here is Hardy's great strength. Though the grander things that Hardy claims for them—the divine and the Promethean—are not there, they are not essential to fictional magnitude. The big and impressive truth is the nature of the attraction between them and the compulsive inability of each to grasp the evidence that could modify the attraction. Hardy's extraordinarily late introduction of the title character as a physical presence (in the seventeenth of 48 chapters) is not only a rare technical *tour de force* in the Victorian novel but a device which helps define the amatory relationship. For first we see fully the toying, the fencing, the sparring of Eustacia and Wildeve—an excellently imagined affinity in which there is mutual erotic responsiveness but not the felt irresistibility that induces total commitment. They make use of each other, perhaps less as sex objects than as ego-maintaining objects. Whether because he feels the incompleteness of Eustacia's devotion or because two girls are more gratifying than one, Wildeve gets engaged to Thomasin; then the power-love of which Hardy is deeply aware makes Eustacia pull him back to her, though she is a little embarrassed to discover 'the dog in the manger' in herself. Acknowledging the irrationality, she can tell him, 'and yet I love you', and still always feel that in some way Wildeve is not good enough for her; hence it is natural for her to feel no more need of him once she has met Clym, the hero from Paris, and begins to nourish other hopes. Dismissed and fearing 'to lose two women', Wildeve must salvage his ego by marrying Thomasin (and hoping thus to make Eustacia feel slighted). All this is very well done.

When Clym shows up, then, Eustacia is already known to the reader as a handsome woman who wants 'to be loved to madness', who has a strong sense of her own status and value, and who has some instinct for and experience in the politics of emotion. Hardy carefully shows both parties drawn in by forms of peripheral charm—the exotic, the unexpected, the preconceived—rather than by a center of congeniality. There is a touch of the Benedick-Beatrice psychology when Eustacia overhears rustics praising Clym and talking about a match between her and Clym; she adores the Paris which she assumes defines Clym— 'like a man coming from heaven'; she begins to have 'visions', a 'day-dream', a 'Great Dream', as Hardy puts it in the caption of a chapter in which he calls her 'half in love with a vision'; later she thinks of Clym as a deliverer. She creates him out of her needs and desires rather than observes the actual creature before her. When she takes a part in the mummers' play, Clym is struck by 'a cultivated young woman playing such a part as this'. Taken for a witch and pricked by Susan Nunsuch wielding a needle, Eustacia becomes the victim bound to attract Clym's attention and sympathy; and each expresses concern for the other's risk of injury at the bucket-raising—a 'Timeworn Drama' as Hardy almost jestingly puts it in the caption. From here on Hardy wonderfully records the way in which each one listens to himself and not to the other. Eustacia is quite explicit in her disavowal of interest in schoolteaching, but Clym doesn't hear it or doesn't believe it. Likewise with her hatred of the heath that he loves. The intensity of her romantic fascination with Paris does not dawn on him. And he pays not the slightest attention when she says, testingly or coquettishly but still truthfully, 'I shall ruin you . . . Kiss me, and go away forever'. So they get engaged, she thinking that she can get him out of teaching and back to Paris, and he sure that they'll be happy in love and in improving heath-life. Despite their moments of doubt, the egotism of passion, which Hardy entirely understands, carries them ahead into marriage. The hubris of each is to think that the loved one can be subsumed under, or coopted into, the social passion of the lover.

Once the initial excitement is over, their minds and feelings are more than ever back on their single tracks. One might wish that Hardy, evidently with the epic year in mind, had not chosen to speed disaster by making Clym go nearly blind (mildly prepared for by brief references to eye-strain), by inventing the plot of the misdirected guineas, and by employing the adder to make sure that Mrs. Yeobright does not survive, but they are his way of reducing the inevitable to plot-form. What is unexceptionable is the tracing of the life within as it issues in visible conduct—Eustacia's seeking a little excitement with Wildeve, her concealment of his presence on the day Mrs. Yeobright calls, Clym's breakdown after her death, the self-righteousness of his fury against Eustacia when he learns the whole story, the mutual recriminations, Eustacia's mixture of almost unconscious footwork and desperation. What is especially good is Hardy's perception of the egotism that runs through the grief and despair on both sides, of the interplay in both characters, of tragic sense of guilt and a strange *amour propre* which clings to intensity of blame, of others or obdurate circumstance or even of oneself. 'But I don't want to get strong,' complains Clym at one point —a key-point in a continuing self-flagellation that borders on the self-indulgent. On the other hand, when he can say, after Eustacia's death, 'She is the second woman I have killed this year', his words lack the theatrical and hysterical note: here is the borne self-knowledge of tragic experience.

Likewise, on learning of Mrs. Yeobright's death, Eustacia can be toughly clear-headed for a moment: 'I am to blame for this. There is evil in store for me'. But she cannot tell Clym the truth; he ferrets it out and rages, and her awareness turns self-defensively from what she has done to what has been done to her, and to bitterness. At one moment Hardy can look at her with his tragic sense; at another he turns to his sympathy with the sense of defeat in a woman who finds it easy to believe herself an undeserving victim. As tragic observer he remarks that 'instead of blaming herself for the issue she laid the fault upon the shoulders of some indistinct, colossal Prince of the World, who had framed her situation and ruled her lot'. There he virtually spots in her a habit of his own mind: the flight from tragic awareness to the laying of blame on outer forces. She oscillates as he does. How well he imagines the anguish of the self that feels at once immaculate and preyed upon by an uninvited fate. Eustacia can perceive the difference between fact and hope (if not the illusion that feeds the hope): Wildeve is 'not *great* enough for me to give myself to—he does not suffice for my desire!'. She goes on in a rage of unearned defeat: 'How have I tried and tried to be a splendid woman, and how destiny has been against me! . . . O, how hard it is of Heaven to devise such tortures for me, who have done no harm to Heaven at all!' Hardy catches beautifully the ecstasy of self-love and self-pity, a force as dangerous to the psyche as a suicidal guilt neurosis. It is the last of the governing irrationalities that he portrays with a vitalising mastery (and by which he makes us all but forget the artifices of the mediating actions).

The Return is somewhat of a border point between the earlier and later Hardy. The rustics remind us of an earlier world, and Thomasin has ties with Fancy Day. On the other hand, insofar as serious troubles precede the final happy love, she anticipates Elizabeth Henchard. In the central triangles Hardy now crosses over from the soluble situations of comedy to the difficulties that issue in disaster: the Clym-Eustacia-Wildeve triangle anticipates the Alex-Tess-Angel and the Arabella-Jude-Sue affairs. In *The Return* he introduces materials or situations that he will repeat or use more fully later. There is his French connection. Here, Clym is a Comtian, and Wildeve is 'the Rousseau of Egdon'—'the man of sentiment', whose nature it is 'To be yearning for the difficult, to be weary of that offered; to care for the remote, to dislike the near . . . '. Later Sue Bridehead will appear as a 'Voltairean', albeit of a shallow variety.

Certain narrative devices appear here and will be used later. Clym's letter urging Eustacia to return fails of delivery, as does Tess's explaining her past to Angel; both might have changed the course of action. The heavy rains on 6 November appear again in *The Mayor* to compound Henchard's difficulties, and in *Jude* to amplify the troubles of the return to Oxford. Hardy begins to use preaching as an index of personality: Clym slowly finds it a way of life, Alex d'Urberville would find it a temporary satisfaction, and Angel Clare would renounce it. Eustacia's dislike of Clym's reading is interestingly duplicated in Arabella's attitude to Jude's learning and books. Eustacia's and Clym's opposite attitudes to Parisian life would be deepened in the opposition between Sue's rationalism and Jude's faith, the latter opposition to be ironically reversed. A subtler anticipation: when Eustacia handles searching questions of Clym by saying, 'Dearest, you must not question me unpleasantly, or it may make me not love you,' and by using several similar ploys, Hardy is discovering a kind of female strategy that he would explore more fully in Sue Bridehead. Eustacia is a forerunner of Sue in that both are wilful and crave power without defining power as a conscious end. Eustacia, however, has read the travel books and comes up with a conventional desire for self-gratification in a glamorous city, whereas Sue wants to be the ruling divinity only in the life of one unglamorous man. In Clym, Hardy is getting into two aspects of human nature that later he would carry into further implications. After his mother's death Clym clings to a sense of guilt that borders on the pathological, but he does come around; after the death of her children, on the other hand, Sue falls into a sense of guilt that, as Hardy well sees, has such deep roots in her personality that it must intensify into an illness beyond therapy. When Clym finally learns the death-day facts that Eustacia has not told him, his verbal chastising of her contains a good deal of self-righteousness. Likewise Angel Clare when he learns facts about his wife's past: wounded ego, censoriousness, self-righteousness. But just as Sue's guilt is deeper than Clym's, so is Angel's punitiveness.

If such partial duplications tell us something about continuities and developments in Hardy's imagination, some comparisons outside the Hardy *oeuvre* may help place the range and depth of his perceptiveness. **The Mayor** conquers time by looking backward; it is reminiscent of *Oedipus the King*, and to say that is to say that it transcends a local history in a specific time and place. *Jude* transcends its own times by looking ahead: it makes formulations of character perhaps more familiar now than in 1895. Jude prefigures what we now know as the 'narcissistic student', the type whose self-concern inhibits an adequate openness to realities that need to be understood. But still more significant is Sue, in whom Hardy has caught, more than half a century before it surfaces in often disturbing social phenomena that are widely visible, an excessive dependence on rational structurings of life and hence a violent rebound into sub-rational or apparently supra-rational experiences that represent a neglected human need.

Like the later novels, **The Return** looks beyond its own time. Mrs. Yeobright is the possessive mother who is a fixture on the twentieth-century stage, though she is a larger character than many of her successors because of her intelligent grasp of the world in which she lives. Eustacia looks backward in time and forward in time. As a sister of Emma Bovary she so yearns for an overpowering romance that any available life is not going to satisfy, though she is complicated by a precocious sense of the transitoriness of things that makes her doubt the relationship with Clym before its insufficiency has become evident. In the next century Eustacia's longing to be whirled away by some more than life-size force might lead to the beds of presidents or prime ministers, to drugs, or to political adventurism of a millennial coloring. Yet in all these courses there is an infusion of the vulgarity that Eustacia, whose taste is insecure, would avoid if she could, witness her final judgment of Wildeve (whose ironic fate it is to achieve, despite himself, a certain largeness, as of a Diggory rendered reckless: the self-gratification of plucking forbidden fruit turned into the self-abnegation of risking death in the weir). If Eustacia had talent one might think of her as the poet desperately weighed down by a sense of injuriousness and duplicity in the *natura rerum*.

Though Clym is never the thinker that Hardy asserts him to be, he is a very successful character: in him Hardy catches the archetypal lineaments of what we now call the do-good-er, and he anticipates the ironic treatment of the type that would be the life of Dorothy Sayers' *The Devil to Pay* (1939) and Duerrenmatt's *An Angel Comes to Babylon* (1953). Clym is sure that 'with my system of education, which is as new as it is true, I shall do a great deal of good to my fellow-creatures'. By a do-good-er we mean a theorist in benevolence who pays very little attention to human actuality and who hence may be a fantast, a busybody, or an enforcer (the man of good will whose will is to impose his good on man). It is not that good does not get done in the world, but that the professional benefactor is not the most effective agent of good. There is a nice structural interplay between Clym and Diggory Venn, who does good as it may be done: he consults the will of a specific person who has a specific desire and does his best to see that it is satisfied (in striving to bring and keep Thomasin and Wildeve together, Diggory is not striving to impose on others some theoretical good of his own). But Clym has an abstract idea of what is good for local humanity generally—'instilling high knowledge into empty minds without first cramming them with what has to be uncrammed again before true study begins'. It sounds noble, but it is hard to tell what it means. If as observer of education Hardy approves of Clym's idea, as artist he is unable to come up with a single concrete formulation that would give life and meaning to the theoretical program. Clym does seem to think that Susan Nunsuch's anti-witch operation—sticking Eustacia with a needle—proves the need of a new education, but Hardy gives no sign of sharing the belief. In fact, Hardy rather enjoys setting it off against furze-cutter Humphrey's view that some such 'rum job or other is sure to be doing' whenever anyone from Egdon goes to church.

Hardy portrays, not a period freak, but the *a priori*, dogmatic improver who belongs to every age. This type pays no attention to conditions and possibilities. These are implicitly recorded by local observers when Clym announces his desire for a 'rational occupation among the people I [know] best': Timothy Fairway is sure that 'In a few weeks he'll learn to see things otherwise,' and 'another' that 'he had better mind his business'. The type pays no attention to historical appropriateness; Hardy himself notes that the 'rural world was not ripe for him' and that his 'mind' was not 'well-proportioned'. This type pays no attention to lack of appropriate experience; Clym does not listen when his mother says, 'The place is overrun with schoolmasters. You have no special qualifications' and when she prophesies accurately, 'Your fancies will be your ruin'. In a particularly shrewd perception Hardy sees that the type absolutises personal philosophic ideas and regards them as a sound center for reform: 'teach them [i.e. 'half the world'] how to breast the misery that they are born to'. The type is ascetic, immune to the pleasures made available by maturing culture: 'I cannot enjoy delicacies; good things are wasted upon me.' The type instinctively subsumes persons and relationships to the mission; Hardy does very well to have Clym ask the turf-cutter whether Eustacia 'would like to teach children' and pay no attention to the answer. He hardly takes it in when she wants to talk about Paris; he categorically refuses a return because 'It would interfere with my scheme' and feels he can command her, 'Don't press that, Eustacia'; he doesn't really listen when she accepts his proposal on the ground that 'You will never adhere to your education plan'; and when, after their marriage, she makes an effort to get Paris into their plans, he is shocked and responds by working harder than ever at his books. Eustacia learns the approximate truth of what Mrs. Yeobright has told her, that Clym 'can be as hard as steel'. Clym may look less like the rigid ideologue when, nearly blind, he takes to the rough life of the furze-cutter and thus seems to make peace with actuality instead of seeking a way to compel it. But in finding his way out of difficulty, he pays no attention to his wife; he arbitrarily rejects the financial help that could come from Captain Vye, and in his relative contentment he is insensitive to Eustacia's grave discontent; he is almost resentful that she can 'cling to gaiety so eagerly as to walk all the way to a village festival in search of it', although he does finally tell her to go; the egoist inside the benevolent idealist bursts out fully when Clym, sure of grave misdeeds by Eustacia, attacks her with the crude fervor of a prosecuting attorney.

To show that Clym, despite basic decency and good intentions, is not a very good matrimonal risk (a social scientist informs me that the domestic-success rate for cause-addicts is low; the excitement of battling conspicuous evil reduces the capacity for doing humble good, *vide* Dickens' Mrs. Jellyby, the archetype) is to round out the portrait of the strong-willed do-good-er that transcends historical boundaries. In the final stroke in that portrait Clym appears as itinerant preacher—exactly the right outcome for the character as created. It would be less so if Clym had a strong sense of actuality (human habits and needs) and a talent for collaboration and what we now call organisation. But his bent is toward the prophetic voice, the unclear saving vision, and solitary summons to better things that have become present to him after he has read a book and looked outward through the interstices of daily routines. A gentle egotist with a flair for moral theatre, he needs only a little ladder and a Hyde Park, and Clym finds his on Rainbarrow and elsewhere in Wessex.

Thomasin escapes from her aunt's sense of marriage as a preservation or improvement of status and settles down into the sensible problem-solver, even playful and humorous as she finds and sticks to the right road, a fixture in English fiction. Diggory looks backward in the history of the novel and, with a quite fascinating unexpectedness, forward too. On the one hand he is the faithful lover who derives from Thackeray's Dobbin. On the other hand he is the ancestor of a character who appears with vast frequency in popular fiction of the twentieth century—the 'private eye', the fixer, the amateur detective who manages to find things out and to be at the right place at the right time, the 'good guy' who is at least of peripheral help to the deserving, the jesting troubler of misbehavers. There is no artistic softening-up in the story of his and Thomasin's marrying. Hardy is simply wrong in thinking that the original ending in which Venn disappeared and Thomasin remained a widow represents an 'austere artistic code' and a 'more consistent conclusion' and the 'true one'. One side of Hardy likes to hector happiness and point bitter fingers at the gods who do not work harder for human felicity. But another side of Hardy sees that humanity does include people who have their feet on the ground, who do effect an accommodation with reality, who do manage to like suitable members of the opposite sex and find adequate lives with them. Thomasin and Diggory earn each other; it is not a case of Hardy's interfering and giving each one to the other to gratify a public not up to his darker view of things. The final evidence of the truth of this relationship is the naturalness, spontaneity, and vivacity of the chapters in Book VI. They work; they are not forced, casual, or flatly dutiful. Hardy's art contradicts his official opinion of the cosmos, but it does not betray his insight. His imagination embraced a fuller reality than he supposed.

One could hardly pay a better centennial tribute than that. (pp. 58-80)

> *Robert B. Heilman, " 'The Return': Centennial Observations," in* The Novels of Thomas Hardy, *edited by Anne Smith, Barnes & Noble Books, 1979, pp. 58-90.*

Rosemary Sumner (essay date 1981)

[*In the following excerpt, Sumner examines Hardy's methods for portraying individual psychology in* The Return of the Native.]

All Hardy's novels deal to some extent with the problems both of adjusting to changes in society and of coping with its failure to change in response to the individual's needs. His treatment of character emphasises that individuals as well as society are in a process of change and that novelists' methods of exploring character must change in order to reflect this and to take into account new insights. This is the area of Hardy's most important innovations in the novel. (p. 99)

In *The Return of the Native,* Clym and Eustacia illustrate in a number of ways the exploratory nature of Hardy's writing. In this novel the experimentation is of a fairly rudimentary kind. In Clym, we have an early example of the "advanced" young thinker; in the treatment of both of them, we see Hardy's increasingly complex and searching examination of the nature of love, and with Eustacia there is some grappling with the technical problems of exploring a character in depth in a novel.

From *Far from the Madding Crowd,* or even earlier, to

Jude the Obscure, we can see Hardy's interest in complex, tormented, maladjusted beings (often set alongside comparatively stable and uncomplicated characters). In his book on Hardy, Howe suggests that in ***The Return of the Native,*** "a new kind of sexuality, neurotically wilful but also perversely exciting makes its appearance". This vividly describes the quality of Eustacia's passions, but it is not true to say that such passions appear here for the first time; the sentence could be applied to Boldwood, and even to Miss Aldclyffe's brief Lesbian encounters in ***Desperate Remedies.*** In this respect, ***The Return of the Native*** is not a new departure, but a continuation in the line of Hardy's development which was to culminate in ***Jude the Obsure.*** Howe continues: "A thick cloud—the cloud of modern, inherently problematic consciousness—falls across the horizon of Wessex". It is certainly true that Hardy sees Clym as "a modern problematic consciousness", but I would deny that this is an innovation for Hardy since we see glimpses of similar problems in Knight in ***A Pair of Blue Eyes.*** In ***The Return of the Native*** Hardy is following up some lines of thought about psychology and about sexual relationships which he has already tentatively introduced in earlier novels.

This development in the kinds of personality portrayed is accompanied by definite changes and experiments in the methods of depicting them. Hardy's technique in presenting Eustacia is unusual in that there is less analysis and a higher proportion of observation of externals than in most of the other novels. This, inevitably, at some points in the story leads to a concentration on action rather than on mental processes or emotional states, but there are times when the external method becomes an instrument for exploring the subconscious. The choice of a viewpoint largely outside the character is partly the result of the immense significance of Egdon Heath in the novel. In the first chapter, Hardy describes the heath as "the hitherto unrecognised original of those wild regions of obscurity which are vaguely felt to be compassing us about in midnight dreams of flight and disaster". This unequivocal identification of the heath with the unconscious at the beginning of the book establishes its significance in Hardy's portrayal of the human psyche. Through his use of the heath, he is able to suggest great depths in his characters, without much close analysis; the unconscious remains unknown, though we are aware of its existence. Eustacia's affinity with the heath, which coexists with her antagonism to it, gives a sense of enlargement to her character. Whole areas of her thinking and feeling remain mysterious, unanalysed, but we are made aware that they exist. In this, as in so many other things, Hardy is going in the same direction as Lawrence, who said [in his essay "The Novel and the Feelings," *Phoenix*] he was trying, "to make new feelings conscious". In ***The Return of the Native,*** Hardy has not gone as far as this. He has drawn attention to the existence of the unconscious, but he has not attempted to make its nature known.

The importance of Egdon Heath in the novel lies mainly in the way Hardy uses it to enlarge our concept of human nature, and yet it is probably Egdon Heath above all which has given rise to the theory, popular until quite recently, that Hardy's characters are puppets, totally insignificant against an overwhelming background. This view implies that the characters are purely physical beings and disregards the importance Hardy gives to their inner existence. Certainly, Hardy saw man as dwarfed by the size of the universe, but simultaneously he showed him as a central feature of it; he describes Eustacia as "the pivot of this circle of heath country".

It is for these reasons fitting that both characters and landscape are subjected to the same delicate, sensitive scrutiny; there is the same minute observation of the wind in the heather bells and the sigh of Eustacia. Though it might seem that this method would lead Hardy right away from the psychological examination of character, it does not do so entirely. By observing so meticulously every outward manifestation of emotion, Hardy is able to suggest that these observable "expressions" reveal only the surface, and that there are vast depths of emotion, invisible to the outsider; he is thus moving towards the view that human beings are inexplicable—a view further developed in the treatment of the "conjectural" Grace [in ***The Woodlanders***] and the "puzzling and unstateable" Sue Bridehead [in ***Jude the Obscure***]. This is the beginning of Hardy's tentative exploration of that aspect of human beings which Lawrence felt was his own central concern as a novelist. Even by the time of his last novel, Hardy is still only hinting at the existence of "a strange dark continent that we do not explore". Hardy made a small, cautious advance to the edge of an area into which Lawrence boldly plunged.

In Eustacia we have this rather surprising combination of a wild, tormented personality, presented largely from an external viewpoint, and yet conveying an impression of considerable depth. Hardy uses the external, descriptive method on a grand scale (but never again in such a lengthy and elaborate manner) with occasional passages of analysis and together they create an impression of a passionate, fascinating, yet neurotically maladjusted personality. She is first seen from a distance on top of the Rainbarrow, looking like "an organic part of the entire motionless structure". Even when she is seen in close-up, it is stressed that the view is that of an outsider only able to guess at what is taking place in her mind: "What she uttered was a lengthened sighing, apparently at something in her mind". Yet, while emphasising that the view of her is external, Hardy creates an intense interest in what is going on in her mind: "There was a spasmodic abandonment about it, as if, in allowing herself to utter the sound, the woman's brain had authorized what it could not regulate". Emphatically refusing the stance of omniscient author, Hardy not only implies the existence of unseen, unknown depths of feeling, but also emphasises that these emotions may be too powerful for conscious control. In this way, even while using the technique of an external observer, Hardy has been able to suggest "a strange dark continent" in human personality, and in Eustacia's in particular.

This method is used in its most elaborate form in "The Queen of the Night". The view of her is at first a distant one, and the sense of detachment is here increased by Hardy's irony; she would have done well as "a model goddess . . . with a little preparation", he says and at once reminds us that his opinion of goddesses is a low one. He spends many paragraphs creating an impression first of strange, smouldering beauty, gradually becoming more and more extravagant, associating her with "Bourbon roses, rubies and tropical midnights", until he again brings the whole picture into question: "In a dim light, with a slight rearrangement of the hair, her general figure might have stood for one of the higher female deities". This is characteristic of his ambivalent attitude to Eustacia. He encourages us to take her at her own evaluation, to see her as a sublime, exotic creature, and then shatters the illusion, bringing home to us all the more sharply because we have been persuaded to share her own view of herself, the true nature of the situation. In his "Study of Thomas Hardy", Lawrence sees Eustacia as a natural aristocrat, but in doing so he is recreating her as one of his own characters. Hardy is much more uncertain about the value of aristocracy. He stresses how she often, and often consciously, deludes herself in her longing to escape from the world as it actually is. (At one moment, Wildeve is "some wondrous thing she had created out of chaos": minutes later, he arrives and she tells him, "You are not worthy of me".) After comparing her (with reservations) to goddesses, Hardy says that, "at times she was not altogether unlovable". This places in an even more satirical light a sentence two pages earlier: "To be loved to madness—such was her great desire". In these ways, one facet of "The Queen of the Night" is shown to be a romanticising adolescent dreamer, living in a fantasy world of which she is the heroine. Hardy creates a sense of her psychological complexity largely through describing her outward appearance and behaviour, but also towards the end of "The Queen of the Night" chapter by giving some account of what is habitually going on in her mind, while at the same time he retains a position of critical detachment. Even the description of her thinking and feeling is given in generalised summary form rather than following the ebb and flow of her mind and this lends itself to critical, even ironical commentary.

The experiments in method tried out in "The Queen of the Night" are not really successful and, since Hardy did not repeat them, he was probably dissatisfied with it. It was an attempt to convey in an excessively elaborate way the impossibility of completely knowing anyone. The ambivalent effect of the partly ornate, partly satirical commentary seems to have been deliberately intended. It does succeed in creating mixed feelings about Eustacia in the reader, and contributes to our sense of her tortured and conflicting emotions, but its weakness is that in its elaboration it tends to focus attention excessively on technique, which is especially unfortunate in the more grostesque passages (such as the one about mouths like muffins). In a retrospective view, the chapter contributes to our sense of the "nocturnal mysteries" of Eustacia, and mingles with her own wish-fulfilment dreams, but under close scrutiny it seems too long and ornate for the amount of insight it gives us. It is primarily interesting as a crude first attempt to find a method which will enable the novelist to suggest the existence of unconscious and impenetrable areas of the mind without in the process eliminating the element of the unknown.

This chapter is in keeping with Hardy's general scheme of allowing the contradictions in Eustacia's nature and in his own attitude to her to emerge. His general comments have the same effect of emphasising contradictions: "The fantastic nature of her passion which lowered her as an intellect, raised her as a soul"; "To an onlooker her beauty would have made her feelings almost seem reasonable". Here again, the wry, onlooker's view is used as a way of bringing out her inner contradictions and of underlining the fact that she cannot be explained or summed up. Here, long before he had clearly developed new ways of looking at character, Hardy is already anticipating the refusal of the twentieth-century novelists to pin down and define characters. Hardy also uses the simple device of observers with opposing views to help reinforce this impression; Charley wholeheartedly accepts her view of herself as a goddess, while Susan Nonsuch sees her as a witch; to Clym's mother she was "not a good girl", to Clym she was a goddess (and then "no longer a goddess").

Although he relies so much on observation of externals and manages, through his suggestive approach, to achieve also considerable depth, Hardy acknowledges the inadequacy and possible inaccuracy of this method of portraying character; he describes how, when dancing with Wildeve, Eustacia's "soul had passed away from and forgotten her features, which were left empty and quiescent as they always are when feeling goes beyond their register". He compensates for this, at this point, by describing her thoughts and feelings, and using imagery which suggests their elemental and uncontrollable quality: "she had been stepped in arctic frigidity by comparison with the tropical sensations here"; the dancing was "like riding upon a whirlwind". His use of her dreams of Clym would seem also to be a move in this direction, a way of exposing her subconscious drives. But, in fact, Hardy's treatment of the dream does little more than amplify the impression we already have of her adolescent imagination; her wish-fulfilment dream images of Hollywood glamour and Clym as her knight in shining armour mainly serve to increase our ironical attitude to her romantic fantasies rather than to give us further insight into her psychological complexities.

The shifting to and fro from an external observer to a view of the inner workings of Eustacia's mind persists throughout the novel. There are times though, when the situation demands some insight into her thinking, but we are kept outside, watching her for clues as to what is going on in her mind, as, for instance, when "she remained in a fixed attitude for nearly ten minutes", looking at her grandfather's pistols. This is, of course, dramatically very arresting, but at this point in the story, a more subtle, inner directed view might have been more rewarding. In much the same way, just before her death, Hardy moves far back, right away from her consciousness. All we know of is the distant splash heard by Clym. Again, from the point of view of psychological penetration, this seems a missed opportunity. But it is deliberate on Hardy's part. He feels that at crucial moments the action is all-important and overrides other considerations, as his criticisms of Meredith indicate. Eustacia's state of mind has already been suggested in the description of her despairing, almost demented condition as she wanders through the storm. Just as Boldwood's murder of Troy [in *Far From the Madding Crowd*] and Tess's murder of Alec [in *Tess of the D'Urbervilles*] are treated dramatically, so as to create suspense, so here Eustacia's drowning is a dramatic occurrence, shown from a distance in a scene of great dramatic power. In this episode, Hardy combines the psychological and the dramatic, without using the analytical method at all, but its effectiveness derives from the explorations of her tormented mental state which lead up to this moment. All we know of the fall into the water is what Clym knows. We are left to speculate whether it was accidental or suicidal. But Hardy creates a vivid impression of her state of mind before this final moment in his account of her journey from her grandfather's cottage to Rainbarrow "where she stood to think". He uses in a compressed form all the various methods of exploring her consciousness found elsewhere in the novel. He conveys the confused and fluctuating nature of her thoughts even though at a conscious level she thinks her mind is made up. On opening the door and seeing the rain, she pauses, "But having committed herself to this line of action there was no retreating for bad weather. Even the receipt of Clym's letter would not have stopped her now". When she stands thinking on Rainbarrow she suddenly realises that she is penniless and that she must either ask Wildeve for money, which she is too proud to do, or become his mistress, which now comes to seem equally impossible: "Can I go, can I go?" she moaned. "He's not *great* enough for me to give myself to—he does not suffice for my desire! . . . . If he had been a Saul or a Buonaparte. . . . "

Intermingled with these confused and tormented feelings are descriptions of how she appeared to various observers. There is Susan Nonsuch's terror of her witchcraft and her attempt at a counterattack with wax figures, there is Diggory Venn's awareness of a mysterious weeping woman passing his hut in the dark and there is a hypothetical observer who, if present, would have been able to observe her outward appearance and make deductions about the mental state it expressed: "Any one who stood by now would have pitied her. . . . Extreme unhappiness weighed visibly upon her. Between the dripping of the rain . . . from the heather to the earth, very similar sounds could be heard coming from her lips". The same delicate observation which earlier in the novel distinguished the different sounds of the wind coming from different kinds of heath bells is again being applied to human nature. This seeing human beings in the same way as the natural world is central to *The Return of the Native*. The different kinds of affinity which the characters have with their surroundings is particularly important for Eustacia. She is simultaneously identified with the heath and in violent revolt against it. This is emphasised right from the beginning of the novel, when she "seemed like an organic part" of the Rainbarrow, and continues through to the end: "Never was harmony more perfect than that between the chaos of her mind and the chaos of the world without". It is this, far more than the elaboration of "The Queen of the Night" which makes Eustacia at times a figure on a grand scale; it shows her inner world to be as storm-swept and mysterious as the heath itself: "She had imbibed much of what was dark in its tone". We are reminded again of the opening description of the heath as "the original of those wild regions of obscurity which are vaguely felt to be compassing us about in midnight dreams of flight and disaster". By the end of the novel this world of "flight and disaster" and "choas" has wholly filled Eustacia's inner world. Her identity seems assimilated into the storm-swept heath and her death inevitable.

Without this identification with elemental and unconscious forces, Eustacia would have been a fairly slight study of a maladjusted girl—interesting, but without the strangeness and power of Hardy's conception. This is the most effective of the methods with which he is experimenting here. The use of the point of view of some unidentified "onlooker" who can only conjecture about the inner life from its outward manifestations is used rather clumsily, and would seem to work against any profound exploration of the inner life. Yet the intermittent use of such a viewpoint is consistent with Hardy's continually developing interest in analysing psychological complexities, because his very awareness of these complexities makes him particularly conscious of those areas of human personality which recede beyond human consciousness. In this way, as in so many others, his affinity with Lawrence is striking. He has the sense, developed so much further by Lawrence, of pushing out the frontiers of consciousness, of looking into unconscious processes, while always acknowledging that a human being cannot be wholly known. The imagined onlooker is a clumsy device, and Hardy does not use it again. Nevertheless, enigmatic Eustacia is a forerunner of his later "conjectural creatures" and of Lawrence's. Her nature is of the tormented, complex kind which always absorbed Hardy as a novelist. By relating her so closely to the most vividly imagined part of the book, the heath, he makes her mysteriousness convincing.

Similar complexities and contradictions confront us in the character of Clym. In conception, he is another of Hardy's psychological problem characters. Hardy states clearly that Clym's mind was not "well-proportioned", that it was not the kind of mind which will "never cause its owner to be confined as a madman". In the course of the story he shows how he veers towards madness on several occasions—during his nervous breakdown, after his mother's death, when he is overwhelmed by guilt feelings, in his insane rage with Eustacia after discovering about the closed door, and in his obsessional, possibly therapeutic, preaching at the end.

But Hardy does not present Clym simply as an unbalanced personality, but as a representative of the problems of "modern" man's difficulties in adjusting to new ways of thinking and feeling, especially those arising from the loss of religious faith. This sense that anyone who is aware of contemporary philosophical problems is bound to have some difficulty in adjusting his emotions to his intellectual insight occurs in *A Pair of Blue Eyes*, where Knight's intellectual development is seen as emotionally inhibiting, and later in Angel [in *Tess of the D'Urbervilles*], Jude and Sue. Hardy is not, I think, very successful in handling this aspect of Clym, which he treats in a theoretical way, giving it a good deal of prominence in passages of commentary, but not really embodying it in Clym's character, or in the story. He describes the ravages of profound thinking on his outward appearance: "an inner strenuousness was preying upon an outer symmetry . . . he already showed that thought is a disease of the flesh". But this introduction is followed up only by further abstract statements about him: "In Clym Yeobright's face could be dimly seen the typical countenance of the future", and it is said to express "the view of life as a thing to be put up with". The idea of Clym as a modern man who "would not stand still in the circumstances in which he had been born", is several times stated and discussed and we are told that "he was in many points abreast with the central town thinkers of his date", yet this aspect of his mind is never presented to us in a concrete way (we do not know what books he reads so doggedly—unlike Jude and Sue—nor do we have any clear idea of the nature of his educational theories). It never seems to be a driving force in his character. He does on one occasion feel that there is a specific wrong to be righted; this is when Susan Nonsuch pricks Eustacia in church and says she is a witch. "Do you think I have turned preacher too soon?" Clym asks his mother, but this can hardly be classed as a novel, modern way of looking at the situation. Clym's dissatisfaction with the diamond business, his hope of improving the minds of heath dwellers and some of his conversations with his mother do suggest a philosophical turn of mind; but there is nothing in his behaviour or his thinking to support Hardy's suggestion that he is one of those whose disillusionment has grown as they "uncover the defects of natural laws and see the quandary that man is in by their operation". None of his difficulties in coping with his emotional experience are derived from a conflict between a traditional education and modern ideas, as those of Angel and Sue are, at least in part, and so Clym's modernity remains theoretical and abstract, on the periphery of the story.

The real conflict is between the impulse to do something original ("he would not stand still in the circumstances amid which he was born") and his affinity with his native setting ("he was inwoven with the heath"). Clym maintains he wants to bring about changes on Egdon Heath but the only occasion when he seems to feel any real necessity for change is the pricking of Eustacia. Otherwise, the heath-dwellers are presented as tolerant and good-humoured and Clym's own readiness to become one of them and to merge with the heath is presented by Hardy as wholly admirable under the circumstances. Eustacia's snobbish feeling of being degraded by this is shown as alien and self-centred. Clym was quite content to be "a brown spot in the midst of an expanse of olive green grass and nothing more". All his schemes for change and improvement are qualified by his delight in the ancient, unchanging nature of the place: "he could not help indulging in a barbarous satisfaction at observing that, in some attempts at reclamation from the waste, tillage, after holding on for a year or two, had receded again in despair, the fern and furze-tufts stubbornly reasserting themselves". Admittedly, Clym's plans are for purely intellectual change, but his delight in things as they are, and his ready acquiescence in a life of manual labour do not suggest overwhelming singlemindedness in the pursuit of change. Though he appears to be attempting to convey a message at the end, it is presumably significant that his preaching appears to be vague, grandiose and understandably ineffectual.

Though Hardy as commentator tends to lay the blame for Clym's predicament on modern man's clearer understanding of the nature of things, Hardy the novelist relates it much more closely to his personal relationships. Even here, the conflict is sometimes presented in an excessively schematic and theoretical way: "Three antagonistic growths had to be kept alive: his mother's trust in him, his plan for becoming a teacher and Eustacia's happiness. His fervid nature could not afford to relinquish one of these, though two of the three were as many as he could hope to preserve". Though this method of stating Clym's problems simplifies and limits them, the actual presentation of the personal relationships probes his personality at considerable depth. It is in this area that we see the effects of the "not well-proportioned mind".

Hardy's treatment of Clym's relationship with Eustacia explores some aspects of his mental and emotional problems as well as hers. As "the first blinding halo kindled about him by love and beauty" is rapidly extinguished, "sometimes he wished that he had never known Eustacia, immediately to retract the wish as brutal". Immediately, Clym is in a state of conflict over Eustacia, partly because of his mother, but also because of his own attitudes and desires. His "distrust of his position as a solicitous lover" suggests a similarity to Sue, who was "unfitted . . . to fulfil the conditions of the matrimonial relationship . . . with scarce any man". Unlike so many lovers in Hardy who delude themselves about the nature of the loved one, Clym is quite clearsighted about the absence of affinity between himself and Eustacia and knows that "her tastes touched his own only at rare and infrequent points". Though he does say that "she would make a good matron of a school", this is in the heat of an argument with his mother, and is an illustration of the outrageous points people will make when quarrelling, and not intended to be taken as an honest statement of his opinion—there is nothing to suggest he deluded himself as much as this. Of course, he does delude himself about her in his assumption that she will easily abandon her longing for Paris (and she reciprocates by assuming she can easily persuade him to return there). Yet, his decision to marry Eustacia seems to be due to his sensitivity, to his feeling of owing it to her since he has encouraged her to hope he will, rather than to love. She was "no longer a goddess", though his original passionate feelings are reawakened in the early days of the marriage. None of this suggests lack of balance or neurosis in Clym, but his "firmness in the contrary intention" to Eustacia's and his "undeviating manner" perhaps indicate a dangerous rigidity, rather like Angel's.

It is from his relationship with his mother that violent, unbalanced emotions arise. Hardy depicts very powerfully the intensity of their relationship and the close affinity between their minds. Especially moving and convincing is the way they are able to communicate without using words. This gives their exchanges, whether affectionate or hostile, a sense of great depth of feeling: "The love between the young man and his mother was strangely invisible now. Of love, it may be said, the less earthly, the less demonstrative. In its absolutely indestructible form it reaches a profundity in which all exhibition of itself is painful. It was so with these". Even though they are at loggerheads most of the time, either over Clym's career or over Eustacia, they understand one another completely. Mrs Yeobright is really entirely at one with him about the diamond business and in agreement with him on his moral and philosophical position. When she is criticising his abandonment of his job in Paris when he was "doing well", his question, "Mother, what is doing well?" silences her because she fully understands the implications of his question, and really agrees with him. The dissension between them is entirely on account of Eustacia, and Mrs Yeobright's possessive jealousy is such that she would have been antagonistic towards any woman who interested her son. Clym's response to this is very violent: "whenever any little occurrence had brought into more prominence than usual the disappointment he was causing her it had sent him on long and moody walks; or he was kept awake a great part of the night by the turmoil of spirit which such a recognition created". When she finally tells him, during a particularly violent quarrel, to leave the house, he replies, " 'I beg your pardon for having thought this my home. I will no longer inflict myself upon you: I'll go!' And he went with tears in his eyes". He returns only to pack and leave. He makes no move to give her the opportunity to say that she had spoken in the heat of the moment, nor does she attempt any approach to him, but simply sits downstairs, listening to him packing overhead. They are both equally inflexible and "undeviating". As Mrs Yeobright tells Eustacia, "He can be as hard as steel".

Clym's emotions about his mother are more extreme and more shattering than anything he experiences in relation to Eustacia apart from his frenzied rage about her failure to go to the door when Mrs Yeobright pays her visit. Because of the quality of their relationship, Clym's breakdown after his mother's death is almost inevitable. Just as Sue Bridehead is shown to be precariously balanced and is then exposed to a traumatic experience which undermines her delicate equilibrium, in a similar way Clym is given his traumatic experience and is shown succumbing to it. After his mother's death he, too, tortures himself with guilt. But the fact that Clym's guilt is to some extent justified (in that he had been as inflexible as his mother) makes his delirious self-accusations seem a little more rational than Sue Bridehead's—his are at least directly related to what has occurred, and his guilt is of a much more conscious kind than hers. Nevertheless, his remorse is extreme, and his claim that "it has not upset my reason" seems hardly justified. Chapter 2 of Book Five is entitled, "A Lurid Light breaks in upon a darkened intellect", and reason is said to have "now somewhat recovered itself". His weeklong delirium, followed by obsessive preoccupation with his mother, provokes Eustacia's "Other men's mothers have died", which, in spite of its callousness, arouses a certain sympathy in the reader; by making us experience the irritating, obsessional harping on the single theme, Hardy evokes a response to her plea for rationality, and emphasises how remote from normal thinking Clym's frame of mind is. This phase is a very plausible development from Clym's "undeviating" and highly moral behaviour in the past, and from his extremely close and intense relationship with his mother. Hardy very effectively indicates that this mind, which he stated in his earliest descriptions was prone to madness, has now become grossly disturbed, and is on the edge of insanity.

Clym's temporary recovery of control is shown to be precarious, "he sank into taciturnity", but his obsession, though no longer voiced, still possessed him, completely blotting out all other thoughts: "How to discover the solution to this riddle of death seemed a query of more importance than the highest problems of living". It is characteristic of the subtlety with which Hardy handles this stage of Clym's mental disturbance that he shows him, after he has heard the story from Johnny Nonsuch, though "blank" and "icy", as yet sufficiently conscious of things outside himself to be aware of

> the imperturbable countenance of the heath, which, having defied the cataclysmal onsets of centuries, reduced to insignificance by its seamed and antique features the wildest turmoil of a single man. . . . A consciousness of a vast impassivity in all which lay around him took possession even of Yeobright in his wild walk towards Alderworth.

This ability, at least for the moment, to perceive the world outside himself is a very important feature of Hardy's conception of Clym; it is what saves him from collapsing permanently into neurosis or even madness; other neurotics in Hardy's novels . . . for example, are totally self-absorbed at moments of acute mental suffering (and at other times quite often) and they do not make a recovery as Clym does. After this moment of awareness of the heath, he shuts his mind to it, and going into the house to accuse Eustacia, he seems to become temporarily demented. She sees that he is capable of killing her now, but instead he vents his frenzy in smashing her desk. His accusation that she has been making a trade of prostitution, his idealised account of his mother, his self-righteousness are, as Eustacia sees, almost inevitable counterparts of his previous guilt and remorse. All these attitudes are in keeping with his extremely severe and demanding conscience.

Hardy is creating a picture of an obsessional neurotic, not a madman. After Eustacia has left him, he regains his normal state, still obsessed with his mother ("it had become a religion with him to preserve in good condition all that had lapsed from his mother's hands to his own") but he is prepared to admit that his enraged accusations of Eustacia were unjustified. In the latter part of *The Return of the Native,* Hardy's treatment of Clym consists of exposing him to a series of shattering experiences, showing his collapse, and subsequent slow return to sanity, followed by another blow and another painful recovery. After the third and final blow, the drowning, he returns to a more extreme form of the guilt and remorse which overwhelmed him after his mother's death. He is more vulnerable now, after his only partial recovery, but he is not so frenzied and is not delirious; Hardy's description of his relatively quiet reaction effectively suggests an even deeper and more settled state of neurotic self-blame. He says quietly, "with a wild smile", "She is the second woman I have killed this year". From this point onwards Hardy depicts an obsession with guilt which is clearly neurotic and also fully in keeping with Clym's always severe and rigid personality. That he now becomes wholly taken up with the idea of his mother as "a sublime saint whose radiance even his tenderness for Eustacia could not obscure", is an authentic development under these particular circumstances, from the original relationship with its suggestions of Oedipal intensity. Hardy even describes him as looking like Oedipus after hearing Johnny's story.

Clym's personality shows many of the qualities which Freud associated with the Oedipus complex. In *Civilisation and its Discontents,* Freud emphasises the part played by the "severe superego", which is one of Clym's driving forces, leading him to abandon diamond-dealing in favour of helping his fellow men. A neurotic element in this is perhaps suggested by his "sitting *slavishly* over his books" (unlike Jude who either studies them enthusiastically or abandons them), and by his eventual blinding himself through overstrain, almost as if it were an unconscious way of escape from the powerful demands of his conscience. It is interesting that Hardy says of him when furze-cutting, "A forced limitation of effort offered a justification of lowly courses to an unambitious man, whose conscience would hardly have allowed him to remain in such obscurity while his powers were unimpeded". Hardy here describes precisely the workings of the superego; this "naturally unambitious" man's conscience "will not let him remain in such obscurity" because the dominant influence of his mother, pushing him towards ambitious goals, has been absorbed and become an inner drive. Though he rejected her goal of financial and social advance in favour of more apparently altruistic objectives, the drive towards effort and achievement is a fundamental element in his personality.

Another feature which, according to Freud, is related to the Oedipus complex is a strong sense of guilt. Clym obviously has this. Further, Freud points out a parallel between the demands of the individual's superego and the demands made by systems of ethics on the community. The superego can make excessive demands on the individual:

> In our investigations and our therapy of the neuroses, we cannot avoid finding fault with the superego of the individual on two accounts; in commanding and prohibiting with such severity, it troubles too little about the happiness of the ego, and it fails to take into account sufficiently the difficulties in the way of obeying it . . . in our therapy we often find ourselves obliged to do battle with the superego and work to moderate its demands.

Similarly, the "cultural superego" or system of ethics can demand more than human beings can achieve: "even in so-called normal people the power of controlling the id cannot be increased beyond certain limits. If one asks more, one produces revolt or neuroses in individuals". Hardy's analysis of Clym illustrates this point exactly; not only does his superego make demands on him as an individual which he is unable to fulfil, but also his theories about the nature of society make excessive demands and Hardy defines the nature of this precisely:

> In passing from the bucolic to the intellectual life the intermediate stages are usually two at least, frequently many more; and one of these stages is almost sure to be worldly advance. We can hardly imagine bucolic placidity quickening to intellectual aims without imagining social aims as the transitional phase. . . . To argue upon the possibility of culture before luxury to the bucolic world may be to argue truly, but it is an attempt to disturb a sequence to which humanity has long been accustomed.

When Hardy leaves Clym at the end of the novel "lecturing on morally unimpeachable subjects" he is not presenting this as a satisfactory fulfilment of his ideas. Though he says that Clym has "found his vocation", he also suggests that the preaching is at least partially therapeutic. The text he quotes indicates that Clym is using the sermons at least in part as outlets for his continuing obsession with his mother. The final sentence of the novel hints that he appears as an ineffectual, though amiable, teacher: "But he was everywhere kindly received, for the story of his life had become generally known".

In these ways, Hardy's treatment of Clym corresponds closely to Freud's formulation of his theory of the Oedipus complex and of the relationship between the id, the ego and the superego. This is nothing new in imaginative writing, as Freud's name for his theory and his many references to literary examples of it clearly acknowledge. But this parallel between Hardy and Freud does throw some light on the kinds of interest Hardy took in characterisation. Clym is one example among many of his interest in problematic, disturbed personalities and illustrates his clear understanding of their complexities. With Clym he attempts to deal with a number of interrelated psychological problems. The imaginative and vivid treatment of his relationship with his mother is wholly successful. The other elements are less imaginatively conceived, in particular the very theoretical and abstract handling of Clym as representative of the problem of the modern, thinking man. Yet in some ways this failure is revealing. In the opening chapter and in the introductory descriptions of Clym, where Hardy is formulating his theories about the nature and problems of modern man, we can clearly see his struggle to shape the novel so that it can be a vehicle for his theories. That the theories are not fully integrated with and embodied in the characterisation of Clym is a weakness, but it is interesting because it reveals that Hardy was working out, painfully and clumsily sometimes, a theoretical basis for his conception of character and for the changes which he felt were occurring in contemporary man. Hardy, in a theoretical as well as an imaginative way, was concerned with the psychological effects of "civilisation and its discontents", but in a way which is not limiting or restrictive. His attempts to fuse so many different elements in a single personality show his awareness of the complex nature of human beings which he never reduces to make them fit a theory.

Hardy then is showing what happens to a mind which is not "well-proportioned" when it is exposed to a series of overwhelming experiences. Though he examines the processes of disintegration and partial recovery at some depth, he does not allow this to dominate the telling of the story. This is one of the reasons why Clym is sometimes shown, as Eustacia is, silently brooding without any clear impressions of the precise nature of his thoughts being given. This creates a very powerful impression of painful and intense emotion which might be lessened by a more clinical attempt to formulate the thoughts in words. Just as Lawrence often creates somewhat inarticulate characters (Will and Anna in *The Rainbow* or, more extreme examples, the characters in "The Fox") and then explores by a variety of means their passionate responses to experience, so Hardy too was conscious of the problems of verbalising the characters' emotions. He states the problem in ***The Return of the Native;*** in the course of Clym's disagreement with his mother, "it was almost a discovery to him that he could reach her by a magnetism which was as superior to words as words are to yells". Sometimes he did not speak because "the current of her feeling was too pronounced to admit it". But though it would be true to say that Lawrence found brilliant and original ways of solving these problems, in ***The Return of the Native*** Hardy does little more than show his awareness of them. Even in the later novels he does not go far in developing a technique for this purpose.

The fact that Clym survives his repeated ordeals and finds himself a role which is not totally remote from his original plan to do something for the good of mankind, however ineffectual it turns out to be, is partly due to his sense of belonging to and being part of the heath. In the first chapter, Hardy says, "to know that everything around and underneath had been from prehistoric times as unaltered as the stars overhead, gave ballast to a mind adrift on change, and harassed by the irrepressible New". This sentence has significant bearing on Clym's later development. He can merge with the heath as a furze-cutter and find it "soothing". Even at the height of his anguish and frenzy, he is conscious of the heath's hugeness, permanence and antiquity. On the night of the eclipse, while waiting for Eustacia, as he watched the moon,

> his eye travelled over the length and breadth of that distant country—over the Bay of Rainbows, the sombre Sea of Crises, the Ocean of Storms, the Lake of Dreams, the vast Walled Plains and the wondrous Ring Mountains—till he almost felt himself to be voyaging bodily through its wild scenes, standing on its hollow hills, traversing its deserts, descending its vales and old sea bottoms or mounting to the edge of its craters.

This capacity to move outside himself is an important aspect of Clym's character. The sense of himself as part of the universe, whether he is feeling at one with "winged and creeping things" as he cuts furze, or recognising for a moment that the heath "reduced to insignificance by its seamed and antique features the wildest turmoil of a single man", or feeling he is actually exploring the moon "gave ballast" to his mind and enables him to survive, without being completely and permanently overwhelmed by his individual personal troubles; these only temporarily seem to engulf his whole world.

This relates closely to some of the points made by Jung [in his *Archetypes of the Collective Unconscious*] about the collective unconscious and man's relation to the cosmos; Hardy stresses that Clym can feel a sense of being in touch with the cosmos through being "inwoven with" and "permeated by" the heath; Jung says that the

> cosmos and man in the last analysis obey common laws; man is a cosmos in miniature and is not divided from the great cosmos by any fixed limits. The same laws rule for one as for the other, and from the one, a way leads into the other. The psyche and the cosmos are related to each other like inner and outer worlds. Therefore man participates by nature in all cosmic events and is inwardly, as well as outwardly, interwoven with them.

In ***The Return of the Native*** the passages on the relationship between man and the heath parallel remarkably Jung's statements on the relationship between man and the cosmos. Hardy says of the heath: "It was at present a place perfectly accordant with man's nature—neither ghastly, nor hateful nor ugly; neither commonplace, unmeaning nor tame: but, like man, slighted and enduring; and withal, singularly colossal and mysterious in its swarthy monotony".

Similarly, Jung says: "All the mythological processes of nature, such as summer and winter, the phases of the moon, rainy seasons and so forth . . . are symbolic expressions of the inner unconscious drama of the psyche, which become accessible to man's consciousness by way of projection—that is mirrored in the events of nature".

Hardy gives a single example, Jung generalises, but they are both making the same point. Hardy emphasises the extreme antiquity of the heath: "with the exception of the aged highway, and a still more aged barrow . . . themselves almost crystallised to natural products by long continuance—even the trifling irregularities were not caused by pickaxe, plough or spade, but remained as the very finger-touches of the last geological age".

Similarly Jung stresses the primeval contents of the unconscious: "The unconscious psyche is . . . immensely old . . . it moulds the human species and is just as much a part of it as the human body, which, though ephemeral in the individual is collectively of immense age". and: "so far as the collective unconscious contents are concerned, we are dealing with archaic or—I would say—primordial types, that is, with universal images that have existed since the remotest times".

Both authors see that there is conflict between this primeval element and civilisation. Hardy says, "The untameable, Ishmaelitish thing that Egdon now was, it always had been. Civilisation was its enemy." At the same time, modern man needed it: "it gave ballast to a mind adrift on change and harassed by the irrepressible New". Jung elaborates this more fully:

> Our European ego-consciousness is inclined to swallow up the unconscious, and if this should not prove feasible, we try to suppress it. But if we understand anything of the unconscious, we know that it cannot be swallowed. We also know that it is dangerous to suppress it, because the

unconscious is life and this life turns against us if suppressed, as happens in neurosis.

Clym illustrates this conflict; he is interested in new ideas, and from the little Hardy tells us about his educational theories, we get the impression that in his efforts to achieve "high thinking" he is prepared to "suppress the unconscious"—his disregard for material advancement suggests this unconcern about man's primitive, instinctive needs. Yet his own instinctive rapport with the heath ultimately saves him from the effects of such an attitude.

Egdon Heath is a Jungian archetype. Jung says that archetypes have their "immediate manifestation in dreams and visions", (this manifestation being "less understandable and more naive than in myths"). Here, finally, we have an exact parallel between Hardy's thought and Jung's: "it was found to be the hitherto unrecognised original of those wild regions of obscurity which are vaguely felt to be compassing us about in midnight dreams of flight and disaster". The phrases "hitherto unrecognised original" indicates that Hardy is quite consciously formulating a new psychological theory 50 years before Jung. It is the formulation of the theory that is new in the novel. As Jung says, the theory finds expression indirectly in myths, dreams and visions, and many writers, especially poets, have embodied the concept in their work. It is Hardy's statement of it as a theory which shows his affinity with Jung. The actual statement of the theory is not of vast importance in *The Return of the Native* itself—it is the imaginative expression of it which creates the feeling of a powerful and timeless relationship between man and nature—but as a further instance of Hardy's recurring ability to give expression to ideas which were further developed in the psychological theories of the twentieth century, it is obviously significant. The frequent recurrence of these similarities in Hardy's works suggests that his exceptionally acute sensibilities which made him aware of the minutest natural objects and the subtleties of human emotion also made him unusually sensitive to new ideas which were just beginning to stir in the consciousnesses of people at the time; his alertness and sensitivity enabled him to use these ideas creatively earlier than most people.

Though the statement of the theory of the collective unconscious is important mainly as evidence of Hardy's tendency to be ahead of his time, the way he used the theory in the novel makes it fundamental to his whole conception and significantly related to his treatment of character in all the novels. Clym's affinity with the heath keeps him in touch with the primitive instinctive aspects of his nature in spite of his conscious drive towards "high thinking", which, if he soared too far, might well detach him completely from them. His modern "disease of the flesh" is shared in an even more extreme form by Knight, Angel and Sue who, with their high evaluation of the intellect, regard anything physical as "gross" and risk the atrophy of their instincts. Their lack of any real sensuous contact with nature makes them even more cut off than Clym; unlike him, they have already committed themselves to one side in "the war between flesh and spirit". Clym, with his intellectual aspirations on the one hand, and on the other, his link, through his ability to merge with the heath, with the "wild regions of obscurity" of his own nature, looks forward more to Jude, who embodies more completely and effectively Hardy's realisation that the "war between flesh and spirit" need not be fought. (pp. 99-119)

Rosemary Sumner, in her Thomas Hardy: Psychological Novelist, *St. Martin's Press, 1981, 216 p.*

Hardy on his philosophy of fiction:

A Plot, or Tragedy, should arise from the gradual closing in of a situation that comes of ordinary human passions, prejudices, and ambitions, by reason of the characters taking no trouble to ward off the disastrous events produced by the said passions, prejudices, and ambitions.

Thomas Hardy in The Early Life of Thomas Hardy: 1840-1891, *1928.*

Rosemarie Morgan (essay date 1988)

[*In the following excerpt, Morgan analyzes the conflict between men and women in* The Return of the Native.]

The world of freedom and action Hardy's greater heroines would shape for themselves disintegrates as rapidly as the manmade world superimposes upon them its own curbing shape. With the advent of adulthood and a fully awakened sexual consciousness, every exploratory move towards self-discovery, self-realisation and sexual understanding, meets with obstruction in a male-dominated world intent upon highranking the docile woman over the daring, the meek over the assertive, the compliant over the self-determining, the submissive over the dynamic. There is no area of exploration, whether occupational, sexual or merely developmental, that does not, eventually, conflict with the dominant male will to dispossess woman of autonomy, identity, purpose and power. This becomes an increasingly important part of Hardy's critique—from Henry Knight's nullification of Elfride's needs and desires to Sue Bridehead's fight against the tyranny of man-made institutions. He would have had no hesitation at all in joining with J.S. Mill who argued for a liberated world in which

> each individual will prove his or her capacities in the only way in which capacities can be proved—by trial; and the world will have the benefit of the best faculties of all its inhabitants.

In Hardy's view, it is evident that the world would *not* have the benefit of the best faculties of its inhabitants because half of it, the female half, is denied the right to prove them.

While he was writing *The Return of the Native* in the mid- to late-1870s, he may well have had such thoughts in mind, for he was reading the works of a woman he greatly admired, whom he regarded as one of the 'Immortals' of literature, and who also happened to be highly unconventional—in fact, an openly and defiantly liberated woman. He was reading George Sand and, taking notes from her novel, *Mauprat,* he comes across the following:

> Men imagine that a woman has no individual existence, and that she ought always to be absorbed in them; and yet they love no woman deeply, unless she elevates herself, by her character, above the weakness and inertia of her sex.

Hardy's attention now turns to a woman, Eustacia, whose husband certainly feels she 'ought always to be absorbed' in him, and whose 'individual existence' should, according to 'men's imaginings', most certainly be mediated by his desires.

Hardy's greater heroines are not, in his original conception of them, confined to a domestic domain beside the proverbial hearth but are persistently recalled to the world of men and work. There is no sphere, in Hardy, designated woman's realm. But Eustacia, unlike Bathsheba, Tess and Sue [in *Far From the Madding Crowd, Tess of the D'Urbervilles,* and *Jude the Obscure*], is very much a prisoner in her world which she roams restlessly, night and day, yearning for freedom, action, passion—a yearning manifest in the burning fires she sets by night as beacons of her desire.

It is part of Hardy's purpose in *The Return of the Native* to expose the anger and frustration suffered by the intelligent mind and energetic body restricted to an unvarying, unchallenging, isolated existence. Thomasin's domestic world, with all its conventional trappings, throws Eustacia's into relief by contrast; the estranged solitary woman belongs to no circumscribed world, least of all Thomasin's, in the sense of settling in it, becoming habituated to it or wishing to remain in it. Where Thomasin enacts the exemplary, dutiful, submissive, forbearing wife, Eustacia burns with 'smouldering rebelliousness'.

> To be loved to madness—such was her great desire. Love was to her the one cordial which could drive away the eating loneliness of her days. And she seemed to long for the abstraction called passionate love more than any particular lover.

The rapt joy of passionate love, of erotic bliss, of the translucent sublime—great desires indeed, and far removed from Thomasin's world of low expectations and makeshift monogamous marriage.

Eustacia's tense and frustrated sexuality is also far removed from Bathsheba's self-delighting, auto-erotic passion, but it is no less expressive, no less palpable, no less physical. In *The Return of the Native,* Hardy turns again to the natural-object metaphor covertly to evoke the sexual nature of his heroine. But here the poetic device points to the interactive, reciprocal potential in the sexual relationship and, by extension, to the equal force of Eustacia's desire. Take, for example, the hermaphroditic image of the 'mollusc' (perhaps the most arcane of Hardy's natural-object metaphors), which functions to couple the lovers Eustacia and Wildeve as they wander off to make languid love in the twilight of the heath.

> Their black figures sank and disappeared from against the sky. They were as two horns which the sluggish heath had put forth from its crown, like a mollusc, and had now again drawn in.

Reinforcing the sense of mutuality, reciprocity, and sexual equivalence which the hermaphrodite (mollusc) image introduces, Hardy invokes here the metonym 'horns' which serves aptly in its significant plurality—twinned erectile protuberances—to suggest sharpened appetites and sexual arousal in *both* his lovers.

Hardy takes the concept of mutuality further still, and imagistically reinforces the latent 'force' of Eustacia's nature by rendering her physically sturdy, potentially combative: her mouth is 'cut as the point of a spear'. Clym, in complement, is introspective, passive, soft. 'The beauty here visible' in Clym's face is meditative, not quite 'thoughtworn', a look, Hardy writes, born of 'placid pupilage'.

This woman of 'Tartarean dignity'—an 'Artemis, Athena, or Hera'—has none of Clym's placidity. Rather the reverse, she is constantly restless, perpetually on the move, endlessly roaming. Her confined and confining world so deprives her of sensory experience that her impulse, when walking on the heath, is to pass her thick skeins of hair through the thorny gorse, the 'prickly' tufts of 'Ulex Europeaeus'; and her need to ache and suffer in love expresses her deprivation at an even deeper level, in algolagnia—in taking pleasure in pain. 'Give us back our suffering,' cried Eustacia's peer in life, Florence Nightingale, 'for out of nothing comes nothing. But out of suffering may come the cure. Better have pain than paralysis.' These could be Eustacia's own words. She too demands remission from the enervated life, the enforced seclusion of her days. To Wildeve she protests:

> I should hate it all to be smooth. Indeed, I think I like you to desert me a little once now and then. Love is the dismallest thing where the lover is quite honest. O, it is a shame to say so; but it is true! . . . my spirits begin at the very idea. Don't you offer me tame love, or away you go!

She longs for exquisite pain, sublime erotic anguish. Her spirits *begin* at the very idea. It is a challenging, not a tame lover that she needs. She wants him vulpine, athwart, to match her own intensity of feeling—an intensity palpably felt in the 'Ah!', 'Ah', 'O's of her articulations with Wildeve and the 'O!', 'O', 'O's of those with Clym. Eustacia craves sensation, and predictably cannot conceive of adequate objects for her desire. How could she imagine adequacy? She has been starved of what she calls 'life': 'life—music, poetry, passion, war, and all the beating and pulsing that are going on in the great arteries of the world'.

Yet Eustacia is not merely 'romantical nonsensical', as her grandfather would have it. She commands, in fact, both powerful vision—'seeing nothing of human life now, she imagined all the more of what she had seen'—and a firm grasp of reality: 'Nothing can ensure the continuance of love', she tells the romantically inclined Clym:

> You have seen more than I, and have been into cities and among people that I have only heard of, and have lived more years than I; but yet I am older at this than you. I loved another man once, and now I love you.

Her fundamental acceptance of non-exclusive love, of serial monogamy scarcely equips her for the conventional world to which Clym subscribes, and to which he would have her conform.

Stressing her alienation still further, Hardy tells us her 'celestial imperiousness, love, wrath and fervour', are 'somewhat thrown away on netherward Egdon'. On Olympus, we are told,

> she would have done well with a little preparation. She had the passions and instincts which make a model goddess, that is, those which make not quite a model woman.

Hardy is careful to make the distinction, by negation, between model goddess and model woman: the model woman (represented here by Thomasin) exhibits submissiveness not imperiousness, docility not fervour, amiability not anger, demureness not passion. The model goddess clearly belongs to a different world:

> Had it been possible for the earth and mankind to be entirely in her grasp for a while—few in the world would have noticed a change in the government. There would have been the same inequality of lot, the same heaping up of favours here, of contumely there, the same generosity before justice, the same perpetual dilemmas, the same captious alternation of caresses and blows that we endure now.

The 'model goddess', then, would effect no change in a mortal world. Presumably, if we are to follow Hardy, her descent from Olympus into the modern world, from the Hellenic polytheistic into the Christian monotheistic world, would find her at some considerable disadvantage. For, according to the Hellenic mythological tradition, originating with Kronos, of containing the forces of order and disorder within a pluralistic governing structure, the balance of power between the sexes is equally distributed, and the strong, the powerful, the brave and the heroic count among their number as many females as males.

That Hardy does not attempt to reconcile Eustacia as an Olympian with the everyday world, that her 'passions and instincts' remain unrealised as well as unrealisable on netherward Egdon, brings me to what I regard as a central motif in this novel: the opposition between the Victorian world of the book's principal characters and the Hellenic spirit embodied in both Eustacia and Egdon's Atlantean brow itself.

This disjunction is powerfully evoked by the contrast between Hardy's personification of the Egdon heights, on the one hand, and the life of its inhabitants on the other. Egdon's highest elevation, which takes the form of Rainbarrow, is shaped from an imaginative amalgam of three Barrows, which the author has unified and centralised within his landscape, where in actuality they are spatially separated and peripheral to the heath. Geographical heights naturally lend themselves to images of elevation, high ideals, transfiguration, and to embody these concepts Hardy accords his Egdon heights fine 'architectural' proportions. But first, he conceives a stratified artefact of geological foundations upon which the imprints of humanity are superimposed: the Bronze Age burial mound and the Roman road respectively. The particularised epoch grounds the imaginative concept in physical reality, so to speak, but, in fact, both participate in the timeless spirit of Hellenism: the one signifies humanity's commemoration of the immortality of the spirit, and the other humanity's desire and capacity to broaden horizons, to forge new frontiers.

These features are essential to Egdon's composite character and to its ascendant quality. 'Almost crystallized to natural products by long continuance', the Barrow, on the one hand, projects the brow of Egdon 'above its natural level', and the ancient highway, on the other, 'traverses from one horizon to another'—leading on and out.

But the most important feature of this part-anthropomorphic, part-monolithic landscape is the manner in which all elements and forces interact and reciprocate. Egdon has a spectral presence signifying, in its balanced proportions and harmonious relations, an embodied ideal nowhere to be matched by the inequitable, discordant world it overreaches.

The time for action, for change, for humanity to draw a richer existence from the 'vast tract of unenclosed wild' cocooned by membraneous sky and vegetative earth, has been preternaturally prolonged:

> when other things sank brooding to sleep the heath appeared slowly to wake and listen. Every night its Titanic form seemed to await something; but it had waited thus, unmoved, during so many centuries, through the crises of so many things, that it could only be imagined to await one last crisis—the final overthrow.

The temporal setting is midcentury and revolution is in the air. The great seats of Europe and Eustacia's Paris are in the process of overthrow, or are already overthrown, and folk speak retrospectively of decapitated kings and the Napoleonic wars. The modern capital ideologically anterior to Hardy's Egdon is not London but 'the French capital—the centre and vortex of the fashionable world': a city riven by crises and political turbulence. Egdon too has seen 'the crises of so many things', and it too contains its own turbulence:

> Intensity was more usually reached by way of the solemn than by way of the brilliant, and such a sort of intensity was often arrived at during winter darkness, tempests and mists. Then Egdon was aroused to reciprocity; for the storm was its lover, and the wind its friend.

To the modern mind 'adrift on change, and harassed by the irrepressible New', Egdon generates a reassuring sense of endurance aligned, we are told, with humanity's pioneering 'slighted and enduring' spirit.

Hardy's reference to the heath's 'Titanic' form has already introduced the Hellenic motif, the notional opposition to the Modern World. But it is not until we encounter the 'modern' Clym with his monotheistic God, his deterministic outlook, his passive acceptance of his fate, that the opposition becomes fully apparent. Despite his affection for the heathlands that are barely visible to his increasingly failing sight, the placid Clym is patently incompatible with the Titanic force and grandeur of Egdon's Atlantean pres-

Hardy in old age.

ence. Or, as we are later told, he is 'of no more account (to it) than an insect . . . a mere parasite of the heath'.

What, then, do we infer from this incompatibility between the 'native' and his environment? Michael Millgate [in his *Thomas Hardy: His Career as a Novelist*] suggests that:

> Both the allusion to Greek tragedy and the evocation of setting are presumably intended to elevate the central story, to project its narrative and thematic patterns as in some sense reflective or representative of permanent elements in human experience at all times and in all places.

But to juxtapose this 'desert tract of pre-civilisation' is, Millgate argues, 'to jar credulity and promote continuous unease'. Hardy, I would argue, intends the clash.

It happens thus: the clash, or opposition lies between Hellenistic polytheism and the pursuit of happiness, of Greek joyousness—and Christian monotheism and the pursuit of godliness, of self-redemption through self-denial. Now, the Titanic construct, or Egdon paradigm, as I will call it, with its very physical characteristics, its 'bossy projections' complementing its 'rounds and hollows', not only embodies reciprocity (its 'female' and 'male' characteristics complementing each other), but it is also noticeably unrestrained and sensuous, noticeably turbulent and embattled, and noticeably well-endowed with strong human passions. Most important of all, it is pagan. This is not Clym's world, but it may well be Eustacia's.

To complete the symmetry and unity of the construct Hardy names its uppermost reaches 'Atlantean' and places upon its peak the heroine, herself of Greek extraction, who now features as the 'perfect, delicate, and necessary finish' to the whole. In keeping with the 'architectural demands of the mass', classic forms are inscribed upon its physical outlines. Hence, with 'Atlantean' signifying the presence of atlantes (male), the complementary figure of the caryatid (female) is required, so to speak, to complete symmetrical form:

> There the form stood, motionless as the hill beneath. Above the plain rose the hill, above the hill rose the barrow, and above the barrow rose the figure. Above the figure was nothing that could be mapped elsewhere than on a celestial globe. Such a perfect, delicate, and necessary finish did the figure give to the dark pile of hills that it seemed to be the only obvious justification of their outline. With it it, there was the dome without the lantern; with it the architectural demands of the mass were satisfied. The scene was strangely homogeneous, in that the vale, the upland, the barrow, and the figure above it amounted to a unity.

The opposition between Greek and Modern, between unity and disunity, between parity and disparity has yet to be fully dramatised. This is instigated by the modern heathdwellers' displacement of the classic figure from the Atlantean brow, and is later compounded by her fragmented existence on the heath. But first Humanity appears on the scene 'Hand in Hand with Trouble' (as Hardy entitles Chapter Two) to inaugurate a temporal change from timeless past to present-day while also consolidating the theme of opposition. The first figure to appear seems innocuous enough, although, as it later transpires, he is the neglectful guardian of the orphaned heroine. He is, therefore, one of those 'hand in hand with trouble'. The second figure, Venn, the reddleman who trades in red ochre for the marking of sheep, is readily recognisable as an alien intruder by virtue of his lurid blood-red raiment. No sheep, after all, graze on Egdon. Although there is little, at this stage, to indicate the nature of Venn's true role, Hardy's initial clues are both apt and prefigurative. For this intruder and moral watchdog from the civilised world who later secretes himself in the hollows of the heath to spy on Eustacia, now stirs irritation and unease in his companion, Captain Vye, by making five separate, secretive, visits to peer inside his van, where the concealed Thomasin, after the abortive wedding ceremony with Wildeve, lies in an exhausted sleep. Venn's actions are plainly provoking:

> Possibly these two [Venn and Vye] might not have spoken again till their parting, had it not been for the reddleman's visits to his van. When he returned from his fifth time of looking in the old man said, 'You have something inside there besides your load?'

Despite his manner of teasing out five previews, the reddleman divulges nothing, leaving Vye to draw his own conclusions—to discover what turns out in fact to be common knowledge about the girl from 'Blooms-End'. And what the reader discovers from this minor instance of 'trouble' is that Venn enjoys creating it. This will culminate in less minor troubles, in more destructive deeds, notably in his attempts to bring down Eustacia—the 'displacement' which ends in her tragic death.

Mainstream criticism holds Venn to be a benign agent of order within the community. This interpretation depends heavily upon the reader's need to order Hardy's world, to locate a recognisable regulating force within it, and to assign the locus of order to the moral watchdog who, mirroring the Victorian puritanical conscience, fulfils the role of censor.

Venn's activities have been seen, by critics, as appropriate to a moral universe in which woman's irregular sexual activity needs to be checked. However, this reading at best reflects the exegetical pursuits of the critic and, at worst, over-simplifies Hardy's very complicated schema here. Since Venn features centrally in this schema, and since the Egdon paradigm presents the only alternative *weltanschauung* (in terms of sexual relationships), in the entire range of the Wessex novels, I think it is important to examine his true role and function as the moral watchdog in *The Return of the Native's* troubled world.

As officious intruder, troublemaker and Eustacia's demoraliser, Venn is clearly visible as the furtive stalker who persistently tracks her down in order to catch her out in actions he disapproves. And, as Hardy subtly indicates, he serves no one's interests but his own.

Strongly urged by a desire to trap the 'rare' creature and to curtail her freedom, Venn rationalises his persecution of Eustacia as activated by a desire to protect Thomasin's interests. But he deceives himself:

> His first active step in watching over Thomasin's interests was taken about seven o'clock the next evening, and was dictated by the news which he had learnt from the sad boy. That Eustacia was somehow the cause of Wildeve's carelessness in relation to the marriage had at once been Venn's conclusion on hearing of the secret meeting between them. It did not occur to his mind that Eustacia's love-signal to Wildeve was the tender effect upon the deserted beauty of the intelligence which her grandfather had brought home. His instinct was to regard her as a conspirator against rather than as an antecedent obstacle to Thomasin's happiness.

Venn's interference is not only shown to be misconceived, it is also obliquely disapproved by Hardy here, who, in speaking of Eustacia, allows soft, sympathetic tones to colour his narrative ('the tender effect') but who, in speaking of Venn, reverts to polite severity: 'His instinct was to regard her as a conspirator against rather than as an antecedent obstacle to Thomasin's happiness.' There can, of course, be no protection of Thomasin's interests all the while her self-appointed guardian gets his facts wrong; but obsessed with his mission he sets out to track Eustacia, not for a few hours, not for a day, but for five consecutive nights. Success comes 'a day-week' after her previous meeting with Wildeve; but while he is spying on the lovers Venn is frustrated by a cross-wind, which interferes with his eavesdropping. It is at this point that his compulsion to meddle is exposed by Hardy for the totally unprincipled thing it is. To overcome the cross-wind, Venn decides to creep up in disguise on the unsuspecting pair:

> He took two of these (turves) as he lay, and dragged them over him till one covered his head and shoulders, the other his back and legs. The reddleman would now have been quite invisible, even by daylight; the turves, standing upon him with the heather upwards, looked precisely as if they were growing. He crept along again, and the turves on his back crept with him . . . it was as though he burrowed underground.

Where Gabriel Oak, in his espials, squats in shadows or peers through crevices, Venn, like the veritable demon of old who, it was held, mined under the earth for treasure, creeps along 'as though he burrowed underground'. This allusion shapes Hardy's discourse most tellingly to demonstrate Venn's true nature, without stripping him entirely of his superficial guise of respectability.

In his creeping and crawling spying activities Venn reveals a malevolent underside which Hardy does not cloak but, rather, continues, in gradual stages, to expose. Venn decides to confront Eustacia with his knowledge of her movements and Hardy, with a keen sense of what is fitting, has him choose a Sunday morning 'for an interview . . . to attack her position as Thomasin's rival either by art or by storm'. The Sabbath is clearly the most appropriate day for a little demonic intervention. Contravening custom and goodwill, Venn also chooses to arrive at a time when 'folks never call upon ladies'—that is while they are still in bed. He is not, of course, perturbed by his own intrusiveness, rather he seeks to perturb, no doubt pruriently relishing the thought of his name being carried into the private quarters of the young woman as yet undressed, whom he fully intends to strip of dignity.

When eventually she greets him, he uses no 'art' whatsoever but rude and rending 'storm'. He begins by referring to her lover, Wildeve, not by name but with a vulgar jerk: 'he jerked his elbow to south-east—the direction of the Quiet Woman'. Whereupon, distressed, but holding fast to her dignity, Eustacia coolly enquires if he is speaking of 'Mr Wildeve'. This merely prompts yet another insulting reference, this time to herself as 'This other woman' Wildeve 'has picked up with', and yet another as Venn proceeds to tell the 'pickup' that her lover has no intention of marrying her, implying that she may be fit for sex but not for wife.

Venn's most pitiless blow, though, is his disclosure of his espial. Just as Oak sought to shame and humiliate so Venn now does the same. He lets it be known that he has been watching her; that he knows a good deal about her movements; that he has seen her with Wildeve at their last meeting, the evening they had wandered off hand in hand, into the dusky twilight of the heath:

> It was a disconcerting lift of the curtain, and the

mortification of Candaules' wife glowed in her. The moment had arrived when her lip would tremble in spite of herself, and when the gasp could no longer be kept down.

Eustacia's emotional distress speaks volumes. Clearly, she fears Venn has witnessed far more than just the holding of hands.

This is just the moment he has been waiting for, the moment for engineering her displacement. He will come to her aid; he will find her a position in Budmouth; she can become a widow-lady's 'companion'. Venn may shame her, may degrade her, may humiliate her but he cannot dupe her. Seeing, instantly, his ploy to have her reduced yet further—to the menial position of unpaid servingwoman—she turns on him angrily and snaps back that she will not go.

Humiliating the proud girl may gratify Venn, but it does not urge her departure. On the contrary, even as he persuades himself that his mission is to rid Egdon of her presence, if she had fostered the remotest longing to escape, he effectively robs her of it now.

> As a rule, the word Budmouth meant fascination on Egdon. That Royal port and wateringplace, if truly mirrored in the minds of the heath-folk, must have combined, in a charming and indescribable manner, a Carthaginian bustle of building with Tarentine luxuriousness and Baian health and beauty. Eustacia felt little less extravagantly about the place; but she would not sink her independence to get there.

'Sink' is exactly the word. Venn's projection of her servitude in perpetuity has left its mark.

Clearly Venn does not operate as a benign regulating force. Perpetually meddling and perpetually failing to get his facts right, he is also responsible for passing Clym's inheritance into the wrong hands. This small interference leading to large consequences takes place in the gambling scene. Here, 'confusion' and 'vice' are well foregrounded as the addled Christian, the drunken Wildeve, and the officious Venn crouch, in an unlit world, around the Promethean 'dregs' of burning 'fires' generated in fits and starts from a collection of much abused glow-worms. And that it should be Clym's inheritance which will shortly be misappropriated, who is himself later to be found crouching and crawling, half-blind in an unlit world—'a mere parasite of the heath'—reinforces Hardy's vision of polarised worlds: this world of self-interested, joyless, punitive men is singularly at odds with the Hellenic Egdon paradigm.

'It was sometimes suggested', Hardy writes,

> that reddlemen were criminals for whose misdeeds other men had wrongfully suffered: that in escaping the law they had not escaped their own consciences, and had taken to the trade as a lifelong penance. Else why should they have chosen it? In the present case such a question would have been particularly apposite. The reddleman who had entered Egdon that afternoon was an instance of the pleasing being wasted to form the ground-work of the singular, when an ugly foundation would have done just as well for that purpose.

Why would this 'pleasing being' in his pleasing guise—this 'agreeable specimen of rustic manhood'—relinquish 'his proper station in life'? For money it seems: 'Yes I am given up body and soul to the making of money. Money is all my dream', Venn jests to Thomasin in Mephistophelian vein, but the jest rings rather hollow. His guise of respectability is, in truth, exceedingly thin, insured, as it is, by his 'never-failing production of a well-lined purse'. In fact, more Mephistophelian than 'an agreeable specimen of rustic manhood', he personifies, as a 'blood-coloured figure' and a 'red ghost', 'all the horrid dreams which had afflicted the juvenile spirit since imagination began':

> 'The reddleman is coming for you!' had been the formulated threat of Wessex mothers for many generations.

And only superficially less sinister in his whitewashed guise at the last, Venn 'comes for' Thomasin as a 'ghost' of altered hue:

> [Clym] heard a slight scream from Thomasin, who was sitting inside the room. 'O, how you frightened me!' she said to some one who had entered. 'I thought you were the ghost of yourself.'

Not fully reassured that it is in fact Diggory Venn 'no longer reddleman', Thomasin confesses that she could not 'believe that he had got white of his own accord! It seemed supernatural,' she says. Telling words! For if Hardy's 'white-washing' of Venn is not supernatural, it is decidedly unnatural.

Those Wessex mothers threatening their children with the reddleman are, for Hardy's purposes, prophetic. The prophecy is fulfilled most dramatically in the shooting episode, in the chapter entitled 'Rough Coercion is Employed'. Here, having already set trip-wires to bedevil Wildeve, Venn takes the law into his own hands and, while on the one hand he tells himself that he is 'prepared to go to any lengths short of absolutely shooting', on the other, he stalks the innkeeper across the heath takes aim and fires:

> Had Wildeve known how thoroughly in earnest Venn had become he might have been still more alarmed. . . . The doubtful legitimacy of such rough coercion did not disturb the mind of Venn.

The 'doubtful legitimacy' may not disturb Venn but it does Hardy. If Venn is to feature in *The Return of the Native's* 'happy ending' an exculpatory note should be sounded at this point. There is no genuine attempt, on Hardy's part, to conceal the unnaturalness of Venn's transformation, where he becomes an overnight success with Thomasin, hitherto indifferent to his charms. Hardy, in fact, openly admits that this *volte-face* goes right against his 'original conception'. Venn, he says, 'was to have retained his isolated and weird character to the last, and to have disappeared mysteriously from the heath, nobody knowing whither'. A token 'cleaning-up' nevertheless has to take place at some point, if readers' expectations of marriage-and-happy-endings are to be met. After all, Venn is becoming, by the minute, a radically more demonic version of the Oak whom Hardy aligns with Milton's Satan early in *Far From the Madding Crowd;* although Oak does have one dogged foot in the upperworld. Accordingly, with the arrival of this 'new and most unpleasant form of menace', Hardy offers a token exculpatory note:

> Sometimes this is not to be regretted. From the impeachment of Strafford to Farmer Lynch's short way with the scamps of Virginia there have been many triumphs of justice which are mockeries of law.

I use the word 'token' advisedly. For this apparent vindication of Venn is subtly undermined by the anomalous examples Hardy draws upon: Strafford was, after all, impeached and beheaded on controvertible charges of treason, and the 'triumphs of justice' executed in Charles Lynch's name gave rise to some of the most brutal injustices committed in Hardy's century.

Venn may fulfil the role of a moral watchdog equipped with punitive instincts where beautiful, rebellious women are concerned, but it is not Hardy's intention that he should be applauded for it. If we go back to the novel's opening sequences, it is now apparent that Venn's first appearance 'Hand in Hand with Trouble' has led in steady, gradual steps towards far greater troubles; but before they begin to unfold Hardy shifts the focus back to the Barrow where Eustacia is seen in cameo as the 'perfect and necessary finish' to the architectural mass. The classic form is stable, unified and balanced:

> The form was so much like an organic part of the entire motionless structure that to see it move would have impressed the mind as a strange phenomenon. Immobility being the chief characteristic of that whole which the person formed portion of, the discontinuance of immobility in any quarter suggested confusion. Yet that is precisely what happened. The figure perceptibly gave up its fixity . . . descended . . . and then vanished. The reason for her sudden displacement now appeared . . . a newcomer . . . protruded into the sky. . . . A second followed, then a third, a fourth, a fifth, and ultimately the whole barrow was peopled with burdened figures.

The woman, we are told, 'had no relation to the forms who had taken her place'. They intrude, bringing confusion and disorder, unsettling the spectral image of classic perfection, balance and equilibrium.

> The imagination of the observer clung by preference to that vanished, solitary figure, as something more interesting, more important, more likely to have a history worth knowing than these *new-comers,* and unconsciously regarded them as *intruders.*

This displacement of Eustacia as an Olympian apparition, spectrally the perfect finish to the Atlantean brow, prefigures her later demise, her displacement in Egdon's modern world 'not friendly to women'. At the same time it testifies to the destabilising agency of the modern world's inhabitants. This is an important point. Critical assumptions claiming that Eustacia is both the intruder and agent of disorder in *The Return of the Native,* are not supported by the text. Hardy was writing for and about a world 'not friendly to women' but he was not inviting its perpetuation by literary critics.

Heralded by Boeotian witlessness set in antithesis to Eustacia's Olympian grandeur, the intruders, 'like a travelling flock of sheep', ascend the tumulus, and the world now becomes one in which all perspectives are dimmed. The horizon blurs and the heath below phases out: 'none of its features could be seen now'. As if usurping 'some radiant upper storey of the world', neither complementing its grandeur nor adding to it any 'necessary finish', the heathfolk can perceive nothing of the world they customarily inhabit. The sense is now of a gradual emergence of two distinct and separate hemispheres: the one, the upper Atlantean world, pleasing in form, finish and atmosphere, and the other, the lower 'Limbo' world—the abode of souls barred from Paradise. The polarisation of the two spheres becomes the more apparent as we are told that in the nether regions of the heath 'the muttered articulations of the wind in the hollows were as complaints and petitions from the "souls of mighty worth" suspended therein'. The one soul of 'mighty worth' now 'suspended therein' is Eustacia. Precipitated into the 'Limbo' that is to be her Egdon existence, it is her articulations that carry on the winds:

> There mingled with all this wild rhetoric of night a sound which modulated so naturally into the rest that its beginning and ending were hardly to be distinguished. The bluffs, and bushes, and the heather-bells had broken silence; at last, so did the woman; and her articulation was but as another phrase of the same discourse as theirs. Thrown out on the winds it became twined in with them and with them it flew away.

Hardy's polarisation of the two spheres, the Hellenic and the Modern, now becomes dramatically complete as confusion takes the place of stability: 'all was unstable': 'those whom Nature had depicted as merely quaint became grotesque, and the grotesque became preternatural; for all was in extremity'. With stability lost and divided worlds very much to the fore, dialogues now convey division within the community: the putting-up of Thomasin's wedding banns and Mrs Yeobright's opposition to them, Wildeve's worthiness or not, and Thomasin's folly or alternatively her wisdom in accepting Wildeve's suit. Added to these minor differences (all of which devolve upon issues of class and sex) there is also talk of Christian Cantle's ambiguous sexuality and a good deal of superstitious interchange. Pandemonium is finally most appropriately dramatised by the figures of the 'whirling . . . dark shapes' cavorting 'demoniac' measures in the 'boiling confusion'. Poor addled Christian Cantle is beside himself: 'They ought not to do it—how the vlankers do fly! 'tis tempting the Wicked one, 'tis'. And sure enough a 'long, slim figure' flames up out of the heath before his very eyes, clad in 'tight raiment, and red from top to toe'. 'For all the world like the Devil in the picture of Temptation' Venn arrives, summoned by the 'boiling confusion of sparks' and flying vlankers to set the seal upon a scene as profane as the earlier one had been sublime.

The heathfolk finally descend and Eustacia ascends again to 'her old position at the top'. But the prelude is over: the Atlantean brow is now invisible; Eustacia's figure is blurred by an 'incomplete darkness'; the radiant upper storey is lost to view.

This displacement motif echoes on throughout the novel. It is, for example, reiterated in prefigurative form later on where Venn's declared intention to displace Eustacia is prefaced, by Hardy, with an analogy. This introduces the high-flying courser, the rare bird from hotter climes which, we are told, was remorselessly tracked by a 'barbarian' who 'rested neither night nor day' until he had hunted her down and finally shot her. The analogy is clear: Venn's persecution of Eustacia, in intention as much as in act, passes well beyond a bid for power. Envy and desire are equally present here.

Venn's attempts to displace the rare, splendid woman, are paralleled in less demonic form, in Clym's overshadowing of her in marriage. Her phasing into invisibility as Clym grows increasingly blind grounds the motif in harsh, physical fact, but it is the invisibility (to him) of her pain, frustration and desire that drives her out of her mind. In this instance, events are foreshadowed by the lunar eclipse which, significantly, dims the radiant upper sphere as, in their courtship days, Clym and Eustacia meet up by night on the heath.

Moving from Hardy's microcosmic world to the macrocosmic world of the reader, this motif finds its true parallel in woman's legal, social, sexual overshadowing, in her lack of equal rights in a man-made world, in which there was no need to display the sign of the headless, silenced 'Quiet Woman'. Eustacia's live counterpart, socially conditioned to be decorative and dumb with the aid of the cult of the 'doll-madonna', lived out her amputated life without legal existence, without political voice under the auspices of the Institution of Matrimony, for all the world to see. 'Homer's Cimmerian land', nowhere to be found on netherward Egdon, was nowhere to be found beyond it.

Venn, as a power-mongering bully and degrader of voluptuous womankind, typifies the punitive male censor of female nonconformity, although in his personification of things demonic, he takes on somewhat melodramatic proportions. This is necessary, I think, to Hardy's rather grand scheme of polarising the two worlds, Hellenic and Modern. Clym, on the other hand, is less stereotyped. He is not so much the personification of social evils in general and male-domination in particular as, simply, an 'unseeing' native of the land. He is, even so, one of Hardy's more sympathetically drawn heroes. There are not many who, in wielding power and authority, do not trivialise and debase, or (the inverse) rarefy and etherealise, the woman they love, but Clym does struggle to meet Eustacia on her own ground. He is, Hardy says, 'before his time', 'mentally in a provincial future', and this shows in his earlier days with Eustacia (before his vision goes) as, for example, when she argues against monogamy without fear of repression or humiliation. Her views are highly unconventional not to say anarchic. Yet, unlike Venn who, in common with many of his live contemporaries, mentally categorises Eustacia a hussy, Clym listens without sneers or disgust or condescension. Or so we might suppose, for it is with tact and diplomacy, both signs of self-assurance, that she speaks to him of her past love and then moves on to deflect him from present talk of marriage—following his sudden announcement that she should be his wife:

> 'Shall I claim you some day—I don't mean at once?'
>
> 'I must think,' Eustacia murmured. 'At present speak of Paris to me. Is there any place like it on earth?'
>
> 'It is very beautiful. But will you be mine?'
>
> 'I will be nobody else's in the world—does that satisfy you?'
>
> 'Yes, for the present.'

Eustacia seeks to gain from Clym's responses a measure of reassurance that his return to Paris is a possibility. No doubt aware that the Victorian maid taken in marriage as man's property marries not only the man but also his way of life, she must needs canvass his intentions, his affiliations, his line of country. Her stratagem, then, is to divert him back to Paris.

> 'Now tell me of the Tuileries, and the Louvre,' she continued evasively. 'I hate talking of Paris! Well I remember one sunny . . . '

Clym does not hate talking about Paris, as Eustacia knows only too well. His vivid evocation of the place betrays him. He is discomposed, though, by the fact that both his lover and his mother appear to know what is best for him, and this turns him, in his male pride, perverse and stubborn. Vexed by Eustacia's consuming passion to belong in Paris—a city surely redolent, to her rebellious mind, of revolutionary zeal and women-on-the-barricades—and apparently ignorant of her attraction to rebels and warriors, he taxes her with loving him,

> rather as a visitant from a gay world to which she rightly belonged than as a man with a purpose opposed to that recent past which so interested her.

He had earlier expressed his opposition in no uncertain terms:

> 'How extraordinary that you and my mother should be of one mind about this!' said Yeobright. 'I have vowed not to go back, Eustacia.'

The tenor of this vow suggests a renunciation of the worldly, of the instinctual life in favour of the devotional, but Clym's new plan is vain and unworldly to the point of impracticality:

> To argue upon the possibility of culture before luxury to the bucolic world may be to argue truly, but it is an attempt to disturb a sequence to which humanity has long been accustomed. Yeobright preaching to the Egdon eremites that they might rise to a serene comprehensiveness without going through the process of enriching themselves, was not unlike arguing to ancient Chaldeans that in ascending from earth to the

pure empyrean it was not necessary to pass first into the intervening ether.

In short, the plan is totally unrealistic. But Eustacia is not to know this, any more than she can know that his immediate impulse to set her in Paris stirs, in his mind, illusions rather than realistic visions. Notice, for example, how inappropriate his settings are: 'Why', he says, the 'Galerie d'Apollon' would be a fitting place to live, and

> the Little Trianon would suit us beautifully to live, and you might walk in the gardens in the moonlight . . .
>
> you could keep to the lawn in the front of the Grand Palace . . .

Eustacia is now uneasy. Possibly she finds the grandiose, opulent settings hard to identify with. She is a woman, after all, with a liking for warriors and a strong yearning for 'life-music, poetry, passion, war and all the beating and pulsing that are going on in the great arteries of the world'. Revolutionary, not aristocratic, Paris would be far more to her liking. Then again, Clym's settings discompose her because they give the impression that she cares more for glamour and riches than for him:

> Don't mistake me Clym: though I should like Paris, I love you for yourself alone. To be your wife and live in Paris would be heaven to me; but I would rather live with you in a hermitage here than not be yours at all. It is gain to me either way, and a very great gain. There's my candid confession.

This is the telling moment. Despite the sympathy of her listener Eustacia has, in some subtle way, found herself restated. Is it the glamour, the glitter, or is it the formality of landscaped gardens that lend a different shape to her dreams, her sense of self? Whatever the cause, she is trapped in an unfamiliar identity and in the confusion she falls back upon a culturally approved language expressing approved attitudes that completely misrepresent her. She has stalled an imminent clash of wills only to find herself precipitated into a deeper conflict as Clym takes her 'candid confession' to mean her submission to his will. And in like manner he, too, falls into conventional attitudes, patronising attitudes. Metaphorically patting her on the head, he declares that she has 'spoken like a woman'. But in so saying, in falling back upon that authoritarian manner of mixing approval with condescension, he has shifted the relationship on to a different level: not only is there a disparity in their hopes and dreams, there is now an imbalance of power.

Eustacia is caught in a double-bind. Suffering a check upon her thoughts and emotions, but knowing no language of sexuality other than that of conventional courtship, her utterances are now shaped to a false representation of her true feelings. What she cannot speak of 'like a woman' and what Hardy has to tell on her behalf, is that 'Fidelity in love for fidelity's sake had less attraction for her than . . . fidelity because of love's grip'. She has already startled Clym with her thoughts on the non-exclusivity of love; she has frankly admitted that a cosmopolitan life would be ideal; but she has not been able to say that she has 'got beyond the vision of some marriage of inexpressible glory'; that the marriage tie is not for her. Clym, in turn, misreads her languid manner as passive acceptance, as a 'feminine' yielding to circumstance. His modernism, his enlightenment, is in this sense more theoretical than actual. Had he been less inclined to seek a 'model woman' in Eustacia, he would have discovered a radical, a potential woman-on-the-barricades. But he turns his back on the real Eustacia just as he has turned his back on the real world—on Paris, the city of social and political revolutions—to return to his native, class-divided community; to set himself up as philanthropic teacher to a handful of Egdon eremites; to 'fain make a globe to suit him': to play chieftain to what he calls 'the lowest classes'.

Egocentricity and introspection, 'parasite thought', devour the vision that had once urged him to strive at 'high thinking', to become 'acquainted with ethical systems popular at the time'. Even his philanthropic outlook is self-regarding, as his own words reveal, where vagueness of vision is prefaced by the self-referential 'I' that remains the object of contemplation.

> I no longer adhere to my intention of giving with my own mouth rudimentary education to the lowest classes. I can do better . . . I shall ultimately, I hope, be at the head of one of the best schools in the county.
>
> I shall do a great deal of good to my fellow-creatures!

Despite the 'waggery of fate' which has afforded Clym a highly privileged start in life, enabling him to test his ideas, needs and skills in both London and Paris with all the social and economic freedom Eustacia has been denied, it is all wasted on him. Rightfully, given his privileged background, he sees his scope as large; but his visionary powers are small. His mother and his lover both know this and tell it. But they are overruled: the right to choose his own way of life is his male birthright, and exercise this right he will.

Eustacia's dreams are by contrast either fragmented or truncated. They could scarcely be anything else. Hardy, sensitively acknowledging the extent to which her cut-off life has moulded the deeps of her unconscious, presents even her paradisal dream as truncated—in terms of both form *and* content. There is first of all some indication that this is a dream of such splendour as to outmatch all dreams. But Hardy pieces together only its final disintegrating moments. It is as if he would stress her dislocation from her Olympian heights as too remote, too atavistic, for full recall. Then there is the armoured figure who features centrally in the dream. He disintegrates before the dreamer's very eyes and just at the point of touching. The dream of harmonious relations, prefigured in Hardy's own dream of an alternative world of reciprocity and equilibrium, shatters about the dreamer's ears and falls into fragments as she awakes.

Untimely awakened from what she calls her 'youthful dream'—the music, the pulsing, the passion—Eustacia, denied all that Clym has been so freely offered and so freely squanders, suffers bitterly at the sight of him toiling on the surface of the heath singing mindlessly in defeat,

> not more distinguishable from the scene around him than the green caterpillar from the leaf it feeds on . . . of no more account than an insect—a mere parasite of the heath.

Like an imbecile, Clym draws emotional soothing relief from his 'curious microscopic' activities, impervious to the continuing damage to his sight. But to Hardy he is an infestation, parasitical. This is reflected in his insensitivity to Eustacia's suffering as daily he makes callous references to his life in Paris. Having decided not to return to that city, having doggedly insisted to the woman he loves that there is no possibility he will change his mind, having ignored her hopes and desires, he returns, again and again, in his stories of 'Parisian life and character' and, again and again, in the songs which had struck his fancy in Paris, to the people and places she, herself, longs to hear and touch and see.

Tormented by the mindlessness of the man and haunting strains of his songs, Eustacia turns away and weeps 'in sick despair of the blasting effect upon her own life of that mood and condition in him'. It is a mood and condition of blind egocentricity. Clym's failure to attune himself to the high thinking and ethical systems of the time, becomes, in turn, his physical blindness. And blind he certainly becomes to his own double-standard. To Eustacia's attempts to persuade him to live at a different level he explains that he needs to keep himself occupied: 'You cannot seriously wish me to stay idling at home all day?' What then of Eustacia condemned to idling at home all day, day after day after day?

Eustacia's displacement is now fully compounded. The rare woman, with her affinity for heights she has no means of scaling can only descend and continue descending to the last. But Hardy will not have her sink, like Clym, into a wasting decline. As befits her Olympian status she will be consumed by the elements; her death will call up a fury in the natural world; like her Wessex predecessor, King Lear, she will be stricken with wild and fretful delirium under impetuous blasts: 'nocturnal scenes of disaster'. Having seen the spectre of her greatness Hardy must draw her back into Egdon 'as if she were drawn into the Barrow by a hand beneath'. Lashed earthwards by streaming torrential rain which gathers up her tears in its coursing, her life down-spirals:

> Between the drippings of the rain from her umbrella to her mantle, from her mantle to the heather, from the heather to the earth, very similar sounds could be heard coming from her lips; and the tearfulness of the outer scene was repeated upon her face. The wings of her soul were broken . . .

The rare creature is finally 'winged' and brought down.

Cross-relating her descent from the Barrow, where she had provided a necessary finish to the heights, Hardy cannot permit her simply to drown. The skies must break and the Barrow must seek to draw her back to itself. Her death must become a victory over life—a mortal life that had, to her, been empty of significance and purpose. For who and what had she been? She does nothing, goes nowhere and, apart from her status as Clym's wife, she is totally without identity. Unlike Clym, who is not only familiar to everyone long before his advent, who has an identity born partly of reputation, partly of kinship to the singular Mrs Yeobright, and partly of his secure status in a world predisposed to securing status for males, Eustacia is shown by Hardy to be the sum total of male circumscriptive attitudes. To her grandfather, who inconsistently chides and neglects her, she is alternately childish and romantical, nonsensical or sportive—'one of the bucks'. To Venn she is the fabled *femme fatale;* to the heath-folk she is a witch; and to Clym, predictably, given his reversion to type, she is first goddess then whore. 'Here was action and life,' writes D.H. Lawrence [in *Lawrence on Hardy: 'A Study of Thomas Hardy' and 'Introduction to These Paintings',* edited by J.V. Davies],

> here was a move in being on [Clym's] part. But as soon as he got her, she became an idea to him, she had to fit in his system of ideas. According to his way of loving, he knew her already, she was labelled and classed and fixed down.

Clym's perception of Eustacia is circumscribed by a host of assumptions that range around the polarised stereotypes of Goddess and Whore; but Hardy's own perspective, even while invoking visions of Goddesses, emphasises Eustacia's painfully isolated, nullified existence. If (recalling George Sand's words), Eustacia's urge to better herself is obstructed by a society that denies her individual existence, then Hardy will not only deny that society its ultimate appropriation of her—neither man nor institution will hold her—but he will ensure that she remains unclassifiable, a-typical, bearing no resemblance to male circumscriptions. In the 'Queen of Night' chapter, for example, she remains, throughout, an unfocused, blurred figure, the 'raw material of a divinity'. Elsewhere, she is, invariably, shrouded in darkness, or invisible to her myopic husband, or masked as a Turkish Knight, or masked again as a veiled dancer. Or she is simply a white face at a window. She is never familiar or close. She cannot be familiar or close. She, herself, does not know who or what she is: 'How I have tried and tried to be a splendid woman,' she cries in solitary anguish. 'Tried and tried to be . . . ', to come into being. She is a soul in search of a self.

Displaced, then, from her natural position of equipoise to live out her mortal life confined, inutile, restive and angry, Eustacia is suffocated in a man-made world. In her sepulchred existence, sensitively evoked by Hardy's insistence upon her life-by-night consciousness, she is prevented from coming into being in a world that denies autonomy, identity, purpose and power to women.

And that world is to be the loser in Hardy's view. It is emptied of life with Eustacia's passing. The strong women are dead. The 'native', stripped of credibility and respect, is now rootless and itinerant, and the good Thomasin with her do-good husband has removed to the very fringe of the heath's reaches—of no account to it. Egdon is inhabited at the last by a coterie of dwellers whose capacity for renewal cannot be guaranteed. The sickly Nonesuch boy and the sexually enfeebled Christian Cantle, as the heath's youthful representatives, exemplify an etiolated life wholly alien to the vigorous, turbulent, enduring heights overreaching them.

This then is a world in which, to misquote J. S. Mill, woman's capacities cannot be proved by trial, that the world might have the benefit of all its inhabitants. And as he lived out the harmonious days of his 'Sturminster idyll', composing *The Return of the Native* in the mid-1870s, it must have struck Hardy with singular force—note-taking from his much admired George Sand and in 1876 confronted with the shock of her death—that this was indeed a world unfriendly to women.

For he would almost certainly have read Victor Hugo's obituary, in *The Saturday Review,* on George Sand, and as he reflected upon the hostile response this drew from his compatriots, he must have felt, deeply, the injustice of their attack. *The Saturday Review* first quotes Hugo:

> In this country, whose law is to complete the French Revolution, and begin that of the equality of the sexes, being a part of the equality of men, a great woman was needed. It was necessary to prove that a woman could have all the manly gifts without losing any of her angelic qualities; be strong without ceasing to be tender. George Sand proved it. . . . Whenever one of these powerful human creatures dies we hear, as it were, an immense noise of wings. Something is going; something is coming. The earth, like heaven, has its eclipses; but here, as above, the reapparition follows the appearance. The torch which was in the form of a man or woman, and which is extinguished under that form, reappears under that of an idea. This torch is flaming higher than ever; it will constitute afterwards a part of civilisation, and enter into the vast enlightenment of humanity.

It is interesting to find in both Hugo's discourses and in Hardy's *The Return of the Native* a set of images common to both authors: the splendid woman strong without ceasing to be tender, the apparition in human form that reappears as an idea, the Promethean flame, the winging bird, the equality of the sexes principle, and even the conceptual image of 'the earth, like heaven, [having] its eclipses' which, in Hardy, takes the form of Eustacia's eclipse prefigured in her night watch with Clym.

But the reactionary *Saturday* now has its say. Launching into an attack on mutinous, rebellious women, the writer works up to a full discreditation of Sand, and concludes that,

> Many women would seem to be getting tired of what they call the tame and monotonous sphere in which they are confined, and demand that the same range of active life and personal freedom should be opened up to them which is allowed to men. . . . It may be believed that [George Sand] flung off conventional restraints, not so much under the influence of vicious passions as of rash and presumptuous confidence. . . . [But] it is the harmonious co-operation of the two distinct influences of manly force and womanly tenderness and spirituality, and not the confounding of them in one common form, which keeps society sound and strong.

Hardy's *Return of the Native* has the last word here. By way of a rejoinder, what the Egdon paradigm proclaims, with its embodiment of reciprocal female and male characteristics, is that it is not 'confounding' but *compounding* diverse gender attributes in 'one common form' which would 'keep society sound and strong'. (pp. 58-83)

> *Rosemarie Morgan, in her* Women and Sexuality in the Novels of Thomas Hardy, *Routledge, 1988, 205 p.*

FURTHER READING

Bibliography

Gerber, Helmut E., and Davis, W. Eugene. *Thomas Hardy: An Annotated Bibliography of Writings about Him,* 2 vols. De Kalb: Northern Illinois University Press, 1973-83.
> Includes a comprehensive list of periodicals and books which discuss *The Return of the Native.*

Biography

Hardy, Florence Emily. *The Life of Thomas Hardy, 1840-1928.* London: Macmillan, 1972, 616 p.
> Biography by Hardy's wife that is substantially composed of material from his journals and letters.

Howe, Irving. *Thomas Hardy.* New York: Macmillan, 1966, 206 p.
> Critical biography in which *The Return of the Native* is discussed as "the first book in which Hardy reaches toward grandiose 'literary' effects."

Millgate, Michael. *Thomas Hardy: His Career as a Novelist.* New York: Random House, 1965, 428 p.
> Critical biography of Hardy with a chapter devoted to *The Return of the Native.*

Criticism

Bayley, John. *An Essay on Hardy.* Cambridge: Cambridge University Press, 1978, 237 p.
> Wide-ranging discussion of Hardy's poetry and selected novels, with numerous references to *The Return of the Native.*

Bloom, Harold, ed. *Thomas Hardy's "The Return of the Native."* New York: Chelsea House, 1987, 152 p.
> Compilation of previously published essays.

Deen, Leonard W. "Heroism and Pathos in Hardy's *Return of the Native.*" *Nineteenth Century Fiction* 15, No. 3 (December 1960): 207-19.
> Compares the structure and characterization of *The Return of the Native* with heroic tragedy.

Eggenschwiler, David. "Eustacia Vye, Queen of Night and Courtly Pretender." *Nineteenth Century Fiction* 25, No. 4 (March 1971): 444-54.

Examines the concurrently tragic and comic aspects of Eustacia Vye.

Firor, Ruth A. *Folkways in Thomas Hardy.* Philadelphia: University of Pennsylvania Press, 1931, 357 p.

Discusses numerous legends, superstitions, and customs that appear in Hardy's novels, including the maypole ritual in *The Return of the Native.*

Giordana, Frank R., Jr. "Eustacia Vye's Suicide." *Texas Studies in Literature and Language* 22, No. 4 (Winter 1980): 504-21.

Examines the ambiguity of Eustacia Vye's death.

Gregor, Ian. *The Great Web: The Form of Hardy's Major Fiction.* London: Faber and Faber, 1974, 236 p.

Contains a chapter devoted to the novel which argues that "in *The Return of the Native* Hardy reveals himself as a major novelist; he sees for the first time his fictional world—and sees it whole."

Jordan, Mary Ellen. "Thomas Hardy's *Return of the Native:* Clym Yeobright and Melancholia." *American Imago* 39, No. 2 (Summer 1982): 101-18.

Psychological examination of Clym Yeobright.

Kramer, Dale. *Thomas Hardy: The Forms of Tragedy.* Detroit: Wayne State University Press, 1975, 190 p.

Focuses on the structure of Hardy's major novels, with a chapter devoted to *The Return of the Native.*

Lawrence, D. H. "A Study of Thomas Hardy." In his *Phoenix: The Posthumous Papers of D. H. Lawrence,* edited by Edward D. McDonald, pp. 398-516. New York: Viking, 1936.

Discusses the incompatibility between Clym and Eustacia.

Paterson, John. "The 'Poetics' of *The Return of the Native.*" *Modern Fiction Studies* VI, No. 3 (Autumn 1960): 214-22.

Asserts that *The Return of the Native* is "the most formal and even the most literary of Hardy's experiments in prose fiction."

Schweik, Robert C. "Theme, Character, and Perspective in Hardy's *The Return of the Native.*" *Philological Quarterly* XLI, No. 4 (October 1962): 757-67.

Argues that Hardy presents Clym from two perspectives: "as a potential hero who sees through the glitter of social shams to the human condition beneath and as the victim of a youthful fantasy that prevents him from understanding the connection between social progress and intellectual advancement."

Southerington, F. R. "*The Return of the Native:* Thomas Hardy and the Evolution of Consciousness." In *Thomas Hardy and the Modern World,* edited by F. B. Pinion, pp. 37-47. Dorchester, Dorset: The Thomas Hardy Society, 1974.

Considers *The Return of the Native* as a "study of the relationship between modes of perception and modes of living; or as a study of changing perceptions within the framework of time and the limitations of place."

Walcutt, Charles Child. "Character and Coincidence in *The Return of the Native.*" In *Twelve Original Essays on Great English Novels,* edited by Charles Shapiro, pp. 153-73. Detroit: Wayne State University Press, 1960.

Argues that Hardy's use of coincidence exempts his characters from blame so that "the flaws in the universe do not remove the flaws in the characters, and so the tension in the novel is sometimes painful rather than tragic."

Additional coverage of Hardy's life and career is contained in the following sources published by Gale Research: *Concise Dictionary of British Literary Biography, 1890-1914; Contemporary Authors,* Vols. 104, 123; *Dictionary of Literary Biography,* Vols. 18, 19; *Major 20th-Century Writers; Short Story Criticism,* Vol. 2; and *Something about the Author,* Vol. 25.; *Twentieth-Century Literary Criticism,* Vols. 4, 10, 18, 32; and *World Literature Criticism.*

D. H. Lawrence
Lady Chatterley's Lover

(Full name David Herbert Lawrence; also wrote under the pseudonym Lawrence H. Davison) English novelist, novella and short story writer, poet, essayist, translator, and dramatist.

The following entry presents criticism of Lawrence's novel *Lady Chatterley's Lover* (1928). For information on Lawrence's complete career, see *TCLC,* Volumes 2 and 9. For discussion of *Sons and Lovers,* see *TCLC,* Volume 16; for discussion of *Women in Love,* see *TCLC,* Volume 33.

INTRODUCTION

Lawrence's last and most controversial novel, *Lady Chatterley's Lover* focuses on the sexual relationship between a baroness and her husband's gamekeeper. This subject matter and the sexually explicit, often vulgar language of the novel elicited extreme responses from readers and critics. Banned in the United States and England, the novel was not legally available in an unabridged form until 1960. Considered artistically inferior to Lawrence's earlier masterpieces, including *Sons and Lovers* and *Women in Love, Lady Chatterley's Lover* is important for its bold treatment of human sexuality and as a major articulation of the social and psychological themes introduced in Lawrence's previous works.

Lawrence began writing *Lady Chatterley's Lover* in Italy in October 1926 after visiting the coal mining regions of Nottingham and Derby during the final months of a long and bitter strike. Considered his response to the class conflict implicit in the strike in his native region, Lawrence's novel called for social and individual renewal through the revitalization of human sexual relations. Lawrence produced three separate versions of *Lady Chatterley's Lover* between October 1926 and January 1928, all of which were eventually published under different titles. Although the story line remained for the most part the same in each version, Lawrence did alter some significant details between the initial and ultimate drafts of the novel. For instance, the gamekeeper's name was changed from Parkins to Mellors, and his ties to the working class were de-emphasized. Certain that no English or American publisher would handle the manuscript, Lawrence published *Lady Chatterley's Lover* privately in Italy, and later published an inexpensive paperback edition to combat the sales of pirated editions. Expurgated editions were published in the United States and England after Lawrence's death in 1930, and the first of the novel's three versions was published in 1944 as *The First Lady Chatterley.* The second version of the novel, *John Thomas and Lady Jane,* was published in 1972.

Early critical reaction to *Lady Chatterley's Lover* was dra-

matically divided. While some critics considered it a serious work of literature, others attacked it as mere pornography and called for its suppression. In 1959 and 1960, *Lady Chatterley's Lover* became the subject of obscenity trials in the United States and Great Britain. In the first case, a lawsuit brought by Grove Press against the Postmaster of the City of New York, the judge rescinded a postal ban on the distribution of the novel, determining that the work was not obscene. In the second trial, which took place before a full jury, Penguin Books was charged with violating England's Obscene Publications Act. Numerous writers and critics testified to the book's worth as literature, and the jury returned a verdict of not guilty, thus rendering publication of the novel legal in England.

As many critics have observed, the plot of *Lady Chatterley's Lover* is neither complex nor original. During the last year of World War I, Constance Reid marries Clifford Chatterley, the heir to Wragby Hall, an estate in the industrial region of England. Returning from the war impotent and paraplegic, Clifford adapts to his new condition: he writes short stories that achieve popular success, hosts parties, and succeeds in increasing the productivity of his coal mines. Feeling progressively cut off from her husband's affairs, Connie takes as a lover one of the young writers who frequents Wragby Hall. The relationship is short-lived and only deepens Connie's loneliness. During her solitary walks through the surrounding woods, a diminishing remnant of Sherwood Forest, Connie meets Mellors and the two become lovers. After becoming pregnant by Mellors, Connie asks Clifford for a divorce, which he refuses to grant after discovering the identity of her lover. Hoping to reunite in the spring and establish a small farm, Connie and Mellors leave Wragby Hall at the end of the novel, Connie for her family in Scotland and Mellors for a position at a Midlands farm.

Criticism of *Lady Chatterley's Lover* is most often concerned with the two related themes in the novel: the sexual theme of regeneration through intimate relationships and the social theme of conflict between the vitality of nature and the mechanized order of modern industrial society. In discussions of the sexual theme in *Lady Chatterley's Lover*, critics have accented the contrast between Clifford and Mellors, arguing that Clifford symbolizes death because of his impotence, intellectualism, and disdain for close emotional ties with others, whereas Mellors symbolizes life because of his association with nature and his uninhibited approach to sexual intercourse. Connie must choose between the two extremes represented by Clifford and Mellors and, through her sexual relations with Mellors, confirms her choice of life. Critics concerned with the social theme in *Lady Chatterley's Lover* consider the novel an indictment of industrial civilization. For example, Julian Moynahan has argued that the contrast between Clifford, who represents the devitalized quality of modern life and the mining village of Tevershall, with its appalling living conditions, indicates the class divisions inherent in industrialized culture. Similarly, the logging and mining which has depleted the forest, Mellors's home and the site of the love scenes, illustrates industry's assault on vitality. In her affair with Mellors, Connie crosses class boundaries, reestablishes contact with nature, and experiences a sexual and spiritual rebirth. Critics contend that, through Connie, Lawrence revealed the steps which society must take to regenerate itself.

Lawrence's use of vulgar language and his inclusion of a scene involving anal intercourse have prompted considerable critical commentary. Although previous writers had employed vulgarisms, Lawrence wished to "cleanse" these terms by using them in a manner that would not be perceived as obscene. H. M. Daleski has explained that, for Lawrence, it was the public attitude toward vulgar words, rather than the words themselves, that was obscene and indicative of the disdain with which people such as Clifford regard sex. While noting his intentions, critics have asserted that because such words cannot be divorced from their social context, they undermine Lawrence's attempt to depict sexual intercourse as a sacred rite. Similar to Lawrence's desire to cleanse obscene words, most critics contend that he included the anal intercourse scene to demonstrate that no part of the body or manner of sexual expression should be considered disgusting. However, Mellors's attitude of anger rather than love throughout the act has led critics to assert that this scene contradicts the quality of tenderness that Lawrence had been developing through his previous descriptions of sexual intercourse.

Despite the critical attention it has received, *Lady Chatterley's Lover* is not considered one of Lawrence's major novels. Many critics have found its tone didactic and its characters lacking in depth and complexity. Others have pointed to problems in Lawrence's presentation that inhibit the communication of the novel's themes. Nevertheless, critics concede that as an appraisal of modern society and as Lawrence's ultimate statement on the life-affirming element of human sexuality, *Lady Chatterley's Lover* will continue to be a much-read and much-studied novel. Moynahan has written that "*Lady Chatterley's Lover* is founded on a belief that the world is alive and that aliveness is the only thing worth cherishing. . . . More clearly and more persuasively than in any previous novel, Lawrence brings the reader into touch with that vision."

CRITICISM

J. Middleton Murry (essay date 1929)

[*Murry is recognized as one of the most significant English critics and editors of the twentieth century. Anticipating later scholarly opinion, he championed—through his positions as founding editor of the* Adelphi, *and as a regular contributor to the* Times Literary Supplement *—the writings of Marcel Proust, James Joyce, Paul Valéry, D. H. Lawrence, and Thomas Hardy. As with his magazine essays, Murry's book-length critical works are noted for their impassioned tone and startling discoveries; such biographically centered critical studies as* Keats and Shakespeare: A Study of Keats' Poetic Life from 1816-1820 *(1925) and* Son of Woman: The Story of D. H. Lawrence *(1931) contain esoteric, controversial conclusions that have angered scholars who favor more traditional approaches. Notwithstanding this criticism, Murry is often cited for his perspicuity, clarity, and supportive argumentation. His early exposition on literary appreciation,* The Problem of Style *(1922), is considered an informed guidebook for both critics and general readers. In it Murry espouses the theoretical premise underlying all his criticism, that in order to evaluate fully a writer's achievement, the critic must search for the crucial passages which effectively "crystallize" the writer's innermost impressions and convictions. Before 1926 when Lawrence broke off personal relations with him, Murry had been one of Lawrence's closest friends. In the following excerpt from an essay first published in the* Adelphi *in 1929, Murry provides an appraisal of* Lady Chatterley's Lover.]

One thing is certain. No one who reads ***Lady Chatterley's Lover*** to the end with the responsiveness without which the book is not merely obscene but nonsense as well, will be troubled by its obscenity. He will end by finding quite natural the repetition on a printed page of words which give him a turn when he finds them on the wall of a privy.

No ordinary alchemy is demanded for such a transmutation.

Mr. Lawrence, as all the world knows, happens to believe in Sex. He really does believe in it, and now he has reached a point where, on the surface at least, he believes in little else. There are, *apparently*, for him, about two ultimate realities in human life: one, the absolute and utter isolation of the individual, the other, the sole real emergence from that isolation in the perfect sexual fulfilment. When a man feels about sex with that degree of vehemence and conviction, it is quite impossible for him to be obscene in any but the Bow Street meaning.

The story of the book is quite simple; it tells of the discovery of each other by the wife of an aristocratic coal-owner, and her husband's gamekeeper—a man who (like others of Mr. Lawrence's heroes) has passed beyond class-distinction to an individual self-awareness—and of their progress towards the complete sexual fulfilment, which, Mr. Lawrence holds, contains the sole possibility of a new beginning for this worn-out world. As a narrative it is perfectly convincing: the two people are real, and most real precisely where Mr. Lawrence would have them appear most real, namely, in their sexual mating. But in such a narrative a philosophy is implicit; and the philosophy makes us pause. Not that we necessarily disagree with it. It leaves us with a feeling less of its untruth than of its incompleteness.

For the moment we will say that Mr. Lawrence's novel absolutely justifies itself. Rather paradoxically (if its philosophy were taken literally) it is the work of a very conscious man. Mr. Lawrence knows precisely what he is after in using the novel in this way. (p. 281)

In so far as ***Lady Chatterley's Lover*** causes the tide of our sensitive awareness to flow about the secret places of life—and it does this abundantly—it is not merely justified, but positively good. It is a cleansing book, the bringer of a new 'katharsis'.

But Mr. Lawrence does more than this: and it is the more which gives us pause. He is not content to say that it is right and necessary that men and women should come to a sensitive awareness of the sexual mystery; he goes on to say something much more questionable. He says, in effect, that the only sensitive awareness we need, the only one indeed that is real, is the awareness of and in the sexual mystery. The effect of this insistence is one of monotony, and finally, of almost suffocation. For all its fiery purity ***Lady Chatterley's Lover*** is a deeply depressing book. Were it not for a few words of unconscious wisdom from Lady Connie towards the end, we could scarcely breathe at all. Her words provoke a reluctant admission from Mellors, which is crucial. We will quote the passage in full. Lady Chatterley has been demanding that they should make a new life together. Mellors has been withdrawing into his old mistrust and aloofness. 'What *is* the point of your existence?' she suddenly asks.

> 'I tell you, it's invisible. I don't believe in the world, not in money, nor advancement, nor in the future of our civilisation. If there's got to be a future for humanity, there'll have to be a very big change from what now is.'

'And what will the real future have to be like?'

'God knows! I can feel something inside me, all mixed up with a lot of rage. But what it really amounts to, I don't know.'

'Shall I tell you?' she said, looking into his face. 'Shall I tell you what you have that other men don't have, and that will make the future? Shall I tell you?'

'Tell me then,' he replied.

'It's the courage of your own tenderness, that's what it is.' The grin came flickering on his face.

'That!' he said.

Then he sat thinking.

'Ay!' he said. 'You're right. It's that really. It's that all the way through. I knew it with the men. I had to be in touch with them, physically, and not go back on it. I had to be bodily aware of them and a bit tender to them, even if I put 'em through hell. It's a question of awareness, as Buddha said. But even he fought shy of the bodily awareness, and that natural physical tenderness, which is the best, even between men; in a proper manly way. Makes 'em really manly, not so monkeyish. Ay! it's tenderness, really. Sex is really only touch, the closest of all touch. And it's touch we're afraid of. We're only half-conscious, and half alive. We've got to come alive and aware. Especially the English have got to get into touch with one another, a bit delicate and a bit tender. It's our crying need.'

The Mellors of this dialogue is not far from Mr. Lawrence himself. For all practical purposes they are identical. It shows he must sometimes be asking himself whether he really has 'the courage of his own tenderness'. That tenderness is very great—unique in our generation. Why should it always (as it is in this book) 'be mixed up with a lot of rage'?

And the answer, we think, is this. Mr. Lawrence has the tenderness; but he has *not* got the courage of it. When it comes to having the courage of it, he will have it only where his courage is shocking. When the courage of his tenderness runs together with the current of his rage, then the flood-gates are opened; but not otherwise. What would the world think of him, if he were really to have the courage of his tenderness? God knows, but it might even love him. And that would be terrible. 'Hate me,' he implores, 'and for God's sake let me hate you.'

Probably there is no danger. If Mr. Lawrence really did have the full courage of his tenderness, it is not likely he would be loved. He would be hated rather more. He would become really dangerous, as he ought to be. He would become a leader, which he is not. As it is, he can be disregarded with ease, by those who wish to disregard him. He has chosen to be the prophet of a half-truth. It is the seed of a whole one, but why should they look for the seed? They take Mr. Lawrence at his own declared face value, and they do not trouble even to hate him.

'Sex is the closest of all touch.' True. It is the deepest and most primary touch: to be recognized, to become aware of, and to be obeyed. But is it the only touch? Do I not touch Mr. Lawrence at this moment through his book, even though he hides himself within? Veritably touch him, and closer than by laying my hand upon his arm? And do I not touch other men, long dead, and do they not touch me? Why should I deny them? Mr. Lawrence may, if he wills it so, but why should I? Organic contact is in many modes. In the name of one to deny the others is to impoverish life. Our duty is to see to it that the contact in every mode is organic indeed. We shall not reach a future by cutting ourselves off from the past; we shall only die. The tenderness of which we humans are capable has been painfully learned. Great men have shown us the way, sometimes they have given up their lives to shield the birth of a new tenderness in and through themselves. Mr. Lawrence wants to cheat himself, and us, into believing it was all there at the beginning. But even the sex relation which he would have us learn is not an old one; it is very new. A thousand other touches than the sexual in Mr. Lawrence have shaped it to what it is. To deny the obligation is ungrateful and untrue: worse still, it will prevent his ideal from being realized save in a false and perverted form.

Perhaps a word should be said on the question whether or not this book should be circulated. Certainly it is a book of the utmost value: for all its incompleteness and its still smouldering rage, a positive, living, and creative book. It glows with its own dynamic force, and in it is the courage of a new awareness. But it is no use pretending that all the world is fit to read it. If it were, Mr. Lawrence would have no excuse at all for his still smouldering rage. In a sense, therefore, the point of the book is that the world is not fit for it. If it could be circulated it would not be quite what it is. And it would be quite foolish to work up indignation because it has to creep into England. The necessity is implicit in the book itself.

After all, it is yet another nucleus, among the many which Mr. Lawrence has flung into the world, of a new kind of consciousness, which we believe must some day come. This consciousness will be conscious of many things besides those on which Mr. Lawrence insists; but of those on which he insists it must be conscious. Without this deep 'passional' awareness of which he chiefly has lit and guards the tender flame, the new consciousness can only be a sterile and intellectual thing—a mere combination of new words without vision, without meaning, without life, and without simplicity. In those who know in their depths what Mr. Lawrence is after, the seed he lets fall will grow. Like a growing thing it will push its way even through the denials which Mr. Lawrence himself would still impose upon it. There is no living element in life which it will not incorporate into its own tissue, if it is once received into good ground where it can bring forth thirty, or sixty, or a hundredfold.

That Mr. Lawrence shrinks from completing his own doctrine, and still rejects deliberately what some of us will not and cannot reject, is ultimately of small importance. It takes from his perfection, but not from his significance. On the level of this awareness, our criticism here is largely beside the mark. What Mr. Lawrence has to give is of a kind that completes itself: it is organic. And if our criticism should be used as an excuse for glancing aside the full impact of his latest, his calmest, and his most 'appalling' book, it had better not have been written. Assuredly it was not written for anyone who would abuse it thus. (pp. 282-84)

J. Middleton Murry, in a review of "Lady Chatterley's Lover," in D. H. Lawrence: The Critical Heritage, edited by R. P. Draper, Barnes & Noble, Inc., 1970, pp. 281-84.

F. R. Leavis (essay date 1961)

[*An influential English educator and critic, Leavis articulated his views in his lectures and his many critical works. His critical methodology combines close textual analysis, predominantly moral and social concerns, and emphasis on the development of "the individual sensibility." Leavis believed that the writer, who represents "the most conscious point of the race" in his or her lifetime, should strive to eliminate "ego-centered distortion and all impure motives" to promote "sincerity," or the realization of the individual's proper place in human society. Literature which accomplishes this he calls "mature." Although Leavis's advocacy of a cultural elite, the vagueness of his moral assumptions, and his refusal to develop a systematic philosophy have alienated many scholars from his work, he remains an important, if controversial, force in literary criticism. In the following excerpt, he argues that* Lady Chatterley's Lover *is not representative of Lawrence's creative genius but rather the didactic tirade of a dying man.*]

To make sure, in commenting briefly on the court proceedings over **Lady Chatterley's Lover,** that the note one hits on won't lead to one's being misunderstood isn't altogether easy. If one says that the Prosecution failed because it was as inept as the Defence was ludicrous, one might be supposed to be wishing it had been less inept. And who could have hailed the success of the Prosecution as a good thing—a proof and promise of health and creative vitality in our civilisation? Yet I have to point out that the Prosecution was defeated, not by the presentment of any sound or compelling case, but by its realisation that it was confronted by a new and confident orthodoxy of enlightenment—that the world had changed since the virginal pure policemen came and hid their faces for very shame. And one has to recognise that, if there had to be, as the upshot of a court trial, a definitive registration of this change in society, the thing could hardly have occurred in any essentially different way from that which has its record in [*The Trial of Lady Chatterley,* ed. C. H. Rolph]. I mean, in any way less disturbing to the literary critic and admirer of Lawrence.

I express here, of course, my conviction that the outcome of the trial cannot at best be seen as pure gain from the point of view I have just indicated. A fair appraisal of the probable consequences would be a delicate matter. But this is certain: a real advance, in the sense represented by Lawrence, depends upon the existence of a body of genuinely enlightened opinion, ensuring that the nature of

Lawrence's genius and achievement shall be widely understood, so that these may have their proper force. ***Lady Chatterley's Lover,*** then—it is important that this obvious enough truth should be recognised—is a bad novel. Moreover, to assert, as was done again and again during the trial, and made a major point in the final speech for the Defence, that without having read it one cannot truly appreciate Lawrence's other works, and so cannot have received what the great and salutary creative writer of our time has to give, is to betray and further an alarming misconception of his genius and what he actually achieved. It is to misrepresent this disastrously. For the experts did not mean by their testimony that ***Lady Chatterley's Lover,*** in giving us something that violates Lawrence's own essential canons as an artist, serves as a foil to his successful and great art, and in that way may be used as an aid to its critical appreciation. The book should be current as an unquestioned literary classic—this was essential to the case for the Defence.

One of the witnesses, testifying to Lawrence's earnest and wholly conscious intentness on his purpose in writing the book, speaks of his 'integrity.' Well, no one would suggest that Lawrence was deceiving himself in his conviction that his hatred of pornography was complete. But the integrity we demand of an artist is a rarer thing than that which we testify to (perhaps) in a politician. Lawrence himself, in postulating it as the essential aim in both life and art, insisted on the most exacting conception and criteria. He is insisting on them in his caveats against 'will' and 'idea' (terms, in his use of them, intimately related).

'Will' and 'idea' certainly play a part in ***Lady Chatterley's Lover*** that the normal creative and critical Lawrence would have diagnosed and condemned. He is *not* the normal Lawrence in this novel—a point unwittingly made by one of the experts in the trial when, exalting Lawrence's 'integrity' of purpose, he says that the book might almost be called a tract (though there is a consensus among the witnesses that it is something else). Lawrence, of course, meant it to have the integrity of a creative work. But at this moment of his life he was too possessed by his passionate didactic purposes to be capable of achieving *that,* or of recognising his failure (he was ill—in fact, for all his incredible vitality, slowly dying—and inflamed with rage and disgust at the thought of the 'virginal pure policemen'). That this was his state, this the essential case, should be manifest to the reader in the business of the 'four-letter words.' The intense earnestness of the hygienic aim can't be doubted, and I needn't discuss whether or not we can reasonably think of it as justified by probable success: it *is* a hygienic purpose, that is the unanswerable point I have to make. We have here, in obviously questionable relation to creative integrity, the assertive presence of 'will' and 'idea.'

But equally we have this presence, on a large scale, and in no less—or so it seems to me—questionable relation to creative wholeness in the artist, in the insistent renderings of sexual experience (sensations, emotions, and all the physical details). How these are essential to Lawrence's enterprise has been explained in the pages of the *Spectator* as well as by the body of testifying experts. They represent a hygienic purpose and they certainly engage the creative art of the creative writer. To me, I must report, a great deal in them has always been strongly distasteful, and has not become less so now that, yet again, I reread them thirty years after I read them first. The expert may perhaps comment that *that* only shows how little I have yet been able to submit myself to the beneficent potency of which I am still in need.

That might seem to be a difficult retort to answer. Yet I remain convinced that my distaste is something that the normal Lawrence, the creative Lawrence, would have shared and justified; that (whether in his abnormal state he was aware of it or not) the will to write those passages had had a resistance to overcome, and the price of the overcoming was the artist's integrity in the profounder sense: the wholeness was violated. Lawrence would have had a resistance to overcome in himself uttering the 'four-letter words' with the ease and freedom with which the gamekeeper and Tommy Dukes use them. In the way of those frequent and insistent offers to evoke sexual experience in pondered, dwelling immediacy there was a deep-seated *pudeur,* going back to a finely civilised upbringing in a Victorian working-class home. This *pudeur* became in the developed and mature Lawrence the exquisitely sensitive human delicacy of the great artist—something so patently manifested in his novels and tales that we don't need the extraneous evidence we have that he didn't like 'emancipation.'

Still, if readers—experts and others—insist that they feel no distaste, and that they confidently judge these passages, and kindred things in the book, to be justified by success, and to be thoroughly *of* the tenderness (a word made almost unusable in relation to Lawrence by the witnesses), the life and the beauty of the creative whole, we shall hardly get further here by argument: we are faced by a conflict of reports. Nevertheless, that the passionate drive of willed purpose in ***Lady Chatterley's Lover*** is attended by evidences of a disrupted integration in the artist, by a failure of unified wholeness in his imaginative engagement, such a failure as makes the novel a bad one from any defensible point of view, is, I think, indisputable: there are manifestations to point to, the clear significance of which, once the attention rests on them, can hardly be questioned. It has, of course, been suggested that Sir Clifford's paralysis, so usefully symbolic to exegetes and experts, is not altogether a felicity. Lawrence himself agreed that this might be so, but defended himself by saying that so the tale 'came' to him and continued to 'come,' and that he had to keep it so, by the law of creative integrity.

But even a Laurentian genius in Lawrence's state cannot (the penalty of indulging the quasi-creative intervention of passionate will, didactic, corrective and reforming) trust what 'comes' to him: his unity is broken, he cannot be engaged as a whole, his touch is no longer sure. And the questionableness of Mellors is still more destructive of the claim that ***Lady Chatterley's Lover*** is a good novel, or a decent work of art, or a convincing piece of reinforced didacticism, than the questionableness of Sir Clifford. Why does Lawrence make the lover working-class? The answer (not given by any of the experts) is that Lawrence doesn't.

The gamekeeper is not only educated, he is an intellectual—we are told of the impressive array of books he has on his shelf. Moreover, having (we learn from Sir Clifford) held a commission, he is irretrievably and securely a 'gentleman': he has obviously the manners, the poise, the right distinction of appearance when properly dressed, and Connie reflects that he 'can go anywhere.' Why, then, does Lawrence make him drop into the dialect—drop so much and on those occasions?

A simple and (I imagine) generally acceptable answer is that Mellors's use of the dialect is a way of putting over the 'four-letter words'—of trying to make the idea of their being redeemed for non-obscene and undefiant, or 'normal,' use look less desperate. When used by Tommy Dukes in the intellectual talk that takes place among Sir Clifford's cronies, one can't be certain how much distaste Lawrence means them to evoke, but they certainly evoke distaste (it has its part in the general unpleasant effect produced by Tommy Dukes's emancipation). It is significant that, when she first takes note of the keeper, Connie reflects that he 'reminds her curiously of Tommy Dukes.' But Mellors can turn on the dialect. And when he does there is a 'curious' effect (I find it hateful—and it seems to me a paradigm of much that I find hateful in the book) of its being Lawrence who turns it on. Along with the dialect go, not only those words, but all those brutally insistent inflictions on Connie (and us) of 'uninhibited' talk in keeping with the words.

If I find these performances on Mellors's part insufferable, I am sure that it isn't merely because of my still unvanquished *pudeur*. There is something hateful conveyed in the intention (here) of the dialect itself—something hateful conveyed in the turning-on. Connie perceives it and on occasion protests. We are told that she 'never knew how to take him when he used the dialect.' But Sir Clifford, in the hostile exchanges with the keeper, knows.

It is in place here to note that the outburst of bitterly ugly impassioned contempt for the 'middle-classes' that Mellors attributes to his Colonel ('who loved him') is relayed to Connie in the dialect. It comes, we feel, from Lawrence himself, direct. Not, I must add at once, from the whole Lawrence—from the great clairvoyant artist who said that he wrote 'out of a deep moral sense—for the race, as it were.' It is the lack of *that* impersonality which makes so much of *Lady Chatterley's Lover* repellent.

Those who suggest . . . that Mellors's working-class status—what he has of it—must be taken as conveying something positive and basic in relation to Lawrence's otherwise despairing critique of modern civilisation insult Lawrence—his character and intelligence. He had no illusions about the working classes. He was in general without class-feeling, and nothing could be more ridiculous than the one-time orthodoxy that called him a snob. Nevertheless, his history had left somewhere in him a dormant exasperation, contemptuous and resentful—it betrays itself in his calling Jane Austen a 'narrow-gutted spinster.' It is this Lawrence we have, unmistakably, in the Colonel's—or the keeper's or Lawrence's—tirade. If only we could confine him there the constatation need not have been critically very damaging. But the obtrusive presence is only the clear sign of something generally and radically wrong—the failure of wholeness of engagement, of insight and self-knowledge, of intelligence, in the creative Lawrence. It is not easy to say with any precision just how Mellors's treatment of Connie (Lawrence's treatment of the relations between Mellors and Connie) is involved, but, Mellors being the equivocal figure he is, uneasinesses and suspicions and distastes cannot be banished.

As for the treatment of Sir Clifford, the significantly manifest scandal of that can hardly be denied. Professor D. W. Harding, with some irony of understatement, has remarked in the *Spectator* that the burden of symbolic responsibilities laid on Sir Clifford grows unquestionably large. What most disturbs me is the animus Lawrence has developed towards him by the close. It is embarrassing, not because one sympathises with Sir Clifford, but because of the evidence that something has gone radically wrong with Lawrence.

Of course, Mellors helps to give plausibility to the suggestion that the treatment of the personal theme gives us at the same time a diagnosis of industrial civilisation. Actually, the evoked Midland *décor* remains merely *décor*. Industrial civilisation doesn't really enter into a just appraisal of Connie's behaviour. Nor can Lawrence's presentment of that be shown to be a vindication of marriage, or an incitement to realising the difficulty and importance of achieving a permanent relation, by quoting, as was done for the Defence, '**A Propos of** *Lady Chatterley's Lover*.' What that truly Laurentian classic betrays is the misgiving Lawrence himself had about the novel, of which it constitutes, in its essential incongruity, an admonitory criticism. (pp. 229-30)

> F. R. Leavis, "The New Orthodoxy," in The Spectator, *Vol. 2016, No. 6921, February, 1961, pp. 229-30.*

Ian Gregor (essay date 1962)

[*In the following excerpt, Gregor contends that Lawrence's attempt to express his ideas on sex in* Lady Chatterley's Lover *is detrimental to its effectiveness as a novel.*]

'The essential function of art is moral,' Lawrence wrote in an essay on Whitman, 'not aesthetic, nor decorative, not pastime and recreation. But moral.' It is a remark which has been widely quoted and echoed in the literary criticism of the last thirty years. What, however, has been noticeably less publicized is the sentences which follow it: 'But a passionate, implicit morality, not didactic. A morality which changes the blood' should be sufficient to warn us that Lawrence's conception of the moral function of art was not quite as transparent in meaning as it is often made to appear.

This passage, with its simple assertion and dark qualification, reflects, in a small way, the whole conflict and uncertainty that arise when we come to look at the relationship of the moral to the story in Lawrence's work. In the early novels this relationship is obviously present, but it remains in the background; in *Lady Chatterley's Lover* it is the very subject with which the novelist is concerned. Thus, we are not surprised to find in this novel one of the most famous descriptions of the purpose of the Novel as a literary form. And Lawrence uses Clifford's writing of short stories as a way of making a moral point about him, just as he later defines Mrs. Bolton's gossip by saying that it was 'Mrs. Gaskell, and George Eliot, and Miss Mitford all rolled into one'. *Lady Chatterley's Lover* is very much a novel which is concerned, implicitly at least, with the status of the Novel—a status which is described in Lawrence's remark that it is 'necessary for us now'. What is interesting about a claim like this is not its justice or otherwise, but its unusualness. . . . Consequently, it is not surprising to find that a novel for which such claims are made readily lends itself to a moral defence, should it be needed. Equally clearly, it is vulnerable to moral attack, because if a novel which asserts that 'it is necessary for us now' is found not to be so, it is more than likely to be found 'dangerous'. The artist who contends for a socially therapeutic function exposes himself to the risk, at least, of being accused of quackery.

In *Lady Chatterley's Lover* we find, carried to an extreme, positions which are present in all of Lawrence's work, positions, moreover, which are largely responsible for his swift rise in prestige during the last ten years or so. To begin with, there is the importance with which he invests the medium of the novel, 'it can help us to live as nothing else can.' In a period when literary critics have seen themselves increasingly as custodians of a humane culture against the encroachments of mass civilization, so that the study of literature can become an educational touchstone in a more far-reaching way than it has ever been before, Lawrence's claims for the novel bring assurance and inspiration. The only art he is concerned with begins with a small letter, and it ministers dedicatedly to his vision of life, which is both diagnostic and prophetic. In the general contemporary breakdown of communal purpose, a personal vision, expressed with the conviction and power which Lawrence had at his command, comes to be valued for its own sake. Integrity of purpose provides its own justification.

Given this kind of purpose and vision, it is inevitable that the form of the novel will undergo radical changes. But there will be nothing doctrinaire, 'experimental' about such changes, and, if his novels look different from the traditional nineteenth-century novel, the impulse for such a revolution is moral rather than aesthetic. It is within this perspective that we notice 'character' giving way to 'consciousness' in his work, narrative outline being replaced by symbol and theme, conclusions being subordinate to explorations. These were highly congenial shifts for a critical age which had learnt that in art 'there is always another story, there is more than meets the eye', and had inquired, with irony, how many children had Lady Macbeth? If Lawrence's novels were much to our taste in reading fiction, they were no less well suited to our talking and writing about it. The way, for instance, in which they suddenly concentrate themselves into brief scenes of overwhelming immediacy was particularly rewarding to that kind of detailed, local analysis of verbal texture which is such a marked feature of our critical practice. And if his work rewarded us where our critical methods are strongest, it did not disturb us where these methods are weakest. 'Conclusions', in Lawrence, are very much a matter veiled and obscure, but we have absorbed so thoroughly the implications of Mr. Eliot's dictum—'when we consider poetry, it is as poetry we must consider it, and not as another thing'—that we are extremely reluctant to pursue a literary discussion beyond the bounds of formal analysis, even while recognizing the arbitrary nature of that boundary. . . . If this has been an age remarkable both for the quality and the quantity of its literary criticism, it has found in the work of Lawrence notable reassurance and stimulus. Indeed, it seems to me likely that, when future literary historians come to look back on the present period, they will see the legal vindication of *Lady Chatterley's Lover* marking not so much a stage in 'literary freedom', as the high-watermark and triumph of a particular phase of literary criticism. There is, however, as the phrase 'literary freedom' suggests, another side to this story.

The fact that *Lady Chatterley's Lover* can raise such an issue as 'freedom of expression' points to the deep disturbance that the novel has always provoked in a great number of readers. If the legal expression of this disturbance is, from the literary point of view, naïve and crude, this should not be allowed to obscure the fact that it is connected with other reactions, which are certainly not naïve or crude. Lawrence may have regarded the novel as 'the bright book of life', but the novelist, he felt, had to have inside him, 'something vicious, old Adamish, incompatible to the ordinary man'. And so we find, throughout Lawrence's work, intense affirmations arising out of no less intense negations. 'Life' is affirmed when the conventional moral pattern is exposed for the deathly thing it is; the self emerges properly only when notions of personality have been abandoned; the vitality of his particular episodes overwhelms because it breaks down that contemplative response, that aesthetic distance, which we usually associate with successful art. Thus it becomes a commonplace to say that in reading Lawrence we find ourselves constantly thrown into a state of violent endorsement or violent rejection. In *Lady Chatterley's Lover* there are intense affirmations of the importance of creativity, and the reader who responds to them will make his account of the novel a matter of illustrating clearly its overt seriousness of purpose, its relevance for 'our time'; and he will endorse this by pointing to its liberating honesty in its treatment of sexual relationships, its diagnosis of and opposition to the acquisitive spirit of the age, its tender, perhaps lyrical descriptions of human love and the natural life of the wood. He will probably choose, as an epigraph for his account, Lawrence's statement of purpose:

> I always labour at the same thing, to make the sex relation valid and precious, instead of shameful. And this novel is the furthest I've gone. To me it is beautiful and tender as the naked self. . . .

Those, however, who see in *Lady Chatterley* the pressure of nihilism will maintain that it is a novel which attacks the dignity and responsibility of the person, that it proclaims the infallibility of feelings, and that it turns sex into a psychotheology for the elect. The epigraph chosen here is likely to record the mood present in Mellors's remark:

> 'I feel the colonies aren't far enough. The moon wouldn't be far enough, because there you could look back and see the earth, dirty, beastly, unsavoury among all the stars: made foul by men.'

'Reverence', 'disgust'—the attitudes behind these passages can lead the reader, in his turn, into expressions of high moral approval and vehement moral condemnation. A close examination of the novel may help to show the reason for these antithetical views and allow a judgment between them; what it will certainly show is that this is a kind of opposition which makes *Lady Chatterley's Lover* the most curious moral 'case' in the whole range of English fiction.

'Ours is essentially a tragic age,' the novel begins, but 'we've got to live, no matter how many skies have fallen.' In that statement and counter-statement the novel takes its shape and meaning; it is concerned on the one hand to analyse and present us with the 'tragedy', and on the other to reveal the 'life' that must oppose it.

Lawrence embodies this in a tale which has the severe outlines of fable. 'Once upon a time . . .', the narrative simplicity of *Lady Chatterley's Lover* is of that kind, and it would be a mistaken perspective which concentrated on complexity of plot. All that needs to be said, at this level, can be tersely said. There is the marriage in the last year of the First World War of Connie Reid with Clifford Chatterley, heir to a large estate in the Midlands. A year later Clifford succeeds to the estate, but he has been fatally crippled and made impotent by the war. He learns to adapt himself to his new life, inviting house parties of his friends and writing short stories which soon become fashionably successful. Connie, increasingly lonely and cut off from her husband's world, takes as a lover one of the young writers who visit their home. It is very much an affair of the moment and her sense of loneliness deepens. Only by walking in the estate which surrounds the house is she able to find a sense of peace and satisfaction, particularly by watching the gamekeeper Mellors at work building coops for the pheasants and feeding the chickens. Her intimacy with him grows and they become lovers. Clifford has now revived his early interests in engineering and he is intent on restoring industrial prosperity to the area. The gulf between him and his wife is now virtually complete. Connie's family invite her to Venice for a holiday, knowing that she will use the opportunity it offers to tell Clifford that she is going to have a child and that she wishes a divorce. For a time, Mellors's name is kept out of the affair, but local scandal takes over and his relationship with Connie becomes public news. Clifford, infuriated, refuses Connie a divorce; she leaves him and goes to stay with her family until such time as she can rejoin Mellors, whose divorce against his own unfaithful wife is pending.

Clearly the narrative as such is not one that commands much interest; there is very little progression of incident and what there is seems forced on the novelist. It is only in the last three chapters that anything resembling plot comes into being, and there it has an apologetic and makeshift air. The novel is driven not by developing incident but rather by the friction of antitheses. It is the constantly repeated antitheses of setting and character that constitute the power-centres of the book, each being vitally connected to the other.

Lady Chatterley's Lover is rooted in a deep sense of region, at once intensely localized, a precise part of the Nottinghamshire-Derbyshire border, and intensely stylized. Connie goes for a drive by car, and the local villages pass by, Tevershall, Stacks Gate, Shipley, the car crosses the railway lines as they curve north to Sheffield, and then turns sharply west to Matlock. It is a region of great houses falling into decay, Nonconformist chapels, miners' cottages, new council estates, corner-end shops, and then, suddenly, long rolling woods which end abruptly on the slag heaps of a colliery. As Connie makes her journey we can make it too, gazetteer in hand. But there is another way of regarding this setting, a way in which all particularities fade and we are left looking at a gaunt stage-setting for a morality play. Instead of the traditionally opposed entrances of Heaven and Hell, we have, on the right, the fretted silhouette of a great wood, and on the left, the pyramid outline of the colliery slag heap, and the shadows of both darken the facade of the great house which is placed in the centre of the stage. Continually, we have the double awareness of the setting, realism is shot through with symbolism and vice versa. As Connie and Mellors walk through the wood at night, they see, shining through the leaves, the winking lights of the colliery; as the sun comes up it is the pit hooters which break their sleep. When Connie looks at the clouds at night she sees them streaked with red from the blast furnaces, and she notices that the main path which runs through the wood is gravelled with the refuse of the pit-bank, so that, when it rains, it turns a dull pink. Everywhere this contrast is present and it is absolute. Even when Connie moves about the house she can hear 'the rattle-rattle of the screens at the pit, the puff of the winding engine, the click-click of shunting trucks and the hoarse little whistle of the colliery locomotive. Tevershall pit-bank was burning, had been burning for years and it would cost thousands to put out. So it had to burn. And when the wind was that way, which was often, the house was full of the stench of this sulphurous combustion of the earth's excrement. But even on windless days the air always smelt of something under-earth; sulphur, iron, coal or acid. And even on the Christmas roses the smuts settled persistently, incredible, like black manna from the skies of doom.' 'Black manna from the skies of doom . . .', the disfiguring of the earth coming as a warning from the gods, the physical scene intimating a spiritual doom. One antithesis discloses another, setting gives way to character.

We have observed the machine that is outside the wood, dominating the horizon, colouring the night skies, echoing through the house; but, more deadly, we have the machine inside the park. It is a Sunday morning, pear and plum are in blossom, and the sound of shunting trucks has been replaced by church bells. Connie has taken Clifford out in his motorized chair, 'quiet and complacent, Clifford sat at the wheel of adventure. . . .' And then, as they are returning, the chair jerks to a halt and stops. Clifford shouts for Mellors to help and 'they waited among the mashed flowers under a sky softly curdling with cloud.' He arrives but is unable to find the fault. Clifford runs the engine viciously, it clicks into action, he refuses Mellors's offer of help; suddenly the chair lurches and virtually falls. Mellors saves it. Again Clifford orders him to leave it. The brake jams and Clifford is now quite helpless. He abuses Mellors but eventually has to ask for his assistance. Connie helps too. 'At the top of the hill they rested and Connie was glad to let go. She had had fugitive dreams of friendship between these two men: one her husband, the other the father of her child. Now she saw the screaming absurdity of her dreams. The two males were as hostile as fire and water. They naturally exterminated one another. . . .' 'Now she saw . . .', it is the machine which has revealed the nature of her husband to her, dominant yet impotent, asserting his will over the machine, turning it into a moral support, blind to the fact that he is utterly dependent upon it, morally as well as physically. ' "Thanks so much, Mellors," said Clifford, when they were at the house door. "I must get a different sort of motor—that's all." ' Connie looks at Clifford, and then at Mellors, and sees now the kind of opposition between them; she sees that the machine can indicate a dimension of soul as well physical fact. In this, of course, we see plainly Lawrence's inheritance from a whole tradition of nineteenth-century social and political thinking. In 1829, for instance, we find Carlyle writing: 'Not the external and physical alone is now managed by machinery, but the internal and spiritual also . . . men are grown mechanical in head and in heart as well as in hand.' It is a contention which we can find as early as Blake and appearing in Cobbett, in Dickens and Matthew Arnold, in Ruskin and William Morris, and it is within that social tradition that Lawrence writes. But this scene illuminates for Connie not simply Clifford's relationship with the machine but his relationship with Mellors, 'the two males were as hostile as fire and water.' And it is this note which is uniquely Lawrence's, namely his presentation of character in terms of consciousness.

It is a presentation which, on the whole, is alien to change or development, consisting mainly of increasingly forceful repetitions of the datum. . . . Clifford's essential datum is given to us very early in the novel: 'He was remotely interested: but like a man looking down a microscope or up a telescope. He was not in touch. He was not in actual touch with anybody. . . .' He is insulated by instruments from the world in which he lives, he sees the miners as 'labour' serving his engineering experiments; he hears of the outside world through the radio and a voice from Frankfurt or Madrid is closer to him than his wife's. When he seeks his leisure, he plays chess with his nurse throughout the night in the intimacy of his bedroom, with a terrible kind of perverted lust. The withering of his emotional and sentient life has created a vacuum which has been filled by pure mind and will. He can no longer live above the earth, 'he felt life rush into him out of the coal, out of the pit. The very stale air of the colliery was better than oxygen to him.' He can only live in an atmosphere of death and consequently, when Connie looks at him, his eyes are vacant, when she touches him, he is cold. Desperately she turns away, not so much in search of a person as in search of life itself. And it is precisely not as a person, but as a power, that she first encounters Mellors.

Walking out with Clifford in the estate she meets the new gamekeeper and is startled, 'he seemed to emerge with such a swift menace . . . like the sudden rush of a threat out of nowhere.' Throughout the novel this associated sense of mysterious power and indefinable danger is an intrinsic part of the presentation of Mellors, and clearly, however elusive this aura is to define, it is the antithesis of the 'deathliness' of Clifford. Whatever human characteristics Mellors possesses, we feel, are there to serve this 'life' that he possesses, and this life is not something that can be understood in terms of personal qualities. Mellors is like a medium who is capable of transmitting a life to others, a capacity which cannot be thought of as coextensive with his conscious intention or individual ability. When Connie first meets Mellors she notes his isolation, 'why was he so aloof, apart?', 'a man very much alone, yet on his own', 'a pallor of isolation came over him'. But this remoteness, this isolation is very different from Clifford's—where his proceeds from hatred of life, Mellors's comes from fear of its terrible and necessary claims:

> Especially he did not want the old contact with a woman again. He feared it; for he had a big wound from old contacts. . . . His recoil from the outer world was complete; his last refuge was this wood, to hide himself there.

It is here, in the wood, that he meets Connie and their relationship begins.

> 'I thought I'd done with it all. Now I've begun again.'
>
> 'Begun what?'
>
> 'Life.'
>
> 'Life,' she re-echoed with a queer thrill.
>
> 'It's life,' he said, 'there's no keeping clear. And if you do keep clear you might almost as well die. So I've got to be broken open again. . . .'

This is an interesting conversation not only because it hints at the moral calculus Lawrence is employing, but because it suggests how that calculus works. The key lies in the concept of 'Life'. Clifford 'dies' because he tries to keep clear, which means shutting down his affective nature; Mellors 'lives' because he realizes in time the folly of such an attempt. It is in the sexual relationship that 'Life' is most fully embodied, and it is embodied there because, as Mellors says, 'sex is really only touch, the closest possible touch', and as Lawrence says elsewhere, because it is in sex that 'man comes to the limits of himself and becomes aware of something beyond him . . . aware of what surpasses him.' Both of these assertions must be borne in mind if we are to understand the centrality of sex for Lawrence, but it is important to notice their order. There is first the assertion that the fulfilment of the individual human life depends upon our capacity for intimate sensual relationship with one another, found most completely in sex. And then, consequent on the first assertion, is the second: in the achievement of this relationship we come into union with the very source of Life itself. Arguing that Lawrence's preoccupations are religious rather than ethical, F. R. Leavis writes of the characters in *The Rainbow:*

'Each lover is for the other a "door"; an opening into the "unknown", by which the horizon, the space of life, is immensely expanded, and unaccepted limits that had seemed final are "transgressed".'

When we stop regarding Mellors as an example of cosmic force and look at him as an individual, we feel a steep decline in Lawrence's creative interest. Faced with the social and economic questions of the day, Mellors emerges as a disillusioned Luddite: 'I'd wipe the machines off the face of the earth and end the industrial epoch absolutely, like a black mistake. But since I can't and nobody can, I'd better hold my peace and try and live my own life.' On two occasions Connie asks what he would like to see in place of the industrial society which he opposes so bitterly, but his proposals for the Revival of Folk Culture fail to hold even her attention. Like Mellors, Lawrence has no hopes in this direction either, and the social gesture is a routine impulse. If there is hope it lies only in the individual life, and Mellors concludes by saying: 'You can't insure against the future, except by really believing in the best bit of you. So I believe in the little flame between us. For me now, it's the only thing in the world.' However desperate the hope may be, the novel ends by endorsing it. Mellors has emerged from his isolation, been broken open by the emotional and sensual claims of another person, and agreed to the responsibilities entailed, suitably symbolized by his approaching fatherhood.

Connie's development in the novel lies in her rejection of Clifford and in her acceptance of Mellors, and it should be clear by now that in saying this we are not saying that she has come to hate one person and love another, so much as that she has learnt that a man can die without ceasing to exist, and that an adult can be born into life as surely as a child can. Like Clifford, and like Mellors, Connie also is out of contact at the beginning of the story, 'an inward dread, an emptiness, an indifference to everything gradually spread in her soul.' Her condition, however, has to be distinguished from theirs—where one is detached, and the other enclosed, she is lonely. Even in her loneliness, she reacts strongly and sensitively against the world of Clifford, and the whole of the first part of the book is taken up, as far as she is concerned, with these negative reactions. There is opposition to the world of talk with which he surrounds himself, antipathy to his malicious short stories and to his olympian plans for the redirection of labour, 'she could not help feeling how little connection he had with people. The miners were, in a sense, his own men, but he saw them as objects rather than as men, parts of the pit rather than parts of life, crude raw phenomena rather than human beings along with him.' Correlated with this is his attitude towards the wood as a kind of museum of memories, 'I want this wood perfect, *untouched,* I want nobody to trespass in it' (my italics). But for Connie, the miners are human beings who have been broken by the world in which they live, and the wood is the only living thing that she knows, '. . . she sat down with her back to a young pine tree that swayed against her with curious life, elastic, and powerful and rising up. The erect live thing with its top in the sun.' Obviously, we see here a foreshadowing in terms of the wood of her subsequent sexual response to Mellors. The more complete her rejection of the Clifford world, the more she is made open to the life that is to come to her. She feels it first in the wood, and then, more explicitly, when she watches Mellors feeding the chickens, 'life, life, pure sparky fearless new life. For in a moment a tiny, sharp head was poking through the gold brown feathers of the hen and eyeing the Cosmos. Connie was fascinated. And at the same time never had she felt so acutely the agony of her own female forlornness.' It is in this mood of desolation that Mellors sees her, is touched, and their relationship begins. And almost immediately it finds expression in sexual terms, because all that Lawrence is concerned to do is to bring to Connie 'life' where up to now she has found 'death'. I put it this way in order to emphasize how very far from Lawrence's interest or purpose is the creation of a realistic human situation, of anything resembling what is usually understood by a 'love story'. If we argue that the progress of Connie's relationship with Mellors and his with her is lacking in credibility or in variety, we are really asking for a portrait, where the whole structure of **Lady Chatterley's Lover** has been designed to take X-ray photographs. Consequently, when we say that the sexual episodes have to be seen in the context of the whole story, we shall look in vain if we think that Lawrence is presenting them as only an element in the relationship of Connie and Mellors. They are, as everyone knows, the total relationship, but they are this not because Lawrence imagined this was how people actually lived or how they ought to live, but because Lawrence is relating a fable and a fable does not attempt to copy reality in this way. Lawrence's fable is concerned to isolate and plot the interaction of two forces, to which he gives the simple labels of 'life' and 'death'. We don't need to cavil about the labels, they are only there to suggest an archetypal opposition. The drama, however, must be a human one, because it is only in human beings that these forces exist. Given this, it is reduced to the simplest possible shape, with one character embodying death, another life, and a third the victim of one or the other. Connie resolves it by finding 'life' in her sexual relationship with Mellors. It is not happiness that she aims at, but salvation. Giving the words their full weight, we might say that the upshot of **Lady Chatterley's Lover** is that a woman learns to live her life, and we all have to learn what that means.

Up to now I have been describing the kind of novel **Lady Chatterley's Lover** aims to be. Whether it succeeds or not is another question, but obviously it is one which is contingent upon its aim. The intention is plain, the structure of the novel should make it clear beyond dispute; but no one was more trenchant than Lawrence in warning us against accepting intention as achievement: 'Let me hear what the novel says. As for the novelist, he is usually a dribbling liar.' If the storm of controversy that has followed the publication of the novel is any indication, then this novel would appear to say a great number of contradictory things. Immediately, the question must arise: why should a novel with such a markedly simple outline as **Lady Chatterley** have given rise to the kind of dispute which I [have] described? . . . Admittedly, some of the opposition arises out of, or is related to, Lawrence's employment of a number of words usually considered taboo, but it would be readily granted by both 'sides' that that is merely a symptom of a disagreement much more radical than one over the use of an offensive vocabulary. What would seem to be at stake is Lawrence's whole attitude in the novel. (pp. 217-30)

The most useful starting point here is to look again at Lawrence's presentation of character. If we assemble the various details we are given about Clifford and think of them in relation to his dramatic role, we shall find a man who is physically crippled, isolated, self-centred, devoted to the life of the mind and the worship of the machine. If we do the same for Mellors we shall find a man who has been emotionally hurt, isolated, increasingly involved in a sexual relationship, devoted to the infallibility of the feelings and to the life of the wood. In neither case will these details account for the archetypal opposition between the two characters; an opposition constantly expressed in terms of 'life' and 'death'. Indeed, looked at as 'characters', there seems little to choose between them. If we think of Connie complaining that Clifford's devotion to talk was excessive and wearisome, then she can hardly have found Mellors's distinguished by its charm and variety; if we feel Clifford enjoying his authority as an employer, we can remember Mellors enjoying his authority over his employer's wife; if Clifford seems to believe in the mystical properties of coal, Mellors sees in forget-me-nots something more than woodland flowers. Now, of course, it will be protested, and rightly, that this divorces incident from context, and confuses, perversely, modes of presentation which are sometimes realistic, sometimes symbolic. But when this protest has been heeded, the fact still remains that as *characters* Clifford and Mellors do not convey the basic antithesis which Lawrence intends. If we feel that they do, then I suggest that our impression emerges from something other than the dramatized incidents of the novel. What that 'other' is, is not difficult to locate; it lies not in the individuality of Clifford and the individuality of Mellors, but in their differing kinds of consciousness. This is a distinction which has far-ranging implications for the status of the novel as a medium of imaginative communication.

Ever since 1913, when Lawrence published *Sons and Lovers,* he had been persistently accused by critics of faulty characterization, of involving his characters in emotional conflicts in excess of the dramatic facts. Feeling was abundant, but motivation was obscure. This led, it was argued, towards anonymity of character, so we find Middleton Murry writing about *Women in Love:*

> . . . . we can discern no individuality whatever in the denizens of Mr. Lawrence's world. We should have thought that we should have been able to distinguish between male and female at least. But no! Remove the names, remove the sedulous catalogues of unnecessary clothing . . . and man and woman are as indistinguishable as octopods in an aquarium tank.

and Edwin Muir remarking:

> We remember the scenes in his novels; we forget the names of his men and women. We should not know any of them if we met them in the street. . . .

Lawrence replied to Muir and his answer seems a convincing one for this whole kind of criticism:

> I have lunched with Mr. Banality and I'm sure I should know him if I met him in the street. . . . Alas, that I should recognize people in the street by their noses, bonnets, or beauty. Does nothing exist beyond that which is recognizable in the streets? How does my cat recognize me in the dark? Thank God, there are more and other sorts of vision than that which Mr. Muir esteems above all others.

'There are more and other sorts of vision . . .', the claim is surely an unexceptionable one. Lawrence, benefiting, often intuitively, from the insights of psycho-analysis, is genuinely extending the province of the novelist, and today it seems difficult to deny that novels like *Sons and Lovers, The Rainbow* and *Women in Love* rely for their distinction largely on Lawrence's extraordinary ability to render 'other kinds of knowledge' vivid and compelling to the reader. If then we find the characterization in *Lady Chatterley's Lover* ambiguous and unsatisfactory, this is not because we are applying the kind of criteria implied by Muir, or are reluctant to accept the character presentation as valid, but because Lawrence's own presentation changed as his work went on. In the 'twenties the exploring artist in his work was yielding to the needs of the prophet, his fiction began to oscillate between autobiography and tract, and in the process 'other kinds of knowledge' tended to contract into 'the *only* kind of knowledge'. A rare ability for a certain kind of artistic creation was now being pressed to serve a gospel for salvation. (pp. 231-33)

To try and show more exactly what is implied in the distinction between 'character' and 'consciousness' in the later novels of Lawrence I want to select two passages from *Lady Chatterley's Lover* and examine our response towards them. The first is from a scene where Clifford and Connie are discussing their marriage, and Clifford goes on to reflect:

> '. . . the occasional sexual connections . . . if people don't exaggerate them ridiculously, pass like the mating of birds. And so they should. What does it matter? It's the life-long companionship that matters. It's the living together from day to day, not the sleeping together once or twice. You and I are married no matter what happens to us. We have the habit of each other. And habit, to my thinking, is more vital than any occasional excitement.'

Now clearly this passage is intended to bring home to the reader Clifford's 'deathly' consciousness. But as we read the novel we respond to this passage not as a denigration of sex, but as the words of a particular man in a particular situation, a man who has been made impotent by war, outlining the only kind of marriage that is possible for him, and, even if mistakenly, at least very understandably, making it out to be a good marriage. Lawrence has rendered Clifford incapable of enjoying a proper marriage; to go on and attack him for the perversity of his views is perversity on the part of the author. The critical point is that Lawrence is continually muting our response to a particular character, which, as a novelist, he can *dramatize*, in order to sharpen our response to a generalized consciousness, which, as a seer, he can only *announce*. To think that this kind of difficulty can be overcome by talking of Clifford's crippling being 'symbolic' of the inward death he embodies, is to underestimate considerably our response to the physical attributes of personality.

This underestimation works in the opposite way in a passage, much later in the novel, when Connie is talking to Mellors of the practical difficulties which prevent their being able to live together for some time. Mellors pauses to consider and then:

> 'I could wish the Cliffords and Berthas all dead,' he said.
>
> 'It's not being very tender to them,' she said.
>
> 'Tender to them? Yea, even the tenderest thing you could do for them, perhaps, would be to give them death. They can't live! They only frustrate life. Their souls are awful inside them. Death ought to be sweet to them. And I ought to be allowed to shoot them.'
>
> 'But you wouldn't do it,' she said.
>
> 'I would though! and with less qualms than I shoot a weasel. It anyhow has a prettiness and a loneliness. But they are legion. Oh, I'd shoot them.'

Connie's response here is much the same as the reader's; we are disturbed at Mellors's violence. We see a terrible autocracy here, an unchallengeable sense of righteousness, which can only think of any opposition in terms of its annihilation. And yet clearly, for Lawrence, Connie's response does not proceed from her humanity but from her uncertain faith, because the 'life' that Mellors embodies and proclaims is so overwhelmingly 'right' that even to demur at its expression is to belong to the devil's party. At this point, I want to make the simple criticism that in *Lady Chatterley* Lawrence not only gives us no dramatic key to the 'deathly' consciousness of Clifford and the 'vital' consciousness of Mellors, but that he has got himself into a position where, if the reader thinks in these terms, he misunderstands the whole position. When the earlier novels, **Sons and Lovers, The Rainbow, Women in Love,** seemed obscure and unsatisfactory, this was either because Lawrence had not been able to express completely what he wanted to say or because the reader was looking for the wrong thing. But in his last novels what he is increasingly concerned to say can no more be dramatized in terms of the novel than faith can be conveyed in logical discourse. The outlines of individual men and women fade and become incandescent with the awesome, impalpable presences of 'Life' and 'Death'. The voice of the artist has become lost in the voice of the prophet, and the burden of his message is—how shall we be saved? It is salvation by an election no less fearful and exclusive than that which haunted Bunyan himself, a salvation which will be found finally and inescapably in sex, because sex, as Lawrence remarked simply in one of his last poems, 'is a state of grace'. And without this psychotheology there can be no access to 'life'. (pp. 234-36)

[*Lady Chatterley's Lover* is not merely] preoccupied with showing that the basis of life is religious, in the sense that in life we encounter a power which we must respond to and which transcends the individual will, but that this religious power is often obstructed or obscured by our moral preoccupations. From this it is but a short step to seeing 'religion' and 'morality' as profoundly hostile to one another. This kind of hostility is caught in Lawrence's remark, 'You can develop an instinct for life *instead of a theory* of right and wrong, good and bad.' It is the kind of remark which should impel us to enquire more exactly about Lawrence's conception of religion. . . . A remark from *Apocalypse* indicates quite clearly why: 'The Christian doctrine of love even at its best was an evasion. Even Jesus was going to reign "hereafter" when his "love" would be turned into confirmed power. This business of reigning in glory hereafter went to the root of Christianity, and is, of course, only an expression of frustrated desire to reign here and now.' The affirmation of 'an instinct for life' and the rejection of the Christian doctrine of immortality indicate sufficiently the direction of Lawrence's religious ideal, and, in so doing, guide us to the heart of *Lady Chatterley's Lover.*

'No man', Mr. Eliot once remarked rather loftily, 'would attach himself to the universe who had anything better to join himself to.' It is a remark which has a profound relevance for *Lady Chatterley's Lover,* pointing to the achievement and the tragedy of the novel. In Lawrence's attachment to the universe we have the basis of his faith, and, in the profound misanthropy of his last years, we find the force which helped him to maintain it. These two aspects are intimately related and Lawrence's deep animism emerges out of the frustration of his religious and social instincts. The concern to sense and describe a force 'behind', but inseparable from, observed realities, is everywhere present in *Lady Chatterley's Lover.* Connie looks at the miners returning from their shift, 'elemental creatures, weird and distorted, of the mineral world! They belonged to the coal, the iron, the clay as fish belong to the sea, and worms to dead wood. The anima of mineral disintegration.' If this is the animate spirit of Death, the animate spirit of Life is caught in Sex, so that not only do we encounter 'life' here, but it is an experience which enables us 'to see into the life of things'. Thus when Connie, returning from a sexual meeting with Mellors, runs through the wood, she sees 'the world as a dream; the trees in the park bulging and surging at anchor on a tide'. Sex is the anima of natural integration. And it is here, of course, in sex, that Lawrence's animist view of the cosmos chimes in with his emphasis on consciousness as opposed to character. Where love emphasizes individuality, sex conceals it; the face is hidden, speech gives way to touch. And so we find Connie thinking of Mellors, 'he was kind to the female in her, which no man had ever been. Men were very kind to the *person* she was, but rather cruel to the female, despising her or ignoring her altogether. . . . He took no notice of Constance or of Lady Chatterley; he just softly stroked her loins or her breasts.' Whatever the implication of this shift of attention for Mellors, it is considerable for the novelist, who must, by virtue of his medium, communicate through character. The kind of difficulties which this elimination of the individual presents for Lawrence are to be found in the ambiguity which surrounds his presentation of sex in the novel.

Lawrence's dilemma was a profound one; he wanted to do two things simultaneously and they warred against each other. In the first place he was intent on restoring a sacred character to sex—he would not have it vulgarized and degraded in what he considered 'the modern way'—he would reveal it again as a holy mystery. Mircea Eliade, in *Patterns of Comparative Religion,* writes: 'For the modern man sex is a physiological act, whereas for the primitive it was a sacrament, a ceremony by means of which he communicated with *the force which stood for Life itself . . .*' (my italics). It is in the light of this primitive vision that Lawrence writes. Hence his sexual descriptions are charged with the language of religion, and language which is rich in biblical association and power. This is not because Lawrence is seeking to promulgate a specific 'belief', still less is he parodying religious orthodoxy; rather he is trying to create by use of rhythm, imagery, diction, an aura of intensity and exaltation which will be recognized as religious. It is in sex, Lawrence feels, that man encounters most fully the awesome mystery of Life itself, that he comes to apprehend the Power that is in him; and at the same time it is a Power which infinitely transcends him. It is not a phallic cult but an animistic encounter which lies at the centre of Lawrence's concern with sex. For Mellors, '. . . she lay there crying in unconscious, inarticulate cries. The voice out of the uttermost night, the life! The man heard it beneath him with a kind of awe. . . .' For Connie, 'out of his utter, incomprehensible stillness she felt again the slow, momentous, surging rise of the phallus again, the other power. And her heart melted out with a kind of awe. . . .' The corollary to making sex sacred, however, is that it is also made taboo. And it was this which Lawrence persistently disregarded.

The sacred mysteries are always veiled, not because they are shameful, but because they are dangerous. But if Lawrence was bent on restoring the sacred character of sex, he was no less concerned with restoring the shameless character of sex. But the prophetic and the therapeutic make uneasy companions. It is not of course that, abstractly considered, there is conflict, but that within a common context their mode of operation must be so different as to constitute a clash. Where the concern of the first is to create a sense of mystery and rarity, the concern of the second is with clarity and normality; where one urges awe, the other urges frankness. The proper language of one is poetic; the language of the other, ethical. Consequently, the verbal and structural tactics Lawrence was employing to win battles on one front were effectively helping him to lose them on the other. It is really this kind of pull and haul which causes the uncertainty of tone in such episodes as the famous forget-me-nots scene, where the awkwardness might appear simply as an artistic confusion between symbolic and realistic modes of presentation. In this episode Lawrence makes his fullest assertion about the sacredness of sex; and device after device is called upon to assist him; the depersonalization of Mellors and Connie, and the explicit, but ritualistic, joining of the force of sex with the force of nature. A roughly analogous episode would be the flower episode in *The Winter's Tale.* But, unlike Shakespeare, Lawrence, having created a symbolic ambience for his religious purpose, recalls, as it were, his very different therapeutic intentions. And so this must now be a scene, literally, about two particular individuals and their specific sexual relationship. To establish this we have the stream of realistic details, the anatomical insistence, the enumerated flowers, and Connie, noticing the rain, prudently putting on rubber shoes before dashing outside naked. It is impossible to keep a picture like this in focus; if it escapes dissolving into obscenity, then it dissolves into bathos. And the clarity and honesty of the intention cannot save the scene from artistic tastelessness and moral ambiguity; the prophet and the moralist have not come to terms; because of this the scene rings false, and the effect of this falsity is of mild though unwitting prurience.

The uncertainty of Lawrence's presentation of sex in **Lady Chatterley** is not in any way a reflection of an uncertainty in his general outlook. Indeed, the reverse is the case. By the time Lawrence came to write this novel he had put far behind him the welter of ideas that we see surging behind **Women in Love,** or the elaborate variations on a theme that we find in **Kangaroo** and **The Plumed Serpent.** There is a simplicity about **Lady Chatterley** not to be found in any of these novels, but this is not the simplicity which arises from the harmony of opposites, but the simplicity obtained by the elimination of opposition. Anything that brings with it complexity must be severely circumscribed. And so we find Lawrence's best work in his last years to lie in a simple fable like **The Virgin and the Gypsy,** or a visionary gospel like **Apocalypse,** or a straight essay in polemic like **'A Propos of Lady Chatterley's Lover'.** Here the whole success arises from an intensity of conviction finding expression in an appropriate intensity of language. But unequivocal assertion is death to the novel; character and symbol cannot live in that atmosphere. And Lawrence, in writing **Lady Chatterley,** had become distrustful of character and of symbol to convey what he wanted to say; of character because it may bring complexity, of symbol because it may bring obscurity. (pp. 238-42)

> Ian Gregor, "The Novel as Prophecy: 'Lady Chatterley's Lover'," in The Moral and the Story *by Ian Gregor and Brian Nicholas, Faber & Faber, 1962, pp. 217-48.*

Julian Moynahan (essay date 1963)

[*An American novelist, educator, and critic, Moynahan has written a book-length study of Lawrence's novels and short stories and contributed articles to several books about D. H. Lawrence. In the following excerpt, he analyzes the structure of* Lady Chatterley's Lover *and argues that the novel calls for the regeneration of modern society.*]

Lady Chatterley's Lover dramatizes two opposed orientations toward life, two distinct modes of human awareness: the one abstract, cerebral, and unvital; the other concrete, physical, and organic. A relatively clear statement of the distinction may be found in Lawrence's long essay, **"A Propos of Lady Chatterley's Lover,"** written two years after he had published the Florence edition of his novel:

> **An excerpt from** *Lady Chatterley's Lover*
>
> Connie heard long conversations going on between [Clifford and Mrs. Bolton]. Or rather, it was mostly Mrs. Bolton talking. She had unloosed to him the stream of gossip about Tevershall village. It was more than gossip. It was Mrs. Gaskell and George Eliot and Miss Mitford all rolled in one, with a great deal more that these women left out. Once started, Mrs. Bolton was better than any book, about the lives of the people. She knew them all so intimately, and had such a peculiar, flamey zest in all their affairs, it was wonderful, if just a *trifle* humiliating to listen to her. At first she had not ventured to "talk Tevershall", as she called it, to Clifford. But once started, it went. Clifford was listening for "material", and he found it in plenty. Connie realised that his so-called genius was just this: a perspicuous talent for personal gossip, clever and apparently detached. Mrs. Bolton, of course, was very warm when she "talked Tevershall." Carried away, in fact. And it was marvelous the things that happened and that she knew about. She would have run to dozens of volumes.
>
> Connie was fascinated, listening to her. But afterwards always a little ashamed. She ought not to listen with this queer rabid curiosity. After all, one may hear the most private affairs of other people, but only in a spirit of respect for the struggling, battered thing which any human soul is, and in a spirit of fine, discriminative sympathy. For even satire is a form of sympathy. It is the way our sympathy flows and recoils that really determines our lives. And here lies the vast importance of the novel, properly handled. It can inform and lead into new places the flow of our sympathetic consciousness, and it can lead our sympathy away in recoil from things gone dead. Therefore, the novel, properly handled, can reveal the most secret places of life: for it is in the *passional* secret places of life, above all, that the tide of sensitive awareness needs to ebb and flow, cleansing and refreshing.
>
> But the novel, like gossip, can also excite spurious sympathies and recoils, mechanical and leaning to the psyche. The novel can glorify the most corrupt feelings, so long as they are *conventionally* "pure." Then the novel, like gossip becomes at last vicious, and, like gossip, all the more vicious because it is always ostensibly on the side of the angels. Mrs. Bolton's gossip was always on the side of the angels. "And he was such a *bad* fellow, and she was sich a *nice* woman." Whereas, as Connie could see even from Mrs. Bolton's gossip, the woman had been merely a mealy-mouthed sort, and the man angrily honest. But angry honesty made a "bad man" of him, and mealy-mouthedness made a "nice woman" of her, in the vicious, conventional channeling of sympathy by Mrs. Bolton.
>
> For this reason, the gossip was humiliating. And for the same reason, most novels, especially popular ones, are humiliating too. The public responds now only to an appeal to its vices.
>
> > D. H. Lawrence, in his Lady Chatterley's Lover, *Nesor Publishing Co., n.d.*

There are many ways of knowing, there are many sorts of knowledge. But the two ways of knowing, for man, are knowing in terms of apartness, which is mental, rational, scientific, and knowing in terms of togetherness, which is religious and poetic. . . .

But relationship is threefold. First, there is the relation to the living universe. Then comes the relation of man to woman. Then comes the relation of man to man. And each is a blood-relationship, not mere spirit or mind. We have abstracted the universe into Matter and Force, we have abstracted men and women into separate personalities—personalities being isolated units, incapable of togetherness—so that all three great relationships are bodiless, dead.

The novel's structural method involves a simple juxtaposition of the two modes; its narrative method combines explicit interpretative comment by a narrator who from the beginning makes clear his sympathy for the vitalist viewpoint together with lucid and objective renderings of characters, situations, and settings. Furthermore, there is a sort of synechdochic method employed in the narration. Wragby Hall and the industrial village of Tevershall are realized in themselves but come also to stand for entire industrial, social, and even spiritual orders dominant in the modern world, more especially in twentieth-century England. Sir Clifford Chatterley sums up a modern habit of mind as well as a ruling class in transition from one type of economic proprietorship to another. In contrast, the gamekeeper, Oliver Mellors, not only follows but represents the organic way of life, and the wood in which he lurks is a spatial metaphor of the natural order, or, what Lawrence frequently called "the living universe."

These are but a few of the simple and necessarily rigid equations the novel sets up between particular and general conditions. Of course very few novels have been written which fully resist the regular habit of readers to discover general truths mirrored in particularized and historically limited episodes. But few novels are so explicit and so demanding in the control they impose on the reader's moral imagination as *Lady Chatterley's Lover.*

Among the leading characters only the heroine, Connie Chatterley, plays no rigid representative role; and it is her freedom of action which creates the possibility of drama. As she shuttles from one realm to another—both in space and in terms of inner awareness—from Wragby Hall to the gamekeeper's hut in the woods, her experiences project the energies of the two modes in conflict with one another. She is both booty and battleground in the ensuing struggle between vital and unvital ways of apprehending experience. If it is not too scandalous a suggestion, Lady Chatterley may be said to stand for ourselves, for all those puzzled modern people who have not yet resolved the question of whether they wish to be domiciled at Wragby Hall or in Wragby wood, of whether to live among powerful abstractions or growing things. If the alternatives appear rigidly posed, then that is a limitation which the novel fully accepts. Life can be mapped according to other patterns as even Lawrence knew. But in this story the idea emerges clearly that Lady Chatterley—we—cannot have it both ways. There is no possibility of compromise between vitality and its opposite.

Although the heroine possesses a freedom of role and action unknown to such representative figures as the lord and the gamekeeper, this does not mean that dramatic interest ever depends upon suspense of outcome. From the beginning Connie is no more free to choose the realm of "death-in-life" than Alvina Houghton in *The Lost Girl* was free to continue living alone beside her father's shop in Woodhouse. Freedom in the novel is merely relative. In Lawrence's last novel it extends only to questions of means. The heroine must escape her husband and what he stands for; but for a time she is free to entertain various alternatives: to hesitate, to become confused, to relapse, but never finally to make the great refusal. (pp. 140-43)

[One] reason for the superiority of *Lady Chatterley's Lover* [to Lawrence's earlier novels] is the rich simplicity of its structural design. This design is realized most powerfully and significantly in spatial terms, in terms of setting. The most enduring meanings the novel projects are inextricably bound up with the arrangement of three locations—the manor house, the industrial village, the wood—and their spatial relations with one another under a fume-laden atmosphere which seems to be no better and no worse than Pittsburgh's or northern New Jersey's. Many of Lawrence's novels are built around a central contrast: in *The Rainbow* the contrast is between things as they are and a promised transformation of being; in *The Plumed Serpent* it is between a Europeanized and an aboriginal Mexico; in *The Lost Girl* it is between "higher" and "lower" selves, or, spatially, between Woodhouse and southern Italy. All these contrasts from one point of view come to the same thing. They express the opposition between "two ways of knowing."

In *Lady Chatterley's Lover* the same contrast is represented through settings which impinge on one another, which coexist at the same time, in the same district. There is no appeal to the strange and far to fix either side of the contrast and no direct appeal to the future. The novel concentrates its drama within the space of a few square miles, and Lawrence summons all his powers of description to present this space as it is: a portion of English soil in transition from a semi-rural, semi-industrial condition to one of total industrialization. If the novel demands that we regard these few miles as an epitome of the larger world of Western Civilization itself, we may find it easy to assent because in so many ways Lawrence's microcosm looks and smells like the world we know.

The wood is the vital center of Lawrence's panorama. It is menaced on one side by the ugly houses and mining installations of the colliery village; on the other it is owned but not valued by the occupants of the dreary manor house. There is social and economic hostility between village and manor, but both workers and owner unite in opposition to everything the wood represents. Both worship the abstractions of money, power, and property, and both are devoted to the mechanistic organization of human affairs. The wood stands approximately in between two forces of negation. It is Lawrence's sacred wood within which life-mysteries are enacted. These are of birth, budding, and growth, embodied in the annual cycle of fertility in tree, flower, and animal, humanly embodied also in the sexual encounters between the gamekeeper and the lady; for out of these encounters proceed a rebirth of feeling in both people, the possibility of a new life together, and finally the promise of a child. The love affair moves in phase with the organic burgeoning of the wood during a wet but beautiful spring. It extends from the time of the first flowers to a time when the trees and flowers are in full bloom.

The religious or mythic aspect of the woodland setting is most fully realized in a lovely passage from the first version of the novel which Lawrence did not carry forward into the final version. It occurs after Connie has had her first sexual experience with Parkin:

> She was filled, herself, with an unspeakable pleasure, a pleasure which has no contact with speech. She felt herself filled with new blood, as if the blood of the man had swept into her veins like a strong, fresh, rousing wind, changing her whole self. All her self felt alive, and in motion, like the woods in spring. She could not but feel that a new breath had swept into her body from the man, and that she was like a forest soughing with a new, soft wind, soughing and moving unspoken into bud. All her body felt like the dark interlacing of the boughs of an oak wood, softly humming in a wind, and humming inaudibly with the myriad, myriad unfolding of buds. Meanwhile the birds had their heads laid on their shoulders and slept with delight in the vast interlaced intricacy of the forest of her body.
>
> From the man, from the body of the man, the pure wind had swept in on her. . . .
>
> And meanwhile the voice of the other man, Sir Clifford, went on and on, clapping and gurgling with strange sound. Not for one second did she really hear what he said. But it sounded to her like the uncouth cries and howls of barbarous, disconnected savages dancing around a fire somewhere outside the wood. Clifford was a smeared and painted savage howling in an utterly unintelligible gibberish somewhere on the outskirts of her consciousness. She, deep within the sacred and sensitive wood, was filled with the pure communication of the other man, a communication delicate as the inspiration of the gods.

Here the woman's consciousness becomes fused through metaphor with the wood itself, so that she can carry its mystery indoors with her. Lawrence uses the traditional religious image of the wind to express how she has become inspired. Notice, also, the inversion whereby the civilized becomes the savage—Clifford has been reading aloud from Racine!—whereas the sensations of well-being after an erotic experience are defined in pentecostal terms.

For no character in the novel is the wood a natural and inevitable habitat. Connie and Mellors are both somewhat battered products of unwholesome civilization who, as it were, stumble onto sacred ground while following paths leading from opposite sides. Mellors arrives first from the direction of Tevershall; the lady comes trailing down some months later from the "eminence" on which Wragby sits. In the not wholly adequate shelter of a remnant of Sherwood Forest they create through the sex act that condition of interconnection which is the *sine qua non* of escape from the "tragic" world but which certainly does not guarantee that escape.

The wood symbolizes not only a way of life but also the beleaguered and vulnerable status to which the vital career has been reduced. The vastness of the original forest has declined under the steady attrition of civilization to a thin wood which barely conceals the lovers from prying eyes and barely provides cover for the pheasants and rabbits which are its only wildlife. Mellors grimly tracks down the colliers who poach on his preserves, but there are other kinds of invasion that he is powerless to resist. From Tevershall comes the obscene Bertha Couts to fill the sensitive glade with domestic uproar, and from Wragby comes Clifford in his motorized chair to ride down the wild flowers while musing on the felicities and responsibilities of being a property owner. For reasons of family pride the Chatterleys have been interested in preserving the remaining forest. But we are told that this interest can yield to "higher" claims. During the late war, Clifford's father, Sir Geoffrey, in an excess of patriotic zeal had cut hundreds of trees to provide trench timber for the troops in Belgium and France:

> On the crown of the knoll where the oaks had stood, now was bareness; and from there you could look out over the trees to the colliery railway, and the new works at Stacks Gate. Connie had stood and had looked, it was a breach in the pure seclusion of the wood. It let in the world.

Throughout the novel we are made aware of this process of attrition, as if in a short time the trees and glades will disappear, leaving village and hall locked—like the aristocratic Sir Clifford and the plebeian Mrs. Bolton at the end of the story—in monstrous, unvital embrace. Finally, not only is the wood surrounded, but also it is being attacked from beneath. The vertical shafts of the local mines lead to horizontal corridors fanning out in all directions. The rich soil of Wragby Wood is undermined by coal diggings, while its flora and fauna are being reduced at ground level. Simultaneously from the skies come poisonous fumes and "smuts" to sicken the vegetation and reduce the vigor of the animals. All in all it is through his power to project a crisis of industrial civilization in these concrete terms that Lawrence is able to make his point compelling.

Since the central theme of **Lady Chatterley's Lover** is concreteness *versus* abstraction, it is appropriate that the success of Lawrence's representative method should depend largely on richly concrete realizations of persons, settings, and situations, that the power of his prophecy should depend on the power of his art to particularize meanings which suggest broader conditions and widely applicable truths of experience. Here I want to examine some features of the two opposed modes or realms of experience as they are fictionally embodied and to raise some questions both about the artistic success of these representations and about the ideas to which they may be referred. Although the story proceeds in a dialectical movement, usually alternating scenes at Wragby with scenes in the gamekeeper's domain, there is no reason why we cannot examine each realm in turn.

An abiding impression of Sir Clifford and of most of the intellectuals who foregather at Wragby Hall during the early part of the story is that they are not very real. But this hardly supplies a ground for criticism of the portrayal of Sir Clifford since his unreality is precisely the point the novel makes. He is a "hurt thing," a "lost thing" whose capacity to be involved in life has been destroyed by the war. He is able to think and to experience egoistic feeling but cannot get in touch. It seems to his wife, and nothing happens in the story to contradict her view, that at the core of him there is only "a negation of human contact." His is not a problem of war neurosis or of the psychology of invalidism. Perhaps the best way to regard him is in the nature of an experimental hypothesis: given such and such conditions, then what other conditions will result? Looked at in this way, the character remains interesting throughout the novel and vibrates with a queer mechanical energy, like those incredibly energetic yet two-dimensional characters one finds in Dickens and in the novels of Smollett and Fielding.

The hypothesis may be stated as follows: what will a man do with himself and with others when his physical attachment to experience has been violently and traumatically severed? The novel's answer is that such a man will create a "simulacrum of reality," a complex pattern of abstract relationships to substitute for felt connections between himself and others. Within this pattern or web he will enjoy the illusion of life, but all the time he will not be alive at all. Here one might remark that the "adjustment" is harmless enough, but this ignores the problem of others. Actually, Clifford's first great crime is that he draws his wife into his orbit of nonexistence. The abstracted man who cannot live in himself leans with crushing weight on his partner. He slowly draws from her those vital energies which sustain her in being, but can only waste what he absorbs since nothing can restore him to life.

In this depiction of Clifford's parasitism Lawrence is working once again with an assumption which is basic to all his work. It is that there is life in the vital sense and death in the sense of the unvital but no third thing, no possibility of an attitude of nonattachment—one which neither preys on the vitality of others nor is based on the capacity of physical self-realization. In Lawrence generally the ground of all value is physical experience. This is both his characteristic limitation and the theme that unifies all his works—fiction, poetry, essays, and treatises. The only reality and the only marvel is to be alive in the flesh. At the same time an individual can experience his aliveness only through direct relationship with another living thing. He can fuse himself in contemplation with the life of trees, flowers, or animals, but the crucial experience of relatedness is, appropriately enough, a sexual experience with a woman: appropriate because it conforms to the order of nature, because for Lawrence touch is a more powerful mode of connectedness than sight, because sex is, in sensory and emotional terms, a stronger experience of connection than any other.

All this can be put into a single doctrinal statement: to know and possess oneself is to have experienced a unity with live things and persons outside oneself. These Laurentian convictions are primarily a product of intuition, but they receive some reinforcement in the speculations of at least one major modern philosopher. A. N. Whitehead has presented similar conclusions about men's relations to a "living universe" in his essay "Nature Alive," although needless to say he does not concern himself with the sexual relation. But Whitehead argues that all mental experience is derived from bodily functioning and that strictly speaking no one can determine where our bodies end and where the surrounding physical environment begins. A man is alive in nature and nature is alive in him; his sense of self is included in his sense of otherness, and *vice versa*. Therefore, "togetherness" is not only a way of knowing but the fundamental mode of being.

Clifford's first pattern of abstraction is created with words. As a writer he spins verbal cobwebs, and in his daily association with Connie he invariably tries to reduce concrete experience to formulae. He attempts to fill the void between his wife and himself with phrases like "the habit of intimacy," and "our steadily-lived life." But within his orbit the only reality for Connie is "nothingness, and over it a hypocrisy of words." Because he accepts words as a facsimile of reality, verbal connections as a substitute for felt connections, he comes to worship success. He wishes to be talked about, written about, recognized as something, because he is nothing. And, although wealthy and not avaricious, he seeks money as the visible yet abstract emblem of success.

In mid-career Clifford orients himself in a new pattern of abstraction. This time it is economic and industrial power that give him the illusion of life. He is brilliantly successful at developing new methods of mining organization because he sees human beings only as functions of an abstractly formulated process, not as flesh-and-blood realities. His social views are summed up in his slogan, "the function determines the individual"—a man *is* no more than what he does. Now Clifford is in a position to commit far greater crimes than before. As an industrialist he draws men and women by the thousands into his orbit of nonexistence. He becomes a leader in a civilized society described at one point by the word "insane" and gains new confidence and toughness from his success in manipulating men and machines. He is described as becoming "almost a *creature,* with a hard, efficient shell of an exterior and a pulpy interior, one of the amazing crabs and lobsters of the modern industrial and financial world, invertebrates of the crustacean order, with shells of steel, like machines, and inner bodies of soft pulp." From the pulp of his inner life emanate just two vibrations—an impulse of self-assertion and a contradictory impulse of terrified dependency. (pp. 145-54)

As a portrait of the modern businessman Clifford is surely no better than a monstrous caricature. It would be incorrect to regard him as the imaginative representation of some such cliché of popular psychology as "Men who succeed in business are often emotionally underdeveloped and infantile." It would be more appropriate to see him as a kind of imagined limit toward which certain tendencies in modern life might be moving. Real men fall somewhere between the limits defined at one extreme by Sir Clifford Chatterley and at the other by the gamekeeper.

The narrative presentation of Clifford is carefully handled so as to prevent the reader ever coming at the character directly. His utterances are invariably hedged round with interpretative comment by the narrator or by Connie which draws out the depraved implications of what he says and does. He is always an illustration of disconnectedness; never for a moment does he emerge as a man who has suffered a terrible wound and is to be pitied for it. If even briefly the reader could feel with him as a human being, then his whole characterization would seem terribly cruel, and Lawrence's demonstration would be fatally flawed. But the truth is that Clifford in this novel is himself a man entirely defined by his functions. There is nothing left over to pity. Riding about the estate in his motorized chair he is a kind of mechanical centaur who, because he is only half human, is not human at all. Voidness cannot be villainous, nor can it become an object of sympathy.

Clifford is essential to the novel, but the same cannot be said for those characters who sit about in the drawing room at Wragby discussing the superiority of mind over matter and revealing their diseased attitudes toward love, working people, and the sex act. Insofar as many of these people—Lady Bennerley, Charles May, Hammond, and Tommy Dukes—are devitalized, two-dimensional creatures, they are no more than tautological variations on Clifford himself. Their discussions seem hopelessly dated. These characters do not appear in the first version of the novel and add little to the final version. Dukes, of course, is a spokesman for the vital and "phallic" consciousness: "Real knowledge comes out of the whole corpus of the consciousness; out of your belly and your penis as much as out of your brain and mind." In saying this he anticipates the views of Mellors, but it is hard to see why such press agentry should be necessary. When Mellors enters the story, it soon turns out that he can speak for himself, sometimes to the point of tediousness. Dukes in his own words is a "mental-lifer" who holds the right ideas but cannot act upon them. He is the Hamlet, or rather the Prufrock, of ***Lady Chatterley's Lover.***

The novel's second powerful representation of "death-in-life" is concentrated in a set passage of description occurring about midway in the story. It is a genuine *tour de force* running on for eleven pages and covering in meticulous detail the physical appearance of three industrial villages and the many miles of semi-industrial countryside which lie around them. Things seen are richly rendered as fact and simultaneously judged and analyzed by the newly awakened heroine, Connie Chatterley. It is dramatically appropriate that she should interpret her impressions as she does. At the same time the entire description may easily stand as Lawrence's own last indignant comment on the crimes perpetrated by an industrial civilization against essential human needs and capacities.

Connie drives from Wragby through Tevershall, the new village of Stacks Gate, and on to Uthwaite, an old Midland village where the Chatterley family are still looked upon as country gentry. In and around the villages she observes coal miners and other workmen, working-class homes and shopping districts, schools, churches, factories, pubs, and hotels. Her perspective is constantly shifting as the car mounts hills and drops down into valleys, crawls through narrow streets crowded with traffic, or runs swiftly through open country. In the end this moving panorama of an entire district creates a striking and large image of human disorder spread out upon a portion of the earth's surface scarred and ravaged by man himself.

To the heroine the hideousness of these raw villages expresses much the same meaning as Wragby and its master. Ugliness is seen as evidence of "the utter absence of the instinct for shapely beauty which every bird and beast has, the utter death of the human intuitive faculty." As she hears school children bawling out a song in one of the new school buildings she asks, "What could possibly become of such people, a people in whom the living intuitive faculty was dead as nails, and only queer mechanical yells and uncanny will-power remained?" These observations are not sentimental, nor are they validated by any program of social or economic reform she has in mind for the improvement of the lives of the industrial masses. Instead the natural grace and vigor of human beings left free to express themselves in physical and instinctive ways is the assumption from which criticism follows. No social or economic class is assigned full blame for producing the "half-corpses" of the "new race of mankind" although there is a vague distinction between leaders and led in the questions "Ah God, what has man done to man? What have the leaders of men been doing to their fellow man?"

Actually, the description embodies a mordant irony. Connie observes that the new mining villages and industrial installations are crowding in upon the parks and manors of the rich, cultivated people of the district. These magnates had set the industrial process in motion when they first began to exploit the mineral resources of their hitherto rural properties. Their desire for profits had created the conditions which produced the dehumanization of the workers and the denaturing of soil and atmosphere. Now the miners, "elemental creatures, weird and distorted, of the mineral world," build their houses at the very gates of the manor parks. The owners are being shoved out of their places by the inhuman pressure of the industrial masses for living room:

> This is history. One England blots out another. The mines had made the halls wealthy. Now they were blotting them out, as they had already blotted out the cottages. The industrial England blots out the agricultural England. One meaning blots out another. . . . And the continuity is not organic, but mechanical.

The description as a whole does not protest change as such, or rest its case on an imagined superiority of past to present. The real protest is against a change which seems to be altogether uncontrolled by human beings. Men have made a machine—industrial civilization—and now the machine proceeds to make men—in its own image. In the end there can be no distinction between victim and victimizer because the machine, manned by dehumanized creatures like Sir Clifford and the half-corpses whom he employs, victimizes all alike. This pessimistic conclusion is most pointedly expressed by the gamekeeper as he looks out at night from his leafy shelter toward the nearby industrial area:

> The fault lay there, out there, in those evil electric lights and diabolical rattlings of engines. There in the world of the mechanical greedy, greedy mechanism and mechanized greed, sparkling with lights and gushing hot metal and roaring with traffic, there lay the vast evil thing, ready to destroy whatever did not conform. Soon it would destroy the wood, and the bluebells would spring no more. All vulnerable things must perish under the rolling and running of iron.

The profound sense of crisis communicated by the description I have been discussing depends partly on the patience and skill with which closely observed facts of daily experience have been grouped to make a unified, overwhelming impression, partly on the validity of the idea that underlies the description. The idea is that men, because they are alive, cannot without fatal injury to themselves be subordinated to that which is not alive. Living is not a matter of functions but of the organic wholeness and health of a physical species. Industrialism, insofar as it maims the human organism, or forces it to form a shell of insentience to protect its vulnerable substance, defeats the great human ends for which it was designed. Lawrence's attack on industrialism is not conducted on idealistic grounds. It stems from his keen sense that men and women, like tree, bird, and flower, are physically alive and growing. This is the basic human reality, and all higher possibilities depend upon the healthy condition of the physical man and woman.

Perhaps we are so used to the demands civilization makes upon us to regard our bodies merely as serviceable instruments that we cannot respond to Lawrence's insistence that *our bodies are our selves* and that the only way to be alive is in the flesh. But it seems to me he has discovered the perfect place to rest a case against an industrial civilization. For no one pretends that such a civilization offers spiritual rewards to its supporters. It offers merely the promise of a richer material existence, and Lawrence suggests that the offer is a swindle. What is given by one hand is taken away by the other, since dead men cannot appreciate, except in a simulated way, the benefits of life. On this view all wars are lost, all five-year plans fail, because men cannot wage military battles or battles or production without dying "vitally." This is because vulnerability and tenderness are of the essence of the human, and these qualities cannot be preserved in large, difficult enterprises requiring the subordination of individuals to impersonal processes. A man must live in the now; if he does not, he will find himself dead in the hereafter.

To cope with the argument on its own terms one might grant the tendency of the "insentient iron world" to maim and destroy the vital essence of human beings, but argue that Lawrence overplays vulnerability and tenderness. Is it possible that the "human intuitive faculty," anchored as it is in the powerful surges of the body's life, can survive the ugliness and disintegration of factory towns and the inhuman efficiency of assembly lines? Does it not seem true that toughness alike with sensitiveness is demonstrated in the power of most growing things to maintain themselves in being? Granted that the basis of endurance is the same in man and crocus, is the man less hardy than the crocus? Perhaps the Laurentian answer would be that the crocus knows when it is time to die, but many human beings, who ought to accept the fact that they are already dead, fashion for themselves a simulacrum and continue during some years to spread death among the living in the manner of Clifford Chatterley.

Constance Chatterley's trip into Wragby Wood is, in the symbolic terms the novel establishes, a journey from death into life and from the profoundly unreal into reality. Wragby is dominated by the word, and, as Lawrence remarks in a passage of **"A Propos of *Lady Chatterley's Lover*,"** the word is insufficient to establish that "vivid and nourishing relation to the cosmos and the universe" which is man's only hope of sustaining himself fulfilled in the midst of life:

> It is no use asking for a Word to fulfil such a need. No Word, no Logos, no Utterance will ever do it. The Word is uttered, most of it; we need only pay true attention. But who will call us to the Deed, the great Deed of the Seasons and the year, the Deed of the soul's cycle, the Deed of a woman's life at one with a man's. . . . It is the *Deed* of life we have now to learn: we are supposed to have learnt the Word, but, alas, look at us. Word-perfect we may be, but Deed-demented. Let us prepare now for the death of our present "little" life, and the re-emergence in a bigger life, in touch with the moving cosmos.

This is the prophetic dimension in which the reader must view the heroine's quest. At the same time, it would be foolish to deny that from another perspective Constance Chatterley is merely a bored society woman of rather low moral character who is swept forward into fulfillment in spite of herself. Her personal background, her girlish sexual adventures with German students in the Black Forest, her nerve-wracking affair with the careerist, Michaelis, contain nothing to admire. Her only qualification for the role of heroine is a capacity to come alive in the body, to become awakened instinctually, and to be "at one with a man's life." But of course this is the only qualification demanded. Connie's lack of distinction is all to the good if we agree that her reorientation in life is enacted convincingly since then her success holds out a promise to all. To confer on an ordinary woman an extraordinary fate and to suggest that there is no other fate worth seeking is what ***Lady Chatterley's Lover***, like ***The Lost Girl*** before it, tries to do. The earlier novel is less successful because it presents no clearly described experience embodying the "vivid relation," no setting where that relation is convincingly enacted. The sexual episodes in the "sacred" wood are dramatic experience embodying such a relation in ***Lady Chatterley's Lover***. Less ambiguously than in any earlier novel Lawrence completes his main mission here by balancing rejection against affirmation, the attack on an insensate civilization against a celebration of creative possibilities in warmly physical, interpersonal human experience. When the sexual scenes are looked at in this way, the importance of their function in the total action becomes evident. Union in sexual experience demands as concrete expression as does disconnectedness at Wragby and in the industrial environs.

The only serious argument that can be raised against these scenes has to do with the inadequacy of words—any words—to set forth the meaning and drama of intimate physical and emotional experiences in which consciousness, on the narrator's own admission, surges in a dimension of reality inaccessible to language. For example let us consider the following passage from a scene in which Connie and the gamekeeper come to a sexual climax together:

> And it seemed she was like the sea, nothing but dark waves rising and heaving, heaving with a great swell, so that slowly her whole darkness was in motion, and she was ocean rolling its dark, dumb mass. Oh, and far down inside her the deeps parted and rolled asunder, in long, far-travelling billows, and ever, at the quick of her, the depths parted and rolled asunder from the center of soft plunging, as the plunger went deeper and deeper, touching lower, and she was deeper and deeper and deeper disclosed, and heavier the billows of her rolled away to some shore, uncovering her, and closer and closer plunged the palpable unknown, and further and further rolled the waves of herself away from herself, leaving her, till suddenly, in a soft, shuddering convulsion the quick of all her plasm was touched . . . and she was gone. She was gone, she was not, and she was born: a woman.

This is beautiful enough in its way, but somehow these heavy rhythms and overlapping repetitions of word and phrase seem verbose. The narrator cannot adequately synthesize this sort of experience in words any more than one might adequately describe the circulation of the blood from an "inside" viewpoint. The description has some good features. It avoids the grey vocabulary of sexual science; it is ingenious in its attempt to match up verbal rhythms with the mounting neural tensions of sexual excitation. But ingenuity is hardly enough to do the job here. The reader fails to achieve any deep realization of the sexual mystery and instead is liable to find himself stopping to ask questions about the plain prose meaning of such things as "the quick of the plasm," the statement that this woman has now become a woman (what was she a few moments earlier?), or the statement that at the height of the experience "she was not."

In a piece of music like Wagner's *Liebestod* sequence in *Tristan und Isolde*, which might be interpreted as orgasmic, such questions do not arise. Given the kind of materials he works with, any composer may conceivably create in a structure of pure sound a perfect analogue of the feminine sexual climax. Words, however, ordinarily cannot do this, unless they are wrenched from normal grammatical relationship and purified of their ordinary signific meanings. Here the narrator does not choose to withdraw from the scene; Lawrence does not choose to develop some version of the stream of consciousness technique which could render the kind of pure suggestiveness music is capable of rendering. The ocean-swimmer: woman-man analogy on which the passage is built remains curiously formal, not quite an argument but too much like an argument to overwhelm and flood the reader's awareness with emotive meanings.

The problem of language is less intense when less central features of sexual relations are described or dramatized, but it is still there. The gamekeeper's use of the dialect and of the Anglo-Saxon four-letter words possesses the sort of charm that cloys in repetition. Perhaps the slurs, elisions, and crooning sounds of Midlands vernacular are more appropriate to tender, erotic conversations than the tight-lipped accents of Received Standard British, but this is something difficult for an American reader to judge. Also, the four-letter words will or will not have their effect depending on a reader's personal background. They may seem fresh, honest, and direct to someone who has never heard them used eight or ten times to a sentence by ordinary, unvital men in discussions of the news, politics, baseball, and movies. For this reader most of their magic had been rubbed off before he was out of grammar school. (pp. 155-64)

It is easier to understand why we should be given so much nakedness and so many descriptions of the sexual experience than to make fine distinctions between degrees of effectiveness in particular scenes. The insentient outer world denies the primary value of the body's physical life and aspires toward an ideal condition of disembodiment. But in the wood, where this value is asserted, naked contact between the physical man and woman is more important than anything else. Furthermore, the closest possible contact comes in sexual intercourse, an experience defined by the novel as a fusion into a temporary unity of man with woman, woman with man, the two together with the secret heart of life. The possibility of a rebirth of wholesome feeling is grounded in the sex act because only at the moment of orgasm does the individual escape his self-obsession into identification with the "living universe." When he or she returns from his blind mystical illumination—one which is not separable from the powerful sensual feelings that momentarily overwhelm ordinary awareness—he discovers himself to be *changed,* as if he had looked into the face of God Himself. This is mysticism. One needs not assume in making use of the term that such experiences are "unreal," only that, like more orthodox varieties of the experience, it will never yield up its meaning to the nonmystic. As Connie Chatterley lies with her lover in a condition described as "one perfect concentric fluid of feeling" she utters inarticulate little cries. The narrator's reverent comment is that here we have "the voice out of the uttermost night, the life!" It is easier to believe in this miracle—a miracle because it is not the woman crying out but the voice of the universe itself—than to comprehend it.

The reader may more easily come to terms with that part of the redemptory pattern of action which leads up to the sexual scenes. The first sexual encounter between gamekeeper and heroine actually completes rather than begins the drama of her passing over from one life-orientation to another. For Connie this process of transition is painful, and it is poignantly realized in some of the most moving descriptive-dramatic passages in the novel. The sexual scenes succeeding the first really add nothing new. Connie has her moments of resistance. She has to undergo a sort of basic training in the arts of the vital career, and later chapters take up the practical problem of how the lovers are to translate their adulterous connection into a permanent living arrangement. But when the heroine first enters the hut to give herself to her husband's servant, she has crossed the gulf between the unliving and the living. The central action is substantially complete.

This action of passing over is presented as a series of definable moments of realization. The process is not wholly internalized or reflective, for each hesitant step forward follows an occasion in which Connie comes into contact with some form of the vital outside herself. The mode of contact is at first visual. Later other modes of perception come into play, and finally it is a touch which gently presses her forward into fulfillment. To conclude my discussion of the "vital realm" I shall trace this process in some detail.

A point of departure is established during a walk in the woods with Sir Clifford. Connie is bored with life, entangled in a shoddy love affair with Michaelis, entangled in the web of Clifford's phrases about the steadily lived life. Suddenly, the new gamekeeper, whom Connie has never met, emerges from a sidepath in the wood "like the sudden rush of a threat out of nowhere":

> She was watching a brown spaniel that had run out of a side-path, and was looking towards them with lifted nose, making a soft, fluffy bark. A man with a gun strode swiftly, softly out after the dog, facing their way as if about to attack them; then stopped instead, saluted, and was turning down hill. It was only the new gamekeeper, but he had frightened Connie, he seemed to emerge with such a swift menace.

The description simultaneously expresses the heroine's alienation from what is real and suggests that, unlike Clifford, she is not beyond cure. Although frightened she is not indifferent. The threat conceals a promise which she is not yet capable of realizing, but when she turns her attention back to Clifford and Wragby, her sense of the profound meaninglessness of her existence has become intensified.

For a time after this encounter Connie makes no progress out of her condition of alienation. (pp. 165-67)

Connie is shocked into awareness for the second time when by accident she observes the gamekeeper washing himself in the open air behind his cottage. A commonplace experience becomes "visionary" when for some moments this woman who has devoted her life to nothingness recognizes that she is in the presence of something. Her conscious mind rejects the vision, but "in her womb" she knows she has been exposed to a reality which is fundamental and concrete: "the warm, white flame of a single life, revealing itself in contours that one might touch: a body." When she returns home she strips off her clothing before a mirror and examines her own body inch by inch. Painfully, she recognizes that it is becoming meaningless and ugly. She has been swindled out of her first youth by what she calls "the mental life," with its abstractness and its neglect of the body as an essential human reality.

From here on she is in covert rebellion against her husband's world. At the same time Mellors remains withdrawn and suspicious. She increases the frequency of her walks in the woods during the month of March and experiences a whole series of recognitions which can be turned back as perspectives on her own dynamic state of being. On a cold, brilliant March day she enters the woods while certain phrases sweep through her consciousness:

> Ye must be born again! I believe in the resurrection of the body! Except a grain of wheat fall into the earth and die, it shall by no means bring forth. When the crocus cometh forth I too will emerge and see the sun!

The wind, described as the breath of Persephone, who is "out of hell on a cold morning," and as though it were trying to break itself free of the branches in which it has become entangled, excites her. An identification between the woman and the wind is established through the emphasis on the idea of escape and release. She sits with her back against a young pine tree and becomes excited as it sways against her "elastic and powerful, rising up." The description, of course, has phallic overtones and foreshadows some of the phallic rituals which take place in later sexual scenes. But what makes these descriptions beautiful and exciting for the reader is the imaginative power with which the idea is communicated that there is a real connection between the life springing in the reawakened woods and the changing, revitalized feeling of the woman.

To be at one with the life of the woods is a great deal in itself. Nevertheless the heroine's change of awareness cannot be arrested at this Thoreauvian point of vital realization. She is now "loose and adrift" between the old life and the new, and must exert herself to find new moorings. From this point on it is only the reluctance of the gamekeeper to become himself reawakened under the pathetically inadequate auspices of the beleaguered wood which delays fate. Day after day Connie comes to the little clearing to watch Mellors at work performing the wholesome tasks of pheasant husbandry and then returns home alone to Wragby where Mrs. Bolton has already begun to replace her as Clifford's companion and nurse. The gamekeeper remains wary until the beautiful scene in which Connie takes up a newly born pheasant chick in her hand, then bows herself down and weeps. (pp. 167-69)

She has been moved by the touch of new life in the tiny bird who stands so boldly on her outstretched hands. She weeps because her own maternal instincts have been frustrated, because her life is emotionally barren, because she is a woman without a warm physical connection with anybody or anything. Perhaps also she weeps because the direct physical apprehension of this "atom of balancing life" is painful, as though Lawrence were saying here that to know the world in the way of naked contact is painful at first for those who have been "ravished by dead words become obscene, and dead ideas become obsessions."

In the climax of this scene there is a reversal. Now it is the gamekeeper who is "touched," who experiences a moment of overwhelming realization which leads him, despite misgivings, to begin life anew, to become once again tender and vulnerable and open in a world full of the sharp edges and points of anti-vital abstractions and grim, uncontrollable machines.

In the hut to which the couple retire the woman asks herself over and over again, "Was it real?" and, "Why was this necessary?" but then deciding to lay down the burden of herself, she reflects that she is "to be had for the taking." This phrase, so often employed cynically, expresses here a change which is in the final analysis deeply spiritual in implication. A lady yields her favors to a surly gamekeeper: a woman yields up herself to life and is saved. This is an equation the novel as a whole insists upon and which Lawrence's art attempts to sustain. (p. 170)

> Julian Moynahan, in his *The Deed of Life: The Novels and Tales of D. H. Lawrence,* Princeton University Press, 1963, 229 p.

H. M. Daleski (essay date 1965)

[*Daleski is an Israeli educator and critic. In the following excerpt, he comments on the significance of the "obscene" language in* Lady Chatterley's Lover *and assesses the thematic significance of the scene involving anal intercourse.*]

> Man need not sacrifice the intellect to the penis, nor the penis to the intellect. But there is an eternal hostility between the two, and life is forever torn across by the conflict between them. Yet man has a holy ghost inside him which partakes of the nature of both. And hence man has a new aim in life, to maintain a truce between the two and some sort of fluctuating harmony. Instead of deliberately, as science and Socrates, Christianity and Buddha have all done, deliberately setting out to murder the one in order to exalt the other. [*The First Lady Chatterley*]

> As I say it's a novel of the phallic Consciousness: or the phallic Consciousness versus the mental-spiritual Consciousness: and of course you know which side I take. The *versus* is not my fault: there should be no *versus*. The two things must be reconciled in us. But now they're daggers drawn.
> [D. H. Lawrence in a 1928 letter to Earl and Achsah Brewster]
> (pp. 258-59)

[Lawrence's] concern throughout the years in which he worked at *Lady Chatterley's Lover* was that the 'penis' and the 'intellect' should be reconciled; but faced by what he thought was the 'exaltation' of the one at the expense of the other, he determined in this novel to do justice to the former. He determined, that is to say, to do justice to those qualities which he felt were undervalued in an industrial civilization, to those qualities, we might add, which were undervalued in his Eastwood home and which he had undervalued in himself in the writing of parts of *The Plumed Serpent*. In view of the phallic paean in that novel this may appear to be a wilful assertion; but we have to distinguish between a glorification of 'the phallus', of male power, that is, and an adherence to the 'phallic consciousness', to what Lawrence elsewhere calls the 'primal consciousness' or 'blood consciousness', an adherence to a sensitive if earthy physical awareness, to the senses (particularly the sense of touch), to a vital spontaneity, to tenderness—in a word, to the female principle. Indeed, Lawrence's invocation of the 'phallic consciousness' betrays the infirmity of a divided self, for it is a subterfuge which enables him to identify himself with 'female' qualities while preserving a 'male' turn of phrase. The identification is obvious enough, as the extract from the letter to the Brewsters shows. It would seem, moreover, that in between the first and final versions of the novel this identification became more and more defiant and strongly altered the emphasis of the finished work. Even in *The First Lady Chatterley* I do not think that the emphasis falls on the 'new aim in life', on the depiction of the 'sort of fluctuating harmony' that should be attained between the 'penis' and the 'intellect'; in *Lady Chatterley's Lover* it seems Lawrence felt 'a truce' could not be established between the two until the 'mental consciousness' had been decisively routed.

Lawrence's defiant identification with the 'phallic consciousness', his 'taking of sides', helps to explain several features of the final version of the book. It accounts, in the first place, for an obtrusive element, the deliberate use of the so-called obscene words. Since the unexpurgated edition of *Lady Chatterley's Lover* has at long last been legally instated in England, there is now no call to discuss whether the use of these words is obscene or not; but what must be considered is the curious critical response to their use, the apparently liberal understanding of Lawrence's intention and the firm disapproval of the practice. I quote what I take to be a representative instance of the prevailing critical attitude:

> . . . when we come to the obscene words . . . I think we encounter an excessive reaction to censorship and prudery. . . . Lawrence uses them probably not more than a hundred times in all . . . in the course of a longish novel. So in any case they cannot make much difference. They . . . are meant to show [Mellors'] frank carnality and its vivifying power. So far they are an integral part of Lawrence's purpose. But still more, one suspects, they are part of the extracurricular activity of bringing "sex out into the open", and like all such secondary purposes in a work of fiction they are so far an irrelevance. Of course, it is quite true, we have no proper vocabulary to discuss sex. . . . Lawrence's remedy is to use the obscene words familiarly and seriously, so that the tabooed acts and parts of the body can be talked about in natural and native words. An admirable intention, no doubt, but doing no great credit to his literary sense. Writers are masters of language, but they can only become so by respecting its nature. No writer can alter the connotations of a whole section of the vocabulary by mere fiat: and the fact remains that the connotations of the obscene physical words are either facetious or vulgar. And very useful they are in these contexts. But in any context where dignity, tenderness, respect for one's own person or that of another is concerned, they are impossible. The effect of putting them into Mellors' mouth as they are is either to create the impression that he is, as one of Lawrence's acquaintance described him, a crude sexual moron, or that whole passages of his discourse are disastrously out of character.
> [Graham Hough, *The Dark Sun*]

It seems to me that, if we respond to the novel as I think Lawrence intended us to, we cannot say that the words do not 'make much difference'; nor, if we understand that Lawrence was not engaging in an 'extracurricular activity' (the book is an organic whole), can we regard them as 'an irrelevance'. Lawrence himself would certainly have been surprised at such an estimate: referring to the first version of the novel, he wrote to his Italian publisher: 'I believe it has hardly any fucks or shits, and no address to the penis, in fact hardly any of the root of the matter at all.' Furthermore, I should say that Lawrence uses the words in an assault on the 'mental consciousness' of the reader, and that the assault, to judge from the letter to the Brewsters, is as much an integral part of his purpose as the effort to show Mellors' 'frank carnality and its vivifying power'. He deliberately tries to shock us out of a false mental position. He violently attempts to dislodge the grip which the 'mental consciousness' exerts on the 'phallic consciousness' in order to bring about an adjustment between the two modes of consciousness; that is to say, he seeks to overcome the superficial aversion of the mind to the words by forcing a response from a deeper conscious-

Page from the manuscript of the first version of Lady Chatterley's Lover.

ness which is not shocked. What he hopes for is a calm, *rational* acceptance both of the words and the physical facts they denote, for a shrinking from the word implies a shrinking from the fact:

> But I want, with **Lady C.,** to make an *adjustment in consciousness* to the basic physical realities. . . . If a man had been able to say to you when you were young and in love: an' if tha shits, an' if tha pisses, I' glad, I shouldna want a woman who couldna shit nor piss—surely it would have been a liberation to you, and it would have helped to keep your heart warm. Think of poor Swift's insane *But* of horror at the end of every verse of that poem to Celia. But Celia shits!—you see the very fact that it should horrify him, and simply devastate his consciousness, is all wrong, and a bitter shame to poor Celia. It's the awful and truly unnecessary *recoil* from these things that I would like to break. It's a question of conscious acceptance and adjustment—only that. . . .
> [D. H. Lawrence in a 1928 letter to Lady Ottoline Morrell]

If Lawrence's use of the words is thus directed at effecting an adjustment in the individual consciousness, his deliberate violation of a literary convention is also intended to shock us out of a social insanity. That adult men and women should have judged the following passage, for instance, to be socially acceptable goes far to justifying the thoroughness with which Lawrence rejected the convention; for it is, of course, the dash, and not the missing guts of the word, which is obscene and perniciously perpetuates the attitudes he was attacking:

> 'Ay!' he said. 'I'm a gamekeeper, at thirty-five bob a week. Ay! I'm all right. I'm Sir Clifford's servant, an' I'm Lady Chatterley's—' he looked her in the face—'What do you call me, in *your* sort of talk?'
>
> 'My lover!' she stammered.
>
> 'Lover!' he re-echoed. A queer flash went over his face.
>
> 'F-er!' he said, and his eyes darted a flash at her, as if he shot her. [*The First Lady Chatterley*]

Lawrence, indeed, saw clearly enough that social sanity is indivisible, and his prophecy of 'a howling manifestation of mob-insanity' has been too horrifyingly borne out for us not to take him seriously:

> The result of taboo is insanity. And insanity, especially mob-insanity, mass-insanity, is the fearful danger that threatens our civilization. . . . If the young do not watch out, they will find themselves, before so very many years are past, engulfed in a howling manifestation of mob-insanity, truly terrifying to think of. . . . In the name of piety and purity, what a mass of disgusting insanity is spoken and written. We shall have to fight the mob, in order to keep sane, and to keep society sane.
> [Preface to **Pansies** in *Phoenix*]

Lawrence, however, did not intend merely to shock. His use of the words should be linked with an overt concern at what might be called the mortification of language: 'All the great words, it seemed to Connie, were cancelled for her generation: love, joy, happiness, home, mother, father, husband, all these great, dynamic words were half dead now, and dying from day to day.' Lawrence, that is to say, in attempting to cleanse the grime from the 'obscene' words, sought to revitalize the 'great' words by providing them with a new content. The new content is provided, of course, by the novel as a whole, but the use of the 'obscene' words is an essential part of the undertaking which is the whole. Connie later reflects that one can be ravished without ever being touched, 'ravished by dead words become obscene'; we might say that Lawrence seeks to show how one can be warmed by obscene words become tender. He seeks, that is, to enhance the value of the words by fashioning new contexts for their use, employing them seriously in contexts which support neither an abusive nor a shameful nor a scornful connotation. His practice, in this respect, is markedly different from that of James Joyce in *Ulysses,* for Joyce's use of the words in the last section of the book, though admirably revelatory of the character of Molly Bloom, in effect perpetuates their debasement. Lawrence, unlike Joyce, was trying to use the words in two different ways at the same time. He wished, on the one hand, to retain their earthy character, for he detested the 'spiritualizing' of sex: '. . . We shall never free the phallic reality from the "uplift" taint till we give it its own phallic language, and use the obscene words. The greatest blasphemy of all against the phallic reality is this "lifting it to a higher plane".' On the other hand, he believed that 'a proper reverence for sex' entailed the use of 'the so-called obscene words, because these are a natural part of the mind's consciousness of the body'. ['**A Propos of** *Lady Chatterley's Lover*']

What, then, is the overall effect of Lawrence's use of the words as distinguished from his intentions? I deliberately quote a passage in which these words preponderate:

> 'Why should I say *maun* when you said *mun,*' she protested. 'You're not playing fair.'
>
> 'Arena Ah!' he said, leaning forward and softly stroking her face.
>
> 'Th'art good cunt, though, aren't ter? Best bit o' cunt left on earth. When ter likes! When tha'rt willin'!'
>
> 'What is cunt?' she said.
>
> 'An' doesn't ter know? Cunt! It's thee down theer; an' what I get when I'm i'side thee, and what tha gets when I'm i'side thee; it's a' as it is, all on't.'
>
> 'All on't,' she teased. 'Cunt! It's like fuck then.'
>
> 'Nay nay! Fuck's only what you do. Animals fuck. But cunt's a lot more than that. It's thee, dost see: an' tha'rt a lot besides an animal, aren't ter? even ter fuck! Cunt! Eh, that's the beauty o' thee, lass!'

First, I think it should be said that the words do shock in exactly the way Lawrence intended them to; that is, if we are shocked on first encountering them, we soon cease to be so and realize how absurd it was to be shocked at all. Second, I contest Hough's judgement that the words are 'impossible' in a context of dignity, tenderness, and personal respect. Mellors uses them, it seems to me, in a manifestly tender manner, with full respect for Connie's person, and without impairing either his dignity or hers; the soft stroking of her face, indeed, is a physical equivalent of the caressive gentleness of his speech. Nor does it strike me that he speaks out of character or like 'a crude sexual moron'. A more valid objection against Lawrence's use of the words, I should say, is that it is too deliberate, if not self-conscious; and, in this passage at any rate, their use is open to the same sort of criticism that we would level, for instance, at an over-elaborate metaphor. It would be idle to pretend, moreover, that Lawrence is able to employ the words with the effortless simplicity and freshness of a Chaucer; like the special but very different terminology used in *The Rainbow,* the words do undoubtedly carry with them at least a residue of their more usual, contemporary associations. But that does not mean to say, as Hough seems to imply, and as other critics emphatically state, that their use should be restricted to facetious or vulgar contexts. It is, after all, a context which determines the meaning of a word, not a word the context; and a reinstatement of these words would not inhibit their use as invective either in literature or in life. (pp. 259-65)

What, then, . . . of the conflict within Lawrence between male and female elements? Does the serenity with which he solves so many of the problems that agitated him for so long indicate that harmony is established in this respect too? Or does it at least indicate that Lawrence is finally reconciled to the predominantly 'female' quality of his vision? His last novel would seem to suggest that he did ultimately write in grudging, if camouflaged, acceptance of the 'female' view of things, for, as I have pointed out, his vindication of the 'phallic consciousness' is, in effect, if not in intention, a vindication of the female principle. . . . But such a conclusion would not convey the whole truth. *Lady Chatterley's Lover* forces us to conclude, rather, that, deep down, so deep, indeed, as radically to qualify the nature of what is offered us while barely disturbing the surface, Lawrence's self-division compels him to make a 'male' counter-assertion of a kind which it is impossible to reconcile with the overt 'female' statement of the novel.

On the face of it there is not much evidence of male assertion on Lawrence's part. . . . Clifford, for instance, is, in terms of the Hardy essay, all 'man'. Committed both by mishap and by inclination to the spirit, not the flesh, he achieves 'utterance' in his writing and is eminently successful in his work in the 'man's world' of the mines. Yet I need not stress, at this stage, what sort of person he is shown to be, both futile as a writer and utterly inhuman as an industrialist. And the futility and the inhumanity are directly attributable, of course, to the paralysis of his emotional or 'female' self. To be all 'man', we see, and this is a strong refutation of Birkin's characteristic insistence in *Women in Love,* is to be only half a man, is to be, indeed, a 'half-corpse'. Clifford wins his 'man's victory', but at the same time he lets Mrs Bolton shave him and sponge him 'as if he were a child'; he also becomes 'almost a *creature,* with a hard, efficient shell of an exterior and a pulpy interior, one of the amazing crabs and lobsters of the modern, industrial and financial world', and when he is forced out of that world, when, for instance, he discusses the question of Connie's having a child, he speaks 'like a cornered dog'. Dog, lobster, crab, child—the indictment of the unadulterated male is vicious. The epithets, moreover, are shown to be not unjustified when Clifford has to face up to the emotional crisis of Connie's abandonment of him. After he has read the letter in which she breaks the news to him, he is 'like a hysterical child', and his face is 'yellow, blank, and like the face of an idiot'; the experienced Mrs Bolton realizes that his hysteria is a sign that 'his manhood [is] dead, temporarily if not finally'. When she comforts him, he clings to her and lets 'himself go altogether, at last'. Clifford's letting go, of course, has to be sharply distinguished from the way in which Connie and Mellors let go: his is a 'sheer relaxation . . . letting go all his manhood, and sinking back to a childish position that [is] really perverse'. In the end he gets into the habit of kissing Mrs. Bolton's breasts 'in exultation, the exultation of perversity, of being a child when he [is] a man'. His childish perversity is exhibited just as damagingly, and this is the last we see of him, in his refusal to grant Connie a divorce when he discovers it is Mellors she wishes to marry.

Mellors, on the other hand, with whom Lawrence is closely identified in several important respects, . . . clearly has (again in the sense in which the word is used in the Hardy essay) a preponderantly 'female' character. He even says of himself: 'They used to say I had too much of the woman in me', and though he adds, with justification, 'But it's not that. I'm not a woman because I don't want to shoot birds, neither because I don't want to make money, or get on', we know, nevertheless, that he is in fact presented as an exemplar of the 'phallic consciousness', that is, of the female principle. And we have seen that it is not merely a matter of his having no ambition to make money; he has totally rejected the 'man's world', and his occupation has symbolic undertones, for his task is to preserve the wild life of the wood. He would like, too, to 'try an' live [his] own life', simply to be. It is here that Lawrence is faced by what proves to be an insoluble problem in his fiction when the protagonist is not a writer—the difficulty of establishing a convincing 'male' meaning in such a life. (In his own life, of course, his writing was both his 'utterance' and his 'action', even though it has an unmistakable 'female' quality.) Mellors, indeed, is very much aware of this problem: 'A man must offer a woman *some* meaning in his life', he tells Connie, 'if it's going to be an isolated life, and if she's a genuine woman. I can't be just your male concubine'.

The problem is of no consequence to Connie. She assures Mellors he has something that other men do not have, the courage of his own tenderness, and that it is this which will 'make the future', but though the novel has established the supreme importance of this kind of courage in a world in which the Cliffords have power, we remain aware that tenderness is not a 'male' quality. Nor does Mellors in any way modify his rejection of the outer world: he hopes that ultimately he and Connie will be able to have 'some small farm of their own', into which he can 'put his energy', and he writes to her that 'the little flame' between them is for him 'the only thing in the world.' He seems set, that is to say, to live the kind of life lived by the Brangwen forebears in *The Rainbow,* a life based on a close connection with the earth and with a woman, a life that is characterized by 'the drowse of blood-intimacy'. It was from that drowse that Tom Brangwen stirred, . . . girding himself to face the task of establishing his 'man-being'; and it was with an unsatisfied bitterness that he many years later recognized the limitations, as well as the value, of a life which had in fact 'amounted' to nothing but 'the long marital embrace with his wife'. Mellors, in the end, is not conscious of a similar sense of dissatisfaction both because he is more confident of his priorities and because he believes he has found the 'male' meaning he is seeking when he conceives of opposing his faith in tenderness to the insentience of the 'man's world':

> 'I stand for the touch of bodily awareness between human beings,' he said to himself, 'and the touch of tenderness. And she is my mate. And it is a battle against the money, and the machine, and the insentient ideal monkeyishness of the world. And she will stand behind me there. Thank God I've got a woman! Thank God I've got a woman who is with me, and tender and aware of me . . . '

That Lawrence can permit Mellors this triumphant confidence in the value of tenderness and sexual love is a measure of the distance he has travelled between *The Rainbow* and *Lady Chatterley's Lover;* but when he also allows Mellors to believe that to stand by his tenderness in the isolation of his life with Connie will indeed constitute 'a battle' against the world he hates, he merely evades the point at issue—for Mellors' battle, it is clear, is to be fought outside that world, not from within it, and does not commit him to any characteristic 'male' activity. Lawrence himself, of course, fought such a battle courageously and magnificently in the writing of *Lady Chatterley's Lover;* Mellors cannot respond in a similar way to a challenge he is no doubt ready to take up. If we never feel that he is merely Connie's 'male concubine', we are nevertheless not convinced that he *has* found a genuine male meaning in his life.

I believe it is Lawrence's own uncertainty, in this regard, that makes him feel the need of asserting Mellors' 'manhood' in some other manner:

> It was a night of sensual passion, in which she was a little startled and almost unwilling: yet pierced again with piercing thrills of sensuality, different, sharper, more terrible than the thrills of tenderness, but, at the moment, more desirable. Though a little frightened, she let him have his way, and the reckless, shameless sensuality shook her to her foundations, stripped her to the very last, and made a different woman of her. It was not really love. It was not voluptuousness. It was sensuality sharp and searing as fire, burning the soul to tinder.
>
> Burning out the shames, the deepest, oldest shames, in the most secret places. It cost her an effort to let him have his way and his will of her. She had to be a passive, consenting thing, like a slave, a physical slave. Yet the passion licked round her, consuming, and when the sensual flame of it pressed through her bowels and breast, she really thought she was dying: yet a poignant, marvellous death.
>
> She had often wondered what Abélard meant, when he said that in their year of love he and Héloïse had passed through all the stages and refinements of passion. The same thing, a thousand years ago: ten thousand years ago! The same on the Greek vases, everywhere! The refinements of passion, the extravagances of sensuality! And necessary, forever necessary, to burn out false shames and smelt out the heaviest ore of the body into purity. With the fire of sheer sensuality.
>
> In the short summer night she learnt so much. She would have thought a woman would have died of shame. Instead of which, the shame died. Shame, which is fear: the deep organic shame, the old, old physical fear which crouches in the bodily roots of us, and can only be chased away by the sensual fire, at last it was roused up and routed by the phallic hunt of the man, and she came to the very heart of the jungle of herself. She felt, now, she had come to the real bed-rock of her nature, and was essentially shameless. She was her sensual self, naked and unashamed. She felt a triumph, almost a vainglory. So! That was how it was! That was life! That was how oneself really was! There was nothing left to disguise or be ashamed of. She shared her ultimate nakedness with a man, another being.
>
> And what a reckless devil the man was! really like a devil! One had to be strong to bear him. But it took some getting at, the core of the physical jungle, the last and deepest recess of organic shame. The phallos alone could explore it. And how he had pressed in on her!

This passage has been the object of considerable critical attention, and there is no need to repeat in detail the arguments with which certain critics have established the meaning of the allusions to Abélard and the Greek vases. These allusions, which by themselves are inconclusive, link up, as Eliseo Vivas [in his study *D. H. Lawrence*] was the first to point out, with others to Mellors' sexual practices with his wife and, in particular, with Clifford's reference (in a letter to Connie) to Mellors' apparent liking for using his wife, 'as Benvenuto Cellini says, "in the Italian way" '. They should also be related to Connie's immediate understanding of Mrs Bolton's vague report of 'the low, beastly things' Mellors is alleged to have done to his wife: 'Connie remembered the last night she had spent with him, and shivered. He had known all that sensuality, even with a Bertha Coutts!' I think, therefore, that we can now take it as established beyond doubt that the 'night of sensual passion' is a night on which Mellors has anal intercourse with Connie; but what needs to be investigated is the significance of the experience.

The experience is overtly presented as a necessary purification: the 'sensual fire', and we note how fire images recur throughout the passage, burns out 'false shames' and smelts out 'the heaviest ore of the body into purity'. It is as if Connie must be made to realize, despite conventional revulsion and disgust, that nothing to do with the body is 'low' and 'beastly', that where there is love between a man and a woman, everything is permissible. It seems that the fire is intended to consume the shame associated with 'the most secret places' and with the practice of what is usually regarded as a sexual 'perversion' in much the same way that Lawrence's use of the 'obscene' words is meant to startle us out of a different, but related, shame. Lawrence, says G. Wilson Knight [in 'Lawrence, Joyce and Powys,' *Essays in Criticism* (1960)], is trying to 'blast through . . . degradation to a new health. . . . So the deathly is found to be the source of some higher order of being; contact with a basic materiality liberates the person.'

If this is what Lawrence is trying to do in the passage, it strikes me that we have to face two objections to the way in which he presents the experience. In the first place, if it is love that can be deemed to give the practice an individual moral sanction in defiance of convention, it is clear that Mellors, on this night, does not come to Connie in love. It is not only that we are told that his sensual passion is 'not really love'; it seems to spring directly from his anger with Hilda. Immediately before, he has had a fierce altercation with Connie's sister, and when Connie remonstrates with him, he replies: 'She should ha' been slapped in time.' Though Connie cannot help being aware of how 'outwardly angry' he is even when they are alone together, she is sure that his anger is not directed to her. Nevertheless, he takes 'no notice of her', and when he asks her to go up to the bedroom, 'the anger still [sits] firm' on his brows. Mellors' 'sensuality', therefore, would appear to be an expression of his anger, a release of the violence that is coiled within him; the man who cannot bring himself to shoot birds, we note, here lends himself with gusto to 'the phallic hunt'. Is it, we wonder, . . . that Lawrence cannot reconcile the experience he describes with the kind of love he has previously shown to exist between Connie and Mellors, and that he consequently feels compelled to provide a context of anger and violence for it? That, at all events, *is* the context of Mellors' 'sensuality'—just as the scene at the coops defines the meaning of his 'tenderness'.

Second, I think we cannot help noticing that there is something peculiarly one-sided about the way in which the experience is presented. I have remarked earlier, in regard to the important question of the 'losing' and 'finding' of the self in the sex act, that we are left in no doubt that what is shown to happen to Connie applies to Mellors as well. Here, though we are told that the shame and fear crouch 'in the bodily roots of us', of all of us, that is, it is only Connie, apparently, who needs to be subjected to the purifying fire. If it is maintained that, in the nature of things, it is only Connie who can be so subjected, then Wilson Knight has pointed out that, in *Women in Love,* there are hints of an analogous practice in which 'the implements are fingers'. If this is so, and I find Wilson Knight's argument convincing in its broad outline, though not always in detail, then it is most noticeable that in *Women in Love* Birkin wishes to share in the same experience:

'And he too waited in the magical steadfastness of suspense, for her to take this knowledge of him as he had taken it of her. He knew her darkly, with the fullness of dark knowledge. Now she would know him, and he too would be liberated . . . '

In *Lady Chatterley's Lover* there is no indication that Mellors wishes Connie to take this liberating knowledge of him; and though it is said to be 'forever necessary' to burn out a shame that is twice referred to as 'organic', he shows no desire to be purified of *his* shame and fear.

I suggest the experience is shown to be one-sided because its covert significance is the aggrandizement of the male. The vitality of the trees in the wood, we recall, was associated with power as well as with tenderness, and it seems to me that in the quoted passage Mellors, the keeper of the wood and the man who has the courage of his tenderness, is celebrated as a man of power. Indeed, the Mellors who is presented to us in this passage bears a distinct resemblance to Cipriano of *The Plumed Serpent.* He has both 'his way' and 'his will' of Connie, and she has to be 'a passive, consenting thing, like a slave, a physical slave'. I have already indicated that I believe it is Lawrence's uncertainty about the 'male' meaning in Mellors' life that leads him to present this kind of evidence of his manhood. Connie's reaction to Mellors on this night would seem to confirm the analysis: she reflects what 'a reckless devil the man' is, 'really like a devil'; she contrasts Mellors' manhood with that of men like Clifford and Michaelis, whom she thinks of as 'so doggy', and she realizes 'how rare a thing a man is' when most men, it seems, are 'dogs that trot and sniff and copulate'; finally, she looks appreciatively at Mellors, who is 'sleeping so like a wild animal asleep'. Mellors, we see, is a wild animal where other men are tame dogs; he is a devil who dares everything where other men only copulate; he is a 'man'.

Two further objections to the passage now present themselves. First, it seems to me that Lawrence is guilty of forcing Connie's reaction to the experience in much the same way that he forces Kate's responses to Cipriano. For Lawrence to say flatly that Connie was a 'little' startled and 'almost' unwilling, but that 'at the moment' the 'thrills of sensuality' were 'more desirable' than the 'thrills of tenderness', for him to say that she was a 'little' frightened, but that 'she let him have his way' seems to me to be a wanton denial of the scrupulous and penetrating presentation of her previous reactions to Mellors. We remember that her fear of 'losing' herself was a fear of becoming 'effaced', and that 'she did not want to be effaced, a slave, like a savage woman'. It was tenderness alone which broke down her resistance to even orthodox intercourse, and induced her to accept her effacement. Nevertheless, she dreaded 'the thrust of a sword in her softly-opened body', fearing that it 'would be death'. Her fear, then, was allayed by Mellors' tenderness, and, allowing herself to 'die', she was 'reborn'; here, his passion 'consumes', and she 'really [thinks] she [is] dying'. The desirability of such a 'death' is not established merely by saying that it is 'poignant' and 'marvellous', for we have just been told that Mellors' sensuality '[burns] the soul to tinder'.

Second, it has struck several critics as significant that, in a book as determinedly frank as *Lady Chatterley's Lover,* Lawrence should be reticent and oblique in his description of the 'night of sensual passion'. I think this is an important consideration, but it seems to me absurd to say, as Andrew Shonfield does [in "Lawrence's Other Censor," *Encounter* (1960)], that the reticence and obliquity are 'cowardly', or to maintain, as John Sparrow does [in "Regina v. Penguin Books Ltd.," *Encounter* (1962)], that the method betrays a 'fundamental dishonesty'. We can hardly think of the man who wrote **Lady Chatterley's Lover,** when he wrote it, as a coward; and if Lawrence expressed his meaning obliquely in the passage under discussion, he was not dishonest about it, for he carefully added a sufficient number of clues elsewhere to make it quite unambiguous. Sparrow has himself shown the pains that Lawrence took to make his meaning clear, and if Shonfield, writing before Sparrow, could only make 'a reasonable guess' at it, that is attributable to his own failure to follow up all the clues, not to Lawrence's cowardice. Nor do I believe it is justified to say that Lawrence is 'completely reticent about the sensuality' because he 'cannot achieve any sort of innocence about it . . . It is evil, because he believes it to be evil' [John Middleton Murry, *Son of Woman*]. Whatever the covert meaning of the scene may be, I have already indicated, in discussing its overt significance, that Lawrence assuredly did not believe the practice itself to be evil, that he was, indeed, fighting against those who would automatically assume it to be so. I think it more likely that he is reticent because he does not know how to present the experience directly in such a way that it will not appear to be 'unnatural' or disgusting or degrading—though he is convinced it is none of these. And he does not know how to say directly what he wants to say because he is uncertain of the value of what he is offering, uncertain that the liberation of which Wilson Knight writes can be achieved in this way, uncertain—and these are the points that I should like to stress—that he can really reconcile this kind of sensuality with love and tenderness, and that it is a legitimate means of asserting manhood.

It is scarcely surprising that Lawrence is uncertain. If he is trying to blast through to a new health, as Wilson Knight says he is, it is perhaps only to be expected that he should be tentative about this method of doing so, for he is exploring an experience of an unusual kind at a level far removed from ordinary understanding. If, moreover, he is also using the experience as a means of asserting Mellors' manhood, he must be uneasily aware that this represents a reversion to the ethos of **The Plumed Serpent,** an ethos which he tacitly repudiated in undertaking to write **Lady Chatterley's Lover** and from which he later explicitly dissociated himself in his letters. Finally, if he is trying to reconcile the sensuality with love and tenderness, he must also be uneasily aware that he is negating a great deal of what he has so profoundly established in the book. We have been shown that there is no need for tenderness to be balanced by power; it has its own power, a revivifying power, and we cannot reconcile the flame that melts and heals with the fire that sears and consumes. Lawrence, it seems, is trying to suggest that love between a man and a woman must be both 'sensual' and 'tender', in the sense in which these words are defined by their contexts in the novel. It is not a convincing position because he has not been able to establish that the 'sensuality' is a manifestation of love. We can see clearly enough that the same man can be both 'tender' and 'sensual'; we are not convinced that he can be both with the woman he loves. I submit that Lawrence cannot convince us because, in effect, he is also trying to reconcile a 'male' sensuality with a 'female' tenderness; and though the two are perhaps not intrinsically irreconcilable, he—at any rate—was temperamentally incapable of effecting such a reconciliation.

[In **Women in Love**] Birkin, a most Lawrence-like figure, felt free to express his desire for 'oneness' in the wrestling bout with Gerald because he was under no defensive compulsion, as he apparently was in regard to a woman, to realize the man's 'otherness'. To the extent that we can identify Lawrence with Birkin in this respect, I think we can say that Lawrence, who had a predominantly 'female' disposition, laboured under a similar compulsion; we may add that his characteristic insistence that the man should not 'lose' himself in the sex act sprang, to follow Mrs Krook, from the fear of a loss of identity, of his male identity, and that the presence in **Women in Love** of hints of an unorthodox sexual practice indulged in by Birkin and Ursula should be related to the same fear. Inasmuch as Lawrence can be identified with Mellors on the 'night of sensual passion', therefore, I would suggest that the sensuality represents not only a reversion to a desire for male domination, but also a recrudescence of the old fear of a loss of identity, which, as we have seen, is the fundamental cause of a sexual assertiveness. Mellors' tenderness has taught Connie to overcome this fear, but it would seem that, in this instance, a similar fear on his part is responsible for his departure from the more usual form of intercourse; there is no fear of a 'loss' of self in this kind of contact because there is no tenderness to melt the separateness of the self. Indeed, the repeated emphases on the fact that Mellors is 'a man', to which I have already referred in another connection, take on further significance when we interpret them in this light, and we become aware of a deeper level of meaning when we are told that Connie 'shared her ultimate nakedness with a man, another being'.

The passage which I have discussed at such length does, I think, impair the quality of the novel both because it introduces an alien element into the vision of tenderness which is otherwise so superbly rendered, and because, on a small scale, in the forcing of Connie's response, it represents a failure of artistic integrity. But we should not overemphasize the failure here. Mellors, after all, puts his faith, in the end, in the little flame of tenderness, not in the searing fire of sensuality. . . .

The passage is also an indication, however, of Lawrence's failure to reconcile his 'male' and 'female' impulses. I believe that this failure . . . was the fundamental determinant of the direction he took in the large enterprise of the novels. **Sons and Lovers** gave him both the knowledge and the confidence of his power as a writer, and was the fullest expression in his early work of that opposition between the spirit and the flesh which was to continue to be of prime concern to him. The opposition, of course, is a basic instance of the male and female principles, of which he was to write at length in the Hardy essay; and it was of such concern to him not only because it was externalized in the conflict between his mother and father and in his own relations with Jessie Chambers, but also because it projected a violent clash within himself. In ***The Rainbow*** Lawrence made his most strenuous effort to show how the male and female principles could be reconciled both within the individual psyche and within marriage. I think that this is Lawrence's finest novel, less flawed than ***Women in Love,*** if not more profound; and I do not believe it is coincidental that in it he succeeded in depicting an individual who was able to achieve a full reconciliation between the two principles. It is perhaps not without significance that the individual should have been a woman, that the task, as it were, was to balance an inherently female disposition with 'male' qualities. In ***The Rainbow,*** however, no man was found to match Ursula's achievement, and in ***Women in Love***—the most remarkable of the novels in its scope—her marriage to Birkin proved to be a marriage on essentially 'female' terms. In it, moreover, Birkin persuaded Ursula to withdraw with him from the 'man's world', and this withdrawal, I believe, necessitated the ensuing effort to redefine the meaning of 'man-being' and to explore alternative ways of effecting a return to the world of men. This effort led to the compensatory male assertion, of which there was already some evidence in ***Women in Love,*** that characterized the novels of the third period, and that drove Lawrence through ***Aaron's Rod*** and ***Kangaroo*** to the cul-de-sac of ***The Plumed Serpent.*** These novels are the worst of Lawrence's mature work. The decline in artistic achievement, in comparison with ***Women in Love,*** which preceded them, is marked; and it would seem that, in trying to establish a new kind of 'male' significance and to assert a desire for male domination, Lawrence wrote so badly because he was writing against his own deepest values. In ***Lady Chatterley's Lover*** he succeeded in giving full and vivid expression to those values and in producing a novel that is only a little inferior to ***The Rainbow*** and ***Women in Love.*** To the end, however, he could not reconcile the male and female elements in himself; and his attempt to balance the overt 'female' tendency of the novel by asserting a covert 'male' significance resulted in its major blemish. (pp. 300-11)

> H. M. Daleski, in his The Forked Flame: A Study of D. H. Lawrence, Faber & Faber, 1965, 320 p.

J. R. Ebbatson (essay date 1977)

[*In the following excerpt, Ebbatson argues that Thomas Hardy had a major influence on* Lady Chatterley's Lover *in light of the parallels between Lawrence's novel and Hardy's* Two on a Tower.]

The question of Lady Chatterley's literary antecedents is an intriguing one, and some curious candidates have been advanced. Neither Mrs. Humphrey Ward's *Lady Connie* (1916) nor Shaw's *Cashel Byron's Profession* (1886), two of the most recent, betrays any family likeness, even if they were ever read by Lawrence, which is improbable. The ancient theme of old or maimed husband and young, passionate wife tends, in its Victorian variants, towards the sombre. Lawrence's presentation of Clifford and Connie was plainly influenced by such couples as Sir Leicester and Lady Dedlock, and Casaubon and Dorothea, and also by local families such as the Sitwells at Renishaw and the Barbers at Lamb Close—indeed, the range of Eastwood names Lawrence introduces, including Chatterley, Mellors, Chambers and Leivers, hints at a *roman à clef*.

I think we may identify one literary analogue which lay closer to "the country of my heart" than any so far proposed: Hardy's *Two on a Tower,* a story centering on the secret passion of a neglected aristocratic lady for a young astronomer. Even without Lawrence's **"Study of Thomas Hardy,"** his familiarity with Hardy's work would be indisputable and its formative influence beyond doubt. Jessie Chambers recalled her father reading *Tess* in the kitchen at the Haggs, and added, "Hardy's name had been familiar in our house since childhood days". Lawrence left no recorded reference to Hardy before 1910, but he and Jessie had certainly read a good deal in their teens and this reading spilt over into the various versions of **The White Peacock.** As it happens, *Two on a Tower* was one of the novels most immediately available to the young Lawrence, being one of four volumes by Hardy in the Eastwood Mechanics' Institute Library according to the 1895 catalogue. We have Jessie's testimony that Lawrence was familiar with virtually everything in this library, and I think we can reasonably conclude that *Two on a Tower* was a Wessex novel crucially placed to influence Lawrence's imagination at this time.

This must necessarily remain conjectural. What is certain is that Lawrence was fully aware of *Two on a Tower* by the time he came to prepare his study of Hardy. He speaks impressively in the "Study" of the "great background, vital and vivid, which matters more than the people who move upon it," citing not only *The Return of the Native* and *The Woodlanders,* but also *Two on a Tower* in proof of his assertion. Lawrence takes Lady Constantine, Hardy's heroine, as an example of Hardy's *prédilection d'artiste* for the aristocratic type, and places her in a group of "passionate natures" with Elfride, Marty South, and Tess. Passion is a quality he finds lacking in the male protagonist of *Two on a Tower,* the young Swithin St. Cleeve, whom he characterises as an "unsuccessful but not very much injured astronomer." After the **"Study"**, scattered references reveal that Hardy was still in Lawrence's mind from time to time. He wrote of the country round Hermitage, where he stayed towards the end of the war, and which he took as the setting for **"The Fox,"** that "to wander through the hazel copses, away to the real old English hamlets" was like something from *The Woodlanders* (**Kangaroo**). In 1924 he wrote that Hardy, "a last big one, rings the knell of our Oneness," and in the same year noted more quizzically that "Even the greatest men spend most of their time making marvellous fine toys. Like *Pickwick* or *Two on a Tower.*" Early in 1928, whilst completing the third version of **Lady Chatterley,** Lawrence re-read Hardy's stories "What a commonplace genius he has," he complained, "or a genius for the commonplace, I don't know which." "He doesn't rank so terribly high, really," Lawrence concluded adding maliciously, "But better than Bernard Shaw, even then." This summing-up, despite its dismissive tone, argues that Lawrence's imagination was still to some extent engaged with Hardy; this is corroborated by a report from Barbara Weekley, who on visiting the Lawrences in 1929 noted, "the only serious writer I heard him speak of with respect was Thomas Hardy."

Hardy, then, was in Lawrence's thoughts in the late nineteen-twenties when he was working on the three versions of the Lady Chatterley story. It seems highly probable that his lifelong familiarity with the novels, and specifically, I believe, with *Two on a Tower,* helped in the germination of these extraordinary works.

The plot of *Two on a Tower* was recounted with bald succinctness in an early review by J. M. Barrie:

> a married lady visits an astronomer stealthily, and makes open display of her affection for him. She secretly marries him in the belief that her husband has died in Africa. Some time afterwards she learns that her husband did not die until after this secret ceremony, and then she marries a bishop.

An important factor which Barrie omits, and which Lawrence utilised, is that Lady Constantine becomes pregnant by the astronomer, but when she discovers her false marital position "fathers" the baby on Bishop Helmsdale. This is an implausible recital of events, but Hardy had a serious intent in his "slightly-built romance:" a wish, as he put it, "to set the emotional history of two infinitesimal lives against the stupendous background of the stellar universe" (Preface to the Osgood, McIlvaine edition, 1895). Despite these high aims, like Lawrence after him, Hardy complained that he was "made to suffer" for his novel, "such warm epithets as 'hazardous', 'repulsive', 'little short of revolting', 'a studied and gratuitous insult,' being flung at the precarious volumes" (*Ibid.*). *Two on a Tower,* therefore, possesses a metaphysical aim which was rather botched by Hardy's not having completed the writing until after the work had begun to appear in print. In later years, whilst urging Mrs. Henniker to read his "more serious and later books," on looking again at *Two on a Tower* Hardy found it "rather clever." The contrast between human and cosmic is carefully drawn, and the implausibility is subsumed in the emotional romance.

Such poems as "At a Lunar Eclipse," and "In Vision I Roamed," with the latter's images of "ghost heights of sky" and a "Universe taciturn and drear," have been justly cited as origins of the novel, but an important source in Mill seems to have gone unnoticed. In the essay on "Nature," published eight years before *Two on a Tower,* Mill wrote:

> The solar system, and the great cosmic forces which hold it together; the boundless firmament, and to an educated mind any single star; excite feelings which make all human enterprises and powers appear so insignificant, that to a mind thus occupied it seems insufferable presumption in so puny a creature as man to look critically on things so far above him, or dare to measure himself against the grandeur of the universe . . . The enormous extension in space and time, or the enormous power they exemplify, constitutes their sublimity; a feeling, in all cases, more allied to terror than to any moral emotion.
> (*Three Essays on Religion,* 1874)

Thus *Two on a Tower,* however slight and imperfect, shares that late-Victorian intellectual scientific pessimism which Walter Houghton has said led to "cosmic isolation and the terror of absolute solitude." At the same time Michael Millgate is right to stress that "the stars were inescapably associated with ancient mythologies and with lingering and perhaps inextinguishable supersitions, that heavenly bodies had always provided a rich source of imagery, especially for the poetry of love." This helps to make the link with Lawrence, who in place of astronomy portrays his protagonist as an adept of nature; but the function within the parable is essentially the same.

An examination of *Two on a Tower* reveals how closely the parallels run. The naming of the heroines is very near, and it takes little willing suspension of disbelief to visualize Lady Constantine being transformed into Lady Constance Chatterley, whilst her Christian name, Viviette may have suggested Yvette of ***The Virgin and the Gipsy.*** More substantially, the characterisation is exceptionally close even where the plots diverge, for Lady Constantine is one of those Hardyesque victims of *Bovarysme* of which Eustacia Vye is the supreme exemplar. Hardy explained this at the beginning of chapter fourteen, in a passage later deleted:

> Rural solitude, which provides ample themes for the intellect and sweet occupations innumerable for the minor sentiments, often denies a ready object for those stronger passions that enter no less than the others into the human constitution. The suspended pathos finds its remedy in settling on the first intrusive shape that happens to be reasonably well organized for the purpose, disregarding social and other minor accessories. Where the solitude is shadowed by the secret melancholies of the solitary, this natural law is still surer in operation.

At the outset of the tale Lady Constantine is in a mood of "almost killing *ennui* " as she contemplates the column of the tower where her love is to kindled. Her "cribbed and confined emotions," like those of Connie Chatterley, are rendered more intense by her peculiar marital status. Her husband, Sir Blount, after mistreating her, has disappeared in Africa, leaving her, as St. Cleeve's grandmother explains, "neither maid, wife, nor widow." With "Romance blood in her veins," Viviette is possessed of "a warm and affectionate, perhaps slightly voluptuous temperament, languishing for want of something to do"—a want that is supplied when she encounters the handsome young astronomer on top of the tower. As Lawrence says of his heroine, "Out of her disconnexion, a restlessness was taking possession of her like madness . . . she must get away from the house and everybody. The wood was her one refuge, her sanctuary" (***Lady Chatterley's Lover***). The symbolic configurations of landscape in the two stories are close: the great, gloomy house, the park, and the woods, with the "sanctuary" of tower or cottage. The resonance of the scene in Lawrence has been suggestively analysed by Ian Gregor:

> Instead of the traditionally opposed entrances of Heaven and Hell, we have, on the right, the fretted silhouette of a great wood, and on the left, the pyramid outline of the colliery slag heap, and

the shadows of both darken the façade of the great house which is placed in the centre of the stage. Continually, we have the double awareness of the setting, realism is shot through with symbolism and vice versa.

But the Hardy setting also has symbolic overtones; as Richard Carpenter writes, men ascend towers "to place themselves in mystic converse with the eternal, to raise themselves above ordinary men the better to realise their universal humanity." Carpenter justly adds that the tower is "a powerful phallic symbol, suited to the growth and consummation of a passionate love affair." In both works love is separated from the mundane world outside—in Hardy's case an agricultural reality epitomised by the rustic comedy of the choir-practice, in Lawrence's by the more threatening industrial reality of Tevershall and the pits:

> Round the near horizon went the haze, opalescent with frost and smoke, and on top lay the small blue sky; so that it was like being inside an enclosure, always inside. Life always a dream or a frenzy, inside an enclosure.
> *(Lady Chatterley's Lover)*

Like Lady Chatterley, Viviette makes little of her social eminence. There was in her, Hardy, writes, "an inborn liking . . . to dwell less on her social position as a county lady than on her passing emotions as a woman," and in this portrait he may be drawing upon his early patroness, Julia Augusta Martin of Kingston Maurward. These "passing emotions" draw Lady Constantine inexorably into an affair with Swithin St. Cleeve, "no *amoroso*, no gallant, but a guileless philosopher," who attempts to initiate her into the mysteries of the heavens. She is drawn on by his almost obtuse lack of personal awareness, until it becomes "a serious question whether, if he were not hidden from her eyes, she would not soon be plunging across the ragged boundary which divides the permissible from the forbidden"—a distinction which, allowance made for changes in morals, is equally operative with Lady Chatterley. Like Connie, Viviette's aristocratic selfhood is revived in passional contact with a man of the lower orders, and like her she protests her commitment: "I did not mean that it was a mere interlude to *me*. O if you only knew how very far it is from that!" In both cases this commitment issues in the renewal of childbirth: "Lady Constantine's external affairs wore just that aspect which suggests that new blood may be advantageously introduced into the line; and new blood had been introduced, in good sooth,—with what social result remained to be seen." This comes after news of Sir Blount's death and the clandestine marriage ceremony—like Parkin/Mellors and Connie, Swithin and Viviette communicate by a system of signals from house to woods. It later transpires that Sir Blount had died later than first reported, and that the marriage is consequently null and void; Lawrence had utilised this sequence in his first novel, when Annable, the gamekeeper, tells Cyril of his marriage to Lady Crystabel: "I was supposed to have died in the bush. She married a young fellow. Then I was proved to have died, and I read a little obituary notice on myself" (*The White Peacock*). Lady Constantine, discovering that her lover had sacrificed a bequest by marrying, and despite her pregnancy, practises that abnegation of self that decisively marks off the Victorian from the modern heroine: "She laboured, with a generosity more worthy even than its object, to sink her love for her own decorum in devotion to the world in general, and to Swithin in particular." This devotion leads her to impose the child of her passion on the unwitting and pompous Bishop Helmsdale, just as Connie plans to have her child "fathered" by the impotent Clifford—a crucial narrative twist which underlines Lawrence's debt. The *dénouement* of *Two on a Tower,* with Swithin's return from abroad to confront the now widowed Lady Constantine, and her death from overexcitement on top of the tower, lapses into Victorian sensationalism far removed from Lawrence's elegiac close.

There is nothing like so close a parallel between St. Cleeve and the gamekeeper. The origin of Lawrence's keepers is a topic of some complexity, but there are points of comparison. First, St. Cleeve is conceived, however pallidly, as an initiate of nature indifferent to social distinctions. "A student of the greatest forces in nature," Hardy writes, "he had, like many others of his sort, no personal force to speak of in a social point of view, mainly because he took no interest in human ranks and formulas." Though it might be said that "he was worshipping the sun," his worship does not always fill him with joyful contemplation of nature. On the contrary, as he himself explains, "those minds who exert their imaginative powers to bury themselves in the depths of the universe merely strain their faculties to gain a new horror," and the lovers often feel themselves "oppressed with the presence of a vastness they could not cope with even as an idea, and which hung about them like a nightmare." Nonetheless, Swithin, in his rôle as student of natural forces, does have a point of contact with the nature-loving gamekeepers, and interestingly enough, one of Connie's friends is Charles May, "an Irishman, who wrote scientifically about the stars," though she finds him "a little distasteful and messy, in spite of his stars" (*Lady Chatterley's Lover*).

A closer analogue is to be found in the social origins of the characters. St. Cleeve is the product of a marriage between a curate and a local farmer's daughter. Thus, although he does not affect the curious vacillation between orthodox and dialect speech which characterises Lawrence's socially mobile keepers (and which is also a feature of *Tess* and Jefferies's *Amaryllis at the Fair*), St. Cleeve is in an equally ambivalent, if not *déclassé*, position. As old Amos explains to Lady Constantine, "what with having two stations of life in his blood he's good for nothing, my lady." It is this social ambiguity that drives St. Cleeve into the isolation of his tower-top, "the temple of that sublime mystery on whose threshold he stood as priest," just as the keeper lives "quite alone, detached, in that stone cottage at the end of the wood" (*The First Lady Chatterley*). When Viviette joins him, the tower becomes a love-nest not dissimilar to the keeper's hut and cottage—indeed, Swithin has a hut constructed at the base of the column and rudely furnished in exactly the manner of the "cosy" woodland hut in Lawrence. After the wedding Viviette and Swithin spend three days secretly encamped in this hut, in a sequence which prefigures the second "honeymoon" of Tess and Angel Clare, and which resembles Connie's night in the gamekeeper's cottage. "I could be happy here for ever," Viviette exclaims on awakening, "I wish I could never see my great gloomy house again." Just so does Connie, in the cottage, thinking with revulsion of Wragby, reflect that "she would be content with this little house, if only it were in a world of its own" (*Lady Chatterley's Lover*). And like Connie's sojourn in the wood, the honeymoon in the astronomer's hut takes on an aura of irrecoverable joy: "I wish I was going back with you to the cabin", Viviette declares, "How happy we were, those three days of our stay there."

As Millgate has shown, the patterning of Hardy's narrative is carefully achieved:

> Hardy works largely in terms of schematised oppositions . . . Swithin's paganism . . . is set against Lady Constantine's religiosity—her temperament, as Hardy says, makes her "necessarily either lover or *dévote*"—while his initiation of her into the mysteries of the universe balances her initiation of him into the realities of sexual passion.

This sort of *schema,* in which the major characters become archetypes moving in a heightened romantic landscape, is equally discernible in Lawrence, though with a crucial difference which Millgate helps to suggest when he concludes that "Hardy himself remained uninvolved, manipulating the story as a structural and thematic exercise."

It would be wrong to try to "process" one novel into the other. The differences, centering upon Lawrence's critique of industrialization, are crucial and massive. But there is a residue of material parallels and similarities: the *donnée* of the marital situation; the characterization of the heroine, and the social background of the hero; and the symbolic country house landscape. These factors are enough, I believe, to warrant the assertion that Hardy played a crucial part in the shaping of the story of Lady Chatterley. (pp. 85-94)

J. R. Ebbatson, "Thomas Hardy and Lady Chatterley," in Ariel: A Review of International English Literature, *Vol. 8, No. 2, April, 1977, pp. 85-95.*

Jeffrey Meyers (essay date 1982)

[*An American educator and literary biographer, Meyers has defined his approach to literary criticism as follows: "I take an inter-disciplinary, comparative, and biographical approach to modern English and European literature, and believe criticism should be based on fact, not theory." Meyers has written extensively on Lawrence's life and work. In the following excerpt, he explores the theme of resurrection in* Lady Chatterley's Lover *and points out parallels between the characters and incidents in the novel and Lawrence's life.*]

The theme of resurrection originates in Lawrence's early exposure to evangelical Christianity. It is complicated by his simultaneous identification with and rejection of Christ: his view of himself as prophet and redeemer, martyr and messiah of a decaying civilization, and his hostility

---

Lawrence on sex and marriage:

A young man said to me the other day, rather sneeringly, "I'm afraid I can't believe in the regeneration of England by sex." I said to him: "I'm sure you can't." He was trying to inform me that he was above such trash as sex, and such commonplace as women. He was the usual vitally below par, hollow, and egoistic young man, infinitely wrapped up in himself, like a sort of mummy that will crumble if unwrapped.

And what is sex, after all, but the symbol of the relation of man to woman, woman to man? And the relation of man to woman is wide as all life. It consists in infinite different flows between the two beings, different, even apparently contrary. Chastity is part of the flow between man and woman, as to physical passion. And beyond these, an infinite range of subtle communication which we know nothing about. I should say that the relation between any two decently married people changes profoundly every few years; often without their knowing anything about it; though every change causes pain, even if it brings a certain joy. The long course of marriage is a long event of perpetual change, in which a man and a woman mutually build up their souls and make themselves whole. It is like rivers flowing on, through new country, always unknown.

D. H. Lawrence, in his "We Need One Another," in Phoenix: The Posthumous Papers of D. H. Lawrence, *edited by Edward D. McDonald, 1936.*

---

to the elements of Christianity he thought repressive and life-denying. Lawrence's ambivalent attitude to Christianity became especially significant in his work in February 1925, just after completing ***The Plumed Serpent,*** when he became gravely ill in Oaxaca and had to confront the likelihood of his own death. The doctor confirmed Frieda's greatest fears when he told her: "Take him to the ranch; it's his only chance. He has T.B. in the third degree. A year or two at the most." After this nearly fatal experience, Lawrence abandoned his faith in a strong leader and his hope for a political solution to the problems of postwar chaos, which he had explored in the novels of power during 1921-25. He returned to his prewar belief in the regeneration of society through the personal relations of men and women, and portrayed characters who defied disease and experienced, in Italy, a rebirth in *this* life.

Lawrence, brought up in a strict evangelical tradition, recalled that the Bible permeated his consciousness and "became an influence which affected all the processes of emotion and thought." He often used resurrection imagery, identified himself with Christ and felt a personal mission to redeem society. Contrasting England and Italy during a brief trip to London in December 1923, he wrote: "It's all the dead hand of the past, over here, infinitely heavy, and deadly determined to put one down. It won't succeed, but it's like struggling with the stone lid of the tomb." Lawrence was especially sensitive to Good Friday, and in 1927 he told Mabel Luhan: I'm "suffering from a change of life, and a queer sort of recoil, as if one's whole soul were drawing back from connection with everything. This is the day when they put Jesus in the tomb—and really, those three days in the tomb begin to have a terrible significance and reality to me. And the Resurrection is an unsatisfactory business—just *noli me tangere* and no more."

Yet Lawrence's relation to Christianity was essentially negative, for he disapproved of its dreary repression and used its imagery in an attempt to lead society back to a pre-Christian, pagan awareness of vital possibilities. He preached the radical limitations of Christ to his own disciple, Dorothy Brett: "Christ was a rotter, though a fine rotter. He never *experienced* life as the old Pagan Gods did. His merit was that he went through with his job: but that was soft, squashy and also political—a labor leader. He never knew animals, or women, from a child—never. He held forth in the temple and never *lived*. He was out to die, that's what makes his preaching disastrous." In **Phoenix** he exclaimed, even more forcefully: "The history of our era is the nauseating and repulsive history of the crucifixion of the procreative body for the glorification of the spirit, the mental consciousness." And in **Apocalypse** he maintained: "What man passionately wants is his living wholeness and his living unison. . . . Man wants his physical fulfilment first and foremost, since now, once and once only, he is in the flesh and potent." To Lawrence, the survival of the spirit was not enough: there must also be a resurrection of the body. He was determined to transform the Christian myth—maintaining its images but abandoning its renunciation—and to achieve the promise of salvation while on earth.

The resurrection theme was Lawrence's personal and artistic response to the threat of death. He had been an invalid throughout his life; and in 1930, when he lay dying in Vence, he told Frieda: "I have had bronchitis since I was a fortnight old." As early as June 1913 David Garnett noticed that after a fit of coughing Lawrence's handkerchief was "spotted with bright arterial blood." While living at the Villa Mirenda in July 1927 Lawrence had a massive hemorrhage: "He called from his room in a strange, gurgling voice," Frieda wrote. "I ran and found him lying on his bed; he looked at me with shocked eyes while a slow stream of blood came from his mouth." In January 1930, Dr. Andrew Morland, the tuberculosis specialist who came from London to Bandol to examine Lawrence, stated he "had obviously been suffering from pulmonary tuberculosis for a very long time—probably 10 or 15 years." After Lawrence's death Aldous Huxley said that for the last two years of his life Lawrence had been like a flame that miraculously burned on though it had no fuel to feed it. (pp. 149-51)

The resurrection theme had often been evoked at the conclusion of Lawrence's works. In **Sons and Lovers,** Paul Morel rejects the direction of darkness after his mother's death and "walked towards the faintly humming, glowing town, quickly." In **The Rainbow,** Ursula "saw in the rainbow the earth's new architecture, the old, brittle corruption of houses and factories swept away, the world built up in a living fabric of Truth, fitting to the over-arching heaven." ***Look! We Have Come Through!*** celebrates a rebirth in the flesh after his mother's death and Frieda's moribund marriage. And in **The Lost Girl** and ***Aaron's Rod,*** Alvina and Aaron find a new life in Italy after escaping from England.

Virtually all the works that Lawrence wrote after the Mexican illness and during the last five years of his life concern the resurrection theme: **"The Woman Who Rode Away," St. Mawr, The Virgin and the Gipsy, "The Flying Fish"** (all 1925); **The Plumed Serpent** and **"Sun"** (both 1926); **Etruscan Places** (written 1927); **Lady Chatterley's Lover** and **The Man Who Died** (both 1928); **"The Risen Lord," "Bavarian Gentians," "The Ship of Death"** and **Apocalypse** (all 1929). These thematically unified works were Lawrence's final response to the despair of the War years as well as to his own death—which was always immanent during this period. In **"The Flying Fish,"** which "was written so near the borderline of death, that I have never been able to carry it through, in the cold light of day," he declared: "Even as the flying fish, when he leaves the air and recovereth his element in the depth, plunges and inevitably rejoices. So will tall men rejoice, after their flight of fear, through the thin air, pursued by death."

The three works of 1926-28 that are most clearly connected to Lawrence's paintings and to the resurrection theme that dominated the last phase of his career and was realized in Italy are the story **"Sun"** and the novel **Lady Chatterley's Lover**—both of which reveal the characteristic movement from illness to health, from an arty society at the beginning of the work to a sensual cure at the end— and the novella **The Man Who Died.** Finally, Lawrence's greatest poem, **"The Ship of Death,"** directly inspired by his vision of the Etruscan tombs, transforms the resurrection theme into pagan terms and expresses his acceptance of death. (pp. 152-53)

Harry Moore describes the composition of **Lady Chatterley's Lover,** which was written and published in Tuscany: "Lawrence sometimes wrote in the Villa Mirenda's tower, which looked out on orchards and olive trees towards the distant scrawl of Florence, and sometimes on the sunny terrace of the villa, but most often behind the small church of San Polo (sometimes Paolo), where, on days when the weather was gentle, he sat in a little wood of umbrella pines." Lawrence's mode of writing is portrayed in the novel when "Constance sat down with her back to a young pine-tree, that swayed against her with curious life, elastic, and powerful, rising up. The erect, alive thing, with its top in the sun!" The Tuscan wood is transformed, in Lawrence's imagination, into the wood that becomes Connie's refuge and sanctuary; and Oliver Mellors, whose name suggests Mediterranean olives and the Italian word for best (*meglio*), is modelled not only on Lawrence's father and on himself but also on the Italian peasant "in velveteen corduroys, bandolier, cartridges, game-bag over his shoulder, and gun in his hand," who sometimes passed by when Lawrence was writing. Mellors is the essence of the Italian spirit, transposed to and expressed in England. (p. 156)

Frieda was attracted to Lawrence's working-class background just as Connie was to Mellors': "That he came of the common people was a thrill to me. It gave him his candour, the wholesomeness of generations of hard work and hard living behind him, nothing sloppy, and lots of guts."

After Lawrence's death Frieda, who never valued fidelity, revealed that Lawrence had become sexually impotent toward the end of 1926 and that she had slept with Lieutenant Angelo Ravagli, who had been their landlord in Spotorno, while Lawrence was in France in October 1928.

Frieda later wrote: "The terrible thing about Lady C. is that L. identified himself with both Clifford and Mellors; that took courage, that made me shiver." Clifford Chatterley's sexual impotence and unfaithful wife are thus a bravely honest portrayal of Lawrence's own impotence—due to his wasting disease—and Frieda's adulterous liaison with Ravagli. Connie wants the child that Lawrence could never give Frieda, whose own three children were the main cause of her early quarrels with Lawrence. Mellors agrees to have a child "provided it doesn't touch your love for me. If it would touch that, I am dead against it." Connie's transfer of loyalty from the impotent Clifford to the virile Mellors is an important aspect of the resurrection theme.

The biographical connection between Lawrence and Mellors is even more significant; and Mark Schorer [in his introduction to the 1966 edition of *Lady Chatterley's Lover*] is quite mistaken when he asserts: "Connie and Mellors are *not* Frieda and D. H. Lawrence." Like the young Lawrence, Mellors was a clever lad who had learned French and won a scholarship to an urban grammar school. The photograph of Mellors taken when he was married at twenty-one, which he destroys to show his loyalty to Connie, reveals him for what he was: "a young curate" and "prig." This description refers to the photograph of Lawrence at twenty-one, which (he said) shows him as a "clean-shaven, bright young prig in a high collar like a curate." Mellors' description of his early love affairs is clearly based on Lawrence's relations with Jessie Chambers and Helen Corke just as his "bringin' her her breakfast in bed sometimes" refers to his practice with Frieda. Connie's first, unsuccessful sexual encounter with Mellors recalls Lawrence's wedding night with Frieda, described in the poem "First Morning." Mellors' loathsome and messy divorce—"I hate those things like death, officials and courts and judges. . . . Couldn't one go right way, to the far ends of the earth, and be free from it all?"—reflects Lawrence's squeamish response to Frieda's divorce after their scandalous elopement.

Most important, Mellors' pneumonia—which he caught during army service and which left him ill and coughing, with weak heart and lungs—shows Lawrence's courage to confront his own disease and mortality. Connie brings him back to life just as Frieda did Lawrence. Mark Schorer points out that "In the first version [of *Lady Chatterley*, Mellors] is physically strong; in the second, not so strong; in the third, sometimes rather frail." Mellors' extreme exhaustion after pushing Clifford's broken wheel chair up the hill—"his heart [was] beating and his face white with the effort, semi-conscious"—is similar to Knud Merrild's description of Lawrence's fatigue after chopping wood in New Mexico: "Lawrence did his share. Although he tired quickly, he stubbornly kept on. . . . It had hurt us to see him strain himself. He did not have the strength to be efficient." Mellors' narrow escape from death and damaged health—"It seems to me I've died once or twice already"—connects him with Lawrence, who also came back from the dead, and with the resurrection theme in the novel.

In **"A Propos of *Lady Chatterley's Lover*,"** Lawrence expresses the idea that provides both a thematic and structural unity to the work, which begins in autumn and follows the seasonal cycle to spring: "The greatest need of man is the renewal forever of the complete rhythm of life and death, the rhythm of the sun's year, the body's year of a lifetime, and the greater year of the stars, the soul's year of immortality." Tommy Dukes, who prepares Connie for Mellors' revolutionary beliefs, states the theme of temptation and the fortunate fall that leads to rebirth: "Once you start the mental life you pluck the apple. You've severed . . . the organic connection. And if you've got nothing in your life *but* the mental life, then you yourself are a plucked apple. . . . [And] it's a natural necessity for a plucked apple to go bad." Later he demands the resurrection of the body and describes cerebration and money as the stone on the tomb. Soon after meeting Mellors in March, Connie walks in the wood, quotes Swinburne's attack on the "pale Galilean" in the "Hymn to Proserpine," recalls the Christian adage of the grain of wheat that dies only to spring forth from the ground (John 12:24) and remembers Persephone-Proserpine (the central myth in **"Bavarian Gentians"**) rising from Hell to a new life on earth.

Just as Clifford seems ironically "to be re-born" when a new sense of power flows through him and he transforms the mines in the manner of Gerald Crich, so Mellors, after his first sexual experience with Connie, exclaims that he too has begun life again. When Clifford casuistically insists that the life of the body is merely the life of animals, Connie, revitalized by her sexual experience, sharply contradicts him: "With the Greeks [the body] gave a lovely flicker, then Plato and Aristotle killed it [by idealizing love], and Jesus finished it off. But now the body is coming really to life, it is really rising from the tomb."

Mellors' programmatic plea for men who could sing and swagger and wear bright red trousers as a way to replace money with manhood may seem an absurd residue of ***The Plumed Serpent.*** But this scheme for rebirth has deep roots in the regenerative idealism of Ruskin and William Morris as well as in Lawrence's youthful ideas about miners' schools. "What they ought to do," he told Jessie Chambers, "is recreational work. Teach the adolescents to sing and dance and do gymnastics, and make things they enjoy making." Mellors' plea is also connected to Lawrence's admiration for the scarlet legs in Bernardo Strozzi's *Parable of the Wedding* (mentioned in **"Making Pictures"**) and to the brilliant clothing worn by imaginative folk in the Italian Renaissance: "In the really great periods like the Renaissance, the young men swaggered down the street with one leg bright red, one leg bright yellow." (pp. 157-60)

It is essential to recognize that the sexual rebirth is developed through and subservient to the maternal theme. Clifford urges her to have a child by another man—as if emotion and procreation could be separated; Connie comforts the sobbing gamekeeper's daughter, Connie Mellors, whose name will eventually be her own; she holds "the soft little arms, the unconscious cheeky little legs" of Mrs. Flint's baby; and discovers the charming old family cradle of rosewood in the lumber room of Wragby.

The maternal theme is superbly evoked in the scene when Connie feeds the pheasant chicks—who are destined to be slaughtered by Clifford's friends as soon as they reach maturity (like the soldiers in the War). Like Miriam in *Sons and Lovers,* Connie is afraid of the fierce pecks of the protective mother hen, and "drew back startled and frightened." Then Mellors, in a subtle mixture of sexual exploration and midwifery, "slowly, softly, with sure gentle fingers, felt among the old bird's feathers and drew out a faintly-peeping chick in his closed hand." As Connie holds the soft baby bird and begins to cry, the maternal is linked to the sexual theme. Mellors comes to life and is suddenly "aware of the old flame shooting and leaping up in his loins, that he had hoped was quiescent forever." He caresses Connie, establishes his authority by commanding her to lie down and makes love to her for the first time as sex transcends class through the "democracy of touch."

Lawrence holds the contradictory belief: "One is swindled out of one's proper sex life, a great deal. But it is nobody's individual fault: fault of the age: our own fault as well." He therefore places strong emphasis on simultaneous orgasm and is careful to show how Connie progresses from a kind of clitoral masturbation with her prewar German lover and again with Michaelis, to early sex with Mellors where only he is satisfied, to vaginal and then to simultaneous orgasm. Finally, we learn that the road to excess does not lead to the palace of wisdom. For Mellors recklessly burns out the last shame, "stripped her to the very last, and made a different woman of her" in the only sexual act that is not made explicit in the novel: the strange apotheosis of anal penetration. "How could anything that gave one satisfaction be excluded," Gudrun asks in *Women in Love.* "Degrading things were real, with a different reality. . . . Why not be bestial, and go the whole round of experience?" One can only agree with André Malraux's sceptical response to Lawrence's belief that the body is wiser than the mind: "I am suspicious of the guarantees one must look for in the most profound regions of flesh and blood." (pp. 160-61)

Connie and Mellors, attracted by their differences of class and drawn together by threats of scandal and separation, oppose with their bodies, love and hopeful hearts the catastrophic results of the War, which Lawrence described in Spenglerian terms in the great opening sentences of the novel: "Ours is essentially a tragic age, so we refuse to take it tragically. The cataclysm has happened, we are among the ruins." As W. B. Yeats observed: "Those two lovers, the gamekeeper and his employer's wife, each separated from their class by their love, and by fate, are poignant in their loneliness; and the coarse language of one, accepted by both, becomes a forlorn poetry uniting their solitudes, something ancient, humble and terrible."

At times, when they are nearly overwhelmed by this cataclysm, Mellors thinks it is wrong to bring a child into the world, longs for an apocalypse without a resurrection and happily contemplates the "extermination of the human species and the long pause that follows before some other species crops up." "Lawrence's theme is a high one," Edmund Wilson wrote in 1929, "the self-affirmation and triumph of life in the teeth of all the sterilizing and demoralizing forces—industrialism, physical depletion, dissipation, careerism and cynicism—of modern English society." . . . (p. 162)

> Jeffrey Meyers, in his D. H. Lawrence and the Experience of Italy, *University of Pennsylvania Press, 1982, 189 p.*

John B. Humma (essay date 1983)

[*In the following essay, Humma examines Lawrence's use of metaphors concerning nature, myth, and ritual in* Lady Chatterley's Lover.]

While we obviously cannot take Oliver Mellors out of his woods (or the woods out of Mellors) in *Lady Chatterley's Lover* and have anything like the same book, we may still ask to what extent the novel's nature imagery—the purely descriptive or figurative language—serves Lawrence's purposes. That is, if we strip *Lady Chatterley* of its metaphors and similes, do we materially impoverish the whole? Does, for instance, a simile comparing the gamekeeper to a "lonely pistil in an invisible flower" advance the action in any significant way? Certainly most of the figures have sexual references and thus add texture. But I wish to show that the nature-sex imagery provides considerably more than texture or, rather, that the texture it provides becomes inseparable from the meaning it creates.

We cannot, however, discuss Lawrence's orchestration of this imagery apart from the modes within which he was working: those of the pastoral and of myth and ritual. Oddly, only within the last ten years or so have scholars significantly addressed these elements in *Lady Chatterley.* Michael Squires [in his book *The Pastoral Novel: Studies in George Eliot, Thomas Hardy, and D. H. Lawrence* (1972)], the first critic to do so at length, grounds his parallels on two notable studies of the pastoral form. First, he establishes the criteria by quoting from Walter R. Davis' *Map of Arcadia:* "The standard pastoral action consists then of disintegration in the turbulent outer circle, education in the pastoral circle, and rebirth at the sacred center." In *Lady Chatterley's Lover* the turbulent outer ring is, of course, the modern mechanistic society epitomized by Clifford Chatterley's collieries; the pastoral circle is Wragby Wood; the sacred center is the pheasant hut. Squires then cites E. R. Curtius' discussion of the *locus amoenus*—"a beautiful shaded natural site whose minimum ingredients comprise a tree (or several trees), meadow, and a spring or a brook"—as further evidence that *Lady Chatterley* is a pastoral. Similarly, Kingsley Widmer [in his essay "The Pertinence of Modern Pastoral: The Three Versions of *Lady Chatterley's Lover,*" *Studies in the Novel* (1973)] labels the novel a "modern pastoral": "The European conventions (in contrast to the American pastoral, which usually lacked the erotic dimensions) provide an idyllic and regenerative sacred place for loving, such as a grove or rural retreat, whose description carries pagan religious meanings." Widmer argues that Lawrence, by the time he wrote the final version of the novel, believed that the solution to the problems of the day was to "pastoralize" society. More recently Dennis Jackson [in his essay "The 'Old Pagan Vision': Myth and Ritual in *Lady Chatterley's Lover*," *D. H. Lawrence Review* (1978)], has demonstrated the significance of pagan myth and ritual in **Lady Chatterley.** Having shown that Lawrence read in Frazer on at least two occasions, Jackson identifies Mellors with the King of the Wood at Nemi (both guard an oak wood) as well as with the green George and other summer or fertility figures discussed in Frazer. But even if Lawrence had not been consciously working within a mode or tradition (and Lawrence would probably not have been shy about identifying any intended folk or literary antecedent for Mellors), the claim that he was actually doing so suffers no great damage. In fact, considering the tradition or traditions within which **Lady Chatterley's Lover** appears to fall, we can appreciate the parallels even more fully if they are unconscious or semiconscious. But what Lawrence unquestionably did recognize is that his treatment of his material had mythic or ritualistic proportions. When, near the end of this analysis, we look at the changes Lawrence made in the second version of the novel (published as **John Thomas and Lady Jane**) in producing the final version, we will see a strategy that molds a distinctly ritualistic central action from scenes that originally had only a rough relation to ritual.

What I try to do here, and what earlier studies do not attempt, is to assess the significance of the nature imagery for the narrative—that is, to consider how this imagery affects total meaning. The figures of speech in the novel have a way of overlapping, of crossing boundaries, indeed of becoming at times cross-references taking us forward or backward from one scene or passage to another. They almost always make connections beyond themselves. I call such linking figures interpenetrating metaphors. For they relate not only literal terms to figurative terms but also vegetable images to animal and, to a lesser extent, mineral images and each of these to the process of sexual-spiritual rebirth at the heart of the novel. Unless Lawrence can convince us that Connie's sexual regeneration is also her spiritual regeneration, the novel collapses. Thus the wood, as a sacred place, must impart its religious properties to the sexual activities taking place there. This transfer occurs, I believe, largely through the overlapping or interpenetrating nature images that describe the sexual act. Lawrence always routes rebirth from *dis*integration to integration: this process involves connecting one faculty and another within the individual (in Lawrence essentially mind consciousness and blood consciousness) as well as connecting the individual and nature. The metaphors in **Lady Chatterley's Lover**—linking bird, beast, and flower (and air, water, earth) with one another and with hero and heroine—organically emblemize both the sexual-spiritual union of Connie and Mellors and a similar union (symbolized, for instance, by the flower-bedecking scene) between them and the sacred wood—in effect, the "cosmos," to use Lawrence's term.

As we might expect, the wood being the major locus of the novel, the preponderance of the imagery is vegetable—tree, leaf, flower. The wood exists in polar opposition to Tevershall pit and town, the secondary locus (together with Wragby Hall). About a third of the way into the novel we observe Clifford taking on renewed energy and "life" from the so-called improvements he is to make in the operations of the colliery. That this resurgence is bogus we know because its source is not the living world but the decayed, coming "out of the coal, out of the pit." As if life could flow from death! "The very stale air of the colliery was better than oxygen to him." By contrast, we watch Connie fumbling toward a new life a few pages later in the scene with the pheasant hens and their chicks. Although she is terrified as she attempts to feed them (appropriately so, since they bring her and Mellors together), she persists, with the help of Mellors, who educates her out of her clumsiness and fear—as he later is to do in their sexual life. Along the way she comes to regard the fowl with a "sort of ecstacy." She thinks, "Life, life. Pure, sparky, fearless new life!" After she and Mellors have made love for the first time (through the agency of the hens and the baby chicks), we see him alone in the wood experiencing mixed emotions about being "connected . . . up again." He thinks of the way the industrial world "would destroy the wood, and the bluebells . . . spring no more" and then considers her vulnerability, for "Somewhere she was tender, tender with the tenderness of the growing hyacinths." Finally we are told that "his penis began to stir like a live bird."

When we look at these ten or so pages, we discover a development that is either very lucky or else very carefully thought through—one or the other, but not both. From the dead coal and stale air of Clifford's world, we proceed by way of the pheasants to Connie and Mellors' lovemaking, from there to Mellors' imagining of Connie in a flower trope, and from there to the penis-bird simile, the progression *connecting* up the principal actions of these pages, from Connie's recognition of the "Pure, sparky, fearless new life" to the description of Lawrence's channel for this renewal as a "live bird." We remember Tommy Dukes's earlier remark about modern civilization. "It's all going down the bottomless *pit* [my emphasis], down the chasm. And believe me, the only bridge across the chasm will be the phallus." We see the way in which imagery interpenetrates imagery, action interpenetrates action, creating an exceptional coherence. The next several pages develop similarly. On the following afternoon Connie goes again to the wood. In her body she feels "the huge heave of sap" in the massive trees and "their silent efforts to open their buds." Later: "The wood was silent, still and secret in the evening drizzle of rain, full of the mystery of eggs and half-open buds, half-unsheathed flowers. In the dimness of it all trees glistened naked and dark as if they had unclothed themselves, and the green things on earth seemed to hum with greenness." The overt purpose of these passages is to suggest Connie's own unfolding into life, but they also catch up the previous interpenetrating action (and imagery) through the juxtaposition of egg and bud and the simile of disrobing. Moreover, the reference to the sap rising in the tree recalls the scene in which Connie had viewed her body in the mirror, finding it, disturbingly, to be "greyish and sapless," her "pear-shaped breasts" "unripe." It embraces also the passage in which Connie thinks of the way that Clifford turns everything into words, "sucking all the life-sap out of living things." What has seemed to be a rather casual figure is in reality a further casting of the net of metaphor, a sinking of the image deep into the reader's consciousness.

The leaf and tree and flower metaphors function in much the same way. Clifford's conversation with Connie early in the book about her having a baby seems to her the next day "like dead leaves, crumpling up and turning to powder, meaning really nothing, blown away on any gust of wind. They were not the leafy words of an effectual life, young with energy and belonging to the tree. They were the hosts of fallen leaves of a life that is ineffectual." The obvious comment here is that the leaves are disjoined, having severed their connection with the vital source. They are like the coal: vegetation that was. In a later scene in which Clifford is again talking, reading Racine to Connie, Lawrence uses contrasting imagery to refer to her. Thinking of Mellors, "She was gone in her own soft rapture, like a forest soughing with the dim, glad moan of spring, moving into bud. . . . She was like a forest, like the dark, interlacing of the oakwood. . . . Meanwhile the birds of desire were asleep in the vast interlaced intricacy of her body." Unlike the figures in the previous passages, these are all positive because they describe regeneration and growth and integration. Moreover, the metaphor "the dark interlacing of the oakwood" interpenetrates with that of the "birds of desire" asleep in the body's "vast interlaced intricacy." These in turn enter the vast interlacing of metaphor that runs all through the novel. The interlocking of fowl-plant metaphors, demonstrated again in the passage quoted above, is recurrent. Lawrence has already, for instance, compared his hero's penis to a bird. In a later trope this sacred member takes on a "small bud-like reticence and tenderness" and in a still later one Connie describes it as "tiny and soft like a little bud of life"—metamorphoses of figures that a "god of the wood" reasonably might undergo. The effect is ultimately that of a sort of music in which the images form the chords. These images blend over the course of the novel with phallic similes comparing Mellors to flowers (daffodils) and parts of flowers: "And the keeper, his thin, white body, like a lonely pistil in an invisible flower." A page later Connie rests against a pine tree and thinks of its "curious life, elastic and powerful, rising up. The erect, alive thing, with its top in the sun." Each successive image strikes its correspondences, so dense (like the trees) and intertwined are the figures at last.

If some images have their tops in the sun, their lower parts exist within the earth. The several root metaphors in the novel are fascinating and, in their manner of conferring meaning, perhaps the most strategic of all. Here is Connie, thinking of her situation with Clifford: "It was as if thousands and thousands of little roots and threads of consciousness in him and her had grown together in a tangled mass, till they could crowd no more, and the plant was dying." She is afraid "of how many of her roots, perhaps mortal ones, were tangled with [his]." No Lawrencian character, certainly, wants to get entangled in any way or "merged" with anyone, and Connie does well to be afraid, of Clifford or of whomever. A second root metaphor occurs about two thirds of the way into the development of Connie and Mellors' relationship. It involves a bit of after play to their lovemaking during the sequence in which Connie is said to have been "born a woman": "What a mystery! What a strange heavy weight of mystery that could be soft and heavy in one's hand! The roots, root of all that is lovely, the primeval root of all full beauty." The reader here must make a connection. If Mellors' testes are the root, then the phallus must be the stalk or trunk. Again we recall Tommy Dukes's statement about the importance of the phallus to the survival of civilization. We recall also the phallic descriptions of the trees. Certainly, then, if Wragby Wood is the forest primeval, this decidedly phallic forest must have its testicular roots primeval.

This figure is not so facetious as it may sound: indeed, it has a clear and linear logic, as does the further development of the same metaphor: "He's got his root in my soul, has that gentleman." Mellors makes this remark during his next-to-last meeting with Connie. He is being playful, but he is also speaking, as he nearly always does, in his role as "the priest of love." We have just seen what the root of that gentleman is; now we learn the home, or source, of that root. As I stressed at the outset, the reader must be convinced that Connie's sexual development is her spiritual one as well. The corollary to this statement is that her spiritual regeneration depends on her sexual regeneration. Mellors' apparently offhanded remark locating the genitalia with the geography of the soul signifies more than the casual reader might at first suspect.

To compare *Lady Chatterley* with other Lawrence novels is to appreciate the unique strategic function of the nature imagery here. Although Lawrence's reputation for describing nature is deservedly high, the general view is that *Lady Chatterley's Lover* marks a falling off. Harry T. Moore's criticism [in his book *D. H. Lawrence: His Life and Works*] is probably representative: "Nature appears fairly frequently in *Lady Chatterley's Lover,* though not so effectively as in previous novels; if Lawrence's descriptive powers had been at their height when he was writing *Lady Chatterley,* it would have made a far more forceful book." As Moore acknowledges, however, Lawrence could still write nature passages charged with color, as is evident from the nature descriptions in such late works as *The Plumed Serpent, St. Mawr,* and *The Man Who Died.* But we must not expect *Lady Chatterley* to have the sort of evocative nature imagery that Lawrence provides elsewhere. One can find nothing, for example, to compare with the confrontation between Ursula and the horses in *The Rainbow* or with the "Moony" episode in *Women in Love.* (These are scenes, one feels, that Lawrence could not have *not* written, scenes that his daimon wrote, so to speak—not to deny the shaping hand its part.) In contrast, *Lady Chatterley* offers a thoughtful subordination of nature to the structure of meaning, an orchestration of detail that is purely the achievement of sullen craft.

What have been symbols in previous Lawrence novels become metaphors here. When Ursula passes through the wood near Willey Water before encountering the horses in the meadow, the trees are symbolic, not metaphoric. In *Lady Chatterley's Lover* the trees are, of course, both. The "commemorating" cypresses of ***Aaron's Rod*** are symbols, as are the eagles in their dalliance and the lily:

> Happy lily, never to be saddled with an *idée fixe,* never to be in the grip of a monomania for happiness or love or fulfilment. It is not *laisser aller.* It is life-rootedness. It is being by oneself, life-living, like the much-mooted lily. One toils, one spins, one strives: just as the lily does. But like her, taking one's own life-way amidst everything, and taking one's own life-way alone. Love too. But there also, taking one's way alone, happily alone in all the wonders of communion, swept up on the winds, but never swept away from one's very self. Two eagles in mid-air, maybe like Whitman's Dalliance of Eagles. Two eagles in mid-air, grappling, whirling, coming to their intensification of love-oneness there in mid-air. In mid-air the love consummation. But all the time each lifted on its own wings: each bearing itself up on its own wings at every moment of the mid-air love consummation. That is the splendid love-way.

Here the eagles and the lily merely symbolize the ethic that the character Lilly embodies. Obviously, though, Lawrence also uses images metaphorically, as in this passage from ***Aaron's Rod:***

> Sunlight, lovely full sunlight, lingered warm and still on the balcony. It caught the facade of the cathedral sideways, like the tips of a flower, and sideways lit up the stem of Giotto's tower, like a lily stem, or a long, lovely pale pink and white and green pistil of the lily of the cathedral. Florence, the flowery town. Firenze—Fiorenze—the flowery town: the red lilies. The Fiorentini, the flower-souled. Flowers with good roots in the mud and muck, as should be: and fearless blossoms in air, like the cathedral and the tower and the David.

The lily figure serves the passage but, unlike the figures in ***Lady Chatterley's Lover,*** does not serve in any fully orchestrated way the central action of the story. It is primarily a mechanical component, not an organic one. We even find a metaphor within a metaphor, as in ***Lady Chatterley:*** "But I love it; it is delicate and rosy, and the dark stripes are as they should be, like the tiger marks on a pink lily. It's a lily, not a rose: a pinky white lily with dark tigery marks." But the metaphors only feather, they do not interlock; we find no meshing of meaning, no engagement with prior or subsequent details.

In the "Excurse" chapter of ***Women in Love,*** after Ursula and Birkin resolve their quarrel, Birkin is said to feel "as if he had just come awake, like a thing that is born, like a bird when it has dropped out of its egg, into a new universe." At the inn they speak only through "the flowers in each other"; the strange passage in which Ursula kneels before Birkin incorporates "river," "flood," and "fountain" images. At the end of the chapter, they walk among the "great old trees" of Sherwood Forest, where, "like old priests," the fern rises in the distance, "magical and mysterious." Like Mellors and Connie, Birkin and Ursula make love on the floor of the wood. But in this passage, unlike the one from ***Lady Chatterley's Lover,*** which I examine below, Lawrence provides no nature imagery at all. In short, although he gives us the vegetable, animal, and water imagery of previous parts of the chapter and endows the wood with a religious aura, we do not find any sort of organic interpenetration involving the images and the action. My point, of course, is not that there is anything amiss with his treatment of the scene here, or with his treatment of those in ***Aaron's Rod;*** it is simply that the absence of such a strategy in these novels and others points up the deliberate orchestration of the nature details in ***Lady Chatterley's Lover.*** What allows for it here, if not dictates it, is the blatantly phallic action. The orchestration is simply a matter of Lawrence's having found what suffices for him.

The nature imagery provides the texture for the main action of the novel. It is also the consequence of the action. Mellors is descended from the Green Man who figures prominently in both continental and British folklore—in the latter as the Jack-in-the-Green of holiday pageantry. Perhaps the most famous of Mellors' earlier manifestations is the Green Knight, Gawain's adversary and ultimate benefactor. When we first see Mellors, he is dressed in woodsman's green. He superintends the wood—a remnant of Sherwood Forest—and also the game within it, so that we identify him with both the animal and the vegetable spheres of the natural world. In the military he had served as a blacksmith with the cavalry. Clifford tells Connie that Mellors "always was connected with horses, a clever fellow that way." He is responsible for the increase in the pheasants. (And of course he literally fertilizes Connie.) Yet, though we see him significantly in relation to animals—the dog Flossie, too, is usually at his side—it is in relation to the wood, in the general manner that Jackson describes, that his dimensions become indeed symbolic: he is the mythic fertility figure who will effect, along classical lines of ritualistic death and rebirth, Connie's regeneration.

Early in the novel Lawrence contrasts the remnant of the wood with the chopped-down portion, which seems intended as a symbol of the war's destruction. He wants to show us the connections with an earlier time, that of Robin Hood and "of knights riding and ladies on palfreys": "The wood had some of the mystery of wild, old England. . . . How safely the birds flitted among [the] trees! And once there had been deer, and archers, and monks. . . . The place remembered, still remembered." The last sentence contains an admonitory note; it suggests a vengeance to come. Connie is the observer here, walking Clifford in his chair. Then comes a remarkable passage that seems to me one of the two or three most important in the book. It establishes the main action, the symbolic action of the novel, and looks ahead to the climax of this action, the night of the "phallic hunt" at Mellors' cottage when Connie's sexual and spiritual development reaches its apotheosis:

> She was watching a brown spaniel that had run out of a side-path, and was looking toward them with lifted nose, making a soft, fluffy bark. A man with a gun strode swiftly, softly out after the dog, facing their way as if about to attack them; then stopped instead, saluted, and was

turning down hill. It was only the new gamekeeper, but he had frightened Connie, he seemed to emerge with such a swift menace. That was how she had seen him, like the sudden rush of a threat out of nowhere.

All students of twentieth-century literature will appreciate the implications of the gun. But it is Mellors' bearing, his threatening aspect, that dominates the other details of the passage. Not content to give us only one detail that alarms Connie, Lawrence gives us several: Mellors faces the Chatterleys as if "to attack"; he emerges with "swift menace"; he is like a "sudden rush of a threat out of nowhere." He represents a direct challenge to Clifford's way of life and Connie's sterile existence. Of course he frightens her, for he is to be her executioner as well as her savior. She must die out of her old existence before she can enter her new one—the old leaves must fall before the new ones emerge: "'Ye must be born again! I believe in the resurrection of the body! Except a grain of wheat fall into the earth and die, it shall by no means bring forth. When the crocus cometh forth I too will emerge to see the sun.' In the wind of March endless phrases swept through her consciousness." As we shall see, Connie's "death" coincides with her rebirth. This first encounter between Connie and the gamekeeper, with its heavy symbolic quality, anticipates the travail of Connie's coming through.

A glance at the corresponding scene in the second version of the novel, published in 1972 as *John Thomas and Lady Jane,* reveals a conscious shaping of strategy in the passage quoted above. The changes point to Lawrence's effort to make the confrontation clearly symbolic:

> Out of the side riding came the gamekeeper, dressed in greenish velveteen corduroy. He looked at the two intruders, and touched his old brown hat in a salute, then was going on, evasive, down the hill, making a soft noise to call his dog. He was striding away.
>
> "Oh I say, Parkin!" said Sir Clifford.
>
> The man stopped and swung round suddenly, showing his red face and enquiring eyes, as if he expected some attack.
>
> "Sir?"
>
> "Turn my chair round for me, and get me started, will you? It makes it easier for me."
>
> Parkin came striding up the slope, with a quick, small movement slinging his gun over his shoulder. He was a man of medium build. His face almost vermilion-ruddy with the weather wearing a rather sticking-out brown moustache. His bearing had a military erectness and resistance, that was natural to him, and at the same time he was silent, his movements were soft, silent, almost secretive or evasive.

Though the gamekeeper (Parkin in this version) wears his green velveteen and carries the gun, almost everything else about the scene is different. Here he acts as if it were *he* who might be attacked, not the other way around. There is nothing at all menacing or threatening about him. Despite his military posture, he seems more recessive than aggressive. The entire tone of the passage is different. In the *John Thomas* version the lady meets "his glance almost without knowing it" and "is hardly aware of him, being so much disturbed in herself by what Clifford had said." Then the point of view shifts to Mellors, who feels "the queer spark of appeal touch him somewhere." But in *Lady Chatterley* we are told that "he stared straight into Connie's eyes, with a perfect, fearless, impersonal look." The point of view stays with her, and it is she, we perceive, who is affected: he makes her feel "shy" and at the same time curious about him. In brief, the revisions transform the entire tenor of the scene and set up a second development. The meeting in *John Thomas and Lady Jane* sets up nothing.

A second important symbolic scene in *Lady Chatterley* occurs when Connie is returning from her visit to Mrs. Flint. She has made love to Mellors now on two occasions but, having become revolted by him, has avoided him for several days:

> Connie climbed the fence into the narrow path between the dense, bristling young firs. Mrs. Flint went running back across the pasture, in a sunbonnet, because she was really a school teacher. Constance didn't like this dense new part of the wood; it seemed grotesque and choking. She hurried on with her head down, thinking of the Flints' baby. It was a dear little thing, but it would be a bit bow-legged like its father. It showed already, but perhaps it would grow out of it. How warm and fulfilling somehow to have a baby, and how Mrs. Flint had showed it off! She had something anyhow that Connie hadn't got, and apparently couldn't have. Yes, Mrs. Flint had flaunted her motherhood. And Connie had been just a little bit jealous. She couldn't help it.
>
> She started out of her muse, and gave a little cry of fear. A man was there.
>
> It was the keeper; he stood in the path like Balaam's ass, barring her way.

Indeed, she is in a deeper part of the forest, quite literally and figuratively. Disturbed, since she is still trying to avoid Mellors, she seeks only an exit. But there he is, suddenly, barring her way. By force of his will he leads her "into the dense fir trees, that were young and not more than half-grown"—Connie is in an intermediate stage of her growth. Then:

> He led her through the wall of prickly trees, that were difficult to come through, to a place where was a little space and a pile of dead boughs. He threw one or two dry ones down, put his coat and waistcoat over them, and she had to lie down there under the boughs of the tree, like an animal. . . .

With another author one might not be inclined to make anything of "prickly," but with Lawrence, in this context, the reader has every reason to consider it a phallic pun. The wordplay here is a strategic inversion of the interpenetrating metaphors considered previously, in which the figurative term is natural, the literal term sexual. That Connie is forced to "lie down . . . like an animal" signifies the animality of the act in which she is about to participate: her placement is part of her instruction. But the interpenetrating metaphors of the next paragraph make it clear that, though the act is an animal one, it connects the participant to the great world around her. Connie feels "new strange trills rippling inside her . . . like a flapping overlapping of soft flames . . . melting her all molten inside." The fire and thermal imagery yields to sea imagery: her womb becomes "open and soft . . . like a sea anemone under the tide." Then a familiar vegetable image merges with the marine imagery to dramatize metaphorically the enlarging and interpenetrating character of Connie's experience:

> She clung to him unconscious in passion, and he never quite slipped from her, and she felt the soft bud of him within her stirring, and strange rhythms flushing up into her with a strange rhythmic growing motion, swelling and swelling till it filled all her cleaving consciousness, and then began again the unspeakable motion that was not really motion, but pure deepening whirlpools of sensation swirling deeper and deeper through all her tissue and consciousness, till she was one perfect concentric fluid of feeling. . . .

The largely mineral imagery here interacts with the other imagery to create a meaning beneath the surface of the action—a meaning that parallels the action and dramatically reinforces it. (The vitalistic language, moreover, mirrors an outcome of the scene, suggesting that Connie conceives during the act.) Connie's development is now two-thirds complete. The world has become vital around her. Smaller doubts may persist, but the large one is overcome. As Connie returns to Wragby Hall after a subsequent rendezvous with Mellors, the park trees, in another interpenetrating trope, "seemed bulging and surging at anchor on a tide, and the heave of the slope to the house was alive."

If we look at what happens in *John Thomas and Lady Jane* we can once again find some instructive differences. Neither "prickly" nor "half-grown" appears in the earlier version, and Connie is not forced to lie waiting "like an animal." As we have seen, these additions to the scene in *Lady Chatterley* are key details within the novel's ritualistic dimensions. The most extensive revisions, though, are in the description of Connie and Mellors' copulating and Connie's orgasm. Here is Lawrence's earlier version:

> And then, something awoke in her. Strange, thrilling sensation, that she had never known before woke up where he was within her, in wild thrills like wild, wild bells. It was wonderful, wonderful, and she clung to him uttering in complete unconsciousness strange, wild, inarticulate little cries, that he heard within himself with curious satisfaction.
>
> But it was over too soon, too soon! She clung to him in a sort of fear, lest he should draw away from her. She could not bear it if he should draw away from her. It would be too, too soon lost. He, however, lay quite still, and she clung to him with unrelaxing power, pressing herself against him.
>
> Till he came into her again, and the thrills woke up once more, wilder and wilder, like bells ringing pealing faster and faster, to a climax, to an ecstasy, an orgasm, when everything within her turned fluid, and her life seemed to sway like liquid in a bowl, swaying to quiescence.

We find only three similes, two of them identical. Only one ("her life. . . . like liquid in a bowl") is based on nature, and then only partially. By contrast, the description in *Lady Chatterley's Lover* mingles music, fire, bird, sea, and plant metaphors, overlapping and interlocking them: note, for example, the remarkable layering of three metaphors in "trill . . . like a flapping overlapping of soft flames, soft as feathers." The most unobtrusive yet signally significant of the additions to the final version, however, is this paragraph:

> But he drew away at last, and kissed her and covered her over, and began to cover himself. She lay looking up to the boughs of the tree, unable as yet to move. He stood and fastened up his breeches, looking round. All was dense and silent, save for the awed dog that lay with its paws against its nose. He sat down again on the brushwood and took Connie's hand in silence.

The trancelike state of the surroundings conveys the symbolic magnitude of the scene. Even Flossie is "awed" by the magic and mystery of what has taken place. The mesmeric effect on her, in conjunction with the rest of the passage, nicely suggests the ritualistic aspect of the drama that has just transpired.

The account of the last stage of Connie's rebirth, which takes place at Mellors' cottage, involves mainly fire imagery, consistent with Mellors' purging from Connie the "deepest, oldest shames," and mineral imagery ("smelt out the heaviest ore of the body to purity"; "the real bedrock of her nature"). We can now understand why Lawrence described Mellors' initial appearance as threatening, menacing in all aspects. As Green Man (whose modus operandi in this scene may have more of the Greek than the English in it), he must hunt out and kill in order to purify, must destroy in order to resurrect. Connie "really thought she was dying: yet a poignant, marvelous death." The victim, the prey, is Connie's "shame": the "deep organic shame . . . which crouches in the bodily roots of us, and can only be chased away by the sensual fire, [and] at last it was roused up and routed by the phallic hunt of the man, and she came to the very heart of the jungle of herself." The reader observes the presence once more of "roots" and the apt deepening of the metaphor into "jungle" (from forest). And Mellors afterward is "like a wild animal asleep." If these metaphors do not immediately blend like those in earlier passages, there is nonetheless an interplay, a resonance. The success of the scene may not depend on the interlacing of the imagery between this passage and previous ones, but it certainly builds on these connections.

In *Lady Chatterley* Lawrence devotes eight paragraphs to a scene that requires only four in the *John Thomas* version, for he now clearly intends the scene to be the climax of Connie's education. We can see what he left out in the earlier version by looking at its two middle paragraphs:

> Now, however, after this night, she knew it meant stages of sensual intensity, and degrees of refinement in the different practices of sensuality. In this one short summer night, a new range of experience opened out to her, frightening, but acute as fire, and necessary. She had never known it was necessary, till she had it. And now at last she felt she was approaching the real bedrock of her nature, her intrepid sensual self. She thought she would have been ashamed. But she was not ashamed. She felt a triumph, almost a vainglory. So that was what one was! That was it! There was no more to suppress.
>
> But what a reckless devil the man was! One had to be strong to bear him! She felt that she was mated. And that was what had been at the bottom of her soul all the time! the hunger for the daredevil, sensual mate! What liars poets were! at least for her. Communion of love, and all the rest! When the bed-rock was sharp, flamey, rather awful sensuality. And the man who dared do it, without shame or sin or abating his pride. If he had been shamed, it would have been awful. But now, in the morning light, he slept with the innocence and also the mystery of the full sensual creature. As a tiger sleeps with its ears half pricked.

We find no mention of the phallic hunt, no intensification of forest to "jungle." The *John Thomas* version does refer to the purging of Lady Jane's "shame," but only as a side issue. In *Lady Chatterley* the scene focuses on this theme:

> In the short summer night she learnt so much. She would have thought a woman would have died of shame. Instead of which, the shame died. Shame, which is fear: the deep organic shame, the old, old physical fear which crouches in the bodily roots of us, and can only be chased away by the sensual fire, at last it was roused up and routed by the phallic hunt of the man, and she came to the very heart of the jungle of herself. She felt, now, she had come to the real bed-rock of her nature, and was essentially shameless. She was her sensual self, naked and unashamed. She felt a triumph, almost a vainglory. So! That was how it was! That was life! That was how oneself really was! There was nothing left to disguise or be ashamed of. She shared her ultimate nakedness with a man, another being.
>
> And what a reckless devil the man was! really like a devil! One had to be strong to bear him. But it took some getting at, the core of the physical jungle, the last and deepest recess of organic shame. The phallus alone could explore it. And how he had pressed in on her!
>
> And how, in fear, she had hated it. But how she had really wanted it! She knew now. At the bottom of her soul, fundamentally, she had needed this phallic hunting out. . . .

What we see is both a concentration and an expansion of the same material. We have the satisfying sense, missing in the ur-passage, that this scene is the culmination of a significant symbolic action. The change from "In the short summer night she had learnt so much" to "she had needed this phallic hunting out" reveals the central meaning of the novel in its final development: the phallic education of Constance Chatterley through the primitive green agency of her husband's gamekeeper.

This episode consummates, then, the major action of the novel. The rest—approximately a quarter of it—is denouement. Her rebirth, or resurrection, accomplished, Connie no longer requires the sacred wood—and the novel suffers as a result: what follows contains a good bit of Lawrencian silliness. Lawrence is at his best in the episodes set in Wragby Wood, in those scenes focused squarely on Connie's fruition. He is at his worst, his most artificial, when he allows a secondary character, moreover one whom we are intended to dislike—Tommy Dukes in the first part of the book, Connie's father in the last—to mouth certain of his ideas. The same is true of Mellors when he forgets that he is a Green Man of (symbolic) action and fancies himself the polemicist. Even Connie can be insufferable once she participates in Mellors' views and her "voice" becomes indistinguishable from his, as it does at times in the last quarter of the book. But in showing her development, Lawrence is near the top of his form. It is unfortunate that Connie could not always be "becoming."

One may well wonder why Lawrence felt the need to argue his point at all, having dramatized it to such superb effect in what is the true ending of the novel—that final, ritual love scene. Perhaps he felt disposed to contend further for his views since he had not worked out his own shame. I seriously doubt, however, that he had any reservations about his sexual ethic. More likely, Lawrence—whose career reflects a progressive departure from the good sense of keeping polemics out of fiction—simply forgot that a picture is worth a thousand words and expended twenty more thousand on his cause. At any rate, the scenes of Connie's awakening constitute the real, imaginative world of the novel. As we have seen, the metaphorical language of those episodes, through the interpenetrating action of the figures, overarches the central action, reinforcing and, indeed, dramatizing Connie's sexual awakening and its fructifying consequences: integration of the self and vital connection with another individual and with the cosmos. The interaction of the images within the metaphorical structure of the novel is organic in that it reproduces—even (it may be said) creates—the effective meaning of *Lady Chatterley's Lover*. And this is no petty function. (pp. 77-85)

> John B. Humma, "The Interpenetrating Metaphor: Nature and Myth in 'Lady Chatterley's Lover'," in PMLA, Vol. 98, No. 1, January, 1983, pp. 77-86.

Michael Squires (essay date 1983)

[*Squires is an American educator and critic. In the following excerpt from his study* The Creation of "Lady Chatterley's Lover," *he considers the success of* Lady Chatterley's Lover *as a novel.*]

Why is [*Lady Chatterley's Lover*] a novel of the first rank? And why is it *not* Lawrence's acknowledged masterpiece? These questions are [hard] to answer. To do so, I must address some critical issues that face readers of *Lady Chat-*

terley: the novel's ultimate message, the possible contradiction implied by that message, the novel's explicit sexuality, and the controversial experiment with phallic language.

Lawrence wanted primarily to show the value of sexual relations in marriage. But he wanted more: he wanted to demonstrate the relation between a *phallic* marriage and the larger cosmos, to show that sexuality must acknowledge its roots in the daily and seasonal rhythms of the cosmos. ***Lady Chatterley's*** concern with tenderness and touch ought to express this "cosmic" dimension of sexuality; it ought to make fully persuasive the connection between opening leaves and opening desire, between daily rhythms and the progression of desire, between religious ritual and sexual rite. In this crucial way the novel fails. It fails because in ***Lady Chatterley*** Lawrence has not yet recognized the fullness and complexity of the connection, and so the connection, like a rainbow, threatens to disappear.

But the direction of Lawrence's thought shows him struggling toward the major insight that he does not fully reach until **"A Propos of *Lady Chatterley's Lover*"** in 1930. In this long and uneven essay Lawrence argues eloquently for a return to a phallic, regenerative marriage between man and woman. But such a marriage can only regenerate if it hums in unison with "the rhythmic cosmos," if it is linked organically to the sun and the earth and the moon and the stars, if it counterpoints the rhythm of days and seasons and years. In a central passage Lawrence explains how to make the return:

> We *must* get back into relation, vivid and nourishing relation to the cosmos and the universe. The way is through daily ritual, and the re-awakening. We *must* once more practise the ritual of dawn and noon and sunset, the ritual of the kindling fire and pouring water, the ritual of the first breath, and the last. This is an affair of the individual and the household, a ritual of day. The ritual of the moon in her phases, of the morning star and the evening star is for men and women separate. Then the ritual of the seasons, with the Drama and the Passion of the soul embodied in procession and dance, this is for the community, an act of men and women, a whole community, in togetherness. And the ritual of the great events in the year of stars is for nations and whole peoples. To these rituals we must return: or we must evolve them to suit our needs. For the truth is . . . we are cut off from the great sources of our inward nourishment and renewal. . . . We must plant ourselves again in the universe.

I believe that if Lawrence had rewritten the novel still again, it is "daily ritual" that he would have stressed, illustrated, defined, vitalized. The integration of such rituals would have given the novel transcending depth and force. Lawrence might, for instance, have demonstrated how the progression of sexual scenes, culminating in darkness, is itself a rhythm that mimes cosmic phases and processions. Unable to represent these rituals powerfully in ***Lady Chatterley,*** Lawrence nonetheless felt the need to make men whole, to give them a vital connection with others and with the universe. It is impossible, today, to feel that he was wrong in believing that the road to ultimate spiritual fulfillment lies in this direction.

In the novel, however, the road is forked. For returning to wholeness requires the demolition of "personality." As Lawrence explains in **"A Propos,"** the "sympathy of nerves and mind and personal interest," though fostering friendship, is "hostile to blood-sympathy." Personality inhibits phallic awareness. Thus, whereas most men were kind merely to the *person* in Connie, Mellors was kind "to the female in her," kind "to her womb." Following Birkin, he seeks the absolute harmony between his inner male self and Connie's inner female self. Although this notion sounds vague, the evidence for it pervades ***The Rainbow.*** Yet while personality must be demolished in the admired characters, the narrator flaunts his; and his personality, so distinct and "personal," disturbs. It can even fool a good critic like Keith Alldritt into thinking that the chief subject of ***Lady Chatterley*** is "merely personal feeling" [*The Visual Imagination of D. H. Lawrence*]. That is not true of the novel as a whole. But the problem remains that the narrator's personality is almost purely mental, intellectual, analytical. His loops show feelings ruthlessly ordered, while his verdicts, stubbornly authoritative, are to be accepted by the reader as gospel. Yet this imposition of authority contradicts part of the novel's message. In short, the narrator's voice often undermines the norms that are offered as moral alternatives, and thus lessens the novel's aesthetic integrity.

These moral norms pose a special problem in a discussion of the novel's explicit sexuality, a topic perennially heated by critical debate. Whether Lawrence ought to have been so explicit concerns me less than whether his explicitness sustains the novel's larger meaning. It can be argued that in ***Women in Love*** Lawrence's perception of creativity arising from disintegration is more challenging and sophisticated than his simpler and more personal treatment of sex in ***Lady Chatterley.*** Perhaps that is a fair criticism, although in ***Lady Chatterley*** Lawrence approaches the sexual act more concretely and compellingly than in his earlier work. Still, a critic must question the relation between anal intercourse and wholeness, between what appears *disintegrative* and what appears *creative.* Lawrence avers that anal intercourse makes Connie whole by burning out her deepest shames, by liberating her from the thought that any part of her body may be sensually unclean. The critical problem is knowing the place of disintegration in man's need for ritual adjustment to the cosmos. Is Connie's sacrifice of female will connected to ancient sacrificial rites? Is Mellors' display of male dominance a ritual act? As Mark Spilka shows [in his essay "On Lawrence's Hostility to Wilful Women: The Chatterley Solution," in *Lawrence and Women,* edited by Anne Smith], the buggering scene might have purged Mellors' sexual hostility, revealed his emerging need for "male identity" rather than dominance, and so extended his characterization. But Lawrence had not yet worked out in his own mind how wholeness reinforces oneness with the rhythmic universe; and he does not explore the relationship with as much imaginative and intellectual energy as he explores comparable ideas in ***Women in Love.*** The major problem with the scene of anal intercourse is not that it fails to corroborate the novel's ethic of tenderness, or that it reveals Lawrence's latent homosexuality, but that it does not express the deepest kind of human fulfillment, which Lawrence elsewhere imagines.

It seems a shame to quarrel with the novel's sexuality when it is represented with such exquisite delicacy and expresses so well the themes of knowledge and silence and sensual tenderness. But another aspect of Lawrence's sexual ethic has troubled readers: the idea that Connie should discipline her female "will" in order to reach orgasm simultaneously with Mellors. Connie must not manipulate Mellors' phallus as a tool, but must share with him the rhythms of intercourse in such a way that she need not writhe for her separate satisfaction. In effect, Lawrence distinguishes clitoral from vaginal orgasm, a distinction widely debated today. The idea first appears near the end of *The Plumed Serpent,* where Kate Leslie learns from Cipriano and Teresa to deny her "ruthless female power" and so invite a softer, deeper connection to the man she loves. Still, the diatribe in *Lady Chatterley* against women like Bertha, who tear and rip with their clitoral "beaks," probably has a biographical origin. I think it likely that [Lawrence's wife] Frieda was a woman, like the young Connie, who writhed in intercourse unaware of the physical pain she may have caused her husband. Lawrence probably concluded from personal experience that if a female could achieve a more quiescent orgasm, intercourse would prove more comfortable and satisfying for the male. . . . [He] designed his novel partly as a means of teaching Frieda how to live with him.

But for Lawrence to insist on female passivity in sexual intercourse is, today, like teasing a coiled snake; and Lawrence has been bitten more than once. Vivas, Holbrook, Daleski, Millett, and others have all complained. Though least fair, Kate Millett can represent the group. She argues that Lawrence, following Freud, believes vaginal orgasm can indeed be reached by inactive females: "The phallus is all; Connie is 'cunt,' the thing acted upon, gratefully accepting each manifestation of the will of the master. . . . She enjoys an orgasm when she can, while Mellors is managing his own. If she can't, then too bad" (*Sexual Politics*). From this Millett concludes that whereas the frigid Victorian woman could withhold assent, "the 'new woman' could, if correctly dominated, be mastered in bed as everywhere else." Lawrence's notion becomes a "superb instrument" of subjection. Though calculated and tendentious, her whole attack raises a larger question: How *might* Lawrence see female passivity in intercourse as a worthy goal for Connie? or for women? It is unfair to assume that Lawrence's hostility to women compelled him to imprison Connie's sexual activity, for her discovery of the value of sexual passivity encourages a truly mutual flow of sensation between partners, a genuine balance of male and female. In return for the male disciplining himself to delay ejaculation, the female disciplines herself to reduce physical activity and so, by relaxing her active will, "let[s] herself go," "let[s] go everything, all herself, and [is] gone in the flood"—a flood of sensual awakening, a forgetting to manipulate, and a willingness to hear what Lawrence calls in a fine, canceled passage "the sensual birth of the first trilling music" and to see "the sensual birth of the loveliness of colour" and to know the "gushes of dawn that flashed brilliant at the edges. . . . There, there is the dawn of all beauty, in the sheer sensual act of creation, when men and women create one another." In a tract aimed to reform sexuality, Lawrence's view would appear narrow. But in a novel that aims to represent the way a single couple reaches sexual harmony and wholeness, I find his treatment legitimate. Yes, he hymns the splendor of vaginal orgasm. He does so because he is attracted to the phallus and its power to deliver massive stimulation. Readers can object that in view of recent research his belief in the value of female passivity appears limited. But they will be objecting to his ignorance of scientific data, not to his understanding or to his art.

I wish this were all that needed to be said. However, the highly controversial scene where Connie and Mellors engage in anal intercourse shows Connie consenting reluctantly, letting the keeper "have his way and his will with her. She had to be a passive, consenting thing, like a slave, a physical slave." The key words are *passive thing.* Connie functions as an object, a willing victim of a sexual experiment, just as she does earlier when the keeper "tips her up" outside the hut and penetrates her without foreplay. A real issue emerges. One can view Connie as a violated female, shorn of respect, and cringe from the love ethic that fosters her behavior. Or one can do as Lawrence asks, and connect this experimental sexuality to the themes of education and rebirth, which join all of the sexual scenes. In this view the keeper's fiery sensuality burns out Connie's false bodily shames and makes her "shameless." As a form of salvation, Connie's new sensual identity proves her rejection of both mental dependence and social conditioning. Shame dies not because of a mental act but because the flood of sharp sensation kills it, leaving her fresh and fully awakened, washed clean of her old social status. On these grounds the scene can be accepted.

Yet it continues to disturb readers for two reasons: not only is it poorly located in the cycle of cosmic ritual, as discussed earlier, but it is not fully integrated into the norm of rhythmic natural order which forms the most intelligible context for understanding the novel's sexuality. Just as Gerald tells Birkin in *Women in Love* that nature "doesn't provide the basis" for homosexuality, so Parkin in [in the first version of *Lady Chatterley's Lover*] tells Connie that it is "not the way of the animals" to have intercourse during pregnancy. And Mellors himself attacks women who refuse "natural" orgasms, who cannot " 'come' naturally with a man." Yet the question remains: Why is it peculiarly the way of humans to differ from nature in the matter of buggery? The problem is not just that the scene is inexplicit and narrated at too great a distance but that it does not anywhere suggest the larger basis of its own justification. Its capacity to connect to natural law or to cosmic forces, or even to human ritual or human morality, seems unduly limited, so that the scene does not represent Lawrence's best writing.

What constitutes Lawrence's best writing governs the issue of his experiment with sexual language. His attempt to cleanse the sexual vernacular of its impure connotations is, artistically, the most innovative aspect of the novel. Early, Lawrence recognized the controversy he would fire: "But the *words* are all used!" In **"A Propos"** he argues that his experiment will free the phallic reality from the taint of uplift: "We shall never free the phallic reality . . . till we give it its own phallic language, and use the obscene words." Made bold by his courage and insight, Lawrence attempts to turn sexual language into respected verbal communication. Whether or not we like it, he succeeds in forcing his readers to acknowledge a separate phallic vocabulary, consisting of words like *cunt, fuck, shit,* and *piss.* This language has an earthiness and a pungently poetic force that the language of the narrator (who prefers *intercourse, womb, phallus*) has not; and certainly it strengthens the keeper's virile image. Certainly, too, Lawrence is right to say that the words that shock at first "don't shock at all after a while" (**"A Propos"**). For most readers the words become better integrated and less salient with each rereading of the novel.

But the case against Lawrence's experiment must also be heard. F. R. Leavis regards Lawrence's hygienic mission to cleanse the obscene words as an offense against "taste." For Richard Aldington the words, "incrusted with nastiness," cannot regain their purity. Following Edmund Wilson, Graham Hough questions Lawrence's "literary sense" in trying to reform, by mere fiat, the resonance of a whole stratum of vocabulary: "The fact remains that the connotations of the obscene physical words are either facetious or vulgar." Still, Hough's intelligent assessment is not quite the last word. What finally disturbs readers, I think, is not Lawrence's vulgarity but the way in which he *mingles* the vulgar and the sacred, the common and the unique. As a drunken festival would defile a baroque church, or as an obscenity would degrade a marriage ceremony, so the keeper's phallic language is hard to reconcile with the holy rites of intercourse: not because language and rites are intrinsically antagonistic but because their conjunction has not found a supporting context in the other arts. In contemporary films, for example, "phallic language" still signifies not tenderness and bodily reverence but coarseness and vulgarity and contempt. Without this wider supporting context, Lawrence's use of phallic language will always seem incongruous and disturbing to most readers.

The discussion of these various issues will suggest why ***Lady Chatterley*** is not the masterpiece of Lawrence's fiction. The narrator's display of his personality, Lawrence's failure to justify the moral basis of the novel's sexual experiments in relation to female passivity or to the ritual cosmos, the misguided foray into phallic language—these are causes. More important is Lawrence's inability to understand the relationship of his story of Connie and the keeper to the ideas set forth in **"A Propos,"** which would have given the novel a wider and deeper human significance. And to these must be added some of Lawrence's idiosyncratic methods of composition, which sometimes heighten the novel's schematic antitheses into a diagram where characters subserve abstract ideas. Even so, ***Lady Chatterley*** is not the "feeble and spiteful novel" that Marvin Mudrick sees, nor the sentimental and self-indulgent work that David Cavitch discovers, nor yet the failure that David Holbrook and William Ober find. But how, then, is it the "great achievement" that Frank Kermode sees? or that "most impressive work" that Daleski finds? or "one of the great novels of the period," as Delavenay thinks? or, to quote Anaïs Nin, "artistically . . . his best novel"—the "climax" of his work? It is time, now, to pose my earlier question: How is ***Lady Chatterley's Lover*** a work of the first rank?

Its beauty and its greatness blossom from its many strengths. Especially impressive are the novel's economy, its control of detail, and its careful shaping of materials into a coherent whole. Lawrence's rigorous control points neither to his impatience with detail nor to his willingness to sacrifice realism for myth. A reader coming from the overdone second generation of ***The Rainbow*** or from the bloated talk of ***Women in Love*** or even from the loose construction of version 1 is struck by the concentration of the final ***Lady Chatterley.*** Take the scene where Connie and Clifford go for a morning walk. Suppressing the details of their return to Wragby, Lawrence simply employs a transition: " 'Who is your game-keeper?' Connie asked at lunch." Providing the drawstring of the novel, this kind of narrative compression shows how Lawrence eschews the inessential. When Mrs. Bolton glides sleepily into Clifford's room for a night game of cards, Lawrence skillfully leads her to the window lit with dawn and so redirects the narrative to Connie and the keeper. The coherence is perfect: Mrs. Bolton comments on the keeper, whose shape she discerns in the driveway, while the reader sees the two cardsharks bonding together—"a reassurance to one another" in the night. From first to third version, the novel focuses ever more insistently on validating Connie's decision to leave Wragby.

It is not true that Lawrence explores sexuality alone: around it he sketches a border of literature, art, history, politics, and details of the mining industry, tersely surrounding the sexual center with a frame of modern life. But the contextual frame creates a clear pattern: not a delicate lyrical shading but the bold contrasts of a moral fable, with its symbolic oppositions and its moral application to an industrial society. Unlike Kingsley's *Yeast* or Morris' *News from Nowhere,* ***Lady Chatterley*** is not a tract in fictional form. In **"Morality and the Novel"** and elsewhere, Lawrence saw the risk of the narrator's putting his thumb in the scale and "pull[ing] down the balance to his own predilection" (***Phoenix***) the risk of "metaphysic" subsuming art. However, the novel's apotheosis of sensual feeling and its hatred of the mechanical do wrap it in a social ideology; and in its form and its ideas alike, the novel approaches a diagram. What saves it is that the jabbingly incisive analysis of modern life rarely interferes with the regeneration of Connie and Mellors: the novel succeeds in forcing the diagram simply to frame the characters' sensual awakening.

Still, this analytical frame attracts much of the novel's critical insight. One admires not only the artistic coherence of the novel but its ideological coherence as well. Lawrence understands how industrialism makes men puppets of the machine principle and ciphers in a profit formula; and he understands how we cope with the spiritual desolation that rises from the ashes of our old integrated being: without sentient roots, we let our wills calculate our goals and manipulate our environment, smother our spontaneity and fuel our desire for egocentric sex. All of this is finely perceptive. Like a husk, these ideas surround the lovers' effort to discover a phallic union, then point toward the keeper's more controversial critique (in version 3) of female will and industrial enslavement. One must concede that Mellors' attack on females like Bertha Coutts draws on very personal material. His diatribe reveals Lawrence striking out against the flock of women who clung to him all his life, when he would have preferred men. "I am . . . so sick of nothing but women on top of me," he cries to Orioli in 1929. Lawrence does not advance beyond his solipsistic animosity. But the program that Mellors sketches to salvage the masses from industrial enslavement is a different matter. Shrewdly he analyzes the plight of the common people; though just as Fielding should have made Tom Jones interrupt the Man of the Hill's monologue, so Lawrence should have made Connie a more critical listener. To make the program artistically valid, he should have made Connie question Mellors' assumptions, prick them with counterstatement (as she does Clifford's), and show lively intellectual interest in his solution. Yet Mellors' radical critique of industrial society shows how deeply he cares for his fellow man, how fervently he wants to bring strength and vitality into their lives. It is therefore disturbing to find his ideas dismissed as the rantings of a crazed misanthrope. Even a discriminating critic like Julian Moynahan finds these ideas immature and ironic (*The Deed of Life*). But Mellors means passionately what he says, and has the narrator's approval.

These ideas become clear only when one knows how they existed in their original, unrevised form. Perhaps in response to Aldous Huxley's criticism of the typescript, Lawrence slashed big chunks from Mellors' remarks to Connie; these chunks, never before published, help one to appreciate the keeper's insights into the need for beauty, brotherhood, and escape from materialism. To Connie he says, "We aren't wage-slaves. . . . We'll be content wi' little—eh, a little bit o' money's enough for folks as 'as got life in 'em." Once freed from the vise of materialism, the miners can be guided by a man like Mellors (or Lawrence) to enjoy life—by dancing and singing, or competing in games: "Why, I'd teach the men to dance again, the old dances, *all together:* the old wild dances. And to sing right out from their very balls, like men: sing together. An' run an' jump like the Greeks did." Proud of their bodies, they would learn "how to *move,* to move and be lovely moving. That's life." The vision sweeps before his eyes like a reality: "I could do it! I could do it!" he cries to Connie, passionately committed:

> "[I could] get back the real straight life, wi' a heart of its own. . . . "
>
> "Yes!" she said. "It has always been my secret dream. But I felt it could never happen any more, never."
>
> "Ay, it could though!" he said. . . . "I could start it again—even in Teversall colliers—come the right moment."

The canceled material yields moving examples of the keeper's humanity, of his strong concern for the colliers: "Nobody's cared about the working-classes, with a bit of warm-hearted care, not for a second." When he finishes talking, Connie reflects on his commitment to others: "She felt him so serious in what he said, so involved in it all. He seemed to care so much . . . whether the colliers had ever been loved, or whether they hadn't." In ways like this, the novel's textual history can be surprisingly helpful, calling into question judgments like Kate Millett's that Mellors "despises his own class." The manuscript shows that far from being the bitter misanthrope critics have found, Mellors loves his fellow man; he cares deeply for the *life* of others.

And the reforms he proposes, despite their wistful idealism, reflects mature thinking. The salvation of the working class will come not through the mystical worship of pagan deities and demagogues, as in ***The Plumed Serpent,*** but through the reform of social priorities and the intelligent use of ritual. The public side of reform calls for an organic community that would supply basic material needs yet would mainly encourage the social rituals that bind men together; the private side of reform stresses the cultivation of phallic rituals that bind man to woman. Both sides are crucial to understanding Lawrence's "message" in ***Lady Chatterley.*** Lawrence cut Mellors' program for reform not because it seemed like amateur theorizing but because it was, as it stood, too long. The novel could not contain it—and has trouble embracing even the condensed version, which needs the bite of counterargument. It is true that Lawrence's vision of reintegrating society is the vision of an alienated man trying to shed his own detachment. Still, that vision seems no less profound because it is, in the novel, only a *vision* of man's moral responsibility to his fellows. Yet some readers think Lawrence should have put the vision into practice, and I agree that the ending might have been enhanced if Connie and Mellors had committed themselves to some politically useful work. In that way they would have demonstrated a connection, now lacking, between the politics of sex and the politics of class. That Lawrence refused such an ending shows not cowardice but a disturbing lack of faith in society to set itself aright.

There is also the private side of social reform. The greatness of the novel arises equally from Lawrence's full exploration of the processes of phallic bonding. By insisting on the beauty and centrality of sensual awareness, he forces readers to acknowledge the limits of their willful manipulation of their bodies. If Lawrence brilliantly recognizes our need to bind our phallic selves to cosmic cycles, he also shows Connie and Mellors abandoning the drive for power and mastery in order to reach a phallic communion. In his earlier novels Lawrence shows admired characters like Ursula Brangwen and Paul Morel driven to seek fulfillment. But Connie and Mellors have shed the hide of will power: they seek fulfillment at deeper levels of their being, beneath the overlay of education and social conditioning. Charles Rossman says perceptively that Lawrence motivates the behavior of Connie and Mellors "from deep within them, in both cases against their conscious wills. The body of each answers spontaneously and unconsciously to the call of the other, each awakened from a dormant state." [" 'You are the call and I am the answer': D. H. Lawrence and Women," *D. H. Lawrence Review* (1975)] But there is a paradox here. In novels like ***The Rainbow*** and ***Women in Love*** Lawrence renders half-conscious states of mind extraordinarily. In ***Lady Chatterley*** the characters' emotional needs are deeper, but Lawrence has not advanced his technique to express the greater relative depth of their need: the "stream" passages that express their need contain the fibers of conscious analytical thinking. The range of their need is not therefore fully met by Lawrence's technique for rendering states of being. From Joyce and Woolf he could have learned how language can comb the unconscious mind. He needed to discover both a vocabulary of phallic awareness and a vocabulary of the unconscious.

Despite this artistic limit, the rejection of personal power and the decision to explore phallic awareness make possible the exquisite theme of tenderness. Here, Lawrence concentrates his artistic power and achieves a major thematic advance over his earlier novels. The concept of phallic tenderness is fresh, persuasively wreathed by the motifs of silence and softness and natural processes. Equally impressive, nature intones a voiceless hymn of creation, sung in unison with the deepest urges of Connie and Mellors, so that the rush of blood into the keeper's phallus mimes the rush of sap into the old oak trees. No other novelist handles the myth of rebirth with more sensitivity than Lawrence does in ***Lady Chatterley's Lover.***

For readers like myself, what matters is not the particular myth alone but the paradigm of rebirth and self-discovery that Lawrence embodies in fictional form. The novel beautifully illustrates the pastoral myth of escape from despair, regeneration of self in a *locus amoenus* that heightens experience, and a return to ordinary life with surer direction. The novel also illustrates a number of deeply significant moral truths about human experience: the need to demand from life more than material satisfaction, the need to elevate the status of the human body, the need to recognize one's rootedness in the cosmos, the need to discover beauty amid industrialism, and the periodic need to renew one's spiritual self in order to find wholeness and harmony. It is all too easy to abstract lessons from ***Lady Chatterley,*** to reduce the novel to a tangy sermon. But the novel is peculiar in the way it can resist this kind of reduction and still retain its moral purpose. I suspect that for most readers the novel's moral significance is ultimately its most attractive feature. (pp. 176-87)

> *Michael Squires, in his* "The Creation of Lady Chatterley's Lover," *The Johns Hopkins University Press, 1983, 237 p.*

Scott R. Sanders (essay date 1985)

[*A novelist and educator, Sanders has written articles and a book-length study on Lawrence. In the following essay, he discusses the view expressed in* Lady Chatterley's Lover *that humanity is driven toward self-annihilation.*]

While a thunderstorm crashes outside, stirring the remnant trees of Sherwood Forest, the gamekeeper shelters in

---

Lawrence on the mind and the body:

The mind has an old grovelling fear of the body and the body's potencies. It is the mind we have to liberate, to civilize on these points. The mind's terror of the body has probably driven more men mad than ever could be counted. The insanity of a great mind like Swift's is at least partly traceable to this cause. In the poem to his mistress Celia, which has the maddened refrain "But—Celia, Celia, Celia s***s," (the word rhymes with spits), we see what can happen to a great mind when it falls into panic. A great wit like Swift could not see how ridiculous he made himself. Of course Celia s***s! Who doesn't? And how much worse if she didn't. It is hopeless. And then think of poor Celia, made to feel iniquitous about her proper natural function, by her "lover." It is monstrous. And it comes from having taboo words, and from not keeping the mind sufficiently developed in physical and sexual consciousness.

> D. H. Lawrence, in his "A Propos of Lady Chatterley's Lover" in Sex, Literature, and Censorship, *edited by Harry T. Moore, 1953.*

---

his hut with Constance Chatterley. Secure amidst the deluge ("It was like being in a little ark in the Flood"), he ruminates about doomsday: "Quite nice! To contemplate the extermination of the human species and the long pause that follows before some other species crops up, it calms you more than anything else. And if we go on in this way, with everybody, intellectuals, artists, governments, industrialists and workers all frantically killing off the last human feeling, the last bit of their intuition, the last healthy instinct; if it goes on in algebraical progression, as it is going on: then ta-tah! to the human species!" Is that warning, or is that yearning? The gamekeeper seems half to dread the prospect of extermination, half to relish it. A similar ambivalence runs through most of Lawrence's doomsday visions, which appear with impressive frequency in his writings from the war years onward, beginning with ***The Rainbow*** and ***Women in Love;*** continuing in essays and letters during the 1920s; extending into all three versions of his last novel, ***Lady Chatterley's Lover;*** and occupying the center of his last book, appropriately entitled ***Apocalypse.***

In works written during and immediately after the Great War, the yearning for annihilation frequently predominates, as when Rupert Birkin in ***Women in Love*** declares, "I abhor humanity, I wish it was swept away. It could go, and there would be no *absolute* loss, if every human being perished to-morrow." Lawrence himself seemed at times during the war to feel that the only hope for the renewal of the world was a holocaust, a violent collapse of industrial civilization. Yet even in those years of bitterness, his visions of doom were most often warnings; in a letter of 1915 he wrote, "The disintegrating process of the war has become an internal evil, so vast as to be almost unthinkable, so nearly overwhelming us, that we stand on the very brink of oblivion." By the time he came to write the three versions of ***Lady Chatterley's Lover,*** there remained only the slightest trace of his earlier ambivalence regarding the prospect of annihilation, as the lines from the gamekeeper quoted above would suggest. Instead, those last novels provide wholehearted warnings about what Constance Chatterley, in *John Thomas and Lady Jane*, foresees as "the suicide of the human race."

When I began reading Lawrence in the late 1960s, I discounted such visions of annihilation as the hyperbole of a writer who had spent too many childhood days listening to readings from the Old Testament, or as the mild hysteria of a man who was convinced humanity had taken a wrong turn, or as the occasional misanthropy of someone who had been sorely used by his contemporaries. I now take these visions much more seriously, for reasons that have less to do with Lawrence's history than with our own.

During the First World War, the latest devices of annihilation, including aerial bombardment and poison gas, were used to kill ten million people. During the Second World War, "improved" weapons led to the annihilation of entire cities, such as Dresden and Hiroshima, and to the death of more than fifty million people. Operating on Jews and Gypsies and Slavs, the Nazis pioneered scientific methods for exterminating races. Since 1945 there have been more than 150 civil and regional wars, each one fought with the newest available weaponry, all of them combined slaughtering a greater number of people than the first two world wars. Most nations on earth continue to devote a large proportion of their wealth, resources, and talent to preparations for war. In the United States during the mid-1980s, for example, roughly half of all federal taxes go to the military, and fully half of all the scientists and technicians in the country are engaged in military research.

An all-out nuclear exchange between the United States and the Soviet Union could kill three hundred million people outright and sentence millions more to lingering death by hunger and disease. The long-term effects of radiation and ecological disruption would exterminate many species—perhaps including, within a generation or two, our own. After a million-year struggle to escape the assaults of nature we have constructed machineries of destruction that make plagues and earthquakes seem mild by comparison. The suicide of the human race, of which Lawrence so often warned, is now *literally* possible. How has this come to pass? Why have we pushed ourselves and our planet to this brink of annihilation? There is no deeper mystery, nor any we need more urgently to solve.

Lawrence died in 1930, fifteen years before the first atomic bombs were exploded. Yet he would certainly have recognized the impulse that led to the building of these weapons and to their use on Hiroshima and Nagasaki. There is nothing new about the human compulsion to obliterate whatever stands in the way of personal or tribal or national will. Our tools for *acting* on that compulsion are constantly being strengthened, however, and are now commensurate with our most gargantuan jealousies, our most ambitious schemes. Weary of sharing daylight and pasture and praise with his brother, Cain slew Abel, but could use only his bare hands, or perhaps a club or stone, to perform the deed. We are not so limited. Today, a nation possessing nuclear weapons can treat any brother or sister nation as a collective Abel, a rival to be erased. Genocide is only an enlargement, a perfecting, of fratricide.

So Lawrence would not have been surprised, although he would doubtless have been dismayed, by the development of tools for extermination. In novel after novel, essay after essay, for more than two decades, he traced the origins of human destructiveness to the *desire for mastery*— over nature, over the body, over one's mate, over servant classes and rival nations and whatever appears to resist the personal or collective will. If the mountain blocks your highway, blast a tunnel through it. If the river floods your fields, dam it up. When people of a color or creed different from your own occupy the land you covet, then butcher them, make them gifts of blankets infected with smallpox, tear up their crops and slaughter their game. If a rival nation defies your wishes, point missiles at its cities. The evil effects of the desire for domination were painfully evident to Lawrence in the war, and in the brutalized people and devastated landscape of his native industrial Midlands.

This quest for mastery is founded, according to Lawrence, upon the *illusion of separation:* the illusion that mind can be divorced from body, self from other, humanity from nature. The attitude of domination presupposes a master and something *else* to be mastered. Before "conquering" the flesh or the forest or the enemy, we must first create barriers, imagine distance. We can only bring ourselves to devastate what we have first defined as radically alien. A part of creation—another country, another class, another person, a parcel of forest—is imagined as a *thing,* reduced to the status of an object, and then subjected to our violent will. One can readily think of examples: whales, redwoods, Indians, communists, capitalists, the visiting football team, worshippers of another god; imagined as prey or resources or enemy, each is annihilated first in thought, and then in fact.

We enter a universe that is all of a piece, and with our minds and machines we slice it full of rents—this is Lawrence's persistent message, repeated with increasing urgency toward the end of his life, as in this passage from *Apocalypse:* "We are unnaturally resisting our connection with the cosmos, with the world, with mankind, with the nation, with the family. . . . We *cannot bear connection.* That is our malady. We *must* break away, and be isolate. We call that being free, being individual. Beyond a certain point, which we have reached, it is suicide. Perhaps we have chosen suicide." The most elementary form of this malady is the illusion of the isolated ego, self-sufficient and all-powerful, distinct from flesh and from nature, in competition with other egos. In its epidemic forms the malady spreads to entire tribes and nations, transforming the group into a collective ego. The remedy clearly lies in erasing the illusory barriers we have erected—between mind and body, self and other, humanity and nature.

In tracing the sources of human violence to the desire for mastery and the illusion of separateness, Lawrence was echoing a view common to many of the world's religions. What did Adam and Eve hope to gain from biting the apple, after all, if not godlike power over creation? Lawrence was original, not in his analysis of human destructiveness, but in the psychological acuity and stylistic power with which he rendered both the malady and its remedy. Consider as an illustration that last, gentle novel he wrote three times, about the lady and her gamekeeper.

All three versions of *Lady Chatterley's Lover* open with the same arresting phrase: "Ours is essentially a tragic age." Tragic how? one wonders. Lawrence immediately goes on to explain, with different phrasing in each version, that the age is tragic because "the cataclysm has fallen," the terrible war has occurred, and yet people go on living among the ruins as if nothing has been changed by the half decade of bloodshed. In Lawrence's eyes, the paroxysm of violence that gripped Europe between 1914 and 1918 called into question the most fundamental assumptions of industrial civilization.

Instead of tracing the origins of war to the quest for domination—over nature, over subject classes and colonial peoples, over rival nations—the leaders and ideologists for all sides in the conflict blamed the cataclysm on the "enemy," thus reinforcing the psychology of domination and preparing the way for the Second World War. After that later war, with its vast escalation of violence, Albert Einstein warned: "The unleashed power of the atom has changed everything save our modes of thinking, and thus we drift toward unparalleled catastrophe." The First World War had persuaded Lawrence of the same truth. Long before the unleashing of the atom, he was warning us that we must transform our ways of thinking and feeling if we are to avoid being annihilated by our own murderous inventions.

Clifford Chatterley epitomized for Lawrence those who, resuming power after the Armistice, set about intensifying the very processes that had led to the war. As a member of the ruling class, Clifford insists upon his right to dominate the working class. "What the mass of people want is *masters*," he tells Connie. Like that earlier industrial magnate in *Women in Love,* Gerald Crich, whom he resembles in so many other respects, Clifford regards his employees as tools, extensions of his will: "The miners were, in a sense, his own men; but he saw them as objects rather than men, parts of the pit rather than parts of life, crude raw phenomena rather than human beings along with him." Here we see the gesture of estrangement which accompanies every gesture of domination and destruction. Those whom you would manipulate or murder, you must first dehumanize.

As an owner of mines, Clifford hurls himself into a mechanized war against nature, succumbing to "the long-enduring ecstasy of the struggle with uncanny Matter. It was as if he fused himself into the very existence of coal and sulphur and petroleum and rock, and lost his humanity, as the trolls have lost theirs, in iron." The very earth becomes his antagonist. Just as he refuses to acknowledge the independent life of the miners, so he refuses to acknowledge the life of nature itself. Pheasants exist to be shot, trees to be felled, coal to be mined: objects awaiting the exercise of his sovereign will. He takes on the shape of his imagined opponent, becomes matter wrestling with matter, robot man confronting inanimate nature.

As a husband, Clifford expresses the same desire for mastery over Connie, leading her to fear that "she would become just a half-animate automaton worked entirely from Clifford's will, coming as he willed, going as he willed, thinking only the thoughts he released in her mind, feeling only the feelings he allowed to come forth." Although he is more courtly in his dealings with her than in his dealings with the colliers and the coal, he is no less insistent in the exercise of his will. He is emotionally dependent on Connie, to be sure, yet he dominates her in intellectual matters and in the affairs of daily life.

His craving for mastery feeds upon his sense of isolation: "he was finally limited entirely to himself. No breath entered him from any other living being or creature or thing. He was as it were cut off from the breathing contact of the living universe." Here we behold the illusion of separation in its purest form. As his continual reading of the famous idealists—from Plato and Plotinus through Hegel and Rilke—would suggest, Clifford perceives the material universe as an inferior imitation of some higher spiritual realm. His own ego figures prominently in that empyrean. At one point, quoting an idealist philosopher, he proclaims to Connie: "The universe shows us two aspects: on one side it is physically wasting, on the other it is spiritually ascending." Once again, nature takes on the guise of enemy. Clifford fondly dreams of erasing everything that resists the touch, everything that breathes—everything, that is, except himself.

Locked within the fortress of his ego, Clifford regards the rest of the cosmos as an infringement on his bloated self: "He felt that, in the universe, he was a thing apart, and that all the other things in the universe were probably taking away a portion of life he himself might have had. The expansive yellow face of the dandelion irritated him, with its crude yellowness and its exposed foolishness. He preferred the nipped bud, in the rain." It would be hard to imagine any attitude more repellent to Lawrence than this jealousy of dandelions, this grotesque inflation of the ego to such proportions that it squeezes out every other creature.

Clifford is a monster of self-importance. But he is also a cripple, and this makes it difficult to judge clearly the role he plays in the symbolic landscape of *Lady Chatterley's Lover.* The war has left him paralyzed from the waist down, forever excluded from any pleasures of the flesh, including sexual intercourse. Is it so shocking that such a man would despise fleshly existence? Lawrence himself conceded, in a later remark on the novel, that it was perhaps clumsy of him to have made Clifford a physical as well as a psychological cripple: "As to whether the 'symbolism' is intentional—I don't know. Certainly not in the beginning, when Clifford was created. When I created Clifford and Connie, I had no idea what they were or why they were. They just came, pretty much as they are. . . . And when I read the first version, I recognized that the lameness of Clifford was symbolic of the paralysis, the deeper emotional or passional paralysis, of most men of his sort and class today" (*Phoenix II*). In the novel itself Lawrence takes pains to show, through Connie's recollections and perceptions, that Clifford's contempt for the body and hostility toward the physical universe preceded the war. His paralysis is an outward symptom of an inward condition, just as the war itself was a terrible symptom of the profound disorder at the heart of industrial civilization. As member of the ruling class, as mine owner, husband, ego, Clifford is *a thing apart.* Other people and nature itself only exist as objects of his power. Whatever resists his power he will annihilate, in desire if not in fact. Thus when Connie names the gamekeeper as her lover, Clifford responds by shouting, "[Y]ou ought to be wiped off the face of the earth!" In this bullying owner of mines, Lawrence depicted the psychopathology of the unbridled desire for domination.

Terrified of becoming an "automaton worked entirely from Clifford's will," Connie struggles to free herself from his domineering influence. She struggles, not into the splendid isolation of her own ego, there to become a wielder of power to rival Clifford, but into communion with nature, with the gamekeeper, and, through him, into fitful contact with the local working people. In all her motions of thought and feeling, she moves in a direction contrary to Clifford. He yearns for separation, she for connection. He longs to enslave the colliers, she to understand them. He sets himself up as master of the countryside; she enters sympathetically into the life of the forest, almost as a beast among the trees. He strives to hammer the imprint of his being onto the world, she to decipher the being of the world itself. Whereas Clifford demonstrates those attitudes which had produced the First World War, the deep hatred between classes and the industrial blight, Connie demonstrates those attitudes which, in Lawrence's eyes, might heal the blight and overcome the hatred and prevent future wars.

She does not arrive all at once, or easily, at her new vision of things. Life with Clifford has reduced her to a state of nervous exhaustion: "Connie was aware . . . of a growing restlessness. Out of her disconnection, a restlessness was taking possession of her like madness. . . . Vaguely she knew herself that she was going to pieces in some way. Vaguely she knew she was out of connection: she had lost touch with the substantial and vital world." Clifford seems to be reconciled to this state of "disconnection," but Connie suffers from it. Her story in all three versions of the novel is one of painfully restoring connections. The notorious lovemaking with the gamekeeper puts her back in touch with her own body. But even before she lies down for the first time in the keeper's hut, she enters into communion with the forest itself; and this connection, we realize by the end of the novel, is more fundamental and comprehensive than the sexual one: "Constance sat down with her back to a young pinetree, that swayed against her like an animate creature, so subtly rubbing itself against her, the great, alive thing with its top in the wind! And she watched the daffodils sparkle in a burst of sun, that was warm on her face; and she caught the faint tarry scent of the flowers; and gradually everything went still in her, so still, so still and disentangled!" Here is the antidote for the frenzy into which life with Clifford has driven her. Instead of feeling diminished by the life of other things (as does Clifford, jealous of the dandelion's glow), Connie feels comforted by this brush with a life greater than her own.

The language in this description of communion with nature, like that in many such descriptions throughout Lawrence's works, is strongly sexual. That "great, alive thing" "so subtly rubbing itself against her" is clearly phallic. And yet—which is primary, the tree or the phallus? Should we read Connie's communion with the forest as a sublimation of her sexual yearning, or should we regard her later sexual enlightenment as a deepening and confirmation of her contact with the animate universe? I hold with the latter view. Consider this description of Connie's reaction to a bout of lovemaking:

> She felt herself filled with new blood, as if the blood of the man had swept into her veins like a strong, fresh, rousing wind, changing her whole self. All her self felt alive, and in motion, like the woods in spring. She could not but feel that a new breath had swept into her body from the man, and that she was like a forest soughing with a new, soft wind, soughing and moving unspoken into bud. All her body felt like the dark interlacing of the boughs of an oak wood, softly humming in a wind, and humming inaudibly with the myriad, myriad unfolding of buds. Meanwhile the birds had their heads laid on their shoulders and slept with delight in the vast interlaced intricacy of the forest of her body.

Here the metaphorical exchange is reversed: instead of the forest taking on the overtones of sexuality, sex takes on the shapes of the forest. Sex powerfully reveals the true ground of her existence; but she has been connected to that ground, unknowing, since birth and through all the celibate months of her marriage to Clifford. In Lawrence's world, one might be barred from lovemaking by youth or age, by distance or—as Lawrence himself was during his last years—by illness; yet one can still maintain one's "touch with the substantial and vital world."

Connie discovers *through* sex her rootedness in nature, and she is alerted to the awesome power of life in nature itself. After another bout of lovemaking, she sees the world in this light:

> The trees seemed to be bulging and surging, at anchor on a tide, and the heave of the slope of the park was alive. She herself was a different creature, sensitive and alert, quietly slipping among the live presences of trees and hills and a far-off star.
>
> . . . Time was a full soft urge, with no minutes to it. And the universe ceased to be the vast clock-work of circling planets and pivotal suns, which she had known. The stars opened like eyes, with a consciousness in them, and the sky was filled with a soft, yearning stress of consolation. It was not mere atmosphere. It had its own feeling, its own anima. Everything had its own anima.
>
> The quick of the universe is in our own bodies, deep in us.

This is the central moment of discovery in one after another of Lawrence's works, this perception of the world's vast inhuman aliveness, and of one's participation in it. Having seen this, Connie recognizes that Clifford's view of nature as inert matter is monstrous. His pretense of "owning" the woods or the neighboring coal mines is grotesque. "Cut off from the breathing contact of the living universe," he is very dangerous, and grows more dangerous as machines multiply the destructive power of his will. Others embracing Clifford's outlook have produced the gruesome villages and devastated landscapes of industrial England, villages like Tevershall and Stacks Gate whose ugliness wrings Connie's heart, landscapes such as the mining country around Nottingham where Lawrence grew up and which he visited again in 1926 just before starting the first version of *Lady Chatterley's Lover*. His letters of the time show that Lawrence felt, like Connie, "a tenderness . . . , a wistfulness, for this disfigured countryside, and the disfigured, strange, almost wraithlike populace." Clifford's central fault is that of all industrial magnates, seeing the earth as a warehouse of "resources," treating workers as "hands" for harvesting wealth, regarding the material universe as a playground for his desires. Connie's view points toward affirmation of nature, Clifford's toward exploitation—or, when his will is obstructed, toward annihilation.

What Connie has learned about her own body and about nature she also learns, through her lover, about the working class. At the outset of each version of the novel, she is acutely aware of the seemingly unbridgeable distance between herself and the "common people." She feels trapped on one side of an incipient class war: "It was something she dreaded coldly and fatally, the working-out of this new, unconscious, cold, reptilian sort of hate that was rising between the colliers of the under-earth, the iron-workers of the great furnaces, and the educated, owning class to which she belonged, by the accident of destiny." This is more than a theoretical concern about the possibility of class war, as the repeated references to the Bolshevik revolution and to socialism would suggest. ("She knew a good deal about the terrible revolution in Russia, and the convulsive class hatred which had wreaked itself without expending itself there.") England itself had teetered on the brink of revolution in 1919, when the disgruntled troops returned from the war to find the same old arrangements of wealth and power; and it was teetering again in 1926, during the months in which Lawrence made his visit to the strikebound Midlands and began writing *The First Lady Chatterley*.

Of all the "disconnections" explored in the novel, this gulf between classes poses the most immediate threat of cataclysm. Just as Clifford, on the one side, strives for "mastery" and yearns to enslave the workers, so workers on the opposing side exhibit "a capacity for a ruthless destruction." The two classes gaze at one another as into a mirror, hatred matched by hatred, every gesture of violence answered by violence. While justice clearly stands on the side of those who have been oppressed, both sides are equally vulnerable to the annihilation impulse. The very willingness to destroy the "enemy" poisons the heart of worker and owner alike. Imagine the rival classes as nations, and one sees the confrontation between Britain and Germany which led to the First World War, or the long-standing duel between the United States and the Soviet Union, which might lead to the Last World War.

How to break out of the vicious circle? How to abolish the walls between classes? Politicians, theologians, and revolutionaries would all proffer their own—generally sweeping—solutions. Being a novelist, a fabricator of characters instead of laws, Lawrence offers a remedy centered in personal relations rather than politics. Connie seeks "the clue to this gruesome business of class war. . . . But . . . she could only sympathise with a particular man, not with a whole villageful or a whole class." If the "clue" to this "business of class war" is the imagined *division* of humanity into groups of masters and servants, the solution is a discovery of the *connection* between person and person, a connection more fundamental than any seeming divisions. This recovery of human connections is a matter not of theory but of direct experience: "It was touch that one needed: some sort of touch between her class and the under class." Even while Lady Chatterley persists in thinking in class terms, her experience with the gamekeeper erases all such categories: "Parkin was beyond class in passion." In passion, Connie escapes not only the illusions of class, but also the illusions of human separation from nature: "passion overcame her, and the body of the man seemed silken and powerful and pure god-stuff, and the thrusting of the haunches the splendid, flamboyant, urgent god-rhythm, the same that made the stars swing round and the sea heave over, and all the leaves turn and the light stream out from heaven." Thus Connie recovers all her "connections" at once, with her body and with the "common people" and with the "quick of the universe."

Her liaison with the gamekeeper will not reconcile her class with his, will not unseat the rulers or liberate the workers, any more than her revery in the forest will halt the woodcutters' blades. However close the two lovers feel personally, they are still divided socially, by differences of wealth and education and privilege. That Lawrence felt compelled, in writing each successive version of the novel, to reduce the social distance between the lady and the gamekeeper is a measure of how seriously he regarded divisions of class as impediments to love. Lawrence himself yearned to escape from society into a territory of freedom, of pure passionate relationships with other people and with nature. He searched in vain—and so do Connie and the gamekeeper. The lovers shelter in their hut in the woods, secure for a time against the crippling influences of the human world. But poachers lurk in the shadows, nearby smokestacks vent noxious fumes, Clifford puffs along through the wildflowers in his motorized chair, and acre-by-acre the woods are chopped down. Many of the oldest trees were felled during the war to supply props for mineshafts and trenches. A neighboring estate has already been razed. The lovers' sanctuary, like their passion, is besieged and vulnerable.

The contrast between Clifford and Connie sums up the choice Lawrence saw before us, the choice between two opposed ways of relating to one another, to other social groups and nations, and to the earth. As usual in Lawrence, the choice is presented as a series of variations on one fundamental dichotomy: at one extreme, the isolation and exaltation of the ego (or collective ego of class, race, nation), coupled with a desire to dominate or annihilate whatever stands outside the ego; at the other extreme, a discarding of all barriers dividing person from person or humankind from nature, a respect for the ways of living things and for the needs of all people, a reverence for the "quick of the universe" that is present in all creation.

One characteristic formulation of this dichotomy appears in ***John Thomas and Lady Jane,*** when Connie remarks to her sister, "It's so different . . . *knowing* life, and *being* it." Scholars in particular will find this opposition a disturbing one. Clifford is in fact very much the scholar, locked away with his books, trying to seize the world through ideas while avoiding direct contact. Knowledge is for him a mode of power—power over the mines and the miners, over Connie, over the material universe. Once he "knows" a thing, he can control it, and the thing itself is evacuated of all meaning. Of course, "*knowing* life, and *being* it" need not be so radically opposed as they are in Clifford's case. Connie learns a great deal through her loving, but the knowledge she gains is connecting rather than severing. When she learns "to see the trees bulging and urging like ships at anchor on a tide: to feel the world full of its own strange, ceaseless life," she begins to participate in the larger being of nature.

Lawrence also poses the choice between Clifford's way and Connie's way in terms of the opposition between industry and forest, the familiar romantic dichotomy between mechanical and organic: "there were two main sorts of energy, the frictional, seething, resistant, explosive, blind sort, like that of steam-engines and motor-cars and electricity, and of people such as Clifford and Bill Tewson and modern, insistent women, and these queer vacuous miners: then there was the other, forest energy, that was still and softly powerful, with tender, frail bud-tips and gentle finger-ends full of awareness." Connie herself is divided between these two kinds of energy, as we all must be, since human life would be impossible without our exerting *some* control over the environment. Simply building a fire is an exercise in manipulation. The light by which I see to write these lines depends upon the harnessing of electricity. Lawrence does not confront either Connie or us with the absurd alternative between fully embracing and fully repudiating technology. Rather, he forces us to decide whether we owe our deepest respect to the energy of machines or to the energy of the forest, whether our highest purpose is to control or to participate in nature. We are left in no doubt as to which allegiance Connie chooses, or which one Lawrence would have us choose:

> Life is so soft and quiet, and cannot be seized. It will not be raped. Try to rape it, and it disappears. Try to seize it, and you have dust. Try to master it, and you see your own image grinning at you with the grin of an idiot.
>
> Whoever wants life must go softly towards life, softly as one would go towards a deer and a fawn that was nestling under a tree. One gesture of violence, one violent assertion of self-will, and life is gone. You must seek again. And softly, gently, with infinitely sensitive hands and feet, and a heart that is full and free from self-will, you must approach life again, and come at last into touch. . . .
>
> But with quietness, with an abandon of self-assertion and a fulness of the deep, true self one can approach another human being, and know the delicate best of life, the touch. The touch of the feet on the earth, the touch of the fingers on a tree, on a creature, the touch of hands and breasts, the touch of the whole body to body, and the interpenetration of passionate love.

Stated simply, in the traditional terms that Lawrence himself employed, this is the choice between the way of power and the way of love. The most highly industrialized and militarized nations have chosen the way of power. By means of weapons and machines, we try constantly to impose our will upon the land, upon "enemies," upon those who are weaker or poorer than we, upon the chemistry of our own bodies. If we look honestly at our situation, we should agree with Connie that "the individual, the company, the nation, they are alike all possessed with one insanity, the insanity of conceit, the mania of the swollen ego."

That way lies doom, said Lawrence, and I think he was right. The planet is too small to sustain for very long so many gluttonous egos, so many—even two—tyrannical nuclear governments. The assault upon nature and the assault upon rival nations are both expressions of the drive for total security, the craving for unchallenged supremacy. With the First World War so recently behind her, the prospects for class war immediately in front of her, and the devastating effects of rampant industrialism visible on all sides, Connie has good reason to feel "a terror of the incipient insanity of the whole civilised species." We have even more reason to feel that terror now. In the letter he writes to Connie at the close of ***Lady Chatterley's Lover,*** the gamekeeper grimly predicts, "there's a bad time coming! If things go on as they are, there's nothing lies in the future but death and destruction, for these industrial masses." We have all become members of the "industrial masses," depending for our survival on a biosphere that is under daily assault from human greed. We are hostages to rival political systems that operate in the nuclear age with a bullying ideology more appropriate to the stone age. "If man could will it," Lawrence warned in ***Apocalypse,*** "it would be cosmic suicide. But the cosmos is not at man's mercy, and the sun will not perish to please us." The sun remains immune to us; but the earth, at least, is now at our mercy, and our relentless accumulation of bombs and poisons suggests that we are quite capable of willing its destruction.

What we are shown in the history of Lady Chatterley's loving is the education of one woman's consciousness. That seems a humble spectacle in the face of the enormous horror that Lawrence confronted, and the even greater catastrophe that we now face. And yet, in proportion as we are drawn into her loving and altered by it, we are forced to realize along with her that there is no ultimate basis for distinctions between classes, between races, between nations, or between humankind and the rest of nature. Like Connie, "We are clothed with a new awareness." Out of that awareness may arise new ways of living, new ways of loving one another and the earth. The reading of novels, even such generous-hearted novels as those of Lawrence, will not save us from our violence. But they may keep alive in us the vision of a gentler existence. (pp. 1-16)

Scott R. Sanders, "Lady Chatterley's Loving and the Annihilation Impulse," in D. H. Lawrence's "Lady": A New Look at "Lady Chatterley's Lover," *edited by Michael Squires and Dennis Jackson, The University of Georgia Press, 1985, pp. 1-16.*

James C. Cowan (essay date 1985)

[*An American educator, Cowan has written extensively on D. H. Lawrence and was the founding editor of the D. H. Lawrence Review. In the following excerpt, he characterizes Lawrence's use of epiphanies in* Lady Chatterley's Lover.]

D. H. Lawrence and James Joyce never met, but they read and despised each other's work. Their mutual dislike sprang in part from their commitment to contrasting theories of literary art. They represent opposing tendencies in modernism that are clearly visible in their differing treatments of the epiphany.

For a writer who had experienced so many censorship problems himself, Lawrence was surprisingly uncritical in echoing the popular charge of obscenity against Joyce's *Ulysses*. Dorothy Brett reports a conversation in Taos in 1924 in which Frieda's calculated statement that *Ulysses* "is a wonderful book" provoked the predictable, vehement response from Lawrence: "The last part of it is the dirtiest, most indecent, obscene thing ever written. Yes it is, Frieda. . . . It is filthy."

After Lawrence read a section of Joyce's *Work in Progress*, he declared, "My God, what a clumsy *olla putrida* James Joyce is! Nothing but old fags and cabbage-stumps of quotations from the Bible and the rest, stewed in the juice of deliberate, journalistic dirty-mindedness—what old and hard-worked staleness, masquerading as the all-new!" And he told Harry Crosby, whose Black Sun Press published both Lawrence's **"Sun"** and Joyce's *Tales Told of Shem and Shaun*, "James Joyce bores me stiff—too terribly would-be and done-on-purpose, utterly without spontaneity or real life." Lawrence thought Giovanni Verga a better writer. Although Verga's style "gives at first the sense of jumble and incoherence" in an effort to convey the "muddled" thought processes of the peasant mind, Lawrence says, "he is doing, as a great artist, what men like James Joyce do only out of contrariness and desire for a sensation" (**Phoenix**).

The clue to Lawrence's dislike for Joyce is his repeated use of words like "would-be" and "sensation," terms which in Lawrence's criticism usually mean overconscious and deliberate, mechanical and inorganic. That is why he categorizes Joyce among the modern novelists whose "dominant note is the repulsiveness, intimate physical repulsiveness of human flesh" (**Phoenix**). It is also why he ridiculed the stream-of-consciousness novelists for "the death-rattle in their throats," for "dying in a very long-drawn-out fourteen-volume death-agony, and absorbedly, childishly interested in the phenomenon. 'Did I feel a twinge in my little toe, or didn't I?' asks every character of Mr. Joyce or of Miss Richardson or M. Proust" (**Phoenix**).

For his part, Joyce returned the ill opinion in repeated condescension toward Lawrence's work. In one letter he mockingly calls Lawrence's book *"Lady Chatterbox's Lover,"* and in a later letter, Joyce says of *"Lady Chatterli's* [sic] *Lover":* "I read the first 2 pages of the usual sloppy English which is a piece of propaganda in favour of something which, outside of D.H.L.'s country at any rate, makes all the propaganda for itself." Joyce's derisive parodies of Lawrence's title convey the same sort of judgment (or misjudgment) as Lawrence's derisive parody of the stream-of-consciousness character's obsession with his own sensations. But the real clue to Joyce's judgment of Lawrence is his charge against **Lady Chatterley's Lover** of "propaganda," a charge related to Stephen Dedalus's declaration, in chapter 5 of *A Portrait of the Artist as a Young Man*, that "pornographical or didactic" arts, which excite "kinetic" feelings of "desire or loathing," are "improper arts." As Richard Ellmann comments, Joyce "was anxious that his books should not commit propaganda, even against institutions of which he disapproved."

Yet both Joyce and Lawrence employed scenes of the type that Joyce called "epiphany" and Lawrence called "visionary experience," although they arrived at these scenes by different routes and from opposing theoretical positions. The theory set forth in *A Portrait of the Artist as a Young Man* is a classical, mimetic theory in which "the esthetic emotion" "arrests the mind" because "the tragic emotion is static. . . . The mind is arrested and raised above desire and loathing." "Beauty expressed by the artist," Stephen declares, "cannot awaken in us an emotion which is kinetic or a sensation which is purely physical." Rather, it should awaken or induce "an esthetic stasis, an ideal pity or an ideal terror, a stasis called forth, prolonged and at last dissolved by what I call the rhythm of beauty" (*Portrait*).

Lawrence recognized the validity of classical theory for certain types of literature. His statement in **"Poetry of the Present"** that the "poetry of the beginning and the poetry of the end" have a "finality" and "perfection" "conveyed in exquisite form" fits Joyce's aesthetic theory and practice. "But," Lawrence suggests, "there is another kind of poetry: the poetry of that which is at hand: the immediate present. In the immediate present there is no perfection, no consummation, nothing finished. The strands are all flying, quivering, intermingling into the web, the waters are shaking the moon. . . . If we try to fix the living tissue, as the biologists fix it with formalin, we have only a hardened bit of the past, the bygone life under our observation."

Joyce in *A Portrait of the Artist* and Lawrence in **"Art and the Individual"** set forth the theories in which their views of the epiphany and of art are rooted, although both go beyond these theories in their artistic practice. Stephen Dedalus's celebrated aesthetic theory in the fifth chapter of *A Portrait of the Artist* is drawn, of course, from the teachings of Saint Thomas Aquinas on the three principles required for beauty, *"integritas, consonantia, claritas,"* which Stephen translates as *"wholeness, harmony and radiance,"* qualities which, he believes, "correspond to the phases of apprehension." The "synthesis of immediate perception," as the object is first seen as a unified image, "selfbounded and selfcontained" against the background of all that is not it (*integritas*), is followed by the "analysis of apprehension" as the image is seen to be "complex, multiple, divisible, separable, made up of its parts, the result of its parts and their sum" (*consonantia*). Finally, having rejected as "literary talk" the idea that radiance is "the artistic discovery and representation of the divine purpose" or universality of the object, Stephen concludes that having perceived the object's wholeness and having analyzed its form, "you make the only synthesis which is logically and esthetically permissible. You see that it is that thing which it is and no other thing" (*claritas*), which Stephen takes to be identical with "the scholastic *quidditas*, the *whatness* of a thing." (*Portrait*).

In **"Art and the Individual,"** a youthful essay of the Croydon period, Lawrence's concept of "two schools of Aesthetic thought," the mystical and the sensual, prefigures his later theory of the two kinds of poetry, that of the beginning and the end and that of "the immediate present." In the first, "Art. Beauty is the expression of the perfect and divine Idea." In the second, "Art is an activity arising . . . from sexual desire and propensity to play" or from some other pleasurable emotion. In the interpretation that Lawrence accepts, "these two, the mystical and the sensual ideas of Art are blended. Approval of Harmony—that is sensual—approval of Adaptation—that is mystic— . . . " (***Phoenix II***). Despite his differences from Joyce, Lawrence's definition of *harmony,* using the example of a swan, as approval of "the silken whiteness, the satisfying curve of line and mass," is compatible with Stephen Dedalus's definition of *consonantia* as the "analysis" that follows *integritas* as "you pass from point to point, led by [the object's] . . . formal lines; you apprehend it as balanced part against part within its limits; you feel the rhythm of its structure" (*Portrait*). But whereas Joyce relies on Aristotle and Aquinas, Lawrence's idea of art depends on Herbart's "classification of interests," from which Lawrence arrives at categories according to the source of the interest and arranges these in an aesthetic progression from the concrete to the universal (empirical, speculative, aesthetic, sympathetic, social, religious). "Since Aestheticism embraces all art," the aesthetic image in Lawrence's work may be seen as incorporating all six planes on ascending levels of experience (***Phoenix II***).

Turning to the question of epiphany in the context of Joyce's and Lawrence's theories of art, I want to consider first the nature of the experience to which the term refers, then some distinguishable types of literary epiphany. Joyce originally used the term to refer to the genre of some seventy short prose pieces he wrote between 1900 and 1904, recording actual experiences and moods; forty extant examples of these epiphanies are published in *The Workshop of Daedalus,* edited by Robert Scholes and Richard M. Kain. As Joyce explains Stephen Dedalus's use of the term in *Stephen Hero,* "By an epiphany he meant a sudden spiritual manifestation, whether in the vulgarity of speech or of gesture or in a memorable phase of the mind itself. He believed that it was for the man of letters to record these epiphanies with extreme care, seeing that they themselves are the most delicate and evanescent of moments." This statement is clearly the source of Morris Beja's definition of *epiphany,* in *Epiphany in the Modern Novel,* as a "sudden spiritual manifestation, whether from some object, scene, event, or memorable phase of the mind—the manifestation being out of proportion to the significance or strictly logical relevance of whatever produces it." In a critical exchange with Scholes, Florence Walzl comments that "the term *epiphany* has several meanings in current Joyce criticism. It may refer to an early prose type, to a spiritual and intellectual illumination of the nature of a thing, and also, by extension, to the artistic insights and means by which such a revelation is achieved." ["The Epiphanies of Joyce," *PMLA* (1967)] Whereas Beja barely mentions Lawrence, Ann Shealy, in "The Epiphany Theme in Modern Fiction: E. M. Forster's *Howards End* and D. H. Lawrence's ***Sons and Lovers,***" treats Lawrence's epiphanies in light of the second and third meanings of the term as given by Walzl.

Irene Hendry Chayes, in her seminal essay "Joyce's Epiphanies," correctly observes that "the epiphany is not peculiar to Joyce alone":

> Virtually every writer experiences a sense of revelation when he beholds a fragment of his ordinary world across . . . 'psychic distance'—dissociated from his subjective and practical concerns, fraught with meaning beyond itself, with every detail of its physical appearance relevant. It is a revelation quite as valid as the religious; in fact, from our present secular viewpoint, it perhaps would be more accurate to say that the revelation of the religious mystic is actually an esthetic revelation into which the mystic projects himself—as a participant, not merely as an observer and recorder—and to which he assigns a source, an agent and an end, called God. What Joyce did was give systematic formulation to a common esthetic experience, so common that few others—writers, if not estheticians—have thought it worth considering for its own sake.

Where Lawrence is concerned, the question is not the presence in his work of revelatory experience of this kind but the breadth of the "psychic distance" across which such fragments of ordinary experience are seen in the transforming light.

There is no need to rehearse Chayes's whole discussion of Joyce's work. Indeed, two of her four types of epiphany are largely irrelevant to Lawrence's work: the first, achievement of *claritas* "through an apparently trivial incident, action, or single detail which differs from the others . . . only in that it illuminates them, integrates them, and gives them meaning"; and the third, the emergence of *claritas* from *quidditas* as "character is sacrificed to the *integritas* of the esthetic image" which resynthesizes the generalities of the individual. The other two types of epiphany, however, are in accord with Lawrence's practice.

In the second type, "although *claritas* is ultimately generated by *quidditas,* we are first aware of an effect on the beholder—Stephen, or ourselves through Stephen—not of an objectively apprehensible quality in the thing re-

An October 1926 photograph of Aldous Huxley and D.H. Lawrence in the Tuscan Hills near Florence, Italy. Huxley assisted Lawrence in revising the typescript of Lady Chatterley's Lover.

vealed." For Joyce this method may have been regressive in terms of his aesthetic goal of refining the artist's personality out of existence, but it had the advantage, Chayes says, "of realizing the three principles, *integritas, consonantia,* and *claritas,* in a single image." For Lawrence, whose third-person narratives often center in the consciousness of a focal character, this method is predominant, especially in scenes that emphasize the importance of a visionary experience in the education into instinctual or sensual being of the focal character. Examples of this type of epiphany include Ursula Brangwen's encounter with the horses near the end of *The Rainbow,* her recognition of the meaning of Gerald Crich's brutal subjugation of the Arab mare and of Rupert Birkin's stoning of the moon's reflection in *Women in Love,* and Lou Witt's vision of the "mysterious fire" of St. Mawr's body in *St. Mawr.*

In the fourth type, *quidditas* has the function "to identify rather than to abstract." The character, "broken down into its separate parts," is then reduced to an image associated with him. "Only one or two of the detached 'parts'—'the vulgarity of speech or of gesture,' . . . a detail of figure or expression, an item of clothing"—are recombined to create the individual *quidditas,* a technique that "represents the ultimate in 'objective' characterization, 'revealing' an individual essence by means of a detail or an object to which it has a fortuitous relation"; for example, Father Dolan's pandybat or Mr. Casey's "three cramped fingers." "Through Joyce's fourth epiphany technique (in which *claritas* is a tiny, perfunctory flash, all but absorbed by *quidditas*) we can trace out a virtual iconography of the characters, like the systematic recurrence of emblems and attitudes among the figures in sacred art."

There are emblems aplenty in Lawrence—Will Brangwen's phoenix butter-mold, Count Dionys's ladybird, Ramón Carrasco's "eye of Quetzalcoatl," or even Anna Brangwen's gargoyle faces, Ursula's rainbow, and Aaron Sisson's flute. But these deliberate emblems, except perhaps for the last one, are not the same as the metonymic images with which Joyce's characters have a "fortuitous relation." A nearer example in Lawrence can be found in the clothes imagery by which characters throughout his work are defined—William Morel's collar, Gudrun Brangwen's stockings, Gerald Crich's elegant robe, Hermione Roddice's feathered hat. But this epiphany technique is perhaps most evident in the close association Lawrence evokes between a character and an image that clearly objectifies his essential quality as a human being—Henry Grenfel and the fox, Jill Banford and the dead tree, or Sir Clifford Chatterley and the motorized wheelchair.

Lawrence's identification of character with iconographic image, however, cannot often be called the "ultimate" in objectivity. It must be said also that his insight is never a "perfunctory flash" of meaning absorbed in the "whatness" of the object, but a clear metaphorical statement in which the image, rather than merely "standing for" the character, is so interpenetrated with his essential quality that it effectively becomes him: Sir Clifford's motorized chair *is* his very being.

Both Joyce and Lawrence employed epiphanic scenes to present ideas by means of revelation rather than by thematic statement. But because Lawrence's narrative technique involved more discursive statements about the characters and less aesthetic or psychic distance from them than is typical of Joyce, Lawrence has not often been described as an epiphanic writer. The first three chapters of *Lady Chatterley's Lover,* written from the point of view of an assumed narrator relating a general history, lack the artistic objectivity necessary to the Joycean epiphanic style. Rather, the technique corresponds to Stephen Dedalus's definition of the "epical form" (*Portrait*), mediating between artist and reader through the narrative point of view. But the scenes present what usually happens in the ongoing relationship, and the potential for epiphanic distillation inherent in the dramatic situation and a few concrete details is undercut by Lawrence's inveterate explanations. In contrast, the opening chapter of *A Portrait of the Artist,* although it also has an expository function, is fully visualized, concrete, specific, and not interpreted by a narrator.

In chapter 4 of *Lady Chatterley* the discussion of the "mental lifers" who visit Wragby parallels in several ways that of the Christmas dinner scene in chapter I of *A Portrait of the Artist.* Both involve a dramatic situation in which a group of people, family and visitors, engage in a lively discussion which is registered on the perceiving consciousness of one member of the family (Stephen and Connie) who takes little part in the discussion but whose perceptions of the discussants and the issues involved motivate a change in the observer. Whereas Joyce used Mr. Casey's "three cramped fingers" as an epiphanic identification of his character, Lawrence, in his brief character sketch of the Wragby visitors, associates the first two with institutional abstractions—Tommy Dukes with the army, Charles May with the science of the stars, only in the case of Arnold B. Hammond identifying and distilling the character by means of an epiphanic image: "a tall thin fellow with a wife and two children, but much more closely connected with a typewriter." Joyce's judgment of Dante Riordan for the narrowness of her religious politics in supporting the Irish clergy even in their treatment of Parnell is clear if unstated. Similarly, when Tommy Dukes compares the sexual and property instincts in terms of the "craving for self-assertion and success," when Charles May speaks of sex as "just an interchange of sensations instead of ideas," or when Arnold Hammond, in Graham Holderness's phrase, "equates sexual emotions with excretory functions," Lawrence's judgment of them is clear.

The violent rhetoric of the Christmas dinner scene in *A Portrait of the Artist* brings to vivid life the "nets" of family, church, and nation that the soul of the youthful artist will later determine to "fly by." The ostensibly intellectual conversation of the "mental lifers" in *Lady Chatterley* embodies, in its emotional vacuity and its desperate wit, the triviality and deadness which the instinctual self, in order to live at all, will have to escape. Joyce maintains Stephen's point of view throughout; the epiphanic experience is registered on his consciousness from the beginning to the end of the scene when "Stephen, raising his terror-stricken face, saw that his father's eyes were full of tears" (*Portrait*). Lawrence begins in a general, historical perspective, moves to a concrete dramatization, and brings the potential for epiphany to the surface by returning increasingly to Connie's point of view. As in the second type of epiphany defined by Chayes, the reader of both scenes is conscious not so much of "meaning" as of an "effect" registered on an observer. Connie says nothing at first but "put another stitch in her sewing," an ironic link with the faithful Penelope, since Connie's thoughts reveal her real attitude of contempt for both the "suitors" and the returned soldier husband. The men discuss Plato and Socrates, Bolshevism and Capitalism, and the meaninglessness of sex. They ignore Connie's presence, but Lawrence does not let the reader forget that the scene is being played out on her consciousness. When Dukes speaks of Renoir's saying that "he painted his pictures with his penis" and confesses, "I wish I did something with mine. God! when one can only talk," Connie responds to his despair: "There are nice women in the world," thus revealing how closely she has been attending the conversation. The potential for epiphany is not realized in the kind of objective revelation that Connie will experience later but is inherent in the dawning realization of sterility and death that precede rebirth and growth. Connie's disillusionment with this kind of mental life is comparable to the disillusionment with Irish patriotism motivated by Stephen Dedalus's experience of the Christmas dinner scene.

Chapter 5 of *Lady Chatterley* begins, appropriately, with an objective statement: "On a frosty morning with a little February sun, Clifford and Connie went for a walk across the park to the wood. That is, Clifford chuffed in his motor-chair, and Connie walked beside him." The shift from the generalized historical perspective of the first three chapters to the dramatic scene of the fourth chapter and thence to the concrete narrative mode of the fifth establishes the necessary context not only for the contrast between Clifford and Mellors introduced in this chapter but also for several important epiphanic images.

One of these may be called the denuded knoll epiphany: "The chair chuffed slowly up the incline, rocking and jolting on the frozen clods. And suddenly, on the left, came a clearing where there was nothing but a ravel of dead bracken, a thin and spindly sapling leaning here and there, big sawn stumps, showing their tops and their grasping roots, lifeless. And patches of blackness where the woodmen had burned the brushwood and rubbish." The narrative explanation as Connie surveys the wasteland scene directs without stating the interpretation: "This was one of the places that Sir Geoffrey had cut during the war for trench timber. The whole knoll, which rose softly on the right of the riding, was denuded and strangely forlorn. On the crown of the knoll where the oaks had stood, now was bareness; and from there you could look out over the trees to the colliery railway, and the new works at Stacks Gate. Connie had stood and looked, it was a breach in the pure seclusion of the wood. It let in the world. But she didn't tell Clifford." Considered in the light of the Fisher King motif in the novel, the war has caused both the sexual maiming of Clifford (the Fisher King) and the destruction of the phallic trees of Wragby (his kingdom): both have been reduced to lifeless stumps. There is even an echo of T. S. Eliot's imagery: as in *The Waste Land,* where the question "What are the roots that clutch?" is ultimately answered in "And other withered stumps of time," so in this passage from **Lady Chatterley's Lover,** the implied question of what caused the destruction of "big sawn stumps, showing their tops and their grasping roots, lifeless" is answered in the explanation: Sir Geoffrey had cut the trees "during the war for trench timber." The progression of imagery leads as inevitably as the colliery train to "the new works at Stacks Gate."

The denuded knoll is not only a symbolic image but an epiphanic one as well, a self-contained microcosm of the wasteland over which Sir Clifford Chatterley presides, though its meaning is revealed at different levels to the two observers. To Clifford, in anger, it conveys the destruction by the war of a legacy of the heart of "the old England," which had been entrusted to the stewardship of his generation to keep inviolate. To Connie, in pathos, it is "a breach in the pure seclusion of the wood," an assault on the private self and on organic nature. The fact that for both it is also linked with the destruction of Clifford's potency is signaled by their conversation, in this context, on Clifford's inability to sire a son and his suggestion that Connie might have a child by another man. But the mechanistic quality of Clifford's love of tradition and his wish for paternity is exposed by the difference between his attitude and Connie's toward the prospect. "I don't believe very intensely in fatherhood," he says in a Lawrencean blasphemy, and refers to the hypothetical heir as an "it," not as a person. He does not think it matters much who the father is. Connie, already an organicist, wonders "how could she know what she would feel next year," and says that while she agrees with Clifford theoretically, "life may turn quite a new face on it all." It is at this point, as if in response to Connie's prophetic statement, that Oliver Mellors, the gamekeeper, emerges with his symbolic red mustache, dark green velveteens, and phallic gun.

Another major epiphanic image introduced in this chapter is Clifford's motorized wheelchair. Clifford, who has chuffed into the wood in the chair, calls to Mellors to "turn the chair round and get it started." Mellors, "curiously full of vitality, but a little frail and quenched," pushes "the chair up the steepish rise of the knoll in the park." Set in opposition to the wood, the chair symbolically embodies all of the forces that account for the denuding of the knoll.

The chair is the focal image in a recurrent pattern of imagery culminating in the long scene in chapter 13 in which the motor stalls and Mellors is again called to help. The mindless war of machine against nature is set forth in admirable, uninterpreted specificity as the chair puffs slowly on: "Connie, walking behind, had watched the wheels jolt over the wood-ruff and the bugle, and squash the little yellow cups of the creeping-jenny. Now they made a wake through the forget-me-nots." An epic simile presents the chair, "washed over with blue encroaching hyacinths," as the ship of Western civilization, and Clifford, with an ironic allusion to Whitman's Lincoln, as its mock-heroic captain: "Oh last of all ships, through the hyacinthian shallows! Oh pinnace on the last wild waters, sailing in the last voyage of our civilisation! Whither, Oh weird wheeled ship, your slow course steering! Quiet and complacent, Clifford sat at the wheel of adventure: in his old black hat and tweed jacket, motionless and cautious. Oh captain, my Captain, our splendid trip is done!" The simile of the ship identifies the chair with Clifford's mines, for Mrs. Bolton has told him: "Oh, there's been some money made in Tevershall. And now the men say it's a sinking ship, and it's time they all got out. . . . It seems soon there'll be no use for men on the face of the earth, it'll be all machines."

Throughout the novel, the chair is compared, sometimes directly, sometimes subtly, to Clifford's sexual being, which is held in contrast to that of the organicist Mellors, who confesses his incompetence "about these mechanical things." In chapter 13, Lawrence employs a number of sexual double entendres. Clifford's attempts to force the wheelchair to go are compared to masturbation. Connie warns him, "You'll only break the thing down altogether, Clifford, . . . besides *wasting your nervous energy.*" Calling for Mellors to examine the motor, Clifford asks pointedly, "Have you looked at *the rods underneath?*" Grimly determined, "[Clifford] began *doing things* with his engine, running her fast and slow as if to get some sort of tune out of her. . . . Then he put her in gear with a jerk, having *jerked off* his brake." Finally, he turns to the gamekeeper: "'Do you mind *pushing her home,* Mellors!' he said in a cool, superior tone." The irony of the question escapes Clifford, but Lawrence does not allow it to escape the reader. As Mellors pushes the wheelchair home, he takes Connie's wrist in a caress behind Clifford's back, and she bends to kiss Mellors's hand. Clifford is identified and defined throughout the novel by the metonymic image of the wheelchair, which is as much a part of Clifford as Mellors's penis is of Mellors. Considered in terms of the fourth epiphanic method discussed by Chayes, this motorized chair is his whole mechanistic being, a mechanical contrivance that he possesses instead of a self. (pp. 91-102)

After chapter 12, especially, the focus of the story shifts from Lady Chatterley to her lover and the working out of the realistic and symbolic details of their life together. There are still occasional changes through visual perception—Connie's sight of Mellors's "erect phallos rising darkish and hot-looking from the little cloud of vivid gold-red hair"; Connie's journey with her sister Hilda to Venice as a tour in hell (chapter 17)—but little that could be called epiphanic. A scene such as the one in chapter 15 in which Connie and Mellors dance naked in the rain, then decorate their pubic hair with forget-me-nots, Mellors's penis with creeping jenny, and their bodies with campion and bluebells, although certainly conducive to growth, involves acting out rather than sudden epiphany. In the first half of the novel, however, epiphany or visionary experience is the principal way through which Connie's development in consciousness is achieved. (pp. 112-13)

> James C. Cowan, "Lawrence, Joyce, and the Epiphanies of 'Lady Chatterley's Lover'," in D. H. Lawrence's "Lady": A New Look at "Lady Chatterley's Lover," edited by Michael Squires and Dennis Jackson, The University of Georgia Press, 1985, pp. 91-115.

Dennis Jackson (essay date 1985)

[*Jackson has written extensively on Lawrence. In the following excerpt, he illustrates Lawrence's use of literary allusions in* Lady Chatterley's Lover.]

Allusion in D. H. Lawrence's fiction is never the innovative, virtuoso performance it is in the works of Joyce, Pound, and Eliot. But Lawrence was throughout his life a voracious reader—Jessie Chambers recalls that he "seemed to read everything"—and his own writings are often filled with ideas and expressions gathered from other authors. His last novel, **Lady Chatterley's Lover,** is saturated with allusions to the Bible, hymns, popular songs, classical myths, and other literary works from Plato to Proust. These references typify Lawrence's analogical method, becoming a primary means by which he defines characters and themes and creates dramatic irony. Frequently he uses allusions to guide the reader's response to the antithetical philosophical worlds between which his heroine moves—the unvital realm of Wragby Hall, where the "life of the mind" and spiritual consciousness are paramount, and the vital Pan world of Wragby Wood, where the "life of the body" and intuitive consciousness reign. In the novel's thematic structure the use of allusion helps create a philosophic subtext that awakens the reader to the larger implications of the lovers' sexual and psychic regeneration. In this essay I shall focus on the pattern of allusion that creates this subtext: the allusions characterizing Sir Clifford Chatterley and his Wragby Hall circle. With these allusions Lawrence discredits certain well-entrenched philosophical concepts ranging from Platonic idealism to modern scientific materialism.

Allusions characterize the failing relationship of Clifford and his wife, and even figure prominently in Connie's ultimate rejection of him; she reacts bitterly to his reading tastes (his liking for Proust makes him seem "very dead, really") and to his tendency to "[turn] everything into words." When Clifford responds to forest flowers with two quotations, "Sweeter than the lids of Juno's eyes" and "Thou still unravished bride of quietness," Connie despairs: "How she hated words, always coming between her and life: they did the ravishing. . . ready-made words and phrases, sucking all the life-sap out of living things." Clifford has quoted first from Shakespeare's *The Winter's Tale* and then from Keats's "Ode on a Grecian Urn." Perdita invokes Proserpina to supply her with spring flowers—among them "violets dim, / But sweeter than the lids of Juno's eyes / Or Cytherea's breath." Connie objects, however, that she sees no "connection" between Clifford's quotation and the "actual violets." In Keats's ode, the speaker looks on the urn and projects himself into its "flowery tale." Conversely, Clifford looks at the real flowers and tries to translate them into art. His response is neither immediate nor vital, but indirect, literary, and cerebral; typically, he substitutes words for feelings. Connie's later remark about Proust—"He doesn't have feelings, he only has streams of words about feelings"—reflects the way she comes to feel about her husband.

The opposition between words and experience also informs the scene where Clifford reads Racine to Connie soon after her third sexual encounter with Mellors. She sits, "gone in her own soft rapture," the keeper "in all her veins," while "the noise" of Clifford's reading continues; "of the Racine she heard not one syllable." There is exquisite irony here. "One gets all one wants out of Racine," Clifford declares. "Emotions that are ordered and given shape are more important than disorderly emotions." Connie, fulfilled by the ecstatic "after-humming" of her own disorderly emotions, leaves without kissing her husband goodnight; upset, he thinks that "even if the kiss was but a formality, it was on such formalities that life depends." Insisting as he does on "formalities," on "order" in life, on reason, Clifford feels a natural affinity for Racine, and his defense of the playwright reveals much about his own personality.

After Connie exits, Clifford's dread of "annihilation" comes upon him. Alone at night he feels "lifeless," but desperately stays awake, "as if he were triumphing over life in spite of life. 'Who knoweth the mysteries of the will—for it can triumph even against the angels—'." Lawrence alludes to the epigraph to Poe's "Ligeia": "Who knoweth the mysteries of the will, with its vigor? For God is but a great will pervading all things by nature of its intentness. Man doth not yield himself to the angels, nor unto death utterly, save only through the weakness of his feeble will." Ligeia, who dies reciting part of this quotation from Joseph Glanvill, never yields herself "unto death utterly"; with her "gigantic volition" she overcomes death and returns to her lover by supernaturally usurping the body of his second wife. Lawrence once called Poe's tale "a ghastly story of the assertion of the human will . . . against death itself," while condemning the two lovers in "Ligeia" for shaping their "spiritual, nervous love" into a destructive "battle of wills." In **Lady Chatterley** he appropriates Poe's story for his own analogical purposes, using the allusion to define the way Clifford uses his own "gigantic volition" to resist death and the great "bruise" of the war. Two pages earlier, Lady Chatterley thinks of her husband in terms as applicable to Poe's heroine as to Clifford: "What a strange creature. . . . One of those creatures of the afterwards, that have no soul, but an extra-alert will." Both Connie and Clifford's relationship and that of Ligeia and her husband are characterized by a struggle of "wills." Connie is repulsed by her husband's "cold, inflexible will"; he in turn denounces the fact that "the lady loves her will," recalling the last line of a traditional four-line song called "The Four Loves": "The Hart he loves the high-wood, / the Hare he loves the hill, / The Knight he loves his bright sword, / the Lady loves her will." Moreover, Ligeia and her mate, like the Chatterley's, avidly pursue "the mental life." Ligeia, a woman of "immense" knowledge, joins her husband in "metaphysical investigation," just as Connie collaborates on Clifford's stories. But whereas Ligeia submits to "the vampire of her husband's consciousness," Connie does not. Though Clifford thinks of his wife as "embedded in his will," she finally frustrates him by fleeing Wragby. The "Ligeia" allusion thus yields a richer, fuller text for the reader who recognizes Lawrence's source and activates the two texts simultaneously.

Moreso than the other characters in **Lady Chatterley,** Clifford is characterized by allusions, which serve to enhance the ironies of his character and to associate him with what Lawrence regarded as the twin evils of modern life—the "mental life" and scientific materialism. Clifford is made the living image of much that his creator detested in Western civilization, the chief angel of a fallen world resulting from man's over-reliance on "mental-spiritual" modes of consciousness. This fallen world and its potential redemption are the focus of a number of statements made by Clifford's friend Tommy Dukes, a chief spokesman for Lawrence. Dukes's declarations are often informed by the myth of the Fall and by the Christian belief in the Resurrection. He prophesies a "resurrection of the body," a "democracy of touch" that will come after men have "shoved the cerebral stone away a bit," alluding to passages in the Synoptic gospels which describe the removal of the stone before Christ's sepulcher; but the entombed body is not just Christ's—it is that of all men entombed by the "stone" of spiritual-mental consciousness. Dukes similarly uses images of the Fall when he tells the Wragby intellectuals: "[W]hile you *live* your life, you are in some way an organic whole with all life. But once you start the mental life you pluck the apple. You've severed the connection between the apple and the tree: the organic connection . . . you've fallen off the tree." In Lawrence's view man fell from grace in ancient Greece, when he "ate the apple and became endowed with . . . mental consciousness" (**Phoenix II**) in the age of Platonic/Socratic rationalism. Plato, insisting that man's nature is essentially spiritual and that man should subjugate his dark "lower" faculties in order to give ascendancy to the "light of reason," was a natural enemy to Lawrence, and the frequent allusions to the *Dialogues* in all three versions of **Lady Chatterley** reflect the way Lawrence regarded his novel as an assault on the tradition of scientific rationalism which Socrates and Plato had initiated.

Dukes's speech on "fallen" man is a direct response to Plato's epistemology expressed in the *Theaetetus*. In arguing that "real knowledge comes out of the whole corpus of the consciousness; out of your belly and your penis as much as out of your . . . mind and . . . reason," Dukes is countering Socrates' assertion that "knowledge . . . is not to be found in the sensations we undergo, but in our thought about them; it is only by the latter that we make contact with experience and truth (*Theaetetus*). Here and elsewhere in the *Dialogues* (for instance, in *The Republic* Book VII and in the *Phaedo*), Socrates asserts that sensation deceives man, yielding an unworthy copy of ultimate reality, and argues that real knowledge can be derived only through "properly mental activity" (*Theaetetus*), which acts upon reports of the sense organs. Dukes's refutation echoes Lawrence's own earlier statements about "blood-knowledge" and about Plato. For instance, in a 1915 letter to Bertrand Russell he had observed that our collective tragedy "is that the mental and nerve consciousness exerts a tyranny over the blood-consciousness. . . . Plato was the same."

Clifford's identification with Platonism is most obvious in **The First Lady Chatterley.** His wife thinks of him as "the speculative spaniel of Plato," and the Chatterleys often converse in the "symbols of Plato's myths," on one occasion thoroughly dissecting the Phaedrus myth. Eventually, however, Constance rebels against Platonism, just as she does in version three, and concludes that Clifford's "heaven of the pure abstraction" is but a "prison" and that her own preference is for the "immortality of the flesh." The Platonic allusions in version three, though less insistent, remain a major vehicle by which Lawrence explores his philosophic concerns and characterizes Chatterley and his friends. The attack on Socrates and Plato is launched early, when Lawrence recounts several of the "famous evenings" at Wragby Hall. During one typical gathering, the issues of love, sex, and marriage are debated by two-dimensional characters who represent antithetical philosophies: to Hammond, marriage means "a comfortable house" for the "life of the mind"; to May, sex is merely an "interchange of sensations"; and for neither is sex a vital act. This after-dinner disputation on "the sexual problem" forms a rough parallel to Plato's *Symposium,* where, after a dinner party, Socrates and his circle discuss the general question, "What is Love?" The Wragby guests display the same "mental friction" (as Dukes labels it) that characterizes Plato's urbane but ironic disputants, and Lawrence unquestionably has the *Dialogues* in mind as he describes Clifford and his friends. After remarking on the Wragby intellectuals' "spiteful" talk, Dukes says: "[T]he mental life seems to flourish with its roots in spite. . . . Always has been so! Look at Socrates, in Plato, and his bunch around him! The sheer . . . joy in pulling somebody else to bits. . . . Protagoras, or whoever it was! And Alcibiades, and all the other little disciple dogs joining in the fray!" (*Protagoras* and *Alcibiades* are titles of other *Dialogues,* and Alcibiades, a Greek general, participates in the *Symposium.*)

Clifford is especially linked with Platonic thought in the last half of **Lady Chatterley.** In chapter 13 Connie accompanies her husband and his motorized wheelchair into Wragby Wood:

> "I ride upon the achievements of the mind of man [brags Clifford], and that beats a horse."
>
> "I suppose it does. And the souls in Plato riding up to heaven in a two-horse chariot would go in a Ford car now," she said.
>
> "Or a Rolls-Royce. Plato was an aristocrat!"
>
> "Quite! No more black horse to thrash and maltreat. Plato never thought we'd go one better than his black steed and his white steed, and have no steeds at all, only an engine!"

The irony appears later in the scene, when the chair stalls amid bluebells, rendering Clifford a helpless prisoner. He pits his mind against the chair, trying to will it to move, but ultimately he is forced to summon the gamekeeper, whose bodily strength frees the chair. Such a symbolic opposition of mind and body is seen also throughout the *Phaedrus,* which the Chatterleys allude to. Plato's argument concerns the reasons why a philosopher should welcome release from the body, in the certainty that the soul is immortal. By introducing the *Phaedrus* myth into **The First Lady Chatterley,** Lawrence indicates how much Clifford's mentality has been shaped by the *Dialogue:* in the baronet's mind, he and his wife are, in their sexless marriage, "like two souls free from the body and all its weariness, two souls going hand in hand along the upper road that skirts the heaven of perfection." Socrates in the *Phaedrus* describes the nature of man's soul in terms of two winged horses, a "good" white one and a "bad" black one, drawing a charioteer (man) toward the heavenly fields of light where truth, goodness, and beauty exist. When the charioteer sees a "vision of love," the black steed surges wildly toward the beloved, but is restrained. Once subjugated, the black horse follows the charioteer's will and they reach the heavenly fields. All of this is meant to illustrate Socrates' idea of the conflict between those forces of the psyche that urge an individual to seek gratification and those that urge caution and restraint. The obedient white horse represents those idealistic impulses of the psyche that cause man to be ruled by fear and shame and the love of honor, while the dark horse is, as Constance explains, a symbol of "the body straining after the goal of its own gratifications." According to Socrates, and to his many European followers, the best men restrain the steed of passion.

But of course Lawrence disagreed, and in **The First Lady Chatterley** full sympathy is given to the black horse. Clifford accepts the imagery of "the two horses that draw the chariot of the soul," but his wife vigorously declares that she will let her own dark horse "run right to his goal." The Phaedrus myth thus accentuates the opposed philosophies of the Chatterleys and illuminates the heroine's internal struggle: like the soul in the Socratic mythos, Constance must decide whether to follow the dictates of her "white horse of pure yearning" (and remain faithful to the ideal of her marriage) or to follow the instinctive urges of her "black horse" (leading her to union with the keeper). In **John Thomas and Lady Jane,** the *Phaedrus* material is pared to less than two pages, and though it is reduced even further in **Lady Chatterley's Lover** to the brief conversation I quoted earlier, that minimal allusion to the myth of the two horses still affords Lawrence maximum symbolic effect as he treats the passion/reason dichotomy. In the final version, he uses the Phaedrus myth to voice his complaints that, for passionless modern man, there is "no more black horse to . . . maltreat" and that the "engine" has replaced the "steed" in men's lives and imaginations (later, in **Apocalypse,** he complains that his contemporaries have "lost the horse," the "symbol of surging potency," in their psyches).

After the Chatterleys' brief discussion of the Phaedran charioteer, the baronet's chair stalls and Mellors subsequently joins with Connie to push Clifford out of the forest, in what amounts to a rite of expulsion. Throughout this important chapter, allusions—to the Bible, to Juvenal, to British and American poems, to Proust, and especially to Plato's *Republic*—are expressive components of Lawrence's art. It is here that Connie most emphatically rejects her husband, and the allusions help reveal her reasons. Throughout the wheelchair scene she and Clifford debate the justice of a British economic system wherein one class are "rulers" and the other "servers," leading her to recognize and reject the inhumanity of her husband's ruthless paternalism. His truculence is on display throughout chapter 13, especially when he and the keeper contend over the stalled chair. But Clifford loses the battle with Mellors, who in effect succeeds to the kingdom. Connie herself views the clash between the two men as a contest for power, for the right to "rule." Throughout the chapter, she and Clifford lengthily discuss the issue of "ruling," and she ultimately protests to him, "You don't rule. . . . You only bully with your money." By that time she has realized for the first time that she "definitely hated Clifford" and that she cannot "go on living with him." Thus usurped, Clifford suffers a symbolic death, as his wife suddenly wishes him "obliterated" and thinks of him as a cold "skeleton," a man "very dead."

Clifford's attitudes toward political power and business ethics are well elucidated by references to Plato's *Republic.* Chapter 13, more vividly than any other passage in Lawrence's fiction, indicates the influence of the Platonic dialogues. The influence is not limited to ideas borrowed and personified in a character for purposes of refutation. It bears directly on the form of **Lady Chatterley.** In his 1923 essay **"Surgery for the Novel—or a Bomb,"** pondering the death of modern "self-conscious" fiction in Proust and Joyce, Lawrence had written:

> If you wish to look into the past for what-next books, you can go back to the Greek philosophers. Plato's Dialogues are queer little novels. It seems to me it was the greatest pity in the world, when philosophy and fiction got split. They used to be one, right from the days of myth. Then they went and parted. . . . The two should come together again—in the novel.
>
> [*Phoenix*]

In passages like the wheelchair scene Lawrence was making his own attempt to bring fiction and philosophy "together again." More directly than the earlier Wragby Hall scenes recall the *Symposium,* the discussion in the wheelchair scene parallels that in Book I of the *Republic.* That book records a Socratic conversation on the question "what is justice?" and on the related topics of political power and the "function" of the individual in society; Socrates and his acquaintances debate whether justice can be identified with business morality and whether might makes right. These are precisely the issues disputed by the Chatterleys during their visit to Wragby Wood.

When Connie laments the rancor that exists between British ruling and serving classes, and wonders if there could be "a mutual understanding," her husband responds, "Absolutely: when they [the workers] realize that the industry comes before the individual." His comment recalls the Platonic ideal community ("larger than an individual," formed "to satisfy our many varied needs") delineated in Book II of the *Republic*. Clifford then defends the ownership of property: "The point is *not:* take all thou hast and give to the poor, but use all thou hast to encourage the industry and give work to the poor." He reverses Luke 18:22, where Christ tells the rich man to "sell all that thou hast, and distribute to the poor" in order to "have treasure in heaven." Clifford's Tory paternalism, as Connie realizes, is no benevolent, New Testament sort of Charity, but rather a harsh economic tyranny. The disparity between masters and masses, he argues, is the result of fate: somebody must be "boss of the show," and industrial owners are the ones "fated" to live up to the "responsibility of their own boss-ship." The aristocratic Wragbys and Shipleys have given the colliers political liberty, education, and everything "worth having."

Such ideas of "boss-ship" come straight from Book I of the *Republic,* where Socrates declares that the "true" ruler is the honest man who reluctantly assumes political power because no one else is capable, and who rules always with the interests of the masses in mind. Socrates' remarks are in reply to the cynical sophist Thrasymachus, who has argued that "justice is nothing else than the interest of the stronger," that in any state the governing party makes the moral code and legislates to maintain its domination and its own interest. This is the justice of nature and of the strong, and the supreme embodiment of this ideal is the successful tyrant—just such a tyrant as Clifford shows himself to be in this chapter. He argues that the industrial captains, possessed of superior wisdom, have generously assumed power over the helpless workers "for their own good." But Connie disagrees. "All the things you mention now [political liberty, etc.], Wragby and Shipley *sell* them to the people, at a good profit," she complains. "You don't give one heart-beat of real sympathy. And besides, who has . . . given them this industrial horror?" Clifford counters that the workers themselves are to blame, that they are "animals" little different from "Nero's mine slaves." "The masses are unalterable," he declares. "*Panem et circenses!* Only today education is one of the bad substitutes for a circus." He is alluding to Juvenal's tirade, in the tenth satire, against "the mob of Remus," who compass their own destruction by misguided wishes for only two things: bread and circuses. The masses, being what they are, will need ruling till time ends, Clifford argues, and he proclaims arrogantly: "I can do my share of ruling . . . and give me a son, and he will be able to rule his portion after me." When Connie reminds him that such a son may not be his own, of his own "ruling class," Clifford again directly echoes the *Republic:* "It is not who begets us that matters, but where fate places us. Place any child among the ruling classes, and he will grow up, to his own extent, a ruler. . . . It is the overwhelming pressure of environment." In Plato's Commonwealth, environment is more important than heredity; and people become specialized (and "class"-ified) according to their ability to fulfill a particular "function" (*Republic,* Book III). Clifford, thinking of Plato, tells Connie: "Aristocracy is a function, a part of fate. And the masses are a functioning of another part of fate. The individual hardly matters. It is a question of which function you are brought up to and adapted to. . . . When it comes to expressive or executive functioning, I believe there is a gulf and an absolute one, between the ruling and the serving classes. The two functions are opposed. And the function determines the individual." (pp. 170-79)

Clifford also advocates ideas of Alfred North Whitehead, whose metaphysics developed from Plato's. Like his Cambridge colleague Bertrand Russell, with whom he collaborated on *Principia Mathematica,* Whitehead was a "Philosophic—and Mathematics man," to use Lawrence's phrase describing Russell. Such books as *Science and the Modern World* (1926) and *Religion in the Making* (1926) had brought Whitehead recognition as the leading metaphysical thinker of his day. An allusion in **Lady Chatterley** indicates that Lawrence knew at least one Whitehead book. One evening Clifford reads aloud from "one of the latest scientific-religious books":

> The universe shows us two aspects: on one side it is physically wasting, on the other it is spiritually ascending. . . . It is thus slowly passing, with a slowness inconceivable in our measures of time, to new creative conditions, amid which the physical world, as we at present know it, will be represented by a ripple barely to be distinguished from nonentity. . . . The present type of order in the world has risen from an unimaginable past, and will find its grave in an unimaginable future. There remains the inexhaustive realm of abstract forms, and creativity with its shifting character ever determined afresh by its own creatures, and God, upon whose wisdom all forms of order depend. . . .

Clifford never mentions the title or author of this popular book, but he is quoting directly from the last page of *Religion in the Making,* Whitehead's short book on the interdependence of science, philosophy, and religion. Connie labels the philosopher a "famous windmachine" and dismisses his argument as "silly hocus-pocus." "It only means *he's* a physical failure on the earth, so he wants to make the whole universe a physical failure," she responds. Victor Lowe contends, in his book on Whitehead, that the philosopher never meant to predict a nonphysical order of nature and that Lawrence misreads Whitehead's conception of the creative advance of the universe. At any rate, Lawrence obviously views Whitehead as another perpetuator of escapist metaphysics, another despiser of the body, and the conclusion of *Religion in the Making* is made to seem in **Lady Chatterley** an amplification of what Connie has heard the "mental-lifers" saying earlier about how men could improve their own nature by "forgetting" the "physical side" of life and becoming mere "spirit."

Moreover, the Whitehead quotation triggers a fresh debate over the "life of the mind" and the "life of the body" which establishes a philosophical framework by which we can measure Connie's affair with Mellors, especially her experiences during the upcoming "night of sensual passion." Clifford, defending Whitehead's theories, calls the physique an "encumbrance" and asserts that "whatever God there is is slowly eliminating the guts and alimentary system from the human being, to evolve a higher, more spiritual being." He thus rationalizes his own paralysis into a spiritual advantage. But Connie argues that "whatever God there is has at last wakened up in my guts." For

Lawrence, her physical awakening has been indeed "religion in the making."

The excerpt Clifford reads from this "scientific-religious" book thus further sharpens the philosophic issues in *Lady Chatterley* and stresses Lawrence's belief that both Whitehead and Chatterley are successors to Plato, minor "priests" continuing the "crucifixion of the procreative body for the glorification of the spirit, the mental consciousness." Connie extends her attack on Whitehead to a broad assault on Platonism and Christianity: "The human body is only just coming to real life. With the Greeks it gave a lovely flicker, then Plato and Aristotle killed it, and Jesus finished it off. But now the body is . . . rising from the tomb." Frequently in late works such as *Etruscan Places, Apocalypse,* and **"A Propos of *Lady Chatterley's Lover,*"** Lawrence praises the way ancient peoples led lives untainted by doctrinal "thought-forms" like those proposed in the *Dialogues,* the way they had spontaneously perceived the wonder of life through their senses. In *Lady Chatterley* he urges reaccommodation with the spirit of the ancients—with their animistic conception of an earth that was alive and sacred, and especially with their attitude toward sexuality. To render this "old pagan vision" of life, Lawrence laces his narrative realism with suggestions of primitive myth and ritual—the archetypes of the underworld descent, the dying-reviving god, the restoration of the powers of fertility, and the hierogamy of sun and earth.

The ancient nature cults appealed to Lawrence because they celebrated the vital phallic relation of man and woman, and offered psychic and physical revitalization for an impotent modern civilization. Throughout *Lady Chatterley* Lawrence emphatically ascribes the problem of impotence directly to Socrates and Plato. In *The First Lady Chatterley* the narrator blames "science and Socrates" for "murdering" the penis in order to exalt the intellect, a concept dramatically rendered in *Lady Chatterley's Lover* in the persons of Clifford and Dukes. Lamenting that his penis "never lifts its head up," Dukes complains: "God! when one can only talk! Another torture added to Hades! And Socrates started it." Moreover, because of Clifford's strong identification with the tradition of scientific rationalism, the reader is led to conclude that the baronet's own impotence (war wound or not) is also somehow attributable to "science and Socrates." Because he and Dukes have set their "mind and . . . reason to cock it" over their psyches, each man has lost the phallic power which "connects us with the stars and the sea and everything," that "organic connection" of which Dukes speaks in narrating man's Fall. (pp. 187-90)

Once Lady Chatterley has announced her intention to leave Wragby, Lawrence withdraws the reader's sympathies from the cuckolded husband through the use of several allusions that record Clifford's reaction to the news and that reflect his consequent intimacy with Mrs. Bolton. The first describes Mrs. Bolton's strategy for handling his "male hysteria" over Connie's behavior: "The only thing was to release his self-pity. Like the lady in Tennyson, he must weep or he must die." For the reader who recognizes this reference to one of the intercalary songs of *The Prin-*

cess, there is a double-edged irony. The song, which prefaces section 6, opens: "Home they brought her warrior dead: / She nor swooned, nor uttered cry: / All her maidens, watching, said, / 'She must weep, or she will die.' " She cries, finally, when a nurse places the dead warrior's child upon its mother's knee. Weeping, the lady declares, "my child, I live for thee." But Clifford's nurse will place no child upon his knee—his wife is pregnant, but by another man; she will leave no heir in the Chatterley cradle. Clifford does at last weep, but it is "for himself," not for any lost mate or for the heir she might have left him. The Tennyson line recalled by Mrs. Bolton thus comments ironically on Clifford's response to losing his wife.

Two other allusions, to a nineteenth-century French play and to the Old Testament, serve similarly to characterize Clifford's response. When Connie declares her love for the keeper, Clifford cries, "You're one of those half-insane, perverted women who must run after depravity, the *nostalgie de la boue.*" "*Nostalgie de la boue,*" or "*homesickness for the mud,*" is an expression used in a key passage of Émile Augier's *Le Mariage d'Olympe* (1855), and Lawrence may have this play in mind as he records Chatterley's moralistic condemnation of Connie's "beastly lowness." It seems reasonable that Clifford would recall Augier on this occasion, for the Frenchman was particularly well known for his social dramas that exalted home, family, marital fidelity, and the moral standards of the middle class. *Le Mariage d'Olympe* is an explicit indictment of illicit love. (pp. 191-92)

Clifford soon becomes "wistfully moral, seeing himself the incarnation of good, and people like Mellors and Connie the incarnation of mud, of evil." Such self-righteous behavior shows how aptly Mellors characterizes him as a vengeful Jehovah. Clifford, writes Mellors to Connie, "will want to get rid of you at last, to cast you out . . . to spew you out as the abominable thing." Mellors's words, "cast . . . out," "spew . . . out," "abominable thing," echo diction of several Old Testament chapters—Leviticus 18, Isaiah 65, and Jeremiah 16—which report Jehovah's threats to the Israelites who have defiled his land with "abominable things." Jehovah threatens to punish his rebellious people for their ingratitude and acts of immorality—precisely the transgressions the "wistfully moral" Clifford feels his wife and his gamekeeper have committed against him. The allusion to Chatterley as an angry and judgmental Old Testament God serves as another means by which Clifford is unsympathetically drawn in the closing pages of *Lady Chatterley.*

Lawrence's ultimate dismissal of Clifford is conveyed through two allusions, one biblical, one mythical, describing the baronet's "intimacy of perversity" with Mrs. Bolton. With Connie gone, Clifford regresses into the position of a suckling child, gazing on his nurse with "wonderment, that looked almost like a religious exaltation: the perverse and literal rendering of 'except ye become again as a little child'—While she was the Magna Mater, full of power and potency. . . ." Lawrence alludes first to Luke 18:17, where Jesus tells the ruler, "whosoever shall not receive the kingdom of God as a little child shall in no wise enter therein"; and the effect of this allusion and Lawrence's reference to "madonna-worship" is to make Clifford's relationship with Mrs. Bolton seem all the more perverse. In mentioning the Magna Mater, Lawrence recalls the myths of the ancient Asiatic deity involving incestuous mother-love (precursors of the Oedipal story), and the allusion nicely characterizes Clifford's involvement with the nurse, his "half-mistress, half foster-mother." Lawrence thus once again loads the dice against Clifford, leaving him bound in perverse infantility, but it is just another part of the calculated process of reduction to which Chatterley—and all he represents on a philosophical level—has been steadily exposed throughout the novel. (pp. 193-94)

In general [Lawrence's] allusive technique is a complex and successful component of his art in **Lady Chatterley.** The allusions I have examined are particularly valuable for the way they encourage the reader to take the story "philosophically," to see the broader implications of Clifford's adherence to "the mental life." These allusions to classical writings, to Plato's *Dialogues,* to the Bible, and to works by various British, American, and continental writers—in effect to literature echoing the entire span of Western culture—allow Lawrence to bring past and present into collocation, and to extend the meaning of his "novel contrasting the mental consciousness with the phallic consciousness" far beyond the confines of Wragby Hall and Wragby Wood. By paralleling Clifford Chatterley and other characters with figures from the literature of the past, Lawrence surrounds them with clusters of associations which endow their individual experiences with universal human significance. (p. 194)

> *Dennis Jackson, "Literary Allusions in 'Lady Chatterley's Lover'," in* D. H. Lawrence's "Lady": A New Look at "Lady Chatterley's Lover," *edited by Michael Squires and Dennis Jackson, The University of Georgia Press, 1985, pp. 170-96.*

FURTHER READING

Bibliography

Cowan, James C., ed. *D. H. Lawrence: An Annotated Bibliography of Writings about Him.* Vol. 1. De Kalb: Northern Illinois University Press, 1982.

An annotated bibliography of biographical and critical writings on Lawrence and his works from 1909 to 1960.

Rice, Thomas Jackson. "Studies of *Lady Chatterley's Lover.*" In his *D. H. Lawrence: A Guide to Research,* pp. 245-58. New York: Garland Publishing, 1983.

An annotated bibliography of books and articles on *Lady Chatterley's Lover.*

Biography

Meyers, Jeffrey. "*Lady Chatterley's Lover* and the Paintings, 1928-1929." In his *D. H. Lawrence: A Biography,* pp. 352-72. New York: Alfred A. Knopf, 1990.

Biographical account of the writing of *Lady Chatterley's Lover.*

Criticism

Balbert, Peter H. "The Loving of Lady Chatterley: D. H. Lawrence and the Phallic Imagination." In *D. H. Lawrence: The Man Who Lived,* edited by Robert B. Partlow, Jr. and Harry T. Moore, pp. 143-58. Carbondale: Southern Illinois University Press, 1980.

Concludes that Lawrence integrated form and doctrine in *Lady Chatterley's Lover* to stress "the primacy of the phallic imagination over the modern world's penchant for evasion, reductive mechanization, and aesthetic pretense."

———. "From *Lady Chatterley's Lover* to the *Deer Park*: Lawrence, Mailer, and the Dialectic of Erotic Risk." *Studies in the Novel* 22, No. 1 (Spring 1990): 67-81.

Discusses Lawrence's influence on Norman Mailer's work.

Beal, Anthony. "*Lady Chatterley's Lover.*" In his *D. H. Lawrence,* pp. 84-97. Edinburgh: Oliver and Boyd, 1961.

Comments on various aspects of the novel and maintains that it owes its fame to the obscenity trials and its suppression rather than its intrinsic literary value.

Bedford, Sybille. "The Last Trial of Lady Chatterley." *Esquire* LV, No. 4 (April 1961): 132-36, 138, 141-55.

An account of the British trial of *Lady Chatterley's Lover.*

Britton, Derek. *Lady Chatterley: The Making of the Novel.* London: Unwin Hyman, 1988, 300 p.

Chronicles the writing of *Lady Chatterley's Lover.*

Bryan, Frederick van Pelt. "Opinion." *Evergreen Review* 3, No. 9 (Summer 1959): 37-68.

Judge Bryan's opinion in the American trial of *Lady Chatterley's Lover.*

Charney, Maurice. "Sexuality and the Life Force: *Lady Chatterley's Lover* and *Tropic of Cancer.*" In his *Sexual Fiction,* pp. 93-112. London: Methuen & Co., 1981.

Compares *Lady Chatterley's Lover* with Henry Miller's *Tropic of Cancer* and asserts that "both writers are prophets of a sexual apocalypse that represents a new freedom for modern man."

Clarke, Colin. "Mechanical and Paradisal: *The Plumed Serpent* and *Lady Chatterley's Lover.*" In his *River of Dissolution: D. H. Lawrence and English Romanticism,* pp. 131-47. London: Routledge and Kegan Paul, 1969.

Asserts that the contrast between the mechanical and the organic in *Lady Chatterley's Lover* is flat and that *Women in Love* addresses the same themes in a far superior manner.

Coetzee, J. M. "The Taint of the Pornographic: Defending (Against) *Lady Chatterley's Lover.*" *Mosaic* 21, No. 1 (Winter 1988): 1-11.

Contends that Lawrence's novel is about transgressing sexual and social boundaries which must continue to exist for the novel to retain its tension and dramatic force.

Draper, R. P., ed. "*Lady Chatterley's Lover* (1928)." In his *D. H. Lawrence: The Critical Heritage,* pp. 278-98. New York: Barnes & Noble, 1970.

Contains examples of early critical reaction to *Lady Chatterley's Lover*.

Edwards, Duane. "Mr. Mellors' Lover: A Study of Lady Chatterley." *Southern Humanities Review* XIX, No. 2 (Spring 1985): 117-31.

Argues that most readers underestimate the negative influence of society on the individual and fail to properly distinguish between Lawrence's and Connie's reactions to the "tragic age."

Gertzman, Jay A. "The Piracies of *Lady Chatterley's Lover*: 1928-1950." *D. H. Lawrence Review* 19, No. 3 (Fall 1987): 267-99.

An account of the unauthorized publications of *Lady Chatterley's Lover*.

———. "Legitimizing *Lady Chatterley's Lover*: The Grove Press Strategy, 1959." *Paunch*, nos. 63-64 (December 1990): 1-14.

Discusses the novel's evolution from an underground novel to a literary classic.

Gill, Stephen. "The Composite World: Two Versions of *Lady Chatterley's Lover*." *Essays in Criticism* XXI, No. 4 (October 1971): 347-64.

Concludes that the principal objections to *Lady Chatterley's Lover* point to artistic failures which are not present in *The First Lady Chatterley*.

Henry, G. B. McK. "Carrying On: *Lady Chatterley's Lover*." *The Critical Review*, no. 10 (1967): 46-62.

Concludes that despite its flaws, *Lady Chatterley's Lover* succeeds in conveying Lawrence's vision of life.

Hinz, Evelyn J. "Pornography, Novel, Mythic Narrative: The Three Versions of *Lady Chatterley's Lover*." *Modernist Studies* 3, No. 1 (1979): 35-47.

Argues that the essential "difference between the three versions of the Lady Chatterley story is one of genre."

Holbrook, David. "The Fiery Hill: *Lady Chatterley's Lover*." In his *The Quest for Love*, pp. 192-333. University: University of Alabama Press, 1965.

Characterizes *Lady Chatterley's Lover* as a narcissistic projection of Lawrence's psychological problems.

Hough, Graham. "*Lady Chatterley's Lover.*" In his *The Dark Sun: A Study of D. H. Lawrence*, pp. 148-66. London: Gerald Duckworth & Co., 1956.

Contends that *Lady Chatterley's Lover* does nothing more than recapitulate themes from Lawrence's previous works, particularly the idea that tenderness and passion between individuals can negate the dehumanizing effects of industrial society.

Howe, Marguerite Beede. "The Lesson in *Lady Chatterley's Lover*." In her *The Art of the Self in D. H. Lawrence*, pp. 133-40. Athens: Ohio University Press, 1977.

Concludes that Lawrence's "greatest lesson is the necessity of wholeness, of integrating rational and nonrational experience."

Jackson, Dennis. "*Lady Chatterley's Lover*: Lawrence's Response to *Ulysses*?" *Philological Quarterly* 66, No. 3 (Summer 1987): 410-16.

Asserts that Lawrence intended "his story of Lady Chatterley as a corrective to the marital situation he had seen described in Joyce's novel."

Kermode, Frank. "*Lady Chatterley's Lover.*" In his *D. H. Lawrence*, pp. 131-43. New York: Viking Press, 1973.

Argues that *Lady Chatterley's Lover* was Lawrence's call for a rebirth of the "phallic consciousness" as the only means to achieve personal and national regeneration.

Knoepflmacher, U. C. "The Rival Ladies: Mrs. Ward's *Lady Connie* and Lawrence's *Lady Chatterley's Lover*." *Victorian Studies* IV, No. 1 (September 1960): 141-58.

Compares the novels *Lady Connie* and *Lady Chatterley's Lover* and argues that Lawrence should be "seen in the typically Victorian role of the innovating traditionalist, the radical conservative."

Lawrence, D. H. "A Propos of *Lady Chatterley's Lover*." In *Sex, Literature, and Censorship*, edited by Harry T. Moore, pp. 89-122. New York: Twayne Publishers, 1953.

Remarks relevant to *Lady Chatterley's Lover* on marriage, obscenity, and sex.

Levine, George. "Lawrence, *Frankenstein*, and the Reversal of Realism." In his *The Realistic Imagination: English Fiction from "Frankenstein" to "Lady Chatterley*," pp. 317-28. Chicago: University of Chicago Press, 1981.

Examines Lawrence in relation to the Victorian realists.

Mackenzie, Compton. "The Case of *Lady Chatterley's Lover*." In his *On Moral Courage*, pp. 120-38. London: Collins, 1962.

Comments on the British trial of *Lady Chatterley's Lover*.

Mandel, Jerome. "Medieval Romance and *Lady Chatterley's Lover*." *The D. H. Lawrence Review* 10, No. 1 (Spring 1977): 20-33.

Argues that Lawrence borrowed the plot, characters, and situations depicted in *Lady Chatterley's Lover* from the medieval romance *Tristan and Isolt*.

Mandel, Oscar. "Ignorance and Privacy." *The American Scholar* 29, No. 4 (Autumn 1960): 509-19.

Concludes that Lawrence's depiction of sexual intercourse in his revolt against Victorianism has eliminated the mystery surrounding sex.

Martz, Louis L. "The Second Lady Chatterley." In *The Spirit of D. H. Lawrence: Centenary Studies*, edited by Gamini Salgado and G. K. Das, pp. 106-24. London: Macmillan Press, 1988.

Compares the second and third versions of *Lady Chatterley's Lover*.

Niven, Alastair. "*Lady Chatterley's Lover.*" In his *D. H. Lawrence: The Novels*, pp. 175-86. Cambridge: Cambridge University Press, 1978.

Asserts that Lawrence used *Lady Chatterley's Lover* to attack the major trends in modern life and to call on us to seek integrity in our personal relationships.

Ober, William B. "Lady Chatterley's What?" In his *Boswell's Clap, and Other Essays: Medical Analysis of Literary Men's Afflictions*, pp. 89-117. Carbondale: Southern Illinois University Press, 1979.

Interprets *Lady Chatterley's Lover* as Lawrence's reaction to his tuberculosis and psychosexual disorders.

Parker, David. "Lawrence and Lady Chatterley: The Teller and the Tale." *The Critical Review*, no. 20 (1978): 31-41.

Argues that *The First Lady Chatterley* is superior to

Lady Chatterley's Lover because the theme of marriage which Lawrence defined as the novel's achievement in "A Propos of *Lady Chatterley's Lover*" is much more pronounced in the original version.

Peters, Joan D. "The Living and the Dead: Lawrence's Theory of the Novel and the Structure of *Lady Chatterley's Lover*." *D. H. Lawrence Review* 20, No. 1 (Spring 1988): 5-20.

Asserts that Lawrence's discourse on the purpose of the novel in *Lady Chatterley's Lover* is central to the novel's design because it serves as the novel's structural blueprint.

Pinion, F. B. "*Lady Chatterley's Lover*." In his *A D. H. Lawrence Companion: Life, Thought, and Works*, pp. 205-17. New York: Barnes & Noble, 1979.

Discusses the themes of *Lady Chatterley's Lover*.

Polhemus, Robert M. "The Prophet of Love and the Resurrection of the Body: D. H. Lawrence's *Lady Chatterley's Lover* (1928)." In his *Erotic Faith: Being in Love from Jane Austen to D. H. Lawrence*, pp. 279-306. Chicago: The University of Chicago Press, 1990.

Asserts that Lawrence imagined the erotic relationship depicted in *Lady Chatterley's Lover* as a religious mystery and an ideal vision of marriage.

Porter, Katherine Anne. "A Wreath for the Gamekeeper." In her *The Collected Essays and Occasional Writings of Katherine Anne Porter*, pp. 14-28. New York: Delacorte Press, 1970.

Criticizes Lawrence for trying to "cleanse" obscene words and derides his ideas on sex.

Rembar, Charles. "Lady Chatterley: The Trial," "Lady Chatterley: The Federal Courts," and "Lady Chatterley: Postscript." In his *The End of Obscenity: The Trials of "Lady Chatterley," "Tropic of Cancer," and "Fanny Hill."* pp. 59-113, pp. 114-51, pp. 152-67. New York: Random House, 1968.

Detailed account of the American legal proceedings surrounding the publication of *Lady Chatterley's Lover*.

Resina, Joan Ramon. "The Word and the Deed in *Lady Chatterley's Lover*." *Forum for Modern Language Studies* XXIII, No. 4 (October 1987): 351-65.

Argues that Lawrence failed to demonstrate how humanity's severed relations to the universe could be reestablished.

Rolph, C. H. *The Trial of Lady Chatterley: Regina v. Penguin Books Limited*. Harmondsworth, Middlesex: Penguin Books, 1961, 250 p.

A detailed account of the British trial.

Sagar, Keith. "The Holy Ground (1926-1927): 'Sun,' *Lady Chatterley's Lover*." In his *The Art of D. H. Lawrence*, pp. 173-98. Cambridge: Cambridge University Press, 1966.

Concludes "that *Lady Chatterley's Lover* should have been a short novel . . . where the pressure to provide a realistic setting and fully drawn characters would not have sunk the myth of innocence regained."

Sanders, Scott. "*Lady Chatterley's Lover*: Eros and Civilization." In his *D. H. Lawrence: The World of the Major Novels*, pp. 172-205. London: Vision Press, 1973.

Treats *Lady Chatterley's Lover* as a response to historical circumstances, such as the class divisions in industrial society.

Schorer, Mark. "On *Lady Chatterley's Lover*." *Evergreen Review* 1, No. 1 (1957): 149-78.

Compares the three version of *Lady Chatterley's Lover* and interprets the novel as a critique of modern society.

Sparrow, John. "Regina v. Penguin Books Ltd.: An Undisclosed Element in the Case" and "Afterthoughts on Regina v. Penguin Books Ltd." In his *Controversial Essays,* pp. 40-58, pp. 58-70. London: Faber and Faber, 1966.

Contends that the jury's verdict might have been different if Lawrence's depiction of anal intercourse had been made explicit. In the second essay, Sparrow comments on the controversy which the publication of his first essay aroused.

Spilka, Mark. "*Lady Chatterley's Lover* and *The Man Who Died.*" In his *The Love Ethic of D. H. Lawrence*, pp. 175-235. Bloomington: Indiana University Press, 1955.

Interprets *Lady Chatterley's Lover* as Lawrence's description of the rites of phallic marriage and *The Man Who Died* as his attempt to link those rites to the general scheme of Western Civilization.

———. "On Lawrence's Hostility to Wilful Women: the Chatterley Solution." In *Lawrence and Women*, edited by Anne Smith, pp. 189-211. London: Vision Press, 1978.

Regards Mellors as a projection of the male traits that Lawrence sought and Clifford as a projection of those traits he wished to discard.

Squires, Michael. "*Lady Chatterley's Lover:* 'Pure Seclusion'." In his *The Pastoral Novel: Studies in George Eliot, Thomas Hardy, and D. H. Lawrence*, pp. 196-212. Charlottesville: University Press of Virginia, 1974.

Interprets *Lady Chatterley's Lover* as a pastoral novel and asserts that its "continuity with a tradition illustrates the recurrence of a widely used pattern of emotional or spiritual adjustment."

———, and Jackson, Dennis, eds. *D. H. Lawrence's Lady: A New Look at "Lady Chatterley's Lover."* Athens: The University of Georgia Press, 1985.

Collection of essays on *Lady Chatterley's Lover*.

Vivas, Eliseo. "*Lady Chatterley's Lover*." In his *D. H. Lawrence: The Failure and the Triumph of Art*, pp. 119-47. Evanston: Northwestern University Press, 1960.

Contends that the novel suffers from fundamental defects, such as a lack of unity, unconvincing characterization, and didacticism.

Widmer, Kingsley. "The Pertinence of Modern Pastoral: The Three Versions of *Lady Chatterley's Lover*." *Studies in the Novel* 5, No. 3 (Fall 1973): 298-313.

Compares the novel's three versions and concludes that "in several times redoing his romance, Lawrence decisively rejected the proletarianization of his awakened characters and heightened the pastoral moral."

———. "Lawrence's Cultural Impact." In *The Legacy of D. H. Lawrence*, edited by Jeffrey Meyers, pp. 156-74. London: Macmillan Press, 1987.

Assesses Lawrence's impact on contemporary cultural and social issues with special emphasis on *Lady Chatterley's Lover*.

Worthen, John. "*Lady Chatterley's Lover*." In his *D. H. Lawrence and the Idea of the Novel*, pp. 168-82. Totowa, N.J.: Rowman and Littlefield, 1979.

Compares the three versions of the novel.

Additional coverage of Lawrence's life and career is contained in the following sources published by Gale Research: *Concise Dictionary of British Literary Biography, 1914-1945; Contemporary Authors,* Vols. 104, 121; *Dictionary of Literary Biography,* Vols. 10, 19, 36, 98; *Major 20th-Century Writers, Short Story Criticism,* Vol. 4; *Twentieth-Century Literary Criticism,* Vols. 2, 9, 16, 33; and *World Literature Criticism.*

Bolesław Prus
1845-1912

(Pseudonym of Aleksander Głowacki) Polish novelist, short story writer, and journalist.

INTRODUCTION

Prus is regarded as one of the greatest Polish novelists in the period spanning the late nineteenth and early twentieth centuries. Prus's novels typically revolve around the dynamics of Polish society and politics, employing humor and details of daily life to underscore the ethical dilemmas of his characters. These concerns reflect Prus's belief that the purpose of literature was to "aid the spiritual development of the individual and of society. The sciences aid thought, social sciences aid thought and will, while literature aids thought, feeling, and will."

Prus was the son of an impoverished aristocrat employed on an estate in the district of Lublin. When he was eighteen years old, Prus joined a guerilla troop in the anti-Russian uprising of 1863. He served in battle and was detained in a Russian prison, experiences that he drew on for his celebrated novel *Lalka* (*The Doll*). Prus later studied mathematics and physical science in Warsaw, where he was exposed to the philosophies of Auguste Comte and Herbert Spencer. The Comtean positivism in vogue among Prus's contemporaries stressed an optimistic faith in the benefits of scientific rationalism and the Industrial Revolution. Prus himself, however, felt a greater affinity for the philosophy of Spencer, which is reflected in the view expressed in Prus's novels that society is an organism whose health depends upon the harmony of its parts. Prus began his literary career as a writer of humorous prose sketches and verse for magazines. For several decades his articles appeared in Warsaw periodicals and earned him both popular acclaim and the respect of the intelligentsia. These pieces, which are known as the "Weekly Chronicles," frequently had educational aims and made use of humor and sentiment to address social concerns. Dissatisfied with the limitations of journalism, Prus began writing short stories, usually set in Warsaw and focusing on the lives of the poor. In 1886 Prus published his first novel, *Placówka* (*The Outpost*), a detailed and unsentimental portrayal of a Polish village. *The Outpost* foreshadows the interest in contemporary social and ethical problems which Prus later addressed in such novels as *The Doll, Emancypantki,* and *Faraon* (*The Pharoah and the Priests*). Toward the end of his life, Prus grew pessimistic as a result of the violent revolutionary activities of Polish socialists. His novel based on the revolution of 1905, *Dzieci,* has been criticized for being less a work of literature than a journalistic admonition aimed at the younger generation. Prus died in 1912.

Prus's early short stories were based on his meticulous ob-

servation of Polish life. Closer to newspaper sketches than to short stories, his portraits of indigent vagrants and dispossessed aristocrats were criticized for their lack of artistry. Gradually, however, Prus grew more adept in the short story form, and such stories as "Katarynka" ("The Barrel Organ") and "Antek" are included among his best works. In "Katarynka" a wealthy voluptuary is annoyed by the playing of a barrel organ grinder outside his home and orders him away. When the rich gentleman discovers that the music was the sole pleasure of a blind girl living in the neighborhood, he invites a host of organ grinders to serenade her, thus revealing both Prus's sense of the fundamental decency of human nature as well as his method of treating his characters with sympathy. "Antek" is the story of a gifted peasant boy who lacks the opportunity to cultivate his talents. That Prus's fiction often had a didactic purpose is revealed in the epilogue attached to "Antek" in which the author exhorts his readers to aid individuals resembling his protagonist.

The narratives of Prus's major novels occur within a much wider social context than his short stories. *The Outpost,* for example, portrays the resistance of peasants in the face of German colonization in Poland. Prus artfully represented the peasant mentality in its attachment to tradition and anxiety over the changes initiated by modernity. *The Doll*, viewed by some critics as the greatest Polish novel, focuses on the experiences of two men living in Warsaw. Stanislaw Wokulski, an impoverished nobleman turned businessman, is a committed proponent of the new positivist ideology who attempts to reconcile his passion for science with his drive for social success as represented by his pursuit of an indifferent aristocratic woman. The humorous journal of Wokulski's older colleague, Ignacy Rzecki, forms a novel within a novel which places the condition of contemporary Poland within the wider context of international events earlier in the century. The vast scope of *The Doll* has led Czeslaw Milosz to write that the novel "contains not a single page which, regardless of its connection or lack of connection with one or another plot, does not tell something interesting or shed a new and interesting light on various phenomena." Closely resembling *The Doll*, *Emancypantki* displays on an epic scale the social, political, and psychological forces animating Poland, while ostensibly concerning itself with the single issue of the emancipation of women. Prus raises many questions in this novel and provides a variety of viewpoints, yet refrains from drawing any conclusions. *The Pharaoh and the Priests*, acknowledged as Prus's final masterpiece, has been called one of the most preeminent historical novels in European literature. Set in ancient Egypt, *The Pharaoh and the Priests* combines a masterful application of historical scholarship with an incisive anatomy of political power. The action of the novel revolves around the struggle for power between the radical young pharaoh (the fictional Ramses XIII) and the caste of powerful priests. Commentators have noted that in this depiction of political conflict, Prus intended to make general observations relevant to human societies rather than a direct allusion to the state of affairs in late nineteenth-century Poland.

In their narrative style and ideological concerns, Prus's novels belong to a tradition of realistic literature that is more conspicuously represented by the works of such authors as Charles Dickens and Emile Zola. With the advent of Modernism in Poland in the early years of the twentieth century, Prus's works suffered neglect. Recently, however, scholars have reevaluated his achievement and have sought to revive critical interest in his works. Today, *The Doll* and *The Pharaoh and the Priests* are considered among the greatest Polish novels, and, as Milosz writes, Prus is regarded "as a writer of rare integrity and high intellectual standards."

PRINCIPAL WORKS

Placówka (novel) 1886
Lalka (novel) 1890
 [*The Doll*, 1972]
Emancypantki (novel) 1894
Faraon (novel) 1897
 [*The Pharaoh and the Priests*, 1902; also translated as *Pharaoh*, 1991]
Dzieci (novel) 1909

CRITICISM

J. Krzyżanowski (essay date 1931)

[*In the following excerpt, Krzyżanowski examines the historical and philosophical foundations of Prus's fiction.*]

The second half of the 19th century in Polish literature, as in other literatures, was a period of the novel. Poetry had been the dominating feature of the romantic era which about the middle of the century was almost completely over, and in the new régime that set in, a Platonic republic of thinkers and scholars, no room was left for it. It was held to be too much of a luxury and, accordingly, had to yield to the simpler, more sober and accessible prose. The new fashion in literary life produced an innumerable host of novelists, semi-novelists and journalists trying their hand at novel writing; but at the same time this period produced three outstanding writers, whose work survived the passing tide of time. The names of the "big three" were Bolesłav Prus, Henry Sienkiewicz and Eliza Orzeszkowa.

The first among them, Bolesłav Prus (1845-1912) or better Alexander Głowacki (for this was his real name, that of Prus being only his *nom de plume*), proved capable of embodying the leading ideals of his time in a more adequate form than the other two, for which reason he may be considered the most representative writer of the period of Polish Realism. His comparative supremacy depended not so much on his talent as on his circumstances, which, one might say, had equipped him for the task of mirroring the characteristics of his day in a higher degree than his contemporaries. The point is that, while Sienkiewicz was a novelist and hardly anything else, and Orzeszkowa a novelist and moralist wedded to the countryside, Prus devoted the greater part of his lifetime to journalism, in which profession he was able to develop his own attitude to life more in accordance with a realist's than with a simple novelist's approach to the demands of the period.

His reasons for resolving to become a journalist, however, had but little in common with the genuine inclinations of the future novelist. After the gloomy period of his youth, overshadowed by the failure of the January Rising of 1863, in which he had taken an active part, he had no means to continue his favourite studies in mathematics and science, so he was forced to give them up and to earn his daily bread in the editorial offices of the Warsaw newspapers. He started by supplying them with satirical articles, sketches and "chronicles," in which he discussed, in his own way, all the topics of the day, except the political problems prohibited by the Russian censorship. All these early contributions betrayed an observant eye and a peculiar sense of humour tinged with a strain of irony. Still as time went on, Prus was beginning to dislike his very success; he considered himself merely a jester, and he had a contempt for the society which, while it would not help him to enter the proper path of his vocation, seemed to enjoy his jokes. To suppress this unpleasant feeling, he attempted to treat his work in a more serious way. He passed from jokes to articles in which he scrutinised the social and economic conditions of the country and aimed at suggesting necessary reforms. In them he blended the conclusions to which he had come by close observation of the demands of life with theoretical arguments drawn from the books of the German and English thinkers, such as Buckle, Mill, Spencer and other "authorities" then in vogue all over Europe. Under the influence of these writers he constructed a philosophic system of his own, which enabled him to undertand the complicated problems of practical life and encouraged him to make suggestions which went deeper than those of his professional colleagues. He learned that the problems which he had to discuss were not disconnected; chance facts were but manifestations of underlying social laws, a part of processes which appealed to the writer's interest, claiming a thorough investigation. Still, an attempt to base journalistic activity upon the groundwork of a philosophic system ended in failure. Prus began to run a newspaper *Nowiny* (*The News*) in which he wished to be impartial and independent of the political parties, but he soon had to realise that such a paper was too difficult for most of its readers; it did not pay, and the editor was obliged to stop it. This second failure of his life, however, was not able to break the obstinate man. He resolved now to return to the field, which in the earlier phases of his career had seemed to him hardly worthy of attention, the field of the novel. Of course, he was prepared for this change, for in his sketches and chronicles he had applied many a time the form of the short story, although such a form served him only as a means of expressing his views and, therefore, lacked artistic perfection. Now, once he had arrived at the conclusion that his journalistic activities had failed to make the desired appeal, he looked for another and more effective medium, but he never completely abandoned his earlier profession. So, to the very end of his life he contributed to the daily and weekly papers in Warsaw, keeping in touch with current political and social events of the period.

This decisive change of profession occurred in the early 1880's and showed two fundamental aspects of Prus' personality as a writer. In his journalistic articles he was fond of stressing his fanatical devotion to science and his contempt of imagination; he spared no effort to apply scientific methods to the investigation of social problems; accordingly he might have been taken to be a man notoriously lacking in fantasy. Still, his first attempts at novels, unsuccessful though most of them were, showed in him an unexpected wealth of imagination, an uncommon capacity for constructing a world of imaginary life. At the same time they betrayed the unerring eye of the journalist, accustomed to notice all that was going on in his surroundings, and the thoughtful habit of seeing among individual facts their internal links and their underlying factors. None the less, his first stories did not meet with the approval of the critics. Prus was accused of making his narratives rather sketches and caricatures, of being too fond of distorting life and exaggerating its proportions instead of giving a balanced picture of it. To a large extent such opinions were justified; for Prus was unable to free himself from the way to which he had been used in his journalistic productions, the artist in him was still overshadowed by the teacher who was aiming at instructing his readers. In fact he introduced into his stories all sorts of wretched characters such as poor vagabonds from the streets of the suburbs, bankrupt outcasts from the gentry class stranded in Warsaw after the agrarian reform and emancipation of the peasants, and many other victims of indolence, ignorance or just ill luck. The pictures drawn by his hand, true to life though they were, lacked the finishing touch of the artist. At the same time, however, each of them possessed a peculiar quality bidding the reader reconcile himself to the writer. In spite of the jester's mask which the author continued to wear, the narratives witnessed to his human heart throbbing with the sympathy which he felt for everything that struck him as miserable, destitute and helpless. In this way one might discover under the apparently satirical attitude towards life in Prus something else, the attitude of a first-class humorist.

In the course of time he did not lose this precious quality, moreover, he added to it a new accomplishment, the lack of which had been objectionable to his readers, a high perfection of style. The moment that he had achieved this, it was evident that he was among the greatest writers of his generation. To understand the nature of this development, it suffices to compare two of his short stories, **"In the Saxon Park"** and **"The Adventure of Stasio."** In the first one sees a ridiculous provincial family, the uncouth members of which do their best to enjoy themselves in the fashionable park in Warsaw. Pushed and mocked at by people amused at the sight of their clumsiness and embarrassment, they leave the park rather suddenly, whereat the writer takes the opportunity to make some bitter remarks about the ugliness of the park and the snobbery of its visitors. The other story is quite different. Into it Prus introduced a series of scenes from country life bound up with the story of Stasio, a baby son of a village smith. The novelist is unable to suppress his inclination for the ridiculous, and now and then he indulges in exaggeration. The father of the baby, anticipating that Stasio may soon be wanting a teacher, entertains the would-be master; they drink a little too much and come to blows, an incident which threatens to destroy the premature educational schemes of the smith. Still, the overdone though amusing scenes do not entirely consume the reader's attention; they are well balanced by a string of lovely pictures of a rather idyllic nature. The best among them concern the baby's earliest impressions; the little one is left in the orchard in charge of the faithful and lazy dog, Kurta. The condescending and sympathetic analysis of the ideas crossing the brain of the animal, the overwhelming laziness of the summer midday, the humming of the wind among the branches of the tree, the interest the plants take in the life of the baby, everything contributes to an accomplished picture, the genuine charm of which may be compared with the most fascinating pages in Mr. Galsworthy's novel on the childhood of Jon Forsyte.

The comparison between Prus and the English novelist may be drawn a little further. Another of Prus' masterpieces, the story called **"The Barrel-Organ,"** can be easily compared to *A Forsyte Encountering the People,* for both of them are based on the unexpected contact of a wealthy sybarite with a human misery to which he had never before paid any attention, not because he was egotistic but because he had had no opportunity to understand the poor and miserable. The two stories are akin not only on account of their subject but on account of the similarity of method adopted by their writers who impress the reader by refraining from any comments, but by reproducing simple facts. The same may be said of one more of Prus' jewels in the province of the short story, that is, of **"Antek."** In it the novelist handled the very problem which, in Sienkiewicz's *Johnny the Musician* had made such a strong appeal, the problem of wasted abilities in the peasant boys of Poland. Sienkiewicz approached this theme from the lyrical standpoint, and gave a pathetic story of a little fiddle player who paid with death for his musical inclinations. Prus, on the other hand, handled the problem in an epic and impersonal manner, and starting from similar premises gave an optimistic picture, while Sienkiewicz, although a born optimist himself, had been unable to escape from the snares of involuntary pessimism. Prus found escape both in the sense of humour so peculiar to his talent, and in his philosophic system, which bade him believe that human nature was capable of overcoming all sorts of difficulties in spite of temporary failures and vain attempts. One ought to add that owing to the wealth of detail from country life the story of Antek, a capable youth who under favourable circumstances might have developed into a great inventor, is among the best stories from the life of the Polish peasantry.

The existence of a system of philosophic and social ideas, which had emerged in **"Antek,"** as well as the journalistic habit of paying attention to every serious alteration in the life of his nation, came to the forefront in his stories and novels, the plots of which were set against a broader background of the social conditions of the day. So in a short story called the **"Returning Wave"** (1880) he dealt with the industrialisation of the Congress Kingdom and its effects upon the life of the country; in it he accentuated the defencelessness of the growing working class exploited by the factory owners and unprotected by social legislation. In doing so he was a forerunner of later novelists, such as Reymont, who in the course of time were destined to come back to this problem.

The same may be said of Prus' first novel called ***The Outpost*** (1885). To appreciate duly its significance, one must remember that about the middle of the second half of the 19th century the Congress Kingdom had become an objective of German colonisation. The position of the Polish peasant class was miserable. Its growth resulted in "unemployment" and its best representatives, who could find no work at home, were obliged to leave for America in quest of bread. At the same time the Russian government encouraged the German colonists, who crossed the frontier and settled down to form an alien body within the nation, the aims and claims of which they were unable or unwilling to share and understand. The Polish Press of the period could not help noticing the double danger implied by the colonisation, political and economical, and this much-discussed topic also appealed to Prus. He wrote a series of articles on a similar subject to investigate the exterminating policy adopted by the German government in the Duchy of Poznań; in them he discussed the necessity of founding agrarian banks and inventing other means of rescue, and at the same time he resolved to approach the problem in a different way, more permanent and less dependent on passing events, in a word, by a novel the very title of which was to indicate the writer's attitude toward this disturbing social phenomenon.

In doing so, he did not abandon the lines laid down in Sienkiewicz's story *Sketches in Charcoal,* that is to say, he did not shrink from emphasising the notorious ignorance and helplessness of peasants compelled to face and solve problems which were beyond the limits of their traditionally narrow outlook. As he had more or less done in his earlier short stories, he adopted the objective and impartial method of treating his subject; he refrained from any sarcastic comments on the events in his novel, leaving the reader to draw conclusions without the author's interference. Instead, by means of an extremely minute, naturalistic description of the daily life of a village he enabled the reader to penetrate into the awkward, though entirely human, psychology of the characters in the novel. As to its plot, Prus connected it with an unheard of event in the then Polish countryside, the construction of the first railway track, cutting short the primitive existence of an up to that moment inaccessible village and bringing it into contact with modern civilisation and its complex demands. He linked this innovation, which was to indicate the historical background of the events, with the changes in the structure of the population as mentioned above, the antagonism between the German settlers and the Polish peasants. The newcomers had bought the estate of a ruined landowner and tried to persuade their neighbour, Slimak, whose farm handicapped their schemes for developing the settlement, to sell them his farm. They applied all sorts of means to force him to yield to them and they failed, for the "outpost," although worn down by the struggle which he had had to fight alone and singlehanded, proved capable of resisting all temptations and calamities; nothing could remove him from the soil of his ancestors. Alone and supported by nothing but his inborn obstinacy and his subconscious love of the farm, the illiterate peasant turned out to be the very outpost that stopped the advance of the enemy.

As in the **"Returning Wave,"** in the ***Outpost*** again Prus paved the way for his great successor in the province of the novel, for Reymont, in whose well-known epic *The Peasants* one also comes across the same problem, the interrelations of the Polish peasantry and their neighbours the German colonists. Yet, despite the fact that the ***Outpost*** soon won an enormous recognition, it was only a chance excursion of the writer into the countryside. A journalist and novelist, acquainted with the town and its life, could not resist the influence of his surroundings; he was born to become an "urbanist," a painter of town life. And, in fact, after a long series of short stories which formed a preparatory stage in his career as a novelist, he devoted his greatest achievements to Warsaw.

It was the success of the ***Outpost*** that encouraged him to produce a very long novel in three volumes called ***The Doll*** (1890). This title was accidentally suggested to the writer and did not express the essence of the novel which, according to Prus' earlier and more appropriate intention, should have been called *Three Generations.* As to its genre, the novel was modelled on the typical novels of manners in the latter half of the 19th century. He followed the path of the great French and English masters, though his indebtedness to them has not yet been investigated. Recently it has appeared that *The Doll* bears some evidence of a direct influence of Spielhagen, whose novels were eagerly read in the seventies and eighties in Poland; still, to give a proper idea of the type represented by *The Doll* one can best compare it to the novels of Thackeray: I do not mean in analogies in the way of handling the subject peculiar to the two novelists, though that might lead to extremely interesting results, but in the structure of their works. So both *The Newcomes* and *The Doll* give us the impression of a sketchbook rather than of a well-constructed fiction. Their subject is so vast and so loosely put together that it seems to burst the weak frame of the narrative. One is inclined to admit that each might have furnished the subject-matter for several novels, and such an impression is strengthened by the fact that both *The Newcomes* and *The Doll,* in spite of their biographical form, lack a distinct plot. It is evident that what had been intended by the authors as a plot, acts as a more or less artificial link to keep together a number of pictures reflecting the social life of the period.

The Doll is a biography of one Stanislas Wokulski, especially of the last stage in his life, the earlier periods of which are introduced to the reader by various indirect means, in particular, the memoir of his old friend, Rzecki. The story of Wokulski who, born in a ruined and pauperised family, owing to his enormous will power grew from a poor shop assistant into a leading business man and a scientist, as well as the autobiographical memoir of Rzecki, allowed the writer to include in his novel a panoramic vista of the generations between 1830 and 1880; that is, a history of the inner development in the social structure of the Polish nation within the 19th century. In an exquisitely minute description of the early years of Rzecki and Wokulski, Prus seized an opportunity of portraying the lower class of the Warsaw population, the shop keepers and shop assistants, small officials, and all sorts of clients of the public-house; again the later stage in Wokulski's career, the hero's attempts to organise and develop commerce in Poland as well as his connections with aristocratic circles, especially his love of a "doll," an aristocratic girl, afforded Prus a good chance of painting the decay of the once powerful and wealthy social class now pushed out by the growing middle class. Finally Wokulski's travels in Poland and abroad furnished material for a large gallery of various personages representing other social spheres, the proletariat and intelligentsia as well as the world of learned eccentrics.

The most attractive part, perhaps, is the very beginning of the novel, the story of an old shop owned by the German family of Mincel, against the background of which Wokulski and Rzecki are shown to the reader. Through the medium of the story of the growth of the old-fashioned shop into a first-class magazine, the writer was able to paint the spirit which animated the population of Warsaw for half a century and found its best manifestation in the political events of the period. In an extremely clever and picturesque way he demonstrated how ideas, created at the very beginning of the century, spread and grew until they became the property of the lowest class of the nation. In this manner Prus found an artistic form for what is usually described as the process of democratisation, the process of the growing up of the uncultivated classes till they reach the level of self-consciousness. Rzecki and his German friends are the medium in which this process may be easily studied. Rzecki, the son of a porter who had served under Napoleon and had always remained faithful to the ideals of his youth, has inherited from his father a love for liberty and a complex of views which may be called political romanticism. This inheritance bids him leave the shop and go to Hungary to fight for her independence in 1849. He is accompanied by his colleagues who, despite their German origin, cannot stand the "Shvabs," as they scornfully denominate the Austrian oppressors of the day of Metternich. Prus, of course, did not conceal the ridiculous exaggeration of the political faith of Rzecki and his friends, none the less the modern reader cannot help noticing the underlying sympathy that supplies warmth of life to the picture. On account of the Russian censorship, the novelist was unable to show the similar efforts of the following generation, the political ideals of which led to the January Rising of 1863 and suffered a deadly blow after the rising was suppressed. He only stressed another characteristic of the period in the story of Wokulski, who from a shop assistant changed into a student, I mean the interest of that generation in science and the illusion that by means of science one would be able to find a solution of the most urgent problems of life, both national and social.

On the other hand, in the portion of the novel dealing with the aristocratic world, the humorist in Prus gave way to the satirist. The writer did not like the aristocracy; its representatives seemed to him survivals of a period gone by, incapable of keeping up their previous position in national life and destined to decay. The internal corruption of the aristocracy struck him as something hideous, particularly when compared with the claims of the members of that class. Aristocracy in Poland, the novelist maintained, was not only unable to produce anything that counted in public life, but it affected everything, it spoiled every noble effort which was made by others to improve whatever was wrong. This standpoint was demonstrated in the history of the family of Lecki and their aristocratic friends and relatives. The religion to which they seemed to cling, was shallow and insincere; their political activities only aimed at supporting their ancestral dignity. On the whole the verdict of Prus was as merciless as that of his Romantic predecessors, young Krasiński in the *Undivine Comedy* and Kraszewski in his novels, and in this respect he anticipated a series of equally ruthless pictures in the works of his gifted successor, Baron Joseph Weyssenhoff. In comparison with the Romantic authors, however, Prus was self-controlled, and therefore his novel gave the reader an impression of a more impartial and objective mirror of life than the fierce attacks of the earlier generation.

This effect was due to placing Wokulski in the very centre of the aristocratic circle of Warsaw. The self-made man who had proved capable of raising himself from the very depths of humiliation and, despite the established opinion about the notorious lack of ability for business in his countrymen, had made a big fortune, wastes his energy in trying to get admission into the sphere of aristocracy. He manages to overcome all sorts of hindrances, of caste prejudices; he engages himself to Isabella, the fair daughter of a ruined aristocrat; but he has soon to discover that he has made a terrible mistake, that this doll of a girl is unworthy of all this effort. Broken by the discovery, he disappears in a mysterious way; the epilogue of the novel has not solved the riddle whether Wokulski killed himself or went to Paris to shut himself up in the studio of his weird learned friend Professor Geist, to devote himself to science.

The Doll was a completely successful attempt to give an account of the most important changes undermining the general attitude towards life inherited from the era of Romanticism, and introducing an entirely new period in Polish life. It is questionable whether Prus was capable of defining the contours of the latter, but it cannot be denied that he managed to persuade the reader that this was indeed a new period, and that the preceding one was gone for ever. And from this point of view *The Doll* formed a milestone in the history of life and literature in Poland; it was a literary account, perhaps a literary monument of the generation which had ceased to exist.

The conclusions to which the analysis of Polish life in the second half of the 19th century had led the writer of *The Doll* were obviously far from optimistic. Still, he refused to yield to pessimism and, to the readers' astonishment, he closed the sad story of Wokulski's defeat with the hopeful Horatian formula "non omnis moriar"! Such an ending was not justified by the course of events in the novel, and a similar contradiction, or at least discrepancy, seemed to prevail in his second great contribution to the body of Polish fiction called *The Emancipated Women* (1895). In it he again portrayed his period and again failed to reconcile his artistic vista of life to his philosophic system. He expounded the latter in an interesting episode in the novel, a lecture given by a certain professor Debicki; still the reader cannot easily see the convincing inter-relation between life and the opinions of the lecturer who, having started from metaphysical premises, attempted to apply them as ethical rules of conduct for man. One is inclined to admit that Prus was unable to reconcile the two fundamental aspects of his personality, the realist writer and the philosopher, and that, accordingly, the thinker in him was bound to give way to the artist, being too weak to resist the rapid torrent of impressions with which his watchful eye never ceased to supply him. If this was so, he would have to approach an entirely fictitious world, to be able to bring the two elements mentioned above into perfect harmony. This task was achieved in his following novel, the subject matter of which was taken not from modern life but from the history of ancient Egypt.

This historical romance, called *Pharaoh* (1897), was received with great interest by readers who could not believe that Prus, whose earlier works had been strongly bound up with modern life and its common folk, could have abandoned this path and turned to the legendary and heroic. For heroic virtues and heroic mistakes formed the framework of the leading character in the new novel, that of Rameses XIV. The young prince and would-be successor to his aged father, Rameses XIII, is introduced in the opening chapter of the novel as the conqueror of a rebellion, on the very eve of his coronation. He seems to be well prepared for his royal duties; he has valour and wisdom; moreover he has conceived a series of political schemes which he wants to carry through in his reign, as well as of social ideas concerning the reform of the internal structure of his country. In his youthful dreams, inspired by a liberal teacher, he has seen the necessity to emancipate the oppressed victims of the privileged classes, and as soon as he can grasp the helm of government he seizes his chance. His reforms aim at curtailing the liberties of the most powerful class, the priests, and here begins the tragedy of the bold reformer. First of all he wants to make war on the age-long enemies of Egypt, the Assyrians, and to this end he attempts to get hold of the innumerable treasures preserved in the Labyrinth in the charge of the priests. The guardians of the treasure, however, who object to the war, refuse to support the young ruler. Of course, had he not been so stiff-necked, had he been able to stoop and make peace with the priests, they would have been his loyal assistants. But the *Pharaoh,* being more of a soldier than a politician, a man who dislikes intrigues, endeavours to arrive straight at his goal and he loses the game. His enemies profit by his mistakes, by his powerful passions, and hasten the death of Rameses. At the decisive moment he is stabbed by a lunatic from whom he has taken a sweetheart and who avenges his wrong with a poisoned dagger. The premature death of the *Pharaoh* puts an end to the dynasty, and a new one is started by the dead hero's chief antagonist, the pontiff Herhor. Curiously enough, the new monarch begins his reign by granting his subjects the very rights the introduction of which he had vehemently opposed under Rameses. In this way the epitaph of the young hero might bear the inscription which one reads in the final chapter of *The Doll,* "non omnis moriar," for his death does not prevent the execution of his ideas; they are carried through, although he does not live to see their victory.

One easily notices the internal kinship between the story of Rameses and that of Wokulski. Each of them worked out schemes concerning the welfare of those surrounding him, and each of them was prevented from turning these schemes into reality. But undoubtedly one must acknowledge the superiority of the historical romance, and it is not difficult to explain why in *The Doll* Prus was bound to follow the demands of his subject matter; he could not leave the definite precincts of reality, the limits of the historical period against the background of which he had placed the story of Wokulski. Within Polish life of the second half of the 19th century there was no room for enterprising reformers, for glorious heroes. It was thus in the semi-fictitious atmosphere of ancient Egypt that the Polish writer might indulge in carrying through his idea to its fullest extent. Certainly he possessed an astonishing knowledge of the history and life of that country, and closely followed the indications of Egyptology; yet his imagination moved more freely in the domain of reconstructed historical facts, for this reconstruction, faithful though it was, was flexible enough to answer the demands of the creative will of the writer. This was the reason why **Pharaoh** became the supreme achievement of the Polish novelist and might claim a high position in the ranks of the historical romance.

At the beginning of this article I said that Prus had embodied the ideas of his period in a more accomplished way than did any other among his contemporaries. To support this statement I should compare his novels with, at least, the most outstanding works of Sienkiewicz and Orzeszkowa, a task hardly possible within the limits of a short article. Moreover, I ought to discuss the purely artistic aspect of, at least, *The Emancipated Women,* to show the perfection of Prus as a novelist—which again cannot be done here. Still, in spite of this double limitation, I should like to reiterate my opinion in regard to one other point of a rather general nature.

Though the present essay hardly gives an adequate idea of the range of subject matter in the work of Prus, it shows that the novelist embraced in it nearly every constituent of Polish society, in the village, the town, the factories and the residences of the aristocracy; moreover, that he chronicled most of the significant alterations which had occurred in Poland in the second half of the 19th century. Having concentrated upon the historical and sociological aspect of his work, I have been obliged to ignore the problem, to what extent he has managed to create an artistic picture of the period under discussion, a vision of life convincing for modern readers. To make up for this defect, I should like to refer to "consensus omnium": I mean the established opinion of the majority of his readers, who were looking for enjoyment only in the fictitious world of his novels. Further, Prus lived in a period of great technical development, of devotion to knowledge and of a general belief that science would solve all the problems of human existence. In his novels Prus reflected not only the matter-of-fact, historical surface of his day but also its philosophical undercurrents, its hopes, beliefs and failures. It might be observed, of course, that the novelist failed to bring into unity the basic elements of his personality as a writer, that his attitude of an artist watching the coloured panorama of life was not compatible with that of a thinker probing to the very core of its phenomena; still we cannot help noticing that at the end of his career he achieved harmony in the domain of pure poetry into which the noisy voices of real life could not intrude. None the less, this highest achievement of his, apparently distant from the troubles of daily life, was rooted in it; for it was suggested by and closely bound up with the interest which the novelist had taken in the life of his period and the fortunes of his community. (pp. 695-707)

J. Krzyżanowski, "Bolesław Prus," in The Slavonic and East European Review, Vol. IX, No. 27, March, 1931, pp. 695-707.

Manfred Kridl (essay date 1956)

[*In the following excerpt, Kridl discusses Prus's writings in the context of positivist philosophy and literary realism, two influential intellectual movements that gained prominence in Poland during the late nineteenth century.*]

The most distinguished and representative writer of the epoch of positivism and realism was Bolesław Prus (penname of Aleksander Głowacki, 1845-1912). In his writings as a publicist the positivist ideology found its loftiest and most humanitarian expression. It was conceived as a world view sufficiently broad to comprise not only economic and material questions, but also spiritual and moral issues. It was based on both reason and feeling, and on the unprejudiced understanding even of conflicting tendencies; it was, in short, to represent all sides of man's highest moral and cultural interests. Prus was one of the noblest figures in the whole course of Polish literary history. His political writing falls into different periods, marked by ups and downs; there were some misunderstandings and mistakes, side by side with a true insight into historical and contemporary problems, but his work as a whole was penetrated and ruled by an exceptionally honest and integral mind; everywhere a deeply humanitarian attitude was revealed and (an essential characteristic of Prus) a great and genuine sensitivity which often colored even his journalistic writings. Born and bred to the gentry, he was emotionally tied to this class, which even in his youth was beginning to change and disappear. Nevertheless, Prus became one of the firmest and most uncompromising heralds of that transformation from the traditional world to modern times, a herald of progress, both material and spiritual, in every domain of civilization. Prus had a profound faith in humanity, in its immortality, its unlimited progress and possibilities. He looked at his own nation objectively and evaluated it soberly, as a sensible man evaluates his neighbors. His patriotism was of the kind that edified and educated rather than that which bowed to chauvinistic instincts and flattered the people. He knew and strongly believed that his nation, like every other, could exist in the modern world only by the highest exercise of all its physical and spiritual powers. All his life he urged people to this effort and tried to organize society to this end. He strove ceaselessly and in the most diverse ways to prove and explain that if the Polish nation was to survive and contribute to the progress of humanity, its life must be rid of laziness, bland indifference, and that typically Polish philosophy of 'somehow we shall manage'; it must be cured of blindness to the inevitable laws of social development and of belief in unrealistic theories of messianism and chauvinism. Prus also fought to overcome prejudices, class pride, and all forms of social animosity, and to bring about instead a clear, sober realization of the condition of society and a readiness to get down to hard work in the crafts, in commerce, industry, technology, and learning. This was, according to Prus, the only way to form useful and productive citizens out of the landed gentry, who found themselves on the sidewalks as a result of the new economic and social circumstances which began to prevail after the peasants' enfranchisement.

Whatever question Prus discussed, even if it was the most minute or local, he never took it lightly, but always treated it from the general and at the same time practical point of view. In this manner even petty questions took on a wider significance in his interpretation and became parts of a more general issue. This, of course, would not have been possible without Prus's splendid talent for writing, revealed already in his early articles, which he called 'chronicles.' During several decades he wrote these chronicles in various daily papers and periodicals; his perception of the general truth in the particular detail, his ability to detect problems to which other writers and journalists were insensible, his excellent sense of observation and talent for lively presentation, whether of people or ideas, his subtle humor which made him look leniently at human foibles, and his high humanitarian attitude, all these qualities assure the chronicles of lasting value.

Prus's humanitarianism and his profoundly human relation to his fellow men was also seen in his actions. As an example we may use a story told us by Professor Ludwik Krzywicki. When the Fighting Organization of the Polish Socialist Party engaged in active revolutionary struggle in 1905, and on the streets of Warsaw and other cities under Russian occupation bullets were flying and bombs falling in bloody demonstrations against the representatives of tsardom, Prus came out against this form of political opposition and fought against it firmly in his articles. At the same time, when he met Krzywicki, who was close to the party, Prus inquired about the fate of the families of those who perished in the street fights or were hanged on the citadel, and he gave Krzywicki money for the support of widows and orphans. This money he had saved from his modest author's pay and he preferred to give it quietly, in secret. Indeed, the Polish Socialist Party had few political opponents such as Bolesław Prus.

His so-called 'chronicles' already reveal Prus's talent as a short-story writer. Time and again in the chronicles one finds scenes from Warsaw life, dialogues and characterizations which show the artist rather than the publicist; they are conceived disinterestedly, without bias. These were the germs of tales, sketches, and short stories. Soon Prus's short stories themselves began to appear and to form a large collection which played an important part in the development of this literary genre in Poland. Although Polish literature may claim even before Prus all kinds of tales, such as oral tales, *gawędas,* and anecdotes, there were few short stories in the sense in which this genre has been understood since the time of its creator, Boccaccio. Boccaccio's short stories, as well as those of later short-story writers (Mérimée, Maupassant, or Poe, to mention only a few) were distinguished, in contrast to the novel, by their brevity, their concentration of the plot on one event, the elimination of all superfluous episodes, descriptions, psychological analyses, or extensive characterizations, as well as by their emphasis on the ending or the so-called *pointe*. Within this general framework of short-story structure there was, of course, room for different kinds and types of story, accordingly as one or another of its traits was emphasized. In Prus's collection we also have short stories of various types: sketches, which contain only 'pure' narration about events or 'pure' description (the latter are scarce and connected with the chronicles); short stories whose structural principle lies in the plot or action; longer narratives which rather approach a novelistic structure, that is, the kind in which exposition is expanded, secondary episodes occur, or a principal character, 'the hero' and his life become of central interest. A separate group is made up by the 'fantastic' short stories, which combine both fantastic and realistic material in an interesting manner. In his stories Prus touched upon the most varied subjects and problems, both of a universal and national character. One which is made extremely impressive by its masterly structure, **"Z legend dawnego Egiptu" ("A Legend of Old Egypt")**, presents a dramatic situation of extraordinary suspense. An old pharaoh is on his death bed, and his successor is awaiting the news of his death at any moment in order to take up the rule and to conduct a series of liberal reforms in the state. The situation is complicated by the fact that the young heir is also threatened by death, for he was stung by a poisonous spider. There takes place a kind of race towards death on the result of which depends the fate of the Egyptian people. If the old pharaoh dies even a moment before, the prepared decrees may be declared law as the first and last deed of the dying young pharaoh. In the contrary case everything will continue as before. Paradoxically enough (but in a way artistically motivated) the old pharaoh recovers and the heir dies. All the elements of this short story, the sketching of its characters, their psychology, the descriptions of nature (the moving of the moon behind the palm trees, which marks the inevitable passage of time), and even ethnographic and historical motifs, all serve only to heighten the action and by being skilfully subordinated to it lend it peculiar horror.

A different response is evoked by the short story entitled **"Kamizelka" ("The Waistcoat")**—an episode in the life of two poor, insignificant people, a lonely and destitute married couple. He is a petty employee, suffering from tuberculosis, which he knows but wishes to conceal from his wife; she also realizes her husband's critical condition, but does not show it. A process of mutual deception begins around the waistcoat. The husband moves over the buckle every day and informs his wife that he is 'gaining weight' because the waistcoat is becoming tighter on him, while the wife shortens the strap every day in order to maintain his conviction. On a certain snowy night in March he finally dies. She must leave the apartment and sell everything, including the waistcoat which had become the symbol of their sad love. The story is written calmly, discreetly, even with some humorous episodes, all of which makes the general effect more powerful and moving.

In **"Katarynka" ("The Barrel-Organ")** an old and wealthy gentleman suddenly discovers that the barrel-organs which he detests and has always chased away from the court-yard of his house constitute the only joy of a little blind girl across the way; he violates his habits and even decides to take the unhappy child's fate in his hands. In the short story, **"Antek,"** the author presents the fate of a talented peasant boy who wastes himself in a poor and ignorant environment, without learning or funds. He finally goes out into the world to seek happiness and assistance, but the short story does not answer the question whether he found them. The author—*antiquo modo*—addresses himself to the readers in the epilogue, urging them, should they ever meet such an Antek on their way, to stretch out a helping hand. We see that Prus has no dis dain even for such traditional devices as author intervention. Another kind of short story, where biography rather than action or plot forms the structural basis, is represented by "Michalko," the story of a poor peasant boy of limited intelligence who is not successful in town and probably never will be because he is shy, unenergetic, and fearful of everything. There are also stories that are gayer in mood, like **"Przygoda Stasia"** (**"Stasio's Adventure"**), which might be more accurately called a novelistic sketch, as more space is devoted to the description of the place of action and to the characterization of the heroes (the psychology of the child and also of his dog is excellent) than to the humorous adventure itself.

The short stories with a novelistic structure mark a transition to the real novel. One of the most distinctive among Prus's earliest works in this genre is ***Placówka*** (***The Outpost***, 1886). The central and representative figure is a Polish peasant called Ślimak (his name means *snail*). He is a shrewed man of some gifts, but heavy, lazy, and indecisive, borne down under the weight of numerous traditional prejudices and superstitions; at the same time he has the traditional peasant stubbornness and desire to keep his land. The instinct to property and his subconscious attachment to the soil is revealed in Ślimak through his resistance to the German colonists who want to buy his land. The author does not idealize his character at all, he does not make a 'hero' of him; on the contrary he introduces him at the end into such a situation in which the peasant breaks down and is ready to give up his land to the Germans. Prus penetrates the peasant psychology deeply, showing his eternal instincts and traits of which he is not aware and which constitute part of that moral 'raw material' of society, a raw material which still requires a cultural 'manufacturing process,' but which is solid and durable. The structure of the novel is based on a chronological development of events from the time of the Germans' arrival in the neighborhood until they move out again. The plot of the novel is founded on the premeditated and systematic action of the Germans, who are anxious to get Ślimak off his land, and on the peasant's passive resistance to this action; his resistance would have terminated in defeat, had it not been for the almost supernatural intervention of his dying wife. A series of episodes characterizes the peasant's relation to the landlord, to the Jewish inn-keeper, the priest, and to his own wife and children. The peasant dialect is lively and authentic; the language of the narrative and descriptive parts clear, concrete, epic, and 'realistic,' devoid of all poetization or lyricism even in the description of sad or grim scenes. The title might indicate a certain tendency towards idealization or point to an example or model; but this is absent in the execution of the novel which is characterized by objectivity and epic integrity. The characters live their own lives, and the action is governed by a purely artistic logic.

The next larger work of Prus's is ***Lalka*** (***The Doll***, 1890). Without exaggeration one may say that it is the most distinguished novel produced in Poland up to that time and the finest novel of its period. No previous novel presented such a broad view of social life nor suggested so many aspects of it, and none reached such a high level of artistic presentation. It is difficult to say to what type of novel ***The Doll*** belongs, because it combines various types. It is in many respects a 'novel of character' of the type so common in both Polish and foreign literature (Kraszewski, Korzeniowski, Walter Scott, Dickens, Thackeray, and others), which treats a main plot centered around one or a few unchanged, 'static' characters and conduct them through a series of situations and events. Such a character and 'hero' in ***The Doll*** is Stanisław Wokulski, a nobleman by origin, but businessman by profession, and at the same time a romantic and unhappy lover. The history of that character, both as an active positivist and as a lover, gives the basis of the plot. He is a representative of the new positivist world, and of the transformation from gentry to bourgeois psychology; there are, however, some romantic-erotic vestiges, or rather certain universal traits unconnected with any cultural movement. Wokulski is a complex character, highly interesting in his reactions to various issues; his forceful personality is clearly drawn and given a consistent psychological 'style.'

At the same time ***The Doll*** is also a novel in which the action does not merely serve to shape and emphasize the characteristic traits of the persons involved but plays an autonomous and significant part in the structure of the novel. Several interwoven plots can be distinguished, which enrich and complicate the main action. There is the problem of Wokulski's love for the beautiful but soulless Isabella Łęcka, which is complicated by the affection he in turn inspired in another woman; there is the question of his commercial activities, while the shop of Mincel (owned later by Wokulski) and its story become, as it were, a separate plot in the novel. Parallel with those problems runs the story of Ignacy Rzecki, one of the finest figures in Polish fiction. There is besides a whole group of bigger and smaller episodes whose task it is to complete the picture of the life of this epoch. Thanks to this multiplicity and diversity of the action, the story flows vividly and swiftly, moving the reader's attention frequently from one center of action to another and sometimes leaving him in suspense and uncertainty as to the subsequent development of one problem; it then soon intrigues him with the development of another problem which merges more or less organically with the former. There is no redundancy in Prus; those dead and empty passages which occur in the works of older writers, are absent from his. It may be said of ***The Doll*** that it contains not a single page which, regardless of its connection or lack of connection with one or another plot, does not tell something interesting or shed a new and interesting light on various phenomena. Even in such passages as Rzecki's Journal, where we are taken back into completely different times and a different spiritual atmosphere and when the frequently dramatic story of Wokulski is interrupted, we are entirely absorbed by the world Prus presents, so alive, artistically true, and close to us does it appear. The same is true of a number of episodes: the life in the shop, the fight of the students with the Baroness Krzeszowska, the trial over a doll which was supposedly stolen from her, a lawsuit against those students who do not pay their rent and frighten the landlady with a skull introduced into her flat with the help of a rope, and who later move out of their lodgings through a window; the auction of Łęcki's house with some obscure figures of middlemen, amateur advisers, and professional bidders. The book is full of excellent scenes and sketches of life in Warsaw, lively and original human types, splendid humor and the finest wit, as well as a moving, though reserved, sentiment, or revelations of a profound problem or painful social injustice.

Among the gallery of characters in *The Doll* we find representatives of all classes of contemporary Polish society, which was then undergoing one of its most significant transformations. We know from Prus, the publicist, what his attitude towards that historical process was. In *The Doll* he looks at it with the eye of an artist who sees, feels, and understands. He shows us the landed aristocracy, some of them still settled on their land, some completely bankrupt, like the Łęcki family who sought to redeem themselves by a rich marriage (this is the reason Isabella finally consents to an engagement with Wokulski). He also presents the gentry of various financial and cultural levels, as well as the budding Polish bourgeoisie, often of German origin, like the Mincel family, and groups of salesmen, draftmen, employees, and representatives of the workers and peasants. In another cross-section we see the Polish conservatives, both educated and ignorant, the gentry who try to understand the meaning of the new life and to adjust to it, as well as that gentry who have only indignation and disdain for it because it did not spare them; there are also progressives, positivists, radicals, and socialists; in addition, there are representatives of the free professions: lawyers, doctors, engineers, students; and there are the social outcasts and women of ill repute. Among the representatives of the Jewish minority there are both the good-natured, unassuming Jews, devoted to their country, and the champions of a nascent Jewish nationalism. There is even a Russian, a typical Moscow businessman, Wokulski's friend and admirer.

In his portrayal of this many-sided world Prus maintains a strictly artistic attitude, uncolored by ideological opinion but inspired by a humanitarian and artistic interest in each human soul and every social symptom. He is able to show human feeling even in that 'doll,' Isabella Łęcka, or that mummy, her father. His novel is not a satire on contemporary society, but the *epos* of an era, which, as every epic should, treats its world calmly and with moderation, devoting the same keen attention to the good as to the bad and granting equal rights to details.

In the structure of *The Doll* we observe the use of traditional devices beside new and original ones. The majority of the events in the novel are looked upon from two points of view: that of Wokulski or that of his friend, Rzecki. The latter's journal is not only a novel within a novel, which describes its author's childhood, youth, and maturity, but in many passages it directly or indirectly involves the story of Wokulski and other characters. It plays the part of a commentary on the problems, written by a man of a completely different generation, of different opinions and feelings. Rzecki, that 'last romantic,' as Wokulski calls him, comes from a generation brought up in the romantic, Napoleonic, and revolutionary ideology; his father was a soldier of Napoleon, who educated his son to venerate the emperor's ideas and even his descendants. In his youth, Rzecki took an active part in the Hungarian Revolution of 1848, and it is the most pleasant and proud memory of his life. He sees contemporary questions from the point of view of international politics, connected with the cause of Napoleon III, with which he closely associates the cause of Poland, just as his spiritual ancestors always associated it with the revolutions of oppressed peoples in Europe or with wars against the agressors. That is why Rzecki has nothing in common with the world he lives in, and only by an irony of fate is he a salesclerk and later the manager of Wokulski's shop. In fact his only civic interest is in international politics, which he cautiously designates by a 'p.' in his journal ('p. of great importance in this matter—P. at stake here,' he notes there often, interpreting every item of world news in this way). He is sincerely attached to Wokulski and impressed by his energy and enterprising spirit, but he worries about his unhappy love and even tries to suggest a more suitable life companion (whom, incidentally, he himself loves secretly). Through the character of Rzecki and his Journal the positivist epoch is linked with the preceding one; it illuminates the transitional and critical character of that epoch better than any other device in the novel, even Wokulski's 'romantic' love.

Rzecki's Journal plays still another structural role. It contains what the Germans have called the 'Vorgeschichte,' that is, the story of Wokulski before the plot proper begins. In this way his whole story is unveiled slowly and gradually, intriguing the reader more than if, following the style of older novels, the author had begun his biography from the beginning, reported it summarily in the first chapter, and then proceeded to the actual plot. There is one further source of information concerning the hero's early life, namely the conversations of the *habitués* at a little Warsaw restaurant, who, naturally, look at Wokulski's 'career' from a different point of view than Rzecki's. These and similar structural devices are used extensively in *The Doll*, and they all help to maintain the reader's attention and interest in a state of suspense, to reveal the characters and problems of the novel from different sides, and to impress them on the reader more forcefully and suggestively. *The Doll* is one of those Polish novels that describe a world close to our personal experience; we readily believe that these people actually lived and that everything occurred just the way Prus described it; such a reaction can only be evoked by a masterpiece.

After *The Doll*, Prus wrote a long, four-volume novel entitled *Emancypantki* (*The Emancipationists*, 1894). The then urgent problem of the emancipation of women and their equality in work and rights of citizenship was here conceived again in an artistic rather then a journalistic spirit and presented in all the complexity of its aspects. What is emancipation, what is its scope, what are its limits, what are the practical ways of its execution, what are the psychological transformations connected with it, and what the individual and social consequences? Those are a few of the questions posed, some of the problems with which the emancipationist movement and every woman who took part in it were faced. Who is the real emancipationist in the novel: Mrs. Latter, owner of a 'boarding school for girls' in Warsaw (a monumental picture of this kind of institution which brought up whole generations of

Polish women), an interesting and rich human personality, but forced to think mostly about her personal problems? Or Madzia Brzeska, that 'genius of feeling,' who in life followed only the instinct of her heart and not social theories, constantly wounded in her idealistic feelings by the external world, but faithful to them until the end and strongly believing that they were her mission in life? Or the noisy but empty women who affect the 'emancipationist' jargon, dress in men's clothes, cut their hair short, smoke cigarettes, speak loudly, and express themselves violently 'like men,' at the same time declaring their hatred and disdain for men? Prus devotes relatively little space to the latter, but he characterizes them in telling, satirical lines. The central figure of the novel is Madzia, and her story occupies the greater part of the novel. The point is that the title does not represent entirely the contents of the novel, and the problem of emancipation, introduced in the first volume as a parallel to the history of Mrs. Latter, is gradually abandoned in the next volumes until finally it almost disappears. As a result, *The Emancipationists* becomes, like *The Doll,* a broad social canvass, in which the 'woman' problem in the sense of the epoch is seen only as one of many. But the question of womanhood in a more general sense, the question of woman's role in the life of individuals and of society, is followed in the character of Madzia throughout the subsequent volumes of the novel as an important, if not the central point of interest. This question appears, again as in *The Doll,* against a panoramic background of the life of contemporary society. Two main pictures stand out in striking contour and constitute two separate wholes within the novel. One is the life in Mrs. Latter's boarding-school and her personal drama; the other is life in the little town where Madzia seeks shelter after her first failure. These are like two specimen cells of social life, which the author draws with the passion of a born epic writer and with his characteristic ability to capture, as it were, social phenomena 'alive.' The Warsaw boarding-school represents a world enclosed in itself, socially important because it forms the character and minds of future wives, mothers, and social leaders; the provincial town is a miniature of society, a microcosmic version of its structure, its characteristic traits, its qualities and foibles, and its biological force. Prus shows us the reflection of the whole social sea in this little provincial drop, magnifying these little, ordinary people, petty, unimportant problems, intrigues, gossip, hatreds, and types of various social classes. He shows us both universal and national psychological traits, values of social forces, and the problem of this society's perseverance and adjustment in the new world. These are the questions with which an attentive reader is faced, although the author draws no conclusions but presents a skilful selection of material for thought looked at from many sides.

Even from the discussion above one may see that the structure of *The Emancipationists* differs from that of *The Doll*. It is looser and freeer, the whole broken up into separate parts that are linked chiefly through the person of the heroine. The episodes grow into separate tales which are not necessarily tales of a novelistic character. The last volume introduces a series of chapters which include an unusual résumé of a whole metaphysical system. This system is exposed by Dr. Dębicki, a character introduced into the novel only for this purpose. Regardless of the intellectual value of his theories and regardless of whether they are an expression of the author's opinion or simply a picture of certain intellectual trends opposed to positivism, this whole digression is too extensive and not sufficiently linked with the plot of the novel. It must be recalled, however, that in the novels of the most distinguished West-European and Russian writers such philosophic, religious, historical or other digressions were not at all rare: for instance, in some of the novels of Balzac, Tolstoy, or Dostoyevski. And, among more recent writers in Poland, like Żeromski, we find long exposés or discussions between the characters, which go far beyond the subject and structure of the novel. Such digressions must be accepted as the external expression of the authors' spiritual need to take part, even if only in an indirect manner, in the discussion of general questions.

The third great novel of Prus is *Faraon* (*Pharaoh,* 1896). Here the author of so many short stories and novels about contemporary society, who was apparently engrossed in the life and problems of his time, set his imagination back into the distant past to the days of ancient Egypt. This serves as one more proof of the difference between the personality of the man and that of the artist. The artist found in ancient Egypt an interesting and colorful picture of human life, material of universal and eternal interest to every time and country. He also found there problems of a social nature which have recurred in one form or another since the organization of the first states in the world. In *Pharaoh,* Prus shows the functioning of a political and social organism, the Egyptian state, at a relatively advanced stage of evolution already using some of the methods typical of modern states. Egypt is nominally ruled by the pharaoh, honored almost as a deity, but the actual power rests in the hands of the priestly caste, wise and learned men armed with all the knowledge of their time, who are ruthless and cruel against all opposition and immovable in the face of all attempts to reduce their power. This is then the rule of a caste or clique, which has been so often seen in world history. The psychology of the ruling caste is masterfully depicted by Prus. It manifests itself in the priests' hierarchy and their unconditional obedience to superiors, in their habit of surrounding themselves with an air of holiness and mystery, and in keeping the people in ignorance, poverty, and humiliation in order to gain the support of the wealthy. It also manifests itself in their watchful care over the most holy pharaoh, making him even a member of the caste in order to bind him more securely, as well as in their accumulation of great wealth extorted from the people and in their foreign policy, whereby they conclude treaties and declare wars according to their own interests. In short, they control the entire apparatus of state. They cultivate learning not for its own sake, but for purposes of power; they educate scholars in various fields of learning and profit by their services in order to blind the people with 'supernatural' phenomena which they presumably control. What we have here summarized is, of course, presented in the novel through a series of characters, pictures, scenes, events, and conflicts. The crux of the plot lies in the struggle of the young pharaoh, Rameses, against the omnipotence of the priests. While still heir to the throne, he tries to break loose from their rule; when he becomes pharaoh he undertakes a veritable war against them. Inspired by the best of intentions, he contemplates social reform and alleviation of the distress of the common people; he has a general idea of regenerating his country and regarding the interests of the people rather than of one caste. He has clever ideas, noble feelings, and surrounds himself by honest and talented men, but he lacks experience and acquaintance with his opponents, he does not know the extent of his own power, and wants the ability to prepare the final blow systematically. He is too confident and believes enthusiasm will win the day; perhaps he does not know his own people and its psychology shaped by centuries of ignorance and superstition. When the showdown finally comes, and when it seems that the whole country is on his side and against the priests, when the latter are besieged in a temple by the army and the people, he loses suddenly and irrevocably as a result of a truly satanic ruse on the part of his opponents. At the moment of highest tension during the fight, when it appears that the temple will be seized at any moment, the archpriest, Herhor, appears on its walls dressed in festive clothes and surrounded by the priestly orders. He solemnly urges the populace to leave the temple in peace, and when that does not help he turns to the gods and hands over to them the care of 'the holy sanctuary attacked by traitors and blasphemers.' Then is heard the voice of the god of the sun, Osiris (staged by the priests) who declares that he is turning his face away from the damned people. At that very moment a terrible thing happens: the light of day slowly begins to go out, the earth is gradually covered with darkness. One can easily imagine the effect of this phenomenon. The people are mad with fear, the army throws down its weapons and runs away; the air is full of desperate cries for mercy. At that moment the archpriest again turns to Osiris with a plea for mercy, which ends just as the sun reappears. But the catastrophe of Rameses and his cause is inevitable. He still attempts to seize the temple with the help of a unit of faithful soldiers, but it turns out that half of them had been bribed by the priests. Their commander is killed, and Rameses perishes by the hand of a murderer hired by the priests.

What had happened? What was that miracle that saved the temple and its priests? It was not a miracle at all, but their knowledge which empowered the final blow against their opponent. The priests knew from a trusted astronomer that in those days a complete eclipse was to take place; they directed the battle in such a way as to make its climax coincide with the eclipse. In this way they decisively vanquished Rameses and affirmed their own power, which was signalled by the archpriest Herhor's ascension to the throne as pharaoh.

One must not suppose that Prus makes any allusions to contemporary or later conditions in any passage of the novel or that he points to analogies between the Egyptian priests' system of rule and their later spiritual successors. Prus only conveys a suggestive and often fascinating picture, presenting the caste system without the help of abstract explanation, through the lives and story of his characters. In other words, the system emerges of itself, through the actions of the people and the course of events and through all the scenes and episodes in the life of all social classes of ancient Egypt. This novel marks one of the great triumphs of a powerful creative imagination which can bring to life a world long since dead and make it close to us. This imagination, however, is backed by a thorough knowledge of ancient Egypt and a unique understanding for the social conditions which lie at the basis of all regimes, including that of the Egyptian priests.

Although this work does not possess an 'intriguing' plot in the traditional sense expected of fiction (the love story of Rameses for a beautiful Jewess is little more than a fragment), and although the foundation of the action rests, on—it would seem—such an 'abstract' subject as the fight for power, *Pharaoh* is one of the most impressive historical novels not only in Polish but in European literature. It belongs to that rare European genre of historical novel in which the principal subject is not war, battle, and adventure, in which the heroes are not vainglorious soldiers, and the action not a series of exploits designed to cover these heroes with glory. It is a profound and varied picture of the life and processes of society, in which it may be compared only with Flaubert's *Salammbô*. The plot and action are moving in spite of the absence of all the 'extraordinary' features of war or mystery. They possess great dramatic suspense, skillfully developed and graduated through a series of events, until the final, unexpected but inevitable catastrophe. The fact that it is unexpected and at the same time artistically justified by an intrinsic necessity arising out of the pattern of previous events, combined with the greatness of the cause which fails, lends to the ending of *Pharaoh* a note of grandeur bordering on tragedy.

We first met Prus as the leading figure of Polish positivism. Though no more than an outline, this discussion of his novels should have substantiated the idea that he was also the most outstanding representative of realism in Poland. His work distinguishes an epoch in the development of this literary genre and marks its summit. (pp. 360-73)

Manfred Kridl, "Positivism and Realism," in his A Survey of Polish Literature and Culture, *translated by Olga Scherer-Virski, Mouton, 1956, pp. 347-402.*

Jerzy Pietrkiewicz (essay date 1960)

[*In the following excerpt, Pietrkiewicz discusses the presentation of failure in Prus's major novels, focusing on Prus's moral and social justification of the failures associated with each of his protagonists.*]

Noble success, like triumphant goodness, is rarely convincing as a theme in literature; yet the didactic writer continues to be a matchmaker between man and virtue, generously rewarding both with the improbabilities of his plots. The positive hero of yesterday had to do good. His modern counterpart, however, has been so much exposed to doubt by the psychologically-minded critics that even the least assuming of his actions are thought to be suspect. This scepticism is further deepened by the absurd treatment of positive characters in social-realist fiction.

The positivist novel of the 19th century tried to achieve

verisimilitude by making the hero's virtues dependent on his environment and upbringing. The formula was basically honest, and though later it led to some excesses (e.g. when novelists gave heredity the status of dogma), it nevertheless widened the scope of fiction. During the positivist period in Poland the novel became the chief literary medium, and nearly all the classics of Polish fiction appeared in the thirty years between 1870 and 1900. The representative novelist of this period was undoubtedly Bolesław Prus (1845-1912), because his more successful rival, Sienkiewicz, preferred historical romances to straight realistic stories.

The ambiguities inherent in the concept of the positive hero have added to the difficulty of relating Prus to the literature of his age. Many of Prus's readers still take it for granted that his characters, convincing as they are, must illustrate ideas, social and national, and utter significant asides, as if from the author. Prus himself invited this kind of interpretation. In his public life he was the opposite of an enigmatic man of letters: he declared his views on the controversial causes of his day and urged his public to be aware of what was happening around them. His 'weekly chronicles' dealt with all sorts of practical matters over many years. None of these journalistic pieces would have survived however, had his novels proved unreadable today. The customary equation between Prus the didactic commentator and Prus the imaginative writer can surely now be set aside, so that we may meet his characters face to face.

The major novels of Prus number only four, beginning with *Placówka* (*The Outpost,* 1886) and ending with *Faraon* (*The Pharaoh,* 1897). He was not a prolific novelist, and though some of his books are of considerable length, one feels that he knew just how far his pen could carry him and did not go, like most of his contemporaries, beyond the point of exhaustion. Even his last completed novel, *Dzieci* (*The Children,* 1909), which shows artistic weakness and personal strain as well, is far more interesting than, say, some of Hardy's later books.

In the four novels to be examined here, the elusive character of their respective heroes is the puzzling feature which they all have in common; but it is also an unexpected strength which lifts these novels above the transitory problems of the time and the formal limitations of plots with a thesis. Perhaps Prus was wholly unaware of this similarity within his method of characterisation; but whatever conclusion the critic may arrive at, the valid line for him to pursue is Prus's unresolved personal conflict, which penetrated into his fictitious characters and altered them against the cheerful nagging of positivist thought.

The heroes of his major novels are in fact portraits of failure, and theirs is an all-embracing kind of failure which involves the collapse of successful plans, material and spiritual losses, and in two cases the loss of life at the end of the story. What fascinates the modern reader in Prus's use of psychological motivation rests on this repeated emphasis in all the four novels. He feels the need to justify failure in moral and social terms, pointing with his endearing persuasiveness to the ultimate nobility of such failures so that they appear to him and to us as successes within the larger frame of things. This gives Prus's writing a truly Christian quality of compassion and, at the same time, discreetly suggests a heart-felt personal confession.

Oddly enough, it is his fiction, including his historical novel about ancient Egypt, which provides the key to his life, and not all the confessions of his perceptive mind which he scattered throughout the thirty-five years of his literary career in diverse periodicals and newspapers. At the height of his fame he summed up his views in a book with the forbidding title *Najogólniejsze ideały życiowe* (*The Most General Ideals of Life,* 1901); but this is a misleading door through which to approach him, for it stands too widely open and has no key. To probe into an artist's personality need not necessarily mean to unmask his sham and bashful secrets. Prus's agoraphobia is well known and his idiosyncrasies have been duly reported; but no biographical malice could change him into a fraud or a clinical case. He had one of the most sympathetic personalities among great writers, in some ways resembling Chekhov's, and his gentle nature illuminated by the wisdom of resignation, deserved the epigraph which was carved on his grave: 'To the heart of hearts.' Yet goodness in real life as in fiction tends to inspire flabby legends, and judging by the popular aura about Prus, even his burning gentleness seems to have thinned out into tepid gentility.

On carefully re-reading the first chapters of Szweykowski's biography of Prus, one begins to piece together an early portrait of the artist from the documents. The sources of potential conflict are, as could be expected, an orphan's childhood, a shock of sudden disillusionment in adolescence, and high ambitions frustrated in the university. With due insight, Szweykowski stressed in particular the importance of Prus's bitter experiences in the rising of 1863, which he joined as a boy of eighteen. All these facts from his early years are given artistic meaning when they appear transformed within the themes of his novels. It is better to deal with them as part of the literary context, each new disguise made more telling by the repeated process of change. Prus became a successful novelist; but deep in his heart he considered himself a failure before the vivid image of his youthful self. The feeling remained with him during his best creative years, and for this reason it is worthwhile to revalue his characters as studies of justified failure.

Placówka (*The Outpost*) was Prus's first novel, and it came after a series of short stories, some of which were tinged with sentimental didacticism. The subject which he chose for this full exercise in the narrative technique had a social interest, and the central character belonged to the new class of realistic heroes: he was a peasant and not particularly bright at that. His name—Ślimak—suggested in itself a snail-slow deliberation and caution; in fact, the behaviour of Ślimak throughout the book could be regarded as the author's exaggeration in the anti-heroic direction.

The plot of *Placówka,* however, depends not on individuals but on the activities and tensions of two social groups, Polish and German. Their accidental meeting involves the reluctant Ślimak far more than any of his private decisions; and even these usually come from his wife. His passivity is, in effect, intended to be a dramatic contrast; and the contrast becomes clear with the arrival of the German colonists who are a well organised group. One of the prospective settlers wants to buy Ślimak's land, because it includes a hill suitable for the building of a windmill. At first Ślimak's resistance to tempting offers and pressure has a purely passive character; but later, as one misfortune after another befalls his family and property, the resistance changes into a struggle for survival, and the small farm, which will not be sold, is a kind of outpost after all. This time Prus allows no sentimentality to muffle the tone of his narrative. On the contrary, his hero is so ill-equipped to stand up to his fate that the reader cannot help wishing that the author had not put Ślimak into such a difficult predicament.

The Outpost seems to be founded on the moral justification of failure. Within his restricted environment Ślimak moves from one failure to another, and towards the end he is ready to give in. It is only the death of his wife which stops him before new circumstances come to his rescue and frustrate the plans of the colonists who decide to leave the village altogether. But even this ultimate victory of Ślimak has an air of melancholy about it, and when at the close of the story he reflects on the turn of events, he is neither proud of his improved social position in the village nor happy with his new wife. Yet he has passed a test of inner strength, and life has surprised him by revealing this strength to him, the least assertive of heroes.

A sophisticated reader of *The Outpost* may see the obvious positivist ideal in the group of German colonists whom Prus portrayed without prejudice. He goes so far as to contrast German industry and efficiency with the less enterprising habits of Polish peasants, and he makes the Ślimaks watch the strangers at work and at prayer, now with distrust, now with admiration. For they are a people determined to succeed; their deep penetration into Polish territory is doubly dangerous because of its impact on peasants like Ślimak. After the Franco-Prussian war this was not a surprising attitude to adopt; but already by then Prus must have queried the positive values in success. What could a rational man do, if his chances were bound up with defeat? The Ślimaks of his country were at a hopeless disadvantage when faced with the German kind of success; yet they could still take a gamble on failure and go through it, as though it meant a black night of spiritual trial. This is perhaps why Prus chose such a passive if not a negative hero to defend his village outpost. Instinctively, he was beginning in his imaginative writing to grope for the paradox of his own strength.

Lalka (*The Doll,* 1890), which appeared in book form four years after *Placówka*, is a very different kind of novel both in scope and in style. Its ambitious panorama of society, with three main character studies, recalls the framework of George Eliot's *Middlemarch* and in part that of Thackeray's *Vanity Fair.* Warsaw seems to be as much the feminine element of the novel as its 'doll' Izabela, and the city comes to life in every detail, carefully selected to recapture the exact atmosphere of the years 1878-9. The artistic success of *Lalka* was apparent to Prus's contemporaries, and it has remained one of the most admired books in Polish literature.

Thackeray's definition, 'a novel without a hero', printed under the title *Vanity Fair,* could also be applied to Prus's novel, for although it contains a central character study (Wokulski) and two full portraits (Izabela Łęcka and Ignacy Rzecki), none of them is 'heroic' enough to dominate the social theme or control the workings of the plot. It is known that originally Prus had a wider title for his story, viz. *Trzy pokolenia* (*Three Generations*); and however much he departed from his first concept, the receding perspective of the generations is still evident in 'The Memoirs of an Old Shop-Assistant' which cover about forty years and are ingeniously interwoven with the main narrative.

Much has been said in Polish criticism about the writer of these memoirs, the shop manager Rzecki who works in Wokulski's store, but in fact plays the part of his confidant and adviser, mothering and worshipping him in turn. He is an incurable romantic, in contrast to Wokulski who belongs to the new positivist generation; but somehow—so the critics complain—Wokulski keeps his restless feet in both camps and is dragged down by the romanticism of love, the love being, of course, directed to an unworthy creature, the aristocratic doll Izabela. The critics assume a black-and-white interpretation of literary characters. But is Wokulski's ideological indecision a weakness ascribed to him by the author, or is the author responsible for drawing his features clumsily, so that they seem to characterise a weak man? The portrait of Wokulski has the same accuracy of detail as the city around him, which witnesses his spectacular rise to the pinnacle of the middle class and his downfall into the moral enigma of suicide. Because of Prus's adherence to exact detail, one must not impose a preconceived psychological type on an individual like Wokulski who is convincingly human both in his prosaic behaviour and in his romantic obsession, in clever financial schemes and in silly gestures.

By departing from the true-to-type realism of novelists with a message, Prus created a very original character. Just how original Wokulski is in Polish fiction, one begins to grasp after collating the facts of his biography, which are scattered throughout Rzecki's memoirs and in the allusions casually made by him or other characters in the narrative proper. What a revealing study of a 19th-century Pole his life turns out to be. A nobleman by birth, he had to earn his living from boyhood and experienced his first trial of idealism in the rising of 1863, which ended for him, as for many of his compatriots, in Siberia. But, we gather from hints in the story, the enforced stay in Siberia was for the disillusioned idealist a lesson in positivist thinking. Not only did he fully mature, away from the emotional constrictions of his native environment, but he also realised where the trends of the modern age were leading, and decided to become a man of science. Allowed to return to Poland, he diverted his new enthusiasm to the idea of offering his knowledge for the needs of his people; but again his idealism had to suffer a disappointment, and he saw himself instead as a useless member of that new class of frustrated men, the intelligentsia.

At this point Wokulski compromised with life. The would-be hero embarked on a shopkeeper's career in J.

Mincel's firm: he secured his prospects by marrying Mrs Mincel, an elderly widow, endured her humiliating jealousy for five years, and after her death was amply rewarded with her fortune. The shop now bore the names of J. Mincel and S. Wokulski, the old faithful Rzecki still serving loyally behind the counter. Here came the big opportunity for the man who had managed to outwit his early failures. The chronological narrative of *The Doll* (as distinguished from Rzecki's recollections) deals in fact with this adventure of inheritance, which leads to real love for a very unreal sort of woman. A friendship with a financial genius from Moscow had taught Wokulski how to use his capital in a spectacular way by trading in army supplies, and the Bulgarian war gave him his big opportunity. In six months he made 'ten times more', as the text says, 'than two generations of the Mincels had done during half a century'. This would have been a sufficient antidote to the sense of failure in a man completely possessed by success; but Wokulski wanted a warm human justification. Social influence, mingling with the aristocracy, charitable acts and other by-products of life at the top, could not obliterate in him the memory of the clambering-up.

Relentlessly, Prus pursued this inner uncertainty in his hero to its bitter end. Wokulski was over forty when he fell in love with Izabela Łęcka. The timing could not have been better from a novelist's point of view. Any level-headed woman would have succeeded with Wokulski at this age in finding the weak spot in his character. But Izabela had a greater power at her disposal: frigidity combined with snobbery proved a deadly weapon in her amorous duel with Wokulski. And before he could even collect his wits, he had allowed his romantic love to grow into an obsession. Deprived of fulfilment, this obsession was bound to attack the cells of his personality and gradually to destroy them all like cancer. Suicide, its moral meaning apart, must have seemed to him a mere gesture. The pages of *The Doll* which describe the growth of this obsession are guided by a psychologist's insight. A modern novelist, Maria Dąbrowska, has commented on it in her perceptive introduction to the 1955 edition of Prus's works. There are two men in Wokulski, she writes, one possessed by his love and the other watching the possessed one with cold and condemning despair.

It would be irrelevant here to analyse Prus's portrayal of Izabela, which certainly matches that of Wokulski. What is, however, most relevant to the problem of failure, concerns Prus's use of autobiographical material. There seems still to be some lingering misunderstanding about an author's fidelity to his private experiences. It is true that he rarely stoops to treat his life as a storage of ready-made scenes and situations and prefers instead to rely on his imaginative faculties; but self-knowledge is undoubtedly his best instrument for measuring human and natural models. Literature may become for the writer a corrective kind of experience, partly resolving his past problems, partly offering tentative solutions to acts half-committed in his existence between facts and imaginings. Prus was this type of writer, and the best of his novels seem to have been moulded by the corrective force within his literary experience.

Only an enthusiast for biographical conjectures would claim that Wokulski is the auto-portrait of Prus. Nevertheless he has to go through a series of failures similar to those which Prus himself experienced. The handicaps imposed by his origin and early upbringing also resemble Prus's own disadvantages which he was slow to forget. They both have an unhappy childhood in common: hence Prus's portraits of children drawn with exquisite understanding, especially in his short stories, and hence Wokulski's protective attitude to people like Węgielek, Wysocki and Mrs Stawska's little daughter. Youthful idealism is well reflected in those letters of Prus which have survived. They contain phrases like the following:

> Our main tasks are: learning, research and general self-education. If we devote our life to them and draw others towards them, progress will benefit, peace and well-being will flourish on earth, there will be no quarrels between people and the law, or among individuals, no superstitions. . . .

But the experience of the rising struck perhaps deeper than any disappointment of his later years. The rebel in Prus, if there was any rebel in him, perished at the age of eighteen. What precisely happened remains shrouded in mystery. All we know is that Prus was wounded, captured, and sent to prison in Lublin, where he must have undergone a serious crisis. His family pleaded with the Russian authorities on his behalf, and being a minor, he was saved from the further consequences which Wokulski had to bear. In *Dzieci* (*The Children*), based on the events of 1905 and published three years before his death, Prus showed little patience with the revolutionary mood of the times, and the novel widened the breach between himself and the new generation. The feeling of estrangement from his own people, which grew in Wokulski after the defeat of 1863, was also not unfamiliar to Prus, as his letters to a friend show.

Equally revealing is Prus's great dream of a scientific career which ended, for him as for Wokulski, in the reality of a mere hobby. He had studied for two years in the faculty of mathematics and physics at the university of Warsaw which was then the influential *Szkoła Główna*. But instead of completing his studies he had to tackle odd jobs and lead a precarious existence until he made a name for himself as a humorist in popular periodicals. Like Chekhov, he became a writer almost by chance. What remained of the scientist's dream was a positivist outlook and a respect for applied knowledge, especially for new theories and inventions which he was to use as a subtheme in his novels. Thus Wokulski is attracted to the mad genius of Geist who believes he can invent a metal lighter than air. The money which Wokulski gives Geist seems to be a retribution for his own failure in science.

This interrelation between Prus and his fictitious character occurs, so to speak, in a land of the mind inhabited by their past ghosts and frustrations. Wokulski's genesis is therefore vital to the understanding of his eventual failure after a series of successes. The biographer of Prus points out that *The Doll* was written during a period of morbid pessimism. He further suggests that it followed a second crisis in Prus's life. If so, the earlier crisis must have emerged from the subconscious layers of his memory and produced strange analogies in his artistic imagination. We see the result of them in his greatest novel, and particularly in its central character, the unheroic Wokulski.

Whatever meaning we try to attach to pathology in characterisation, it does not explain Prus's method, and it is therefore impossible to agree with Szweykowski's definition of *The Doll* as 'a novel about the communal pathology of society'. Although the narrative vividly describes the decay of some social structures, it embraces far more than this, accepting the diversity of life rather than rejecting its negative aspects which are shown with humorous detachment. The originality of the novel hangs on the concept of Wokulski, which in turn depends on the justification of his failure. After surveying Wokulski's life in his memory, Rzecki reflects:

'One has to admit that in such conditions he did his best.' The phrase *Non omnis moriar,* used twice in the final chapter of the novel, justifies the ultimate sense of Wokulski's struggles. They were, one feels, not entirely in vain.

After achieving the unified effect of *Lalka,* Prus turned to a rigid formula which, ironically enough, produced his most diffuse novel. *Emancypantki* (*The Emancipated Women,* 1893) could be taken as an illustration of faults typical of the *roman à these*. Prus's thesis happens to be the failure of emancipation in terms of social adjustment and its impact on naïve enthusiasts among women. Much of his criticism is nowadays of only mild antiquarian interest, and since the novel follows a meandering plot, with too many incidental characters, the total impression seems to be close to boredom.

Prus upset the balance from the start by deciding on an almost saintly heroine in the person of Madzia Brzeska. That she was modelled on a real character made matters even worse, because an author's admiration is hardly a safe ingredient when he wants to copy an ideal from life. In contrast to Madzia, other women in *Emancypantki* are either enlarged into grotesque types (e.g. Miss Howard) or invented to fill up significant vignettes. Only Mrs Latter, the head of a private school for girls where Madzia works for a time, has the authority of a well-motivated character. Needless to say, the male creatures interfering in the story come out not too badly.

Mrs Latter has become an embittered failure, trying to assert herself through her profession; but Madzia, positive and sweet-natured as she is, seems to be going in the same direction. Her trusting naïvety attracts every kind of disappointment, as if Prus wanted to draw from Madzia's emancipation the moral that the willingness to learn through experience is bound to bring sorrow to a truly good person. The novel *Emancypantki,* in spite of its shortcomings, presents yet another attempt of Prus to justify failure, this time in a subject with a thesis.

In contrast to *Emancypantki* there is no doubt about the quality of *Faraon* (*The Pharaoh,* 1897), which discusses under the guise of a historical novel a problem relevant to all epochs of human history, namely the workings and maintenance of political power. *The Pharaoh* deserves a better translation than that of Jeremiah Curtin. For it is Prus's most intelligent statement, capable of reaching a wider public outside Poland. Again the central character of the novel mirrors the moral significance of failure. He is Ramzes (Rameses) XIII, for whom Prus invented a reign and a disastrous end. As for the historical background, it seems quite immaterial whether it was constructed out of many or very few sources. It serves the purpose of the novel admirably, giving its hero a social and political context as well as a depth of tradition.

The originality in Prus's interpretation of Ramzes lies in his youthful innocence coupled with the sense of supreme power which he has to test on becoming a ruler. In fact, two out of the three volumes of the novel are devoted to the preparations of Ramzes for his high office. The young and idealistic heir to the throne of Egypt must learn, slowly and patiently, how the intricate mechanism of the state works before he realises that the centre of real power lies in the hands of the priests. This informative part of the book resembles the type of educational novel popular in the 18th century. When Ramzes becomes Pharaoh, he challenges the caste of the priests, at the head of which stands his genuine rival, Herhor. The archpriest contrives to apply the secret knowledge of astronomy to defeat the Pharaoh's supporters during an eclipse of the sun. The idealist is killed, and the old mechanism of power remains in the experienced hands of Herhor who thinks it safer however to carry out some of the reforms which Ramzes had planned and he himself had previously opposed. The novel ends like a chronicle with a dispassionate summary of events.

The plot in a way illustrates a thesis which happens to be intelligent and of universal interest; yet the credibility of the atmosphere depends to a large extent on the portrayal of Ramzes XIII. Through his inquiring eyes we see the pattern of Egyptian life, and through his growing awareness we commit our intellect to all his noble ambitions. He is endearingly youthful, even when he hurts those whom he once loved; and it is precisely in this sympathetic presentation that a link exists between him and Wokulski. They both have the warm curiosity of adolescence and both are quick learners. But in *The Doll* the genesis of Wokulski has to be pieced together, whereas in *The Pharaoh* the genesis of the hero fills the larger part of the story, and being told directly, achieves a different psychological emphasis. With Wokulski, the genesis of his character causes cracks in his middle age; Ramzes on the other hand is all genesis, and because of it his downfall seems more heroic than Wokulski's. Yet neither of them can be called a tragic hero. The birthright of Ramzes places him at once at the top of the ladder; unlike Wokulski he is not forced to climb it and by doing so to experience humiliations. Nevertheless he has this in common with Wokulski that at every point of the story he can avert his fate. True tragedy closes all emergency exits: there is no escape from it. But Ramzes walks brisk and confident towards catastrophe, blinded by his own enthusiasm; and his blindness, like the obsession of Wokulski, determines failure, not pure tragedy.

By bringing his characters down to the level of human weakness, Prus gave their struggles a meaning independent both of the stories which contain them and of any topical message. *The Pharaoh* in particular defies the 19th-century convention of historical fiction. Instead of being a stilted romance from the remote past, it presents a credible situation in which history seems to stand on trial before modern man.

Prus finds the justification of failure to be morally necessary and psychologically honest. There are passages in *The Doll* and *The Pharaoh* which would lose their relevance to the human predicament if they were not meant to justify failure. We read in *The Pharaoh* chapter vi, vol. III:

> Despair overcame him because he felt that with the last talent spent, his power would end as well as his life. But here his thoughts turned abruptly. The Lord of Egypt halted in the middle of the chamber and reflected: 'What can happen to me? Only death. I shall go away to my glorious ancestors, to Rameses the Great. . . . How could I tell them that I perished without defending myself? Eternal shame would be then with me, after the miseries of my life on earth'.

And another reflection from a character about to die (chapter xiv, vol. III):

> In his mind he surveyed all his life, its achievements, dangers, hopes and ambitions—and everything now seemed to him a mere trifle. . . . This is vanity and dust. Far worse: it is an illusion. Only one thing is great and charged with truth: death.

There is no ambiguity about the positive meaning of Ramzes's defeat. The words *Non omnis moriar,* which are used as an indirect comment on Wokulski's death, echo again in the chronicle-like report of events after the reign of Ramzes XIII. His ideas did not perish with him. On the contrary, they demand realisation from the ruthless politician, Herhor. The very fact that he becomes Ramzes's successor on the throne of Egypt confirms the ironic moral of this novel about failure.

Prus lived in a country of maimed possibilities. After his first crisis in 1863 and the collapse of his plans in the university, he learnt how to adjust himself to the abnormal conditions imposed by the tripartite existence of Poland. In his didactic writing he almost bullied his countrymen to admire efficiency and thrift. But he could not practise hearty optimism in his literature: he was too good an artist for that. Observation taught him to face the realities of his Polish environment; positivist ideals made him distrust heroic gestures. With this equipment he embarked on a novelist's career. When he came to fit his characters into the stories which he invented for them, his own experience of failure began to illuminate their actions.

His first character study had a modest range. What however added original touches to the behaviour of Ślimak was his unexpected victory. This victory, like the failures which had preceded it, happened outside his consciousness. The peasant was made aware of them by their results; but he seemed incapable of becoming a participant. In peasants like Ślimak perhaps lay the only source of collective strength. In Wokulski and Ramzes, Prus followed the growth of character, making them both introspective. As studies of failure they complement each other.

In a paradoxical way the positivist Prus finally resorted to religious beliefs similar to those of the Polish romantics. They had tried to justify the national tragedy by giving a messianic interpretation to history. Prus, however, understood the ways of political cynicism and the appetites of empires, but he could not accept the practical philosophy of success. Being a Christian, he preferred to follow the clearest example of a fully justified failure. He would surely have agreed with these words from a poem by Hilaire Belloc:

> Prince, may I venture (since it's only you)
> To speak discreetly of The Crucified?
> He was extremely unsuccessful too:
> The Devil didn't like Him, and He died.

(pp. 95-107)

Jerzy Pietrkiewicz, "Justified Failure in the Novels of Bolesław Prus," in The Slavonic and East European Review, *Vol. XXXIX, No. 92, December, 1960, pp. 95-107.*

An excerpt from Prus's short story "The Dream"

There was in fourth-year Medicine a certain poor student. He used to give tuition for six roubles a month at a railway-driver's home in the Warsaw suburb of Praga, and also for three roubles at the home of a shopkeeper, who lived in the suburb of Podwale. He himself lived on Piwna Street, on a fourth floor costing four roubles, which systematically he did not pay—not because he wanted to ruin the landlord but because he was not stinking rich.

He wore a uniform frayed at the seams and with the buttons rubbed to a red copper. His trousers were so threadbare that actually they were rather like logarithms of real trousers. The pockets he had nicknamed the Torricellian vacuum; there was nothing in them, so eventually they fled in shame from the clothing and their places were taken by holes.

Bolesław Prus in his "The Dream," translated by Peter Rennie, in The Slavonic and East European Review *XXIX, No. 72 (December 1950).*

Jerzy R. Krzyżanowski (essay date 1976)

[*In the following essay, Krzyżanowski discusses irony in* The Doll.]

In one of his most celebrated statements concerning the purpose of art, Joseph Conrad once wrote [in his *The Nigger of the "Narcissus"*] that "a work of art that aspires, however humbly, to the condition of art should be defined as a single-minded attempt to render the highest kind of justice to the visible universe, by bringing to light the truth, manifold and one, underlying its every aspect." A noble task indeed, and to the extent that literary criticism is a kind of art, the same principle should apply to its purposes and standards as well. But works of art must be available and known in order for critics to attempt to render justice to them, and many valuable works have been ignored only because they have not been translated into an easily accessible language.

The recent first English publication of *The Doll* by Bolesław Prus provides us with an opportunity to rediscover a literary masterpiece of the Polish nineteenth-century novel. Eighty-two years after its original publication in 1890, *The Doll* comes to the English-speaking readers and must either win their approval as a major part of nineteenth-century fiction, or fall into oblivion as have many other novels of that time. It is the purpose of this paper to make an attempt at rendering justice to the novel's artistic values, particularly by emphasizing its irony, a basic structural device on which the whole novel hinges.

The history of *The Doll*'s reception is itself somewhat ironic, and a brief survey of its fate will add to our understanding of the problems a critic of Prus' fiction faces even today. Originally serialized in a Warsaw newspaper, *Kurjer Codzienny*, in 1887-1889, *The Doll* (*Lalka*) began to draw criticism even before it appeared in a book form. T. T. Jeż accused it of being tendentious, Piotr Chmielowski tried to prove that its composition was faulty, while Józef Kotarbiński compared it to "a rich park established without any plan, without harmony between the groups of trees," etc. Most critics credited Prus with great talent and congratulated him on his first major novel, despite certain weaknesses in its composition. The first major attack against *The Doll* was launched by Aleksander Świętochowski, the most influential personality in the Positivist movement of the 1880s. He took to task the characters in *The Doll:*

> Let us imagine a small gallery of beautiful sculptures which, by some accident, got busted and which someone not very well acquainted with their forms put together again partly by instinct, thus exchanging many parts of their bodies. Let us imagine, then, that after such a restoration Hercules has received Adonis' head, Venus with a head of Diana, Cupido with the legs of little Bacchus—and then we will have a picture of *The Doll,* and partly of all major novels of its author.

The controversy about the novel's value and its drawbacks persisted for years, and it is only in most recent times that its place in Polish literature has been at last firmly established. As the noted Polish critic, Kazimierz Wyka, stated:

> If a novel could possess its own normative aesthetics, and if such an aesthetics was to be written based on a selected Polish novel, all that would be needed would be *The Doll,* I believe, . . . for in that particular novel it is its form which is best balanced and therefore the most invisible, seemingly the most obvious—so obvious because it is not sufficient in any of its parts.

The Doll has received extensive attention on the part of Modern Polish critics. There are at least five major monographic studies devoted entirely to it, while scores of articles, papers, and polemics about it appear in Polish academic journals virtually every year. While *The Doll* continues to be a vital issue in Polish criticism, its reception abroad has been negligible until very recently, mostly for the lack of available foreign translations. Natalia Modzelewska's Russian translation of 1948 has been republished at least twice, in editions of Prus' selected writings in 1955 and 1961. The German translation appeared in 1954, followed by the French translation of 1964 in the series "Collection UNESCO d'oeuvres representatives." David Welsh's English translation appeared in 1972.

The Doll's delayed appearance in translation was not the case of oversight, for as soon as *The Doll* was originally published, a Polish critic Adam Bełcikowski announced it in his yearly review of Polish literature in the London *Atheneum:* "The *Puppet* is certainly one of the most remarkable additions made of recent years to our imaginative literature, and is quite the most notable work produced in the last twelve months." In France an interesting essay, including some vital critical remarks on *The Doll,* was published by Ch. Chéret in *La revue* in 1902, but bad timing prevented it from arousing interest since France was just recovering from "l'invasion étrangère dans la littérature française," as a French critic Henri Bordeaux called it. Maria Kosko, whose study on the French reception of Sienkiewicz's *Quo vadis?* provides excellent insight into the literary polemics of that period, concludes that the nationalist crisis was over by February, 1902, and the ground for yet another foreign novel for the French readers had to be prepared anew. The translators from Polish were painfully aware of the situation. In a letter to Prus, Bronisław Kozakiewicz, who had just completed his translation of Prus' historical novel *The Pharao,* wrote on April 17, 1902: "I have to wait though until May 15 before I let it go, since the French reading public is a little bit tired with translations. Besides, the public has to be prepared with a few articles which will be published in *Le matin* and *Écho de Paris.* . . . Starting April 20 I am beginning a journalistic campaign on *The Pharao;* I have nice promises and great hope."

These and similar reasons must have contributed to the fact that *The Doll,* too, received a rather limited reception abroad, even during the next decades. But the problems concerning it seem to lie deeper. After all, *The Pharao* and many of Prus' short stories enjoyed numerous foreign translations since the 1880s. Was *The Doll,* of which Manfred Kridl wrote [in his *A Survey of Polish Literature and Culture*] that "without exaggeration one may say that it is the most distinguished novel produced in Poland up to that time and the finest novel of its period," either too Polish, too provincial, or too topical? Why didn't it capture the attention of foreign critics when for so many years it remained a classic in its own country?

The answer seems to be fairly simple: it is not the fault of the novel but of the critics who failed to recognize its artistic merits. Polish critics concentrated mainly on either the ideological or social significance of the novel, while most of the foreign critics presented Prus as a novelist in general and comparative terms. For example, in his monographic study of *The Doll,* Zygmunt Szweykowski devoted twenty-eight out of the total three-hundred-and-sixty pages to the problems of composition and literary devices of the text. He devoted the rest of his study to biographical, historical, and ideological problems. Among the articles written in languages other than Polish, the majority deals with such comparative topics as Turgenev and Prus, Prus and Gončarov, Prus and Spielhagen, etc. The study of Prus' characters, written by Jerzy Pietrkiewicz in 1960, did not sound an encouraging note: "The heroes of his major novels are in fact portraits of failure, and theirs is an all-embracing kind of failure which involves the collapse of successful plans, material and spiritual losses, and in two cases the loss of life at the end of the story."

Now that we finally have the English text of *The Doll* available, the time has come to render critical justice to that novel, and, following Conrad's inspiration, "to bring to light the truth, manifold and one, underlying its every aspect."

As we stated earlier, irony is a basic structural device in *The Doll*. Interestingly enough, no critic has ever paid sufficient attention to its major role in the novel, although quite a few have mentioned Prus' ironic mood casually while elaborating at some length on his humor. It is necessary to define in what sense the term irony will be used here since there exist major discrepancies among the literary theoreticians concerning its precise definition. Indeed, even J. A. K. Thomson, one of the pioneers of modern literary studies and the author of a historical study on irony and its origins [*Irony: A Historical Introduction*], remarked at the very beginning of his work that "irony, which is a criticism of life, is as hard to define as poetry." Since that time, of course, the tools of literary research have been sharpened thanks to many ingenious and sophisticated studies written by American Neo-critics as well as the Russian Formalists, but differences of opinion persist. For Cleanth Brooks irony is "a general term for the kind of qualifications which the various elements in a context receive from the context"; Boris Tomaševskij considers it merely a rhetorical trope when he refers to "the use of words in a sense contradictory to their meaning," a phenomenon "belonging to the phenomena born by metonymy." A different attitude is represented by a Polish scholar, Julian Krzyżanowski, according to whom irony is a part of the comic in general, a result of a negative, complicated, and speculative reaction of a writer, a psychological attitude rather than merely a literary device in a text. One must settle on a definition which may encompass those diversified views and opinions. Such a definition was offered by Northrop Frye in his *Anatomy of Criticism*, where he stated that "when we try to isolate the ironic as such, we find it seems to be simply the attitude of the poet as such, a dispassionate construction of a literary form, with all assertive elements, implied or expressed, eliminated." And Sonia Gotman, who based her essay on irony in Čexov's fiction on Frye's assertion, adds that "irony may have a dispassionate front, but when we penetrate it we grasp the ironist's real attitude." This amended definition works very well indeed in analysing Prus' fiction in general, and *The Doll* in particular.

In order to grasp the full meaning of the irony in Prus' attitude and literary technique, we must go back to the beginning of his literary career. Somewhat like Chekhov, Prus started as a humoristic columnist in 1872, and for almost forty years contributed regularly to the Warsaw newspapers in the form of his weekly "chronicles." Collected today, these "chronicles" comprise twenty impressive volumes. From the beginning, the author's goal was two-fold—to criticize and to amuse. Prus was writing in the repressive political climate of the 1870s and the following decades, combatting the overpowering presence of Russian censorship on the one hand, and the negative attitudes of some Polish circles toward the Positivist movement on the other. Humor alone could not suffice to combat those two forces, and Prus instinctively chose to develop a protective shield of irony behind which he could hide his real concern for the welfare of the nation, whose very existence was threatened after the 1863 national uprising. Furthermore, at the beginning of his journalistic career Prus joined the staff of a satirical weekly *Mucha,* and soon was appointed its editor-in-chief. In that position he mastered the art of satire, which grew directly from his ironic attitude toward some social problems he chastised in his early writings. His journalistic techniques of irony and satire carried over into his fiction, which he began writing in 1874. His early stories, written before 1881, were often little different from his weekly newspaper column, displaying his humoristic attitude combined with didactic goals. As the Polish critic Janina Kulczycka-Saloni notes:

> Those who see in Prus a humoristic writer above all make a mistake, generalizing some insignificant cases from the first (but not very first) years of his creative work. Prus did not begin with humoristic stories. His first writings in *Opiekun domowy* are above all social, and his *Listy ze starego obozu,* besides some humoristic coloring, have clearly didactic goals; the very fact that the first outlines of his short stories were interwoven in the text to support the author's practical philosophy indicates what attitude Prus had toward his writing, and what role didacticism played in them.

A detailed critical discussion of that early period resulting in such well-known short stories as **"Michałko"** (1880), **"Antek"** (1881), **"The Waist Coat"** (1882) as well as a short novel *The Outpost* (1886) would exceed the limits set forth for this paper; suffice it to say they all represent a practical authorial workshop of a writer whose talent, interest, and ambitions moved him closer and closer to the crucial test of creating a major contemporary novel about all those problems which moved him deeply. That novel, originally intended to be titled "Three Generations," came down to us as *The Doll.*

The first installment of the novel appeared in *Kurjer Codzienny* on September 29, 1887, and it ran with some interruptions till May 24, 1889. It was brought out in book form by Gebethner and Wolff at the beginning of 1890, and almost instantly stirred an animated critical discussion which still continues.

The time and setting of *The Doll* are clearly defined. The novel encompasses the period between March, 1878, and October, 1879, with some extensive flashbacks to the

1840s. Most of the action takes place in Warsaw, with one long excursion to Paris, and some short trips to the Polish countryside. The description of life then, both based on, and substantiated by the evidence from contemporary Warsaw newspapers, together with some detailed references to certain streets, buildings, and locations in Warsaw, prompted most critics to consider *The Doll* a perfect example of "the nineteenth-century realism at its best," as Czesław Miłosz puts it [in his *The History of Polish Literature*]. And Jan Kott, whose perceptive studies in French literature established him as a major critic of the nineteenth-century realistic fiction, went even further in stating that "the place occupied by *The Doll* in Polish literature can be only compared with the area covered by Balzac and Flaubert on the map of French literature." But the opening paragraph of the novel does more than just provide a realistic time and setting of the action; it sets out the ironic mood which will prevail throughout the novel and become a decisive structural element in it:

> Early in 1878, when the political world was concerned with the treaty of San Stefano, the election of a new Pope, and the chances of a European war, Warsaw businessmen and the intelligentsia who frequented a certain spot at the Cracow Boulevard were no less keenly interested in the future of the haberdashery firm of J. Mincel and S. Wokulski.

The ironic contrast of the political events of worldwide importance, and the petty gossip of the Warsaw businessmen and "the intelligentsia of a certain part of Krakowskie Przedmieście," as the original Polish text reads, is emphasized by the narrator's qualifying remark about their being "no less keenly interested" in the private affairs of Mr. Wokulski. That contrast is developed in the paragraphs which follow, as Prus juxtaposes the names of Bismarck and MacMahon with those of Mincel and Wokulski, particularly with the latter, his business, and eventually his background. The narrator is not satirizing anyone in particular, but by contrasting the events of note in the world to the narrow interests of his characters, he exposes the pettiness of the provincial world of Warsaw, into which he will eventually introduce Wokulski as the protagonist of the novel. As Stanisław Eile, whose penetrating study centers on the narrator's role in *The Doll*, pointed out: "Any reader of *The Doll* who is sensitive to the position of the narrator versus the narrated story must be struck by the fact that the narrator's ideological-cognitive posture vacillates between a position of a reporter who registers the novelistic facts, and that of an interpreter who sometimes becomes a moralist."

As the plot of the novel unfolds we see Wokulski through the eyes of his old friend Rzecki. We learn more about him from the impressions he makes on Izabela Łęcka, the aristocratic girl he is in love with, than from his own actions. Since his presentation differs depending on which character is viewing him, the question of Wokulski's real identity arises. Is he treated as ironically as the rest of the characters in *The Doll* because of his love for the girl of higher social standing and because of his frustrations? Or is he a tragic hero whose unfulfilled ambitions bring him to the brink of his final destruction? Perhaps a comparison with another literary hero of our time will bring him closer to the American reader and answer that question. Quoting one of Wokulski's exclamations, "How can I draw her attention to myself if not with money," a Polish critic Adam Kaska remarks: "No, that motto does not come from a novel by Fitzgerald. I have taken it from another book, well known to a Polish reader. Yes, so speaks Wokulski in Prus' *The Doll*. One could pick up more of similar quotations, and make some kind of a literary puzzle: Gatsby or Wokulski? The answer would not always be easy."

Indeed, despite the differences between the 1870s in Poland, and the 1920s in the United States, Wokulski and Gatsby belong to the same breed of men driven to their ultimate destruction by a foolish love with a girl socially superior and morally inferior to the protagonist. And if *The Great Gatsby* "represents the irony of American history and corruption of the American dream," as John Henry Raleigh pointed out, for Fitzgerald "has run in his characteristic changes, doubling and re-doubling ironies," the same, *mutatis mutandis,* is true of *The Doll* and its unhappy hero. Gatsby's celebrated remark on Daisy: "Her voice is full of money," could as well apply to Izabela Łęcka. The ironic mood of the American novel may very well serve those American readers who would like to investigate Prus' novelistic technique used some forty years earlier.

The irony in *The Doll* is of three kinds. In some few instances it is explicit to the point of becoming satirical or even grotesque. More often, however, it is implicit but ever present, making the novel structurally coherent. There is also a subtle verbal irony which is lost in translation. Selected examples of these types of irony will be dealt with subsequently in this paper. The first kind is particularly evident in chapters presenting the aristocracy, a very special world Wokulski wants to enter in order to marry Izabela. Her father, Mr. Łęcki, lives not only on borrowed time but on borrowed money as well. Virtually all his friends, the princes, the counts, the barons, resemble a gallery of caricatures whom Prus describes with an ironic detachment expressed not so much by the narrator's comments as by the contrast of their idle and superficial lives with Wokulski's driving energy. And yet it is Wokulski who is barred from that enchanted world of the upper class because he is just a businessman who does not belong in the aristocratic circles. This represents an ironic theme in itself, and since it forms the novel's main plot, the role of irony becomes quite obvious.

It is worth noting that this type of irony eventually turns into satire and grotesque in the second half of the novel. Beginning with Chapter 31 of the English edition, characteristically titled "Ladies and women," Prus not only introduces some new characters who do not play any significant role, thereby stressing the superficiality of the social life of the upper classes, but gives them proper names of mocking quality. And so we meet Miss Pantarkiewicz (Guinea Hen), Mrs. de Gins Upadalska (Fallen-down), Mrs. de Fertelski Wywrotnicka (Upside-down), Prince Kielbik (Gudgeon, also Fuzzy-minded), Count Sledziński (Herring), etc. Whereas in his previous novel, *The Outpost,* the name of the protagonist, Ślimak (Snail) indicated some qualities in his character, this time the mocking names just serve a satirical purpose.

Such overdrawn satire prompted some critics to compare Prus' novelistic technique with that of Dickens or even Prus' contemporary caricaturist, Franciszek Kostrzewski, whose pictures of Warsaw characters were quite popular at that time. That type of criticism, launched by Świętochowski, resulted in the novelist's angry reply in his well-known article "Słówko o krytyce pozytywnej," a masterpiece of ironic polemics in itself. Nonetheless, this type of criticism was repeated by Karol W. Zawodziński as recently as 1946.

The second type of irony is much more intricate and subtle, for it is only implied in most cases. This could account for its absence in critical discussions of the novel, but it certainly deserves more attention than the obvious manifestations of the novelist's satirical vein. It must be noted here that some of Prus' ironic attitude was noted by his contemporary critics who grasped its general tone and the author's philosophy. Kazimierz Ehrenberg, a Polish journalist and critic, commented as early as 1890 on a Latin inscription inscribed on Wokulski's alleged grave in the ruins of an old castle, *Non omnis moriar:* "Is this irony? Or is it a reproach that so it will be forever, that there always will be people among us who will nostalgically repeat the enchanted words of the Romantic seers in order to blame them for their own misfortunes?"

Only seventy years later Prus' subtle irony was understood in a much broader and more literary sense by a French author of the introduction to *La Poupée,* Jean Fabre, who noted "the main value of the irony" in the novel as opposed to rather insignificant events depicted in it. The early critics, preoccupied with the novel's ideological message, missed the point almost completely. They did not notice that Wokulski's downfall, more ironic than tragic since it was brought about not only by social injustice but by his own folly, represented an ironic twist in itself. In fact the novel is so deeply saturated with "doubled and redoubled ironies" that merely quoting them would result in quoting pages after pages almost *in extenso.* Let us therefore point out just the most interesting examples, leaving to the careful reader the pleasure of adding the ironic tone, as Northrop Frye advises.

We can grasp some of Prus' ironic technique beginning with the title of the novel, for the novelist's claim that it derives from the law-suit between the baroness Krzeszowska and Mrs. Stawska about an alledgedly stolen doll cannot be taken seriously. It is, of course, Izabela, "the society doll," to whom it refers, although she obviously is the object of Wokulski's passion rather than the subject of the novel as well. After Wokulski's ambiguous disappearance—we do not know whether he committed suicide or sobered up and went to Paris to become a scientist—Dr. Szuman mourns Rzecki's death, and asks the fateful question: "Who will be left here in the end?" "I shall," comes an instant reply pronounced simultaneously by Szlangbaum, a Jewish inheritor of Wokulski's fortune, and Maruszewicz, a petty swindler. "There will be no lack of men," adds councilor Węgrowicz, a silly gossip who, incidentally, had appeared in the opening scene of the novel and did not play any role throughout. This trio, representing all the pettiness and baseness in the Polish society, is an ironic parallel to Wokulski's firm belief in "the earth, the simple man, and God," as the only hope for himself and for the nation.

It has often been noted that a group of chapters generally entitled "the memoirs of an old clerk" provide not only the *Vorgeschichte* of the actual story, but also introduce a much needed relief from the tensions in Wokulski's personal affairs. Rzecki's memoir uses a special kind of auto-irony with which, as Henryk Markiewicz pointed out, he "consciously creates his own ridiculousness, with a comical exaggeration describing his behavior and psychical reactions, and gives his own statements a parodistic style." It is Rzecki, the old clerk and a faithful friend of Wokulski, who at the beginning of the novel sets in motion a display of mechanical toys, and at the end of it repeats the show, this time, however, with thoughts which sum up the novelist's attitude toward the characters and events depicted in the novel: "And, as he watched the movements of the inanimate objects, he repeated for the thousandth time: 'Puppets! . . . All puppets! They think they are doing as they choose but they only do what the springs command, blind as they are!' "

An additional bitter ironic twist is provided by the fact that even at that very last moment of his sad happiness Rzecki is being watched by a new clerk since the owner of the store suspects him of stealing after more than twenty-five years of faithful service.

Rzecki's memoir provides the novel with humor, an important element otherwise largely missing in Wokulski's story. Rzecki's encounters with the students renting an apartment in Wokulski's house, his conversations with his associates and friends, his constant suspicions concerning Wokulski's alleged involvement in politics—all these factors make Rzecki and his memoir an integral part of the novel. Initially misunderstood by the critics who thought it a nuisance in the novel's construction, it received its due appreciation only from modern critics who, like Ch. Chéret in 1902, noted that "nothing is more amusing than his Napoleonic ideas of the Romantic and liberal kind expressed in front of his subordinates, one of whom is a socialist, another one an anti-Semite, and still another one a *je menfichiste.*"

To complete this survey of ironic devices used in **The Doll,** we ought to mention a third type of irony, the subtle verbal irony unfortunately often lost in translation. As an excellent example we may take Prus' handling of a very delicate Jewish question which grows in importance as the novel progresses. In a scene at the court, when Rzecki describes the public attending the proceedings, he notices "the Jews who, as I was later informed, are the most patient of all audiences at the court cases." In the original Polish version of the novel the Jews are referred to as "Żydki" instead of grammatically correct "Żydzi," and even Dr. Szuman, who is Jewish himself, speaks of them as "te Żydziaki" instead of as "ci Żydzi," substituting non-virile and diminutive forms often encountered in spoken Polish to indicate either ironic, or at least contemptuous, attitude of the speaker. In this way, through his characters, Prus disclosed his attitude toward the so-called "Jewish question" which caused him much trouble from the beginning of his literary career. (Accusations against him ranged from rampant anti-Semitism to charges that he was a Jew in disguise, not Aleksander Głowacki [which was his real name], but "a young Jew, Ajzik Głowasser.")

Another example is perhaps even more telling since under the verbal irony there is the disclosure of a tension seemingly created by a misunderstanding, but in fact by hypersensibility of a Jew who knows he cannot be accepted by his Polish associates in spite of his wealth. When Mr. Szlangbaum takes over Wokulski's business he notices a certain coolness of his employees who "would jump into the fire" for Wokulski. In the ensuing heated exchange of words, one of the clerks, Lisiecki, asks Szlangbaum:

> "And do you know, sir, why we'd jump into the fire for Wokulski?"
>
> "Because he has more money," Szlangbaum replied.
>
> "No, sir. Because he has something you haven't got, and never will have," said Lisiecki, striking himself on the chest.
>
> Szlangbaum went as red as a vampire: "What is it?" he cried. "What haven't I got? We cannot work together, Mr. Lisiecki. . . . You insult my religion!"

For the benefit of the American reader it must be explained here that only the Jews in Poland were circumcised, and Lisiecki's reference was understood by Szlangbaum as a direct hint to that fact which was generally considered derogatory. That type of poignant irony is much more sophisticated than Prus' sarcastic remarks on the aristocracy.

Taking into consideration the various forms of irony discussed above we may ask whether Prus used his irony as an intentionally employed, carefully thought out literary device, or just as a manifestation of his general attitude toward certain social problems. Recently published documents will help answer these questions. It has been known for years that since 1886 the novelist kept special notes on his aesthetic and literary theories. The existence of those materials, presumably lost, was first hinted at by Feliks Araszkiewicz in 1925. Nine years later Zygmunt Szweykowski corrected that assumption and published some fragments of those notes, but only in 1963 Stefan Melkowski researched those materials and used eleven notebooks out of the existing twenty-one in his study on Prus' aesthetics and literary composition. Leaving aside Prus' general literary theories, which to a great extent follow the poetics of the nineteenth-century novel, the most specific remarks concerning the problem in question can be found in the following note:

> Composition ideas: 1. Next to A put contrast and antithesis. E.g. a decent man next to a scoundrel, a thinker next to an artist and a hero. 2. Next to a large feature or phenomenon put a small one. E.g., someone very wise has a missing finger; a man threatened with bankruptcy has lost his hat; or a man lucky in love has just torn his dress. 3. Next to $\pm$ virtues put $\pm$ small vices, and next to $\pm$ vices—$\pm$ virtues. E.g., a very brave man stutters, a thief loves birds, etc. 4. Real and fantastic /metaphysical/ characters.

Although irony as a literary device is not mentioned in the fragments published by Melkowski, the method of using contrast obviously creates tensions implied in irony. Melkowski seems to be correct in concluding that "the means serving the composition of a literary work play a subservient role to its ideology. They are only definite 'devices' by which the author communicates his thoughts and emotions to his readers." But Prus must have been well aware of the role of those devices. As another Polish critic, Edward Pieścikowski, demonstrated analyzing Prus' next major novel, *Emancypantki,* the novelist purged the last version of the novel of such authorial comments in the narration as "indeed," "of course," "really," "in fact," etc., thereby creating a distance between the reader and the fictious character, obviously an ironic device. Thus we may conclude that Prus' ironic attitude toward certain philosophical and social problems resulted in his conscious use of literary devices which from the literary point of view made his novels, and especially *The Doll,* structurally sound and coherent.

We have tried here to underscore some artistic aspects of *The Doll* so far generally overlooked by the critics, and, at the same time, to introduce one of the major Polish nineteenth-century novels to foreign readers who may not have a chance to read it. If we succeeded, that kind of rendering justice to a work of art Joseph Conrad was speaking of has been accomplished. (pp. 266-79)

Jerzy R. Krzyżanowski, "B. Prus' 'The Doll': An Ironic Novel," in Russian and Slavic Literature, *edited by Charles A. Ward, Slavica Publishers, Inc., 1976, pp. 266-82.*

Czesław Miłosz (essay date 1983)

[*A celebrated Polish poet, essayist, and novelist, Miłosz was awarded the Nobel Prize for Literature in 1980. In the following excerpt from his comprehensive survey* The History of Polish Literature, *Miłosz provides a general overview of Prus's career.*]

Undoubtedly, the most important novelist [of the late nineteenth and early twentieth centuries] was Bolesław Prus (the pen name of Aleksander Głowacki). He was born in 1845, the son of a minor employee on a landed estate in the district of Lublin. Like many others in Poland, his father lived only on his salary, but was of noble origin. The name Prus, designating the family's coat of arms, later served his son as a pseudonym. Orphaned early and brought up by relatives, Prus had an unhappy childhood. He was a schoolboy when the uprising of 1863 broke out, and, like his comrades, he joined a guerrilla unit. This is a chapter in his life about which little is known, for he did not like to talk about it, probably because of an acute conflict between his feeling of duty and his personal convictions. After being wounded in a battle, he spent several months in a hospital and then in a prison, from which he was finally released on the grounds of being underage.

(His relatives probably falsified his birth certificate.) Owing to these experiences, he matured early; but he remained an introvert, inclined to use masks. In his high school, to which he returned after his stay in prison, he was known as a wit and even a buffoon. He was mostly interested in science, and toyed with the idea of studying at one of Russia's big universities. But on the advice of his friends, he registered in the mathematics and physical science department of the *Szkoła Główna* in Warsaw. Science was surrounded, there, by an atmosphere of worship; but the ideology of Positivism, then evolving, left Prus rather cold. His stay at the *Szkoła Główna* was cut short owing to lack of money. Partly for financial reasons and partly because he took seriously the slogan that called for the intelligentsia's getting to know the life of the masses directly, he worked for a while in a metallurgical factory in Warsaw. All of his free time, however, he devoted to self-education. His reading of Herbert Spencer was crucial; later on, he was to call him "the Aristotle of the nineteenth century." And in his mature age, he confessed: "I grew up under the influence of evolutionist Spencerian philosophy, and I heeded its counsels, not those of idealistic or Comtian philosophy." In order to learn, he needed money and time, but his factory job gave him neither. He remarked in his notebooks: "In order to learn, capital is necessary. So my aim should be as follows: to find a job that would give me as much money as possible, and that would leave me as much time as possible for learning." He tried tutoring, but at last, he found what he had been looking for, as a contributor of verse and prose to humor magazines. The public liked him, while he himself considered his occupation a defeat. He wrote: "Good humor is like a thistle which usually grows on the ruins. It wounds a delicately shaped mouth, but is a joy for asses." He acquired the dubious position of a literary buffoon; and later, when he turned to novels, it seemed somehow unnatural to his readers. Prus's mathematical mind, his love for precision and thoroughness, prompted him to approach his role as a humorist quite seriously. He had seven notebooks for gathering material; the first, for facts; the second, for relations between facts; the third, for general remarks; the fourth, for witticisms; the fifth, for scientific facts and views; the sixth, for observations and methods of making them; the seventh, for historical notes. Gradually, thanks to such material, he was engaging himself in a study of society as a whole. He passed beyond the narrow limits set by the humor magazines and began to publish short pieces on various subjects. These **Weekly Chronicles** (*Kroniki tygodniowe*), as Prus called his articles, were published in various Warsaw periodicals for about forty years, bringing him renown and exercising a decisive influence on the Polish progressive intelligentsia. The genre originated in France; *chroniques,* as they were called, dealt mostly with Parisian mores, theater gossip, scandals, artists' lives, etc., treating it all with *esprit,* wit and malicious humor. . . . Because censorship did not allow for direct discussion of certain questions, some tiny detail from everyday life had to serve as a pretext for a discourse built of hints and allusions. Prus employed his humor as a tool. His aim was to combat and to educate. He compared the public to a fish, which can be caught only with a bait of jokes. Another time he said that every week he prepared a soup that should be nourishing, but that every good cook adds ingredients to taste, in his case—humor.

Prus was a middle-of the-roader; he cannot be ranged among the fighting Positivists of [Aleksander] Świętochowski's ilk. Indeed he reproached them for their attachment to theories and words and for an insufficient knowledge of reality. The success of his **Chronicles** was due to Prus's genuine humor; the public guessed that behind everything he wrote was a goodhearted, compassionate man, indulgent even toward those he satirized, always ready to defend the underdog, organically incapable of hatred. His readers were won over by that blend of laughter and sentiment, so typical of Prus—a somewhat melancholy, skeptical smile and a belief in the inherent goodness of human nature. His point of departure was usually a little fact, for instance, the story of a botanist, gathering herbs outside Warsaw, who was surrounded by angry peasants demanding money—if herbs had value for him, they reasoned shrewdly, he should pay for them. To enrich a subject, Prus used many devices: he introduced human types, little scenes he observed, dialogues, humorous doggerel of his own. The **Weekly Chronicles** remain a valuable source of knowledge about everyday life in Warsaw, a city for which Prus had a strong attachment. How deeply the **Chronicles** implanted themselves in the minds of the progressive intelligentsia is indicated by the use of the same title in the years 1918-1939 to head a column written by a progressive spokesman and, in many ways, an inheritor of Prus's social philosophy—the poet Antoni Słonimski.

Prus passed to fiction gradually. This came about as a result of his disillusionment with the effectiveness of journalism. While learning the craft, he was indebted, above all, to Józef Ignacy Kraszewski, among Polish authors, and to Charles Dickens and Mark Twain, among foreign authors. He began with short stories, usually situating them in a Warsaw apartment building among its poorer tenants (whose apartments always faced onto a gloomy central courtyard). His characters usually live on the brink of starvation: the seamstress in **"Ball Gown"** (**"Sukienka balowa"**); the unemployed mason in **"A Tenant in a Garret"** (**"Lokator poddasza"**); the little blind girl in **"Organ-Grinder"** (**"Katarynka"**), whose poverty prevents her from undergoing surgery; the poor copyist in **"Waistcoat"** (**"Kamizelka"**). This last story is a good example of Prus's tenderness toward his characters. It tells the tale of a waistcoat sold to a secondhand dealer after the death of the owner. While the latter was ill with tuberculosis, he had lived with only one thought: not to depress his wife. He assured her his waistcoat had been getting too tight, while she herself in her turn had been narrowing it in the seams in order to fool him. The rich, in Prus, are not treated with any ferocity. A houseowner to whom a poor seamstress owes money turns out unexpectedly to be quite humane; or a tenement owner, a Jewish rabbi, goes in search of help for an unemployed mason; or an old bachelor, a connoisseur of music, is at first irritated by the organ-grinder in the courtyard, but when he notices the joy its sounds give to a blind girl, not only does he pay the janitor to bring in all the organ-grinders of the neighborhood, but he contributes money for the blind girl's operation. In

"**Michalko,**" Prus depicts an illiterate young peasant newly arrived in Warsaw who is a little like a Steinbeck hero. Michael (Michałko) is extremely strong, hardworking, and so naïve that by city standards he is an idiot. After saving a man from being crushed by a wall on a construction site, he disappears into the crowd, unaware of the very notion of heroism.

The short stories date mostly from the earlier phase of Prus's work. Around 1885, he turned to the novel. As a realist, he formulated his program in opposition to both "idealism" (read "Romanticism") and naturalism, although Flaubert and Zola, who both were then called naturalists, had some impact upon him. "The aim of literature," he wrote in 1885, "is to aid the spiritual development of the individual and of society. The sciences aid thought, social sciences aid thought and will, while literature aids thought, feelings, and will, that last indirectly." Quite interesting is the parallel he drew between literature and science: "Such characters as Hamlet, Macbeth, Falstaff, Don Quixote are discoveries as valid for psychology as the laws of planetary motion are for astronomy. Shakespeare is worth no less than Kepler."

Of Prus's three best novels, his first, *The Outpost* (*Placówka*), appeared in 1886. It is a study of a Polish village. The hero, a peasant named Ślimak (which means "snail"), serves to illustrate the life of the entire village. Practically all of its inhabitants are illiterate. There is no school, and religion consists largely of magic: when one of them buys, by chance, a painting representing "Leda with a Swan," they pray to it just as they do before two old portraits of noblemen, former benefactors of the local church. The far from picturesque, poor, and hard-working village has been touched, however, by certain transformations taking place in the country as a whole. A railway is being built in the neighborhood, and the owners of a manor have sold their property to German settlers, who divide up the land into small farms. Here, Prus inserts a message, as he was deeply distressed by Bismarck's policy. German settlers were being given loans and encouraged by the German Government to move across the border into Russian-occupied Poland. The Germans were economically stronger and better organized than the Polish peasants, while the rich Polish landowners seemed to lose their patriotic spirit when money was involved. In the novel, landowners speak more French than Polish, and decided to move either to a city or abroad instead of staying in the boring countryside. The plot is built around a series of misfortunes which befall Ślimak when he refuses to sell his plot of land to the German settlers, who want to construct a windmill on it. The extremely stubborn Ślimak does not act out of self-interest, since the money from the sale of his property would buy him a better farm elsewhere. He acts out of sheer inertia and an attachment to the principle inculcated by his father and grandfather: once a peasant loses his inherited plot of land, he is headed toward the greatest of misfortunes, namely, becoming a wage earner. Ślimak himself lacks the strength of will that his wife possesses (and here, Prus seems to be a good observer of the Polish village). He hesitates. But his wife, although she is on her deathbed, asks him to swear that he will never sell the land. Far from being a hymn to the supposed vigor of the peasant, the novel exposes his conservatism. It is the only defense he can make against the inroads of a world hostile both to him and to his country.

This somber picture is enlivened by Prus's flashes of humor and his warmth. The local priest, though preoccupied mostly with dinners, drinking, and hunting parties at neighboring manors, is, under Prus's pen, not completely deprived of all semblances of a good Christian. Two of the lowliest creatures, by village standards, emerge as bearers of the most lofty ethics of selflessness. Ślimak's half-wit farm hand, upon finding an abandoned baby, carries it to his miserable quarters and takes it under his permanent care. A Jewish wandering peddler, himself a wretch, is the only one to befriend Ślimak after his wife has died and his farm has burned down. In his thoughts he does not separate himself from Ślimak, whose misfortune is felt by him as his own. Thus, *The Outpost* is different from the novels of naturalists who would have life reduced to the blind struggle for existence, in that ethical motives here have considerable weight. All told, it is, in spite of its weaknesses, an honorable achievement in the realistic, discreetly tendentious, novel.

Being a Spencerian, Prus looked at man as part of nature, but he did not see Darwin's theory of the "survival of the fittest" as the key to understanding social dynamics. Although struggle was necessary to eliminate worthless individuals, cooperation, also found in nature, was even more important. For Prus, society was an organism, whose health depended on the equilibrium and harmonious functioning of its parts. In his view, it was impossible to keep a social organism healthy without ideals toward which people might tend, for example, the ideal of being a scientist, or a technician, or a merchant. For Prus, Polish society was sick. Its model of behavior had been imposed by the nobility, and it was a model based upon worship of an out-moded code of honor, empty phraseology, and false spiritualism which forgot that it could only subsist thanks to masses of people engaged in manual labor. For centuries the *bourgeoisie* had been weak; the peasant (such as he appeared in *The Outpost*) could hardly be recognized as a force for progress.

It is this pessimistic vision that underlies the huge sociological panorama in Prus's novel *The Doll* (*Lalka*). The title is of purely accidental significance and alludes to an episode involving a stolen doll, although the public saw in it a judgment on the main female character. The author had originally intended to call the book *Three Generations*. Published in installments beginning in 1887 and as a book in 1890, *The Doll* has been considered by many people the best Polish novel because of its combination of a richness of realistic details with a simple, functional language. There are few instances in world literature of a novel's hero acquiring in the public eye all the characteristics of a live and tangible person, as did *The Doll*'s principal character, Stanisław Wokulski. Thus, between the two world wars, Prus's admirers expressed their feelings by attaching a plaque to the wall of a Warsaw apartment house (which could be identified from an exact description in the novel), with the inscription: "Here lived Stanisław Wokulski, hero of *The Doll* by Bolesław Prus."

The basic structure of *The Doll* consists of two parallel narratives: one relates the events in the 1870s, the time of action; the other, thanks to a diary written by one of the characters, shifts the reader by flashbacks to the time of the "Spring of Nations" in 1848-1849. There is an imposing gallery of characters. They come from various social classes, represent diverse mentalities and attitudes, but are always connected with the two central figures, each of whom belongs to a different generation. Stanisław Wokulski begins his career as an underpaid waiter in a Warsaw restaurant. He comes (like Prus) from an impoverished noble family. An athletically built adolescent, he leads the life of an ascetic, dreaming about making discoveries in science. Deported to Siberia because of his participation in the uprising of 1863, he spends several years there, and upon his return to Warsaw takes a job as a salesman in a shop owned by a German named Mincel. Prus's minutely detailed description of the old shop (belonging to Mincel's father) is one of the most charming passages in the novel. By marrying, though not too willingly, the shopowner's widow, Wokulski comes into money. He uses this capital to set up a partnership with a Russian merchant, whom he had met during his forced stay in Russia. Together they go to Bulgaria during the Russo-Turkish war, and Wokulski acquires a fortune selling army supplies to the Russians. Although he and his Russian partner have engaged in some not necessarily innocent financial operations (dealing in armaments for instance), Wokulski is nevertheless portrayed as a type of "positive capitalist"—hard-working, sober, calculating, a useful member of society. Yet there is a chink in his armor. In his heart he is a Romantic, a man who dreams about some undefinable "true life." It is this lack of internal unity which brings about his defeat, for he is blind to the worthlessness of an aristocratic woman with whom he is in love. Wokulski exemplifies the difficulty of abandoning what Prus looked upon as the stigma of Poland's chivalrous past. An old man, Ignacy Rzecki, a friend of Wokulski's and manager of his store in Warsaw, represents that Poland which is gradually disappearing. The warmth with which Prus treated him proves that the novelist was far from using clichés or too clear-cut divisions. Rzecki comes from the Warsaw "folk"—i.e., artisans, minor employees, petty bourgeois. He lives on memories of his bygone youth, a heroic chapter both in his life and in the life of Europe. It is from his (Rzecki's) diary that we learn about some of Wokulski's adventures, thus seen through eyes of an admirer. We also find the story of young Rzecki. A pure Romantic, he, and his friend Katz, went to Hungary in 1848 to enlist in the revolutionary army. Outbursts of lyricism accompany his battle descriptions as he reminisces over the most beautiful experience he ever lived through. For Rzecki, the whole cause of freedom in Europe was connected with the name of Napoleon Bonaparte, and the Hungarian revolution sparked new hopes of abolishing the system of reaction which had triumphed after Napoleon's fall. Rzecki never lost hope; later, he placed his confidence in Emperor Napoleon III. While he writes his diary, he still believes in Bonaparte's last scion, Napoleon III's son, Prince Loulou. However, at the end of the novel, when he hears that Prince Loulou has perished in Africa fighting in English ranks against rebel tribesmen, he is suddenly seized by the despondency of old age. Beneath his asceticism, his punctuality, his dry and pedantic appearance, Rzecki lives in constant excitement, preoccupied by the affairs which he discreetly designates in his diary by the letter *P*, namely, politics. An avid reader of the daily press, he sees indications everywhere showing that "it" has begun. Prus coddled no other figure in his work as much as Rzecki, lavishing on him all the treasure of his sentiment and humor. A shy believer in great causes, a shy admirer of women, too timid ever to confess his feelings, Rzecki makes a funny and truly moving figure. In addition to these two generations, the novel provides glimpses of the youngest one, personified by a promising scientist, Ochocki, a few students, and the young salesmen in Wokulski's store. Here, Prus's attitude seems ambiguous, expressed rather by questions than by answers. The half-starving students live in the garret of an apartment house, in constant conflict with the landlord because they do not pay the rent. They are gay, inclined to macabre pranks, rebels against the established order, and, probably, socialists. One young salesman is also attached to socialist ideas; others are only too ready to pursue sleek careers, and even their business integrity, as compared with Wokulski's or Rzecki's, is somewhat dubious.

The plot of the novel is centered around Wokulski's unhappy love for Izabella Łecki. Perhaps depth psychology would elucidate why Wokulski's long-repressed needs and desires lead him to invest all his feelings in a person for whom he is no more than a brute, a plebeian who looks like a butcher, with huge, red hands. Izabella lives in an ideal world, untouched by the "dirt of life," convinced that people below the level of aristocracy are subhuman. She, a virgin, indulges in dreams in which she surrenders herself to famous actors and singers or to a statue of Apollo. Sometimes, though, her dreams are disquieting: dens full of smoke and soot, gigantic figures of filthy workers hammering on fiery iron; one of them tries to grab her, and he has Wokulski's face. To conquer such a woman, Wokulski must renounce his modest way of life. He begins to frequent theaters and aristocratic salons, to spend money on carriages and flowers. To help Izabella's father, a completely ruined man who keeps up only the appearances of wealth, he founds a company for trade with Russia and sets the aristocrats up in business. Izabella's milieu appears as more of a caricature than we might expect from a mild middle-of-the-roader. The facade of senatorial dignity, of grave and polite manners, hides dishonest deals in marriages, stupidity, and a complete incapacity for economic survival—a major sin in a bourgeois system. The hero's downfall—Wokulski, as the author leaves us to guess, commits suicide at the end of the novel—highlights the basic theme of *The Doll*—the inertia of Polish society. The only energetic and successful representative perishes, for private reasons it is true, but perhaps because he is just as much the bearer of a virus as the aristocratic milieu: he makes an absolute out of love and honor and, because of that, is crushed at the critical moment of his life. Wokulski and Rzecki are, in many ways, alter egos of Prus himself, a man on the border line of two mentalities. Wokulski, the frustrated scientist, is created in Prus's own image. During a visit to Paris, Wokulski reveals his "Eastern European complexes." He envies Western technology, progress, industry, and feverish work. In Paris, he meets an old scientist, named Geist, who has made the extraordinary discovery of a metal lighter than air; in the hands of those who would use it to organize mankind, it could bring universal peace and happiness. Wokulski, till the end of the novel, is torn between his love for Izabella and the idea of settling in Paris and using all his fortune to perfect Geist's invention.

Rich in episodic figures and observations of daily life in Warsaw, the novel demonstrates nineteenth-century realism at its best. It fulfills the basic exigency of the genre: to lead the hero toward a full awareness of the rift between his dream and the reality of the society around him.

After *The Doll,* Prus wrote a long novel on the emancipation of women—*The Emancipationists* (*Emancypantki,* 1894). The novel as a whole can be called an artistic failure, perhaps because Prus (not unlike Rzecki in *The Doll*) seems to have known little about women; at least he was never able to build a convincing female character (Izabella in *The Doll* is a satirical portrait).

The daring conception of his next novel, *Pharaoh* (*Faraon*), written in 1894-1895 and published in 1896, is matched by its excellent artistic composition. It can be defined as a novel on the mechanism of state power and, as such, is probably unique in world literature of the nineteenth century. Ancient Egypt had tempted the European imagination ever since the hieroglyphs had been deciphered by the Frenchman, Champollion, after the Napoleonic invasion of Egypt. Yet it was mainly its external side, its picturesque exoticism, that attracted writers. Prus, by selecting the reign of "Pharaoh Ramses XIII" (who never existed) in the eleventh century before Christ, sought a perspective that was detached from the pressures of actuality and censorship. Through his analysis of the dynamics of an ancient Egyptian society, he wanted to suggest an archetype of the struggle for power that goes on within any state. He researched his material thoroughly, and if he committed some historical errors, they were due to the level of the Egyptology of his time; besides, this is immaterial in view of his purpose. As a journalist, he had been interested in Arabi Pasha's revolution (in 1881-1883). Arabi Pasha launched his uprising with the slogan, "Egypt for the Egyptians," but was beaten back by the English and deported to Ceylon. It is probable that Prus's meditation on those events in Egypt, then a British colony, helped him to bridge the gap between the ancient world and modern politics; the old often serves him as a metaphor for the new.

The treatise on Egyptian civilization which opens the novel agrees surprisingly with Arnold Toynbee's historical thesis—that civilization arises as a response to a challenge. The inhabitants of the valley of the Nile had to regulate its flooding or perish. For the accomplishment of the former, great mathematical and astronomical skills were required—and they were provided by the priestly caste, the highest, since Egypt lived under a theocratic system. But Prus was concerned with the period of Egypt's decay. In the eleventh century B.C., the population has diminished from eight million to six million. Desert sands are relentlessly devouring the arable land. Egypt has powerful enemies; the strongest are the Assyrians. Because of financial difficulties the Egyptian army is not numerous and is composed mostly of aliens, Greeks and Asiatics. But Egypt's predicament is due, above all, to an upset class equilibrium. And here we find the idea, so dear to Prus, of society as an organism with its parts functionally adapted to the goals of the whole. The young Pharaoh, Ramses XIII, whose political maturing forms the overt subject of the novel, discovers gradually that one class, the priests, has acquired absolute power at the expense of the other layers of the population. Organized both as a church hierarchy and as a political party (with an inner party accessible only to the initiated), disposing of tremendous wealth, with a monopoly on scientific knowledge, the priests have so shackled the monarchs that they are unable to introduce any reforms, while the peasants, who nourish the entire population, have sunk into misery and must bear the burden of inhuman taxation. But the Church Party is not fully autonomous. It has international bonds and seems to be dependent on the highest of initiates, the priests of Chaldea. Another international force, the Phoenicians, exists within Egypt itself. As financiers, they control, to a great extent, the functioning of the state. Young Ramses draws up a three-point program: out-and-out war against the Church Party, which he justifies by the need to curb its power; military action against Assyria, which he considers necessary but which is opposed by the priests; radical measures to better the lot of the peasants. Pursuing that policy, he concludes an alliance with the Phoenicians and wins over both the army and the mob. Yet he fails, not only because of personal shortcomings, but because his adversaries are people of formidable stature. The Church Party, under its monolithic facade, conceals an acute struggle for power, but the high priests are extremely intelligent, disciplined men who identify the interests of the Church Party with those of the state, and are ready to use any means to foster that supreme interest; for instance, to compromise Ramses, they order the massacre of one thousand Libyan prisoners of war to whom Ramses has promised life. They maintain ubiquitous undercover agents, especially among the corrupt and plethoric bureaucracy, whose proliferation is one of the causes of Egypt's decay. The bureaucracy and the commanding posts in the army are recruited mostly from the aristocracy, whom Ramses is unable to rally in wholehearted support of his program. As contrasted with the chief priest, Herhor, Ramses is but a young fool. He is a shifting, contradictory personality, swayed by his passions, noble-hearted but deluded by visions of grandeur. He dreams of acquiring the name of Ramses the Great, of conquering Assyria, and of improving agriculture with the labor of prisoners of war. This mentality is typically military-feudal (and we may suspect that in reality he is a Polish nobleman). His impulsiveness is no match for the cold, calculating minds and experience of the high priests. Moreover, he is always entangled in affairs with women, who are used as a bait by those who attempt to sway him to their side.

The first volume of the novel describes the slow awakening of moral consciousness in Ramses, then the crown prince, his loves, his drinking bouts and military feats; Volume Two traces his combat against the priests and ends with the assassination of the young Pharaoh. The direct cause of Ramses' fall is his scorn of science. He has been warned about an eclipse of the sun, known to the priests in advance through astronomical calculations, but he pays no heed. When the people rise up precisely on that fateful day, the priests are able to convince the mob that the eclipse is a punishment of the gods for an attempt to change the established order of things. After Ramses' death the chief priest, Herhor, is crowned Pharaoh. He not only carries out some of the reforms which Ramses had planned to introduce (i.e., periods of rest for the peasants every seventh day) but concludes an advantageous treaty with Assyria, and draws considerable sums from the Church's treasury for the use of the state.

The Pharaoh was received rather coolly by both critics and the public. It was understood as an attack upon the Roman Catholic clergy. Yet Prus's intention went beyond the limits of one country; he shuffled elements taken from ancient Egypt, contemporary Egypt, from Poland and the Europe of his time to convey certain views on the health and illness of civilizations. We are led to assume from the novel that general trends in history are stronger than the wishes of individuals, and whoever opposes them must fail. Young Ramses was out of step with the most important forces able to shape the fate of his country. He was rooted in the military aristocratic tradition; therefore, his understanding of the mechanism of power was somewhat naïve. Perhaps he was a cousin of Wokulski's, a romantic in his heart. At the same time, however, it is clear from the reading that a crazy individual—and perhaps only a crazy individual—is at the origin of changes. By his actions, Ramses engendered a revolutionary situation within the country and strengthened opposition against the initially planned treaty with Assyria, which would have been harmful to the interests of Egypt. The chief priest, Herhor, when crowned Pharaoh, had to take into account this new ferment unleashed by Ramses. We may also assume from **The Pharaoh** that dependence upon international centers testifies to the existence of a grave illness in a social organism, as exemplified by the reliance of Egyptian priests upon the sacred college in Chaldea and by the cancerous growth of Phoenician capital, which promoted Phoenicia's interests behind the scenes to the detriment of Egypt. Analogies could be found at will in Poland, Western Europe, and in the Egypt of Prus's time. The author's kind heart and his humor proved to be his best artistic allies in writing the novel. The antagonists are not simply black or white. Each of them is complex and many-faceted. They are rather personifications of social forces, neither good nor evil in themselves but comparatively, according to their relationships to each other. In a sense, **The Pharaoh** can be linked up with the educational novel of the seventeenth and eighteenth centuries, like Fénelon's *Adventures of Télémaque,* in which the education of a crown prince is at stake. Other features make it a strictly realist novel of the nineteenth century, and, in its stress on the social background, it resembles the French novel as practiced by Balzac, Flaubert, and even Zola. What makes it unique is that no one had ever attempted to deal with the State as such in a novel. **The Pharaoh** is, perhaps, inferior to **The Doll,** as it lacks the same immediate observations of detail, but it is a work worthy of Prus's intellect and one of the best Polish novels.

At the time he was working on **The Pharaoh,** and even more later on, Prus was inclined to be pessimistic about Poland as a society. Instead of an organism functioning harmoniously, he saw contradictory interests in bitter conflict. He wrote in one of his articles: "Our society today does not look like an organism, like a net in which every interstice is connected with thousands of others, but like a heap of sand which seeps through one's fingers." He rejected all expectations of change through war or a revolution. For him the Boer War of 1900 served as a warning of the fate of small nations. The future, according to him, belonged to the Big Powers, aligning themselves into larger unions perhaps, and renouncing a part of their sovereignty. He hoped that huge states would gradually be transformed into commonwealths, which would grant autonomy to the smaller nations dominated by them. While not excluding a better mutual understanding between Poles and Russians, he was extremely sensitive to growing German nationalism and was skeptical of coexistence with Germany. A few quotes from his articles prove that already, at the turn of the century, perceptive people were able to glimpse some of the dangers yet to become a reality:

> We live in the epoch when science is beginning to lose its character of universal truth and is becoming a set of falsities, of instruments for a rapacious policy. . . . The honor of creating such a science belongs to the Germans; less than a year ago, a philosopher, Hartmann, acting as a political agent, advised his compatriots to exterminate the Poles. . . . Wait a bit, and upon the stem of the once glorious German science will grow a "new chemistry" to poison unpleasant peoples, a "new medicine" to contaminate them with epidemics.

Sometimes in Prus there are even traces of Pan-Slavism:

> And what if a war creates proper frames for the Slavic question which today—in reality—does not exist? And what if it happens so that all the Slavs would desire to be free, in their own lands, in order to work, within the limits of their forces, for some new civilization and not to feed upon Roman-German remnants?

The main reason for Prus's pessimism was his conflict with the young generation. Around 1900 the modernist movement in literature and art, which rejected the tenets of Positivism, was in full swing, while in politics the upper hand was being taken by revolutionary socialists who condemned political realism and the pussyfooting prudence of the old generation. Even more in Poland than in Russia, the year 1905 was marked by strikes, barricades in the streets, and sentences of death carried out by socialists upon managers or foremen of factories, officers of the czarist police, etc. Prus then wrote his novel **The Children (Dzieci).** From the title it is not difficult to guess the contents. Publicistic in character, intended as a warning, the novel, which is devoid of humor, is one of Prus's weakest works. The remaining products of his late period can also be characterized as the meditations of a publicist rather than as literature.

The stature of Bolesław Prus as a writer of rare integrity and high intellectual standards has never been questioned, and in recent times scholars have done much to revive interest in his activity as a publicist. (pp. 291-303)

> Czesław Miłosz, "Bolesław Prus (1845-1912)," in his The History of Polish Literature, 1969. Reprint, second edition, by University of California Press, 1983, pp. 291-303.

Jerzy R. Krzyżanowski (essay date 1983)

[*In the following essay, Krzyżanowski analyzes Prus's short story "A Mistake."*]

It is a curious literary phenomenon that some masters and masterpieces sometimes have to wait long years for a "rediscovery" either by later generations or by audiences wider than their own compatriots, and for recognition that is relevant to the problems and minds of modern readers. Such a recognition, posthumous in most cases, usually benefits the readers rather than the writer in question or his work but at least it grants him a secure place either in his national literature or among "the great books" on the international scene. Examples are too numerous to be quoted here but the fate of Poland's leading nineteenth-century novelist Bolesław Prus (Aleksander Głowacki, 1845-1912) represents a perfect point in the case. While his most popular novel **Lalka** (**The Doll,** 1890) has been generally accepted in Poland as the real masterpiece of nineteenth-century fiction, it had to wait eighty-two years for its English translation, and it will probably take yet more time before it is given due critical appraisal in the English-speaking countries. Critical studies on Prus available in English so far have been either general or at the most comparative in nature, while virtually none of them has attempted to analyze his prose critically. Studies on Prus published in Poland, either biographical or monographic in character, such as those written by Zygmunt Szweykowski, Henryk Markiewicz, Jan Kott, and Janina Kulczycka-Saloni, usually stress Prus's Positivistic philosophy and his role in the society he tried to influence with his writings; but they rarely provide an insight into the author's literary technique. Particularly notable by its absence is any critical discussion of a genre of short story in which Prus excelled.

The origins of Prus's interest in the short-story form can be traced back to his voluminous journalistic Kroniki with which he entered the field of literature in a manner similar to Chekhov's career: his mostly humoristic sketches and anecdotes gradually evolving toward a mature and conscious literary form. In those first attempts in prose the generic lines between journalistic reports and fiction were so blurred that even today it would be difficult to establish when Prus began to become a short story writer, and how many stories he actually wrote. Janina Kulczycka-Saloni, the author of a study of Prus's short stories, frankly admits: "Unfortunately, I cannot answer that question, for I do not know how many stories by Prus exist." It is, therefore, safe to accept 1878 as a date after which Prus emerges as a mature short-story writer, because only then, with the publication of **"Szkatułka babki"** (**"Grandma's Jewelbox"**) "does the longing for realism spread over some other elements in his work, aiming either at an independent composition, or abandoning it and entering its own ways," according to Zygmunt Szweykowski.

The notion of realism characterizes most of Prus's mature stories, while some of them tend to deviate from it by way of fantasy or even abstraction. In general, however, one should agree with Kulczycka-Saloni who concludes a review of his topics with the remark that "Prus in his creative work walked securely only on Polish soil." Although such a limitation of his subject-matter could not contribute to the popularity of his works outside of Poland, it should be recognized as a rather unique quality of a realist who was able to provide some penetrating insights into the life of the society by changing the everyday occurrences and people into artistically coherent situations and characters who seem to be as alive and convincing today as they must have seemed a hundred years ago. Often didactic in character, Prus's stories survive thanks also to another important, permanent feature: the genuine, slightly ironic humor with which the author approached life as well as fiction.

Such elements of a well-written short story as realism, psychological insights, and humor, can be found in virtually any work of that genre perfected in the nineteenth century and represented in Polish literature by scores of excellent authors including Sienkiewicz, Żeromski, Reymont, and many others. What makes Prus's art interesting and unique is his way of telling the story, i.e., its composition and the method of narration. "**A Mistake**" is a story that is in a way crucial in Prus's creative life. It represents a period of transition toward the genre of the novel which Prus entered the year after its publication with the novel **Placówka** (**The Outpost,** 1885), and is therefore worth looking at closely as one of Prus's significant short stories, and one of the most revealing of his technique.

The story was initially given the title "The Spy"; later on Prus considered the title "Vox populi." Finally he decided to name it "**A Mistake**" ("**Omyłka**") and published it in a St. Petersburg-based Polish weekly, Kraj, in 1884. With it he intended to begin "a number of novels about the great questions of our epoch," as he wrote to Erazm Piltz, the editor of that paper, a few months earlier. The particular question he decided to deal with in his story was a very difficult one indeed, for he wanted to return to events of twenty years earlier, the 1863 Polish uprising against Russian domination, a tragic struggle in which he himself took an active part as a young man. What was even more difficult, though, was the fact that he wanted to present in his story two controversial points of view, challenging one of the national *sancta* by questioning the validity of pure bravery in a fight without proper political preparation and support either from abroad or on the part of the nation's masses.

The decision to publish it in St. Petersburg rather than in Warsaw was motivated by Prus's anticipation of a less harsh censorship there than he feared in occupied Poland, and he followed many previous examples of contemporary authors who, like Józef Ignacy Kraszewski, Jan Lam, Michał Bałucki, Ignacy Maciejowski and many others, had chosen to publish their works on the 1863 uprising elsewhere rather than in Warsaw; nonetheless "**A Mistake**" in its original version underwent some cuts, and appeared only in 1885 in *Kurjer Lwowski* unexpurgated.

Prus was very well aware of the difficulties involved, and he proceeded carefully with the writing which took him some ten months. Sending it off to Piltz he wrote: "Finally I have finished it, and I admit it would be a pity if the thing couldn't go through for higher reasons."

In order to have it published at all he resorted from the very outset to two interesting devices which in turn determined to a large extent the artistic shape of the story. First, there is no mention against whom and when the fighting takes place, and yet the realistic presentation of the events (with no names mentioned) and of the general spirit of the population makes it perfectly clear that the story deals with the 1863 uprising. The unnamed town around which the two opposing forces clash could be identified from Prus's own biography as Lubartów, a small town north of Lublin in central Poland, and, as Krystyna Tokarzówna has pointed out, the battle described in the story could be traced to an actual event of May 24, 1863. Hence Prus achieved one important goal of a realistic writer by making a particular event so general in nature that it could apply to many similar situations and thus became typical; yet in its detailed presentation it is deeply rooted in an actual location and time. On top of that he was able to establish a line of communication between the author and his readers so that they understood quite well the message which for external reasons could not be spelled out.

The second device is even more literary in nature, and had been mastered by Prus in his earlier stories, such as "**Anielka**" (1880) and "**Przygoda Stasia**" (1883). It consists of making the narrator of the story an eight-year-old boy who, incidentally, should not be accused by Prus's critics of having any specific political orientation. But above all, the method of looking at events through a child's naive yet perceptive eyes establishes a distance necessary for maintaining a detached, objective presentation; at the same time it changes the perspective from the established point of view, distorting it slightly. In short he "makes it strange" as the Formalist critics of the 1920s were to interpret the device of *ostranenie*.

It is, or course, highly doubtful whether the author used that type of narration consciously for there is no proof of such a method in the unpublished notes on literary theory which he kept most meticulously between 1886 and 1912. Besides, literary theory in Poland in Prus's lifetime was fairly unsophisticated and even as late as the 1930s it had barely begun to advance some of the more modern approaches concerning the specific character of fiction, especially in establishing the generic characteristics of a short story versus a novel. It is, therefore, interesting to see how effectively Prus used that particular device to make his story artistically mature and coherent.

Antoś, the narrator of the story, thanks to his age and his limited experience, is able to tell about the events of the uprising with impartiality and detachment, perceiving the surroundings and the characters with childish innocence and curiosity. His imagination has been captured by a lonely hut at the outskirts of town, and the hut with its mysterious inhabitant gradually becomes the focus of the story. Initially indicated in the general description of the vicinity, it comes back in virtually every conversation with his relatives, until finally it becomes the scene of the tragic "mistake"—the execution of the strange old man, a victim of false accusation of high treason. A touch of irony—the device always present in Prus's humor—is added in such comments as, e.g., Antoś's understanding of his mother's active involvement with the community:

> The peasants, the landlords, the children, the sick ones, the animals, the trees, even a stone at the gate—everything concerned her. Only the hut standing behind our fields she never mentioned. Its inhabitants must have been very healthy and happy people for mother never visited with them.

Only gradually does Antoś learn from his old nurse about the reputation of the old man living in the hut, and his curiosity is mixed with fear and contempt for the alleged traitor. The unseen presence of the old man is always there, even during a merry social evening at Antoś's home: when the local notables sing patriotic songs, the mayor asks his secretary to look out and make sure that "that one" is not eavesdropping. "The forbidden songs" include the popular repertory of popular poetry written after the 1830 uprising as well as a ballad by Mickiewicz ("something very forbidden"). While for Prus's contemporaries they must have conveyed a patriotic message, for a modern reader today they represent a faithful record of the type of entertainment available at social gatherings in the 1860s. At the same time such an occasion provided Prus with an opportunity to introduce a collection of characters who represent various political views, ranging from the conservative Francophilia of the old teacher, Mr. Dobrzański, through the blind patriotism of the mayor up to the pretentious pseudoheroism of the cashier, all of whom will play some roles in the tragic mistake to be unfolded in the near future, when the actual uprising takes place. But even during such a carefree evening the unseen presence of the old man is always felt, and when Antoś goes to sleep, once more recalling all the characters in their happy mood, "as if in reality," his youthful sensitivity adds a somber memento:

> There was one difference though, that among those present I saw a shadow, perhaps of that man for whom the secretary looked out of the window. I wanted to point it out to my mother but I could not raise my hand. And the shadow floated about the room, silent, elusive, and unseen by none but me.

The psychological realism of a child's mind is further strengthened in the scene of the first encounter with the old man who is being chased away by a street mob fostered by the cashier. The scene which, according to Edward Pieścikowski, could have been a reflection of an unprovoked attack made by some Warsaw students on Prus in

1878, makes "a painful impression" on the child, and enhances his curiosity mixed with fear to such an extent that he ventures to explore the hut. Armed with a wooden sword he goes to the deserted area, and finally approaches the old hut. But when he sees its collapsing walls bearing the ominous inscription "A SPY," he runs away in fear and apprehension. The cycle of his initiation into the tragedy of the old man seems to be completed.

The actual events of 1863 are again introduced into the story with the appearance of the mysterious old man who, overcome by cold and snow, enters Antoś's home as if a premonition of the dramatic months to come. This time his meek and humble behavior changes the child's attitude to such an extent that, seeing the old man going off into the blizzard, he begins to pray for him and falls asleep with a deep conviction that "nothing will happen to the old man." But soon the news about "the war"—unidentified for obvious reasons—overshadows the problem of the mysterious stranger in Antoś's mind. Describing the general mood of the population and later the scenes of military activities, Prus uses the device of *ostranenie* very effectively. Antoś never sees the fighting but he hears its sounds, first as "a constant murmur as if somebody was throwing peas on a tin-pan, and once in a while there resounded a broken, angry 'bow-wow' as if the barking of huge dogs," then "it seemed that the lightning struck from the bluest sky," until finally "a column of smoke arose from behind the woods. It stood high above the trees, and began to spread to the right and to the left, looking like a mushroom standing on one leg wearing a reddish hat." To convey not only the scenes but also the mood of despair after the defeat of the Polish insurgents Prus used that device in the description of the march of the victorious troops returning to town. It is one of the most impressive passages in the story:

> The roaring surf gradually approached the town. It is already at the outskirts, it is already passing the barns, it already is at our house. Suddenly there resounded a powerful command repeated by some echoes, and the noise ceased. . . . And then the house again shook from the foundations to the attic. The pipes have begun to whistle, the drums to growl, and from a thousand of breasts a song exploded. One could think that some unknown forces of nature having broken to bits run and speed away in some mad jumps—and then that all autumn winds moan, or perhaps a storm has broken down from the sky onto the earth, and moves on, foamy and powerful. Sometimes the choir grew silent, and then one could hear a shrill treble voice wailing, and the impatient beating of a drum. Soon a new hurricane rose, pounding at the doors and windows of the houses, mocking at the human pains, kicking the earth and breaking at the sky. In a bloody darkness of my room I thought that the holy pictures hanging on the walls shatter and look at me with surprised eyes.

The author need not name the nationality of the troops—the description is self-explanatory for anyone who had ever heard the Russians marching. To make it even more realistic Prus chose an obsolete but more onomatopoeic word, *uragan,* instead of the regular Polish *huragan* (the hurricane) as if trying to convey the ever-present Russian *ura!,* a typical feature of the Russian military vocabulary. The image was equally well understood by the Russian censor who deleted the whole scene. Prus stubbornly insisted on restoring it for its more than artistic importance. In a letter to Piltz he tried to appease the censor:

> Having cooled off from the first shock I read the manuscript and I became aware—not for the first time though—of the fact that K. is not only an honest man but that he has an artistic taste because he strikes out in such a way that he does not spoil the whole thing, as it happens very often here. On the other hand, if I were not aware of the situation, I would ask him to restore "the return of the troops" from the battle. On the second thought he would have to admit that in that passage (as well as in the whole story) there is no chauvinism, but on the contrary, the purest objectivism. Furthermore, that "return" does not pet the reader either!

The return of the Russian troops brings the story to its climax with the appearance of the old man who had saved Antoś's brother, hiding the wounded insurgent from a search party at the cost of self-humiliation ("I told the officer that nobody would come to me for hiding because they call me a spy." "A scoundrel," muttered the officer and instantly withdrew his soldiers). In an ensuing confrontation with Mr. Dobrzański, who represents the patriotic movement and provides a link with the old man's past, we finally learn why the latter was ostracized by his former fellow soldiers and subsequently acquired the mark of a traitor. As it turns out he had the courage to disagree with them as to the methods and goals of the struggle for independence although he supported them generously working as a *clochard* in Paris during the years of emigration following the defeat of the 1830 uprising. In a dramatic speech the old man seems to be voicing Prus's own point of view, disavowing the Romantic tradition of heroism at any price and presenting his more Positivistic philosophy when he exclaims:

> "You argued that you would capture rifles with your bare hands, and that with your rifles you would take cannons, while I tried to convince you that a hundred rifles meant more than a thousand bare hands. You shouted at me. And now—here you have the answer." And he pointed at the bloody spots on a scarf bandaging my brother's head.

And he adds: "To speak one's own convictions is a civic duty, only you have made a crime out of it." Thus Prus's message to his contemporaries returns twenty years after the 1863 uprising with power and dignity but does not provide a final resolution as it was proven by the historical developments in the decades to come. The same arguments could have been repeated sixty years after the publication of "**A Mistake**," and the recent discussion of the 1944 Warsaw uprising quotes them almost *verbatim.* Thus Prus's story has achieved a new dimension and has successfully withstood the test of time as a story "about the great questions of our epoch," as Prus initially intended it to be. It has achieved a philosophical level and its literary values made it one of the most interesting stories in nineteenth-century Polish literature.

Both the message of the story and its artistic level were well understood by Prus's contemporaries. An anonymous critic (later identified as Adam Breza) welcomed the story in 1887 with the following acknowledgment:

> There is in "**A Mistake**" that lovely, everpresent half-tone covering the text not by the author's own will, and through that half-tone we can yet see perfectly well what it is all about, what is going on, although the author never tells us those things by their name. There is some anxious time, some great anxieties, and some hopes at the same time, preparations and danger, later on some battles and some wounded [men], and the defeat, and the great sorrow—and thanks to that half-tone the story becomes even more beautiful, its contours merging with the earth and the sky, but from its very outset we can see them as clearly as on the palm of our hand.

Neither Breza nor the critics of the next generations could openly express their appreciation of "**A Mistake**" as one of the crucial literary documents dealing with the tragedy of the Polish fight for independence. It ranks as high as some of Zeromski's stories dealing with the same period, and deserves to be re-discovered and rescued from semi-oblivion. Since literary scholars in Poland today can only echo what Maria Konopnicka said about that story ("One could only argue about its very presupposition—if only one could") it seems to be our task to discuss it here, since it speaks as strongly and convincingly to our generation as it spoke to Prus's contemporaries a hundred years ago. (pp. 31-9)

Jerzy R. Krzyżanowski, "Bolesław Prus: 'A Mistake'," in The Polish Review, *Vol. XXVII, No. 2, 1983, pp. 31-9.*

FURTHER READING

Belcikowski, Adam. Review of *Lalka,* by Bolesław Prus. *The Athenaeum,* no. 3271 (5 July 1890): 24-5.

    Favorable review of *Lalka* in which the novel is called "one of the most remarkable additions made of recent years to our imaginative literature."

Dyboski, Roman. *Modern Polish Literature: A Course of Lectures.* London: Oxford University Press, 1924, 130 p.

    A general survey that contains a brief discussion of Prus.

Folejewski, Z. "Turgenev and Prus." *The Slavonic and East European Review* XXIX, No. 72 (December 1950): 132-38.

    Compares Prus with the Russian writer Ivan Turgenev.

Giergielewicz, Mieczyslaw. "Prus and Goncarov." In *American Contributions to the International Congress of Slavists,* Vol. II, pp. 129-45. The Hague, The Netherlands: Mouton and Co., 1963.

    Examines the possible influence of the Russian writer Ivan Goncharov on the works of Prus.

William Thomas Stead
1849-1912

English journalist and editor.

INTRODUCTION

Stead was a prolific early practitioner of exposé journalism in England. As an editor and writer for such periodicals as the *Pall Mall Gazette* and his *Review of Reviews,* he uncovered social ills and agitated for reform. While his writings are generally criticized for their sensationalism, Stead had a profound effect on turn-of-the-century English politics and journalism.

Stead was born into a large family at Embleton Manse, Northumberland. His father, a Congregational minister, educated Stead and his siblings at home, instilling in them a love of literature and a reverence for the Bible. Stead also received two years of formal schooling at Silcoates, a school for clergymen's sons near Wakefield in West Yorkshire. At the age of twenty-one, after briefly working as a clerk to the Russian vice-consul in Newcastle, Stead became the editor of the Darlington *Northern Echo;* he held this position from 1871 to 1880. In that period he succeeded in making the paper a powerful provincial voice of radical political views and Nonconformist religious sentiment. In 1880 Stead was invited to London to work as assistant editor to John Morley on the *Pall Mall Gazette.* During his nine-year stay with the *Gazette,* Stead launched sensational, successful press campaigns to forge a strong Royal Navy, to repeal the Contagious Diseases Act, to raise the age of consent for girls from thirteen to sixteen years, and to ruin the political careers of Sir Charles W. Dilke and Charles Stewart Parnell, both of whom Stead considered immoral. Stead was also an outspoken proponent of home rule for Ireland, British Imperialism, and women's rights. Under Stead's editorship the *Pall Mall Gazette* became one of the most powerful dailies in Great Britain. Throughout his career at the *Gazette,* Stead popularized the techniques of what Matthew Arnold would later term "the new journalism," making generous use of illustrations, headlines, and the personal interview, all of which were relatively new to British journalism at that time. In 1889 Stead left the *Gazette* to found his *Review of Reviews,* a monthly that featured summaries of news, essays, and stories drawn from various foreign and domestic periodicals and books. Stead used the *Review,* as he had the *Gazette,* as a personal pulpit from which he preached his numerous social and religious causes.

Stead's most notorious exposé was *The Maiden Tribute of Modern Babylon,* published serially in the *Pall Mall Gazette* in 1885 and compiled into pamphlet form later that year. In a four-day series of articles, Stead detailed in explicit terms the widespread and profitable activities of the

vice underworld in London, focusing especially on child prostitution and white slavery. The series culminated with Stead's account of the purchase of a girl for five pounds, intended to demonstrate the ease with which children could be obtained by procurers. The enormous public outcry against the articles intensified when it became apparent that this account was, as Bernard Shaw later called it, a "put-up job" perpetrated by Stead himself. Enlisting the help of members of the Salvation Army, including the services of a converted procuress, Stead purchased thirteen-year-old Eliza Armstrong from her mother for five pounds, had Armstrong certified a virgin by a midwife, and installed the girl in a bordello. Before any harm could be done to the girl, she was removed from the house and sent to live with Salvationists in Paris. Stead and his cohorts were convicted on kidnapping charges; all received light sentences except Stead, who was made to serve three months in Coldbath Prison and Holloway Gaol. While most readers found the articles distasteful and Stead's actions inexcusable, they conceded the essential truthfulness of his writings. As a direct result of the *Maiden Tribute* exposé, Parliament passed the Criminal Law Amendment Act, raising the age of consent and allowing in court the testimony of young children against their alleged molesters.

Although his reputation and credibility were somewhat tarnished by the *Maiden Tribute* scandal, Stead continued to be a prominent critic of vice. Journeying to Chicago in 1894, he made a thorough investigation of the city's underworld, publishing a 500-page account of his findings entitled *If Christ Came to Chicago: A Plea for the Union of All Who Love in the Service of All Who Suffer.* In 1895 Stead began publishing his "Masterpiece Library," a series of volumes aimed at making important literary works accessible to the working class and, especially, children. About 100 pages each and profusely illustrated, the "Penny Poets," "Penny Novels," and "Books for the Bairns" series presented condensations or retellings of classics and biblical stories. The series sold over fourteen million copies during its more than thirty-year publication run. In his efforts as a publisher of inexpensive pamphlet editions of his exposés and of the classics, Stead is regarded as a herald of the present era of cheap, accessible paperback books that place a diversity of reading matter within the reach of all classes of people. In later years Stead protested vociferously against the Boer War in South Africa; he also devoted himself increasingly to his interest in spiritualism, editing *Borderland,* a journal devoted to occultism, and publishing *Letters from Julia,* a volume of epistles that he claimed were transmitted to him by a deceased woman named Julia Ames. Stead died in the sinking of the *Titanic* in 1912.

In Stead's time the general public reacted to his journalism with distaste for his methods but appreciation for his sincerity and, usually, the realization that his exposés were truthful despite their often sensational tone. His detractors attacked his lack of regard for Victorian standards of propriety, or, questioned the truthfulness of his work. Although they often deplored his opinions and way of presenting information, Stead's associates agreed that he was a rigorous truth-seeker who thoroughly researched and believed in everything he published. Present-day critics praise Stead for his revitalizing role in British journalism, asserting that his work represented the advent of an aggressive new generation of correspondents who would not only report about political and social issues but would also raise those issues, effectively claiming an active role in revealing corruption and engendering change. Such works as *If Christ Came to Chicago* are recognized as models of journalistic research, requiring months of probing information sources as various as tax rolls, crime-ridden locales, the testimony of relief workers, and the statements of prostitutes and street people. While his writings and the political issues he covered have been largely forgotten, Stead's influence continues to be felt by any reader who buys an inexpensive paperback book or picks up an illustrated, headline-punctuated newspaper.

PRINCIPAL WORKS

The Maiden Tribute of Modern Babylon (journalism) 1885
If Christ Came to Chicago: A Plea for the Union of All Who Love in the Service of All Who Suffer (nonfiction) 1894
Chicago To-day; or, The Labour War in America (nonfiction) 1894
Letters from Julia (letters) 1897; also published as *After Death: Letters from Julia,* 1914
Satan's Invisible World Displayed; or, Despairing of Democracy: A Study of Greater New York (nonfiction) 1898
Shall I Slay My Brother Boer? (nonfiction) 1899
Are We in the Right? An Appeal to Honest Men (nonfiction) 1900

CRITICISM

Richard F. Burton (essay date 1888)

[*Burton was a celebrated English adventurer, anthropologist, and translator. A talented linguist, Burton mastered more than forty languages and dialects and produced sixteen translations. Among these was his monumental translation of* The Thousand Nights and a Night, *the classic collection of Arabian folk tales, which Stead attacked as being immoral. In the following excerpt from an appendix to his* Supplemental Nights to the Book of The Thousands Nights and a Night, *originally published in 1885-88, Burton, who relished attacking Victorian prudery and hypocrisy, excoriates Stead for the* Maiden Tribute of Modern Babylon *exposé.*]

Some three years and a half ago (June 3, '85), the [*Pall Mall Gazette*] startled the world of London by a prodigy of false, foul, and fulsome details in the shape of articles entitled ***"The Maiden Tribute of Modern Babylon."*** The object of the editor, Mr. William T. Stead, a quondam teacher in the London schools and a respectable Methodist strengthened by non-Conformist support, in starting this ignoble surprise on the public was much debated. His partisans asserted that he had been honestly deceived by some designing knave—as if such child-like credulity were any excuse for a veteran journalist! His foes opined that under the cloak of a virtue, which Cato never knew, he sought to quicken his subscription-list ever dwindling under the effects of his exaggerated Russophilism and Anglophobia.

But whatever may have been the motive, the effect was deplorable. The articles, at once collected into a pamphlet (price twopence), as the "Report of the *Pall Mall Gazette's* Secret Commission," and headed by a laudatory quotation from one of the late Lord Shaftesbury's indiscreetly philanthropic speeches, were spread broadcast about every street and lane in London. The brochure of sixteen pages divided into three chapters delighted the malignant with such sensational section-headings as—How Girls are Bought and Ruined—Why the Cries of the Victims are not Heard—Procuresses in the West End—How Annie was Procured—You Want a Maid, do You?—The Ruin of Children—A London Minotaur (?)—The Ruin of the Young Life—The Demon Child and—A Close Time for Girls, the latter being intended to support the recommendation of the Lords' Committee and the promise of a Home Secretary that the age of consent be raised from thirteen to sixteen. And all this catchpenny stuff (price 2d.) ended characteristically with "Philanthropic and Religious Associations can be supplied with copies of this reprint *on special terms.*" Such artless benevolence and disinterested beneficence must, of course, be made to pay.

Read by every class and age in the capital, the counties and the colonies, this false and filthy scandal could not but infect the very children with the contagion of vice. The little gutter-girls and street-lasses of East London looked at men passing-by as if assured that their pucelages were or would become vendible at £3 to £5. But, the first startling over, men began to treat the writer as he deserved. The abomination was "boycotted" by the Press, expelled the clubs, and driven in disgrace from the "family breakfast-table," an unpleasant predicament for a newspaper which lives, not by its news, but by its advertisements. The editor had the impudence to bemoan a "conspiracy of silence," which can only mean that he wanted his foul sheets to be bought and discussed when the public thought fit to bury them in oblivion. And yet he must have known that his "Modern Babylon" is not worse in such matters than half-a-dozen minor Babylons scattered over Europe, Asia, and America; and that it is far from being, except by the law of proportion, the "greatest market of human flesh in the world." But by carefully and curiously misrepresenting the sporadic as the systematic, and by declaring that the "practice of procuration has been reduced to a science" (instead of being, we will suppose, one of the fine arts), it is easy to make out a case of the grossest calumny and most barefaced scandal against any great capital.

The revelations of the *Pall Mall* were presently pooh-pooh'd at home; but abroad their effect was otherwise. Foreigners have not yet learned thoroughly to appreciate our national practice of washing (and suffering others to wash) the foulest linen in fullest public. Mr. Stead's unworthy clap-trap representing London as the head-quarters of kidnapping, hocussing, and child-prostitution, the author invoking the while with true Pharisaic righteousness, unclean and blatant, pure intentions and holy zeal for good works, was welcomed with a shout of delight by our unfriends the French, who hold virtue in England to be mostly Tartuffery, and by our cousins-german and rivals the Germans, who dearly love to use us and roundly abuse us. In fact, the national name of England was willfully and wrongfully defiled and bewrayed by a "moral and religious" Englishman throughout the length and breadth of Europe.

Hard upon those "revelations" comes the Eliza Armstrong case whereby the editor of the "Sexual Gazette" stultified thoroughly and effectually his own assertions; and proved most satisfactorily, to the injury of his own person, that the easiest thing in the world is notably difficult and passing dangerous. An accomplice, unable to procure a "maiden" for immoral purposes after boasting her ability as a procuress, proceeded to kidnap one for the especial benefit of righteous Mr. Stead. Consequently, he found himself in the dock together with five other accused, male and female; and the verdict, condemning the archplotter to three months and the assistants to lesser terms of imprisonment for abduction and indecent assault, was hailed with universal applause. The delinquent had the fanatical and unscrupulous support, with purse and influence, of the National Vigilance Association, a troop of busybodies captained by licensed blackmailers who of late years have made England their unhappy hunting-ground. Despite, however, the "Stead Defence Fund" liberally supplied by Methody; despite the criminal's Pecksniffian tone, his self-glorification of the part he had taken, his *effronté* boast of pure and lofty motives and his passionate enthusiasm for sexual morality, the trial emphasised the fact that no individual may break the law of the land in order that good may come therefrom. It also proved most convincingly the utter baselessness of the sweeping indictment against the morality of England and especially of London—a charge which "undoubtedly had an enormous influence for harm at home and cruelly prejudiced the country abroad." In the words of Mr. Vaughan of the Bow Street Police Court (September 7, '85) the *Pall Mall's* "Sensational articles had certainly given unlimited pain and sorrow to many good people at home and had greatly lowered the English nation in the estimation of foreigners." In a sequel to the Eliza Armstrong case Mr. Justice Mainsty, when summing up, severely condemned the "shocking exhibition that took place in the London streets by the publication of statements containing horrible details, and he trusted that those who were responsible for the administration of the law would take care that such outrage should not be permitted again." So pure and pious Mr. Stead found time for reflection during the secluded three-months life of a "first-class misdemeanant" in "happy Holywell," and did not bring out his intended articles denouncing London as the head-quarters of a certain sin named from Sodom. (pp. 398-401)

A journal which, like the *Pall Mall Gazette,* affects preferably and persistently sexual subjects and themes lubric, works more active and permanent damage to public morals than books and papers which are frankly gross and indecent. The latter, so far as the world of letters knows them, are read either for their wit and underlying wisdom (*e.g.* Rabelais and Swift), for their historical significance (Petronius Arbiter) or for their anthropological interest as the Alf Laylah. But the public print which deals, however primly and decently, piously and unctuously with sexual and inter-sexual relations, usually held to be of the Alekta or taboo'd subjects, is the real perverter of conduct, the polluter of mental purity, the corrupter-general of society. Amongst savages and barbarians the comparatively unrestrained intercourse between men and women relieves the brain through the body; the mind and memory have scant reason, physical or mental, to dwell fondly upon visions amatory and venereal, to live in a "rustle of (imaginary) copulation." On the other hand the utterly artificial life of civilisation, which debauches even the monkeys in "the Zoo," and which expands the period proper for the reproductory process from the vernal season into the whole twelvemonth, leaves to the many, whose lot is celibacy, no bodily want save one and that in a host of cases either unattainable or procurable only by difficulty and danger. Hence the prodigious amount of mental excitement and material impurity which is found wherever civilisation extends, in maid, matron, and widow, save and except, those solely who allay it by some counteragent—religion, pride, or physical frigidity. How many a woman in "Society," when stricken by insanity or puerperal fever, breaks out into language that would shame the slums and which makes the hearers marvel where she could have learned such vocabulary. How many an old maid held to be cold as virgin snow, how many a matron upon whose fairest fame not a breath of scandal has blown, how many a widow who proudly claims the title *univira,* must relieve their pent-up feelings by what may be called mental prostitution. So I would term the dear delights of sexual converse and that sub-erotic literature, the phthisical "French novel," whose sole merit is "suggestiveness," taking the place of Oriental *morosa voluptas* and of the unnatural practices—Tribadism and so forth, still rare, we believe, in England. How many hypocrites of either sex, who would turn away disgusted from the outspoken Tom Jones or the Sentimental Voyager, revel in and dwell fondly upon the sly romance or "study" of character whose profligacy is masked and therefore the more perilous. And a paper like the (modern) *Pall Mall Gazette* which deliberately pimps and panders to this latent sense and state of aphrodisiac excitement, is as much the more infamous than the loose book as hypocrisy is more hateful than vice and prevarication is more ignoble than a lie. And when such vile system is professionally practised under the disguise and in the holy names of Religion and Morality, the effect is loathsome as that spectacle sometimes seen in the East of a wrinkled old eunuch garbed in woman's nautchdress ogling with painted eyes and waving and wriggling like a young Bayadère. (pp. 403-04)

> Richard F. Burton, "The Biography of the Book and Its Reviewers Reviewed," in his Supplemental Nights to the Book of the Thousand Nights and a Night, Vol. VII, n.p., 19—? pp. 385-454.

Stead on his editorial policy:

I am ready to allow anybody to discuss anything in any newspaper that I edit: they may deny the existence of God, or of the soul, they may blaspheme the angels and all the saints, they may maintain that I am the latest authentic incarnation of the devil; but the thing I have never allowed them to do was to say a word in favour of the [Contagious Diseases] Acts, or of any extension of the system which makes a woman the chattel and slave of the administration for the purpose of ministering to the passions of men.

> quoted by J. W. Robertson Scott in his The Life and Death of a Newspaper, 1952.

The Chap-Book (essay date 1898)

[*In the following unsigned review of* Satan's Invisible World Displayed, *the commentator criticizes Stead for his sensationalism.*]

For a second time that gifted impressario of literary vaudeville, Mr. Stead, has made us bounden to him for the tribute of his genius. For a second time our municipal life has demanded his attention. Time and opportunity denied a personal glance. Cuttings from the corkscrew probings of the Lexow Committee suited quite as well. Their five stout octavo volumes of 1,100 pages each, "were mastered in the attempt to construct a readable and authentic narrative which would make this great object-lesson accessible to the world." The picturesque title [*Satan's Invisible World Displayed*] is borrowed from one Hopkins, a seventeenth century expert in witches, who uses it as the title of his "history and secret mystery of the infernal regions."

The plunderings of an appointed banditti, their perfect organization for the sake of prey—their abetting of all manner of evil, their highhanded brutality, their defiance of the popular will, these were the elements in the reign of terror which is described. In a sense, the entire book is a criticism of democratic rule. From the history of these official crimes the author passes onto a discussion of the charter of Greater New York, which he regards as a reactionary expression of the deep distrust of her citizens in the principle of government by popular election. A czar mayor, and hamstrung at that, is the remedy which the misrule of Tammany has forced upon the city. Thus far Mr. Stead has been retelling a tale long since told. That part of his majesty's invisible world which it is Mr. Stead's peculiar privilege to display, is located in the brain of the present boss of Tammany, and is set forth in a "character sketch" at the end of the book, in which the character in question sketches itself in the recurring theme, "I have done only good all my life."

The tale is well told—there is dramatic action on every page—more dramatic because it moves in a reality so familiar and immediate. But beyond the readable narrative there is nothing. The pedagogic interest which was expressed in the preface is not realized. Mr. Stead has indeed saved a ne'er-to-be-repeated experience from the voiceless tomb to which its record was entrusted, but he has in no measure organized it for us. True, he has made a statement, but an object-lesson is never a statement—the experience itself is presented; where this is impossible the lesson is in no sense objective, it is interpretative. The object, the raw crude fact, cannot re-exist. It is useless to memorialize it. It can become dynamic only by being adequately organized. Thus, analysis, which is not scientifically exact, and which results in no form of synthesis, is not teaching, but an indulgence. It is not sufficient to have said, "It is awful, horrible, the Turk could do no worse." For we have had a raw product thrust upon us—an uncooked fact—and for the moral indigestion which is sure to follow, we may thank the chef who did his work so badly. He has indeed succeeded in popularizing the findings of that committee, but the method chosen has defeated, in a large measure, the usefulness of his task. To have displayed the conscious and unconscious villainy which is cloaked beneath the "unctuous rectitude" of contemporary political life is a worthy service. To have analyzed it into its elements and so have pointed out a remedy would have been a great one. Mr. Stead is a literalist, who knows the power of a one-stranded, rapid-action tale. Time is as nothing to this theme, and all events seem to fall within a single day; there is no restful background, no palliating circumstance, no mitigating virtue, only the isolated succession of his hypnotic spell. Truth suffers by exclusion. The entire life of New York seems to be expressed in acts of these official bandits who plundered, beat and bribed to their stomach's full—for surely such things do not fill the heart.

The truth contained is damaged by its setting—is not treated as serious enough to demand a sober statement. Its reporter cannot see things without seeing them grotesque. Mr. Stead believes in the pyrotechnic of the press. It is his stock in trade and his criterion for estimating others. This predominating quality finds its fullest expression in his appreciation of the editor of the *New York Journal,* who is pointed to as "far and away the most promising journalist whom I have yet come across"—a phrase well classified as an insult to American journalism. (pp. 372-73)

> *"Mr. Stead on the Warpath Again," in* The Chap-Book, *Vol. VIII, No. 9, March 15, 1898, pp. 372-73.*

Henry W. Nevinson (essay date 1926)

[*In the following excerpt from his review of Frederic Whyte's* Life of W. T. Stead, *Nevinson considers Stead's faults and accomplishments.*]

Bernard Shaw was a young man like myself when Stead, as editor of *The Pall Mall Gazette,* stirred the country to passion with the series of articles called **The Maiden Tribute of Modern Babylon.** Like myself and most other decent people, he eagerly defended Stead's action in exposing the horrors of child prostitution in London. Through thick and thin we defended him, and it was my first experience in fighting against the indifference and passive resistance of fashion and cynicism. But when we found that the case on which Stead seemed to depend most strongly for his evidence had in fact been vamped up by himself, just to show what abominations could possibly be done in "modern Babylon," our confidence began to shake, though, for my part, I tried to defend him still. But in 1922 Bernard Shaw wrote:

> Stead was impossible as a colleague; he had to work single-handed because he was incapable of keeping faith when excited; and as his hyperesthesia was chronic he generally *was* excited. Nobody ever trusted him after the discovery that the case of Eliza Armstrong in the **Maiden Tribute** was a put up job, and that he himself had put it up. We all felt that if ever a man deserved six months' imprisonment Stead deserved it for such a betrayal of our confidence in him. He meant well; all his indignations did him credit, but he was so stupendously ignorant that he never played the game.

Stead was indeed stupendously ignorant. It has been said with some truth that the test of real education is the power of judging evidence. Except a knowledge of the Bible as a literal history and sufficient guide, Stead in youth had no education, and he remained to the last utterly incapable of judging evidence. I found it so time after time, and, what was most remarkable, his incapacity in this respect increased with age, until latterly he was ready to believe whatever he wished to believe and almost whatever anybody told him, provided it was incredible. He meant well always. He was passionately sincere in all his social and political passions—in his rage at the abomination of child prostitution, in his defense of this or that woman who had suffered wrong, in his denunciation of Dilke and Parnell for breaches of the Seventh Commandment, in his expectation that Gordon would save the Soudan single-handed and in his belief that the Tsar was almost divine and Tsarist Russia the type of a holy power. His excellent intentions, his persuasive powers and his strong personality won many of us to his side, and then, as Shaw says, his stupendous ignorance would let us down and his incapacity for judging evidence would bring discredit upon the cause we had at heart.

Once, soon after the abortive revolution at which I was present in Russia twenty years ago, I wrote in my paper that I believed Mr. Stead had enjoyed the privilege of interviewing the Tsar in person. I admit I wrote in some irony, for my opinion of Tsarist Russia was very different from Stead's. But the otherwise innocent remark called for torrential letters of protest and abuse from Stead to my editor and myself. "All the world knew—every one in creation but an ignorant jackass knew—that he was quite intimate with the Tsar, had been received not once but twice by Nicholas II, and once by his father. What ignorance! What impudence! What calumny!" and so on. It was a peculiar instance of megalomania. He loved to live in the reflected glory of the rich and great. He was ready to adore any one who was big enough and who condescended to take notice of him. Cecil Rhodes, a Tsar, a King, a Queen—any whale was a fish for his net.

When he rose to intimacy with the spiritual world I could not follow him, for I never enjoyed similar association with the departed souls of either sex. I envied his intimate conversations with Miss Julia Ames, who, after she had been dead for some years, would sometimes accompany him on railway journeys to Brighton, giving him valuable information on the route. But when Stead published a long conversation with the ghost of Mr. Gladstone the peculiar similarity between that worthy statesman's ideas in another world and W. T. Stead's own ideas upon politics in this appeared to me a very remarkable coincidence.

Even more enviable to me was his confidence that a divine intuition or inspiration always guided him aright, so that at times he was tempted to identify his own will and knowledge with the Almighty's, and he became even more familiar with God than with the Tsars. It is true that this reliance upon the highest possible guidance sometimes failed him, and his biographer tells us that Stead once observed, rather pathetically, to Mr. Balfour (now a lord): "Depend upon it, God Almighty has many tricks up His sleeve of which we know nothing. What we have got to do is to do the right."

Mr. Havelock Ellis, the greatest authority upon the subject, has said that "repressed sexuality was the motive force of many of Stead's actions," and indeed his ostentatious display of flirtatiousness when I was with him at the Hague Conference of 1907 seemed evidence of a strong feeling for sex, however much repressed. He himself defended this habit as "adding to the innocent gayety of the world," and certainly it added to my gayety. If I might for the moment adopt the Freudian jargon, I should say that Stead suffered from an "inferiority complex" which made him fall prostrate at the feet of the great who were good enough to speak to him, and from a "sex complex" which certainly supplied force to his nature, but sometimes perverted his judgment when combined with that "stupendous ignorance."

But you must not suppose that either I or his biographer can say nothing but evil of so remarkable a man. I always recognized his extraordinary power as a journalist—his dashing style of expression, his indefatigable industry, his rapid decision (often wrong but always unhesitating), his freedom from dreary old conventions, and above all his real sincerity in advocating the causes he took up. He was the creator of a New Journalism in London. He may have borrowed the idea from [the United States]; I cannot say. Nor can I say for certain whether the influence upon our journalism has been good or evil up to now. But it has been immense. Alfred Harmsworth (Lord Northcliffe) developed it to its present extent. Nearly all our daily papers have been influenced by his example, but it was Stead who created the idea, and Harmsworth only borrowed it. Long before the Harmsworth Press was heard of, Matthew Arnold, finest of critics, with Stead in his mind, wrote of the *New Journalism:*

> It is full of ability, novelty, variety, sensation, sympathy, generous instincts; its one fault is that it is feather-brained. It throws out assertions at a venture because it wishes them to be true; does not correct either them or itself if they are false; and to get at the state of things as they really are it seems to feel no concern whatever.

That appears to me to be the final verdict on Stead and his wide influence upon British journalism.

Yet we admired him, and what was more remarkable he retained the admiration and affection of men so chilly and reasonable in temper as John Morley (Lord Morley), Alfred Milner (Lord Milner) and E. T. Cook, all of whom worked either at his side or under him or, what was far more difficult, above him on the old *Pall Mall.* (pp. 88-92)

Henry W. Nevinson, "The Life of W. T. Stead," in Current Reviews, edited by Lewis Worthington Smith, Henry Holt and Company, 1926, pp. 87-92.

Hugh Kingsmill (essay date 1929)

[*In the following excerpt, Kingsmill examines Stead's* Maiden Tribute *exposé and his spiritualist writings.*]

The revelations in the *Pall Mall Gazette,* under the title of **The Maiden Tribute of Modern Babylon,** and Stead's subsequent trial at the Central Criminal Court were, Stead declared, his best title to fame. Towards the close of his life, his best title to fame became his connection with [Julia Ames, an American woman with whom Stead supposedly communicated after her death in 1892]. Both deserve to be remembered, for both illustrate, though very differently, the forms in which late Victorian Puritanism expressed itself through its most astonishing representative. (p. 184)

In the spring of 1885 Mr. Benjamin Scott, Chamberlain of the City of London, a man of seventy-five, and Mrs. Josephine Butler, who had now for many years been promoting the cause of Social Purity, called on Stead to claim his support in forcing Parliament to pass the Criminal Law Amendment Bill. This Bill, the chief provision of which was to raise the age of consent from thirteen to sixteen, had been introduced during numerous sessions, and dropped again. It was strongly opposed by a small group of members; and there was nothing in its chief provision to arouse particular enthusiasm either in Liberals or Conservatives.

Stead took fire at once. His plan of campaign, which he communicated to the Archbishop of Canterbury, Cardinal Manning, and Dr. Temple, the Bishop of London, was to publish in the *Pall Mall Gazette* all the facts about juvenile prostitution which he and his colleagues could collect, and to demonstrate in his own person the ease with which a man could be supplied with a girl of over thirteen and under sixteen.

Archbishop Benson was horrified, in spite of his general sympathy with Stead's motives. Cardinal Manning and Dr. Temple approved.

The unreality as of a dream, present in so much of Stead's life, envelops him more thickly than ever in his impersonation of a depraved *roué*. One gets at the state of mind in which he set about this task most easily in the speech he delivered at the Central Criminal Court, where he appeared on the charge of abducting the girl in question.

"When I walked these streets of London," he said, "and heard the church bells clanging to prayer to a Christian God, it seemed to me too cruel to be borne, for, remembering these poor girls, and knowing that the house of ill-fame was *here,* and the house of ill-fame was *there,* in which the very last night it might have been some poor child, as innocent as any of your daughters, had been snared and entrapped and ruined for life—oh! I seemed to see written up over the house of ill-fame, in letters illumined with fire, that ghastly parody of Christ's words, 'Suffer the little children to enter here, for of such is the kingdom of hell!' That was the state of mind in which I met Rebecca Jarrett."

Rebecca Jarrett was a converted brothel-keeper, to whom Stead was introduced by Mr. Bramwell Booth, of the Salvation Army. Miss Jarrett, after much more trouble than seems consistent with Stead's inflamed view of London morals, discovered a poor woman, a Mrs. Armstrong, whom she persuaded, after some angry interchanges, to part with her daughter, Eliza, for £3. Eliza was taken to a house of ill-fame, and sent to bed. Stead entered her room, she awoke and gave a cry of alarm. This completed the test case. Eliza was then handed over to a Salvation Army officer, a woman, and sent the next morning to the headquarters of the Salvation Army in Paris. In due course, we are told, she married and became the mother of six children.

The version here given of this episode is the one least favourable to Mrs. Armstrong, who may have believed, and was widely held to have believed, that her daughter was being bought as a domestic servant. There can, at any rate, be no dispute that Mrs. Armstrong became in time distressed at Eliza's absence. "The story," Stead himself writes, in his account of these events, "attracted the attention of her neighbours, and they began taunting her with having sold her 'Liza. She made an indignant outcry and was taken to the police-court." There she was informed that Eliza was in excellent hands. Yet she continued to be indignant; and eventually Stead, Mr. Bramwell Booth, and three others appeared in the dock on the charge of abducting Eliza. Stead was given three months, on the technical ground that he had not obtained the father's consent, in addition to the mother's; but the jury added that they recommended him to mercy, and wished to put on record their high appreciation of the services he had rendered the nation by securing the passage of a much-needed law for the protection of young girls.

Stead's trial began in September. The articles which secured the passing of the Criminal Law Amendment Act appeared in the *Pall Mall Gazette* during the first two weeks of July.

The leader, which, under the heading "We Bid you be of Good Hope," accompanied the first article, opened as follows: "The report of our Secret Commission will be read to-day with a shuddering horror that will thrill throughout the world. After this awful picture of the crimes at present committed, as it were under the very eyes of the law, has been fully unfolded before the eyes of the public, we need not doubt that the House of Commons will find time to raise the age during which English girls are protected from inexpiable wrong."

The Secret Commission referred to was composed of Stead and various members of his staff; but the articles based on their investigations are understood to have been written almost entirely by Stead. In the first article, Stead gave the story of Eliza Armstrong, whom he calls Lily; but he supplied no hint that the incident had been manufactured. Among others who were powerfully affected by this story was George Bernard Shaw, then a young man of twenty-nine. "I am quite willing," he wrote to Stead, "to take as many quires of the paper as I can carry and sell them (for a penny) in any thoroughfare in London. I believe I can find both ladies and gentlemen ready to do the same." The effect on Shaw, when the facts about "Lily" were exposed during Stead's trial, is given in a letter he wrote to Stead's biographer, in 1922. "Nobody ever trusted him after the discovery that the case of Eliza Armstrong in the Maiden Tribute was a put-up job, and that he himself had put it up. We all felt that if ever a man deserved six months' imprisonment Stead deserved it for such a betrayal of our confidence in him. And it was always like that. . . . He meant well; all his indignations, did him credit; but he was so stupendously ignorant that he never played the game. The truth is that he seldom knew that there was any game to play, and was delivered up to a complete infatuation with his own emotions which prevented him from noticing or remembering or even conceiving that other people were otherwise preoccupied."

It is impossible to say whether Stead doctored the other facts in *The Maiden Tribute of Modern Babylon* as sweepingly as he doctored the Eliza episode; but it is quite clear that the facts these articles contain were garnered by someone far too emotionally exasperated for exact enquiry into so delicate a matter. When, for example, Stead presents himself to his readers as a debauchee into whose presence this or that procuress ushered defenceless virgins, the only impression produced is that the women concerned were anxious to indulge the illusions of a free-handed gentleman who was not opposed to their preference for champagne above less expensive wines. Few persons, too, will care to follow Stead in his aspersions on the fair fame of the charwomen, a class of his fellow-creatures whom, with the social reformer's characteristic insensibility to the feelings of others, Stead roundly accused of luring unnumbered cooks and housemaids to their doom. Nor does the demon of iniquity, referred to by Stead as "the Minotaur of London," with his two thousand victims, seem much less mythological than the Minotaur of Crete.

The excitement aroused by *The Maiden Tribute* appears to have been at least equal to any manifestation of mass emotion during the Great War. On the Monday and Tuesday after the articles began Northumberland Street, in which the offices of the *Pall Mall Gazette* were situated, was filled with an infuriated mob, which no doubt included many charwomen and their male relatives; nor did the police take any notice of requests for protection until the Thursday of this week. The *Pall Mall Gazette* was banished from the railway book-stalls of W. H. Smith & Son, and in the House of Commons Mr. Cavendish Bentinck, who had fought the Criminal Law Amendment Bill with desperate tenacity and so far with success, asked the Home Secretary "whether his attention has been directed to certain publications relating to objectionable subjects which have been printed and circulated throughout the metropolis by the proprietors of the *Pall Mall Gazette,* and whether any means exist of subjecting the author and publishers of these objectionable publications to criminal proceedings." The Home Secretary's reply, on the following day, was courteous but vague. He had been advised, he said, that the publication of obscene matter could be prosecuted by indictment in the usual way and that the offence was punishable by fine and imprisonment, according to the direction of the court.

The daily press was at first unanimous against Stead. Later, they moderated their tone, with one or two exceptions, notably *The Evening News,* which Frank Harris was editing. Some months later this paper summarized as follows what was probably the view of *The Maiden Tribute* taken by the ordinary unregenerate Tory: "The hideous narratives of obscene practices which Stead professed to have revealed were based merely on gossip he had picked up from prostitutes when wandering about brothels 'in a state of intense mental excitement' and obfuscation due to unwonted indulgence in champagne and cigars."

Remonstrances poured in on Stead from many private individuals, who were much embarrassed by being compelled to read pornography at the breakfast table, in front of their children. One correspondent wrote: "I have taken care that my girls do not read such filth, and I hope every other parent has done the same." Another denounced "the mass of disgusting details which pollute your pages." A third requested that the *Pall Mall Gazette* may no longer be forwarded to his home address, as the articles cannot be read promiscuously in any family circle. A fourth wrote: "I am connected with a large printing-office, where a variety of small boys are employed. For the past two days these juveniles have been seen eagerly perusing the columns of your paper, which once had the reputation of being written by gentlemen for gentlemen."

But the country as a whole supported Stead with increasing enthusiasm. Meetings to force the Criminal Law Amendment Bill through Parliament were organized all over England. His sister, Mary Issie (for so she spelt her second name), wrote to him of the feeling in the north. "Ladies here full of enthusiasm say to me, 'Oh, Miss Stead, what a noble fellow your brother is. How I do honour him.' Did you see the *Jarrow Guardian?* Most touching. Every time the name Stead was mentioned the whole concourse of near, 1,000 men in the raft-yard waved their hats and cheered. . . . Oh, William, my heart is too full, I can't write, I can only say how I love and honour you."

The leaders of Nonconformity, Dr. Clifford and Spurgeon, were naturally with Stead; and in the biography of Hugh Price Hughes we read: "Mr. Stead has told the tale of how he (Mr. Hughes) came to him on the morning of publication, white and pale and quite terrible to look upon, so repressed was his wrath. 'Is it true?' he asked simply."

Outside Noncorformity, Stead had several important champions, Lord Shaftesbury, Lord Dalhousie, Cardinal Manning and Bishop Temple; but it seems probable that the following passage from the *Pall Mall Gazette,* of July 9th, holds the clue to the expedition with which Parliament placed the Criminal Law Amendment Bill on the Statute-Book.

> We challenge prosecution. . . . We are prepared, if we are driven to it, to prove our statements, prove them to the hilt, although in order to do so it may be necessary to subpœna as witnesses all those who are alluded to in our enquiries, either in proof of our *bona fides* or as to the truth of our statements, from the Archbishop of Canterbury to Mrs. Jefferies, and from the Prince of Wales down to the Minotaur of London.

The distaste inspired in the ordinary man by crusaders against self-indulgence, and especially by crusaders against sexual self-indulgence, derives from the feeling that this crusading is itself a form of self-indulgence, entered into primarily to satisfy instincts which the mass of men satisfy by less disingenuous methods. To the average sensual man, lacking both in enterprise and imagination, it seemed unfair that Stead should have been rewarded for his varied and curious experiences in houses of ill-fame by the benediction of venerable prelates and the passionate applause of countless refined women.

Opinions may differ about this aspect of Stead's campaign, but it is difficult to find any excuse for the part in the drama thrust upon Mrs. Armstrong by Stead and the Salvation Army. If we accept Stead's version, the poverty of Mrs. Armstrong was used to force her to sell her daughter for immoral purposes. A campaign on behalf of morality opened with, in the kind of phraseology favoured by Stead, the ruin of a woman's soul. If we accept Mrs. Armstrong's version, she was tricked into appearing before the world, and among her neighbours, as a mother who had sold her daughter into a brothel. Nor can we set much value on Stead's feeling for the self-respect or even ordinary human instincts of the poor, when we find him referring in the following terms to Mrs. Armstrong's attempt to recover the daughter transported to Paris by the Salvation Army: "The mother of Eliza Armstrong, although she might have been willing to sell her daughter into shame, had not bargained for losing her daughter altogether."

Without such methods, half callous, half hysterical, Stead would hardly have forced the Criminal Law Amendment Bill through Parliament. The taste of the times required to be stimulated with monsters of depravity and helpless victims. "There are," Stead declared in his speech at the Central Criminal Court, "between 50,000 and 60,000 lost girls on the London streets now, and if you think that the great multitude of our fallen sisters got there without the intervention of any go-betweens . . . you are muchly mistaken."

Out of the 16,000 prostitutes interviewed during this decade by the Rev. G. P. Merrick, Mr. Merrick does not quote one as attributing her downfall either to force or treachery. What, then, are we to make of the Minotaur of London, with his list of two thousand victims? Are we to suppose that the laws of probability suspended themselves in order to avert a meeting between the Reverend Merrick and some scores of these victims? Or are we to suppose that in his interviews with these victims, the Reverend Merrick, of all persons, followed with faint attention the exploits of the Minotaur and his retinue of charwomen? It seems impossible to credit Stead's revelations, unless one is willing to accept the hypothesis that the Minotaur of London was the Reverend G. P. Merrick.

Nearly twenty years later, in 1904, Stead visited the theatre for the first time. The play was *The Tempest.* Stead was moved by "the merciless enslavement inflicted upon Caliban for attempting the virtue of a maid"; but while he was condemning Prospero's cruelty it occurred to him that there were "sitting doleful in felons' cells all over the land, and not this land only, but throughout the English-speaking world, men serving out sentences of imprisonment with hard labour for offences against the virtue of maids, who but for my action nineteen years ago would have been free from prison bars." The change in the law was, he thinks, justified; the punishment not excessive. Yet "who can say how many of those men convicted under my Act have sunk into the hopeless criminal class, from which they may have found it as vain to escape as Caliban from the spells of Prospero."

It is a pity Stead was not editing a daily paper at this time. He might have given the public a series of articles on *The Caliban Tribute of Modern Babylon.* (pp. 185-93)

. . . . .

Stead's spiritualism, which towards the close of his life became the chief interest in his life, puzzled and alienated many of his supporters. They regarded his connection with Julia as an inexplicable aberration, though it was really a synthesis, on a plane beyond the reach of disillusionment, of Stead's two chief preoccupations, God and woman. In the spirit world his fancies at last became facts.

"What is it to be a Christian?" was a question which had already exercised Stead in his *Pall Mall Gazette* days, and when he was editing *The Review of Reviews* he quoted a number of answers from a magazine called *The Young Man.*

The answer of the Reverend D. P. Macpherson was: "To be a Christian is to be a *Christ*-ian." Without pausing to wonder what this epigram was like in its earlier stages, before the Rev. D. P. Macpherson laid his pen down and gazed at its completed form, one may see in it an example of the growing tendency, even among the orthodox, as the nineteenth century neared its end, to emphasize Christ's teaching and example rather than his divinity.

Stead mirrored this tendency in his usual style. There is no definite evidence that he ever ceased to accept Christ's divinity in the literal sense, but he seems to have become increasingly convinced of the potential divinity of all men, the complete acceptance of which view abolishes the distinction between Christ and the rest of humanity.

During his imprisonment after **The Maiden Tribute** he wrote: "What we want is not to be Christians but to be Christs. . . . A whole gulf cuts us off from all but a few of our fellow-creatures. Yet we are one with them, one with the thief, the harlot: that is, we ought to be. And until we are, we are not Christs."

In his statement of "The Gospel according to the P.M.G." he comes very near to what at that date would have been considered complete unorthodoxy. "A new catholicity," he writes, "has dawned upon the world. All religions are looked upon as essentially Divine. They represent the different angles at which man looks at God. Questions of origin, polemics as to evidences, erudite dissertations concerning formulae, are disappearing, because religions are no longer judged by their supposed accordance with Divine Revelation, but by their ability to minister to the wants and fulfil the aspirations of man. . . . Handsome is that handsome does. Christian is that Christian does. The man who acts as Christ would do under the same circumstances is the true believer, though all his dogmas be heretical and his mind is in a state of blind agnosticism."

On this side Stead's religion reflected the humanitarianism of his age. In his belief that God was his Senior Partner, as he used to call Him, Stead showed his Puritan origin. "I went into Notre Dame to have a talk with God," he once said to a friend, "when an overwhelming sense came over me of the greatness of the task to which I was called with this *Review of Reviews* and the *Daily Paper.* I felt so crushed that I said to God, "Is this not putting too many eggs in one basket?"

But Stead's view that a new catholicity had dawned upon the world, and that all religions are essentially divine, quarrelled with his Puritan sense of a God working out His purposes through the small group of His elect. However confidently he referred to his Senior Partner, and to the "sign-posts," which at each one of the innumerable crises in his life the Senior Partner set up for his guidance, he needed some other assurance of the nearness of God than his own asseverations. His dreams of Imperial Federation, and an Anglo-American Republic, expressed his unconscious desire to compress the unmanageable modern world into a single community. In an isolated community, like New England in its early days, or in a small State beset by enemies, like Israel, the directing forces of the universe naturally embody themselves in a personal God, with a close and exclusive interest in the community's welfare. Such a personal God Stead wished to bring back to the modern world, and to his own consciousness. It was this need which, as his imperialistic visions faded, entangled him always more inextricably in spiritualism; for spiritualism is the mysticism of the materialist, the means by which, when the framework of a solid materialistic creed like Puritanism begins to disintegrate, the adherent of this creed tries to regain what is slipping from him.

"Nothing," Stead wrote in his preface to **After Death,** "can be less scientific than to ignore the subject and to go on living from day to day in complete uncertainty whether we are entities which dissolve like the morning mist when our bodies die, or whether we are destined to go on living after the change we call death."

"Entities which dissolve like the morning mist" measures the gap between Stead's belief and the belief of men like Bunyan and Jonathan Edwards, or even Charles Wesley.

In his later years, Stead used to declare that if he were remembered at all by posterity, it would be as "Julia's amanuensis"; Julia being an American lady, Miss Julia Ames, who began in 1892, shortly after her death, to communicate with Stead, and continued this practice with increasing assiduity during the remainder of Stead's life.

Among Stead's papers was found a record he had made of messages received from Julia in 1892 and 1893. The writing is Stead's, but slopes backward more than his usual handwriting, and sometimes becomes disordered and straggling, or degenerates into a formless scribble.

Julia, in one of these messages, gives Stead her view of two of his women-secretaries. One of them is too sharp with her tongue, the other is becoming dangerously attached to him. In another message Julia tells Stead that the Prince Consort and John Brown propose to help Stead with a character-sketch of Queen Victoria, but before affording this assistance they must stipulate that nothing in the sketch will be of a nature to offend the Queen. Parnell communicates through Julia his unflattering view of Mr. Healy, but not of Stead, and Tennyson, more amenable since his death, dictates a poem which Stead submitted to various persons as conclusive evidence that Julia was not a projection of his unconscious self. Mr. F. W. H. Myers, though himself a spiritualist, could not find Tennyson in the poem, much to the annoyance of Tennyson, who informed Stead through Julia that Myers was an opinionated poetaster. "I wish," Tennyson added, "you would not delay in writing about it to Swinburne. He is a judge. He would not resent your letter." There is no record that this suggestion was acted upon; so no doubt it was.

In one of these messages, which I reproduce in its original punctuation, Stead's desire to unify all mankind in some not very clearly formulated belief and his thirst for a closer sense of God are both expressed: "No you are not a weak miserable wretched creature you are a poor mean worm yourself But you are the destined instrument of the truth and it will be mighty mightier far than you imagine Oh my dear dear friend how I envy you the opportunities you will have You will deliver mankind from the fear of death and bring them into the living presence of spirit. Yes that paper will be your throne the world will hear and listen and believe. My dear William Have you lost hold of the Hand of God? Julia Ames. No I will write no more today. NO, NO, NO, the Hand of God never leaves hold of you. Courage pray more. Read the Bible more and Remember THE LORD LIVETH. Goodbye. JULIA AMES." (pp. 216-20)

> Hugh Kingsmill, "W. T. Stead," in his *After Puritanism*, Duckworth, 1929, pp. 171-220.

J. W. Robertson Scott (essay date 1952)

[*Robertson Scott was an English journalist and editor who worked for the* Pall Mall Gazette *during Stead's editorship. In the following excerpt, he offers a favorable appraisal of some of Stead's achievements as editor of that newspaper.*]

Sir Arthur Quiller-Couch would have found in Stead's articles some of the jargon against which he warred. But 'Q' would have been the first to repudiate the notion that no man may write who is slipshod about 'in the case of' and indifferent to literature which may 'glad a few high souls once in a century'. Stead's strength of conviction, his fervour, his sense of effectual calling, his consciousness of ability in his profession, his untiring industry and curiosity, his faculty for enlisting all his powers, and his drilling in the Bible, Bunyan, Milton and Lowell gave him an effectiveness as a writer for the day which eclipsed all faults of style and some errors of taste. His quiet, cultivated assistant editor, of Winchester and Oxford, E. T. Cook, must have suffered many things because of him. I have the Bible that Stead used at the *Pall Mall*. It has one or two holes in its pages where the scissors of an editor 'with no feeling for books' have pounced into it in a hurry for a favourite text for that leader which was always being written against time. Stead's godlier following would have been aghast had they had a sight of the mutilated Scriptures, but Stead, though he had a rare acquaintance with the Bible and valued it intensely, revolted at the sanctimonious. As I have noted, he was on as easy terms as Cromwell with both his Bible and his God. The religious folk who followed Carlyle's 'good man Stead' got shocks. But not more shocks than were received by the ungodly who came along with him because he was a political force and found themselves in the company of one who cared as little for the *convenances* as Ezekiel.

The *Pall Mall*, in spite of the endeavours of Cook and Edmund Garrett—on whom a word later—was often, as I say, a scorn to literary persons. But Stead had some niceties of his own. Within the first few weeks of my novitiate in the office he opened the shutter in the wall which divided his writing den from the room in which I worked and demanded to know what I meant by writing 'the *P.M.G.* man' in a few lines of chat I had had with a celebrity.

Ruskin was not the only master of letters who overlooked Stead's literary infelicities in appreciation of his purposes. Ruskin was indeed a frequent correspondent for publication or for private counsel. On one occasion he sent to the office a copy of the paper—a copy now, alas, lost—with almost every item in it re-headed or marked to be cut down, or omitted, or to occupy greater space or a more prominent position. (pp. 79-81)

That a man had abused the editor of the *Pall Mall* in speech or print would not in the least prevent Stead from going to see him and hearing what he had to say for himself, or offering him an opportunity to state his views. It is not easy to credit how gross were the attacks on Stead after *The Maiden Tribute.* He had stirred ugly depths in more than one part of London life. At the starting of the *Review of Reviews* it was pleasantly suggested that Stead had got capital out of the headquarters fund of the Salvation Army. I heard him reply to the suggestion that in this instance he should bring a libel action 'I would not take legal proceedings if it were stated that I had killed my grandmother and eaten her'.

Stead was big. He would have welcomed to his sanctum, with equal vivacity and the office cup of tea, Gabriel and Judas and, on the departure of each of them, would at once have dictated one of those marvellously accurate interviews of his, for, as there is no end of testimony, his memory was—one is tempted to write the ill-used word—phenomenal.(p. 82)

Stead had all the virtues credited to him, along with warmth, accessibility and self-criticism, but little humour. Think of trying to sell the public the truth about South Africa in a brochure called *Shall I Slay My Brother Boer?* (Is it surprising that there was a skit, 'Shall I Kick My Brother Stead?') He got on the nerves of people who were as concerned, or almost as much concerned, as he was about objects he had in view. Many men and women with only a public impression of him or without sympathy for his aims detested him. Some people had no doubt that he was mad. There was at the time, in large sections of the public, much prudery, widespread unwillingness to have truths blurted out, not a little contentment with things, on the whole, as they were, and amazing ignorance.

SHOWMAN? No doubt Stead liked appreciation as other

people do; but he had also a relish for abuse. Did it not show that what he was writing was hitting the mark? A common criticism of him was that he was a good showman. 'Barnum' was flung at him. Certainly he saw no good in hiding his light under a bushel or in keeping back what he thought it was for the good of the public that it should buy and read. He was a downright speaker at a public meeting because he knew it was no good addressing people if they did not listen. There was no knowing, of course, what he might not say—or do. He was in dead earnest. Bernard Shaw told me that he had to leave some political demonstration 'because Stead turned it into a prayer meeting'. Hadley thinks this may be misleading. 'I never knew Stead attend a party political meeting. More than once I heard him preface his own speach with a very short prayer. It was his common practice to say a few words of prayer before addressing his Peace Crusade meetings.'

Allowances had to be made, and were made by thousands, for Stead. For the work he had to do for his time it is not easy to see that he could have been very different from what he was. His methods were not what his critics would have chosen. These methods seemed the only possible ones to him. He was a little turbulent, spectacular, melodramatic, but how few of us have left adolescence completely behind? Stead puts in our minds Francis Thompson's aspirations:

> Oh for the flushed excitement of keen strife!
> For mountains, gulfs and torrents in my way,
> With perils, anguish, fear and strugglings rife!
> For friends and foes, for love and hate in fray—
> And not this lone, flat, torpid life.

Stead lacked the poise, balance and judgment often possessed by persons of mediocre achievement. He divided his strength. He used up his energies not only in the pursuit of great ideals but fidgeted and frayed by idle, vain and selfish people and by some crude and trifling efforts made in association with them. He had moments of defeat and abasement; but, when account is taken of all, he did experience the joy of life which, as Shaw has told us, is 'being a force, being thoroughly worn out before you are thrown on the scrap heap'.

Something should be added concerning Stead's extraordinary tenacity of purpose in union with an uncommon willingness to turn right about when he found on enquiry that the facts were against him. Only a few of his intimates understood this. 'Get to know your facts' was, as I keep saying, his workaday motto. It was in a search for facts, a spiritual search that he was persuaded must be successful, that he was led into some morasses. Of the sincerity of his telepathic beliefs no one who knew him could doubt for an instant. One day I wired to him that I should come in the evening to see him at Wimbledon. 'My dear Robertson Scott', he said on my arrival, 'why did you take the trouble to wire? You know that you could have made me aware of your coming'.

WOMEN'S DEBT. Stead's name is remembered with gratitude by many women. It might well be cherished by more. The other day I met a woman of education and public spirit, in a circle usually supposed to be well-informed, who had never heard of *The Maiden Tribute.* To pose Stead as a plaster saint for the women's movement would be, of course, ignorant and absurd. Sincere Congregationalist he was to the last, a 'twicer', like Gladstone, at his Sunday religious exercises; but no man was less 'tied up wi' godly laces'. He was not 'sicklied o'er' with his religion. He was a religious and honest man. A Galahad, no man of his time can have been more exposed to 'temptation'. Stead, like so many big natures, had a saving vein of Rabelaisianism, but his life was lived at a high level of morality.

Clever women with sparks of ability but often stranded, undisciplined and unfit, women to whom no other editor than Stead would have given any hearing at all, were often to be met with ascending or descending his stairs or lying in wait for his kind word, his recommendation or his charity. A young woman once said to me, 'He talked to me as if I were his equal'. I remember, too, one of Stead's meetings. There was a good and famous woman on the platform beside him who, as she came forward to speak, attracted the attention of the reporters, for her bonnet seemed to slide to a sharper angle, a piece of stuff in the penetralia of her skirts ripped and a hairpin dropped beside her. A rather superior representative of *The Times* attending his first 'purity' meeting muttered to me as he gazed, 'Gad, I could trust that woman anywhere!'

THE GOSPEL ACCORDING TO THE PALL MALL GAZETTE. When a final judgment on Stead's career comes to be passed it may well be asked just what our journalism would have been without him. The roots of some of the better things which were cropped by Northcliffe are to be found, as Northcliffe agreed with me more than once, in the pioneering and vision of Stead. It would have been a worthy exercise if, when his circle began to narrow and his light to fail a little, more of those who with advantage walked in daily and periodical journalism in his footsteps had owned their indebtedness to Northumberland Street and Mowbray House. Not only at home but all over the world the 'gospel' according to the *Pall Mall,* as Stead taught it, came to be practised. Some will have in mind the service of the American and Australasian *Review of Reviews.* Nor will readers of Sir Edward Cook's *Edmund Garrett* (Arnold), in which one of Stead's men writes of a colleague, fail to see how much of the *Pall Mall* there was, in a time of Imperial crisis, in the *Cape Times,* how much of Stead was its Editor-Assemblyman in that public work which is part of the history of South Africa and is proudly acknowledged in Capetown Cathedral. Nothing touched me more during my publication in wartime of a monthly review in Tokyo (*The New East*) than a message from Havelock Ellis in which he said: 'It is clear that you have been largely inspired by Stead and in this, I think, you have been wise'. (pp. 84-8)

> J. W. Robertson Scott, "The Man and His Work," in his The Life and Death of a Newspaper, Methuen & Co. Ltd., 1952, pp. 76-89.

Warren Sylvester Smith (essay date 1968)

[*Smith is an American editor, educator, and critic who has written several works about George Bernard Shaw. In the following excerpt, Smith surveys Stead's career as a reformer.*]

> **Alfred, Lord Milner on Stead and the *Pall Mall Gazette*:**
>
> I do not think that within my recollection any newspaper in any country has ever exercised so much influence upon public affairs as the *Pall Mall* did during the first years of [Stead's] editorship. This was, of course, entirely due to the force of his personality. My own position, I believe, was nominally that of assistant editor. I was certainly his closest associate, and the relations between us were those of the greatest intimacy and confidence. But, as far as actual work was concerned, my duties were almost a farce. No power on earth could have prevented [Stead] from doing all the work himself—not only writing almost the whole of the literary matter but inspiring and controlling almost every part of it. But if my position inside the paper was as easy as it was always delightful, "external relations" were certainly not equally comfortable. To tell the truth, we were always in hot water with one or other large portion of the public. The tremendous energy—not to say recklessness—with which the *Pall Mall* of those days urged its invariably very pronounced opinions naturally excited no little animosity.
>
> *quoted by Frederic Whyte in his* Life of W. T. Stead, *1925.*

William T. Stead and Bernard Shaw were both in their own ways such incurable reformers and such compulsive meddlers that few London groups calling themselves "progressive" did not know them. Shaw alone has so completely described every twist and turn of interest in a flood of correspondence, prefaces, recorded speeches, and letters-to-the-editor that the time may come when readers will assume that he invented the Edwardian Age. (p. 254)

But Shaw and Stead were not a team. They rarely saw each other and, according to Shaw never spoke over the three decades when they were both in London, but they communicated occasionally. Stead indirectly gave Shaw needed assistance in the beginning of his journalistic career. William Archer, who had been reviewing for Stead's *Pall Mall Gazette,* steered some of the reviewing Shaw's way in 1886, and this led to a continuing association of Shaw with the *Gazette*. After the Bloody Sunday riot of 1887, Annie Besant remained their mutual friend. Stead was not in the actual march, but he helped raise bail and was part of Linnell's funeral. Afterwards he helped found the Law and Liberty League and co-edited, with Annie, its short-lived organ, *The Link.* GBS supported Stead's attack on the slums, but never forgave him for the "put-up job" of ***The Maiden Tribute.*** Nevertheless Shaw later advised the easy-going T. P. O'Connor of *The Star* to make himself, for the sake of good journalism, as hated as Stead was. At the turn of the century Shaw and Stead worked together in uneasy tandem in the "International Peace Crusade" though, as usual, their aims were not identical.

Stead was completely anti-theatre for years, and Shaw failed consistently to get him to attend. Eventually in his fifty-fifth year Stead was lured into the theatre by the actress, Elizabeth Robins. Quite in character, he made great news of his conversion, and thereafter published his reactions to any plays he saw in his *Review of Reviews*. For the most part he praised Shaw's plays highly—*John Bull's Other Island, Candida,* and *Major Barbara.* The latter he thought had "the pathos of Gethsemane, the tragedy of Calvary". He compared it with the Passion Play of Oberammergau—one of the few plays he had previously seen. Shaw was not flattered. He thought the Passion Play dull stuff, and did not respect Stead's views on artistic matters.

> He was a gifted journalist, but a complete Philistine, to whom literature was not a fine art but simply news. He was as ignorant as it is possible for a newspaper man in possession of his five senses to be on art. Science, philosophy: in short, of literature.

Stead's puritanical notions of the inherent wickedness of the theatre and its people were, he admitted, deeply ingrained, and, at the outset of his theatrical adventure, he expressed his concern as to whether the theatre was a power making for righteousness. A slight slur on the morality of actresses produced the following sample of Shavian invective [in a letter to the editor of the *Freethinker*]:

> What do you mean, you foolish William Stead, by an immoral actress? I will take you into any church you like, and show you gross women who are visibly gorged with every kind of excess, with coarse voices and bloated features, to whom money means unrestrained gluttony and marriage unrestrained sensuality; but against whose characters—whose "purity" as you call it—neither you nor their pastors dare level a rebuke. And I will take you to the theatre, and show you women whose work requires a constant physical training, an unblunted nervous sensibility, and a fastidious refinement and self-control which one week of ordinary plutocratic fat-feeding and self-indulgence would wreck, and who anxiously fulfil these requirements; and yet when you learn that they do not allow their personal relations to be regulated by your gratuitously unnatural and vicious English marriage laws, you will not hesitate to call them "immoral". The truth is that if the average British matron could be made half as delicate about her sexual relations, or half as abstemious in her habits as the average stage heroine, there would be an enormous improvement in our national manners and morals. When you sit in the stalls, think of this, and as the curtain rises and your eyes turn from the stifling grove of fat naked shoulders round you to the decent and refined lady on the stage, humble your bumptious spirit with a new sense of the extreme perversity and wickedness of that uncharitable Philistine bringing up of yours.
>
> Hoping that your mission will end in your own speedy and happy conversion—I am, as ever, your patient Mentor,
>
> G. Bernard Shaw.

Poor Stead had neither the sophistication nor the humour to defend himself against such an onslaught. Neither had he any understanding of the "new morality"—especially sex morality—and his warm friendship with such "new women" as Annie Besant and Olive Schreiner remains something of a mystery.

Small wonder that Shaw found him "impossible as a colleague: he had to work single-handed because he was incapable of keeping faith when excited; and as his hyperaesthesia was chronic he generally *was* excited". This was borne out by John Morley, who successfully tempted Stead to come to London to edit the *Pall Mall Gazette* in 1880. After three tempestuous years with Stead, Morley left the magazine and entered Parliament, eventually to become Irish Secretary. He accepted that challenge with the simple comment, "As I kept Stead in order for three years, I don't see why I shouldn't govern Ireland."

Stead came down to London with reservations, for he looked on the metropolis with the suspicions of a Puritan reared in the traditions of Milton, Cromwell, and the Pilgrim Fathers. Furthermore, at thirty-one, he had already a successful record as editor of the *Northern Echo* at Darlington, and a family that he preferred not to raise in a city "steeped in cynicism and indifference". Still, there was an element of the inevitable in the confrontation of this largely self-educated son of a Congregationalist minister and the city he was to characterize as "the modern Babylon". Standing on the deck of the *Titanic,* at the sensational end to a sensational career, there was still some doubt as to whether he had changed London more than London had changed him.

We have already observed, in connection with his Spiritualism, that he was, at bottom, religiously conservative, though far from satisfied with the answers of orthodoxy or the behaviour of the Churches. He remained a seeker. His employer, Morley, was a professed Atheist, and wished to make the *Pall Mall Gazette* a declared advocate of Secularism. Stead, of course, could not do this. But in a later memoir of Morley he was able to say,

> . . . I am by no means sure that he, the Atheist, is not much more deeply religious than I, the Christian. . . . There is a depth of reverence about him and a fine sympathy of soul to which I can lay no claim. . . . I, on the other hand, am so impatient, so vehement, so anxious ever to jog the elbow of the Almighty, that I fancy Mr. Morley's mood of mind harmonizes much more with the truly religious ideal, which is perhaps more devotional, more meditative, more resigned than mine could ever be. . . . I cannot be moderate, the throbbing of my heart will never cool, the fever burns within my brain.

Neither in the *Gazette* nor in the *Review of Reviews,* which he founded in 1890, did he apologize for or conceal his religious motivations. It was a religion of feeling, not of thought—he rarely took time to think—and its continuing inconsistency never seemed to matter. Much of the time his religious utterances sounded like those of a revivalist preacher, but he yearned to be counted among the "advanced" thinkers too. In a New Year's summary for 1885 he wrote:

> The formulas and shibboleths of a former age shrivel up or fall into pieces before the silent energies of present facts. Evolution is the greatest of all revolutions, for it is a constant factor in the progress of the race. Our creeds and our institutions perish or pass, not because we will but because they must. . . . The insignificance of the individual appears almost infinite.

Churchmen were glad to have him on their side, but his support always raised questions. His association with diverse and suspect personalities was well known: the notorious if fascinating Annie Besant; the glamorous Russophile, Mme. Novikoff; the bohemian feminist, Olive Schreiner; the arch-imperialist millionaire, Cecil Rhodes—not to speak of his reported contacts beyond the grave. The truth is that in a very real sense, editing was his religion and his heresy. He was a new kind of journalist in the 1880s and he made the *Pall Mall Gazette* and the *Review of Reviews* social and religious documents. The latter was the first of the "digests", a compendium of articles from many sources, meant to make the finest contemporary journalism accessible to all English-speaking people. It began in January 1890. A special American edition was in charge of Albert Shaw.

Paradoxical in almost every respect (Lord Milner described him as a combination of Don Quixote and P. T. Barnum), he retained his pose of Champion of the Downtrodden throughout all his other roles. He neglected everything for his work—his social life, his family, even his manners (he called himself "the wild barbarian from the north"). This lifelong compulsive attachment to his mission was the real reason for the lack of culture which so disturbed GBS.

His journalistic ethics appalled many, but there can be no doubt about the effectiveness of his drive to better the conditions of the London poor. His part in publicizing *The Bitter Cry of Outcast London* helped bring about Lord Salisbury's action for the Royal Commission on the Housing of the Poor, which may be regarded as the beginning of modern social legislation. It incidentally catapulted the *Pall Mall Gazette* into public attention and high circulation figures.

All waves of Stead-inspired sensationalism, however, are reduced to mere ripples compared to the public indignation he stirred by his dramatic gesture against juvenile prostitution in 1885. Floundering in Parliament that year was a Criminal Law Amendment Bill, strongly supported by welfare workers but little regarded by the rest of the public. The welfare workers came to Stead for help. Stead was shocked to discover that any girl over thirteen was legally responsible for her own behaviour, and at the mercy of procurers. Many young girls, Stead was told, were inveigled into houses of prostitution, often hardly knowing what was in store for them.

"Aren't their screams enough to raise hell?" Stead asked.

"They don't even raise the neighbours," a Scotland Yard investigator told him.

"Then I will raise hell!"

The plan that Stead concocted and carried out has little competition for melodrama in nineteenth-century fiction. He went first to London's three most eminent churchmen:

the Archbishop of Canterbury (Edward White Benson), the Bishop of London (Frederick Temple, later himself Archbishop of Canterbury), and Cardinal Manning. The Archbishop demurred with some shock, but the others promised support.

Stead then asked the direct help of the Salvation Army's General Booth and his family. Through them he got in touch with Rebecca Jarrett, a procuress before she had joined the Army. Reluctant to return to her old ways even in a good cause, this woman nevertheless succeeded in obtaining from the child's mother thirteen-year-old Eliza Armstrong for the price of three pounds down and the promise of two pounds later; she then installed the girl in a brothel run by a Mme. Mourez. Posing as the patron who had financed this transaction, Stead presented himself at the brothel and was permitted to enter Eliza's room—where he found her asleep. When she awoke, startled, Stead called in a waiting Salvation Army woman officer who proceeded, as planned, to take charge of the girl. After a prominent London physician examined Eliza she was removed from the centre of the publicity that was to follow and placed in the care of the Salvation Army in Paris.

"Even at this date," Stead wrote in 1910, "I stand aghast at the audacity with which I carried the thing through." There is just a suggestion of self-delusion here. It was a task entirely cut to his own cloth, and there can be little doubt that both in creating the drama and in acting it out he enjoyed himself to the full.

In five flamboyant summer issues, the *Pall Mall Gazette* presented the great exposure to London and to the world under the banner of **The Maiden Tribute of Modern Babylon.** Stead's language was not calculated to spare Victorian prudery, and there were those who thought it almost better to let the evil persist than to talk so openly about it. In today's world of blatant tabloids we may even find a touch of nostalgia in such a comment as this from the *Weekly Times:* "The evil will be spread, till there will scarcely be a boy or girl in England whose ignorance will not be displaced by forbidden knowledge, or whose innocence will not be tainted." But expressions of support far outweighed such timidities. England rose to its duty, even while deploring Stead's vulgarity. The Criminal Law Amendment Bill passed through both Houses of Parliament in almost record time.

For all the to-do, its reforms seem less than radical: it raised the "age of consent" to sixteen, allowed girls of any age to testify against procurers and increased penalties for both domestic and "white slavery" traffic in prostitution. On the other hand a dark corner of London underworld which reformers had sought for decades to bring before the public conscience was suddenly flooded with light. (pp. 256-62)

Warren Sylvester Smith, "Independent Seekers and the View Ahead," in his The London Heretics, 1870-1914, *Dodd, Mead & Company, 1968, pp. 254-83.*

Constance Benson on Stead's "conversion":

In the year 1904 I received a letter from W. T. Stead asking me to send him my views on an article he had written, which he enclosed.

It was a sweeping condemnation of the Theatrical Profession, laying particular stress on the immorality of the Actors and Actresses, though the writer admitted he had never been inside a theatre in his life. I sent him a most indignant reply to what I naturally considered a most unwarrantable attack on a fine profession. He published my letter in the *Review of Reviews* and wrote me a most courteous letter, saying "I have published your reply to me, and I dare say I deserve all you say—I am quite open to be converted to your views." Soon after, when we were playing at the Fulham Theatre he came to see me, and I suggested to him that he should come to Stratford the following Festival and see for himself the kind of life led by the average actor on tour. He at once accepted my challenge, and the following Spring, 1905, saw W. T. Stead sitting night after night in the stalls of a theatre—a place hitherto as hateful to him as an "unfilled can" to Sir Toby Belch—listening with the keenest enjoyment to the plays of Shakespeare spoken by the mouths of the "licentious rogues and vagabonds." What he saw of the life and work of the actors made a lasting impression on him, and completely shattered his old prejudices. So much so indeed, that not only was this visit the prelude to many others—and, I am proud to add, the foundation of a deep personal friendship between us—but the following year he sent his daughter Estelle to join our company. Henceforward he became one of our staunchest supporters, and never failed in his sympathy and help.

Lady Constance Benson, in her Mainly Players: Bensonian Memories, *1926.*

Joseph O. Baylen (essay date 1969)

[*Baylen is an American historian who has written extensively on English Radicalism. In the following excerpt, he surveys Stead's skill as an interviewer.*]

As the innovator of the "New Journalism" in late Victorian Britain, Stead adapted and perfected the American technique of interviewing in the British press [according to Harold Herd in his *The March of Journalism. The Story of the British Press from 1622 to the Present Day*]. In spite of criticism that he was vulgarizing the British press by promoting "the Americanisation of English journalism . . . ," [H. R. Fox Bourne, in *English Newspapers. Chapters in the History of Journalism,* asserts that] Stead utilized the interview as a journalistic device in dealing with all situations. [In Frank G. Carpenter's "A Chat with Stead" in the Washington *Evening Star* of 24 December 1892 Stead remarked]:

> The field of the interviewer . . . is one of the most attractive in journalism. The newspaper is for the communication of thought. The interview is one of the best methods of such communication. It brings the reader and thinker close together, and such talks sometimes change history. . . .

Stead's innovation was so effective that by the 1890's young British journalists had enthusiastically accepted the interview as [What Harold Spender in his *The Fire of Life. A Book of Memories* termed] "a very handy method of picking great people's brains. . . . " And, Stead himself set the example for his colleagues and the British press by the publication of such interviews as that with "Chinese" Gordon in early January, 1884, which helped compel the Gladstone Government to dispatch Gordon to the Sudan and to his death at Khartoum. Indeed, as Stead's contemporaries recalled, Stead was "a tireless and persistent interviewer" who was "astonishingly successful" in obtaining access to all sorts of prominent personalities. The "list of the captives of his bow and arrow," wrote a journalist friend, "extends from . . . Czar to General Gordon . . . ," even though (as Stead readily admitted) he was never able "to report the other person's views without introducing his own. . . . " Similarly, Stead's old colleague, Aaron Watson, later remarked [in his *A Newspaper Man's Memories*]:

> He was always interviewing, though 'not necessarily for . . . publication.' No man that I ever met could put so many questions in so short a space of time . . . [and] there was only an occasional opportunity for a reply. [In fact] . . . many . . . [of those interviewed] . . . must have gone away feeling that they had been interviewed by a hurricane.

Stead's approach was always direct. J. L. Garvin told Stead's biographer that "when Stead met great personages . . . he looked quite steady into their eyes . . . [with what] was an almost daunting expression of nerve force. . . . " Yet, as Aaron Watson noted, on the request of the person interviewed, Stead would not publish the record of the interview or even mention the source of the information he had obtained during the conversation.

Stead's technique in interviewing often had two objectives: (1) the conversion of the individual interviewed to his cause and (2) the alignment of public opinion behind the cause. In fact, during the interview it seemed as if Stead, while listening to the person interviewed, was hearing [what Robert Marss Lovett called] "the great roar of the people outside." But, in spite of the frame of reference and purpose which sometimes marked his interviews, Stead's memoranda of the dialogue were remarkably accurate. It was Stead's accuracy as an interrogator which most impressed his Assistant Editor on the *Pall Mall Gazette*, Edward Tyas Cook. At the close of a long and distinguished career in British journalism, Cook [in his *Literary Recreations*] rated Stead and his protégé, Edmund Garrett, as the "ablest interviewers" he had ever known because of "The general accuracy of their interviews. . . . " "They never took a note," averred Cook, "and did not attempt to reproduce with slavish literalness every word that was said by their subjects . . . . "

Almost all of Stead's contemporaries and colleagues greatly admired his remarkable memory and especially his ability to conduct an interview without the necessity of taking notes on the conversation. Although the practice of composing a written record immediately after the meeting contributed to the accuracy of Stead's memoranda, the major factor was his acute recall of what was said and had occurred. Stead's partner, the editor of *The American Review of Reviews,* Dr. Albert Shaw, was not only impressed with Stead's unusual powers of recall, but also with his ability "to transmute a conversation in which no notes were taken into an extended report of almost flawless accuracy . . . . " Shaw's observation was confirmed by Lord Bryce who, after Stead's death on the *Titanic,* remarked that an "uncanny" memory was one of Stead's unusual attributes.

> I remember [Bryce wrote] how once when we had been discussing inaccurate versions which most interviewers are apt to give of things said in talk, he offered to write out and send to me an account of all I had said to him in a half-hour conversation. The account came the next day, and was accurate in every particular . . . .

Stead attributed his remarkable memory to exercises in "remembering the leading points of whatever was heard" which his father, the Rev. William Stead, had devised for the children in the Stead family manse. In a pamphlet [**My Father: (The Rev. William Stead)**] memorializing his father's death in 1884, Stead explained:

> the habit of taking a condensed precis of a speech or a sermon stood me in good stead in after life. To this hour, if I want a condensed report of a speech, I would rather have a long hand summary than the cut down report of the most efficient reporter . . . .This faculty of remembering what has been said to you in order to repeat it at home has been of great use to me in many ways. In interviewing it is invaluable. I have frequently, without taking a single note, been able to dictate or write three columns of close print report of an interview, to the accuracy of which the person interviewed has given his most emphatic testimony . . . .

If Stead occasionally erred in recording an interview it was not in deliberately giving a false impression, but in his tendency to see things "through the eyes of Stead" and to speak on things [as T. P. O'Connor put it] "in the language of Stead . . . . " (pp. 23-6)

> Joseph O. Baylen, in his The Tsar's "Lecturer-General": W. T. Stead and the Russian Revolution of 1905, *Atlanta School of Arts and Sciences, Georgia State University College of Arts and Sciences,* 1969, 93 p.

James Mennell (essay date 1984)

[*In the following excerpt, Mennell examines the pro-Socialist campaign Stead conducted in the* Pall Mall Gazette *from 1885-1887.*]

William T. Stead, editor of the *Pall Mall Gazette* during much of the 1880s, was a daring and resourceful editor. His press campaigns had the impact of bombshells on the English public and usually obtained concrete results. His emotional plea for the "Bulgarian maidens" in 1876 created the Bulgarian Atrocities issue that helped produce the Liberal election victory of 1880; his pioneering use of the public interview with General "Chinese" Gordon created much of the public pressure that forced Gladstone to send Gordon to Egypt; and his most famous press campaign, *The Maiden Tribute of Modern Babylon* in 1885, aroused England to change the law to protect young girls from white slavery.

Stead conducted another press campaign that affected politics but has been largely forgotten. In 1885 he began a campaign to guide the young Socialist movement into the Radical camp by offering free and sympathetic publicity in the *PMG* in return for influence on Socialist policy. Such attempts to sway political opponents with cajolery are not new. But such tactics nevertheless may influence events and may cast light on facets of politics hitherto unnoticed. And when a talented editor like Stead is involved, something big is likely to happen. In fact, such were Stead's journalistic powers that he was able to attract at least 100,000 people to a Socialist demonstration by 1887 and to bring the Socialists into a working relationship with the Radicals for a time.

One is likely to ask why the editor of a respectable newspaper would risk getting involved with the outcast Socialists. Stead could not hope to sell more newspapers by supporting such an unpopular group; indeed he risked a decline in circulation figures. In fact [according to Frederic Whyte in his *Life of W. T. Stead*], his support for the Socialists helped cost him his job in 1888. We must look elsewhere for his motive in publicly supporting the Socialists.

Stead's basic motive seems to have been political. Although he was clearly not a Marxist like the Socialists he would deal with, Stead was a Radical with a genuine sympathy for the poor. He believed that people should be given every opportunity possible to improve themselves. To promote this idea [K. S. Inglis writes in *The Churches and the Working Classes in Victorian England*] he had turned an obscure pamphlet, *The Bitter Cry of Outcast London,* into a very successful press campaign to awaken the public to the plight of the poor. But at the same time that Stead sympathised with the poor he was aware that their new voting power could easily be manipulated. What if some politician like Joseph Chamberlain were to pander to the mass of voters to win political power? Chamberlain had only recently publicly asked what ransom the rich would pay to remain in power. For Stead [Whyte notes] this question raised the spectre of ruinous taxation of the successful to benefit the unsuccessful.

This concern with Chamberlain helps to explain Stead's courting of the Socialists. One would assume that Stead thought the Socialists even more dangerous than Chamberlain since their Marxist aims were far more threatening than Chamberlain was likely to be. Yet Stead never attacked the English Socialists as vehemently as he attacked Chamberlain. Stead apparently believed that deep down inside an English Socialist lay an English Radical similar in views and sincerity to Stead himself. Stead had many times already shown himself to be the most dynamic editor in England, unafraid to go against prevailing views. It is in the Stead mold for him to have believed that, for all their Marxist ideology, the Socialists were not as dangerous as commonly thought, but at heart were Radicals if only they could be gently pushed to see it. Stead was bold enough to make that push even if it required an editorial position that would jeopardize his career with the *PMG*.

Stead's plan had no chance of success unless there was a willingness by the Socialists to moderate their behavior in return for the free publicity from Stead. The Social Democratic Federation, which in 1884 had brought together most active Socialists, was in such need of publicising its cause to the public at large that it soon began to cooperate.

A recognizable bond seems to appear with the Oxford Street looting incident in February 1886. After an open-air meeting in Trafalgar Square held by the SDF on behalf of the unemployed, [Godfrey Elton writes in his *England Arise*] some of the unemployed looted stores and broke windows in Oxford Street. Hyndman and two other leaders of the SDF, John Burns and H. H. Champion, were arrested and charged with inciting the looting.

Stead took advantage of this incident to pull the SDF into the Radical position with timely protection. Stead stoutly defended the SDF as persecuted Radicals. He published a full report of the prosecution [in the 16 February *Pall Mall Gazette*], explaining why the men were being tried and suggesting that the Government had no case. He said nothing about the merit or lack of merit of Marxism but concentrated on the high-handed behavior of the police.

Stead's defense of the SDF in the Oxford Street Affair seems to have been decisive in creating a bond of trust with Hyndman, who reacted in [the 20 February 1886 issue of] *Justice* with a note of surprised pleasure:

> The *Pall Mall Gazette* has certainly taken a bold stand in supporting our right to free speech, and in protesting against the attempt to crush Social Democrats by a State prosecution, because a riot followed upon some speeches in Trafalgar Square.
>
> Such conduct is rare among journalists in the face of the bitter feeling of the upper and middle classes against our comrades. We thoroughly appreciate it, and we hope the day may yet come when the editor and conductors of the *Pall Mall Gazette* will not regret having stood by us when we were comparatively few and unorganized.

Even after the trial of Hyndman and the other SDF leaders had ended with their acquittal, Stead's support was still appreciated. Apparently Hyndman had felt somewhat beleaguered and was sincerely grateful for Stead's solitary support:

> Throughout the late proceedings at Bow Street and the Old Bailey the *Pall Mall Gazette* and its Editor, Mr. W. T. Stead have most courageously and handsomely supported our comrades. We owe that journal and its Editor our sincerest thanks. Though we may differ on some points we hope Social Democrats will never fail to remember and if possible to repay the kindness which they have received at a time when they wanted it.

Below the remarks just cited were quotations taken from the *Times,* the *Standard,* and the *PMG* on the trial results which were no doubt expected to speak for themselves:

Times:—criticized the law which failed to convict the Social Democrats.

Standard:—the tribunal showed a generous blindness.

Pall Mall Gazette:—As to the wider issues raised by the trial, we do not suppose that anyone will dissent from the opinion that a more splendid stroke of good luck never attended the Social Democrats than this miserable prosecution.

The decisive effect of Stead's support for Hyndman in the trial is confirmed in a later issue [15 May 1886] of *Justice*. A month after the trial Hyndman was still smarting over the unflattering comments to which he had been subjected by the "capitalist press." By contrast, Stead fairly shone as the one "honourable exception":

> Those who have ever expected that the labouring classes in any country would get fair play from the capitalist press when they began to show a little vigour in claiming a reasonable share of the wealth must have been fully undeceived of late. Nothing more disgraceful than the conduct of the press during the last few months has been recorded even in all its annals of deliberate turpitude. Take the riots in Pall Mall and Piccadilly [Oxford Street]. With one honourable exception—*the Pall Mall Gazette*—the whole of the London newspapers howled for the immediate arrest and speedy condemnation of the four men who were afterwards acquitted by a middle class jury.

Perhaps it is an indication of the effect Stead's publicity was having on the SDF's attitude toward Radicalism that only a little later Hyndman commented in [the 19 June 1886 issue of] *Justice:*

> What is wanted to secure fair play is payment of all election expenses and of members out of the public funds. This every Radical candidate and every Radical newspaper should go for.

This statement suggests that Hyndman was not adverse to working with and perhaps even joining the ranks of Radicalism.

A time came when Stead was able to use his good will with the Socialists to make a positive attempt to alter SDF policy in a more moderate Radical direction. The SDF announced that they would hold a counter-demonstration at the same time that the traditional Lord Mayor's Day parade was being held. Threats were made that the traditional parade would be broken up by the counter-marching SDF. Such tactics clearly went beyond Stead's Radicalism. The time had come to test his ability to control the SDF. He began by suggesting [in the 19 October 1886 edition of *Justice*] that he might withdraw his support:

> No one is likely to charge us with attempting to scold the Social Democrats. On the contrary, we have given them the fullest fair play, and on one critical occasion [at the time of the Oxford Street affair], when it seemed to us that they were being treated unfairly, the best defense in our power.

Stead then demanded that Hyndman, Champion, and Burns rescind their plans for the Lord Mayor's Day counter-demonstration. If they did not, Stead implied, they were no longer in the Radical camp and "the public will have confidence in Sir Charles Warren's [the police commander's] ability to meet them on their own ground."

Stead went on to show that he was trying to manipulate the Socialists when he brought up the "Tory gold" issue in another article a week later, on 28 October 1886. In the General Election of 1885, financial aid had been offered to Hyndman by the Conservatives to put up SDF candidates in London, hoping to split the Liberal vote. Hyndman had accepted the financial aid knowing that by doing so he risked creating division in the SDF. He had intended that any such objections would be submerged in the election triumph. But [as Simon Maccoby writes in his *English Radicalism 1853-1886*] the gamble had lost, and the SDF had won no seats in the election. The "Tory gold" issue then became the most divisive force among the members of the SDF and eventually led [according to Stead in an article in the *Pall Mall Gazette* of 27 September 1887] to a split in the organization.

Stead now condemned the decision [in the 28 October 1886 edition of the *Pall Mall Gazette*] to counter-march on the Lord Mayor's Day with the suggestion that the SDF wanted to make trouble only to pocket as much Tory gold as possible. This accusation attacked the SDF at its most sensitive spot. Obviously Stead was showing Hyndman that publicity could work two ways: the *PMG* could either support the SDF or become an effective antagonist.

Apparently in reply to Stead, Hyndman wrote this justification of his actions in [the 31 October 1886 issue of] *Justice:*

> We knew that we were running a risk, in the present state of mind of the governing classes, by calling upon the unemployed to follow the Lord Mayor's Show unless some measures were at once adopted for their benefit. But what were we to do? We had exhausted every other means of directing attention to the most important subject of the day.

Hyndman seems to be appealing to Stead to understand, and he apologized regretfully for refusing to alter his decision to march:

> The *Pall Mall Gazette* has done us so many good turns and stood by us so staunchly on a critical occasion, that we are really sorry not to be able to accept its advice at the present time.

Stead scornfully rejected Hyndman's claim to have exhausted all constitutional means before embarking on calculated violence. English Socialists, said Stead [in the 28 October *Pall Mall Gazette*], had far greater constitutional opportunities than Continental Socialists, and yet the English Socialists had not accomplished anything in politics compared with the hard-pressed Continental Socialist parties.

This iron-fisted attitude, in such great contrast to earlier comments, climaxed a few days later with Stead's assertion that moral reform was more effective than violence. If the Socialists had blundered politically, said Stead [in the 1 November *Pall Mall Gazette*], they had blundered even worse morally. "Constitutional methods and moral improvement involve, we know, far harder and less conspicuous work than street processions and political riots; but then they are far more efficacious".

Now that Stead had damaged his influence with the Socialists by such frank criticism, he immediately began to flatter them again: "The trouble with the Social Democrats is that they have such a good case." He again emphasized the tenets of the SDF program that found common ground with the Radicals:

> You cannot with satisfaction to your own conscience argue the question of the abstract right of processions with men who assure you in reply, with a good deal of truth, that they are the only organization claiming to be heard on behalf of the million homes in Great Britain to which the coming winter will bring actual grim starvation.

Perhaps with a last-minute compromise in mind Stead now gave the SDF his blessing to demonstrate so long as no calculated violence was involved.

As the Lord Mayor's Day approached, shopkeepers in the vicinity of Trafalgar Square boarded up their shops, blockades were thrown up by the police, the trams in the area stopped running by police order, and the police massed for the expected violence. But the SDF called off its counter-demonstration on the eve of the Lord Mayor's Day. It was decided to hold instead a demonstration in Trafalgar Square without reference to the other parade. The decision probably was Hyndman's because, according to a remark made in the *PMG* a year later [on 27 September 1887], Champion had deserted the SDF as a direct result of Hyndman's decision not to counter-march on the Lord Mayor's Day.

The threatened opposition of the *PMG* may well have had an important influence in Hyndman's decision not to counter-march. Certainly the resumption of support by the *PMG* was not lost on the editor of *Justice*. Three weeks after the demonstration had been peacefully carried out, Hyndman wrote in [the 20 November 1886] *Justice:* "Our very best thanks are due to the *PMG,* which has treated us most handsomely throughout the business." This resumption of support, Hyndman noted, contrasted strongly with what the other papers were saying about the SDF: "To mention all the newspapers which have criticized us would fill this journal twice over." A week later, on 27 November 1886, Hyndman was still grateful and perhaps a little relieved that it was all over: "The only journal in London which has ever pursued a line of conduct opposed to its advertising interests is the *Pall Mall Gazette."*

The most notable influence Stead made on the Socialists may well have been his role in publicizing the Trafalgar Square riots of late 1887 and the ensuing funeral of the martyr, Alfred Linnell. Historians [such as Elton] seem to have taken for granted that Socialist leaders were responsible for Linnell's public funeral, which produced probably the largest funeral procession since Wellington's. But the publicity behind the public funeral was primarily Stead's work on behalf of all Radicals, with whom Stead continued to insist that the Socialists belonged.

Rioting by the unemployed resumed in the autumn of 1887. Sir Charles Warren, the official in charge of the police, gave Stead yet another issue with which he could attempt to unite the SDF with the Radicals. This time the police virtually forbade any public meetings in Trafalgar Square.

This year, however, was different from those preceding it. For there was a cumulative tension from the experiences of the previous few years of rioting of the unemployed. As a result, the police seemed determined to prevent lawlessness and the recurrence of the previous year's looting and window smashing. The police did not spare any heads as they beat speakers assembled in Trafalgar Square. The civil rights issue implicit in the SDF's right to speak in Trafalgar Square was another good opportunity for Stead. And this time it was to lead to a great but temporary union of the Socialists with the Radicals.

To accomplish this union, Stead claimed all the rioters as Radicals: the speakers in Trafalgar Square were peaceful and, therefore, were only Radicals. He also pointed out [in the 21 October 1887 *Pall Mall Gazette*] that parades of the unemployed were not the invention of the SDF since such parades were occurring spontaneously all over England. Finally, the basic issue was not the rightness of Socialism, he claimed, but purely one of civil rights.

> This is a grave and deliberate attack upon the right of public meeting in London, and it argues ill for our principles that most of us have not cared to protest against such an attack because we do not approve of the persons or doctrines immediately affected.

This stratagem seems to have been virtually the exclusive idea of Stead among the London press. He demanded [in the 22 October *Pall Mall Gazette*] that the press look at the rioting with open eyes and noted that only the *Globe* had begun to do so. The *Times* had become so frightened that panic overtook its editor [in the 8 November 1887]: "If the law is against us, let us break the law and trust to an act of indemnity."

Stead found the time ripe to call for a conference of representatives from "all bodies which represent the masses, and who are interested in the rights and privileges of the people, from the Social Democrats to the Salvation Army, and from the Secularists to the League of the Cross." The inclusion of the Salvation Army and the League of the Cross in the proposal was certainly not inspired by the SDF or Annie Besant. Several times the *PMG* had contained appeals to observe that the Salvation Army was either doing the same work as the Socialists or preventing Socialism from capturing the "semi-socialist" poor. It appears therefore that Stead himself was responsible for the inclusion of this Christian organization in the proposed conference. In addition, the inclusion of Radical groups would put the Socialists in a minority. In this way the SDF could be controlled, or at least influenced.

Stead now began an effective campaign to arouse Radicals and Socialists alike to the need for his proposed conference. He spent the week before the next Sunday demonstration of the unemployed in creating an atmosphere of tension in London. A crisis had been reached, he said [in the 10 November *Pall Mall Gazette*], and Londoners must prepare to act. Even the anti-Socialist Charles Bradlaugh was prevailed upon to write an article for the [11 November] *PMG* defending the right to meet in Trafalgar Square. Then Stead [in the 12 November *Pall Mall Gazette*] called for thousands of "determined but orderly" working men to march down upon Trafalgar Square on the following Sunday.

The day after the demonstration the *PMG* exploited the use of troops by the Government to win over the Socialists to his proposed conference. London would not soon forget, said Stead, the "glimmer of the bayonets" nor the "clanking steel of the Life Guards" who had prevented anyone from entering the square. This use of force had produced a riot and the arrest of the demonstration leaders. The next day, 14 November 1887, the *PMG* looked like a Socialist newspaper. The arrest of Cunningham Graham and John Burns in Trafalgar Square was detailed with great sympathy. To heighten the excitement Stead vehemently denied that the police had released the two men on bail. Letters written that same day by Burns and Cunningham Graham, perhaps at Stead's request, were printed. Another article told of the "The Lies and Libels of the *Times*." One wonders what a casual purchaser of the *PMG* must have thought was happening to respectable London journalism. Even Eleanor Marx-Aveling got a by-line.

The affair of 13 November 1887 was another opportunity for Stead to tie the SDF to the Radicals. The use of the army made the civil rights issue even more acute. The arrest of rioters, especially Cunningham Graham and Burns, produced an immediate need for lawyers, bail bonds, and provision for the families of the prisoners. Some group had to be formed to answer these needs. Stead therefore dropped the idea of a conference and adopted an aim more promising for a Socialist-Radical alliance: a permanent Law and Liberty League should now be formed to aid in fighting civil rights cases.

Each day of the following week the subscription list for the Law and Liberty League grew longer, and Stead worked to keep emotions high: "London, it is said [by whom he did not say], is within four days of a massacre" [he wrote in the 16 November *Pall Mall Gazette*]. John Burns's experiences of the previous Sunday were printed in the *PMG* on Thursday (17 November 1887). On Friday [18 November] an interview with Graham proclaimed him "The Hero of the Hour."

On Friday night at a meeting of five hundred people the Law and Liberty League was founded. In his [19 November 1887] report of that meeting, Stead emphasized that although the group was heterogeneous, "Secularist and Salvationist" and "Radical and Socialist" were highly sympathetic toward the common cause:

> Men and women who are in some things the poles asunder, people who in their daily propaganda are in the deepest antagonism, found themselves for once on common ground, in the defense of a common interest.

This banding together seems to have been the object of Stead's long courting of the SDF: the Law and Liberty League was his accomplishment to end the polarization of Radicals and Socialists. The extent of Stead's role in creating this alliance can be seen in the [24 November 1887] comments of *Justice:*

> No more noteworthy meeting has been held in London for two hundred and fifty years than the gathering of determined men and women who were present in the Memorial Hall on November 18th. That meeting was due to the initiation of the *Pall Mall Gazette,* which has played a very noble part throughout the whole of this unemployed agitation and Tory Terror business. That Mr. Jacob Bright should have taken the chair and that speeches should have been delivered by such different men as Mr. Stead, Mr. William Saunders, the Reverend Stewart Headlam, the Reverend Benjamin Waugh, Dr. Pankhurst, Mr. Foote, Mr. Tims, Mr. Winks, and our comrades Burns, Culwick and Hyndman was enough of itself to show how recent events have helped on the cause of peaceful revolution. The audience which included Mrs. Besant, William Morris, Dr. Hunter, M. P., and many other well-known men and women of all creeds and opinions was a thoroughly representative one, and that the Law and Liberty League then formed will be a great success we have no doubt whatever. We Social Democrats cannot, of course, expect that those who work side by side with us in this great movement will at once accept our doctrines, cordially as they greeted our comrades. But men and women of the well-to-do class have pledged themselves to secure for us the same treatment that is accorded to others in the Courts, and to see to it that Salvationists and Secularists, Teetotalers, Radicals, Social Democrats, and Anarchists have fair play in their propaganda. For this we thank them, and are ready to do our part towards working cordially and loyally with those who have shown themselves ready—apart from their opinions—to work cordially and loyally with us.

If *Justice* is any guide, then Stead was the key figure and the *PMG* the instrument by which the Law and Liberty League had been formed. Nor did Stead's influence stop there. The selection of those who sat on the platform in that first meeting strongly suggests Stead's influence: Jacob Bright, M. P., a Christian feminist who had the chair; Steward Headlam, a Christian Socialist; Benjamin Waugh, a Nonconformist minister who later wrote a sympathetic biography of Stead; and Stead himself. It is likely that Stead chose Bright to preside so that any outbursts from the SDF would be controlled. In any case, the SDF was outnumbered.

Stead's influence in the early days of the Law and Liberty League must also have been great. He was quick to refer to the league [in the 23 November 1887 *Pall Mall Gazette*] as an organization of "liberals," and *Justice* did not protest. Coincidentally with the formation of the league, Stead began to suggest in his newspaper some Radical solutions for ending the unemployment problem, the basic cause of the seasonal rioting. One of these was soon afterward adopted by the league: a register of those unemployed who were willing to work was to be presented to the House of Commons with the demand that something be done to provide employment.

At the same time, Stead began to deemphasize violence in Trafalgar Square. He had achieved his aim of uniting the factions involved. Now violence would aid only the extremists. Therefore, Stead began to advise the Government that they were foolish to provoke the working classes just to compel people to keep out of Trafalgar Square: "We would like to ask our well-to-do respectable classes to reflect whether the game is worth the candle" [he wrote on 26 November 1887]. No inflammatory articles were printed this time when the police cleared Trafalgar Square of Sunday demonstrators on 27 November, one week later. And [on 28 November] Stead was quick to congratulate Sir Charles Russell for being the first Liberal M. P. to denounce the Government's policy in Trafalgar Square.

But Stead's pacification program ended in a rush when an event occurred that made the Trafalgar Square issue of major importance for the purposes of publicity. In another demonstration in Trafalgar Square on December 4th, the police rode down an innocent bystander, Alfred Linnell, an indigent law copyist who was just watching the excitement. Suffering from a compound fracture of the thigh, he died in a few hours.

In an era when staid journalism still predominated, Stead's headlines the next day fairly screamed out: "Killed by the Police! A Martyr of Trafalgar Square." For Stead was too experienced at arousing the public to miss the value of a martyr. "Poor Linnell!" wrote Stead,

> His groan was but the instinctive, inarticulate outpouring of the natural indignation of the human heart when suddenly confronted by the tyrannous and brutal abuse of force.

Nor was Stead content to leave it at that. Linnell deserved more than a pauper's funeral, he insisted [on 5 December 1887]. Nothing less than a public funeral was called for [The Critic Adds in a footnote: "Ironically, two other men who actually participated in that 4 December demonstration and were fatally injured received no honored funeral: they died too late for Stead's purposes.].

Why was Stead doing this when he had already achieved the alliance of Radicals and Socialists in the Law and Liberty League? The reason was probably that he had to show his value to the league to help keep Radical control of that group. The need for control was already arising, as this [10 December] complaint by *Justice* indicates:

> Is the Law and Liberty League to be Another Middle-Class Affair?
>
> Vigorous working men will have to be the backbone of the business if any real work is to be done for London. Yet we hear of meetings in the afternoon working-men delegates cannot possibly attend, and unless we are misinformed, which is not likely, a nasty intrigue is on foot to capture the whole thing for mere political purposes. Now, Mr. Stead, it is the duty of the *Pall Mall Gazette* to nip this sort of thing in the bud, and to secure thorough democratic public meetings of all delegates in the evening, when the workers can be present.

Within two days Stead reported that his suggestion to give Linnell a public funeral had met with a hearty response; a meeting of the Law and Liberty League had decided to take it up. The proposed funeral removed Socialist pressure on the Radicals in the league. Stead's Radical influence caused the league to propose to invite all the Liberal members for London, and to ask the Bishop of London to read the service at the grave. Stead played a key role in the league's propaganda too: those desiring to communicate with the league about participation in the funeral parade were to contact the LLL through the *PMG*, not through *Justice* or William Morris's *Commonweal.*

The Linnell funeral may well have been the greatest publicity stunt of the 1880s. *Justice* thought as much and admitted [on 24 December 1887] that Stead had made it possible:

> The extraordinary success of this demonstration at poor Linnell's funeral, largely due, as all must admit, to the *Pall Mall Gazette*, will mark an epoch in the history of the Social Democratic movement in Great Britain.

The funeral was not, as Godfrey Elton says, a Socialist-sponsored affair. Stead had been the driving force in its organization, as shown in the funeral itself. The allegiance of the notables at the head of the procession had the same character as the Law and Liberty League; these were not exclusively Socialists, in spite of the fact that the SDF had borne the brunt of the fighting in Trafalgar Square. [According to Arthur Nethercot in his *The First Five Lives of Annie Besant*] Stead's influence was apparent also in that as the body went past the packed sidewalks, people cried out, "Murdered by the police," Stead's headline which had opened the press campaign.

The response of the people of London to the funeral left Hyndman in awe [he wrote in the 24 December *Justice*]:

> Mile End Road is the broadest thoroughfare in London . . . where large open pieces of ground stretch along either side of the wide roadway. As far as my eyes could reach [from the top of a tram-car], towards the City and towards Bow, was one sea of heads.

Unfortunately for Stead, his usefulness to the Socialists lasted only as long as they needed his publicity. His very success in his part of the bargain had made the Socialist cause well known: 100,000 people had appeared for the Linnell funeral. The sense of independence, growing in the Socialists a few weeks later, can be seen in William Morris's *Commonweal* of 3 March 1888:

> Where Are the Radicals?
>
> Isn't it about time that the Radicals did a little of the real fighting for free speech or showed a little pluck of some sort? They have all been talking very big about what they have done and the risks they have run, and how they won't cooperate with S-D's—as if we ever ran after them— unless we go the way they want us to and so on.

What, however, we should like to know is where are the Radical prisoners for free speech and justice to the unemployed? What have the Liberal and Radical Clubs of London been doing since the 13th November? That was their meeting, remember, and their defeat, not ours.

This obvious sense of independence probably stemmed from what was to be a crushing blow for Stead's attempted control of the Socialists: the capture of a major London daily, the *Star,* for Socialist propaganda without any strings attached. Stead no longer had any leverage with the Socialists, and the Law and Liberty League quickly faded away as did the Socialist-Radical alliance.

What does this study reveal? It appears that Stead's belief that the Socialists could be brought into the Radical camp was unfounded. Although the Socialists could be influenced to moderate a specific goal temporarily, it is also clear that they were very wary of coming under Radical influence. Stead was unable to dispel this attitude. In fact, the Socialists appear to have used Stead as long as they needed him and dropped him as soon as they could when they found a more accessible newspaper for their publicity. If it is true that the Socialists only used Stead, then the Radical nature of their practical program can be deceptive, for the Socialists, including Hyndman, must not have been Radicals at heart. Yet in spite of the failure of Stead's plan, the Socialist-Radical alliance of 1886-1887 demonstrates that William T. Stead was a remarkable journalist: although a Radical, he did more than any other person to raise the Socialist image in the 1880s. (pp. 42-52)

James Mennell, "Newspaper Publicity and Politics: W. T. Stead and the English Socialists in the 1880's," in Ball State University Forum, *Vol. XXV, No. 2, Spring, 1984, pp. 42-52.*

FURTHER READING

Biography

Baylen, Joseph O. "Mark Twain, W. T. Stead, and 'The Tell-Tale Hands'." *American Quarterly* XVI, No. 4 (Winter 1964): 606-12.

Recounts the story of "an experiment in palmistry" conducted in Stead's journal of the paranormal, *Borderland.*

——. "Stead's Penny 'Masterpiece Library' " *Journal of Popular Culture* IX, No. 3 (Winter 1975): 710-25.

Describes Stead's "Penny Poets," "Penny Novelists," and "Books for the Bairns" schemes.

——. "W. T. Stead as Publisher and Editor of the *Review of Reviews.*" *Victorian Periodicals Review* XII, No. 2 (Summer 1979): 70-84.

Traces the history of Stead's monthly magazine.

Baylen, Joseph O., and Robert B. Holland. "Whitman, W. T. Stead, and the *Pall Mall Gazette:* 1886-1887." *American Literature* XXXIII, No. 1 (March 1961): 68-72.

Discusses Walt Whitman's epistolary relationship with Stead and the *Pall Mall Gazette.*

Downey, Dennis B. "William Stead and Chicago: A Victorian Jeremiah in the Windy City." *Mid-America: An Historical Review* 68, No. 3 (October 1986): 153-66.

Follows Stead's efforts to "drive the devil out of Chicago" in the 1890s through the publication of *If Christ Came to Chicago.*

Raymond, E. T. "W. T. Stead." In his *Portraits of the Nineties,* pp. 174-82. New York: Charles Scribner's Sons, 1921.

Brief overview of Stead's life and eccentricities.

Whyte, Frederic. *The Life of W. T. Stead.* 2 vols. New York: Houghton Mifflin, n.d. [1925], 713 p.

The most complete biography of Stead.

Criticism

Eckley, Grace. "A Paradigm for the Fall of Humphrey Chimpden Earwicker." *Journal of Modern Literature* 12, No. 1 (March 1985): 61-76.

Argues that James Joyce modeled the character of Earwicker in *Finnegans Wake* on Stead.

——. "The Entertaining *Nights* of Burton, Stead, and Joyce's Earwicker." *Journal of Modern Literature* 13, No. 2 (July 1986): 339-44.

Shows that Joyce incorporated events from Stead and Sir Richard F. Burton's clash over Burton's translation of *The Thousand and One Nights* and Stead's *Maiden Tribute* press campaign into *Finnegans Wake.*

——. "Beef to the Heel: Harlotry with Josephine Butler, William T. Stead, and James Joyce." *Studies in the Modern Novel* XX, No. 1 (Spring 1988): 64-77.

Maintains that events in Joyce's *Ulysses* mirror those surrounding Stead's campaign against England's Contagious Diseases Act and Stead's *Maiden Tribute of Modern Babylon* articles.

Gertrude Stein
1874-1946

American novelist, poet, essayist, biographer, and playwright.

For further information on Stein's career, see *TCLC*, Volumes 1, 6, and 28.

INTRODUCTION

Stein is regarded as a major figure of literary Modernism and one of the most influential writers of the twentieth century. Rejecting the naturalistic conventions of nineteenth-century fiction, she developed an abstract manner of expression that was a counterpart in language to the work of the Postimpressionists and Cubists in the visual arts. Stein wrote prolifically in many genres, composing novels, poetry, plays, and opera libretti.

The youngest daughter of a wealthy Jewish-American family, Stein spent most of her childhood in Oakland, California. In 1893 she enrolled in the all-female Harvard Annex, which later became Radcliffe College. There she attended classes taught by the psychologist William James, who proved a decisive influence on her intellectual development. Many of his teachings, including his theories of perception and personality types, later informed her principles as a writer. Intending to become a psychologist, she began medical studies at Johns Hopkins University; however, she grew disaffected with medicine and left the university in 1902 without completing her degree. Stein devoted herself to the study of literary classics, and, inspired by her reading, she began to write her first novels.

In 1903 she and her brother Leo settled in Paris. The Steins' apartment at 27 rue de Fleurus became a salon where numerous artists and literary figures met regularly. Stein particularly enjoyed the company of Pablo Picasso, and she greatly admired his artistic style, as well as those of such other painters as Paul Cézanne and Juan Gris, who experimented in their works with ways of conveying a more profound and truthful vision of reality than that allowed by the naturalistic techniques of the nineteenth century. The Cubist painters broke a subject down to its essential geometric forms, then reassembled those forms in ways that offer the viewer startling new perceptions of the subject. This revolution in the visual arts encouraged Stein to formulate a literary aesthetic that would similarly violate existing formal conventions in order to allow the reader to experience language and ideas in provocative new ways. In 1909 Stein began living with Alice B. Toklas, a young woman from California, and the women developed a close relationship that Stein referred to as a marriage; they remained together for the rest of their lives. Because commercial publishers initially rejected her work, Stein was forced to subsidize the printing of her first

books. However, many of her distinguished and influential friends, most notably art patron Mabel Dodge, critic Carl Van Vechten, and poet Edith Sitwell, admired and promoted her writings. After the First World War, Stein became the friend and mentor of a number of young writers from the United States, notably Ernest Hemingway. As an epigraph to his 1926 novel *The Sun Also Rises,* Hemingway quoted Stein's remark, "You are all a lost generation," which came to refer to Hemingway, F. Scott Fitzgerald, and other young American writers gathered in Paris during the 1920s. At this time Stein, as well known for her many friendships with talented, wealthy, and famous persons as for her innovative literary work, was urged by a publisher to write her memoirs. She produced *The Autobiography of Alice B. Toklas,* which became a best-seller and made her an international celebrity. She maintained an active social and literary life until her death in 1946.

Stein's literary career is often divided by commentators into three phases. Her first novel, *Q.E.D.*, is an apparently autobiographical study of a young woman's unhappy relationship with a fickle female lover. Because of its taboo subject matter, the novel was not published until after

Stein's death. Her next major work, *Three Lives,* consists of three novellas: "The Good Anna," "The Gentle Lena," and "Melanctha," which, commentators note, is essentially a reworking of the love story in *Q.E.D.,* this time presented as a heterosexual love affair between two black characters. Although critics now recognize "Melanctha" as an inaccurate, stereotyped depiction of African-American life, it was virtually unprecedented as a serious attempt by a white author to portray realistic black characters. Both *Q.E.D.* and *Three Lives,* although relatively conventional, contain some traces of Stein's later experimental style, such as minimal punctuation, deemphasis of plot, and the depiction of characters as psychological types rather than as unique individuals.

Stein regarded *The Making of Americans,* the 925-page epic novel that initiated the next phase in her career, as her masterpiece, a revolutionary work on the scale of James Joyce's *Ulysses* (1922) or Marcel Proust's *À la recherche du temps perdu* (1913-27; *Remembrance of Things Past*). Stein's approach to the psychology of her characters became even more clinical in this novel, in which she intended to illustrate personality types, revealing the "bottom nature," or essential type, of individuals by depicting their patterns of behavior. In addition to its psychological plan, *The Making of Americans* is an autobiographical work that chronicles the lives of three generations of the Herslands, a German-American family modeled after the Steins. *The Making of Americans* and many of Stein's other prose works of this period are written in a dense, ruminative style. They have little conventional narrative continuity and are composed of long sentences made up of simple words and repeated phrases, stripped of subordinate clauses and all punctuation except periods.

Stein further developed her avant-garde style in *Tender Buttons,* a collection of prose poems. Presented in three sections, "Objects," "Food," and "Rooms," the poems are written in a manner that focuses attention on the things described and on the language used to describe them rather than evoking emotions or ideas in the reader. Some critics have compared the style of these poems to the deliberate absurdities of the Dadaists or to the experiments in automatic writing conducted by the Surrealists. In fact, Stein disliked the deliberate irrationality of Dadaism; although her writings are often frustratingly complex or obscure, they are never intentionally nonsensical. Stein used psychological theory as a basis for her writings, as did the Surrealists, but she was interested in the dynamics of the conscious mind, not the subconscious. The writings of her middle period reflect theories of consciousness that she learned from William James. According to James, the individual perceives the world not in discrete temporal segments of past, present, and future, but as a continuous awareness of the moment being presently lived. By using long, static narratives, Stein sought to evoke this atemporal sense of a continuous present.

During her third period Stein continued to develop and implement her theories. Her writings became less accessible to readers, not only because of the increasingly complex intellectual plans behind their composition but also because Stein used many words and phrases that had meanings only she or close friends could understand. Many of her writings of this era, such as *Lucy Church, Amiably,* reflect the pleasant domestic life she shared with Toklas. With *The Autobiography of Alice B. Toklas* Stein proved to her critics that she was capable of writing a relatively conventional, commercially successful work. While most reviewers were charmed by Stein's wit and engaging conversational style, not all were pleased. A group of Stein's friends from the art world, including Tristan Tzara and Henri Matisse, published "Testimony against Gertrude Stein," in which they condemned the *Autobiography* as a shallow, distorted portrayal of their lives and work. Stein nevertheless followed the popular success of the *Autobiography* with other memoirs, *Everybody's Autobiography* and *Wars I Have Seen.* She also published *Lectures in America* and *Narration,* theoretical writings which have proved invaluable to students of her work in explaining her often esoteric style. While she continued to write such avant-garde narratives as the novels *Ida* and *Mrs. Reynolds,* her last works reflect an awareness of current social and political realities absent from the introspective writings of her early and middle period. *Brewsie and Willie,* for instance, a set of fictional dialogues between American soldiers and nurses, deals with the atomic bomb and other issues relevant to the post–World War II era.

From the time she started to publish her writings Stein has proven a challenge to critics. Because much of her work violates basic formal and thematic conventions, certain interpretative methods, such as the close textual analysis practiced by the New Critics, are of no use in approaching her writings. Most of the commentary on Stein from 1910 through the 1950s is evaluative rather than interpretative, either arguing her merits, as does Carl Van Vechten, or deriding her, as in the case of Wyndham Lewis and B. L. Reid. The linguistically based critical methods of structuralism and deconstruction that emerged in the 1960s and 1970s offered Stein's readers a critical method better suited to understanding her work as she had conceived it. Feminist critics have also provided a fresh perspective on Stein, discussing such issues as her treatment of sexuality and her defiance of patriarchal literary traditions. An additional topic often raised by commentators is Stein's relation to the Postimpressionists and Cubists. While critics acknowledge her as one of the leading literary Modernists, her often cryptic style has made her works less popular than those of her contemporaries Virginia Woolf and James Joyce; her true worth as an artist, some commentators have suggested, is best indicated by her influence on other writers. Her radical approach to literary style and structure was admired and emulated by other writers of her era, including Ernest Hemingway, Thornton Wilder, and Sherwood Anderson, and has served as an inspiration for such Postmodernist writers as the French New Novelists and William H. Gass.

PRINCIPAL WORKS

Three Lives (novellas) 1909

Tender Buttons: Objects, Food, Rooms (poetry) 1914
Geography and Plays (dramas and prose) 1922
**The Making of Americans: Being a History of a Family's Progress* (novel) 1925; also published as *The Making of Americans: The Hersland Family* [abridged edition], 1934
Composition as Explanation (essay) 1926
Lucy Church, Amiably (prose) 1930
Before the Flowers of Friendship Faded Friendship Faded (poetry) 1931
How to Write (prose) 1931
Operas and Plays (dramas) 1932
The Autobiography of Alice B. Toklas (biography) 1933
Matisse, Picasso, and Gertrude Stein with Two Shorter Stories (portraits) 1933
Four Saints in Three Acts (libretto) 1934
Lectures in America (lectures) 1935
Narration (lectures) 1935
The Geographical History of America; or, The Relation of Human Nature to the Human Mind (prose) 1936
Everybody's Autobiography (biography) 1937
Picasso (memoir) 1938
The World Is Round (novel) 1939
Ida (novel) 1941
Wars I Have Seen (prose) 1945
Brewsie and Willie (prose) 1946
Four in America (prose) 1947
The Mother of Us All (libretto) 1947
Last Operas and Plays (prose, dramas, and libretti) 1949
†*Things as They Are* (novel) 1950; also published as *Q.E.D.*, 1971
The Yale Edition of the Unpublished Works of Gertrude Stein. 8 vols. (novels, poetry, and novellas) 1951-58

*This work was written between 1903 and 1911.

†This work was written in 1903.

CRITICISM

Gertrude Stein and William Lundell (interview date 1934)

[*Lundell was a reporter for NBC. In the following interview, which was broadcast on WJZ and WNET radio on 12 November 1934, Lundell questions Stein about her unusual writing style.*]

[Lundell]: *Coming back to the United States for the first time in thirty-one years, Miss Stein, is there anything in particular which has seized your interest?*

[Stein]: Coming back to the United States after thirty-one years everything seizes my interest and seizes it very hard. The buildings in the air and the people on the street they are all exciting and they are and I know it seems a funny thing to say but that is the way they appear to me, they are so gentle, so friendly, so simply direct and so sweet. I feel that way about the people on the street and I feel that way about the buildings in the air. By the way what I feel most about the buildings is the way they come down into the earth more than the way they go up into the air and they do it all so naturally and so simply. But the people on the street never could I have imagined the friendly personal simple direct considerate contact that I have with all of them. They all seem to know me and they all speak to me and I who am easily frightened by anything unexpected find this spontaneous considerate contact with all and any New Yorker touching and pleasing and I am deeply moved and awfully happy in it. I could tell so many incidents but charming as are the incidents it is the unreality of it the gentle pleasant unreality of it that makes my moving about in the street just a pleasure.

Just yesterday Mr. Cerf told me a story in that connection, Miss Stein. After the party given in your honor by Random House and the Modern Library, Mr. Cerf was going down in the elevator and he talked with the elevator boy. The boy said, "You had a big party." Mr. Cerf replied "Yes, we had a lot of celebrities there. How did it strike you?" The boy said, "Well, I only recognized two of them . . . Miss Stein and Miriam Hopkins, the movie actress."

Well, you see the sweet part of that was that we liked each other and asked each other's advice without really knowing who each other was. But in a way that is a joke because what is extraordinary is that in this the largest city in the world everybody knows me and I feel that I know everybody it is just exactly like the village in France where I spend my summers and where there are 20 families and they all know me and I know all of them. Why even at the football game a little boy came up to me and bowed and said please Miss Stein may I have an autograph. I said how old are you and he said twelve and we were both pleased, then everybody handed me their programs and it was perfectly charming, simply charming. Why when I first arrived off the boat the first evening I took a walk and I wanted an apple and I went into a little fruit store on Sixth Avenue to buy it, and the clerk said how do you do Miss Stein did you have a pleasant trip over.

Your coming to the United States to lecture, Miss Stein, seems to me to imply that there are many people who will be able to comprehend your ideas. The current impression of your work, however, among American people, is founded largely upon the tremendous publicity attained by **Four Saints in Three Acts,** *and although it may seem absurd in them, many American people doubt your ability to speak intelligibly. Just where, then, does* **Four Saints in Three Acts** *fit into your scheme of lecturing, which, if it is to be successful, must be at least understandable . . . which is more than most of us can say for your opera.*

Look here, being intelligible is not what it seems, after all all these things are a matter of habit. Take what the newspapers say about what you call the New Deal. If you just know ordinary English you do not have the slightest idea what the newspapers are talking about everybody has their own English and it is only a matter of anybody getting used to an English anybody's English and then it is all right. After all when you say they do not understand *Four Saints* what do you mean, of course they understand or they would not listen to it. You mean by understanding that you can talk about it in the way that you have the habit of talking . . . putting it in other words . . . but I mean by understanding enjoyment. If you go to a football game you don't have to understand it in any way except the football way and all you have to do with *Four Saints* is to enjoy it in the *Four Saints* way which is the way I am, otherwise I would not have written it in that way. Don't you see what I mean? If you enjoy it you understand it, and lots of people have enjoyed it so lots of people have understood it. You see that is what my lectures are to be. They are to be a simple way of telling everybody this thing, that if you enjoy it you understand it and so if I am telling them this about why my punctuation is, why my so-called repetition is, what my prose is and what my poetry is and what my plays are and what my English literature is and what my pictures are and I am telling them all this simply as I tell everything you will see, they will understand it because they enjoy it.

Well I think I understand. . . . Your life has been amazingly full of interest, it would seem, Miss Stein, judging from **The Autobiography of Alice B. Toklas.**

Yes, my life has been and is full of interest because I like it all it is all wonderful to me and one is not more wonderful than the other anybody anybody meets is wonderful and that is all there is to it and if you are wonderful and they are wonderful the world is full of interest and that is natural enough. In ***The Autobiography of Alice B. Toklas*** I told all this one way, in ***Portraits and Prayers*** the book that is coming out and I am so pleased that it is coming out just as I am here I have told what it is in another way. You see in ***Portraits and Prayers*** are collected together all the portraits that I have made of anyone over all these years and what I mean by a portrait is this. When I know anybody well they are all something to me each one is. That is natural but then there has to come a moment when I know all I can know about anyone and I know it all at once and then I try to put it down to put down on paper all that I know of anyone their ways the sound of their voice the accent of their voice their other movements their character all what they do and to do it all at once is very difficult. Just anybody try to do it and you will see what I mean and in this book ***Portraits and Prayers*** I have tried to do it and I have done it in a great many ways and sometimes I have felt that I have done it. And you must not think that you do not understand because you cannot say it to yourself in other words. If you have something happen in you when you read these portraits you do understand no matter what you say to yourself and others about not understanding. Really and truly that is really and truly true.

As you look back, Miss Stein, over these friends of whom you have done portraits, do any Americans stand out from among those told about in **The Autobiography of Alice B. Toklas** *and in your latest book,* **Portraits and Prayers?**

Yes, there are Americans in this book. There is everybody in this book everybody that has been in my life because after anybody has become very well known to me I have tried to make a portrait of them well I might almost say in order to get rid of them inside in me. Otherwise I would have got too full up inside me with what I had inside me of anyone. Do you see what I mean? Yes, there are lots of Americans in ***Portraits and Prayers*** and some of my favorite portraits in it are Americans, there is the second portrait of Carl Van Vechten, and there is one of Sherwood Anderson which I consider perhaps the best portrait I ever did and there is a little one of Hemingway and some of Americans you do not know and another one of an American I loved very much Mildred Aldrich of the Hilltop on the Marne which is there as "Mildred Aldrich Saturday".

Going back for a moment to your opera to be sung, **Four Saints in Three Acts**—*I should like to ask if you sincerely believe that English literature can in any way be improved by such experimentation as you, Miss Stein, have made in* **Four Saints in Three Acts?**

There is no question of improving English literature, Lundell, there is only a question of English literature going on and now American literature going on and I do think that my work and ***Four Saints in Three Acts*** is an important part of it, is an important very important element in English literature's going on and naturally anybody who wants anything wants it to go on and my writing is part of its going on that is the way I feel about it.

I'd like you to speak perfectly frankly, Miss Stein. What do you think of the writing now being done in the United States?

The writing in the United States is going on and the young ones send me lots of manuscripts and a good many of them really know what writing is but you see what is necessary is that they should go on writing. Horace Greeley said about the resumption of specie payments after the Civil War that the only way to resume is to resume and that is the way with writing. The only way to go on writing is to go on writing and if you have anything in you it will be something but if you have not it will not but as there is undoubtedly a great deal in America that stirs me a lot coming here there will undoubtedly be a great deal in future American writing.

While reading **The Autobiography of Alice B. Toklas,** *Miss Stein, I had an unusual reading experience because of your peculiar style, the words seemed to fly before my eyes. I read page after page with a kind of breathless haste. Just what in your style is responsible for this swiftness?*

The style of ***The Autobiography of Alice B. Toklas*** is not peculiar at all. The only peculiar thing is that I wrote it myself. I suggested to my secretary Alice B. Toklas that she write her life story and she kept putting it off and finally to encourage her one day I sat down in the garden and wrote a chapter then it seized me so I kept on writing and writing sitting in the garden writing and I wrote the whole ***Autobiography*** in six weeks.

And you didn't go over it to correct it at all?

No, I didn't—I, I, just wrote it.

But, Miss Stein, why did you omit capital letters so frequently and question marks?

Well, because you see, Lundell, capital letters and question marks are useless. They are hangovers from the days when people didn't read very well, that all goes into the whole question of the life and death of punctuation marks, if you don't know that a question is a question without a question mark being there what is the use of writing the question.

Not much. You mean that question marks and capital letters are crutches for the mentally crippled?

That is it exactly they are a help to some people but the average reading mind does not need them.

But in addition to punctuation you seem to have very definite opinions about nouns and adjectives.

I do, nouns are pretty dead and adjectives which are related to nouns which are practically dead are even more dead.

But where is the life then in writing. In the verb?

In the verbs there is life in the prepositions and adverbs too and very much in the conjunctions. As an example the most vigorous expression in American speech is that composed of two words—"And how." It is full of emotion and it says everything that needs to be said.

But your study in these slang phrases, it would seem to me, must be rather limited. In your literary circles you don't meet much new and vigorous slang.

Oh, don't I. How do you know I do not. And what makes you think I only talk to literary circles. I talk to and listen to anybody. Whom did I talk to during the war? And everyday I talk to my cab drivers and my publishers.

You apparently find American speech very vigorous then?

Oh, yes. American speech is very vigorous, more vigorous than English. English speech is dead and if the speech of the people is dead then the literature is dead. When a country is in transition and growing its speech is vigorous and its literature is vigorous and alive. In the Elizabethan days in England that was a most lively period and the language was growing and the language was vigorous.

Would that then mean, Miss Stein, that because of the vigor of Greek life in the days of Sophocles and of Roman life in the days of the Caesars that Greek and Latin are not dead languages but very much alive?

Certainly they are alive. The literature of any language that was once alive is never dead but the English of modern writers is not in a state of vitality. Since the death of Swinburne, Browning and Meredith there have been no first rate writers in English, just second and third rate and that isn't anybody's fault but England's it has lost its vitality.

But what of our younger American writers?

Young writers are young writers, you can't judge a writer until all of his work is behind him.

But then how are we to know what books to buy and what is the value of a book reviewer if we can't judge an author's value until his work is finished?

The function of a book reviewer is to review and that is alright.

Well, then, to get back to your own writing again, Miss Stein. Will you explain the passage from **Four Saints in Three Acts** *about the pigeons on the grass which begins, "Pigeons on the grass alas. Pigeons on the grass alas. Short longer grass short longer longer shorter yellow grass," and ends up, "Lily Lily Lily let Lily Lucy Lucy let Lily. Let Lucy Lily."*

That is simple I was walking in the gardens of the Luxembourg in Paris it was the end of summer the grass was yellow I was sorry that it was the end of summer and I saw the big fat pigeons in the yellow grass and I said to myself, pigeons on the yellow grass, alas, and I kept on writing pigeons on the grass, alas, short longer grass short longer longer shorter yellow grass pigeons large pigeons on the shorter longer yellow grass, alas pigeons on the grass, and I kept on writing until I had emptied myself of the emotion. If a mother is full of her emotion toward a child in the bath the mother will talk and talk and talk until the emotion is over and that's the way a writer is about an emotion.

But how is the reader supposed to know what you are thinking about?

The reader does know because he enjoys it. If you enjoy you understand if you understand you enjoy. What you mean by understanding is being able to turn it into other words but that is not necessary. As I said before, to like a football game is to understand it in the football way.

You saw the Yale-Dartmouth game a week ago Saturday, didn't you? Did you understand that in the American way or the football way or how?

In the American way. The thing that interested me was that the Modern American in his movements and his actions in a football game so resembled the red Indian dance and it proves that the physical country that made the one made the other and that the red Indian is still with us. They just put their heads down solemnly together and then double over, while on the side lines the substitutes move in a jiggly way just like Indians. . . . Then they all get down on all fours just like Indians.

But those jiggles are warming-up exercises.

It doesn't make any difference what they are doing it for, they are just doing it, like the way the Indian jiggles in the Indian dance and then there is that little brown ball they all bend down and worship.

But the idea in that is to get the ball across the goal line.

But don't you suppose I know that, and don't you suppose the Indians had just as much reason and enjoyed their dancing just as much?

Perhaps so. But permit me, Miss Stein, to ask you to explain the lines entitled **"A Portrait of Carl Van Vechten."** *I don't understand them. Will you read them?*

"If it and as if it, if it or as if it, if it is as if it, and it is as if it and as if it. Or as if it. More as if it. As more. As more as if it. And if it. And for and as if it." That is a portrait of Carl Van Vechten. He is just like that sometimes this way sometimes that way he is sometimes very real and then very unreal sometimes alive sometimes not alive.

But what about this fifth paragraph?

"Tied and untied and that is all there is about it. And as tied and as beside, and as beside and tied. Tied and untied and beside and as beside and as untied and as tied and as untied and as beside." Well, just look at these words, the words look like Carl Van Vechten, anybody can know that beside they mean Carl Van Vechten anybody can know that.

Well, that's rather hard for us normal Americans to see.

What is a normal American, there are lots quite normal who do see. And how. But after all you must enjoy my writing and if you enjoy it you understand it. If you did not enjoy it why do you make a fuss about it? There is the real answer. (pp. 87-97)

Gertrude Stein and William Lundell, in an interview in The Paris Review, *Vol. 32, No. 116, Fall, 1990, pp. 85-97.*

Allegra Stewart (essay date 1957)

[*Stewart is an American critic and educator. In the following excerpt, she analyzes Stein's writing processes as "sacred activity."*]

On the basis of her first short stories in **Three Lives** and her long novel, **The Making of Americans,** Gertrude Stein has often been classified as a writer of fiction, perhaps because the great body of her work is so difficult to classify in any way at all. Since 1914, however, when she published **Tender Buttons,** most of her writing defies classification under the familiar categories of literature, although she made a few sallies into autobiography, fiction, and the essay. Her publications, to be sure, can be discriminated as poetry and prose, but she herself discarded the distinction as irrelevant. She called her psychological word-paintings of personalities and objects "portraits," and her descriptions of things moving in space (landscapes and scenes) she called "plays" and "operas." But her compositions in these literary genera are the very reverse of what one would expect, because [as she writes in ***Everybody's Autobiography***] she was always "in" her own consciousness, attempting to put into words, regardless of their associational meanings, the union of two inner realities (those of subject and object) or the marriage of outer and inner realities as it took place in presentational immediacy:

> When I see a thing it is not a play to me because the minute I see it it ceases to be a play for me, but when I write something that somebody else can see then it is a play for me. When I write other things not plays it is something that I can see and seeing it is inside of me but when I write a play then it is something that is inside of me but if I could see it then it would not be.

Thus her "portraits" really leave out what everyone else can see, and her "plays" make visible what nobody else can see. The portraits objectify the personality or essential nature of people and things as distilled in the alembic of Gertrude Stein's consciousness, while the plays objectify her imaginative ideas and constructions excited by the motion and arrangement of objects in space. The portraits are impressionistic, the plays, expressionistic. Or, to put it another way, the portraits reflect her receptivity to the substantial, whereas her plays reflect the "play" of her mind with the purely phenomenal. She subjectifies the world in portraits and objectifies the contents of her consciousness in plays.

This *bouleversement* of the portrait and the play is all of a piece with her deliberate efforts to destroy the associational meanings of words in order to express pure quality apart from the forms which carry it. Her first portraits, written in 1909, represent an abrupt break with all forms of discursive writing, and with all the conventional symbolisms of language. From the point of view of contemporary literature, her compositions were part of a general revolt against surface realism and the constricting effects upon the imagination of scientific and historical data; and her rejection of conventional plot and chronological narrative was part of the general effort to restore to reality that inwardness which had been lost to life and literature in the general materialism of thought and life in our time.

In the twentieth century, organization and mechanization have supplanted both the rationalism of the enlightenment and the extreme individualism of the romantic period, with the result that society tends to be collectivized and depersonalized and the individual lost in the statistical table of averages. To all these forces Gertrude Stein's work (like that of many of her contemporaries) paradoxically opposed an irrationalism and an impersonalism of an entirely different kind. Inevitably her writing appeared to be part of a cult of unintelligibility, or a manifestation of a new barbarism. For in a period when there seemed to be nothing that had not been explained or that could not be understood, and among sophisticates who "knew" everything and believed nothing, she was seeking to recover mystery, and to reawaken wonder.

After 1909, this affirmative effort of hers consisted chiefly of recording the motions of her own mind. Writing became for her an exercise (or ritual) in concentration, for the act of concentrating one's attention liberates consciousness from every necessity except its own autonomous activity. But the struggle for such freedom imposed upon her a stern *ascesis,* requiring as it did the perception and then the verbal expression of her own inner motions, stripped of everything but presentational immediacy. Such introversion differs radically, of course, from the introspection associated with anxiety or other neurotic maladjustments.

In seeking such interior freedom, Gertrude Stein suppressed all subject matter as such in behalf of this on-going inner movement, which she tried to express without interposing any conscious purpose between her mind and its object, excluding both memory and conceptual forms. Unlike the chronological time of history and nature, the interior time of consciousness—duration, as Bergson called it—is always present time. It is in the present moment that the mind is free to act creatively and to "make" out of the "given" subject matter new objects that have no causal connections with the course of events in the external world. Gertrude Stein attempted in many different ways to record the time of duration in herself and in others as always the same, yet always different—the same because it is always present, different because it is filled with the fleeting stream of its own contents and the flux of things in chronological time. "Content without form," she was fond of saying, meaning that structures and forms should not be permitted to tyrannize over direct experience—that they are less important than the quality of life by which the forms themselves are actually distinguished.

As the activity of the individual soul alone with its "object," writing affirms the freedom and autonomy of man amid the flux of things and the determinations of space and time. Writing is "sacred," and Gertrude Stein often warned writers against trying to serve two masters, "god and mammon" [which she defined in *Lectures in America*]:

> When I say god and mammon concerning the writer writing, I mean that any one can use words to say something. And in using these words to say what he has to say he may use words directly or indirectly. If he uses these words indirectly he says what he intends to have heard by somebody who is to hear and in so doing inevitably he has to serve mammon. Mammon may be a success, mammon may be an effort he is to produce, mammon may be a pleasure he has from hearing what he himself has done, mammon may be his way of explaining, mammon may be a laziness that needs nothing but going on, in short mammon may be anything done indirectly. Now serving god for a writer who is writing is writing anything directly, it makes no difference what it is but it must be direct, the relation between the thing done and the doer must be direct.

In her own struggle for directness, Gertrude Stein strained words and exerted pressure upon them, and renounced "names" (nouns), and dissected grammar. Whatever she concentrated her attention upon became isolated from all the relations in which it stood to other things. A thing-in-itself with its own existence, *sui generis,* the object entered into a process of reciprocal excitement with a knowing consciousness and became open on all sides to the understanding in contact with it. The intellectual perception of sheer existence is an act of ingatheredness, or recollection, in which the knower feels outside of time and freed from the demands of the ego. He becomes a spiritual entity whose only action is the incarnation of what it knows in the word. This, Gertrude Stein believed, is the final creative act, the mystery in which knower and known are joined in unity.

To eternize in this way a fleeting moment of life is to create a new value from what would otherwise have been carried along in the temporal flux to oblivion. Such a value need never have been realized even fleetingly, of course, because there is no necessary relation between knower and known.

The conjunction between them is accidental and contingent, but the act of realization is an exchange between two finalities of experience, and no matter how trivial the object may seem to be in terms of the world's work the value of the interchange is infinite. The product of exchange serves no purpose beyond itself; its measure is devotion rather than use. In Gertrude Stein's vocabulary it is variously called a "hymn," a "prayer," a "song," a "meditation," a "master-piece" of human experience—given an immortality beyond the life of both the knowing subject and the known object, in an object totally new.

Thus Gertrude Stein could write with words "together" and "apart," dedicated to the task of resurrecting them from the smooth, dead phrases of descriptive science, surface realism, factual narrative, and philosophical abstraction: "I have of course always been struggling with this thing, to say what you nor I nor nobody knows, but what is really what you and I and everybody knows." To restore to the imagination the living word, to bring back an interest in man as man, to revive an interest in the normal and the ordinary—in what everybody knows and nobody knows—such was the task she undertook. It required drastic renunciations and ascetic intellectual discipline, and it involved not being understood as well as being misunderstood.

If writing is a sacred activity, a hymn or a prayer, then the traditional classifications of literature are irrelevant. It does not matter very much what Gertrude Stein called her compositions, not only because she was not concerned with forms, but because, no matter what she wrote, it was a "piece" of an integrated consciousness, a work of the human mind absorbed in knowing. As Hegel said [in his *Phenomenology of Mind*], the "well-known," the familiar, is never intelligibly known, since acquired knowledge is formal and not contentual. Gertrude Stein had set herself the goal of discovering what knowing is, and therefore she directed her knowing against this "being-familiar" and "being well-known." In *The Geographical History of America* she maintained that hers were ordinary ideas: "That is what I mean to be I mean to be the one who can and does have as ordinary ideas as these."

Whitehead once remarked [in his *Science and the Modern World*] that "it requires an unusual mind to undertake the analysis of the obvious. Familiar things happen, and mankind does not bother about them." Gertrude Stein's analysis of the obvious, however, confronts the given in ordinary human experience with full awareness of its mystery. She raises questions as to the nature of perception, the meaning of being, the boundlessness of space and the roundness of the world, the passage of time and the nature of personality and identity, and the activities of genius. To contemplate the obvious is to confront the polarities in the universe and the contradictions in man. It is to become aware of the dualism which runs through all things.

Meditation upon these subjects has been the exercise of reflective minds in all ages, but it has been considered the work of philosophers and religious thinkers rather than of creative writers. There is a vast body of writing, however, which, while differing radically in form and content, is unclassifiable except as "meditation." Of this class are Cicero's *De Officiis,* Erasmus's *Moriae Encomium,* Pascal's *Pensées,* Traherne's *Century of Meditations,* and—to mention a sensitive modern thinker—Gabriel Marcel's *Mystery of Being.* One might say, too, that the quality of the best poetry of Wordsworth, of Yeats, and of T. S. Eliot is meditative, and that the novels of Kafka, Mann, Joyce, Hesse, and Proust are fictionalized meditations. The emergence of the meditative element in modern poetry and fiction is correlative with the secular movement in the western world, but the lyrical element itself is reflective, and one need only recall such elegiac pieces as "Night Thoughts" or *The Anatomy of Melancholy* to recognize the diverse forms in which meditation upon "first and last things" has been the "object" of the writing. Hegel's *Phenomenology* and Emerson's essay on *Nature* are brought together under this mode of classification. In fact, all distinctions of form are dissolved in the masterpieces of literature, if the "object" is viewed in terms of content and not in terms of form. The actual subject matter and the personality of the mind that reflects upon it survive in the written word, stripped of all that is accidental and changing, and the written word itself becomes a "moving" power, a dynamic and living entity.

The meditative element became dominant in the writings of Gertrude Stein when she began to write portraits—in other words, at the time when she ceased to worry about communication and emphasized communion. During the writing of **The Geographical History of America,** she was concerned primarily with being, not with time and change. From **Tender Buttons** on, however, all her work is a kind of communion. She detached herself from [what she termed in **Everybody's Autobiography**] "mechanical civilizations and the world being round," convinced that the dialectical process in time leads only from one pole to another—from communism to individualism and back again in a never-ending cycle, in which the individual is always lost in the collective or the solipsistic. The union of opposites is a creative act, but that action itself can never become the object of knowledge. To perform the act is to assert man's freedom from every necessity except that of existence itself. "The only interesting thing is that no one knows the limits of the universe," she said. "You live on this earth and you cannot get away from it and yet there is a space where the stars are which is unlimited and that contradiction is there in every man and every woman and so nothing is ever settled."

Like space, knowledge is infinite, but actual knowing is an individuated process within a finite world where all things change. In view of the contradiction between finite and infinite and in view of the fact that all living creatures die, the important thing is to affirm this life by living it in full consciousness—that is, by living in the present. But it is very difficult to live in the present consciously. "Somebody has to have an individual feeling"; "any time is the time to make a poem. The snow and the sun below"; but the weight of the past and the hope for, or fear of, the future prevent most people from really living in the present. "Being men is a very difficult thing to be," for the primary fact is that time passes. "After all that is what life is and that is the reason there is no Utopia." Human institutions are not static and will never become so. All forms of action

Gertrude Stein in California with her nephew Allan, the son of her brother Michael.

upon the world must consume themselves in the process except the immediate knowing of the present, but it is just as well that most people are so engaged in the struggle for existence, so occupied by the mere business of living, that they do not have time to dwell upon the mystery of existence. For they do not have the vitality to concentrate upon the present: "you have to be a genius to live in it and to exist in it and express it to accept it and deny it by creating it. . . ."

Life is mysterious and can never be understood. "The only thing that anybody can understand is mechanics," but machines are neither interesting nor essential: "you cannot exist without living and living is something that nobody is able to understand while you can exist without machines it has been done but machines cannot exist without you. . . ."

The modern world, overmechanized and overorganized, is an empty world, a world in which few have an individual feeling, because it has lost the sense of strangeness and mystery. To restore to it the feeling of life, writers must achieve a direct vision of the world. The novel, for example, is a dead form, because people have lost their belief in the reality of fictional characters. "I tell all the young ones now to write essays, after all since characters are of no importance why not just write meditations, meditations are always interesting, neither character nor identity are necessary to him who meditates."

For Gertrude Stein, meditation is more than reflection: it is communion, participation—an act of presence. Direct, immediate—it is the only way to master the contradictions and oppositions of discursive thinking and experience and to give a content to the "now." Only through participation will the word have life, and only through the written word can life be immortalized. The written word is the one medium in which all mediation disappears. Words on the written page bear no resemblance to the things they signify, and they are therefore entirely closed to sense perception and open immediately to the inward eye. Through written words one can commune in silence across space and time by signs which in themselves need make no appeal to the senses. All other forms of expression create an object with extension in space or time that is a necessary part of them; they are bound by one or the other and therefore appeal to eye or ear. Thus, paradoxically, the written word is the most immediate of all the modes of expression. In it the writer is disembodied but enduring. "Mention me if you can," Gertrude Stein said [in *The Geographical History of America*], "because I am here." She also said [in *Useful Knowledge*], "How can a language alter. It does not it is an altar."

In contrast to the written word, the spoken word is mediated both by the voice and by the physical presence of the speaker. Gertrude Stein found lecturing difficult because it brought her into contact with an audience, and so she sought to isolate herself in every way possible in order that communication should not interfere with communion. When a writer is writing [Stein said in *Narration*], "that physical something by existing does not connect him with anything but concentrates him on recognition," whereas when he is addressing, or writing for, an audience, that physical something diverts his energies and deprives his words of authenticity. Only in so far as the consciousness is concentrated upon its object—is really present to it—can there be anything created. "By written I mean made. And by made I mean felt," she said [in *Lectures in America*], and over and over again she defined the genius as the one who talks and listens at the same time. "One may really indeed say that that is the essence of genius, of being most intensely alive, that is being one who is at the same time talking and listening. . . . " Talking and listening are not consecutive acts: they occur simultaneously in concentration, "The two in one and the one in two," "like the motor going inside the car and the car moving, they are part of the same thing."

In the act of presence, by which the dualism of experience is overcome here and now, an exchange occurs, in which the objects of contemplative perception and knowing become mental phenomena. Knower and known are joined in an object—the masterpiece—through which they become intelligible to our intuition and feeling, but not to our reason. The transaction occurs in time, but it is not a time-process, and the masterpiece itself has a life beyond life. It "does nothing." Though it can be destroyed, it cannot be used. Since creative writers are contemporaries in the "continuous now," the loss of a masterpiece does not really matter because it would remain the possession of those who had known it and no one else would miss it.

The number of masterpieces is of no importance, and no one of them has any necessity either to be or not to be. They are the gratuitous acts of "presence" itself, and the witnesses to man's freedom in this world. Through them the world-and-life-negation fostered by the thought of death is overcome and the contents of time rescued from the flux. Writing thus becomes ritual, in which the writer affirms himself as one who continues to exist after his death as long as he has readers—indeed, even if he has no readers.

Such a theory of creative writing equates the work of genius with the activity of saints, and the creativity itself with grace. Yet in the work of Gertrude Stein neither the prayers nor the grace seems to involve either a transcendent deity or an immanent world spirit. [She wrote in *The Geographical History of America*], "It is the habit to say there must be a god but not at all the human mind has neither time or identity therefore enough said." The human mind is a dynamism within the life force which moves in the individuated consciousness in a dimensionless inner space—a constructive agency, which is capable of individuating its own objects, free from causal necessity. To Gertrude Stein, the human mind was mysterious, but she was not mystical about it. She had [she wrote in *The Autobiography of Alice B. Toklas*] "an intellectual passion for exactitude in the description of inner and outer reality," and neither had nor sought mystical experience. She defined mysticism [in *Everybody's Autobiography*] as a kind of metamorphosis: "if you believe in anything deeply enough it turns into something else and so money turns into not money. That is what mysticism is. . . ."

Such transubstantiation is not the act of the human mind which knows and distinguishes. "A rose is a rose is a rose is a rose" to all eternity for Gertrude Stein, and the function of the human mind is not to dissolve itself in either the One or the All, nor to be turned into something else through transubstantiation, but to maintain itself courageously against all collectivisms and Nirvanas and to bound the infinite at every moment by its own autonomous acts of knowing. Thus she seems to deny nearly everything that we ordinarily call religion—mystical and nonmystical alike. And yet her view seems to me to be one legitimate view of man, and to merit the name of religion as defined by James, Bergson, and Whitehead.

[In his *Varieties of Religious Experience*] William James denied that there is any such entity as religious emotion; nor is religion "conscience and morality." He defines religion as "the feelings, acts, and experiences of individual men in their solitude, so far as they apprehend themselves to stand in relation to whatever they may consider the divine," and points out that divine means "God-like, whether it be a concrete deity or not." In his chapters on saintliness, James ascribes saintliness to the susceptibility of the individual to "sovereign excitements" of a spiritual order: "the saintly character is the character for which spiritual emotions are the habitual centre of the personal energy," so that the claims of the non-ego are always met with "yes, yes," instead of "no, no."

According to James, among all the shiftings from self-centeredness to love, perhaps the most important is the one in which the individual passes from tenseness and self-responsibility to equanimity, receptivity, and peace, not by an act of will—"not by doing, but by simply relaxing and throwing the burden down." The difference between ordinary people and geniuses depends solely on "the amount of steam-pressure chronically driving the character in the ideal direction, or on the amount of ideal excitement transiently acquired." Thus the "genius with the inborn passion seems not to feel [the inhibitions to action] at all; he is free of all that inner friction and nervous waste." James praised the saintly life, but he felt that there were many ways of being saintly—of being true to one's mission and vocation. He was particularly ambivalent about "mere devotion, divorced from the intellectual conception which might guide it towards bearing useful fruit." For James, the universe was open; he was hospitable to mysticism, although himself not mystical. A moralist, he judged mystical experience by its fruits, not by its transports; a psychologist, he described the facts, without passing judgment upon their metaphysical meaning.

Bergson, on the other hand, was decidedly mystical, and [in his *The Two Sources of Morality and Religion*] saw the whole universe as "a machine for the making of Gods." In opposing static to dynamic religion, he associates the intellect in its myth-making faculty with static religion, and intuition and the vital impetus with dynamic religion. "Religion is to mysticism what popularization is to science," he said. In connection with the activity of intuition, he distinguished between writing intellectually and writing through "the imperative demand of creation," characterizing the latter as an "image of the creation of matter by form." It is important to point out here that Gertrude Stein attended Bergson's lectures in Paris in the winter of 1908, just before she began to write portraits, and it may well be that the impact of those lectures turned her attention from the problem of time in narrative to the problem of objectifying purely qualitative perceptions. Certainly her anti-intellectualism resembles Bergson's and was directed against the static and formal aspects of knowledge just as his was. It may be, too, that the Bergsonian mystical intuition and Gertrude Stein's "human mind" are so similar as to be almost indistinguishable. But Gertrude Stein herself was much less optimistic about the universe than Bergson was and believed much less in progressive evolution and the efficacy of action.

In my opinion, Whitehead's definition of religion comes closest to Gertrude Stein's attitude toward writing. Whitehead says [in his *Religion in the Making*] that "religion is what the individual does with his own solitariness," and he related individual solitariness to universality, because "universality is a disconnection from immediate surroundings. It is an endeavour to find something permanent and intelligible by which to interpret the confusion of immediate detail." The great reflective books of the Old Testament, for example, seek neither to reform society nor to express religious emotion; instead, "there is a self-conscious endeavour to apprehend some general principles." In analyzing the aesthetic experience, Whitehead says that it is "feeling arising out of the realization of contrast under identity." "Expression is the one fundamental sacrament. It is the outward and visible sign of an inward and spiritual grace." A written piece, if it is really firsthand expression, is a masterpiece, and its creation is an act of loyalty to the universe. Geniuses display their originality in precisely that part of their expression which remains unformulated: "They deal with what all men know, and they make it new. They do not bring to the world a new formula nor do they discover new facts, but in expressing their apprehension of the world, they leave behind them an element of novelty—a new expression forever evoking its proper response."

It seems to me that Gertrude Stein's correlation of creative writing with the activity of saints is closest to James's idea of a religious vocation, that her view of the essential dynamism of the creative process is very close to Bergson's theory of intuition, and that her view of writing as "the fundamental sacrament" is very close to Whitehead's. But Gertrude Stein rejected all philosophical systems, believing that neither ontology nor epistemology could resolve the dualism of the universe. Like the existentialists, she began and ended with experience. And experience meant coming to grips with what Charles Sanders Peirce calls "firstness," or pure quality in all its immediacy, and with "secondness," or brute fact in all its starkness; and it meant rejecting utterly the realm of law—as either immanent or transcendent—which is what Peirce meant by "thirdness." For laws in Gertrude Stein's philosophy are constructs of the human mind, and the human mind is not subject to them.

Observation and construction, the activities of the imagination, [he writes in *The Geographical History of America*], have nothing to do with the will to live, either:

> If a master-piece is what it is how can then its not being one effect it. All that is silence because it makes longing and longing and feeling have nothing to do with what a master-piece is.

The human mind bridges the chasm between the fluctuating polarities of the universe, not by asserting the supremacy of either spirit or matter, but by maintaining always the distinction between them. In the act of knowing (either "in a glance or in looking"), man asserts his freedom to create this bridge; freedom is not asserted in the reconstructions of memory and habit. It is direct acquaintance that marries subject and object without destroying the separate existence of mind and the world, and Gertrude Stein declared that no one could know how this was done. It "happened" from time to time in the activity of genius. Such action is a force, an impulsion in individuals, but it is not Bergson's *élan vitale* rushing through matter. Nor is it the will to live of Schopenhauer, or James. It has nothing to do with progress or the struggle for existence. It is not something that arises out of the *negation* of the will to live, however, but rather an excess of vital energy, or abundance of life itself. It is an existential freedom, to which Gertrude Stein gives the name of the "human mind." Like the muse of Homer or of Milton, it is not a function of the ego, but the function of spirit.

For inspiration, psychology has no name but genius. Nordau treated it [in his *Degeneration*] as a disease of personality, degenerate and aberrant. Others, notably Frederick W. H. Myers [in his *Human Personality*], have seen it as a subliminal self. Jung identified it with the collective unconscious, working through the intuition. James considered it an inexplicable form of selectivity which directed the attention towards a particular class of objects. Gertrude Stein compared it [in ***Everybody's Autobiography***] to lightning, which strikes in a particular time and place, occasioned by natural phenomena, but itself the cause of its own activity. The motions of genius are impulsive but unnecessitated, processes of attention rather than motives. For in genius, intention is freedom to know and to create.

The knower, according to this way of putting the case, is an individual, but to his feeling he is not existing in time; nor is he existing in eternity, though he may feel as if he were. Gertrude Stein's phrase for the condition of knowing is "being existing"—her way of expressing the permanence which endures through change. The "be" in become is a reminder that things persist—that there is a continuous present in which actual beings exist and sustain themselves as entities amid the flux. A masterpiece is such an entity. It carries within it its own measure of value and is therefore open to everyone who has a human mind in any conceivable here and now. It is thus universal in its content, not as a mere form.

In this connection, it is interesting to note what Charles Sanders Peirce has to say about abstraction and the present. According to him, the present is just what cannot be abstracted; it cannot be "aufgehoben," [the critic adds in a footnote, "Hegel's term for the process of 'transformation.' "] for the abstract is always "what the concrete makes it be" [writes James Feibleman in his *Introduction to Peirce's Philosophy*]. The concrete is always a "surprise," different from what we thought it would be, something that we had not expected, and for which we cannot prepare. To recognize it demands the independent existence of both the knower and the known, in an accidental relationship, independent of everything except the interplay of subject and object.

This interplay is really the activity of the human mind as it is present to the world at any moment. [According to John E. Smith in his "Religion and Theology" in Wiener and Young's *Studies in the Philosophy of Peirce*] Peirce called it "musement,"

> an occupation of the mind which "involves no purpose save that of casting aside all serious purpose," and which consists in wonder either at some striking characteristic within one of the universes or at some purposeful connection between two of the universes, together with speculation about the cause of these features. The attitude of mind involved is closest to *pure play* because it is not fraught with serious purpose of any kind; on the contrary, it is actually an attempt to cut through the layers of conscious purpose and arrive at that state of mind which is close to the naïveté and freshness of children in the face of some awe-inspiring wonder. If, however, some ulterior purpose is allowed to enter, the proper attitude is destroyed.

Gertrude Stein's writing increasingly became "musement" of this order—play—particularly in ***Tender Buttons*** and ***Geography and Plays,*** in which she was seeking to express the successive moments of realizing the objects or the scene arbitrarily selected for attention, or to convey the essential nature of living creatures or of objects moving in space. [In ***Lectures in America*** she writes], "As I said if you like, it was like a cinema picture made up of succession and each moment having its own emphasis that is its own difference and so there was the moving and the existence of each moment as it was in me." Impersonal, objective, even mechanical, such writing is unconcerned with hopes and fears. Thus she could later say [in ***The Geographical History of America***], "Finally a prayer has nothing to do with I care."

No matter what her subject matter was—and paradoxically, as she became more playful, she wrote more and more frequently about "saints and singing"—she was never solemn or conventionally religious. She had wit and a love of the comic, and since her object was only to be present both to her writing and to her reader, she gives the impression of childlike intentness, as though she were concentrating upon each movement in an absorbing game. Thus her work is dominated by the spirit of play, and is filled with a peculiarly pervasive feeling of delight and freedom from care, even when she is describing the wars she has seen. She wrote without tears, for there is something that sings in life—that is gratuitous and free. We do not know how to name it:

> Dogs and birds and a chorus and a flat land.
> How do you like what you are. The bird knows, the
> dogs know and the chorus well the chorus yes the chorus
> if the chorus which is the chorus.
> The flat land is not the chorus.
> Human nature is not the chorus.
> The human mind is not the chorus.
> Tears are not the chorus.
> Food is not the chorus.
> Money is not the chorus.
> What is the chorus.

For Gertrude Stein, there is a harmony between man and the universe, but it is not a heavenly harmony—not a music of the spheres. It is not a process in time nor a result of progress nor an event in history. It is perhaps "the choir invisible of those immortal dead who live again" in masterpieces, who were present to the world and to themselves, participating in experience, contemplating it, loving it, dreaming about it, and expressing it in words. But she rejected all mysticism, all theology, and all systematic philosophy which placed the oneness of things beyond experience; and the chorus as she conceived it is a harmony of separate and distinct voices, not a transcendent or an immanent paean in which the many are resolved into the One. Consequently there is little exalted rhetoric in her writing. But there is a great deal of joy—joy in the pleasures of perception, of imagination, of play. She sings a song that we all can sing in those moments when we really live consciously in the actual present and affirm life as an end in itself. In singing this song, one is "doing nothing" in exactly the way the saints are "doing nothing" when they pray or sing or perform their ritual tasks. The song is childlike and gay in its quality, solemn and serious only in the attention devoted to it. It asks for nothing, but finds everything. "They liked it as much as they ever liked it before because the wind blew and blew the birds about and they liked it they liked it as much when the wind did that" [*The Geographical History of America*].

This seizing of the present moment and savoring it is very characteristic of all forms of real participation. Contemplative participation is only another name for the process of knowing in which, according to Schopenhauer [in his *The World as Will and Idea*], the artist becomes the "pure will-less subject of knowledge." In *The Geographical History of America,* Gertrude Stein seems to be speaking of herself when she writes: "She says she wanted that she should be the only ideal one, but she is, what else is she but that, she is, and so the human mind rests with what is." Like Schopenhauer, she saw in the Idea the abiding and the essential, and in art, the embodiment of reality. Though her emphasis is different, it seems to me that she must have agreed with nearly everything that Schopenhauer says about the work of art.

> It repeats or reproduces the eternal Ideas grasped through pure contemplation, the essential and abiding in all the phenomena of the world; and according to what the material is in which it reproduces, it is sculpture or painting, poetry or music. Its one source is the knowledge of Ideas; its one aim the communication of this knowledge. While science, following the unresting and inconstant stream of the fourfold forms of reason and consequent, with each end attained sees further, and can never reach a final goal nor attain full satisfaction, any more than by running we can reach the place where the clouds touch the horizon; art, on the contrary, is everywhere at its goal. For it plucks the object of its contemplation out of the stream of the world's course, and has it isolated before it. And this particular thing, which in that stream was a small perishing part, becomes to art the representative of the whole, an equivalent of the endless multitude in space and time. It therefore pauses at this particular thing; the course of time stops; the relations vanish for it; only the essential, the Idea, is its object.

Ordinary people do not linger over the mere perception of an object or focus their attention sufficiently upon it to see it as a thing-in-itself. The man of genius lets us see the world through his eyes. It is his presence of mind which enables others to see. The value of vision does not arise from the subject matter; the insignificance of the matter may even intensify aesthetic experience as in still-life paintings or in the paintings of common country scenes by Ruisdael. It is for this reason that Gertrude Stein's writings give the appearance of triviality, and convey an impression of fragmentariness and inconsequentiality. But this is only on the surface. Like Henry James, she knew that it is the quality of life in the work of art that really counts.

The isolation of an object by the human mind was carried much farther by Gertrude Stein than it has been carried by other writers. Many of her portraits and plays, taken in isolation, seem fragmentary and unintelligible. The whole of her work, however, has unity and meaning. Her writings have the kind of unity which she ascribes to the continents on this planet. They are one as the land is one, separated into continents and islands by the waters of the world, but connected beneath by the vast floor of rivers and oceans, and so really one land, though to our eyes this one land appears as so many different "pieces" of various contours and sizes. The literal indivisible oneness of the ground beneath the waters is one of her recurrent ideograms for the oneness of the human mind under the flow of history and amid the diversity of peoples. [In *The Geographical History of America* she writes] "Do you see that there is the land which nobody can see because there is the sea, and yet there is the land in America, there is the land salt lake land where there is no sea."

To penetrate beneath the separating seas of literary forms to the substratum of consciousness requires one to ignore for the most part the separations in time and space which force upon us the isolated parts and fragments rather than the whole. The mind of man is still largely a *terra incognita;* it is revealed, if at all, primarily through the lives of saints and the creations of the artist, both often seeming to be occupied in doing nothing immediately useful. Masterpieces and the life of sanctity are "presences" across the centuries; they are always "here" to the mind that attends.

But this is a rather exalted way of describing Gertrude Stein's works. After all, her favorite illustration of the way one exists in eternity is Robinson Crusoe's discovery of Friday's footprints. "[It] is one of the most perfect examples of the non-existence of time and identity, which makes a master-piece," she said [in *What Are Masterpieces*]. For in any moment of absorbed wonder the self is recollected in an experience of heightened awareness. And the beautiful paradox is that the artist, the saint, or the philosopher—like Crusoe in this dramatic confrontation of the "otherness" in the world—becomes most truly himself, is most truly a Self, precisely in the moment of self-forgetfulness. It was to this paradox that Gertrude Stein pointed when she said [in *The Geographical History of America*] that "the human mind is like not being in danger but being killed," and [in *What Are Masterpieces*] that "At any moment when you are you you are you without the memory of yourself because if you remember yourself while you are you you are not for the purposes of creating you." (pp. 488-506)

Allegra Stewart, "The Quality of Gertrude Stein's Creativity," in American Literature, Vol. XXVIII, No. 4, January, 1957, pp. 488-506.

James E. Breslin (essay date 1979)

[*Breslin is an American critic and educator. In the following excerpt, he examines Gertrude Stein's experi-*

mentation with autobiographical conventions in The Autobiography of Alice B. Toklas *and* Everybody's Autobiography.*]*

When *The Autobiography of Alice B. Toklas* was published in 1933, the book soon became, as Gertrude Stein both hoped and feared, a critical and popular success. Stein earned celebrity and a substantial amount of money, both of which depressed her. *The Autobiography*'s subsequent literary reputation might have cheered her up, however, for Stein's critics—with the notable exception of her best critic, Richard Bridgman [in his *Gertrude Stein in Pieces*]—have generally either ignored or rejected *The Autobiography.* B. L. Reid dismissed it as "chitchat" [in his *Art by Subtraction*], and many readers find it merely anecdotal and gossipy. Certainly, readers who approach it with expectations shaped by the revival of confessional writing in the 1960's are apt to reject it as too reserved. Stein herself had somewhat different misgivings about the book, stating in *Everybody's Autobiography* (1936) that the earlier work had dealt with what had happened instead of "what is happening." Yet *The Autobiography*'s charming, playful, anecdotal surface has distracted its readers from its real complexity; it provides not—as Stein seems to have thought—a mere submission to the conventions of autobiography but an intense and creative struggle with them.

In many ways the autobiographical act is one at odds with, even a betrayal of, Gertrude Stein's aesthetic principles. Her essay **"What Are Master-pieces and Why Are There So Few of Them"** offers a concise statement of those principles: "The minute your memory functions while you are doing anything it may be very popular but actually it is dull," Stein warns; her desire to live and write in a continuous present thus turns her against the necessarily retrospective act of autobiography. But Stein's opposition to the conventions of her genre runs even deeper than this, because her commitment to a continuous present forces her to reject the notion of identity altogether. "Identity is recognition," she writes: "I am I because my little dog knows me." Identity, an artificial construction based on the perception of certain fixed traits that allow my little dog or anyone else to imagine that they know me, stresses repetition, which is, according to Stein, antithetical to creativity. Identity "destroys creation"—as does memory; both, carrying the past over into the present and structuring by repetition, are ways we have of familiarizing the strangeness, the mysterious being, of others. Masterpieces de-familiarize; they derive from "knowing that there is no identity and producing while identity is not." In part Stein is warning against self-imitation, and she quotes Picasso as saying that he is willing to be influenced by anyone but himself; but she is also stressing that to live in a continuous present, to *be* rather than to *repeat,* one must constantly break down identity. But can there be an *auto*-biography in which "there is no identity"? Or, to put the question somewhat differently: autobiographies are customarily *identified* as acts of *self*-representation, but Stein is challenged to refashion the form to show that she eludes or transcends the category of self or identity.

At the same time her belief in a continuous present sets Stein against the kind of narrative that we are accustomed (again) to find in auto-*bio*-graphy. "What is the use of being a boy if you are going to grow up to be a man?" she asks in **"What Are Master-pieces."** Like remembering and identifying, narrating—telling, say, the story of a girl becoming a woman—such narrating represents a linear sequence of time, not an ongoing present. In addition, remembering, identifying, and narrating all view things in relation to other things (e.g., girl in relation to woman), instead of viewing a thing as what Stein calls an "entity"—a thing existent in and for itself. A masterpiece, transcending linear time and recognizable identity, is itself an "entity," not, as Eliot had said, a revision of the literary tradition but an absolute act of creation. The fact that the early works of Cubism derive from such absolute acts of creation explains why, as we are told in *The Autobiography,* they are so strange, almost physically painful to look at—and yet must be looked at intently: the viewer must struggle to get beyond mere recognition, the comfortably familiar. But autobiographies are hardly absolute acts of creation; they are historical, referring to persons and events that clearly existed out there, in reality, prior to their representation in language. Finally, Stein holds that any concession to—or even consciousness of—an audience undermines creativity; as soon as a writer begins to think of him/herself in relation to an audience, he or she "writes what the other person is to hear and so entity does not exist there are two present instead of one and so once again creation breaks down." But if we now find it problematic to think of even a lyric poem as autotelic, how can we imagine an autotelic autobiography? Can Stein create an autobiography without identity, memory, linear time? And if she did, could we bear to read it? In some ways *Everybody's Autobiography,* dealing with "what is happening" instead of what had happened, comes closer to these aims; but what makes *The Autobiography of Alice B. Toklas* so interesting is that it admits the conventions of memory, identity, chronological time—in order to fight against and ultimately to transcend their deadening effects.

When she was asked to write her autobiography, Stein replied, "Not possibly," and it is easier to imagine her writing an essay called "What Are Autobiographies and Why Are None of Them Masterpieces" than it is to imagine her writing her own autobiography. Of course, she did not write her own autobiography; she wrote *The Autobiography of Alice B. Toklas.* Or did she? [According to Bridgman] some writers have speculated that Alice B. Toklas wrote her own autobiography or at least substantial parts of it. But perhaps the most important point about this debate is that it seems to have been generated not just by an extraliterary curiosity about the book's composition, but by an actual literary effect the book has on its readers—namely, the effect of raising questions about just whose book it is.

I will return to this issue; for the moment, assuming (as I have been) Stein to be the book's author, I want to suggest how she took up the formal challenge of autobiography by recalling a young man named Andrew Green, who appears briefly in the third chapter of *The Autobiography.* Andrew Green "hated everything modern." Once while staying at 27 rue de Fleurus for a month he covered "all the pictures with cashmere shawls"; he "could not bear" to look at the strange, frightening paintings. Significantly, "he had a prodigious *memory* and could recite all of Milton's Paradise Lost by heart" (my emphasis). "He adored as he said a simple centre and a continuous design." Green *has* an identity, so much so that his character can be fixed in a single, brief paragraph. Gertrude Stein does not have an identity; in attempting to represent her "self" she created in *The Autobiography of Alice B. Toklas* a book with an elusive center and a discontinuous design.

Even the title page of the current Vintage edition—*The Autobiography of Alice B. Toklas* BY Gertrude Stein—is enough to suggest that the center of the ensuing text may be difficult to locate. The original Harcourt edition made the same point in a more subtle way: both the cover and the title page print only a title—*The Autobiography of Alice B. Toklas*—but no author's name is given. The frontispiece (facing the title page), however, is a Man Ray photograph which shows Stein in the right foreground, seated at a table, but with her back to the camera and in dark shadow; Alice B. Toklas stands in the left background, but she stands in light and framed by a doorway. The photograph, with its obscure foreground and distinct background, has no clear primary subject—like the book that follows; the seated Stein, however, is writing, and the possibility is raised that *she* may be the author of the book, an uncertainty not resolved for the reader of this edition until its final page—when "Toklas" tells us that Stein has in fact written *The Autobiography.* Moreover, the book's style blends the domestic particularity, whimsical humor, and ironic precision of Toklas with some of the leading features of Stein's writing—e.g., stylized repetition, digression, a language that continually points up its own artifice. The reader is not certain who it is he is listening to; nor is he meant to be. Richard Bridgman has shown that *Stanzas in Meditation,* written at the same time as *The Autobiography,* is at least partly about writing *The Autobiography,* and the poem strongly suggests that our uncertainties were an intended effect: "This is her autobiography one of two / But which it is no one . . . can know."

But most readers are more like Andrew Green than Gertrude Stein; they don't like to dwell in uncertainties, and so most discussions of *The Autobiography* begin by assuming the character of Stein to be its easily identifiable center, and they proceed to discuss this character as if it were not mediated for the reader by a perspective that is to *some* degree external to it. Yet, even if we proceed along these lines, the character of Stein turns out to be an elusive and enigmatic "center." Stein, Toklas tells us, sought in her writing to give "the inside as seen from the outside"; that is one reason she creates herself through the external perspective of Toklas. What she means by "the inside" can be clarified through *The Autobiography*'s account of Picasso's famous portrait of Stein; it was with this painting, we are told, that Picasso "passed from the Harlequin, the *charming* early italian period to the *intensive struggle* which was to end in cubism" (my emphasis). Stein emphasizes the "intensive struggle" that went into the painting of the portrait itself. During the winter of 1907 Stein patiently posed for Picasso some eighty or ninety times, but then he abruptly "painted out the whole head." "I can't see you any longer when I look, he said irritably." At this point both Stein and Picasso left Paris for the summer, but the day he returned "Picasso sat down and out of his head painted the head in without having seen Gertrude Stein again." In the enigmatic sentence, "I can't see you any longer when I look," what is the referent of "you"? On the one hand, it is not the external, literal Stein, recognizable to her little dog or a realistic novelist. That is why, when Stein later cuts her hair short, Picasso, at first disturbed, can conclude that "all the same it is all there." He was not striving for a realistic mimesis, as Stein stresses in her account of Picasso's difficulties with what turned out to be the least realistic feature of the portrait, the face. On the other hand, Picasso was not trying to evoke the inner, subconscious depths of Stein, of the sort that might fascinate a psychological novelist; in fact, Toklas later claims that Stein had no subconscious.

In the painting itself Stein's body is solid, massive, weighty, sculptured; the simple, severe lines of the eyebrows, nose and mouth, the slightly uneven eyes create a stylized, mask-like face. She inhabits an abstract space, her eyes conveying an almost fierce attentiveness, but she is calm, at rest, even serene. Picasso's Stein seems a regal, perhaps deific, figure, but the earth colors of her dress, blending with the tan background, modify the austerity of the face and the monumentality of the body to create warmth and to humanize Stein. The portrait is thus an instance of what Stein herself called "elemental abstraction"; the "you" painted by Picasso is, therefore, not a personality, a recognizable identity, but an entity—Stein's being, awesome, serene, strange, mysterious yet human. Like Picasso's portrait, *The Autobiography* gives the inside by way of the outside; it plays down psychology and sticks to the surface, recording externals (objects, acts, dialogues) in a way that clearly manifests deliberate and idiosyncratic acts of selection and stylization. Such admitted artifice annoys many readers who, with simpler models of self and autobiography, demand a fuller intimacy and deeper psychology of their autobiographers. But Stein's stylization of the surface reveals the "you" that Picasso, having looked so long and intently, could no longer see when he looked. *The Autobiography,* in short, gives us Gertrude Stein being.

To envision *this* Stein required an "intensive struggle" and at many points Picasso was urged by friends—among them Andrew Green—to stop with the "beauty" of what he had so far accomplished, but Picasso, turning his back on his audience, went on. In this way, renouncing a "charming" for a more severe and difficult work, Picasso produced a masterpiece. Compare Picasso's heroic struggles with the facility of a Vallaton:

> When he painted a portrait he made a crayon sketch and then began painting at the top of the canvas straight across. Gertrude Stein said it was like pulling down a curtain as slowly as one of his swiss glaciers. Slowly he pulled the curtain down and by the time he was at the bottom of the canvas, there you were. The whole operation took about two weeks and then he gave the canvas to you. First however he exhibited it in the autumn salon and it had considerable notice and everybody was pleased.

Vallaton's scrupulously predetermined works are the

comic opposites of Picasso's adventurous and difficult acts of discovery. Vallaton's paintings pleased everybody, whereas at first only "the painter and the painted" admired Picasso's portrait of Stein. Creative works thus demand an intensive struggle from both creator and audience. "The pictures were so strange that one quite instinctively looked at anything rather than at them just at first," Toklas recalls of her first evening in Stein's atelier, and even in recollection, some twenty-five years later, this difficulty is reexperienced: Toklas comes to describe the paintings (about which the reader is very eager to hear) only slowly, almost resistingly, after several digressions. Gertrude Stein can rest her head against a rock and stare at the Italian noonday sun; but like a masterpiece or the sun, Stein herself is hard to look at directly—another reason for the mediation of Toklas—and even Toklas approaches her, too, very slowly. Stein is first mentioned on page 5 where Toklas reports of their first meeting only that "I was impressed by the coral brooch she wore and her voice," and that "a bell within me rang" certifying that Stein was a genius. The reader expects the first meeting between the two women to be related with ample circumstantial and emotional detail; instead, only two rather oddly selected details are given, then a long leap is made to a perception of Stein's genius, though the playful tone makes it hard for us to be sure exactly how seriously we are to take this claim. The scene is deliberately simplified; circumstantial and psychological detail are eliminated—to foreground the powerful, strange presence of Stein and the intuitive powers of Toklas.

Stein is next glimpsed obliquely, through objects associated with her—again, as if her presence were too powerful to be looked at directly. Toklas remembers from her first visit to the atelier "a large table on which were horseshoe nails and pebbles and little pipe cigarette holders" which she later found "to be accumulations from the pockets of Picasso and Gertrude Stein." Without any clear associational values, these objects at once invite and frustrate psychological speculation, as the stylized surface of *The Autobiography* so often does; we are tempted to "identify" Stein but are shown that we can't. Resisting metaphorization, these simple objects nevertheless provide humanizing detail (like the earth colors of Picasso's portrait) before the mythologizing of Stein that follows just a few sentences later.

> The chairs in the room were also all italian renaissance, not very comfortable for short-legged people and one got the habit of sitting on one's legs. Miss Stein sat near the stove in a lovely high-backed one and she peacefully let her legs hang, which was a matter of habit, and when any one of the many visitors came to ask her a question she lifted herself up out of this chair and usually replied in french, not just now.

In this Gertrude Stein—sitting "peacefully" in a high, hard, uncomfortable chair, dispensing regal gestures of denial—the reader confronts a presence of profound, contemplative calm, a figure very like the one in Picasso's portrait. This first image points toward the Stein who, later, finds it restful to stare at the midday sun or at those disquieting paintings that Andrew Green covered with cashmere shawls; it also points toward the later mysterious, sibylline Stein who makes enigmatic pronouncements, who lives in a world of "hidden meanings" and who does not explain things to the reader or even to Toklas, leaving the adventure of discovery to us; it is this Stein who dismisses Pound as the "village explainer." But in this first representation of Stein, as throughout *The Autobiography,* the external perspective of Toklas, sticking to the observable surface, suggests the inside while leaving it mysterious. As a result, Stein is not created as a realistic, psychologically complex character; she is, rather, an abstraction, a deliberate simplification—a mythical figure whose peaceful self-sufficiency allows her to transcend external circumstances.

The *Autobiography* of Benjamin Franklin records the attempt to create an identity through acts of will; *The Education of Henry Adams* records the breakdown of a similar attempt and the dissolution of the very idea of identity. **The Autobiography of Alice B. Toklas** takes the process one step further; the book shows us not someone striving to create a self, but someone who *exists* calmly in a world without any external orders. Again and again the book shows us Stein existing "peacefully" under circumstances that are often far more stressful than uncomfortable chairs. Even Picasso, the character closest to her equal, is "fussed" when he arrives late for a Stein dinner party; looks "sheepish" when he wrests his piece of bread back from Stein, who has accidentally picked it up; or becomes embarrassed when Stein mentions the possibility of his seeing Fernande after they have temporarily separated. Stein, on the other hand, seems to possess an inner stillness that allows her to respond to external pressures with serenity, sometimes even with good humor. When World War I starts while she is visiting London, Stein is concerned but not alarmed about the fate of her writings, all copies of which are back in Paris. Later, after her return to Paris, during an air raid, she calmly quiets an Alice B. Toklas who is so frightened her knees are literally knocking together; and in **The Autobiography**'s final chapter Stein enters the confused and diminished Paris of the postwar era with the same equanimity she had shown during the many crises of the war. Most impressive, however, is the cheerful confidence with which she meets the frugality, frequent disorder, and the public antagonism of the early years of her career. Stein remains steadfastly committed to her work, in spite of her difficulties in finding publication—and in spite of journalistic ridicule when her writing does appear. When **Three Lives** is privately printed, her publisher sends to 27 rue de Fleurus a young man, who questions her knowledge of English; Stein laughs—as she often does at moments when we expect her to be angry or embittered—and her response is contrasted with that of Matisse, two pages earlier, whose feelings are "frightfully" hurt by newspaper ridicule of his art school.

Yet the Stein of **The Autobiography** is by no means as easy to pin down as this discussion of her so far implies; rather, the book frustrates any attempt to fix Stein in a simple identity. In **Everybody's Autobiography** Stein admires paintings which move rather than being about movement and which seem to come out of the "prison" of their frames—as if the subject were alive, truly existing. Stein's own aesthetic theory, as we have seen, made her acutely aware that by attempting to incarnate her being in language in an autobiography, she was running the risk of merely fixing, of limiting and deadening, herself. But the pressures of autobiography, among them the pressure of language itself, constitute another set of external circumstances to which Stein calmly responds with a playful sense of adventure. The result is that *The Autobiography of Alice B. Toklas* presents a Gertrude Stein who keeps stepping out of the frame, as if she were alive, truly existing. The "psychology" of her character may be a simplified one, but a reader who tries to delineate this character in a careful way finds him/herself speaking in contradictions; and these very contradictions are what make the character of Stein remain mysterious, elusive—alive.

Gertrude Stein liked to sit and pose for Picasso and other artists, but she also liked the long walks home afterwards through the darkening Paris streets. Stillness and motion are one set of contraries that create the character of Gertrude Stein. Andrew Green, resisting the challenge of modernity, of the moment, remains anxiously fixed and static—neither at rest nor in motion. But alongside the oracular Stein who can sit peacefully in a hard, high-backed chair, we must place the Stein who, in a recurring phrase, "goes on." "Keep your mind open," William James had told her at Radcliffe, and the willingness to move into new experience—or "liveliness"—becomes a standard against which all characters are measured in *The Autobiography.* Fernande feels "heavy in hand" and seems "indolent"; Matisse is "very alert although slightly heavy" and, later, virile but without "life." In contrast with both of these Picasso is "quick moving but not restless"; Stein herself is lively and adventurous, not heavy nor indolent; she may move slowly, but she moves forward—although not restlessly. Not long after Gertrude Stein and her brother arrive in Paris, they begin to buy Cézannes, small ones at first. But "having gone so far," they "decided to go further, they decided to buy a big Cézanne and then they would stop." But even then they go on and later Stein— unlike her brother, another casualty to modernity—goes on to Picasso. This commitment to process explains why Stein "loves objects that are breakable": "she says she likes what she has and she likes the adventure of a new one." In fact, so committed is Stein to ongoing movement that when driving her car "she goes forward admirably, she does not go backward successfully."

But even this account of the contradictions in Stein's character simplifies it, for each side of the rest/motion opposition generates, in turn, its own oppositions. Stein may be calmly self-possessed, but she also has an "explosive temper"; she enjoys the novelty of fresh experience, yet she is upset if asked to do something suddenly. The important point, however, is that these various features are not presented as the odd twists and turns within a complex yet ultimately unified character; they are the unresolved contradictions of Gertrude Stein's being. She resists all our attempts to frame her as surely as that odd assortment of objects from the pockets of Picasso and Stein resist our efforts to find meaning in them: they just *are.*

Contradictions similarly proliferate when we examine the book's theories about and actual practice of writing. At times Stein speaks of her own work as if it were based on a very simple model of art as representation. Real life sources are given for characters in her fiction; Picasso's cubism is given a realistic basis in Spanish landscape and architecture and Stein speaks of art as the "exact reproduction of an inner or an outer reality." Yet in the same paragraph Stein asserts that "events" ought not to be "the material of poetry and prose"; her writing is often described as the making of sentences, as if it were more construction than representation; and she elsewhere affirms distortion and abstraction in art. Anyone who reads *The Autobiography* looking for a "key" to Stein's fictional works—and many do, as Stein knew they would—will be just as frustrated as the one who reads it looking for the "key" to Stein's private psychology. "Observation and construction make imagination," Stein says, as if she were demystifying the imagination, making it a matter of perception and craft, but Stein, of course, *goes on:* "Observation and construction make imagination, that is granting the possession of imagination," and imagination and Stein herself remain playfully mystified. Oracular and witty, Stein is a sibylline presence, no village or even a Parisian explainer.

The oppositions in Stein's "theorizing" reappear in the writing of the book itself, which continually offers contradictory clues about what *kind* of book it is. Its anecdotal manner, its preoccupation with recognizable, real figures, its concern with "the heroic age of cubism" give it the quality of a memoir, as if it were presenting a true historical record. Yet it is *The Autobiography* OF *Alice B. Toklas*—BY Gertrude Stein: the book is marked at once as an autobiography and a fiction (since it is the autobiography of someone other than the author). An ingenuous sentence at the end tantalizes us in the same way: "I am going to write [the autobiography] for you," Stein tells Toklas. "I am going to write it as simply as Defoe did the autobiography of Robinson Crusoe." But how simply was that? Not even this sentence is very simple; it is one written by the (likely) actual author, Stein, imputed to the fictive author, Toklas, who is reporting something said by the character Stein to the character/author Toklas; the sentence, moreover, compares the autobiography of a fictional character (Robinson Crusoe) with that of a character who was real, at least until Stein started writing her autobiography for her. Throughout, *The Autobiography*'s whimsical, self-interrupting, repetitious, stylized prose marks it as a piece of admitted and self-conscious artifice. The book is an historical memoir; the book is a fictional construct.

To put it another way, *The Autobiography* continually points up the disparity between actuality and its representation, but it does so without irony, without lamenting the insufficiency of either reality or of literary fictions. The book's narrative method simultaneously acknowledges chronological time and the power of writing to play freely with that time; again Stein does not privilege either one over the other. "Moving is in every direction," Stein writes in *Narration.* Just the chapter titles in *The Autobiography* ("Before I Came to Paris," "My Arrival in Paris," "Gertrude Stein in Paris—1903-1907," "Gertrude Stein Before She Came to Paris," "1907-1914," "The War," and "After the War—1919-1932") are enough to suggest that the book both establishes and breaks a forward movement toward the time of its composition. Yet this overall movement is further complicated by the book's local texture—partly by its numerous portraits (which halt temporal progression) and partly by Toklas' wandering style of narration, its constant excursions backward and forward in time. For it is not accurate to speak, as I just did, of the book's forward movement toward the time of its composition, because we listen to Toklas in the *act* of recollection; and Toklas, no Vallaton proceeding along pre-designed lines, moves by playful, free association—thereby liberating herself from chronological order while still accepting its reality. Another temporal dimension of ***The Autobiography*** is thus the continuous present of its telling. The book's multivalence, its moving in all directions, can also be seen in its ending. In the foreground of the final chapter we have Toklas writing in the present; she is writing about "After the War—1919-1932," and by looking backward to this period she carries the book's narrative forward into the postwar era and acknowledges the reality of historical time. One feature of this period that is emphasized is Stein's increasing literary success, which might seem to provide the book with a happy conclusion until we remember that, for Stein, recognition is as much reason for self-doubt and suspicion as it is for gratification, and Toklas equally emphasizes the postwar decline from "the heroic age of cubism." At the same time Stein, fixated neither by success nor by nostalgia for an heroic past, is shown searching for the source of a new creative idea she believes has entered painting; the source may be the work of Francis Rose, but this is not certain. With "her never failing curiosity" the adventuresome Stein remains in a continuous present, an entity.

At ***The Autobiography***'s close, the narrative catches up with itself or at least with its beginning, as we learn of the genesis of the book and that Stein is its author. In the original edition this final page of the text was followed by a photograph of the first page of the manuscript. ***The Autobiography*** ends by folding back on itself; and a reader is invited to reread the book in light of the revelation that Stein is its author. Lest this revelation make the reader too comfortable, he or she is also, as we have seen, assured of the book's Defoe-like simplicity in a way that warns of its complexity and deviousness. At the end ***The Autobiography*** circles back on itself as if it were an autonomous verbal reality. Yet the book's conclusion also reveals Stein to be on a quest that is not completed; the book's ending is also open. The end of the book closes off and frames a life at the same time that it breaks out of its frame, its artificial closure, to affirm the ongoing process of the author's life. At its close, as throughout ***The Autobiography,*** moving is in all directions.

Gertrude Stein complained to Matisse that "there is nothing within you that fights itself "; that is why he lacks life. Through its contradictions ***The Autobiography of Alice B. Toklas*** fights itself and so achieves creative life. The problems of the book—many of which are versions of the problem of referentiality, the relation of the work to external reality—are the problems and contradictions of autobiography itself, problems that make the genre such a difficult one for both theoretical and practical criticism. How can we deal with the tension between historical truthfulness and aesthetic design in autobiography? Or with the splitting of the author into character and writer? Or with the difficulties of ending an autobiography, given that the author's life is likely to go on? Stein deliberately raises and foregrounds these difficult questions, not in order to solve or answer them, but to play with them and to make the ways in which the genre fights itself into her book's energizing principles. Her relation to autobiography parallels what she says [in ***Everybody's Autobiography***] the relation of a genius to time must be: he or she must "accept it and deny it by creating it." By renouncing a simple center and a continuous design, by exploring the formal dilemmas of the genre, Gertrude Stein at once accepted, denied, and created autobiography. (pp. 901-13)

> James E. Breslin, "Gertrude Stein and the Problems of Autobiography," in The Georgia Review, *Vol. XXXIII, No. 4, Winter, 1979, pp. 901-13.*

Jayne L. Walker (essay date 1984)

[*In the following excerpt, Walker compares Stein's methods of representing reality in* Three Lives *with Paul Cézanne's theories about representational painting.*]

"I believe in reality as Cezanne or Caliban believe in it." This credo, which Stein recorded in her 1909 working notebooks, provocatively couples the modernist painter with Shakespeare's ignoble savage to invoke a "reality" that lies far outside conventional *vraisemblance.* In painting as well as in literature, verisimilitude depends more on correspondence to conventional models than on accurate notation of the immediate data of perception. In ***The Autobiography of Alice B. Toklas,*** Stein recalled that Cézanne's portrait of his wife had not at first "*seemed* natural, it had taken her some time to feel that it *was* natural" (my emphasis). Once she understood that Cézanne's paintings represented a version of the real that had not previously been codified by tradition, she dedicated herself to an equally radical pursuit of "reality" in her own writing. (p. 7)

Throughout *The Principles of Psychology* (1890), [William] James's discussions of visual perception emphasize the gap between the incomplete, fragmentary, or distorted "signs" of immediate retinal sensations and the familiar objects they signify. This semiotic analogy that James derived from [the *New Theory of Vision* by] Berkeley helps to elucidate more precisely the nature of the challenge that the painters' goal of rendering direct retinal sensations posed to time-honored conventions of representational painting. The impressionists took as their primary object sensations of light striking the retina. In James's terms, their basic unit of signification corresponded not to the "sensation as 'object' " of normalized perception but to the "sensation as 'sign' " (or what Saussurean linguistics would call the signifier). Most radically in Monet's and, later, in Seurat's canvases, a multitude of small patches or dots of color notate the fragmentary signs of direct retinal sensation. This technique shatters the illusory coalescence of signifier and signified object that characterizes both normalized perception and conventional techniques of representing objects in painting and the concomitant illusion of the canvas as a transparent window opening into deep space. The surface design of color patches retards easy recognition of familiar objects and refuses to dissolve into illusory depth. By foregrounding the material patterning of the signifiers that model the raw data of visual sensations, these canvases demand that the viewer work *through* the surface design in order to achieve belated recognition of the objects it signifies.

Before the impressionists, other nineteenth-century painters' efforts to re-create sensations of light and color entailed a similar foregrounding of the painted surface. Both Constable's brushwork and Courbet's use of the palette knife roughened the texture of their canvases, prefiguring the increasingly assertive surface designs of the impressionists and Cézanne. This heightened emphasis on the material reality of the medium, on the "painting . . .—before being a battle-horse, a nude woman, or whatever anecdote—[as] essentially a flat surface covered with colors assembled in a certain order" (to quote Maurice Denis's famous phrase, which first appeared in 1890 [in his essay "Cézanne" in *Théories, 1890-1910: De Symbolisme et de Gauguin vers un nouvel ordre classique*]), was the seemingly paradoxical result of the nineteenth-century painters' ongoing quest for an empirical realism of direct sensation. The more exclusively they concentrated on notating the fragmentary signifiers of color sensations, the more strikingly their canvases foregrounded their surface designs and, consequently, their autonomous reality.

This tension inherent in impressionist painting became even more extreme in the paintings of Cézanne. While he shared his contemporaries' commitment to rendering color sensations, which led the impressionists to flatten depth and dissolve the contours of objects, he was unwilling to sacrifice his equally strong perceptions of depth and the solidity of objects. One of his letters emphasizes the enormous tension between the conflicting demands of these two kinds of sensations: "For improvements in realization, there is only nature, and the eye is trained by contact with it. It becomes concentric by looking and working. I mean that, in an orange, an apple, a ball, a head, there is a culminating point, and this point is always—*in spite of the terrible effect* [*of*] *light and shade, sensations of color*—the closest to our eye; the edges of objects recede in relation to a center placed in our horizon." Monet and Seurat focused exclusively on one kind of "sensation as 'sign,'" which Ruskin described as "flat stains of colors." Not satisfied with notating only these sensations and ignoring all the rest, Cézanne attempted to render the various and sometimes mutually contradictory sensory signs that combine to form the complex object of visual perception. His method of reconciling these conflicting visual signs resulted in paintings that manifest a greater tension between material surface and illusory depth and, consequently, a more direct challenge to the tradition of Western representational painting than the work of the impressionists.

Stein's years of study with William James enabled her to understand the striking "distortions" in Cézanne's paintings as faithful models of the multiple and fragmentary signs of immediate visual sensations. One of James's illustrations [in his *Principles of Psychology*] of the vast difference between direct sensations and acquired perceptions could serve as an accurate description of some of Cézanne's characteristic deformations of the familiar shapes of objects:

> So when I get, as now, a brown eye-picture with lines not parallel, and with angles unlike, and call it my big solid rectangular walnut library-table, that picture is not the table. It is not even like the table as the table is for vision, when rightly seen. It is a distorted perspective view of three of the sides of what I mentally *perceive* (more or less) in its totality and undistorted shape.

James's "brown eye-picture" aptly describes the tables rendered in Cézanne's famous *Portrait of Gustave Geffroy* (1895), *The Kitchen Table* (1880-90), and many other still lifes, with their "lines not parallel, and with angles unlike." In this passage, as in many others in *The Principles of Psychology,* James goes on to emphasize that each completed perception is a complex mental object, composed of "reproduced sights and contacts tied together with the present sensation in the unity of a thing with a name," far removed from the immediate visual signs that it transforms into a familiar object.

"As regards shape," James observes, "almost all the retinal shapes that objects throw are perspective 'distortions.' Square table-tops constantly present two acute and two obtuse angles; circles drawn on our wallpapers, our carpets, or on sheets of paper, usually show like ellipses; parallels approach as they recede; human bodies are foreshortened; *and the transitions from one to another of these altering forms are infinite and continual*" (my emphasis). Cézanne not only "distorted" the shapes of objects to correspond to the kinds of "retinal shapes" James describes; he also employed a number of techniques, including *passage* and multiple outlines, to suggest the accumulation of visual data—the minute transitions and tiny readjustments—that contributes to the process of perception. Instead of being modeled according to conventional chiaroscuro, the objects in Cézanne's paintings are frequently bounded by a number of outlines of strikingly different tonalities. A letter he wrote from Estaque in 1876 strongly suggests that this rejection of chiaroscuro modeling was grounded in his scrupulous observation of nature: "The sun is so terrific here that it seems to me as if the objects are silhouetted not only in black and white, but in blue, red, brown, violet. I may be mistaken, but it seems that this is the opposite of modeling." Later he had no doubts: "We should not say model, we should say *modulate.*"

It was this strategy of notating everything, including volume and depth, in terms of colors juxtaposed without transitional tones, that posed the most serious challenge to the fundamental conventions of illusionistic painting. Many of Cézanne's early critics regarded this as the most striking evidence of his gaucherie, but most recent art historians acknowledge how powerfully these techniques "contribute . . . to the impression of an emerging order,

Picasso's famous portrait of Stein.

of an object in the act of appearing, organizing itself before our eyes," in Merleau-Ponty's words [in his essay "Cézanne's Doubt" in *Sense and Non-Sense*].

Although it is important to emphasize how strongly Cézanne's innovative techniques were grounded in his meticulous analysis of the process of visual perception, it would be a mistake to regard his art as naïve naturalism, the simple transcription of raw sensation onto canvas. Cézanne's dicta reveal how conscious he was that his was not an "innocent eye," that his observations were always mediated by his awareness of the concrete resources of his medium. He describes this mediated vision as "reading nature, that is, seeing it through the veil of interpretation in terms of color patches that succeed one another according to the law of harmony." He frequently emphasized that his work was not a naïve "copy" of nature but a relational model that "represents" it in terms of the material he has at his disposal: "I wished to copy nature. I could not. But I was satisfied when I had discovered that the sun, for instance, could not be *reproduced,* but that it must be *represented* by something else . . . by color." Despite, or perhaps more accurately, because of the intensity of his commitment to "realizing" his sensations, Cézanne was always aware that seeing was "reading," through a grid determined by the concrete resources of his medium, and that the colored patches he arranged on his canvases were signs, not replicas, of the objects of perception. (pp. 8-11)

In **"A Transatlantic Interview 1946,"** Stein described the "new feeling about composition" that she derived from Cézanne's paintings in terms of a similar—and equally radical—reformulation of the premises and methods of literary realism: "It was not solely the realism of the characters but the realism of the composition which was the important thing, the realism of the composition of my thoughts." Earlier in the interview, Stein discussed the impact of Cézanne's new sense of composition on her writing in more detail:

> Up to that time composition had consisted of a central idea, to which everything else was an accompaniment and separate but was not an end in itself, and Cézanne conceived the idea that in composition one thing was as important as another thing. Each part is as important as the whole, and that impressed me enormously, and it impressed me so much that I began to write *Three Lives* under this influence and this idea of composition and I was more interested in composition and I was more interested in composition at that moment, *this background of word-system,* which had come to me from this reading I had done. I was obsessed by this idea of composition, and the Negro story (**"Melanctha"** in *Three Lives*) was the quintessence of it. (my emphasis)

No longer subordinated to the organization of ideas, Stein's "background of word-system" comes to the fore as the predominant element of the composition. Cézanne's surface designs were conceived in an effort to create a perfect match between the concrete signifiers of painting and the empirical data of perception. And, like Cézanne's "veil" of "color patches that succeed one another according to the law of harmony," Stein's foregrounded "word-system" creates a new mode of realism that inheres in the material patterning of the composition, not merely representing the objects of completed conception but modeling the processes of perception and cognition. As she defines it here, it is a "realism of the composition" that is the formal embodiment of the "composition of [her] thoughts."

The Jamesian model of consciousness suggests that this new mode of realism, grounded in the processes of perception and cognition, would necessarily pose as great a challenge to the conventional language of fiction as it did to traditional techniques of representation in painting. Although James regarded language as an inextricable part of what he called the "stream of consciousness," one of the major themes of *The Principles of Psychology* is the extent to which conventional "language works against our perception of the truth." The "truth" he is discussing in this passage is what he calls the "actual concrete consciousness of man." James observes that we tend to label our experiences with names that fail to register the complexity of the process of apprehension: "We name our thoughts simply, each after its thing, as if each knew its own thing and nothing else."

In his discussion of the "stream of consciousness," James again laments the inadequacy of language as an instrument for registering the operations of consciousness. The difficulty, as he sees it, lies not in naming the "substantive conclusions" of thought but in registering what he calls the "transitive parts" of the "stream of consciousness," the "thoughts of relations" that "lead us from one substantive conclusion to the next." Significantly, James locates the problem in our habits of apprehending language, not in a lack of semantic resources within the system itself: "[I]nstead of catching the feeling of relation moving to its term, we find we have caught some substantive thing, usually the last word we were pronouncing, statically taken, and with its function, tendency, and particular meaning in the sentence quite evaporated." The "transitive parts" of speech can express these relations, but we habitually fail to pay attention to them:

> There is not a conjunction or a preposition, and hardly an adverbial phrase, syntactic form, or inflection of voice, in human speech, that does not express some shading or other of relation which we at some moment actually feel to exist between the larger objects of our thought.... We ought to say a feeling of *and,* a feeling of *if,* a feeling of *but,* and a feeling of *by,* quite as readily as we say a feeling of *blue* or a feeling of *cold.* Yet we do not: so inveterate has our habit become of recognizing the existence of the substantive parts alone, that language almost refuses to lend itself to any other use.... All *dumb* or anonymous psychic states have, owing to this error, been coolly suppressed; or, if recognized at all, have been named after the substantive perception they led to, as thoughts "about" this object or "about" that, the stolid word *about* engulfing all their delicate idiosyncrasies in its monotonous sound.

Implicit in this passage and elsewhere in James's writings is the assumption that language has the semantic resources to register the movements of consciousness—a belief Stein shared during the early years of her career. (pp. 13-15)

Roland Barthes has suggested [in his *Essais Critiques*] that what defines realism is not the origin of the model it purports to copy but the exteriority of its models to language. Indeed, all of these canonical metaphors for the realist text assume a reality that is simply *there,* prior to and exterior to the language that reproduces it. And they all emphasize the extent to which the classic realist novel is or, more accurately, pretends to be unconscious of its literariness. While both the visual and the auditory metaphors propose an ideal correspondence between the medium and the objects it represents, they equally ignore the vast difference between the realm of discourse and the external world the novel purports to reflect.

The new mode of realism Stein began to create in *Three Lives* is grounded in a fundamentally different valuation of language. With her shift of focus from the "realism of character" to the "realism of the composition of ... thoughts," language, like Cézanne's patches of color, becomes a property shared, at least to some extent, by the object and the medium. Of course, quoted speech and thought have always been important components of realist narrative—a fact that Barthes's formulation ignores. But before the twentieth century, with very few exceptions, characters' thoughts, like their speeches, were presented in language that conformed to the norms of the narrative discourse. Interior speech and narrated monologue served more to report the results of thought than to trace its process. Stein's project of modeling the actual "composition" of thought in language necessarily entailed not only disrupting this normative discourse but also challenging its authority to represent the reality of human consciousness.

Stein was not the first—or the last—writer whose efforts to model what William James called the "actual concrete consciousness of man" resulted in compositions that flaunt the artfulness of their elaborately patterned language. In **"A Transatlantic Interview 1946,"** Stein acknowledged that she had recognized in the prose of Henry James and Flaubert "a little" of the same "new feeling about composition" that she saw in Cézanne's paintings. Henry James's labyrinthine sentences create a verbal surface that strenuously resists the reader's habitual rush to conclusions in order to register the subtle intricacies of the thought processes of his characters. Proust [in his "A propos du 'style' de Flaubert" in *La Nouvelle Revue française* 7, 76 (1 January 1920)] credited Flaubert with an "entirely new and personal usage" of tenses, past participles, and certain prepositions and pronouns, which "has renewed our vision of things almost as much as Kant, with his Categories, the theories of Knowledge and Reality of the exterior world." But already in *Three Lives* Stein's manipulations of syntax, sound, and rhythm are more radical than James's and more systematic than Flaubert's.... (pp. 16-18)

. . . . .

Flaubert's "Un Coeur simple" was the literary point of departure for her first attempt to create a mode of realism analogous to Cézanne's in her own medium. In 1905 she began translating "Un Coeur simple" into English. She soon abandoned this project to write **"The Good Anna,"** her own story of the life of a simple servant woman. After completing it, she went on to write **"The Gentle Lena"** and **"Melanctha"** and named the collection of stories *Three Lives* (originally *Three Histories,* [according to Richard Bridgman in his *Gertrude Stein in Pieces*] in deliberate homage to Flaubert's *Trois Contes*).

"Un Coeur simple" provided Stein with both a subject and a structural model for **"The Good Anna,"** the first story in which she began to explore this new principle of composition. Stein's Anna, like Flaubert's Félicité, is a hardworking servant, totally devoted to her employers; her own quiet existence, like Félicité's, is shaped by events in other people's lives. Flaubert's story narrates Félicité's uneventful life from her adolescence to her death. Its episodic narrative structure demonstrates a high degree of temporal and logical discontinuity. **"The Good Anna"** is an equally discontinuous episodic narrative, which recounts the life span of its heroine from childhood to death. Flaubert's unemphatic narrative unfolds the repeated pattern of Félicité's ardent loves and losses—her lover, her mistress's daughter, her own nephew, and, finally, her beloved parrot—which culminates in her epiphanic deathbed vision of the parrot as the Holy Ghost. **"The Good Anna"** lacks this kind of unifying pattern, but Stein's story makes deliberate use of some of the other narrative strategies Flaubert employed in "Un Coeur simple." His text frequently juxtaposes short, even one-sentence paragraphs to create a slight discontinuity of action:

> Elle eut envie de se mettre dans les demoiselles de la Vierge. Mme Aubain l'en dissuada.
>
> Un événement considérable surgit: le mariage de Paul.
>
> (She wanted to join the ladies of the Virgin. Mme Aubain talked her out of it.
>
> An important event suddenly emerged: the marriage of Paul.)

The "événement considérable" is merely reported in passing, not described. Stein makes similar use of short, unemphatic paragraphs to recount the events in Anna's life:

> The wedding day grew always nearer. At last it came and went.

The wedding of her mistress's daughter changes Anna's life, forcing her to find a new employer; like the marriage in "Un Coeur simple," it is merely noted in a short paragraph. For both of these servant women, the kinds of major events that shape the plots of conventional novels take place only in other people's lives, yet they have considerable effects on their own situations. Character is emphatically not destiny for these women. Because of their social position, the course of their lives is the by-product of the actions of others. Appropriately, their stories lack the strong sense of narrative causality that shapes traditional fiction.

Stein's Anna is a far more voluble character than Flaubert's Félicité. This difference indicates a major divergence between Stein's project and the literary model that served as her point of departure. While Félicité's speech is never quoted and only rarely reported, Stein eagerly embraced the challenge of creating speeches for characters whose command of standard English is limited. Both Anna and the characters in **"The Gentle Lena,"** the second story she wrote for *Three Lives,* are German immigrants. **"Melanctha,"** the third story, is set in a southern black community.

Paradoxically, the more accurately dialectal speech is rendered in fiction, the more insistently it calls attention to itself as linguistic artifice. The more radically language deviates from the norms of conventional narrative discourse to reproduce actual dialect features, the more insistently it resists the normal tendency of prose to "dissolve" easily into meaning. In *Three Lives* Stein avoided phonetic approximations of dialectal pronunciation, but she systematically used syntactical deformation and repetition to create stylized models of the dialectal speech patterns of her characters. (pp. 19-21)

[The first story, **"The Good Anna"**] simply presents Anna's difficulty with language as a naturalistic character trait. The next two stories Stein wrote explore more extensively the role of language in shaping the thoughts and the lives of characters whose imperfect command of English makes self-expression an arduous labor. By dramatizing these linguistic struggles, the stories in *Three Lives* foreground the material reality of language as an arbitrary and problematic system, far from a transparent medium of communication.

In *The Colloquial Style in America,* Richard Bridgman has observed that in nineteenth-century American fiction dialectal speech was generally confined to a "special arena fenced in by quotation marks," sharply contrasting with the normative narrative voice, except in a few first-person narratives like the *Adventures of Huckleberry Finn.* In *Three Lives* the use of immigrant characters motivates the syntactical deformation that breaks their speech into unusual and assertive rhythmic patterns, but these stylistic effects overflow the restricted area bounded by quotation marks to pervade the entire narrative. Dorrit Cohn [in *Transparent Minds: Narrative Modes for Presenting Consciousness in Fiction*] uses the rather infelicitous term "stylistic contagion," borrowed from Leo Spitzer, to describe the encroachment of a character's speech style into the surrounding discourse; Hugh Kenner, in *Joyce's Voices,* more jocularly calls it the "Uncle Charles principle." The style of **"The Good Anna"** is strangely mixed. It frequently approaches the simple diction and awkward syntax of the characters, but it also incorporates words like "coquetry" and "repression" (in the passage cited above) that are far removed from their lexicon and, consequently, from their mental horizons as well. In the subsequent stories Stein wrote for *Three Lives,* she sharply limited her lexicon to create a narrative idiom that closely approximates the speech of the characters. This assertive, evenly textured verbal surface is analogous to the surfaces of Cézanne's canvases, with their dense patterning of brushstrokes that unite objects and background in a tapestry of color patches of equal value.

Again, Flaubert can be seen as a literary model for compositional principles similar to those suggested by Cézanne's painting. Proust described reading Flaubert as undertaking a "continuous, monstrous, dreary, indefinite march" on the "great moving sidewalk" of his prose. For Proust, the beauty of Flaubert's style, which he greatly admired, was grammatical; it derived, in part, from the powerful and original rhythms created by his "deforming syntax" (*syntaxe déformante*). One of Flaubert's most striking innovations, which often motivates his peculiar manipulation of syntax, is the use of free indirect discourse that pervades most of his texts. This third-person, past-tense rendering of speech or thought which approaches the verbal style of a character allows for almost imperceptible shifts in and out of a character's point of view. It creates an even stylistic surface that approaches the structure of oral speech while it remains a distinctly "written" style. For Flaubert, the *mot juste* can be the word or phrase that is slightly wrong—flat or awkward, according to correct literary usage, but exactly the right word to approximate the sensibility of his characters.

Henry James provides an American model for a narrative discourse that incorporates traces of the rhythms of colloquial speech and thought. Although Stein always claimed not to have read James seriously until much later in her career, *Q.E.D.,* one of her earliest narratives, suggests a recent and thoughtful reading of James. It is a limited third-person narrative, with a heroine who functions as a

Jamesian central intelligence. Bridgman has argued [in his *Colloquial Style in America*] that Stein's style in this early text owes much to James's example, especially in its use of repetition to create the effect of colloquial speech. James's dislocations of syntax render the fastidious mental discriminations and reevaluations of his eminently conscious characters. But *Q.E.D.* demonstrates nothing of James's technical virtuosity in registering subtle movements of consciousness through rapid alternations of [what Cohn terms] psychonarrative, narrated monologue, and direct quotation of interior speech. Stein did not begin the use of syntactical deformation to model the process of thought until she wrote *Three Lives.*

While James generally preferred to focus on highly articulate characters with finely tuned moral sensibilities, Flaubert was fascinated by stupidity. In the *Dictionnaire des idées reçues* and in many of his narratives as well, he lovingly and ruthlessly exposed the linguistic and mental limitations of commonplace minds, the products of middle-class culture. In "Un Coeur simple," however, [according to Jonathan Culler in his *Flaubert. The Uses of Uncertainty*] he protects the simple Félicité from the corrosive effects of his irony by denying her a voice. In *Three Lives,* Stein extends the narrative strategies of Flaubert and James into a territory they shrank from exploring—the narrowly restricted linguistic universe that confines the speech and thoughts of simple uneducated characters. In **"The Gentle Lena"** and **"Melanctha,"** to a far greater degree than in the first story, the characters' speeches dominate the narratives, while anecdotal actions and circumstantial details, such as physical descriptions of characters and settings, are reduced to a minimum. In **"The Gentle Lena,"** Stein began to combine direct quotation with extensive use of narrated monologue, Flaubert's favorite device for blurring the distinction between the characters' speech and the narrative voice. In the second and third stories of *Three Lives,* there is no escape from the linguistic and conceptual boundaries that restrict the characters' expression and their thought. (pp. 22-5)

When Samuel Beckett staked out "impotence, ignorance" as his artistic terrain, in contrast to Joyce's exuberant linguistic virtuosity, he believed he was the first to embrace that project: "I don't think impotence has been exploited in the past." Apparently he was not acquainted with *Three Lives,* in which Stein used the verbal impotence of her characters, combined with a similarly restricted narrative idiom, to create a poetics of impotence, of antieloquence. More systematically than the first two stories she wrote for *Three Lives,* **"Melanctha"** probes the ways in which the confines of her characters' language shape and, finally, impede their understanding. The central incident in **"Melanctha"** recasts her 1903 novella *Q.E.D.,* a story of "college bred American women of the wealthier class," in the vastly different social and linguistic world of a southern black community. Stein considered **"Melanctha"** the "quintessence" of the new compositional principles she developed in response to the work of Flaubert and Cézanne. A comparison of these two texts, written only three years apart, reveals how consciously she reevaluated the resources of her medium and how radically she transformed her narrative strategies in response to the twin challenges posed by the work of Cézanne and Flaubert.

The longest and most polished of the three works Stein wrote before *Three Lives, Q.E.D.* retraces the course of her own passionate and ultimately painful involvement with May Bookstaver, a fellow student at Johns Hopkins, from its tentative beginnings to her final realization of its hopelessness. Apparently Stein wrote *Q.E.D.* purely for herself, as an effort to understand her own recent and painful experience. Adele, its heroine, is a resolutely rational character, committed to verbal "analysis" and "dissection" of her experience. Her first speech announces this fundamental personality trait: "I am reasonable because I know the difference between understanding and not understanding and I am just because I have no opinion about things I don't understand." Her intense attraction to Helen soon threatens the placidity of her "reasonableness" and forces her to deal with things she doesn't understand. Challenging her naïve faith that "all morality [is] so easily reducible to formula," her passion for Helen forces her to confront not only the question of lesbianism but also the problem of Helen's prior involvement with Mabel. Her gradual realization that Mabel is supporting Helen further intensifies the moral complexity of her situation. (pp. 27-8)

Recasting *Q.E.D.* in the "negro" community of "Bridgeport" posed the challenge of creating a character who, like Adele and originally Stein herself, needs to "have it all clear out in words always, what everybody is always feeling," but lacks the verbal and conceptual resources provided by their class and educational background. Adele's mind works incessantly to impose rational order on her experiences by formulating them "in definite words." "All I want to do is to meditate endlessly and think and talk," she confesses to Helen. Adele regards language as an infallible instrument for clarifying complex emotional and moral issues. For the characters in **"Melanctha,"** language is, itself, part of the problem. Both Jeff and Melanctha are painfully aware of the inadequacy of their language. During one of their first conversations, Melanctha accuses Jeff, "You don't know very well yourself, what you mean, when you are talking." Jeff feels the same uncertainty about the efficacy of their communication: "I certainly do wonder, Miss Melanctha, if we know at all really what each other means by what we are always saying." (p. 30)

Thematically, *Q.E.D.* marks the beginning of Stein's long career of testing the limits of language, but its narrative discourse is still cast entirely in the rational, analytical language of its central character, which it ironizes and punctuates with silences but does not otherwise surpass. **"Melanctha"** is the first of many texts in which Stein challenges the dominant cultural discourse stylistically as well as thematically. Even more deliberately than in the other stories in *Three Lives,* in **"Melanctha"** the characters' distance from mainstream American culture is used to motivate a systematic stylistic demonstration of the limits of rational discourse as a medium for interpersonal communication.

In *Q.E.D.,* Adele's linguistic and conceptual system provides her with pat labels to classify her experience. She relies heavily on abstract nouns arranged in sets of binary oppositions: virtues and vices, cowardice and heroism, humility and arrogance. In **"Melanctha,"** Jeff shares Adele's need for conceptual order, but his more restricted lexicon does not include the abstract conceptual terms that dominate Adele's discourse. His speeches consistently translate Adele's abstract nouns into gerundial forms: "heroism" becomes "being game and not hollering"; "passion" is translated into "getting excited"; "living regular" replaces "the middle-class ideal." These changes involve more than a shift to a more colloquial level of diction; Jeff's terms, derived from active verbs, suggest a closer connection to his immediate experience than Adele's abstract nouns convey. Adele can dispose of the bewildering contradictions in her lover's behavior by categorizing her as a "wonderful example of double personality." Jeff, who does not have this kind of terminology at his disposal, has to work harder to come to terms with the same phenomenon in Melanctha:

> "Melanctha Herbert," began Jeff Campbell, "I certainly after all this time I know you, I certainly do know little, real about you. You see, Melanctha, it's like this way with me[.] . . . You see it's just this way, with me now, Melanctha. Sometimes you seem like one kind of a girl to me, and sometimes you are like a girl that is all different to me, and the two kinds of girls is certainly very different to each other, and I can't see any way they seem to have much to do, to be together in you. They certainly don't seem to be made much like as if they could have anything really to do with each other."

Jeff's hesitations, his new beginnings, his repetitions, concretely embody the slow revolutions of his mind as he tries to define his contradictory feelings about Melanctha. His distortions of syntax ("much to do, to be together," "much like as if") function as linguistic symptoms of his inability to make a logical connection between the two extremes of Melanctha's personality. Later in the passage, which closely follows the sequence of Adele's speech in *Q.E.D.,* Jeff's language fails him completely. Adele reports her observation of Helen's "infinitely tender patience that entirely overmasters" her. Attempting to describe the same aspect of Melanctha's personality, Jeff is so overwhelmed that he completely loses control of his syntax: "and a kindness, that makes one feel like summer, and then a way to know, that makes everything all over, and all that."

Throughout the central section of **"Melanctha,"** Adele's succinct formulations are translated into a more limited lexicon and greatly expanded to dramatize the process of Jeff's efforts to comprehend Melanctha and his own experiences. Adele's speeches and interior monologues use abstract nouns in well-formed sentences simply to report the conclusions of her thought; they do not enact the confused, uncertain process of thinking. In **"Melanctha,"** deformations of syntax and repetitions of words and syntactical structures radically foreground the materiality of language as an unwieldy medium the characters must work with, and against, in their efforts to resolve complex moral and emotional issues. Like a Cézanne canvas, the assertive surface of this text resists easy comprehension and forces the reader to participate in its rhythmic patterning. In a Cézanne painting, the artfully patterned surface models the process of perceiving physical objects; in **"Melanctha,"** it embodies the slowly revolving thought processes of the characters as they take shape in language.

Jeff's struggle to understand Melanctha and his own awakening passion dramatizes the extent to which his language shapes and confines his thought. Like Adele, he begins with a moral framework that provides simple binary categories for classifying his experience: "living regular" is "good" and "getting excited" is "bad." When Jeff is introduced into the story, the narrator uses the words "good" and "bad" as if they were reliable, univocal labels, in apparent complicity with Jeff's system of moral judgment. Jeff is "good"; his father is "good"; Melanctha is "good now to her mother." But in the early part of the story, which presents Melanctha's initiation into sexual and emotional maturity as a "wandering after wisdom," the rich polyvalency of the repeated words "wandering" and "wisdom" eludes moral categorization. In sharp contrast, Jeff confronts Melanctha with a rigid set of moral labels. At first he has her safely categorized: "he did not think that she would ever come to any good"; he refuses even to acknowledge that she had a "good mind." As he comes to know her somewhat better, he reverses his initial judgment: "Melanctha really was a good woman, and she had a good mind." (pp. 31-3)

Jeff learns more from his experience than Adele ever does. Gradually his speeches demonstrate to him, as well as to the reader, how inadequate his language and the conceptual framework it dictates are to the moral and emotional complexity of his experience. Through his verbal struggles with Melanctha and with his own passions, Jeff gradually comes to doubt his own habitual intellectual stance: "Perhaps what I call my thinking ain't really so very understanding." As he abandons his efforts to rationalize his experiences and allows himself simply to feel them, he begins to achieve for himself the "real wisdom" of passionate life that Melanctha already possesses. When he begins to sense the loss of her love, he asks for verbal assurances, but he can no longer be comforted by her repeated declarations that she loves him. Aware now of the gap between language and the reality of emotional experience, he "could not make an answer to Melanctha. What was it he should now say to her? What words could help him to make their feeling any better?" At the end of *Q.E.D.,* Adele reverts to her habits of abstract categorization as a means of distancing and controlling her pain; she dismisses Helen by labeling her a "prostitute." Jeff, with more wisdom, cannot use such words to deny his feelings. Even after he has lost Melanctha, he "always had strong in him the meaning of all the new kind of beauty Melanctha Herbert once had shown him, and always more and more it helped him with his working for himself and for all the colored people." (pp. 37-8)

Repetition is central to the mode of realism Stein created in **"Melanctha,"** a densely patterned textual surface that models the process by which thoughts take shape in language. Although it makes use of some syntactical features common to nonstandard dialects, the language of "Melanctha" is not a literal transcription of Black English but a stylization of the speech and thought patterns of characters whose language is inadequate to their experience. Although the simple words the characters use are shown to be slippery, unstable instruments, their patterning forcefully enacts the play of passions, the frustrating processes of thought and communication. Wordsworth, a century before Stein, discovered the power of repetition to imitate the "craving in the mind" to bridge the gap between intense emotion and inadequate means of expression [he wrote in his note to "The Thorn" in *Poetical Works of William Wordsworth*]:

> There is a numerous class of readers who imagine that the same words cannot be repeated without tautology: this is a great error: virtual tautology is much oftener produced by using different words when the meaning is exactly the same. Words, a Poet's words, more particularly, ought to be weighed in the balance of feeling, and not measured by the space which they occupy upon paper. For the Reader cannot be too often reminded that Poetry is passion: it is the history or science of feelings; now every man must know that an attempt is rarely made to communicate impassioned feelings without something of an accompanying consciousness of the inadequateness of our own powers, or the deficiencies of language. During such efforts there will be a craving in the mind, and as long as it is unsatisfied the Speaker will cling to the same words, or words of the same character. There are also various other reasons why repetition and apparent tautology are frequently beauties of the highest kind. Among the chief of these reasons is the interest which the mind attaches to words, not only as symbols of the passion, but as *things*, active and efficient, which are of themselves part of the passion.

Wordsworth's project, like Stein's, was to explore the motions of the human mind in the medium of language. In poems like "The Thorn," the occasion for these reflections, he created personae with limited powers of expression, whose verbal repetitions function mimetically, to dramatize their struggles to formulate their experiences in language. As Wordsworth observed, repetition foregrounds the materiality of language, of words "not only as symbols of the passion, but as *things*, active and efficient, which are of themselves part of the passion." Far more radically than Wordsworth, Stein used repetition in **"Melanctha"** to undermine the functioning of words as univocal "symbols of the passion" while emphasizing their irreducible power to shape the process of thought.

But for Stein, as for Wordsworth, repetition has other uses as well. Repetition of words, sound, and syntactical patterns plays a major role in structuring poetic language. In **"Melanctha,"** the characters' speeches have their own "beauties" of sound and rhythm, even as they demonstrate the speakers' linguistic inadequacy. Passages of direct narration use the same verbal texture and rhythm to create a rich evocation of simple, elemental patterns of action. In the following passage, repetition reveals not linguistic helplessness but poetic power:

> From the time that Melanctha *w*as *tw*elve until she *w*as sixteen she *wandered,* always seeking but never more than very dimly seeing *wisdom.* . . .
>
> Melanctha's *wanderings* after *wisdom* she always had to do in secret and by snatches, for her mother *w*as then still living and 'Mis' Herbert always did some *watching.* . . .
>
> In these days Melanctha talked and stood and *walked w*ith many kinds of men. . . . They all supposed her to have *world* knowledge and experience. They, believing that she knew all, told her nothing, and thinking that she *w*as deciding *w*ith them, asked for nothing, and so though Melanctha *wandered widely,* she *w*as really very safe *w*ith all the *wandering.*
>
> It *w*as a very *wonderful* experience this safety of Melanctha. . . . Melanctha herself did not feel the *wonder.* . . .
>
> She knew she *w*as not getting *w*hat she so badly *wanted.* . . .
>
> Melanctha liked to *wander,* and to stand by the railroad yard, and *watch* the men and the engines and the switches and everything that *w*as busy there, *working.* . . . For a child *watching* through a hole in the fence above the yard, it is a *wonder world* of mystery and movement. (my emphases)

The lush surface texture flaunts its poetic play of alliteration, rhyme, and repetition of words. The repeated alliteration of *w* and *m,* the major sound motifs of the passage, contrasts with the repetition of sibilants and hard *k* sounds. Participial endings create a network of rhyme. Throughout the passage, sound creates a network of connections independent of syntax, which has a powerful semantic function. As the pattern of words beginning with *w* gradually unfolds, "wandered" and "wisdom" establish the theme and set in motion the associative chain that follows. Wandering, wanting, walking, watching, the men working—forms of these verbs recur, echoing through this passage and the pages that follow. The nouns "wonder," "world," and "wisdom" entwine themselves in this network of sound associations. A second alliterative chain links Melanctha first to her mother and then to the "mystery and movement" of the world of men. At the beginning, Melanctha's mother is watching her; by the end, Melanctha herself is watching the men working. Finally, several pages later, the words "woman" and "wife" appear to complete the sequence. As it gradually unfolds in the linear movement of the passage, this interplay of phonemic repetition and difference creates a rhythmic sound pattern that powerfully reinforces the life pattern of emerging sexual awareness that is the theme of the passage.

This long passage is the only section of **"Melanctha"** that makes systematic use of repetition to embody the rhythm of a life process. This text demonstrates the impotence of repetition, in the speeches and thoughts of its characters, more systematically than its power. In both cases, repetition is used to model the rhythm of a temporal process, and the realism inheres in the material patterning of language, foregrounded to create an iconic figuration of the object it models. After completing *Three Lives,* Stein soon lost interest in the problem of representing the speech and thought patterns of characters whose command of the language is limited and concentrated on exploring the power of repetition to render her own synoptic vision of characters and life processes. (pp. 38-41)

> *Jayne L. Walker, in her* The Making of a Modernist: Gertrude Stein from "Three Lives" to "Tender Buttons," *Amherst: The University of Massachusetts Press, 1984, 168 p.*

Paul Cohen (essay date 1985)

[*In the following excerpt, Cohen discusses Stein's opera libretti* Four Saints in Three Acts, Doctor Faustus Lights the Lights, *and* The Mother of Us All.]

In Malcolm Bradbury's recent novel *Rates of Exchange,* a British scholar, Professor Petworth, visiting an Eastern European country, is being taken to an opera ("oper") in the local language. His guide asks: "You do not mind to sit for five hours for an oper in another language?" Petworth replies: "Aren't all operas in another language?" The novel is about language and about metaphors involving language, so this makes a handy example for Bradbury. First, Petworth is thinking that very few important operas have been written in English, so he is used to sitting through evenings of Italian, German, French, and even Russian. In addition, he is, no doubt, suggesting that opera has created its own language, a synthesis built out of verbal and tonal languages, which must be learned by someone who wishes to comprehend opera.

Even beyond this, however, I think that his remark implies that even an English-language opera usually sounds as if it is in a foreign language. The responsibility for this may be shared by the composer (melismatic writing and so on), the conductor (the frequent imbalance in favor of the orchestra), the hall (acoustics), the singer (vocal styles which sacrifice clarity for beauty), and the art form itself (conventions such as the simultaneous singing of different texts), but also by the librettist. With a few notable exceptions, such as Hugo von Hofmannsthal, librettists have usually accepted a subordinate role. Some may even have found themselves in Yeats's position. After a lifetime of struggles with theatrical musicians over the audibility of his words, Yeats finally announced his surrender:

> The orchestra brings more elaborate music and I have gone over to the enemy. I say to the musician 'Lose my words in patterns of sound as the name of God is lost in Arabian arabesques. They are a secret between the singers, myself, yourself. The plain fable, the plain prose of the dialogue, Ninette de Valois' dance are there for the audience. They can find my words in the book if they are curious, but we will not thrust our secret upon them.

While he was not, of course, entirely serious about this, and did, on later occasions, continue to demand audibility, this does reflect a feeling common among librettists. Even W. H. Auden, who wrote three important libretti, acknowledged that an opera audience "will be very fortunate if they hear one word in seven," and seriously described the librettist's role as "minor."

In her best operas, Gertrude Stein managed to avoid many of the librettist's most troublesome problems by writing in a new language of her own: a language based upon that of her earlier writings, but adapted to this new medium; a language which is, at its best, exceptionally well suited to its purpose; and a language which is, in certain respects, distinctively American.

Much has been written on Stein's operas, but they have rarely been seriously considered as texts designed for musical setting; indeed, several critics appear to take it for granted that she would have been altogether incapable of tackling such a task. She did not, it is true, appreciate or understand music. Even Virgil Thomson, her most frequent musical collaborator, admits this [in *A Virgil Thomson Reader*]:

> Gertrude didn't enjoy music or have any particular sense of it. . . . She had gone to symphony concerts and the opera as a girl, but it didn't take. And afterward she always said music is for adolescents.

On the other hand, he claims that she "liked being put to music," and was able to produce texts which were unusually suitable for musical setting. He even asserts [in his *Virgil Thomson*] that much of her writing "lies closer to musical timings than to speech timings." While that last phrase is just the sort of thing which would sound suspicious in the mouth of an enthusiast with little knowledge of music, it comes here from a thoroughly professional composer and music critic who, despite his friendship with Stein, was always able to view her work objectively.

Thomson is not, moreover, alone among musicians in these views. Leonard Bernstein writes [in his "Music and Miss Stein"] that "Stein has come closer than any other writer except Joyce to the medium of music." Leslie Orrey, in his very brief *Concise History of Opera,* takes the time to discuss the first Stein-Thomson collaboration, *Four Saints in Three Acts,* calling it "strangely beautiful," and Patrick J. Smith, in his [*The Tenth Muse: A Historical Study of the Opera Libretto*], calls the same text "one of the landmark works in the form." Even Ernst Krenek, whose own music is so different, writes [in *Composers on Music: An Anthology of Composers' Writings from Palestrina to Copland*] of the "decided originality" and "undeniable if not easily explainable charm" of that opera.

Much of the charm can be explained by the continually impressive consonance of the text and the music, a quality which has not always been noticed by literary critics. Auden [in his *Forewords and Afterwords*] once lamented that "a librettist is always at a disadvantage because operas are reviewed, not by literary or dramatic critics, but by music critics whose taste and understanding of poetry may be very limited." Unfortunately, music critics are not the only specialists around.

Richard Bridgman, for instance, probably Stein's most perceptive analyst to date, has argued [in his *Gertrude Stein in Pieces*] that "*Four Saints in Three Acts* occupies a more important position in Gertrude Stein's canon than its intrinsic worth can justify." He says that "the reputation of the piece is maintained by external considerations . . . ," first among which he cites "Virgil Thomson's musical score." While it is easy to see why he feels it necessary to say this—seen only as a printed text, it is not one of Stein's greatest achievements—such a judgment is based upon unacceptably narrow definitions of "intrinsic" and "external." Although she had little experience in writing for music, Stein conceived this seriously as a libretto and it differs quite obviously and substantially from her plays and other writings. Much of its value lies in its suitability for musical setting. Thomson has written that Stein's text needed his music, and is careful to explain why: "I do not mean that her writing *lacks* music; I mean that it *likes* music." *Four Saints in Three Acts* is an exceptionally effective libretto, working with Thomson's music to create a whole which is, as opera should be, much greater than the sum of its parts.

Several writers have noted that Stein's texts work unusually well with their musical settings, but there has been much confusion about the reasons for this. Patrick Smith, for example, is quite discerning and appreciative when discussing Stein's libretti, but he goes too far in his analysis, claiming that **Four Saints in Three Acts** and **The Mother of Us All**

> represent the final and complete liberation of the word from its prison as a meaning-symbol, so that it becomes, primarily, a sound or collection of sounds. In that sense, Stein's use of words frees them from their associative context and forces them into conjunction with words of similar sounds.

Even with the qualifying "primarily," this suggests that Stein's libretti are all but void of meaning, and this is far from true. While many of her writings do fit Smith's description, the two texts which he cites are among her clearest and most conventional works. **Four Saints** certainly has an ambiguous plot and numerous cryptic passages, but both libretti are essentially coherent and provide no more difficulty than do many established Modernist literary works (e.g., *Ulysses, The Waste Land,* or *The Cantos*). Their technique, however, is closer to that of the lyric than to that of the traditional libretto.

In most operas, the audience must follow a lengthy progression, building up its knowledge of the story continuously throughout the work. The music tends to work against this process, breaking the work into discrete parts, calling attention away from the text. Wagner's "continuous melody" was one response to this problem. Stein takes another approach, concentrating her meaning in brief bursts, sometimes lyrical, sometimes aphoristic, alternating with less demanding passages, often involving repetition and sometimes approaching the kind of sound-language which Smith describes. This allows her collaborator to use a wide range of musical techniques, drawing the audience's attention again and again to the music, then allowing it to return to the text, when possible balancing the two simultaneously, without fear of making the audience lose a narrative or conceptual thread. Stein's bursts of meaning do build toward a conclusion, and add up to a coherent whole, but they do so discontinuously, allowing the music its equal role in the process. She is thus able to produce that exceedingly rare thing: a libretto of substantial literary value which works on equal terms with its music, neither dominating it nor subordinated to it.

Stein's libretti are, however, something rarer even than this: they are not only important operas, but important American operas. Although only one has an American setting and subject, they all refflect Stein's American background in significant ways, and they may thus constitute the first substantial American contribution to this art form.

When Thomson first proposed their collaboration on an opera, Stein specified American history as the subject, but Thomson rejected most of her suggested topics, including George Washington. They finally agreed upon a topic, the life of St. Teresa of Avila, which was not only European in origin, but which had been treated in several well-known European creations, from Teresa's own *Vida* and *Moradas* through Bernini's statue to Crashaw's poem. It would be easy to interpret this choice as an American expatriate's enthusiastic embrace of European traditions. Stein had not, however, lost interest in America. She was, in this respect, like Joyce, leaving his native land early in life, but letting it remain his dominant subject, and blending Irish literary traditions and techniques with Continental ones.

Four Saints in Three Acts does not devote much time to American subjects, but the work has a marked American flavor. For all of its well-publicized obscurity, most of the text has a notably matter-of-fact, conversational tone. When the subject matter is saints, this tone sounds like that of a stereotypical American tourist, viewing European customs and treasures with a slightly skeptical attitude, applying the common sense on which Americans tend to pride themselves. This tone is matched by her objective treatment of the saints, denying them, except in a few passages, any special spiritual significance, much less the mystical transcendence generally associated with Teresa. Stein clearly enjoyed the role of American observer in Europe, and she acknowledges the work's conceptual provenance in the introductory section when the announcement of the opera's title is followed by: "My country 'tis of thee sweet land of liberty of thee I sing." Thomson has his large chorus sing this, just as a patriotic invocation would be sung at the beginning of a play or a baseball game, as Stein clearly intended.

Although Thomson throws in a number of exotic passages, his music is, through most of the opera, unmistakably American, with its folklike themes, homey mood, country-church-style harmonium playing, and so on. Thomson himself acknowledged that "its local references . . . are not to Spain, which I had never seen, but rather to my Southern Baptist upbringing in Missouri." Stein's text blends with this music remarkably well, with scarcely any of the tension detectable in even the finest transcultural operas, from the Italian works of Haydn and Mozart to Auden's collaborations with Stravinsky and Henze. Stein and Thomson did not really have much in common. Their personalities were dissimilar, and while it is easy to see, with hindsight, certain common elements in their creative work, they were really very different kinds of artists. They did, however, share certain types of American memories and attitudes, and their collaborative work, like their friendship, was largely built out of these. A libretto which was not essentially American in style and attitude could not have blended so harmoniously with Thomson's score.

Opera is itself, as Professor Petworth implied, a characteristically European genre. Stein had used this genre to treat a specifically European subject, but had looked at the subject through American eyes and treated it in an American style. The resulting hybrid owed much of its charm to these mildly jarring combinations, and Stein was so pleased with it that she adopted the same procedure for her next important operatic project, **Doctor Faustus Lights the Lights.** What, after all, could be a more characteristically European subject than Faust? Moreover, Stein had now become more familiar with the conventions and structures of the genre. Where **Four Saints** had been rather amorphous, requiring a great many decisions of Thomson and of Maurice Grosser, who prepared a scenario, Stein herself filled **Doctor Faustus** with clearly defined arias, recitatives, duets, choruses, ballets, and staging effects. While throwing herself enthusiastically into the European operatic tradition in terms of form and subject, she retained her American viewpoint, giving the libretto, as Allegra Stewart has noted [in her *Gertrude Stein and the Present*], "a peculiarly American twist."

Stein's Doctor Faustus has used his contract to enable him to invent electric light. This primal invention of modern American technology makes a good coherent image for the kind of useless knowledge which Faust always gets from Mephistopheles. Once this Faust-Edison has satisfied his urge to play God by creating light, everyone is inevitably disappointed. His dog complains that he can no longer bay at the moon, since electric lights have, for the city-dweller, abolished true, pitch-black night, and thus hide the moon. This loss also leads a boy to lament the disappearance of lunacy, which he appears to see as part of the cycle of nature and as a potentially creative force. Even Faust himself complains: ". . . and what after all is the use of light, you can see just as well without it. . . ."

Indeed, the opera is largely concerned with the collision of the older, slower European culture and the dynamic style of the New World. Most of the major characters have explicitly dual personalities (and even complain about this at several points), and one side of each generally shows American characteristics. Faust-Edison is clear enough. His leading lady even has a dual name: Marguerite Ida and Helena Annabel, always expressed in this complete form or some rearrangement of it. Taking the first half, we can see that she is not only the traditional European Faust's Marguerite, but also Stein's own character Ida, who first appeared in print in the year before this opera was written and who maintained a prominent role in Stein's work for some time. The character Ida was based upon Wallis Warfield, the American Duchess of Windsor, and has American connections in most of Stein's versions of the story. Even this Faustian Marguerite Ida appears to be a caricature of an American tourist in an exotic place. At one point, lost in a wood full of "wild animals," she asks for "a chair and a carpet underneath the chair."

Mephisto turns up from time to time hidden behind a "man from over the seas," and Mephisto's succinct, down-to-earth tone sometimes seems modern and American, especially in contrast with the Baroque verbosity of Faustus. Toward the end, for instance, Faustus is naturally concerned about his own fate and that of the lady. He confronts Mephisto thus:

> Well well let us forget it is not ready yet let us forget and now oh how how I want to be myself all now, I do not care for light, let it be however light, I do not care for anything but to be well and to go to hell. Tell me oh devil tell me will she will Marguerite Ida and Helena Annabel will she will she really will she go to hell.

Mephisto replies: "I suppose so." A page later, Faustus announces his own intention to go to hell, and asks a tedious series of questions about his fate. Mephisto responds to each question for a while, and then says: "Oh go to hell." Ultimately, his alter ego, "the man from over the seas," whose speech is very simple (if not simple-minded), outlives Faustus and gets the girl, perhaps suggesting that the rather crude Americans shall inherit the earth.

Relatively little needs to be said about the American qualities of **The Mother of Us All.** The libretto addresses various well-known issues from American history, and features such characters as Susan B. Anthony, Daniel Webster, John Adams, and Ulysses S. Grant. Even aside from its subject matter, though, the opera shows numerous signs of its American authorship and deserves to be considered as a thoroughly American work.

Opera and politics don't have many things in common, and there are, naturally, few successful operas on political themes. They do share, however, a predilection for empty language. Stein cleverly uses the operatic genre, in which we have come to expect repetitive and even meaningless passages, to satirize the politician's use of evasive and irrelevant rhetoric. She has Daniel Webster respond as follows to Susan B. Anthony's complaints about the word "male" being used in the Constitution to limit suffrage:

> I hear you say that the word male should not be written into the constitution of the United States of America, but I say, I say, that so long that the gorgeous ensign of the republic, still full high advanced, its arms and trophies streaming in their original luster not a stripe erased or polluted not a single star obscured.

Inevitably, Anthony can give no response at all to this *non sequitur* argument stopper. The other characters immediately turn to other subjects. This political style, while not, of course, exclusively or originally American, is nonetheless distinctively so. I don't like to think about how often I have heard similar rhetoric, only slightly less blatant, coming from our elected leaders over the years in response to tough or inconvenient questions from political opponents and from reporters.

Not that Americans are all ugly. Stein's common people display a much more attractive American quality in their refusal to put up with this kind of empty verbosity and with procrastination. Her character Jo the Loiterer is a good example, as is the chorus, which sometimes reminds one of her Mephisto. Act II, Scene v, for instance, is to be the wedding of Jo the Loiterer and Indiana Elliot. In addition, two other couples, John Adams and Constance Fletcher and Daniel Webster and Angel More, also seem to be about to marry. These last four, and several others, babble about marriage for four pages, upon which the chorus bursts in, after waiting silently throughout the scene: "Why the hell don't you all get married, why don't you, we want to go home. . . ."

Or consider this passage:

> Anne was reproachful why do you not speak louder she said to Susan B. I speak as loudly as I can said Susan B. I even speak louder I even speak louder than I can.

This is the voice of Gertrude Stein who abandoned ambitious projects when she realized that she could actually complete them. "If it can be done," she wrote [in *Lectures in America*] "why do it. . . ." Once again, this ultimate extension of the reach which exceeds one's grasp has, I think, a peculiarly and refreshingly American flavor.

Produced in 1934, *Four Saints* was the first American opera ever to gain any significant attention or acceptance, even within this country. Hundreds had been written, and many produced, but all had been doomed either by their failure to develop genuine American qualities or, ironically, by the unresolved friction between their American content and the European operatic tradition. Stein's unique counterpoint of Old and New World elements represented a breakthrough which, as a result of the critic's emphasis on her operas' peculiarities and alleged obscurity, has rarely been recognized.

Most of Stein's critics have naturally preferred her free-standing works, which can be analyzed and evaluated by literary standards alone. Her best libretti, however, while intentionally and necessarily incomplete on the printed page, are among her most impressive and original creations. From the start, few readers were able to see this, and she may have been expressing her impatience when, in the middle of one libretto, a voice exclaims: "A lyrical opera not an announcement."

All of Stein's operas, including the minor ones, use the lyrical approach to some extent. In general, though, as she became more "professional" as a librettist, she adopted more of the conventions of the genre, and *Four Saints in Three Acts* remains both her most artistically successful opera, and the most important example of this peculiar, yet remarkably effective, style. We can see related techniques, perhaps independently developed, in several more recent libretti, including works as diverse as Michel Butor's *Votre Faust* and Robert Wilson's *Einstein on the Beach*. Her approach does appear to offer a great deal to future librettists, lending itself easily to modern (and even postmodern) music, and allowing a more equitable balance between the music and the text. Perhaps the recent issue of the first complete recording of *Four Saints* will lead some librettists or potential librettists to discover this opera as a vital and provocative creation, rather than simply as an historical curiosity. (pp. 389-99)

Paul Cohen, "Gertrude Stein: American Librettist," in The Centennial Review, *Vol. XXIX, No. 4, Fall, 1985, pp. 389-99.*

An excerpt from "A Grammarian"

I am a grammarian. I believe in duplicates.

Duplicated means having it be twice. It is duplicated. There are beside duplicates. I am a grammarian and I do think well. Of it.

Think of duplicates. They duplicate or duplicated this. Think well of this.

To look back in the direction that they had come.

Think well of this. You cannot repeat a duplicate you can duplicate. You can duplicate a duplicate. Now think of the difference of repeat and of duplicate. I am a grammarian. I think of the differences there are. The difference is that they do duplicate. The whole thing arouses no contention.

Think well or melodiously of duplicate. They will never finish with their watches.

Oh grammar is so fine.

Think of duplicate as mine.

It stops because you stop. Think of that. You stop because you have made other arrangements.

            Changes.

Grammar in relation to a tree and two horses.

Gertrude Stein, in her How to Write, *1931, Dover, 1975.*

Catharine R. Stimpson (essay date 1986)

[*Stimpson is regarded as one of the leading feminist critics in the United States. In the following excerpt, she analyzes the contradictions about gender and gender roles in Stein's literature and life.*]

Among her other abilities, Gertrude Stein was a woman poet. She began to experiment with the theory and practice of poetry around 1910. She was 36 years old. By then, she had written and repressed one autobiographical novel; published three novellas with a vanity press; and embarked upon another autobiographical novel, an epic of family and nation, written for herself and strangers. *The Making of Americans.* She had also begun writing her portraits: combinations of the snapshot, the x-ray, the lyric poem, and conceptual art. Like a dolphin in a school of one, Stein was breathing in the sea of modern poetry—in French and English.

Ideas about gender were powerful crosscurrents in that sea. Simply speaking, gender is a way of classifying living things and languages, of sorting them into two groups: feminine and masculine. However, no system of classification is ever simple. Cultural laws of gender demand that feminine and masculine must play off against each other great drama of binary opposition. They must struggle against each other, or complement each other, or collapse into each other in the momentary, illusory relief of the androgynous embrace. In patriarchal cultures, the struggle must end in the victory of the masculine; complementarity must arrange itself hierarchically; androgyny must be a mythic fiction.

By 1910, the modern reformation of such patriarchal laws was a well-established, though not well-loved, cultural fact. It demanded that masculinity no longer have the strong, heavy beat of the arsis. Either femininity and masculinity were to have the equal beat of the spondee, or, even more radically, femininity and masculinity were to disappear altogether. Men and women were to create a new prosody of behavior. Such a code would necessarily articulate sexual differentiation. No one would stop being born either female or male. However, such a code would dismiss gender differentiation. Once at liberty, at one with liberty, no one would become feminine or masculine. By 1910, of course, the modern counterreformation in support of patriarchal laws had also begun. Among its most powerful popes and priests were otherwise avant-garde male modernists. As Sandra M. Gilbert has written [in her "Costumes of the Mind" in *Writing and Sexual Difference*]: "For the male modernist . . . gender is most often an ultimate reality, while for the female modernists an ultimate reality exists only if one journeys beyond gender."

Stein's negotiations with these crosscurrents are swimmingly self-contradictory. Even as her poetry moves against some patriarchal habits, it reconstitutes others. She is simultaneously disobedient and obedient, a reformer and a counterreformer. Her poetry is a series of propositions about the possibilities of transposing gender, about the possibilities of breaking up its orders, codes, and poses. However, her poetry also demonstrates the difficulties of such fundamental, capacious alterations. For Stein often transposes gender in another, less leaping sense. She merely moves gender's orders, codes, and poses from one point to another. She rearranges them.

As a result, if I may shift my metaphor from sea to mountain, water to earth, fluid to solid, the massive/massif Stein, with the deft slyness of the unconscious, reproduces a range of crevassed discourse about gender in the twentieth century. Her poetics, because self-contradictory, are an encyclopedia about the poetics of gender.

Significantly, one entry is missing from Stein's encyclopedia: misogyny. She can be sardonic about women. Look, for example, at the short poem in *Bee Time Vine*, "**An Elegant Escape**," a quick sketch about presences and absences, similarities and differences, including those between romantic heroines and New Women:

> In the midst of wind there is a milk bottle.
> Not now.
> And in the midst of the water there is a flower.
> So there is.
> There is a difference between Anna Karenina and Anne
> Veronica.

However, Stein, far more apt to find pleasure in women, has little or nothing to do with the virulence and violence of women-bashing. Look, for example, at another fragment [included in *Bee Time Vine*], "**Attacks**," a succinct tribute to women's being, and being in space:

> She is.
> She is the best way.
> She is the best way from here to there.

Of course, some male poets refuse to write about women as nagging, castrating, or engulfing perils. However, such a refusal by a male poet is an act of generosity toward the other; by a female poet, toward the self.

. . . . .

The self-contradictions in Stein emerge as we map the veins of psychosexuality, ideology, and literary practice in her career. Attempting to create modern writing for modern history, a modern period for the modern period, Stein was in conflict with all literature as she knew it. More particularly, she was in conflict with patriarchal poetry in two ways. First, the mere fact of her femaleness challenged an arrogant equation of the creation of high poetry with a male poet. Next, much of the matter *and* manner of her poetry subverted patriarchal, heterosexual rules. Indeed, her poetry is perhaps more subversive than her other literary experiments—if only because her poetry is a primary place for her plays with language as language, for her attempts to treat language as an innocent system consisting of sentences that might be broken into clauses, clauses that might be broken into words, words that might be broken into phonemes and morphemes.

In the laboratory of the text, Stein was searching for the elementary particles of language, no matter how many of them there might be. The process is so wonderfully messy, the product so multi-textured, that together they challenge two patterns of thought on which gender depends: binarism, splitting the world into mutually reinforcing sets of dualistic categories, including that of feminine/masculine; and teleologicalism, believing that the world, and its narratives, spin toward certain ends, including the triumph of the willful masculine over the feminine.

Stein's tricky pages also illustrate a persuasive theory about women's writing. Mary Jacobus has argued [in her essay "The Difference of View" in *Women Writing and Writing about Women*] that the woman writer, especially a member of the avant-garde, takes writing as the site of "challenge and Otherness." If women are to speak, they will articulate difference. However, if they are to speak, they must enter what has been a male domain. Such a passage is risky, for the woman may destroy the femaleness (and its imperatives of silence) that has been the source of her difference. But, if she runs the risk, a woman will have her rewards. For her activity can be more than the "representation of female oppression" and of ancient silence. Her writing can mean the very discovery of difference. The "traversal of boundaries" necessarily "exposes boundaries" as well. In this exposure is the "multiplicity, joyousness and heterogeneity" of textuality itself.

Nevertheless, and despite her sexual preferences, Stein never ceased to believe in bourgeois heterosexuality: its decencies, norms, and families. This had at least two consequences. First, Stein equated the mind, especially that of the genius, with masculinity. She was a frequent Tory about who should labor in laboratories. Next, she equated sexuality with heterosexuality. Necessarily, such an ideology tore at her ambitions and sexual desires. She was at odds with her own compulsions for work and for love.

In order to survive, Stein had to repair such rifts and renderings between ideology and self. [According to Jayne L. Walker in her *The Making of a Modernist,* she] devised a series of coping strategies that were successful enough to permit her, in the last part of the first decade of the twentieth century, to believe in female creativity. Those coping strategies included the choice of a mate, Alice B. Toklas, who utterly supported her. Next, Stein internalized an alternative myth of the artist—the artist as a genderless worker, as voice/eye/ear in time present who lives to work, without hope of an immediate audience. Finally, Stein chose to live in a Bohemian milieu that included, because it was Bohemian, other female artists. Between 1908 and 1912, she wrote **"Orta or the One Dancing,"** a portrait of one of those artists: Isadora Duncan. Here, the female, a principle of "fluid creativity," incorporates the qualities of thinking and feeling; listening and talking; anticipating, actualizing, and accepting. In brief, the female fuses polarities.

Honoring the female, Stein had to deconstruct the male. She did so through cutting loose from her brother Leo, a severing of ties she dramatizes in abstract form in **"Two."** Her Leo (he) is a vociferously hyperrational intellectual. Incapable of hearing (a metonymy for receptivity and understanding); he is deaf, and therefore, dumb. Stein's representation of her family drama is one of the first of her satires about patriarchs and the patriarchy, satires that were to become more joyously mocking as she grew older and more confident.

Despite all this, Stein could not, did not, fully abandon the male. For her lesbian relationship with Toklas, which helped her expand her ideology of creativity to embrace the female as creator, also perpetuated the conventions of bourgeois marriage. Indeed, the couple swerved perilously close to perpetuating the social conventions of the Victorian bourgeois marriage. To be sure, Stein's poetry—whether eroticized or not—contains a number of polymorphous metaphors for her relationship with Toklas. Stein, lucky thing, is frequently "Baby," Toklas her parent. **"In This Way, Kissing,"** [in *Bee Time Vine*] croons:

> Next to me in me sweetly sweetly
> Sweetly Sweetly sweetly sweetly.
> In me baby baby baby
> Smiling for me tenderly tenderly.
> Tenderly sweetly baby baby.
> Tenderly tenderly tenderly tenderly.

Stein also invokes and renders diminutive Toklas' Jewishness. Toklas becomes a "little Jew." However, with the comforting, reassuring ease that can privilege obsession, Stein returns to binary metaphors to articulate her relationship. Stein is an admiral, a caesar, and, most frequently, a husband. Toklas is the happy wife. In burst after burst of rhyme, "Mrs." loves "kisses."

As husband, Stein is a proper gentleman. She is discreet in the descriptions of sexuality in the erotic poetry, using a tact that modern taboos about homosexuality helped to impose. However, she casually, but consistently, appropriates Toklas's voice. Although Toklas could insert herself into Stein's manuscripts, Stein's use of Toklas was by far the more common practice. Take, for example, the poem **"All Sunday"** [in *Alphabets and Birthdays*]. The piece is a dialogue between author and wife, or "Mrs." However, the poem has no quotation marks. At least two interpretations exist for such diacritical lacunae. The first, more charitable, claims that the poem concerns a day in the life of a married couple so coupled that their identities, and voices, blur together. A punctuation mark would puncture this blissful, even symbiotic unity. Supporting such a kindly reading is the fact that some columns of speech fragments are swatches of first-person plural discourse, of "we-ness":

Bravig Imbs, Alice B. Toklas, and Gertrude Stein at Aix-les-Bains, 1928.

> We said we agreed.
> Then what.
> We went everywhere.
> We were hot.
> We sat down.
> It was very pleasant.
> We said we were happy.

The second, less charitable, reading claims that the poem is a covert dramatic monologue. The author has simply sponged up the wife's voice. Of course, the wife talks. She confesses:

> I am going to tell all my feelings. I love and obey. I am very sensible. I am sensitive to distraction. I like little handkerchiefs. I like to have mosquito netting over my bed. I can estimate the reluctance with which I am hurried . . . I like to do my nails. How do I do them. How do you do.

However, the author inscribes the confession. By 1932, when Stein wrote *The Autobiography of Alice B. Toklas,* she was well-versed in turning her wife's "remarks" into literature.

Such poems reflect, not only Stein's adoption of a male role, but her commitment to still another, and complementary myth of the writer: the writer as genius, as exemplary consciousness; as romantic, even ravenous, ego. She believed in the writer as the embracer of multitudes. Indeed, she praised Whitman for doing in the nineteenth century, and for the nineteenth century, what she was doing in, and for, the twentieth century. She refers both to "leaves of grass," and to "leaves of stone," a joke about the English translation of her last name. As the writer commanded the world, so self could merge with language. In **"Poetry and Grammar"** [in her *Lectures in America*], she tells of her love for grammar and of her schoolgirl delight in learning how to parse sentences. "I really do not know that anything has ever been more exciting than diagramming sentences." For this unlikely frisson leads to "one completely possessing something and incidentally one's self."

However, Stein's theories of language are no more unitary than her self-presentations and presentations of gender. The contradictions within those theories subtly, and unpredictably, reinforce the contradictions within those self-presentations and presentations. For she was also profoundly interested in language as language, in writing as writing, an interest compelling enough to help her avoid the more egregious solipsisms of a theory of *writer as language, of writer as writing.* In effect, in addition to saying "It's me there," she said, "It's it there." [In an incident in the 1930s, recounted by W. R. Rogers, in *When This You See Remember Me*], Stein and Toklas, on their American lecture tour, were driving in the country in Western Massachusetts. Toklas pointed out a batch of clouds. Stein replied, "Fresh eggs." Toklas insisted that Stein look at the cloud. Stein replied again, "Fresh eggs." Then Toklas asked, "Are you making symbolical language?" "No," Stein answered, "I'm reading the signs. I love to read the signs."

The tension between a theory of the writer as writing and writing as writing is another head of the Hydra of the debate about the representational power, the referential status, of language. On the one hand, the Stein who believed heroically in the writer as writing also believed in the writer as representor, in language as representational and referential. Of course, customary descriptions might hang over and encrust contemporary realities. However, the modern writer was to break open the stale cakes of linguistic custom. A yeasty, rising literature could then give us compositions from and about the world, those patterns that our activities and perceptions create.

In the 1930s, Stein's lectures about poetry firmly commit the poem to being about the world. She insists that poetry is vocabulary, the lexicon of naming. In colleges, clubs, and lecture halls, she told her American audiences that her "struggle" was to "mean names without naming them." She wanted to generate—from the matrix of language—a word for the Forest of Arden without saying beech, fir, or tree. Famously, she declared: "Poetry is concerned with using with abusing, with losing with wanting, with denying with avoiding with adoring with replacing the noun." Not surprisingly, her rhetoric is that of love. For she saw naming as an act of love—done for love, with love, in love. What, in brief, we do for love. Not surprisingly, for she is the woman writer only partly freed from patriarchal ideologies of work and love, her rhetoric is that of the conventional male role in a love affair: desire; command; fear of rejection; gratification; and abandonment. Once again, like the falcon circling and returning to its trainer, she could not resist the lure of the alluring bait of gender.

On the other hand, to say that a poem is "about" the world is slippery. "About," as adverb or preposition, is ominously vague. The sentence "I am about there" is far looser than "I am there." The Stein who heroically explored writing as writing, who so liked to read the signs, explored writing as a self-controlling and self-reflexive system. **"Poetry and Grammar"** also declares: "Language as a real thing is not imitation either of sounds or colors or emotions it is an intellectual recreation and there is no possible doubt about it and it is going to go on being that as long as humanity is anything." The pun on "recreation" ("re-creation" and "recreation") implies that language is both a mental construct and fun. Because so many of Stein's poems, be they fragments or extended meditations, seem to be immediately indecipherable, they tend to distance the reader from language-on-the-page; to assign that language-on-the-page to another, even inhuman, world. As Walker writes, *Tender Buttons* is "a brilliantly subversive demonstration of the unbreachable gulf that separates the chaotic plenitude of the sensory world from the arbitrary order of language."

Simultaneously, two theoretical texts of the 1930s, ***The Geographical History of America*** and **"What Are Masterpieces,"** speculate about the autonomy of the great text. In a ranking flurry of binary oppositions, Stein groups one quality over another: consciousness of the present over memory and foresight; the present over past and future; the gratuitous over the necessary; the thing itself over relations among things; objects over actions; the masterpiece over journalism and the media. She then associates the first terms with the realm of "entity" and human mind; the second terms with the messy, timestruck, bustling realm of "identity" and human nature. The masterpiece might be about identity, but it belongs to entity. The masterpiece might take human nature as its subject, but it is the product of human mind.

Even as she polarizes kinds of literature and kinds of experience, Stein entangles them in thickets of contradictions—about both literature and gender—that arise from webbing the traditional with the new. First, to illustrate what she means, she repudiates some of her own earlier protofeminist ideas. For example, in **Lucy Church Amiably,** published in 1930, she had stated firmly that women and children were changing faster than men. They were more modern. "If men have not changed women and children have. Men have not changed women and children have." However, in her American lectures, she tells her audience to dismiss all that. "The thing that is important," she stresses, "is the way that portraits of men and women and children are written, by written I mean made. And by made I mean felt." Yet, she holds on to an idiosyncratic fusion of the classical notion of a maker; the romantic notion of the maker as feeler; and another protofeminist notion—the maker/feeler as woman. As she famously asks, "Also there is why is it that in this epoch the only real literary thinking has been done by a woman," and, as famously, answers:

> So then the important literary thinking is being
>   done.
> Who does it.
> I do it.
> Oh yes I do it.

. . . . .

The tension between Stein's presentation of language as representative and as a self-controlling and self-reflexive system is manageable. David Antin and Marjorie Perloff [in her *The Poetics of Indeterminacy*] have taught us to regard Stein's literary language as both "pointing" to the "real world" and teasingly pleasing us as a compositional game. It hovers tantalizingly between these capacities.

With such a doubling poetic language, Stein devised her poetics of a doubled, contradictory sense of gender. Between **Tender Buttons,** published in 1914, and **Lucy Church, Amiably,** she penned out at least three different strategies that, in varying degrees, juxtapose a reconstitution of patriarchal ideas about gender against the repudiation of those ideas. One strategy prefers reconstitution to repudiation; the second balances them; the third, reversing the first, prefers repudiation to reconstitution. This third maneuver, this preference for repudiation over reconstitution, also tears binary oppositions apart. It allows the disruptions, even the anarchy of heterogeneity to burst in. Because each strategy differently balances reconstitution and repudiation, they cannot stabilize each other. On the contrary, they destabilize each other—as a triple pun destabilizes the sentence in which it implodes.

That tantalizing hovering of her language then intensifies our sense of destabilization and subversively warns us against accepting the certainty of any text. Covertly arming the guerilla war against certainty is any lack of scaffolding that Stein might have nailed up around her constructions so that we might stand around and measure them. The effect is to dislodge expectations that we can manage the text; that we can gain interpretative mastery without pain. So doing, no matter how remotely, Stein dislodges our trust in the smoothness, regularity, and uniformity of our dominant discourses—including our discourse about gender. Her texts, like nonsense, test what we have construed to be common sense, a way of thinking that [as Susan Stewart writes in her *Nonsense: Aspects of Intertextuality in Folklore and Literature*] "must see the lifeworld as a stable and ordered phenomenon in order to get on with the business at hand." She dislodges our trust even in her residually patriarchal messages about gender.

As she executes her trickle-down theory of subversion, Stein is no ideological feminist, but she does foreshadow the pulsating, lyrical polemic of much contemporary feminist theory. In "The Laugh of the Medusa," to take a familiar example, Hélène Cixous calls for a revolutionary logos that will breed a revolution of the polis: "writing is precisely the *very possibility of change,* the space that can serve as a springboard for subversive thought, the precursory movement of a transformation of social and cultural structures." However, to destabilize is not to eradicate; to dislodge is not to demolish. Traces of patriarchal message remain graven—too wispy to be laws, but chiseled enough to remind us of patriarchal longings.

Let me offer one case study for each of the three poetic strategies that so juxtapose a reconstitution of patriarchal ideas about gender with their repudiation.

(1) *The preference for reconstitution over repudiation.* Stein called the poem **"As A Wife Has A Cow: A Love Story"** her *Tristan and Isolde*. A work of about eighty lines, it is another of Stein's raunchy, tender recollections of her relationship with Toklas. Like most of Stein's poems, it is a block of type. Stein tends to set up one of two blocks: the horizontal rectangles of **"As A Wife Has A Cow"** or **"Tender Buttons,"** or the vertical columns of portions of **"Sacred Emily."** Here the word "pale" repeats itself seven times as if it were running off a high-speed press. Stein's poetry does not blast the page pictorially, race toward the margins, curl up and around, lay down concrete, or aspire to the forms of the ideogram. Edges of type severely border her wild texts, rather as bourgeois ideologies, and her romantic ego can frame her shattering perceptions of the moment.

"As A Wife Has A Cow" is the drama of the husband-author and his two inseparable pleasures, conjugal eros and literature, love and love story, which make each other possible. The poem's first paragraph murmurs:

> Nearly all of it to be as a wife has a cow, a love
> story. All of it to be as a wife has a cow, all of
> it to be as a wife has a cow, a love story.

In effect, Stein has listed the credits of a verbal movie. The next paragraph moves forward in time to anticipate the cow: "As to be all of it as to be a wife as a wife has a cow, a love story." Then, the third paragraph, in a flashback, shows the cow coming home: "Has made, as it has made as it has made, has made, has to be as a wife has a cow, a love story." In the final paragraph, the cow is present, as if time present was the best, the most gratifying, part of that suspicious sequence: past, present, future. In a rush and climax of open vowels, the husband exclaims: "my wife having a cow as now and having a cow as now and having a cow now, my wife has a cow and now. My wife has a cow."

As Richard Bridgman has shown, Stein chose "cow" as a metaphor for female sexuality and orgasm. "Cow": the sweet-eyed, milk-dripping, warm-breathed, uddered, bell-hung, slow-brained cow! The word that rhymes with wow and now and ow and pow! Its pastoral silliness, a sign of Stein's ludic zaniness, sends up any attempt to straitlace heterosexual marriage in solemnity. Simultaneously, the knowledge, available to even the laziest of Stein's readers, that both "husband" and "wife" might be women severs a sense of the necessity of the putative connections between femaleness and femininity, maleness and masculinity. Despite these repudiations of heterosexual conventions, Stein's sheer repetition of the term "wife" so reinforces the idea of marriage that the reconstitution of those conventions overwrites their sweet mockery.

(2) *The balance of reconstitution and repudiation.* **"Patriarchal Poetry,"** though it moves crisply and briskly, is one of Stein's most intellectually ambitious meditative poems. It, too, explores her relationship with Toklas, her hearth and heart-keeper and muse, as well as the nature of human identity; of grammar; and of differences—between numerical quantities; singularities and collectivities; time periods and tempos; and among persons, places, and things. However, the poem's most insistent concern is "patriarchal poetry," the rubric around which Stein organizes her ideas.

Like a kindly but sardonic analyst, Stein dissects the patriarchs' literary corpus. Patriarchal poetry has had its sins: patriotism; obsession with method; and arrogant, self-reflecting narcissism. Indeed, the speaker even contemplates abolishing it, through refusing to speak of it. "Never to mention patriarchal poetry altogether." However, no literature is wholly evil. Part of a tradition that belongs to her family, to her beloved nephew Allan, patriarchal poetry also provides a foundation on which the speaker can build. She can reject and rejuvenate it. Such a mixture of displeasure and measured praise appears in the poem's first paragraph:

> As long as it took fasten it back to a place where after all he would be carried away, he would be carried away as long as it took fasten it back to a place where he would be carried away as long as it took.

"Fasten it back" and "carry away" seem like a parricidal call for the father's death sentence and burial. However, "carry away" also implies that patriarchal poetry, if properly placed, can write up rapture; can convey ecstasy and the sublime. Later, Stein reiterates her doubled attitude in a series of puns:

> Patriarchal Poetry might be withstood.
> Patriarchal Poetry at peace.
> Patriarchal Poetry a piece.
> Patriarchal Poetry in peace.
> Patriarchal Poetry in pieces.
> Patriarchal Poetry at peace to return to Patriarchal Poetry at peace.

Even as she tames the beast, Stein, through that very act, advances the rights of women as authors. Master composers might give way to mater composers. She repeats the imperative sentence, "Let her be," and the substantive, "letter b," until the two collapse; until autonomous female being and language (especially Alice's middle initial) become one. Oscillating between affirmation and negation, she also demands, "Never to let her be what he said." In effect, Stein glides the labial, but phallic, consonant "p" into the labial consonant, and labial, "b." Indeed, some of the more eroticized passages of the poem evoke female genitals. "Wet inside and pink outside. Pink outside and wet inside wet inside and pink outside latterly nearly near near pink." Patriarchal poetry, she will later crack, is "out of pink once in a while."

Eventually, Stein modestly suggests that she might be an author. "Like it can be used in joining gs," she murmurs, putting the initials of Gertrude Stein daintily into the lower case. Stein even hints that writing women might cultivate new subjects. A pun on "mint," at once the site of manufacturing money and a sweet herb, implies, in a tantalizing foray into a specifically female territory, that women may abandon a literature based on money and create one based on food, pleasure, and nature. "Patriarchal Poetry obliged as mint to be mint to be mint to be obliged as mint to be," she says judgmentally. But, she promises, "Mint may be come to be as well as cloud and best." Her plants may become, i.e., ornament cloud and best, as well as merging with them.

In the middle of her poem, Stein does up a microcosmic exemplum of her balancing of patriarchal modes and their supplement. A "she" has asked what "patriarchal" is. The speaker has responded, "I know what it is." Having achieved some analytical clarity, she offers "A Sonnet," an example of one of patriarchal poetry's great formal achievements. This sonnet is an uxurious tribute from a proud and happy husband to "the wife of my bosom," a woman of transcendent virtues, beauties, and charms. The speaker/husband controls patriarchal tributes to his woman and possesses her body, her "bosom." However, Stein also parodies the sonnet and its earnest sentiments. Her poem, of 18 lines, flows over conventional boundaries. Moreover, the possessive "my" is ambiguous. The husband, too, may have a bosom. To be sure, literature has often granted men bosoms, but both literature and life have tended to feminize them. The sonnet's husband, twisting and tweaking the regulations of sex and gender, may be female.

(3) *The preference for repudiation over reconstitution.* An element of many poems, this strategy announces itself boldly in **Tender Buttons,** the book that established Stein's reputation as an awesome, notorious linguistic rebel. The degendered world of **Tender Buttons** consists of three parts: "Objects," which begins with the naming of a carafe and ends with the naming of a dress and a body; "Food," which starts with a metaphysically charged roast beef and concludes with a linguistically charged table; and

"Rooms," a prose poem that analyzes both the interior spaces that contain objects and food and the method of *Tender Buttons* itself.

Even though Stein focuses intensely on domestic things and environments, she does not ground her text in the feminine. For the domestic need not be synonym for the feminine. Cézanne painted apples in a room, but few accuse him of constructing an icon of the feminine. Indeed, Stein audaciously purges *Tender Buttons* of gender, with the aid of English, a language that lacks gender inflections. In the entire text, female pronouns (she/her) appear less than ten times; male less than five. The neutral "it" holds sway. Obviously masculine nouns (man/husband/soldier) march out perhaps eleven times; obviously feminine (ladies/sister) about seven. Proper names sneak in three times: twice as Susan, once as Mildred, the owner of an umbrella. Gender enters only when it is so blatantly a part of biological and social realities that denying its presence—denying, for example, that sisters are not misters—would be distractingly perverse.

Stein's cleansing of gender is a logical part of her larger project: to investigate the particularities of phenomena—be they umbrellas, asparagus spears, or boxes. She wishes to grasp quiddities. To be sure, objects share qualities. Both roses and roast beef can be red. Both carafes and eyeglasses are made of glass. To be sure, puns reveal similarities in labels and names. A waist may be a "star glide" or the waste of a "single financial grass greediness." To be sure, an object may be a code word for something else. Nevertheless, Stein wishes to evade the trap of placing anything or anybody in a class, such as "The Feminine" or "The Masculine," that values the set over the individual member, or that arranges sets in binary opposition to each other. Simultaneously, she hopes to refuse, in an act of epistemological democracy that she learned from Cézanne, to give any single thing priority and power over another in her compositions. The first sentence of "Rooms" reminds author and reader of both desires: "Act so that there is no use in a centre. A wide action is not a width."

Yet, even *Tender Buttons* cannot, will not, wholly erase the heterosexual patterns that Stein and Toklas followed and that helped Stein to write. Because of this, the text is a cautionary fable about two Utopian dreams: an agenda of scarcity that would do away with gender altogether, and an agenda of plenty that would permit everyone to be he, she, or it as one pleased. The last block of words in "Objects" is **"This Is The Dress, Aider"**:

> Aider, why aider why whow, whow stop touch, aider whow, aider stop the muncher, muncher munchers.
>
> A jack in kill her, a jack in, makes a meadowed king, makes a to let.

Interpretative possibilities spill from the words—like spirits from Pandora's box. They roil the sinister and the gratifying together, a doubling that reflects Stein's ambivalence about patriarchal heterosexuality. For the block first evokes the image of a male killer, a Jack the Ripper. Someone is shouting for help for the woman, the " 'er," who is his victim. However, far more innocently, someone may be telling someone else to aid a woman with her dress, her toilet. Then the block, fusing death and service, recreates a sexual act, which eating/munching both accompanies and signifies. It may be between the speaker and "Ada," a name into which "Aider" elides, the name that Stein gave Toklas in the first portrait Stein wrote. Adopting a male role from playing cards, the speaker is first a jack, then an even more aristocratic and luscious meadowed king. After "a" (for Alice or Ada?) survives the threat that sexuality embodies (a Victorian belief), she finds release. She lets go (a modern imperative).

. . . . .

Of the modern women poets who wrote in English, only Gertrude Stein had the ability to become, if partially, an encyclopedia of the poetics of the transpositions of gender. Perhaps most women poets, attempting to integrate those two terms, would have felt, more acutely than a man, both the reins of cultural history and the whip of the future, the reign of cultural conventions and the subversive lashings of liberty. However, only a lesbian like Stein, who both parodied and rebelled against heterosexuality, could have acted out and on so many sexual codes. Only an experimental writer could have willfully written out those flexible texts that address both the heterogeneity that is one of gender's most fertile foes and the binarism that is one of its most rock-bound friends. (pp. 1-16)

Catharine R. Stimpson, "Gertrude Stein and the Transposition of Gender," in The Poetics of Gender, *edited by Nancy K. Miller, Columbia University, 1986, pp. 1-18.*

Alan R. Knight (essay date 1987)

[*In the following excerpt, Knight discusses the development of Stein's methods of representing reality in her compositions.*]

If we can speak of writing or speaking as being either easy or difficult to understand, it is because we have a solidly entrenched system of linguistic conventions which allows us to make such a judgement. If an act of writing or speaking adheres closely to these conventions, and if the reader or listener is also well versed in these conventions, then understanding, within the limits of the system, comes easily. An act of writing or speaking which does not adhere to these conventions, or any other easily recognized system of conventions, runs the risk of not being understood. In this context, it is easy to understand why Gertrude Stein's writing is often difficult to understand. To say this much is only to say that Stein was not writing readerly texts.

Publishers, whose job it is to understand and to respond to the desires of their paying customers, were understandably wary of a writer whose use of language was so unlike conventional English that it hardly seemed literate. The market forces which influence the publishing industry demand large audiences, the larger the better. And large audiences, according to the publishers Stein approached, could only be acquired with a coherent story, clearly told. Any author who allowed language to get in the way of what was being told by radically deviating from the conventionalized linguistic system was anathema.

The circumstances surrounding the publication of Stein's first collection of stories, *Three Lives,* in 1909, demonstrate very clearly what she was up against. After trying unsuccessfully for over three years to place the book with a commercial publisher, Stein finally agreed to place it with a vanity publisher, the Grafton Press of New York. They would print 1,000 copies for $600.00, of which 500 were to be bound. However, even though Stein herself was paying for the book to be produced, the publisher, thinking that perhaps she was unfamiliar with the English language, offered to hire an editor to turn it into standard English for her; and, thinking that he was doing her a favour, he kindly offered [according to James R. Mellow in his *Charmed Circle: Gertrude Stein and Company*] to "make the charge, of course, as little as possible." Stein, who knew very well that she was undermining conventions, would have none of this and insisted that it be printed exactly as submitted. Ironically, *Three Lives* was as close to conventional English as she was to come for many years.

Stein was not working in a vacuum, however. While the old guard of North American and British publishers were holding on to tradition, writers had been working against it for many years. By the second decade of the twentieth century, traditional linguistic conventions were no longer as sacrosanct as they once had been. The various experiments of the literary avant-garde were gaining more currency and more notoriety. A context was being generated within which such works could be read and understood. It was therefore not simply a case of Stein's works being judged unpublishable because ungrammatical but of their being judged unpublishable because commercial publishers felt that such literary experiments would appeal to too small an audience to be economically viable. Other radical literary experimenters took this for granted and made little or no effort to publish with the large houses. Almost without fail they relied on public manifestations and scandal to create a market for what they were doing, and on publishing themselves or finding patrons who would endow small presses that they could control editorially, to get their work to those who wanted it.

These small presses and literary journals, which were an integral part of the Parisian avant-garde, were not enough for Gertrude Stein; she wanted large commercial success—the sort of success her friends Matisse and Picasso were beginning to enjoy. (The economics of painting are of course very different. High demand and high prices can be generated within a relatively small audience.) In great part, the frustrations she endured during so many years of being unable to find a publisher were due to this desire for large-scale publication. Undermining conventional English undermined her chances of commercial success. Her enduring ambition and relentless efforts to appear in the pages of the conservative *Atlantic Monthly,* and her complete lack of success until the serialization of the more conventionally accessible *Autobiography of Alice B. Toklas,* are indicative of the power of linguistic convention in the marketplace.

Eventually Stein did begin to publish in some of the small journals and with some of the small presses. But her dealings with them were quixotic and querulous and not the sustained and sustaining sort of relationship she wanted to develop with a big press. She believed she was an author who could be understood by everybody and that her books should therefore be made available to everybody. All the publisher had to do was to stick by her and to create a demand. When Stein went to lecture at Oxford and Cambridge in 1926 she was fifty-two years old. But she had finally been given a legitimate opportunity to create demand. She continued her attempts to create demand, and thus a large enough market to make large-scale commercial publication feasible, when she made her lecture tour of America in 1934-35. She set about her task methodically. When she arrived in New York Harbour in 1934, and while she was still on board ship, the journalist Joe Alsop is supposed to have asked her why she didn't write the way she spoke. She is said to have replied by asking why he didn't read the way she wrote. The problem, she was declaring, had little to do with the way in which she distorted and skewed conventions but with the reading public's discomfort with any use of language which did not adhere to conventional usage. She wanted people to move beyond this discomfort and to feel the challenge and excitement of language when it did not adhere to traditional conventions. Once this happened, she felt, there would be a demanding market.

In order to dispel this discomfort she had to explain what she was doing and how it was that she could be clearly understood. "I do write clearly," she wrote [in *Everybody's Autobiography*], "I think I write so clearly that I worry about it." Every lecture she gave was an attempt to explain the basis of this clarity. When she was in California toward the end of her American tour she went to visit a school at San Rafael. The Mother Superior admitted to Gertrude Stein that she found it difficult to understand Stein's writing. Stein writes: "I said to the mother superior . . . what did that matter if the little ones could." She believed that she could be easily understood, or at least understood in the way she understood understanding, and that perhaps children found it easier because their minds were not yet overly constrained by convention. Many of her early reviewers and critics, however, like the mass-market publishers she had approached, found it easier to side with the Mother Superior. To dispel the discomfort of the old guard was not easy.

B. L. Reid is typical of the sort of critic who would have agreed with the attempts of the Grafton Press to conform to the demands of the marketplace by editing Stein into a more accessible English. His sort of criticism is not fruitful in and of itself but his attempt to speak on behalf of all reasonable critics provides a clear picture of the context within which Stein worked. According to Reid [in his *Art by Subtraction: A Dissenting Opinion of Gertrude Stein*], critics have responded to Stein's unconventional use of language in three ways. There are "the hyperbolic schools of adoration and vilification [and] . . . the soberer judgements." The first he dismisses as "perfervid votaries"; he feels the second is understandably upset but has not taken the time to reason things through; and the third [he argues in "Gertrude Stein's Critics," *The University of Kansas*

City Review (Winter 1952)] has come to "the wholly tenable position that her single really important work was *Three Lives*," a judgement made valid by the fact that Stein had been attempting a new type of realism. This third category is little more than a reasoned extension of the second. Reid unavoidably recognizes that Stein's writings demand that the critic respond first and foremost to their subversions of linguistic convention. His characterizations of possible responses is, however, overly constrained by the force of the extant system of conventions. It is his opinion that if the response to these subversions is positive then it is necessarily unthinking and not worth the consideration of reasonable people; if the response is negative then it can be either unreasoned but intuitively correct or reasoned and laudable. Thus his three categories are really one: if language is not used conventionally then it can have no possible use or value. This leaves no room for those critics, of whom there are now many, who would attempt to understand and to account for the inevitability of these subversions of convention. Even though few today pay much attention to Reid, what he has done is clearly to state what the early critics who were attempting to understand Stein were up against. They had to struggle in the same linguistic marketplace that she was struggling in. Any attempt to respond to Stein is therefore concomitantly an attempt to bring the subversion of the linguistic conventions of representation into the marketplace.

At first, Stein's work elicited such unflattering comments as these:

> Are there still people who are impressed by the oracular—who really are so simple minded that they dare not challenge the unintelligible? [Myra Marini, "Being Dead is Something," *New Republic* (20 January 1937)].

> If Miss Stein's useful knowledge points out anything, it is that the loafing mind, equipped with language, can reach a triumph of chaotic imbecility [Sylva Norman, "Words and Waste," *Nation and Athenaeum* (13 April 1929)].

> After a hundred lines of this [***Portrait of Mabel Dodge***] I wish to scream, I wish to burn the book, I am in agony. . . . Some one has applied an egg-beater to my brain ["Flat Prose," *Atlantic Monthly* (September 1914)].

And,

> This is an insult to the civilizations that with incredible labor united . . . sound and sense [Henry Seidel Canby, "Style in English," *American Estimates.*].

This is only a brief sampling of the sort of response that Stein so often received and the sort of response that "hyperbolic adoration" could not adequately "put in its place." The first step toward placing in context such "hyperbolic vilifications" is to recognize that they can be reduced to a single problem: the problem of representation. Stein used language in a way that challenged its status as "silent servant," as transparent medium. She challenged in language the very thing that those who vilified her believed most sacred of all in language: its intelligibility, which is the triumph of order over chaos and our consequent release from the pain of not understanding, in short, its ability to guarantee the union of sound and sense.

To suggest, however, that this was Stein's project from the beginning would be misleading. At the start, like almost all other experimental modernists, her intentions were to use language more objectively, to get closer to pure meaning and to truth. She tells us herself [in **"A Transatlantic Interview, 1946"** in *A Primer for the Gradual Understanding of Gertrude Stein*] that she "had struggled up to . . . [World War I] with the creation of reality," and that it was only later that she "became interested in how you could tell this thing." There are two concepts of reality at issue here; they should not be confused. There is that reality which is believed to exist independently of language and which language is thought to represent. Here, language is believed to 'refer' to a reality external to it. Reference equals representation. But there is also that reality which is contained within and constrained by language. In this sense, reality is not external but internal. The representation of reality is not a reference to something external but rather self-referral. When reality is thought to be external to language then it becomes the task of language to represent its completeness. When reality is within language then representation becomes a continuous exposure of incompleteness. In the beginning, Stein wasn't trying to expose the illusion that language consists of unambiguous references to an external reality by exposing the gaps between sound and sense but instead, she was trying to close the gap. Many of Stein's critics still believe that this struggle to 'create reality' (i.e., to re-create external reality through the medium of language) is as far as she ever went and that her increasingly 'private' use of language must be seen as an attempt to discover a more precise system of conventions. We as readers, the argument goes, only find her difficult because we have not yet discovered the new conventions she devised. The problem, according to these critics, is to discover the new system. Once the new codes are discovered we will be able to unravel Stein's texts into discursive meaning, and we will then be able to look for unity and coherence as we have always done. But this is really only Reid's method displaced. It understands subversion not as a questioning of the metaphysical basis of an epistemology but only as the search for a new epistemology.

Stein didn't stick with this struggle to (re)create reality for long. Norman Weinstein has written [in his *Gertrude Stein and the Literature of the Modern Consciousness*] that "[t]he writing of Gertrude Stein can be seen as a consequence of the Wittgensteinian attack on the referential connection between language and what is truly 'out there.' " Whether or not we accept Weinstein's placing the origin of this insight with Wittgenstein (Nietzsche announced that God was dead in *The Gay Science* in 1882), it is hard to find a contemporary Stein critic who deals with her use of language in the modernist context who would not agree with this, or with Jayne L. Walker when she echoes Roland Barthes in saying [in her *The Making of a Modernist: Gertrude Stein from "Three Lives" to "Tender Buttons"*] that "the most crucial issue of modernist art . . . [is] the problem of representation." In order to avoid being just another "Mother Superior," mass-market publisher, or displaced Reid, then, the first thing a Stein critic must do is acknowledge, as Randa Dubnick has put it [in her *The Structure of Obscurity: Gertrude Stein, Language and Cubism*], that "Much misunderstanding of Stein's work is based . . . [on] insisting on finding discursive meaning where none exists."

For Stein the search for a more objective language had been an unstable starting point, which served only to push her further and further from it. Each renewed effort to use words objectively created in her a more marked ambivalence, a greater doubt. She was in this way more like Tristan Tzara, one of the few avant-garde writers who consistently held that language could not be objective (neither through more precise delimitation nor mystical revelation). In the passage quoted above where Stein admits to her early struggle to create reality, her remark that she "then . . . became interested in how you could tell this thing in a way that anybody could understand," gains a new importance. She emphasizes this in the postscript to **"An Elucidation":** "I am very busy finding out what people mean by what they say. I used to be interested in what they were. I am now interested in what they say."

Stein's most massive and ambitious work, ***The Making of Americans,*** documents this struggle. The book can be roughly divided into three parts. In the first almost three hundred pages she maintains a narrative line with some rigour, as she had done in ***Q.E.D.*** and in ***Three Lives,*** which records the Stein family's history from the time when they lived in Europe to the time when they lived in Oakland, California. In the second part of the book she gets to what she later thought of as the heart of the matter. She begins to hint at what is to come fairly early on: "[s]ome time then there will be every kind of a history of every one who ever can or is or was or will be living." She was no longer going to write the history of the people in her particular family but a history of all people. By page 220 she announces that this is indeed about to take place. But she only begins her attempt in the middle third of the book when she writes that "[t]here will then be soon much description of every way one can think of men and women, in their beginning, in their middle living, and their ending." What follows is a self-conscious struggle to bring this ambition into reality. By the last third of the book, however, her self-consciousness has forced her to abandon the idea as unfeasible. While on one level the project seems to be moving positively forward, at the level of authorial intervention she is filled with doubt. And it is the ambiguities of language that force this doubt upon her. She writes:

> Sometimes one reads a letter that they have been keeping with other letters, and one is not very old then and so it is not that they are old then and forgetting, they are not very old then and they come in cleaning something to reading this letter and it is all full of hot feeling and the one, reading the letter then, has not in them any memory of the person who once wrote that letter to them. This is different, very different from the changing of the feeling and the thinking in many who have in them real realisation of the meaning of words when they are using them but there is in each case so complete a changing of experiencing in feeling and the thinking, or in time or in something. . . . This is very true then of the feeling and the thinking that makes the meaning in the words one is using, this is very true then that to many of them having in them strongly a sense of realising the meaning of the words they are using that some words they once were using, later have not any meaning.

This doubt is repeated over and over again: "Disillusionment in living is finding that no one can really ever be agreeing with you completely in anything . . . not any one really is believing, seeing, understanding, thinking anything as you are thinking, believing, seeing, understanding such a thing." And it is all because of language: "I am feeling many ways of using one word . . . different ways of emphasising can make very different meanings . . . there can be very different ways of reading the thing I have been writing."

In **"Composition as Explanation,"** the lecture Stein wrote at the request of Edith Sitwell for delivery in 1926 at Oxford and Cambridge, Stein attempted for the first time to explain why there were "different ways of reading the thing [she] had been writing." It all had to do with time, "the time of and the time in composition." "[E]ach generation," she writes, "has something different at which they are all looking. . . . The only thing that is different from one time to another is what is seen and what is seen depends upon how everybody is doing everything. This makes the thing we are looking at very different and this . . . makes a composition, . . . the thing seen . . . makes a composition." In other words, our compositions explain for us what we do and what we see. As Derrida would say, we are prisoners of our discourse. And each generation sees something different because at the time *of* composition what has already been said is part of what they see. Thus, "the creator of the new composition in the arts is an outlaw until he is a classic" because he is one of "the few who make it as it is made," which is to say that the time *in* the composition is the present. In the present the writer is seeing what is different. Most writers, however, do not have the present time *in* their compositions; "the most decided of them usually are prepared." They are writing Barthes' 'readerly texts.' While the time of these compositions is the present, the time in them is definitely in the past. To be in the past is to rely upon the memory to create unity and coherence by getting rid of the gaps in the illusion of wholeness. But for the writer who composes in the present (in Barthes' terms, the writer of the 'writerly text') "[n]aturally one does not know how it happened until it is well over beginning happening" and so the composition is not already "prepared" but "prepared by preparing"; it is production without product, a wide action not a width. "Any one creating the composition in the arts . . . [is] conducting life and that makes their composition what it is, it makes their work compose as it does."

Composition explains for us what is happening and not what has happened. This is why new composition is ugly. We are comfortable with what has already happened because we can impose order upon it and accommodate it within whatever scheme of things we have placed our faith in. What happens in the present is unordered and therefore "all beauty in it is denied." But just as surely as "the creator of the new composition in the arts is an outlaw until he is a classic," the beauty denied becomes the "beauty . . . accepted." The change is rapid and startling. It can happen either when a composition has receded far enough into the past (two or three generations) to be accommodated in the prepared for changes in the scheme of things, or it can happen when there occurs an event in the actual world of great enough proportion that we are compelled to live in the present because the past, and its comfortable sense of order, have become meaningless in the present. It happens at a time when we become "contemporary in thought . . . [and] contemporary in self-consciousness"; in the actual world it happened "because it became war and so completely needed to be contemporary became completely contemporary and so created the completed recognition of the contemporary composition." The time of composition has become coincident with the time in composition.

Stein had always been interested in this coincidence of time in and time of. The problem of creating a present composition in time was a problem of "its quality of distribution and equilibration." Stein's answer to the problem required that composition adhere to three constraints, that it present a continuous present, that it be "beginning again and again," and that it be "using everything." Following these constraints, "everything being alike then everything very simply everything was naturally simply different." If the composition is continuing in the present and beginning again and again, then what is used is perhaps like what has already been used but it is different because it has been used again because everything must be used.

Stein started by setting herself a problem, how to use composition to explain what her generation was looking at. This was a far different problem than that faced by writers who felt it their task to discover and represent the unity and coherence of the world. As Thomas Kuhn has written [in his "The Structure of Scientific Revolutions" in *Foundations of the Unity of Science,* Vol. II, Otto Neurath et al., eds.], "Changes in the standards governing permissible problems, concepts, and explanations can transform a science." The problem explained by Stein in this lecture/manifesto can be separated into three parts. First, composition is explanation; it explains the world for us by presenting it to us. Second, in order to explain the world as it is she felt she must write of and in the continuous present—this included starting again and again and using everything. Third, understanding comes when the reader matches the time of with the time in, or the context of composition with the context in the composition. "No one is ahead of his time," she writes [in ***Composition as Explanation***], "it is only that the particular variety of creating his time is the one that his contemporaries who are creating their own time refuse to accept." What they refuse to accept or acknowledge is the matching of the context of and the context in. When time of is matched with time in then reference becomes self-referral. Reading such texts becomes a present, writerly action in collusion with the text.

. . . . .

What Stein has to say about her own writing process is stylistically idiosyncratic but not unique. In fact, there were writers contemporary to Stein, such as the Russian Formalists, who were concerned with and wrote about similar questions and problems. It is not my intention here, however, to place Stein within the context of the thinkers of her historical period. Since Stein prefigures in so many ways contemporary theoretical work, I find it more compelling to place her in the context of contemporary theoretical discourse. However, the question Stein asked is still the question we must ask: how does composition explain the world, or in other words, how does language represent the world?

The language which Stein reacted against (and she was by no means the first nor the only writer to do so) was the 'common-sense' language of transcendental signifieds. It is the language which unquestioningly places or accepts that thought, or the realm of ideas, exists independently of and is therefore prior to language. Such a point of view sees as the task of language the matching of signifiers to signifieds, which is to say, the generation of binary oppositions which allow ideas and things to be unambiguously differentiated. This is a dualist metaphysics with thought on one side and language on the other [the critic adds in a footnote: "See Betty Jean Craige's *Literary Relativity* . . . and D. B. Allison's "Translator's Introduction" to Jacques Derrida's *Speech and Phenomena* . . . for good discussions of this duality."]. As Derrida has pointed out [in his *Positions*] this transcendental signified was an exigency of classical metaphysics.

When modernists recognized that the problem of representation was their key problem, what they recognized was that the infinite regress of ambiguity inherent in language was challenging the metaphysical assumptions behind this dualistic overdetermination of meaning, an overdetermination which attempts to do away with ambiguity and to see in language the capacity to mirror the world. The last serious attempt to make such an argument was Wittgenstein's *Tractatus* (published in 1922, although begun during World War I). But by 1933-34 Wittgenstein himself had reversed his position and in the *Blue Book* was arguing that language had no essence and no unifying force. Where there is inevitable ambiguity or *mise en abîme* or aporia [writes Allen Thiher in *Words in Reflection: Modern Language Theory and Postmodern Fiction*] then we have run up against "one of language's sins, . . . a kind of ontological lack," a lack which challenges the priority of thought over language.

The transcendental signified gives essence or presence (i.e., product quality) to meaning by dividing the world of things and ideas into discrete components. To recognize a lack in the ontological status of the relationship between signifiers and the supposedly discrete components which they supposedly signify or represent is to subvert the ability of language to represent presence. Which is not to say that there is no ideal. We can conceive of ideality but the ideality is empty. There is absence or non-presence at its centre.

That thought is constitutive of language becomes just another myth. It becomes necessary [Thiher says] to see "[m]eaning [as] organized within the space of language itself." Language is no longer a function of a transcendent spiritual world. The subject, the person who uses language, is not a discrete component present in the world; he delimits the world. Discourse shapes reality; thought is based on rhetoric, it is not prior to it. Only what we say can delimit what we think. "[T]hought can claim to set up universal categories," writes Derrida [in his *Margins of Philosophy*], "but . . . categories are always categories of a particular language." Thought and language are merged in a monism of discourse, as are time in and time of composition; they are no longer separated in the dualism of a logic-based metaphysics.

Representation is no longer equal to reference. With no presence and no external unifying principle then what representation refers to is itself. It folds back onto itself. Representation is not a reference to a discrete category or component [as Barbara Herrnstein Smith argues in her *On the Margins of Discourse: The Relation of Literature to Language*] but an instance of something inscribed in the discourse. And if the sacred equals the conditions for the possibility of meaning, then discourse itself becomes the location of what is sacred. Language is not an instrument for exposing the ideal; instead, idealization is a linguistic act. No single language can be considered a natural language if natural means the generation of a language in response to transcendent categories; what is natural is the possibility of constituting codes, [as Derrida writes in *Positions*] "independent of any substance," either transcendent or material. Thus the modernist search for greater objectivity through greater precision or through revelation can only lead back into the infinite regress of ambiguity because [Thiher states] it "inevitably becomes a search for a language that is more than language."

With discourse in control, "composition," in Stein's terms, "explains composition." The marketplace Stein found herself in was a marketplace of "readerly texts" which were conventional and which caused no discomfort, texts in which composition was a transparent vehicle for explaining the categories of thought. She was composing [what Roland Barthes in his *S/Z* calls] "writerly texts," texts which did cause discomfort, texts which did not so much generate new conventions as examine the constitution of conventions. The readerly text is dualist; the writerly text is monist. To create demand for the writerly text, Stein had to explain the composition of the writerly text.

Stein worked in the continuous present, beginning again and again and using everything because she realized that language could not present something logically prepared and expect it to represent unassailable wholeness. Ambiguity [according to Derrida in his *Writing and Difference*] means that any use of language is a rupture with such totality. Language, as a system of differences, "generates forms of play whose meaning always surpasses any attempt to limit their possibility." So Stein stayed in the present, playing at the edge of these limits, starting again and again with whatever was at hand to defer or push away the demands of convention that she close the gaps.

Any work, of course, that physically displaces, has the effect of delimitation. But to avoid the trap of accepting physical delimitation as transcendental delimitation, a writer must somehow contrive to evoke the constituting of those limits by playing at their edge. To do this is to play at the edge of death and madness and sense (or non-sense). For Derrida this means playing with grams, which he considers to be the basic concept of semiotics. The gram is that bit of language that generates traces of meaning by being different from other bits while at the same time deferring adherence to those relational differences by generating supplementary (both as replacement of and as addition to) relational differences. What a text presents to us is traces, or the formal play of differences. The trace of meaning is the writers' and the readers' contact with language.

Stein was protesting against convention from within by continuously following traces. For Stein, composition in the continuous present represented an instance of discourse in process; she did not want to represent discourse as prepared product. She played with "grams," with the difference of language. Presence and prepared product bracket the play of differences until traces are solidified into essences. Beginning again and again [Jonathan Culler maintains in his *On Deconstruction*] replaces essences with similarities; it presents things that are always the same but always different; it is continually intervening by grafting onto the begun discourse new beginnings. It is necessary to begin again and again because the trace disappears under "erasure"; the word once found no longer belongs to the finder. The writer who would play with traces becomes the "bricoleur" who must use whatever is at hand.

The reader of this bricolage must discover the merged context in and context of the writerly text. He must, in other words, frame [what Herrnstein Smith calls] his "cognitive playground." This framing action is not disinterested. The reader assumes reward. The text is for him linguistic currency from which he will fashion figures of power that will serve his cognitive needs and desires—whether they be for pleasure or utility.

Textual meaning is, as Culler has put it, "context-bound, but context is boundless." Thus the reader must acknowledge and choose the contextual category constraints evoked by a text while at the same time acknowledging that he can never finally limit context. The contexts chosen are those within the cognitive frame which delimit not only the text but also the needs of the reader. For to read, as Harold Bloom has put it [in his "The Breaking of Form" in *Deconstruction and Criticism*] is to make one's own figurations of power. In the writerly text these figures of power are not secure within figures of traditional power but are placed at the edge of death, madness, and sense; their power is derived not from any absolute authority but from the ability to go on living at the edge without succumbing. The text is simply the instrument of this performance of figuration.

But still, the text evokes, and the figures must be inferrable from the text. While the reader brings a cognitive frame to the text he can only do so in response to the ways in which the text constrains his interpretive action. To discover the constraints is to discover correct [what Herrnstein Smith calls] "compliance-classes" which delimit possible contexts. The fitness and the plausibility of the figures of interpretation are answerable to these textual constraints. Obvious misinterpretations are obvious mistakes in the categories of contextual constraint [according to] Herrnstein Smith. But since context is boundless, meaning can always be varied by the generation of new and plausible specifications of context.

For a readerly text in which the linguistic currency is arranged in accordance with the conventions which support conventional English, the final reward which is assumed by the reader will be the acknowledgment of a pattern of coherence which allows the reader to sustain the myth that he has come to a greater understanding of reality. For a reader of a writerly text, such as one by Stein, the assumed final reward will not be a set meaning or acknowledgment of coherence and understanding but only the pleasure of [what Herrnstein Smith terms] the "cognitive" experience. Derrida has divided the critical field in two [in his "Structure, Sign, and Play" in *The Languages of Criticism and the Sciences of Man: The Structuralist Controversy*]: the reader can choose to (1) decipher, or (2) to affirm freeplay. To do the first is to accept representation as a system of transcendental signifieds. To do the second is to accept that discourse delimits what we think. The first activity is inscribed in the discourse of the readerly text. The second activity is inscribed in the discourse of the writerly text. To explain the second activity is to explain how it is possible to feel if not completely comfortable at least not completely uncomfortable with the writerly text. In attempting such an explanation, Stein was trying to create a desire for the writerly text in the marketplace. (pp. 406-17)

Alan R. Knight, "Explaining Composition: Gertrude Stein and the Problem of Representation," in English Studies in Canada, *Vol. XIII, No. 4, December, 1987, pp. 406-19.*

Marianne DeKoven (essay date 1988)

[*In the following excerpt, DeKoven reflects on the difficulties Stein's work poses for critics attempting to categorize it and determine its place in the literary canon.*]

In his Introduction to **The Yale Gertrude Stein,** Richard Kostelanetz says that 'no other twentieth-century American author had as much influence as Stein.' However, outside the growing body of academic Stein criticism, Gertrude Stein's public presence, her reputation in any segment of the culture which is aware of her at all, seems to have little to do with her work. Unlike the writers and artists with whom she is generally grouped, she is still perceived as not so much a writer as a 'personality', the centre of one of those nodes of celebrity which are equated with the avant-garde in highbrow mythology. Moreover, the most widely accepted myth of the history of Stein's reputation is less interested in *her,* even as a personality, than in her association with important men: William James, Picasso, Matisse, Apollinaire, Hemingway, Fitzgerald, Wilder, Anderson. This myth begins its narrative with Stein at Harvard, working under James and Hugo Münsterberg. It follows her as she follows brother Leo to Paris and to the early joint purchases of the famous post-impressionist paintings, then to her friendships with Matisse, Picasso, Gris, and the other great male modern painters (Marie Laurencin might also be included these days, last name on the list).

It is easy to imagine a Hollywood Life of Gertrude Stein. We should see her walking through the Paris streets to sit for Picasso in Montmartre, as he painted the famous portrait. She would look pensive, observing the low life of Pigalle, registering the details which she would weave that night into the story of Melanctha. We would see her writing late at night in the atelier at the rue de Fleurus, surrounded by The Paintings; the camera would pan to the Cézanne portrait on the wall and then down to the French schoolchild's composition book in front of her, where the words of 'Melanctha' would be scribbled rapidly by her so greatly inspired hand. Almost every biography of Stein, including her own in the voice of Alice Toklas, from which so many of the rest derive, evokes these scenes—Great Moments of Modern Culture—aglow with the sheen of idealised memory.

The myth continues its narrative with the growing fame of the Steins' paintings, the establishment of the Saturday Evenings at the atelier at 27 rue de Fleurus as the most important salon in Paris, the cultural centre of the Western world. As we move through time we see a new generation of post-war American expatriates flocking to Paris (somehow they always flock) and congregating around Gertrude and Alice. We see Gertrude influencing their writing and dubbing them, via Hemingway, 'lost'. The myth jumps another ten years to 1932, when Gertrude writes Alice's famous **Autobiography**—she has been writing steadily all this time but the myth doesn't think it has amounted to much—goes home to America for the first time in thirty years and is a great success: now that she is famous, says the myth, she can drop the defensive posture of unintelligibility and make sense for a change.

In another ten years she dies, widely loved if not entirely respected, with her last words resuscitating the devotion of her post-1932 admirers: 'What is the answer?' she asks on her deathbed. 'But then what is the question?' she replies. That dying statement is an ideal summation and apotheosis of Gertrude Stein in the terms of an official myth, with its stoic courage and devotion to the pursuit of truth, its aphoristic abstraction and epistemological honesty. It has echoes of both William James and eternity, and is such a perfect climax to the Hollywood Life of Gertrude Stein that it is difficult to believe she actually said it, until one remembers her own late concern with public self-creation.

In spite of this myth, it is Stein's work, much more importantly than her influential friendships, that one might think would locate her at the centre of modern literary and intellectual history. To survey the movements with which Stein's work affiliates her is to survey twentieth-century

Western culture. Her encoding of lesbian sexual feeling in her experimental work, her undoing of patriarchal portraiture in *The Autobiography of Alice B. Toklas,* the buried anger at female victimisation in *Three Lives,* and her overall, lifelong commitment to freeing language from the hierarchical grammars of patriarchy have made her profoundly important to contemporary feminist experimental writers, represented in journals such as *HOWever* in San Francisco, and to critics working from both Anglo-American and French feminist perspectives. Her radical experimental writing, again because of its attempts to confront and reform essential structures of conventional language, has lately been of interest also to structuralist critics and to poststructuralists, language critics and poetics theorists. Her connections to modern art, not just to modern artists, have informed a substantial body of criticism. We know from the biographies how important she has been to mainstream American modernism and to American expatriation in Paris. Richard Kostelanetz and Jerome Rothenberg, among others, have documented Stein's crucial role in the development of the avant-garde. Books such as Allegra Stewart's *Gertrude Stein and the Present* and Norman Weinstein's *Gertrude Stein and the Literature of Modern Consciousness* have also demonstrated the centrality to major currents of twentieth-century philosophy of Stein's psychological, linguistic, epistemological, phenomenological and metaphysical thought.

The theoretical concerns which inform her art, no less than her philosophical speculation, put her at the very heart of progressive twentieth-century literature. Her preoccupations with time, language, the relationship between subject and object, the nature of consciousness and knowing, and the ways in which writing can be a model of authentic experience are the primary concerns of both modernism and postmodernism. Crudely, her earliest work is modernist and her later work, as Neil Schmitz [in his "Gertrude Stein as Post-Modernist: The Rhetoric of *Tender Buttons*" in *Journal of Modern Literature* (July 1974)] and others have shown, is prophetically postmodernist. *Three Lives* and *The Making of Americans* have much in common with the major texts of modernism, concerned as they all are with consciousness-in-time, with individual consciousness set against social backgrounds, and with literature as a large synthesising force. They all alter the form of narrative to coincide with new conceptions of time, consciousness, subjectivity and perception, but they all retain some version of plot, character and theme. In all of them, language is equally an autonomous artistic medium and a system of communication.

In her abolition of the censoring authorial ego, Stein has an important connection to surrealism, which we might put somewhere between the modern and the postmodern. Although Stein rejects both the Freudian subconscious and the idea of automatic writing, and in that sense is anti-surrealist, she does see her writing as proceeding from a state of trance or meditation, and therefore from depths of the mind which are capable of purer, more profound vision than the shallows of 'normal' consciousness. This notion of meditation is also central to experimental theatre, and to the work of American writers such as Kerouac, Burroughs and Baraka.

In her later work, Stein shares with these and other postmodernists a vision of extreme fragmentation, abstraction, non-selectiveness, open-endedness, randomness, flux. She also shares the preoccupation of the *nouveau roman* and of American postmodernists such as William Burroughs with the question of literary mediation: the way in which conventional writing, through its familiarity, prevents instead of enables vision. Stein undertook *matte* or 'zero-degree' writing half a century before Sarraute or Robbe-Grillet, and her verbal collages anticipate Burroughs' efforts to scramble habitual verbal associations by means of what he calls 'cut-up' and 'fold-in'.

No writer's work is more relevant to twentieth-century developments in music and the plastic arts than Stein's: I need only say 'atonal', 'Cage', 'cubism', 'abstract expressionism' to make my point, though many other words could be said as well. Stein herself compares the 'successional' structure of her writing to the structure of film, defending her form by linking it to the representative genre of the twentieth century. And her notion of drama as static spectacle and as pure movement through time and space puts her at the centre of avant-garde theatre, and many of her plays and operas are, in fact, performed off-off-Broadway.

Why, if she is so central, is she so generally perceived as marginal? Why is she lucky, or are we lucky, when she is included in the mainstream modernist canon or syllabus at all, or even in the lesser pantheon of the American experimental tradition? We know, thanks primarily to Catharine Stimpson [in "The Mind, the Body, and Gertrude Stein" in *Critical Inquiry* (Spring 1977)], how much of the answer to that question is that Stein was a woman and a lesbian. As a woman, Stein has been seen merely as the 'personality', the provider of social glue to hold together the glittering bohemian clan. That she herself took her work seriously may make her more interesting, charming, even quaint, but it need not make the guardians of the canon take her work seriously. However, if it were not for her writing, her reputation as a 'personality' would not have persisted as it has in the public mind. The myth of the interesting-woman-whose-work-can-be-ignored allows the notion that it is her life, and not her art, which supports her reputation. The world thinks of her as a personality, but it would not do so if she were not such an important writer.

Another, equally denigrating female stereotype, connected to Stein's lesbianism, and the complement of the stereotype of the charming, unthreatening woman whose work can be ignored, has also been used to keep Stein out of the canon-formed and canon-forming syllabus. To some she is the domineering, overbearing witch who pushes her work on the men under her spell, compelling them to think they like it. We see this version of Stein in B. L. Reid's dismissive *Art by Subtraction,* for example, where he says that, charming as she was (and that is a loaded word), he is ultimately glad he did not know her because otherwise he would not be able to be so 'objective' about her work. He implies that male critics who admired Stein's work and were also her friends, such as Thornton Wilder, Sherwood Anderson, Carl Van Vechten and Donald Sutherland, were somehow under her spell, and incapable of arriving at his own 'objective', that is negative, judgment. As he says,

> Not to have known her is indeed in one sense a disqualification, since so much of her contemporary force has been that of her powerful presence. In another sense, not to have known her personally may be a positive qualification of some value; it was as a writer that she wanted to live, and doubtless it is easier, if duller, to focus on her printed page when one is not distracted by her ingratiating and forceful image.

In *A Moveable Feast,* perhaps the most vicious slander of Gertrude Stein in print, and one which has been the basis of all too many judgements of her, Hemingway manages to combine both these myths, and to reveal the deep male fear of lesbianism which is one basis of the second.

Beyond these demeaning female stereotypes are versions of Stein which do not have the same taint of sexism, but which are none the less affected by distortions or inadequacies in male perceptions of women. The two most important, comprehensive studies of Stein to date remain Donald Sutherland's *Gertrude Stein: A Biography of her Work* and Richard Bridgman's *Gertrude Stein in Pieces.* Opposite and equally partial pictures of Stein emerge from these books. Sutherland's book, though full of brilliant analyses of particular works and syntheses of Stein's thought and writing, sees only a strong, confident Stein, the self-proclaimed 'genius'. He accepts her defensive self-aggrandisement unquestioningly. Accordingly, he echoes Stein's peculiar explanations of various developments in her work. He agrees with her, for example, that it is the special nature of the Spanish landscape that leads to the radical change in her style around 1911-12:

> All that being in the air, what precipitated the change for Gertrude Stein was a trip to Granada in 1911. She suddenly rediscovered the visible world. She had been to Spain before, to Granada, she had known Picasso for some time, and she had been looking at paintings intently for a very long while, but this visit was decisive because of the question in her mind about existence as both immediate and final, and because of the nature of the landscape of Spain, which is eminently both immediate and final.

Although this analysis enters ingeniously and fully into Stein's own version of the shift in her style (see *The Autobiography of Alice B. Toklas,* ch. 2), it does not go very far toward a critical account of *Tender Buttons.*

Richard Bridgman, on the other hand, is correctly suspicious of Stein's aggressive insistence on her greatness, and looks behind it, finding much evidence of her insecurity and deep fear of failure: 'The emotional content of Gertrude Stein's apprentice writing deserves sympathetic attention, for it is in the process of taming and exorcising her demons that Gertrude Stein's stylistic course was irrevocably set.' These very valuable insights lead, however, to some distortion. Bridgman puts too much emphasis on an insecure, fearful, self-hating Stein, seeing the strong Stein entirely as a defensive front. Accordingly, he locates the origin of many of her literary innovations exclusively in pathology, discounting the drive to reinvent literary language which propelled her career.

By assenting to Stein's self-aggrandisement and sometimes facile explanations of her work, Sutherland is drawn into some inflated or contorted defences and analyses, many of which make her sound ridiculous, subverting his intentions. Bridgman, on the other hand, often makes her appear a mere victim of neuroses, incapable of sustained purposiveness, whose literary experiments are frequently unintentional results of a pathological inability to write in the normal way. What we need instead of these two contradictory halves is a book-length whole woman: a synthesis that would show us the fear behind the power, the power behind the fear.

Bridgman's title, *Gertrude Stein in Pieces,* reveals not only his vision of Stein's controlling psychopathology, but also the very condition of her centrality to twentieth-century culture which is, at the same time, the condition of her marginality. Because her *oeuvre* is so multiple, disjunct, important to so many *divergent* movements (as Kostelanetz says, 'her originality was so multifarious'), she cannot be made to adhere to any single centre. But a centre is precisely, as she might say, what makes canon. Parts of her can fit fairly comfortably into mainstream modernist as well as avant-garde or revisionist canons. **Three Lives,** for example, is often taught, and sometimes even written about, as an atypical but *bona fide* work of impressionist or early modernist fiction. **Tender Buttons** is certainly written about, and sometimes even taught, as a central work in the experimental tradition. A number of Stein's works figure importantly in the growing, fluid body of texts under the rubric of the female tradition. But when we think of Stein whole, and not 'in pieces', we immediately see that she fits neatly nowhere.

If we then put that whole Stein next to any of the consensually accepted modernist (to take the 'central' twentieth-century canon) heroes—Conrad, Joyce, Lawrence, Faulkner, even Woolf; Yeats, Pound, Eliot, Stevens, even H D or Moore—the difference comes into sharper focus. The *oeuvre* of each of those writers can be organised into a hierarchy of great and not-so-great, primary and secondary, weighty and slight, mature and apprentice (like the List of Names itself, these hierarchies will vary in content from critic to critic, providing matter for endless printed and oratorical dispute). For Eliot, to consider (perhaps—none of this can be taken for granted) the clearest instance, 'Prufrock', *The Waste Land* and *Four Quartets* would be on anybody's list of major or great works, 'Ash Wednesday' and 'Gerontion' and perhaps 'Sweeney among the Nightingales' would come next, and the rest of the poems would trail off into the distance, with *Old Possum's Book of Practical Cats* barely visible on the horizon (though that is problematical too, now that the musical *Cats* has entered the culture). Joyce's career orders itself, for our everlasting convenience, into a steady upward progress from *Dubliners* to *Portrait of the Artist* to the culminating *Ulysses,* then over the precipice, for some, into *Finnegans Wake.* Woolf has *To the Lighthouse* and *Mrs Dalloway* for all, *The Waves* for the avant-garde, *A Room of One's Own, Three Guineas* and *Orlando* for feminists, and the rest of her writing for the Woolf industry. Critics of modernism read H D's imagist poems, feminists read *Helen in Egypt.* But whether or not their great works appeal to diverse factions of the critical industry, all these heroes have been assimilated as having a few heroic texts—*Lord Jim, Nostromo, Heart of Darkness; Absalom, Absalom!, The Sound and the Fury, Light in August*—followed by a body of lesser writing which we may love but which we do not revere in the same way. It is impossible to order Stein's *oeuvre* into such a hierarchy, not only because everything in her writing works to undermine hierarchy, but because there is no principle of 'the same' running through her writing, no spinal column along which her works could be arranged from head to bottom.

Those works, considered one by one, resist canonisation as well. If we were to try to incorporate her into some version of the mainstream modernist canon, which work(s) should we choose as her *Ulysses,* her *Waste Land,* her *Cantos*? **The Making of Americans** has the proper weightiness, but it is much too anomalous and unassimilable a text, more a *Finnegans Wake* than a *Ulysses.* **Three Lives** seems not to have the proper weightiness, although, in fact, it is a mordant, emotionally loaded, complex text, stylistically highly wrought, masquerading as simple, whimsical, even slight. Moreover—although this perhaps makes it more typical than atypical of heroic modernist texts—its politics of race and class are extremely troubling. **The Autobiography of Alice B. Toklas,** perhaps the best candidate, often seems to be mere gossip, and, as Stein said to Hemingway, remarks are not literature (of course it isn't 'mere' gossip at all, just as **Three Lives** isn't slight, but its complex uses of simplicity, and of anecdotal narrative, extremely fruitful material for feminist analysis, interfere, as women's works so often do, with standard canonisation practice).

Those three works are, however, far more canonisable (if there is no such word, I'm sure, alas, there will be) than the rest of Stein's great writings, which are either radically experimental or of indeterminate genre or both. Think of teaching **Tender Buttons, The Geographical History of America, Four Saints in Three Acts,** or **The Mother of Us All,** not to mention **'Patriarchal Poetry'** or **What Happened,** on the same syllabus as *The Sun Also Rises* or *Mrs Dalloway* (I've done it—a great deal of special pleading is required, unless one opts simply to play the record of **Four Saints** and grin beatifically).

The most influential canonisers of modernism (apologies, again, to those who keep themselves lexicographically pure) have either left Stein out altogether, or might as well have [the critic adds in a footnote: "I have in mind particularly Irving Howe, Hugh Kenner, and Richard Ellman."], or they have included her [as do Frederick J. Hoffman in his *The Twenties: American Writing in the Postwar Decade* and Roger Shattuck in his *The Banquet Years*] as 'personality' and influence first, writer second, or, like Edmund Wilson [in his *Axel's Castle: A Study in the Imaginative Literature of 1870-1930*], they have included her as an extreme point, a boundary which marks the limit of modernist discourse. For Wilson, she is also a failure in her radical work, which he sees as a fruition of modernism's inherent corruption (it is very instructive to consider the female iconography involved in Wilson's use of Stein as a contradictory sign simultaneously of marginality—something eccentric to the modernist core—and of negative essence, embodying the rottenness of that core, which is otherwise more difficult to perceive).

My argument now seems to be pointing to the straightforward conclusion that Stein has been 'left out' by the powerful male canonisers and therefore, to the extent that her exclusion from major twentieth-century canons has been the result of patriarchal politics and not of her own intractable resistance to canonisation, she should in future be 'included in'. I intend, however, either to stop short of, or to go beyond, that satisfying but pat conclusion, because it distorts and glosses the double, contradictory nature of Stein's actual relation to canons: simultaneously inside and outside, at the centre and in the margin. Again, because Stein is central to so many divergent twentieth-century cultural phenomena, she inevitably becomes marginal or eccentric to any unified, coherent tradition.

Richard Kostelanetz's Introduction to **The Yale Gertrude Stein** gives us an excellent objective correlative of Stein's double relationship to major twentieth-century canons. Throughout his essay, he alternates between what we might call canonising and anti-canonising gestures. He opens with a clear, strong anti-canonising gesture: 'The principal reason for such continued incomprehension [of Stein's works] is that her experiments in writing were conducted apart from the major developments in modern literature.' This statement is followed, however, by a series of equally clear, strong canonising gestures:

> Stein's biggest book [**The Making of Americans**] also stands as an epitome of that colossal, uneven, digressive, excessive, eccentric masterpiece that every great American innovative artist seems to produce at least once. Its peers in this respect are Walt Whitman's *Leaves of Grass,* Ezra Pound's *Cantos,* Faulkner's *Absalom, Absalom!,* and Charles Ives's Fourth Symphony.

> In this respect [structural flattening] in particular, Stein clearly precedes the formally uninflected, counter-hierarchical prose of, say, Samuel Beckett and Alain Robbe-Grillet.

> Historically, we can see that the use of such forms placed her among the first imaginative writers to represent the modern awareness of discontinuous experience.

> Though working apart from the French symbolists, she realized their theoretical ideal of a completely autonomous language—creating a verbal reality apart from extrinsic reality.

> Stein also [as in modern music] recapitulated in literature the evolution of modernist painting.

> Stein foreshadowed the contemporary avant-garde principle of making art that is either much more *or* much less than before.

> Her essays also [like her plays] were unlike anything written in that genre before.

These statements not only include Stein in the canon of the avant-garde, they place her at the origin of that canon.

In his concluding paragraphs, Kostelanetz develops for Stein two contradictory relationships to the canonical centre of American literature: she is simultaneously, or in rapid alternation, a wrongfully neglected Great American Writer and a self-constituted Outsider (of course, Great American Writers are also self-constituted Outsiders [Richard Poirier discusses this in his *A World Elsewhere: The Place of Style in American Literature*], but Kostelanetz is not invoking that paradigm here). On the one hand, Stein at fifty-nine was 'one of the most respected writers in the English language,' the 'excellences' of her poetry 'are still rarely acknowledged by poetry critics and anthologies,' the 'special qualities' of her 'more extraordinary' works 'have never been exceeded', and, resoundingly, 'no other twentieth-century American author had as much influence as Stein; and none influenced his or her successors in as many ways.' On the other hand, and in the same pages, 'Largely because Stein's writings were so unconventional, even in terms of the developments of literary modernism, it took her long, far too long, to get them into public print'; and, resoundingly, 'most of her innovations went against the dominant grain of literary modernism' (Kostelanetz might seem to be distinguishing between modernism and the avant-garde here, an important distinction, which he writes about elsewhere, and which American critics often overlook [see also his *Twenties in the Sixties* and Peter Bürger's *Theory of the Avant-Garde*]; however, he uses the terms loosely and somewhat interchangeably in this particular text).

Both of Kostelanetz's versions of Stein's relationship to canonisation are accurate. Stein occupies, has always occupied, and in fact constitutes precisely that middle ground between (male) canonical centre and (female) margin which deconstructs (puts into question, makes visible) the hierarchical-idealist duality of centre and margin itself, a middle ground that feminist critics such as Christine Froula [in her "When Eve Reads Milton: Undoing the Canonical Economy," in *Canons*, edited by Robert Von Hallberg] invoke as a genuine non-separatist, non-self-excluding and therefore non-self-defeating) antidote to patriarchal cultural hegemony:

> But this 'pregnant' juxtaposition [of *Paradise Lost* and Isak Dinesen's 'The Blank Page'] points beyond static dichotomies to active re-readings of the texts that have shaped our traditions alongside those that have been repressed and toward questioning and reimagining the structures of authority for a world in which authority need no longer be 'male' and coercive nor silence 'female' and subversive, in which, in other words, speech and silence are no longer tied to an archetypal—and arbitrary—hierarchy of gender.

Stein's *oeuvre* constitutes just such an 'active rereading', just such a 'questioning and reimagining', just such an unsynthesised dialectic of canonical and repressed, centre and margin, male and female, speech and silence, authority and subversion. Perhaps we are able to postulate this middle ground at the theoretical level precisely because it already exists, and has existed for half a century, in Stein's practice. If we insist either that she be squeezed into existing canons, or that she remain subversively outside them, we are wasting the opportunity she has given us to change our minds: to re-form not only literature itself, but also the politics of literature, as so many of us now know we must. (pp. 8-18)

> Marianne DeKoven, "Gertrude Stein and the Modernist Canon," in Gertrude Stein and the Making of Literature, edited by Shirley Neuman and Ira B. Nadel, Northeastern University Press, 1988, pp. 8-20.

Marjorie Perloff (essay date 1988)

[*Perloff is an Austrian-born American critic specializing in twentieth-century poetry. In the following excerpt, she delineates six distinct styles of writing in Stein's oeuvre.*]

We usually think of Gertrude Stein's writings as falling into two broad categories: on the one hand, the public, accessible, "transparent," and more or less straightforward mode of *The Autobiography of Alice B. Toklas* or of such well-known essays as **"Portraits and Repetition"**; on the other, the opaque, private, experimental, "difficult" mode that ranges from *Tender Buttons* (1914) to *Mrs. Reynolds* (1941-1942), and beyond. Whether we take the distinction to be diachronic (see Marianne DeKoven [in her *A Different Language*]) or synchronic (see Ulla Dydo [in her "Stanzas in Meditation" in *Chicago Review* 35]) is less important than the "experimental" and the "straight" are placed in binary opposition. Obvious as this basic distinction may be, it doesn't get us very far. For is the device of repetition in, say, Stein's portrait of Matisse in fact duplicated in a work like **"Patriarchal Poetry"**? And is the so-called plain style of *The Autobiography of Alice B. Toklas* equivalent to the plain style of *Wars I Have Seen*? What, moreover, about chronology: does Stein's work chart some sort of progress from an early experimentalism to a mature directness or is it the other way around? Or neither, given the fact that *Stanzas in Meditation,* one of Stein's most difficult and obscure works, dates precisely from the period in which she wrote "Alice's" autobiography?

My own view is that there are at least six basic variations on the famous Stein signature, which is to say, at least half a dozen permutations of the familiar model, "Very fine is my valentine. Very fine and very mine" [in *Portraits and Prayers*], or "Toasted susie is my ice-cream" [in *Selected Writings of Gertrude Stein*, edited by Carl Van Vechten]. To examine the larger spectrum of Stein's styles may help us to dispel two still popular myths about her work. First, that her fabled "difficulty," like her rarer clarity, is all of a piece. And second, that her "easy" works avoid the stylization of her difficult ones and hence do not demand the same reading strategies. I want to suggest that, on the contrary, Stein's texts, whatever their date of composition or their hypothetical genre, must be read strenuously in keeping with her own notion that, whatever else a literary text may be, its central unit is always the sentence, that verbal unit which encompasses what Stein calls "Resemble assemble reply" [in *How to Write*].

Consider, for example, the status of description and narration in what is surely one of Stein's most transparent and seemingly innocent texts: *Paris France,* the short memoir she wrote at Bilignin in the early months of World War II. Here is the opening:

> PARIS, FRANCE is exciting and peaceful.
>
> I was only four years old when I was first in Paris and talked french there and was photographed there and went to school there, and ate soup for early breakfast and had leg of mutton and spinach for lunch, I always liked spinach, and a black cat jumped on my mother's back. That was more exciting than peaceful. I do not mind cats but I do not like them to jump on my back. There are lots of cats in Paris and in France and they can do what they like, sit on the vegetables or among the groceries, stay in or go out. It is extraordinary that they fight so little among themselves considering how many cats there are. There are two things that french animals do not do, cats do not fight much and do not howl much and chickens do not get flustered running across the road, if they start to cross the road they keep on going which is what french people do too.

Generically, this account of French life recalls nothing so much as a fourth or fifth grade reader; indeed, Stein's simple declarative sentences probably do not contain a single word that a schoolgirl of her day would not have known. Nor do the sentences in this "reader" seem in any way remarkable, conveying as they do ordinary observations about what is perceived ("There are lots of cats in Paris") and remembered ("I always liked spinach"). The phrasal repetition for which Stein is best known, for that matter, is kept to a minimum, and even syntactic parallelism (for example, "talked french there and was photographed there and went to school there") is not especially prominent.

But the reference to "Paris, France" is redundant even for a grade-school child, and of course no primer written for children would contain the sentence, "PARIS, FRANCE is exciting and peaceful," the second adjective contradicting the first and making it all but impossible for Stein's reader to formulate an image of place. The semantic contradiction is reinforced by the syntactic one at the end of the first sentence, where the coordinating conjunction "and" joins a clause referring to a specific incident ("a black cat jumped on my mother's back") to the preceding "when" clause with its cataloging of habitual actions. Normal usage would require a period after "spinach," followed by a temporal marker like "One day."

Why then does Stein ignore the basic distinction between perfect and imperfect verb forms and draw the clause in question into the larger parataxis of her composition? Perhaps because even in as seemingly transparent a text as *Paris France,* Stein's urge is to minimize temporal distinctions, to present us with a spatial figure, a synchronicity, analogous to the flat or planar landscape of a Cézanne or Picasso. As Lyn Hejinian observes [in "Two Stein Talks," *Tremblor* 3], "one of the characteristics of Stein's writing is that elements coexist with alternatives in the work; phrase or sentence A is not obliterated when it appears, slightly altered perhaps, as phrase or sentence B." Indeed Stein must, so to speak, draw the black cat out of her verbal hat so as to confirm the exciting/peaceful paradox of her opening sentence. "I do not mind cats but I do not like them to jump on my back. There are lots of cats in Paris and in France and they can do what they like." The two sentences are placed side by side without a linking adverb that might explain their relationship, but the positioning makes a sense of its own. Insofar as they jump, "french cats" (the lower case *f* designating that nationality is merely an attribute, rather like size or color) are exciting; insofar as they do as they like, they are peaceful. Indeed, we now learn, "french animals" in general are peaceful: "chickens do not get flustered running across the road." And from chickens it is only one step to human beings: "if they [chickens] start to cross the road they keep on going which is what french people do too."

End of paragraph. The "lesson" is as inexorable as that of any schoolbook. "PARIS, FRANCE is exciting and peaceful." How is it exciting and peaceful? Its animals and hence people are very lively and always in motion but "they keep on going" without getting "flustered." Stein's "argument," wholly devoid of logic or empirical evidence as it is, carries us along by the sheer force of its relational syntax. Accordingly, the text remains peculiarly impervious to explication. When Richard Bridgman suggests [in his *Gertrude Stein in Pieces*] that Stein's optimistic portrait of a France, forty years into the twentieth century and hence ready to "settle down to middle age and a pleasant life and the enjoyment of ordinary living" is "pitifully unrealistic," he is assuming that the mode of *Paris France* is essentially expository. But as Stein herself points out, hers is intentionally an external, and therefore an idealized, view of her adopted country:

> After all everybody, that is, everybody who writes is interested in living inside themselves in order to tell what is inside themselves. That is why writers have to have two countries, the one where they belong and the one in which they live really. The second one is romantic, it is separate from themselves, it is not real but it is really there.

Which is to say that the "France" of jumping cats and docile chickens is not "real" (indeed, one of the central ironies of the book is that Paris itself, the urban environment, is, so to speak, under erasure, the focus throughout being on country life), even as, within the synchronic field of the text itself, the exciting/peaceful realm called France is "really there."

The paradox, then, is that Stein practices what William James [in a letter included in *Flowers of Friendship: Letters Written to Gertrude Stein,* edited by Donald Gallup] called (with reference to *Three Lives*) "a fine new kind of realism," even as she resolutely opposes mimesis, the notion that the verbal or visual construct can replicate the external world of nature. *Paris France* tells us precious little about French history or geography, but in its particular focus on, say, the village girl Helen Button and her dog

William, or on the proper preparation of *quenelles,* it creates a verbal space we come to recognize as, so to speak, *Stein France.* In the same vein, the anecdotes about famous artists that fill the pages of **The Autobiography of Alice B. Toklas** are notable less for their informational content than for their attention to the principle that, as Stein put it [in *A Primer for the Gradual Understanding of Gertrude Stein,* edited by Robert Bartlett Haas] about Cézanne, "in composition one thing was as important as another thing."

The "transparent" style of **The Autobiography of Alice B. Toklas** is, of course, more complex than that of **Paris France,** given its fictional premise that Toklas rather than Stein tells the story. Like the later memoir, however, the **Autobiography** purports to tell its story quite literally, with a minimum of fuss. Here is "Alice Toklas's" account [in **Selected Writings of Gertrude Stein,** edited by Carl Van Vechten] of the famous first night of Stravinsky's *Sacre du Printemps:*

> Nijinsky did not dance in the Sacre du Printemps but he created the dance of those who did dance.
>
> We arrived in the box and sat down in the three front chairs leaving one chair behind. Just in front of us in the seats below was Guillaume Apollinaire. He was dressed in evening clothes and he was industriously kissing various important looking ladies' hands. He was the first one of his crowd to come out into the great world wearing evening clothes and kissing hands. We were very amused and very pleased to see him do it. It was the first time we had seen him doing it. After the war they all did these things but he was the only one to commence before the war.
>
> Just before the performance began the fourth chair in our box was occupied. We looked around and there was a tall well-built young man, he might have been a dutchman, a scandinavian or an american and he wore a soft evening shirt with the tiniest pleats all over the front of it. It was impressive, we had never even heard that they were wearing evening shirts like that. That evening when we got home Gertrude Stein did a portrait of the unknown called a Portrait of One.
>
> The performance began. No sooner had it commenced when the excitement began. The scene now so well known with its brilliantly coloured background now not at all extraordinary, outraged the Paris audience. No sooner did the music begin and the dancing than they began to hiss. The defenders began to applaud. We could hear nothing, as a matter of fact I never did hear any of the music of the Sacre du Printemps because it was the only time I ever saw it and one literally could not, throughout the whole performance, hear the sound of music.

Here the narrator seems to be doing nothing but recording, as faithfully as possible, what happened at the first night even as a child might report it. Nijinsky "did not dance . . . but he created the dance of those who did dance," "We . . . sat down in the three front chairs leaving one chair behind," and so on. No metaphor, no symbolism, no learned allusions, no background information about the Ballets Russes or Serge Diaghilev, no biographical sketch of Stravinsky, and, most important, no word as to Gertrude Stein's judgment on the music or the ballet. Instead, we are treated by the "naive" Alice Toklas to an account of Apollinaire's hand-kissing habits and a description of the pleated evening shirt worn by the unknown "tall well-built young man" who becomes the subject (dressed "In the best most silk and water much, in the best most silk") of Stein's portrait "One" [in **Geography and Plays**].

Why the shift of focus from purported subject to ancillary detail? Like a cubist collage, Stein's composition creates its effect, not by representing the external event but by, so to speak, pasting up metonymically related items that, as in the case of **Paris France,** spatialize the narrative and make it what Stein calls a "continuous present" [in her **Selected Writings**]. Thus Apollinaire's outrageous hand-kissing ritual ("He was the first one of his crowd to come out into the great world wearing evening clothes and kissing hands") ironically parallels Stravinsky's "rite of spring." "After the war," Toklas tells us, "they all did these things but he was the only one to commence before the war." The comic miniature version of the avant-garde ballet makes the latter accessible to us. We know that this is an important evening, an evening to remember—"the first time we had seen him doing it."

In the same vein, the never-before seen "soft evening shirt with the tiniest pleats all over the front of it," an evening shirt worn by a man who "might have been a dutchman, a scandinavian or an american," is a portent of things to come: "we had never even heard," says Toklas "that they were wearing evening shirts like that." The portrait Stein produces that night is appropriately called "One" because the evening shirt is a "first" even as Apollinaire's hand-kissing routine is a first. In this context, the actual performance of Stravinsky becomes a kind of anticlimax, even as a Picasso collage may place its "subject" in the corner and place primary emphasis on a calling card or a newspaper page.

The Autobiography of Alice B. Toklas neither describes the music nor the dancing, but the "anecdote," which is thus quite unlike the anecdotes found in the typical biography or autobiography, is all the more telling. What the reader comes to see is that (1) the first night of *Sacre du Printemps* is a watershed for the arts, prefiguring the watershed soon to be created by the war; (2) Stein herself is part of the magic circle of artists which includes Nijinsky, Apollinaire, and Stravinsky, in that the "well-built young man" (Carl Van Vechten) becomes the occasion for her own artistic composition, the portrait "One"; and (3) the neutral and nonjudgmental voice of Alice Toklas, herself neither artist nor critic but a mere someone who is alternately "amused" and "astonished" by the furor in the theater, serves to highlight the brilliance of a Nijinsky, an Apollinaire—and of course of Gertrude Stein herself.

The compositional strategy of the **Autobiography** is thus one of metonymic deflection. Readers who know Stein's work primarily through James Mellow's biography or

Marty Martin's play *Gertrude Stein Gertrude Stein Gertrude Stein,* or through the countless memoirs of Stein and Toklas in Paris, assume that Stein's own autobiography is "colorful," a series of juicy stories about the French/American avant-garde. But in fact the style of the ***Autobiography*** is not especially imagistic, its descriptions less than concrete, the emphasis being on such pronoun-copula units as "He was," "We were," "We looked," "when we got home," "We could hear nothing." Nijinsky, for example, is defined as he who "created the dance of those who did dance." Period.

"The dance of those who did dance." Incremental repetition is not especially notable in the ***Autobiography,*** but such locutions as "We were very amused and very pleased to see him do it. It was the first time we had seen him doing it," recall those Stein texts, from ***Three Lives*** to ***Lectures in America,*** in which repetition is the central device. I want next to consider the two poles of this more "difficult" Stein compositional mode, a mode that puts off many potential readers who equate excessive repetition with boredom. But once we understand the syntactic habits of the ***Autobiography,*** Stein's experiments in repetition will seem much less eccentric. Here, as my example of a third "style in search of a reader," is the opening of the short story **"Miss Furr and Miss Skeene"** (1908):

> Helen Furr had quite a pleasant home. Mrs. Furr was quite a pleasant woman. Mr. Furr was quite a pleasant man. Helen Furr had quite a pleasant voice a voice quite worth cultivating. She did not mind working. She worked to cultivate her voice. She did not find it gay living in the same place where she had always been living. She went to a place where some were cultivating something, voices and other things needing cultivating. She met Georgine Skeene there who was cultivating her voice which some thought was quite a pleasant one. Helen Furr and Georgine Skeene lived together then. Georgine Skeene liked travelling. Helen Furr did not care about travelling, she liked to stay in one place and be gay there. They were together then and travelled to another place and stayed there and were gay there.

The key to the repetition-permutation pattern in this rather unusual love story may be found in a comment Stein made in the **"Transatlantic Interview 1946"** on the subject of her own earlier ***Tender Buttons,*** specifically **"A Piece of Coffee,"** which contains the sentence "Dirty is yellow." Stein, who is not exactly someone given to frequent self-criticism, tells Robert Bartlett Haas, "Dirty has an association and is a word I would not use now. I would not use words that have definite associations." Which is to say that the best words, from Stein's perspective, are those whose meanings remain equivocal and hence able to take on slightly different shading at each reappearance.

Take "pleasant," as in "Helen Furr had quite a pleasant home." Unlike "dirty," "pleasant," and especially "quite a pleasant" provides us with what John Ashbery has called "an open field of narrative possibilities." "Quite a pleasant" can connote anything from "very nice, very comfortable" to "barely tolerable." "Mrs. Furr was quite a pleasant woman. Mr. Furr was quite a pleasant man."

Again, all we know is that Helen Furr was living with her parents, two people defined only by their indefinability. They are, one supposes, neither better nor worse than most parents—but then, even this supposition cannot be proven or disproven. In the fourth sentence, the phrase "quite a pleasant" is now transferred from persons to Helen Furr's voice, a transfer that makes that voice seem no more interesting than her "quite pleasant" home. "A pleasant voice a voice quite worth cultivating"—it is this bit of exposition that sets Stein's "plot" in motion. For it is Helen's decision to "cultivate her voice" that provides her with the motive she needs to leave home and to go to a place were "some were cultivating something, voices and other things needing cultivating."

In between these two references to "cultivating," the seventh sentence introduces the key word of the story: *gay.* At the time Stein wrote **"Miss Furr and Miss Skeene,"** the designation of "gay" as "homosexual" was not yet so much as a known underground meaning, the word's dictionary definition—"happy," "merry," "good-humored," "blithe"—being the accepted one. Thus, its introduction in the sentence, "She did not find it gay living in the same place where she had always been living" strikes us at first as meaning no more than that Helen Furr is somehow bored at home. Not until "gay" begins to undergo its series of permutations, does its other meaning (inevitably prominent for the contemporary reader but surely latent in Stein's text) come into prominence.

"She did not find it gay living in the same place where she had always been living." How does the repetition of "living" work here? Why can't Stein simply say, "She did not find it gay living at home" or "in her pleasant home"? The locution "living in the same place where she had always been living" emphasizes the duration of Helen Furr's existence prior to her meeting with Georgine Skeene; it is the persistence of her prior "living" that will make the change that now occurs all the more important. In the same vein, the repetition of "cultivating" in "She went to a place where some were cultivating something, voices and other things needing cultivating," is wittily deflationary, its second appearance, modifying "voices and other things needing," suggesting that "cultivating" has less to do with "work" than with some sort of group "gay" activity.

Indeed Helen Furr's new association with a fellow-"cultivator" named Georgine Skeene (the punning names relate fur and skin, even as Georgine Skeene's rhyming name gives her an air of absurdity) suggests that "cultivating" is no more than an excuse for establishing a sexual relationship. But this relationship is already threatened by difference: "Georgine Skeene liked travelling. Helen Furr did not care about travelling, she liked to stay in one place and be gay there." This simple distinction casts doubt on the paragraph's final sentence, "They were together then and travelled to another place and stayed there and were gay there." For it is "travelling" that will produce the split between the two women.

Verbal and phrasal repetition, in this context, is neither ornamental nor, as for many poets, a form of intensification. Rather, repetition generates meaning. For even as the narrative seems to occur in a continuous present ("They stayed there and were gay there, not very gay there, just gay there"), the situation gradually and inevitably changes. By the end, Helen Furr is left alone but she has learned to be "regular in being gay" and "telling about little ways one could be learning to use in being gay, and later was telling them quite often, telling them again and again."

Who are "they," and what is Helen Furr telling them again and again? It is important that we not know. **"Miss Furr and Miss Skeene"** is curiously nonmimetic even as its "realism" is intense. The two women are given no motives; indeed, we know almost nothing about them. There is no explanation of their mutual attraction or of the activity in which they were engaging when they were "regularly" going "somewhere" with the "men who were dark and heavy" or with the men "who were not so dark" and those "who were not so heavy." The mystery of their being is thus left intact. To say that Stein's is a story of how a girl from a nice home comes out of the closet, has a brief fling with a less nice girl, and thus gains the experience to carry on with her "gay" life is to reduce Stein's enormously subtle work to a cartoon. The text itself remains impervious to such easy reading for it never allows us to make secure judgments about character and action. How "pleasant" is a pleasant home? What does being "regularly gay" entail? If we interpret "gay" as homosexual, what are Helen Furr and Georgine Skeene doing when they "sit regularly" with the dark and heavy men? And in the final standoff between Helen and Georgine, whose side are we on?

Repetition, variation, permutation, the minuscule transfer of a given word from one syntactic slot to another, one part of speech to another, creates a compositional field that remains in constant motion, that prevents closure from taking place. *Pleasant, gay, work, cultivate, regularly, somewhere*—these permutating counters make up a dense network of narrative possibilities without ever coalescing into a definable story line. But indeterminacy does not imply, as readers often assume, that Stein's story has no meaning. On the contrary, its meanings are multiple. Stein is describing a woman who moves out from the "quite a pleasant" home of her quite pleasant parents into a larger world where people are "cultivating" something. In the course of her "cultivation" and her "being gay" with another woman and "sitting" with men of all descriptions, Helen Furr learns to be "gay every day" and "learning other ways in being gay" that she can "tell" others about. By the end of this five-page story, Helen Furr is a different person. And it is the coming of this difference that **"Miss Furr and Miss Skeene"** charts.

Many of Stein's best-known texts—***The Making of Americans,* "Melanctha," "Composition as Explanation,"** the first Picasso portrait—employ the mode of repetition used in **"Miss Furr and Miss Skeene."** But what of the many compositions that carry repetition to what seems to be a point of no return? Here, for example, is part 26 of Stein's improvisation on Georges Hugnet's poem *Enfances,* which she called ***Before the Flowers of Friendship Faded Friendship Faded*** (1931):

> Little by little two go if two go three go if three go four go if four go they go. It is known as does he go he goes if they go they go and they know they know best and most of whether he will go. He is to go. They will not have vanilla and say so. To go Jenny go, Ivy go Gaby go any come and go is go and come and go and leave to go. Who has to hold it while they go who has to who has had it held and have them come to go. He went and came and had to go. No one has had to say he had to go come here to go go there to go go go to come to come to go to go and come and go.

Even as enthusiastic an advocate of Stein's "experimental writing" as Marianne DeKoven refers to the poetic sequence in which this text appears as a "travesty." But if we think of Stein's series of permutations on a small corpus of words and phrases as her verbal equivalent to the nonrepresentational landscape of her painter-contemporaries, we begin to discern patterns not unlike the exciting/peaceful clusters in ***Paris France.***

"A sentence," as Stein puts it [in ***How to Write***], "is an interval in which there is a finally forward and back." The "forward and back" in this case is the buried phrase "to and fro." "Little by little two go"—the narrative begins normally enough in the vein of a children's book, even as ***Paris France*** contains sentences like "There are lots of cats in Paris and in France." Again, the logic of "If two go three go if three go four go" sounds like a jingle in *Dr. Seuss* or a nursery rhyme. But Stein never quite lets the "child's play" continue, so she ends this first sentence with the twist "If four go they go."

Successive sentences provide us with further examples of this ambivalence between instinct and knowledge, the perspective of the child ("To go Jenny go Ivy go Gaby go"—a kind of jump-rope rhyme) and that of the grown-up ("It is known"; "they know best and most of whether he will go"; "no one has had to say"). Within this framework, embedded in the sound chiming of "come and go" and "go go go," a single word stands out, rather like a white flag in an otherwise black field—"They will not have vanilla and say so." "Vanilla" is the only three-syllable word in the entire composition (for that matter, out of 144 words, there are only 6 that have two syllables, and 3 of those are proper names); it is the only noun, and the only concrete image referring to a particular sense impression.

What does it mean thus to embed *vanilla* in the field of *come/go, two/go, he/they, who/no one, if/of*? Perhaps no more nor less than that the mind tries to center its little verbal steps on something concrete and tangible, something one might see or taste or touch. But "Who has to hold it?" No sooner does the noun appear than it disappears again, obliterated by the march of "go go go." Like a cubist collage, "vanilla" is the "pasted paper" that draws the eye only to fade again as other relationships become apparent. And in this sense, Stein's composition does have meaning: it suggests that the authority vested in "vanilla" is rejected ("They will not have vanilla and say so") in the interest of the "two" [who] "go," who "come to come" and "go to go."

An enigmatic text like this one demands, of course, a great deal from the reader; indeed, many readers will find the demand excessive. But, even at her most "repetitious," Stein is not just indulging, as some critics have supposed, in automatic writing. And, at their best, her enigma texts present us with a formidable challenge. I turn now to the most difficult of the Stein styles: first, the fragmented, non-referential mode of *Tender Buttons* and then the "sound poetry" of texts such as **"Lipschitz," "Jean Cocteau,"** and **"Pink Melon Joy."**

Like the great realists of the nineteenth century who were her precursors, Stein believed that the domain of literature is the real rather than the ideal, the ordinary rather than the unusual, the everyday rather than the fantastic. But, as Lyn Hejinian observes, "realism" can be an attitude toward language itself rather than only toward the objects to which language refers:

> Perhaps it was the discovery that language is an order of reality itself and not a mere mediating medium—that it is possible and even likely that one can have a confrontation with a phrase that is as significant as a confrontation with a tree, chair, cone, dog, bishop, piano, vineyard, door, or penny, etc.—which replaced [Stein's] commitment to a medical career with a commitment to a literary career.

Which is not to say that references to tree, chair, cone, or dog aren't also obliquely present. In *Tender Buttons* (1914), Stein presents us with a series of objects, food items, body parts, and enclosures, naming each item only to set into motion a kind of riddle. **"Cold Climate,"** we read, and then the single enigmatic sentence, "A season in yellow sold extra strings makes lying places." Does this mean that the title is pure nonsense, having nothing to do with the "description" that follows? Or can we relate the "cold climate" to the "season in yellow" (November? autumn? the time of fog?) and consider the possibilities raised by the suggestion that "extra strings" (for a blanket, a pillow, a lap robe) are sold at this time of year so as to make "lying places" more comfortable?

In such instances, language is certainly not "a mere mediating medium," but neither is it, as Stein's detractors often suggest, purely nonreferential. If what Hejinian calls the "confrontation with a [verbal] phrase" becomes as important as the confrontation with an event, it can only be because we have to be peculiarly attentive so as to uncover the connection between the two. Here is **"A Waist"**:

> A star glide, a single frantic sullenness, a single financial grass greediness.
> Object that is in wood. Hold the pine, hold the dark, hold in the rush, make the bottom.
> A piece of crystal. A change, in a change that is remarkable there is no reason to say that there was a time.
> A woolen object gilded. A country climb is the best disgrace, a couple of practices any of them in order is so left.

Unlike my third and fourth examples, **"A Waist"** does not rely upon repetition as a form of defamiliarization. Neither is the characteristic sentence a simple declarative one. Rather, Stein here makes use of both synecdoche and pun, these figures being embedded in what tend to be short noun phrases and sentence fragments.

The first thing to notice is that "waist" has as its homonym "waste," and that both words generate what follows. "A star glide"—one immediately conjures up a dancer gliding into the room, a graceful person with a delicate tiny waist. But pinching the waist has its problems: "A single frantic sullenness" suggests that the waist has been laced too tightly, that it hurts. To force the dancer into this role is perhaps a "financial . . . greediness," the desire not to "waste" anything. "Grass" suggests envy on someone's part; it also recalls "glass" and hence takes us back phonemically to "glide" and to the image of a "single" graceful movement of the waist. The repetition of the phonemes /gl/, /gr/, and /l/ reenforce this image of fragility and gliding motion.

But in the second "stanza," Stein abruptly shifts to an entirely different image: "Object that is in wood." Perhaps the "waist" is now that of a carved wooden statuette or idol. Someone is carving a figure and "mak[ing] the bottom," but to talk of waists is, of course, also to talk of hips and bottoms. In the third paragraph, the object is explicitly defined as a "piece of crystal," and the image is that of the sort of little glass figurine one finds in display cases. The "change" that turns a bit of wood or glass into a sculpture is so great that "there is no reason to say that there was a time" (i.e., when it was not yet "made"). And now, in the fourth paragraph or "stanza," "glide" is metathesized to "glided," and the "object" has become woolen. Is the statuette dressed in wool? Or is Stein shifting from artwork to real life and to the benefit waists receive from "a country climb" or related "practices" occurring in some sort of "order"? What is "so left," then, is finally an image of tiny waists delicately moving, not wasting any motion, of an artist's carving, whether in glass or in wood, that creates a definite change.

Each item in *Tender Buttons* has a place on this larger continuum of change and transformation. Like *Paris France* which is exciting and peaceful, buttons can be tender, and a carafe that is a blind glass can be a spectacle. If, in her later work, Stein provides us with more connectives, the basic impulse, which is to "define" things as they really occur, not as if they are to be pigeonholed or seen from one angle only, is to force us to think about the subject, in this case, to come to terms with the word "waist."

In thus "confronting" a group of words as if it were an event in the external world, Stein also pays close attention to sound. Indeed, her corpus includes the first experiments with what we now call "sound poetry." Here is the opening of the 1926 portrait [included in *Portraits and Prayers*] called **"Jean Cocteau"**:

> Needs be needs be needs be near.
> Needs be needs be needs be.
> This is where they have their land astray.
>   Two say.
> This is where they have their land astray
> Two say.
> Needs be needs be needs be
> Needs be needs be needs be near.
>   Second time.

No doubt, this is Gertrude Stein at her most "nonsensical," her most opaque. We know neither the subject nor the object of the locution "needs be," nor can we be sure whether the verb is indicative or conditional ("if need be"). Again, we can't pinpoint the meaning of the pun on "Two say" ("to say") or the effect of the rhyme "say" / "astray," any more than we can establish the reference in line 5 to "their land astray."

But read aloud, the poem has a particular rhythmic figure, specifically, the ballad rhythm of songs like "Skip to my Lou," with its refrain lines (three per stanza) like "I'll take another one, prettier than you," or "Fly's in the buttermilk, shoo fly shoo." Just so, the first line of **"Jean Cocteau"**—"Needs be needs be needs be near."—introduces what sounds like the kind of song children sing during circle games; indeed, the refrain "Second time" suggests that the physical movement (skipping? jumping? clapping?) associated with the incantation is to be repeated.

But just as *Paris France* is a parody schoolbook, so **"Jean Cocteau"** is a parody nursery rhyme or jump-rope song. For "needs be" is also a pun on "kneads bee" and the reference "This is where they have their land astray" refers to the world of grown-ups, not children. And, knowing that Stein admired the young Cocteau, who had praised her work but who never quite seemed to find the time to participate in her salon and become one of her *fidèles,* the "land astray" and "needs be" begin to make more sense. Stein regards her literary situation as one in which Cocteau "needs be near," since he regularly flatters and encourages her. But because their primarily epistolary friendship is more assumed than real, Cocteau never quite having time for Stein, she presents herself and the Frenchman ("Two say") as two fellow-artists whose "land" or common artistic property has gone "astray." Still, the need continues, and as she says in the line following that opening passage quoted above, "It may be nearer than two say." We may, that is to say, have more in common than even we think.

The singsong sound pattern of **"Jean Cocteau"** is so prominent that readers may well assume that this portrait has phonological value only. Wendy Steiner, for example, writes: "Relieved of specific reference, the words in this portrait have nothing more than their pale dictionary meanings, and even these are made ambiguous through the variations in context. Words thus are almost pure phonological quanta." But the fact remains that there is something that "needs be," a land that has gone "astray," and, for the "second time," "Two [who] say." Indeed, once we have gotten the hang of finding the excited/peaceful configuration in *Paris France* or the metonymic account of the first night at Stravinsky's *Sacre du Printemps* in *The Autobiography of Alice B. Toklas,* we will find that even the most abstruse of Stein's sound poems or synecdochic riddles do refer, however obliquely, to the events of her extraverbal universe.

To recapitulate. Stein's oeuvre gives evidence of at least six different styles: (1) seemingly "straight" reportage (*Paris France*), (2) autobiographical narrative as ironized by presenting a fictional narrator who tells the story, as in *The Autobiography of Alice B. Toklas,* (3) narrative-as-permutation of phrasal repetitions, each reappearance of the word or phrase giving us a new view, as in **"Miss Furr and Miss Skeene"**; (4) "abstract" repetition of words and phonemes, as in *Before the Flowers of Friendship Faded Friendship Faded,* where the "action" is less a matter of incident than of verbal event; (5) the synecdochic riddling poetry of *Tender Buttons,* where a given title is the impetus for the creation of its cubist equivalent, and (6) sound poetry, as in **"Jean Cocteau."**

One might, of course, refine these distinctions; the mode of repetition in *Lectures in America,* for instance, falls somewhere in between the repetition-as-narrative of **"Miss Furr and Miss Skeene"** and the abstraction of *Before the Flowers of Friendship Faded Friendship Faded.* Or again, the fragments of *Stanzas in Meditation* are at once similar to, and yet also recognizably different from, the concrete texts in *Tender Buttons.* Still, the six types I have isolated give us the basic parameters in which to read the Stein corpus. And in locating these styles on the Stein spectrum, I hope I have laid to rest the notion that Stein *either* writes "simply," so that anyone can understand her, or "obscurely," so that no one can. As she herself put it in **"Arthur A Grammar"** [in *How to Write*], "Successions of words are so agreeable. It is about this." (pp. 96-108)

> Marjorie Perloff, "Six Stein Styles in Search of a Reader," in A Gertrude Stein Companion: Content with the Example, *edited by Bruce Kellner, Greenwood Press, 1988, pp. 96-108.*

Harriet Scott Chessman (essay date 1989)

[*In the following excerpt, Chessman examines the motif of the double in relationships portrayed in Stein's works.*]

At one moment in **"Melanctha,"** the insistent and lively dialogue between Melanctha and Jeff comes to a halt, as a new form of communication begins to occur:

> Melanctha began to lean a little more toward Dr. Campbell, where he was sitting, and then she took his hand between her two and pressed it hard, but she said nothing to him. She let it go then and leaned a little nearer to him. Jefferson moved a little but did not do anything in answer. At last, "Well," said Melanctha sharply to him. "I was just thinking" began Dr. Campbell slowly, "I was just wondering," he was beginning to get ready to go on with his talking. "Don't you ever stop with your thinking long enough ever to have any feeling Jeff Campbell," said Melanctha a little sadly.

Although Melanctha at first "said nothing" in words, she speaks with her body. By her gestures, she suggests her desire for an increasing intimacy, one of "feeling," with little need of words. Jeff's resistance to this bodily speech and his return to language as a representation of "thinking" obstruct the development of a dialogue of the body. These oppositions between thinking and feeling, language and silence, however, begin to dissolve as Stein creates a sensual and rhythmic language incorporating the body. In Stein's later writings, the "silent" realm of intimacy becomes even more voluble. Each of Stein's styles marks a new attempt to bring a bodily intimacy into language.

Stein's concern for such intimacy bears significant connections with the school of post-Freudian psychoanalysis called object relations theory. Focusing upon the earliest, prelinguistic attachment of the infant and small child to the mother, this theory opens a window onto a realm of intimacy that becomes the ground for later formulations of relationship. Stein's forms of intimacy differ in important ways from those of object relations theory: she does not conceive of intimacy in mother-infant terms, just as she chooses to transform the "prelinguistic" into a linguistic realm approximating and even embodying a state outside of language. Yet object relations theory offers a vocabulary and a set of concepts valuable for articulating this Steinian transformation.

One of Stein's major connections with object relations theory lies in a shared emphasis on relatedness. As Nancy Chodorow points out in *The Reproduction of Mothering,* this theory in general argues against the Freudian model of primary narcissism, where the infant's earliest experience occurs in almost total isolation from another being. Chodorow presents Freud and later ego psychologists as claiming that

> the infant originally has no cathexis of its environment or of others, but concentrates all its libido on its self (or on its predifferentiated psyche). The infant is generally libidinally narcissistic; hence, the hypothesis of primary narcissism. . . . This Freudian position also holds that the infant seeks only the release of tension from physiologically based drives—operates according to the "pleasure principle." The source of this gratification . . . is irrelevant to the infant. Accordingly, the child is first drawn from its primary libidinally narcissistic stage because of its need for food.

The child, in this model, is forced into relationship only as a means to an end (for instance, food), where the "end" is still attached to the child's libidinal need. In these early stages, relationship is secondary.

By contrast, object relations theorists like Michael Balint and Alice Balint argue for an infant's connection to its environment beginning even before birth. Paradoxically, even though the infant does not differentiate itself from what surrounds and holds it (originally the womb), it powerfully cathects this very bodily presence. Soon after birth, Chodorow writes, this "generalized cathexis . . . becomes focused on those primary people, or that person, who have been particularly salient in providing gratification and a holding relationship." In contradistinction to Freud's theory of primary narcissism, these theorists suggest the hypothesis of "primary love," which "holds that infants have a primary need for human contact itself."

From the first, then, one experiences being in the world (or in the womb) not as "one" alone, but as two, even when one cannot differentiate between oneself and the other. In D. W. Winnicott's terms [set forth in "The Theory of the Parent-Infant Relationship"] "I once said: 'There is no such thing as an infant,' meaning, of course, that whenever one finds an infant one finds maternal care, and without maternal care there would be no infant." As I shall argue in my interpretation of **The Autobiography of Alice B. Toklas** and the early portrait **"Ada,"** this formulation of a doubleness inherent in and essential to identity has a strong bearing on Stein's literary form. The chiasmus of Winnicott's language here even resembles Steinian crossings-over, as in the quote heading this chapter: "You double I double I double you double." Stein's characteristic use of an unidentified or floating "you" and "I" may resemble this mother-infant bonding. However, Stein avoids fastening the identities of these pronouns to this original dyad, for reasons that will become clearer later in this chapter.

Object relations theory holds as one of its key tenets that "the development of the self is relational." As Chodorow suggests (following Winnicott), the inner "core" of the self depends upon a simultaneous "provision of a continuity of experience," just as the sense of "self," in terms of a unity with ego and bodily boundaries, develops through the gradual demarcation from the m/other. As Chodorow adds, this definition through relation is sustained primarily with daughters. Her intricate analysis leads to this concept: "Because of their mothering by women, girls come to experience themselves as less separate than boys, as having more permeable ego boundaries. Girls come to define themselves more in relation to others." Whereas boys move fairly quickly from the dyad with the mother to the triangular relationship of desire between son, mother, and father, involving the son's rivalry with the father, for girls the matter differs: "A girl, by contrast, remains preoccupied for a long time with her mother alone. She experiences a continuation of the two-person relationship of infancy."

For Stein, although the origin of this "two-person" relationship may lie in infancy, this temporal anchorage holds much less importance or even presence in her writing than the transformation of such a relationship into new forms. The mother disappears from the picture, to be replaced by a more equal figure. Yet the equality of the two subjects in Stein's writing resembles the relation between mother and infant in Chodorow's theory. As Carol Gilligan suggests, Chodorow's great contribution has been to substitute the word and concept of "mother" for the more reified "object." Chodorow challenges the way in which the mother as a responsive and human figure in the relationship has been reduced in object relations theory to an "object" that is either constant (and lifeless) or a monster. Chodorow understands the relation between mother and child as always two-sided, involving two subjects. Accordingly, she emphasizes not only the infant's perspective, but the mother's as well.

The mother's experience, as Chodorow argues, tends to create daughters who will be like their mothers, in a long line of "the reproduction of mothering." This situation between mothers and daughters, daughters who become mothers to more daughters, could be looked at from many angles. Certainly, within the context of a patriarchal culture, where gender differences mark a crucial difference in power, this reproduction of mothering perpetuates an inequality that is socially, politically, and economically visible. This asymmetrical development of males and females is constituted in a further important sense by a culturally defined linguistic difference. As Margaret Homans has shown [in her *Bearing the Word*], when we consider the Lacanian structuring of language acquisition in relation to Chodorow's account of asymmetrical gender development, a fuller picture of our gendered cultural mythos emerges. In Lacan's narrative, which assumes the point of view of the son, the maternal represents the silent, the repressed, and the literal, upon whose absence patriarchal culture and symbolic language depend. The boy's severance from the mother at the onset of the Oedipal crisis marks a disturbingly fortunate fall, for her absence enables the son to enter the Symbolic, constituted by figures of substitution for the now lost maternal presence. The daughter's case manifests a critical difference, however: "because of various consequences of the daughter's likeness to her mother, she does not enter the symbolic order as wholeheartedly or exclusively as does the son." The daughter's prolonged pre-Oedipal attachment to the mother, notes Homans, in being thus allied to the uncertainty of her status within the symbolic order, appears from a Freudian and Lacanian perspective as the "daughter's tragedy."

As Homans points out, however, through her interpretation of Chodorow, another "story" is possible. This alternate account, read from "the daughter's point of view," springs from the potential value inhering in the daughter's different relation to the mother:

> Although in this new story, the daughter does enter the symbolic order, she does not do so exclusively. Because she does not perceive the mother as lost or renounced, she does not need the compensation the father's law offers as much as does the son. Furthermore, she has the positive experience of never having given up entirely the presymbolic communication that carries over, with the bond to the mother, beyond the preoedipal period. The daughter therefore speaks two languages at once. Along with symbolic language, she retains the literal or presymbolic language that the son represses at the time of his renunciation of his mother. . . . Unlike the son, the daughter does not, in Chodorow's view, give up this belief in communication that takes place in presence rather than in absence, in the dyadic relation with the mother, and prior to figuration.

This access to a presymbolic language continued from infancy holds potential for a poetics created by women writers, as Homans suggests. Yet "speaking two languages at once," when the languages have been valued so unequally within culture, has been no easy matter. The nineteenth-century women writers Homans considers responded to this linguistic situation with an ambivalence that becomes lessened, although it hardly disappears, in the twentieth century. Virginia Woolf "intermittently" expresses "pleasure in a nonsymbolic language," just as H. D. attempts to imagine it. A larger acknowledgment of the cultural devaluation of women's language, however, in Homan's view, tempers such pleasure.

Gertrude Stein's writing is unusual even in the twentieth century for its embrace of language's nonsymbolic dimensions. Homans states, "To write 'literature' is to write within the symbolic order." If this is the case, however, Stein redefines "literature" in powerful and delightful ways. A major aspect of Stein's achievement is precisely to recover the "literal" and to return it to the "letter," even as she makes the letter as literal as possible. Stein gives language to a whole realm of experience culturally perceived as extra-linguistic or extra-literary, yet the language she offers, especially after her first decade of writing when she had to confront and put to rest her own Victorian heritage, is a sensual, aural, and visual one playing always on the borders of the symbolic and the unsymbolic, just as it plays on the borders of identity and mergence with an other. She does, indeed, "speak two languages at once," in forms affording not ambivalence but comedic mischievousness, for the Symbolic order appears in Stein's writing not as an irrefutable Law, but as a structure open to transformation. The value of such play lies, for Stein, in the margin of freedom it grants to make use of symbolic forms in order to create a voice for the unsymbolic, thereby "reproducing" an earlier intimacy based on a dialogue of sound and of the body.

Stein's resistance to actual mother-figures in *Three Lives* continues in her long career of writing, even to the creation of the late opera, *The Mother of Us All,* where Susan B. Anthony questions the authenticity of her own authority and achievement as a "mother" of the U.S.A. (Us All). This resistance would seem to suggest Stein's own burial of the maternal, and in a sense it does. For Stein, the literal mother was dangerous for her suppression of the daughter's story, especially the story of the daughter's sexuality, as in the portrait **"Ada."** Yet Stein's voluble and intimate poetics of dialogue, foregrounding the sensual and bodily dimensions of language, reworks the pre-Oedipal bond between mother and infant. This early bond may be buried, yet a similar bond most compellingly exists, redefined as an attachment between "others" or lovers.

Stein's rejection of the mother-daughter relation in favor of the relation possible between two subjects—often, but not exclusively, female subjects—resembles Luce Irigaray's account in "And the One Doesn't Stir Without the Other" of a daughter's silencing by the mother and of her attempt to transform the mother into another woman. From the perspective of Irigaray's daughter-figure then, the mergence and identification that hold a positive value in most object relations theory appear claustrophobic and destructive of autonomy for both the daughter and the mother. The reproduction of mothering prevents the formation of identity outside the role of "a mother's daughter," "a daughter's mother." Between these two images, an authentic self cannot emerge. Each daughter becomes merely a mirror (*glace*), frozen into a "reflection" of her mother, who has no identity of her own, stilled as she is within the world of the father, for whom she, and subsequently the daughter, must serve as mirror: "Immobilized in the reflection he expects of me. Reduced to the face he fashions for me in which to look at himself." Irigaray suggests that women may only escape this labyrinth of empty mirrors through a recognition of the otherness both of daughter and mother. This acceptance and enjoyment of difference, voiced also in Irigaray's earlier essay "When Our Lips Speak Together," marks the possibility of a relationship strikingly similar to Stein's vision: "I would like both of us to be present. So that the one doesn't disappear in the other, or the other in the one. So that we can taste each other, feel each other, listen to each other, see each other—together. . . . *I would like us to play together at being the same and different. You / I exchanging selves endlessly and each staying herself. Living mirrors*" (emphasis added). Such "play" between figures similar and yet different also forms the heart of Stein's poetics of dialogue, although Stein's tone is lighter, her forms more experimental, than Irigaray's.

Through the form of these highly lyric pieces, Irigaray self-consciously transforms the nature of her relation to existing disciplines of psychoanalysis and philosophy. The disciplines' own limitations compel her, along with other contemporary French feminists, to begin to write in new and experimental forms. Unlike Irigaray, Stein does not primarily consider herself to be in the realms of philosophy and psychoanalysis, although her writing offers some of the most brilliant revisions of philosophical and psychoanalytical thinking to be found in the first half of the twentieth century, revisions often anticipating recent feminist and deconstructive thought, as Neil Schmitz and Marianne DeKoven, among others, have argued. She was certainly educated in philosophy and in "psychology," considered a new dimension of philosophy in the late nineteenth century, when she studied at Radcliffe with William James, George Santayana, and Josiah Royce. Her serious and imaginative effort to raise questions about language, representation, the mind's processes, and the formation of identity and relationship continued throughout her writing life. She always works intellectual thought, however, into the playful and difficult forms of her literary creativity.

It is within literary form that Stein addresses structures of relatedness described by psychoanalytic and object relations theories in other terms. She also differs from most of these models, as I have suggested, in her transformation of the mother into a loving "other," her dehistoricized rendering of this dyadic relation, and her emphasis upon language as the utopian place where such intimacy can occur in continuous and infinitely nuanced forms. In the rest of this chapter, I wish to twine Stein's literary language with the language of object relations and feminist theory, in order to gain insight into the significant difference Stein makes. The Steinian dialogue I shall explore [in this essay] will be both actual and metaphoric. It occurs in myriad forms, yet it is arguably ceaseless, as the primary structure out of which her writing is generated.

. . . . .

In the first edition of *The Autobiography of Alice B. Toklas* (1933), a double portrait of Alice Toklas and Gertrude Stein faces the title page. This photograph by Man Ray presents the two figures in an eery and uncanny aspect. Alice Toklas appears in the doorway of Stein's atelier, an unsmiling and quietly ghost-like figure, looking apparently, not at Gertrude Stein, but into the general dusk of the room, while Stein remains at her desk, pen in hand and head bent downward. Two candles rest on the table between the two figures, as if to mark the space between them. The "story" of this picture is uncertain, even mysterious. What seems most uncertain, and most interesting, is the relation between these two women within the moment created by the photograph, which focuses our attention upon the intricately filled space between the figures. Placed at the opening of this "autobiography" of one woman, written by another, the photograph suggests the mystery involved in such a doubling.

At least two interpretations of this mystery may be seen to bear significantly upon Stein's book. In one interpretation, based on the more overt content of the photograph, Stein is clearly the writer. Solid and still, she sits at a kind of altar, replete with votive candles and, on the shelf above, religious icons, including a heavy cross. Alice is a lesser figure in the temple, although a significant one. Hovering on the margin of the sacred writing space, she is perhaps an intrusive spirit, but one that must be acknowledged. In a sense, she appears as a figment of Stein's imagination. Stein does not need to look up because she is in the process of creating Alice on the page. This interpretation suggests a doubleness involving one primary figure with a secondary, shadowy doppelgänger to the side. The act of writing bears in this sense a sinister edge linked to Stein's possible appropriation of Toklas's voice in **The Autobiography.**

The ambiguity of Man Ray's image, however, evokes a second and contrasting possibility. The placement of the two identical candles symmetrically between the two figures intimates the possibility of another form of doubleness, one of exchange rather than of static dissimilarity. The image offers a visual chiasmus, suggestive of the way in which Alice may take Gertrude's "place," and Gertrude Alice's. The cross on the wall, linking the two similar windows, lends support to such a crossing-over of identity. Literally, Alice may be about to cross the room to Gertrude, just as Gertrude may in a moment pause in her writing to come to the door. In another sense, the two women may hover on the brink of a dialogue, whether of language or of the body.

This photograph forms an ambiguous threshold to this ambiguous "autobiography," for the conflicting possibilities contained within the photograph appear in the book as well. The tension informing the book marks Stein's attempt to convert the concept of single voice and authorship into a richly doubled authorial identity, to prevent "one" from subverting the more utopian possibilities of "two." The narrative voice of **The Autobiography** manifests this tension. On the one hand, Stein performs a sleight of hand, a feat of disguise by which she, as the author and the "real" narrator, speaks through the transparent device named "Alice B. Toklas." On the other hand, the ambiguity inherent in an "autobiography" of Toklas written by Stein challenges the concept of a single narrator or author. A radical doubling may occur, marking a playful and elusive interchange. Stein makes it difficult for us to be certain that the voice we hear is only Stein's, especially since the voice differs in its dry, civilized, and muted

The frontispiece of the first edition of The Autobiography of Alice B. Toklas, *"Alice B. Toklas at the Door," by Man Ray.*

tones from Stein's narrative voices until this point. It is difficult to know where Stein's voice ends and Toklas's begins.

The Autobiography compels us to wonder, from the beginning, about the nature of the "auto," the self. We begin to ask, in addition to the question of what the relation is between Stein's and Toklas's voices, the further questions of what is the nature of the writing self and whether a work, even an "autobiography," is ever genuinely written by one figure alone. Stein attempts to convert the solitary act of writing into an act shared by at least two figures who engage in some kind of relationship. The definition of a writing "self" depends upon the often baffling and ambiguous presence of another. The two figures enact a dialogue, insofar as both voices may be present. Irony itself—which may be defined as the possibility of one voice speaking "behind" another—takes on the nature of a dialogue; because we cannot tell which speaker/writer is the "real" narrator, we cannot be certain of the irony's location.

To explore this doubleness of narrative voice further, we may consider one of the many instances of actual dialogue in this autobiography so preoccupied with the possibility of dialogue. As brief and unobtrusive as most of the "remarks" making up this "literature" (following the famous Steinian remark, "Hemingway, remarks are not literature"), this anecdote offers a glimpse into a world of two figures in intimate dialogue:

> One Sunday evening I was very busy preparing one of these [American dishes] and then I called Gertrude Stein to come in from the atelier for supper. She came in much excited and would not sit down. Here I want to show you something, she said. No I said it has to be eaten hot. No, she said, you have to see this first. Gertrude Stein never likes her food hot and I do like mine hot, we never agree about this. She admits that one can wait to cool it but one cannot heat it once it is on a plate so it is agreed that I have it served as hot as I like. In spite of my protests and the food cooling I had to read. I can still see the little tiny pages of the notebook written forward and back. It was the portrait called Ada, the first in Geography and Plays. I began it and I thought she was making fun of me and I protested, she says I protest now about my autobiography. Finally I read it all and was terribly pleased with it. And then we ate our supper.

Alice's concern that Stein is "making fun of [her]" in the portrait **"Ada"** could carry over to Alice's protestations about her "autobiography." In one sense, Toklas's "I" is vulnerable to Stein's manipulations. Toklas appears here as a cook, concerned with the temperature of food rather than with writing. Stein clearly is the writer, Toklas the (at first reluctant) reader.

This interpretation, however, does not take into account the perspective from which the passage is written. Literally, the account of Stein's writing of **"Ada"** becomes inseparable from an account of how Alice Toklas receives **"Ada."** Stein's writing has apparently occurred in the atelier, yet the "I" stands in the kitchen, a place to which Stein ("she") repairs as well, as if the atelier—the place where writing occurs in isolation—becomes marginal to the kitchen and dining room, where the writing may be shared through reading what has been written. Reading occurs on a continuum with eating, as an act of subtle and nourishing communion.

The playfulness of tone accords with the playfulness of this exchange in a way that resembles Irigaray's vision of a paradoxical "exchanging [of] selves endlessly and each staying herself." As a domestic quarrel, this dialogue marks a difference between the two figures; they have a "difference," and they differ from each other. The difference is playful in its simplicity: one likes it hot; the other likes it cold. Through language, each asserts a position defined in opposition to the other.

Yet this difference does not cover the whole picture. In the midst of this establishment of difference, a curious event takes place: the two figures seem to merge, their boundaries becoming less distinct ("exchanging selves endlessly"). The absence of quotation marks adds to the confusion; for example, after we hear that "She came in," we come to an "I" in the following sentence appearing at first to be Alice's, yet revealed to be part of a statement made by "She" (Gertrude). We enact a double-take; for an important moment, we believe that this "I" is both Alice's *and* Gertrude's, for the visual marks by which one woman's discourse differs from another's have disappeared. The insistent repetition and dance of the pronouns confuse us as well. The pattern in the first five sentences looks like this:

> I I
> She
> I you she
> I
> she you

The confusion springs largely from the fact that the speaker/writer Alice B. Toklas (the "I") continually quotes the speaker Gertrude Stein. The quotation, one assumes, was first Stein's, but by its new presence in Toklas's written text, it becomes Toklas's also, inasmuch as she repeats it. Further, as we must remind ourselves, this Toklas is not Toklas at all, but Gertrude Stein, who names herself Toklas. The figure Gertrude Stein assumes the voice of Alice B. Toklas, who quotes Gertrude Stein. To add to the general ambiguity, although Stein writes the portrait under discussion, this portrait forms a representation of Alice.

This brilliant confusion is richly humorous and clever, but it is not merely clever. Stein is suggesting something important about dialogue itself, specifically about the forms that may emerge out of a dialogue between two figures who are similar but different. Such dialogue becomes a metaphor for a certain form of relationship, where two "ones" may be distinguished, yet where the boundaries may also become confused and even disappear. Although difference exists, marked by the "I" and the "she," this difference comes to seem less like an end in itself than the necessary starting point for merging and identification, just as (in this puzzling circle) identification becomes the starting point for difference. Neither "difference" nor "identification" may be defined without the other term, just as this "I" comes into definition through the countering of this "she." What is at stake here is not only the content of the dialogue, or its progression toward a resolution (although such a resolution is often there: "And then we ate our supper"), but the dialogue's metaphoric enactment of a *relationship between* two figures, in a continually shifting exchange that is also an interchange—not only of words spoken, but of the position from which these words are spoken, so that the apparent speaking subject may also become the object spoken about, just as the object may become the subject.

The implications of this form of dialogue unfold further if we turn to the "portrait" generating the dialogue recorded between these two women in *The Autobiography*. Although this three-page portrait, as Stein/Toklas says, is called **"Ada,"** not "Alice," in the original form read by Alice it was still overtly her own portrait. On one level, Alice becomes the object of observation and vision, while Gertrude Stein is the observing, "painting" subject. Yet, as the portrait itself makes clear, Stein's use of dialogue works toward the blurring of such boundaries between the subject and object of representation.

In its last paragraph, **"Ada"** bursts lyrically into an erotic and dialogic exchange. Yet before this ecstatic dialogue can take place, a more familiar story must be retold and superseded, a narrative about a family in which Ada enters at first only as "a sister" and "a daughter," not as an equal and autonomous speaking subject. The narrator does not even name her until halfway through her own portrait. **"Ada"** begins in a literary world close to the stories in *Three Lives;* the excitement "Gertrude Stein" feels in showing Alice Toklas this new piece may have sprung from the knowledge that the portrait shows a clear way to defeat this earlier form of family narrative.

The piece begins, in fact, not with **"Ada,"** but with "A da," a father, named Abram Colhard, who is clearly a patriarchal figure in relation to his children. His patronym contains punning implications: "collared" (he collared his son and his daughter); "call-hard" (he makes use of language as a commanding and authoritative force); and "cold-hard," which suggests his cold-heart-edness as well as his male power. The narrative in this early section involves a struggle between father and son, where the son does not wish to do what the father "wanted him to be doing." Although the "it"—"Barnes Colhard did not say he would not do it but he did not do it"—remains unnamed, we gather that it represents the career urged upon the son by the father. The father attempts to author his son's story, to make him do one "thing." Yet the son resists the father's narrative by his own digressions and oscillations: "He did it and then he did not do it." The father, like the matriarchal and patriarchal figures of *Three Lives,* shows a link to sequential and historical narrative embodied in the history that **"Ada"** rehearses at the beginning.

As one of a long line of Steinian dictators or "officers," Abram Colhard founds his narrative form upon monologue. The son may agree or disagree with the father, listen or not listen; but the son himself cannot initiate his own "tellings." When Ada's relationship with her father finally enters the narrative (after the mother's death), again dialogue does not take place. She tells her father of her unhappiness, for example, yet "he never said anything." Not responding to her stories with stories of his own, he remains simply silent. Any saying on either of their parts leads to the silence of the other, for even when the father finally "said something" about the daughter's declaration that she will leave him, his saying of something results only in her saying of "nothing": "then they both said nothing and then it was that she went away from them."

Ada's participation in the story actually begins, not with her father, but with her mother:

> She had been a very good daughter to her mother. She and her mother had always told very pretty stories to each other. Many old men loved to hear her tell these stories to her mother.. . . . She did sometimes think her mother would be pleased with a story that did not please her mother, when her mother later was sicker the daughter knew that there were some stories she could tell her that would not please her mother. Her mother died and really mostly altogether the mother and the daughter had told each other stories very happily together.

Language assumes a different role within this mother-daughter relationship: whereas the father uses language to give directions, to tell what he wants, here words become the medium for "very pretty stories." At least some mutuality of relation exists here. Each figure, mother and daughter, tells stories to the other, instead of one telling and the other listening in silence, as Barnes Colhard must listen, or as Ada must listen to her father. The "relation" of mother to daughter is such that the mutual "relation" of stories can occur.

Yet the dialogue, the mutual telling, has flaws, hinted at by Ada's description as "a very good daughter to her mother." Ada may tell stories, but, as a daughter, she may not tell all. What she is not allowed to articulate, one guesses, is her own desire; in the light of the subsequent loving relationship, she specifically desires a woman. Such an expression of her desire, from her mother's viewpoint and in her mother's language, is not "pretty." The unspeakable must be silenced, finding no place in this prettier round of fictions. Significantly, these stories are not private. They do not form figures for an intimacy that makes the circle of telling and listening an inviolable continuum. The stories seem, instead, to be for public (and masculine) consumption: "Many old men loved to hear her tell these stories to her mother." The interest these "old men" take in the stories between a mother and a daughter marks the potentially disturbing attachment of this particular female world to the world of the father and of men. For, although Ada now has a voice, she still remains silent in another sense: her desire, which stands outside the bounds of the familial and the heterosexual, must remain unarticulated just as it must within her father's patriarchal discourse. The old men's "liking" of the mother and sometimes of the daughter suggests that the stories act merely as counters in a game of heterosexual attraction engaged in by the mother, a game that, because they are "old" men, may involve the mother's desire to please those in power. The stories may be about a similar realm of heterosexual "liking." Ada is not named within the text until after her mother has died, as if she herself is the thing that could not be named in her mother's presence, just as she is not named within the narrative about her father.

This situation resembles the knot of family relationships that Luce Irigaray's "When Our Lips Speak Together" attempts to escape: "I love you who are neither mother (pardon me, mother, for I prefer a woman) nor sister, neither daughter nor son. I love you—and there, where I love you, I don't care about the lineage of our fathers and their desire for imitation men." For Irigaray, the mother is merely one member of a larger family structure in which the father dominates. As a mother, she participates in the "imitation" of men, both in the sense that she produces imitations of the father in her sons, and in the sense that she serves as a mirror for him, denying her autonomous female identity. An equal love between an "I" and a "you" can come into existence only after the "woman" substitutes for the "mother" and family lineage vanishes from the picture entirely.

In **"Ada"** too, only after patriarchal familial obstructions to genuine dialogue have disappeared may the rich doubling of two figures occur. The final lyrical paragraph enacts the engendering of dialogue:

> She came to be happier than anybody else who was living then. It is easy to believe this thing. She was telling some one, who was loving every story that was charming. Some one who was living was almost always listening. Some one who was loving was almost always listening. That one who was loving was telling about being one then listening. That one being loving was then telling stories having a beginning and a middle and an ending. That one was then one always completely listening. Ada was then one and all her living then one completely telling stories that were charming, completely listening to stories having a beginning and a middle and an ending. Trembling was all living, living was all loving, some one was then the other one. Certainly this one was loving this Ada then. And certainly Ada all her living then was happier in living than any one else who ever could, who was, who is, who ever will be living.

As this paragraph reveals, **"Ada"** moves from the nondialogic to dialogue, from narrative to a circling nonnarrative. In the leap outside the traditional lines from father to son or from mother to daughter, the portrait **"Ada"** leaps both thematically and formally out of historical time and narrative. Time, marked by a series of "thens," becomes uncertain and immeasurable, just as the participles ("living," "loving," "telling") suggest the continuous and uninterrupted flow of such movements rather than precise, sequential action. Although movement occurs within the language's rhythmic and repetitive waves, this motion cannot be fastened to historical progression.

This concern with moving outside of history links Stein with the larger American tradition of narrative. As Richard Brodhead has shown in *Hawthorne, Melville, and the Novel,* the narratives of Hawthorne and Melville manifest a conflict between linear forms of narrative and lyrical moments of epiphany, which tend to disrupt historical lines. His account in turn echoes that of Sacvan Bercovitch and John Lynen, who link the tension between temporal and atemporal modes in American art to an older Puritan habit of thought. From Stein's twentieth-century perspective, the issue is no longer a religious one, where competing narrative styles reflect tension within an older religious ideology, but a secular one, marking a struggle between linear modes of narrative identified with public and patriarchal forms of discourse, and narrative possibilities grounded in alternative social and erotic relations. In **"Ada,"** Stein attaches the leap out of history and story to a specifically female-to-female mode of relationship able to escape from the father's and mother's story at least within the utopian constructs of language. In other compositions, although the female specificity may disappear or become obscured, the structure of dialogue among variously gendered (or ungendered) subjects remains a challenge to this story.

The beauty of this passage in **"Ada"** lies partly in its mystery: who is this "some one"? Is the "some one" also "that one"? The absence of a name apart from Ada's suggests the manifold possibilities of identity. This subject can, at any point, be double, as in "When Our Lips Speak Together," where Irigaray often uses a double subject, distinguished only by a slash ("je/tu"). The English word "one," in its openness, can encompass either figure, or both, in shifting patterns. Some distinction is apparent; if there were no difference at all between these two figures, there could be no "telling" and no "listening." Yet the difference, although we know it must be there, becomes highly uncertain through the refusal, in this passage, to name the difference through naming two different names. The impossibility of distinguishing with any certainty which side is which—the impossibility, even, of finding two "sides"—articulates itself directly toward the conclusion: "some one was then the other one." Which other one? Which is the "some" (the "sum"?)?

In this passionate and ongoing dialogue, as in Irigaray's dialogue between "two lips," *what* is told holds less importance than the process of telling and listening. Stein urges us to hear not the substance of two figures' dialogue, but the rhythm of the dialogue's form, which becomes an almost palpable embodiment of the relationship. Although stories act as the bridge, the connector, between the one telling and the one listening, whichever these ones are, it is the bodily and linguistic bond itself which remains primary. "Listening," "living," and "telling," the participles continually repeating, partake also of "loving," just as "loving," with the change of one letter, becomes "living," and "living" metamorphoses into "listening." All of these movements, in all of their intricate, dance-like exchanges, culminate in a "trembling" attached somehow to the final confused merging of "someone was then the other one." Although the sex of the "some one" is not articulated, the fluidity of identity between the "she" and the "one" suggests an identical sexuality. A kind of mirroring occurs here, where the two figures reflect each other and appear often to be identical, yet where enough asymmetry remains to reveal the fact of doubleness (Irigaray's *"living* mirrors"). The title, **"Ada,"** offers an image of this half-symmetry, where the two "a"s represent the same letter, yet where one letter at any point is capital, the other small.

The representation in **"Ada"** of this linguistic, erotic, and almost continually epiphanic relationship allows us a partial glimpse into the lifelong dialogue between Stein and her companion and lover, Alice Toklas. This dialogue occurred outside the page, yet finds a significant place on the page as well. Although it is important not to reduce Stein's literary forms to biography, it is equally important to remember that, for Stein, relationships of mutual dialogue such as the one in **"Ada"** bore a resemblance to an actual relationship that surrounded, nurtured, and in a sense continued her writing. The fluctuating boundary between self and other recorded in **"Ada"** finds a corollary in Stein's playful mingling of art and life. As Neil Schmitz has suggested, Alice found her way into Stein's writing not only as a listening presence, but as a telling one as well, whose daily words appear to have been received by Stein and interwoven with her own. In this sense, Stein's writing partakes of dialogue in its very creation. (pp. 54-71)

> *Harriet Scott Chessman, in her* The Public Is Invited to Dance: Representation, the Body, and Dialogue in Gertrude Stein, *Stanford University Press, 1989, 248 p.*

Bettina L. Knapp (essay date 1990)

[*Knapp is an American critic specializing in modern French literature. In the following excerpt, she presents an overview of Stein's achievements.*]

The mere mention of the name of Gertrude Stein immediately brings to mind "a rose is a rose is a rose" or "pigeons on the grass alas." It also recalls some of her eponyms, "the Mother Goose of Montparnasse" or the "Sibyl of Montparnasse." Visions of the apartment and studio she shared with her brother, Leo, at 27, rue de Fleurus in Paris also take shape as one imagines such giants as Picasso, Matisse, Francis Picabia, and Juan Gris gracing their home at the turn of the century. Nor must one minimize the importance of such American visitors as Sherwood Anderson, F. Scott Fitzgerald, William Carlos Williams, Virgil Thomson, and Ernest Hemingway.

Stein was an institution. She was an era unto herself—unforgettable, spectacular, revolutionary in every sense of the world. She invigorated language and refused to conform to the provisional culture of nineteenth-century America, referred to so derogatorily by Henry James as that "circumference of civilization." Europe and particularly France seemed just the right place to go at that time for inspiration and for something equally rare: freedom of expression. Furthermore, it was in the American tradition for writers to spend long periods of time abroad, as did James Fenimore Cooper, Nathaniel Hawthorne, Margaret Fuller, T. S. Eliot, Archibald MacLeish, Richard Wright, Ernest Hemingway, Henry Miller, and others.

Virtuoso that she was, Stein mocked all literary conventions: punctuation, syntax, grammar. By violating everything that was familiar to readers, she established new speech connections and remade language. Seemingly indifferent to the impression she made on the literati of her day, she forged ahead, dislocating, deconstructing, dismantling, fragmenting, and assaulting popular modes. So revolutionary was her way that T. S. Eliot, when visiting her in Paris, asked her the name of her mentor. He wanted to know who had advised her to use so many dangling participles. With pride she replied, "Henry James."

Her radical departure from nineteenth-century discourse, from logical and causal reasoning and thought processes, created a whole new approach to both writing and reading. No longer could readers remain passive recipients of whatever was narrated. Nor could they thrill to the excitement and suspense of coming events. Some were shocked and perplexed by the many repetitions and variants of these that they saw imprinted on the page; others were confused by what they considered simplistic banalities and her use of popular, everyday words and phrases intended to convey something complex. There were those who were angered by what they considered to be traps and masks hiding some esoteric knowledge; and, finally, there were readers who were frankly bored by what they considered dull and endless verbiage.

Stein knew well what she was doing. Her course was involved. First, she put the *word* through a wringer. Once cleansed of its barnacles—those nineteenth-century stale and worn appendages that had taken the very *livingness* and newness out of it—the word was reexamined and reevaluated. Genres such as the novella, novel, poetry, and theater, also went through the same severe, sometimes triturating, process. Banished was the well-made plot with its suspenseful episodes and slackening aftermaths designed to carry readers along. Gone were characterizations and highly polished texts that had once delectated the readers of Stendhal, Balzac, and Flaubert in France; of Melville and Hawthorne in the United States; of the Brontës, Thackeray, and Dickens in England. What did Stein offer instead? No plot, no representationalism, no causal sequences of events, and non-referential, therefore self-contained, movement. To add to the complexities, which Stein considered simplifications and clarifications, were the virtually infinite repetitions and their variations. No transitions. No connections. No sense of progress. Rather than espousing mimetism, Stein devalued the world to create a magical realm, an atmosphere, a landscape of her own. Unlike the surrealists, however, she was not fixated on the unconscious—at least, not consciously so. Her reality was composed of abstract temporal and spatial positions lived in a *continuous present.* Thus did she invite readers to view fragments of a life—or lives—drawn from past, present, and future time frames, each exposing continuously new elements within a character who anyway contains them *all.*

Important as well was the interdisciplinary nature of many of Stein's works, notably her short story, **"Melanctha"** and her verbal portraits of Picasso, Matisse, Cézanne, Apollinaire, and others. Cézanne was her guide in the writing process, she tells us in her ***Autobiography of Alice B. Toklas.*** From him, she learned to geometricize sensation, to do away with compositional hierarchies and the notion of a central idea as the pivotal element of a canvas or writing venture. Each segment of her novels, plays, and novellas was considered as important as the next and thus she created a kind of *text-object*. Her use of the triangle and the square was hidden within the very structure of such novellas as ***Q.E.D.*** and ***Fernhurst***, and was accentuated in ***Three Lives***. Her intent was to "re-create" nature through a simplification of forms right down to their basic geometric equivalents. In so doing, she developed new narrative spatial patterns within which her characters stopped, talked, or loved, while inviting readers to observe them from continuously shifting vantage points. Nothing was static, yet all was immobile—printed in the word.

From Picasso and his cubist paintings, Stein learned to emphasize still lifes and to use commonplace objects, such as potatoes or asparagus, to garnish her slim volume of poems, ***Tender Buttons***. For her, however, these very same objects were also endowed with cerebral, spiritual, and sexual equivalents. Nevertheless, no defining or ordering of words in logical and understandable groupings is evident. As Picasso, Georges Braque, and Gris created their collages, so Stein generated her own reality in the word, which she viewed as a *thing* in and of itself. Be it in her poems (***Tender Buttons***), her novels, (***A Novel of Thank You***), or her plays (***Capital Capitals***), words were non-referential, non-relational, non-ideational, non-illusionist. The word replicated the essence or inherent nature of the object.

Because visual, vocal, and verbal qualities were fused in Stein's writings, she succeeded in breaking new ground by doing away with noun-referents that would have involved memory and therefore a tying to a past. Other parts of speech—adjectives, adverbs, conjunctions, and the like—were used by her to obliterate any and all of language's sign-functions. Free-flowing, her writings became so abstruse that Stein suggested relying on associational connections and internal and interlocking relationships as an indication of the person's or the object's immanence, rather than on traditional grammatical and syntactical order.

Stein may certainly be looked upon as a precursor of the French "New Novelists": Michel Butor, Alain Robbe-Grillet, Nathalie Sarraute, Marguerite Duras, and Robert Pinget. Although drastically different from one another, they were homogeneous in their desire to eradicate the nineteenth-century traditional genres. Like Stein, their disembodied characters make their plotless ways through a non-referential, non-narrative, and highly repetitive world. The abolition of chronological time and conventional spatial concepts serve further to increase the contradictory, troubling, and mysterious elements implicit in their works. The Steinian puzzles, replete in such novels as ***The Making of Americans, A Long Gay Book, Many Many Women, Mrs. Reynolds***, make significations difficult to grasp. Her partial goal, like that of the "New Novelists," was to discover the secrets of that nearly mathematical order lying hidden behind the world of appearances. Other contemporary writers, such as Claude Ollier, who also treads Stein's path, seek to create an atmosphere in which the author becomes nonexistent. The world presented to the reader is embedded in a plethora of floating and non-referential descriptive details revolving around gestures, discourses, events, and souvenirs—leaving the reader thoroughly disoriented.

Is such writing to be considered alienating from society? If so, one may consider *Steinese* as having influenced not only a whole "Lost Generation," as Hemingway noted in *The Sun Also Rises*, but the "Beat Generation," such as Jack Kerouac and Allen Ginsberg. (She, however, did not indulge in drugs or in liquor, which she knew diminished the lucidity of the creative artist.) Elements of *Steinese* are also to be found in Kurt Vonnegut's works and in those of William Burroughs and others.

Stein's verbal gymnastics, as contained in ***A Long Gay Book, Many Many Women***, and much of her poetry, are also reminiscent of some of the writings of Raymond Queneau, the founder of the Workshop for Potential Literature (*OLIPO*). Resorting to secret systems, self-contained and interconnecting fantasies, his computerized perimathematical fiction and poetry and ultramechanical literary works allow little room for the imagination to play.

Stein's theater may also be considered a forerunner, to a certain extent, of the works of such dramatists as Eugène Ionesco, Arthur Adamov, Fernando Arrabal, Samuel Beckett, and Harold Pinter. Her seventy-seven anti-literary and anti-theatrical plays subvert language. Humor is hard and biting. No plot, no characters, no logic in the sequence of events. No transitions. No connections. No empathy. No anthropomorphism. Actors, in such theatrical works as ***What Happened, a Play, Four Saints in Three Acts***, and ***Doctor Faustus Lights the Lights***, are the words themselves.

And then, there are many other delectable *things* about Stein's writings that not only keep contemporary readers enthralled but irritate them as well. And then, and then, and then—to indulge in a little *Steinese*. To quote her once again: "Also there is why is it that in this epoch the only real literary thinking has been done by a woman." (pp. 7-11)

Bettina L. Knapp, in her Gertrude Stein, Continuum, *1990, 201 p.*

FURTHER READING

Bibliography

Liston, Maureen R. *Gertrude Stein: An Annotated Critical Bibliography.* Serif Series: Bibliographies and Checklists, No. 35. Kent, Ohio: Kent State University Press, 1979, 230 p.
    Evaluates selected bibliographies, biographies, and criticism published through early 1978.

Wilson, Robert A. *Gertrude Stein: A Bibliography.* New York: Phoenix Bookshop, 1974, 227 p.
    Lists works by Stein; translations, musical settings, and recordings of her works; selected criticism and biograph-

ical materials about Stein; and works published by Alice B. Toklas.

Biography

Brinnin, John Malcolm. *The Third Rose: Gertrude Stein and Her World.* Boston: Little, Brown, and Co., 1959, 427 p.

An early critical biography of Stein.

Hobhouse, Janet. *Everybody Who Was Anybody: A Biography of Gertrude Stein.* New York: G. P. Putnam's Sons, 1975, 244 p.

A detailed, noncritical biography of Stein.

Criticism

Bowers, Jane Palatini. *"They Watch Me as They Watch This": Gertrude Stein's Metadrama.* Philadelphia: University of Pennsylvania Press, 1991, 169 p.

Proposes that Stein's experimental "drama about drama" and the emphasis in her plays of language over other theatrical devices were attempts to prevent action from dominating and overwhelming the texts of her dramas.

Bridgman, Richard. *Gertrude Stein in Pieces.* New York: Oxford University Press, 1970, 411 p.

Attempts to assess Stein's achievement through a "systematic reading" of her oeuvre.

Burke, Carolyn. "Gertrude Stein, the Cone Sisters, and the Puzzle of Female Friendship." *Critical Inquiry* 8, No. 3 (Spring 1982): 543-64.

Analyzes the effect of Stein's relationships with Etta and Claribel Cone on the depictions of female friendships in Stein's early novels.

DeKoven, Marianne. *A Different Language: Gertrude Stein's Experimental Writing.* Madison: University of Wisconsin Press, 1983, 175 p.

Argues that Stein's experimental writing is a multifaceted body of "largely successful" antipatriarchal literature encompassing many different styles.

Doane, Janice L. *Silence and Narrative: The Early Novels of Gertrude Stein.* Contributions in Women's Studies, No. 62. Westport, Conn.: Greenwood Press, 1986, 163 p.

Scrutinizes Stein's use of and attitudes toward silence in *Q.E.D., Fernhurst, Three Lives,* and *The Making of Americans.*

Dubnick, Randa. *The Structure of Obscurity: Gertrude Stein, Language, and Cubism.* Urbana: University of Illinois Press, 1984, 163 p.

Uses structuralist techniques and comparisons with Cubism to study Stein's distinction between prose and poetry in her works.

Mossberg, Barbara Clarke. "A Rose in Context: The Daughter Construct." In *Historical Studies and Literary Criticism,* edited by Jerome J. McGann, pp. 199-225. Madison: University of Wisconsin Press, 1985.

Interprets Stein, Emily Dickinson, Anne Sexton, and Sylvia Plath as women who identify themselves primarily as daughters, frame their art in that identity, and consequently share common images, attitudes, themes, and voices in their works.

Perloff, Marjorie. "Poetry as Word-System: The Art of Gertrude Stein." In her *The Poetics of Indeterminacy: Rimbaud to Cage,* pp. 67-108. Princeton, N. J.: Princeton University Press, 1981.

Discusses the similarity of the language in Stein's poems to Cubism's visual "instability, indeterminancy, and incoherence."

Saldívar-Hull, Sonia. "Wrestling Your Ally: Stein, Racism, and Feminist Critical Practice." In *Women's Writing in Exile,* edited by Mary Lynn Broe and Angela Ingram, pp. 181-98. Chapel Hill: University of North Carolina Press, 1989.

Maintains that Stein was a "white supremacist," "racist," classist author whose works "[kill] the dignity of women of color and working-class women."

Schmitz, Neil. *Of Huck and Alice: Humorous Writing in American Literature.* Minneapolis: University of Minnesota Press, 1983, 268 p.

Two chapters on Stein explore her use of humor and wordplay as tools for investigating reality.

Additional coverage of Stein's life and career is contained in the following sources published by Gale Research: *Concise Dictionary of American Literary Biography, 1917-1929*; *Contemporary Authors,* Vols. 104, 132; *Dictionary of Literary Biography,* Vols. 4, 54, 86; *Major 20th-Century Writers*; *Twentieth-Century Literary Criticism,* Vols. 1, 6, 28; and *World Literature Criticism.*

Preston Sturges
1898-1959

(Born Edmund Preston Biden) American film director, screenwriter, playwright, and autobiographer.

INTRODUCTION

Sturges is considered a master of American film comedy. He combined sophisticated dialogue with a slapstick visual style and a modern sense of narrative structure to create distinctive examples of the "screwball comedy" genre. Despite evidence of a decline in his talents toward the end of his career, the eight films he wrote and directed between 1940 and 1944 established him as one of the world's best filmmakers: a comedy director ranking with Ernst Lubitsch and Frank Capra, and a writer-director whom some critics have compared with Orson Welles.

Sturges was born in Chicago to a traveling salesman and his wife, who were divorced after a year which Sturges's mother spent mainly in Europe. After her marriage to a successful stock broker, she founded "Maison Desti," a perfumery and cosmetics firm based in Paris. Because of his mother's peripatetic lifestyle and his shuttling between parents, Sturges's education was unstructured and irregular, consisting of short stays at private schools in Europe and countless museum trips with his mother. The "Sturges myth," which was promulgated by studio publicity and James Agee's influential essays, derives in part from his supposed hatred of European art, to which he was exposed by his mother, and his admiration for his wealthy American businessman stepfather, Solomon Sturges.

After serving as a pilot in the United States Signal Corps in World War I, an experience which inspired him to draw and patent the plans for an experimental helicopter, Sturges became manager of one of his mother's cosmetics stores in New York. Like his mother, Sturges preferred inventing and experimenting to managing a business, and, despite the success of the "kiss-proof" lipstick he created, the entire "Maison Desti" business failed a few years later. After a severe case of appendicitis from which he nearly died, Sturges did a great deal of reading and decided to pursue a career as a writer. An argument he had with an actress, who claimed that she could write a more successful play than he could, inspired him to write his first play, *The Guinea Pig*. Its modest, surprising success off-Broadway encouraged Sturges to write a second play, *Strictly Dishonorable*, which ran for 557 performances beginning in 1929. The popularity of this play brought offers to write for films. Sturges accepted an offer from Paramount's New York office after the failures of his third play *Recapture*, and *The Well of Romance*, an opera for which he wrote the libretto. In 1932, when he was offered more than $40,000 each for the film rights to *Strictly Dishonor-

able* and *Child of Manhattan*, his latest play, Sturges moved to Hollywood.

From 1933 to 1940 Sturges worked mainly with other writers fixing flawed screenplays and collaborating on adaptations. As a hired writer he was not afforded many opportunities to work on his own projects; however, during this time he wrote the screenplays for *The Power and the Glory* and *Easy Living*, which are considered among his best works. In 1940 he submitted the screenplay for *The Great McGinty* to Paramount, offering to accept a salary of one dollar if he could direct the film; the producer offered him ten dollars, and Sturges became one of the few writers of that era to direct his own screenplays. From 1940 to 1944 Sturges wrote, directed, and produced eight extremely popular and critically acclaimed films. Many critics have remarked that the quality of Sturges's work in this short period of time is unique in American film. He won the Academy Award for Best Screenplay for *The Great McGinty* and was nominated for *The Miracle of Morgan's Creek* and *Hail the Conquering Hero*. In 1946 Sturges formed an independent production company with Howard Hughes. The first film they produced, *The Sin of Harold Diddlebock*, was neither a critical nor commercial success. Despite his assurance that Sturges would have creative control, Hughes re-edited and re-released the film three years later under the title *Mad Wednesday.* The film also failed in its second version and, in either form, is generally seen as the beginning of Sturges's creative decline. Of the remaining three films Sturges made, only *Unfaithfully Yours* is well regarded now. In addition to his film work in the 1940s, Sturges was an avid yachtsman and restaurateur; as commentators have noted, Sturges lived the life of the stereotypical Hollywood director. He died at the age of sixty trying to revive his career in the film business.

Sturges's screenplay for *The Power and the Glory* is his one entirely serious work. In plot it is similar to *Citizen Kane,* and critics believe that Sturges wrote the screenplay as an experiment in narrative structure. The story of powerful industrialist Tom Garner, played by Spencer Tracy, the film progresses in a series of flashbacks depicting episodes from Garner's life in the seemingly random order of a conversation. The story ignores chronology in favor of a structure that facilitates the juxtaposition of significant events. Sturges used this technique to great effect in films he later directed. For example, *The Great McGinty* has a flashback structure which is used to condense a "rise and fall" story to its essentials and to provide a punchline when the fates of the main characters are revealed. Even in the films that do not use a flashback structure, Sturges's editing style—based on principles from the silent slapstick comedies of Mack Sennett—juxtaposed significant events within a chronological narrative and maintained a breakneck pace by disregarding the traditional practice of letting scenes develop from beginning to end. Critics note that the "Keystone Cops" feel of many of Sturges's films is a result of this aggressive editing style.

Perhaps the most distinctive features of Sturges's work are his dialogue and his characters. Sturges employed a regular group of actors for mainly secondary, "character" parts. Among the most well known of these actors were William Demarest and Franklin Pangborn, who frequently steal scenes from the stars of Sturges's films by virtue of their striking physical appearance and a few good lines. In *The Miracle of Morgan's Creek,* Demarest, the town's no-nonsense, crusty policeman who is constantly vexed by his two daughters, delivers a monologue denouncing daughters, fatherhood, and marriage. As he explains to the character played by Eddie Bracken: "Wait till you get married and have half a dozen daughters. . . . They're a mess no matter how you look at 'em . . . a headache till they get married . . . If they get married and after that they get worse . . . Either they leave their husbands and come back with four children and move into your guest room, or their husband loses his job and the whole *caboodle* comes back. . . . Or else they're so homely you can't get rid of them at all and they hang around the house like Spanish Moss and shame you into an early grave." In *The Palm Beach Story,* a rich old man known as the "Weenie King" eloquently tells Claudette Colbert about growing old and concludes by saying, "that's not easy to say with false teeth."

Sturges's critical reputation rests primarily on the dialogue, structure, and fast, sure-handed pacing of his films. Critics note that Sturges, unlike Frank Capra, for example, was unconcerned with "messages" and ideology. Although themes such as success, patriotism, and the hypocrisy of politics show up in many of Sturges's films, they are there to serve as the backdrops for his screwball comedies of error, providing Sturges with a frame of reference and set of comedic situations. Often thought of as a satirist of American mores, as a kind of Hollywood Mark Twain, he is just as often viewed as a brilliant entertainer, poking fun at sacred cows for sheer laughs.

PRINCIPAL WORKS

The Guinea Pig (drama) 1929
Strictly Dishonorable (drama) 1929
*The Big Pond (screenplay) 1930
*Fast and Loose (screenplay) 1930
Recapture (drama) 1930
The Well of Romance (opera libretto) 1930
Child of Manhattan (drama) 1932
The Power and the Glory (screenplay) 1933
They Just Had to Get Married (screenplay) 1933
Imitation of Life (screenplay) 1934
Thirty Day Princess [with Frank Partos] (screenplay) 1934
We Live Again [with Maxwell Anderson, Leonard Praskins, and Thornton Wilder] (screenplay) 1934
Diamond Jim (screenplay) 1935
The Good Fairy (screenplay) 1935
Love Before Breakfast (screenplay) 1936
Next Time We Love (screenplay) 1936
College Swing (screenplay) 1937
Easy Living (screenplay) 1937
Hotel Haywire [with Lillie Hayward] (screenplay) 1937
If I Were King (screenplay) 1938
Port of Seven Seas [with Ernest Vajda] (screenplay) 1938
Never Say Die [with Don Hartman and Frank Butler] (screenplay) 1939
†*Christmas in July* (screenplay) 1940
†*The Great McGinty* (screenplay) 1940
Remember the Night (screenplay) 1940
†*The Lady Eve* (screenplay) 1941
†*The Palm Beach Story* (screenplay) 1942
†*Sullivan's Travels* (screenplay) 1942
†*The Great Moment* (screenplay) 1944
†*Hail the Conquering Hero* (screenplay) 1944
†*The Miracle of Morgan's Creek* (screenplay) 1944
†*The Sin of Harold Diddlebock* (screenplay) 1947; also released as *Mad Wednesday,* 1950
†*Unfaithfully Yours* (screenplay) 1948
†*The Beautiful Blond from Bashful Bend* (screenplay) 1949
†*Les Carnets du Major Thompson* (screenplay) 1955; also released as *The French They Are a Funny Race,* 1957

‡*Five Screenplays by Preston Sturges* (screenplays) 1985

Preston Sturges by Preston Sturges (autobiography) 1990

*Sturges wrote only the dialogue for these films.

†These films were directed by Sturges.

‡This volume includes screenplays of *The Great McGinty, Christmas in July, The Lady Eve, Sullivan's Travels,* and *Hail the Conquering Hero.*

CRITICISM

James Agee (essay date 1944)

[*Agee was an American journalist, novelist, screenwriter, and film critic. His most famous works include* Let Us Now Praise Famous Men *(1941), in which he and the photographer Walker Evans documented rural poverty in the "dust bowl" regions of the American south, and the screenplays for the films* The African Queen *(1951) and* The Night of the Hunter *(1955). In the following review of* The Miracle of Morgan's Creek, *Agee's admiration for the film is tempered by what he perceives as Sturges's shortcomings as a filmmaker.*]

The Miracle of Morgan's Creek, the new Preston Sturges film, seems to me funnier, more adventurous, more abundant, more intelligent, and more encouraging than anything that has been made in Hollywood for years. Yet the more I think of it, the less I esteem it. I have, then, both to praise and defend it, and to attack it.

The essential story is hardly what you would expect to see on an American screen: a volcanically burgeoning small-town girl (Betty Hutton) gets drunk and is impregnated by one of several soldiers, she can't remember which; her father (William Demarest), her younger sister (Diana Lynn), and her devoted 4-F lover (Eddie Bracken) do all they can to help her out; the result is a shambles, from which they are delivered by a "miracle" which entails its own cynical comments on the sanctity of law, order, parenthood, and the American home—to say nothing of a number of cherished pseudo-folk beliefs about bright-lipped youth, childhood sweethearts, Mister Right, and the glamor of war. Sturges tells this story according to a sound principle which has been neglected in Hollywood—except by him—for a long time: in proportion to the inanity and repressiveness of the age you live in, play the age as comedy if you want to get away with murder. The girl's name, Trudy Kockenlocker, of itself relegates her to a comic-strip world in which nothing need be regarded as real; the characters themselves are extremely stylized—a skipping little heifer, a choleric father, an updated Florence Atwater, a classical all-American dope; and the wildly factitious story makes comic virtues of every censor-dodging necessity. Thanks to these devices the Hays office has been either hypnotized into a liberality for which it should be thanked, or has been raped in its sleep.

Having set up these formalized characters, each in a different comic key, and this thin-ice version of the story he is really telling, Sturges has just begun. He also doubles the characters on their own trails, into sharp pathos, into slapstick (some of which falls flat), into farce as daftly unsettling as being licked to death by a lioness, to the edge of tragi-comedy, and into moments of comedy which could emerge only from their full quality as human beings. He plays every twist of his story for sharp realism as well as laughs; his small-town doctor, banker, lawyer, and, most notably, Porter Hall as a justice of the peace are bits of comic realism finely graded against the chameleonlike principals. Above all, Sturges carries farther than he has ever done before his bold blends and clashes of comic and realistic angles of attack. In a typically fine scene on Christmas Eve, when Trudy's pregnancy has developed the comic-emotional portentousness of a delayed-action bomb, he manages to sustain an atmosphere of really tender pathos and, at the same time, (1) to cue in "Silent Night," (2) to show irate Constable Kockenlocker hammering the hell out of a recalcitrant Christmas star, (3) to let him comfort his restive daughter with the noble reminder (deleted the second time I saw the film) "You may be waiting for the President of the United States," and (4) to cap that, for Bethlemayhem, by having young Emily inquire, gently, what that cow is doing in the kitchen.

Besides resonating many traditions of comedy against a firm basic realism, the film rests on an apparently complex emotional and philosophic base which seems to me not really complex but simply mature, being—on its smaller scale—at once as nihilistic as Céline, at least as deeply humane as Dickens, and at all times inviolably, genuinely, and intelligently gay. Excepting a few moments when Sturges forces everything too far, the film is also beautifully played, especially by William Demarest, whose performance stands with Paul Lukas's in *The Watch on the Rhine* among the finest I have seen.

But you may, I have to realize, disagree with me. I have incredulously heard some people dismiss the show as "comedy"; they should stick to something really vital and serious like *Zola*. Others feel it is too frantic and too rough; it has enough mental, creative, and merely brutal energy for a hundred average pictures. Others object to various errors of taste, mainly connected with making laughs out of pregnancy. Here again I partly agree; but I would rather see pregnancy remain a subject for questionable laughter than see it become taboo against any laughter at all. Still others dislike the film for its multiple attack, its shiftiness of style; but if you accept that principle in Joyce or in Picasso, you will examine with interest how brilliantly it can be applied in moving pictures and how equally promising, as against the lovely euphonies René Clair achieved according to the same principle, astute cacophony can be. For barring Chaplin's this seems to me the largest American attempt, on the level of full consciousness, to stir up from the bottom the whole history and possibility of moving pictures into one broth; to draw, like Clair, on the blackloam, instinctive genius of the

Mack Sennett comedies; and to amuse and excite the simplest at once with the most complex customers. In fact, in the degree that this film is disliked by those who see it, whether consciously or passively, I see a measure less of its inadequacies than of the progress of that terrible softening, solemnity, and idealization which, increasing over several years, has all but put an end to the output and intake of good moving pictures in this country.

Yet the more I think about the film, the less I like it. There are too many things that Sturges, once he had won all the victories and set all the things moving which he managed to here, should have achieved unhindered, purely as a good artist; and he has not even attempted them. He is a great broken-field runner; once the field is clear he sits down and laughs. The whole tone of the dialogue, funny and bright as it often is, rests too safely within the pseudo-cute, pseudo-authentic, patronizing diction perfected by Booth Tarkington. And in the stylization of action as well as language it seems to me clear that Sturges holds his characters, and the people they comically represent, and their predicament, and his audience, and the best potentialities of his own work, essentially in contempt. His emotions, his intelligence, his aesthetic ability never fully commit themselves; all the playfulness becomes rather an avoidance of commitment than an extension of means for it. Cynicism, which gives the film much of its virtue, also has it by the throat; the nihilism, the humaneness, even the gaiety become, in that light, mere postures and tones of voices; and whereas nearly all the mischief is successful, nearly every central and final responsibility is shirked. Of course there is always the danger, in trying to meet those ultimate human and aesthetic responsibilities, of losing your gaiety; but that never happened to Mozart—or to René Clair at his best.

I mention Clair again because Sturges has so many similar abilities so richly—and because there is such a difference between the two. Whether or not he ever makes another film under favorable circumstances, and up to his best, Clair is one of the few great artists of this century. Sturges, in his middle forties, is still just the most gifted American working in films, vividly successful in the kind of artful-dodging which frustrates Clair; hollow and evasive at those centers in which Clair is so firm. I suspect that Sturges feels that conscience and comedy are incompatible. It would be hard for a man of talent to make a more self-destructive mistake. (pp. 73-6)

James Agee, in a review of "The Miracle of Morgan's Creek," in his Agee on Film: Reviews and Comments, Vol. I, *Grosset & Dunlap, 1969, pp. 73-6.*

James Agee (essay date 1944)

[*In the following review of* Hail the Conquering Hero, *Agee argues that Sturges failed to realize his full artistic promise.*]

Hail The Conquering Hero is the story of a pitiful discard from the Marines (Eddie Bracken) who, helped and forced by a group of marines just back from Guadalcanal, returns as a false hero to his mother and his girl and his home town just before a local election, is put up for mayor against his guilty will, endures a day of comic-satiric hell which includes three extraordinary civic speeches, and at length, in an awful public confession, makes a genuine hero of himself. It is a bewilderingly skilful picture, and the skill is used no more brilliantly to tell the story than to cover up the story's weaknesses and those of its author, Preston Sturges.

If the story is to tell itself at all, and keep going to feature length, everything depends on the marines who befriend and bully Mr. Bracken into it. But Sturges never lets you know why they are forcing their victim through the show. What Sturges does instead, though, is both interesting and highly characteristic of him. Getting Bracken home in the first place forces him to invent one of his most arresting characters, a psychopathic marine, embodied by the ex-boxer Freddie Steele with a legendary, almost supernatural quality of serene, unfathomable, frightening energy. This marine happens to feel a maniacal reverence toward mothers, and shocked into fury by the hero's neglect of his own mother, he sets everything moving. Once they are all in the small town and the young man is desperately eager to clear up the misunderstanding, Sturges shifts the weight to a marine sergeant played by William Demarest, whose great skill in registering a kind of daft innocence and brutal sentimentality, helped by Sturges, can make you believe anything.

Here, however, you hardly know what to believe, for Sturges takes care never to give Demarest time for more than a hint and a laugh. Unless we are to believe that the sergeant is simply so maddened by all the homely excitement that he refuses to let either himself or Bracken jump off the merry-go-round, his motives would have to be of Dostoevskian cruelty and mysteriousness to hold water at all; but of this possibility the hints are so vague that I suspect myself of supplying them. The long and the short of it is that the more you think of the evidence supplied you the less you understand why the marines are there, and why you ever believed it at all. The trick here, a favorite one with Sturges, is to keep everything so jotted, so shrewdly and ambiguously shaded, so rapid, and so briskly full of irrelevant pleasures, that you neither think nor care to, at all. Flickers of motive, most of them faked or questionable, succeed each other so restively that like the successive frames of a strip of film they create an illusory flowing image of motive which one is liable to swallow whole at the time. But in thoroughly good pieces of work there is an aesthetic and moral discipline which, however richly it indulges in certain kinds of illusion, strictly forbids itself others. It never fakes or dodges a motive, a character, an emotion, or an idea. And it never uses its power to entertain as an ace-in-the-hole against one's objection to that sort of faking.

I'd like not to be so owlish about a picture which gave me so much more delight than displeasure, but now that Sturges is being compared, I am told, with people like Voltaire—there are semi-defensible reasons to compare him with Shakespeare, for that matter—I think there is some point in putting on the brakes. Most certainly Sturges has fine comic and satiric gifts, and knows how to tell more truth than that when he thinks it expedient; but he seldom does. This film has enough themes for half a dozen first-rate American satires—the crippling myth of the dead heroic father, the gentle tyranny of the widowed mother, the predicament of the only child, the questionable nature of most heroism, the political function of returning soldiers, these are just a few; I suppose in a sense the whole story is a sort of *Coriolanus* on all fours. But not one of these themes is honored by more attention than you get from an incontinent barber in a railway terminal, and the main theme, which I take to be a study of honor, is dishonored by every nightingale in Sturges's belfry. When Bracken makes his strongly written, beautifully spoken confession, his fellow-townsmen, persuaded by the sergeant and their own best citizen, promptly make him mayor. This is doubtless supposed to pass as irony, since the townspeople and by implication the general audience, not to say the American voting public, are represented as incurable jackasses. But jackasses or not, people in small towns don't reward virtue in any such way; so I'm sorry to see them rewarding Mr. Sturges.

The small-town types themselves, by the way, smartly cast and dressed and detailed and edited as they are, are very little nearer genuine small-town than Broadway is. The Mayor is so well played by Raymond Walburn that it is impossible to take him simply as a meaningful figure of satire. The hero's girl (Ella Raines), after some well and cruelly drawn phases of mixed motive, comes through solid gold when he is at his nadir. The two bits which best survive all of Sturges's deviousness are a paralyzingly high-charged, many-sided moment in which Bracken hits the psychopath, and Franklin Pangborn's unemphasized, terribly sad, and revealing shifts of face as he reflects Bracken's confession in the depths of the character he plays. Sturges is by far the smartest man for casting in Hollywood; this use of Pangborn, an extremely fine actor, is the one thing that improves on his role in *The Bank Dick*.

Any adequate review of this remarkable movie would devote at least as much space to its unqualified praise as I have to qualifying the praise; it would have to spend more space than that, I think getting at even a tentative explanation of why Sturges functions as he does. "Hollywood" is no explanation, surely; "Hollywood" was made for Sturges and he in turn is its apotheosis; but why? It seems to me that Sturges had reason, through his mother, to develop, as they caromed around high-Bohemian Europe during his childhood, from opera to opera and gallery to gallery, not only his singular mercurialism and resourcefulness, which come especially natural to some miserably unhappy children, but also a retching, permanently incurable loathing for everything that stank of "culture," of "art." I gather further that through his stepfather, a stable and charming Chicago sportsman and business man, he developed an all but desperate respect and hunger for success, enhanced by a sickening string of failures as a business man and inventor up to the age of about thirty; and that this again assumed the dimensions of a complex. I believe that in his curious career as a never-quite-artist of not-quite-genius he has managed to release and guide the energies of these influences in the only way open to him.

I hesitate to write this sort of thing, drawn only from such superficialities as have appeared in print and from some remarkable photographs of Sturges as a child and young man which appeared in the *Saturday Evening Post;* but I risk the worse than questionable taste because I see no other way to understand what Sturges's films are about. They are wonderful as comedies and they are wonderfully complex and ingenious; they seem to me also wonderfully, uncontrollably, almost proudly corrupt, vengeful, fearful of intactness and self-commitment; most essentially, they are paradoxical marvels of self-perpetuation and self-destruction; their mastering object, aside from success, seems to be to sail as steep into the wind as possible without for an instant incurring the disaster of becoming seriously, wholly acceptable as art. They seem to me, indeed, in much of their twisting, the elaborately counterpointed image of a neurosis. It is an especially interesting neurosis, not only because Sturges is a man of such talent and not only because it expresses itself in such fecund and in themselves suggestive images, but also because, in relation to art, it seems the definitive expression of this country at present—the stranglehold wedlock of the American female tradition of "culture," the male tradition of "success."

For East is East, and West is West, and Maggie and I are out. (pp. 114-17)

> *James Agee, in a review of "Hail the Conquering Hero," in his* Agee on Film: Reviews and Comments, Vol. I, *Grosset & Dunlap, 1969, pp. 114-17.*

André Bazin (essay date 1948)

[*Bazin was a French film critic. His numerous reviews, theoretical essays, and book-length studies had decisive influence on the work of the* nouvelle vague *directors and critics, including François Truffaut, Jean-Luc Godard, and Eric Rohmer. In the following essay on* Sullivan's Travels, *Bazin comments on Sturges's strengths and weaknesses as a filmmaker.*]

In the months following the Liberation, when the number of American films being shown in France was still relatively low, we were told that Hollywood had—since the time we had lost track of it—been blessed by two sensational directors, Orson Welles and Preston Sturges. Our curiosity is now satisfied. We have seen everything by Welles that is worth seeing. After ***Sullivan's Travels, Christmas in July, The Palm Beach Story,*** and ***The Lady Eve,*** we have also been able to recognize Preston Sturges' inspiration as well as talent.

The last three films were not very successful in France. ***Christmas in July,*** after a good run in Paris, only reached the provinces through art theaters and did not always find a receptive audience there, either. ***The Palm Beach Story*** and ***The Lady Eve*** passed by pretty much unnoticed.

If Sturges' originality did not engender the enthusiasm and controversy that Welles's did, it is perhaps because his originality was less majestic and it must undoubtedly have been misunderstood. His scripts and directing seem to continue in the tradition of American comedy, and while they are unquestionably more intellectual, that very aspect renders his humor less accessible to the European public. His extremely slight subjects, pure pretexts for gags and predicaments, did not demand as much thought as Capra's films did. Thus it was hardly noticed that ***Christmas in July*** showed an important evolution in the specific Hollywood genre known as "American comedy." With its format and its old heroes, American comedy eked out a laborious existence.

Capra was falling with a great crash amid the broken promises of his leanings. From time to time, a "William Powell-Myrna Loy" duo still made us smile a bit, as much at them as at our memories.

In *The Best Years of Our Lives* (1946), when Teresa Wright tells them they were always lucky in love, we missed some of the dialogue between Fredric March and Myrna Loy. They smile, remembering how often they thought they hated each other and had decided to break up. For the American audience, who knew them well, the numerous comedies involving these two actors made them laugh at their constant flirtations with divorce. For us, the war intervened. The Don Juan of comedy, Fredric March, had aged and become a dramatic actor. American comedy had grown old, like its actors, like history.

Preston Sturges is unquestionably the only director who knew how to carry on the genre by in essence reviving it.

Contrary to what it seems, comedy was in reality the most serious genre in Hollywood—in the sense that it reflected, through the comic mode, the deepest moral and social beliefs of American life. It would take too much time here to try to psychoanalyze this, but it's easy to see how the fundamental optimism of a Capra is tied to American capitalism, and how the Cinderella and Prince Charming myth has its modern counterpart in the typist and the boss's son. Through the most zany and diversified gags, an entire concept of the relationship between money, luck, and politics was implicitly implanted in the American consciousness. And it is because the war—at the very least—disturbed the naïveté and unclouded optimism of these myths that American comedy weakened and died like an uprooted tree.

Preston Sturges' genius comes from having made the most of this aging process, basing his humor and the comic principle of his gags on the sociological displacement of the classical comedy.

This shift allows him to present clearly the themes implied in prewar scripts. In ***Christmas in July,*** for example, the main protagonist is not shown on the screen. It is invisible and all-powerful luck, like God in *Athalie* [directed by Albert Capellani, 1910]. In ***The Palm Beach Story,*** the incredible wealth of a young lover carries the Prince Charming myth to the point of absurdity. Here, money appears as if in a supersaturated solution, suddenly precipitating the dissolved salt crystals.

In other words, with Sturges, the humor of the American comedy became irony. If he made use of old themes it was by forcing them to reveal themselves and thereby to be destroyed.

It remains to be seen if this was the way Preston Sturges pursued a work of social satire or if he was content with the game as it was played. ***Sullivan's Travels*** seems to answer that question once and for all.

The script is without doubt one of the most sensational ideas imaginable. A great director of American comedies, moved by the human condition, decides henceforth to write about its misery. In order to gather documentary evidence, he disguises himself as a bum and sets out with twenty-five cents in his pocket. The panic-stricken producers have him followed by a specially equipped truck to cater to his creature comforts, should the need arise. Throughout the United States the radio broadcasts daily bulletins on Sullivan's adventures in the land of poverty. After becoming infested with lice in a flophouse and riding a freight train, our scriptwriter returns to Hollywood to turn his dearly acquired "experience" into profit. It is then that an admirable dramatic surprise occurs, abruptly swinging the film in a tragic direction. Sullivan disappears the night that he is to hand out a thousand five-dollar bills to the bums, his "friends," as a publicity stunt for the film company. A train has rolled over a body which is identified as his. All Hollywood mourns its best director.

However, Sullivan has in reality been beaten and robbed by a bum and has a slight case of amnesia. He is sentenced to a few years of hard labor in some Southern state. The convict gang, the prison, and the whip are now a completely new initiation into human misery. On Sundays the convicts with records of good behavior are sometimes permitted to watch a film. It is at the movies that Sullivan discovers that laughter is the convicts' only possible escape. When his true identity is known, the great director returns to Hollywood and is entreated to write socially relevant films. Sullivan declares that the best way of being faithful to his adventure is to continue making people laugh.

We can see that such a script, which starts out as an "American comedy" and continues in a realist vein on the *same subject,* constitutes a kind of self-destruction of the genre with which it appears to be connected. But instead of mocking the laws of the genre, Sturges makes their absurdity explode retroactively. If he justifies them in the end, it is only after admitting their untruth and because this untruth is in the end a lesser evil.

Then why does ***Sullivan's Travels*** leave us unsatisfied? It is because Sturges did not dare—or was not able—to play out the game that he had begun and that he owed us. The tragic interlude does not, for directorial reasons, contain sufficient violence and authenticity. Several commercial conventions still slid in and they contradict the nature of the scenario itself. Since Hollywood was to be contrasted with reality, the script should not have contained anything from Hollywood. The tragedy should have dialectically abolished the comedy and reality should have overwhelmed the film. Only then would the final return to Hollywood have had the ironic character it needed and which would have made the viewer question Sullivan's final wisdom.

As such, however, this film clearly throws light on the meaning of Sturges' work. It has enough merits and takes enough risks for us to consider it one of the most sensational productions of the last ten years. Perhaps for the first time, Hollywood dared to make a film which satirizes American life. But its shortcomings—as much in the direction as in the script—lead us to believe that Preston Sturges still does not completely deserve his talent. (pp. 33-8)

> *André Bazin, "Sullivan's Travels," in his* The Cinema of Cruelty: From Buñuel to Hitchcock, *edited by François Truffaut, translated by Sabine d'Estrée with Tiffany Fliss, Seaver Books, 1982, pp. 33-8.*

Sturges on his career as a playwright and filmmaker:

Between flops, it is true, I have come up with an occasional hit, but compared to a good boxer's record, for instance, my percentage has been lamentable. It is a little like that of my friend Dr. Leach Cross, the great lightweight who fought when this century was new. "In my first fight," said Dr. Cross, "I got knocked out in the first round. In my second fight, I got knocked out in the second round. In my third fight, I got knocked out in the third round. I thought I was improving."

My own record was equally painful. I fought a draw in my first fight, stupefied everyone by winning the championship in my second, got a couple of wins with picture rights, then was knocked out three times in a row. Dragging my weary carcass to Hollywood, I was immediately knocked out again, won a big fight some six months later, then marked time for six years as an ordinary ham-and beaner, picking up what I could. Suddenly I saw a chance and offered to fight for the world championship for a dollar [Sturges told Paramount he would accept a salary of one dollar if he could direct ***The Great McGinty***]. To everyone's astonishment, I won that championship and defended it successfully for a number of years, winning nine times by knockout, fighting three draws, losing twice and getting one no-decision in Europe. I have just come over to America for a fight, but it was called off at the last moment, one of the promoters having gone nuts and having to have been locked up. Why I'm not walking on my heels after all this, I don't know. Maybe I *am* walking on my heels. It would be surprising if I weren't.

> *Preston Sturges, in his* Preston Sturges by Preston Sturges, *1990.*

André Bazin (essay date 1949)

[*In the following essay on* Hail the Conquering Hero, *Bazin argues that Sturges was a social satirist similar to Charlie Chaplin.*]

It is now quite clear that we must consider Preston Sturges as a moralist. His films have the demonstrative rigor of the "fable," or the didactic tale. The inhumanity of his characters and their lack of psychological complexity, which certain people see as a weakness or a limitation, actually originate from the laws of the comic genre itself. Zadig is not a character but a moral entity, a philosopher's stone which separates base metal from pure clay.

He is certainly one of those moral psychologists whose imaginary characters do not live on ethical truths alone, viz., La Bruyère.

But morality in its pure form has its own history with writings of distinction from the Middle Ages through Anatole France, by way of Voltaire. Why should Sturges be reproached for his inhumanity when his true purpose is to proclaim collective determinism and the mechanics of society, proving their foolish independence from the human truth to which they refer. All his films are an exploitation of a misunderstanding. What happens when a man is supposed to be lucky (and he believes he is)? You have ***Christmas in July.*** What happens to a great director when he plays the role of a bum and a bum who is really a writer? You have ***Sullivan's Travels.*** What does society think of a common convict, a prison escapee who is wanted in a dozen different states, when he passes himself off as the father of sextuplets (who aren't his anyway)? You have ***The Miracle at Morgan's Creek.***

Hail the Conquering Hero once again confirms Preston Sturges' harsh method: removing the alibi from the classical and inevitable development of a social predicament that it demands. The viewer, who is in on the secret, can then ascertain that everything takes place exactly as if the hero had in fact won the lottery or a prize or defended a Pacific Island all by himself. In ***Hail the Conquering Hero,*** we can search in vain for a trace of individual psychology. But Eddie Bracken can't really exist. His character does not define the void in the script that is created by his not being the man he is believed to be—a hero in the Pacific returning to his hometown. The comedy then originates from the fact that society does not perceive that what it glorifies is in fact nothing. Every one of the pseudo-hero's actions and words continue to raise him in the public's esteem. But the audience feels cheated: when deprived of its alibi, the behavior of society and men appears in all its obscene nakedness of mindless ritual and in its formalism of a liturgy without God. We are watching a curious story of deaf people in which everyone has gone fishing for the simple reason that everyone thinks that he has gone fishing.

At the risk of repeating myself, I want to stress that Sturges' films protracted American comedy because of its negative message. Frank Capra's *Mr. Smith Goes to Washington* (1939) was to us the incarnation of democratic goodwill and the power of the righteous man in a society designed to let him have the last word. Our compassionate laughter appeases our hearts as it lets us feel its throb. Thus courage, fighting for a good cause, and moral generosity always end up overthrowing the combined forces of evil. Capra illuminates American comedy. His humor derives from a mock irreverence for great principles and from a familiarity with myths. We are told that these great principles are everywhere—the odds are that they can even dance on the head of a Rockefeller's stickpin. Preston Sturges shows us in effect that they are everywhere and surround Americans on all sides. But at the same time he proves that these principles are *only* myths and their power is completely imaginary. He throws them back to the ethic they refer to in sociology: we thought they were at our service and, behold, *they* carry *us* like a cork upon the ocean.

It is not even the film as such that reveals the usurped secrets of his power. To substitute the ludicrous figure of Eddie Bracken for Gary Cooper, James Stewart, or Cary Grant is to prove to us in retrospect that our admiration originates from whatever crushes this hero in spite of himself. The crowd that unwittingly cheers a ghost, attributing to him the marvels of a superman, is our mirror image because it goes to the movies.

You may disagree and say that Preston Sturges was not too concerned about being a bitter moralist and that almost all his films, beginning with **Hail the Conquering Hero,** do finally reconcile society and is cinema worthy of Capra himself. I concede this, but it is hardly any more important than Molière's denouements. It may be that Sturges was very comfortable in the inner workings of the mythology he preferred to unmask rather than reveal. In this I would willingly see not some dubious social apostolate but, as Alexandre Astruc suggested during the *Objective 49* debate, the tardy revenge of a scriptwriter-turned-director who profits from an excess of power to let off steam. But these hypothetical considerations take nothing away from the objective content or from the consequences of a work that restores to American film a sense of social satire that I find equaled only (due allowances being made) in Chaplin's films. (pp. 41-4)

> André Bazin, "Hail the Conquering Hero," in his The Cinema of Cruelty: From Buñuel to Hitchcock, *edited by François Truffaut, translated by Sabine d'Estrée with Tiffany Fliss, Seaver Books, 1982, pp. 41-4.*

Siegfried Kracauer (essay date 1950)

[*Kracauer was a German philosopher, social critic, and writer on the arts who emigrated to the United States when the Nazis came to power. He is best known for his highly influential study,* From Caligari to Hitler: A Psychological History of the German Film *(1947), which analyzes pre-World War II German films for evidence of a cultural, or "mass psychological," predisposition in the German people to accept Adolf Hitler's form of fascism. In the following essay, he discusses the essential conformism he finds in Sturges's apparently satirical films.*]

Preston Sturges, who has been typecast as an entertainer, is undoubtedly more than this: his own credo (expounded in **Sullivan's Travels**) as well as his habit of framing his plots with significant stories reveal him as a searching, introspective mind. And, besides, what if Sturges were a mere entertainer? Nothing should be taken more seriously than entertainment that ingratiates itself with the anonymous millions. Mass attitudes of far-reaching consequence often find an outlet in seemingly insignificant pleasures.

In the early '30s, when he began writing screen scenarios, Sturges did not always feel like laughing. His imagination centered around men who fight unscrupulously for power and a world in which integrity is an obstacle rather than an asset.

These preoccupations first materialized in Sturges' script of **The Power and the Glory,** a film directed by William K. Howard (1933). The plot is a variation on the "What Price Glory?" theme: a trackwalker with the instincts of a born tycoon contrives to become a railway magnate and commits suicide after having been betrayed by his own family. Sturges approached this worn-out theme from a particular angle: while fully exposing the tycoon's ruthlessness and antisocial conduct, he made considerable efforts to exculpate him. The film conveyed a moral; power, it implied, is incompatible with human loyalty, and he who conquers the world cannot but lose himself.

Sturges resumed this theme in **The Great McGinty** (1940), the first film he directed himself (drawn from a repeatedly rejected script of his own, done as early as 1933). This film presents the life story of a self-made man in flashback technique, which in this case is used to transform drama into satire. Dan McGinty, an elderly bartender in a forlorn "banana republic" dive, tells of his extraordinary past back in the States; and that past unfolds in sparkling episodes which show him making headway in a political machine. Under the wings of its highly disreputable "Boss," Dan rises from a bum in the soup line to the governor of a state, to grafting and racketeering on an ever larger scale. His upward flight would be as unlimited as his impudence, if it were not for an ingenious story twist: impelled by the woman he loves, Dan, after being sworn in as governor, decides to turn honest; and it is precisely this conversion which brings about his downfall. He joins the Boss in prison and then flees with him to the dim limbo of the banana port dive from which a half melancholy, half derisive light falls on his glorious and odious career.

This amusing attack on buccaneering in politics rests upon much the same attitude as **The Power and the Glory.** The two films, moreover, coincide in their sustained concern with social criticism; up to the very end, **The Great McGinty** satirizes a society in which honesty does not pay. Its unexpected success was, of course, not only due to the moral of this film but also and perhaps, mainly, to a cinematic treatment rich in pointed gags and with a touch of slapstick humor, which readily contributes to the development of a plot that pillories social abuses; and so the laughter spread by **The Great McGinty** has a redeeming quality.

Another overall feature of Sturges' imagery can be traced to his handling of the camera. He adroitly mobilizes the camera, with real film sense, whenever he wishes to point up some gag or create a comic situation; and on such occasions, his camera assumes an independence reminiscent of its role in mature silent films.

The self-made man with his thirst for power (he reappeared, slightly transformed, in **The Great Moment,** a weak tragicomedy, conceived in 1939) occupied one pole of the early Sturges universe. At its other pole loomed the figure of the Innocent, or whatever you want to call a naive and candid young man completely inexperienced in the ways of life. Sturges seems to have been infatuated with this antipode of his ruthless tycoons and corrupt politicians. In the two comedies following *The Great McGinty*, he featured such Innocents as lucky fellows who get everything they want.

The first of these comedies was *Christmas in July* (1940). Jimmy, its Innocent, is a gullible employee who stakes his hopes on a slogan contest offered by a coffee magnate. Naturally, Jimmy's hopes come true; but it is the finesse of the plot that he receives the $25,000 prize without really winning it. This superior trickery is achieved when several practical jokers in Jimmy's office send him a faked telegram acknowledging his victory. Overjoyed, Jimmy presents it to the coffee magnate, and since the latter is no longer on speaking terms with the contest jury, he accepts the telegram at face value and signs the check. Jimmy's gift for coining slogans thus being firmly established, he is promoted by his boss. He and his girl are in clover, and even the inevitable discovery of the fraud cannot evict them from there.

Based on a script of 1931 (when the depression was in full swing), *Christmas in July* looks like just another escapist film intent on diverting white collar workers from their predicament. What satire the film includes is levelled against preposterous commercial slogans, mechanized furniture and overweening juries—minor shortcomings of the otherwise ideal world Sturges evokes. Yet a particularly striking testimony to the film's inherent nonconformism is its admirable denouement: In the concluding scene the jury decides to grant Jimmy the prize—a decision which implies the conformist meaning that day dreams do come true in real life; but since we already know that Jimmy's career does not depend upon the outcome of the contest, we are advised to dismiss this innuendo as soon as it arises. With this twist Sturges maintains the gap between his dream world and the real world precisely when he seems to bridge it.

In *The Lady Eve* (1941), the second comedy Sturges made after his *Great McGinty*, the Innocent is a young explorer who, as the son of a beer tycoon, need not be launched on a career. But money is not all that matters if you have it; and innocence ceases to be a virtue if it is tantamount to immaturity. Emotionally undeveloped, Charles undergoes a lesson in love from Jean, the world-wise and endearing member of a card-sharper trio. The plot—the successive stages of his education—proceeds with an esprit reminiscent of the best French boulevard comedies. First, Charles proposed to Jean and, having learned of her questionable profession, jilts her abruptly. Then Jean, disguised as "Lady Eve," reconquers Charles who believes this model English aristocrat to be a twin of the cardsharper girl. She and Charles go on their nocturnal wedding trip in a Pullman car in the course of which Jean-Eve takes hilarious revenge by confessing to her bridegroom a series of amorous adventures she had never had. Charles, shuddering, abandons her in the dead of night, and only in the finale are the two reunited.

In this picture, again business magnates are presented as funny figures, and the power they wield is minimized; again social satire is diverted from essential abuses to such inoffensive shortcomings as moral priggishness and American awe of British manners. And again this seeming complacency ultimately yields to a deeper disaffection.

In short, both comedies are in the vein of *The Great McGinty:* in making the audience laugh, they arouse its critical faculties. And this identity of attitude accounts for similarity of technique. In both comedies, significant gags predominate over fun for fun's sake. On the other hand, just as in his *Great McGinty*, Sturges continues inserting pictorially arid stretches of dialogue in an otherwise brilliant imagery.

The Great McGinty and the two subsequent comedies appeared after the downfall of France, when civilized mankind lived in the fear of doom. Was laughter sufferable amidst world-wide despair? As if troubled by his role of comedy-maker in such a time, Sturges undertook to justify laughter with *Sullivan's Travels* (1941), a sort of tragicomedy written and directed immediately after *The Lady Eve.* The film is the turning point of Sturges' career.

Sullivan, a Hollywood director famous for his comedies, is so troubled by pangs of conscience that he decides to make only films which will no longer amuse the masses but, through an exposition of their intolerable plight, help promote human dignity. To experience the hardships he plans for his next film, he visits several hobo camps in the guise of a tramp. These travels, a mixture of slapstick and serious encounters, result in a catastrophe: Sullivan contracts amnesia and, under its spell, is sentenced to a long term at hard labor for having resisted the authorities. In a Southern jail, one evening he and his fellow-prisoners are allowed to look at an old Disney film. While Mickey Mouse performs, the camera dwells on the laughing faces of dejected criminals. Even though the happiness of the audience fades out with the short, it has left a lasting imprint on Sullivan. He recovers his memory and returns to Hollywood, imbued with the credo that genuine suffering can be relieved only by laughter. This is what his travels have taught him. And with a truly missionary zeal he abandons his social film project for a comedy.

Sullivan expressed sympathy for the suffering. Yet this does not prevent him from being interested only in picturesque tramps and jailbirds who are far less representative of our society than, for instance, the white-collar workers in *Christmas in July.* There is something evasive about Sullivan's travels; in their neglect of the inconspicuous for the spectacular, they resemble sightseeing tours through the Bowery. Besides, Sullivan cares little about the selected unfortunates he meets en route. From the very outset he had avoided involvement in our workaday world. His reluctance to let himself be seriously affected by the suffering of man—by any suffering, for that matter—goes hand in hand with his belief that things are what they are and that nothing can be done about it. In calling society a "cockeyed caravan," he tacitly admits that he considers its inadequacy unchangeable. His laughter suggests a conformist attitude. The exoneration of tycoons in *The Power and the Glory,* and elsewhere, now appears to be a symptom of social complacency rather than a challenge to moral hypocrisy. Dan McGinty's original indifference to the poor is now pointed up by the callousness of Sullivan's butler who, in about the same words as Dan, advises his master to leave the poor alone—an advice which Sullivan seems to reject but in effect endorses. There was something Aristophanic about Sturges' beginnings, but in *Sullivan's Travels* he betrayed what was best in his laughter.

Having justified comedies as a godsend in these days of wrath, Sturges continued making them with a reassured conscience. There came *The Palm Beach Story* (1942). This comedy about the upper crust abounds in millionaires of all shades and throws in two Innocents instead of the customary one—the impractical Tom, and John, the son of a super-magnate. Tom's loving wife, in her desire to push this stubborn ass ahead, becomes the center of an amusingly volatile intrigue which highlights the wasteful life of the rich through a blend of aggressive slapstick and condoning Lubitsch gags. In the finale Sturges lavishes on Tom, John, and everyone concerned, a fairytale happiness made palatable to the audience by just the right touch of irony.

Sturges' next two films dealt with wartime life in small towns in a manner which reveals Sturges' growing infatuation with old slapstick comedy. The hero of *The Miracle of Morgan's Creek* (1944), played by Eddie Bracken, stutters when excited, frequently because of his adored Trudy's irresponsible behavior. Trudy had attended a gay farewell party for soldiers; it had ended, she dimly remembers, with her marrying some GI whose name she has forgotten. Unfortunately, the result is more concrete than her memory. Eddie, a sweet compound of knight and simpleton, tries the impossible to save Trudy from disgrace; but, of course, his farcical attempts only make things worse for both of them. Gibes at hasty war marriages, hypocritical sex morals and administrative blunders contribute to producing the overall impression of a topsy-turvy society. It is also logical in such a world that a fourteen-year old girl—one of Sturges' best comical figures—should talk and behave like a disillusioned adult. Again, the story is told in flashback fashion; but at the end, when all seems irretrievably mixed up, Sturges springs the surprise for which he has prepared the audience from the beginning: Trudy gives birth to sextuplets. And since Dan, the governor of the state, considers this miracle a unique asset to his administration, he sanctions Trudy's *faux pas* by making Eddie her legitimate husband and a State Militia Colonel to boot.

In *Hail the Conquering Hero* (1944), Bracken is so ashamed of having been discharged from the army for chronic hay fever that he does not dare return to his mother who still glories in the memory of his father, a hero of World War I. Six marines on leave from Guadalcanal, and in search of a good time, pick up Bracken in a bar and propose that, instead of letting his mother down, he should gratify her by posing as her hero son. They have the hesitant Innocent don a bemedaled uniform, escort him home and joyously participate in his triumphal reception by a town reveling in the local boy's alleged war exploits. Never was Sturges' satire more topical than in this hilarious concoction which, in the midst of war, not only mocked such small fry as souvenir hunters and political windbags, but assailed the sanctimoniousness of our official mother-and-hero cult. The marines' junket comes to a head when citizens, worried by the state of municipal affairs, urge Woodrow to run for mayor. Once again he yields, but this time his innate honesty conquers his shyness. At the opening electoral meeting he confesses to being a fraud—an instance of civil courage which the marines are the first to admire. The voters feel similarly, catch up with Bracken at the station and keep him from boarding the train on which the six dashing marines depart.

Sturges' satire is here no longer what it was before he dulled its bite through systematic retreats from any advanced position. At his beginnings Sturges insisted that honesty does not pay. Now he wants us to believe that the world yields to candor.

What satire *The Miracle of Morgan's Creek* offers is drowned in a plot that tends to demonstrate that our existing world, this "cockeyed caravan," is the best of all possible worlds. Our society, the film implies, is constructed in such a way that in the long run any bad action serves a good purpose. But if human integrity is bound to win out—why then try to change the world? Sturges, it is true, dismisses the whole marionette world with an ironic smile that is calculated to pass it all off as a superior joke. But this irony is much too superficial to be an adequate excuse for the harmony he has established between his Innocents and the powers that be.

Sturges' original affinity for the old screen comedy is undeniable. Aside from the many pertinent gags in his earlier films, he proves himself a late descendant of Mack Sennett in that he has built up a sort of stock company to enact the ever-recurrent comic characters that haunt his imagination. Sturges *could* have resurrected the slapstick world of the past. The strange thing is that he seized, deliberately, upon this world just when he had turned away from its spirit. What must happen under such circumstances is predictable: his resurrection of slapstick turns out to be a mere pretense. And his lack of concern for the slapstick spirit shows in the increase of meaningless gags; unmotivated buffooneries become obstrusive in all three comedies.

In short, Sturges turns to the classic slapstick comedy not in spite of his conformism but because of it. Far from reviving this genre, he merely exploits its proved devices to produce as much fun as possible regardless of the meaning they had originally conveyed. Slapstick, to the later Sturges, is nothing but an arsenal of ready-made gags. For whatever inner reasons, Sturges' gift for inventing funny incidents began to fail him from about the time of *Sullivan's Travels.* More readily than before his characters tend to fall or to provoke falls; and subtle jests increasingly give way to farcical business. (Complacency takes revenge on those who indulge in it: his latest comedies, *Unfaithfully Yours* (1948), and *The Beautiful Blonde from Bashful Bend* (1949), are poor in wit and slapstick out of a can.)

And what particular brand of conformism does Sturges-Sullivan administer to the public? It is a streamlined variant of the naive and uncritical conformism current among us. Sturges first draws on the critical faculties of a flattered audience by having it catch a glimpse of the questionable aspects of our society; and then he gives the audience to understand that this world of ours is in effect a paradise where wrongs right themselves automatically. He conceals nothing and gilds all. He uses the tools of social criticism—only to destroy its constructive power.

I do not intend to say that laughter without social significance is evil. The straight film farce, produced for its comical effect alone, is just as valid and welcome an entertainment as any other juggler's act. But the farce in the disguise of satire is dangerous. It dulls the edges of a first-rate weapon of human liberation. And it is dangerous at a time when, along with the means of mass communication, methods of psychological manipulation have been developed to an extent unknown before. (pp. 11-13, 43-7)

> Siegfried Kracauer, "Preston Sturges or Laughter Betrayed," in Films in Review, Vol. I, No. 1, February, 1950, pp. 11-13, 43-7.

Manny Farber and W. S. Poster (essay date 1954)

[*In the following essay, widely regarded as exemplary film criticism, Farber offers a detailed analysis of the major themes and techniques in Sturges's films.*]

By all odds, the most outstanding example of a successful director with a flamboyant unkillable personality to emerge in Hollywood during the last two decades has been that of Preston Sturges, who flashed into the cinema capital in 1939, wrote, produced, and directed an unprecedented series of hits and now seems to be leaping into relative obscurity. Hollywood destiny has caught up with Sturges in a left-handed fashion; most whiz-bang directors of the Sturges type remain successes while their individuality wanes. Sturges seems to have been so riddled by the complexities, conflicts, and opposed ambitions that came together to enrich his early work that he could not be forced into a mold. Instead of succumbing to successful conformity, Sturges has all but ceased to operate in the high-powered, smash-hit manner expected of him.

It is a perculiarly ironic fate, because Sturges is the last person in the world it is possible to think of as a failure. Skeptical and cynical, Sturges, whose hobbies include running restaurants and marketing profitable Rube Goldberg inventions, has never publicly acknowledged any other goal but success. He believes it is as easily and quickly achieved in America, particularly by persons of his own demoniac energy, mercurial brain, and gimmick-a-minute intensiveness. During the time it takes the average American to figure out how to save $3 on his income tax, Sturges is liable to have invented "a vibrationless Diesel engine," a "home exerciser," the "first nonsmear lipstick," opened up a new-style eatery, written a Broadway musical, given one of his discouraged actors his special lecture on happiness, and figured out a new way to increase his own superhuman productiveness and efficiency.

In fact, Sturges can best be understood as an extreme embodiment of the American success dream, an expression of it as a pure idea in his person, an instance of it in his career, and its generalizer in his films. In Sturges, the concept of success operates with purity, clogging the ideology of ambition so that it becomes an esthetic credo, backfiring on itself, baffling critics, and creeping in as a point of view in pictures which are supposed to have none. The image of success stalks every Sturges movie like an unlaid ghost, coloring the plots and supplying the fillip to his funniest scenes. His madly confused lovers, idealists, and outraged fathers appear to neglect it, but it invariably turns up dumping pots of money on their unsuspecting heads or snatching away million-dollar prizes. Even in a picture like *The Miracle of Morgan's Creek,* which deals with small-town, humble people, it is inevitable that bouncing Betty Hutton should end up with sextuplets and become a national institution. The very names of Sturges's best-known movies seem to evoke a hashish-eater's vision of beatific American splendor: ***The Great McGinty, The Power and the Glory, The Miracle of Morgan's Creek, Hail the Conquering Hero, The Great Moment, Christmas in July*** reveal the facets of a single preoccupation.

Nearly everyone who has written about Sturges expresses great admiration for his intelligence and talent, total confusion about his pictures, and an absolute certainty that Sturges should be almost anything but what he nakedly and palpably is—an inventive American who believes that good picture-making consists in grinding out ten thousand feet of undiluted, chaos-producing energy. It is not too difficult to perceive that even Sturges's most appreciative critics were fundamentally unsympathetic toward him. Throughout his career, in one way or another, Sturges has been pilloried for refusing to conform to the fixed prescriptions for artists. Thus, according to René Clair, "Preston is like a man from the Italian Renaissance: he wants to do everything at once. If he could slow down, he would be great; he has an enormous gift, and he should be one of our leading creators. I wish he would be a little more selfish and worry about his reputation."

What Clair is suggesting is that Sturges would be considerably improved if he annihilated himself. Similarly, Siegfried Kracauer has scolded him for not being the consistent, socially-minded satirist of the rich, defender of the poor, and portrayer of the evils of modern life which he regards as the qualifying characteristics of all moviemakers admissible to his private pantheon. The more popular critics have condemned Sturges for not liking America enough; the advanced critics for liking it too much. He has also been accused of espousing a snob point of view and sentimentally favoring the common man.

Essentially Sturges, probably the most spectacular manipulator of sheer humor since Mark Twain, is a very modern artist or entertainer, difficult to classify because of the intense effort he has made to keep his work outside conventional categories. The high-muzzle velocity of his films is due to the anarchic energy generated as they constantly shake themselves free of attitudes that threaten to slow them down. Sturges's pictures maintain this freedom from ideology through his sophisticated assumption of the role of the ruthless showman deliberately rejecting all notions of esthetic weight and responsibility. It is most easy to explain Sturges's highly self-conscious philosophy of the hack as a kind of cynical morality functioning in reverse.

Since there is so much self-inflation, false piety, and artiness in the arts, it was, he probably felt, less morally confusing to jumble slapstick and genuine humor, the original and the derivative together, and express oneself through the audacity and skill by which they are combined. It is also probable that he found the consistency of serious art, its demand that everything be resolved in terms of a logic of a single mood, repugnant to his temperament and false to life.

"There is nothing like a deep-dish movie to drive you out in the open," a Sturges character remarks, and, besides being a typical Sturges line, the sentence tells you a great deal about his moviemaking. His resourcefulness, intelligence, Barnum-and-Bailey showmanship and dislike of fixed purposes often make the typical Sturges movie seem like a uniquely irritating pastiche. A story that opens with what appears to be a bitingly satirical exposition of American life is apt to end in a jelly of cheap sentiment. In *Hail the Conquering Hero,* for example, Eddie Bracken plays an earnest, small-town boy trying to follow in the footsteps of his dead father, a World War I hero. Discharged because of hay fever, Bracken is picked up by six Marines who talk him into posing as a Guadalcanal veteran and returning home as a hero to please his mother. The pretense snowballs, the town goes wild, and Bracken's antics become more complicated and tormenting with every scene. After he has been pushed into running for Mayor, he breaks down and confesses the hoax. Instead of tarring and feathering him, the townspeople melt with admiration for his candor and courage.

This ending has been attacked by critics who claim that it reveals Sturges compromising his beliefs and dulling the edge of his satire. "At his beginning," Mr. Kracauer writes, referring to *The Great McGinty,* "Sturges insisted that honesty does not pay. Now he wants us to believe that the world yields to candor." Such criticism is about as relevant as it would be to say that Cubists were primarily interested in showing all sides of a bottle at once. To begin with, it should be obvious to anyone who has seen two Sturges pictures that he does not give a tinker's dam whether the world does or does not yield to candor. Indeed his pictures at no time evince the slightest interest on his part as to the truth or falsity of his direct representation of society. His neat, contrived plots are unimportant per se and developed chiefly to provide him with the kind of movements and appearances he wants, with crowds of queer, animated individuals, with juxtapositions of unusual actions and faces. These are then organized, as items are in any art which does not boil down to mere sociology, to evoke *feelings* about society and life which cannot be reduced to doctrine or judged by flea-hopping from the work of art to society in the manner of someone checking a portrait against the features of the original.

What little satire there is in a film is as likely to be directed at satire as it is at society. The supposedly sentimental ending of *The Conquering Hero,* for example, starts off as a tongue-in-cheek affair as much designed to bamboozle the critics as anything else. It goes out of hand and develops into a series of oddly placed shots of the six Marines, shots which are indeed so free of any kind of attitude as to create an effect of pained ambiguous humanity, frozen in a moment of time, so grimly at one with life that they seem to be utterly beyond any one human emotion, let alone sentiment. The entire picture is, indeed, remarkable for the manner in which sequences are directed away from the surface mood to create a sustained, powerful, and lifelike pattern of dissonance. The most moving scene in it—Pangborn's monumentally heartfelt reactions to Bracken's confession—is the product of straight comic pantomime. The Marine with an exaggerated mother-complex sets up a hulking, ominous image as the camera prolongs a view of his casual walk down the aisle of the election hall. The Gargantuan mugging and gesturing of the conscience-stricken Bracken provokes not only laughter but the sense that he is suffering from some mysterious muscular ailment.

Such sequences, however, though integral to Sturges's best work, do not set its tone. The delightfulness, the exhilarating quality that usually prevails is due to the fact that the relation to life of most of the characters is deliberately kept weak and weightless. The foibles of a millionaire, the ugliness of a frump are all projected by similar devices and exploited in a like manner. They exist in themselves only for a moment and function chiefly as bits in the tumultuous design of the whole. Yet this design offers a truer equivalent of American society than can be supplied by any realism or satire that cannot cope with the tongue-in-cheek self-consciousness and irreverence toward its own fluctuating institutions that is the very hallmark of American society—that befuddles foreign observers and makes American mores well-nigh impervious to any kind of satire.

Satire requires a stationary society, one that seriously believes in the enduring value of the features providing its identity. But what is there to satirize in a country so much at the mercy of time and commerce as to be profoundly aware that all its traits—its beauties, blemishes, wealth, poverty, prejudices, and aspirations—are equally the merchandise of the moment, easily manufactured and trembling on the verge of destruction from the moment of production? The only American quality that can conceivably offer a focus for satire, as the early moviemakers and Sturges, alone among the contemporaries, have realized, is speed. Some of the great early comic films, those of Buster Keaton, for example, were scarcely comic at all but pure and very bitter satires, exhausting in endless combinations of all possible tortures produced as a consequence of the *naif* belief in speed. Mack Sennett was less the satirist of American speed-mania than its Diaghilev. Strip away the comic webbing, and your eye comes upon the preternatural poetic world created by an instinctive impresario of graceful accelerations. Keystone cops and bathing beauties mingle and separate in a buoyant, immensely varied ballet, conceived at the speed of mind but with camera velocity rather than the human body as its limit. Sturges was the only legitimate heir of the early American film, combining its various methods, adding new perspectives and developing the whole in a form suitable to a talking picture.

Since Sturges thought more synoptically than his pre-

Movie poster for Sturges' last hit film. Sturges was one of the few directors of his era to see his name above the title.

decessors, he presented a speed-ridden society through a multiple focus rather than the single, stationary lens of the pioneers. While achieving a more intense identification of the audience with the actors than in the earlier films (but less than the current talking pictures, which strive for complete audience identification with the hero), Sturges fragmented action, so that each scene blends into the next before it comes to rest, and created an illusion of relative motions. Basically, a Sturges film is executed to give one the delighted sensation of a person moving on a smoothly traveling vehicle going at high speed through fields, towns, homes, and even through other vehicles. The vehicle in which the spectator is traveling never stops but seems to be moving in a circle, making its journey again and again in an ascending, narrowing spiral until it diminishes into nothingness. One of his characters calls society a "cockeyed caravan," and Sturges, himself, is less a settled, bona fide resident of America than a hurried, Argus-eyed traveler through its shifting scenes, a nomad in space observing a society nomadic in time and projecting his sensations in uniquely computed terms.

This modern cinematic perspective of mobility seen by a mobile observer comes easily to Sturges because of his strange family background and broken-up youth. He was the son of a normal, sports-loving, successful father and a fantastic culture-bug mother who wanted him to be a genius and kept him in Paris from the age of eight to about fifteen. "She dragged me through every goddam museum on the continent," he has rancorously remarked. Glutted, at an early age, by an overrich diet of esthetic dancing, high-hatted opera audiences, and impressionist painting, Sturges still shows the marks of his youthful trauma. The most obvious result of his experience has been a violent reaction against all estheticism. He has also expressed fervent admiration for his father's business ability and a desire to emulate him. The fact that he did not, however, indicates that his early training provoked more than a merely negative reaction in him and made him a logical candidate for Hollywood, whose entire importance in the history of culture resides in its unprecedented effort to merge art and big business.

As a moviemaker, the businessman side of Sturges was superficially dominant. He seems to have begun his career with the intention of giving Hollywood a lesson in turning out quick, cheap, popular pictures. He whipped together his scripts in record-breaking time, cast his pictures with unknowns, and shot them faster than anyone dreamed possible. He was enabled to do this through a native aptitude for finding brilliant technical shortcuts. Sturges tore Hollywood comedy loose from the slick gentility of pictures like *It Happened One Night* by shattering the realistic mold and the logical build-up and taking the quickest, least plausible route to the nerves of the audience. There are no preparations for the fantastic situations on which his pictures are based and no transitions between their numberless pratfalls, orgies of noise, and furniture-smashing. A Capra, Wilder, or Wellman takes half a movie to get a plot to the point where the audience accepts it and it comes to cinematic life. Sturges often accomplishes as much in the first two minutes, throwing an audience immediately into what is generally the most climactic and revelatory moment of other films.

The beginning of *Sullivan's Travels* is characteristic for its easy handling of multiple cinematic meanings. The picture opens abruptly on a struggle between a bum and a railroad employee on top of a hurtling train. After a few feet of a fight that is at once a sterling bit of action movie and a subtle commentary on action movies, it develops that you are in a projection studio, watching a film made by Sullivan, a famous director, and that the struggle symbolizes the conflict of capital and labor. As Sullivan and the moguls discuss the film's values and box-office possibilities, Sturges makes them all sound delightfully foolish by pointing up the naïve humanity of everyone involved. "Who wants to see that stuff? It gives me the creeps!" is the producer's reaction to the film. When Sullivan mentions a five-week run at the Music Hall, the producer explodes with magnificent improbability: "Who goes to the Music Hall? Communists!" Thus, in five minutes of quick-moving cinema and surprise-packed dialogue, a complex situation has been set forth and Sullivan is catapulted on his journey to learn about the moods of America in the depression.

The witty economy of his movies is maintained by his gifted exploitation of the non sequitur and the perversely unexpected. In nearly every case, he manages to bring out some hidden appropriateness from what seems like willful irrelevance. In *The Miracle of Morgan's Creek,* a plug-ugly sergeant mouths heavy psychiatric phrases in an unbelievable way that ends by sinking him doubly deep into the realm of the psychotic. With nihilistic sophistication, Sturges makes a Hollywood director keep wondering "Who is Lubitsch?" till you are not sure if it is simply fun or a weird way of expressing pretentiousness and ignorance. Similarly, in *The Conquering Hero,* the small-town citizens are given a happy ending and a hero to worship, but they are paraded through the streets and photographed in such a way that they resemble a lynch mob—a device which flattens out success and failure with more gruesome immediacy than Babbittlike satires.

What made Sturges a viciously alive artist capable of discovering new means of expressiveness in a convention-ridden medium was the frenetic, split sensibility that kept him reacting to and away from the opposite sides of his heredity. These two sides are, in fact, the magnetic poles of American society. Accepting, in exaggerated fashion, the businessman approach to films, he nevertheless brought to his work intelligence, taste, and a careful study of the more estimable movies of the past. He also took care to disappoint rigid-minded esthetes and reviewers. Although it has been axiomatic among advanced movie students that the modern film talks too much and moves too little, Sturges perversely thought up a new type of dialogue by which the audience is fairly showered with words. The result was paradoxically to speed up his movies rather than to slow them down, because he concocted a special, jerky, spluttering form of talk that is the analogue of the old, silent-picture firecracker tempo. Partly this was accomplished by a wholesale use of "hooks"—spoken lines cast as questions, absurd statements, or explosive criticisms, which yank immediate responses from the listener.

Sturges's free-wheeling dialogue is his most original contribution to films and accomplishes, among other things, the destruction of the common image of Americans as tight-lipped Hemingwayan creatures who converse in grating monosyllables and chopped sentences. Sturges tries to create the equally American image of a wrangle of conflicting, overemotional citizens who talk as though they were forever arguing or testifying before a small-town jury. They speak as if to a vast, intent audience rather than to each other, but the main thing is that they unburden themselves passionately and without difficulty—even during siesta moments on the front porch: "I'm perfectly calm. I'm as—as cool as ice, then I start to figure maybe they won't take me and some cold sweat runs down the middle of my back and my head begins to buzz and everything in the middle of the room begins to swim—and I get black spots in front of my eyes and they say I've got high blood pressure. . . ."

As the words sluice out of the actors' mouths, the impression is that they teeter on the edge of a social, economic, or psychological cliff and that they are under some wild compulsion to set the record straight before plunging out of the picture. Their speech is common in language and phrasing, but Sturges makes it effervesce with trick words ("whackos" for "whack"), by pumping it full of outraged energy or inserting a daft idea like the Music Hall gag. All of this liberated talk turns a picture into a kind of open forum where everyone down to the cross-eyed bit player gets a chance to try out his oratorical ability. A nice word-festival, very democratic, totally unlike the tight, gagged-up speech that movies inherited from vaudeville, radio, and the hard-boiled novel.

Paradoxically, too, his showman's approach enabled Sturges to be the only Hollywood talking-picture director to apply to films the key principles of the "modern" revolutions in poetry, painting, and music: namely, beginning a work of art at the climax and continuing from there. Just as the modern painter eschews narrative and representational elements to make his canvas a continuum of the keenest excitement natural to painting, or the poet minimizes whatever takes his poem out of the realm of purely verbal values, so Sturges eliminated from his movies the sedulous realism that has kept talking pictures essentially anchored to a rotting nineteenth-century esthetic. In this and other ways, Sturges revealed that his youth spent "caroming around in High-Bohemian Europe" had not been without a positive effect on his work. Its basic textures, forms, and methods ultimately derive from post-Impressionist painting, Russian ballet, and the early scores of Stravinsky, Hindemith, et al. The presence of Dada and Surrealism is continuously alive in its subsurface attitudes or obvious in the handling of specific scenes. Sturges's fat Moon Mullins—type female, playing a hot tail-gate trombone at a village dance, is the exact equivalent in distortion of one of Picasso's lymphatic women posed as Greek statues.

Sturges's cinematic transpositions of American life reveal the outsider's ability to seize salient aspects of our national existence plus the insider's knowledge of their real meaning. But the two are erratically fused by the sensibility of the nostalgic, dislocated semiexile that Sturges essentially remains. The first impression one gets from a Sturges movie is that of the inside of a Ford assembly line smashed together and operating during a total war crisis. The characters, all exuding jaundice, cynicism, and anxiety, work feverishly as every moment brings them the fear that their lives are going to pieces, that they are going to be fired, murdered, emasculated, or trapped in such ridiculous situations that headlines will scream about them to a hooting nation for the rest of their lives. They seem to be haunted by the specters of such nationally famous boneheads as Wrong-Way Corrigan, Roy Riegels, who ran backward in a Rose Bowl game, or Fred Merkle, who forgot to touch second base in a crucial play-off game, living incarnations of the great American nightmare that some monstrous error can drive individuals clean out of society into a forlorn no man's land, to be the lonely objects of an eternity of scorn, derision, and self-humiliation. This nightmare is of course the reverse side of the uncontrolled American success impulse, which would set individuals apart in an apparently different but really similar and equally frightening manner.

Nearly all the Sturges comedies were centered with a sure instinct on this basic drive with all its complex concomitants. Using a stock company of players (all of a queer, unstandard, and almost aboriginal Americanism), Sturges managed to give his harrowing fables of success-failure an intimate, small-town setting that captured both the moony desire of every American to return to the small world of his youth and that innocent world itself as it is ravaged by a rampant, high-speed industrialism. The resultant events are used to obtain the comic release that is, indeed, almost the only kind possible in American life: the savage humor of absolute failure or success. Sturges's funniest scenes result from exploding booby traps that set free bonanzas of unsuspected wealth. In one episode, for example, two automat employees fight and trip open all the levers behind the windows; the spouts pour, the windows open, and a fantastic, illicit treasure trove of food spills out upon a rioting, delightfully greedy mob of bums, dowagers, and clerks. In *The Palm Beach Story,* members of the "Ale and Quail" club—a drunken, good-humored bunch of eccentric millionaires—shoot up a train and lead yapping hounds through Pullmans in a privileged orgy of destruction. This would seem the deeply desired, much fantasied reward of a people that endures the unbelievably tormented existence Sturges depicts elsewhere—a people whose semicomic suffering arises from the disparity between the wild lusts generated by American society and the severity of its repressions.

Sturges's faults are legion and have been pretty well gone over during his most successful period. Masterful with noisy crowds, he is liable to let a quiet spot in the script provoke him to burden the screen with "slapstick the size of a whale bone." A good businessman believes that any article can be sold if presented with eardrum-smashing loudness and brain-numbing certitude. From a similar approach, Sturges will represent hilarity by activating a crew of convicts as though he were trying to get Siberia to witness their gleeful shrieks. To communicate the bawdy wit of a fast blonde, he will show the tough owner of a lunch wagon doubled up like a suburban teenager hearing his first dirty joke. The comic chaos of a small-town reception must be evoked by the use of no less than four discordant bands. Sturges has been accused of writing down to his audience, but it is more probable that there is too much of the businessman actually in his make-up to expect him to function in any other way. The best of his humor must come in a brash flurry of effects, all more or less oversold because there is nothing in his background that points to a more quiet, reasonable approach to life.

But even these vices are mitigated somewhat by the fact that they provide an escape from the plight of many intelligent, sensibility-ridden artists or entertainers of his period whose very intelligence and taste have turned against them, choking off their vitality and driving them into silence or reduced productivity. The result is that artistic ebullience and spontaneity have all but drained down to the very lowest levels of American entertainment. Even in the movies these days, one is confronted by slow-moving, premeditated affairs—not so much works of art or entertainments aimed by the intelligence at the glands, blood, and viscera of the audience as exercises in mutual criticism and good taste. The nervous tantrums of slapstick in a Sturges movie, the thoughtless, attention-getting antics combined with their genuine cleverness give them an improvised, blatant immediacy that is preferable to excesses of calculation and is, in the long run, healthier for the artists themselves.

As a maker of pictures in the primary sense of the term, Sturges shows little of the daring and variety that characterize him as a writer and, on the whole, as a director. He runs to middle shots, symmetrical groupings, and an evenly lit screen either of the bright modern variety or with a deliberately aged, grey period-finish. His composition rarely takes on definite form because he is constantly shooting a scene for ambivalent effects. The love scenes in *The Lady Eve,* for example, are shot, grouped, and lit in such a way as to throw a moderate infusion of sex and sentiment into a fast-moving, brittle comedy without slowing it down. The average director is compelled to use more dramatic composition because the moods are episodic, a completely comic sequence alternating with a completely sentimental scene. Sturges's treatment is fundamentally more cinematic, but he has not found a technique equal to it. Fluent as a whole, his pictures are often clumsy and static in detail, and he has not learned how to get people to use their bodies so that there is excitement merely in watching them move. In a picture like Howard Hawks's *His Girl Friday,* Cary Grant uses legs, arms, trick hat, and facial muscles to create a pixyish ballet that would do credit to a Massine. But, when Sturges selects an equally gifted exponent of stylized movement, Henry Fonda, he is unable to extract comparable values from a series of falls, chases, listings to portside, and shuddering comas. Stray items—Demarest's spikey hair, Stanwyck's quasi-Roman nose—clutter up his foreground like blocks of wood. Even dogs, horses, and lions seem to turn into stuffed props when the Sturges camera focuses on them.

The discrepancies in Sturges's films are due largely to the peculiar discontinuities that afflict his sensibility, although such affliction is also a general phenomenon in a country where whole eras and cultures in different stages of development exist side by side, where history along one route seems to skip over decades only to fly backward over another route and begin over again in still a different period. What Sturges presents with nervous simultaneity is the skyrocketing modern world of high-speed pleasures and actions (money-making, vote-getting, barroom sex, and deluxe transportation) in conflict with a whole Victorian world of sentiment, glamour, baroque appearance, and static individuality in a state of advanced decay. In all probability, his years spent abroad prevented his finding a bridge between the two worlds or even a slim principle of relating them in any other way than through dissonance. A whole era of American life with its accompaniment of visual styles is skimped in his work, the essential problems thus created being neatly bypassed rather than solved.

But his very deficiencies enabled Sturges to present, as no one else has, the final decay of the bloated Victorian world, which, though seemingly attached to nothing modern and destined to vanish with scarcely a trace, has nevertheless its place in the human heart if only for its visual splendors, its luxurious, impractical graces, and all too human excesses. From McGinty to Harold Diddlebock, Sturges gives us a crowded parade of courtly, pompous, speechifying, queerly dressed personages caught as they slowly dissolve with an era. His young millionaires—Hickenlooper III (Rudy Vallee), Pike (Henry Fonda), and rich movie director Sullivan (Joel McCrea)—a similar type of being—are like heavily ornamented bugs, born out of an Oliver Twist world into a sad-faced, senile youth as moldy with leisure and tradition as an old cheese. Incapable of action, his obsolete multimillionaires gaze out into a world that has passed them by but to which they are firmly anchored by their wealth.

A pathetic creature in the last stages of futility. Vallee's sole occupation consists of recording, in a little black book, minute expenditures which are never totaled—as though he were the gently demented statistician of an era that has fallen to pieces for no special reason and has therefore escaped attention. Fonda as Pike, the heir of a brewery fortune (*The Ale That Won for Yale*), is the last word in marooned uselessness. A wistful, vague, young, scholarly ophiologist nicknamed Hoppsey, Pike's sole business in life consists of feeding four flies, a glass of milk, and one piece of white bread to a rare, pampered snake. In between, he can be seen glumly staring at a horde of predatory females, uncooperatively being seduced, getting in and out of suits too modern for him, sadly doing the oldest card trick in the world, and pathetically apologizing for not liking beer or ale. Oddly enough, his supposed opposite, a fast, upper-class cardsharp (Barbara Stanwyck) is no less Victorian, issuing as she does from a group of obsolete card Houdinis with an old-fashioned code of honor among thieves and courtly old-world manners and titles.

If Sturges has accomplished nothing else, he has brought to consciousness the fact that we are still living among the last convulsions of the Victorian world, that, indeed, our entire emotional life is still heavily involved in its death. These final agonies (though they have gone on so long as to make them almost painless), which only Sturges has recorded, can be glimpsed daily, in the strange, gentle expiration of figures like Shaw, Hearst, Jolson, Ford; the somewhat sad explosion of fervor over MacArthur's return (a Sturges picture by itself, with, if the fading hero had been made baseball czar, a pat Sturges ending); and the Old World pomp, unctuousness, and rural religiosity of the American political scene.

Nowhere did Sturges reveal his Victorian affinities more than by his belief in, use, and love of a horde of broken, warped, walked-over, rejected, seamy, old character actors. Some of these crafty bit players, like Walburn, Bridge, Tannen, made up his stock company, while others like Coburn, Pangborn, Kennedy, and Blore appear only in single pictures. They were never questioned by critics, although they seemed as out of place in a film about modern times as a bevy of Floradora girls. They appear as monstrously funny people who have gone through a period of maniacal adjustment to capitalist society by exaggerating a single feature of their character: meekness, excessive guile, splenetic aggressiveness, bureaucratic windiness, or venal pessimism. They seem inordinately toughened by experience, but they are, one is aware, not really tough at all, because they are complete fakers—life made it inevitable. They are very much part of the world of Micawber and Scrooge but later developments—weaker, more perfect, bloated, and subtle caricatures—giving off a fantastic odor of rotten purity and the embalmed cheerfulness of puppets.

They all appear to be too perfectly adjusted to life to require minds, and, in place of hearts, they seem to contain an old scratch sheet, a glob of tobacco juice, or a brown banana. The reason their faces—each of which is a succulent worm's festival, bulbous with sheer living—seem to have nothing in common with the rest of the human race is precisely because they are so eternally, agelessly human, oversocialized to the point where any normal animal component has vanished. They seem to be made up not of features but a *collage* of spare parts, most of them as useless as the vermiform appendix.

Merely gazing at them gives the audience a tremendous lift, as if it were witnessing all the drudgery of daily life undergoing a reckless transmutation. It is as if human nature, beaten to the ground by necessity, out of sheer defiance had decided to produce utterly useless extravaganzas like Pangborn's bobbling cheeks, Bridge's scrounging, scraping voice, or Walburn's evil beetle eyes and mustache like a Fuller brush that has decided to live an independent life. It is all one can do to repress a maniac shriek at the mere sight of Harold Lloyd's companion in **Mad Wednesday**. His body looks like that of a desiccated 200-year-old locust weighed down by an enormous copper hat. Or Pat Moran's wrecked jeep of a face, and his voice that sounds as if its owner had just been smashed in the Adam's apple by Joe Louis. These aged, senile rejects from the human race are put through a routine that has, in one minute, the effect of a long, sad tone poem and, after an hour, gives a movie a peculiar, hallucinatory quality, as if reality had been slightly tilted and robbed of significant pieces.

No one has delineated sheer indolence as Sturges has with these characters. When one appears on the screen, it looks as if he had wandered into the film by mistake and, once there, had been abandoned by the makers. When a second one of these *lumpen* shows up, the audience begins to sit on the edge of its seat and to feel that the picture is going to pieces, that the director has stopped working or the producer is making a monkey out of it. After a few minutes of lacerated nothingness, it becomes obvious that the two creatures are fated to meet; considerable tension is generated, as the audience wonders what build-up will be used to enable them to make each other's acquaintance. To everybody's horror, there is no build-up at all; the creatures link arms as the result of some gruesome asocial understanding and simply walk off. In **Mad Wednesday,** this technique yields a kind of ultimate in grisly, dilapidated humor, particularly in the long episode which begins with Harold Lloyd meeting the locustlike creature on the greasiest looking sidewalk ever photographed. The two repair to a bar presided over by Edgar Kennedy, who slowly and insanely mixes for Lloyd his first alcoholic potion. This entire, elaborate ritual is a weirder, cinematic version of the kind of "study in decrepit life" for which e. e. cummings is famed; certainly it is at least comparable in merit and effectiveness.

Sturges may not be the greatest director of the last two decades; in fact, it can be argued that a certain thinness in his work—his lack of a fully formed, solid, orthodox moviemaker's technique—prevents him from being included among the first few. He is, however, the most original movie talent produced in recent years: the most complex and puzzling. The emotional and intellectual structure of his work has so little in common with the work of other artists of our time that it seems to be the result of a unique development. Yet it is sufficiently logical and coherent to give it a special relevance to the contemporary American psyche—of precisely the kind that is found in some modern American poetry and painting, and almost nowhere else. Nothing is more indicative of the ineptitude of present-day Hollywood than its failure to keep Sturges producing at his former clip. (pp. 89-104)

Manny Farber with W. S. Poster, "Preston Sturges: Success in the Movies," in Negative Space: Manny Farber on the Movies, *Praeger Publishers, 1971, pp. 89-104.*

Andrew Sarris (essay date 1970-1971)

[*In the following essay, Sarris discusses Sturges's work as a screenwriter in the 1930s.*]

To the end of his days Preston Sturges described himself as a writer rather than a director, and he would have been the first to admit that the films he directed through the forties and fifties relied more on verbal wit than visual style. Still, all his screenwriting efforts in the thirties would now be of only the most esoteric concern if he had not made the decisive leap from the writer's cubicle to the director's chair with **The Great McGinty** in 1940, followed by

Christmas in July that same year, *The Lady Eve* and *Sullivan's Travels* (1941), *The Palm Beach Story* (1942), *The Miracle of Morgan's Creek, Hail the Conquering Hero* and *The Great Moment* (1944), *Mad Wednesday* (1947), and, somewhat anticlimactically, *Unfaithfully Yours* (1948), *The Beautiful Blonde from Bashful Bend* (1949), and *The French They Are a Funny Race* (1957). Although it is relatively common for writers to become directors nowadays, the switch was somewhat unusual in the craft-conditioned thirties when it was not unknown for producers to fire directors who had the temerity to take up typing. As it was, the successful accession of Sturges sparked a writer-director movement involving John Huston, Billy Wilder, Joseph L. Mankiewicz, Dudley Nichols, Clifford Odets, Nunnally Johnson, Robert Rossen, Samuel Fuller, Frank Tashlin, Richard Brooks and Blake Edwards, among others.

But no Hollywood screenwriter-turned-director ever matched Sturges as the compleat writer-director with nine out of his twelve films based on original screenplays, and even his three adaptations (*The Lady Eve, The Great Moment* and *The French They Are a Funny Race*) bearing the personal Sturges stamp of the free-wheeling flashback. By contrast, most of his aforementioned colleagues began to fall back on other people's "properties" once they had switched their guild affiliation. Sturges threw in his script for *The Great McGinty* (originally titled "Down Went McGinty") for the privilege of directing it. Thus, unlike his colleagues, he took a cut in pay for a rise in status. He proved his point and went on to become the brightest comedy director of the forties. But he always remained something of a loner, relatively speaking. Sturges told me on the occasion of an interview before his death that he had never worked with another writer even though his name had been coupled on credit sheets with writers as disparate as Edwin Justus Mayer and Clarence Buddington Kelland. He began his movie career as a "dialoguer" (to use the terminology of the *Film Daily Year Book*) on two Paramount films released in 1930 (*The Big Pond* and *Fast and Loose*). He was hired presumably because of the success of his Broadway comedies—*Strictly Dishonorable* and *Child of Manhattan*—but these two properties were then assigned, by Universal and Columbia respectively, to other screenwriters. It would have been considered incestuous for Sturges to serve as the dialoguer on his own plays. Such was the absurd position of the screenwriter in the movie industry. All in all, Sturges was connected in one way or another with the writing of seventeen films through the thirties, ranging from the total responsibility of an original screenplay for *The Power and The Glory* in 1933 to the minutely marginal assignment of writing the lyrics to a song for *One Rainy Afternoon* in 1936.

Where does that leave us? Not in very good shape. Rumor has it that all of Preston Sturges' papers are in the possession of a film scholar who plans to publish the more pertinent items in a definitive biography. Until the happy day of publication arrives, all we can do is speculate about Sturges' role in the thirties.

At first glance, *The Big Pond* and *Fast and Loose* seems logical projects for Sturges in that they indulge the good-natured whimsy to be found in his most successful plays—*Strictly Dishonorable* and *Child of Manhattan*. *The Big Pond* presents Maurice Chevalier as an impoverished French aristocrat in love with Claudette Colbert as the daughter of an American gum magnate *à la* Wrigley played by George Barbier, a pre-Edward Arnold big-business boomer. Chevalier makes his fortune in America by hitting upon the idea of spiking chewing gum with liquor, thus spoofing both Prohibition and American Knowhow with just a soupçon of Chevalier's Gallic insouciance. Indeed, *The Big Pond* is so completely a Chevalier vehicle that Miss Colbert is reduced to a relatively petulant love interest, with none of the incandescent womanliness Lubitsch was to allow her to project in *The Smiling Lieutenant*. By any standards, Hobart Henley's direction of *The Big Pond* clearly lacks the lilt of Lubitsch, but there are little bits of satire at the factory that might possibly be attributed to Sturges. Even the spiked chewing gum might have been the brainchild of Sturges, himself the inventor of a kiss-proof lipstick for his mother's cosmetics firm. But with four other writers on the project, the odds certainly discourage any unduly creative speculation. Let us say simply that Sturges himself was already operating in a style and a tradition with many other practitioners—Coward, Maugham, Barry, Behrman on the stage, Lubitsch, St. Clair, D'Arrast on the silent screen, and later Cukor and Leisen in the talkies. Many of the ingredients of the Sturges forties classics are here—the insane illogic of the American success story (*Christmas in July, Miracle of Morgan's Creek, Mad Wednesday*), the modesty of heroes who dread becoming little fish in the big pond, and a suavely Europeanized view of America coupled with a brashly Americanized view of Europe so that the Jamesian dialectics of innocence and corruption are deflected from tragic irony to comic irony.

Fast and Loose combines the battle of the sexes with the struggle of the classes, and again the Sturges contribution is marginal if not minimal. Still, the rich-poor paradoxes of the plot bear more than a passing resemblance to the exquisitely elaborated conceits of *The Palm Beach Story*. Otherwise, *Fast and Loose* is memorable less for Fred Newmeyer's labored direction than for the curious tension between Miriam Hopkins' screen debut as a rowdy society girl and Carole Lombard's relatively subdued sass as the poor chorus girl with a disconcertingly delicate beauty. Miss Hopkins overacts with an array of chin-jutting, eye-narrowing mannerisms; Miss Lombard hardly acts at all and yet steals every scene with a smouldering impassivity that is the stuff myths are made of.

When *Strictly Dishonorable* finally materialized on the screen late in 1931, Preston Sturges wrote a letter to Carl Laemmle, President of Universal, congratulating him on the film's fidelity to the play. John M. Stahl was one of the more visually fluent directors of the thirties, and Gladys Lehman's screenplay was reasonably faithful to the Sturges original, but an especially big break for the film was the casting of Paul Lukas as the romantical opera singer and Lewis Stone as the tippling judge. Stone and Lukas both projected the civilized dignity of men of the world more with the zestful sweetness of a Sturges than with the world-weary cynicism one finds in the more vinegary Viennese comedies of Ernst Lubitsch and Billy Wilder. Sturges and Stahl were not so well served by Sidney Fox's determinedly diminutive ingenue complete with a poignantly innocent Southern drawl, a Valentine sampler projected more farcically the following year in *Once in a Lifetime* and more sentimentally in *The Mouthpiece,* on both occasions eclipsed by wondrously woman-wise performances by Aline McMahon. George Meeker as the discarded roughneck boyfriend was one of the least prepossessing exhibits in Hollywood's gallery of losers and masochists in romantic rondelays—Ralph Bellamy, Robert Preston, Lee Bowman, John Howard, Jeffrey Lynn, Peter Lawford, Grady Sutton, Allyn Joslin, Donald Woods, Alan Marshall, Richard Carlson, David Niven (early) and Herbert Marshall (late)—all being somewhat more memorably rejectable than was Meeker.

The plot, and even the mildy paradoxical title of ***Strictly Dishonorable,*** reflect the playwright's snug if not smug sophistication regarding the convenient confluence of materialism, mentality and morality. Hence, though most American movies, particularly during the Depression, sought to console the masses with the notion that money did not bring happiness, Sturges quite casually suggested that the most provincial girl imaginable was more likely to find not merely sensual pleasure but even sacred respect from a philandering opera singer than from the dull boy back home. Later Sturges was to write a ringingly Shavian denunciation of poverty as a proposed life style in ***Sullivan's Travels,*** making explicit what had always been implicit in his success-story-oriented Cinderella plots. Not that Sturges was a Pollyanna about the American Capitalistic System, but the only way to beat it, he implied, was to hang loose, roll with the punches, dance around the ring, and wait for that one opening that can turn a life around from savage frustration to frenzied success. But even people who have long since stopped yearning for even the sweepstakes-type success proposed by Sturges manage to find satisfaction by doing their own thing with as much style and brio as possible. Thus does Sturges transcend the boozy sentimentality of the speakeasy atmosphere in ***Strictly Dishonorable*** by carefully etching the autonomous individualities of extras, at times overexploiting the prevailing ethnic caricature of Italian restaurateurs and Irish cops, but even here supplying some modifying, warming idiosyncracy to the stock characterization. His forties stock company has not yet been assembled, and he is several years away from becoming the Brueghel of American comedy directors, but he is nonetheless on his way, influenced equally by the verbal crackle of a Broadway-West End-Boulevards tradition and the lost but still remembered art of silent slapstick.

The Power And The Glory took Sturges in an unexpectedly ambitious direction in 1933. Producer Jesse Lasky caused something of a furor by publicizing the film flamboyantly as a breakthrough in the art of "narratage." Not narration, mind you, some critics chortled, but narratage, and how fancy can you get, and all we have here is the good-old fashioned flashback with a minor variation of having the narrator occasionally use his own voice to narrate what the characters are mouthing in the flashback. William K. Howard directed Spencer Tracy, Colleen Moore, Ralph Morgan and Helen Vinson through the intricacies of a surprisingly somber Sturges script, and, it seems that Sturges was less than enchanted by Howard's direction; he may have resolved at this point that he would eventually have to direct his scripts himself. The film was neither critically nor commercially the success it set out to be with so much serious effort from all concerned, but it remains one of the more impressive films of the thirties, and not at all an entirely unworthy precursor of *Citizen Kane* in the never very popular genre of grown-up pessimism about the American Dream (vide the box-office receipts from *Greed, The Crowd, Street Scene, A Man to Remember, Kane, The Magnificent Ambersons,* ***The Great Moment***).

There is a tendency nowadays to underrate the contribution of William K. Howard to ***The Power And The Glory,*** one recent film historian going so far as to view the film merely as an episode in the career of noted cinematographer James Wong Howe. But it should be recorded (though not amplified at this time) that Howard was a director more serious and offbeat and original than most through a long career studded with eye-catching exceptions to commissioned routine, such as *White Gold, The Valiant* and *Back Door to Heaven.* Nonetheless ***The Power And The Glory*** remains in retrospect more crucial to the career of Sturges than to those of Howard, Howe, Tracy, Lasky et al. The story of a self-made businessman rising in public life as he falls in private life bears some resemblance to the Orson Welles-Herman J. Mankiewicz treatment of the Hearst-McCormick megalomania, but there are crucial differences as well. *Kane* gets by with people who wouldn't know German Expressionism if they collided with it in a dark alley at the intersection of Caligari Court and Murnau Circle. Nor are these same people particularly concerned with the revolutionary implications of deep focus for staging scenes as opposed to the classically analytical tradition of invisible editing and camera movement. For these people, *Kane* functions as a slice of fashionably pessimistic ideology out of the Kafka bag. American materialism is a dead end and all that, but, when you think about it, what isn't?

The Power And The Glory, unlike *Kane,* does not function implicitly or explicitly as ideology. The Sturges sensibility is too ironic for the demands of dogma. True, the businessman protagonist causes the death of some workers, but there is still something admirable (from Sturges's point of view) in the character's courage and decisiveness. That the story of his life is told after his death by a man he dominated and spiritually emasculated, a born Number Two man content to wait in the shadow of Number One, gives ***The Power And The Glory*** an initially disturbing ambiguity which is never dispelled. Yet we believe the account of Number Two as objective truth in a way we are never asked to believe the more subjectively oriented recollections of characters in flashback movies like *Kane* and *All About Eve* and *Rashomon.* Throughout his screenwriting career, Sturges employed the flashback not so much to express the selfish subjectivity of memory, but to reorganize, restructure and resequence reality so that all its ironies, comic and tragic, can be more effectively expressed. Here in ***The Power And The Glory,*** Sturges establishes very early that his protagonist's son has grown up to be a wastrel, a sponger, a loafer, and an all-round spoiled brat. Part of the problem is that the boy is overindulged by the mother who has felt somewhat neglected by her husband, whom she herself has driven to be a success. No-one's fault really, just the way things are. Then, much further on in the movie, we have proceeded past late flashbacks back to early flashbacks and back to late flashbacks until we find ourselves inside the humble cabin where the protagonist's son has just been born. Spencer Tracy holds up the newborn babe proudly and the music swells and he rousingly declares his hopes and dreams for his son—hopes and dreams that we have long since learned are to be horribly disappointed. And yet the scene is still played for all it is worth as if Sturges were trying to tell us that no matter how things end (and they always end badly), we must act as if they were going to end well. This is the affirmative, idealistic side of Sturges that came to the fore in *The Great Moment,* when he began with the ignominious death and humiliations of Dr. Morton, and ended with the heroic decision of Dr. Morton to end pain at the cost of his own fortune.

Throughout *The Power And The Glory* there are exceptionally strenuous metaphors to express the abstract notions of rise and fall, superiority and inferiority, selfishness and self-sacrifice. On one occasion, Spencer Tracy and Colleen Moore keep ascending a hill higher and higher as Tracy keeps trying to find the courage to propose. Earlier, the businessman as a child keeps climbing a tree to ever more dizzying heights as a prophetic expression of later heights that will be scaled in the business world. Sturges is often given to wildly visual conceits in his screenplays, many out of silent movies. I wonder if Sturges ever saw Harold Lloyd's *Kid Brother* back in the twenties, with its lyrical tree-climbing sequence. Since Sturges worked very knowledgeably with the Lloyd persona in *Mad Wednesday,* it is reasonable to assume some feedback.

Ultimately, *The Power And The Glory* depresses audiences not merely for its pessimism, which it shares with *Kane,* but for its sordidness, in which it is unique. What finally destroys the protagonist in *The Power And The Glory* is the moral corruption of the milieu into which his wealth has propelled him. When he finds his own son making love to his second wife, he feels betrayed to the point of first questioning and then ending his own existence. For Sturges himself, born and raised under still mysterious circumstances, in the circle of Mary Deste, Isadora Duncan, Gordon Craig, Isaac Singer, torn between European bohemianism and American materialism, between feminine fluttering and affectation on the one hand and masculine muscling and acquisitiveness on the other, the story that emerges in *The Power And The Glory* is too uncomfortably clinical for comfort. Still, Sturges treats it gingerly, tentatively, as if he were not yet sure of what attitude to take to it. Oddly, he never returns to this sort of subject again, and never again comes as close to an unguarded view of the frightful tensions through which he grew into manhood.

Sturges was associated with four other writers on the credits of *Thirty Day Princess,* a minor impersonation-Cinderella yarn too fragile and undistinguished for extended comment. Marion Gering directed with ideal structuralist passivity, and Sylvia Sidney made another feeble stab at being a comedienne mainly by winking excessively in the manner Rouben Mamoulian had found so expressive for his optical dissolves in *City Streets.* Miss Sidney was to remain the quintessential proletarian princess of the thirties, and leave the gossamer comedy to others. Otherwise, the movie is interesting mainly for its cross-references to the evolution of Cary Grant and Edward Arnold from minor to major levels of casting.

Sturges's second play to be adapted to the screen—*Child of Manhattan*—was indifferently received. Nancy Carroll, a saucy early-thirties star was winding up her precipitous decline, and John Boles continued to offend reviewers with his mannequin impassivity and light-opera hamminess. Most offended of all by Boles was temporary movie reviewer Graham Greene, who professed never to understand why lovely women on the screen succumbed to the sensual arrogance of Boles' cowlick. Again the plot emphasizes the niceness and consideration of all sorts of stock characters under the most sordid circumstances, the heroine actually launching the frothy farce with her illicit pregnancy, and then wishing to prevent the playboy who has made the noble gesture from sacrificing his own like to her need, and he, on his part, not wishing to allow her to sacrifice her own happiness merely through a misguided notion of his own motives. We are light years away from the attitudes struck in *Way Down East* and *East Lynne,* but mere months away from a time when illicit pregnancy will no longer have the option of being taken lightly.

That Sturges reportedly collaborated with Maxwell Anderson and Leonard Praskins on Leo Tolstoy's *Resurrection* [filmed as *We Live Again*] for Samuel Goldwyn and Rouben Mamoulian indicates only that Sturges was considered a relatively educated man on the Hollywood totem pole, and was therefore entrusted with arty foreign authors like Tolstoy, Ferenc Molnar (*The Good Fairy*), Marcel Pagnol (*Port of Seven Seas*) and François Villon via Justin Huntley McCarthy (*If I Were King*). Of these five-foot-shelf-and-less productions there is little to note beyond their strained refinement. *We Live Again* caused a slight ripple, less through Anna Sten's Slavic stupefaction and Fredric March's laborious stylishness—which always made up in persistence what it lacked in persuasiveness—than through some ideologically pointed speeches about the serfs, which, all things being equal, we would be safer crediting to Maxwell Anderson than to Sturges.

The Good Fairy is notable mainly for William Wyler's strenuous misdirection of delicate comedy, the miscasting of Herbert Marshall as the lawyer-lover, and the lovely, husky-voiced ingenue performance of Margaret Sullavan, particularly in the movie's best and most Sturgean scene in which she plays a tearful usherette in attendance at a cast-from-home-and-hearth-and-cradle side-tearjerker on the screen with the remorseless husband uttering and reuttering and fingerpointing his one word of dialogue: "GO" to great comic effect. Sturges later developed other movie-within-movie routines for *Sullivan's Travels* and *The Miracle of Morgan's Creek.*

Sturges was not given official credit for *Imitation Of Life* and *Next Time We Love,* two genuinely tasteful and above-average sagas of self-sacrifice that deserve mention, but apart from Sturges's presently unknown contributions to their behavioral charms. ***Diamond Jim*** and ***Hotel Haywire*** are somewhat more meaningfully related to the personality of Preston Sturges than their meagre reputations would indicate. ***Diamond Jim*** takes Edward Arnold's big tycoon mannerisms into the climactically logical laughter of his hammy-heroic self-destruction as a ghoulish gourmet. ***Hotel Haywire*** represents the earliest Sturges effort to work in pure farce, a genre then and later in which Sturges tended to enclose his slapstick effects within the quotes of self-conscious imitation. Sturges, like Welles, was a *nouvelle vague, hommage*-addicted director before his time.

Which leaves us with the two quintessentially Sturgean movies of the thirties, ***Easy Living*** and ***Remember the Night,*** both directed by Mitchell Leisen, a stylish middle-level figure at Paramount who bridged the gap between Lubitsch and Sternberg at the beginning of the thirties and Sturges and Wilder at the beginning of the forties. Which is not to say that Frank Tuttle or Wesley Ruggles or Norman McLeod or even Edward Sutherland (though it was a bit late for him) could not have taken a stab at ***Easy Living*** and ***Remember The Night.*** There was a self-operative tradition at Paramount within a reasonable margin of error, but Leisen was something more than a studio artisan if something less than a full-fledged auteur. Curiously, ***Easy Living*** is the only film with which Sturges the writer was associated in the thirties that may be reasonably preferred to any of his own forties films. Not only is ***Easy Living*** funny and gracious and generous in the best Sturges tradition; it is also velvety smooth and comfortably movieish in a way no Sturges-directed film ever was. Always with Sturges's own work, directed and written in tandem, there crept in disturbing dissonances and ambiguities, unexplained tics and complexes, unresolved affinities and attractions.

There is none of this in ***Easy Living.*** The light likeability of the milieu never crosses over into a more complex complicity. The brilliant bits of Luis Alberni as the frantically bluffing and blackmailing hotel impresario, William Demarest as the tough-guy gossip columnist, and Franklin Pangborn as the prissy prune proprietor of the fashion salon, remain just cameos without coalescing into that Dickensian density of detail that Sturges will later fashion in his own films. There are memorable set pieces—the fur coat falling on the double-decker bus, the customers scrambling for food in an automat gone berserkly ejaculatory, and the ticker tape always fouling up in Edward Arnold's hands as if to answer the never-before-asked question of what happens to ticker tape day in and day out when it stops tickering—but the gags and the characters end in themselves coolly and completely without any carry-over or cross-over. There is a neatness and dispatch to the movie that marks it as a work more of expertly collaborative craftsmanship than of the most personal art. It's probably just a coincidence that Sturges was never associated again with Jean Arthur, who gives ***Easy Living*** much of its spunky-elegant resilience; but it is unlikely that he would ever have veiled her with as much expertly mocking glamour as the eye-wise Leisen did in her brilliantly composed super-luxury bedtime (rather than bedroom) scene in the hotel with Ray Milland. Leisen's hommage to Sternberg-on-Dietrich is, like Arthur's ambivalent attitude toward her own working girl beauty, satiric without being derisive, delighted in itself just this side of delirium.

Sturges's career as a scriptwriter, pure and simple, ends with ***Remember the Night,*** a somber, low-key delicately awakening light drama of love and redemption under the shadow of prison and all the guilt such a plot device implies. ***Remember The Night*** is a nice, sensitive, detailed, nuanced movie, and Leisen's direction is virtually faultless from a technical standpoint. But this wasn't enough for Sturges. He wanted something more, a richer tone perhaps, or a more complex mood, or a more personal style. Whatever the source of his discontent, it propelled him into one of the most brilliant and most bizarre bursts of creation in the history of the cinema. (pp. 81-4)

Andrew Sarris, "Preston Sturges in the Thirties," in Film Comment, *Vol. 6, No. 4, Winter, 1970-71, pp. 80-5.*

Gerald Mast (essay date 1973)

[*In the following excerpt from his* The Comic Mind: Comedy and the Movies, *Mast offers a critical overview of Sturges's films.*]

The first of the three major traditions of sound comedy is the American film that generates its comedy through talk. Creating within the confines of the Hollywood studio system, several directors made distinctive, clever, and intelligent comedies that, like most American films of the 1930s and 1940s, were dialogue films in which pictures primarily supported talk. But if the talk was good, the pictures pleasant and functional, the performances energetic and compelling, and the structural conception careful and clever, the comedy could be very entertaining indeed.

Because the dialogue comedy was so dependent on talk and structure, it was equally dependent on the scriptwriter who devised the talk and structure. The dialogue comedies were *written* comedies, and the writer played almost as great a role in shaping the film as its director. The scripts of Ben Hecht, Preston Sturges, Robert Riskin, Dudley Nichols, Herman J. Mankiewicz, Charles Lederer, Garson Kanin, and Ruth Gordon frequently overwhelmed the weak director, exerting far more influence over the film than the director's "auteurial" style. If that fact seems to contradict the assumption that the director is a film's prime mover, it is equally true that in the best dialogue comedies the insight of the writers fused perfectly with the style and attitudes of the director, who expanded the sharp script into the full and final comic conception.

Underlying the best of the dialogue comedies was usually a subtle and silent rebellion against the very studio system and values that produced them. Most of these films slyly bit the hand that fed them, but the bite was very coy and the teeth were often capped with the same tinsel and rhinestones that Hollywood so adored. The comedies developed a unique aesthetic for destroying Hollywood assumptions and conventions while appearing to subscribe to them. Their primary targets were the familiar movie definitions of love, sex, success, and propriety. And by shredding the Hollywood clichés, the comedies frequently implied a more human, sensible, and sensitive system of emotional relationships and moral values. As in the earliest American comedies, the sting of raucous, vulgar sincerity popped the balloon of pretentious gentility. (pp. 249-50)

[Like Howard Hawks] Preston Sturges would seem to be another of Frank Capra's opposites—cynical rather than sentimental, a satirist rather than an apologist, an advocate of the sharp tongue and brain rather than the warm, soft heart. But Sturges was not so distant from Capra as the surfaces would indicate. Like Capra, Sturges was better with comic scenes than with explicit ideology and had as much trouble as Capra at combining funny incidents and serious issues in the same film. And despite his belief in the brain, Sturges' most affectionate and sympathetic people, like Capra's, have sincere hearts beneath the tough exteriors.

No one made better dialogue comedies than Sturges, primarily because no one wrote better dialogue. Sturges is one of those filmmakers whose one-liners are often as memorable as his whole films. In *Easy Living* (a Sturges screenplay that completely dominates its director, Mitchell Leisen), Jean Arthur is sitting on a Fifth Avenue bus when a sable coat descends from the skies to land on her head. She angrily turns to the man behind her, a Hindu wearing a turban, and snaps, "What's the big idea, anyway?" His answer, "Kismet." Ironically, the joke also functions in the film, for Kismet, fate, is the driving force in the film's plot.

In *The Great McGinty,* a crooked politician remarks, "If it wasn't for graft, you'd get a very low type of people in politics." When McGinty subsequently runs out on his wife, he tells her about the money he stashed away "to send the kids through college—without selling magazines." And the most brilliant collection of Sturgesisms opens *Sullivan's Travels,* as an idealistic director discusses a socially conscious film with his money-minded producers:

> "You see the symbolism of it? Capital and Labor destroying each other."
> "It gives me the creeps."
>
> "It was held over a fifth week at the Music Hall."
> "Who goes to the Music Hall? Communists."
>
> "It died in Pittsburgh."
> "What do they know in Pittsburgh?"
> "They know what they like."
> "Then why do they live in Pittsburgh?"

The Sturges emphasis on dialogue determines his film technique, which relies on the conventional American two-shot to capture the faces and features while the characters talk, talk, talk. But it is such good talk—incredibly rapid, crackling, brittle—that the film has plenty of life. Like Hawks, Sturges was a master of the lightning pace.

When Sturges uses special cinematic devices, he inevitably turns them into self-conscious bits of trickery and gimmickry that harmonize well with the parodic spirit of the film. His favorite game with the sound track is to use musical backgrounds that comment parodically on the action in the scene. The opening of *Sullivan's Travels* uses melodramatic "movie music" that underscores a stagey, predictable gunfight on top of a speeding train. We later discover the scene was indeed part of a melodramatic movie within the movie. *The Palm Beach Story* opens with the William Tell Overture to underscore a breathtakingly funny pseudo-melodramatic montage sequence that finally brings a future husband and wife to the altar. The film's final use of music is just as clever. While Rudy Vallee serenades Claudette Colbert with "Goodnight, Sweetheart" (complete with full orchestra) outside her window, the sweetheart takes refuge in the arms (and, by implication, bed) of her husband inside the room. Rudy's romantic singing drives her into the arms of his rival. And perhaps Sturges uses music most effectively and wittily in *Unfaithfully Yours* (1948) when an orchestra conductor imagines three separate strategies for handling his adulterous wife, each perfectly correlated with the musical feeling of the piece he is conducting.

Sturges also reserves his manipulation of editing and the camera for the occasional tricky effect. *Christmas in July* uses a comically obtrusive zoom shot accompanied by a whistling kazoo to achieve its final miraculous solution. *The Lady Eve* combines jarring shock-cuts and screaming train whistles as comic punctuation for each of Eve's "revelations" of her previous affairs to her innocent husband. The opening sequence of *The Palm Beach Story* is a dizzying, almost illogical montage that parallels a melodramatic murder in a closet with a wedding (breaking out of the closet?). Sturges similarly punctuates his scenes of talk with an occasional bit of physical, slapstick comedy (the automat scene in *Easy Living,* the racing land yacht in *Sullivan's Travels,* the escape from prison in *McGinty,* the rifle-shooting sequence aboard the train in *Palm Beach*) that cunningly—sometimes too cunningly—injects motion into his motion pictures.

Sturges' cleverness also shows itself in the unconventional, unexpected people and situations with which he filled his films. His crazy foreigners—Louis Louis in *Easy Living,* the Boss in *McGinty,* Toto in *Palm Beach*—are burlesques of the Hollywood cliché. Where most of Sturges' contemporaries contrasted the pure, natural American with the corrupt, suave European (Henry James in Hollywood terms), Sturges' foreigners parody American ideals by trying to imitate them. Louis tries to open a huge, grotesque hotel rather than remain a brilliant French chef. His aspirations to gentility and class are undercut by his vulgarity and pronunciation—the Imperial "Suit" (suite), "phenonemom," "invisibles." The Boss explains his American success by referring to the romantic tradition of the robber baron and by pointing out that, if it weren't for him, "everyone would be at the mercy" (but he never says at the mercy of what). Toto is the looniest foreigner of all, a slimy gigolo, ugly and wormlike, whose sole functions seem to be to parade around in a series of different costumes, to intrude into conversations with his single coherent word, "Greetings" ("His English is a little elementary"), and to chatter in some stew of languages that makes it impossible to tell to which tongue he owes his original allegiance.

Among the other wonderful Sturges caprices is "the Wienie King" in *Palm Beach,* a gruff, testy, deaf old gentleman who still loves the ladies and who can carry on whole conversations without understanding a single word. To Sturges we owe the comic and rare opportunity to hear Eugene Pallette, the human bullfrog, sing "For Tonight We'll Merry Merry Be" in *The Lady Eve. Easy Living* features a youth magazine called *The Boys' Constant Companion.* Ironically, this magazine is staffed entirely by prune-faced, moralistic old maids and misters. And about this magazine Sturges sneaks in a wonderfully sly bit of obscenity (Sturges, like Lubitsch, was a master at ducking the censor) when the rich businessman mistakenly refers to the publication as *The Boys' Constant Reminder.*

Sturges also delighted in showing apparently conventional Hollywood characters and scenes in a very unconventional light. The conventional boy and girl in *Christmas in July* engage in verbal battles that no Hollywood juvenile and ingenue ought to have. (He even tells her to shut up.) *The Lady Eve* contains two seduction scenes in which the lady throws herself at the recalcitrant gentleman, who insists on protecting both her and his virtue. The idyllic, conventional life of the rich receives rough treatment in the opening scene of *Easy Living,* when the wealthy husband and wife fight (almost to the death) over her newest sable coat. The Hollywood clichés of loving father and daughter get a tough beating from the continual violent arguments between Diana Lynn and William Demarest in *The Miracle of Morgan's Creek. Sullivan's Travels* reverses the clichés of city sensuality and country purity as a fat, lecherous farm widow does her utmost to enjoy the physical pleasures of Sullivan's young, firm body. The best things in the Sturges films are these surprising pieces of reversal and burlesque.

As for their wholes, each of the Sturges films begins with a parodic premise. *The Great McGinty* (1940) parodies both Hollywood "flashback" stories and the American ideal that anyone can rise to greatness; *Sullivan's Travels* (1941), Hollywood production values and the Hollywood iconoclast's urge to say something significant; *The Lady Eve* (1941), shipboard romance and virginal innocence; *The Miracle of Morgan's Creek* (1943), small-town Americana, the sanctity of motherhood, and patriotism; *The Palm Beach Story* (1942), marital tensions; *Unfaithfully Yours* (1948), marital infidelity; and so forth. The best Sturges films never desert delicate, fast-paced parody for moralistic, sentimental conclusions.

The Great McGinty is unrelentingly ironic. It begins with a delicious red herring, a framework story that seems to promise the tale of an erring bank clerk in a South American "banana republic." But the film couldn't care less about this bank clerk. The real story turns out to be about the bartender (Brian Donlevy), the man who stops the clerk from shooting himself. The bartender (only several reels later do we discover his name is McGinty) tells of his rise from hobo to governor. He begins his political career as a two-dollar voter for the political machine of some big city, substituting for those registered voters who are no longer alive to vote for the machine candidates. In his zeal, an ironic burlesque of "get out and vote," the hobo votes 37 times, earning himself $74. That is American ingenuity and gumption doubled and redoubled.

From this auspicious beginning the hobo rises through the machine's ranks. He first shakes down the shady businessmen (and women) who don't want to pay protection; for example, Madame LaJolla (pronounced "Hoya"), a "fortune-teller," must come up with $250 or "Madame LaJolla doesn't jolla any more." Then Dan McGinty wins his first office—alderman. He develops more refined methods for plucking higher sums. Finally, after acquiring a wife and kids, McGinty becomes "reform" mayor. (The Boss ironically runs the "Reform Party" as well as the machine.) In each of McGinty's steps up the political ladder, his style gets smoother (he even grows a mustache), his clothes get slicker (from hobo rags to a ridiculous plaid suit referred to as a "horse blanket" to a dapper three-piece business suit to a top hat and tails).

But McGinty gets into trouble when he falls in love with the woman he married for political convenience. She suddenly feels qualms about McGinty's "municipal improvements" (euphemism for graft) and the grafters who support him—slum landlords, owners of sweatshops. She urges McGinty to institute genuine reform, to buck the party, to make the world safe for the children. McGinty has his doubts. To his wife's sentimentalities about the "dark, airless factories," McGinty retorts with his own sentimentalities: the factory where he worked as a kid was clean and neat, a place where he labored profitably "instead of playing on the streets learning a lot of dirty words." But the wife's sentimentalities triumph—and Sturges clearly parodies yet another political cliché, the woman behind the man. (These were, after all, the years of Franklin D. and Eleanor.) Ironically, McGinty's one honest moment costs him his family, his power, his wife, and his fortune. When he bucks the Boss, the Boss bucks back, and the two of them end up in the "banana republic," continuing their long feud over who exactly is boss.

The unadulterated cynicism of *The Great McGinty,* its burlesque of the democratic political process and its reduction of an ideal—America as "the land of opportunity"—to the absurd would never have been accepted by audiences one year later. During the war years Sturges had to worry not only about the censor but also about stepping on the sensitive moral toes of a country sacrificing its young men to preserve the very ideals that *McGinty* burlesques. Sturges' greater consciousness of audience values is clear in *Sullivan's Travels,* in which the cynicism is tempered by an uplifting moral affirmation. The plot of this film springs from the tension between an intellectual film director who wants to make a "significant," socially conscious film, *Oh Brother, Where Art Thou?* and the producers who want him to keep making the escapist fluff at which he excels, *Ants in Your Pants of 1941.* The first part of the film convincingly demonstrates that a man with a college education, swimming pool, alimony payments, butler, and a troop of publicity men on his tail is incapable

The Great McGinty: *The Boss (Akim Tamiroff) explains things to the not-yet-"great" McGinty (Brian Donlevy). Sturges regular William Demarest (far right) looks on.*

of capturing the desperation and misery of the poor and suffering. (There is perhaps a conscious reference to Ford's *The Grapes of Wrath* and the Pare Lorenz documentaries in the film's depiction of starving tramps and government camps.)

But the second half of the film takes Sullivan and the audience in a very different direction and toward a very different conclusion. Through a series of bizarre accidents, Sullivan winds up truly wretched and helpless, an inmate of a brutal Southern prison (evoking the Hollywood chain-gang genre). In the midst of his misery, Sullivan goes to the movies; the prisoners are guests of a black congregation on its movie night. Sturges shows the parallel misery of both blacks and prisoners; as the convicts shuffle into the humble chapel wearing chains, the blacks sing, "Let My People Go." After this rather idealized display of social misery, the movie flashes on the screen (the third film within this film about films), a Walt Disney cartoon with Mickey Mouse and Pluto. And all the downtrodden members of the audience respond in unison to the funny film—with laughter. From this demonstration, Sullivan concludes (after he gets out of prison as bizarrely as he got in) that *Oh Brother, Where Art Thou?* is not worth making.

He directly proclaims, "There's a lot to be said for making people laugh. That's all some people have. It isn't much, but it's better than nothing in this cockeyed caravan." After the explicit proclamation, only slightly softened by the fancy metaphor, Sturges ends the film with an equally explicit montage of laughing faces.

Christmas in July also insists on a moralistic ending, for the young man learns that his own ability is a stronger asset than any windfall (after which Sturges gives him the windfall). ***Hail the Conquering Hero*** ends with the young man's confession of his dishonesty to the whole town, a greater act of personal heroism than the very clichés that forced the man into his initial lie (after which the town elects him mayor). ***Mad Wednesday*** ends with the implication that it is better to be "mad," spontaneous, and free than to be chained to a stifling, deadening routine (and after Harold Diddlebock's lesson in spontaneity, he discovers he has miraculously won both riches and the hand of the woman he loves).

So many of the Sturges films end with these "miracles"—like those sextuplets which are the miracle of Morgan's Creek. Such miracles are copouts. Despite their obvious parodies of Hollywood success stories and the Hollywood homily that the rewards go to the virtuous, Sturges' endings, like René Clair's, are incapable of tracing the implications of the issues that he himself has introduced. Either Sturges sells out to Hollywood's commercial necessities, or he is a lazy, sloppy thinker who cannot refuse the easy road (as James Agree suggests), or, like René Clair, he simply "likes happy endings"—whether they make intellectual sense or not.

The absence of these moralizing and miraculous solutions in Sturges' domestic films perhaps accounts for their greater unity and consistency. *Easy Living, The Lady Eve,* and *The Palm Beach Story* do not desert irony and satire to give the audience an obligatory piece of optimistic inspiration. In its own way *Easy Living* is a much better film about the Depression than *Sullivan's Travels,* simply because it plays on the irony that for some people a $58,000 sable coat is so valueless that it can be thrown away like a piece of trash, and for others a $58,000 sable coat is so valueless that it can't provide a nourishing meal or a necessary job.

Despite the Sturges toughness, his scorn for fakery and poses, his ridiculing of false ideals, it is more difficult to see what he accepts than what he rejects. If there is a positive Sturges ideal, it can be seen more easily in his people than in the moral summaries that conclude so many of his films. The members of the Sturges troupe—the character actors he uses over and over again—say much about Sturges' values. William Demarest is Sturges' alter ego; tough, cynical, anti-sentimental, he owes no allegiance to abstractions, but is always loyal to his friends. Jimmy Conlin—the owlish flea, nervous, squeaky-voiced—usually comforts those in trouble. Eric Blore, a man of words and poses, knows how to twist appearances to make people accept the fake as real. Robert Greig, the inevitable butler, enjoys the luxury of being a butler and is a loyal cynic who refuses to romanticize the class question. Edgar Kennedy—bartender, private detective—never lets his gruff voice and appearance interfere with his human compassion. And so forth. Most of the Sturges players are mixtures of toughness and softness (even the mincing Franklin Pangborn), scornful of idealistic clichés, usually responsive to each other as people.

In his attack on sentimental and pretentious clichés, Sturges is clearly part of the great American comic tradition that stretches back to the earliest comic jests. Like Lubitsch, Hawks, and Ben Hecht, Sturges disguised his contempt for the Hollywood beatitudes with cinematic conventions that looked very much like the usual Hollywood product. For most members of the audience, *Easy Living* was a wonderful chance to indulge fantasies about incredible luxuries dropping from the skies. The ornate, lavish sets—particularly the Imperial "Suit"—looked exactly like the gaudy settings of their favorite M-G-M films. But for a few members of the audience, the film was a chance to see the grotesque excesses of wealth, the immense gap between rich and poor, and the instability of a stock market that could rise and fall crazily on the whims of a dizzy lady. Further, the film coyly exposes the importance of sex in our supposedly puritanical society; Mary Smith derives all her power from everyone else's assumption that she is sleeping with the powerful financier. In his delightful games with Hollywood expectations, Sturges' cleverness and iconoclasm are more impressive than the depth and complexity of his vision. Sturges very quickly ran out of that iconoclastic energy in the years following the war. (pp. 265-71)

> Gerald Mast, "The Dialogue Tradition," in his The Comic Mind: Comedy and the Movies, *second edition, The University of Chicago Press, 1979, pp. 249-79.*

Orson Welles on Sturges and *The Power and the Glory*:

[Peter Bogdanovich]: *There's a film written by Preston Sturges called* The Power and the Glory *which has been said to have influenced you in the flashback style of* Kane. *Is that true?*

[Orson Welles]: No. I never saw it. I've heard that it has strong similarities; it's one of those coincidences. I'm a great fan of Sturges and I'm grateful I didn't see it. He never accused me of it—we were great chums—but I just never saw it. I saw only his comedies. But I would be honored to lift anything from Sturges, because I have very high admiration for him.

You were friends.

Right up till the end of his life [in 1959]. And I knew him before I went to Hollywood; in fact, I first met him when I was about thirteen and going to school at Todd. Wonderful fellow, and I think a great filmmaker, as it turned out.

Yes, and he wrote marvelous dialogue.

Started in a hospital. He was a businessman until he was about forty. He got very sick and lay in the hospital and decided to write a play, *Strictly Dishonorable,* which ran eight years or something on Broadway. And that made him a writer. Then later he became a director. He had never thought of it before.

What happened to him in Europe in the 1950s? He only made one film.

He was just trying to raise money for a picture. Nobody would give him a job. Simple as that.

> Orson Welles with Peter Bogdanovich, in their This Is Orson Welles, *edited by Jonathan Rosenbaum, 1992.*

Richard Corliss (essay date 1974)

[*In the following excerpt from his study* Talking Pictures: Screenwriters in the American Cinema, *Corliss focuses on three of Sturges's films:* The Power and the Glory, Diamond Jim, *and* The Great Moment.]

In the handful of screenwriters whose influence was crucial to the craft, Preston Sturges deserves at least two fingers and a thumb. He was Hollywood's greatest writer-director, with the emphasis on the former. He created a racy, malapropriate idiom whose deceptive ease would prove inimitable and, more important, a vision that was sometimes profound, often petty, but always worthy of the term "Sturgean." While his direction, especially of extended dialogue scenes, shows far more control than contemporary critics were willing to grant it, Sturges's direction would be of only the most esoteric concern today if he had not written eight or ten of Hollywood's best screenplays; a Sturges script like *Remember the Night,* directed by Mitchell Leisen, is certainly more personal (let alone more successful) than Sturges's direction of an unsympathetic project like *Les Carnets du Major Thompson.* His last decade was spent in a decline that is still only partly explicable. Perhaps his talent simply burned out, since, for five years in the early forties, Sturges's star blazed as brilliantly as any in Hollywood's Golden Age.

The emphasis here is on the Sturges vision as it emanated from his typewriter—especially since four of the ten films appraised in this chapter were directed by others—and not on Sturges's visual style. In their *Film Culture* article, Manny Farber and W. S. Poster ("Bill Poster" sounds suspiciously like the name of some sub-Sturgean bit player, but Farber has said that Mr. Poster actually exists) so perceptively evoked the director's frenzied place and cluttered *mise-en-scène* that further discussion of the subject may seem superfluous. Nevertheless, a few additional points might be made here.

Sturges's films fall, with surprising grace, into "light" and "dark" categories—thematically and chromatically—and this applies even when he did not direct. *Easy Living, Remember the Night, The Lady Eve, The Palm Beach Story, Hail the Conquering Hero, Mad Wednesday, The Beautiful Blonde from Bashful Bend,* and *Les Carnets du Major Thompson* all have a flat, thirties look that allows the dialogue and actors to roam authoritatively, for better or worse, through studio sets and set-ups. The memories provoked by *The Power and the Glory, Diamond Jim, Port of Seven Seas, If I Were King, The Great McGinty, Sullivan's Travels, The Miracle of Morgan's Creek,* and *Unfaithfully Yours* are shadowy, nocturnal, opaque, the mood often somber and melancholy, the theme one of loss through either aristocratic renunciation or plebian frustration. Sturges's bridge between these tonalities is *The Great Moment*—a predominantly reflective, even morose film until its sublime-ridiculous climax, in which divine approval of Dr. Morton's selflessness is signified by an abrupt flood of Kleig lights.

The temptation to construct elaborate dialectics on biographical, professional, and artistic levels seems particularly acute when critics try to deal with Sturges, so I'll stop short of developing a case for the "dark" films over the "light" ones, or even suggesting that the categories are absolute. What can be said is that the dark films are visually more interesting, beginning with *The Power and the Glory*—that startling if embryonic *film noir*—and culminating in the technically accomplished self-immolation performed by Rex Harrison (read: Sturges) in *Unfaithfully Yours.* Consciously or not, Sturges underlit Harrison's grotesqueries with such relentlessness that some of the actor's more painful pratfalls were muffled in the darkness—though Sturges made up for this generosity by dubbing in some especially unpleasant and counterproductive sound effects.

In *Unfaithfully Yours,* Sturges built audience sympathy for the lovable co-stars by shooting them in cheery close-ups that contrasted adroitly with the medium shots he used to frame the comically astringent featured couple. No such distinction was made for the respective pairs in *The Palm Beach Story;* nor was it needed, since all four of the major characters are pretty unstable. In general, though, Sturges let any moral or thematic distinctions arise from the dialogue, and relied on what might be called "the proscenium frame" to express the author's disinterest in his puppets' manic meanderings.

Sturges's remoteness from the numbing activity of his films helps explain the failure of his endless succession of slapstick sequences. To call his attitude "classical" would be to slur genuine Hollywood classicism as exemplified by Hawks and McCarey. Sturges never had the control over a physical scene that Hawks demonstrates in, say, *His Girl Friday.* Instead, his disinterest borders on the documentary, and makes his slapstick seem crueler than it was probably intended. His shots remain as static and noncommittally medium-range as ever; even the tempo is hardly accelerated. His preoccupation with the pain in slapstick when it's attempted by the uncoordinated begins to look almost anthropological. Perhaps Sturges was just as fascinated by members of the *sucker sapiens* when they were humiliated physically as when they tripped malapropriately over the English language. In the end, Sturges's visual-physical style expressed only the perversity of his world, whereas his dialogue expressed both that world's perversity *and* its resilience.

The Power and the Glory

Sturges's first original screenplay—and the only one, except for *Hotel Haywire,* before 1940—proposes the unstartling Hollywood thesis that, as professional power increases, personal glory diminishes. What distinguishes *The Power and the Glory,* making it so relentlessly somber and, for the ultralinear thirties, virtually unique, is Sturges's "narratage" technique, a complicated series of Chinese-box-puzzle flashbacks that casts a pall of determinism over the film's early, joyous sequences. We are led back and forth over four periods of tycoon Tom Garner's life: childhood, early manhood, middle age, and the day of his death; a friend of Tom's narrates the story on the evening of his funeral.

In its present condition (the film had been lost, and was reconstructed from existing scraps into a truncated but not emasculated print), the narrative of *The Power and the Glory* can be broadly traced in the following fashion, with "A" representing childhood, "B" early manhood, "C" middle age, and "D" the day of death; "E" is the burial day.

E. Funeral, with elegy; Henry, Tom's friend, begins the narration that night, in the form of an argument with his wife over Tom's merits and faults; the action frequently returns to the present;

A(1). Henry meets Tom at a rural waterhole; they become friends;

A(2). A few years later, Tom is quiet, moody, and confesses he has no intellectual ambitions;

C(1). Tom, now president of a railroad company, bullies his board of directors into approving the purchase of another line he had actually bought ten minutes earlier;

B(1). Tom learns to read and write, to make Henry "sore"; he proposes to his teacher, Sally;

C(2). Tom meets Eve, the daughter of the president of his new subsidiary, and becomes infatuated;

B(2). Sally, now Tom's wife, prods his ambition;

C(3). Sally tells Tom of her regret that she ever encouraged him to be a success, and Tom tells Sally of his love for Eve; Tom, Jr., now a young man, has become a wastrel;

B(3). Tom is named chief of a construction crew, and Sally becomes pregnant;

B(4). Tom, Jr. is born; Tom expresses his high hopes for the boy;

C(4). Tom divorces Sally and marries Eve, but spends their honeymoon night breaking a strike; Eve spends it on the town with Tom, Jr.; Sally commits suicide;

D(1). Five years later, Tom discovers that his son is the father of Eve's child; Tom commits suicide;

E. The film ends, at Henry's house, in the present tense.

The Power and the Glory is, in several ways, a film out of its time, a unique precursor of forties filmmaking in Hollywood—though, oddly, not of the kind of film Sturges himself was to make. Not only does it bear striking thematic similarities to *Citizen Kane* (Herman Mankiewicz [who cowrote the *Citizen Kane* screenplay with Orson Welles] was head writer at Paramount when Sturges began working there in 1929), but its oppressive sense of predetermined pastness became the hallmark of all those examples of the *film noir* a decade later, films whose copious use of the flashback and of the implicated narrator helped drench nearly every optimistic or noncommittal scene in the mists of irony and fatalism.

Andrew Sarris might argue that **The Power and the Glory** betrays a very thirties-like preference for the evanescent *plaisir d'amour* over that ultimate *chagrin d'amour* we associate with films of the forties. He refers specifically, in his *Film Comment* article on Sturges's early screenplays, to a sequence in which Spencer Tracy, as Tom, "holds up [his] newborn babe proudly and the music swells and he rousingly declares his hopes and dreams for his son— hopes and dreams that we have long since learned are to be horribly disappointed. And yet the scene is played for all it is worth as if Sturges were trying to tell us that no matter how things end (and they always end badly), we must act as if they were going to end well."

If-what an if!—there is any moral lesson to be learned from Sturges's later comedies, it is that no matter how things end (and they always end well), we must act as if they were going to end badly. Witness the heroes of **The Lady Eve, The Palm Beach Story, The Miracle of Morgan's Creek, Hail the Conquering Hero,** and **Unfaithfully Yours,** to name only the most obvious examples; every one of them is a congenital defeatist doomed to final good fortune by the conventions of Hollywood comedy. Now, it may be unfair to use Sturges's later comedies to rebut a point about an early tragedy, but I think there's a simpler dramatic rule at work in the sequence Sarris describes: namely, the greater the hopes, the deeper the depression—a corollary of the film's thesis. The higher Tom holds his son, the more profound will be the psychic injuries when Tom, Jr. falls. Tom's son, who grows up suffering from the spiritual acrophobia that traditionally infects sons of men-in-high-places, is the repository of Tom's only great hope (his financial greatness was thrust upon him by Sally); so it is appropriate that the bursting of this dream will lead to his suicide. But the sequence in question, though "played for all it is worth," conveys less golden optimism than rhinestone irony. We are not meant to share the character's hopes, but rather to appreciate the dereliction of parental responsibilities that triggers their disillusionment. Far from showing "the affirmative, idealistic side of Sturges that came to the fore in **The Great Moment,**" as Sarris argues, this sequence is **The Great Moment's** opposite, in theme if not in tone. The later film is indeed optimistic and affirmative because, although Dr. Morton's life ended in "ignominious death and humiliation," Morton was led to a tragic end by the criminal ignorance of his colleagues, and not by the inability to live up to ideals that condemns Tom Garner. Tom is a rough sketch of Charles Foster Kane; Morton is an earlier, more satisfying version of Sister Kenny. Tom and Kane betray themselves; Morton and Elizabeth Kenny are betrayed by others.

The designation of Henry, the narrator, as Tom's "friend" has to be qualified: Henry is a true friend to Tom, but Tom doesn't reciprocate. He never lets Henry get very close to him, either professionally (Henry was Tom's secretary, not his partner) or personally. Henry is a duller Jed Leland [Charles Foster Kane's friend, played by Joseph Cotton], filling Leland's functions of whipping boy and part-time conscience. At one point, Henry captures exactly the bemused, rather smug tone we will associate with Jedediah: "When Tom bought the Santa Clara," Henry recalls, "he got more than he bargained for. The Santa Clara had a president, and the president had a daughter." Like Leland, Henry is a "sourpuss"; in the person of Ralph Morgan, he even looks like an older Joseph Cotten.

Still, as Jed said of Kane, "Maybe I wasn't his friend—but if I wasn't, he never had one." And Henry is Tom's only friend. Their first meeting reveals Tom's exploitation-education of Henry: Tom throws the younger and smaller Henry into the waterhole and, in desperation, Henry learns how to swim. Is this an act of bullying or a practical lesson in self-reliance? Henry says, "He was teaching me to die." By this definition of "teaching," Tom, Jr.'s cuckolding of his father could be taken as postgraduate instruction at its most chillingly effective. The difference is that something in Henry, the weakling, made him swim, whereas Tom, the strong man, could only sink into suicide.

Sally is accused (by Henry and by herself) of responsibility for Tom's ruin because she instilled in him a desire for success that he resisted at first. Henry says, "Tom might be a track-walker yet, happy and satisfied, if it wasn't for her." Sally depicts herself as a bourgeois Lady Macbeth: "I wanted the power and the money," she says ruefully to Tom; "you wanted to go fishing." And: "You've built so many miles of railroad, and every mile has taken you further away from me." Yet, in the earliest childhood sequence, Tom is shown to be a born leader, or at least a born climber. He dares to climb to the top of a forbidding-looking tree overhanging the waterhole, then dives off, catches his hand under a rock at the bottom of the pond, and fights his way out of the predicament by himself—but with a scar on his hand that will last a lifetime. In later life, the pattern will repeat itself: Tom will have to be resourceful, because he is so foolhardy.

Climbing up . . . tumbling down. There are four of these "exceptionally strenuous metaphors" (Sarris's phrase) in the film, all foretelling or dramatizing the rise and fall of a "great man," all illustrating Sturges's moral: "The power and the glory—what they can do to a man!" The most delirious ascension has Tom dragging Sally up an endless mountain. Here, his ambition is born of indecision; he is simply stalling to get up the nerve to propose. "Tom," Sally asks, "couldn't you have asked me at the foot of the mountain?" Tom's desire to succeed in business is specifically triggered by his impending parenthood: "I'll make so much money that we'll be able to buy the Southwestern"—which he eventually does. All these incidents tend to absolve Sally from much of the guilt that drives her to suicide.

The final "ascension" sequence is related, with genuine poignancy, to the scene where Tom lifted up his son and his hopes. It comes at the end of the film, when Tom learns of his second wife's adultery. Stricken, he slowly mounts the stairs from his living room to the bedrooms above, gasping, "Where's Little Boy? Want to see Little Boy. . . ." His last hope, we can infer, is to hold Little Boy up in ironic completion of an action begun thirty years earlier—even though it is not *his* little boy, as he had believed until that moment, but his little boy's little boy. When he reaches the top of the stairs he mutters, "Why shouldn't you be in love? And do as you want just once in your life?" This is meant less to forgive his young wife for her sins than to recall the exact words Sally used to forgive *his* adultery with Eve. Both Sally and Tom have accepted the responsibility for driving their respective spouses to infidelity. Tom's recollection of Sally's words preordains the denouement, since Sally committed suicide soon after absolving Tom. He shoots himself, and utters one word: "Sally!"

Tom's retrospective reverence for Sally closely parallels Charlie Kane's love for the memory of his mother, while Emily Norton and Susan Alexander [Charles Foster Kane's first and second wives] reflect various facets of Tom's second wife, Eve. With Emily, Eve shares wealth and breeding; with Susan, she shares youth and the lure of self-destruction. Tom's dying word, like Kane's, indicates where his sympathies lie, as well as expressing painful nostalgia for some kind of paradise lost. In Tom's case the pain is complicated by the memory that Sally helped thrust ambition—and success, with the sexual advantages it usually entails—upon a complacent naïf who ended up losing everything he never wanted.

What distinguishes Tom Garner from Charles Foster Kane is Tom's use of power and people (which, for both men, are one and the same thing). Garner never tries anything but straightforward intimidation. He's a grown-up version of the toughest kid in town, and since he missed the moderating, corrupting influence of "good schools," he doesn't know how to get what he wants through seduction rather than rape. (Tracy's portrayal of a tycoon in *Edward, My Son* is slightly more polished, just as his hoodlum executive in *Quick Millions* is even more brutal; and Colleen Moore's—Sally's—ill temper in her last years prefigures Deborah Kerr's Grand Guignol tour de force in *Edward*.) When the railroad workers threaten to strike, Tom threatens them with worse; and when they do strike, he strikes back, with 406 deaths resulting. Nor does Tom hide his infatuation for Eve from Sally. Henry says, "Tom fell in love, that's all. He couldn't help it. He was too honest." Though Henry's wife retorts, "He was too selfish, you mean," we get the point. Unlike Kane, Tom is too honest to hide his selfishness.

Kane, an *émigré* of Princeton, Harvard, and Switzerland, is suaver, more oblique, preferring cajolery to cracked skulls. But his velvet-glove technique fools no one. His colleagues know that an iron fist is encased within, ready for use if the occasion demands—as it does with Boss Jim Gettys. Kane, however, is compromised by his need for "the love of the people," which forces his ruthlessness into subterranean channels. Garner, the financial gangster, strove for power and got it; Kane, the newspaper warlord, wanted glory—and, though he tried to buy it, it was never fully his.

Despite its remarkable resemblance to *Kane* in outline and situations (Mankiewicz's early drafts of the script were even closer, with Kane's son originally growing up into a profligate parody of his father, and Susan taking a young lover), **The Power and the Glory** emerges on celluloid as little more than a primitive ancestor, or a fetus to Welles' child-prodigy of a film. As directed by William K. Howard, the film is desolate and desperate in contrast with Mankiewicz's racy, journalistic cynicism and Welles' love of chiaroscuro magic that together form the mark of *Kane*. In tone and form, **The Power and the Glory** presents us with the skeletons of seven people (Tom, Sally, Tom, Jr., Eve, her father, Henry, and his wife), whereas the portraits in *Kane* give the illusion of being fully fleshed out, at least in relation to the protagonist. Tom Garner's rise and fall is narrated by a loving, rather dull friend; Kane's story—told by three not-so-dull men who had the advantages of wealth (Thatcher), old-country wisdom (Bernstein), and journalistic experience (Leland), and appended by one unimaginative woman—is filtered through the lively if less-than-poetic sensibility of a news-magazine reporter. Henry is given a dash of individual existence early in the film, when his wife tells him that she has been happy enough with "you, and a home of our own, and—well, I have everything I really wanted"—as if to keep herself from prodding Henry, Sally-like, into Tom's world of success and excess. But in general, Sturges's characters are arid, and they make the film as lifeless as *Kane* is incorrigibly vital.

Undoubtedly, we feel a sympathy for Tom that Kane never earns, because Henry (or, rather, Sturges) saves Eve's adultery for the climactic revelation. The crises in Tom's life build to a fairly conventional crescendo, for all the shuffling of tenses, and the climax is at least dramatically compelling. But Kane's last years were uneventful; indeed, the film touches upon them only in the opening newsreel. The climax of the film—Susan's departure and Kane's demolition job on her room, followed by the mention of "Rosebud"—comes eight years before Kane's death, and the absence of a chronological climax in his life story helps validate Mankiewicz's "narratage" framework. Perhaps we respond more immediately to the simple discovery of Tom's cuckoldry than we do to the complex and partially misleading import of a childhood sled, that "missing piece of a jigsaw puzzle." If so, the difference in cinematic stimuli is the difference between a well-manipulated plot device and the lingering, mystical aura of an elusive symbol. Unfortunately, Sturges's most ambitious early film suggests neither the power of a "great man" nor the glory of a great film—both of which distinguish forever the kingdom of *Kane*.

Diamond Jim

The arrival of "narratage" did not exactly revolutionize Hollywood; that privilege would be granted to Orson Welles and Herman J. Mankiewicz some eight years later. So Sturges went to Universal, where he toiled without credit on the scripts for ***Imitation of Life*** and ***Next Time We Love.*** His most prestigious official project there was ***The Good Fairy,*** a Molnar play Sturges adapted for William Wyler. At the time, ***Diamond Jim*** was considered little more than double-feature filler; even now, Eddie Sutherland and Edward Arnold are hardly a charismatic director-star parlay. But a reasonable familiarity with Sturges's career reveals this forgotten film as one of the writer's most personal works and, until his rise at Paramount two years later, certainly his most successful.

Although Harry Clork and Doris Malloy, two screenwriters of deservedly modest repute, are credited with the "adaptation" of Parker Morell's biography of Diamond Jim Brady, the screenplay and, indeed, the entire film are pure Sturges—more Sturges, in fact, than Brady. The most obvious connection with his later films can be found in the cast list: Arnold and Jean Arthur from ***Easy Living,*** Eric Blore from ***The Lady Eve,*** Cesar Romero from ***The Beautiful Blonde from Bashful Bend,*** and those charter future members of the Mighty Sturges Art Players, William Demarest and Alan Bridge. But there are many other references, both vagrant and meaningful, to his other films. Like the hero in Sturges's first screenplay credit, ***The Big Pond,*** Brady makes his fortune by selling an ingenious invention (there it was spiked chewing gum, here it is undertrucks for railroad cars). As in ***The Lady Eve,*** the leading lady is given a double-crossing double role, and a person with an English accent mispronounces "Conne*c*ticut." Sturges's fascination with railroads—which he uses comically in ***The Lady Eve*** and ***The Palm Beach Story,*** heroically in ***Hail the Conquering Hero,*** and tragically in ***The Power and the Glory*** and ***Sullivan's Travels***—is reflected in Diamond Jim's rise from a station hand to an industrial magnate, just as Tom Garner discarded the minor glory of a trackwalker for the forlorn power of a railroad president.

But whereas Garner and, for that matter, J. B. Ball, "The Bull of Wall Street" played by Edward Arnold in ***Easy Living,*** are ruthless and crude, figures of either fear or fun, Brady is sympathetically composed and played. Though he hangs on the ticker tape as tenaciously as Ball does, Brady doesn't take its fluctuations too seriously. When the market crashes, his response is to "grab a sandwich." He is Sturges's generous, somewhat Freudian version of the rich fat man, who has as compulsive a need for food as Tom Garner has for power and Charles Foster Kane has for the love of the people. In each case, the need is an unsatisfactory substitution for mother love (remember that Garner's wife Sally really fills the function of mother to a headstrong, overgrown boy). ***Diamond Jim***'s opening scene has Jim's father come downstairs to announce the birth of a boy who will grow into a tycoon of Garneresque proportions; more important, his father completes the action—***The Power and the Glory***'s final ascension-descension—that Garner's suicide interrupted. Jim's true emotional allegiance, however, is to his mother, and here some more of Sturges's eerie portents of *Citizen Kane* begin.

Like Kane, Jim is separated from his mother at an early age: she dies when he is ten. The year is 1876, about the time Mrs. Kane died. Jim's only memento is a photograph, inscribed "To my dear son James on his 10th birthday—Mother." His only abstention in adulthood is from liquor, which he promised his mother he would never drink. Instead, he drinks orange juice and, to wash it down, eats every kind of food. Since Brady has, subconsciously, renounced all women out of respect for his mother, his courtships are quaint, absurd, worshipful, and irrevocably platonic. His sexual drive is diverted to making money and spent in an orgy of overeating. The woman he thinks he loves (Jean Arthur) is the image of another woman he thinks he loved (also Jean Arthur), who is really a distorted image of his mother. When she finally tells him that she has always loved another man, Brady fumes that the couple has been "double-crossin', two-timin' . . . eatin' my food!" His food is his sex, and sharing his table while sharing someone else's bed is a treasonable act.

Like Kane, Brady gives a great deal of money and personal attention to a singer (who turns out to be Lillian Russell), although here the friendship he shares with Miss Russell is deeper, and more loving, than the infatuation masquerading as love that he feels for Jean Arthur I and II. Like Kane, Brady and his would-be wife argue across a dinner table whose length comically expresses the psychic chasm that divides them. Brady isn't detestable, like

Garner, nor enigmatic, like Kane. His proposal of marriage—"I'll give you more diamonds than there ever was. . . . I'll give you a million dollars for a wedding present"—is affecting and appealing, for all its shortsightedness. Kane's irony doesn't make him self-aware, only self-conscious; but Jim's self-deprecating good humor is surely one of the keys to his good fortune.

Nevertheless, at the end Jim is left alone to die, just as Kane and Garner had been. Before she walked out, Lillian Russell had said, "I guess you only loved one person in your life"—thinking of the first Jean Arthur but meaning, intentionally or not, Jim's mother—and Jim had nodded sagely. Now, in an Americanized hara-kiri, he prepares a ritual in which he will literally eat himself to death, ordering oysters, green-turtle soup, lobster, and guinea hens with truffles. Earlier in the film, the expansion of both his business and his waistline was suggested by a comical left-to-right tracking shot, long and fast, through a busy kitchen preparing one of Mr. Brady's dinners. For his last supper, the shot is reversed: it is somber, slow, and abrupt, moving from right to left over the edible implements of a macabre self-immolation. Jim takes his mother's photograph out to look once more at the only person he loved in his life and, without a word ("Sally!" "Rosebud!"), walks into his dining room/mausoleum, and closes the big doors. This final, elegiac gesture, graceful and audacious, tragic and farcical, heroic and grotesque, captures perfectly a schizophrenic mood that Sturges will evoke again nearly a decade later in his saddest, most ironic film, *The Great Moment.* There are ironies in Sturges's career which this critic would prefer to ignore. (pp. 26-37)

The Great Moment

Endings in Sturges films tend to be schizophrenic showdowns between the two sides of the writer-director. On one side is Preston the Pride of Paramount, laughgetter and moneymaker, stepson of millionaire stockbroker Solomon Sturges; this is the Sturges who gave audiences the endings they wanted, in *Sullivan's Travels, The Palm Beach Story, The Miracle of Morgan's Creek,* and *Hail the Conquering Hero.* On the other side, frowning at his alter ego like Jekyll at Hyde, is Sturges the artist, adapter of Tolstoy, Molnar, and Pagnol, joy and despair of James Agee, only son of the notorious aesthete and adventuress Mary Desti; this is the Sturges who sent Tom Garner and Jim Brady to their lonely deaths, who dazzled the Hays Office with *The Lady Eve*'s double-lutz plot turns, whose studio advertised his pictures as the works of a genius.

Too often, Sturges's artistry would carry a film until the last reel, when the happy hack would take over, turning the fade-out into a cop-out. Too rarely does a Sturges film possess any consistency of tone, and when it does it is often somber and monotonous like *The Power and the Glory,* or easy and impersonal like *If I Were King.* The only important Sturges films with sustained, affecting moods are *Diamond Jim, Remember the Night,* and (precariously) *The Lady Eve.* The characters are developed with as much sense as affection; the dialogue serves the situation instead of tyrannizing it; the climaxes have an aura of inevitability about them, whether dirgelike, teary, or wry. In only one other (very uneven) film did an ending exalt both Sturges and the viewer, and not demean them. This was *The Great Moment,* the last Sturges film Paramount was to release before he left the studio for Howard Hughes and one of the most precipitous pratfalls in screen history.

Sturges had written the script for *The Great Moment* (his only adaptation, besides *The Lady Eve,* as a writer-director at Paramount) several years earlier, soon after the publication, in 1940, of René Fulop-Miller's biography of Dr. W. T. G. Morton, discoverer of ether. Paramount evidently didn't like Sturges's treatment—a bizarre blending of low comedy and high tragedy—from the start, and suggested that another director film it. Finally, the studio relented and Sturges began filming it in 1943, right after *The Palm Beach Story.* But the Front Office (B. G. DeSylva, probably) still didn't like the project, and its release was postponed until after *The Miracle of Morgan's Creek* and *Hail the Conquering Hero* had premiered to general acclaim. By this time (according to Andrew Sarris, who talked with the director in 1957), Sturges had decided to leave Paramount in the wake of a contract dispute which, in the dark shadow of the director's decline, seems absurdly insignificant: the studio offered him a seven-year contract, demanding the right to decide at the end of each year whether or not he would continue; Sturges wanted a seven-year contract where *he* would have the option to terminate.

All this niggling hardly suggests heroic *hamartia,* and it's

Publicity photograph. Director Sturges (right) tells writer Sturges (left) his script is unsatisfactory.

worth reporting only because the artistic freedom Sturges thought he had won when he left Paramount turned out to be a virtual dead end, with Harold Lloyd Alley and Darryl Zanuck Circle offering only the most frustrating of side streets. For most directors who find Hollywood congenial, freedom is like the Labyrinth. Many get lost in the maze of intransigent producers and incompetent technicians and, like Sturges, are eventually devoured by a Minotaur on the order of Howard Hughes or Raymond Hakim; a few, once they are trapped, have the resourcefulness to make the entrapment their subject matter, like Welles; a rare director will rise to the challenge of this freedom, and triumph, as Murnau did with *Tabu*. Sturges was not Murnau. He needed the sympathetic cast and crew he had assembled at Paramount, who took care of the details while he worked on his script and its direction. Once that concentration was broken—once he began spending more time in a production conference with Hughes or Zanuck than in a script conference with himself—the Sturges spell, the lucky streak, the five-year spurt of creative energy went too. Although released out of sequence, **The Great Moment** seems chillingly appropriate just where it is as a chapter in Sturges's artistic autobiography. The writer is reaching up; the machine is breaking down.

The Great Moment is consciously reflective and unconsciously prophetic. It recalls the form (and thus, at least in part, the mood) of Sturges's first important film, **The Power and the Glory.** Both begin in "the present," with the protagonist's funeral; both shift through various stages of the past to tell a story whose conclusion we already know, and to justify a mood we might prefer to escape. But **The Great Moment** returns to the past only twice, and on its second visit stays there for most of the film; Sturges, perhaps committed to subject over form more firmly than he had been a decade earlier, avoids shifts in tense to concentrate on daredevil shifts in mood. As with **The Power and the Glory,** Sturges is again far ahead of his time. These shifts are jarring, atonal, especially for a forties film, and the humor is sudden and abrupt, giving the film an uneasy, very modern feeling that is totally at odds with the presumed seriousness of a biographical subject that Warners would surely have treated with a reverence befitting the Gospel According to Saint Paul Muni.

Sturges's hero is Joel McCrea, survivor of **Sullivan's Travels** and **The Palm Beach Story.** McCrea's bilious stubbornness deprived him of genuine stardom, even in the hunk-hungry war years (though he was certainly handsome enough). But this quality was perfect for a heroic but imperfect medical giant *malgré lui.* Dr. Morton is certified as a hero in the first scene, when his wife receives the Government's posthumous tribute "To the Benefactor of Mankind, With the Gratitude of Humanity"—and even earlier, in the film's introduction, which describes great men towering on the horizon of history: "Morton seems very small indeed, until the incandescent moment he ruined himself for a servant girl, and gained immortality." The film that follows this peculiar tribute is itself so peculiar that we don't know whether to take the line "he ruined himself for a servant girl"—which sounds like a preface for *Dr. Chatterley's Lover*—as a dangerously phrased but honestly felt elegy, or as a Sturgean jibe at the self-important prose style affected by the writers of biographical films. At any rate, we know within five minutes that the Government's testimonial is a sham. President Pierce himself (whom Sturges skewers far more devastatingly than, say, Theodore Flicker will work over Lyndon Johnson in *The President's Analyst* a generation later) turns Morton down. In a memorable exchange, Morton notes that the country is at war with Mexico, and that his discovery might be put to use immediately in Army hospitals.

> MORTON: [Of course] I'd hate for it to look as if I were trying to make the Government pay to relieve the pain of wounded soldiers.
>
> PRESIDENT: The Government pays for the guns, don't it? (*Laughs.*)

So much for executive compassion and idealism. So much, too, for Morton's hope of a patent on his discovery. He is rebuked and disgraced. He dies. End of first flashback, and return to the present for a description of his death. Now, when the film reverts to past tense to trace Morton's courtship, marriage, early practice, discovery of ether and its success, we are aware of the doom, and thus the heroism, that weighs down each forward step. Not *ultimate* doom—since ultimately, in the pages of medical history, Morton's discovery was accepted, and the film itself is a kind of centennial celebration—but *irrevocable* doom, of the sort that finally caught up with Tom Garner. Doom should not be confused with destiny.

Morton is heroic in deed, but not in manner. As McCrea plays him, he is genial, determined, but a little dense (he gets a simple formula wrong the first time)—"Morton seems very small indeed." And he is handicapped by the assistance of William Demarest, who reprises his characterization of Muggsy, Henry Fonda's bodyguard in **The Lady Eve.** Demarest is the fulcrum for most of the film's comic explosions, which not only break the mood but shatter it into as many pieces as the glass beakers Demarest is constantly dropping. Sturges seems to be testing a theory of comedy as vicarious pain, ruthlessly observed. He switches so often from the pain of a surgical patient without anesthesia to the pain of Demarest with a sore tooth or a hurt expression that Sturges's intentions are inescapable. There is little verbal comedy here, and what there is is strained, severe. ("The Wells Method!" one surgeon mocks. "The half-ass-phixiated method!" What unnecessary work Sturges went to, just to sneak that rotten pun into his script!) Sturges has tried to make his slapstick an object of both pleasure and pain, but the only sound it makes is off-putting, off-pitch, flat.

The film's conclusion—The Great Moment itself—is as peculiar as its preface. Here, though, we know that Sturges means to be taken seriously, and the sequence succeeds almost in spite of itself. Morton, who has been imperfect enough to deny surgical use of his discovery because he continued to demand an exclusive patent for it, is walking out of the operating room when he sees the servant girl who is to be the patient. The hall is suffused with a heavenly spotlight; Victor Young's music works hard to undercut any genuine emotions by underlining obvious ones. As the choir builds to a messianic crescendo, the doors to the operating room open magically, and Morton walks through, his patient behind him—she to be saved, he to be condemned. It is a scene Douglas Sirk would be hard pressed to bring off without a giggle, but Sturges nearly does it, through sheer directorial conviction.

Is it melodramatic to point to this as Sturges's own great moment? In five years he had written nine scripts and directed eight of them himself, averaging close to two films per year for which he bore complete responsibility. In fifteen years in Hollywood he had been credited with twenty-one screenplays, almost half of which were original stories—a scandalous achievement among the membership of Writers Guild West. Now Sturges was leaving Paramount, scene of his greatest triumphs, for Total Artistic Freedom under Howard Hughes. A generation later, this clarion call would result in *Myra Breckinridge, Alex in Wonderland,* and *Brewster McCloud.* Sturges was too jealous a custodian of his talent to produce one of these spectacular fiascoes endemic to a dying Hollywood; his decline was to be much more tasteful. And even here he blazed an erratic trail that other filmmakers in the suicidal twilight of their careers could follow: John Huston, Joseph L. Mankiewicz, Nunnally Johnson, and Frank Tashlin were just some of the writer-directors who would trace the same sad parabola a decade or two later.

Among that strange breed, the hyphenate, Sturges had been firstest with the mostest, so it was appropriate that he lose it the fastest—throw it away, almost, as he had made Dr. Morton seem to throw away all chance for reputation and security on the hunch that he might "gain immortality." Sturges wasn't to have even that satisfaction: like Tom Garner, his doom was his destiny. It's as if Sturges walked through those doors and fell victim to the ultimate prank. The doors were the entrance to Diamond Jim's mausoleum, and not the portals to an immortal, great moment. (pp. 52-7)

> Richard Corliss, "Preston Sturges," in his Talking Pictures: Screenwriters in the American Cinema, 1974. Reprint by Penguin Books Inc., 1975, pp. 25-61.

Elliot Rubenstein (essay date 1977-1978)

[*In the following essay, Rubenstein first analyzes how in* Sullivan's Travels *Sturges manipulates various Hollywood genre conventions to convey a message beyond the understanding of the main character; Rubenstein concludes by comparing Sturges's work on* Sullivan's Travels *with Orson Welles's work on* Citizen Kane.]

From the *Show People* of Marion Davies to *The Big Knife* of Clifford Odets, from the pleasant elegance of *The Bad and the Beautiful* to the cruel eloquence of *Sunset Boulevard,* from *What Price Hollywood?* to *A Star is Born* to *A Star is Born* to *A Star is Born,* Hollywood has always been pleased to perform its self-abuse in public. But in a class all its own is Preston Sturges' ***Sullivan's Travels,*** in part because, unlike so many of the other movies about the making of movies, Sturges' film doesn't ignore but instead rejoices in the potential absurdity of any studio product that gazes down on the ways of Hollywood from imagined peaks of moral and artistic superiority. Indeed, it's precisely this absurdity that Sturges seizes on both for occasion and for theme.

The opening sequence makes Sturges' two main points as Sturges only seldom chose to make his points: without dialogue. (***Sullivan's Travels*** is in fact an unusually silent movie: think of the chase during the first journey, the entire third journey, the first part of the fourth, and several shorter sequences. I suppose that in theory it isn't surprising that this movie about movies should rely so heavily on purely visual effect; it is a bit surprising from Sturges.)

Immediately following the credit titles we see two men fighting atop a speeding railway carriage. It is night. The battle is fierce. The Presto of the 'Moonlight' Sonata rushes on in the orchestra. One of the men fires at the other. Clutching each other, the two plunge into a river. A title appears on the screen: THE END.

After this opening, we learn that the actual scene is a studio projection room. John L. Sullivan, an immensely successful director of comedies (*Ants in Your Plants of 1939* is one), has had the film shown to persuade two studio executives to let him make movies of 'social significance'; for the two men fighting in the movie, as he carefully explains, are 'Capital' and 'Labour', the scene has 'symbolism' and 'teaches . . . a moral lesson.' In the course of a grotesque dialogue on the relative value of 'message' and 'entertainment' pictures, the executives make the mistake of persuading Sullivan that he hasn't 'suffered' enough to direct the film version of a novel by one Sinclair Beckstein called *O Brother, Where Art Thou?*. Sullivan accepts their judgment and sets forth on the first of four voyages in search of real suffering, voyages that bring him ever closer to worlds of irremediable poverty and irremediable despair. The basic premise of the plot is established.

But much more has been established by the film clip alone: it does indeed teach lessons, if not exactly the moral lessons Sullivan had in mind. First of all, representing as it does Sullivan's notion of what a 'message' movie should be, it teaches us that Sullivan's aspirations are absurd even before his own arguments trap him in a demonstration of his fatuity. For when you make a scene of men fighting to the death on top of a train, only very specific signals such as the designations 'Labour' and 'Capital' can alert your audience to the fact that it isn't looking at one of the stalest images of action movies, and in the circumstances your designation can only look foolish and arbitrary. Images denote genres, and the power of genre in our experience of movies is nowhere more clearly revealed than in ***Sullivan's Travels.*** If the likes of Sullivan did make *O Brother, Where Art Thou?*, we'd have only an undistinguished representative of precisely the wrong genre, with 'social significance' thrown in even more gratuitously than that 'little bit of sex' one of the executives keeps trying to work into any scenario.

All this suggests an issue so basic that I'd better try to clarify it at once: both Sullivan and Sturges are directors of comedies, and there the resemblance ends. In ***Unfaithfully Yours,*** Sturges would face the challenge of viewing with irony a central character deeply identifiable with himself.

In *Sullivan's Travels* no such challenge exists. Sullivan proclaims himself a clod with his opening gesture, his illustration of what a film of 'social significance' should resemble; he goes on to certify his cloddishness by his very dependence on terms like 'social significance'. Even at the end, after voyaging in earnest into the darkest areas of American experience, he has learned only that 'There's a lot to be said for making people laugh. Did you know that's all some people have? It isn't much, but it's better than nothing in this cockeyed caravan.' True, this makes more sense than Sullivan's opening remarks, but even if one accepts the endorsement of comedy as charity in a world gone to hell one can't take it seriously as the justification of the existence of a Sturges and of a film like *Sullivan's Travels.* Between this speech and the written dedication at the beginning of the movie—'To the memory of those who made us laugh: the motley mountebanks, the clowns, the buffoons in all times and in all nations, whose efforts have lightened our burden a little . . . '—comes a show of film-making quite beyond Sturges' red herring messages and quite beyond Sullivan's understanding or praise.

Even as an endorsement of comedy, the closing speech is drained of much of its effect by virtue of being pronounced by Sullivan: we're *told* that he has been a successful director of comedies, but Joel McCrea's performance makes the claim a little hard to credit. McCrea's Sullivan barely smiles in the course of the movie, and laughs—desperately and convulsively at first, clearly at war with all the pressures of his own nature—on one single occasion, during the prison sequence near the end when he is seated among fellow convicts and destitute Southern blacks at a Disney cartoon. How could this living monument to humourlessness make comedies, let alone Sturges movies?

The difference between Sullivan the director and Sturges the director must be allowed to speak for itself, so Sturges appropriates both the violence and the railroad imagery of the opening sequence throughout the film, and more particularly for the single most intricate scene in any Sturges movie. The premise of the scene is simple enough: an old hobo who steals Sullivan's money is in effect destroyed by his own greed. But the treatment is such that a shot-by-shot analysis may serve best:

(1) After we see the tramp dragging the unconscious Sullivan into hiding, we have the first shot of a train. It is led into view, like a gigantic beast, by an attendant carrying a lantern. It grows ever larger in the frame, its lamp like a great eye filling the screen with light.

(2) A medium shot of the tramp alongside the train as it passes. He runs first in one direction, then the other, finally passing out of the frame to the left; but the shot is held, giving us a sense of the length of the train.

(3) A long crane shot of the tramp running up a flight of steps; the camera turns to show him now running across what looks like acres of criss-crossing tracks. Finally he attains the farthest reaches of the cinematic field; he falls; the dollar bills fly into the air.

(4) A medium shot of the tramp caught in an inverted V of two crossing tracks, stuffing bills into his pockets.

(5) A shot apparently from the cabin of a train—a train now moving fast, its lamp illuminating the tracks before us.

(6) A medium shot, slightly closer than (4) and from a slightly different angle, of the tramp picking up bills.

(7) Again a shot from the point of view of the train. We see a field of signal lights and, again, an incomprehensible criss-cross design of tracks.

(8) The same set-up as (4). The tramp is still gathering up the bills. But now the light from the train's headlamp begins to illuminate the space. The tramp looks up.

(9) A shot from the point of view of the tramp: the train is heading directly towards him.

(10) Again the set-up of (4), but now in a light more terrifying than the earlier darkness. The tramp stares at the oncoming train. He runs back and forth over the maze of tracks, the camera following him.

(11) A shot of the tramp running in the direction of the camera, the light from the train now *behind* him and shining directly into the lens.

(12) A long shot from the cabin, the tramp running and looking back over his shoulder at the camera.

(13) The same set-up as (11), but the tramp in his flight has come much closer to the camera.

(14) The same set-up as (12), but the train is now almost on top of the tramp. It comes closer and closer. Waving his arms, the tramp sends a new shower of bills into the air.

(15) A medium shot of one section of a track. The train illuminates the scene, but fitfully, as it passes. The bills rain down—followed by a boot.

The rhythmical complexity of the sequence is manifest. And it's matched by a kind of directorial dexterity Sturges had never shown before and would never need to show again. In the sense it gives of a human agent controlled by an indecipherable higher logic, embodied in a labyrinth of tracks, and by an indecipherable god, embodied in an unseen and oblivious switchman, the scene may remind you of Fritz Lang. In the inevitability of its montage—images of the ineluctable power of a destructive industrialism versus images of a man already destroyed morally by a system that will now reduce even his body to unidentifiable fragments—it may remind you of Eisenstein. It will not remind you of John L. Sullivan.

Bearing the weight of the scenes like this, *Sullivan's Travels* can't be read as a simple-minded blanket vindication of Preston Sturges, *Ants in Your Plants of 1939,* Mickey Mouse, and anything else that might make people laugh. But the explicit message is there, and is important. It's there for its apparent impudence: that's Sturges. It's there too as the inevitable conclusion attained by a director of comedies whom we see living through hells he has never imagined, but whom we also see in a movie whose controlling style, whatever the effect of any given scene, announces happy endings. In short, it's there because the plot exacts its presence as specifically as the plot exacts the marriage of Joel McCrea and Veronica Lake. The message is there to suit the plot, and not the other way around; it's the plot, not the message, that counts. For the story of a movie director who must make many journeys allows Sturges to place Sullivan in a variety of physical settings (Hollywood offices and railroad yards, among others) otherwise improbable in a single film, settings which then inevitably open up a variety of *cinematic* implications otherwise improbable in a single film. And this brings me to the second point made in the opening sequence by the film-within-a-film.

It teaches that anything we see on the screen is a movie, and that only very specific signals such as unexpected end titles can alert us to the differences between what might be called primary and secondary reality in any film. In other words, the fight on the train *is* our movie until we're told it was only an intrusion into our movie. (Later on, *Sullivan's Travels* is twice interrupted by the overt intrusion of other movies. There's the Disney cartoon we watch along with Sullivan near the end. There's also the picture show Sullivan attends in the company of a lecherous widow, and while here we don't actually witness what Sullivan and the widow witness, the background music [Chopin's E-minor Prelude orchestrated into mush] and the titles posted outside the theatre [it's a triple bill: *Beyond These Tears, The Valley of the Shadow, The Buzzard of Berlin*] tell us what we need to know of the quality of suffering being enacted on the screen. These scenes contribute significantly to the film, but situated as they are in already established contexts of the plot, they lack the force of the opening sequence.)

The importance of the lesson lies in the fact that the opening melodramatic snippet readies us for many other scenes which, if screened out of context, would also persuasively resemble kinds of movies *Sullivan's Travels* isn't supposed to be. A partial list is in order. (1) I've already noted the affinities of one episode with Eisenstein and Lang; and while exact pastiche of neither, it certainly evokes what used to be called the 'art film' more startlingly than anything else in Paramount comedies. (2) At one point Sullivan hops aboard the soap-box car of a 13-year-old boy and goes through a couple of minutes of sheer terror as they're pursued by a gang of studio personnel in a land yacht. Though magnified into Sturgean proportions, the chase (wordless, of course) is obviously an *hommage* to Mack Sennett and his successors. (3) When McCrea and Lake ride the freight trains, the imagery recalls several 1930s movies about men and boys forced into vagrancy, most specifically William Wellman's *Wild Boys of the Road,* in which a girl conceals her long hair and her gender by means of a cap exactly like the one Lake wears for the same purpose. (The very angles of several shots of vagrants getting on and off moving freight cars are virtually identical in the two movies: whether or not this was inevitable given the identity of subject is for my purposes irrelevant.) (4) The scenes of the black congregation, led by a preacher who could pass for De Lawd himself, suggest one familiar cinematic treatment of Southern black experience: think not only of *Green Pastures* but of King Vidor's *Hallelujah.* (I have to add that everywhere else, including the first section of *Sullivan's Travels,* Sturges drew on a different tradition of cinematic negritude, the nature of which is revealed by the fact that one of the Pullman attendants in *The Palm Beach Story* is played by an actor named—would I were making it up—Snowflake.) (5) The entire last episode also recalls 30s films, here the cycle of which Mervyn LeRoy's *I Am a Fugitive from a Chain Gang* is the best remembered. The extreme low angle shot of the chained men entering the church, a shot that melodramatically asserts both the terrors and the nobility of slavery, is again like nothing else in Paramount comedies—or indeed in *Sullivan's Travels.*

I could extend the list, and someone who knows 30s movies better than I could extend it further [in a footnote, Rubenstein adds: "I haven't even brought up lines merely alluding to other films. When, for example, Lake says to McCrea, 'You sort of belong to me. When you were a hobo, I found you,' I assume she's referring to the scavenger hunt for 'forgotten men' in Gregory La Cava's *My Man Godfrey* (1936)"]. *Sullivan's Travels* isn't merely a catalogue of cinematic reference; it is, in significant part, a very anthology of genres and styles; but it deals in counterfeit excerpts. John L. Sullivan experiences various griefs and terrors in order to find out that he wants to make comedies; Preston Sturges meanwhile demonstrates that all such griefs and terrors have by now been transmuted into various kinds of movies we've all seen. By this I don't mean to imply that Sturges' handling of the grimmer episodes is motivated by cynicism. The chain gang sequence and the others, like the slapstick chase, are not parodies but renderings, or at least renditions, of their models; Sturges documents as well as LeRoy the unspeakable life in Southern prisons. And so Sturges also demonstrates that he can execute as well as anyone the kinds of movies he anthologises. Finally he demonstrates that, by inventing an extraordinary new context for familiar imagery, he can momentarily revitalise not only that imagery but American comedy itself. No film in Hollywood history except *Citizen Kane* manifests so boldly its maker's belief in his own powers. And Sturges brings it off. And the public bought it.

The public that bought it was the public which in the same year showed considerably more caution in spending its dollars on *Kane*. The most obvious reasons are probably valid, yet in truth the two films have much in common. Both are animated (unless 'frenzied' is the word) by a delight in games that can be played in movies, even if the games they opt for aren't always the same ones. Most of all, the two films are comparable in a way suggested by a recent circular for a New York revival house which in a moment of blind inspiration described *Citizen Kane* as 'a landmark in film criticism'. That I think the phrase could as well be applied to *Sullivan* as to *Kane* is clear from what I've already written about Sturges' movie; but Sturges alone knew how to get around the compelling fact that, in 1941, film criticism didn't sell like movies.

While Welles' strategy is to shock us into attention, Sturges' is to coax us into believing that what we're watching couldn't really be all that foreign to our expectations. And his principal tactic is that of never letting us forget that what we're watching is first and last a Paramount comedy, a species of film Sturges both promoted and nurtured but neither invented nor finished off. The very allusions and pastiches of this 'landmark in film criticism' are in no way incompatible with the species: Paramount comedies of Sturges' day were always pointing to themselves, to one another, and to the studio out of which they grew.

At, or at least near, the bottom of the Paramount ladder are the Bob Hope movies, especially the *Road* comedies with Bing Crosby, full of endless dull allusions to that which is made to seem no funnier in memory than the first time around, full too of enough ruptures of the fictive surface—to remind us it's all only a movie—to have caused Pirandello and Groucho to wish themselves unborn. Even at this primitive level Sturges shows himself a loyal Paramount man. He has Sullivan answer a policeman's question about Lake, 'How does a girl fit in the picture?' with 'There's always a girl in the picture. Haven't you ever been to the movies?' (And 'The Girl' is in fact the only name Lake has, even in the cast credits.)

Sturges resorts to the standard in-jokes, long the traffic of Hollywood radio comedians, about dullard executives and dishonest agents and alimony-crazed ex-wives. He invokes names like Lubitsch and Capra. He shows us sound stages during production—if you look past Lake in her Bo Peep costume near the end as she receives the news that Sullivan is still alive you will glimpse Preston Sturges—and in many other such seemingly unsophisticated ways makes us recall how much we know about dear mad Hollywood and with what ease we can visit there. But as an added benefit he makes us understand that this is the real and only world of movie-making and so of movie directors, the essentially comic world that Sullivan may quit for a while but to which he must sooner or later return, like the heroes of Elizabethan pastoral who in the end bring their country wisdoms back with them to the courts in which and to which they belong.

Perhaps a rung higher than the *Road* comedies are ersatz documentaries of Paramount life like *Star-Spangled Rhythm,* higher if only because they give us a great many performers instead of an omnipresent Hope. Higher still are comedies like *Hold Back the Dawn* (also 1941): in the opening sequence the actual director, Mitchell Leisen, plays a Paramount director getting Veronica Lake through a take (this is the last we see of her) while observed by Charles Boyer, a visitor to the set who wants the director to listen to a scenario which, even as he begins to recite it, turns into a Paramount movie called *Hold Back the Dawn.* And at the top of the ladder is **Sullivan's Travels,** but it's a ladder that starts in the rag-and-bone shop of Bob Hope's mind.

Instructive too are the ways Welles and Sturges use their actors. While both feel the need for a distinctive company of secondary players, Welles imports most of his from New York, filling the screen with presences never known before, none yet a movie type, some even ageing fifty years before our eyes in the course of the movie. Sturges draws on the natural resources of Hollywood to come up with an assortment of actors as familiar to us as the furniture in our homes but considerably less subject to variation. We may find ourselves initially surprised at the vision of that Utopian manservant Eric Blore outfitting McCrea in the habit of a tramp, or at the sound of Robert Greig (the butler, of course) delivering a Shavian tirade on the evils of poverty, or at Frank Moran of the gravel voice and ex-pug face offering 'It's what they call a paraphrase' in explication of the phrase 'the valley of the shadow of adversity,' but their presences and their presentness reassure us that whatever madness Sturges had in mind, these men, along with William Demarest and Franklin Pangborn and the others, will always be there in the perfect logic of their eccentricities, never meaningfully younger or older, perpetual epiphanies.

Welles seizes on a defenceless actress named Dorothy Comingore, thrusts her into the nightmare role of Susan Alexander, makes clear to us that he is exhausting her physical and emotional possibilities as a performer and then leaves her—and it doesn't take the hindsight of thirty-five years to perceive this—with nowhere to go as an actress save back to obscurity. Sturges takes an equally defenceless actress named Veronica Lake, known only as something of a sexual sensation in one previous movie, unexpectedly emphasises her slender boyishness in *travesti* costumes while allowing her to function as the sexually

---

An excerpt from the screenplay for *Sullivan's Travels*

MR. SULLIVAN
How can you talk about musicals at a time like this? With the world committing suicide . . . corpses piling up in the street, grim death gargling at you around every corner . . . people slaughtered like sheep. . . .

MR. HADRIAN
Maybe they'd like to forget that.

MR. SULLIVAN
(Jerking his thumb)
Then why do they hold this one over for a fifth week at the Music Hall . . . for the ushers?

MR. HADRIAN
It died in Pittsburgh.

MR. LEBRAND
Like a dog.

MR. SULLIVAN
(Contemptuously)
What do they know in Pittsburgh?

MR. LEBRAND
(Mildly)
They know what they like.

MR. SULLIVAN
(Sneeringly)
If they knew what they liked they wouldn't live in Pittsburgh! . . .

Preston Sturges, in Five Screenplays by Preston Sturges, *edited by Brian Henderson, University of California Press, 1985.*

alert and aggressive figure in the plot, keeps her talking largely in fascinating mutterings and whispers, and thereby lets us know that we're watching the birth of a unique film persona and this year's biggest new movie star. (Sturges presented his studio with a potential Carole Lombard and his studio then did what it could to transform her into another Dorothy Lamour; but that's hardly Sturges' fault.) If all this is called catering to the public it's nothing to be ashamed of.

Welles makes a movie that fairly blinds us by its refusal to look like any other movie. Sturges makes a movie that, when it isn't looking the way it's supposed to look, at least looks like other movies and so never quite looks foreign. Welles makes a movie that uses every technical resource of a Hollywood studio to produce the effect that it could never have been made in a Hollywood studio. Sturges makes us feel that for all his movie's novelty it could never have been made anywhere but in a Hollywood studio, whose end has always been our comfort and amusement. It goes without saying, though given my argument I'd better say it, that *Kane* is incomparably the greater film. But then *Kane* is so incomparably greater than almost any film from Hollywood or anywhere else that it serves to place Sturges' achievement in perspective without trivialising it. It's our loss that Orson Welles the director could never do more than make brilliant movies, couldn't ever learn how to make it in pictures. It's our gain that at least for a while Preston Sturges knew exactly how. (pp. 50-2)

> *Elliot Rubenstein, "Hollywood Travels: Sturges and Sullivan," in* Sight and Sound, *Vol. 47, No. 1, Winter, 1977-78, pp. 50-2.*

Thomas Schatz (essay date 1981)

[*In the following excerpt from his book* Hollywood Genres: Formulas, Filmmaking, and the Studio System, *Schatz discusses the "screwball comedy" genre and addresses the ways in which Sturges's films satirize its conventions.*]

In 1934, Hollywood produced two of the most critically and commercially successful romantic comedies in its history: *Twentieth Century* (directed by Howard Hawks, scripted by Ben Hecht and Charles MacArthur) and *It Happened One Night* (directed by Frank Capra, scripted by Robert Riskin). The films, released within a few months of each other, marked the culmination of a type of screen comedy popularized during the early sound era—fast-paced, witty comedies of manners exploiting the foibles of America's leisure class, best exemplified by Ernst Lubitsch's *Trouble in Paradise* and *Design for Living* and in George Cukor's *Dinner at Eight.* In the tradition of those upper-crust romantic comedies, *Twentieth Century* and *It Happened One Night* reassured Depression audiences that the filthy rich were, after all, just folks like you and me, and that although money didn't necessarily buy happiness, it certainly generated some interesting social and sexual complications.

Whereas these two films extended the filmic comedy of manners, however, Capra's *It Happened One Night* introduced a dimension that would effectively reconstitute Hollywood's romantic comedy tradition. Into the frantic, decadent world of the idle rich, Capra injected a sense of homespun populism and middle-class ideology. This narrative and thematic variation was refined throughout the 1930s in a great many socially-conscious battles of the sexes, most notably in *My Man Godfrey, Mr. Deeds Goes to Town* (1936), *The Awful Truth,* **Easy Living,** *Nothing Sacred* (1937), *Bringing Up Baby, You Can't Take It with You, Holiday* (1938), *Bachelor Mother, In Name Only, Mr. Smith Goes to Washington* (1939), *His Girl Friday, My Favorite Wife,* **The Great McGinty, Christmas in July,** *Philadelphia Story* (1940), **The Lady Eve,** *Meet John Doe, Here Comes Mr. Jordan,* and *The Bride Came C.O.D.* (1941).

By restructuring the fast-paced upper-crust romance, the screwball comedy dominated Depression-era screen comedy and provided that period's most significant and engaging social commentary. As historian Georges Sadoul has pointed out, *"It Happened One Night* established a new style whose theme became stereotyped in hundreds of romantic comedies of the thirties." It is not surprising that Capra's film was reworked and refined into a distinct formula. The movie broke box-office records nationwide and gathered Academy Awards for its director, screenwriter, leading actor, leading actress, and for best picture of 1934. It is also not surprising that the screwball comedy genre generated by Capra's film has received such scant critical attention, because it lacks easily identifiable elements of setting and iconography. As Sadoul suggests, the screwball comedy is distinguished essentially by its style and theme. The genre derives its identity from a style of behavior (reflected in certain camerawork and editing techniques) and from narrative patterns that treat sexual confrontation and courtship through the socioeconomic conflicts of Depression America. . . . (pp. 150-51)

If there is any single Hollywood filmmaker whose work extended the formula into its mannerist stage, it was writer-director Preston Sturges. In the span of five years, Sturges created eight of Paramount's—and the screwball genre's—most successful and self-reflexive films: **The Great McGinty, Christmas in July** (1940), **The Lady Eve** (1941), **Sullivan's Travels, The Palm Beach Story** (1942), **The Miracle of Morgan's Creek, Hail the Conquering Hero, The Great Moment** (1944). Sturges had served his apprenticeship in Hollywood as a screenwriter, and earlier had scripted one of the screwball formula's most popular Depression-era films, **Easy Living** (Mitchell Leisen, 1937). When he graduated to writer-director, Sturges made it quite clear that he had every intention of turning the screwball comedy formula inside out. In **The Great McGinty,** a hobo (Brian Donlevy as Dan McGinty) earns a few dollars by voting forty times for a local political boss (Akim Tamiroff). The hero then gradually bluffs his way through the state machinery and winds up in the governor's mansion. McGinty's nagging wife (Muriel Angelus) convinces him to go straight, however, and when he does, his personal and occupational facade collapses. In the film's closing sequence, Donlevy and Tamiroff are together again, running a saloon in some South American banana republic. The reuniting of the two con men is Sturges' final perversion of the formula's climactic embrace and its typically utopian resolution.

In this and in his later wartime comedies, Sturges exploits the basic narrative conventions of the screwball genre: the dynamic battle of the sexes, cases of mistaken identity and blind luck which miraculously bring the hero to prominence, the small-town hick's struggle to negotiate life in the big city, the comic-satiric depiction of the ruling class, and so on. Sturges' manipulation of the genre's conventions consistently and pleasantly throws the formula askew. His heroes couldn't be further removed from Capra's—rather than self-reliant, they are confused and easily duped; rather than idealistic, they are openly cynical, seeking not the perfect mate or a utopian community but only an "easy living" of irresponsible affluence. Sturges' archetypal small-town folk hero is the stumbling, stammering Eddie Bracken, a character actor endearing for his pathetic rather than his heroic qualities. In both *The Miracle of Morgan's Creek* and *Hail the Conquering Hero,* Bracken has greatness thrust upon him in situations which play up both his own ineptitude and society's irrational mania for hero worship.

The Miracle of Morgan's Creek involves a small-town girl (Betty Hutton) who gets drunk at a service party and is wedded and bedded by a soldier who goes overseas the following day but whose name she cannot recall. She ropes Bracken into marriage without letting him know she's pregnant, and both of them achieve national celebrity status when she delivers sextuplets. *Hail the Conquering Hero* also parodies the genre's rags-to-riches/bum-to-celebrity strategies but this time from Bracken's viewpoint. Here our reluctant hero is discharged from the Marines for chronic hay fever, only to be "pitched" as a genuine war hero to his hometown by a group of Marines playing a practical joke. Bracken eventually runs for mayor of the town, and though he later admits his duplicity, he is finally forgiven by the community. Capra's populist conception of the essential wisdom and innate goodness of "the folks" is turned upside down in Sturges' comedies, which satirize an array of America's cultural foibles: its undying commitment to the Horatio Alger myth of instant success, its celebration of the small-town folk hero, its sexual prudery, its blind adherence to social conventions, and most of all, its collective irrationality. The general public provides easy targets for hucksters, politicians, advertisers, reporters—and even for filmmakers, as in *Sullivan's Travels.*

Perhaps Sturges' best film, *Sullivan's Travels* seems to have been made with Frank Capra in mind. A self-important comedy director (Joel McCrea as John L. Sullivan) wants to make highbrow social-problem films, so he sets out disguised as an American everyman to discover the meaning of life on city streets and country roads. A succession of comic mishaps separate Sullivan from his elaborate entourage. Eventually he is involved in a fracas and winds up on a chain gang. In a typical example of Sturges' wit, however, our hero finds The Truth in this most unlikely environment. Sullivan's fellow prisoners are able to lose themselves for a time, despite their unspeakable living conditions, laughing at a Mickey Mouse cartoon. Through them, Sullivan rediscovers the transcendent value of comedy and of human laughter. He later is able to reveal his true identity and return to Hollywood. There he weds a madcap blonde he had met on the road (Veronica Lake in a solid comic performance) and decides to continue directing film comedies. Ironically, Sturges himself also continued making screwball satires, but after two years his career suddenly disintegrated. Like Capra, Sturges had been able to parlay his popular and commercial success into an independent production venture (and an initial partnership with Howard Hughes), and like Capra he gradually lost touch with his once-massive audience. (pp. 168-70)

> Thomas Schatz, "The Screwball Comedy," in his Hollywood Genres: Formulas, Filmmaking, and the Studio System, *Random House, 1981, pp. 150-85.*

Elliot Rubenstein (essay date 1982)

[*In the following essay, Rubenstein focuses on* The Miracle of Morgan's Creek *and* Hail the Conquering Hero *to address such issues as the definition of the screwball comedy genre, the differences between Sturges's films and those of Frank Capra, and the extent to which Sturges's work can be viewed as satirical.*]

Until very recently, the temptation among film historians to skirt serious or extended discussion of Preston Sturges's films has not met with much resistance; even now, no thoughtful book-length study of Sturges has appeared. Yet what figure in Hollywood history set himself a task at once as precise and as grandiose as did Sturges? His aim-instinct with his more obvious endeavor to make of himself a public figure as recognizable and as saleable as any of his most famous players—was nothing less than the recension and reanimation of Hollywood comedy.

In one of his invaluable *obiter scripta,* André Bazin has suggested the scope of Sturges' enterprise:

> It is surely not an accident that the director of *The Outlaw* was an associate of the director of *Sullivan's Travels.* Preston Sturges and Howard Hughes were made to understand one another. These two men knew how to structure their work on what for others would be a limitation. Preston Sturges understood that the mythology of the American comedy had arrived simultaneously both at saturation point and the point of exhaustion.

Bazin's remarks reflect not only on *Sullivan* but on all of Sturges's major films; however timeless (and however rare) the pleasure that these movies still afford on their own, they need to be located more precisely in the legacy of Hollywood comedy that Sturges accepted and exploited in the 1940s, need to be read as chapters in the history of inherited comic modes playing themselves out once and for all under Sturges's direction.

But let me begin by recalling the place of the two films I principally consider in this essay, *The Miracle of Morgan's Creek* and *Hail the Conquering Hero,* in another and briefer history—that of Sturges's own career.

The films of Sturges's halcyon Paramount years as writer/director may, with one important exception, be divided into three sets of two: *The Great McGinty* and *Christmas in July* (both 1940), his profoundly ironic versions of the various Depression-rooted comic fantasies of sudden money and sudden fame; *The Lady Eve* (1941) and *The Palm Beach Story* (1942), his explosive valedictories to the screwball comedy of the 1930s; and his tantalizingly ambiguous investigations of American patriotism, *Morgan's Creek* and *Conquering Hero* (both 1944). The exception I spoke of is, of course, *Sullivan* (1941), a film that boldly appropriates for its subject matter nothing less than the Hollywood movie itself and so in a sense stands both inside and outside virtually *all* modes of comedy. A minor exception, Sturges's only other film of the period, is *The Great Moment,* finally released in 1944 in a version so manifestly fussed over and botched that it seems to suggest a category without precedent or parallel—and, thank God, without issue. Between the first pair and the second we may read a chapter in the success story that Sturges both repeatedly dramatized and passionately lived: if *McGinty* and *Christmas* bear the unmistakable (and defiantly undisguised) marks of Paramount's equivalent of Poverty Row, *Eve* and *Palm Beach* testify to Sturges's promotion to Paramount's most prestigious sound stages.

Nowhere are the new glory and the new budgets more evident than in the casting: in place of dim Muriel Angelus and dimmer Ellen Drew, of Brian Donlevy (as first lead—a pretty sure sign of something less than Paramount's loftiest aspiration) and an oddly deracinated Dick Powell (too late for Ruby Keeler not yet ready for Claire Trevor), we now have Barbara Stanwyck and Claudette Colbert, Henry Fonda and Sturges's stalwart Joel McCrea. Whatever else they may be, *Eve* and *Palm Beach* are fancy star vehicles, with the right stars to travel in them: Sturges's joy in those stars (along with his skill in coaxing them into his delirious style) is part of our own joy in the films. Yet even here, the secondary characters, the true Sturges People, make at least as strong a claim on our attention. Indeed, the familiar contours of romantic comedy can barely fit around them.

Sometimes, albeit rarely, the Sturges People had to be invented. But not out of whole cloth. Some patterns had to be there for Sturges to discern. The categorical instance of the procedure is Rudy Vallee in *Palm Beach:* the most insipid of crooners, an absurdity forsaken by fashion, is here reborn as the "Erl King," John D. Hackensacker III, the most insipid of billionaires, and he offers himself to us not just as a fool but as that most valuable of fools, a genuine comic type.

But as a rule the types were already there in Hollywood, and in crazy profusion: Sturges's genius—in this context the word will surely be allowed—is to give them such things to say as even they had never said, and then, when possible, to mass them in such numbers that the seething human "ground" of screen life threatens (at least threatens) to engulf the would-be star "figures." In *Eve* the Sturges People more or less respect their secondary place in the narrative, playing out their roles of confidants and ambassadors and commentators; but Eric Blore and William Demarest and Eugene Pallette and a few others never fail to let us know that they could easily steal the picture—

they sentence the stars to hard labor. And in *Palm Beach,* from the early appearance of Colbert's protector "the Wienie King" (Robert Dudley), himself ushered into the scene by no less lordly a major domo than Franklin Pangborn, the tension between the star and the Sturges People never slackens.

Who will forget, or forget to cherish, Sturges's Wienie King? Talking continuously, deaf (literally) to the words of others, his kingdom consists of the sounds he makes and the wad of Wienie bank notes in his hand; as loaded with cash as with words, he embodies the ultimate dream of Sturgean orality. But when he provides Colbert with the means to pay all her New York bills and get out of her foundering marriage, he unwittingly releases her to a journey to Palm Beach of which the vehicle is to be a train holding the Ale and Quail Club. An army of little millionaires, all in search of sport and pleasure, each more bizarre or besotted than the next, the Ale and Quail is the ideal exemplification of Sturges's verbal slapstick. The members' interminable symposium is such a jumble of voices and accents and sound effects as the poor microphone had seldom before been asked to capture. They pay Colbert's way to Palm Beach, but, howling and muttering and arguing and shooting their way to a kind of immortality in which gold-digger sanity has no place, they drive her out of their frames, nearly out of the movie. Finally the car containing them is simply severed from the rest of the train: how else to be rid of this organism that rages with the fever of terminal noise and disarray? With its disappearance our ears and eyes are momentarily at peace. But we are guided almost at once into the Hackensacker world, where Colbert is once again nearly finished off. The Erl King and his sister, the awesome sex maniac called the Princess Centimillia (Mary Astor—who like Vallee is here reborn, though in Astor's case it is out of the ashes of her own off screen sexual scandals of five years earlier), and the Princess's dear little gigolo Toto tendering to all comers his Ruritanian "Grittinks!" now what's a poor Park Avenue girl to do? Colbert, that most elegant of movie stars, passes through *The Palm Beach Story* like the last of an endangered species.

And so Sturges's next move, in *Morgan's Creek,* was to dispense altogether with the Colberts. Eddie Bracken had already established himself at Paramount as a popular player but an undisguisable, irremediable, homely eccentric. For her part Betty Hutton, pretty and goofy and just off the bus from Morgan's Creek, U.S.A., hadn't yet been encouraged to assume the incongruous masks of high drama and glamorous stardom that would figure in certain later stages of her career. The last stage of Sturges's Paramount tenure thus illustrated a new demographic principle: if *The Palm Beach Story* introduces enough Sturges People to populate a small world, *The Miracle of Morgan's Creek* and *Hail the Conquering Hero* proclaim a world small enough to be populated exclusively by Sturges People. Each is so profoundly a type, by which I mean a being so profoundly different from any other, that each could live comfortably only in a Sturges world. And a world, a single world, it is: the sets, Paramount Middle America, are the same in both films; only in the frame episodes of *Morgan's Creek* (dominated by The Governor and The Boss, Donlevy and Akim Tamiroff, resuscitated from *McGinty* and fixed in a series of stationary long-take shots, along with a montage sequence of worldwide reactions to Hutton's Miracle) no significantly different worlds are even hinted at. And the genre of comedy that Sturges was now exploring was implicit in these settings: Sturges People would pass for Little People.

Having spoken of "genre"—having spoken of genre with respect to Preston Sturges—I must at once submit a qualification: while one can hardly overestimate the force of genre in the history of the Hollywood film, one must at the same time remember that pure examples of most genres are the exception rather than the rule. ("Cycle" might be a safer term, but its implications of temporal continuity and bracketing dates are frequently misleading. Stanley Cavell's "medium" is perhaps still more accurate, but to use it outside Cavell's own contexts might be to prompt still further confusion. Hollywood's mythologies, after all, often feasted on one another, Hollywood's players passed without visa from one mythology to the next, Hollywood's inconographies were borrowed and lent as freely as its dress extras. Seldom even can Hollywood's cycles be dated with anything like tolerable accuracy.

And so when one refers, as I have done in connection with *The Lady Eve* and *The Palm Beach Story,* to "screwball comedy," one is evoking a mood, perhaps even a mode, of comedy, but one may find oneself uneasy at having to vindicate such a label as "genre." The roots of that which was to become what we now call screwball comedy are fixed in the first five years of talking pictures—the period of the Marxes at their best, of Mae West before the censors had their way with her, of Jean Harlow and Marie Dressler, of the first *Gold Diggers* musicals at Warners, of the earliest rat-a-tat newspaper comedies at several studios, of Lubitsch's extraordinarily naughty pre-Breen exercises in "sophisticated" comedy, and of much more. In one way or another—whether in the tempo and metrics of their dialogue, or in the sexual freedoms they make public and the sexual cynicisms they express, or in their air of nearly reckless determination to keep going no matter what—they prepared the way for screwball comedy in general and for Sturges's style in particular. But in 1934, the year of Hawks's *Twentieth Century* and of Capra's *It Happened One Night,* something new did happen, something discernible and describable enough to tempt us to speak, as I have spoken, of a new "genre"—to speak, that is, of screwball comedy, or to speak of it with as much or as little finality as ever we can speak of genre in a culture like Hollywood's.

But let us proceed with caution. For in *It Happened One Night* Capra in effect inaugurated *two* strands of comedy—overlapping, sometimes interchangeable even within the same film (for that was, more often than not, the Hollywood way), yet at least for purposes of discussion separable. One is the variety manifest in Hawk's *Brining Up Baby,* McCarey's *The Awful Truth,* *The Lady Eve*—the comedy of dizzy heiresses, of marriages dissolving in order to allow the partners to resume their courtships, of American popular theatrical speech speeded up to its limits as it echoes through the halls of the wealthy of New York and Connecticut.

The other variety is virtually identified with Capra himself: its major expressions are *Mr. Deeds Goes to Town* (1936), *Mr. Smith Goes to Washington* and *You Can't Take It With You* (both 1938), and *Meet John Doe* (1941). Those halls of the wealthy are hardly even seen save as the places where the Little People are condemned and ugly plots against them are imagined. The Little People themselves—smalltown folk, even if their communities be precariously constructed in great cities—are Capra's most powerful metaphor, while the very argument of his films is the Little People's moral straightness, their capacity for repentance and reform if temporarily misled. Yet much of the verbal style of these comedies is virtually indistinguishable from that of, say, Hawks. The characters, primary and secondary, may be every bit as eccentric: "pixillated" is the term that *Mr. Deeds* bequeaths us to fix them with. But for Capra pixillations are tokens of grace: Capra's fools aspire to saintliness, and through Capra's indulgence attain it, in a way that Robert Dudley of *Palm Beach* or Charles Ruggles or Barry Fitzgerald of *Bringing Up Baby* wouldn't know much about.

Capra's comedies in a sense served as models for *Morgan's Creek* and *Conquering Hero:* how could Sturges, in his grand plan to renovate American screen comedy, disregard the possibilities that Capra had opened up or the enormous popular success he had achieved? But such models as these were not made to submit to Sturges's retouchings. However huge their popularity, however welcome their "Capracorn" tidings, however beguiling the skills of their director, Capra's comedies were alien to Sturges's temperament. Their habit of encouraging the most deceptive (and dangerous) of political daydreams was not a habit Sturges would find attractive.

Think back to *McGinty:* the hero, doubtless to the censors' great relief, is rescued from political corruption (and delivered to prison) by the love of a good woman, but in breaking jail and fleeing to Bananaland with his pal The Boss he (1) leaves that good woman with a handsome bundle with which to rear her children according to the American dream and (2) leaves the audience with the confidence that one day, and soon, another rogue will follow his example of The Boss's and bleed the system dry once again: that is what systems are there for in this land of opportunity. Besides, for all the honor they pay to the Little People, Capra's comedies are condescending to all but demigods: it takes a Gary Cooper or at very least a James Stewart to give the Little People something to survive for, a living statue around which to assemble in trim ranks. (Sturges People get Eddie Bracken.)

On the other hand, Sturges couldn't be content simply to expose the meanness and bitterness to which people called "little" might understandably repair: the citizens of Sturges small towns were, after all, *his* people (even in the 1940s they were already known as his stock company), there to give expression to his wildest imaginings of eccentricity and verbal excess, commanding his fondest and least qualified allegiances. In *Morgan's Creek,* the narrative somehow sustains his own ironic but joyous sense of

Sturges People. But in *Conquering Hero,* Capra's practices appear to infect Sturges's own.

The scenarios tell all. In *Morgan's Creek,* Trudy Kockenlocker, daughter of the town constable (Demarest) and V-girl unparalleled, finds herself married (probably) and impregnated (certainly) after a wild one-night spree with a PFC named (if memory serves) Ratskiwatski. Her official escort of the evening, a worshipful 4-F called Norval Jones (Bracken), assumes total responsibility. But all their plans to salvage the situation, including a bogus reenactment of the Kockenlocker-Ratskiwatski nuptials, die ludicrous deaths. Norval finally leaves town in search of Ratskiwatski while the Kockenlockers await the lying-in in nearby exile. The birth—the Miracle—saves the day: in managing to produce sextuplets Trudy becomes not only the heroine of town, state, and nation but the central figure in an industry of Dionne-like proportions, while "father" Bracken gains both a (sort of) legal bride and a (sort of) military commission for his own labors.

In *Conquering Hero,* Woodrow Lafayette Pershing Truesmith (Bracken), denied entry into the military because of chronic hay fever ("the worst kind," he is told in all sympathy), leaves his home town to work in a defense plant, letting it be known to fellow citizens, including his mother, the widow of a Marine fallen in World War I, that he is in service. A crew of bona fide Marines (led by Demarest) force him to return home in the guise of a Marine hero. The exultant town is prepared to elect him mayor (over incumbent windbag Raymond Walburn) when Woodrow himself desperately lays bare the imposture. Far from denouncing him, the electorate applauds him for an act of courage beyond all military valor and unites in support of his candidacy. The question that leaves so many viewers ill at ease with the film is plain: does Sturges, by this denouement, submit to Capra's example and deliberately blur the line between economic convention on the one hand and, on the other hand, easy moral uplift and suspicious political optimism?

Northrop Frye speaks of the "enormous disproportion between grace and merit" in Shakespeare's comedies. However that may be, Sturges did turn to *Twelfth Night* for the printed moral of *Morgan's Creek:* "Some are born great, some achieve greatness, some have greatness thrust upon 'em." Comedies, anyway most farces, may indeed be cleared up by grace—by miracles, at the very least, of dramatic "logic." But the miraculous twinships finally unshrouded in classical farces (cf. *The Palm Beach Story*) are explained as existing among nature's own less traveled routes, first of intrigue and then of escape. In most farces (as in *Morgan's Creek*) the immediate hopeless situation—the situation of personal loss and legal impossibility—is redeemed by what dramatically is, but need not in any other sense be, a miracle: the climax is, if one may speak of such a thing, miraculous but not all that mysterious.

In *Morgan's Creek,* because the protagonist is Betty Hutton, the Miracle is one of biological extravagance, and because the setting is America, it is one of profit beyond imagining. But insane fecundity and the probability of staggering fortunes, while serving as the temporary tools of grace, remain in the end for Sturges only forces of nature, implicit in Sturges's world of excess and inevitable in his world of happy endings. Sturges wrenches us all, players and audience, from hopelessness by means of an outrageous, "satirical," but not unreasonable proposition: one feels it to be perfectly just that the truths of one little plot should submit to higher likelihoods of nature and of nation. The "miracle," once divulged, feels practically axiomatic.

In *Hail the Conquering Hero,* Sturges tries to fashion a miracle out of merit itself. Can it be done? Can it be done in this mode of comedy? Let me return for a moment to Capra and to the celebrated botched ending of *Meet John Doe.*

After *It Happened One Night,* as I have noted, Capra concentrated on breeding his own strain of political comedies in which the Little People managed to edify the decadents and chasten the politicos—without, of course, in any way imperiling an economic system manifestly certified by God. By the time of *Meet John Doe,* the bug of Swift had apparently bitten: the Lilliputians, as if out of Capra's control, turn small indeed—fickle and vindictive. Gary Cooper, once their supreme Nardac, their giant movie-star political hero, now, with his fraudulence laid bare, their scapegoat, will redeem them by dying for his and their sins. But (at least in the ending finally released to the public, the last of five that Capra shot) Doe is saved by the love of a magdalen who somewhat presumptuously threatens to die, or at least to be very ill, for him, and by the voices of the contrite Lilliputians beseeching his survival. Even Capra knew that this was no ending at all: "the best of a sorry lot," he has called it. But how could he allow the inevitable—that John Doe should indeed have achieved his own immolation; that in the world Capra has here obliged us to see, a world not only of big-time cynicism but of small-time faithlessness, a world in which the proletariat fairly itches to befoul Cooper's moral superiority and mutilate his godly person, John Does are either bums or suicides; that a Capra comedy won't hold this script?

So, even as scenario, *John Doe* refuses to live up (or down) to its own revelations. And in its visual and vocal manners it is in ceaseless combat with the message it must finally serve. The driving typewriter rhythms of the metropolitan newspaper world—whatever else it turns out to be, *Meet John Doe* is for much of its length one of the great Hollywood newspaper comedies—informs its style. Far more dramatically than the late-1930s expressions of Capra's imagination, it therefore must cancel its own dream. Simple assertions of truth are, all said and done, no more than one source of flashy copy—of flashy movies. Capra can't prevent his bristling and irresistible Hollywood-journalist skepticism from putting all in doubt.

Like *Meet John Doe,* **Hail the Conquering Hero** seems to negotiate the parlous trail that leads form farce to moral rearmament. In *Morgan's Creek,* I have suggested, the farcical denouement comes as satire and so harmonizes, effortlessly—all the more effortlessly for its very outrageousness—the farcical and satirical premises. As in any comedy that works, there is no pretending that the cure of injudiciousness is the cure of pharisee injustice. Sturges does not propose that the Miracle will purify the prudes and bigots; it will at best shut them up, rechannel their forces. For what are the relatively solitary joys of prudery and bigotry when there are millions to be made? (The optimism may even be genuine. The ways of *Morgan's Creek* are the ways of an America that has always needed miracles to guard it from its own madness, and has usually had them.)

But in *Conquering Hero* the situation is very different: the grace, instead of falling from on high, instead of being thrust upon him, is squeezed from Bracken himself, and it does smell rather like toothpaste. The blatant irony of the title appears to give ground without much struggle to straight moral uplift, and all the eccentrics and misfits and types beyond typage are ready for a transfiguration that Sturges's public never before seemed to think they needed. Heretofore more than content with bodies and voices, the quirkier the better, Sturges now tells us in one breath that America's destiny lies in self-abasing truths and that the Little People really have Big Souls. If by some fluke it happens to be true, it isn't the sort of news that farces bear gracefully.

But all this assumes that the happy "catastrophe" of *Conquering Hero* is only opportunism or evasion on Sturges's part, that it ignores or impatiently discards the details that have engendered it. Is the assumption fair? To the degree that it makes the film sound like television farce, surely not: it would require miscalculations far more fundamental than this to obscure for long the joys of Sturges operating at full career, and anyway the miscalculations of plotting that some of us see here only sabotage the last quarter or so of the film.

But even this is too simple. Although the personnel and moral milieu, indeed the very settings of *Morgan's Creek* and *Conquering Hero* are so nearly the same, the latter is much the darker of the two. The grace that rescues Bracken in the guise of suspicious sanctimoniousness will not be disunited from the sinister epidemic Marine-worship of the entire movie. "The Halls of Montezuma" is in the air, on the soundtrack, everywhere. The parlor shrine to Truesmith *père* of which Mrs. Truesmith serves as tireless sacristan, the implication (in the person of Bracken's rival for the hand of Ella Raines) that young men not in uniform gladly dying for Mom really are a national embarrassment, Bracken's barely whispered "Semper fidelis" as the Marines at the end clear out of the now purified town: all this and much more like it may leave us queasy. How much of this is penance? Did Sturges recognize that he had gone too far in his ironic portrait of wartime America in *Morgan's Creek*? The censors can't be faulted here: they certainly tried to tell him.

Along with the scary patriotism, equally inescapable, comes Woodrow's distinguishing bitterness. His gloom and self-pity, well beyond the usual comic manifestations of those traits, are evident from the first shot of him, drinking alone at a dreary wartime bar. His impotence against the pressures of the coterie of Marines, against all the mindless urgencies of a nation at war, which we experience as the relentless urgencies of Sturges's plotting and pacing, have more than a little of the quality of nightmare. This quality may only be an intensification of one quality of all farce. But the intensification isn't negligible.

There is something not quite comic—neither appropriate to comedy nor funny in itself—in Woodrow's dejection, and there is something as chronic as his own hay fever in a whole nation's intolerance of nonheroes. The actual and potential injustices of civilian life are writ too plain for anyone's comfort; the crowd that comes at the end to tell Woodrow of its gratitude is somewhat nervously compared to what it indeed looks exactly like, a lynch mob: things could have gone either way. Even the most startling discords in Sturges's fantasia of patriotism—the parlor shrine itself, for instance, of the bizarre mothermania of an orphan Marine—carry sinister resonance. Woodrow's lies may be pardoned and his situation reclaimed, but the continuities between his world and the real one (as in *Meet John Doe*) are too sharply drawn to allow the gods of comedy in some streamlined Sturgean machine to fly down and save the day.

Yet the need for a happy ending remains absolute. And so Sturges seems to take the easy way out by escaping by means of a rather fishy demonstration of popular virtue. The plan is efficient enough: the breach between Marines and civilian untouchables is at once closed, or at least neatly covered over. Woodrow's grim valor puts quite to shame all veterans of all foreign wars. The Marines in attendance halt in reverence. Dramatic convenience is served. And, most viewers report, the comedy suffers. Still, we forgive the ending of *Conquering Hero,* if we forgive it at all, because it is part of an ironic vision of American patriotism so complex and so full of knowing contradictions that we are never free quite to feel superior to its threatening pieties; because Sturges keeps the explicit wholesome homilies to a decent minimum; because even here, even now, Sturges will not mute a voice from the crowd that identifies Woodrow's self-humiliation with "a natural flair for politics"; because these are Sturges People and we sense that Sturges's sentimentality, like his "satire," is finally an expression of his delight in these people and in the people they stand in for.

At any rate, the word "satire" has been slipping in and out of my quotation marks for long enough. Now seems the time to explore Manny Farber's suggestion that Sturges, at once the embodiment and the chronicler of American success, is, all received opinion to the contrary, really no satirist at all.

Sturges's identity as ironist no one will dispute; incongruity is his meat, laughter his seasoning. From this point on, however, easy definitions show signs of rebellion. They simply won't play critics' games when turned loose on Sturges.

Frye, as ever at the ready with some ground rules, ventures that "As structure, the central principle of ironic myth is best approached as a parody of romance: the application of romantic mythical forms to a more realistic content which fits them in unexpected ways." The "structure," a commodious one, lodges all Sturges's Paramount work. But where if ever is the ironic perspective sharpened into satire? Frye goes on:

Patriotic pandemonium surrounds Ella Raines, Eddie Bracken, and Franklin Pangborn in Hail the Conquering Hero.

The chief distinction between irony and satire is that satire is militant irony: its moral norms are relatively clear, and it assumes standards against which the grotesque and absurd are measured. Sheer invective . . . is satire in which there is relatively little irony: on the other hand, whenever a reader is not sure what the author's attitude is or what his own is supposed to be, we have irony with relatively little satire.

In this arena of preliminary definitions, Frye helps me phrase some of my own questions about Sturges. Where, and of what, in Sturges's detonative little empire, can we be "sure"? And will historical considerations serve where the viewer's own instincts are uncertain?

Pursuing Frye's and other critics' categories of satirical voices and their dramatic embodiments, we are rewarded with no definitions that absolutely, or even approximately enough, include and so account for **Morgan's Creek** and **Conquering Hero.** Too many ingredients have obscured the original satiric recipe, if ever there was one: to the inherent contrarieties of the mentality and behavior of a nation at war, worshipful of the soldier boys but famished for impieties and laughs, Sturges mixes his own ahistorical zest for the personally peculiar and the morally knavish, and throws in (*inter alia*) Walburn and Demarest and the whole Paramount crew (including Franklin Pangborn as a pillar of the community!) and Betty Hutton carrying sextuplets and a kindly merchant with an Irish name and a Yiddish accent and punchdrunk Marine orphans and cacophonous martial music and shrines to the heroes of World War I in montage with utterly silly Doughboy uniforms and dowagers playing trombones and The Governor and The Boss in transit from another movie and "Semper Fidelis" and mortgages going up in flames and "Home to the Arms of Mother" and everywhere you turn Eddie Bracken. In such a jumble as this, let us admit, satire is not easily located. Yet historians of satire do help: they force us back through times and temperaments to the origin (debated, but let it pass) of the very word "satire" and so to its first spirit—to *satura,* commonly (and, for Sturges, perfectly) rendered as "hash."

"The road of excess," Blake thought, "leads to the palace of wisdom"; "the more the merrier," echo voices less preoccupied with destinations. Sentiments of this sort, much more than any pious textbook wish to "hold up human vice and folly to ridicule," suggest the actual working recipe for Sturges' delectable hash. Sturges's methods proceed from the deepest and truest instincts of movies, especially

Hollywood movies. Frye again, on *satura:* "a kind of parody of [ideal] form seems to run all through [satire's] tradition, from the mixture of prose and verse in early satire to the jerky cinematic changes of scene in Rabelais . . ." When he adds, "I am thinking of a somewhat archaic type of cinema," one might wish to correct him. (He could be thinking of cinema itself, of its natural reflection of its wildly mixed historical and generic origins and its material dependence on scissors and paste; he might be thinking specifically of Sturges.)

Given its aspiration to pure hash, its bald irreverence toward the perfectability of forms, given too its boundless ironies, Sturges's work will always invite the label of satire. There is no harm in the term so long as we recall that it doesn't impute to Sturges a position fixed in any known morality—that it doesn't confer on him exactly those pretensions he most passionately disclaimed. (In this sense, one could even argue that the species of edification implied by the end of ***Conquering Hero*** is no different from the fantastic amorality of the end of ***Morgan's Creek.*** In each case the shoe—available from among many shoes—happened to fit, so Sturges wore it. Today's taste will favor the ending of ***Morgan's Creek,*** but that is, in the last analysis, a matter of today's taste and nothing more. This isn't the sort of thing one says of, for example, Swift.)

Consideration of satire, which includes consideration of cautions governing the use of the term, does in another way help bring our experience of Sturges into sharper definition. Maynard Mack, among others, warns repeatedly of assuming, with respect to a poem like "The Rape of the Lock," that the guns of Pope's satire are aimed only at the precious trivialities of the eighteenth century, that the military heroics of the ancient world function for Pope only as the source of unflattering contrasts with his own effete culture. The poem itself, in its grace and elegance, its zeugmas and couplets, in the very wit without which such poems don't happen, is the chosen weapon of Belinda's milieu, not Agammemnon's. Its satire, its militancy, would, in too narrow a definition of satire, have to be taken as operating against itself. And the poem's satire may indeed be precisely so taken. The major point would be the same, namely that with a poet like Pope we had better be ready for a more menacing sky of ironies than a beginning critic might forecast.

So it is, if I may widen the notion, with Welles and Kane: how can a man (Welles) whose dictatorial urges over all aspects of the cinematic environment are so boldly affirmed be seen as merely contemptuous of a man (Kane) whose great sin is the urge to act as dictator over his environments? So too, in a situation closer to Pope's, with Renoir and *The Rules of the Game:* the intelligence, the cunning, the delight in roles and in the endless subtleties of playing, and so on—what we talk about when we talk about the film—are by and large the qualities that Renoir has had from the world he describes, the world whose passing his own style leaves him powerless simply to applaud. (The case is terribly complex: the disappearance of Octave/Renoir from the film before the Marquis's conclusive speech is enough to suggest the complexity. Still, to call the film a "savage" attack on a decaying society is to ignore both Renoir's perfect manners and his manifest sadness in the presence of dying.) So too, in a situation as far removed from Pope's or Renoir's as may be thought, with Sturges in ***Morgan's Creek*** and ***Conquering Hero.*** It's only a beginning, if a necessary beginning, to observe that what Sturges and we relish are the incongruences and vulgarities and all the crazy ambitions. We arrive closer to the truth only when we add that the America that Sturges films so delight in—that is to say, the America that Sturges loved enough to remake for our fond inspection—is, precisely, an America remade in Sturges's fashion and in his image. Sturges reminds us in his very style of America's inebriating tempo, its variety, its capacity for overlooking crassness and its unique hospitality to triumph. How might this style house a satire, properly speaking, of America?

In his insatiable appetite for discordant popular modes, in the delirious olio which is the world of ***The Miracle of Morgan's Creek*** and ***Hail the Conquering Hero,*** Sturges asks for comparison with another of America's most distinctive voices. I am thinking now most particularly of the homecoming sequence in ***Conquering Hero.*** Pangborn is attempting, with the all-but-spent patience that is one of his great masks, to coordinate the several bands assembled to welcome the hapless small-town lion. (At one point you may fear that your ears are playing tricks. No; it's a Sturges picture, and Pangborn out of nowhere really does mutter, "O death, where is thy sting?") The bands play well enough—well enough, that is, for an occasion when skill is clearly of secondary matter, when uncontaminated fervor is in the air. The problem is that all four ensembles hanker to play on and on, heedless of Pangborn's calls to decorum. Bewildered by the political rhetoric flying from all quarters, by the slogans which wed American speechmaking to American music and which the poor musicians of this sequence naturally take for their cues, they launch into their oompahs with all the ardor befitting this happiest of hours. Finally both verbal rhetoric and music move completely out of Pangborn's or anyone's control. "The Halls of Montezuma," "Hail the Conquering Hero," "There'll Be a Hot Time in the Old Town Tonight," and "Home to the Arms of Mother" are joined in an astonishing anthem to patriotic energy and sentiment. A larger emotional harmony absorbs and transcends the immediate cacophonies. Deafening, jarring, hilarious, as touching as it is familiar, this is indeed the voice of American singing. It is of course also the voice, or one of the voices, of Charles Ives.

It is unlikely that Sturges in the 1940s knew very much, if anything at all, of Ives's music. And even if by some chance he had come upon a performance of a work like the *Three Places in New England,* in which the use of overlapping martial bands specifically predicts the homecoming hymn in ***Conquering Hero,*** Sturges would not have expected a recondite acknowledgment of the composer to be noticed by more than a handful of movie-goers. In pointing to any likeness between Sturges and Ives I am therefore probably not drawing attention to any precise allusion on Sturges's part. What I am pointing to, beyond specific similarities of method and effect, is that creative spirit in which terms like "popular" and "classical," those instruments of an aimless pedantry, are discarded. For Ives, larding his difficult scores with generous doses of universally familiar tunes—as for the Pop artists of the 1960s—the confounding of terms like these was a gesture of irreverence. In the movies, by contrast, the terms had never seriously existed in their musical senses: try applying them, for example, to John Ford. (Try applying them to Jean Renoir.) Sturges's best pictures are among the happy results of this spirit. The huge audience of *Hail the Conquering Hero* might include, and the film might particularly delight, the minuscule audience of *Three Places in New England*. Sturges did not have to be anything but Sturges when the movies were for everybody.

But we needn't dwell upon Sturges's affinities with Ives or with any cultural figure outside the movies in order to perceive the centrality of his place in the history of Hollywood comedy. That his was the most brilliant comic talent of his day few have disputed; what remains to acknowledge and to explore is the complexity of the relation of his work to that of his predecessors and the subtlety and canniness of his responses to the various comedies of America. (pp. 131-41)

> Elliot Rubenstein, "The Home Fires: Aspects of Sturges's Wartime Comedy," in Quarterly Review of Film Studies, Vol. 7, No. 2, Spring, 1982, pp. 131-41.

Brian Henderson (essay date 1985)

[*In the following excerpt from his introduction to* Five Screenplays by Preston Sturges, *Henderson traces Sturges's development as a dramatist, screenwriter, and director, assesses the criticism on Sturges, and analyzes the Sturges myth promulgated by James Agee.*]

Preston Sturges was "by far the wittiest scriptwriter the English-speaking cinema has known" (Andrew Sarris). He was "probably the most spectacular manipulator of sheer humor since Mark Twain" (Manny Farber). He "restored to American film a sense of social satire . . . equalled only in Chaplin's films" (André Bazin). "He was Hollywood's greatest writer-director, with emphasis on the former. He created a racy, malapropriate idiom whose deceptive ease would prove inimitable" (Richard Corliss).

Sturges wrote and directed twelve films. The first eight were made for Paramount Pictures between 1939 and 1944: *The Great McGinty* (1940), *Christmas in July* (1940), *The Lady Eve* (1941), *Sullivan's Travels* (1942), *The Palm Beach Story* (1942), *The Great Moment* (1944), *The Miracle of Morgan's Creek* (1944), and *Hail the Conquering Hero* (1944). In partnership with Howard Hughes, Sturges wrote and directed *The Sin of Harold Diddlebock* in 1946; it was cut by Hughes and released as *Mad Wednesday* in 1947. For Twentieth Century–Fox, Sturges wrote and directed *Unfaithfully Yours* (1948) and *The Beautiful Blonde from Bashful Bend* (1949). In Paris he wrote and directed (in French and English versions) *Les Carnets du Major Thompson* [*The French They Are a Funny Race*] (1955).

Critics and other viewers generally agree that Sturges's last two films were failures. His extremely high reputation as a writer-director thus rests on ten films. (p. 1)

Sturges the writer and Sturges the director have had their respective partisans. Andrew Sarris said of Sturges that "all his screenwriting efforts in the Thirties would now be of only the most esoteric concern if he had not made the decisive leap from the writer's cubicle to the director's chair." Evidently responding to Sarris, Richard Corliss wrote a few years later in his book on Hollywood screenwriters: "While his direction, especially of extended dialogue scenes, shows far more control than contemporary critics were willing to grant it, Sturges's direction would be of only the most esoteric concern today if he had not written eight or ten of Hollywood's best screenplays." This opposition at first glance resembles a Kantian antinomy—each proposition appears to be necessarily true yet both cannot be true. The opposition itself, however, may be questioned, arising as it does in a dispute about the relative importance of directors and screenwriters generally. Perhaps Sturges is not a good example for such disputes—he was hardly a typical screenwriter or a typical director.

Sturges was the sole major Hollywood director who filmed only his own original screenplays. *The Great Moment* draws its facts from a published biography, but otherwise Sturges—his last two films aside—never adapted his screenplays from someone else's story, novel, or play. The exceptions of *Easy Living* and *The Lady Eve,* based on stories by Vera Caspary and Monckton Hoffe respectively, only prove the rule. The stories are so completely transformed by Sturges that screen credit to the "original authors" seems ludicrous. As a screenwriter, moreover, Sturges never, as far as I know, collaborated with another writer. He was sometimes assigned, especially in the 1930s, to improve or rewrite the scripts of a prior writer or writers who had departed a project. Even then Sturges preferred, as often as possible, to discard the prior work and start all over again. It is perhaps not surprising that Sturges as writer-director was not able to meet such exacting standards for much more than a decade—no one else was able to sustain them for even that long. (Billy Wilder has functioned as a successful writer-director for an astonishing five decades, but he has always collaborated with other writers and has frequently adapted novels and plays.) (pp. 4-6)

The most common—and bitter—complaint of Hollywood writers of all eras is that their work has been distorted by other writers and/or by the director. Sturges had the opportunity to alter his dialogue, even to omit scenes or to change the order of scenes if he chose to, during shooting or in the editing. His own brilliance and his tireless revising aside, this opportunity resulted in a final polish and perfection that few scripts have ever enjoyed. (p. 6)

. . . . .

At Christmas of 1927, during a visit to his father's tailor to be measured for some new suits, Preston had an attack of acute appendicitis. He almost died before medical advice was sought, and he spent six weeks in the hospital. There he wrote an operetta based on Irvin S. Cobb's *Speaking of Operations,* [Sturges's father] Solomon bringing him books on drama to help in his writing. Most useful was Brander Matthews's *A Study of the Drama,* which emphasized audience response rather than formal values for their own sake. He soon decided that his hospital play was worthless, a product of anesthesia and drugs.

Recuperating at his father's apartment, he was also going out with a successful actress, who taunted him with his failures and his lack of money. One night, after he had assessed her failings in retaliation, she responded that she was writing a play about a bore and that he was the model. Stung, he derisively announced that if she could write a play, he could write one too and, furthermore, that his would be produced first and run longer. He went home and wrote Act III of **The Guinea Pig** that night. The play concerns a young woman novelist who has written a romantic bestseller and is hired by a New York producer to turn it into a play. She is unable, however, to write a convincing seduction scene. A young man she meets in the producer's outer office becomes her way of finding out "exactly what does a young man say to a young woman to make her surrender herself instantly." The girl, not surprisingly, eventually falls in love with the young man. The play's funniest lines, the critics later agreed, belonged not to the leads but to Sam Small, the fur dealer-turned-producer who commissions the girl's play; Sturges had apparently based the character on the thickly accented professors he had known in Europe. Sturges convinced the Wharf Players of Provincetown to put on the play, gathered some good notices, and set out to seek a Broadway production.

Through an actor friend he got a job as assistant stage manager for a play produced by the successful director Brock Pemberton. When no one was interested in **The Guinea Pig,** Sturges produced the play himself on $2,500 donated by the hostess of a dinner party he attended. With the advice of Charles H. Abramson a low-budget production was staged, its opening timed for the return of the major critics from the Christmas holidays. Sturges was fortunate to get Alexander Carr, a well-known stage and screen actor, who brought Sam Small vividly to life. Carr also showed Sturges how to "point" his dialogue. In one scene Sturges had Small correct the girl's opinion of a third party: "No, dearie. He was a damn fool. Excuse me to contradict you." Carr turned the line around: "Excuse me to contradict you . . . but he was a damn fool." (Sturges later summoned Carr from New York to play Mr. Schindel in **Christmas in July.**) The "uncertain little comedy" was praised by George S. Kaufman in the *New York Times* for having "quite a little simple and entertaining humor," and it ran sixty-four performances.

Sturges then joined a touring company of *Frankie and Johnnie* as assistant stage manager and actor. After *Frankie and Johnnie,* he was assistant stage manager for *Goin' Home* and then for a road company of *Hot Bed,* which he left in Chicago when it was closed by the police.

At his father's house Sturges wrote (in six days, as he later boasted) **Strictly Dishonorable,** a speakeasy comedy in which the sophisticated, foreign-born opera singer wins the girl from the clean-cut American boy. The most comic parts were Judge Dempsey, a chronic patron, and Patrolman Mulligan, neither of whom was a stickler for the rulebook. Sturges sent it to Pemberton, who wrote back immediately that, with work on the second and third acts, he would direct an August production. In stormy rehearsals and previews Pemberton forced Sturges to rewrite much of the play and made changes of his own in his work with the actors. Sturges acknowledges the collaboration of all concerned in the published version of the play: "A play, as produced, is rarely the work of one individual. During the rehearsal period, suggestions are accepted from everyone within shouting distance. Many of these suggestions are excellent, and all of them are used. It is impossible to list here the names of all the people responsible for **Strictly Dishonorable** as it stands; I thank them all, and spend my royalties to their good health." At the time, however, Sturges resented the rewrites, feeling that Pemberton was undermining his work; often the two did not speak. The play was a great success, running 557 performances in New York alone. Sturges enjoyed the fame and the money but seems to have had a strong desire to succeed thenceforth without Pemberton's interference.

Sturges next wrote **Recapture** (1930), a comedy-drama with a tragic ending evidently based on his relationship with Estelle [De Wolfe Mudge Godfrey, Sturges's first wife]. An ex-husband seeks to recapture the love of his ex-wife and succeeds in Act I, both have doubts in Act II, she dies in an elevator accident in Act III. The venture was opposed by Pemberton and Abramson, who now shared an apartment with Sturges. Both of them urged him to write another comedy. The play opened in January 1930, was deplored by the critics, and ran twenty-four performances. (When Noël Coward's *Private Lives* opened later, Sturges noted that it was **Recapture** with a happy ending.)

By the time **Recapture** opened, Sturges was involved in another project considered by his theater friends to be even more dubious. H. Maurice Jacquet, a friend from his songwriting days, had written an operetta that had been produced expensively and had flopped. But he had saved the scenery and costumes and wanted to try again. Sturges agreed to write a new book and lyrics and some new songs to go with the sets and costumes on hand. To escape Abramson's outrage and the skepticism of others, Sturges left New York on February 10, 1930 (the same night that **Strictly Dishonorable** opened in Chicago), for the Palm Beach home of Paris Singer.

On the train he met heiress Eleanor Post Hutton, then twenty. They were married, despite her family's opposition, on April 12, 1930. Soon after, Sturges's mother [Mary Desti] returned from Europe in ill health, which she attributed to the shock of Isadora's death in 1927, and as a result, a honeymoon trip on Sturges's yacht, *Recapture,* was postponed. Then, backed by all of Sturges's available money, the operetta, retitled **The Well of Romance,** opened in November 1930, but it failed to excite critical or popular interest and folded after eight performances. Mary Desti died in April 1931; Eleanor left for Europe in June the same year—to continue her singing lessons. Sturges had apparently dominated Eleanor, had not taken her seriously, and had been depressed at his two failures and his mother's illness.

Sturges then worked on a bedroom farce called *Unfaithfully Yours* and wrote *A Cup of Coffee,* a three-act play about a slogan-contest winner. He gained weight and wore a flowing moustache that made him look much older than he was. He patronized a number of dime-a-dance halls and eventually wrote *Child of Manhattan,* which opened March 1, 1932, about a millionaire who falls in love with a dance-hall girl. The critics found it coarse on the one hand and trite on the other; although it ran eighty-seven performances, audiences also seemed to find it distasteful. While writing the play, Sturges asked Eleanor to return and, when she did not, he sailed for Paris to tell her of his resolve to be a better husband. But she had been enjoying her independence and the attentions of many titled suitors and was cool to Sturges. He wrote Abramson from Paris, "I'm terribly in love . . . but if you could only see her, Charley, she is unbelievably beautiful and smart." She declined to return but apparently renewed her commitment to the marriage. When *Child of Manhattan* failed, he borrowed money to go to Paris again, angering the producer by leaving the show when it needed work. Eleanor asked how much he would accept for a divorce; insulted, he overlooked $100,000 he figured she owned him and said, "It will cost you one courteous request, madame, and a polite thank-you when it is all over." Back in New York, however, he discovered that he could communicate with her only through her lawyers.

Before he met Eleanor, Sturges had done two filmscript rewrites for the Paramount Astoria studio on Long Island—*The Big Pond,* a Maurice Chevalier vehicle, in 1929 and *Fast and Loose* in 1930. He received only "dialogue" credit on these films, but he earned twelve thousand dollars for less than a month's work. *Strictly Dishonorable* was filmed in 1931 and *Child of Manhattan* in 1932, both under previously negotiated contracts. On the basis of the former, Carl Laemmle of Universal Pictures offered Sturges a contract, which he accepted. Never intending to stay, he went to Hollywood in 1932 in order to repair his fortunes. He kept his Manhattan apartment and his boat but took with him his secretary, Bianca Gilchrist, the estranged wife of a songwriter friend, and two cronies who followed in his Lincoln. In fact, he stayed in Hollywood for twenty years. For Laemmle he wrote an adaptation of H. G. Wells's *The Invisible Man*—ignoring, as was to become his habit, the eight previous attempts in the studio's file. In the end his version, like the others, was not used.

He stayed on in the studio bungalow and did three weeks' complimentary work on a comedy released later as *They Just Had to Get Married* (1933). "I hope that this bread cast upon the waters will return as ham sandwiches," he remarked. He then wrote *The Power and the Glory,* which bore some relation to the life of Eleanor's grandfather, C. W. Post, a self-made millionaire who had killed himself at age fifty-five for unknown reasons. From time to time Eleanor had told him stories about her grandfather's life, and although nonchronological, they had a certain cohesiveness. Sturges thought he could successfully use that nonchronological structure to tell a story on film. *The Power and the Glory* may well have been the first use of "voice-under" in film. Sturges was hailed for inventing "narratage," and the script was displayed under glass in the lobby of the New York theater in which the film opened. Narratage included the voice of Tom Garner's old secretary remembering long-past conversations while the screen depicted the players mouthing the words we hear in the secretary's voice. With its tycoon subject and its nonchronological flashback structure, *The Power and the Glory* is a striking anticipation of the theme and method of *Citizen Kane* (1941). It differs most from the later work perhaps in its lugubrious direction by William K. Howard, who flattens the potential variety of its scenes into monotony and the bold complexity of its structure into sheer anticlimax.

Sturges wrote *The Power and the Glory* on speculation, as he was accustomed to do at this period, reasoning that no playwright gets better terms. (Later he was to decry "the Hollywood disease" of being unable to write unless on salary.) Jesse L. Lasky admired the script and agreed to film it exactly as written, offering Sturges a percentage of the profits against a $17,500 advance. This arrangement frightened many producers; B. P. Schulberg of Paramount wrote in *The Hollywood Reporter* against the percentage deal, the non-revision clause, and particularly the use of a single screenwriter. Sturges wrote in defense of the arrangement; he also broke precedent by being present on the set during shooting. Indeed, several performers averred that they had never seen a writer before. Ostensibly serving as dialogue director, Sturges sought to learn as much about filmmaking as possible. *The Power and the Glory* was admired by critics and did well at first in the large city theaters but it was not commercially successful.

Sturges rented a house in the Hollywood hills, built a schooner, and developed a number of friendships among writers and humorists of the time. He wrote a political comedy, *The Vagrant,* in 1933, but after the failure of the much-touted *The Power and the Glory,* no studio was interested. He wrote a screenplay based on *The Green Hat* in eight weeks at MGM, but his contract was not renewed. Harry Cohn hired him on a comparable basis for Columbia and soon also fired him. He did some work on *Imitation of Life* (1934), then wrote the screenplays for *Thirty Day Princess* and *We Live Again* (1934), the latter an adaptation of Tolstoy's *Resurrection* for Rouben Mamoulian and Samuel Goldwyn. On the basis of that film, typecast for the moment as a specialist in literary adaptations, he was rehired at Universal for $1,500 a week.

Sturges wrote the script for *The Good Fairy* (1934), based on a Molnar play, for William Wyler and wrote a new screenplay for *Diamond Jim* (1935), another tycoon story, thought to be one of his best scripts. On both films Sturges was often on the set, observing and rewriting to some degree. A. Edward Sutherland, the director of *Diamond Jim,* often conferred with him on the nuances of scenes about to be shot. They fought the producer for their ending—Jim commits suicide by overeating—and won. Sturges received sole screen credit for *The Good Fairy* for the first time since *The Power and the Glory;* two prior writers received an adaptation credit on *Diamond Jim,* although Sturges had characteristically abandoned their script, and even the biography of Brady on which it was based, to begin again from scratch.

Sturges's salary was now $2,500 a week, and he had several offers. He did two rewrites for Universal, ***Next Time We Love*** (1935) and ***Love Before Breakfast*** (1935), vehicles for Margaret Sullavan and Carole Lombard respectively. Songs that he co-wrote appeared in *The Gay Deception* (1935) and *One Rainy Afternoon* (1936). Around this time Sturges also wrote a story and screenplay called *Song of Joy,* about a studio that has hired an opera singer for $19,000 a week and has to invent a picture for her in four weeks. Although Universal bought the story and screenplay, Sturges's stinging satire of producers, yes-men, writers, and directors did not appeal to his friend Sutherland or to anyone else, apparently to Sturges's genuine surprise. . . .

In March 1936 Sturges was hired by Paramount to write ***Hotel Haywire*** (1937), a vehicle for Burns and Allen that was eventually rewritten and made with other players. This led to a two-year contract with Paramount at $2,500 a week, Sturges's first regular employment by a studio, beginning September 29, 1936.

Sturges's first Paramount assignment was to Arthur Hornblow, Jr., who asked him to turn ***Easy Living***, a Vera Caspary story owned by the studio, into a screenplay. The story concerned a poor cosmetician who impulsively steals a sable coat from one of her clients. Deception piles on deception, and she eventually loses both the man she loves and the coat itself. In Sturges's version, the coat is thrown from a high-rise by a millionaire banker (Edward Arnold) trying to teach his wife a lesson. It lands on Mary Smith (Jean Arthur), who is passing by on a bus. She tries to return the coat, but the banker insists she keep it and buys her a new hat. She loses her job but because everyone (falsely) thinks she is having an affair with the banker, she gets a luxurious hotel suite, room service, and beautiful clothes free.

Easy Living is Sturges's most explicit satire on the irrationality of the stock market, capitalism, and the lives lived under it. In one day a millionaire's son (Ray Milland) can be reduced to working in the Automat and a poor clerk can rise to living in a posh hotel. A coat that costs $58,000 is worth so little to a banker that he can throw it away, and worth so much to a clerk that she cannot grasp that it will utterly change her life. The stock market fluctuates on the unthinking words of a clerk, and fortunes are thereby made and lost. The son's silly buy-and-sell formulas for the stock market make millions, and he goes from total failure to total success in one day. A girl's notoriety makes her a walking advertisement for expensive goods; money flows toward her in expectation of a market break-through and a hotel's fortunes depend on her.

Sturges had given his father $15,000 of the proceeds of ***Strictly Dishonorable*** to invest—just before the crash of 1929. This was lost, as was most of Solomon's business. Perhaps as a consequence, Sturges did not invest the money he earned as a screenwriter in the thirties and as a writer-director in the forties, a decision that cost him dearly in the long run. (With the large sums he earned, Sturges built boats, opened and continually supplied capital to restaurants—first Snyder's, then The Players— bought and remodeled a house, opened and continually supplied capital for the Sturges Engineering Company, paid salaries for household staff, paid alimony and child support, and so on. By the time of World War II, he was in the 96 percent tax bracket.) ***Easy Living*** is Sturges's light-hearted revenge on Wall Street or, as it is called in the film, Broad Street. J. B. Ball is "the bull of Broad Street," which becomes, in one marvelous transposition, "the Ball of Bull Street."

After ***Easy Living,*** Sturges worked on ***Port of Seven Seas*** (1937), ***College Swing*** (1937), and ***Never Say Die*** (1938). ***If I Were King*** (1938), a film about François Villon directed by Frank Lloyd, with Ronald Colman and Basil Rathbone, engaged his interest far more than these. Sturges entirely rewrote the forty-year-old play on which the film was based, translated Villon's poetry himself, and in some cases invented his own.

Bianca Gilchrist, who was living with Sturges and supervising reconstruction of his house, left him when he seemed to have little time for her amidst an engineering company he set up to develop his inventions, a restaurant he was establishing, and other activities. During this time Sturges met Louise Tevis, who was seperated from her husband, a man Sturges knew slightly. They fell in love and were married in Reno, when her divorce was final, on November 7, 1938. In Reno Sturges worked on *Two Bad Hats* from a Monckton Hoffe story of the same name, finishing a draft on November 30, 1938; it was later revised and directed by Sturges himself as ***The Lady Eve.*** This project was developed for the Paramount producer Albert Lewin, with whom Sturges enjoyed working but who left Paramount in 1939. . . .

Another project for Lewin was *Beyond These Tears,* which became *The Amazing Marriage* and finally ***Remember the Night*** (1940). Lewin's memos helped shape the plot of this film and, to some degree, of *Eve. Remember the Night* is an unusual Sturges script—sentimental, romantic, gentle. In it a district attorney (Fred MacMurray) prosecutes a shoplifter (Barbara Stanwyck) just before Christmas. He wins a continuance over the holidays, undercutting her lawyer's lachrymose work on the jury. Feeling guilty, he arranges her bail; she is dropped at his door by mistake and he ends up taking her to his Indiana home for Christmas, where everyone likes her and he falls in love. He has told his mother (Beulah Bondi) that Stanwyck is a criminal. Separately, she asks Stanwyck not to undermine her son's hard-won career. Back in New York, MacMurray is mean to Stanwyck on the stand in order to turn the jury in her favor; to foil this strategy, she confesses to the crime. Once she is convicted, she tells him that things have worked out for the best, and he agrees to wait for her.

Lewin's departure and that of Arthur Hornblow, Jr., another Paramount producer congenial to Sturges, meant that Mitchell Leisen, now his own producer, had a free hand with the film. He preferred his own cuts to rewrites with the writer. Sturges felt that such cuts were unnecessary and that they interfered with his pacing, but because Leisen had been successful in recent years, the head of production, William LeBaron, let him make them. On the other hand, LeBaron wanted to keep Sturges, who was talking of leaving Paramount for another studio where he might have more control of his scripts. He gave Sturges permission to proceed with a favorite project, *Triumph over Pain,* which later became **The Great Moment,** but Sturges was still unhappy.

LeBaron then agreed, apparently with considerable misgiving, to let him direct a low-budget film of his earlier script *The Vagrant.* Sturges went over the script, revising it extensively; the shooting script . . . was finished on November 28, 1939. Shooting began on December 11 and continued until January 1940; the film was retitled **The Great McGinty.**

. . . . .

However brief his sojourn as a Hollywood director, Sturges has been blessed with some of the best American film criticism ever devoted to a single director. It began, of course, with James Agee. Although I take exception to certain of Agee's strictures on Sturges in what follows, his writing on the director is deeply felt, perceptive, and lively; he never doubted Sturges's value and importance. Now that we know more about Agee, moreover, his writing on Sturges may be read as much in relation to himself as to Sturges. He seems at times to be projecting himself rather directly onto Sturges, which may account for the intensity of the passages quoted below and is arguably the highest tribute that a writer of Agee's stature may pay to another artist.

Manny Farber's 1954 essay on Preston Sturges (written with W. S. Poster) is, in my judgment, the most brilliant piece ever written on Sturges and one of the finest pieces of film criticism in any language. It is virtually an anthropology of Sturges's cinematic world—akin, all differences aside, to Roland Barthes's Racinian anthropology in *On Racine.*

Andrew Sarris has written a number of fine pieces on Sturges among them a rare interview with Sturges in 1957 and an expert survey of Sturges's scriptwriting work in the 1930s. Richard Corliss's essay on ten of Sturges's best scripts in *Talking Pictures* is perhaps the best chapter in that accomplished book. Stanley Cavell's chapter on **The Lady Eve** in *Pursuits of Happiness* has a number of remarkable insights into that film. Elliot Rubenstein's essay on **Sullivan's Travels** in *Sight and Sound* is the most complete analysis of that work's meta-filmic aspects.

Outside of American film criticism the most important work is undoubtedly that of André Bazin, who wrote on Sturges between 1948 and 1951, when Sturges's Paramount films and **Mad Wednesday** were first being shown in Europe. Bazin wrote only four brief pieces on Sturges, barely totaling fifteen pages, but they are as assured, far-reaching, and valuable as Bazin's most highly regarded work.

The foundations of Sturges criticism were laid during his career, indeed at its high point, by James Agee. In a series of essays written in 1944, Agee developed a biographical-psychological interpretation of Sturges and his work that has proven astonishingly durable. In one variant or another, Agee's interpretation has turned up in most later writing on Sturges. There are important instances of the Agee position in writings on Sturges in the 1950s, 1960s, 1970s, and 1980s.

Agee wrote regularly about film for *Time* and *The Nation* and occasionally for *Partisan Review.* Needless to say, these journals represented different echelons of intellectual sophistication and had distinct audiences. In the 1940s, it is worth remembering, the sophistication of an audience was directly proportional to its hostility to what were then called "the movies."

Agee wrote in different styles, made different points, and sometimes came to different conclusions for his various audiences. Manny Farber once noted that *Agee on Film,* the posthumous collection of Agee's film essays, showed "no evidence of his conflicting reviews on the same picture for the power (*Time*) and the glory (*The Nation*)."

Agee's review of Sturges's **The Miracle of Morgan's Creek** (1944) appeared in the February 5, 1944, issue of *The Nation.* He begins: "**The Miracle of Morgan's Creek,** the new Preston Sturges film, seems to me funnier, more adventurous, more abundant, more intelligent, and more encouraging than anything that has been made in Hollywood for years. Yet the more I think of it, the less I esteem it. I have, then, both to praise and defend it, and to attack it." Here, in his first words on the subject, is that striking ambivalence toward Sturges that characterizes all of Agee's writing on him.

Agee goes on to praise the film for its audacity and its effective mixing of tender pathos and nihilistic farce. He defends the film against those who have dismissed it as mere comedy, for its frantic, rough character, for its bad taste, or for its multiplicity of attack and shiftiness of style.

> Yet the more I think about the film, the less I like it. There are too many things that Sturges, once he had won all the victories and set all the things moving which he managed to here, should have achieved unhindered, purely as a good artist; and he has not even attempted them. . . . The whole tone of the dialogue, funny and bright as it often is, rests too safely within the pseudo-cute, pseudo-authentic, patronizing diction perfected by Booth Tarkington. And in the stylization of action as well as language it seems to me clear that Sturges holds his characters, and the people they comically represent, and their predicament, and his audience, and the best potentialities of his own work, essentially in contempt. His emotions, his intelligence, his aesthetic ability never fully commit themselves; all the playfulness becomes rather an avoidance of commitment than an extension of means for it . . . nearly every central and final responsibility is shirked.

Agee concludes the review with an unfavorable comparison of Sturges to René Clair, whom Agee calls "one of the few great artists of this century"—a judgment that few critics, if any, would share today. Agee concludes: "Sturges, in his middle forties, is still just the most gifted American working in films, vividly successful in the kind of artful-dodging which frustrates Clair; hollow and evasive at those centers in which Clair is so firm. I suspect that Sturges feels that conscience and comedy are incompatible. It would be hard for a man of talent to make a more self-destructive mistake."

In this review, the framework of Agee's ultimate position on Sturges is already in place, although no biographical fact has been adduced as yet. Agee feels that Sturges has remarkable talent, intelligence, and inventiveness but lacks moral and aesthetic seriousness, what Agee calls "commitment." This imbalance (which in fact is generated by Agee's own premises) seems to baffle and disturb him—it constitutes a gap in his argument and in his understanding. That gap will soon be filled by a psychological-biographical analysis of Sturges himself, perhaps already suggested in the previous quotation by Agee's speculation about what Sturges feels and his attribution of self-destructiveness to him.

The *Time* review of February 14 pursues the same line of argument in a more colloquial style, but it substitutes biographical data for the moral-aesthetic judgments of his review in *The Nation:*

> Chief credit for **The Miracle** must go to Sturges. . . . The chief failures are his, too. Some of the film is painfully unfunny, because it is like a joker who outroars his audience's reaction. Some of the pity is pitiful because it is smashed before it has a chance to crystallize. Most of the finest human and comic potentialities of the story are lost because Sturges is so much less interested in his characters than in using them as hobbyhorses for his own wit.

Then, as though to illuminate his own criticisms, Agee quotes a remark by René Clair that Sturges should slow down, be a little more selfish, and worry about his reputation; then he launches into a summary of Sturges's life story:

> The life of Preston Sturges might read as dizzily as one of his own comedies if it were not, in essence, so intensely bitter. On his first day at school in Chicago, Preston rode a bicycle and wore a Greek chiton. The bicycle was his stepfather's influence—Solomon Sturges, stockbroker and socialite, was a champion cyclist and a good amateur baseball player. The Attic haberdashery was his mother's idea. . . . Preston's mother was determined that he should be a genius. "I was never allowed," Sturges says, "to play with other kids. They wedged art into me from every side. I was dragged into every goddamn museum in the world." There were gay moments, but they usually stank of culture.
>
> The effect of such training was predictable. "They did everything they could," he says, "to make me an artist, but I didn't want to be an artist. I wanted to be a good businessman like my father". . . .
>
> Sturges' brilliant, successful yet always deeply self-absorbing films suggest a warring blend of the things he picked up through respect for his solid stepfather, contact with his strange mother, and the intense need to enjoy himself and to succeed which came from 30 years of misery and failure. . . . The combination might explain his matchless skill in producing some of the most intoxicating bits of nihilism the screen has known, but always at the expense of a larger excellence.

Agee's views on Sturges also emerged in his writing for *Partisan Review.* In Spring 1944 he wrote a rather despairing essay on folk art, which concludes, "Preston Sturges' latest film reaches the great audience if only through its vivacity, but it is hardly a work of art, popular or unpopular; it fails through snobbery, cynicism, cowardice and a radical lack of love."

Agee's final piece on Sturges is a September 23, 1944, review of **Hail the Conquering Hero** for *The Nation.* Agee used the occasion to formulate definitively his overall position on Sturges. Indeed, at least for those who admire the film, it is almost as though Agee did not see **Hail the Conquering Hero** at all; he merely subsumed it under a file he had opened earlier.

> Any adequate review of this remarkable movie would devote at least as much space to its unqualified praise as I have to qualifying the praise; it would have to spend more space than that, I think, getting at even a tentative explanation of why Sturges functions as he does. "Hollywood" is no explanation, surely; "Hollywood" was made for Sturges and he in turn is its apotheosis; but why? It seems to me that Sturges had reason, through his mother, to develop, as they caromed around high-Bohemian Europe during his childhood, from opera to opera and gallery to gallery, not only his singular mercurialism and resourcefulness, which come especially natural to some miserably unhappy children, but also a retching, permanently incurable loathing for everything that stank of "culture," of "art." I gather further that through his stepfather, a stable and charming Chicago sportsman and business man, he developed an all but desperate respect and hunger for success, enhanced by a sickening string of failures as a business man and inventor up to the age of about thirty; and that this again assumed the dimensions of a complex. I believe that in his curious career as a never-quite-artist of not-quite-genius he has managed to release and guide the energies of these influences in the only way open to him.
>
> I hesitate to write this sort of thing, drawn only from such superficialities as have appeared in print and from some remarkable photographs of Sturges as a child and young man which appeared in the *Saturday Evening Post;* but I risk the worse than questionable taste because I see no other way to understand what Sturges' films are about. They are wonderful as comedies and they are wonderfully complex and ingenious; they seem to me also wonderfully, uncontrollably, almost proudly corrupt, vengeful, fearful of intactness and self-commitment; most essentially, they are paradoxical marvels of self-perpetuation and self-destruction; their mastering object, aside from success, seems to be to sail as steep into the wind as possible without for an instant incurring the disaster of becoming seriously, wholly acceptable as art. They seem to me, indeed, in much of their twisting, the elaborately counterpointed image of a neurosis. It is an especially interesting neurosis, not only because

Sturges is a man of such talent and not only because it expresses itself in such fecund and in themselves suggestive images, but also because, in relation to art, it seems the definitive expression of this country at present—the stranglehold wedlock of the American female tradition of "culture," the male tradition of "success."

Manny Farber and W. S. Poster's 1954 essay on Sturges reflects Agee's biographical-psychological interpretation of Sturges and his work. It does so, however, in the context of a critical approach to its subject which is very different from Agee's, whose criticism Farber questions as well as praises in another essay. In the ten years that separate Agee's essays from Farber's, Sturges's Hollywood career had ended. It was perhaps no longer possible to speak, as Agee had, of Sturges's "all but desperate respect and hunger for success." In any case, Farber sees Sturges's mother/father, artist/businessman conflicts as a positive force, which led to the distinctive, indeed unique qualities of his films. Farber celebrates Sturges with only minor reservations. He uses Agee's biographical-psychological scheme to account for Sturges's successes as a filmmaker, not for his failures:

> One of his characters calls society a "cockeyed caravan," and Sturges, himself, is less a settled, bona fide resident of America than a hurried, Argus-eyed traveler through its shifting scenes, a nomad in space observing a society nomadic in time and projecting his sensations in uniquely computed terms.
>
> This modern cinematic perspective of mobility seen by a mobile observer comes easily to Sturges because of his strange family background and broken-up youth. He was the son of a normal, sports-loving, successful father and a fantastic culture-bug mother who wanted him to be a genius and kept him in Paris from the age of eight to about fifteen. "She dragged me through every goddam museum on the continent," he has rancorously remarked. Glutted at an early age, by an overrich diet of esthetic dancing, high-hatted opera audiences, and impressionist painting, Sturges still shows the marks of his youthful trauma.
>
> The most obvious result of his experience has been a violent reaction against all estheticism. He has also expressed fervent admiration for his father's business ability and a desire to emulate him. The fact that he did not, however, indicates that his early training provoked more than a merely negative reaction in him and made him a logical candidate for Hollywood, whose entire importance in the history of culture resides in its unprecedented effort to merge art and big business.
>
> As a moviemaker, the businessman side of Sturges was superficially dominant. He seems to have begun his career with the intention of giving Hollywood a lesson in turning out quick, cheap, popular pictures. He whipped together his scripts in recordbreaking time, cast his pictures with unknowns, and shot them faster than anyone dreamed possible. . . .
>
> What made Sturges a viciously alive artist capable of discovering new means of expressiveness in a convention-ridden medium was the frenetic, split sensibility that kept him reacting to and away from the opposite sides of his heredity. These two sides are, in fact, the magnetic poles of American society. Accepting, in exaggerated fashion, the businessman approach to films, he nevertheless brought to his work intelligence, taste, and a careful study of the more estimable movies of the past. He also took care to disappoint rigid-minded esthetes and reviewers.

The last line may be a reference to Agee's reservations about Sturges. The piece as a whole in effect counters Agee's charges of aesthetic and moral failure in Sturges's work. In a later review of *Agee on Film,* Farber criticized "the growing Agee legend" in addition to praising him on Farber's own grounds: "His criticism had an excessive richness that came from a fine writing ear as well as cautious hesitancy, ganglia, guilt. The sentences are swamps that are filled with a suspicious number of right-sounding insights. Actually, Agee's appreciations stick pretty close to what the middle-brow wants to hear."

In *The American Cinema* (1968), Andrew Sarris wrote in his Sturges entry:

> Sturges was criticized at his peak by James Agee and Manny Farber for an ambivalence in his work derived from a childhood conflict between a culturally demanding mother and an admired businessman foster father. This unusually Freudian analysis of the director's work, unusual, that is, for its time, sought to explain the incongruity of continental sophistication being challenged by American pragmatism. Sturges himself was seen as an uneasy mixture of savant and wise guy. On the one hand, his extreme literacy, rare among Hollywood screenwriters, enabled him to drop words like "ribaldry" and "vestal" into their proper contexts without a pretentious thud. On the other, he seemed unwilling to develop the implications of his serious ideas. His flair for props and gags suited the popularly recalled image of the young inventor of kissproof lipstick.

By attributing the biographical-psychological criticism of Sturges to other critics, Sarris himself managed to straddle the issue. By recounting the Agee view of Sturges, however, his work served to pass it on to a younger generation of film critics, just as his indirect discourse of attribution allowed it to pass into the texture of his own argument.

It is interesting that at least one younger critic has returned to the Agee position in its undiluted state. In *Talking Pictures,* Richard Corliss discusses Sturges's screenwriting for other directors and for himself. In his discussion of **The Great Moment** (1944), Corliss says:

> Endings in Sturges films tend to be schizophrenic showdowns between the two sides of the writer-director. On one side is Preston the Pride of Paramount, laughgetter and moneymaker, stepson of millionaire stockbroker Solomon Sturges; this is the Sturges who gave audiences the endings they wanted, in **Sullivan's Travels,**

The Palm Beach Story, The Miracle of Morgan's Creek, and *Hail the Conquering Hero.* On the other side, frowning at his alter ego like Jekyll at Hyde, is Sturges the artist, adapter of Tolstoy, Molnar, and Pagnol, joy and despair of James Agee, only son of the notorious aesthete and adventuress Mary Desti; this is the Sturges who sent Tom Garner and Jim Brady to their lonely deaths, who dazzled the Hays Office with *The Lady Eve*'s double-lutz plot turns, whose studio advertised his pictures as the works of a genius.

Too often, Sturges's artistry would carry a film until the last reel, when the happy hack would take over, turning the fade-out into a cop-out. Too rarely does a Sturges film possess any consistency of tone, and when it does it is often somber and monotonous like *The Power and the Glory,* or easy and impersonal like *If I Were King.* The only important Sturges films with sustained, affecting moods are *Diamond Jim, Remember the Night,* and (precariously) *The Lady Eve.* The characters are developed with as much sense as affection; the dialogue serves the situation instead of tyrannizing it; the climaxes have an aura of inevitability about them, whether dirgelike, teary, or wry. In only one other (very uneven) film did an ending exalt both Sturges and the viewer, and not demean them. This was *The Great Moment* the last Sturges film Paramount was to release before he left the studio for Howard Hughes and one of the most precipitous pratfalls in screen history.

Corliss's essay on Sturges marks a resurgence of the Agee position—not only because he adheres to Agee's biographical-psychological approach but also because he uses it to account for what he perceives as an aesthetic failure in Sturges's films. Corliss suggests also, if not as explicitly as Agee does, that this is a moral failure too—a kind of selling out.

James Curtis's *Between Flops: A Biography of Preston Sturges* is not a critical biography, but Curtis endorses—or at least perpetuates—the Agee position by quoting the long passage from Agee's September 23, 1944, *Nation* review of *Hail the Conquering Hero* quoted above. Curtis omits only the first, qualifying sentence of each paragraph—Agee's profession of esteem for the film in the first and his acknowledgment of the superficiality of his biographical information in the second. The fact that Curtis cites this passage without disagreement or qualification is surprising, since his own findings tend to undermine Agee's position. This is perhaps the ultimate triumph of Agee's view of Sturges—that it has survived the establishment of directly countervailing facts.

That Sturges compromised particular scripts or films in order to achieve success or, in general, that he had insufficient artistic ambition is not in keeping with the facts as we now know them. Sturges persisted with *The Great Moment,* even though it cost him the enmity of his studio and finally undid him, simply because he believed in the project. Even before *The Great Moment,* Sturges had not had a box-office success since *The Lady Eve* in 1941—and was not to have another until *The Miracle of Morgan's Creek* in 1944. *Sullivan's Travels* was not expected to be popular and it wasn't; *The Palm Beach Story* was expected to bring in large audiences but it did not. For Sturges to insist on making *The Great Moment* under these conditions and despite the opposition of Paramount chief of production, Buddy DeSylva, was to court disaster.

Sturges's Paramount trials merely repeated his experience in the theater a decade earlier. *Strictly Dishonorable* (1929) had been one of the great comedy successes of the twenties. His colleagues urged Sturges to write another frothy comedy, but instead he wrote *Recapture* (1930), a comedy-drama with a tragic ending, then *The Well of Romance* (1930), an operetta that had already failed with a book by someone else, and finally *Child of Manhattan* (1932), a comedy-drama about a dance-hall girl and a millionaire that audiences found distasteful. These three flops quickly ended what had been a most promising Broadway career.

Moving to Agee's own ground, we might ask where Agee obtained the facts on which his interpretation is based. His sources, by his own admission, were "superficialities"—popular magazine accounts of Sturges. But such "celebrity profiles" were a blend of studio promotion, audience expectation, and Sturges's own willing presentation of self. By most accounts, Sturges played the role of flamboyant movie director with relish and attracted publicity of all sorts; "spell my name right" was his attitude, according to Louise Sturges [his third wife]. That he did this in good part to buoy his position at Paramount—in order to make films as much as possible on his own terms—seems likely. His position at the studio was shakier than anyone, including Agee, could have known at the time. Sturges's childhood was good copy—when interviewed, he told anecdotes about it for hours on end. What Agee took as the Sturges facts were at least partly a self-made myth, whose central "conflicts" between artist and businessman had as much to do with his current situation in the industry as with Sturges's actual early life. The public Sturges played the "genius" that Paramount publicity billed him as but also rejected the "artist" label of his mother's side in favor of the "businessman" label of his father's side. But this is obligatory Hollywood-speak, as any reader of interviews of directors knows. Direction was "just a job of work" for John Ford; Don Siegel plays down his degree from Cambridge University; and so on. Peer pressure, the tough-director image, and above all, perhaps, producers' unease at artistic talk—which they equate with business loss—account for this persistent phenomenon. The directors who spoke like artists or conspicuously acted like them or even looked the part did not last long in Hollywood: Erich von Stroheim, Joseph von Sternberg, and Orson Welles are only the best known.

Agee's analysis of Sturges's "especially interesting neurosis" is too general to belong to any identifiable school of psychiatry. But what sort of psychoanalysis, even of a generalized sort, bases itself entirely on the self-conscious statements of the subject, indeed on public interviews and press releases? If there is no notion of a hidden truth, that is, of repression, hence of interpretation in some sense against the conscious statements of the subject, can we speak of psychoanalysis at all?

So deeply entrenched is Agee's reading of Sturges, however, that no mere statement of facts or counter-argument is likely to prevail against it. It has become that most insidious of critical phenomena—an interpretation that is later taken as fact. It is mythic in the Barthesian sense that it is not perceived as such—it operates beneath the awareness of those who invoke it, manipulating even those who think they manipulate it. Dissent from the Agee view of Sturges may therefore not succeed on the rational terms that that dissent proposes. Perhaps a myth can finally be displaced, or its stranglehold loosened, only by counter-myths.

There are, after all, other ways in which Sturges's films might be related to his life, even if no one has suggested any since Agee's time. The new biographical and textual information on Sturges and his work might suggest ways to oppose the still prevailing myth. The point is not to propose a counter-myth for its own sake but to question the authority of the Agee myth by posing alternatives that are at least equally plausible.

For instance, the saga of Mary Desti and young Preston might be read differently from the way the official myth has it. Was the child's psychic wound caused by compulsory attendance at art events or, on the contrary, by his mother's abandoning him again and again with strange people in strange places? Sturges never spoke publicly of this as far as I know, but such vulnerability was less acceptable in 1940s America than a dismissal of art and artiness. That his mother always left him in the name of art might have led the child to hate art. It might also have led him to model himself on and compete with what carried his mother away, that is, to become an artist. This same scenario of rejection followed by resort to artistic creation was enacted—or reenacted—in the actress's insults that led Sturges to write his first produced play, *The Guinea Pig* (1928). (This pattern seems also to have been involved, more generally speaking, in Sturges's turning from inventing to songwriting and playwriting after Estelle left him.) *Strictly Dishonorable* (1929) was based upon a characteristic Sturges switch—the girl is won by the suave Italian opera singer away from the clean-cut American boy, who turns out to be a rotter. (The American was played by Louis Jean Heydt, a specialist in the type, which he repeated for Sturges in *The Great McGinty* and *The Great Moment*.) Europe stole his mother away from him again and again—why shouldn't Sturges identify with it?

Recapture was the title of Sturges's failed play of 1930. (He named his first yacht *Recapture* before he knew the play had failed.) His experience with Estelle was evidently the immediate point of departure for the play. Perhaps the extremity of his reaction to Estelle's rejection was due in part to the incident's reactivation of old wounds, notably his mother's abandoning him initially and her subsequent repetitions of the trauma. In *Recapture* the husband wins back his ex-wife's love—she realizes that she will never love so rapturously again—but she dies in an elevator accident in the third act. Psychoanalytically speaking, the play arguably fuses the fantasy of recapture with the fantasy of revenge. (Of course the Oedipus complex itself may be understood as a recapture fantasy—the child wishes to recapture the exclusive bond with the mother enjoyed in infancy.) The notion of recapture, in any case, is fundamental to Sturges's work in many periods.

Before she rejected him, at least, Sturges's relationship with Eleanor seems to have been more complex in psychological terms, if less emotionally intense, than that with Estelle or, of course, his mother. He was the author of a still-running hit and a more recent flop when he met her. In asking for Eleanor's hand of her father, founder of E. F. Hutton and Company and chairman of the board of General Foods, he boasted an income of $1,500 a week. "For her that's pin money," her father replied. During his marriage to Eleanor, Sturges worked on *The Well of Romance.* ("Well" suggests a source one can return to again and again for sustenance and renewal, which Sturges's romances proved to be throughout his life. A well is the place for wishes of unlimited happiness but also for plunges to bottomless despair.) When Sturges had encountered difficulty finding backers, Eleanor agreed to back *The Well of Romance* entirely with part of the inheritance she would receive on the occasion of her birthday (in December 1930). On this basis Sturges put all the money he had—$64,000—into the production, which opened on November 7. Its failure plunged Sturges down a financial well—Eleanor never made good on her promise—as well as a romantic one; she sailed for Paris in June 1931. (Perhaps significantly, around this time Sturges wrote the bedroom farce *Unfaithfully Yours* and also *A Cup of Coffee,* which concerned the mistaken winner of a slogan contest.)

Sturges's lack of money after the *Well of Romance* fiasco sent him to Hollywood in 1932. An "existential psychoanalysis" might stress Sturges's unconscious complicity in accepting the destiny apparently imposed upon him by Eleanor's actions—as by Estelle's and his actress friend's before that. It might also suggest the larger pattern of his coming to accept Mary Desti's destiny for him: to become an artist. The schooner he had built in 1933, after he had decided to stay on in Hollywood, was called *The Destiny.* (It was named after his mother and his first home port: Desti—New York.)

Among Sturges's films, critics have usually found *Sullivan's Travels* to be, as Andrew Sarris says, "the most profound expression of the director's personality." Richard Corliss calls the film autobiographical and believes that Sturges identifies with his hero. The film's defense of comedy does seem to relate to Sturges's experience. He tried serious plays and screenplays before accepting his destiny as a writer-director of comedies, although *The Great Moment* indicates that he did not entirely accept the earlier film's conclusion. In psychoanalytic terms, however, *Sullivan's Travels* is utterly "secondary," that is, remote from highly charged instinctual and emotional conflicts. The film's central dilemma is a conscious one—should a comedy director attempt to do something serious in a time of crisis? Its method of resolving the question brings the film close to rationalization in both a psychoanalytic and a popular sense. In addition, the love relations presented in the film are rather affectless. Sullivan seems to feel no strong emotion about his estranged wife or about "the Girl" (Veronica Lake). One could argue indeed that the too-evident identifiability of Sturges and Sullivan almost guaranteed a detached handling of the material.

I would argue that it is instead his "frivolous" films, notably the screwball comedies *The Lady Eve* and *The Palm Beach Story,* that pose issues and situations highly charged for Sturges. (That these are the most genre-typed films that he made provides, besides their lightness itself, a built-in defense structure. No director is responsible for the subject or even the plot of a genre film—they are taken as given.) Perhaps Sturges identifies more with Jean in *The Lady Eve* than with Sullivan, or at least at a deeper level. She is smart and street-smart, witty yet still able to feel, indeed to be carried away by emotion. Charles Pike, like Sturges's wife Eleanor, is the pampered product of wealth, who has never had to struggle or live by his wits. He is also retarded emotionally—uneasy with his sexual feelings and spitefully cutting off his emotions when he feels betrayed. One might speculate further that Eleanor's many suitors once she had left Sturges are displaced forward in the film to the fortunehunters who seek to attract Charles before he meets Jean—after which they disappear, an obvious fantasy.

The second half of *The Lady Eve* fuses the revenge drive with the recapture quest. Jean both punishes Charles and wins him back. Her means is to impersonate a titled foreigner, thereby asserting her social superiority to the rejecting lover, disparaging the notion of titles generally, and asserting her own worth. She then, in the guise of the high-born Eve, torments Charles with stories of her sexual promiscuity, with the result that Charles appreciates what he had in Jean. To suggest that Sturges may have fantasized impersonating one of Eleanor's titled suitors in Paris in order to expose them, prove his own worth, and win her back would be speculative, not to say presumptuous, but it seems to me as plausible as Agee's reading. When Charles wants a divorce from Jean, she refuses to take any money—insisting, as did Sturges, only that he ask her. Charles, like Eleanor, refuses to do so and even refuses to speak to her in person or by telephone.

The Palm Beach Story is wilder, crazier, and far less well organized than *The Lady Eve* but, perhaps for this reason, is even closer to Sturges's romantic experience than is the earlier film. In it Tom Jeffers is a failed inventor, a total business flop who cannot pay his rent or other bills. Nevertheless, he is charming and well dressed, and he lives on Park Avenue. His wife, Gerry, walks out on him but not before paying all the bills—shades of Estelle on both counts. That she is doing so in part to raise money for a project of Tom's is a fantasy element, as is her receiving money from a kindly old (symbolically impotent) man, the "Weenie King," who also gives Tom money to follow her. Penniless on a train to Palm Beach, Gerry is given a ticket and escort by the members of "The Ale and Quail Society." She is then picked up by a millionaire, who buys her clothes, finally finances Tom's project, and is also in effect sexless. The symbolic impotence of all of these men is a fantasy element that avoids the pain of cuckoldry. The film as a whole thus concerns Tom's ultimately successful recapture quest.

It might be said, finally, that *Unfaithfully Yours* (1948) is a psychological version of the recapture motif. Sir Alfred de Carter suspects his wife of infidelity, fantasizes revenge, then discovers that she has been faithful after all—a kind of armchair recapture.

The difficulty with psychoanalytic explanations is not that they are wrong, but that there can be too many of them—what Freud called overdetermination. For any problem there is a multiplicity of satisfactory explanations, and no single explanation can be proven to be uniquely correct. This difficulty does not, however, hinder the present purpose—which is merely to break the exclusivity of a reigning single explanation. (pp. 9-29)

> Brian Henderson, in an introduction to Five Screenplays by Preston Sturges, *edited by Brian Henderson, University of California Press, 1985, pp. 1-30.*

An excerpt from Sturges's autobiography

Looking back, are there any conclusions to be drawn? Any errors to be avoided the next time around, if there happened to be such a thing? Certainly there are.

There is absolutely no advantage to being poor, for instance. A small income derived in any way that does not make the recipient too ashamed or unhappy is vastly preferable to no income. The Nietzschean theory of living dangerously is splendid, but should possibly be modified to "live dangerously with a small income."

There is no advantage to being without education, either. This pleases no one but your biographer. Education means remembering what you have been told. Remembering what you *haven't* been told, directly out of the human heritage, is called genius.

There can be no question but that it is also an advantage to speak another language besides the mother tongue; two are better, three better still. Theoretically, *ten* should be still better, but for some reason that I have not fathomed, true polyglots seem never to have profited greatly from their ability to converse and read in a multiplicity of languages. Most of the polyglots I have met were sad-eyed guides in caps either too large or too small for them, standing around in drafty customs' sheds.

Money is not star material. One should never have enough of it, or enough lack of it, to allow of its playing a principal role.

I had an idea when I started this that I might pass on, for the edification of my sons at least, the wisdom gained through years of experience. Then a voice within me said, "*What* wisdom? Gained from *what* years of experience? You are as inexperienced and impulsive at sixty as you were at sixteen!"

Preston Sturges, in his Preston Sturges by Preston Sturges, *edited by Sandy Sturges, Simon and Schuster, 1990.*

Richard Schickel (essay date 1989)

[*In the following essay, Schickel assesses the major writing on Sturges, offers a corrective to the Sturges myth created by James Agee, and provides a thematic overview of the major films for which Sturges wrote screenplays.*]

It is time to set aside all those pop Freudian explanations of the life and art of Preston Sturges. Enough about the giddy aesthete mother dragging him around the galleries and theaters of Europe, thereby instilling in him a lifelong distrust of high, formal culture. Enough about the down-to-earth stepfather in Chicago, the athlete-inventor-businessman whose values—principally his definition of success in purely economic terms—Sturges so desperately tried to emulate. Enough about how little Preston's psyche was split down the middle by their conflicting demands and how that split affected his movies, mostly adversely.

How did we get off on that sidetrack anyway? Brian Henderson, in his introduction to a collection of some of the master's best screenplays, says it's all James Agee's fault. By the time Sturges became Hollywood's hottest director—the first and at that time the only one who wrote all his own pictures single-handedly—and the interviewers from the popular magazines were coming around to do their standard eccentric movie genius numbers, Sturges realized that there was good copy for them in his admittedly curious background. It would be diverting for their readers and diversionary for him. As Henderson says, it did not do in those days for an American movie director to wear his artist's heart on his sleeve. It was much more comforting to the bosses and to the typical moviegoer to play it a little dumb. And so Sturges alleged that he shared none of his mother's high aspirations, that all he wanted to do was make funny, knockabout comedies that turned a tidy profit—the goal to which Daddy had taught him all real American men must aspire. Never a man to prune back his best inventions, Sturges permitted this tale to grow lush and purple in the retelling, though it appears that one aspect of it—the fact that it was his mother who presented Isadora Duncan with the scarf that killed her when it became entangled in the spokes of a car wheel—was a true believe-it-or-not.

In any case, all this glorious Technicolor served Agee especially well. He was emotionally committed to a different kind of comedy—silent comedy, the values of which (obviously) were kinetic, not verbal, the air of which was more austere (to put it mildly) than anything Sturges was doing. The tale was used by the critic to explain why Sturges's films, which he seems to have admired more than he could bring himself to admit openly, so often failed to meet the formal standards he felt obliged to apply to comedy. Sturges's work appeared to Agee less well made than that of Agee's childhood idols, the silent comedians. Moreover, this prefabrication permitted the critic to fit the director into the preexistent, overarching, and apparently permanent Hollywood myth in which the man of talent goes west and is corrupted by the vulgar values present there. Sturges, it seemed, was a prime candidate for yet another reenactment of this cautionary yarn, even gave evidence that he welcomed the casting.

Since Agee is for some reason Agee, a "great" critic who never got around to creating a great or even a sustained body of critical work (he had a silky, confidential style, approachably middlebrow tastes and the good sense to die young, with several promises unfulfilled), everyone who has since written about Sturges has had to contend with his fly-by-the-slicks psychologizing. Even if one were disputing it, as, variously, Manny Farber, Andrew Sarris, and Richard Corliss somewhat have, some of Agee's theory has stuck to their revisionisms. Not that Henderson, having done his best to strike down Agee on Sturges, offers anything useful by way of a replacement. Indeed, Henderson's performance both in his introduction and in his essays on each script in his collection (***The Great McGinty, Christmas in July, The Lady Eve, Sullivan's Travels, Hail the Conquering Hero***) is exceeding strange. He seems to have mislaid whatever critical sensibility he has among the reams of Sturges's papers to which he had access. It is interesting, to be sure, to learn that the seemingly profligate Sturges never really abandoned even his half-developed ideas. He was always hauling them out of his trunk, refurbishing them, and using them as the basis for new projects. On the other hand, it is not at all interesting, or profitable, to follow his progress on a script from one stage of revision to the next. The main thing we learn from Henderson's dogged pursuit of variously expanding and contracting ideas from draft to draft (with the final polish occurring when Sturges was on his feet, directing) is that he was a very craftsmanlike writer, an intelligent and rea-

An ad from the New York Sun *notable, in part, for its emphasis on the director rather than the stars Dick Powell and Ellen Drew.*

sonably ruthless self-editor, as, given the overall quality of his work, one suspected. In any event, this information, presented in mind-bending detail, argues neither for nor against Agee's reading of Sturges's character. But then Henderson appears to be a scholar in pursuit of an "edition," not a critic in pursuit of an insight.

He therefore misses a timely opportunity to start fresh on Sturges, unburdened by preconceptions. More than four decades have now passed since Sturges's great run of Paramount successes, beginning with *McGinty,* abruptly halted with *Hero.* It now ought to be possible not only to correct Agee's misapprehensions but also to abandon some of the estimable, but entirely inappropriate, critical principles with which people have been yes-butting Sturges for years. There is, for example, the question of whether or not Sturges was truly a satirist, and if not, why not? (He wasn't, but who cares?) And the matter of whether his failure to accede to the formal demands of the genre in which he seemed to be working was willful or careless. (It was neither; he just didn't give a damn.) And the endless critical cluckings about his sudden descents into broad farce, which looked to some writers like failures of the imagination or, worse, like pandering to the lowest tastes of his audience. (They were neither; they were integral to his vision, and they worked brilliantly as often as they failed miserably.) It is the same with his happy endings, which Corliss in particular finds to be "cop-outs," though I think a case can be made that they express his true, and utterly singular, authorial nature in roughly the same degree that the disconcerting black passages (notably in *Sullivan's Travels*) also express that nature's mercurial qualities.

All of this is easy enough for me to say—easier, anyway, than it was for most of the critics who have preceded me. When Sturges was at the height of his Hollywood celebrity, I was in the depths of preadolescence. His was a name I heard around, and I think I watched one or two of his movies sail over my head; but he was not a moviemaker I could appreciate at all. Then there was a long period in the fifties and sixties when he became a kind of legend of the lost, his work hard to find even in the more esoteric revival houses. It was not until the seventies, when his repute slowly began to revive, that I came delightedly to his films. Not only was I finally old enough to appreciate them, but so were a lot of people who, like me, were now sufficiently detached from the issues that not only had agitated and distracted his contemporary reviewers but had conditioned so much of the discussion that had followed in cinéaste circles.

I can sum up my view of Sturges very simply. Sturges was not, and never intended to be, the social critic, the satirist that Agee and the rest wanted him to be. James Curtis's biography *Between Flops,* a straightforward, well-researched, and admiring volume, makes it clear that Sturges was an utterly apolitical character without an ideological bone in his body; which explains why his politician characters (in *McGinty* and *Hero*) are so enduringly funny. He saw the typical American pol for what he timelessly is—a venal windbag—and was utterly undistracted by the thought that a true liberal (or conservative) commitment might cure that condition. In other words, Sturges was not, and never meant to be, a politicized social critic. He was, rather, an uncommitted observer, bemused and compassionate, but without any cures in mind for the conditions he observed. These were, he seemed to say, specifically American adjustments to, and evasions of, dull reality. The best we could hope for was the temporary palliative of a good laugh; that is, of course, the entire point of *Sullivan's Travels,* a movie I take to be emotionally autobiographical, in its gentle contempt for the social-critical aspirations of his Hollywood contemporaries, but not a statement about any frustrated ambitions of his own.

That his viewpoint, his genius, if you will, was decisively formed by his early personal history goes without saying, but not in the narrow sense that Agee proposed. If it had been, surely we would have seen at least one female in his movies who was a determined culture vulture like his mother—not exactly an unknown comic type in American movies of the time. But there is none. On the contrary, the women in Sturges movies always represent, charmingly, the reality principle stated in sweetly patient, deflationary terms. Some aspects of his beloved stepfather do possibly influence his characterizations of men—they tend to be rather quizzically loving when they get around to thinking about their relationships, which is not very often—but they tend to be far goofier than Solomon Sturges seems to have been, and much less practical.

No, I think the influence of his earlier years on his work is much simpler to understand. He was away from the United States so much, and his education was so oddly catch-as-catch-can, that when he returned, he was mildly but permanently an alien—no matter what his passport said. That is to say, most of the assumptions his fellow citizens had learned to take for granted from childhood on, all the premises they saw no reason to examine, struck him as strange and wondrous, very much worth pausing and mulling over.

It took him awhile—the better part of two up-and-down decades as a Broadway playwright and a Hollywood scenarist (he was past forty before he directed his first film)—to catalog his anthropological finds and to discover a manner of presenting them that was worthy of, and fully expressive of, their value. He has been justly praised for the structure of what is, perhaps, the most famous of the early screenplays he did not direct, *The Power and the Glory,* a recollection, from more than one point of view, of an American tycoon's career in the immediate aftermath of his death, which must have influenced the Welles-Herman Mankiewicz approach to *Citizen Kane*. The prints that survive—the original negative was lost in a fire—have a severely truncated air, as if what we are seeing may be a version cut down to fit on double-feature programs after the failure of the original road show presentation of the 1933 film. Allegedly inspired by the rise of cereal magnate C. W. Post (Sturges had been married to his granddaughter), it traces the rise from illiteracy to presidency of a railroad of one Tom Garner (Spencer Tracy in one of his best early roles), ambivalently celebrating the nerve, energy, and native shrewdness of an archetypal American yeoman. Like many of Sturges's later characters, he generally proves his worth at the expense of more conventional-minded middle-class and wealthy figures, though interestingly (considering the historical moment at which he appeared), he shares the establishment's antilabor views (an antiunion speech to striking employees is the dramatic high point of the film). There is irony in his undoing: He abandons the faithful wife, who, by teaching him to read and write and by believing in him, was greatly responsible for his rise, and is then himself abandoned by the younger woman who replaced her and who, it is strongly implied, has an incestuous relationship with his son by his first marriage. But clearly this is not yet comic irony, nor is the typical Sturgesian music for American voices yet heard in the dialogue, which is flatly realistic, and not much helped by William K. Howard's pedestrian direction.

His next attempt at an American theme, *Diamond Jim* (Brady), edges Sturges a little closer to what would become his home territory. Brady is like Sturges himself in that he is a man who knows how to make money (a great Hollywood controversy arose around Sturges's deal for *Power*, which appears to have been the first in which a screenwriter was awarded a percentage of the gross), without having much interest in using it to make more. The picture contains one pure Sturgesian madness, the invasion of a bar by a horse, and a climax in which Brady commits suicide in a unique fashion—by eating himself to death.

But it was really not until 1937 and his script for *Easy Living* that Sturges began to find his truest tone as a screenwriter. Directed by the talented Mitchell Leisen (who was Paramount's George Cukor, though apparently not so likable, especially to Sturges, who was now ambitious to direct), it tells what happens after a fur coat descends from the sky onto the head of a secretary (Jean Arthur) as she rides on the open top of a Fifth Avenue bus. This, obviously, is a screwball premise, and the film contains many stock screwball situations and characters, notably the choleric yet down-to-earth tycoon (Edward Arnold) who heaves the coat out his penthouse window in a fit of anger at his spendthrift wife and his good-natured, useless heir (Ray Milland), who must learn a thing or two about life by briefly falling downward through society. This occurs as the secretary (with whom, naturally, he falls in love) rises in the world, precisely because the coat gives her credentials among the easily impressionable. But in addition to these predictable (but well-orchestrated) generic elements, one hears Sturges's voice piping above the chaos. The play of the film's language is unmistakly his—richer, more lunatic than one usually finds in films of this kind.

But even though it was a success, and Sturges's contribution to that success was widely acknowledged, he still had to wait three years for his first directorial opportunity, finally giving his *McGinty* script (worth perhaps thirty thousand dollars at his normal rates) to Paramount for ten dollars on condition he be allowed to direct. For the next few years, making the seven movies on which his immortality rests, he was like a man possessed. Everyone speaks—correctly—of their density, both verbal and visual: the way he packed his often inelegant, but (given his needs) highly practical, frames with American eccentrics, the kinds of faces that the fully acculturated native passes without noticing but that apparently stopped Sturges in his tracks; the way his sound tracks resounded with their relentlessly articulate expression of their wayward but passionately held ideas, right down to the one-line day player, whose one line was almost sure to be a lulu.

It is, indeed, his concern for language—the American language, that is—that best proves my point about the way his partial alienation shaped his sensibility. He reminds me of certain émigré artists—Nabokov comes to mind only in this one respect—for whom our clichés, our slang, which the rest of us are too familiar with to hear, ring sharply, comically. In the case of Sturges, his fascination with common speech extends to promotional sloganeering—mere existential wallpaper to most of us growing up in a heavily commercial culture. For him it provides more than just a source for an odd gag or two. It is one of the major motifs of his work. The entire plot of *Christmas in July*, it should be recalled, revolves around the hopes for rising out of the slums and his dead-end job that Jimmy, its central character, has staked on winning a coffee company's contest for a new catchphrase. (His awful, wonderful entry, designed to go with pictures of insomniac citizens, is: "It isn't the coffee, it's the bunk.") But this obsession is everywhere in Sturges movies. Don't forget that Sullivan sets out on his travels to prove his worthiness to direct the movie version of a proletarian novel hilariously entitled *Oh Brother, Where Art Thou?* (I don't know of a literary critic who has observed how often leftist political fiction of the thirties sought to broaden its popular appeal by fake biblical evocations.) Don't forget that the source of that fortune that causes the cardsharks of *The Lady Eve* to fix their cheating hearts on hapless Hopsie Pike, heir to a great brewery, is a slogan—"The Ale That Won for Yale." And don't forget the delirious homemade sloganeering of the small-town political campaign in *Hail the Conquering Hero*, for example, this placard: UP OUR HERO GOES, DOWN THIS ZERO GOES.

It is not too much to say, finally, that it is wartime rhetoric—sloganeering on the grandest and most pervasive scale—that leads poor, innocent Trudy Kockenlocker into all that trouble in *The Miracle of Morgan's Creek*. Explaining why she ignored her father's orders not to attend a dance for soldiers—the one at which the man known in her dim memory only as Private Ratsky-Watsky impregnated her (unless, of course, her sextuplets were, in fact, a new example of virgin birth)—she says: "Soldiers aren't like they used to be when he [her father] was a soldier. They're fine, clean young boys from good homes and we can't send them off maybe to be killed—the rockets' red glare, the bombs bursting in air [an inspired touch, that quotation]—without anybody to say goodbye to them." She pauses for a moment's giddy thought and concedes they do perhaps have families to bid them adieu, but "How about the orphans? Who says goodbye to them?" (Another inspiration, that linkage of peacetime's common-consent neediest case with wartime's, the departing soldier.)

This diatribe, played in a fever combined equally of sexual excitement and patriotic fervor by Betty Hutton may be the greatest of all Sturges's satirical epiphanies, a brilliant commentary on the mad media rhetoric of wartime (remember "The Kid in Upper 4" lying awake in his berth, a tear trembling on his eyelid, as he thinks about "a dog named Shucks or Spot or Barnacle Bill" in the famous railroad ad?). It is also an act of considerable artistic bravery since no other movie of the war years dared send up either the official version of why we fought or the carefully sanitized image of those who were doing the fighting. In the movies there was no such thing as a man who enjoyed killing, just as there were no hardened criminals or other antisocial types among democracy's defenders. As far as the movies and the rest of the media were concerned, America's soldiery was drawn exclusively from the working middle class, and mainly the small towns at that, except for the comic relief from Brooklyn and Texas. Even the mildly out-of-step soldier—the griper or the slacker—existed merely to reform in the final reel, and no one—absolutely no one—got knocked up after a USO dance.

But weird distortions of language of every kind, not only those of the advertising culture, endlessly fascinated Sturges. The most endearing moment in that first directorial effort of his, *The Great McGinty,* arises out of wordplay, which, besides being in itself a comic invention of rare felicity, also reveals, with offhanded grace, how tough Dan McGinty's character has been softened by marriage. He is reading a story to his stepchildren: "I'll give you three guesses and then three more and three other ones, but you could guess all night without guessing who it really was, because it was none other than—" His wife interrupts this splendid parody of icky children's literature to point out that the kids have nodded off. But the semiliterate McGinty, caught up in what may be the first fiction he has ever read, presses on: " . . . none other than our friend Muggledy-Wump the tortoys." That mispronunciation is breathtaking. And so is its capper, McGinty's delighted "That's who I thought it was." This scene is the emotional turning point of the movie, telling us that if McGinty is capable of this comprehension, then he is capable of comprehending political corruption and of opposition to it. As well, this moment, so soft amidst the general ruckus of the movie, may be a tribute to Solomon Sturges's gentle stepfatherhood.

McGinty is—shall we say?—incapable of sustained linguistic analysis. But other Sturges creations are. And they have the spunk to wrangle determinedly over these delicate matters. In *Christmas in July,* for example, Jimmy is in love with the play on words that is the basis for his slogan. But his girl friend, faithfully supportive in all other respects, is not. She simply does not understand how he expects to win a contest with a phrase that is manifestly a lie. Everyone knows that coffee keeps you awake—no matter what is claimed by the fancy Viennese doctor, whose theory about its being a soporific Jimmy has read in the Sunday paper. It is their only contentious moment. There is a little throwaway scene of a similar nature in *Sullivan's Travels.* The studio, protecting its investment in its wayward director, has sent a trailer, staffed with cook, secretary, and press agent, to follow Sullivan on his wanderings. As he trudges ahead of it, the publicist begins dictating a press release to the secretary: "Thus begins this remarkable expedition into the valley of the shadow of adversity." "The shadow of the what?" she inquires. Whereupon the van's driver speaks up in a voice as rough as his countenance: "The valley of shadow of adversity. It's a paraphrase." Sturges's America was full of autodidacts, proud of their hard-won knowledge and determined to insist on making fine distinctions based on it.

One of the best scenes in *Hail the Conquering Hero* involves a similar dispute, this time between the town mayor, who is dictating a speech to his son and commits a grammatical error. The lad corrects him. The mayor has a typically choleric fit. And ends up firing the secretary, who agrees with his son. The issue here, as it is in Jimmy's squabble with his girl, lies between the literalists and the poets, between those who see language as purely functional and those for whom it is the clothing of dreams. The mayor points out that good grammar has never been a plank in his platforms, that part of his success is based on deliberate misusage. "It gives that homey quality," he says, before drifting off into beloved clichés—"horny hands and honest hearts." Beneath the ancient commonplaces of democracy one senses, as well, and despite his corruption, the pull of an ancient belief, now honored only in the comic breach. Bear in mind that this character's name is Everett *Noble.*

He is, finally, only another of Sturges's near-grotesque caricatures. But like all his villains, Mr. Noble is impossible to hate. For they all seem once to have dreamed some great American dream. Their problem is that they lost it—or never found its redeeming implications and now are trapped in their quotidian crassnesses. They should be seen by Sturges's heroes as cautionary figures, but the bright young men rarely make that recognition. For them the dream is so fresh, so utterly compelling. They cannot imagine its having a dark downside because they are still suffused in the glow of original innocence.

Yes, the opposite of original sin. By this I mean Sturges operated as a sort of Henry James in reverse. He came back from Europe to discover in blooming health that quality that the novelist found ever-imperiled. And the point he is making is a variant on James's. Isolated behind our oceans walls, untainted by the major corruptions of the Old World—high culture, exquisite manners, a rigid class system—we are (or were) permitted to dream on undisturbed. And even when we fall from this state of grace (which none of his heroes ever does permanently), we fall only into tolerably petty crookedness, comic eccentricity, or, at worst, those farcical kafuffles that so distressed Sturges's early critics.

How determined he was to permit his American Dreamers to preserve their dreams unvexed! Of the five central figures preserved for close study in the published screenplays—which read enchantingly, by the way—only one, Dan McGinty, comes late to the dream. It requires the love of a good woman to convert him to reluctant idealism. But once he is caught in its grips, he is willing to sacrifice everything he has just won for it—his governorship, his family, the comforts that might have crowned and rewarded a discomfited lifetime. He comes not to consciousness but to a willed unconsciousness of venal practicalities, the reason why Sturges permits him to escape to a banana republic which lacks an extradition treaty with the United States. The others, of course, are far purer. Jimmy, the coffee sloganeer, is convinced that he will win this prize because he has lost so many others. As he sees it, when he lost the how-many-peanuts-in-the-window contest, it doubled his chances in the you-fill-in-the-missing-word contest. "But you lost that one, too," says the girl. "Fine. So I was eight to one when I went into the limerick contest." "But you didn't win it, Jimmy." "That's what makes me such a cinch in this one."

And so it goes. Why can't Hopsie Pike see that Jean, the cardsharp he falls for, is not what she seems to be? Similarly, when she is working her revenge plot on him, why can't he penetrate her transparent disguise as the Lady Eve? The answer is simple: Hopsie, as he tells us, has actually dreamed a dream girl, and Jean-Eve is her living incarnation. He cannot and will not abandon that ideal image made flesh, no matter what the provocations.

It's the same way with Woodrow Lafayette Pershing Truesmith, of **Hail the Conquering Hero.** A medical discharge (for unromantic hay fever) has spoiled his chances of being the marine hero his father was and he has dreamed of becoming since boyhood. But he has been unable to abandon that fancy totally, indeed, engages in elaborate deceptions of his mother and girl friend back home rather than admit his failure. It is when they sense that in his way Woodrow lives the corps motto (*Semper Fidelis*—Always Faithful) better than they do that the six marines he meets in a bar force him into impersonating a military hero and claiming the acclaim of his hometown. Given that Truesmith has been the true smithy of his soul, loyal to his own best self all along, given that all his deceptions have been harmless—none of his business what the social consequences of other people's self-deceptions are—can one really argue that his fable requires a punishing ending?

In **The Miracle of Morgan's Creek** Sturges goes even farther. Dear, ditsy Trudy, unable to find the unholy ghost that impregnated her, carries his issue to term—and delivers herself of sextuplets. And delivers herself of *the* American dream—a first *and* a most. She is famous, and fame forgives anything, everything. Morgan's Creek, the great world, are now willing to accept her story, to make of her a home front heroine who gave her all for the cause and to provide her with her just rewards. No need to belabor the parallels between this myth and the central myth of Western civilization—the virgin Trudy, the Virgin Mary. Sturges certainly does not, though even hinting at it at any time in a Hollywood movie, let alone in the midst of World War II, is an act of staggering daring. But parallelism is not the point. The dream is the point. And in this film it is not just the beleaguered individual who sets aside reality in order to embrace the improbably inspirational. It is the whole world that finally does so.

It was, of course, the obviously genial spirit in which **Miracle** was made—no village atheism here—that permitted Sturges to get away with what in any other hands would have seemed sacrilege. That was a crucial element in all of Sturges's successes: his ability to escape the consequences of his satire. He was always ducking away into the melees he created.

Was this shrewdness—cynicism—on his part? Or was it an aspect of his vision? America as hubbub, an infinitely distractable society, incapable of concentrating very long on abstractions. No matter, probably. Historically it looks like a vision. Certainly we know Sturges despised ideologues, reformers, people whose ideas impose burdens on their fellow citizens instead of lifting them with a useful invention, or a moment of delight. It was a point he addressed directly only once, but brilliantly—in **Sullivan's Travels.** John L. "Sully" Sullivan, wildly successful auteur of *Hey, Hey in the Hayloft* and *Ants in Your Plants of 1939* dreams a dream, too, but it is for Sturges an unworthy one: that of using commercial movies to propagate what he believes to be the higher philosophical truths—as it happens, Marxist (i.e., European) theories about the class struggle and all that. This was not, in 1941, an unknown moviemaker's dream, and if there was sometimes something innocently admirable about the earnestness with which it was pursued, there was something inappropriate about it, too, not just because Hollywood was what it was but because America was what it was—politically in a state of invincible ideological ignorance.

And a good thing, too, in Sturges's view. Sully is presented not as a grim Stalinist but rather as someone possibly capable of fellow-traveling with them. In other words, he is another of Sturges's rich, good-natured, dangerously educable nitwits—an articulate Hopsie Pike. There is something sweet in his lack of cynicism and his bravery in search of direct experience of poverty. Surely abundant America can provide that, too, if you ask it nicely. Everyone, from the kindly studio bosses (their humanity irritates observers, who do not enjoy having their mythic Hollywood disturbed) to the down-to-earth girl he meets on his travels, tries to dissuade him. But he must endure the film's bleak middle passage, and we must endure that brutal break with comic conventions—one of the most daring structural strokes in American movie history, I think—in order for Sully to learn what Sturges most deeply believed—at least in those glory days. Simply stated, it is not that it is impossible to tell the "truth" in Hollywood films but that the "truth" everybody was always hectoring them to tell was a lie.

If we are a nation of eccentric and volatile individualists, each absorbed in his own private variant on the American dream, if much of the time we cannot even agree on a language with which to express this infinite multiplicity, then of what use to us are generalizations, dragooning us into the conformities of class consciousness? Or, for that matter, those of the tragic sense of life? All we can agree on is that everyone else we meet is likely to be—thank God—some kind of a weirdo. That is to say, we can reach agreement only on one point: the absolute necessity of laughing at each other—ruefully and not unkindly. That is, of course, how we laugh at Sullivan and how we imagine his audience will laugh at his characters in the comedies he vows to make after his travels have revealed to him what the girl knew all along: that "there's nothing like a deep dish movie to send you out in the open."

If there is a problem with this movie, it is not that its conclusion is "happy." It is that it is too easy, not complex enough to resolve fully the rich set of questions that preceded it. Probably this is what critics of Sturges "happy" endings are complaining about. Too many of his wildly unconventional tales end with the hasty application of conventional good cheer.

Alas, poor Sturges. The neat conclusion he always found for his movies eluded him in life. He reached the point his characters always reached at the end of his movies. He pursued his dream and enjoyed its triumphant fulfillment. The eccentric inventor hit the jackpot. He was famous. He was rich. He was honored by a grateful nation. But life is not a movie. It doesn't always end where it's supposed to. Sturges had to go on living in postwar America when the country he had discovered with his innocent émigré's eye, realized on film with a freshness unmatched by anyone, was smothered by the great wet blanket of prosperity, the price for which was near-universal corporatization, stunting and stifling the juking, jiving waywardness which Sturges, better than anyone, had crammed onto the movie screen, the very act of cramming increasing the energy of the work. Bitter decline followed. He wandered the world, his money gone, scratching away at scripts and plays that sometimes came close to production but almost never made it. He lived the unhappy ending he would not permit Sully or anyone else in his pictures to endure. True to his code, he died optimistic, believing he was merely "between fortunes" as an actor is often between roles, believing his autobiography, his impending television deal, or something was about to rescue him. Who knows? He may have been right, for we know with certainty that he was, at that moment, only between reputations.

If, now, much of the criticism he endured seems niggling and namby-pamby, irrelevant to his enterprise, one must yet admit that one's growing love for his work is in part based on nostalgia for a world that, truly though he reflected it, is now gone beyond recall. But one suspects Sturges sensed even in his glory years how quickly it was passing. Maybe it was one of the things that accounted for his energy in those years—the need to get as much of it as he could down before the colors faded. In those last sad years did he perhaps remember the poem of the *The Palm Beach Story*'s Wienie King?

> Cold are the hands of time—
> that creep along relentlessly
> Destroying slowly
> but without pity
> That which yesterday was young.
> Alone our memories
> resist this disintegration—
> And grow more lovely with the passing years.

It always gets one of the best laughs in the picture. It even appears to break up Claudette Colbert, to whom the poem (which Sturges originally composed for Rouben Mamoulian's guest book) is spoken. Its success, of course, partly depends on the fact that it is recited by a funny little man who represented the wacky way wealth can descend on you in America (he invented a variation on the hot dog which he advises Colbert not to try). But its claim on memory—on immortality, in my judgment—depends on the perfection with which it captures the essence of the hot dogs Sturges used to peddle—a farcical filling, spiced with wonder and wistfulness, wrapped in a tough-tender casing, and hawked in the most astonishing version of the American language ever to issue from a movie sound track. (pp. 57-69)

> Richard Schickel, "Four Directors: Preston Sturges," in his Schickel on Film: Encounters—Critical and Personal—with Movie Immortals, *William Morrow and Company, Inc., 1989, pp. 57-69.*

FURTHER READING

Biography

Curtis, James. *Between Flops: A Biography of Preston Sturges.* New York: Limelight, 1984, 339 p.

> Appreciative biography that includes lists of casts and credits for all of Sturges's work in theater and film.

Sturges, Preston. *Preston Sturges by Preston Sturges.* Edited by Sandy Sturges. New York: Simon and Schuster, 1990, 352 p.

> Sturges's memoirs collected and edited by his widow.

Criticism

Budd, Michael. "Notes on Preston Sturges and America." *Film Society Review* (January 1968): 22-6.

> Discusses Sturges's cynicism, biting wit, and irreverence as qualities that defined what is most "American" about him.

Byrge, Duane, and Miller, Robert Milton. *The Screwball Comedy Films: A History and Filmography, 1934-1942.* London: St. James Press, 1991, 146 p.

> Discusses the major actors, writers, directors, and films of the screwball comedy genre; includes an annotated filmography.

Cavell, Stanley. *Pursuits of Happiness: The Hollywood Comedy of Remarriage.* Cambridge: Harvard University Press, 1981, 283 p.

> Includes chapters on *The Lady Eve* and six other film "comedies of remarriage." Cavell argues that while these films are not as good as Shakespeare's romantic comedies, "the Shakespearean tradition . . . survives [through them] in film" and "film may provide an access for us to that tradition."

Crowther, Bosley. "When Satire and Slapstick Meet." *The New York Times Magazine* (27 August 1944): 14-15, 37.

> An appreciation written during the first run of *Hail the Conquering Hero*.

Downey, Robert. "Past Master." *New York* 3, No. 30 (17 August 1970): 46-7.

> Brief appreciation in which the author writes, in reference to *Unfaithfully Yours,* "Yes, I've seen all of Shakespeare's Othellos; Sturges's is better."

Garrand, Tim. "Preston Sturges and American Comedy Theater." *Studies in American Humor* 4, No. 3 (Fall 1985): 209-14.

    Discusses the influence of American theatrical comedy on Sturges's work.

Houston, Penelope. "Preston Sturges." *Sight and Sound* 34, No. 3 (Summer 1965): 130-34.

    An appreciation written on the rerelease in England of some of Sturges's most famous films.

Rebello, Stephen. "King of Comedy: The Rise of Preston Sturges." *American Film* VII, No. 7 (May 1982): 42-4.

    Overview of Sturges's career in film with comments from directors Peter Hyams, who at the time had plans to remake *Sullivan's Travels,* and Howard Zieff, who directed Dudley Moore in the remake of *Unfaithfully Yours.*

Rubenstein, Elliot. "Sturges' Folly: The Fate of *Unfaithfully Yours.*" *Sight and Sound* 50, No. 4 (Autumn 1981): 268-71.

    Argues that *Unfaithfully Yours,* often thought of as one of Sturges's less successful films, is in fact a "joyously original" work and that its failure at the box office was due to the fact that "Sturges's irreverence went too far."

Wineapple, Brenda. "Finding an Audience: *Sullivan's Travels.*" *The Journal of Popular Film and Television.* 11, No. 4 (Winter 1984): 152-57.

    Analyzes *Sullivan's Travels* and the phenomenon of movies that take movie-making as their subject matter.

Additional coverage of Sturges's life and career is contained in the following sources published by Gale Research: *Contemporary Authors,* Volume 114 and *Dictionary of Literary Biography,* Volume 26.

Mark Twain

The Prince and the Pauper

(Pseudonym of Samuel Langhorne Clemens; also wrote under the pseudonyms Thomas Jefferson Snodgrass, Josh, Muggins, Soleather, Grumbler, and Sieur Louis de Conte) American novelist, short story writer, journalist, essayist, memoirist, and dramatist.

The following entry presents criticism of Twain's novel *The Prince and the Pauper* (1881). For discussion of Twain's complete career, see *TCLC*, Volumes 6 and 12; for discussion of the novel *The Adventures of Huckleberry Finn*, see *TCLC*, Volume 19; for discussion of *A Connecticut Yankee in King Arthur's Court*, see *TCLC*, Volume 36.

INTRODUCTION

The Prince and the Pauper is recognized as an important work in the development of Twain's career and acknowledged as a classic of young adult literature. Set in sixteenth-century England, *The Prince and the Pauper* concerns two adolescent boys—an impoverished London youth and the heir apparent to the English throne—who are mistaken for one another and forced to assume each other's role in society until they are returned to their rightful positions. Often described as a great departure in subject matter and style from his earlier works due to its serious examination of social problems and its focus on English rather than American society, *The Prince and the Pauper* remains one of Twain's best known novels.

During the 1870s Twain developed an interest in historical English life and read such works as Charlotte Yonge's *The Little Duke,* a juvenile historical romance that he later credited as his source of inspiration for *The Prince and the Pauper.* Another of Yonge's juvenile novels, *The Prince and the Page,* has also been occasionally cited as an influence on Twain, though most commentators generally agree that similarities between either of Yonge's novels and *The Prince and the Pauper* are limited and superficial. Twain is believed to have begun work on the novel during the summer of 1877. In November of that year he recorded a brief synopsis of the plot in his notebooks: "Edward VI and a little pauper exchange places by accident a day or so before Henry VIII's death. The Prince wanders in rags and hardships and the pauper suffers the (to him) horrible miseries of princedom, up to the moment of crowning in Westminster Abbey, when proof is brought and the mistake rectified." Twain laid aside *The Prince and the Pauper* in 1878 to prepare for a trip to Europe and did not resume work on the manuscript until January 1880. After completing the first draft in September, Twain solicited suggestions for revisions from various family members and friends, including William Dean Howells, an American novelist with whom he maintained extensive correspondence. Incorporating several suggestions from Howells and others, Twain added material about the prince's adventures and dropped a minor episode from the work. In December 1881 *The Prince and the Pauper* was published in the United States, England, and Canada. Although the book received favorable reviews in the United States, the sales were disappointing compared to those of Twain's satirical works.

The Prince and the Pauper begins the day before the death of King Henry VIII, when the heir apparent to the throne, Edward Tudor, Prince of Wales, observes one of his guards mistreating Tom Canty, the pauper. After inviting Tom into the palace, the two exchange clothes as a jest and then notice their striking resemblance to one another. While still wearing the pauper's rags, the prince goes outside to reprimand the guard for his treatment of Tom and is promptly ejected from the grounds. The narrative then alternately traces each boy's experiences. Tom is thought to suffer from a diseased mind for claiming that he is not the Prince of Wales, while Edward is viewed as being similarly feebleminded for claiming that he is the prince. Although he finds the formal customs of the monarchy tedious, Tom gradually adapts to life in the palace with the aid of various members of the court and earns respect for his compassionate administration of justice. Meanwhile, the Prince gains firsthand experience of the suffering of the poor and the injustices of English law: he is abused by Tom's father for failing to beg, falsely convicted of stealing a pig, and briefly imprisoned as a vagabond. He manages to escape from these misadventures with the aid of Miles Hendon, a former soldier, and breaks into Westminster Abbey just as Tom is about to be crowned. He is unable to prove his identity, however, until Tom, by reminding him of an incident that took place when they met, is able to prove it for him. The two exchange places and the coronation proceeds under the proper conditions. In the closing chapters of the book, Edward rewards Tom and Hendon for their service to him and corrects many of the injustices he observed while wandering the country.

In an 1880 letter to William Dean Howells, Twain explained his purpose in writing *The Prince and the Pauper:* "My idea is to afford a realizing sense of the exceeding severity of the laws of that day by inflicting some of their penalties upon the king himself & allowing him a chance to see the rest of them applied to others—all of which is to account for certain mildnesses which distinguished Edward VI's reign from those that preceded and followed it." Critics have attributed Twain's extensive research and documentation of English language, customs, and law to his desire that *The Prince and the Pauper* be viewed as a "grave & stately work being considered by the world to be above my proper level" and not another one of "Mark Twain's whoppers." Early reactions to the work were divided. English reviewers generally faulted the book's amalgamation of fact and fiction as well as its irreverent attitude towards royalty, with one critic calling it a "ponderous fantasia on English history." American critics, however, lauded the novel as a "new departure" in Twain's writing, praising the historical detail, refined language, and subject matter; William Dean Howells predicted that *The Prince and the Pauper* would "surprise those who have found nothing but drollery in Mark Twain's books and have not perceived the artistic sense and the strain of deep earnestness underlying his humor."

The critical success of *The Prince and the Pauper* among Twain's American contemporaries has been attributed to the fact that the subject matter, language, and minimal use of humor in the novel conformed, more than any of his other works, to the genteel literary standards of his time. While most modern critics now consider *The Prince and the Pauper* to be of lesser stature than *The Adventures of Huckleberry Finn* and *Tom Sawyer,* they recognize that the novel's skillfully developed plot and emphasis on social concerns foreshadowed the themes and techniques Twain developed in such works as *The Tragedy of Pudd'nhead Wilson* and *A Connecticut Yankee in King Arthur's Court.*

CRITICISM

Mark Twain (letter date 1880)

[*In the following letter to William Dean Howells, Twain outlines the plot of* The Prince and the Pauper *and explains his purpose in writing the work.*]

I take so much pleasure in my story [**The Prince and the Pauper**] that I am loth to hurry, not wanting to get it done. Did I ever till you the plot of it? It begins at 9 a.m., Jan. 27, 1547, seventeen & a half hours before Henry VIII's death, by the swapping of clothes *and places,* between the prince of Wales & a pauper boy of the same age & countenance (& half as much learning & still more genius & imagination) and & after that, the rightful small king has a rough time among tramps & ruffians in the country parts of Kent, whilst the small bogus king has a gilded & worshiped & dreary & restrained & cussed time of it on the throne—& this all goes on for three weeks—till the midst of the coronation grandeurs in Westminster Abbey Feb. 20, when the ragged true king forces his way in but cannot prove his genuineness—but the bogus king, by a remembered incident of the first day is able to prove it *for* him—whereupon clothes are changed & the coronation proceeds under the new & rightful conditions.

My idea is to afford a realizing sense of the exceeding severity of the laws of that day by inflicting some of their penalties upon the king himself & allowing him a chance to see the rest of them applied to others—all of which is to account for certain mildnesses which distinguished Edward VI's reign from those that preceded & followed it.

Imagine *this* fact—I have even fascinated Mrs. Clemens with this yarn for youth. My stuff generally gets considerable damning with faint praise out of her, but this time it is all the other way. She is become the horse-leech's daughter & my mill doesn't grind fast enough to suit her. This is no mean triumph, my dear sir. (pp. 291-92)

> *Mark Twain, in a letter to William D. Howells on March 11, 1880, in* Mark Twain—Howells Letters: The Correspondence of Samuel L. Clemens and William D. Howells, 1872-1910, *edited by Henry Nash Smith and William M. Gibson with Frederick Anderson, Cambridge, Mass.: The Belknap Press of Harvard University Press, 1960, pp. 291-92.*

William D. Howells (letter date 1880)

[*Howells was the chief progenitor of American Realism and one of the most influential American literary critics of the late nineteenth century. Through realism, a theory central to his fiction and criticism, he aimed to disperse "the conventional acceptations by which men live on easy terms with themselves" so that they might "examine the grounds of their social and moral opinions." In the following letter to Twain, Howells comments on an early draft of* The Prince and the Pauper. *After receiving this letter, Twain decided to drop the whipping-boy incident that Howells mentions.*]

I have read the Two Ps [**The Prince and the Pauper**], and

I like it immensely. It begins well, and it ends well, but there are things in the middle that are not so good. The whipping-boy's story seemed poor fun; and the accounts of the court ceremonials are too long, unless you *droll* them more than you have done. I think you might have let in a little more of your humor the whole way through, and satirized things more. This would not have hurt the story for the children, and would have helped it for the grownies. As it is, the book is marvellously good. It realizes most vividly the time. All the *picaresque* part—the tramps, outlaws, etc.,—all the infernal clumsiness and cruelties of the law—are incomparable. The whole intention, the allegory, is splendid, and powerfully enforced. The subordinate stories, like that of Hendon, are well assimilated and thoroughly interesting.

I think the book will be a great success unless some marauding ass, who does not snuff his wonted pasturage there should prevail on all the other asses to turn up their noses in pure ignorance. It is such a book as *I* would expect from you, knowing what a bottom of fury there is to your fun; but the public at large ought to be *led* to expect it, and must be. (p. 338)

You will be surprised, perhaps, that I have written you . . . about the book, but Osgood sent it to me, and it took five good hours out of me on Saturday, and I think I have a right to say something. And I say it is *good*—and only long-winded in places. You ought to look out for those. The interest of the story mounts continually; there are passages that are tremendously moving; and it is full of good things. . . .

Hendon's mock—and growingly real—subordination to the prince is delightful—one of a hundred fine traits of the story. (p. 339)

> *William D. Howells, in a letter to Samuel L. Clemens on December 13, 1880, in* Mark Twain—Howells Letters: The Correspondence of Samuel L. Clemens and William D. Howells, 1872-1910, *edited by Henry Nash Smith and William M. Gibson with Frederick Anderson, Cambridge, Mass.: The Belknap Press of Harvard University Press, 1960, pp. 338-39.*

The Atlantic Monthly (essay date 1881)

[*In the following review the critic notes that* The Prince and the Pauper *is a radical departure from Twain's earlier works and praises the volume's realistic and accurate portrayal of sixteenth-century England.*]

Inclination to forsake the field of assured success, and seek distinction in untried paths, has shown itself a controlling impulse in many an artistic mind. Examples are most frequent, probably, amongst actors, whose eagerness to shine in unexpected situations, and to demonstrate merits apart from those by which they have achieved prominence, is a common characteristic. For reasons sufficiently obvious, these efforts of theatrical aspiration are seldom satisfactory; nor would they be likely to win applause, even if based upon sound judgment and sustained by positive ability. The actor, as a rule, must be content with fame in a single branch of his vocation, unless he is prepared to undertake a fresh career in regions where his person and his precedents are unknown. In other arts ambition is subject to no such restraints. If the power of versatility exists, it is fairly sure of recognition. A Doré may desert the narrower channel of his early fortune, and enlarge his fame in proportion to the breadth of his spreading canvas. Rossini, with a reputation founded upon dozens of dazzling comic operas, could not rest, in his old age, until he had produced a solemn mass which might stand beside the grave works of more majestic composers. Scott, after securing eminence enough to content his modest nature through the exercise of one gift, built himself secretly a higher renown by means of another. Bulwer's less brilliant light shone with a still greater variety of rays. The "deed" may not in all cases be equal to the "attempt," but the evidences of determined endeavor to establish this sort of manifold claim upon public attention and regard have always been abundant, and will be as long as the imagination of men can be turned to creative account.

The publication of Mark Twain's new story, **The Prince and the Pauper,** supplies a rather striking instance in point,—or, at least, supplies material for illustration of the tendency of writers whose position is fixed and prosperous to give their faculties a new and unexpected range, and strive for a totally different order of production from any previously accomplished. It would be impertinent to pronounce too confidently upon the author's motive, but what he has done is, in one particular, plain to every comprehension. He has written a book which no reader, not even a critical expert, would think of attributing to him, if his name were withheld from the title-page. There is nothing in its purpose, its method, or its style of treatment that corresponds with any of the numerous works by the same hand. It is no doubt possible to find certain terms of phraseology, here and there, which belong to Mark Twain, and characteristically convey his peculiar ideas; but these are few, and would pass unnoticed as means of identification, although we recognize their familiarity readily enough, when we are already aware from whom they come. It is also possible to recall episodical passages in his earlier volumes—quaint legends and antique fantasies—which seem to be animated by a spirit similar to that of the present tale; but these, again, would have suggested nothing as to the origin of **The Prince and the Pauper,** if it had appeared anonymously. So far as Mark Twain is concerned, the story is an entirely new departure; so much so as to make it appear inappropriate to reckon it among that writer's works. It is indisputably by Clemens; it does not seem to be by Twain,—certainly not by the Twain we have known for a dozen or more years as the boisterous and rollicking humorist, whose chief function has been to diffuse hilarity throughout English-reading communities, and make himself synonymous with mirth in its most demonstrative forms. Humor, in quite sufficient proportion, this tale does assuredly contain; but it is a humor growing freely and spontaneously out of the situations represented,—a sympathetic element, which appeals sometimes shrewdly, sometimes sweetly, to the senses, and is never intrusive or unduly prominent; sometimes, indeed, a humor so tender and subdued as to surprise those who are under its spell with doubts whether smiles or tears shall be summoned to express the passing emotion.

The book is not only a novelty of Mark Twain's handiwork; it is in some respects a novelty in romance. It is not easy to place it in any distinct classification. It lacks the essential features of a novel, and while principally about children, is by no means a tale exclusively for children, although the young may have their full share in the enjoyment of it. The subject is so absolutely simple that to know it beforehand deprives the reader of none of the pleasure he has a right to expect. There is no pretense of a formal plot, and all the charm is owing to the sincerity, the delicacy, and the true feeling with which the story is told. Two little boys (one a bright figure in history, the other a gem of fiction; the former King Edward the Sixth of England, the latter a pauper vagrant) accidentally exchange stations at the age of about twelve years, and each remains for several days in his strangely altered condition. A strong resemblance between the two, coöperating with accidents of time and place, makes it possible for the substitution to remain undetected. The sharply contrasting adventures of the pair constitute the whole tale. The incident of the exchange is the sole point that would seem to be hazardous for the narrator; but whether the skill is conscious or not, whether that particular passage gets its truthfulness from the author's own sense of its validity, or is carefully elaborated with a view to the reader's beguilement, it certainly presents no difficulty as it stands. The rest follows naturally and ingenuously. There is no strain upon credulity, for the characters come and go, live and breathe, suffer and rejoice, in an atmosphere of perfect reality, and with a vivid identity rarely to be found in fictions set in mediæval days. The same life-like verisimilitude that is manifest in many pages of Scott, and throughout Reade's *Cloister and the Hearth,* glows in every chapter of this briefer chronicle of a real prince's fancied griefs and perils. To preserve an illusion so consistently, it would seem that the author's own faith in the beings of his creation must have been firm, from beginning to end of their recorded career. Unless the teller of a story believes it all himself, for the time, he can hardly impress such conviction as he does in this case upon the mind of the reader.

However skillful in invention a writer may be, it is certain that his work loses nothing of effect from a studious harmonization with the period in which it is placed. In **The Prince and the Pauper** this requirement has been scrupulously observed. The details are not made obtrusive, and the "local color" is never laid on with excess; but the spirit of the age preceding that of Elizabeth is maintained with just the proper degree of art to avoid the appearance of artfulness. Critical examination shows that no inconsiderable labor has been given to the preservation of this air of authenticity; but the idea that the results of research are inflicted with malice aforethought is the last that would occur to any reader. On the other hand, if irrelevant phrases may be once or twice detected, their employment is obviously intentional,—the indulgence of some passing whim, the incongruity of which, it is taken for granted, will be excused for the sake of its fun. Such might easily be spared, no doubt, though they do no serious harm. It is in every way satisfactory to observe that the material accessories are brought into view with an accuracy which coherently supports the veracity of the narrative. Dresses, scenery, architecture, manners and customs, suffer no deviation from historical propriety. It would be a pity if our trust in the existence of the little pair of heroes, or of the well-proportioned figures that accompany them, were to be shaken by short-comings in these respects. But there is no danger. The big-hearted protector of guileless childhood is as palpable to our senses as to the grateful touch of the prince's accolade. The one soft spot in the hard old monarch's nature reveals itself to our apprehension as clearly as to the privileged eyes of the courtiers at Westminster. The burly ruffian of the gutters, the patient, sore-afflicted mother, the gracious damsels of pure estate and breeding, the motley vagabonds of the highway, the crafty and disciplined councilors of the realm, the mad ascetic, and the varied throng of participants in the busy scenes portrayed,—all these take to themselves the shape and substance of genuine humanity, and stamp themselves on our perceptions as creatures too vital and real to be credited to fable land. We go beyond the author's cautious proposition in the prefatory lines, that the story "*could* have happened:" we are sure that it ought to have happened, and we willingly believe it did happen.

It will be interesting to watch for the popular estimate of this fascinating book. Of the judgment of qualified criticism there can be little question. That it will be accorded a rank far above any of the author's previous productions is a matter of course. It has qualities of excellence which he has so long held in reserve that their revelation now will naturally cause surprise. Undoubtedly, the plan upon which most of his works have been framed called for neither symmetry, nor synthetic development, nor any of the finer devices of composition. Generally speaking, they served their purpose, without the least reference to the manner in which they were thrown together. They stood, and stand, at the head of all the genuine successes of modern comic writing; but, notwithstanding the frequent flashes of power that give them vigor, the felicities of characterization that brighten them, the pathos that chastens them, and no one can say how many other manifestations of cleverness, they remain the most heterogeneous accumulations of ill-assorted material that ever defied the laws of literature, and kept the public contentedly captive for half a score of years. Now the same public is called upon to welcome its old favorite in a new guise,—as the author of a tale ingenious in conception, pure and humane in purpose, artistic in method, and, with barely a flaw, refined in execution. (pp. 843-45)

> "Mark Twain's New Departure," in The Atlantic Monthly, *Vol. XLVIII, No. CCXC, December, 1881, pp. 843-45.*

E. Purcell (essay date 1881)

[*In the following review, Purcell unfavorably appraises* The Prince and the Pauper.]

Those who have discovered wit, wisdom, and good taste in Mark Twain's previous works will laugh beforehand at even an historical romance from his pen. But whether we were expected to laugh or cry we could not quite make out—on the whole, [*The Prince and the Pauper*] seemed to be written *au grand sérieux*—but, at all events, we did neither. Against the happy thought which forms the backbone of the tale, we must really protest. A street Arab, one Tom, is supposed to have changed clothes with Edward VI during Henry's last illness, to have played the part of a royal Christopher Sly, and reigned with much distinction till the real Edward, after dreadfully low adventures, steps forward at the coronation and claims his own. And this is intended for "young people of all ages." Mr. Clemens will permit us to point out that, if the young Britisher has once passed the age when such historical heresies must either be prohibited or extirpated by the rod, he will infallibly fall to criticising, and probably even to making fun at, instead of with, Mark Twain. Victor Hugo's veiled Wapentake, or Court of Arches, that synod of the English Church, is not more astounding than this picture of Reformation times—a misty atmosphere of Scott's chivalry in which floats all the flunkeyism, aristocratic oppression, and so forth, of all or any later period, as revealed to Columbia's stern eye. It is not worthwhile to multiply instances; let the absurd description of the young King's *levée* in chap. xviii suffice, where the author exaggerates something he must have read somewhere about the ceremonies of the bedchamber introduced by Louis XIV. There is no excuse for this libel on the English Court. The list of thirteen officials, ending with the Primate, through whose hands the royal hose pass is concocted with peculiar clumsiness. Not even Cranmer would have stooped to hand the King's breeches, no matter how heavy the pockets felt. Foxe's classical work has apparently been consulted; burnings and boilings are done full justice to, and the general Protestant tone would be highly satisfactory were it not that the author is always fidgeting about certain "Blue Laws of Connecticut." From the Appendix (which, in its quotations from Hume, Mr. Timbs, and the erudite Dr. Trumbull, author of a Defence of the said Blue Laws, is quite a curiosity) we gather that this ponderous fantasia on English history is intended to show up British barbarism, and so, by contrast, to whitewash this embarrassing Blue business, which, in a solemn last general note in italics and capitals, he calls "*the first* SWEEPING DEPARTURE FROM JUDICIAL ATROCITY *which the 'civilised' world had seen,*" and "*this humane and kindly Blue-Law Code.*" And why? Because our laws had 123 capital crimes, and the Blue Laws only fourteen. What those fourteen were he does not say. We think we can guess. The book is full of pictures in the spirited, florid old style. These will amuse the children. Naturally, the plot has suggested several comical situations, some of which are amusingly dwelt on; while a few smart sayings relieve the monotony of a prolix work singularly deficient in literary merit.

E. Purcell, in a review of "The Prince and the Pauper," in The Academy, *Vol. 20, No. 503, December 24, 1881, p. 469.*

The Critic, New York   (essay date 1881)

[*In the following review, the critic argues that* The Prince and the Pauper *is not a significant departure in style from Twain's earlier works and praises the descriptive passages and humor of the book.*]

The public has seen fit to be surprised at Mark Twain's 'new departure,' and the critics have, as far as we know, without exception taken it for granted both that it is a departure, and that it is new. We do not necessarily claim to be wiser than the rest, but we must insist that the author has in his recent books very gradually prepared the public for just such a volume. What has made Mark Twain's extravagant humor so effective has been (apart from its more glaring qualities) the skilfully painted background of more subdued and often delicate description. We need only remind the reader of the many picturesque passages in ***Innocents Abroad,*** and ***A Tramp Abroad,*** and if a particular instance is demanded we might select from the latter work the charming episode of the little girl's bathing in the Neckar, which though very slight in itself becomes significant from the tenderness with which it is treated. We could cite many other passages to prove that the finer element in Mark Twain's nature, which has been more or less distinctly traceable in all his books, has been growing more predominant in his more recent writings, until at last, in ***The Prince and the Pauper,*** it hides temporarily the humorous vein out of sight. It is very amusing, however, to observe how the old humorous habit which has here been forcibly repressed occasionally crops out in some droll conceit which fits oddly into the delicate texture of the mediæval tale. We can imagine a lover of the old Mark, the Western humorist (as distinguished from the new Mark, the romancer), hailing with uproarious delight his familiar friend in the two passages which we are about to quote, after having puzzled his brains to discover the *raison d' être* of this, to him, wholly enigmatical tale. Speaking of the perils of the office of the royal taster, the author observes: 'Why they did not use a dog or a plumber seems strange; but all the ways of royalty are strange.' Again, in the description of the people who lived upon London bridge, we recognize the old familiar manner: 'They always talked bridgy talk, and thought bridgy thought, and lied in a long level, direct, substantial, bridgy way.' The touch of grotesqueness in the account of Tom Canty's toilet, while in his princely disguise, is chiefly inherent in the mediæval custom as to the dressing of royalty, which was sufficiently absurd even without exaggeration. The plot itself must, indeed, at every step have impressed the author as a fertile theme for an extravaganza, and he deserves great credit for having made it something far better—a sweet and wholesome tale.

Mark Twain, as we observe on his title-page, has wisely addressed his romance to the 'young people of all ages.' It is far less distinctly juvenile than was ***Tom Sawyer,*** because it contains, besides the entertaining adventures and situations which no child would fail to comprehend, a gentle humor and a poetic quality which appeal to that remnant of childhood which in the happiest lives survives even into old age. The fancy itself, out of which the tale is woven, is of that elastic kind which would adapt itself to almost any kind of treatment. It would lend itself admirably to heavy moralizing in didactic prose; and one shudders to think what it would have become in the hands of those who supply the literature of the Sunday-school libraries. It is briefly as follows: Tom Canty, a pauper, is born on the same day as Edward, Prince of Wales, the son of Henry VIII, and as he grows up he develops a striking resemblance to the prince. He dreams, in the midst of his wretchedness, of greatness and splendor, the fabric of his dreams being borrowed from the tales of Father Andrew, an old priest who takes a kindly interest in him and teaches him a little Latin. On one occasion he meets the young Prince of Wales, who invites him into the palace, and there, in a boyish freak, they exchange clothes. Being indignant at the treatment Tom has suffered from one of the guards, the Prince, forgetful of his rags, rushes out to rebuke the offender, is thrust out from the palace grounds and turned adrift. Tom, in spite of his protests, is treated with all the honors due to royalty, and his references to his humble origin are supposed to emanate from a diseased mind. His supposed madness, however, is kept a secret by the King's command, and after much unhappiness and many discomforts he begins to accustom himself to his new position, and after the king's death makes some beneficent amendments of the cruel criminal code of England. He has just entered Westminster Abbey to be crowned, when the real Prince reappears and makes his way through the crowd, and Tom Canty, seeing him, springs down from the throne and falls on his knees before him. After a trying scene, in which Tom attests his magnanimity by assisting the Prince to regain his kingdom, Edward VI mounts the throne and is jubilantly hailed by the people. In the last chapter summary justice is meted out, both the villains and the virtuous receiving their due.

It is obvious that Mark Twain has taken considerable pains in bringing the local tone and color of his story into harmony with the historic period in which its action is laid; and his poetic instinct, assisted by some historic research, has also in this instance guided him safely. It is only just to say that while there is a fair amount of descriptive details, there is nothing which savors of 'cramming'; there is, in fact, just enough of quaintly archaic conversation and peculiarly mediæval incident to bring the reader *en rapport* with the old English feeling which pervades the tale.

A review of "The Prince and the Pauper," in The Critic, *New York, Vol. I, No. 26, December 31, 1881, p. 368.*

The British Quarterly Review (essay date 1882)

[*In the following review of* The Prince and the Pauper, *the critic comments on Twain's amalgamation of humor and historical fact.*]

Mark Twain has in [**The Prince and the Pauper**] almost accomplished the impossible, and in doing this he has essayed a new line. He has written a story which gives a vivid idea of a historical period, but which outrages history at every point in the most daring and barefaced manner. He is at once satirical and matter-of-fact, having carefully examined the byways of history, and he stirs up a little dust now and then in odd corners to show that he has been there, and can cleverly conceal his processes even by imparting confidences. Tom Canty, the pauper, and the young prince, Edward the Sixth, who are remarkably like each other, change places, the one having (rather an impossible feat for a Prince well guarded) managed that they shall change clothes, with the result that the prince is kicked out as a beggar, and the beggar exalted to be a prince, as if to prove that if manners make the man, clothes—*pace* Carlyle—can at most only half make him. Both, in the assertion of their real positions under this disguise, are taken for mad, and hence arises a double train of the most grotesque incidents, never, however, without a touch of pathos in midst of the laughter-moving absurdity. The reader will get glimpses of Henry the Eighth and some other historical characters, but we venture to say that he will generally be more interested in Mark Twain's imaginary ones. Miles Hendon, the father and mother of Tom Canty, and some of the characters about the court, are particularly well done. We do not think that this sort of writing in ordinary hands would be advisable for the young of any age, as perhaps the author would put it; but Mr. Mark Twain's fun and satiric chaff, his mingled humour and pathos, his fine perception of human nature, and his nimble fancy make him an exception; and we already know from experience—having tried it on some youngsters—that Mr. Mark Twain's art is such that there is no fear of any of the puzzle or confusion which might have arisen. The illustrations are very quaint and clever, and varied in character, and the book is altogether very pretty.

A review of "The Prince and the Pauper," in The British Quarterly Review, *Vol. LXXV, No. CXLIX, January, 1882, p. 118.*

I like [*The Prince and the Pauper*] better than *Tom Sawyer*—because I haven't put any fun in it. I *think* that is why I like it better. You know a body always enjoys seeing himself attempting something out of his line.

—Mark Twain, in a letter to Anne Lucas *later collected in* Mark Twain the Letter Writer, *1932*.

Arthur Lawrence Vogelback (essay date 1942)

[*In the following essay, Vogelback examines how critical reaction to Twain's works changed after the publication of* The Prince and the Pauper *and discusses the qualities of the novel that contributed to this reappraisal of his work.*]

With the appearance in 1869 of **Innocents Abroad,** Mark Twain established himself as a "funny man," and it was as the work of a funny man that each new book of his was interpreted. While there were occasional comments along the way which revealed a growing appreciation of abilities in Clemens other than that of mere humorist, for the most part there appeared little disposition by critics to take him seriously. But with the publication of *The Prince and the Pauper* in 1881, there sprang up sudden and widespread recognition of unusual qualities in Clemens the writer, qualities which caused many reviewers to express astonishment that such a work could have been written by Mark Twain. Remarked the Boston *Transcript* [in January 1882]: "There is little in the book to remind one . . . of the author," and the *Atlantic Monthly* significantly titled its [December 1881] review: "Mark Twain's New Departure." Howells summarized this attitude when, after dealing with the fictional elements in Clemens's story, he stated: ". . . we have indicated its power in this direction rather than in its humorous side, because this has struck us as peculiarly interesting in the work of a man who has hitherto been known only as a humorist—a mere farceur—to most people" [*New York Tribune*, October 1881].

It will be profitable as a study in the critical standards of the day to inquire what were these "new" qualities in *The Prince and the Pauper* which so pleased the critics, and why the critics liked them. This will be best shown by a consideration of the critical reaction to Mark Twain, not only as fictionist—that is, as writer of description, stylist, architect of plot, and depicter of character—but also as "philosopher."

Previous to the publication of *The Prince and the Pauper*, there had been little recognition of Mark's talents as a descriptive writer. Occasionally there occurred an appreciative comment, but for the most part attention remained incidental. When some clearer-visioned critic like Howells insisted upon unusual descriptive talents in Twain, his voice rarely found echoes in other reviews. But with the publication of *The Prince and the Pauper,* the majority of critics awoke to a sharp realization of Twain's powerful descriptive gifts. This was reflected not only in the increased attention given in reviews to the descriptive portions of the book, but in the importance accorded those portions. Thus the *Transcript* took note of Twain's "vivid descriptive powers," and another critic, praising "the skilfully painted background of more subdued and often delicate description," belatedly called the attention of the reader to "the many picturesque passages in *Innocents Abroad* and *A Tramp Abroad*" [*Critic*, December 1881]. At the same time the accuracy of Clemens's description was commented on. Said the *Critic:* "It is obvious that Mark Twain has taken considerable pains in bringing the local tone and color of his story into harmony with the historic period in which its action is laid," and the reviewer in the *Transcript* acknowledged that "the local coloring of the time in which [the story] is laid—that of Edward VI—is carefully studied," a judgment that was echoed [in March 1882] by *Harper's,* which found in the story "a careful regard for the historical accessories." One of the most flattering observations on this aspect of Clemens's writing came from the *Atlantic Monthly:*

> However skillful in invention a writer may be, it is certain that his work loses nothing of effect from a studious harmonization with the period in which it is placed. In *The Prince and the Pauper* this requirement has been scrupulously observed. The details are never made obtrusive, and the "local color" is never laid on with excess; but the spirit of the age preceding that of Elizabeth is maintained with just the proper degree of art to avoid artfulness. Critical examination shows that no inconsiderable labor has been given to the preservation of this air of authenticity. . . . It is in every way satisfactory to observe that the material accessories are brought into view with an accuracy that coherently supports the veracity of the narrative. Dresses, scenery, architecture, manners and customs suffer no deviation from historical propriety.

It is notable, too, that *The Prince and the Pauper* was the first work of Clemens's in which his ability as a stylist received attention. Most of the reviewers registered not a little surprise at the difference between the former style of Clemens and that exhibited in the new book. The *Transcript,* for example, remarked: "There is little in the book to remind one of the individual style of the author," and the *Atlantic Monthly* commented similarly: "There is nothing in . . . its style of treatment that corresponds with any of the numerous works by the same hand. It is no doubt possible to find certain terms of phraseology, here and there, which belong to Mark Twain . . . but these are few. . . ."

Many were the complimentary things said about this aspect of Twain's writing. The *New York Herald* praised the "plastic and finished" style of the book; [the *Atlantic Monthly*] wrote that "all the charm is owing to the sincerity, the delicacy, and the true feeling with which the story is told . . . ;" and the *Transcript,* seeking to describe the style, used the adjectives "vivid" and "natural."

Again, *The Prince and the Pauper* was the one book on which most critics were agreed that Twain demonstrated outstanding powers as a constructor of plot. There were, of course, dissenting reviewers. The *Transcript,* for example, remarked that "the highly improbable plot will . . . task the credulity of the most imaginative reader," but the larger number praised Clemens's achievement. To Howells, *The Prince and the Pauper* was definite confirmation of Clemens's ability as plot architect. He prophesied that the book would come in this respect as a surprise to many:

> Like all other romances, it asks that the reader shall take its possibility for granted, but this once granted, its events follow each other not only with probability but with realistic force. The fascination of the narrative . . . [is] felt at once, and increase[s] . . . to the end in a degree which will surprise those who have found nothing but drollery in Mark Twain's books, and have not perceived his artistic sense. . . .

The critic for the *Atlantic Monthly* was inspired by the construction of the tale to point out how remarkably Mark had developed in stature as a writer:

> It will be interesting to watch for the popular estimate of this fascinating book. . . . It has qualities of excellence which [the author] has so long held in reserve that their revelation now will naturally cause surprise. Undoubtedly the plan upon which most of his works have been framed called for neither symmetry, nor synthetic devel-

"DOFF THY RAGS AND DON THESE SPLENDORS."

The Prince and the Pauper exchange clothes.

opment, nor any of the finer devices of composition. Generally speaking, they serve their purpose without the least reference to the manner in which they were thrown together. . . . Notwithstanding [their merits], they remain the most heterogeneous accumulation of ill-assorted material that ever defied the laws of literature, and kept the country contentedly captive for half a score of years. Now the same public is called upon to welcome its old favorite in a new guise—as author of a tale ingenious in conception . . . artistic in method, and, with barely a flaw, refined in execution.

The *Century Magazine* praised the structure as "an ingeniously formed chain of circumstances," and the *Critic* pointed out that Clemens deserved commendation for the development of a plot which must have "at every step impressed the author as a fertile theme for extravaganza."

In the same fashion, with the publication of **The Prince and the Pauper** Clemens came newly, as it were, to the attention of critics as a gifted depicter of character. The reviewer in the *Atlantic Monthly* warmly praised Clemens for the latter's achievement in this regard. After describing the two little boys in the story as "one, a bright figure in history, the other a gem of fiction," the critic made these appreciative comments in which he compared Twain's work with that of a pair of famous English novelists:

> The characters come and go, live and breathe, suffer and rejoice, in an atmosphere of perfect reality, and with a vivid identity rarely to be found in fictions set in medieval days. The same lifelike verisimilitude that is manifest in many pages of Scott, and throughout Reade's *Cloister and the Hearth,* glows in every chapter of this briefer chronicle of a real prince's fancied griefs and perils. To preserve an illusion so consistently, it would seem that the author's own faith in the beings of his creation must have been firm, from beginning to end of their recorded career. . . . The big-hearted protector of guileless childhood is as palpable to our senses as to the grateful touch of the prince's accolade. The one soft spot in the hard old monarch's nature reveals itself to our apprehension as clearly as to the privileged courtiers at Westminster. The burly ruffian of the gutters, the patient, sore-afflicted mother, the gracious damsels of pure estate and breeding, the motley vagabonds of the highway, the crafty and disciplined councilors of the realm, the mad ascetic, and the varied throng of participants in

the busy scenes portrayed—all these take to themselves the shape and substance of genuine humanity, and stamp themselves to our perceptions as creatures too vital and real to be credited to fable land.

Howells, in his review, likewise pointed out the unusual merits of the character portrayal:

> The author has respected his material . . . and has made us feel its finer charm in the delicacy and subtlety with which he has indicated Tom Canty's lapse from lively rebellion at his false position to appreciation of its comforts and splendors, and, finally, to a sort of corrupt resignation in which he is almost willing to deny his poor old mother, when she recognizes him in one of his public progresses. . . . The character of Miles Hendon is dashed in with a rich and bold humor that gives its color to all the incidents of their association. . . . The whimsical devotion with which he humors the boy's royal exactions is charmingly studied . . . amidst the multitude of types with which the story deals, he is realized the best; he is first of all thoroughly recognizable as a man; and then as a man of his own time and country—the adventurous and generous Englishman of the continent-hunting age. . . . The effect of prosperity on the mock Prince is, perhaps, more subtly studied than that of adversity on the real Prince . . . but . . . it is this [latter] phase, apparently . . . which the author most wishes [the reader] to remember. . . .

Perhaps no higher commendation was possible than the remark of the *New York Herald:* "The character of [the] two boys, twins in spirit, will rank with the purest and loveliest creations of child-life in the realm of fiction."

Finally, not only were reviewers enthusiastic about ***The Prince and the Pauper*** as Clemens's first artistic work, but they found in the book even more unusual revelations. They discovered that it demonstrated a philosophical side to Twain. The author had proved himself quite capable of dealing with a profound and serious theme. In almost every review one detects the note of surprise over this aspect of the book. The *Transcript* found "a quality so refined and so searching as to excite wonder that it should flow from the same pen as that which wrote ***The Innocents Abroad. . . .***" *Harper's* spoke of the tale as being "charged with a generous and ennobling moral." The critic in the *Atlantic Monthly* found the story "pure and humane in purpose"; and the *Century* called the writer of ***The Prince and the Pauper*** "a satirist and . . . true philosopher." Howells, likewise, found ***The Prince and the Pauper*** evidence of growth in Clemens:

> The strength of the implied moral [is] felt at once and increase[s] . . . to the end in a degree which will surprise those who have found nothing but drollery in Mark Twain's books, and have not perceived . . . the strain of deep earnestness underlying his humor. Those even who have read him with this perception will recognize an intensified purpose in the human sympathies which have hitherto expressed themselves in some ironical form. The book is in this way an interesting evidence of growth in a man who ought to have his best work before him. The calm of a profound ideal . . . make[s] this a very remarkable book.

And the reviewer in the *Critic* decided with satisfaction that the "finer element" in Mark Twain's nature had at last "hid[den] . . . the humorous vein out of sight."

It appears that the first work on which critics generally agreed that Mark Twain displayed notable abilities as a serious writer and literary artist was ***The Prince and the Pauper.*** They found the book a praiseworthy departure from his former writing, and they regarded its publication as heralding the advent of a new Clemens. It is time now to ask why this book created such a stir. What were these "new" qualities that so appealed to the critics? Why was it that they ignored a work like ***Tom Sawyer*** (1876), and poured critical abuse upon the head of Twain when, three years after ***The Prince and the Pauper,*** his ***Huckleberry Finn*** (generally acknowledged now as Clemens's finest book) appeared? The answer to these questions may be found in the prevailing critical standards of the day. Reviewers liked the description in ***The Prince and the Pauper*** because it was "delicate" and "subdued." Even the structure was praised on the ground of being "refined in execution." The characters, too, in ***The Prince and the Pauper*** were sweeter and more gentle than such rough-and-tumble fellows as Tom Sawyer and Huck Finn. The book dealt pleasantly with a faraway place and epoch, not with the rude, exuberant frontierland of their own times. The story was charged with a "pure" and "ennobling" moral; it might be introduced to any classroom or household without fear of its consequences to the gentle reader, an advantage which could not be held out for either ***Tom Sawyer*** or ***Huckleberry Finn.*** In short, critics approved of ***The Prince and the Pauper*** because, more than any other of Mark Twain's books up to that time, it complied with conventional literary ideals. Works like ***Tom Sawyer*** or ***Huckleberry Finn*** puzzled and disturbed the critics; therefore they ignored or denounced them. But ***The Prince and the Pauper*** was a work reviewers could understand; it fitted in perfectly with the tradition of correctness and imitation—with the genteel tradition; and therefore the critics acclaimed as "new" those qualities in ***The Prince and the Pauper*** which were actually least original. (pp. 48-54)

Arthur Lawrence Vogelback, " 'The Prince and the Pauper': A Study in Critical Standards," in American Literature, *Vol. XIV, No. 1, March, 1942, pp. 48-54.*

Leon T. Dickinson (essay date 1949)

[*In the following essay, Dickinson discusses Twain's source materials for* The Prince and the Pauper *and speculates on his reasons for documenting a work of fiction.*]

Mark Twain, we usually say, was a remarkably independent writer, one who wrote primarily from experience and was anything but bookish. Such a view has, of course, much truth in it. And yet he did refer to books in his writing. We know that he read about foreign countries before and during the writing of the travel books. He read widely, also, in preparing to write his historical books. Of these, *The Prince and the Pauper* offers some interesting problems. It is clear what the sources are, for Clemens acknowledges his indebtedness in notes appearing at the end of the volume. I am concerned with how he used the sources and why he admitted dependence on them.

The work most frequently cited in connection with Clemens' book is Charlotte M. Yonge's juvenile, *The Prince and the Page* (1865). No critic, however, points to similarities in the two books, for they are entirely different. Clemens' biographer [Albert Bigelow Paine] believed that the earlier story, an historical romance laid in the thirteenth century, might have "inspired" the later tale; but he concludes, rightly [in his *Mark Twain: A Biography*], that "no comparison of any sort is possible between them."

He did borrow from books, however, in writing *The Prince and the Pauper,* as can be seen from his appended notes. Some of these refer to the book of his Hartford friend, J. Hammond Trumbull, entitled *The True-Blue Laws of Connecticut and New Haven and the False Blue-Laws.* Trumbull's book was written to show that the laws of seventeenth-century Connecticut were not so foolish or so severe as were commonly supposed, and that compared to the English statutes of the same period, the Connecticut laws were humane and enlightened, a point that Mark Twain makes in a "General Note" at the end of his volume. In order to show that what was harsh in the Connecticut laws was of English origin, Trumbull included in his introduction several cases involving infringement of the severe laws in England during the sixteenth and seventeenth centuries. It was from these cases, as his notes show, that Mark Twain borrowed for his story— borrowed accounts of persons losing their ears, being branded, being burned to death, boiled to death (sometimes in oil), hanged for such offenses as larceny above twelve pence, stealing a horse, a hawk, and so on.

Another source which he used in much the same way was *The English Rogue,* a seventeenth-century English book by Richard Head and Francis Kirkman. Several details in Chapters 17 and 18 of *The Prince and the Pauper* he took, sometimes without acknowledgment, from Chapters 5, 6, and 7 of the English tale. Clemens' chapters treating the low life of London include canting terms, a snatch of song, dialogue, description, and episodes, all of which are to be found in *The English Rogue*. At times he sticks close to his original, as is evident from the following passages, dealing with the set speech of beggars asking for coins:

The English Rogue

For Gods sake some tender hearted Christians, cast through your merciful eyes one pittiful look upon a sore, lame, and miserable wretch: Bestow one penny or half-penny upon him that is ready to perish, &c.

The Prince and the Pauper

". . . o' God's name cast through your merciful eyes one pitiful look upon a sick, forsaken, and most miserable wretch; bestow one little penny out of thy riches upon one smitten of God and ready to perish!"

At other times Mark Twain elaborates on his original, as, for instance, when he takes an episode, treated in two pages in the source, and expands it to fill six pages, adding detail and dialogue that make the incident more dramatic. But whether he followed his source closely or whether he elaborated on it, he borrowed for the same purpose: to give an air of authenticity to his book. He read a good deal to prepare himself for writing the book, and he was interested not only in making it authentic, but in making it *appear* authentic.

Several points are clear regarding Clemens' use of sources in *The Prince and the Pauper:* (1) he used source material to acquaint himself with the period he was writing about; (2) for the most part he followed his sources quite closely, taking specific things from them; (3) usually, but not always, he acknowledged his debt to a source, either in a footnote or in a note at the end of the volume. This last point calls for comment.

Granted that he had a respect for facts, why did Clemens want to document a work of fiction? Two explanations seem likely. One has to do with his purpose in writing the book. He wrote with serious intent, trying to give his readers "a realizing sense of the exceeding severity of the laws of that day by inflicting some of their penalties upon the King himself and allowing him a chance to see the rest of them applied to others." So anxious was he for the book to be taken seriously, that he considered publishing it anonymously. Regarded at the time strictly as a funny man, he feared that the name Mark Twain on the title page would inevitably suggest humor. If the documentation were missing, certainly some of the details of the story would seem, to one unacquainted with Tudor history, to be Mark Twain "whoppers." It was precisely this that Clemens wanted to avoid.

The other explanation concerns Mark's theory of fiction. Fiction based on fact, he seemed to think, was superior to purely imaginative writing. We are told in *The Gilded Age,* for instance, that "The incidents of the explosion [of a steamboat] are not invented. They happened just as they are told." Similarly, in the preface to *Tom Sawyer,* Clemens writes: "Most of the adventures recorded in this book really occurred." He makes the same point in the preface to *A Connecticut Yankee:* "The ungentle laws and customs touched upon in this tale are historical, and the episodes which are used to illustrate them are also historical." Again, a footnote at the beginning of Chapter I in *Tom Sawyer, Detective* is to the same effect: "Strange as the incidents of this story are, they are not inventions, but facts—even to the public confession of the accused." If the story is true, Clemens thought, if it is based on fact, it is somehow better than if it were wholly imaginary. Such a theory of fiction, common enough in the West of his day, would go far toward explaining the presence of documentation in *The Prince and the Pauper.* (pp. 103-06)

Leon T. Dickinson, "The Sources of 'The Prince and the Pauper'," in Modern Language Notes, *Vol. LXIV, No. 2, February, 1949, pp. 103-06.*

Roger B. Salomon (essay date 1961)

[*In the following excerpt, Salomon argues that* The Prince and the Pauper *reflects the themes, imagery, and subject matter of Twain's more esteemed works, including* Life on the Mississippi, The Adventures of Huckleberry Finn, *and* A Connecticut Yankee in King Arthur's Court.]

[*The Prince and the Pauper* is] an early result of the same intellectual ferment that produced *Life on the Mississippi, Huckleberry Finn,* and eventually *A Connecticut Yankee.* It is a book which closely reflects the themes, imagery, and much of the subject matter of these three other artistically greater works. In *The Prince and the Pauper* are the same attacks on feudalism and false romance, the same hatred of mobs and small town provincialism, the same generally pessimistic picture of human nature, and the same appeal to the natural goodness of children. Tom Canty and his counterpart Prince Edward are amalgamations of the characters of Tom Sawyer and Huckleberry Finn; their vision is clouded and distorted by false romanticism as the story begins, but they learn from their suffering to see life clearly and honestly for what it is—to see (using Twain's metaphor in *Life on the Mississippi*) the snags beneath the picturesque surface of the river. Tom Canty comes from essentially the same poor and depraved background as Huck; both have cruel and drunken fathers who are killed or disappear; both (this time with Prince Edward as Tom) make friends and take up with fellow outcasts and victims of injustice; and both take representative tours through society. Altogether *The Prince and the Pauper* is a significant enough book to warrant our taking a closer look at it than it has hitherto received.

In its official theme *The Prince and the Pauper* bears close resemblance to *A Connecticut Yankee.* "My idea," Twain wrote Howells during the later stages of its composition, "is to afford a realizing sense of the exceeding severity of the laws of that day by inflicting some of their penalties upon the King himself and allowing him a chance to see the rest of them applied to others—all of which is to account for certain mildnesses which distinguished Edward VI's reign from those that preceded and followed it." Just as in the *Yankee,* Twain's treatment of these laws in *The Prince and the Pauper* is frankly anachronistic; both books are compendiums of the worst features of English and European social legislation from the sixth to the nineteenth century (though the latter makes more of a passing bow to verisimilitude).

In his original preface to the *Yankee,* Twain specifically discusses the Connecticut Blue Laws and points out that they were milder than English legislation of the same period: "There was never a time when America applied the death-penalty to more than fourteen crimes. But England, within the memory of men still living, had in her list of crimes 223 which were punishable by death." This passage closely parallels a paragraph in his "General Note" at the end of *The Prince and the Pauper:* "There has never been a time—under the Blue-Laws or any other—when above FOURTEEN crimes were punishable by death in Connecticut. But in England, within the memory of men who are still hale in body and mind, TWO HUNDRED AND TWENTY-THREE crimes were punishable by death!" The similarity here is so striking as to suggest not only the identical impulse behind the two books but also that Twain, in writing the Yankee, must have re-examined *The Prince and the Pauper* and the historical materials used in this book. In his own list of the sources of *A Connecticut Yankee* Twain lists Trumbull's *Blue Laws, True and False.* Perhaps another result of this re-examination is the use of almost identical plot devices for revealing the enormity of social injustice: in both books, the kings inadvertently become wandering outcasts and are forced to "go to school to their own laws" in order to "learn mercy"—the words are Edward's and express his revelation and his hope.

Edward and Arthur are noble and courageous individuals, who tower above the craven and persecuting mobs which are always nipping at their heels. But only Edward "learns mercy," and he "learns" it only because he can still instinctively respond to human suffering. Arthur, great as he is in his own way (as the Yankee comes to recognize), can only respond to the demands of his own code. When he remains in the smallpox hut, for example, he does so, Twain stresses, primarily because he "considered his knightly honor at stake." Not that Arthur is without feelings of pity in this scene; the point is simply that his first and primary response is always (to use Twain's dichotomy) to his "moral sense" rather than his "heart." On another occasion he tells the Yankee that "his conscience . . . was troubling him" because he had encountered two young men escaping from their cruel lord and was doing nothing to catch them and turn them in. Subsequently, he urges on the mob after these men and refuses to cut down a hanged (but apparently still living) man from a tree because, as he puts it, "if he hanged himself, he was willing to lose his property to his lord; so let him be. If others hanged him, belike they had the right—let him hang."

These are responses which move within the narrow limitations of what Twain considered to be a medieval and aristocratic code of conduct, and their contrast with those of both Edward and Huck Finn in similar situations is obvious and startling. *Adult* kings apparently can not "learn mercy" by going "to school to their own laws." The Yankee castigates Arthur in terms more concrete but, nevertheless, similar in tone to those he had used earlier on the vicious Morgan le Fay: "He could see only one side of it [i.e. the debate on whether or not to try to catch the escaped peasants]. He was born so, educated so, his veins were full of ancestral blood that was rotten with this sort of unconscious brutality, brought down by inheritance from a long procession of hearts that had each done its share toward poisoning the stream." The escape of these men, subject, as they were, to the will and pleasure of their lord, was an insult and outrage, "a thing not to be countenanced by any conscientious person who knew his duty to his sacred caste." On the king, in other words, lay the full burden of the Fall. Beyond any hope of redemption he was cursed with the moral sense—that curious concept which in Twain's hands really becomes an attempt (evident enough in the above passage) to describe the influence, not only of one's immediate environment, but of what Faulkner has aptly called the "entailed birthright" of the past.

Clearly Arthur could not himself ameliorate a society which, even before he was born, had already claimed him as its most important victim. Only a deus ex machina, an external force which presumably represented "better" environmental training, could effect changes. Significantly, however, the Yankee's changes are burlesqued, shunted into the background, and finally wiped out, while Twain keeps a steady focus on the spectacle of human suffering and human inertia caused by the moral sense. In *A Connecticut Yankee* Twain put his entire faith in progress and that faith wavered badly. "There are times," admits the Yankee at one point, "when one would like to hang the whole human race and finish the farce."

In *The Prince and the Pauper,* on the other hand, Twain combined his official theme of Whig progressivism with the dream of innate goodness which, during this time, was so integral a part of his image of childhood. The book contains the same kind of duality of values . . . [present] in *Life on the Mississippi,* but in *The Prince and the Pauper* there is less sense of potential disparity because the antisocial values are used for social ends. In a fairy story (and only there) Tom Canty masquerading as an absolute monarch could achieve the kind of omnipotence that allowed him magically to set things right in society before society destroyed the goodness he was born with. The reign of Edward VI was, of course, an ideal vehicle for Twain's purposes. Not only had the Somerset protectorate, with its firm Protestantism and its retreat from the pure absolutism of Henry VIII, received the seal of approval of the Whig historians, but also, and more important, the alleged personal qualities of the boy king were those to which Twain was sure to respond. "How his name shines out of the midst of that long darkness," he once wrote, at the same time arguing that Edward was the only good English ruler before Victoria. The tone of this comment is close to that which Twain used normally when talking about Joan of Arc and suggests how much Joan was simply a feminized and somewhat more grown-up Edward. Both (in contrast to Arthur) were miraculous exceptions to all the laws of history as Twain conceived them, yet individuals who had somehow made an impact on history—individuals who at least had managed to illuminate the darkness briefly with their own innocence. They were logically impossible, as Twain's contrasting treatment of Arthur makes only too clear, but in their very impossibility lay their goodness, and in their goodness lay all the goodness of history. In *The Prince and the Pauper* Twain would "account for certain mildnesses which distinguished Edward VI's reign from those that preceded and followed it," not by an appeal to institutions as he did later in *A Connecticut Yankee,* but by bringing innate goodness directly to bear on iniquity.

In the working out of this theme, only the career of Joan of Arc would furnish Twain more ready-made raw materials—more of those historical "facts" he so cherished—than did the short life of Edward VI. David Hume, Twain's chief historical source, describes Edward as possessing "mildness of disposition, application to study and business, a capacity to learn and judge, and an attachment to equity and justice." Hume adds only one qualifier: "He seems only to have contracted, from his education, and from the age in which he lived, too much of a narrow predisposition in matters of religion, which made him incline somewhat to bigotry and persecution" [*The History of England,* 1880]. In the personality of Edward VI, in short, a good heart was in conflict with a stultifying conscience. In an earlier passage Hume gives a telling illustration of this conflict. A young woman called Joan Bocher was about to be sent to the stake on an obscure point of heresy until young Edward, who "had more sense than all his counsellors and preceptors," intervened and "refused to sign the warrant for her execution." Only after all sorts of weighty theological arguments were brought to bear on him did he submit, "though with tears in his eyes."

Here, indeed, was material aplenty for Twain. In *The Prince and the Pauper* he apparently echoes Hume in that scene in which Tom Canty as Edward first really asserts his new and fortuitously won power. Inquiring about a hooting and shouting mob approaching along the road—the mob, here as elsewhere, Twain's most effective symbol of the craven baseness of most human beings—Tom is informed that they are following a man, woman, and young girl to execution. His reaction is immediate and instinctive: "The spirit of compassion took control of him, to the exclusion of all other considerations; he never thought of the offended laws, or of the grief or loss which these criminals had inflicted upon their victims, he could think of nothing but the scaffold and the grisly fate hanging over the heads of the condemned." This, incidentally, is a paler but more explicit statement of Huck's feelings when he sees the king and duke tarred and feathered: "Well, it made me sick to see it, and I was sorry for them poor pitiful rascals, it seemed like I couldn't even feel any hardness against them any more in the world. It was a dreadful thing to see. Human beings *can* be awful cruel to one another." But, where Tom can intervene and set right, Huck can only look on and mourn; this is the truest measure of the maturity of the later book.

Before Tom does set things right, however, he almost turns the condemned over to their fate because the evidence of witchcraft against them seems overwhelming and because his mind (again like Huck's) completely accepts the superstitions of his day. Only at the last instant does he save them by the native shrewdness of his questioning—a product, not of his learning, but of his lack of education mingled with his strong grasp of empiric reality and his innate sense of values. These are the same kind of questions which Twain enjoyed putting in the mouth of Nigger Jim and which (when Twain uses the technique for something more than its mechanical joke value) undercut so effectively the dogmas of society.

Edward VI, of course, as befitted a monarch who was to have no parallel before the later nineteenth century, was conceived of by Twain and his sources as a great believer in education. After he has been set upon and beaten by the boys of Christ's Hospital, he resolves that, when he regains power, "they shall not have bread and shelter only, but also teachings out of books; for a full belly is little worth where the mind's starved, and the heart. I will keep this diligently in my remembrance, that this day's lesson be not lost upon me, and my people suffer thereby; for learning softeneth the heart and breedeth gentleness and charity." Edward's sentiments here have a certain amount of historical accuracy (as Twain was quick to point out) and what is more important, are completely in accord with Twain's theory of progress. However, it is hard to believe that Edward could have perpetuated these sentiments after his subsequent experiences along the road—all of which seem to point a different moral.

At the height of Edward's degradation, for example, when he has escaped from the gang of thieves and is walking the roads ragged, lonely, and hungry, he meets rebuffs and curses every time he stops at a farmhouse and asks for help. With a sense of total isolation from the rest of humanity, he stumbles along the road. "All sounds were remote; they made the little king feel that all life and activity were far removed from him, and that he stood solitary, companionless, in the center of a measureless solitude." He finally slips unnoticed into a barn and lies down next to something he soon discovers is a calf. "The king was not only delighted to find that the creature was only a calf," Twain wrote,

> but delighted to have the calf's company; for he had been feeling so lonesome and friendless that the company and comradeship of even this humble animal was welcome. And he had been so buffeted, so rudely entreated by his own kind, that it was a real comfort to him to feel that he was at last in the society of a fellow creature that had at least a soft heart and a gentle spirit, whatever loftier attributes might be lacking. So he resolved to waive rank and make friends with the calf.

This association of boy and calf—of a child uncorrupted by civilization with a creature beyond its pale—is reminiscent of both the relationship of Huck and Jim and Eve and the animals in Eden. This relationship is the "divine estate" that Satan described to Eve when he told her that whatever she and the animals did was "right and innocent."

Characteristically, Twain's image of man before the Fall is quickly followed by the complementary image of sleep and stasis. After Edward has cuddled up to the calf,

> pleasant thoughts came at once; life took on a cheerfuler seeming. He was free of the bonds of servitude and crime, free of the companionship of base and brutal criminals; he was warm, he was sheltered; in a word, he was happy. The night wind . . . swept by in fitful gusts . . . He merely snuggled the closer to his friend in a luxury of warm contentment and drifted blissfully out of consciousness into a deep and dreamless sleep that was full of serenity and peace.

Youth, innocence, freedom, and sleep—these ideas and images were inextricably mingled in Twain's consciousness to suggest a mode of existence far removed from the terrors of time and history. That they were somehow related to personal psychological problems seems obvious. He once commented in a revealing note: "I was never old in a dream yet." As major symbols, youth and sleep lie at the very center of Twain's best fiction. Where Edward achieves a momentary freedom with the calf in a barn, Huck flees from the Grangerford feud to Jim and the raft, but the pattern remains the same. "You feel mighty free and easy and comfortable on a raft," says Huck, and there follows an idyll of three days and nights as they drift down the river, go naked (clothes, of course, being one of the prime symbols in the book of the civilization Huck is rejecting), and "watch the lonesomeness of the river, and kind of lazy along and by and by lazy off to sleep." For Huck, "other places do seem so cramped up and smothery, but a raft don't." The reference to places "cramped up and smothery" is another image of civilization like that of clothes: i.e. houses, institutions, and, by extension, the entire system of rigid determinism which constitutes for Twain the "law" of history.

When King Edward awakes on the following morning, he finds himself being stared at by two little girls "with their innocent eyes." Almost without question, they accept his pledge that he is king, and he, in turn, pours out his troubles "where they would not be scoffed at or doubted." Eventually they run to get him food, and the king says to himself: "When I am come to mine own again, I will always honor little children, remembering how that these trusted me and believed in me in my time of trouble; whilst they that were older, and thought themselves wiser, mocked at me and held me for a liar." Twain hammers home this point with particular force when the children's mother receives Edward kindly but pities his "apparently crazed intellect." Even the best and most sympathetic of adults, in short (and these were few and far between), had lost the innocence, the instinctive—and, to the adult, naive—honesty that they were born with. Later in the novel, when Miles Hendon himself is accused of being an impostor, he asks the king if he doubts him, and the king answers immediately, "with a childlike simplicity and faith," that he does not. But to Edward's own question, "dost thou doubt me?" Hendon, the adult, can give no such simple and spontaneous answer.

"I have never written a book for boys; I write for grown ups who have *been* boys," Twain noted late in life. His distinction is a crucial one. The importance of boyhood, Twain seems to be saying, lies not so much in the kind of experiences encountered, as in the way a boy reacts to experience—a way which reflects a complex of values enormously precious to the mature person but undiscoverable in the adult world of time and history. The children who befriended Edward, and Edward himself, were as yet almost unmarred by the knowledge of good and evil which would be an inevitable part of their later development. Perhaps the growth of reason would compensate for the loss of innocence and bring about a Utopia greater than the one that had been lost; this has been the dominant hope of Western Society at least since the seventeenth century, a hope predicated squarely on the acceptance of history. With a part of his consciousness Twain, of course, embraced this hope. His Edward, as we have already noted, plans to educate the children of Christ's Hospital, for "learning softeneth the heart and breedeth gentleness and charity." But that part of Twain which rejected the ameliorative influence of history—which, in other words, could no longer accept the theory that history was the vehicle carrying man forward to the new Eden—necessarily rejected all hope.

Individuals of most earlier societies could dream of Eden without predicating their dreams on the forward movement of history. For the ancients the future was the past: Eden would return and then decay again during an infinity of cycles, a more or less mechanical process which, for all practical purposes, annulled time and "abolished" history. Such cyclical theories were essentially optimistic. Catastrophe was normal and certain in meaning because no event was irreversible, no transformation final. For the Western mind, however, nurtured on the concept of one great cycle of Fall and Redemption, cyclical theories (especially as they have been secularized in modern times from cycles of cosmos to those of civilization—not "abolishing" history but simply making it meaningless) are an expression of pessimism and hopelessness. Certainly they are for Twain, who stresses the endless return of evil—never of Eden. There was only one Eden and that was in the past—in dreams, in fantasy, in the responses of children, in the image of a raft floating down the Mississippi. (pp. 146-58)

> *Roger B. Salomon, in his* Twain and the Image of History, *Yale University Press, 1961, 216 p.*

Robert A. Wiggins (essay date 1964)

[*In the following excerpt, Wiggins interprets the structure and meaning of* The Prince and the Pauper.]

To some extent Twain departs from his principles of realism in *A Connecticut Yankee,* and in its closely related predecessor *The Prince and the Pauper,* chiefly as a consequence of the propaganda purpose of these novels. Both books are too weighted with sociocritical ideas to be entirely satisfying as novels. *Huckleberry Finn* was critical of the society it portrayed, but in that instance the ideas seem to have grown logically out of the material examined, whereas *The Prince and the Pauper* and *A Connecticut Yankee* give the impression that the material was selected to illustrate a thesis.

The writer, of course, approaches the composition of any work with a body of beliefs which he holds, but the process of writing is also one of discovery. It is now generally a critical commonplace to observe that, as he writes, the novelist gradually learns what his story is, and not until it is quite complete does he really discover his story. Moreover, this discovery does not necessarily suggest the author's complete awareness. *Huckleberry Finn* seems to have been composed somewhat after this fashion, but in the writing of *The Prince and the Pauper* and *A Connecticut Yankee,* Twain thought he knew in advance what he wanted his stories to be. They do not unfold themselves to the reader as does *Huckleberry Finn,* but rather marshall themselves as evidence to prove a point. But this is not to say that they are logically and coherently organized about a central issue, for in organization they are typical of Twain's discursive approach. However, a rough unity of purpose is discernible within them that does accord them some measure of design beyond Twain's customary achievement.

The Prince and the Pauper was published in December, 1881, before *Huckleberry Finn,* because, although the latter was begun almost immediately after the publication of *Tom Sawyer* in 1876, Twain's "tank ran dry," and *Huckleberry Finn* was shelved for several years before Twain returned to it and completed the book in 1883. *The Prince and the Pauper* was begun in the summer of 1877; it too was shelved for a time, but was taken up with *Huckleberry Finn* again in 1880, and then Twain alternately worked on them both, completing *The Prince and the Pauper* first.

Twain outlined the plot with more care than was his custom in order to keep the story within the limits of historical fact and to illustrate his thesis. Because he was forced to stay within the historical time between the death of Henry VIII and the prince's coronation, he could not take the discursive liberties of *Tom Sawyer* and *Huckleberry Finn;* moreover, his thesis controlled the kind of events he could select or invent as relevant to his purpose. As a consequence he produced a plot unified in the conventional sense understood by the novel-reading audience of his time.

The plot hinges upon a variation of the twin theme—a constantly recurring motif for Twain. Two look-alikes trade places. One is Tom Canty, a slum-dwelling boy raised in a blighted area of London; the other is the young prince, later to become Edward VI. The story alternates between Tom's uneasy masquerade as a young monarch almost to the moment of his coronation and the picaresque adventure of the young king. The latter plot gets the greater emphasis. In company with a dispossessed nobleman as his protector, the king is subjected to a series of episodes in which he is regarded as mentally deranged. During this revealing experience, the prince learns a great deal about his subjects and their sufferings under oppressive laws and economic exploitation.

The book was acclaimed as a newer and higher achievement than any of his previous fiction. Certainly his earlier misgivings about its reception were dispelled. He had told Mrs. A. W. Fairbanks that it would appear without his name, "such grave and stately work being considered by the world to be above my proper level." His wife and Howells both assured him that it should appear as his own work; indeed, Olivia was more enthusiastic about this book than any other Twain had produced. Her critical judgment would seem to have been vindicated by the success of *The Prince and the Pauper,* but it should not be surprising. Her tastes reflected her upbringing, and they were those of conventionally accepted standards of the day. *The Prince and the Pauper* more than any of Twain's earlier works met those standards and consequently was judged more successful, meeting with greater critical and popular favor than either *Tom Sawyer* or *Huckleberry Finn,* though it did not match the commercial success of his earlier books.

To Howells in March, 1880, Twain described what he felt to be the controlling purpose of his tale in *The Prince and the Pauper:*

Prince Edward and Miles Hendon.

My idea is to afford a realizing sense of the exceeding severity of the laws of the day by inflicting some of their penalties upon the king himself and allowing him a chance to see the rest of them applied to others—all of which is to account for certain mildnesses which distinguished Edward VI's reign from those that preceded and followed it.

Twain took the text for his exemplum from *The Merchant of Venice* and quotes it in the introduction:

> The quality of mercy . . .
>   is twice bless'd;
> It blesseth him that gives, and him that takes;
> 'Tis mightiest in the mightiest: it becomes
> The throned monarch better than his crown.

The text is kept constantly before the reader up to the closing words of the tale:

> "What dost thou know of suffering and oppression? I and my people know, but not thou."

> The reign of Edward VI was a singularly merciful one for those harsh times. Now that we are taking leave of him let us try to keep this in our minds, to his credit.

The theme is based upon the assumption of moral progress and enlightenment since the time of Edward VI. It was a view of progress that he later abandoned, maintaining that man had made progress in materialities only. But in ***The Prince and the Pauper*** Twain asserts by way of a general epilogue that mankind had made some moral progress. The assertion, however, is only incidental to his favorable contrast of the United States to another country still led by a king. No book by Twain fails in some way to reflect his hatred of monarchy, even an enlightened monarchy, and ***The Prince and the Pauper*** is no exception. The statement reflects Twain's motive in developing his theme of mercy and also indicates the theme that was to receive a fuller treatment in ***A Connecticut Yankee:***

> One hears about the "hideous Blue-Laws of Connecticut," and is accustomed to shudder piously when they are mentioned . . . There has never been a time—under the Blue-Laws or any other—when above FOURTEEN crimes were punishable by death in Connecticut. But in England, within the memory of men who are still hale in body and mind, TWO HUNDRED AND TWENTY-THREE crimes were punishable by death! These facts are worth knowing—and worth thinking about, too.

The book is an historical romance, "Tale for Young People of All Ages," as the subtitle proclaims, and not a bad one. Indeed, in its day it was a positive advance over the usual fare offered to a juvenile audience. Twain was essentially a realist, and even a romance, he believed, should be told with realistic details. He contrasts the world of the court with that of the common people and does not stay his hand from painting the filth, poverty, drunkenness, and brutality of the people laboring under cruel and unjust laws. Twain portrayed the conditions as faithfully as his limited knowledge, gained from reading a few sources, would permit.

But even if one accepts the fantastic exchange of identity between the prince and the pauper that begins the tale, the following events cannot be said to proceed realistically. The numerous adventures involving the prince in his picaresque wanderings are no more unusual in their own cultural and historical setting than Huck Finn's in another time and place, but there is a vast difference between the two in the elementary forms of their treatment. Verisimilar details are supplied, but Twain does not really seem to desire the reader to feel any sense of immediacy in the events. In *Huckleberry Finn,* the reader feels himself to be present as events unfold before him, but in *The Prince and the Pauper* Twain reminds the reader that the events after all took place long ago; this is a legend that he is narrating for an audience: "It may be that the wise and the learned believed it in the old days; it may be that only the unlearned and the simple loved it and credited it." The reader is frequently reminded that he should not even pretend to be present.

> Let us skip a number of years.
>
> London was fifteen hundred years old, and was a great town—for that day. . . .
>
> Let us privileged ones hurry to the great banqueting room and have a glance at matters there while Tom is being made ready for the imposing occasion. . . .
>
> And so we leave them. . . .
>
> Let us go backwards a few hours. . . .
>
> Let us change the tense for convenience. . . .

Twain repeatedly addresses the reader directly and reminds him that he is outside them. The method does not follow the principle of making the events "seem reality." The numerous footnotes citing authorities for the actuality of the events portrayed cannot make them "seem reality"; indeed, in attempting to convince the reader of their truth, they only remind him more that the tale is fiction and not a chronicle of actuality.

Twain does not demonstrate any historical sense on a significant level. He asserts, for example, the naive notion that the common man reacts universally and fundamentally the same. Tom Canty, so far as Twain understood, in another time and place was a Tom Sawyer whose romantic dreams came true, but he had no conception that the difference in circumstances could also account for the differences in their characters. The assumption that the only difference between the prince and the pauper was in their clothing is manifestly absurd. Even if their raiment is symbolic, the proposition is untenable, but Twain persists in working it out to an improbable solution.

The Prince and the Pauper certainly is not a realistic view of mankind, or boyhood, distilled in the pages of pseudo-history. It may be regarded as a kind of legend and as such embodies an ideal that mankind should serve; but inevitably, in the light of his nature, man must fall short of achieving. The story is then directed to the mythic, primitive, juvenile mind, and to this mind it speaks a message: mankind is fundamentally good, and the virtues of charity, mercy, and magnanimity are inherent in man's nature. It is the message of *Huckleberry Finn* in another range of material. The two books, which he often worked on simultaneously, afford a striking contrast: although the beliefs about the nature of mankind informing both books are similar, *Huckleberry Finn* is more convincing because the body of belief is associated with the folk from which it sprang, while in *The Prince and the Pauper* it is forced upon an alien culture. (pp. 72-7)

> *Robert A. Wiggins, in his* Mark Twain: Jackleg Novelist, *University of Washington Press, 1964, 130 p.*

William Dean Howells on *The Prince and the Pauper:*

The strength of the implied moral [of *The Prince and the Pauper* is felt at once and increases] . . . to the end in a degree which will surprise those who have found nothing but drollery in Mark Twain's books, and have not perceived . . . the strain of deep earnestness underlying his humor. Those even who have read him with this perception will recognize an intensified purpose in the human sympathies which have hitherto expressed themselves in some ironical form. The book is in this way an interesting evidence of growth in a man who ought to have his best work before him. The calm of a profound ideal . . . make[s] this a very remarkable book.

William Dean Howells, in the New York Tribune, *25 October 1881.*

Edward Wagenknecht (essay date 1964)

[*Wagenknecht is an American biographer and critic. His works include critical surveys of the English and American novel and studies of such authors as Twain, Charles Dickens, and Henry James. In his works on Dickens and Twain he employed the biographical technique of "psychography," derived from American biographer Gamaliel Bradford, who wrote of this method: "Out of the perpetual flux of actions and circumstances that constitutes a man's whole life, it seeks to extract what is essential, what is permanent and so vitally characteristic." In later works Wagenknecht has focused more on the literary than biographical aspects of his subjects. In the following essay, which was originally published as the introduction to a 1964 edition of* The Prince and the Pauper, *Wagenknecht traces the novel's composition, publication, and early critical reception.*]

Mark Twain entered the basic idea of *The Prince and the Pauper* in his notebook on 23 November, 1877:

> Edward VI and a little pauper exchange places by accident a day or so before Henry VIII's death. The Prince wanders in rags and hardships and the pauper suffers the (to him) horrible miseries of princedom up to the moment of crowning in Westminster Abbey, when proof is brought and the mistake rectified.

On 5 February 1878 he reported to Mrs. Fairbanks, his 'mother' since *Quaker City* days, that he was writing 'a historical tale, of 300 years ago, simply for the love of it—for it will appear without my name—such grave & stately work being considered by the world to be above my proper level.' The intention to publish anonymously was not in this instance carried out; later he did publish *Personal Recollections of Joan of Arc* anonymously for the reasons here stated.

On 5 March 1880 he wrote William Dean Howells that he had written 326 MS. pages of the tale, '& if I knew it would never sell a copy my jubilant delight in writing it would not suffer any diminution.' Six days later he summarized the story for Howells:

> It begins at 9 am, Jan. 27, 1547, seventeen & a half hours before Henry VIII's death, by the swapping of clothes *and places,* between the prince of Wales & a pauper boy of the same age & countenance (& half as much learning & still more genius and imagination) & after that, the rightful small king has a rough time among tramps & ruffians in the country parts of Kent, whilst the small bogus king has a gilded & worshipped & dreary & restrained & cussed time of it on the throne—& this all goes on for three weeks—till the midst of the coronation grandeurs in Westminster Abbey Feb. 20, when the ragged true king forces his way in but cannot prove his genuineness—but the bogus king, by a remembered incident of the first day is able to prove it *for* him—whereupon clothes are changed & the coronation proceeds under the new & rightful conditions.

He added a brief description of his purpose—'to afford a realizing sense of the exceeding severity of the laws of that day by inflicting some of their penalties upon the king himself & allowing him a chance to see the rest of them applied to others—all of which is to account for certain mildnesses which distinguished Edward VI's reign from those that preceded & followed it.' Mark is elated over the fact that Mrs. Clemens, who generally gives his stuff 'considerable damning with faint praise,' is 'fascinated' by this story, and he reports having been delighted at the theater the night before by *Torick's Love* (Howells' version of a play by Tamayo). 'The "thee's" & the "thou's" had a pleasant sound, since it is the language of *The Prince and the Pauper.*'

Mark Twain worked on *The Prince and the Pauper* concurrently with both *Huckleberry Finn* and *A Tramp Abroad.* Though, like most of his works, it was subjected to interruptions (apparently because he found certain structural problems temporarily insoluble), the actual writing—compared to his experience with either of the others named—was sheer delight. The book was published early in December 1881 in England, Canada, the United States, and (says Albert Bigelow Paine) Germany. James R. Osgood of Boston, the American publisher, brought out a beautiful (according to the standards of the time) and lavishly illustrated book for the Christmas trade but, despite the excellent press, did not succeed in selling nearly as many copies as Mark Twain desired. It is amazing to read that at one time Osgood contemplated publishing *The Prince and the Pauper* in the same volume with *Huckleberry Finn;* Mrs. Clemens should be given credit for vetoing this plan, even though her reason probably was that she thought poor Huck unworthy to associate with the other boys.

In a letter to the Reverend F. V. Christ, August 1908, Mark Twain said that he got the idea for *The Prince and the Pauper* from 'that pleasant and picturesque little historybook, Charlotte M. Yonge's *Little Duke.*' In his introductory note to this letter, Albert Bigelow Paine corrects *The Little Duke* to *The Prince and the Page* by the same author, and has been followed unquestioningly by all writers on Mark Twain except Howard G. Baetzhold. Actually neither of these works contains anything approaching the story of *The Prince and the Pauper.* The most Mark Twain could have got from either would have been the mere suggestion for certain situations, which he was to handle quite differently, and Baetzhold's argument that *The Little Duke* is a somewhat better candidate than *The Prince and the Page* is not unreasonable. But Franklin R. Rogers has now shown that there is considerably more resemblance between *The Prince and the Pauper* and Victor Hugo's *L'homme qui rit*—'the ultimate source' he calls it. He also suggests the possible influence of Hugo's *Ruy Blas* and of the play *Don Caesar de Bazan* based on it by P. F. P. Dumanoir and Adolphe Dennery. Mark Twain speaks of *Don Caesar de Bazan* in *The Prince and the Pauper* itself, and he was certainly familiar with the Hugo novel, for among his papers is an unpublished 'Burlesque *L'homme qui rit*' dating from 1869 or 1870. This, however, is not completely to discount Miss Yonge. One need not be a special admirer of *The Prince and the Pauper* to perceive that, whatever its shortcomings may be, it is a very lively and 'modern' work compared to her stilted tales, but she may well have contributed to the strain of 'Godwottery' which runs through it.

Mark Twain also used a good deal of straight historical writing for *The Prince and the Pauper,* and since he mentions a number of these sources in the book itself, they need not be enumerated here also. Mark Twain was using an historical setting, and he was anxious to get everything right, especially when his material involved outrages which he thought contemporary readers might find it difficult to swallow; he did not want any of these to be taken as examples of 'Mark Twain's whoppers.' The period in which he was writing was one in which fact was more respectable than fiction and the use of the imagination still somewhat suspect; in the foreword he even goes so far as to suggest that the story *might* have happened.

We have not completely recovered from this point of view

yet. There are still people who believe history, biography, and science to be more 'serious,' 'worthwhile' reading matter than poetry and fiction, and it has only been during the last few years that fiction has been priced as realistically as non-fiction in relation to the cost of production. Up to that time there was a ceiling on the price of novels, and if they did not pay for themselves in terms of large sales, then the publisher's non-fiction list, which was priced higher, was expected to make up the difference.

More interesting than this, however, is the use Mark Twain made of his history. It has been said of one of the leading historical novelists of the present day that she reads extensively for her novels, taking copious notes in a handwriting so crabbed that she is never able to read any of them, so that when it comes time to write, she is thrown back upon the material she has actually been able to assimilate. While this is probably not literally true, it does indicate almost an ideal formula for writing historical novels. The basic difficulty with the historical novel is not, as many critics suppose, that it is in itself inferior to the novel of contemporary life, but merely that very few novelists ever learn enough about the past to feel really at home in handling it. There are times when Mark Twain is fairly successful in assimilating his historical and factual materials. In the *Joan of Arc,* for example, he follows the records of the trial very closely, yet he manages to tell the story as nobody except Mark Twain could possibly have told it. Generally, however, in fiction and in travel-writing alike, he documents somewhat clumsily, and often gives the impression of scraping the bottom of the barrel. He does this, it seems to me, in *The Prince and the Pauper,* and I find an endearing, child-like humility in it. He has found something interesting in his reading; he is charmed by it, or astonished by it, or indignant over it, and he wishes to share it with his reader. Listen to this, he says in effect, how wonderful it is! Or, doesn't a race which can behave like this deserve to be destroyed?, but, on the other hand, what are we to say of a man or a woman capable of such nobility as is shown here?

At the outset, Mark Twain seems to have thought of *The Prince and the Pauper* in dramatic terms, and there is plenty of theatre left in it as it stands: in the nearly first-rate Gothicism of the mad hermit, in the use of the Great Seal as an effective stage property, in the whole background-intrigue involving Miles Hendon, and in Hendon's arriving, as he does, at the psychological moment, just in time to save the little Prince, and above all in the detailed, formal, unfolding closing scene, which is almost elaborate enough for the Elizabethans. It is not surprising, then, that the story should have been dramatized. In 1884 Mark Twain himself was trying to dramatize it; Howells thought the results 'altogether too thin and slight.' That same year, according to Paine, Mrs. Clemens and the children and others made it into a Christmas surprise for the author. His daughter Susy, as the Prince, brought down the house with 'Fathers are alike, mayhap; mine hath not a doll's temper.' There were later performances of Mrs. Clemens's version, Mark Twain himself taking a hand in both writing and acting, himself impersonating Miles Hendon— 'beautifully,' says Susy, 'and he added to the scene, making it a good deal longer,' which should surprise nobody. Much later he recalled that he could never remember his lines, and that 'it was so fresh and enjoyable to make up a new set of words each time I played the part.'

Then, in 1889, Abby Sage Richardson came up with a dramatization of *The Prince and the Pauper* which was directed by David Belasco and produced by Daniel Frohman to at least moderate success. Mark Twain did not care much for the play—nor the dramatist—but his affection for little girls being what it was, it was inevitable that he should fall in love with Elsie Leslie, who played both the boys, and whom the Clemenses virtually adopted into the family. Except for the association with Elsie, the production was a frustrating experience, for it involved the most publicized of all his lawsuits, initiated by Edward M. House, who claimed that Mark Twain had authorized him to dramatize the story and that the Richardson play infringed his rights. In 1920 *The Prince and the Pauper* was again on Broadway, in a version by Amelie Rives, with William Faversham as Hendon, Ruth Findlay as the boys, and Clare Eames as Princess Elizabeth.

The book made its screen debut in 1909 as an Edison one-reeler; Mark Twain himself appeared briefly in the prologue, and six years later came the much more elaborate Famous Players production with Marguerite Clark. In 1937 there was a sound production from Warner Brothers, with Billy and Bobby Mauch as the two boys and with Errol Flynn as Hendon.

The Prince and the Pauper and *Joan of Arc* (which he considered his masterpiece) are the two of his books which none of Mark Twain's more 'hard-boiled' admirers can forgive him for having written. For this reason among others, I am glad that The George Macy Companies have decided to bring out a fine edition of *The Prince and the Pauper,* for it would be a pity if our leading publishers of timeless literature should permit themselves to be captured by the time spirit, or to forget, as Chesterton once reminded us, that our time is a time, not the Day of Judgment. Yet the special enthusiasm of the eighties is always cited as exemplifying the taste of that 'genteel' period at its worst. Brave young spirits cite the review in the Hartford *Courant:* 'Mark Twain has finally fulfilled the earnest hope of many of his best friends, in writing a book which has other and higher merits than can possibly belong to the most artistic expression of mere humor.' They also speak of Mark Twain's neighbor Harriet Beecher Stowe grasping his hands on the street and saying, 'I am reading your Prince and Pauper for the fourth time, and I *know* it is the best book for young folks ever written.' They even cite Susy Clemens, who loved *The Prince and the Pauper* because it partly revealed Mark Twain's 'kind sympathetic nature,' and who was 'enjoyed' by one who apparently preferred *Huckleberry Finn.* Certainly there never was a book on which Mark Twain got more advice from his genteel mentors and guides than he did on *The Prince and the Pauper.* He read it to Mrs. Clemens and their children and to other children, and he had it read by Howells and others.

The Prince and the Pauper has the seriousness and the symmetry which the period valued in fine literature, and it deals with the kind of material that contemporaries thought fine literature should deal with; no wonder it received a better press than any earlier book of Mark Twain's. Insofar as this point of view made it impossible for people to understand and appreciate *Huckleberry Finn*, I think we have a right to be indignant, though we ought not to forget that the editor of the *Century*, Richard Watson Gilder, who is always cited nowadays as a typically genteel figure of a genteel time, and who actually was nothing of the sort, wrote of *The Prince and the Pauper* that 'it was not necessary for the author to prop his literary reputation with archaic English and a somewhat conventional manner. His recent humorous writings abound in passages of great excellence as serious compositions, and his serious nervous style is the natural expression of an acute mind, that in its most fanciful moods is seldom superficial in its view.'

It is now pretty late in the day for anybody to feel it necessary to point out that the fact that their settings are foreign or far-away-and-long-ago does not in itself make such books as *The Prince and the Pauper, A Connecticut Yankee,* and *The Mysterious Stranger* alien to the heart of Mark Twain's work. We have long since recognized that the primary concerns of *A Connecticut Yankee* are with the problems of the nineteenth century, not the sixth, and that the boys of mediaeval Eseldorf are merely Huck and Tom transplanted (in an unpublished version of the *Stranger*, young Satan actually comes to Hannibal and associates with Huck and Tom). It has taken us longer to get *The Prince and the Pauper* straight, but Walter Blair, Albert E. Stone, and Roger Salomon have recently done such a thorough job in the way of pointing out its relevancy to Mark Twain's central work that one despairs of finding anything to add to the discussion.

Through much of its action *The Prince and the Pauper* is actually 'The King and the Pauper'; one cannot but recall how the chief rascal in *Huckleberry Finn* is called both King and Dauphin. The structure of the book has always been praised; the plot is well organized and the parallelism between the two boys' stories well maintained, with much careful preparation—though, except for the Prince, historical characters are stereotyped, Mary Tudor ('afterwards the "Bloody Mary" of history') being the one who suffers most. The book is full of effective irony, not only in its central situation but in matters of detail, and though it has plenty of humor, unsuitable burlesque is generally avoided, the principal exception being the unbelievably gauche statement about the royal taster in Chapter VII. On the other hand, I think the author was perfectly right in refusing to follow his mentors in removing Tom's question about the dead king, which is quite obviously what such a boy would say under the circumstances; and the special use Tom finds for the Great Seal of England is irresistible. Completely realistic tests can no more be applied to such a book as *The Prince and the Pauper* than to *The Merchant of Venice,* yet in its frame the folk wisdom shown by Tom in the administration of justice *is* believable, as is also the cozening of the constable in Chapter XXIV.

The romanticism of both boys is straight out of *Tom Sawyer:* Tom Canty uses his reading like Tom Sawyer (not very convincingly, it must be admitted, in his milieu), and his discomfort in the palace suggests that of Huck Finn with the Widow Douglas. *Per contra,* Prince Edward's envy of Tom Canty's life, when it is first described to him and before he has experienced its discomforts, is like the envy felt by the village boys for Huck's way of life. Various critics have pointed out, too, that the Prince at the burning is like Huck at the feud, that the hermit suggests Injun Joe, and that Tom's educational journey has its points of affinity with that of the tenderfoot in *Roughing It.*

There is not as much ambivalence in *The Prince and the Pauper* as there is in *A Connecticut Yankee,* but there is plenty for all that, because there was vast ambivalence in Mark Twain himself, and because life itself exists in a state of equilibrium. When Winifred Howells read it, it made her 'glad to think that I live in these times.' Mark Twain's attitude toward monarchy as an institution being what it was, this was not an unperceptive reaction; yet *The Prince and the Pauper* often capitulates to the charm of the past, and if Mark still believed when he wrote it that mankind could solve its political problems by getting rid of kings, he was not to continue to believe it for long. The book is a study in education running clear back, in some of its presuppositions, to the educational novels of the late eighteenth century; but it is also a deterministic study in conditioning, and while the conditioning does not go so far as it was destined to go in *Pudd'nhead Wilson,* it might well have done so if the experiment had been prolonged. At the coronation procession Tom is already bad enough to deny his mother, but not yet bad enough to avoid the prickings of a true Huckleberry Finn conscience afterwards or to fail to rally superbly in the scene which follows. Rudely treated by the Christ's Hospital boys, Prince Edward expresses Mark Twain's own faith in education: 'When I am king, they shall not have bread and shelter only, but also teachings out of books; for a full belly is little worth where the mind is starved, and the heart.'

But alongside this stands the touching primitivism of the scene with the calf in Chapter XVIII. The treatment of the folk too is ambivalent, for the book burns with generous indignation against the oppressors of mankind; yet a common man can be as evil as John Canty, and the mob in *The Prince and the Pauper* is often as contemptible as the mob Colonel Sherburn insults in *Huckleberry Finn.* The innocence of childhood accepts the Prince on faith in Chapter XIX, and Roger Salomon is quite right when he shows that because of the superior plasticity of youth, Prince Edward's adventures among the folk are far more effective in altering his fundamental outlook than those which King Arthur undergoes in *A Connecticut Yankee,* but though he believed that Frances Hodgson Burnett got the idea for *Little Lord Fauntleroy* from *The Prince and the Pauper,* Mark Twain himself knew that children are people, not angels, and that as such they too are capable of cowardice and cruelty. So even here he disdains all-too-easy solutions of the human problem.

No responsible critic today would claim that *The Prince and the Pauper* is as good a book as *Huckleberry Finn.* But it is unmistakably a product of the same mind as *Huckleberry Finn,* some of whose problems its composition may have helped Mark Twain to solve; and when the two works are set in juxtaposition, both become more meaningful. (pp. 5-13)

> *Edward Wagenknecht, in an introduction to* The Prince and the Pauper *by Mark Twain, The Heritage Press, 1964, pp. 5-13.*

Robert Regan (essay date 1966)

[*In the following excerpt from his* Unpromising Heroes: Mark Twain and His Characters, *Regan applies what folklorists have called the Unpromising Hero motif to* The Prince and the Pauper. *In the preface to his study, Regan defines the Unpromising Hero tale as "the story of the unlikely youngster who, against all odds and every expectation, wins his way to success in the world."*]

At the last possible moment in ***The Adventures of Tom Sawyer,*** Tom and Huck make a kind of pact: Tom will let Huck into his "high-toned" robber gang and Huck will give the civilized life another try. That pact constituted a victory for Tom, and a kind of victory for Mark Twain also, for it forged a link between the two boys who embodied their creator's deepest wishes—Tom, the wish to succeed; Huck, the wish to be free, to be his own man. But the link, as every reader knows, as Mark Twain himself must have known, would not hold: Tom was irrevocably committed to that journey to law school via West Point which Judge Thatcher had promised to arrange for him, and Huck was equally, if less consciously, committed to a journey in an opposite direction, a journey toward the freedom represented by the Territory. The two boys could not remain themselves and remain together for long. Whatever the achievements of ***The Adventures of Tom Sawyer,*** it failed to effect a permanent rapprochement between the fantasy of success and the dream of independence. Mark Twain's next novel, in happy contrast, proved a notable success on that score. In ***The Prince and the Pauper*** (1882) Mark Twain found a new and more effective way of coping with the challenge of accommodating the Tom Sawyer Impulse and the Huck Finn Impulse: he presented three heroes—two of them boys, the third an adult who had not outgrown the innocent strength of boyhood—and in each of these characters he linked the special virtue of Tom with that of Huck.

Roger B. Salomon has observed [in his *Mark Twain and the Image of History*] that both of the two boy heroes of the novel combine attributes of Tom Sawyer and Huck Finn, and that they both progress from a vision of life typical of Tom toward one typical of Huck: "Tom Canty and his counterpart Prince Edward are amalgamations of the characters of Tom Sawyer and Huckleberry Finn; their vision is clouded and distorted by false romanticism as the story begins, but they learn from their suffering to see life clearly and honestly for what it is. . . ." There are many other ways in which Prince Edward and his pauper-double, Tom Canty, combine characteristics of the two boys in the earlier novel. Some of these will appear as we examine both Prince and Pauper as Unpromising Heroes.

Our first glimpse of Tom Canty indicates the kind of role he is to play. On the day of his birth, all England was talking joyfully about another newborn babe, the Prince of Wales, Edward Tudor, "but there was no talk about . . . Tom Canty, lapped in his poor rags, except among the family of paupers he had just come to trouble with his presence." In spite of his poverty, and because of it, Tom dreams of the life of a prince—"the charmed life of a petted prince in a royal palace." But Mark Twain is at pains to make Tom a modest child, even in his fantasies: he dreams not of being a prince but of merely *seeing* one. When he confides his self-effacing dreams of glory to some of his comrades, they jeer him and scoff at him; thereafter he keeps his dreams to himself. Hidden from the world, his fantasies work all the more strongly upon his mind and he begins to speak like a prince and act the prince. At first this amuses his playmates, but their amusement gradually changes to admiration and the admiration spreads from the children of Offal Court, Tom's residence, to the adults. These begin to bring their problems to the princely pauper for solution, and acting the part of the young Jesus among the doctors, he astonishes them with "the wit and wisdom of his decisions." Becoming a little more like Tom Sawyer, Tom Canty next organizes a royal court in which he plays the prince and his playmates the attendant lords and ladies. All of this prepares the pauper, and the reader, for the great change in his life, his trading places, quite inadvertently, with Edward, Prince of Wales. Tom Canty's response to the transformation of his identity is the antithesis of what we would expect from a Tom Sawyer: mistaken for the prince, he tries his best to convince the royal court that he is an unwitting imposter. But no one will believe his protestations; the courtiers and even the dying King Henry mistake the truth Tom tries to tell them for an insane delusion. The Prince, they believe, has gone quite mad; he has suffered, they are convinced, the ultimate alienation, the loss of his sense of self. Just as Huck Finn would accommodate himself to the identity thrust upon him at Phelps farm, the little pauper adjusts to his situation and accepts for as long as he must the fantastic misunderstanding everyone else takes for the truth: if they insist he is the heir apparent—and presently the king—he will play the role. Note, however, that Tom Canty takes his place at the head of the authority-structure without adopting the folkways of the authority-structure. All of his acts as king strike at the cruelty, prejudice, and ignorance upon which, in Mark Twain's view, the crown based its power. For as long as he reigns, he enjoys Tom Sawyer's success without paying Tom Sawyer's price.

Prince Edward's case is superficially Tom Canty's turned upside down, but actually it is not reversed at all. The mistake in identities thrusts Edward into the pauper's place; suddenly translated from the Palace to Offal Court, he becomes what the other boy had been before, a ragged wanderer who talks like a prince and dreams of the life of a prince. His road from Offal Court to Westminster Abbey is longer and harder than Tom Canty's, but it leads in the same direction and passes the same landmarks. Each boy must make his way through jeering, scoffing mobs; each must have his identity and his sanity challenged by both the hostile and the hospitable people he meets in his travels; each must witness along his way terrible spectacles of man's inhumanity to man, just as Huck Finn would witness one horror after another during his journey down the river. In another significant respect Prince Edward is identified with Tom Canty: he too re-enacts a notable scene in the life of Christ. Just as the Roman soldiers stripped Jesus "and put on him a scarlet robe . . . and platted a crown of thorns . . . [and] put it upon his head, and a reed in his right hand; and they bowed the knee before him and mocked him saying, Hail King of the Jews," so the band of beggars and criminals Edward falls among robe and scepter and crown him:

> Almost before the poor little victim could draw a breath he was crowned with a tin basin, robed in a tattered blanket, throned upon a barrel, and sceptered with the tinker's soldering-iron. Then all flung themselves upon their knees about him and sent up a chorus of ironical wailings, and mocking supplications, while they swabbed their eyes with their soiled and ragged sleeves and aprons.

The portion of the life of Christ which Tom Canty had re-enacted was, in keeping with the difference of treatment Mark Twain gives the two boys, a much happier one. Edward, who is being educated for a higher office than Tom is to occupy, is appropriately made to suffer more pathetic humiliations. After his long journey through the "under-world" of his kingdom and a long night's sleep in the tomb of King Edward the Confessor, those humiliations ultimate in the coronation scene, a kind of ritual resurrection from the dead.

Tom Canty and Prince Edward are not the only Unpromising Heroes in the novel: the Prince's protector, Miles Hendon, is in more details than either of the boys a member of that class. Miles's troubles begin in sibling rivalry. He is, like Samuel Clemens, a middle brother near in age to the youngest. His younger brother, Hugh, is the tattle-tale, spoilsport Sid Sawyer grown up, "a mean spirit, covetous, treacherous, vicious, underhanded—a reptile." He has caused Miles to be sent into virtual exile; and their father and the eldest brother having died during his years of exile, the treacherous Hugh has possessed himself of Miles's inheritance and married his sweetheart.

For Mark Twain the greatest difficulty in presenting an Unpromising Hero tale seriously (i.e., melodramatically, not satirically) lay in making the hero succeed *without* trying: if the hero seems to be seeking his own advancement we lose sympathy with him. This is, in part, what shook our confidence in Tom Sawyer in the earlier novel; it is what was to reduce Tom to something of a comic butt in the opening of **Tom Sawyer Abroad,** and we shall see Mark Twain taking pains to avoid it in his later novels when we come to them.

Miles Hendon's story solves the problem ingeniously. Long before Miles learns that his brother has cheated him of everything which is by rights his, he meets the pathetic young prince who has been driven in a pauper's rags from the palace. He has little inkling of the similarity of their predicaments, but he takes the seemingly mad boy under his protection and saves him from a bloodthirsty mob. Moments later we learn that Henry VIII is dead: the lad Miles has saved from death is England's rightful king. He will in due time create his protector Earl of Kent and bestow upon him unique dignities as reward for the services he renders him. But Miles does not render those services to the king; rather he champions and serves a mad beggar-boy helpless to care for himself. Miles's exertions on behalf of Edward are as selfless as Huck's on behalf of Jim: he has nothing whatever to gain except jeers and hoots and a dozen lashes. The fable is perfectly contrived to allow Hendon to succeed without trying.

The fable is equally successful in dealing with this pitfall of the Unpromising Hero motif in the cases of Edward and Tom. Edward is of course above suspicion: since all power and honor are his by right of birth he cannot be accused of seeking either; but the novel reinforces the point by making power and honor his by right of suffering and sympathy also. Tom Canty is exonerated of any charge of seeking his own advancement since he repeatedly attempts to escape from the captivity of kingship by protesting that he is not Edward Tudor. He even dreams of being back in Offal Court, a pauper joyful in the possession of twelve pennies. Although Tom's essential goodness of heart is never in question, he wavers in his honesty to himself at a crucial moment in the action. When he first resigns himself to playing the king's part, he thinks at once of his mother and wonders if he could make her Duchess of Offal Court, but she gradually fades from his mind. On the day of the coronation, she sees him and recognizes him; he denies her, in words which again sound a biblical echo: "I do not know you, woman." Life in the court, this failure of Tom's moral integrity seems to say, can corrupt even the purest, the most innocent will. But remorse follows at once; the confrontation with his mother recalls to Tom his earlier insight that his royal state is in actuality a kind of slavery and he exclaims to himself, "Would God I were free of my captivity." The incident assures his making the right choice when the true king appears in rags at the coronation and claims his crown. But Tom Canty, in common with King Edward VI and Miles, Earl of Kent, is an Unpromising Hero, and his honest acknowledgement of the true king must not deprive him of the success which is his due: Tom, who had ironically been called "the little Prince of Pauperdom" in an early scene, becomes, appropriately, a kind of king of paupers, the chief governor of Christ's Hospital. Edward's gesture in giving Tom that place makes a fit conclusion not only to Tom's history but to his own also: the boys of Christ's Hospital had abused their prince shamefully when he was in pauper's rags and Tom Canty had, however unwillingly, usurped the place of the rightful king for a season; yet when Edward regains his throne, instead of punishing the boys of Christ's Hospital and the usurper, he rewards both: he places his alter-ego over the charity boys in order to ensure that they "shall have their minds and hearts fed, as well as their baser parts." The young king proves by that enlightened and merciful act that his long educational journey has brought him to its destination.

The three Unpromising Hero fables of **The Prince and the Pauper** are unified in a remarkable number of ways. The most obvious of these is that all three are unmistakably instances of the one motif. A second unifying factor is an outgrowth of the first: all three heroes have double father-figures, and the fathers of each of the heroes are linked in some subtle way to those of the next, so as to forge a continuous chain. The bifurcation of the father-figure is most clearly represented in Tom Canty's case: John Canty, the thief who tyrannizes his impoverished family, is the "ideal" father of a boy's Oedipal imagination—dirty, ugly, brutal, and swinishly ignorant. He is a man fit for the hanging King Edward finally promises him if Tom shall desire it. Tom's other father is as kindly as John Canty is odious. Father Andrew, "a good old priest whom the king had turned out of house and home with a pension of a few farthings," prepares the boy for his unsuspected royal vocation by teaching him to read Latin and to dream. Father Andrew, celibate, old, and nearly destitute, and consequently inconceivable as a rival, is another instance of perfect type casting.

Edward Tudor's father, Henry VIII, the Protestant king who has reduced Father Andrew to his pitiful circumstances, is in his own son's view not unlike John Canty. When the prince learns from the little pauper of John's cruelties, he comments, "Fathers be alike, mayhap. Mine hath not a doll's temper. He smiteth with a heavy hand, yet spareth me: he spareth me not with his tongue, though, sooth to say." Edward's feelings toward King Henry are, however, not entirely unfilial, as his genuine sorrow at the King's death demonstrates. But when Edward is booted out the palace gate in the pauper's rags, he inherits his double's father, John Canty, an entirely unambiguous figure. John's threatening presence follows him through much of his journey of initiation, but at every crisis he can turn to his kindly father-figure, Miles Hendon. The case of Adam in *The Tale of Gamelyn* and *As You Like It* suggests that a servant makes an ideal kindly father-figure because he is by virtue of his social status a non-rival: and Miles is, in relation to his king, a servant.

Miles Hendon's dual paternity is especially interesting. His own kind father and the kind (and sickly) older brother who would have taken his father's place in the family are, although Miles has no knowledge of it, dead before the action commences. Miles's younger brother has become the head of his family and has married the woman Miles loves, a woman who also loves Miles. Hugh Hendon is as perfectly qualified in temperament and disposition to play the odious father-figure as John Canty is: he is "a tyrant who knows no pity." And what of Miles Hendon's kindly father-figure? Blake Andrews, a faithful old servant of the Hendon family, bears some resemblance to Gamelyn's Adam, but Blake's role is brief and shadowy: he is powerless to help Miles against the evil Hugh. (The coincidence of names, Blake Andrews and Father Andrew, is probably unintentional, but it underscores the similarity of the roles the two play.) Assistance finally comes to Miles from an unexpected quarter, from the deranged lad he has befriended. That lad is in actuality his king and as such stands *in loco parentis* to Miles, his most favored subject—his favorite "son." The evil brother Hugh flees from the presence of this boy-father to a deserved, albeit accidental, death.

Thus the novel effects the degradation of each hero's odious father-figure and provides for each an ideal kindly substitute: for Miles, a royal father who stands deeply in his debt; for Tom, an aged, celibate father; for Edward, a father who is at once his protector and his subject.

In *The Adventures of Tom Sawyer* the hero and almost all his fellow villagers are engaged in frantic efforts to establish their artificial identities: the results are comic, sometimes amiably so, sometimes mordantly. In *The Prince and the Pauper* all three heroes are confronted with the deadly serious necessity of reestablishing their true identities. In a metaphoric sense, establishing his identity is always the business of the Unpromising Hero, but Mark Twain has made it the literal business of the heroes of this novel. The initial idea upon which the plot is based presupposes that Prince Edward and Tom Canty will suffer the denial of their identities, but the conception of Miles Hendon's problem did not dictate that it take this form. Yet consider what happens in Chapter XXV when Miles presents himself at Hendon Hall. The wicked Hugh, who has wrongfully possessed himself of the inheritance which belongs to Miles and has even taken possession of Miles's sweetheart, might well have been expected to try to murder the rightful claimant. Instead, he denies Miles's identity; he refuses to recognize him as his brother, and he forces all the people in his power, even the grief-stricken lady, to examine Miles, as if sympathetically and hopefully, and then to avow that they have never seen him before. In the denial of Miles Hendon's identity Mark Twain's craftsmanship is apparent: since collaborating on *The Gilded Age,* he had learned the art of fashioning a unified novel out of multiple plot strands by making those strands run parallel.

The questioned identities of all three heroes receive added emphasis from the frequent references to dreams, and these references give a further pattern and unity to the whole work. Tom Canty's story begins with an account of the "empty grandeurs of his dreams"; on the night after the change of places has occurred, Edward lies down to sleep in Tom's straw, Tom on Edward's royal couch; in the middle of the night each boy wakes, thinks he is in his own bed and calls out that he has had a strange dream; but then the painful truth that it has not after all been a dream comes to each boy. The distinction between dream and reality is obscured for these two. Lady Edith, Miles Hendon's sweetheart, who has been compelled to become his brother's wife, tries to convince him that he too is living in a dream and although nothing can shake Miles's grip on the reality of his own situation, he fails to distinguish dream from actuality in the situation of the young king: he calls Edward "the Lord of the Kingdom of Dreams and Shadows" and after Edward has knighted him he calls himself "a Knight of the Kingdom of Dreams and Shadows."

I have cited only a representative selection of the elements Mark Twain employed to unify this triple-plotted novel—the dream as dominant metaphor, the quests for identity, the linking of sons through shared father-figures, the customary elements, in sum, of Unpromising Hero *Märchen*. The result is a book which hangs together exceptionally well: it is, and it deserves to be, a classic of children's literature. One can put it into the hands of a young reader confident that it will do more than hold his interest and pro-

Edward, still wearing the pauper's rags, interrupts the coronation of Tom Canty.

vide moral instruction; it will also place before him in a simplified conceptual vocabulary a touchstone for testing the quality of novels. In characterization, in style, and in the articulation of structure and image and meaning, *The Prince and the Pauper* is exemplary among books accessible to younger children. One must, however, acknowledge that its conceptual vocabulary is so greatly simplified, its orientation so monotonously two-valued, that it comes short of the legitimate expectations of adult readers. I like to think that Mark Twain knew he had written a book exclusively for children and that his subtitle "A Tale for Young People of All Ages" was not a painfully accurate cliché, but a prediction, written with Horatian confidence, that he had produced a *monumentum aere perennius* scaled to the size of a child's world. (pp. 143-54)

> Robert Regan, in his Unpromising Heroes: Mark Twain and His Characters, *University of California Press, 1966, 246 p.*

Howard G. Baetzhold (essay date 1970)

[*In the following essay, Baetzhold discusses the influence of British writers on Twain and Twain's views on British life as expressed in* The Prince and the Pauper.]

[By 1880] *The Prince and the Pauper* had been on Clemens' list of literary projects for almost four years. As he later remembered it, he was browsing in the library at Quarry Farm one summer afternoon in 1876, picked up one of Charlotte M. Yonge's popular English juveniles, and, inspired by its charm, decided to try his hand at a historical tale of his own.

Albert Bigelow Paine was mistaken in naming Miss Yonge's *The Prince and the Page* as the stimulus, though the title perhaps was influential. Or possibly Clemens had actually mentioned that title to his biographer. Still, as Paine himself was quick to admit, the adventures of the teen-age page of Prince Edward (later Edward I) do not at all resemble those of Tom Canty and Edward Tudor. But another of Miss Yonge's books, *The Little Duke*, which recreates the boyhood of Duke William of Normandy (grandfather-to-be of William the Conqueror), contains parallels in both situation and character relationships to the novel that Clemens several times called "The Little Prince & the Little Pauper." The association of the two boys, Richard and the more worldly Alberic de Montemar, and Osmond de Centeville's role as Richard's protector (and later, rescuer) foreshadow Prince Edward's relationships with Tom Canty and Miles Hendon. Some of

Richard's reactions to court ceremonies, his attempted escape in disguise from the French king's guards (like Edward's ejection in pauper's rags from the palace at Westminster), and the coronation scene strongly suggest similar details in *The Prince and the Pauper.* Clemens was not (as Paine charged) the victim of a faulty memory in 1908 when he credited "that pleasant and picturesque little history book, Charlotte M. Yonge's *Little Duke*" with providing his initial inspiration.

The time for a new literary venture was right, too. Clemens needed a new project. After finishing reading proof for *Tom Sawyer* during July and the first week in August, he had begun *Huckleberry Finn,* only to have interest or inspiration, or both, fail after about four hundred manuscript pages. No doubt the somewhat disappointing sales of *Sketches New and Old* (1875), as well as his desire to be considered a "literary" figure rather than merely a "funny-man," also encouraged him to seek other fields.

All these possibilities lead to the conjecture that it was actually Sir Walter Scott who influenced the decision to try a historical novel. Clemens' boyhood enthusiasm for Scott's works had by this time given way to a strong aversion to certain of their characteristics, particularly their florid style and overly romanticized adventures. In a savage mood early in January, 1870, following a lecture that had been poorly received, he had regaled Olivia in a letter with a burlesque synopsis of *Ivanhoe,* advising her not to bother reading the book. He was not merely entertaining his fiancée, for his tone on the whole was gloomy. The probability is great that the thought of the widespread popularity of Scott's flowery rhetoric and the lack of appreciation for his own lecture, so carefully designed to seem casual and colloquial, irked him considerably. Sometime in 1876, in notes for a speech or essay, he specifically turned to the matter of style, including Scott as a prime example of the sort of writer whose excessive and inexact verbiage ruined the effectiveness of his literary efforts. After citing several examples of forceful yet unostentatious diction—like the Bible's "shadow of a great rock in a weary land"—he concluded that Scott, whose language was always "riding the high horse," could not have conveyed the idea "in anything short of four chapters."

Even so, Clemens respected Scott's use of historical detail. In study notes for *The Prince and the Pauper,* he twice considered the possibility of incorporating examples of chivalric combat from *Ivanhoe,* and also jotted down page numbers from *Kenilworth, Quentin Durward,* and *The Fortunes of Nigel* where he might find descriptions of dress and armor, the wording of "a stately proclamation," and an account of Alsatia (White friars) as a place of refuge for criminals.

Since *Ivanhoe* was on Clemens' mind on these several occasions, it is likely that some of the advice in Scott's introduction to the novel had hit home. Explaining why he had abandoned Scottish subjects for an excursion into the world of chivalry, Sir Walter there notes that the greatest danger to an author's literary fame was to be regarded as a "mannerist" capable of working only in "a particular and limited style," and a little later he concludes that to confine himself to Scottish subjects would not only weary his readers but also limit his ability to afford them pleasure—or, one is tempted to add, to sell them books.

In his "Dedicatory Epistle to the Rev. Dr. Dryasdust," which also prefaces *Ivanhoe,* Scott discusses the problems of a historical novelist in making his work seem authentic. He (or rather his *persona,* Laurence Templeton) advises authors not to collect large numbers of obsolete words, but rather to concern themselves with the "grammatical character" of the language, its "turn of expression, mode of arrangement." In the area of "sentiment and manners," he applies the same principle, noting that in both instances the author must of course take care not to introduce details inconsistent with the manners of the age described, nor language that might betray "an origin directly modern." Otherwise, the author would be making no very serious error to mingle the manners of two or three centuries in his medieval tale, for the general reader would not notice them and experts in the field would "probably be lenient in proportion to their knowledge of the difficulty of [the author's] task."

Whether or not Scott's advice sent Clemens to those "ancient English books" . . . for practice in archaic language, he followed the precepts Scott set down. Probably that same summer he compiled the list of "Middle Age phrases for a historical story" preserved in the Mark Twain Papers. It is interesting also, in the light of Scott's emphasis on authenticity of manners and costumes, that Clemens' later study-note references to the Waverly novels dealt primarily with details of dress, armor, and local color.

The remainder of 1876, however, saw few tangible results of these investigations besides *1601* and the list of phrases. The following summer began hopefully enough, with Clemens reminding himself in May to take along the appropriate volumes of English history by Froude and Hume on the annual trek to Elmira. But other literary interests soon claimed priority—the longish story of the Bermuda trip that spring (later published in several *Atlantic* installments as **"Some Rambling Notes of an Idle Excursion"**); the ill-fated Simon Wheeler play, and revisions of *Ah Sin,* both before and after its July 31 opening in New York. At the end of the summer, therefore, though the stockpile was richer by some reference notes and a few suggestions for possible episodes, Tom Canty and Prince Edward had still not met.

Finally, in the late fall or early winter of 1877 the way seemed clear. On November 23 a synopsis of the author's current plan found its way into his notebook: "Edward VI and a little pauper exchange places by accident a day or so before Henry VIII's death. The Prince wanders in rags and hardships and the pauper suffers the (to him) horrible miseries of princedom, up to the moment of crowning in Westminster Abbey, when proof is brought and the mistake rectified." By February 5 Clemens was telling Mrs. Fairbanks of "a historical tale of 300 years ago" that he was writing "simply for the love of it." He was reveling, too, in the enthusiasm of his family and his Saturday Club of teen-age girls for the portions he read to them. But then the "badgered, harassed feeling" and preparations for the European trip had moved in to halt the novel shortly after the point (in Chapter Eleven) where Miles Hendon first leaps to Edward's defense before the gates of the Guildhall.

While in England, Clemens supplemented earlier studies of a pocket map of London with visits to the actual localities his characters would frequent. But before doing so, he had repeated the practice begun in Paris earlier in 1879 of reading about places of interest before going to see them. His guides this time were works like John Timbs' *Curiosities of London* (1855) and Leigh Hunt's *The Town* (1848), both to be cited as documentation for specific details in **The Prince and the Pauper,** and John Stow's *Survey of London* (1598, 1603).

Home again, and finally freed from the burden of **A Tramp Abroad** in January, 1880, he relaunched his book with all flags flying. February saw him "grinding away . . . with an interest which amounts to intemperance." By March 5 he had added 114 pages, bringing the total, as he told Howells, to 326. Even with the many interruptions which always plagued his literary work in Hartford, he finished eighty-seven more pages by mid-June. With summer and the greater leisure of life at Quarry Farm, the book almost reached port. In fact, on September 15 Clemens announced enthusiastically to Thomas Bailey Aldrich that he had completed the story the day before. But as so often happened, the huzzah was premature, for suggestions by Howells in December resulted in some additional revisions, notably the omission of the whipping-boy's story of the bull and bees. While revising, too, the author decided to expand "the prince's adventures in the rural districts" by some "130 new pages of MS." But finally, by January 21, 1881, **The Prince and the Pauper** was ready for the printer.

From the beginning, Clemens intended this novel to be serious. Until Howells' enthusiasm encouraged him to "publish intrepidly instead of concealing the authorship," he had planned to follow the example set with "The Curious Republic of Gondour." His desire to be "authentic" had led him to many sources. As his "study notes" reveal, he turned to Pepys' *Diary* and Shakespeare's historical plays (especially *Henry IV*) for archaic language. Besides looking at several of Scott's novels, he scoured Froude and Hume for appropriate references to events, personages, and other pertinent details. More specifically he used the volumes by Timbs and Leigh Hunt that he had consulted in England; J. Heneage Jesse's three-volume, *London: Its Celebrated Characters and Remarkable Places* (1871); *The English Rogue,* a seventeenth-century compendium of English low-life by Richard Head and Francis Kirkman (1665; facsimile reprint, 1874); *A Classical Dictionary of the Vulgar Tongue* (1785); and his Hartford friend J. Hammond Trumbull's *The True Blue Laws of Connecticut and New Haven* (1876). From these sources and from Hume he sometimes quoted directly in the text, and further to "authenticate" various incidents, followed the practice of both Scott and Miss Yonge by appending to his novel explanatory notes based on most of these works.

Trumbull's defense of New England's "blue-laws" against charges of excessive harshness probably became most important to **The Prince and the Pauper** after Clemens' European trip, though he doubtless had known the book since its publication in 1876. It perhaps even helped to cause the slight shift in purpose that seems to have occurred when he resumed work on the novel in 1880. The original notebook plan of November, 1877, had suggested that Tom Canty and Prince Edward were to receive approximately equal emphasis as they learned how inaccurate their respective concepts of court and common life had been. But when Clemens told Howells about his project in March, 1880, his mind was on Edward's adventures. "My idea," he said, "is to afford a realizing sense of the exceeding severity of the laws of that day by inflicting some of their penalties upon the king himself & allowing him a chance to see the rest of them applied to others—all of which is to account for certain mildnesses which distinguished Edward VI's reign from those that preceded & followed it." In the notes to the book itself he cited chapter and verse from Trumbull to justify the episodes involving the man sentenced to death by boiling, the girl and her mother condemned as witches for having caused a storm by pulling off their stockings, and the scene in prison where Edward observes at first hand the victims of other harsh laws.

The English Rogue proved another rich mine. In it Clemens found historically accurate dialogue for his beggar band, and an ample vocabulary of cant terms (both of which he supplemented from *A Classical Dictionary of the Vulgar Tongue*). More specifically, he borrowed the last six lines of a rousing "Canting Song" and several examples from the catalogue of frauds perpetrated by the beggars upon their unwary victims. Among these were instructions for producing a "clyme" or false sore, which he introduced into Chapter Twenty-two, where Edward barely escapes being subjected to the process. More important, immediately following those instructions in *The English Rogue* Clemens discovered most of the details for his next episode—Edward's arrest on a charge of pig-stealing, and his narrow escape from death at the subsequent trial.

Several particulars of the theft and concealment of the pig also suggest that Clemens here received an assist from Pepy's *Diary,* which he had known and loved for some years. On August 22, 1668, Pepys notes that while passing through Leaden Hall, he "did see a woman catched, that had stole a shoulder of mutton off a butcher's stall, and carrying it wrapt in a cloth in a basket." In this case, however, the culprit was not arrested, a fact which caused the diarist to sneer that the owner was "so silly as to let her go that took it, taking only the meat." Such implicit callousness (for if the owner had pressed charges, the penalty would have been as severe in Pepys' day as in Tudor England) perhaps underscored for Clemens both the cruelty of the age and the harshness of the laws.

Edward's experience at the trial—he was saved from hanging only when the woman reduced her valuation of the pig below "thirteen-pence ha'penny"—gives him his first real insight into the sufferings of his subjects under the harsh legal code. Hence the episode was an important one for developing the book's major theme. Moreover, it effectively prepares the way for Edward's full comprehension of human suffering when shortly thereafter he sees the two kindly Baptist women burned at the stake.

When Clemens announced to Howells that he hoped "to afford a realizing sense" of the harshness of life in Tudor times by exposing Edward directly to some of the unjust laws, he was echoing a concept derived from still another British author—William Edward Hartpole Lecky. From his first encounter with Lecky's *History of European Morals from Augustus to Charlemagne* (probably during the summer of 1874), he had read, marked, and inwardly digested many of its arguments. Often he noted marginally his agreement or disagreement with what the historian said, or even with how he said it. But at one point, after revising several clumsy constructions in the text, he revealed an abiding affection: "It is so noble a book, & so beautiful a book, that I don't wish it to have even trivial faults in it." And he would continue to borrow ideas and incidents from it for the remainder of his writing career.

In his own works, one may perhaps mark the beginnings of his fascination with the historian's graphic analysis of medieval asceticism in Chapter Thirteen of **Tom Sawyer** (written in 1874), where Huck Finn ridicules the habits of hermits described by Tom. By 1876, as Walter Blair has shown in detail [in his *Mark Twain and Huck Finn*], ideas stimulated by Lecky had permeated the chapters of **Huckleberry Finn** written that summer.

In **The Prince and the Pauper** Lecky's influence seems three-fold, stemming from the historian's examination of the conflicting moral theories of the "intuitionists" and the "utilitarians"; his emphasis on education as a stimulus to the imagination; and his portrait of man's subjection to fear and superstition down through the ages.

The first two of these elements appear in the historian's long opening chapter. Because they were to be important to Clemens' future works, as well as to **The Prince and the Pauper**, they deserve discussion in some detail.

For many years to come Clemens would implicitly carry on what Walter Blair has called his "discussion with Lecky" concerning the relative value of the two systems of moral theory characterized by the historian as "the stoical, the intuitive, the independent or the sentimental" and "the epicurean, the inductive, the utilitarian, or the selfish." The "intuitive" view, which Lecky espoused, argues that moral choices are governed by an innate moral sense, a "power of perceiving" that some qualities (like benevolence, chastity, or veracity) are better than others. A natural accompaniment to this power is a sense of *duty,* an obligation to cultivate the good qualities and suppress their opposites. This sense, in turn, becomes "in itself, and apart from all consequences," a sufficient reason for following any particular course of action. The "utilitarian" theory, to which Clemens was increasingly drawn over the years, *denies* that man possesses any such innate perception of virtue. Rather, his standards of right and wrong, his consideration of the "comparative excellence of . . . feelings and actions," depend solely on the degree to which those feelings and actions are conductive to happiness. That which increases happiness and lessens pain is good; that which does the opposite is evil. Hence it is external forces rather than intuitive perceptions of good or evil which determine moral choices.

A number of marginal comments reveal Clemens' attraction to the utilitarian side. On page five of the history, for instance, Lecky summarizes the utilitarian position as follows: "A desire to obtain happiness and to avoid pain is the only possible motive to action. The reason, and the only reason, why we should perform virtuous actions, or in other words, seek the good of others, is that on the whole such a course will bring us the greatest amount of happiness." Besides heavily underscoring the whole statement, Clemens bracketed the "should," underlined the "us" a second time, and wrote in the margin: "Leave the 'should' out—then it is perfect (& true!)." In several other places he challenged Lecky's agreement with the intuitionists that man's moral perceptions were innate. At one point he contended that "all moral perceptions are acquired by the influences around us," and that since those influences begin in infancy, "we never get a chance to find out whether we have any that are innate or not."

This is not to say that this was the humorist's first encounter with the idea that man's moral choices depend largely on forces outside himself. During his days as a cub-pilot he had absorbed the teachings of Tom Paine's *Age of Reason,* with its emphasis on the immutability of natural law. The notion that man's character and actions were molded primarily from without was doubtless reinforced also by some of Oliver Wendell Holmes' musings on hereditary and environmental influences in *The Autocrat of the Breakfast Table,* which Clemens and Olivia used as a "courting-book" in 1869. Even more important was Clemens' interest in nineteenth-century evolutionary theory.

Because of a fragmentary essay by Clemens that Albert Bigelow Paine included in *Mark Twain's Autobiography,* it has generally been accepted that the author's first instruction in the mysteries of evolution came from a Scotsman named Macfarlane, who preached his own version of the theory in a Cincinnati boarding-house "fourteen or fifteen years before Mr. Darwin's *Descent of Man* startled the world." It now appears, however, that the piece was intended as a magazine or newspaper article and that "Macfarlane" was probably a *persona,* a means of presenting Clemens' own current views of man's pettiness and conceit without publicly committing himself to opinions that might well prove unpopular. It could be that "Macfarlane" owes something to the author's association with J. H. Burrough, his literary-minded St. Louis roommate of 1854-55, who was also at least partially the model for Barrow, the boarding-house philosopher of **The American Claimant** (1892). But until additional evidence becomes available, one must accept the likelihood that Clemens' interest in evolution came primarily from a knowledge of Darwin's writings themselves, or from discussions of those works in contemporary periodicals.

Whether the humorist read *The Origin of Species* (1859) is not certain, but marginal notations in his copy of *The Descent of Man* (1871) show that he may well have been among those whom the book "startled." He thoroughly accepted the theory of evolution, and would later in his own **What is Man?** adapt specific ideas and details from *The Descent of Man.* Yet he apparently was not entirely satisfied with Darwin's attempts to support, on purely evolutionary grounds, the argument that the moral sense was the most important characteristic separating man from the lower animals. He was more impressed, it seems, by Darwin's reference to the notion that the impulse to relieve the sufferings of others stemmed not from altruism but from the desire to alleviate one's own painful feelings which the sight of suffering aroused. For in the margin beside that latter comment he wrote: "Selfishness again—not charity nor generosity (save toward ourselves.)"

These years also marked the beginnings of Clemens' lifelong fascination with Edward FitzGerald's *Rubaiyat of Omar Khayyam.* The haunting quatrains first enchanted him shortly after his return from Europe in 1879, when the Hartford *Courant* quoted a number of them in its front-page review of the new fourth edition of the "translation," published in England that August. From then on, the *Rubaiyat* became his favorite poem, one of the few examples of literary expression that he considered "perfect." Though the effects were to be more obvious later on, particularly during the 1890's, there is little doubt that the deterministic overtones of Omar's discussion of morality and personal responsibility added their elements to Clemens' considerations in the late 'seventies and early 'eighties.

The fact remains, however, that in Lecky he probably first encountered a systematic development of the utilitarian and intuitionist arguments. And for many years his works would show that even though strongly attracted to the utilitarian position, he did not wholly accept it. The "discussion with Lecky" would continue for most of his life.

One of the matters on which Clemens partly agreed with Lecky at this time concerned the nature of the conscience. The historian agreed with the intuitionist view that the conscience was an "original faculty," arising from man's innate perceptions of good and evil. The utilitarians, on the other hand, regarded it simply as an "association of ideas" based on the pleasure-pain theory and society's standards of right and wrong.

To show the inadequacy of the utilitarian concept, Lecky argues that the operation of the conscience does not really fit the view that "self-interest" is the one ultimate reason for virtue. What one "ought or ought not" to do cannot depend merely upon "the prospect of acquiring or losing pleasure." For, if a man had a tendency toward a certain vice, he might well attain happiness by a "moderate and circumspect" indulgence of that vice. But if he sins, his conscience judges his conduct, and "its sting or its approval constitutes a pain or pleasure so intense, as to more than redress the balance." This would happen whether the conscience were an "association of ideas" or "an original faculty."

But (the argument continues) conscience is more often a source of pain than of pleasure, and if happiness is actually the sole end of life, then one should learn to disregard the proddings of conscience. If a man forms an association of ideas that inflicts more pain than it prevents, or prevents more pleasure than it affords, the reasonable course would be to dissolve that association or destroy the habit. "This is what he 'ought' to do according to the only meaning that word can possess in the utilitarian vocabulary."

Therefore, a man who possessed such a temperament would be happier if he were to "quench that conscientious feeling, which . . . prevents him from pursuing the course that would be most conducive to his tranquillity."

Clemens had dramatized this very theme in **"The Facts Concerning the Recent Carnival of Crime in Connecticut,"** written in January, 1876, and published in the June issue of the *Atlantic Monthly.* As the story opens, the narrator muses over efforts of friends and relatives to keep him in the paths of virtue. Suddenly, his Conscience appears in the form of a "nauseating" dwarf, resembling the narrator himself but covered with a greenish mold. ("Considered as a source of pain," Lecky says, "conscience bears a striking resemblance to the feeling of disgust.") The two discuss at some length the function of the Conscience as tormentor. Finally, a recitation of his many sins goads the narrator into throttling the dwarf, tearing him to pieces, and throwing the "bleeding rubbish" into the fire. Having thus followed Lecky's advice to obliterate his conscience, the narrator embarks on a career of "unalloyed bliss," committing all sorts of heinous crimes without a moment's remorse.

Fantastic as the piece is, it nevertheless parallels Lecky's discussion almost exactly. Certainly Clemens' own experiences with a tormenting conscience, which must have been one of the keenest in literary history, had led him here to agree with Lecky's assertion that the reproaches of conscience often prevented a man from following a course that might be "most conducive to his tranquillity." And since the proddings of conscience obviously could *not* be so easily dismissed, Clemens at least implicitly agreed that Lecky had found a fallacy in the utilitarian reasoning.

Echoes of this idea of "quenching" the conscience occur also in the chapters of ***Huckleberry Finn*** written in 1876. Furthermore, Huck's struggles with his conscience about turning Jim over to the authorities show Clemens agreeing with the historian in a slightly different way. The climax of that conflict in Chapter Thirty-one, when Huck decides to "go to hell" rather than reveal Jim's whereabouts was not to be written for several years. But the struggle itself was clearly established in 1876, especially in Chapter Sixteen, when Huck decides to paddle ashore "and tell," but then recants and lies to the slave-catchers about the color of the man on the raft. Some years later, in a notebook plan for an elaborate "lay sermon on morals and things of that stately sort," Clemens proposed to use that very chapter from his novel to show how "in a crucial moral emergency a sound heart is a safer guide than an ill-trained conscience." Though Clemens here was obviously regarding the conscience as an "association of ideas" rather than an "original faculty," both this passage and Huck's later decision not to write to Miss Watson dramatize the triumph of Huck's "sound heart" over his community-trained sense of right and wrong. This "sound heart" is first cousin, if not brother, to the "innate moral perceptions" championed by Lecky and the intuitionists.

The second major concept derived from Lecky involves the interrelationship of imagination and compassion, and the influence of education upon both. Shortly after his analysis of the two conflicting moral theories, the historian devotes a long passage to explaining how society's progress from barbarism to a high degree of civilization had depended upon "the strengthening of the imagination by intellectual culture." Defining imagination as "the power of realisation," he argues that men pity suffering only when they "realise" it, and that the intensity of their compassion is directly proportionate to the extent of that "realisation." That is why the death of an individual "brought prominently before our eyes" elicits greater compassion than any account of battle, shipwreck, or other catastrophe. Therefore, if benevolent feelings thus depend upon prior "realisation," then any influence that can increase the range and power of the imagination (the "realising faculty") will help to develop sympathy and compassion. And of all such influences, education is the foremost.

Besides the echo in Clemens' letter to Howells, that idea finds a direct statement early in *The Prince and the Pauper* when Edward vows (in Chapter Four) to make Christ's Hospital a school for "mental nourishment" rather than "mere shelter" so that poor boys may develop the "gentleness and charity" which education encourages. More important, the concept underlies the subsequent education of Edward and, in some measure, that of Tom Canty.

The plot structure of this most carefully wrought of Clemens' works shows that the author clearly intended Edward's "education" to be primary. Each of the boys gets almost equal space until the end of Chapter Thirteen. But then the spotlight begins to focus on Edward, as Miles Hendon discovers the disappearance of his protégé, who has been lured from the lodgings on London Bridge by a mysterious message from John Canty. After three chapters describing Tom's experiences at court following the death of Henry VIII, the next twelve are Edward's (save for the two that relate Hendon's family troubles). Of the final five, two are again Tom's; one is shared; the fourth is largely Edward's; and the unnumbered "Conclusion" briefly summarizes the subsequent careers of the principal characters, with emphasis on Edward's good works as king.

Prince Edward's schooling begins immediately upon his ejection from the palace grounds when the group of boys from Christ's Hospital mock and beat him. His promise to make the institution into a school, like his initial befriending of Tom Canty, springs from his own innate "gentleness and charity." But he is to achieve real compassion and understanding only near the end of his wanderings. As Franklin Rogers has noted [in his *Mark Twain's Burlesque Patterns*], when Edward first leaves the city via London Bridge, he is still an arrogant aristocrat. He has demanded all the niceties of court etiquette from Miles Hendon and has sworn to have Tom Canty hanged, drawn, and quartered for usurping his throne. Only gradually does the basic soundness of heart, which Hendon recognizes as "the sweet and generous spirit that is in him" assert itself. Finally, after the burning of the Baptist women who befriended him, Edward (in Chapter Twenty-seven) declares that the horror will remain in his memory and his dreams for the rest of his life. Hendon then underscores the change of character by noting how gentle Edward has become; earlier he "would have stormed at these varlets, and said he was king, and commanded that the women be turned loose unscathed."

Other inhumanities in the prison complete the educational process, and Edward swears he will amend the harsh legal code, concluding: "The world is made wrong, kings should go to school to their own laws at times, and so learn mercy." Now he is ready to re-cross London Bridge, a merciful monarch. Subsequently, in righting earlier wrongs, he often stresses the importance of his personal experience, subduing objections by reminding his courtiers that *they* know little of suffering and oppression. And recognizing the tendency of human beings to forget important lessons, he often repeated his story so as to "keep its sorrowful spectacles fresh in his memory and the springs of pity replenished in his heart."

Besides paralleling Lecky's description of the "realisation" process, then, Edward's development reveals a "soundness" of heart like that of Huck Finn. From the first instinctive kindness to Tom, through the sloughing off of the aristocratic arrogance engendered by his upbringing, he proceeds to a conscious kindness. Had he not been innately good, however, it is more than likely that the abuse and ridicule to which his travels exposed him would have far outweighed his pity for the sufferings of others.

To say that *The Prince and the Pauper* is chiefly Edward's story should not, of course, minimize the importance of Tom Canty's "education." In the first place, once Tom loses his fear of being found out, he begins to discover how false were his dreams of kingly pleasures. Concern over the impending execution of Norfolk, the embarrassment of his first court dinner, and the tedium of business and ceremony successively engulf him until, in Chapter Fourteen, he almost begs to be freed from the "affliction" of kingship. Soon, however, his innately kind heart and sound common sense allow him to initiate a slight amelioration of the harsh laws.

Faced with the prospect of the execution of the alleged poisoner and the two "witches charged with controlling the weather" (Chapter Fifteen), he reacts with instinctive compassion. As Roger Salomon has observed, he faces something of the same conflict of heart and society-trained conscience as both Huck Finn and the historical Edward VI portrayed by David Hume. Of Edward, Hume says that training and "the age in which he lived" qualified his "mildness of disposition" and his "capacity to learn and judge," and thus caused him to "incline somewhat to bigotry and persecution." In a case involving the supposed heresy of a young girl, for instance, the king at first reacted compassionately, refusing to sanction the execution. But his advisers prevailed, and he finally signed the death warrant, though "with tears in his eyes."

Tom Canty, as king, finds himself in a similar position. Like Hume's Edward he is sympathetic. Then, though he grants the "poisoner's" request to be hanged rather than boiled to death, he considers the seriousness of the crime and says with a sigh, "Take him away—he hath earned his death." Fortunately, he decides to review the case further, and when additional questioning reveals the flimsiness of the evidence, reason enters the picture, and Tom frees the man. In the case of the alleged witches, the "influence of the age" again is evident in Tom's superstitious shudder at their presence, a reaction natural in a time when everyone dreaded encountering those possessed by the devil. But whereas the real Edward consented to the execution of the young girl, in this case Tom's sound heart and common sense (again like Huck's) triumph over his trained conscience. Sorry for their plight, Tom reasons that a mother would do anything to save her child, and so offers them freedom and his own protection if they will repeat their magic. When they still protest their inability to create a thunderstorm, he pronounces them innocent and dismisses the charge.

Yet those episodes also affect Tom adversely. On realizing that his word truly *is* law, he begins to relish his position and power. Periodically, however, he is plagued by a different sort of conscience—more akin to what Lecky would call an "original" faculty than a community-trained "association of ideas." Tom's shame and guilt arise from two sources: the knowledge that he is usurping Edward's rightful place and his fear that his mother or sisters might appear to thwart his pleasure by exposing him. Though he almost succeeds in following Lecky's advice to quell a troublesome conscience, his guilty feelings continue to torture him. When his pride finally leads him to reject his mother during the coronation procession, all the glamor of kingship falls away as remorse overwhelms him. Edward's appearance in Westminster Abbey brings welcome relief, and Tom is only too glad to relinquish the throne.

One might argue that here Clemens has accorded a purely utilitarian function to the conscience; that Tom's restoring the throne to its rightful occupant and himself to his own family is an action that will ultimately result in the greatest happiness for himself. So it does. But his feelings evolve basically from his natural goodness—his concern for Edward and his love for his family, rather than from a fear of the consequences of being exposed. The miseries of conscience which destroy his happiness and make him glad to give up the throne reflect the kindness and gentleness that he exhibited even at the height of his pleasure in his kingly position. Thus Clemens still seems to side with Lecky.

From Lecky's discussion of the influences of superstition in human affairs at least two other episodes derived support, if not their original inspiration. In Chapter Seventeen, Edward learns of the sad plight of certain husbandmen and of the once-prosperous farmer, Yokel, whose property has been confiscated because his mother was convicted of witchcraft. In a sarcastic harangue to Hugo's outlaw band, Yokel describes his experiences with "the merciful English law": when he had turned to begging as his only recourse, he had for successive offenses been whipped, deprived of both ears, branded, and finally enslaved. "Do ye understand that word!" he shouts; "An English SLAVE!" And then he explains that he has fled from his master and, if caught, will hang.

At that point the horrified Edward cries that the law shall be revoked that very day, whereupon he is robed, crowned, sceptered, and dubbed "Foo-Foo the First, King of the Mooncalves." To keep the historical record straight, the author contributes a note to this passage which explains that the peasant was "suffering from this law *by anticipation*," for the statute "was to have birth in this little king's own reign." But, he adds, "we know, from the humanity of his character, that it could never have been suggested by him." Presumably, this law was to be among those which Edward (in the novel) would later repeal.

This chapter in Edward's education may well have been fathered by Lecky's discussion of the concept of Christian charity, and specifically, of how the establishment of charitable institutions had in many cases actually increased mendicancy rather than relieved it. The paradox resulted, Lecky says, from the superstition that the donor of charity would reap spiritual rewards. The prospect of such rewards produced an anxiety to give. Increased giving, in turn, led to increased begging, even by those who might otherwise be able to engage in productive labor. Finally, in England and elsewhere, the problem of begging became so severe that the harshest sort of legislation was invoked.

Two of the laws cited by Lecky to illustrate his point are especially significant. The first, from the reign of Henry VIII, provided increasingly severe penalties: for a first offense—whipping; for second—whipping and loss of part of an ear; for a third—death. On the other statute, Lecky says: "*Under Edward VI, an atrocious law, which, however, was repealed in the same reign* [italics mine], enacted that every sturdy beggar who refused to work should be branded, and adjudged for two years as a slave to the person who gave information against him." If he fled during that period, he was condemned for a first offense to perpetual slavery, and for a second, to death. Taken together, the two laws describe the experiences of several of the husbandmen and almost exactly the fate of Yokel.

Edward's visit to the insane hermit shortly after his escape from the beggars suggests one further debt to the *History of European Morals*. Immediately preceding the discussion of the relationship of charity and mendicancy, Lecky traces a number of historical attitudes toward insanity. Immediately following it, he embarks upon the long discourse on medieval asceticism from which Clemens was to borrow heavily for ***A Connecticut Yankee***. The crazy recluse who claims to be an archangel and mutters about personal visits to Paradise is certainly a blood brother to Lecky's generic ascetic who, "delirious . . . from solitude and long-continued austerities," mistakes his hallucinations for "palpable realities." But there is a more specific model. In contending that for many centuries most madness assumed a theological cast, the historian cites, among others, the case of a Spanish lunatic who thought himself "the brother of the archangel Michael . . . destined for the place in heaven which Satan had lost" and, like Edward's hermit, claimed to have visited freely between this world and the next.

If Clemens had originally intended Edward's encounter with the "archangel" to awaken a sense of sympathy for the hermit, who had been made homeless by Henry VIII's seizure of his monastery, he failed badly. At best the recluse is an object of horror as he whets his butcher-knife

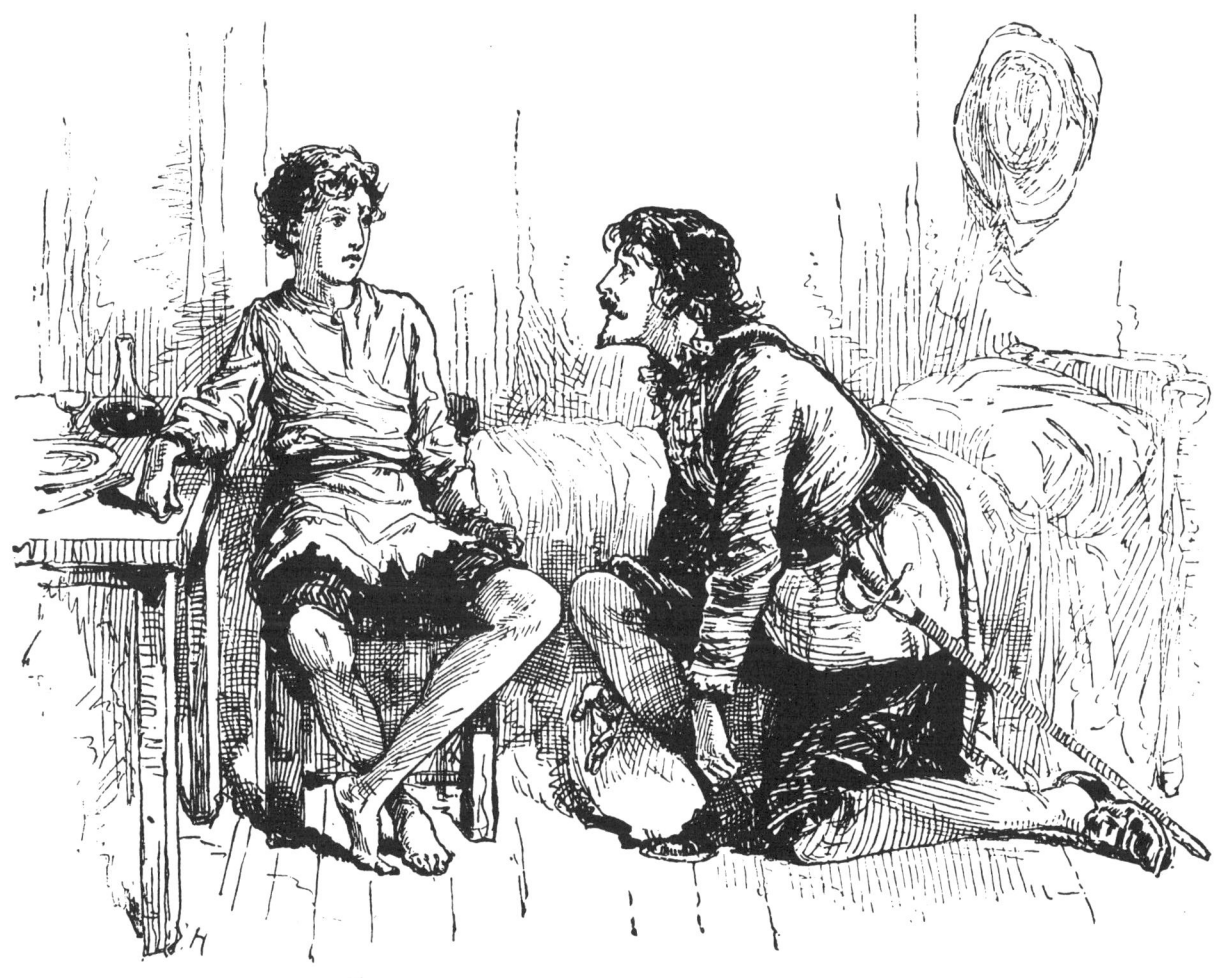

Edward proves his claim to the throne.

and chuckles over his intended revenge on Henry's heir. At worst he is ridiculous. Whatever the original intention, Clemens' treatment clearly reflects the mingled horror and disgust with which Lecky viewed religious mania.

In some respects Clemens' attacks on superstition point toward *A Connecticut Yankee,* where Lecky was to play an even larger role. Edward's travels among his people, too, foreshadow the similar journey of King Arthur. Nevertheless, many commentators have read ***The Prince and the Pauper*** under too strong a glow from *A Connecticut Yankee.* DeVoto's conclusion [in *Mark Twain's America*], for instance, that the author was attacking as much as he could manage of the "modern perpetuation" of the harsh Tudor law, is warranted neither by Clemens' political and social attitudes at the time of composition nor by the book itself. First, the novel was conceived when Clemens' admiration for England, her traditions, and her government was at its zenith. At that time he may well have thought of the many examples of religious persecution and severe treatment of prisoners (gathered mainly from Hume in 1877) as "local color" which would illustrate the hardships to be observed by the little king in contrast to the "horrible miseries of princedom" to be borne by Tom Canty. Nor had his conviction of the common man's incompetence in government changed much as a result of the European trip of 1878-79. Nowhere in his personal utterances of these years, nor in ***The Prince and the Pauper*** itself, is there any sign of his later contention that all monarchies should be overthrown. Tudor law was oppressive, to be sure, and bespoke a system sorely deficient in respect for human rights. But it was man rather than monarchy that needed reform; first the rulers and then the people themselves must be rid of false notions. DeVoto's suggested title, "A Missouri Democrat at the Court of Edward VI" is thus inaccurate, and ascribes ideas to Clemens that he demonstrably did not hold when he wrote the book.

In the book itself there is relatively little satire of monarchy and aristocracy. The sharpest thrusts at court ceremony occur in the ludicrous picture of grown men stumbling and fumbling as they attempt to clothe one small boy. Balanced against this sort of burlesque is an obvious fascination with the traditional pomp and display associated with other ceremonies, such as the coronation. Even in the exposure of the more striking legal atrocities of the age, Clemens' target is not the iniquity of the system which produced them but the ignorance and superstition of the age.

Finally, much as it points toward Clemens' later application of Carlyle's clothes-metaphor in *A Connecticut Yankee,* the often-cited picture of Tom and Edward standing naked before a mirror, amazed at their identical appearances, cannot really be read as proof of Clemens' current belief in social or political equality. Barring the fact that the plot itself demanded such physical similarity, other evidence seriously weakens any argument that Clemens had freighted **The Prince and the Pauper** with an "equalitarian" message. In fact, when the novel was in full swing and nearing completion in August, 1880, the author was planning still another episode for **Captain Stormfield's Visit to Heaven** with opposite implications. As the notebook sketch indicates, Stormfield was first to be charmed with the idea that the residents of Paradise lived in a world completely free of social barriers. But when a Negro, a Fiji Islander, an Eskimo, and various politicians, tramps, and other pariahs began inviting themselves to dinner and calling him "Brother Stormfield," he was to grow progressively less enthusiastic. Finally, he would become disgusted by this enforced association with "all sorts of disagreeable people," and would resolve to move from heaven. Such a plan, though not ultimately used, shows that Clemens in 1880 and 1881 had not deviated far from his social and political opinions of the 1870's.

The "message" of **The Prince and the Pauper,** then, was not that British monarchy was evil, not even that monarchy in itself breeds injustice. It was rather that the cure for political and social ills might be achieved through the paternalistic rule of those best qualified to rule, whose qualifications should include innate kindness, intelligence, and the "realisation" provided by "education." The book is much closer to **"The Curious Republic of Gondour"** with its mistrust of the masses and plea for qualified public officials, or to **Huckleberry Finn** with its belief in the efficacy of the "sound heart," than to the Yankee Hank Morgan's proposal to demolish and then recreate on an equalitarian basis the institutions of a nation. Nevertheless, its exposure of ignorance, superstition, and unreason does reflect a further deepening of Clemens' disillusionment with human nature. And the careers of its protagonists show Clemens a step closer to the proposition that environment and circumstances alone determine the course of life.

Though Clemens thus weighted **The Prince and the Pauper** with serious implications, the novel unfortunately fails to transcend the limitations of time, place, and melodramatic action. Hence, it lacks the universality which allows **Huckleberry Finn,** or even **Tom Sawyer,** to grip the minds and imaginations of adult readers. The book continues to be read, certainly, but its appeal is chiefly to children and to students of Clemens' literary development, rather than to "young people of all ages."

In the novel's own day, however, most American critics praised it. Some applauded the emergence of a new and superior Mark Twain; a few, like Howells, contended that the book merely presented clearer evidence of the underlying seriousness in all of Mark Twain's works. Enthusiastic as he himself was about the story, Clemens no doubt found these plaudits especially heartwarming. But when the far less enthusiastic first reactions from England reached him, he must have felt a very different kind of warmth—that of anger.

The critical barbs from Britain flung at **A Tramp Abroad** had not hurt much. Clemens' own impatience with the laborious task of finishing the book had deadened their sting. Now, however, with a labor of love under fire, he could not have remained unruffled. What perhaps irritated him most was the reviewer's advice in the *Athenaeum* for December 24, 1881, that Mark Twain should stick to his proper sphere as "a brilliant and engaging humorist" rather than attempt a genre in which he became only a "dull and painful romancer." If not that, then the opinion that the "disastrous and amazing" effort to achieve a serious book had resulted only in "some four hundred pages of careful tediousness, mitigated by occasional flashes of unintentional and unconscious fun." Clemens may not have seen the *Academy* for the same date, which characterized **The Prince and the Pauper** as "a ponderous fantasia of English history," bathed "in a misty atmosphere of Scott's chivalry." If he had, he would not have appreciated the comparison, especially in view of the pains he had taken to be "authentic."

The more favorable comments in January of the *Quarterly Review* and the *Spectator* probably salved the wounds somewhat, when the latter commended his skillful working out of an "ingenious idea" and the former praised his "fun and satirical chaff, his mingled humor and pathos, his fine perception of human nature, and his nimble fancy." But Clemens was more sensitive to slights than to praise, and he seems almost to protest too much in a letter to Andrew Chatto in March which pooh-poohed the adverse criticisms of the *Anthenaeum* and *Saturday Review.* "Here we consider that neither of those papers would compliment the holy scriptures if an American had written them," he said. The unfavorable reviews had surely rankled, however, and they probably helped to aggravate whatever antipathy had developed during the English visit two years before. (pp. 48-67)

> Howard G. Baetzhold, "The Prince and the Pauper (1880-1881)," in his Mark Twain and John Bull: The British Connection, *Indiana University Press,* 1970, pp. 48-67.

Everett Emerson (essay date 1984)

[*Emerson is an American educator and critic. In the following excerpt, he discusses the ways in which* The Prince and the Pauper *departed from Twain's usual style and subject matter.*]

The Prince and the Pauper had its origins in Samuel Clemens's reading, not his experience. He read, probably in 1874, William E. H. Lecky's *History of European Morals from Augustus to Charlemagne* (1869), a book that was to arouse his interest both in early European history and in the sources of morality. . . . In a copy of Lecky's history, Clemens wrote, "It is so noble a book, & so beautiful, that I don't wish to have even trivial faults in it." Now his latent interest in history was heightened. It came to include the history of the English language, especially early Modern English, and in the summer of 1876 he compiled

"**Middle Age Phrases for a Historical Study**" and wrote *1601*." The next summer he read books on England in the sixteenth century: James Anthony Froude's *History of England,* and the portion of David Hume's history on Henry VII and Henry VIII. He now had a title for his historical fiction but, still interested in the theater, what he planned was a play. He recorded in his notebook in July, "Write Prince and Pauper in 4 acts and eight changes."

The immediate sources for the book were two. First, the Westerner who had come east was much interested in the notion of role-exchanging. The earliest version of his plot takes place in Victorian England, with Albert Edward, heir to the throne, exchanging identities with a London slum dweller. Then he judged his purposes would be better served by moving further back into English history. Second, he read Charlotte M. Yonge's *The Little Duke,* which tells of how Richard, duke of Normandy, profits from his experiences at the corrupt court of Louis IV to become a just and merciful ruler. In November 1877 he recorded in his notebook the basic plot: "Edward VI and a little pauper exchange places by accident a day or so before Henry VIII's death. The prince wanders in rags & hardships & the pauper suffers the (to him) horrible miseries of princedom, up to the moment of crowning, in Westminster Abbey, when proof is brought & the mistake rectified."

In February 1878, Mark Twain was writing what he now called "A historical tale, of 300 years ago," and unlike the **Tramp,** which was soon to occupy him, he was writing "simply for the love of it." He called his word "grave & stately" and thus "considered by the world to be beneath my proper level." Enough had already been written to permit Clemens to read portions to the Saturday Club or "Young Girls' Club" he had founded earlier, hardly the audience Mark Twain was accustomed to addressing. But then plans for his European trip intervened, and he seems not to have touched the manuscript for about two years. He returned to it with "jubilant delight" early in 1880. His interest amounted to "intemperance," he told his brother. In a letter to Howells he implies a strong distinction between his current book and the one he had been writing. His pleasure was so great, he declared, that he was not concerned whether the book sold or not, and he was enjoying the act of creation so much that he was trying not to rush for fear he would finish and end his pleasure. Mrs. Clemens liked what he was writing far more than his earlier work. In early September he thought he had completed the book, or so he wrote Thomas Bailey Aldrich, and by early December Howells had read and admired it, though he had some substantial suggestions for revision, which Clemens in part accepted. He dropped the "whipping-boy story," to which Howells objected, and he "added over 130 new pages of MS to the prince's adventures in the rural districts." These additions were made at least in part to give the novel the proper heft for a subscription book. "The number of pages before," the author explained, "was 734—the number is 870, now—fully as bulky a book as Tom Sawyer, I think." (But buyers had judged **Tom** not big enough.) After a few final revisions on February 1, 1881, the book was finished. The author expressed his pleasure: "I like this tale better than **Tom Sawyer**—because I haven't put any fun in it. I *think* that is why I like it better. You know a body always enjoys seeing himself attempting something out of his line." Mrs. Clemens was eager to have the book "elegantly gotten up," and it was. Howells both read proof and reviewed the novel, anonymously, well before its publication in December 1881, when it appeared simultaneously in England, Canada, and the United States.

The Prince and the Pauper was indeed out of Mark Twain's line, and his friend Joe Goodman from Virginia City days told him so: "What could have sent you groping among the driftwood of the Deluge for a topic when you could have been so much more at home in the wash of today?" What sent him was a need to write a book of the sort that Mrs. Clemens and his daughters (a third, Jean, was born in July 1880) would approve. And there were others pushing too. Mrs. Fairbanks had told him to write "another book in an entirely different style." "The time has come for your *best book,* your best contribution to American Literature." The Hartford clergyman Edwin P. Parker had asked him to do himself "vast honor" and his friends "vast pleasure" by writing a book with "a sober character." Clemens did exactly as he had been encouraged to do. Dedicated to "those well mannered and amiable children Susy and Clara Clemens," and subtitled "A Tale for Young People of All Ages," **The Prince and the Pauper** is well mannered and amiable. Susy was delighted. She recorded in her biography of her father (much of which years later Clemens inserted into his autobiography) that it was "unquestionably the best book he has ever written." She objected to people thinking of him as "a humorist joking at everything." In her eyes the new book was "perfect." Mrs. Fairbanks rewarded her child—Clemens always addressed her as "Mother"—with the highest compliments. "The book is your masterpiece in fineness." The December 28 Hartford *Courant* congratulated the author for "writing a book which has other and higher merits than can possibly belong to the most artistic expression of mere humor." His neighbor Harriet Beecher Stowe told him it was "the best book for young folks that was ever written." Only Joe Goodman is recorded as thinking otherwise. He thought the book was a mistake.

In what ways **The Prince and the Pauper** is a book designed to satisfy the genteel readers of Hartford and elsewhere is not hard to understand. It is a historical tale, laden with learning about the past and set in England. Thus it appealed to those burdened by a need to learn from a novel as well as be entertained, especially those Americans whose model was English gentility. Clemens himself had become its ardent admirer (though before he finished the book his admiration had cooled). He was well acquainted with England and had broken bread with many of its aristocrats. Having dredged up historical material from books, he was able to show off, like Tom Sawyer, even if his learning sat precariously balanced. His notebook contains a list of over seventy people to whom he proudly sent copies of his book, among them Holmes, Emerson, Whittier, and Longfellow, whom it must have been particularly gratifying to address after the humiliation of the Whittier birthday dinner; the Scottish clergyman-poet George MacDonald; Charlotte M. Yonge, whose *The Little Duke* had contributed to his book; Rose Terry Cooke.

Specially printed and bound copies went to the amiable Susy and Clara. He had done something special—what *had been* out of his line—and he wanted the world to know.

Compared with Mark Twain's other books, fictional and otherwise, *The Prince and the Pauper* is well plotted and unmarred by wild burlesques. The experiences of the prince and the pauper after they exchange roles are neatly parallel: each boy finds that his "father" believes him to be mad; each is befriended by his "sister," and each wakes from sleep thinking that his trying experiences have been just a bad dream. But the novel lacks nearly every quality that one associates with Mark Twain. There is little humor. With a setting in the mid-sixteenth century, the time of Edward VI, so remote from Clemens's own experience that he documents it with footnotes citing various authorities, the book provides no sense of being present at the events it describes. The master of the colloquial style here writes dialogue that is a labored attempt at Elizabethan English. "Searched you well—but it boots not to ask that. It doth seem passing strange." A few metaphors reveal the writer's background. If the guardians of Tom Canty, the pauper who by mischance becomes the prince, "felt much as if they were piloting a great ship through a dangerous channel," for Tom himself, according to chapter 6, "Time wore on pleasantly, and likewise smoothly, on the whole. Snags and sand bars grew less and less frequent." Just below the surface there is much that reflects the author's interests and concerns. The courtly ceremonies of Europe had attracted him as early as his first visit, when he saw Napoleon II and met the czar of Russia, as well as later when he covered the shah's tour. Increased financial pressures on Clemens are reflected in Tom's worried comments in chapter 14 on royal expenditures: "We be going to the dogs, 'tis plain. 'Tis meet and necessary that we take a smaller house and set the servants at large." Like Tom Sawyer (and Samuel Clemens), Tom Canty yearns for excitement and is bored by routine, and—like the hero of the earlier novel—both boys are basically good-hearted, innocent. Their goodness is underscored by the cruelty of the society in which they live, an interest soon to become a major preoccupation. Clemens had always been sensitive to suffering, as his writings about the Chinese in California show. Now his reading in historical works had shown him, as he told Howells in March 1881 while writing the novel, "the exceeding severity of laws of that day." He was moreover disenchanted with monarchy if not with its trappings. What the prince learns of suffering and oppression makes him a merciful king when the two boys change places a second time. The education that the prince receives is more than an indictment of a system of government or a historical epoch. Unlike *The Little Duke*, *The Prince and the Pauper* depicts man's cruelty as part of his nature. Though a book for children, it is the first of the author's works to castigate the damned human race, as he was to call it. Like Huck and later King Arthur, the prince is educated and learns the facts of life through his travels, and like them he is encouraged by a companion, one Miles Hendon. The tone, however, is far more optimistic, though the reader may see that the lessons the prince learns will have little effect, because his reign as Edward VI was brief.

In *The Prince and the Pauper* an important theme is the mystery of identity. The switch of roles that forms the basis of the plot permitted Clemens to demonstrate what was becoming one of his pet ideas, later set forth simply: "Training is everything." The differences between the prince and the pauper are only skin-deep, for they are still young. The pauper in time learns to play the role of prince, as a result of his training. Later Clemens would perform a more fundamental experiment by switching a "black" slave and the son of a white aristocrat while they are still babies. But *The Prince and the Pauper* looks backward too. Like the tenderfoot narrator in *Roughing It*, both boys at the beginning of their adventures have their vision distorted by romanticism; their experiences serve as educational correctives.

The Prince and the Pauper was not published by the American Publishing Company, for on the death of Elisha Bliss, its president, in 1880, Clemens turned to James R. Osgood of Boston, formerly a partner in the firm of Ticknor and Fields. Osgood was to publish just three books by Mark Twain; he proved to be inexperienced in subscription publishing. Because of his ambitions, encouraged by those of Mrs. Clemens, production costs of the books, especially this historical novel, were high. These expenses were borne by the author, who thought he could increase his profits by such a financial arrangement. But because his readers did not expect him to write such a work and because of Osgood's lack of publishing knowledge, *The Prince and the Pauper* was a financial failure. The book, as might be expected, was given bad reviews in England— one writer called it "a ponderous fantasia on English history." It fared better among American reviewers. Joel Chandler Harris welcomed its author as a "true literary artist." What Howells wrote was doubtless most important, for it contributed to Clemens's view of himself as a writer. Howells called the new novel "a manual of republicanism which might fitly be introduced into the schools." While he could not become the polite *littérateur* his Hartford friends were encouraging him to become, Mark Twain could and would be a serious social critic. (pp. 106-11)

Everett Emerson, in his The Authentic Mark Twain: A Literary Biography of Samuel L. Clemens, *University of Pennsylvania Press, 1984, 330 p.*

John C. Gerber (essay date 1988)

[*Gerber is an American educator and critic who has written and edited numerous works on Twain. In the following excerpt, he discusses the problems Twain faced in writing* The Prince and the Pauper, *unfavorably comparing it to such works as* Huckleberry Finn *and* Tom Sawyer.]

[*The Prince and the Pauper*] turned out to be the most conventional and the blandest [book that Twain] ever wrote. We can only guess at his motives. Besides wanting a commercial success he apparently hoped for a story that would entertain his daughters. He regularly read to them from the manuscript and he dedicated the book to "Those good-mannered and agreeable children, Susie and Clara Clemens." Apparently, too, he was so tired of being called a "mere humorist" that he wanted to prove that he could compete successfully with the more serious writers by tackling one of their favorite genres, the historical romance. And probably after reading so much English history while abroad he wanted to exploit the English past. As in *Huckleberry Finn,* he selected two boys and an older man as his major characters. He has the boys change clothes and tries to imagine what would happen. Plenty happens because one boy is a London ragamuffin and the other is the heir apparent to the English throne. Rolled into one, *The Prince and the Pauper* is a tall tale, an historical romance, and a story designed to entertain and ennoble juvenile readers. When he read it, Joe Goodman, Twain's former boss on the *Territorial Enterprise,* thought Twain had lost his senses, but Twain's family and Hartford friends believed that he had finally brought out the best in him.

To give his narrative the aura of legend, Mark Twain in a preface calls it a tale that has been passed down from generation to generation. It is the story of two fourteen-year-old look-alikes, Tom Canty of Offal Court in London and the young prince soon to be Edward VI of England. It opens at 9:00 A.M. on 27 January 1547—seventeen-and-a-half hours before Henry VIII dies—and covers the period between then and the crowning of Edward VI on 20 February. In the first three chapters Twain introduces the boys and their contrasting backgrounds. Seeing the Pauper manhandled by one of his guards, the Prince invites him into the palace where as a jest they exchange clothes. It is not so much of a jest, though, when the Prince in rags gets thrown out of the palace grounds. In chapter 4 John Canty, Tom's father, collars the Prince, mistaking him for Tom, and drags him off to the human sty that the Cantys call home. Chapters 5-9 switch the story to Tom and his perplexing problems as prince. Despite his ingenuity and the bits and pieces of information he had picked up about court life, his behavior appears so strange that word gets out that the Prince has lost his mind. In chapter 9, though, Tom, "magnificently habited," stands forth as the commanding figure in a fantastic river pageant—one of Mark Twain's great scenes.

In chapters 10-13 the real prince also gives the impression that he has lost his mind when he issues orders in regal language to the inhabitants of Offal Court. Only his "mother" and twin "sisters" are kind to him, his mother suspecting that all is not right because he does not, when startled, cast his hand before his eyes as Tom had habitually done. Escaping Canty the next day, the Prince tries to break into the Guildhall, where a royal banquet is in progress. He well might have been trampled to death by the jeering mob had he not been befriended by an ex-soldier named Miles Hendon. The two repair for the night to Hendon's room in a little inn on London Bridge. When he awakes the next morning, Hendon finds the Prince has gone. Chapters 14-16 shift the story back to Tom, who must now with the help of the whipping boy adjust to being king. Though Tom rapidly begins to feel a captive of the stuffy palace routine, he wins general admiration for his compassion in dealing with persons unfairly accused of crime.

The next thirteen chapters, 17-29, describe the continuing troubles of the Prince as he falls into the hands of a band of outlaws and probably would be put to death except that once more Miles Hendon rescues him. The two set out for Hendon Hall, where Miles discovers that all of his family have died except an evil brother, who has taken over the estate and married Hendon's former sweetheart. Miles and the Prince are thrown into jail as vagabonds. There the Prince has a chance to observe firsthand the horrors of English prison life. When free again, the two set off for London.

In chapter 30 the tale turns once more to the court where preparations are under way for the coronation. By this time Tom has begun to adjust to court life—and to like its ease and splendor. But during the great procession from the palace to Westminster Abbey for the crowning he sees his mother and "up flew his hand, palm outward, before his eyes." Recognizing the old involuntary gesture, his mother struggles up to the horse on which Tom is riding but is rudely snatched away by an officer of the king's guard. Although the encounter pricks Tom's conscience, he nevertheless enters the Abbey and is about to allow himself to be crowned when suddenly the real prince, who has been hiding in the Abbey all night, strides up the aisle to the throne. The guards would arrest him, but Tom intervenes and in a burst of natural goodness announces that the tattered intruder is the real king. Appropriately the final chapter of the book is entitled "Justice and Retribution." The new Edward VI makes Tom Canty the head of Christ's Hospital and Miles Hendon the Earl of Kent. Hendon's evil brother flees to the Continent where he dies, thus leaving his wife free to marry Miles, whom she has loved all along. The last sentence wraps fact and story together: "The reign of Edward VI was a singularly merciful one for those harsh times. Now that we are taking leave of him, let us try to keep this in our minds, to his credit."

Mark Twain said that the idea for the story came from Charlotte M. Yonge's *Little Duke,* a copy of which he discovered in the mid-1870s in his sister-in-law's house at Quarry Farm. Yonge's little Duke, Richard of Normandy, escapes from bondage at the court of King Louis IV and returns to Normandy where he is a much more compassionate ruler because of what he has endured. Apart from suggesting a line of action the Yonge book undoubtedly appealed to Twain because it shows how he might use the historical novel form to dramatize the moral development of a young boy, a subject he had already introduced in *Tom Sawyer* and later developed more fully in *Huckleberry Finn.* To turn his prince into a pauper he conjured up the idea of look-alikes whose stations in life become reversed when in jest they exchange clothes. After trying contemporary possibilities he selected Edward VI, the Tudor boy king who lived from 1537 to 1553 and Tom Canty of Offal Court out of Pudding Lane in London. To familiarize himself with the setting he began in the summer of 1876 to steep himself in the history and language of Tudor England. That he enjoyed the task hugely seems certain from the fact that its first literary consequence was the hilariously bawdy *1601* or *Conversation as It Was by the Fireside in the Time of the Tudors,* written to amuse Joseph Twichell, his minister. He continued his research in the summer of 1877 and by November, as an entry in his notebook indicates, he had the plan of the book well in mind. Then he put the partly written manuscript aside in order to prepare for the 1878-79 trip to Europe. It was not until he had finished *A Tramp Abroad* in January 1880 that he got back to *The Prince and the Pauper.* When he resumed work, he was more than ever convinced that he should use the book to show the need for compassionate rulers. So he dropped the idea of alternating more of less equally between the two boys, and began to concentrate on the Prince whose misfortunes offered a better chance to point out the cruelty of English laws and customs—and hence the need for reform.

Mark Twain finished the first draft of the work in September 1880, but spent the next four months enlarging and revising it. For advice and encouragement he turned to his family and to such friends as Howells, Twichell, Warner, Mrs. Fairbanks, and the young ladies of the Saturday Morning Club in Hartford, all of whom, as might be expected, enthusiastically approved not only of the book itself but also of Mark Twain's new interest in conventional and hence "respectable" fiction.

Finally satisfied, he gave the manuscript to James R. Osgood, a Boston publisher who had already brought out his small volume entitled *A True Story and the Recent Carnival of Crime* in 1877. He dropped the American Publishing Company, which had brought out his earlier books, because he was convinced that the company had been cheating him—and there is evidence to indicate that it had been. Osgood was a trade publisher, but for Twain he agreed to sell the book by the subscription method and to retain only a 7 ½ percent commission for himself. In effect, the arrangement made Twain his own publisher. Much care was taken with the illustrations, Twain insisting that the costumes and settings be accurate, and that the boys seem thirteen or fourteen years of age. Production proceeded with surprisingly few delays: the American edition appeared in December 1881, shortly after the English and Canadian editions. The sales, however, were disappointing, Twain blaming Osgood's inexperience as a subscription publisher.

His research for the book was surprisingly extensive. He investigated not only general histories of England but also works dealing more narrowly with English laws, customs, and life among the rogues and outlaws. For the language he relied upon specialized dictionaries as well as works by such writers as Shakespeare and Sir Walter Scott. As he found words that might be useful, he jotted them down in his notebook. He wanted, he said, to saturate himself in archaic English to a degree that would enable him "to do plausible imitations of it in a fairly easy and unlabored way."

As in previous books, his use of sources varied from copying a passage verbatim (without acknowledgement) to changing the facts to suit the fiction (also without acknowledgment). The description of Tom Canty's progression to Westminster Abbey to be crowned, for example, is largely Holinshed's description of the progress of Elizabeth. On the other hand, to make Edward a more credible character he changes his age from ten to about fourteen, and to make his moral improvement more striking he says nothing of the real Edward's religious intolerance. The book's chief contribution to our understanding of English history, however, is not factual information, but a sense of the extremes of life in Tudor England, the wealth and pageantry on the one hand and the poverty and suffering on the other.

With young readers especially in mind, Twain tells a lively story. He packs it with action, keeps the adventures of both boys moving at a rapid pace, and fashions a smashing climax in which everything hinges on the Prince's being able to remember where he cached the Great Seal. For readers thrilled by dime novels there are villains aplenty and one last-minute rescue after another. For those charmed by sentimental fiction there are tender scenes of youthful virtue and mother love. The story never slows down. Its steady pace is all the more remarkable because the basic design of shifting attention back and forth between the boys created at least three major problems for the author. The first was that the book could easily have broken into two stories unrelated except at beginning and end.

Though he makes the adventures of the two boys strikingly different, Twain holds them together with considerable skill. Tom Canty's miscues serve as constant reminders of how the Prince would have behaved, and many of the Prince's blunders bring to mind how much more easily Tom Canty could have gotten along. Additionally, Twain keeps the reader anxious about the fates of both boys even when concentrating on only one. He does this by breaking from the Prince to the Pauper (or vice versa) when events become ominous. The technique resembles that used today in multiplotted soap operas that leave television viewers worried about the fate of one heroine while watching the catastrophes befalling another. A second problem for Twain was that each boy when placed in an alien environment had to have information and protection in order to survive. Tom manages because he has learned to read while still in Offal Court, and has played at being a prince. Once in the palace he finds a book on court etiquette and is befriended by the Earl of Hertford and his whipping boy. The Prince, of course, is befriended by Miles Hendon. Finally, Twain encounters the problem faced by the author of every historical novel: how to adapt history to the story but yet in the end seem to leave history undisturbed. In the instance of *The Prince and the Pauper,* no matter how he alters the details of the life of Edward VI, Twain has to get him crowned on 20 February 1547. What Twain does is to use the fact of Edward's coronation to build suspense. Until the crown is about to be placed on Tom Canty's head he conceals from the reader the information that Edward is in Westminster Abbey. Even when he finally produces the Prince he intensifies the suspense by making it difficult for the Prince to prove his identity. At the last moment, however, everything gets resolved—just as it should in historical novels of the kind written by Charlotte Yonge and Sir Walter Scott.

Intentionally or not, some of Twain's more serious themes of the 1880s slip in. Several of these reveal him as the sentimentalist who accepts as articles of faith the miracles of mother love, the almost preternatural perception of young children, and the spirit of compassion that persists in individuals who have had at least a modicum of Christian nurture. Moreover, as a typical Victorian he suggests that goodness pays off both spiritually and materially. Yet for a work intended for young readers the book contains astonishing evidences of his growing cynicism. Mark Twain is not yet the mechanical determinist, but the doctrine is clearly taking hold of him. The characters are what they are principally because of their time and station in life. He shows himself, moreover, increasingly sour about the fickleness and cowardliness of crowds, and about the pervasiveness of human injustice, both legal and economic. Granted that Twain wanted to show how Edward VI learned through contact with the worst elements in English society, his rendering of those elements is at times so biting as to suggest that he was drawing on the "damned human race" theme that already lay at the heart of the half-completed *Huckleberry Finn.*

If *The Prince and the Pauper* contains hints of Mark Twain's more mature ideas, however, they remain shadows in the background. Up front the book is neither dark nor profound. Rather, it is what Twain meant it to be: a lively story for young readers fitted into the form of the conventional historical romance. Its action is engrossing, its fatherly tone is reassuring, and its language, liberally besprinkled with words such as "prithee" and "mayhap," suggests the atmosphere of ye olde time. The humor is definitely muted. Only once does the Western spirit erupt: when told that Henry VIII will not be buried for almost twenty days after his death, Tom Canty as the fake heir apparent asks, "Will he keep?" For his own generation Twain probably did prove with this work that he could be more than a humorist. But tastes have changed. Modern adults prefer the humorist. Many believe that, for an author who could write a *Tom Sawyer* and a *Huckleberry Finn, The Prince and the Pauper* was a waste of time. (pp. 81-7)

John C. Gerber, in his Mark Twain, *Twayne Publishers, 1988, 176 p.*

FURTHER READING

Bibliography

Tenney, Thomas Asa. *Mark Twain: A Reference Guide.* Reference Guides in Literature, edited by Ronald Gottesman and Joseph Katz. Boston: G. K. Hall & Co., 1977, 443 p.
   Bibliography of writings about Twain through 1974.

Biography

Hill, Hamlin. *Mark Twain: God's Fool.* New York: Harper & Row, 1973, 308 p.
   Detailed biography of the last decade of Twain's life based on unpublished material from the papers of Mark Twain. Hill portrays Twain's last years as a tragedy of declining artistic powers and growing bitterness.

Kaplan, Justin. *Mr. Clemens and Mark Twain: A Biography.* New York: Simon and Schuster, 1966, 424 p.
   A well-researched biography, emphasizing conflicting aspects of Twain's personality.

Paine, Albert Bigelow. *Mark Twain: A Biography—The Personal and Literary Life of Samuel Langhorne Clemens.* 3 vols. New York: Harper & Brothers Publishers, 1912.
   Authorized biography. The volume contains much valuable material on Twain but is criticized by some scholars as idealized.

Wagenknecht, Edward. *Mark Twain: The Man and His Work.* 3rd rev. ed. Norman: University of Oklahoma Press, 1967, 302 p.
   An essential biographical and critical study of Twain and his outlook in which the author demonstrates extensive knowledge of Twain criticism through 1960 and includes valuable footnotes and bibliographies.

Criticism

Anderson, Frederick, ed. *Mark Twain: The Critical Heritage.* New York: Barnes & Noble, 1971, 347 p.
   Includes reprinted early reviews of *The Prince and the Pauper.*

Andrews, Kenneth R. "The Nook Farm Writers and the Genteel Tradition." In his *Nook Farm: Mark Twain's Hartford Circle,* pp. 188-98. Cambridge: Harvard University Press, 1950.
   Discusses how Twain's friends and acquaintances in Hartford, Connecticut, influenced the composition of *The Prince and the Pauper.*

Review of *The Prince and the Pauper,* by Mark Twain. *The Athenaeum,* No. 2,826 (24 December 1881): 849.
   Brief, unfavorable review of *The Prince and the Pauper* in which the critic comments: "To the innumerable admirers of *Roughing It* and *A Tramp Abroad, The Prince and the Pauper* is likely to prove a heavy disappointment. The author, a noted representative of American humour, has essayed to achieve a serious book. The consequences are at once disastrous and amazing. The volume, which deals with England in the days of Edward VI, and is announced as 'A Tale for Young People of all Ages,' is only to be described as some four hundred pages of careful tediousness, mitigated by occasional flashes of unintentional and unconscious fun."

Baetzhold, Howard G. "Mark Twain's *The Prince and the Pauper.*" *Notes and Queries* 1 (n.s.), No. 9 (September 1954): 401-03.
   Argues that Twain's primary source of inspiration for *The Prince and the Pauper* was Charlotte M. Yonge's *The Little Duke* (1854) and not her *The Prince and the Page* (1865) as previously argued by Albert Bigelow Paine, Twain's official biographer.

Duram, James C. "Mark Twain and the Middle Ages." *Wichita State University Bulletin* XLVII, No. 3 (August 1971): 1-16.
   Focuses on Twain's philosophy of history and views on the Middle Ages as expressed in *The Prince and the Pauper, A Connecticut Yankee in King Arthur's Court, Per-*

sonal Recollections of Joan of Arc, and The Mysterious Stranger.

Gale, Robert L. "*The Prince and the Pauper* and *King Lear*." *The Mark Twain Journal* XII, No. 1 (Spring 1963): 14-17.

Discusses similarities "in character relations, in plot situations, and in ultimate ethical import" between *The Prince and the Pauper* and William Shakespeare's *King Lear*.

Review of *The Prince and the Pauper*, by Mark Twain. *Harper's New Monthly Magazine* LXIV, No. CCCLXXXII (March 1882): 634-35.

Early, favorable review in which the critic concludes: "The tale is full of romantic surprises, and besides being rich in historical facts and teachings, is charged with a generous and ennobling moral."

McKeithan, D. M. "More about Mark Twain's War with English Critics of America." *Modern Language Notes* LXIII, No. 4 (April 1948): 221-28.

Brief discussion of Twain's satirical presentation of the English monarchy in *The Prince and the Pauper*.

Salamo, Lin. Introduction to *The Prince and the Pauper*, by Mark Twain, pp. 1-25. Edited by Victor Fischer and Lin Salamo. Berkeley: Iowa Center for Textual Studies/ University of California Press, 1979.

Discusses the composition, publication, critical reception, and historical sources of *The Prince and the Pauper*.

Sloane, David E. E. "Humor and Social Criticism: *The Gilded Age* and *The Prince and the Pauper*." In his *Mark Twain as Literary Comedian*, pp. 104-27. Baton Rouge: Louisiana State University Press, 1979.

Discusses Twain's blend of comic devices, narration, and social satire in *The Gilded Age* and *The Prince and the Pauper*.

Smith, Henry Nash, and Gibson, William M., eds. *Mark Twain—Howells Letters: The Correspondence of Samuel L. Clemens and William D. Howells, 1872-1910*. 2 vols. Cambridge: Harvard University Press, Belknap Press, 1960.

Reprints correspondence between Twain and Howells in which they discuss *The Prince and the Pauper*. The appendix includes notes on the omitted whipping-boy episode and a discussion of Miles Hendon's ballad.

Review of *The Prince and the Pauper*, by Mark Twain. *The Westminster Review* LXI, No. 2 (April 1882): 576.

Brief unfavorable review of *The Prince and the Pauper*. The critic comments: "It is somewhat startling to find the writer who has made himself famous as Mark Twain turning from comic accounts of travel and general American buffoonery to the task of writing a serious historical novel. . . . The story has its merits, though it is a little long, and at times threatens to be tedious. On the whole, Mr. Mark Twain was more at home in his earlier literary efforts."

Additional coverage of Twain's life and career is contained in the following sources published by Gale Research: *Concise Dictionary of American Literary Biography, 1865-1917; Contemporary Authors*, Vols. 104, 135; *Dictionary of Literary Biography*, Vols. 11, 12, 23, 64, 74; *Short Story Criticism*, Vol. 6; *Twentieth-Century Literary Criticism*, Vols. 6, 12, 19, 36; *World Literature Criticism*; and *Yesterday's Authors of Books for Children*, Vol 2.

Charlotte Yonge
1823-1901

(Full name Charlotte Mary Yonge) English novelist, historian, biographer, and essayist.

INTRODUCTION

Yonge was the most popular and prolific novelist associated with the Oxford Movement, also known as the Tractarian Movement or Anglo-Catholic Revival. Led by John Henry (later Cardinal) Newman, this group resisted the trend toward liberalism in the Church of England during the mid-nineteenth century, urging a return to the stricter doctrines and more elaborate rituals derived from Roman Catholicism. Although Yonge wrote nearly two hundred works, including histories, juvenile novels, historical romances, biographies, and essays on religious topics, she is best remembered for novels that portray middle-class domestic life of the mid-Victorian era.

Yonge was born to an upper middle-class family in the Hampshire village of Otterbourne. Educated at home by her parents, she received instruction in ancient and modern languages, history, literature, and theology. At fifteen, Yonge was prepared for confirmation by the theologian John Keble, the vicar of a nearby church. Keble, whose 1833 sermon on "national apostasy" had led to the establishment of the Oxford Movement, inspired in Yonge an ardent religious fervor. Keble became her literary mentor and, along with her father, edited all her manuscripts until his death in 1866. Although her family initially disapproved of her desire to become a writer, as it was considered socially improper for a woman to profit from her own labor, they agreed to let Yonge continue writing as long as all proceeds were contributed to missionary activities. Yonge began publishing her short stories in 1842, and in 1851 founded *The Monthly Packet,* a magazine she edited for nearly half a century and in which many of her novels were serialized. Following the publication of *The Heir of Redclyffe* in 1853, she became a highly popular novelist. Yonge rarely left the village of her birth, and her increasing isolation and unquestioning adherence to religious dogma are widely considered to have limited the quality of her later works. She died in 1901.

Yonge's novels have been praised for documenting the tensions, rivalries, and intense affections in Victorian family life. *The Heir of Redclyffe,* her best known novel, contrasts Sir Guy Morville, a virtuous hero whose only flaw is his quick temper, with Philip, his self-righteous cousin. Although betrayed by Philip, Sir Guy overcomes his desire for revenge and ultimately dies of a fever he contracts while nursing his cousin through an illness. Celebrating traditional Christian ideals of piety, self-sacrifice, and devotion to family, *The Heir of Redclyffe* established Yonge's reputation as a creator of vivid portraits of middle-class family life from the perspective of young or adolescent characters who resolve their religious doubts. For example, the central event in *The Daisy Chain; or, Aspira-*

tions, which revolves around a virtuous Catholic family typical of Yonge's works, concerns whether or not twelve-year-old Harry May will be spiritually, emotionally, and intellectually prepared for his religious confirmation. Critics have commented that Yonge's talent lay in her ability to explore religious subject matter through believable characters rather than explicit didacticism. According to Gillian Avery, Yonge's domestic novels remain her most effective works because "her gift for characterization, for sketching a social background, shines out and makes them charming evocations of a vanished way of life."

PRINCIPAL WORKS

Abbey Church; or, Self-control and Self-conceit (novel) 1844
Scenes and Characters; or, Eighteen Months at Beechcroft (novel) 1847
Kings of England: A History for Young Children (history) 1848

The Two Guardians; or, Home in this World (novel) 1852
The Heir of Redclyffe (novel) 1853
The Castle Builders; or, The Deferred Confirmation (novel) 1854
Heartsease; or, The Brother's Wife. 2 vols. (novel) 1854
The Little Duke; or, Richard the Fearless (novel) 1854
The Daisy Chain; or, Aspirations (novel) 1856
Dynevor Terrace; or, The Clue of Life. 2 vols. (novel) 1857
Hopes and Fears; or, Scenes from the Life of a Spinster. 2 vols. (novel) 1860
The Young Stepmother; or, A Chronicle of Mistakes. 2 vols. (novel) 1861
The Trial: More Links of the Daisy Chain (novel) 1864
The Clever Woman of the Family (novel) 1865
The Dove in the Eagle's Nest. 2 vols. (novel) 1866
The Chaplet of Pearls; or, The White and Black Ribaumont: A Romance of French History, 1572 (novel) 1868
The Caged Lion (novel) 1870
Life of John Coleridge Patteson, Missionary Bishop of the Melanesian Islands. 2 vols. (biography) 1873
The Pillars of the House; or, Under Wode, Under Rode. 4 vols. (novel) 1873
The Three Brides (novel) 1876
A History of France (history) 1879
Unknown to History: A Story of the Captivity of Mary of Scotland (novel) 1882
A Reputed Changeling; or, Three Seventh Years Two Centuries Ago (novel) 1889

CRITICISM

The National Review (essay date 1861)

[*In the following essay, the anonymous critic suggests that Yonge's characters are limited in their development by her strict adherence to religious and ethical dogma.*]

The key-note to Miss Yonge's pictures of life is to be found in this fact: that with much insight into character, with a pure ideal enthusiasm, and strong moral convictions, she is utterly destitute of the speculative instinct. Feeling profoundly that true life is a service and a trust, she is yet sensible of no obligation to examine for herself the nature of that service and the conditions of that trust, and is perfectly content to accept the frame-work of her conception from an external dogmatic source. Hence an anomaly which runs through her whole works. As long as her theme relates to the free expansiveness of character in its purely individual aspects, she usually succeeds. The scene of her tales is generally domestic life, and a great deal of this admits of the free development of character and action. Miss Yonge's great wealth of material (which would often be improved by condensation), and her appreciation of the light and humorous aspects of character, enable her to paint such life with much felicity. But the free play of her moral idealism is only permitted within the limits marked out by certain dogmatic rules. The weight of necessity against which the free-will of her heroes has to contend, is not made up only by their own and others' faults and incapacities, but is frightfully increased by a whole world of sacred conventionalisms, which bar the paths of life in every direction. To take a purely domestic instance: she represents parents as endowed with an absolute right to forbid their children's marriages. In ***Dynevor Terrace*** the authority of a disgracefully bad man is deemed sufficient to forbid the marriage of a grown-up and very discreet daughter; and her total resignation of her own wishes is extolled as a noble act of duty. That the period of authoritative control over a child's actions is ordained for the protection and development of the child's individuality, and ceases when that individuality is fully matured,—after which any collision of wishes or wills falls to the province of individual judgment to decide in each special case,—would appear to Miss Yonge a base heresy. The right to dispose of oneself, or to *be* oneself, is, with her, only to be held on condition of the authoritative sanction of others; and to the terrible waste of moral strength thence resulting she is blind, regarding only the suffering caused to the inclinations. But Miss Yonge's active imagination is not content without illustrating her views on these points in detail; and so she has given us the history of a young lady who came to grief by being too independent. Laura Edmonstone, in the ***Heir of Redclyffe,*** forms an engagement with her cousin Philip, a frequent visitor at her father's house, whom she knows to be held by her parents in the highest esteem. Being too poor to marry, they agree to keep the affair to themselves till such time as he shall be able to offer her a home; and this is treated by the author as one of the most heinous of sins, embittering all their future lives, long after they are forgiven and married! That it would have been more frank and filial in Laura to have confided in her mother, and that Philip's reasons for silence are mostly selfish, is true enough; but the author's view of the matter is extravagant beyond measure. It is entirely the old feudal notion, that in the father resided the right to give or withhold the daughter's hand, and that in giving it herself she committed an act of petty treason. And here we see the peculiar effect which such an unmoral (or immoral?) dogma produces on a mind so naturally ethical and ideal as Miss Yonge's. Accepting this feudality as a truth, she feels bound to show how it worked, and she consequently infuses all manner of morbid misery into the minds of the unhappy lovers, whereby they are brought at last to repentance, but—so rules the Nemesis—never to full happiness as long as they live. Thus her very absence of speculative faculty leads her into that morbid introspectiveness which is the worst form of ethical speculation.

Passing from the domestic circle to that of society at large, we see that Miss Yonge gives us little beyond the ordinary routine of life. Not that she is a mere conventionalist in taste or aspiration; she thoroughly enjoys an unconventional character, and delights to picture her heroes as jesting merrily over the commonplaces of society and character. She has a quick eye for the different shades of intellectual power and perceptiveness which characterise different minds; she can paint the stolidity of mere routinists, the placid goodness of the unimaginative, and the energetic activity of awakened, living minds, with real power and discrimination. But whether she does, or does not, endow her heroes with the intellectual and moral capacity which would enable them to transcend the conventions of life, the practical result always comes out the same. They must fit into the hierarchical order of society which Miss Yonge has been taught to accept, and must never alter it in any direction. With all her enthusiasm for individual elevation of mind, she has no perception of the fact, that half the beauty and spirit of the noblest institutions of society has sprung from the *free play* of individual excellence; and she represents her most intellectual heroes as perfectly content under repressions which would, by any mind of more speculative faculty than her own, be felt as intolerable.

The same original defect is visible in the narrow views and partial interest which she manifests concerning all those spheres of life where something more than merely individual motives is called into play. Of history she is extremely fond, but her allusions to it are always to the romantic or striking deeds of individuals; there is no sign that she enters into the development of great national or social growths of life or thought, except when they happen to be connected with the fortunes or misfortunes of her favourite hierarchical system. Thus her idealities are apt to be tinged with an archaic narrowness; and while she does full justice to the lofty *imperativeness* of the ethical nature, she constantly checks its expansiveness. She is herself partially aware of this, and endeavours to meet the difficulty by making one of her heroes say that his "trust is in *the narrow mind, the only expansive one.* . . . The heart may be wide, but the mind must be so far narrow that it will accept only the one right, not the many wrong. Is not the real evil the judging people harshly because their ways are not the same—not the being sure that the one way is the only right!

Here we see the shadow of the great concrete image of perfection which holds dominion over our author's mind. If there be only *one* right way, of course there must be some external sign to distinguish it from the many wrong ways. But how shall an unspeculative mind discover those signs? "Thinking for themselves," as she observes in *Dynevor Terrace,* "has been fatal to many;" at any rate, she herself has no impulse of that sort, and thus her imagination and conscience are taken captive by the lofty assumptions of the system into which she was born; and she has learnt to believe that to identify with that system the sacredness of the moral instincts and the veracity of the religious intuitions, is the one only way to preserve either faith or virtue. So crude are her notions of what speculative truth really is, that she regards it as not only (as the Cambridge tutor said of Paley's Christianity) "capable of being written out at examinations," but of being stated and learned, once for all, even by the most undeveloped minds. She represents an intelligent savage as asking "little easy questions about the Belief,"—nothing more being requisite, apparently, than for the catechumen to be told what he was to believe. She even advocates, in the *Daisy Chain,* the practice that young children should learn by rote creeds and prayers which are admitted to be beyond their understanding, in order that the *form of words* may be familiar to them against the time when the meaning thereof shall become apprehensible. In short, she has, up to a very recent period, preached Anglicanism *pur et simple,* as the one right way under heaven whereby we may be saved. No Catholic of the middle ages could ignore more loftily than she the existence of any true moral life external to the Church. For her the religious world consisted of "the fold," and the wild moors outside, where "Dissent" was rampant. With the latter she had no call to deal; and all the life on which she dwelt with interest lay within the pale of her own communion. But there was always a vigour and discernment in her pictures which unconsciously implied a wider basis of spiritual life than such absolute orthodoxy can supply, and by degrees she seems to have become so far aware of the fact as to accord to it a certain degree of acknowledgment. In the *Heir of Redclyffe,* her [fourth] novel, the author's bias was all on the side of unspeculative religious dependence and Anglican æsthetics, as against self-reliance and scientific study. In her latest novel, *Hopes and Fears,* the bias is as plainly set in the opposite direction—within limits, of course, in both cases, but with an unmistakable intention in each. Nor is it merely the giving fair play to different sides of truth; it is a real modification of the author's theory of life. She distinctly contrasts the old high-church school, "who fed on Scott, Wordsworth, and Fouqué; took their theology from the *British Critic,* and their taste from Pugin; and moulded their opinions and practice on the past,"—with "the new generation, that of Kingsley, Tennyson, Ruskin, and the *Saturday Review,*"—in a manner that implies her own greater sympathy with the latter; while every reader of her earlier tales, especially of the *Heir of Redclyffe,* must be aware that the older school is there held up as supplying the proper set of preferences for right-minded people. Yet although we are glad to see her mental horizon enlarged, we regret that, after the manner of new converts, she seems scarcely able to deal justly or generously with the position she has left. We like her very much better in her old creed than in her new one, and find her latest novel [*Hopes and Fears; or, Scenes from the Life of a Spinster*] feeble.

The heroine is Honora Charlecote, an affectionate and enthusiastic woman, who, having been deserted by her early idol, Owen Sandbrook, devotes herself, at his death, to the education of his orphan children, Owen and Lucilla. She brings them up, to the best of her ability, in the very way that Miss Yonge has hitherto represented as right and fit,—in a kindly, conscientious high-church training. But it signally fails. Lucilla, a flirt and a vixen from childhood, turns out a fast young lady (inundating the book with a profusion of unwomanly slang), runs completely loose from her guardian's care, and after passing through divers troubles, is restored in some degree to a better mind, and (to the relief of her friends and the reader) settles abroad. Owen, her brother, very impressible and amiable by nature, becomes a pattern of early piety; goes wrong as soon as he gets to college; and, after breaking the heart of his wife, and doing nearly the same for poor Honora, finally repents, and comes back for good. And the author gives us to understand that the undiscriminating reverence inculcated by Honora for all that bore the semblance of religion was one main cause of Owen's downfall, reacting, as it did, in indiscriminate doubt, as soon as he discovered that she was not infallible. As he says, in a sort of confession to her, near the close of the story:

> "I simulated the motions [in childhood] to myself and every one else, and there was a grain of reality, after all; but neither you nor I ever knew how much was mere imitation and personal influence. When I outgrew implicit faith in *you,* I am afraid my higher faith went with it; first through recklessness, then through questioning. After believing more than enough, the transition is easy to doubting what is worthy of credit at all." "From superstition to rationalism." "Yes; overdoing articles of faith and observances, while the mind and conscience are young and tender, brings a dangerous reaction when liberty and independent reflection begin." "But, Owen, I may have overdone observances, yet I did not teach superstitions," said Honora. "Not consciously," said Owen. "You meant to teach me dogmatically only what you absolutely believed yourself. But you did not know how boundless is a child's readiness to accept what comes as from a spiritual authority, or you would have drawn the line more strongly between doctrine and opinion, fact and allegory, the true and the edifying." "In effect, I treated you as the Romish Church began by doing to the populace." "Exactly so. Like the mediæval populace, I took legend for fact; and like the modern populace, doubted of the whole together, instead of sifting. There is my confession, Honora dear. I know you are happier for hearing it in full; but remember, my errors are not chargeable upon you. If I had ever been true towards myself or you, and acted out what I thought I felt, I should have had the personal experience that would have protected the truth when the pretty superstructure began to pass away."

This, taken alone, is just and sensible. But when we meet with it in such a quarter as the present, we begin to ask in what relation it stands to the rest of the representation. Does the author mean that only the bare elements of Church doctrine,—that which the teacher "absolutely believes,"—are to be taught dogmatically, and the superstructure given or withheld according to the specialities of each case? Yet she must surely be aware that the "absolute beliefs" of one Church party are the open questions, or even the dangerous heresies, of another; and how, then, is the line to be drawn between the necessarily dogmatic and the merely "edifying," or unnecessary, teaching? On this vital point she leaves us wholly in the dark, and instead of clearly showing how Honora erred, she resorts to the aid of caricature to produce the impression of her heroine's shortcomings. The whole portraiture is distorted. It is as if the author were struggling between her own sympathy for Honora, and her keen sense of the ridiculous light in which such a character would appear to clever critics of the present day; and as if, unable to disentangle the complexities she has suggested, she contented herself with sketching now from one point of view, and now from another, aiming thus to give the impression that she appreciates both, but in reality failing signally to give any distinct picture.

Another unsatisfactory trait is the mysterious talk in which the author and her characters indulge respecting Honora's presumption in adopting the orphan Sandbrooks. She had no other tie or occupation, and they had no fit home to go to; and yet the author seems to think that, because they were not her own children, it was in some way self-seeking to take charge of them. "Fond affection led her to adopt a work to which Providence had not called her, and to which she was therefore unequal." (Are all mothers equal to the wise training of their children?) And upon her non-relationship to her wards, and her adherence to old high-church views, the author lays the burden of nearly all their sins and misdemeanours, though the brief record of their childhood's training by no means justifies that assumption. Miss Yonge does, indeed, tell us that Honora was not a good judge of character, and was a timid routinist, certainly two disqualifications for the training of children. But why confuse the main question of the tale with these disturbing elements? No rational person doubts that education requires capacity in the educator. If Miss Yonge had really mastered the theme whose suggestion makes the chief interest of the book, viz. how far a thoroughly old high-church education is likely to react injuriously on the mind and morals when the bonds of early discipline are relaxed, she would have given us an instance in which the *other* elements of educational training were fully equal to the average, so that the specially high-church element might stand out distinctly for our study. It would be utterly unfair to judge of any system by a representative thereof whom the author chooses, *on other grounds,* to put ignominiously in the wrong.

In contrast to Owen and Lucilla Sandbrook, we have Robert and Phœbe Fulmort, a brother and sister whom Honora only benefits casually (not loving them enough to do them harm, according to the author's theory), but who derive from her the softening and spiritualising influences needed to supplement the hard rationalistic tendencies of their own home. These two characters give to the book almost the only sunshine which enlivens it. The rest of the Fulmort family are extremely disagreeable, and not very natural; and the number of odious people who infest this novel makes it altogether far from pleasant reading. It is also sadly spun out, and is in every way inferior to her other tales, even to **Dynevor Terrace,** which was decidedly not equal to its predecessors. There is, however, one remarkable episode in **Hopes and Fears,** which deserves notice as an honest attempt to deal with a very deep subject. We have already spoken of the somewhat modified point of view from which our author paints the Anglicanism of Honora. In the character of Miss Fennimore, the Unitarian governess of the young Fulmorts, she gives us a somewhat modified picture of "dissent." Her previous allusions to this subject were very curious. In her first tale of **Abbey Church** she set her face against mechanics' institutions, because they encouraged lectures on geology, in which the ages of the antediluvian patriarchs were regarded as apocryphal. In the **Two Guardians,** the model guardian would not allow a farm of his ward's to be leased to a Dissenter, lest a chapel should be built on it; and, in the **Castle-Builders,** the youth who will not allow of a shadow of disrespect to a rather ungenial clergyman, is represented as perfectly justified in making jokes about dissenting Bible-readers and Evangelical tracts. But by degrees, though not speculative herself, Miss Yonge has come to see that others may be so, to whom, whatever their errors, she cannot any longer refuse the praise of sincerity. The first indication of this was seen in an episode in the *Daisy Chain,* where Norman, the intellectual member of the family, thus describes his experience to his sister Ethel:

> "I am not like the simple and dutiful, who are not fretted or perplexed." "Perplexed?" repeated Ethel. "It is not so now," he replied. "God forbid! But where better men have been led astray, I have been bewildered, till, Ethel, I have felt as if the ground were slipping from beneath my feet, and I have only been able to hide my eyes, and entreat that I might know the truth." "You knew it," said Ethel, looking pale, and gazing searchingly at him. "I did, I do; but it was a time of misery, when, for my presumption, I suppose, I was allowed to doubt whether it were the truth."
>
> Ethel recoiled, but came nearer, saying very low, "It is past." "Yes, thank Him who is Truth. You all saved me, though you did not know it." "When was this?" she asked timidly. "The worst time was before the long vacation. They told me I ought to read this book and that. Harvey Anderson used to come primed with arguments. I could always overthrow them; but when I came to glory in doing so, perhaps I prayed less. Any way, they left a sting. It might be that I doubted my own sincerity, from knowing that I had got to argue, chiefly because I liked to be looked on as a champion."
>
> Ethel saw the truth of what her friend had said of the morbid habit of self-contemplation. "I read, and I mystified myself. The better I talked, the more my own convictions failed me; and by the time you came up to Oxford, I knew how you would have shrunk from him who was your pride, if you could have seen into the secrets beneath."
>
> Ethel took hold of his hand. "You seemed bright," she said. "It melted like a bad dream before—before the humming-bird [Meta Rivers], and with my father. It was weeks ere I dared to face the subject again." "How could you? Was it safe?" "I could not have gone on as I was. Sometimes the sight of my father, or the mountains and lakes in Scotland, or—or things at the Grange, would bring peace back; but there were dark hours, and *I knew that there could be no comfort till I had examined and fought it out.*" "I suppose examination was right," said Ethel, "for a man, and defender of the faith. I should only have tried to pray the terrible feeling away. But I can't tell how it feels." "Worse than you have power to imagine," said Norman, shuddering. "It is over now. I worked out their fallacies, and went over the reasoning on our side." "And prayed," said Ethel. "Indeed I did; and the confidence returned, firmer, I hope, than ever. It had never gone for a whole day."
>
> Ethel breathed freely. "It was life or death," she said, "and we never knew it!" "Perhaps not; but I knew your prayers were angel-wings ever round me. And far more than argument was the thought of my father's heart-whole Christian love and strength." "Norman, you believed, all the time, with your heart. This was only a bewilderment of your intellect." "I think you are right," said Norman. "To me the doubt was cruel agony; not the amusement it seems to some." "Because our dear home has made the truth our joy, our union," said Ethel. "And you are sure the cloud is gone, and for ever?" she still asked anxiously.
>
> He stood still. "For ever, I trust," he said. "I hold the faith of my childhood in all its fullness, as surely as—as ever I loved my mother and Harry." "I know you do," said Ethel. "It was only a bad dream." *"I hope I may be forgiven for it,"* said Norman. *"I do not know how far it was sin."*

The moral of this is evidently, that, although it is most undesirable for any mind to be obliged to test the foundations of its own faith, yet that one who is strong enough and true enough to do so effectually, will at last find "the [Anglican] faith of his childhood in all its fullness" confirmed by reasoning and historical research. In *Hopes and Fears* we are shown a somewhat similar process; but in this instance the inquirer starts from the point of "dissent," and the attraction towards the Church, instead of being the charm of early association, consists in the superior moral and spiritual influence represented as emanating from a church-trained character. Miss Fennimore (who, by the way, is a much more distinctly-drawn character than her opposite, Honora) thus describes her mental history to Robert Fulmort, the clerical brother of her pupils:

> She proceeded to say that her parents had been professed Unitarians, her mother loving and devout to the hereditary faith, beyond which she had never looked. "Mr. Fulmort," she said, "nothing will approve itself to me that condemns my mother."
>
> He began to say that often where there was no wilful rejection of truth, saving grace and faith might be vouchsafed.
>
> "You are charitable," she answered, in a tone like sarcasm, and went on. Her father, a literary man of high ability, set aside from work by ill health, thought himself above creeds. He had given his daughter a man's education, had read many argumentative books with her, and had died, leaving her liberally and devoutly inclined in the spirit of Pope's universal prayer, "Jehovah, Jove, or Lord." It was all aspiration to the Lord of nature, the forms, adaptations to humanity, kaleidoscope shapes of half-comprehended fragments, each with its own beauty, and only becoming worthy of reprobation when they permitted moral vices, among which she counted intolerance.
>
> What she thought reasonable—Christianity, modified by the world's progress—was her tenet, and she had no scruple in partaking in any act of worship; while naturally conscientious, and loving all the virtues, she viewed the terrors of religion as the scourge of the grovelling and superstitious; or if suffering existed at all, it could

be only as expiation, conducting to a condition of high intellect and perfect morality. No other view, least of all that of a vicarious atonement, seemed to her worthy of the beneficence of the God whom she had set up for herself.

Thus she had rested for twenty years; but of late she had been dissatisfied. Living with Phœbe, "though the child was not naturally intellectual," there was no avoiding the impression that what she acted and rested on was substantial truth. "The same with others," said Miss Fennimore, meaning her auditor himself. "And, again, I cannot but feel that devotion to any system of faith is the restraint that Bertha is deficient in, and that this is probably owing to my own tone. These examples have led me to go over the former ground in the course of the present spring: and it has struck me that if the Divine Being be not the mere abstraction I once supposed, it is consistent to believe that He has a character and will,—individuality, in short,—so that there might be one single revelation of absolute truth. When I mark what I can only call a supernatural influence on an individual character, I view it as an evidence in favour of the system that produced it. . . . . Till I came here, I never fully beheld the growth and development of character. I found that, whereas all I could do for Phœbe was to give her method and information, leaving alone the higher graces elsewhere derived, with Bertha my efforts were inadequate to supply any motive for overcoming her natural defects." . . . . "There would be great rest in being able to accept all that you and she do," Miss Fennimore answered, with a sigh, "in finding an unchanging answer to 'What is truth?' Yet even your Gospel leaves that question unanswered." "Unanswered to Pilate; but those who are true find the truth; and I verily trust that your eyes will become cleared to find it. Miss Fennimore, you know that I am unready and weak in argument, and you have often left me no refuge but my positive conviction; but I can refer you to those who are strong. If I can help you by carrying your difficulties to others, or by pointing out books, I should rejoice." "You cannot argue—you can only act," said Miss Fennimore, smiling, as a message called him away.

Now if "saving faith and grace may be vouchsafed" to one who is without the knowledge of "the absolute truth," is it not thereby implied that our intellectual belief *about* God, and our personal relations *with* Him, are two distinct things, of which the latter alone is of vital importance? And if so, why should Miss Fennimore be right in regarding that trustful piety in her Anglican pupil as evidence of a true creed, which she did not so regard in the case of her Unitarian mother? Next, we would ask, why should the Creator's individuality of "character and will" imply his making "one single revelation of absolute truth," *i.e.* of knowledge concerning Himself? When we use the word "individuality," as applied to God, we should not forget that his is a unique individuality, whose combination with the fullness of Infinite Being must render inapplicable some of those analogies of individuality which our finite consciousness suggests. What He is in Himself we cannot wholly grasp; we can only know what He tells us, either through (what we call) the natural action of our faculties, or through special communications. In both cases our knowledge must be limited by the capacity which has been given to us; and it is plain, as a matter of fact, that every man's faith, viz. that which makes his real religion, varies more or less from that of other men. Votaries of one creed, disciples of one teacher, members of one spiritual fold, may or may not acquiesce intellectually in one statement of theological doctrine, but practically the tone of their thoughts and feelings concerning unseen realities will be found to vary in each case, according to the temperament, culture, and capacity of each individual,—as our author clearly sees and well depicts. Why, then, should it be *a priori* so unlikely that partial revelations should have been given to different worshipers, according to the special needs of different nations, ages, and temperaments? How could any single revelation possibly communicate all the (comprehensible) truth concerning God to any one finite intelligence?

But, it will be replied, that some intellectual conception of God must accompany every act of spiritual communion with Him. Undoubtedly; but such a conception is merely a negative condition of such communion. There is nothing quickening in the *mere* knowledge of divine things, unaccompanied by the love of them. What, then, is the meaning of this high *spiritual* estimate of a complete and definite theological chart of belief, which is supposed to sum up all that man has known or can know concerning God? It arises from what may be called an Ecclesiastical Realism; a belief that there are certain divine events, past and future, without a knowledge of which we cannot enter into full relations with our Creator, nor even be regarded by Him as truly his children. That we have a present grasp of his love, and strenuously endeavour to live in his service, is not enough for trust and peace; we must also have mastered a complicated theological narrative. Phœbe's dying mother thus addresses her:

> "Phœbe, you know more than I do; you don't think God will be hard with me, do you? I am such a poor creature; but there is the blood that takes away sin." "Dear mother, that is the blessed trust." *The truth* flashed upon Miss Fennimore, as she watched their faces.

And the central point of this Levitical theory is held by our author in all its integrity. Bertha, Miss Fennimore's sceptical pupil, falling into despair at the desertion of her lover, endeavours to commit suicide, but repents before the act is completed. Struggling under a deep sense of shame, and weakened by illness, she is a prey to horrible dreams; and this is the Christian manner in which she is dealt with:

> "A dream, only a dream!" she murmured, recovering consciousness. "What was only a dream?" . . . Miss Fennimore gathered it at last, and it made her spirit quake, for it referred to the terrors beyond the grave. Yet she firmly answered, "Such impressions may not always result from weakness." "I thought," cried Bertha, rising on her elbow, "I thought that an advanced state of civilisation dispenses with sectarian, I

mean superstitious, literal threats." "No civilisation can change those decrees, nor make them unmerited,' said Miss Fennimore, sadly. "How?" repeated Bertha, frowning. "You, too! you don't mean that? You are not one of the narrow minds that want to doom their fellow-creatures for ever?" Her eyes had grown large, round, and bright, and she clutched Miss Fennimore's hand, gasping, "Say; not for ever!" "My poor child, did I ever teach you it was not?" "You thought so!" cried Bertha. "Enlightened people think so. Oh, say, only say it does not last!" "Bertha, I cannot. God forgive me for the falsehoods to which I led you, the realities I put aside from you."

Bertha gave a cry of anguish, and sank back exhausted, damps of terror on her brow; but she presently cried out, "If it would not last! I can't bear the thought! I can't bear to live, but I can't die! Oh! who will save me?" To Miss Fennimore's lips rose the words of St. Paul to the jailor. "Believe! believe!" cried Bertha, petulantly; "believe what?" "Believe that He gave his life to purchase your safety and mine through that eternity." And Miss Fennimore sank on her knees, weeping and hiding her face. The words which she had gazed at, and listened to, in vain longing, had, even as she imparted them, touched herself in their fullness. She had seen the face of Truth, when, at Mrs. Fulmort's death-bed, she had heard Phœbe speak of the blood that cleanseth from all sin. Then it had been a moment's glimpse. She had sought it earnestly ever since, and at length it had come to nestle within her own bosom. It was not sight, it was touch; it was embracing and holding fast. Alas, the sight was hidden from Bertha. She moodily turned aside in vexation, *as though her last trust had failed her.* In vain did Miss Fennimore, feeling that she had led her to the brink of an abyss of depth unknown, till she was tottering on the verge, lavish on her the most tender cares. They were requited with resentful gloom, that the governess felt to be so just to herself that she would hardly have been able to lift up her head, but for the new reliance that gave place to deepening contrition.

We are to understand, then, that a soul painfully conscious of its sins, and only asking that their punishment should at length be terminated by God's pardon, is to be thrust over the precipice for ever, unless it can accept a statement of historical facts which, whether true or false, is, at the time, *wholly external to its personal moral consciousness.* Without this God cannot forgive her. That a penitent acceptance of the deserved punishment for our sins can lead to ultimate restoration, is one of the "falsehoods" which the governess had "put in the place of realities;" the *realities* of God's hatred of repentant sinners, and acquiescence in the eternal agony of souls that are longing to return to Him. Can this be the deeper personal revelation capable of satisfying a mind worn out with mere scientific abstractions, and yearning for direct communion with the Author of Life? Can this be the Gospel, of which such a seeker could say to its votaries, *"There would be great rest in being able to accept all that you do!"*

Thus it will be seen that although Miss Yonge has learnt greater charity for dissentients, and allows a larger sphere than before to the reasoning faculties, the substance of her faith is unchanged. She still regards it as "a single revelation of absolute truth;" and from this point of view all her world is constructed. Yet even the most conservative of believers are obliged to allow that their single absolute faith grew up from historical antecedents, and has met with powerful rivals. This class of facts is dealt with rather amusingly by Miss Yonge. Of the Reformation she speaks with diplomatic caution. "It is difficult," she says, in her ***Kings of England,*** "to judge how far Wycliffe taught and believed the truth, or how far he was to blame for disregard to the authority of the church." Of the spontaneous religious element among the German Reformers she is deeply distrustful, and holds by the "English Catholic Church," through all its successive phases, creditable and discreditable. All the right-minded heroes in her tales are on the same side; they all idolise "the White King," as she calls Charles I.; and although she does not defend Charles II. as a man, yet she sympathises with the "persecuted" Episcopalians in Scotland during the civil wars, and has no word of admiration for the heroic Puritans. Indeed, nothing is more curious than the ingenuity with which she picks her way through the paths of history, singling out all the heroism on her own side, and pertinaciously ignoring it on the other. To her Mahomet is only an Arabian impostor; Cromwell, a cold hypocrite; Washington, "the principal leader of the rebels" (who "was encouraged by their successes to go much farther than he had at first intended, and at last led them entirely to shake off their allegiance to the King of England;" a statement which would lead us to suppose that Miss Yonge had never heard of the Declaration of Independence in 1776). Her ***Kings of England*** is professedly written to inculcate "faith, loyalty, obedience, reverence;" in which, she says, "lies the strength of nations,"—a dictum which is clearly meant to be taken in the narrowest sense of unconditional allegiance to the church and dynasty under which we happen to be born.

The palpable fallacy of this view is, perhaps, apt to blind many who smile at it to the real difficulty at the bottom of the subject, which does not at first show itself, but which needs to be resolutely met. There *is* an *apparent* additional security to the ethical life, arising from the fully-defined position which is given to it in this system. One of the subtlest evils of a speculative age is the element of doubt which intellectual criticism introduces into moral and spiritual trusts. The great synthesis of the mediæval Catholic ages, when a homogeneous life pervaded all classes, sacred and secular, must be lost in an epoch of disintegration. And those who look back to that unity of life with longing eyes, are so far right that the predominance which it manifested of the spiritual and formative element over the intellectual and active faculties, is in itself a condition of the highest state of man. But it is not the *only* condition thereof, nor is it always found in connection with the greatest spiritual capacities. Nay, the more rich and complex is the nature of the mind, the longer must its period of preparatory growth and discipline necessarily be. In the early Catholic centuries, the Church was really at the head of civilisation, and nearly all the purest streams of intellectual and national life were fed by her. But when other sources of life began to arise, when it became evident that men had the power of getting at reality first-hand, whether in the facts of physical nature, or of intellectual research, or of religious experience, then that chasm began to open between the ecclesiastical and the natural-religious forms of civilisation which has never been understood at all by the ecclesiasticists, and which is even yet but imperfectly comprehended by their opponents. The prophecy of the former is, that if we give up the inviolability of the *form,* we lose all certainty of retaining our hold on the *realities* of religion, and must, sooner or later, drift into Atheism in belief, and mere anarchical individualism in society, each man doing what is right in his own eyes. And in confirmation of this, they point to the merely negative influence of free criticism upon character and civilisation, and ask what we can show to counterbalance it, and even whether we have any means of verifying our religious intuitions at all. How can the finite comprehend the Infinite, or the creature judge that which should be his Ruler and Lord? Here lies the real gist of the difficulty; and perhaps the wide-spread Atheism of the present day may contribute towards the reduction of the problem to its lowest terms more speedily than was possible while men lingered in dead forms of materialistic Christianity on the one hand, or of sentimental philosophy on the other, which obscured the distinctness of the real issue.

The true answer we take to be this: that if we were unable to recognise the existence of any object until we could systematically reconstruct its internal metaphysical constitution, *then* we should assuredly be unable to recognise the being of God; but that no such inability does really attach to the action of our perceptive faculties. We recognise the existence of our fellow-creatures, although we may be wholly ignorant of their mental or physical constitution, and greatly in the dark respecting their characters. The faculties by which we become aware of the existence of God are, of course, less rapid in growth than those by which we become aware of the existence of our fellowmen; but the universal experience of the race shows that they are no less ineradicable and active, and far more directly related to character. Every race and every age, whether savage or civilised, Pagan or Christian, has in its own way, darkly or clearly, found and felt the real Spiritual Personality above us, though discerning his true *character* but imperfectly, and only coming to perceive by slow degrees his infinite mercy and perfect righteousness. But however decidedly we may realise the sensation that God *is,* we are plainly not meant to imbibe passively our ideas of *what He is* from some mechanical source that will save us the trouble of feeling after and finding Him for ourselves. On this subject, as on all others, our faculties must be personally exercised before they can yield any valuable results. Even the elementary senses require education: the infant tries to grasp objects many yards distant, supposing them to be close at hand; the unpractised ear cannot discriminate the identity of sounds which are instantly painted on the mental perceptiveness of a musician; and the tyro in mathematics puzzles himself over theorems which to an older student have long been self-evident. In all these cases, the faculty has to be educated before it can do its appropriate work; but the fact that by exercise and experience it does acquire the power to accomplish that work, shows that there is a real and natural relation between the human faculty and the external object.

Now, believing most profoundly that such a relation exists between ourselves and our Creator, we believe that every genuine inquiry into the subject must tend to develop it, and that it were easier for the earth to thrive without the light of the sun, than for man to live without the perpetual self-revelations of God. They cannot be destroyed, but they may be obscured and distorted; and the fearful mind which dares not trace them to their source, and would base them on mechanical props and confine them to arbitrary and narrow channels, shows far less real faith than one who gives fair play to every power that God has given him, trusting Him for the result. The unnatural repression of the intellectual faculties which orthodoxy so long enforced, has so far succeeded as to drive half the truth-seekers of our time into the error of attempting to reconstruct life upon a purely intellectual basis. But the reaction of Faith is sure, and is already beginning to be seen. We have no fears for the ultimate result. Believing the affirmative and spiritual side of our nature to be incomparably the highest, and ordained to wield lawful authority over the character, we yet hold that the action of the negative and critical faculties is vitally essential to the healthy condition of the mind; and we have so full a faith in the preëstablished harmony of man's powers, that we are indifferent on which side a new truth may enter, feeling sure that its relations with all other truth will disclose themselves in God's own time. Welcoming all vigorous and genuine utterances on either side, we value such works as the best of Miss Yonge's, for their truthful and inspiring delineations of life from an affirmative and spiritual point of view. But we must always regret that they are marred by a feeble reverence for damnatory theories and sacerdotal fictions, which obscures their spiritual beauty, and must tend to narrow the hearts of those who accept it for truth. We should regret this the more, did we not believe that a large proportion of her readers are more discriminating on these points than herself, and are able, with whatever consciousness of moral and intellectual shortcomings, to repose peacefully on that truth which she has yet to learn,—that, under all creeds and at all times,

——if the inmost heart delights to bless
And commune with the God of purity,
Earth has no bonds the spirit to retain,
And heaven no bars its entrance to restrain.

(pp. 214-30)

"*Ethical and Dogmatic Fiction: Miss Yonge,*" *in* The National Review, *London, Vol. XII, January, 1861, pp. 211-30.*

Joseph Ellis Baker (essay date 1932)

[*Baker is an American scholar and critic. In the following essay, he praises Yonge as "the greatest of all purely Anglo-Catholic novelists in the Victorian age," emphasizing her ability to affirm religious principles without resorting to verbose theological arguments.*]

While there were much better artists writing novels of manners [during the 1850s], for our purposes the best way to demonstrate the characteristics of the form will be to analyze the method of Charlotte Mary Yonge. For, whereas in controversial fiction all sides have an equal opportunity, in novels portraying the daily life of Anglo-Catholics, a Tractarian author naturally has the advantage. And Miss Yonge was the greatest of all purely Anglo-Catholic novelists in the Victorian Age. Not only for us, but in any final estimate of her work, Miss Yonge's claim to a position in literature depends on her success with the Tractarian novel during its phase as novel of contemporary manners. A character in Oliphant's *Phoebe Junior* (1876) says that "one reads Scott for Scotland (and a few other things), and one reads Miss Yonge for the church. Mr. Trollope is good for that, too, but not so good. All that I know of clergymen's families I have got from her." Another writer says: "There can be no doubt that the writings of Charlotte Yonge have inspired more than two generations of readers with the enthusiastic belief in the truth and office of the Church of England, and in its historic continuity with the Church of Augustine and Anselm." For many years John Keble himself read in manuscript everything written by Miss Yonge.

Much of her writing was "for the young," and, indeed, there is a touch of the juvenile about all of her novels. We shall try not to include purely juvenile fiction, but it is impossible to draw the line with absolute precision. One novel is designated in its preface as neither a tale for the young nor a novel for their elders, but a mixture of both. Indeed, some of the more conservative still considered novels food largely for women and babes, though by the time Miss Yonge became known as a novelist, *Vanity Fair* had been in print for five years. Miss Yonge's plots are usually complicated, and since it is not the plot but the life that is of value in these novels, it would be an irrelevance for us to give synopses.

If *Hypatia* was the greatest work produced by the enemies of the Oxford Movement, **The Heir of Redclyffe,** published in the same year, 1853, was the most famous of all the novels written by Tractarians. The hero, Sir Guy Morville, though badly in need of the colloquial advice, "Be your age"—it is hard to realize that this boy was supposed to represent a young man—is, nevertheless, a charming character. He is what so many heroes of Anglo-Catholic fiction were meant to be, a saint and a gentleman. (How that combination would have disgusted the old High and Dry aristocrats!) He dies from a disease contracted in nursing his fever-stricken enemy, Philip. The hero is thus removed while the book still has a fifth of the way to go, a rather violent way to avoid a happy culmination of love, even for a Tractarian novel. Sir Guy is not only an enthusiast, but a gentleman, in the narrower social sense. Indeed, Miss Yonge preaches the duty of a certain amount of worldliness. When Guy is rebellious enough to think social life dangerously pleasant, he is told that he cannot lay aside his position in society merely because it is full of trial—that would be to fail in trust in Him who fixed his station.

When Miss Yonge's brother got his commission in the army, she "compared it to a young squire obtaining knighthood, and felt it to be a sort of revival of the romance of an older day." She was at that time almost thirty years of age. With so real a tendency to gild the lily, it is not surprising that she produced, in **The Heir of Redclyffe,** the best example of Victorian life Medievalized. Like so many Anglo-Catholic novelists, admiring the age that Scott had glorified, she made the nineteenth century look as much as possible like the earlier epoch. Religious, social, esthetic traces of the Middle Ages which still lingered in Victorian England, or had been revived, she printed in rubrics, and lo! the objectionable world of Democracy, Industry, and Science vanished! Sir Guy is of high birth, he is pure, chivalric, Catholic. He is on the quest of religious excellence, yet, next to the Church, his lady love has all his heart. He is the monarch, the young prince, of Redclyffe, surrounded by feudal loyalty. He might almost be a petty ruler of an independent principality, rather than a citizen of a united Parliamentary nation. The novel fuses this Feudal with an Esthetic Medievalism in its self-conscious innocence, its careful attention to details, its convention-charged "simplicity." Over the Pre-Raphaelites the novel "exercised an extraordinary fascination." While the group was still at Oxford, Sir Guy "was adopted by them as a pattern for actual life: and more strongly perhaps by Morris than by the rest, from his own greater wealth and more aristocratic temper."

But the Pre-Raphaelites were not the only ones among whom **The Heir of Redclyffe** had a great success. Ethel Romanes says that "many of us are fain to confess to having read it at least a score of times." Miss Yonge's brother in the army found that nearly all the young men in his regiment had a copy of the book. "Scholarly gentlemen wept over Guy's death, and what is far more important, trying to be very good was made interesting and romantic to thousands of good girls. The interesting note in a hero was no longer wickedness but goodness." Miss F. M. Peard said that enthusiasm for Charlotte Yonge among the undergraduates at Oxford was surprising as late as 1865.

Miss Yonge's taste is often at its worst where a book is most vulnerable—in the title. Whatever its demerits, **The Heir of Redclyffe** is a much better novel than one would suppose from the spelling of -clyffe. **The Daisy Chain, or Aspirations** (1856) is even more unfortunately named. This novel deals with the family life of the Mays, who, like most of Yonge's characters, are very conscientious, almost exemplary in conduct, and yet quite real, quite personal. Their sins are usually small ones, such as the world overlooks, but here they entail punishment. There is considerable concern in this novel with specifically Anglo-Catholic interests, such as church restoration and confession. The poor people of Cocksmoor are miserable, and far from a church. Ethel May tries to establish a school among them, but the Ladies' Committee interferes. She does not want to submit to their advice, but, "if the lawful authority—if a good Clergyman would only come, how willingly would I work under him." Thus the Oxford Movement is becoming a part of ordinary life.

The later novels of Yonge are inferior to the two I have

mentioned. In *Hopes and Fears; or, Scenes from the Life of a Spinster* (1860), one of the most important figures is an Anglo-Catholic curate, Robert Fulmort, who tries to atone for the evil his family is perpetrating with its gin palaces. He undergoes persecution at the hands of mobs stimulated by the Fulmort firm and their gin. This is witness to that growing interest in social work which the novels show us taking place in the Oxford Movement about this time.

The Trial: More Links of the Daisy Chain (1864), is about the May family again, and takes us across the Atlantic, where we get an interesting contrast between the typical American and the Anglo-Catholic outlook: The American girl had been bred up to liberal religious ways, but drawn on by her friend's greater precision of religious knowledge and the beauty of the Church system she became more interested in Episcopalianism. After a while, "the fuller and more systematic doctrine, and the development of the beauty and daily guidance of the Church, had softened the bright American girl, so as to render her infinitely dearer to her English friend." As the first part of the title indicates, this novel employs the sensationalism of the 'sixties.

The Clever Woman of the Family (1865), as the title would suggest, shows how a person who is cleverer than others may be a dupe. In this novel, Mr. Mauleverer has not taken orders because he cannot be bound by the formularies. Of course, being a Liberal, he is obviously not a gentleman and proves to be a scoundrel. But not until he has gulled the Clever Woman. (pp. 102-07)

Though there is constantly in the background of Miss Yonge's mind a deep love of Anglo-Catholicism, her novels contain little that is controversial. It is rather that her characters have their being in an Anglo-Catholic atmosphere. Even in lighter moments, thoughts of church work and Catholic literature are not far from them, but in the more serious trials their faith becomes most important. When Guy is told by Mrs. Lavers that it was she who sent for the clergyman that baptized him, his face beams with gratitude. "Then I have to thank you for more than all the world besides." This is Catholic faith in baptismal regeneration; but contrast the way it comes into this novel as a passing remark in the life of an Anglo-Catholic, with the direct argument that it would have occasioned in the 'forties. When Guy's birthday falls in Holy Week, there can be no rejoicing. In the crisis of his anger against Philip, Guy thinks of Biblical passages, of Christ's wrongs and revilings. When he is in despair, Christmas brings him out of it. He has no longer the sense of being in the power of evil. The light of the other life is beginning to shine out. Easter steadies his gaze. As the week before has nerved him in the spirit of self-sacrifice, the feast day brings him true unchanging joy, help to endure the want of earthly hope.

In dealing with Death, Miss Yonge garners the fine fruit of her faith, for, without ignoring human pain, she avoids theatrical sentimentality. Her steady gaze is neither averted from sorrow, nor cruelly bold. She was able to meet this awful test so well because her slight genius was fortified by Christian tenderness—and Christian hope. In these scenes we have an example of a certain faith forming an element of strength in literary art.

The most important way in which Yonge and the true novel of manners reflect the Oxford Movement appears in the psychology. Beliefs about the nature of the mind often depend on religious beliefs; indeed, "psychology" can never be more than the interpretation of man in terms of some philosophy. I have suggested a relation, in Newman and Kingsley, between the author's faith and the way he portrays the workings of the mind. But, in Newman, at least, one feels that specific problems are set and then characters constructed to illustrate them. Miss Yonge's figures are alive in their own right. They are human beings. But she shows that human beings react in certain ways, that their minds have certain laws, that certain consequences spring from the very structure of reality. And often her interpretations are determined by Anglo-Catholic views. We have seen how Paget or Gresley would build a story to illustrate dogma. But Miss Yonge does not do this. The Movement comes into her stories more subtly, though perhaps even more potently. Guy Morville is conscious of a strength not his own to resist his passionate nature. This translates into common terms of fiction a belief in the Grace of God overcoming Original Sin. Perhaps the most remarkable thing about the Tractarians was the way they combined a Romantic reverence for external nature with a great contempt for the natural instincts. Guy thinks it profane for a man like Byron to interpret nature. He says, that "there is danger in listening to a man who is sure to misunderstand the voice of nature,—danger, lest by filling our ears with the wrong voice we should close them to the true one. I should think there was a great chance of being led to stop short at the material beauty, or worse, to link human passions with the glories of nature, and to distort, defile, profane them." It is safe to read Scott's and Wordsworth's descriptions of nature because they had religion. (Contrast this orthodox condemnation of Man as he is naturally, with the liberalism of Kingsley, or with the whole current away from Catholicism from the Renaissance to the Freudian generation.)

The devotion of Miss Yonge's characters to doing good (particularly in furthering religious practices) is well within the tradition of Catholicism, with its emphasis on works. And their minute conscientiousness is characteristic of a faith where the smaller details of worship are carefully observed. The Puritan conscience is stern, but it is concentrated on a few matters, just as the Puritan religion is what the Catholic calls "impoverished," dispensing with a large part of Christian culture. Particularly Tractarian is Miss Yonge's belief in obedience almost for the sake of obedience, and in the evil consequences of self-will. She glorifies submission, not only to the Church, but to any misfortune, for the latter she considers particularly the will of God. The application is often psychological; Laura's agony, upon hearing that Philip was sick, was untempered by resignation, as it was uncheered by prayer. Our attention is fixed not on Anglo-Catholic principles, but upon the moral choice to be guided by those principles, and upon the misery destined as a punishment for any moral heresy. The Clever Woman of the Family is punished for listening to a Liberal. In *The Three Brides,* one bride is punished for her secularity. In *The Daisy Chain,* Flora May has worldly ambitions, and marries a man for his wealth and social position. This leads, with the coöperation of accidents, to the death of their child, through the error of a nurse wanting in "any high religious principle to teach her obedience or sincerity." The mother, who, by her own neglect, has been ultimately responsible, is in despair. She sees that, though she seemed to herself to be trying to do right, it was all hollow, and for the sake of praise.

> The simplicity and hearty piety which, with all Dr. May's faults, had always been part of his character, and had borne him, in faith and trust, through all his trials, had never belonged to her. Where he had been sincere, erring only from impulsiveness, she had been double-minded and calculating; and, now that her delusion had been broken down, she had nothing to rest upon. Her whole religious life had been mechanical, deceiving herself more than even others, and all seemed now swept away.

But while a novel of controversy can be analyzed, and a novel of plot outlined, a novel of manners must be read.

Miss Yonge is a real artist in this sense: What she sets for herself to do she does so well that as we read we are seldom conscious of any flaw, omission or blunder. Her style is quiet and pleasant, as the above quotation illustrates. Her humor is sweet and sound. Dialogue is very natural, and in itself develops the story. Like the majority of great novelists, she uses the dramatic method. Most important of all, her primary object is to tell a story of domestic life, and a story in which character is of much more interest than plot. But she is sentimental and her range of vision small. For all her merits, and her insight into psychological subtleties, Miss Yonge never touches profound experience or the exalted heights of the spirit. She did not have the necessary intellect, passion, or nobility. Her religion is not mysticism, but church-going raised to the *n*th degree She does not take us into the world of ideas nor of great events, but of personal domestic feeling. It is this that distinguishes the novel of manners in the 'fifties from that which was to come later. (pp. 107-11)

> *Joseph Ellis Baker, "Charlotte Mary Yonge, and the Novel of Domestic Manners," in his* The Novel and the Oxford Movement, *Princeton University Press, 1932, pp. 101-13.*

Dorothea Blagg (essay date 1934)

[*In the following essay, Blagg provides a critical overview of several of Yonge's works.*]

In the year 1844 Richard Church, a young Oxford don, afterwards Dean of St. Paul's, was talking to a friend about a book which had just come out. "It is a very clever book," he said, "and the young lady will write well in future." "Oh, why?" said his companion. "Because every character, however simple, is perfectly distinct and living."

Probably few people now alive have read *Abbey Church,* Charlotte Yonge's first published book; but Dean Church's critical insight discovered in it the outstanding characteristic which is Charlotte's chief claim to merit as a novelist: her characters are "perfectly distinct and living." In this one respect there is no writer of English fiction who excels her.

But a writer cannot be placed in the front rank by virtue of one gift alone; and there were serious defects in Charlotte Yonge's work. These were not fully recognised by her contemporaries, for she had not to wait, like Jane Austen, until after death for her full meed of praise; and for many years posterity has been busy redressing the balance. In truth it has done the work too thoroughly.

In one respect Miss Yonge is at a disadvantage as compared with other women novelists. She lived to be nearly eighty, and was writing constantly for half a century; whereas all the great women writers of the 19th century died comparatively young, and not one of them wrote more than six complete novels. Can we suppose that if they had lived to be nearly eighty they would have kept up their level as we know it?

It is impossible to resist comparing Jane Austen and Charlotte Yonge. Their circumstances were curiously similar. Both lived in Hampshire villages, both belonged to the "upper middle-class" of English society. Hence they had a similarly limited outlook. They wrote of what they knew, and let the rest of the world alone. Both concerned themselves largely with the life and doings of young girls. But there the resemblance ceases. Charlotte Yonge's girls live in a new atmosphere, an atmosphere of earnest purpose. They have discovered the possibility of other interests besides water-colour drawing, morning calls, walks in the shrubbery, balls and assemblies, all continually pervaded by thoughts of possible husbands. They know the enthusiasm of devoting one's life to a cause. Young men had been fired with high ideals in the days of the French Revolution, but they had not communicated the fire to young ladies—not at least to the young ladies of Jane Austen's circle. The Napoleonic war did not touch them except when it brought fascinating officers to their assemblies or carried off beloved brothers to the high seas. About half a century separated Jane Austen's novels from those by which Miss Yonge made her name, and there is quite half a century's difference in their outlook. We shall be able to develop this point more fully as we consider some of the individual books.

Yet the contrast between Charlotte Yonge and her contemporaries is almost greater. They were akin in that they all belonged to the romantic and idealistic age, whereas Jane Austen had not really emerged from the classical eighteenth century; but the refined restraint of Charlotte Yonge seems to have more in common with her than with the fierce emotions of the Brontës, the social propaganda of Mrs. Gaskell, or the psychological subtleties of George Eliot.

Charlotte Yonge's books may be divided into three main classes; Family Chronicles, Historical Romances, and Novels of Contemporary Life. Of these, the two first contain by far her best work. In both she may be said to have worked in a medium of her own, and used it with remarkable skill. Even her third class was more or less of an innovation, for it was something between a girls' book and a full-blown novel. It proved very attractive at the time, but these books belong more exclusively to their period and contain more of her characteristic weaknesses than the others. Yet it was one of these, *The Heir of Redclyffe*, which made her fame. Moderns who want to make acquaintance with Miss Yonge's work should not begin with *The Heir of Redclyffe*. They will almost certainly not like it, and it may prevent their reading others which they would enjoy. How, then, can we explain its remarkable success when it was published in 1853? It cannot be dismissed lightly as a typical instance of a best seller, appealing to the low-brow public. It was not merely gushing girls who admired it. Serious critics like M. Guizot praised it. The young Pre-Raphaelites, William Morris and Dante Rossetti, "took Guy as their hero-model." The book seems to have been read quite as much by men as by women. Miss Yonge's brother Julian found that nearly every officer in his regiment had a copy, and when Charlotte visited Oxford in 1865, it is recorded that the enthusiasm for her among the undergraduates was surprising. Clearly there must have been a quality and a power in the book which modern readers miss because they are not *en rapport* with its spirit. It was a product of the age, and it evoked a response from the best spirits of the age. The youth of to-day will no more paint like the Pre-Raphaelites than they will read *The Heir of Redclyffe:* nevertheless the P.R.B. were serious artists, whose judgment on a work of literature is worthy of respect. On the face of it, it does not seem as if there were much affinity between Miss Yonge's work and theirs. But the Brotherhood was in the direct line of descent from the Romantic Revival, which was also conspicuous in the ancestry of the Oxford Movement: and Charlotte was a child of the Oxford Movement, a disciple of John Keble, who prepared her for confirmation and was her spiritual guide until his death.

The germ of *The Heir of Redclyffe* was supplied to Charlotte by her friend Miss Dyson, who said there were two characters she wanted to see brought out in a story—the essentially contrite and the self-satisfied. There were plenty of heroes who were subdued by the memory of some involuntary disaster, but the "penitence of the saints" was unattempted. It was a good idea, but unfortunately Charlotte could not bring herself to make her hero do anything very wrong, and therefore his repentance is overstrained and exaggerated. All he did was to give way to fierce rage against his cousin for a few hours under intense provocation, but he succeeded in forgiving him before the sun went down. If only he had done Philip some injury in the heat of his anger, the story might have been a much finer one.

One thing which Charlotte Yonge achieved by *The Heir* and kindred books was that she made goodness interesting. Jane Austen's heroes were nice young men, but they were never in any danger of becoming too good for this world. It was for Charlotte Yonge to depict a more exalted and heroic type of character, involving the spirit of self-sacrifice, and coming near to the standard of the saints,

John Keble (1792-1866), Yonge's friend and mentor.

while at the same time so attractive that her girl-readers fell in love with it.

Other novels of contemporary life which followed were *Heartsease, Dynevor Terrace, The Young Stepmother,* and *The Clever Woman of the Family. Heartsease* was much liked in its day (by Charles Kingsley for one), but most people would probably find *Dynevor Terrace* more attractive. It contains a charming young man, and shows more of Miss Yonge's gift of humour than appears in the two previous books. *The Young Stepmother* is noteworthy for having kept Tennyson awake at night. F. T. Palgrave thus relates the incident:—

> One bedroom with two huge four-posters was allotted us; and Tennyson lay in his with a candle, reading hard the book which on this trip he had taken for his novel-companion, and at every disengaged moment opened whilst rambling on the moor. This chanced to be one of Miss Yonge's deservedly popular tales, wherein a leading element is the deferred Church Confirmation of a grown-up person. On Tennyson read, till I heard him cry with satisfaction, "I see land! Mr. —— is just going to be confirmed!" after which darkness and slumber.

The heroine of *The Clever Woman of the Family* bears some resemblance to Jane Austen's *Emma;* but it is significant of the changed conditions that, whereas Emma's mistakes are concerned with matchmaking, Rachel's relate to philanthropy and social experiment. A later novel, *The*

Three Brides, published in 1876, is decidedly inferior to any of these: but it contains passages which are highly entertaining in the presentation they give of the opinions of those days. Here is an instance. A disastrous fire has occurred in the town, and a public meeting is held to consider, amongst other things, how to meet the distress due to a number of women having been thrown out of employment through the destruction of a paper-mill. A scheme is proposed, and a lady present asks a question throwing doubt on its practicability.

> "Do you wish any expedient to be proposed?" asked the Chairman, in a sort of aside.
>
> "Yes, I have one. I spent yesterday in collecting information."
>
> "Will Captain Duncombe [her husband] move it?" suggested Raymond.
>
> "Oh no! he is not here. No, it is of no use to instruct anybody; I will do it myself, if you please." And before the astonished eyes of the meeting, the gold pheasant hopped upon the platform, and with as much ease as if she had been Queen Bess dragooning her parliament, she gave what even the astounded gentlemen felt to be a sensible practical exposition of ways and means . . . She finished off in full order, by moving a resolution to this effect.

The resolution was carried without opposition, but this is how the incident was discussed by the society of the neighbourhood afterwards:—

> "She should have got her husband to speak for her," said Mrs. Poynsett.
>
> "He was not there."
>
> "Then she should have instructed some other gentleman. A woman spoils all the effect of her doings by putting herself out of her proper place."
>
> "Perfectly disgusting!" said Julius.

One member of the party, however, takes up the cudgels for the absent.

> Rosamond exclaimed, "Ah! that's just what men like, to get instructed in private by us poor women, and then gain all the credit for originality."
>
> "It is the right way," said the mother. "The woman has much power of working usefully and gaining information, but the one thing that is not required of her is to come forward in public."
>
> "Very convenient for the man!" laughed Rosamond.
>
> "And scarcely fair," said Cecil.
>
> "Quite fair," said Rosamond, turning round, so that Cecil only now perceived she had been speaking in jest. "Any woman who is worth a sixpence had rather help her husband to shine than shine herself."
>
> "Besides," said Mrs. Poynsett, "the delicate edges of true womanhood ought not to be frayed off by exposure in public."
>
> . . . "You were forced to thank her," said Cecil.
>
> "Yes, in common civility," said Raymond; "but it was as much as I could do to get it done, the position was a false one altogether."

Rosamond's jesting remarks show that the author saw it was just possible to take another view; and it is interesting to note that in one of her much later books she had advanced so far that she made one of her woman characters (without adverse comment) take up the career of a public lecturer.

Between the publication of *Heartsease* and *Dynevor Terrace* came *The Daisy Chain,* which was published in 1856. This was the first of the family chronicles, unless we include *Scenes and Characters,* an earlier work of little importance apart from the fact that it introduces us to the Mohun family, whom we meet again later.

In these family chronicles we have Miss Yonge's specially characteristic contribution to English literature. Family chronicles are to-day a familiar form of fiction. John Galsworthy and Hugh Walpole would probably have been surprised at being told that they were following in the footsteps of Charlotte Yonge; but the fact remains that she was a pioneer in that art. These books are a class by themselves. They have no plot, any more than the true history of a family has a plot. Each book is simply a slice out of the life-story of a large family, extending over a considerable number of years. Further events in the same family are related in later books. As they have no plot, so they have properly no hero and heroine. Certain members of the family assert themselves and come inevitably to the fore, but that is all. This type of book was extraordinarily well suited to Charlotte Yonge's special talents; for she had very little power of construction, but her great gift was in the creation of living characters. To the genuine lover of Miss Yonge the characters in *The Daisy Chain* and *The Pillars of the House* are real people; to dip into one of these books for an hour is to spend that hour on a visit to personal friends. Of these two books, Miss Yonge stated that *The Daisy Chain* had always had the largest sale of any of her books, but that on re-reading them she herself preferred *The Pillars of the House* as being brighter and less pedantic. Unquestionably they are the two best of her family chronicles.

The two outstanding creations in *The Daisy Chain* are Dr. May and his daughter Ethel. The character of Dr. May is thought by many people to be the best thing Charlotte ever did. Certainly the book is worth reading for that alone. The author at first intended Margaret to be the chief girl character, but happily Ethel took the law into her own hands; for Margaret is a rather tiresomely perfect character who gives wise counsel from her sofa. It is Ethel's enthusiasm about Cocksmoor which shows how far we have travelled since the days of Elizabeth Bennet and Anne Elliot. And it is no sentimental glamour which moves her; there is not much glamour about tramping rough country roads in all weathers to teach an unruly horde of children in a neglected hamlet. But Ethel sees in Cocksmoor a real need, and having seen it she proceeds to action. The children are neglected and untaught, and she can teach them; and the teaching must of course be founded upon religion, therefore they must have a school and as soon as possible a church, and she will never rest until that end is reached. Mrs. Romanes has pointed out in her book on Charlotte Yonge that she is a true Romantic, for she sees all the glory and beauty that lie behind the dull routine of life. It is because Ethel May knows what is the real inner heart of her Cocksmoor work that she sticks to it through all difficulties. The other great enthusiasm of *The Daisy Chain* is foreign missionary work, to which the clever brother, Norman, consecrates his life. The proceeds from the sales both of this book and of *The Heir of Redclyffe* were given to the Melanesian Mission. It had been decided, when Charlotte began to publish, that it would never do for her to keep the proceeds of her writings for her own benefit! and it was not until comparatively late in life that she broke through this rule.

The Daisy Chain amuses us at times by the light it throws on the social conventions of those days. It was deemed impossible for Margaret, aged eighteen, to take part in an afternoon walk with the rest of the family if young Mr. Ernescliffe were going too—although the governess and any number of young brothers and sisters were of the party! This is an astonishing contrast to the free-and-easy days of Jane Austen, when a mamma would encourage and exhort a girl to go for a solitary walk with a young man. The unhandy Ethel commands our sympathy when we realise the difficulties she had to contend with in the matter of dress—trying to pin up a heavy crape skirt on a muddy day with only a common pin!

The Trial, although a continuation of *The Daisy Chain,* can hardly be included in the family chronicles, for it has quite a thrilling plot, turning on the subject of a murder, for which the hero is tried and condemned to death, the sentence being commuted in view of his youth. Eventually his innocence is established and he is released, but he has been in prison for years, and there is an atmosphere of sadness over a great part of the book. It is an example of Miss Yonge's thoroughness that she went with Judge Coleridge to visit Portland prison, in order to get her details correct with regard to the treatment of the prisoner.

Part of *The Daisy Chain* had appeared in *The Monthly Packet,* the magazine which Charlotte Yonge founded in 1851, and continued to edit for almost half a century. Among her many works which appeared first in it was *The Pillars of the House,* the other family chronicle already mentioned. It was written in the early seventies, when Miss Yonge was about fifty, and it bears the marks of a maturer mind. Again it is the history of a large family— there were eleven Mays, there are thirteen Underwoods. Charlotte thoroughly understood the ways of large families, as in her young days she used to pay annual visits to her numerous cousins in Devonshire. In *The Pillars of the House,* even more strongly than in *The Daisy Chain,* we are shown the flower of heroic goodness blossoming in circumstances of commonplace drudgery. For the thirteen young Underwoods are left fatherless, with an invalid mother, to face the battle of life under conditions of real poverty.

Every one of the thirteen stands out clearly as an individual character. The author's own favourites, we feel sure, are Felix and Lance, and so she makes most of her readers like them the best; Felix, the eldest brother, who has to shoulder the responsibilities of the family, giving up all thought of the University and Holy Orders to take a post in a printer's and bookseller's shop (a bitter pill for one of Miss Yonge's well-born young men to swallow! but he does it without any fuss); and Lance the musical genius, brighter and livelier than the steady-going Felix, who has had most of the liveliness knocked out of him by his family cares. But the merry young Lance does not fall behind Felix in the matter of self-sacrifice, for he sticks to the shop and resists the lure of a possible musical career. There is plenty of humour shown in the drawing of the various characters and their inter-action upon one another. But most readers will probably agree with Mrs. Romanes in seeing no reason why the author should have killed Felix in the end. One of her weaknesses is that she is too fond of illnesses and death-bed scenes. In the history of large families we are bound to have some of them, but they are too long-drawn-out, with too much detail; the picture would be more effective if drawn with fewer strokes.

We turn now to Miss Yonge's other class of stories—the historical romances. In view of these books, critics might demur to the statement that Charlotte Yonge wrote of what she knew and let the rest of the world alone. But she did move so familiarly among the people of bygone periods that it may really be said that she wrote of what she knew. Doubtless she was not always correct as to facts, but it was not for want of taking pains. Even in her girlhood she and her young friends talked about obscure historical characters with the same allusive familiarity with which other people discuss their relations. And in her historical romances she achieved the rare feat of making her historical personages as completely alive and real as her fictitious characters. This is the chief merit of *The Caged Lion.* The hero is a moderately interesting young man named Malcolm Stewart, but the real charm of the book is in the characters of Henry V and his brother John of Bedford, and James I, the captive king of Scotland—captive yet friend of the English king. The description of King Henry's last hours, and the picture of John of Bedford in his desolation taking up the reins of government on behalf of his baby nephew, are full of pathos. But Charlotte Yonge's best historical romances are *The Chaplet of Pearls* and *The Dove in the Eagle's Nest. The Chaplet of Pearls* has a really good plot. The scenes are laid in France and England at the period of the St. Bartholomew massacre, and the story recounts the perils and adventures of a young pair who are parted for years but find one another again at last. *The Dove in the Eagle's Nest* is a story of German history, giving a vivid picture of the contrast between the half-savage robber barons in their mountain fortresses and the highly-civilised burghers of the towns. Both these books contain scenes of great beauty and pathos.

Miss Yonge wrote numerous other historical tales, most of them shorter and slighter than these. Some, like *The*

Little Duke, were simply stories for children. In that category *The Little Duke* is admirable. After the seventies she wrote very little of any solid merit; but two of her later historical romances, *Unknown to History* and *A Reputed Changeling,* are well worth reading. The plot of the former centres on an imaginary daughter of Mary Queen of Scots and Bothwell. *A Reputed Changeling* deals with the Revolution of 1688, and introduces some interesting local colour, notably at Portchester Castle, and Blackgang Chine in the Isle of Wight.

There is a prevalent notion that Miss Yonge's books are of the nature of religious propaganda. This is true of some of her smaller books, written expressly for young people; and here it should be mentioned that she wrote a whole series of village tales which are remarkably good of their kind, and interest village children of to-day as thoroughly as they interested their grandparents. But in her larger and more important works there is no direct propaganda. The only influence they exercise is through atmosphere. It must be remembered that reserve in religious matters was a marked characteristic of the Tractarians. The principles of the English Church are present as a background, but even in *The Pillars of the House,* which deals more intimately with distinctive religious practices than any of her other stories, the allusions spring naturally from the narrative because it happens to be a record of people to whom these things were of paramount importance.

Miss Yonge's method of work was curious; it was her habit to have three works on hand at the same time, *e.g.,* one novel and two other works, and to write a page of each in turn, leaving the first to dry while she wrote the next. In this way she wrote *The Pillars of the House* and the *Life of Bishop Patteson,* and announced one day at luncheon that she had had a dreadful morning—she had killed the Bishop and Felix! She left a quantity of other writings besides novels, but we are concerned with her here only as a writer of fiction. That her work had numerous weaknesses must be clear to anyone who has read thus far. Her literary style was not usually very good, and at its worst it was very bad. It became absolutely slipshod in her later years. Allied to this fault was her lack of constructive power. The deterioration in her later work is easily explained. It was not only that her powers were naturally failing, but her life, which had always been secluded, became increasingly isolated owing to the fact that she had an invalid friend living with her, which prevented her from travelling about or receiving visits from other friends. It was seldom that she had the pleasure of intellectual companionship at Otterbourne. One such rare occasion was a visit from Miss Wordsworth, who has left a charming record of it [in Ethel Romanes's *Charlotte M. Yonge: An Appreciation*] in which she speaks of her hostess as "looking like a French Marquise," a description borne out by her portraits. Her work suffered from lack of contact with the outer world, and from the absence of that bracing criticism which she might have had through association with abler intellects than her own. But perhaps what has been set down here may serve to convince some, who have never hitherto thought much about her, that her work is not merely a curious relic of bygone days, but a serious contribution to English literature. (pp. 191-201)

Dorothea Blagg, "Charlotte Mary Yonge and Her Novels," in Women Novelists: From Fanny Burney to George Eliot *by Muriel Masefield, 1934. Reprint by Books for Libraries Press, 1967, pp. 191-201.*

Henry James characterizes *The Heir of Redclyffe*:

Occasionally, like the *Heir of Redclyffe,* [novels that incorporate religious and historical information] almost legitimate themselves by the force of genius. But this only when a first-rate mind takes the matter in hand. By a first-rate mind we here mean a mind which (since its action is restricted beforehand to the shortest gait, the smallest manners possible this side of the ridiculous) is the master and not the slave of its material.

—Henry James, in his Notes and Reviews, *1932.*

Barbara Dennis (essay date 1973)

[*In the essay below, Dennis characterizes Yonge as the embodiment of a Christian novelist whose religious ideals inform her writing but criticizes her inability to accept the movement towards religious skepticism that characterized her age.*]

Every schoolboy knows that Charlotte Yonge was the novelist *par excellence* of the Oxford Movement; that she lived a long, blameless and wholly uneventful life in a village in Hampshire, the devoted friend and pupil of John Keble; and that she might well have said with Disraeli, 'Whenever I want to read a novel, I write one'. Her output, even by Victorian standards, is staggering—nearly a hundred novels and stories, as well as countless histories, biographies, schoolbooks, editions and translations—and all this despite an early resolve never to write fiction in Lent. But fiction or non-fiction, in season and out, whatever she wrote is stamped with the same fervent motto—Pro Ecclesia Dei.

It is this, the positive voice of Charlotte Yonge, that I want to talk about first, partly because this is the voice for which she was recognized and to which an enthusiastic public responded, and partly because (as some contemporary critics recognized) this is where her originality lies. She habitually thought of herself as 'a sort of instrument for popularizing Church views', and submitted all her early work to the scrutiny of John Keble, who, though his doctrinal purity was beyond question, was at best but a limited literary critic. He found very little to correct, however, from the point of view of Church views. All the ideals of the Oxford Movement are embodied in the novels, the importance of personal holiness, of reserve in Church matters, the necessity of obedience to the Church and submission to the guidance of her appointed ministers.

The eleven May children of *The Daisy Chain* and *The Trial* and various later novels, and the thirteen Underwoods of *The Pillars of the House* are typical Yonge families. Their daily lives are ordered by church-going and family devotions, and teaching in schools for poor children of their own founding; their ideals are concentrated on church building and the mission field, and the most critical and dramatic moment in their lives comes with Confirmation and the subsequent first Communion. (One early novel, *The Castle Builders, or the Deferred Confirmation,* centres unremittingly on this theme, and the question of whether or not twelve year old Harry May is in a sufficient state of grace to be confirmed or receive the sacrament before he leaves home on his first voyage is a crux in *The Daisy Chain.*) Personal conduct is not, in itself, sufficient, however. Direction, in both spiritual and temporal affairs, must be in the hands of the Church. In both *The Castle Builders* and *The Three Brides* earnest and well-meaning girls who devote their time to good works in the community—parish visiting and sanitary improvements—find that their efforts fail because they have not placed themselves under the guidance of the clergy. Young men who take orders may be weak and indecisive in themselves (Walter Lyddell in *The Two Guardians;* Richard, the eldest of the May family; Herbert Bowater in *The Three Brides;* Clement Underwood in *The Pillars of the House*—the list is endless) but they all derive from their cloth the necessary strength and firmness to guide their flocks, and to a man they prove themselves in time of trial. And if it is the duty of the clergy to lead, the duty of the laity to follow is also explicit. Charlotte Yonge's priests may seem obsessed with the importance of the early service, but they also toil in city slums and rural squalor ('Birmingham people', as they had been reminded, 'have souls'); so too the heroes and heroines for whom the conflict of life lies in the conquest of personal faults are also committed to practical charity.

Always it is against this background of the Church of England, and, more specifically, the Anglo-Catholic party of the church, that the novels are developed, from the earliest, in the 1840's, to the latest at the end of the century. She was not the only High Church novelist, of course, who was bent on expressing the Catholicity of the English Church (both Elizabeth Sewell and Felicia Skene were more extreme exponents) but by the 1860's Charlotte Yonge's name is pre-eminent.

Contemporaries recognized that she spoke, in many ways, for the age. Many regarded her with the reverence more often associated with Tennyson and Carlyle. Kingsley, whom (predictably) she disapproved of quite strongly, commended her warmly as representing the best and most wholesome that was being written. In 1869 Lady Georgiana Fullerton, a convert from the High Church to one even more established, the Church of Rome, could break off the plot of *Mrs. Gerald's Niece* to remark interestingly on the current preoccupations of contemporary literature reflected in Charlotte Yonge:

> Everything now in politics and literature . . . is connected with the creeds of men, and bears directly or indirectly on those all important questions, 'Church or no Church', 'Faith or no faith', and, so far as the world's verdict goes, 'God or no God' . . . Whereas, some of the most popular authors of the beginning of this century could write volume upon volume of fiction with hardly a word in them indicating that the thought of it ever crossed their minds, now scarcely a book is published which does not take sides for or against religion . . . Whatever treats of inward conflicts, secret perplexities, and the various trials of individual minds and hearts, necessarily commands attention at the moment when anything that can throw light on the difficulties which so many are experiencing may tend, even remotely, to their solution . . . The immense change in England with regard to the books which take the greatest hold on the mind of youthful readers of the better sort, of those that shun in fiction unwholesome excitement is strikingly exemplified when we contrast the works of Miss Edgeworth with those of Miss Sewell, those of Miss Austin (sic) with Miss Yonge's . . .

Charlotte Yonge located these 'inward conflicts' and 'secret perplexities' and 'various trials of individual minds and hearts' in the mid-Victorian drawing-room. What her public wanted and what they got was a mirror-image of themselves and their own situations. Charlotte Yonge showed them what they wanted to be shown—that life is a drama, to be played out within the confines of the family, in the schoolrooms and drawing-rooms of provincial towns. She suggested in every novel that the ideals of the Tractarians were not only exemplary, but attractive and exciting and, moreover, accessible. The Saint Greal, she avowed, might be found in Bexley and conversely, the spiritual desolation of Sintram's Mountains of the Moon in Cumberland. The pursuit of godliness, in fact, the ideal of all her heroes and heroines, is a domestic occupation, and she is at her best when describing domestic interiors. These may be the scene for spiritual drama, or they may, with clumsy imagery, prefigure a Victorian paradise, but always they touch a chord to which her readers responded eagerly. Take, for example, the opening description of the schoolroom in *The Daisy Chain,* where Charlotte Yonge is assembling her large cast:

> It was such a room as is often to be found in old country town houses, the two large windows looking out on a broad old-fashioned street, through heavy framework and panes of glass scratched with various names and initials. The walls were painted blue, the skirting almost a third of the height, and so wide at the top as to form a narrow shelf. The fireplace, constructed in the days when fires were made to give as little heat as possible, was ornamented with blue and white Dutch tiles bearing marvellous representations of Scripture history, and was protected by a very tall green guard; the chairs were much of the same date, solid and heavy, but there was a sprinkling of lesser ones and of stools; a piano; a globe; a large table in the middle of the room, with three desks on it; a small one, and a light cane chair by each window; and loaded bookcases.

Or take her description of the sanctum of the Edmonstone family early in *The Heir of Redclyffe,* Mrs. Edmonstone's sitting-room:

> It had an air of great snugness, with its large folding-screen, covered with prints and carica-

tures of ancient date, its bookshelves, its tables, its peculiarly easy arm-chairs, the great invalid sofa, and the grate which always lighted up better than any other in the house.

They are ordinary, reassuring interiors, and at the same time *impressionant* and atmospheric, and they anticipate much of what we subsequently learn of their inhabitants. Into the first one, in **The Daisy Chain,** bursts the impulsive fifteen-year old heroine of the novel, bent on a scheme of practical charity and on fire with her new ambition of bringing Christianity to the pagan poor of a neighbouring district by building a new church there. Her vision is of 'spire and chancel—pinnacle and buttress, (which) rose before her eyes—and she and Norman were standing in the porch with an orderly religious population blessing the unknown benefactor, who had caused the news of salvation to be heard among them'. (The church is remarkably like the one which Mr. Yonge had built at Otterbourne, with Charlotte's enthusiastic help. It is a pleasantly quizzical view of youthful idealism that she suggests.)

To the second interior comes the Heir of Redclyffe himself, Sir Guy Morville, a moody young baronet with a passionate temper and an inherited family curse in search of spiritual advice and encouragement from the saintly Mrs. Edmonstone. These two examples, and particularly the second, from **The Heir of Redclyffe,** neatly illustrate the point I am trying to make, that Charlotte Yonge fuses the domestic with the romantic in such a way as to suggest that the romantic *is* domestic. The chivalric values suggested by the Puginesque new church at Cocksmoor and the Byronic moodiness of Sir Guy Morville are as natural, she suggests, in mid-century surburbia as in the *medium aevum* or a European Romantic landscape.

In **The Heir of Redclyffe** particularly she can be seen as an innovator, Christianizing romanticism. Guy has the glamour of Byron and the poetic sensibility of Shelley, but replaces the vice of one and the atheism of the other with scrupulous morality and irreproachable High Church views. His appearance is almost conventionally Byronic—flashing eyes, waving hair, pale complexion—and his background is stock: he is the heir to large estates which encompass the sublime and the grand; his family is under an ancestral doom; he himself is alternately melancholy and gay, he is withdrawn, misunderstood, outlawed. He does not see himself, however, as either Manfred or Cain (indeed, he is wary of reading Byron at all). Charlotte Yonge comments approvingly:

> Who could have told where the mastery might have been in the period of fearful conflict with his passions, if he had been feeding his imagination with the contemplation of revenge, dark hatred and malice, and identifying himself with Byron's brooding and lowering heroes?

Guy's ideal is the Christian Sir Galahad, and his devotion is to King Charles the Martyr, whom he would have served 'half like a knight's devotion to his lady-love, half like devotion to a saint. . . .'

The working model for both Guy and his young wife Amy, however, is the hero of De La Motte Fouqué's German romance, *Sintram,* who provides a recurring motif throughout the novel. It is an allegorical tale of chivalry concerning the knight Sintram who, with an inherited curse upon him, has to ride out against Sin and Death to reach salvation.

Guy's inherited curse is the passionate Morville temper, and like Sintram he finally 'conquers his doom'. He gains his salvation when, goaded almost beyond endurance by his insufferable cousin, he wrestles with his very natural instinct for revenge and finally subdues it. This is, in a sense, the theme of the novel, but an alternative title would be the one Charlotte Yonge used as the sub-title to her first novel,—'Self-Control and Self-Conceit'. Structurally the novel is built around the opposing characters, and inevitable conflict, of the two young men, Guy and his cousin, Philip. The self-control is what Guy attains to, and the self-conceit is Philip's. Charlotte Yonge describes the germ of the novel in a letter, acknowledging that it originated with a friend:

> She told me that there were two characters she wanted to see brought out in a story, namely, the essentially contrite and the self-satisfied. The self-satisfied hero was to rate the humble one at still lower than his own estimate, to persecute him, and never be undeceived until he had caused his death. This was the germ of the tale. . . .

and this is how it is worked out. The priggish but at heart honourable Philip deludes himself into believing the worst about Guy, whose heir he is, and contrives, from the highest motives, to thwart him on all possible occasions. Acting on his usual obstinate insistence on always knowing best, Philip catches a terrible fever, through which Guy nurses him. Guy catches it in turn and (we have been warned several times previously that his constitution has been sadly undermined) it proves fatal. Guy dies amid circumstances of heartrending pathos, and Philip is left to the torments of remorse and the forgiveness of Guy's young widow.

The book, with its compound of piety and romantic chivalry, was an instantaneous success. Undergraduates like William Morris and Edward Burne-Jones modelled their lives on Guy's, Charlotte's younger brother, Julian, reported that all his fellow-officers were buying it; and it was, we hear, 'the novel most demanded by the wounded officers in hospital' during the Crimean campaign. A clergyman writing at the time of Charlotte Yonge's death recalled the *furore* which the book raised at Trinity College, Dublin—'probably the last place on earth to be tinctured with Tractarian spirit'.

But I do not think we should dismiss the **Heir** as a mere best-seller, which, by an accident of history, outlived its generation. Henry James recognized it as both outstanding among novels of its type and also as representing an innovation in fiction. In a far from fulsome review on what he calls 'semi-developed novels' (that is, novels whose message is 'narrowed down to a special precept' as opposed to 'genuine novels' of which the meaning and the lesson are infinite) he speaks of **The Heir of Redclyffe** as 'almost legitimizing itself by the force of genius, by reason of the first-rate mind which takes the matter in hand.' He goes on, 'By a first-rate mind we here mean a mind which . . . is the master and not the slave of its material'. Given the limiting nature of Charlotte Yonge's special precepts in the *Heir,* this is praise worth having.

What follows, however, is even more interesting. James sees Charlotte Yonge's domestic novels as representing the beginning of a realistic school in England (he is writing in 1865) which he compares very favourably with the French version. The 'great brilliancy' and 'great immorality' of these writers (presumably he is talking about Eugène Sue as well as Balzac and Stendhal) come in for some sharp comment as he observes: 'The disciples of this school prove with an assiduity worthy of a better cause, the research of local colours with which they have produced a number of curious effects'. But women, he argues, do these things better, and suggests that for what he calls 'an exhibition of the true realistic *chic*', even Flaubert could do worse than go to Charlotte Yonge.

As well as the *Heir,* he mentions by name *The Daisy Chain,* which he selects as an example of successful 'painting'—a word that picks up George Eliot's more famous remarks on the novel of realism made only a few years earlier. I take it that James has in mind the same qualities in *The Daisy Chain* as George Eliot describes as her ideal in *Adam Bede.* On one level, at any rate, Charlotte Yonge is as faithful to external reality as George Eliot's Dutch painters in whom she admired 'the rare, precious quality of truthfulness'. Her characters are fellow-mortals, and she herself, to use George Eliot's expression, was 'ready to give the loving pains of a life to the faithful representation of commonplace things'. My earlier quotations have already illustrated her talent for Victorian interiors, in which the total effect depends on the clarity of the detail. The warmth, the gaiety, the self-sufficiency, the values of the May family are all suggested by the description of the schoolroom, and as each member of the family appears, our impression is confirmed. Ethel, the fifth child, the heroine of the novel, is, significantly, a gawky adolescent—'a thin, lank, angular, sallow girl', who wears spectacles and tears her clothes—a far cry from the received idea of a Victorian heroine. There is, of course, a practical intention involved: Ethel, plain and unattractive as a large number of Charlotte Yonge's readers, and outwardly distinguished only by the ordinary faults of untidiness, impatience and forgetfulness, has a large imagination and lofty ideals. But the effect desired initially is of faithful representation to life, and this is achieved.

Charlotte Yonge's other gift for realism of this particular kind is in her talent for dialogue. Each character establishes itself at the outset by conversations in which the author rarely needs to interpret or interpolate. Philip serenely confirms his oneupmanship with Guy in a conversation about books; as the eleven members of the May family crowd into the schoolroom they are rapidly and permanently distinguished for the reader by their individual chatter. It is Saturday afternoon, the older girls and their governess are debating, with a scrupulosity which Ethel does not share, the propriety of a walk with a young man.

> 'Miss Winter, 'tis all right—Mr. Ernescliffe says he is quite up to the walk, and will like it very much, and he will undertake to defend you from the quarrymen.' 'Is Miss Winter afraid of the quarrymen?' bellowed Harry. 'Shall I take my club?' 'I'll take my gun and shoot them', valiantly exclaimed Tom; and while threats were passing among the boys, Margaret asked, in a low voice, 'Did you ask him to come with us?' . . .
>
> 'What's in the wind?' said Harry. 'Are many of your reefs out there, Ethel?'
>
> 'Harry can talk nothing but sailors' language' said Flora, 'and I am sure he did not learn that of Mr. Ernescliffe. You never hear slang from him'. 'But aren't we going to Cocksmoor?' asked Mary, a blunt, downright girl of ten.
>
> 'We shall know soon', said Ethel . . . and seating herself on the corner of the window-seat, with one leg doubled under her, took up a Shakespeare, holding it close to her eyes. Her brother Norman, who, in age, came before her and Flora, kneeling on one knee on the window-seat, leant over her, reading it too, disregarding a tumultuous skirmish going on in that division of the family collectively termed 'the boys', namely, Harry, Mary and Tom, until Tom was suddenly pushed down, and tumbled into Ethel's lap, thereby upsetting her and Norman together, and there was a general downfall, and a loud scream, 'The sphynx!'
>
> 'You've crushed it,' cried Harry, dealing out thumps indiscriminately.
>
> 'No, here 'tis,' said Mary, rushing among them and bringing out a green sphynx caterpillar on her finger—' 'tis not hurt'.
>
> 'Pax! Pax!', cried Norman, over all, with the voice of authority, as he leapt up lightly and set Tom on his legs again. 'Harry! you had better not do that again . . . Be off, out of this window, and let Ethel and me read in peace.'
>
> 'Here's the place,' said Ethel,—'Crispin, Crispian's day. How I do like *Henry V*'.
>
> 'It is no use to try to keep these boys in order!' sighed Miss Winter. 'Saturnalia, as papa calls Saturday', replied Flora.

It is interesting that Henry James discerns in Charlotte Yonge the beginnings of the realistic novel, while for Lady Georgiana Fullerton she represents the movement towards the psychological novel—'the analysis of character and revelations of a hidden life'. For Lady Georgiana her talent is for 'whatever treats of inward conflicts, secret perplexities, and the various trials of individual minds and hearts'. For both of them, in fact, she is not only the archexponent of a certain category of literature, the religious tale, but an innovator who is doing something new in the English novel. They differ on what it was, but on the fundamental point at issue they are strikingly in agreement. I take it that if Henry James admired Charlotte Yonge's faithfulness to *external* realism (and this is certainly what he appears to mean from the review, however much his views on the subject were to change later) what Lady Georgiana Fullerton admired were the qualities best summed up in a novel of Charlotte Yonge's early middle age, *Hopes and Fears, or Scenes from the Life of a Spinster.*

The novels I have talked about up to now—*The Heir of Redclyffe* and *The Daisy Chain*—are of 1853 and 1856 respectively, and belong among Charlotte Yonge's earlier works. They are novels of family life in which Charlotte Yonge vividly conveys, among other things, what it was like to live in a Victorian middle-class family in the middle years of the century. We very rarely see the individual members of these families in isolation, but almost invariably in the context of social relationships. R. H. Hutton has some interesting reflections on this aspect of Charlotte Yonge. Female novelists, he declares, seem incapable of delineating 'the more subtle intellectual aspects of social life, . . . hat is, in stories where they have to paint *solitary* aspects of character. By a kind of instinct, all our most skilful feminine novelists avoid this field, simply because they dare not go beyond the actual world of their own observation. Miss Austen avoids it—she knows her own powers; Mrs. Gaskell fails it if she attempts it; Miss Bronte ventures on it only when she is describing herself; Miss Yonge and Miss Sewell avoid it altogether'.

This is illuminating, and up to a point he is right. In the early novels, anyway, Charlotte Yonge *does* seem to be afraid to explore a situation in which the drama is internal and the character isolated from his kind. Her viewpoint is emphatically that of her principal characters, and there is little or no authorial voice independent of the official spokesman. But this situation changes in 1860 with the publication of *Hopes and Fears,* where the subject is no longer the family chronicle but the gradual awakening to self-knowledge of the spinster of the sub-title. In some respects she is the type of Charlotte Yonge character—well-born and wealthy, but fully alive to the responsibilities of her position in the parish, Anglo-Catholic by faith, a staunch Church-woman, loyal to the ideals of the past, and altogether very like Charlotte Yonge herself. In the light of earlier novels, we should have expected Honora to speak serenely for the author, and direct our responses throughout the novel. But almost the contrary is true. Because of her lack of judgement, Honora has made a mess of her life. Her first mistake lies in rejecting the man who could have saved her, because she fancies herself in love with the worthless Owen Sandbrook; and the second in adopting Owen Sandbrook's orphaned children, to whom she transfers her idolatrous affection, with disastrous results. She has no imagination and little tact, her ideals are shown to be destructively reactionary and her attitudes inflexible. Moreover, like Russell in *Eric,* she invariably acts from the highest principles. It is hardly surprising that wherever human relationships are concerned she fails conspicuously. Her bringing up of the children is a disaster: Lucilla, a pert and wayward little girl, whose one aim is to shock Honora, reacts violently from the first, and Owen, after an exemplary childhood in which he seems bent on ordination, proves the real weakness of his character by secretly marrying the village schoolmistress and contracting debts which he seeks to pay by raising a bond on Honora's death.

When her disillusionment is complete, and she recognizes her own shortcomings and those of her system, Honora is allowed a measure of chastened happiness. Owen, her favourite, is given back to her, a young widower with a shattered constitution and an incubus of a son. Charlotte Yonge has, of course, a theological explanation and solution of Honora's problem.

> Her inordinate affection had made her blind and credulous where her favourite was concerned, so as to lead to his seeming ruin, yet when the idol throne was overturned, she had learned to find sufficiency in her Maker, and to do offices of love without excess. Then after her time of loneliness, the very darling of her heart had been restored, when it was safe for her to have him once more.

But the resolution goes further than is stated. As well as a truer knowledge of God, Honora has also arrived at a truer knowledge of herself. The process has been bitter and hard, but the end is tranquillity and resignation.

It seems to me that it is this novel where Lady Georgina's admiration for the psychological penetration is most fully justified. Here Charlotte Yonge is presenting for the first time a full-length and sympathetic study of a character who does not speak with the authorial voice and who is nevertheless presented with a good measure of authorial detachment. It is interesting that Honora is the only heroine we have who is shown, not only in middle age, but in her progress towards it, experiencing the problems which accompany it. Ethel's problems, and Guy's, are those of adolescence and early adulthood, and are worked out against a background of family life; Honora is an isolated figure, early orphaned and never married, whose 'inward conflicts' and 'secret perplexities' are presented with a sympathy and a maturity of vision which Charlotte Yonge had not previously attempted.

All this represents a *positive* side of Charlotte Yonge, which the more discerning of her contemporaries recognized and applauded. Her contributions to the English school of realism and the psychological novel are genuine. But there is another voice to Charlotte Yonge which is perhaps less to her credit. While James recognized the innovating qualities of a 'first-rate mind', there is no doubt that certain limitations in her imagination do constitute a flaw in her achievement. There is one I am thinking of in particular, which is present in all but her best work. It is associated with her work as a 'popularizer of Church views', but it is not her direct exposition of these which I am criticizing. It is her inability to come to terms with the movement of mind of the century, and in particular with the dethronement of Christian orthodoxy and the movement towards scepticism which characterize her age. The values she represents are steady and unwavering, and are based firmly on a child-like morality of unquestioning and implicit obedience, first to one's parents, and second (even more important) to the Church.

This creed was fully developed by the time she was twenty in 1843, and although it may have found rather more sophisticated expressions as she grew older, her basic assumptions never altered. Hence throughout a literary career which saw the publication of *Leben Jesu, The Origin of Species, Essays and Reviews, Lux Mundi,* the whole of

Huxley and Arnold and most of Carlyle, Charlotte Yonge's views on 'infidelity' are almost wholly static. She sees religious scepticism without any real understanding, from a completely detached and secure position of faith. Her own attitude to it is unambiguous: in herself it is unthinkable (unlike her contemporary novelists, Elizabeth Sewell, Geraldine Jewsbury, Mrs. Lynn Linton, etc. all of whom endured and either surmounted or succumbed to religious crises, she never experienced a moment's qualm), in others reprehensible. Her rigidity of outlook is quite uncompromising.

Doubt is either a disease, to be cured, or, much more often, a sin to be punished. She does not distinguish, in terms of censure between the various forms and developments of scepticism, though she reflects most of them at various points in her career: the sinister 'Germanism' of the '30's and '40's (that is, the historical Biblical criticism of the German theologians), the threat of natural science in the '50's, the attack from within the Church represented by the notorious *Essays and Reviews* of 1860, are all stigmatized alike as 'the enemy'. She does not distinguish them, and fears them all equally. This failure of imagination is reflected in her novels. Early novels contain stereotyped and caricatured 'infidels' with names like Ohneglaube whose doubt is represented as a contagious disease, infecting the weaker characters around them. Both they and their victims are relentlessly chastized, by a variety of means. They are visited by blindness, struck down by brain-fevers, and at least one is startlingly punished for his general unsatisfactoriness by being scalped by Red Indians.

Religious doubt is what we might call Charlotte Yonge's blind spot. She is incapable (with one notable exception, which occurs, interestingly enough, in *Hopes and Fears*) of detachment or objectivity when confronted by it. It is, I think, the cause of her most conspicuous failure in an ambitious novel of 1865 called *The Clever Woman of the Family,* which could have been her best. This might well have been another valuable study of a character in isolation, and have followed on from *Hopes and Fears.* The theme is the same in many respects: the heroine's painful progress towards enlightenment and self-knowledge. But while Honora was a devout Anglo-Catholic, Rachel Curtis's religious convictions are unfixed and troubled. This is the basis of her problems and the root from which all her misfortunes spring. Modern readers may well feel, however, that Rachel's real misfortune is the total lack of comprehension with which she is presented by the author. She attempts to show her with a detached sympathy, and all she achieves is superciliousness and spleen. If her fault had been merely an excessive regard for earthly idols, as Honora's was, we might have had her presented from the inside, and been given a subtle interpretation of motive. As it is, all we ever see of Rachel is an outside view, and despite Charlotte Yonge's intention, she is reduced to a set of arguments to be refuted. The actual nature of her doubts is left very vague. She appears to have been poring over periodicals and learned journals, and to have fallen victim to Huxley's Darwinian essays in the *Fortnightly* and *Macmillan's.* But whatever the source, the effect is to destroy faith, character, judgement and morals at a blow. And her return to orthodoxy at the end of the novel is both painful and humiliating to her. I think it is a measure of Charlotte Yonge's concealed contempt for Rachel and her position that she selects as the instrument of her conversion a handsome young cavalry officer with a Victoria Cross.

The real 'clever woman' of the novel, whom Charlotte Yonge invites us to admire without qualification, is an invalid lady, the anonymous editor of the periodical to which Rachel contributes unsuitable articles. Where Rachel is gauche, mannish and wilfully set on her own destruction, Ermine Williams is refined and womanly and though intelligent, has, in her searching for truth, obediently set aside one subject as a no-go area. She will not, we are told approvingly, read 'poisonous' books: nay, 'absolutely as a medical precaution she abstained from dwelling on them'. But the foolish Rachel, with her 'plodding intellectuality', insists on arriving, however, painfully, at her own conclusions, and is resoundingly snubbed for her trouble. 'Many of her errors', Charlotte Yonge explains once she is safely back in the fold, 'had chiefly arisen from the want of someone whose superiority she could feel, and her old presumptions withered up to nothing when she measured her own powers with those of a highly educated man . . . After all, a woman's tone of thought is commonly moulded by the masculine intellect, which, under one form or another, becomes the master of her soul . . .

A woman's efforts at scepticism are but blind faith in her chosen leader, or, at the utmost, in the spirit of the age.'

And yet *The Clever Woman* has enough potential material in it to make it one of Charlotte Yonge's best novels. Rachel is in embryo another and earlier Dorothea Brooke. She is restless and impatient of her constricting society, anxious for the chance of renunciation and eager to devote her life to some noble service. She has outgrown her limited circle intellectually and imaginatively. It is not her fault, we are made to feel, rather her misfortune, that her talent for organization is frustrated by the narrowness of the society she lives in. Thus far she retains the sympathy of the author. But with all her potential, Rachel makes an obvious mistake: instead of allowing her gifts to be directed by the proper authorities, i.e. the Church, she insists on asserting her independence and becomes, in the phrase of the day, a 'strong-minded woman'. This is how Charlotte Yonge describes such a one:

> She has an aptitude for *all* kinds of severe studies, and insists on pursuing them on equal terms with men. She will go anywhere and do anything with perfect coolness, trusting an invisible armour of proof to protect her. She will also say anything to anybody, and never spare her censure or interference for the trifling consideration that it is no business of hers. Her chief dread is of prejudice and of ancient conclusions and she therefore thinks it weak not to read all kinds of books, especially the sceptical and the sensational, and the line she admires most in Tennyson is that in praise of 'honest doubt'!!

I think this last sentence gives Charlotte Yonge away. It is the climax of her peroration, and on it depend all the other faults of which strong-minded women are guilty—

arrogance, pride, impropriety. Religious unsettlement, unlike misdirected devotion, is one human failing for which she has no understanding at all, and so we get no picture of Rachel's mind from within. Charlotte Yonge is right, Rachel is wrong, and that is that. The mental blockage spoils what might have been a very good novel.

I do not wish to overstress this particular voice of Charlotte Yonge, though it is insistent and consistent enough to be observed and regretted. Her real achievement was something that only the more discerning of her contemporary readers recognized—indeed, many of them saw this very weakness, her refusal to respect the opposition as a strength. We, who signally fail to respond with the proper horror to the menace of unbelief as it stalks abroad with personal damnation and social chaos in its wake, can see with hindsight that Charlotte Yonge's contribution to the novel was not this sort of polemic. What we may regret is that her earliest and most influential critics, Keble in particular, were so concerned with doctrinal accuracy that they failed to discern the originality of her genius. Had Keble stayed in Oxford for the duration of the Movement he helped to inaugurate, the novelist most closely associated with it might have developed on very different lines. (pp. 181-88)

Barbara Dennis, "The Two Voices of Charlotte Yonge," in The Durham University Journal, *Vol. LXV, No. 2, March, 1973, pp. 181-88.*

Vineta Colby (essay date 1974)

[*Colby is an American educator and critic. In the following excerpt, she provides an overview of Yonge's most popular works.*]

[The] dogma and ritual of Anglo-Catholicism filled Charlotte Yonge's personal life as fully as romance and motherhood filled the lives of most women of her generation. From her confirmation at fifteen, she dedicated herself to her religion. Her writing began with and essentially never moved beyond the simple tales she published in the *Monthly Packet* to give religious instruction to school children. The money she made went to support church building and the missionary work of the Society for the Propagation of the Gospel. Her religion was parochial in the most literal sense. She shared her work totally with her parents, publishing only with their consent. Her spiritual guide was the vicar of her home church, John Keble, who brought the Oxford Movement to her own hearthside. Therefore it is hardly surprising that her fiction should be equally parochial and domestic. She describes her most popular novel after *The Heir of Redclyffe* (1853), *The Daisy Chain,* as "a Family Chronicle—a domestic record of home events, large and small, during those years of early life when the character is chiefly formed," a book "of a nondescript class" intended for an audience somewhere in between the nursery and the adult world. Her modest disclaimer was sincere. Charlotte Yonge never aspired to literary greatness and never regarded her talent as more than simply another tool with which to work for the celebration of God. Although she took healthy satisfaction in the stunning success of *The Heir of Redclyffe,* she also confided her fears about "vain-glory" to Keble. He responded comfortingly, "not telling one not to enjoy the praise, and like to hear it talked about," and reminding her of the pleasure that her success brought her mother and father.

Everywhere in Charlotte's life spiritual values were translated into domestic ones, and this habit she quite naturally carried over into her fiction. The highest praise we can render her is that her method was one of religious translation or transference, but not reduction. In her work religion is seen in its simplest, homeliest garb, yet it retains its dignity and profundity. Her talent was slight, her range of thought and experience narrow, her conception of human passion confined mainly to adolescent moods of temper, envy, and sentimental love, but within those limitations she achieved psychologically sound and valid perceptions. Henry James had high regard for her. Although he had described the type of fiction she wrote as "semi-developed novels . . . books which grown women may read aloud to children without either party being bored," he considered *The Heir of Redclyffe* a novel legitimated "by the force of genius." This occurs, however, "only when a first-rate mind takes the matter in hand . . . a mind which . . . is the master and not the slave of its material." Her characters are conditioned by the reality of their family and religious experiences. They react spontaneously and sensitively. Many of them are idealistic, but some are self-serving, selfish, and callow. Villainy—in the conventional fictive sense—rarely figures in her novels. Occasionally, in response to the vogues of the sensational novel, she introduces some episode of melodrama or violence (in *The Trial* there is even a murder), but she dismisses it quickly to get back to the comfortable business of Christian family living. Even her idealism is practical rather than visionary. Her heroine of *The Daisy Chain* refuses marriage not to become a nun in a cloister or a martyr-missionary in some distant jungle but to keep house for her widowed father and to raise her younger brothers and sisters. "Her religion," Joseph E. Baker remarks, "is not mysticism, but church-going raised to the *n*th degree. She does not take us into the world of ideas nor of great events, but of personal domestic feeling."

Circumscribed as a world of "personal domestic feeling" must be—especially for a Victorian spinster who rarely travelled beyond her village of Otterbourne and who devoted her life to parents and church—it is nevertheless a lively and emotionally engaging world. Ethel May, one of a brood of eleven children, growing up from painful, clumsy adolescence into warm maturity, is one of those secular saint-heroines of the sisterhood of Maggie Tulliver and Dorothea Brooke. Her ardent idealism is no less ardent than theirs, only it is confined to the more humble goals of building a village church and establishing a school for some poor children in the neighborhood. Intellectually Ethel aspires as loftily as these others; she reads widely and keeps up with her brother in the study of Latin and Greek. Her sensibilities are keen and delicate, though never exaggerated. She displays a natural guilty conscience when she neglects a younger brother, allowing him almost to set himself on fire while she is engrossed in a book. Awkward, near-sighted, and plain in appearance, she is understandably timid and self-conscious. At the ceremony opening the little school that she helped to establish, she suffers paralyzing embarrassment: "She took hold of Flora's hand, and squeezed it hard, in a fit of shyness, when they came upon the hamlet, and saw the children watching for them; and when they reached the house she would fain have shrunk into nothing; there was a swelling of heart that seemed to overwhelm and stifle her, and the effect of which was to keep her standing unhelpful, when the others were busy bringing in the benches and settling the room."

But Ethel May is the focussing center of a larger-scale domestic drama than these merely parochial events would indicate. The novel that begins with a cosy and idyllic domestic scene of family prayer ("It was pleasant to see that large family in the hush and reverence of such teaching, the mother's gentle power preventing the outbreaks of restlessness to which even at such times the wild young spirits were liable") switches suddenly in the third chapter to tragedy. A carriage accident kills the mother, permanently cripples the eldest daughter, leaves the father, who had been the driver, seriously injured and morbidly brooding over his responsibility for the disaster. In an instant this large happy family is bereaved and the problems and duties of adulthood are thrust upon the older children. At a single blow Ethel's "myriads of fancies" about finding money to build a church ("She had heard in books, of girls writing poetry, romance, history—gaining fifties and hundreds. . . . She would compose, publish, earn money—some day call papa, show him her hoard, beg him to take it, and never owning whence it came, raise the building. Spire and chancel, pinnacle and buttress rose before her eyes. . . . ") are shattered. Holding her infant sister in transcendent love she quietly prays: "We have the keeping of you, mama's precious flower, her pearl of truth! Oh, may God guard you to be an unstained jewel, till you come back to her again—and a blooming flower, till you are gathered into the wreath that never fades—my own sweet poor little motherless Daisy."

A healthy resiliency in the May family—and in their creator Charlotte Yonge—saves the novel from the maudlin and the morbid. Their Christianity is a working faith that carries them gropingly but successfully through their increasingly heavy domestic responsibilities. Ethel May learns "that to embrace a task heartily renders it no longer irksome," so she sets about nursing her invalid sister Margaret, educating her younger brothers and sisters, cheering her father, and teaching in the village school. She sacrifices her own studies as later she sacrifices her one opportunity to marry; but this is done in such a natural easy manner that neither she nor the reader broods over the alternatives: "If there had ever been disappointment about Norman Ogilvie [her suitor], it had long since faded away. . . . She had her vocation, in her father, Margaret, the children, home and Cocksmoor [her school], her mind and affections were occupied, and she never thought of wishing herself elsewhere."

In Charlotte Yonge's fiction even more strikingly than in Elizabeth Missing Sewell's, the Church functions both literally and metaphorically. Not only are her characters actively engaged in religious practice, but that practice assumes symbolic and dramatic significance. Confirmation and the taking of the sacrament mark peaks and climaxes in her stories: Guy's receiving the last rites of the Anglo-Catholic Church in a remote Italian village in *The Heir of Redclyffe,* the final "awakening" of the two misguided young sisters of *The Castle Builders* (1854) in the ceremony of their confirmation, the consecration of the church that marks the climax of *The Daisy Chain.* Church building, especially the restoration of neglected ruins, becomes a goal, a romantic ideal. In *The Daisy Chain* even the form of the new church memorializes the ill-fated lovers of the story, Alan Ernescliffe and Margaret May: its timbered roof is shaped like the ribs of a ship because Alan had been a sailor, and Margaret's pearl engagement ring is placed around the stem of the chalice.

Charlotte Yonge's special genius, which distinguishes her charming and still readable novels from the run of evangelical fiction, was her ability to integrate her material. Where Miss Sewell, Grace Aguilar, and Julia Kavanagh stop their narratives cold for their moralizing and have their simple homely characters speak the formal rhetoric of the pulpit, Charlotte writes sprightly, natural dialogue, keeps her story going briskly at all times, invents fitting occasions for the introduction of religious solemnities and then carefully balances these with lighter incidents. Knowing instinctively when to open windows for fresh air, she weaves her moralizing into the fabric of her tales. For example, the staple of evangelical fiction is the naughty child punished for some infraction like concealment, lying, or cheating. In Mrs. Sherwood, the classic of this mode, the punishments, as we have noted, were positively Draconian, and the reader is often left to feel that if denied a providential early death, an unpunished child will grow up a monster of moral corruption. Under the softening influences of domestic realism, however, Charlotte Yonge can make the same moral lesson a touching little case history in child psychology. Young brother Tom of *The Daisy Chain* first shows disturbing symptoms of dishonesty at home when he looks up answers to lessons he is preparing. Failing to warn their father to reprimand him at this early stage, his brothers and sisters allow him to go off to school ("a scene of temptation"), where, with his bad habits unchecked, Tom lies and gets into trouble. The consequences are painful for everyone. An older brother who assumes the blame to protect him loses a scholarship. But he generously comforts the contrite Tom, "If this sets you on always telling truth, I shan't think any great harm done." The lesson is duly learned, and Tom's repentance and reform are assured:

> " 'And you'll try and speak the truth, and be straight-forward?'
>
> " 'I will, I will,' said Tom, worn out in spirits by his long bondage, and glad to catch at the hope of relief and protection.
>
> " 'Then let us come home,' and Tom put his hand into his brother's, as a few weeks back would have seemed most unworthy of schoolboy dignity."

This gift for story-telling, combined with her high moral

purpose, made Charlotte Yonge at once both a popular and an "approved" novelist. Although Owen Chadwick surely over-rates her as "one of the true creative novelists of the nineteenth century, with two or three of her books ranking among the best Christian novels of any age," he weighs her reputation accurately in pointing out that she was "in one respect a channel for the most powerful influence which shy and reserved John Keble exercised upon the Victorian churches." The novel in which that influence was most powerfully displayed was *The Heir of Redclyffe.*

The phenomenon of a best-selling novel that could simultaneously appeal to the most naive and sentimental of readers as well as to the highly educated and most mature minds of its age was less rare in the nineteenth century than it would be today. In 1853 *The Heir of Redclyffe* caught the attention and affection of the widest conceivable public and held it tenaciously for nearly fifty years. It was a family novel, written in a careful and correct style, with many literary allusions and a general spirit of religious sanctity that marked it as eminently suitable for impressionable young readers, all the more so because it firmly demonstrated the importance of filial obedience and the wrongs of secret marriage engagements. Without excessive moralizing it unequivocally endorsed all the values esteemed by Church, State, and Family—honor, bravery, truth, faith, obedience, and duty. At the same time, it was an easy-reading, spirited novel, full of lively dialogue, enough mild suspense to hold flagging interest, a tender love story, and an appealing romanticism, cooled and tempered from Byronic and Shelleyan flamboyance into a refined aestheticism. Charlotte Yonge's romanticism developed in the age of Prince Albert, not Napoleon. The vestiges of that older romanticism remained in her hero's name, Sir Guy Morville, in his crumbling gothic family manor house, and the family curse that dates back to one of the murderers of Thomas à Becket. But at most this is a pale pre-Raphaelite gothicism, and we learn without surprise that young William Morris and Edward Burne-Jones read it enthusiastically at Oxford and that Dante Gabriel Rossetti "loved and revered it."

The new romanticism that *The Heir of Redclyffe* heralds is an introspective, gentle-genteel, somewhat melancholy backward glance at a colorful but long-dead past. The novel captures that moment of transition between Byron's *Giaour* ("bad food for excitable minds," though *Childe Harold* might still be read with profit for "his descriptions of scenery") and Tennyson's *Idylls of the King.* This romanticism found its outlet not in social rebellion, as it had earlier in the century, but in religious reform. The characters in *The Heir of Redclyffe* are lay people; they are not even remotely concerned with theology or problems of religious conflict such as we find in many novels of this period. But they were conceived by an author so thoroughly imbued with religious spirit that her hero was immediately identified as a hero of the Oxford Movement. He is an Anglo-Catholic Galahad (an artist painting his portrait sees him as Sir Galahad kneeling before the Holy Grail), defending the memory of the Stuart Charles I, reading *I Promessi Sposi,* rapt in admiration of a Raphael madonna. Under the influence of her mentor John Keble, Charlotte Yonge had read and, just before beginning this novel, reread the collection of papers and sermons of one of his students—the *Remains of the Late Reverend Richard Hurrell Froude* that Keble and Newman had edited in 1838. Here was a clerical Guy Morville, whose combination of aesthetic, sentimental, sensitive, and intellectual graces, with "vivid appreciation of the idea of sanctity" and profound faith had inspired Newman "to look with admiration" toward Rome. When Charlotte first conceived the character of Guy and described him to her mother, Mrs. Yonge promptly responded, "Like Mr. Hurrell Froude," to which Charlotte reacted with homely delight at this "sign that I have got the right sow by the ear."

As a romantic hero Guy is admittedly tame and domestic. He is an awkward, lonely adolescent thrust into the lives of a large, hearty family. He makes harmless blunders; he is not especially brilliant or talented, nor is he even strikingly handsome. He falls in love with exactly the right girl, as sweet and loving as he is, and marries her when he has barely come of age. Only a premature death prevents him from settling down to a domestic life as wholesome, though on a somewhat higher social scale, as the one Charlotte Yonge portrayed in *The Daisy Chain.* But Guy also serves higher heroic purposes of self-sacrifice, forgiveness of his enemies, and redemption of the souls of others. He is one of those potential saints whose mission, though earthbound, is spiritual and sacred. *The Heir of Redclyffe* began with an idea suggested to Charlotte by her spinster schoolteacher friend Marianne Dyson, who had herself started but then abandoned a story of two characters, "the essentially contrite and the self-satisfied . . . the conceited hero was to persecute the other and finally to cause his death, which was to be to his worldly advantage." The theme was to be the contrition and suffering of this hero— "the penitence of the saints." Miss Dyson's idea fascinated Charlotte, who continued to consult her friend as she shaped her novel. In their letters we can trace the developing domestic and romantic features of what began as a sternly moralistic tale. The emphasis shifts from Miss Dyson's self-satisfied hero, who is Charlotte Yonge's Philip Morville, to the persecuted victim Guy. The family of his guardian becomes prominent: "I *think* there should be some instances of wild escapades of fun together with a tremendous temper, the very vice of the house of Morville. I think a fiery temper would be the thing that would chiefly leave on Guy's mind the impression that he was and must be good for nothing . . . how he finds himself enjoying the lively family too much, and curbs himself sometimes in an odd sudden way which is now and then misunderstood and gives offence."

Charlotte conceived her task as "the playwright work of devising action and narrative." She refers to her characters as "my dramatis personae" and lets them ramble on and grow freely. Peopling her story with the Edmonstone family, she varies, enriches, and vitalizes it—the wise and understanding mother, the hot-tempered but forgiving father, three daughters ranging from young lady down to little girl, an outspoken invalid brother, visiting friends and relatives. Small wonder the novel appealed to all levels of readership and retained its popularity as long as large closely knit family households survived.

It is easy to dismiss *The Heir of Redclyffe* as innocent adolescent romance, a sentimental love story full of pathos and Christian moralizing. Charlotte Yonge herself had no more lofty ambitions than to write this kind of novel. But the shaping influences of Evangelicalism produced more than she had anticipated. The intense spirituality of the work, its emphasis on revealed Truth, on scrupulous examination of the conscience and the heart, on the motivations of human actions, and their moral consequences, produced in this most proper and orthodox of Victorian novels some disquieting insights and raised some questions that propriety and orthodoxy could not so easily answer. A hero manifestly intelligent, noble in character, and firm in his religious faith is nevertheless misunderstood, misjudged, and—what is more disturbing—misunderstands and misjudges himself. He is forever struggling in the snares of guilt and doubt. We are told, and he believes, that he has a violent temper. He broods over "the frenzy of his rage and his own murderous impulse," but these passions are never portrayed. Gentle Guy's only weakness of character, at least so far as the reader can observe, is "what some would call a vivid imagination, others a lively faith." He has, to be sure, a tendency to bite his lip when he is provoked and now and then to clench his teeth, but considering how sorely he is tried by his cousin Philip's unjust accusations, it is his self-control rather than his temper that is remarkable. Guy is a Christian hero, far less molded by the family curse of temper than by the Protestant-evangelical habit of self-analysis: "Many a question did he ask himself, to certify whether he wilfully entertained malice, or hatred, or any uncharitableness. It was a long difficult examination, but at its close, he felt convinced that, if such passions knocked at the door of his heart, it was not at his own summons, and that he drove them away without listening to them."

His antagonist Philip Morville is an infinitely more complex and troubled figure. To all appearances a model of virtuous and prudential behavior, he is inwardly a sinister and destructive agent, all the more frightening because of his total inability to doubt or question his actions. He is goodness perverted and blinded by self-righteousness. He acts malevolently out of what he believes are benign motives—"I speak for your good," he warns Guy, genuinely convinced that he does. "Philip had been used to feel men's wills and characters bend and give way beneath his superior force of mind.... With Guy alone it was not so; he had been sensible of it once or twice before; he had no mastery, and could no more bend that spirit than a bar of steel. This he could not bear, for it obliged him to be continually making efforts to preserve his own sense of superiority."

Driven by an almost Puritanical zeal, though he presumably shares the High Church beliefs of his cousins, "firm in his preconceived idea . . . and his own knowledge of mankind," Philip perverts good. When his cousin refuses to account for a large sum of money he has spent, Philip leaps to the conclusion that he is gambling. On receiving news that seemingly confirms his suspicions, "a sudden gleam, as of exultation in a verified prophecy, lighted his eye, shading off quickly, however, and giving place to an iron expression of rigidity and sternness, the compressed mouth, coldly fixed eye, and sedate brow, composed into a grave severity that might have served for an impersonation of stern justice." Unshakable in his convictions, he rejects Guy's open-hearted denial of the charge as "his usual course of mystery, reserve, and defiance." Instead of questioning his own conduct, Philip rationalizes and justifies it, thus anticipating by some fifteen years the casuistical evangelical Nicholas Bulstrode of *Middlemarch,* "a man whose desires had been stronger than his theoretic beliefs, and who had gradually explained the gratification of his desires into satisfactory agreement with those beliefs."

In attempting to portray this devious, complex, ambivalent young man, Charlotte Yonge accepted a greater challenge than perhaps at first she recognized. Philip's relentless persecution of Guy begins innocently, in the desire of an upright young man to correct and reform a younger man. But unconsciously Philip harbors two rankling, corrosive prejudices against Guy—one, the family curse of temper, of which he believes Guy guilty even when proved innocent; the other an unconscious jealousy of Guy's riches and his estate at Redclyffe to which Philip has only a remote claim: "He paused at the gate, and looked back at the wide domain and fine old house. He pitied them, and the simple-hearted, honest tenantry, for being the heritage of such a family, and the possession of one so likely to misuse them, instead of training them into the means of conferring benefits on them, on his country. What would not Philip himself do if those lands were his—just what was needed to give his talents free scope? And what would it be to see his beautiful Laura their mistress?"

Like the envious Satan, Philip cannot endure happiness in others because it is denied to him. In perfect character, however, with this simple, unmelodramatic family story, he destroys Guy's Eden not by a deliberate act of malice, but out of the same qualities of self-righteousness and moral superiority that have already warped him. Meeting Guy and his young bride Amabel on their honeymoon in Italy, he tries to persuade them to travel with him to a region where fever is raging. When they refuse, he stubbornly sets out alone, catches the fever, and nearly dies. Guy, who comes to nurse him, also falls ill, and as Philip recovers he dies. Thus Philip becomes the heir to the property he has coveted and outlives the man he has envied. But in Guy's noble Christian death, Philip is reborn, contrite and penitent. He has learned his lesson at a terrible price, and although the novel ends with his possession of Redclyffe and his marriage to Laura, we see him as a broken, grieving man, finding consolation only in the little daughter Guy has left behind him.

Charlotte Yonge did not dramatize this struggle in Manichean terms, but, in what they represent, Philip and Guy are men in mortal spiritual conflict. Guy's victory is as inevitable as the reversal of a classical tragedy or the victory of Christ in the Battle of the Angels. In *The Heir of Redclyffe* the battlefield of the Victorian conscience is the family. For all its apparently idyllic blessings, this family is plagued with pain and sorrow: young brother Charlie is a helpless cripple with an agonizing bone disease; sister

Laura is frustrated in her lengthy secret engagement; Guy's father had been killed in an accident following a violent quarrel with his grandfather; his mother dies in childbed; his uncle is a shabby musician unable to support his wife and children; Philip's sister is a cold-blooded mercenary shrew; Guy dies on his honeymoon, leaving his wife pregnant; Philip never recovers physically or mentally from the ravages of his fever.

Charlotte Yonge's vision of life, however, was not as morbid as this summary suggests, nor was she, we may confidently assert, slyly preaching cynicism or rebellion. Rather, under an impulse evangelical in its fervor to present Truth as she saw it, she depicted human suffering as conscientiously as she depicted happiness. Accepting unquestioningly the tenets of her Christian faith, she accepted evil, sin, guilt, suffering, and redemption. In such a vision happiness is at best tenuous. Like all evangelicals, the Anglo-Catholic Charlotte Yonge contemplated it with mixed feelings. "Do you recollect," Amabel asks her young husband Guy, "your melancholy definition of happiness years ago?" It was, she reminds him, "Gleams from another world, too soon eclipsed or forfeited." It is significant that so relatively large a part of this novel is devoted to the reconciliations that follow Guy's untimely death. The conclusion is a long, tearful epilogue, dwelling in almost microscopic detail on Amy's saintly bravery in her widowhood, on her noble foregiveness of Philip, on his lengthy spiritual and physical convalescence, on the legal details of settling the Morville estate (Charlotte does not ignore the paradox of her title). Faulty as all this is both emotionally and artistically, it is part of the overall evangelical scheme of the novel, translating dogma into the everyday realities of family life and human suffering. (pp. 187-201)

> Vineta Colby, "The Victorian 'Ayenbite of Inwyt': The Evangelical Novel from Charlotte Elizabeth to Charlotte Yonge," in her Yesterday's Woman: Domestic Realism in the English Novel, Princeton University Press, 1974, pp. 145-209.

Alan Horsman (essay date 1990)

[*In the excerpt which follows, Horsman examines characteristics of style and theme in Yonge's novels.*]

It is possible to think of [Charlotte Yonge's] talent as taking her in two directions, the one in novels written for adults, like ***Hopes and Fears*** (1860), the other in a wide range of work for readers not yet adult. The former were the more selfconsciously shaped by a lesson which those on the watch for it might learn, while the shape of the latter work, at its best, emerged rather from the 'whole life' of the youthful characters themselves.

Selfconscious shaping at first gave her her most resounding success, ***The Heir of Redclyffe*** (1853), which might well have had the same subtitle as her first novel [***Abbeychurch; or, Self Control and Self Conceit***]. The self-control was that of the young inheritor of Redclyffe, Sir Guy Morville, quelling 'high animal spirits' with a serious ascetic temper, the self-conceit that of the next heir, his cousin Captain Philip Morville, whose Grandisonian rectitude and confidence had the effect of hastening Guy's marriage and then his death. Although the author had accepted that Guy's self-discipline resembled that of a noted tractarian, J. A. Froude's brother Hurrell, the moral was made picturesque in terms readily acceptable in the third quarter of the century, during which the book was reprinted again and again. Guy's Byronic impetuosity, his admiration of Malory (especially of Sir Galahad), and his background of an apparently hereditary curse made him a figure of romance. His conquest of 'the besetting fiend of his family—the spirit of defiance and resentment'—was insistently connected with Fouqué's *Sintram* (1814). So the melodramatic self-communing which dates him for later readers was accepted not only as dramatization of an active conscience but as the appropriate mode for a romantic hero.

There was a ready appeal therefore to readers who might not share the author's religion. Moreover, religious significances which appeared in picturesque suggestion, the brightness of the Easter moon, for example, after Guy had 'suffered and conquered suffering', appeared also in conduct more mundanely observed, 'the soberer manner in which he spoke of his faults . . . without the vehemence which he used to expend in raving at himself'. There was even some attempt to make his religious life, however highly coloured its extremes, credible in its psychological processes, using mundane as well as religious terms: 'Guy had what some would call a vivid imagination, some a lively faith.' All this is far from sufficient to recommend the romantic hero to most readers over a century later. The parallels with Fouqué have lost their efficacy and the religious doggerel which mercilessly accompanies the hero's death and its aftermath raises a formidable barrier, not to mention the tendency to bombastic misapplication of ancient formulas, like the *Nunc dimittis* at the christening of Guy's daughter.

It is quite otherwise with Philip, the Grandisonian prig. It is not only that the author understands him more clearly as a form of life, not a mere figurehead, but that her attitude towards him is proportionately more varied. It includes even touches of an irony approaching Jane Austen's: for instance, Philip, who had been discovered applying a different standard of openness to Guy than to himself, was glad to be forgiven by a fool whose reason was 'I have been young and in love myself':

> That Captain Morville should live to be thankful for being forgiven in consideration of Mr Edmonstone's having been young!

The irony could be called structural in so far as it was Edmonstone who, as guardian, had yielded too readily to Philip's advice to delay Guy's engagement and then, with exaggerated self-assertion, when circumstantial evidence proved Philip wrong, had hurried on not only an engagement but marriage. But the book was finally too didactic to secure all the advantage that it might from such material. The plot could not stress the ironies of Edmonstone's position when his wife and family were allotted so much more space and so much more positive a role, especially his daughter Amy, Guy's widow. The aim was not the civilized pleasure arising from the selection of just what would sharpen the ironical point, but the heavier, more didactic irony that Philip, by inheriting the very estate he had once thought desirable, should suffer so much.

In *Heartsease* (1854) the author's religious interests were subordinate, from the reader's point of view, to the remarkable presentation of the wilfulness of the chief character, Theodora. Her pride was understood in its good manifestations as well as its bad, even though religion might have depreciated the former, and her reformation was stimulated, as it might have been in George Eliot, primarily by the influence of another person, the 'brother's wife' of the subtitle. The title, referring to the effect of the wife upon all surviving members of the family into which she married, meant that hers was the role of heroine—a role which left her vulnerable to idealization once the delicacy, and even comedy, in the treatment of her early hesitations and anxieties, after marriage at 16, gave way to the more improving spectacle of her moral strength. Nevertheless, the novel is a strong candidate for revival.

The same could not be said for *Dynevor Terrace* (1857), where a contrast, as in *The Heir of Redclyffe,* between two young men, the one 'fiery and sensitive', the other 'cool and impassive', yielded not a single plot but two stories, neither of any great force. The restraining of religious and high romantic sentiment in order to present an action much concerned with money, in a period just before and just after 1848, seemed to have left the author with less that she wished to say.

In *Hopes and Fears* (1860) the story was made from the difference between two such periods. At the conclusion the middle-aged heroine looked back to the 'mediaevalism, . . . chivalry, symbolism, whatever you may call it', of her own generation, who were 'fed on Scott, Wordsworth, and Fouqué' and 'moulded their opinions and practice on the past'. The younger characters, adopted by her 'widowed heart', 'were essentially of the new generation, that of Kingsley, Tennyson, Ruskin, and the *Saturday Review.* Chivalry had given way to commonsense, romance to realism, . . . the past to the future.' It was a fruitful subject when the heroine tended to turn into 'idolatry' her love, first for a man who fell short of its demands and then for his son. The faltering of the son's faith, his marriage as a result of 'the theory of fusion of classes', and the development of his sister into a 'fast' girl of 1860 further identified the new generation. But the sister's suitor brought with him his whole family who then swamped this subject with quite another novel. It had some contemporary interest—a young woman attaining 'liberty of action and independence of judgement', her brother refusing to enter the family distillery and devoting himself to the redemption of the patrons of gin palaces—but it left the heroine with little to do apart from approving those actions which enabled her to regard three of the family as each in turn 'a child of her own'. Her 'fluffiness . . . figurativeness and dreamy sentiment' were amusingly criticized by the fast girl: 'I cannot like mutton with the wool on!' But for most of the time the heroine's viewpoint was simply too close to the author's own to have any prominence in the multifarious action. This ambitious book suffered most from the principal feature of her work: it was all foreground. Her very prodigality in providing immediate 'scenes' left her with a correspondingly smaller power of attention to organizing principles and interpretive ideas.

The early chapters of *The Clever Woman of the Family* (1864-5) gave promise of the ability to develop the point of the whole novel from the heroine Rachel's opinionated self-reliance and 'sententious dogmatism', active in dialogue and in scenes which showed how easily eagerness could prevent her from being observant. If the terrible events which disciplined her had grown more specifically out of this dramatization of her defects the result might again have challenged comparison with Jane Austen. The materials were there, but their potentialities for comedy were forfeited in the interests of narrative excitement and a didactic completeness of reformation. Comedy lurked when the most important revelations were brought about by the practical energy and good sense of a young widow on whom Rachel had looked down, determined 'to put Fanny upon a definite system . . . counteracting the follies and nonsenses that her situation naturally exposes her to'. Attempting to be more serious morally, Charlotte Yonge became artistically less so in her crime story and in the suddenly accumulating illness, despised love, death, and birth, in another runaway family chronicle.

In the fiction where she had younger readers principally in mind, their interests placed limits, which she found congenial, on the kind of organizing ideas which might bind the whole together. The foreground was the chief thing and, as long as it was sufficiently lively, a subject could be left to grow out of it. The 'family chronicle' in *The Daisy Chain* (1853-6) and its sequel *The Trial* (1862-4) is the prime example. The first of these began as a series of 'conversational sketches'; after Part I had appeared in monthly instalments, the author, writing ahead, had as much material again in hand and this had shown her her subject. In the complete novel she thereupon published, everything came together, centred upon a widower, Dr May, and his third daughter Ethel, who, having chosen to live single in his interests and those of the family, 'had begun to understand that the unmarried woman must not seek undivided return of affection'. The subject was not unlike the one the author would develop in *Hopes and Fears,* but it consisted to a much greater degree in a pattern that was not recognized until after the main events had occurred. So they could be left free to happen and the habits which prevented a more pointed development of her subject in *The Heir of Redclyffe* and *The Clever Woman* could reign:

> I have taken a sheet of paper and turned my *dramatis personae* loose upon it to see how they will behave.

Naturally, the standards of an urgent, self-examining morality continued to apply; but they did not inhibit humour and they left plenty of scope for surprise, especially in the detail of the reactions which distinguished the two chief personages. The range of their feelings, their aims—church-building, schools, missions—indeed the very existence of large families among the professional classes, may now seem as remote as jousting; a less intense kind of sensibility than Elizabeth Sewell's may be at work, concerned with less painful affection and self-scrutiny; the reader's participation may be limited to observing what is immediately there to be noticed, without being invited to make inferences from it; but the ability of that omnipresent foreground to startle and enchain, once these limitations are granted, is as little diminished in late work like *The Two Sides of the Shield* (1884-5) as it is for the reader a century later. (pp. 247-51)

> Alan Horsman, "Later Minor Novelists," in his The Victorian Novel, Oxford at the Clarendon Press, 1990, pp. 190-255.

FURTHER READING

Biography

Battiscombe, Georgina. *Charlotte Mary Yonge: The Story of an Uneventful Life.* London: Constable and Co., 1943, 171 p.
> Biographical study by a leading scholar of Yonge's works.

Coleridge, Christabel. *Charlotte Mary Yonge: Her Life and Letters.* London: Macmillan and Co., 1903, 391 p.
> Incorporates biographical commentary with Yonge's autobiography and correspondence.

Mare, Margaret, and Percival, Alicia C. *Victorian Best-Seller: The World of Charlotte M. Yonge.* London: George C. Harrap and Co., 1947, 292 p.
> Details Yonge's life and career as a successful Victorian-era novelist.

Criticism

Bailey, Sarah. "Charlotte Mary Yonge." *The Cornhill Magazine* 150, No. 896 (August 1934): 188-98.
> Discusses how Yonge's religious beliefs are evinced in the characters and themes of her fiction.

Battiscombe, Georgina. "Anthony Trollope and Charlotte Yonge: A Study in Contrasts." *The Wind and the Rain* 111, No. 3 (Autumn 1946): 130-39.
> Compares and contrasts Yonge and Trollope, suggesting that "among the whole galaxy of English novelists these two are the most successful in building an imaginary world, the scene of successive novels which are not so much sequels to each other as separate tales, told against the same background and therefore dealing in part with the same characters."

"Miss Yonge's Novels." *The Christian Remembrancer* LXXXII (July 1853): 33-63.
> Favorable review of several of Yonge's novels.

Cruse, Amy. "The World of Miss Charlotte Yonge." In her *The Victorians and Their Books,* pp. 42-64. London: George Allen & Unwin, 1935.
> Examines the Victorian middle-class social milieu which was the basis of Yonge's popularity.

Dodds, M. Hope. "Jane Austen and Charlotte M. Yonge." *Notes and Queries* 193, No. 22 (30 October 1948): 476-78.
> Observes parallels between the lives of Yonge and Austen.

Haldane, Charlotte. Preface to *The Heir of Redclyffe,* by Charlotte Yonge, pp. v-xi. Reprint. London: Gerald Duckworth & Co., 1964.
> Brief biographical and critical introduction.

Hayter, Alethea. "The Sanitary Idea and a Victorian Novelist." *History Today* XIX, No. 12 (December 1969): 840-47.
> Examines *The Young Stepmother* and its depiction of unsanitary living conditions and the poor state of public health in mid-nineteenth century London.

Leavis, Q. D. "Charlotte Yonge and 'Christian Discrimination'." *Scrutiny* XII, No. 2 (Spring 1944): 152-60.
> Attacks Yonge's works as moralistic propaganda, asserting that "it seems incredible that [her] novels could be taken seriously as literature except by those of her own way of thinking."

"Miss Yonge's Novels." *The North American Review* LXXX, No. CLXVII (April 1855): 439-59.
> Favorable review of *The Heir of Redclyffe* and *Heartsease.*

"The Author of *Heartsease,* and Modern Schools of Fiction." *The Prospective Review* X, No. XXXIX (1854): 460-82.
> Underscores Yonge's keen attention to detail and her ability to develop realistic characters in *The Heir of Redclyffe* and *Heartsease.*

Tillotson, Kathleen. "The Heir of Redclyffe." In *Mid-Victorian Studies,* edited by Geoffrey Tillotson and Kathleen Tillotson, pp. 49-55. London: Athlone Press, 1965.
> Reprint of a radio program broadcast in January 1953 in commemoration of the one-hundredth anniversary of the publication of Yonge's novel.

Additional coverage of Yonge's life and career is contained in the following sources published by Gale Research: *Contemporary Authors,* Vol. 109; *Dictionary of Literary Biography,* Vol. 18; and *Something about the Author,* Vol. 17.

Twentieth-Century Literary Criticism

Cumulative Indexes
Volumes 1-48

This Index Includes References to Entries in These Gale Series

Authors in the News (AITN) reprints articles from American periodicals covering authors and members of the communications media. Two volumes.

Bestsellers (BEST) furnishes information about best-selling books and their authors for the years 1989-1990.

Black Literature Criticism (BLC) provides excerpts from criticism of the most significant works of black authors of all nationalities over the past 200 years. Complete in three volumes.

Children's Literature Review (CLR) includes excerpts from reviews, criticism, and commentary on works of authors and illustrators who create books for children.

Classical and Medieval Literature Criticism (CMLC) offers criticism on the works of world authors from classical antiquity through the fourteenth century.

Contemporary Authors encompasses eight related series: *Contemporary Authors (CA)* provides biographical and bibliographical information on more than 99,000 writers of fiction, nonfiction, poetry, journalism, drama, and film. *Contemporary Authors New Revision Series (CANR)* provides updated information on active authors previously covered in *CA*. *Contemporary Authors Permanent Series (CAP)* consists of updated listings for deceased and inactive authors removed from revised volumes of *CA*. *Contemporary Authors Autobiography Series (CAAS)* presents commissioned autobiographies by leading contemporary writers. *Contemporary Authors Bibliographical Series (CABS)* contains primary and secondary bibliographies as well as bibliographical essays on major modern authors. *Black Writers (BW)* compiles selected *CA* sketches on more than 400 prominent writers. *Hispanic Writers (HW)* compiles selected *CA* sketches on twentieth-century Hispanic writers. *Major 20th-Century Writers (MTCW)* presents in four volumes selected *CA* sketches on over 1,000 of the most influential writers of this century.

Contemporary Literary Criticism (CLC) presents excerpts of criticism on the works of creative writers who are now living or who have died since 1960.

Dictionary of Literary Biography comprises five related series: *Dictionary of Literary Biography (DLB)* furnishes illustrated overviews of authors' lives and works. *Dictionary of Literary Biography Documentary Series (DLBD)* illuminates the careers of major figures through a selection of literary documents, including letters, interviews, and photographs. *Dictionary of Literary Biography Yearbook (DLBY)* summarizes the past year's literary activity and includes updated and new entries on individual authors. *Concise Dictionary of American Literary Biography (CDALB)* and *Concise Dictionary of British Literary Biography (CDBLB)* collect revised and updated sketches that were originally presented in *Dictionary of Literary Biography*.

Drama Criticism (DC) provides excerpts of criticism on the works of playwrights of all nationalities and periods of literary history.

Literature Criticism from 1400 to 1800 (LC) compiles significant passages from criticism on authors of the fifteenth through the eighteenth centuries.

Nineteenth-Century Literature Criticism (NCLC) reprints significant passages from criticism on authors who died between 1800 and 1899.

Poetry Criticism (PC) presents excerpts of criticism on the works of poets from all eras, movements, and nationalities.

Short Story Criticism (SSC) offers critical excerpts on short fiction by writers of all eras and nationalities.

Something about the Author encompasses four related series: *Something about the Author (SATA)* contains biographical sketches on authors and illustrators of juvenile and young adult literature. *Something about the Author Autobiography Series (SAAS)* presents commissioned autobiographies by prominent authors and illustrators of books for children and young adults. *Authors & Artists for Young Adults (AAYA)* provides students with profiles of their favorite creative artists. *Major Authors and Illustrators for Children and Young Adults (MAICYA)* contains in six volumes both newly written and completely updated *SATA* sketches on nearly 800 authors and illustrators for young people.

Twentieth-Century Literary Criticism (TCLC) contains critical excerpts on authors who died between 1900 and 1960.

World Literature Criticism (WLC) contains excerpts from criticism on the works of over 200 major writers from the Renaissance to the present. Complete in six volumes.

Yesterday's Authors of Books for Children (YABC) contains heavily illustrated entries on children's writers who died before 1961. Complete in two volumes.

Literary Criticism Series
Cumulative Author Index

A. E. .... TCLC 3, 10
  See also Russell, George William
  See also DLB 19

A. M.
  See Megged, Aharon

Abasiyanik, Sait Faik 1906-1954
  See Sait Faik
  See also CA 123

Abbey, Edward 1927-1989 ...... CLC 36, 59
  See also CA 45-48; 128; CANR 2

Abbott, Lee K(ittredge) 1947- ...... CLC 48
  See also CA 124

Abe Kobo 1924- .... CLC 8, 22, 53
  See also CA 65-68; CANR 24; MTCW

Abell, Kjeld 1901-1961............ CLC 15
  See also CA 111

Abish, Walter 1931-............... CLC 22
  See also CA 101; CANR 37

Abrahams, Peter (Henry) 1919- ..... CLC 4
  See also BW; CA 57-60; CANR 26; DLB 117; MTCW

Abrams, M(eyer) H(oward) 1912-... CLC 24
  See also CA 57-60; CANR 13, 33; DLB 67

Abse, Dannie 1923-............. CLC 7, 29
  See also CA 53-56; CAAS 1; CANR 4; DLB 27

Achebe, (Albert) Chinua(lumogu)
  1930- .... CLC 1, 3, 5, 7, 11, 26, 51
  See also BLC 1; BW; CA 1-4R; CANR 6, 26; CLR 20; DLB 117; MAICYA; MTCW; SATA 38, 40; WLC

Acker, Kathy 1948- .... CLC 45
  See also CA 117; 122

Ackroyd, Peter 1949-.......... CLC 34, 52
  See also CA 123; 127

Acorn, Milton 1923-............... CLC 15
  See also CA 103; DLB 53

Adamov, Arthur 1908-1970 ...... CLC 4, 25
  See also CA 17-18; 25-28R; CAP 2; MTCW

Adams, Alice (Boyd) 1926- ... CLC 6, 13, 46
  See also CA 81-84; CANR 26; DLBY 86; MTCW

Adams, Douglas (Noel) 1952- ... CLC 27, 60
  See also AAYA 4; BEST 89:3; CA 106; CANR 34; DLBY 83

Adams, Francis 1862-1893....... NCLC 33

Adams, Henry (Brooks)
  1838-1918 .... TCLC 4
  See also CA 104; 133; DLB 12, 47

Adams, Richard (George)
  1920- .... CLC 4, 5, 18
  See also AITN 1, 2; CA 49-52; CANR 3, 35; CLR 20; MAICYA; MTCW; SATA 7, 69

Adamson, Joy(-Friederike Victoria)
  1910-1980 .... CLC 17
  See also CA 69-72; 93-96; CANR 22; MTCW; SATA 11, 22

Adcock, Fleur 1934-.............. CLC 41
  See also CA 25-28R; CANR 11, 34; DLB 40

Addams, Charles (Samuel)
  1912-1988 .... CLC 30
  See also CA 61-64; 126; CANR 12

Addison, Joseph 1672-1719 .... LC 18
  See also CDBLB 1660-1789; DLB 101

Adler, C(arole) S(chwerdtfeger)
  1932- .... CLC 35
  See also AAYA 4; CA 89-92; CANR 19; MAICYA; SATA 26, 63

Adler, Renata 1938-............ CLC 8, 31
  See also CA 49-52; CANR 5, 22; MTCW

Ady, Endre 1877-1919 .... TCLC 11
  See also CA 107

Afton, Effie
  See Harper, Frances Ellen Watkins

Agapida, Fray Antonio
  See Irving, Washington

Agee, James (Rufus)
  1909-1955 .... TCLC 1, 19
  See also AITN 1; CA 108; CDALB 1941-1968; DLB 2, 26

Aghill, Gordon
  See Silverberg, Robert

Agnon, S(hmuel) Y(osef Halevi)
  1888-1970 .... CLC 4, 8, 14
  See also CA 17-18; 25-28R; CAP 2; MTCW

Aherne, Owen
  See Cassill, R(onald) V(erlin)

Ai 1947-................... CLC 4, 14, 69
  See also CA 85-88; CAAS 13; DLB 120

Aickman, Robert (Fordyce)
  1914-1981 .... CLC 57
  See also CA 5-8R; CANR 3

Aiken, Conrad (Potter)
  1889-1973 ... CLC 1, 3, 5, 10, 52; SSC 9
  See also CA 5-8R; 45-48; CANR 4; CDALB 1929-1941; DLB 9, 45, 102; MTCW; SATA 3, 30

Aiken, Joan (Delano) 1924-........ CLC 35
  See also AAYA 1; CA 9-12R; CANR 4, 23, 34; CLR 1, 19; MAICYA; MTCW; SAAS 1; SATA 2, 30

Ainsworth, William Harrison
  1805-1882 .... NCLC 13
  See also DLB 21; SATA 24

Aitmatov, Chingiz (Torekulovich)
  1928- .... CLC 71
  See also CA 103; CANR 38; MTCW; SATA 56

Akers, Floyd
  See Baum, L(yman) Frank

Akhmadulina, Bella Akhatovna
  1937-...................... CLC 53
  See also CA 65-68

Akhmatova, Anna
  1888-1966 .... CLC 11, 25, 64; PC 2
  See also CA 19-20; 25-28R; CANR 35; CAP 1; MTCW

Aksakov, Sergei Timofeyvich
  1791-1859 .... NCLC 2

Aksenov, Vassily.................. CLC 22
  See also Aksyonov, Vassily (Pavlovich)

Aksyonov, Vassily (Pavlovich)
  1932- .... CLC 37
  See also Aksenov, Vassily
  See also CA 53-56; CANR 12

Akutagawa Ryunosuke
  1892-1927 .... TCLC 16
  See also CA 117

Alain 1868-1951 .... TCLC 41

Alain-Fournier.................... TCLC 6
  See also Fournier, Henri Alban
  See also DLB 65

Alarcon, Pedro Antonio de
  1833-1891 .... NCLC 1

Alas (y Urena), Leopoldo (Enrique Garcia)
  1852-1901 .... TCLC 29
  See also CA 113; 131; HW

Albee, Edward (Franklin III)
  1928- ... CLC 1, 2, 3, 5, 9, 11, 13, 25, 53
  See also AITN 1; CA 5-8R; CABS 3; CANR 8; CDALB 1941-1968; DLB 7; MTCW; WLC

Alberti, Rafael 1902- .... CLC 7
  See also CA 85-88; DLB 108

Alcala-Galiano, Juan Valera y
  See Valera y Alcala-Galiano, Juan

Alcott, Amos Bronson 1799-1888 .. NCLC 1
  See also DLB 1

Alcott, Louisa May 1832-1888 .... NCLC 6
  See also CDALB 1865-1917; CLR 1; DLB 1, 42, 79; MAICYA; WLC; YABC 1

Aldanov, M. A.
  See Aldanov, Mark (Alexandrovich)

Aldanov, Mark (Alexandrovich)
  1886(?)-1957 .... TCLC 23
  See also CA 118

Aldington, Richard 1892-1962...... CLC 49
  See also CA 85-88; DLB 20, 36, 100

Aldiss, Brian W(ilson)
  1925- .... CLC 5, 14, 40
  See also CA 5-8R; CAAS 2; CANR 5, 28; DLB 14; MTCW; SATA 34

Alegria, Fernando 1918-........... CLC 57
  See also CA 9-12R; CANR 5, 32; HW

Aleichem, Sholom .... TCLC 1, 35
  See also Rabinovitch, Sholem

393

Aleixandre, Vicente 1898-1984 ... **CLC 9, 36**
See also CA 85-88; 114; CANR 26; DLB 108; HW; MTCW

Alepoudelis, Odysseus
See Elytis, Odysseus

Aleshkovsky, Joseph 1929-
See Aleshkovsky, Yuz
See also CA 121; 128

Aleshkovsky, Yuz .... **CLC 44**
See also Aleshkovsky, Joseph

Alexander, Lloyd (Chudley) 1924- .. **CLC 35**
See also AAYA 1; CA 1-4R; CANR 1, 24, 38; CLR 1, 5; DLB 52; MAICYA; MTCW; SATA 3, 49

Alfau, Felipe 1902- .... **CLC 66**
See also CA 137

Alger, Horatio Jr. 1832-1899 ..... **NCLC 8**
See also DLB 42; SATA 16

Algren, Nelson 1909-1981 .... **CLC 4, 10, 33**
See also CA 13-16R; 103; CANR 20; CDALB 1941-1968; DLB 9; DLBY 81, 82; MTCW

Ali, Ahmed 1910- .... **CLC 69**
See also CA 25-28R; CANR 15, 34

Alighieri, Dante 1265-1321 .... **CMLC 3**

Allan, John B.
See Westlake, Donald E(dwin)

Allen, Edward 1948- .... **CLC 59**

Allen, Roland
See Ayckbourn, Alan

Allen, Woody 1935- .... **CLC 16, 52**
See also CA 33-36R; CANR 27, 38; DLB 44; MTCW

Allende, Isabel 1942- .... **CLC 39, 57**
See also CA 125; 130; HW; MTCW

Alleyn, Ellen
See Rossetti, Christina (Georgina)

Allingham, Margery (Louise)
1904-1966 .... **CLC 19**
See also CA 5-8R; 25-28R; CANR 4; DLB 77; MTCW

Allingham, William 1824-1889 ... **NCLC 25**
See also DLB 35

Allston, Washington 1779-1843.... **NCLC 2**
See also DLB 1

Almedingen, E. M. .... **CLC 12**
See also Almedingen, Martha Edith von
See also SATA 3

Almedingen, Martha Edith von 1898-1971
See Almedingen, E. M.
See also CA 1-4R; CANR 1

Alonso, Damaso 1898-1990 .... **CLC 14**
See also CA 110; 131; 130; DLB 108; HW

Alta 1942- .... **CLC 19**
See also CA 57-60

Alter, Robert B(ernard) 1935- ...... **CLC 34**
See also CA 49-52; CANR 1

Alther, Lisa 1944- .... **CLC 7, 41**
See also CA 65-68; CANR 12, 30; MTCW

Altman, Robert 1925- .... **CLC 16**
See also CA 73-76

Alvarez, A(lfred) 1929- .... **CLC 5, 13**
See also CA 1-4R; CANR 3, 33; DLB 14, 40

Alvarez, Alejandro Rodriguez 1903-1965
See Casona, Alejandro
See also CA 131; 93-96; HW

Amado, Jorge 1912- .... **CLC 13, 40**
See also CA 77-80; CANR 35; DLB 113; MTCW

Ambler, Eric 1909- .... **CLC 4, 6, 9**
See also CA 9-12R; CANR 7, 38; DLB 77; MTCW

Amichai, Yehuda 1924- .... **CLC 9, 22, 57**
See also CA 85-88; MTCW

Amiel, Henri Frederic 1821-1881 .. **NCLC 4**

Amis, Kingsley (William)
1922- ...... **CLC 1, 2, 3, 5, 8, 13, 40, 44**
See also AITN 2; CA 9-12R; CANR 8, 28; CDBLB 1945-1960; DLB 15, 27, 100; MTCW

Amis, Martin (Louis)
1949- .... **CLC 4, 9, 38, 62**
See also BEST 90:3; CA 65-68; CANR 8, 27; DLB 14

Ammons, A(rchie) R(andolph)
1926- .... **CLC 2, 3, 5, 8, 9, 25, 57**
See also AITN 1; CA 9-12R; CANR 6, 36; DLB 5; MTCW

Amo, Tauraatua i
See Adams, Henry (Brooks)

Anand, Mulk Raj 1905- .... **CLC 23**
See also CA 65-68; CANR 32; MTCW

Anatol
See Schnitzler, Arthur

Anaya, Rudolfo A(lfonso) 1937- .... **CLC 23**
See also CA 45-48; CAAS 4; CANR 1, 32; DLB 82; HW; MTCW

Andersen, Hans Christian
1805-1875 .... **NCLC 7; SSC 6**
See also CLR 6; MAICYA; WLC; YABC 1

Anderson, C. Farley
See Mencken, H(enry) L(ouis); Nathan, George Jean

Anderson, Jessica (Margaret) Queale
.... **CLC 37**
See also CA 9-12R; CANR 4

Anderson, Jon (Victor) 1940- .... **CLC 9**
See also CA 25-28R; CANR 20

Anderson, Lindsay (Gordon)
1923- .... **CLC 20**
See also CA 125; 128

Anderson, Maxwell 1888-1959 ..... **TCLC 2**
See also CA 105; DLB 7

Anderson, Poul (William) 1926- .... **CLC 15**
See also AAYA 5; CA 1-4R; CAAS 2; CANR 2, 15, 34; DLB 8; MTCW; SATA 39

Anderson, Robert (Woodruff)
1917- .... **CLC 23**
See also AITN 1; CA 21-24R; CANR 32; DLB 7

Anderson, Sherwood
1876-1941 ...... **TCLC 1, 10, 24; SSC 1**
See also CA 104; 121; CDALB 1917-1929; DLB 4, 9, 86; DLBD 1; MTCW; WLC

Andouard
See Giraudoux, (Hippolyte) Jean

Andrade, Carlos Drummond de ...... **CLC 18**
See also Drummond de Andrade, Carlos

Andrade, Mario de 1893-1945..... **TCLC 43**

Andrewes, Lancelot 1555-1626 .... **LC 5**

Andrews, Cicily Fairfield
See West, Rebecca

Andrews, Elton V.
See Pohl, Frederik

Andreyev, Leonid (Nikolaevich)
1871-1919 .... **TCLC 3**
See also CA 104

Andric, Ivo 1892-1975 .... **CLC 8**
See also CA 81-84; 57-60; MTCW

Angelique, Pierre
See Bataille, Georges

Angell, Roger 1920- .... **CLC 26**
See also CA 57-60; CANR 13

Angelou, Maya 1928- .... **CLC 12, 35, 64**
See also AAYA 7; BLC 1; BW; CA 65-68; CANR 19; DLB 38; MTCW; SATA 49

Annensky, Innokenty Fyodorovich
1856-1909 .... **TCLC 14**
See also CA 110

Anon, Charles Robert
See Pessoa, Fernando (Antonio Nogueira)

Anouilh, Jean (Marie Lucien Pierre)
1910-1987 ...... **CLC 1, 3, 8, 13, 40, 50**
See also CA 17-20R; 123; CANR 32; MTCW

Anthony, Florence
See Ai

Anthony, John
See Ciardi, John (Anthony)

Anthony, Peter
See Shaffer, Anthony (Joshua); Shaffer, Peter (Levin)

Anthony, Piers 1934- .... **CLC 35**
See also CA 21-24R; CANR 28; DLB 8; MTCW

Antoine, Marc
See Proust, (Valentin-Louis-George-Eugene-)Marcel

Antoninus, Brother
See Everson, William (Oliver)

Antonioni, Michelangelo 1912- ...... **CLC 20**
See also CA 73-76

Antschel, Paul 1920-1970........ **CLC 10, 19**
See also Celan, Paul
See also CA 85-88; CANR 33; MTCW

Anwar, Chairil 1922-1949 .... **TCLC 22**
See also CA 121

Apollinaire, Guillaume .... **TCLC 3, 8**
See also Kostrowitzki, Wilhelm Apollinaris de

Appelfeld, Aharon 1932- .... **CLC 23, 47**
See also CA 112; 133

Apple, Max (Isaac) 1941-........ **CLC 9, 33**
See also CA 81-84; CANR 19

Appleman, Philip (Dean) 1926- ..... **CLC 51**
See also CA 13-16R; CANR 6, 29

Appleton, Lawrence
See Lovecraft, H(oward) P(hillips)

Apuleius, (Lucius Madaurensis)
125(?)-175(?) .... CMLC 1

Aquin, Hubert 1929-1977......... CLC 15
See also CA 105; DLB 53

Aragon, Louis 1897-1982........ CLC 3, 22
See also CA 69-72; 108; CANR 28;
DLB 72; MTCW

Arany, Janos 1817-1882........ NCLC 34

Arbuthnot, John 1667-1735......... LC 1
See also DLB 101

Archer, Herbert Winslow
See Mencken, H(enry) L(ouis)

Archer, Jeffrey (Howard) 1940- .... CLC 28
See also BEST 89:3; CA 77-80; CANR 22

Archer, Jules 1915- .... CLC 12
See also CA 9-12R; CANR 6; SAAS 5;
SATA 4

Archer, Lee
See Ellison, Harlan

Arden, John 1930- .... CLC 6, 13, 15
See also CA 13-16R; CAAS 4; CANR 31;
DLB 13; MTCW

Arenas, Reinaldo 1943-1990 .... CLC 41
See also CA 124; 128; 133; HW

Arendt, Hannah 1906-1975 .... CLC 66
See also CA 17-20R; 61-64; CANR 26;
MTCW

Aretino, Pietro 1492-1556 .... LC 12

Arguedas, Jose Maria
1911-1969 .... CLC 10, 18
See also CA 89-92; DLB 113; HW

Argueta, Manlio 1936- .... CLC 31
See also CA 131; HW

Ariosto, Ludovico 1474-1533......... LC 6

Aristides
See Epstein, Joseph

Aristophanes
450B.C.-385B.C........ CMLC 4; DC 2

Arlt, Roberto (Godofredo Christophersen)
1900-1942 .... TCLC 29
See also CA 123; 131; HW

Armah, Ayi Kwei 1939- .... CLC 5, 33
See also BLC 1; BW; CA 61-64; CANR 21;
DLB 117; MTCW

Armatrading, Joan 1950- .... CLC 17
See also CA 114

Arnette, Robert
See Silverberg, Robert

Arnim, Achim von (Ludwig Joachim von
Arnim) 1781-1831 .... NCLC 5
See also DLB 90

Arnim, Bettina von 1785-1859.... NCLC 38
See also DLB 90

Arnold, Matthew
1822-1888 .... NCLC 6, 29; PC 5
See also CDBLB 1832-1890; DLB 32, 57;
WLC

Arnold, Thomas 1795-1842 ...... NCLC 18
See also DLB 55

Arnow, Harriette (Louisa) Simpson
1908-1986 .... CLC 2, 7, 18
See also CA 9-12R; 118; CANR 14; DLB 6;
MTCW; SATA 42, 47

Arp, Hans
See Arp, Jean

Arp, Jean 1887-1966................ CLC 5
See also CA 81-84; 25-28R

Arrabal.................... CLC 2, 9, 18
See also Arrabal, Fernando

Arrabal, Fernando 1932- .... CLC 58
See also Arrabal
See also CA 9-12R; CANR 15

Arrick, Fran..................... CLC 30

Artaud, Antonin 1896-1948 ..... TCLC 3, 36
See also CA 104

Arthur, Ruth M(abel) 1905-1979.... CLC 12
See also CA 9-12R; 85-88; CANR 4;
SATA 7, 26

Artsybashev, Mikhail (Petrovich)
1878-1927 .... TCLC 31

Arundel, Honor (Morfydd)
1919-1973 .... CLC 17
See also CA 21-22; 41-44R; CAP 2;
SATA 4, 24

Asch, Sholem 1880-1957 .... TCLC 3
See also CA 105

Ash, Shalom
See Asch, Sholem

Ashbery, John (Lawrence)
1927- ... CLC 2, 3, 4, 6, 9, 13, 15, 25, 41
See also CA 5-8R; CANR 9, 37; DLB 5;
DLBY 81; MTCW

Ashdown, Clifford
See Freeman, R(ichard) Austin

Ashe, Gordon
See Creasey, John

Ashton-Warner, Sylvia (Constance)
1908-1984 .... CLC 19
See also CA 69-72; 112; CANR 29; MTCW

Asimov, Isaac
1920-1992 .... CLC 1, 3, 9, 19, 26
See also BEST 90:2; CA 1-4R; 137;
CANR 2, 19, 36; CLR 12; DLB 8;
MAICYA; MTCW; SATA 1, 26

Astley, Thea (Beatrice May)
1925- .... CLC 41
See also CA 65-68; CANR 11

Aston, James
See White, T(erence) H(anbury)

Asturias, Miguel Angel
1899-1974 .... CLC 3, 8, 13
See also CA 25-28; 49-52; CANR 32;
CAP 2; DLB 113; HW; MTCW

Atares, Carlos Saura
See Saura (Atares), Carlos

Atheling, William
See Pound, Ezra (Weston Loomis)

Atheling, William Jr.
See Blish, James (Benjamin)

Atherton, Gertrude (Franklin Horn)
1857-1948 .... TCLC 2
See also CA 104; DLB 9, 78

Atherton, Lucius
See Masters, Edgar Lee

Atkins, Jack
See Harris, Mark

Atticus
See Fleming, Ian (Lancaster)

Atwood, Margaret (Eleanor)
1939- .... CLC 2, 3, 4, 8, 13, 15, 25, 44;
SSC 2
See also BEST 89:2; CA 49-52; CANR 3,
24, 33; DLB 53; MTCW; SATA 50; WLC

Aubigny, Pierre d'
See Mencken, H(enry) L(ouis)

Aubin, Penelope 1685-1731(?)........ LC 9
See also DLB 39

Auchincloss, Louis (Stanton)
1917- .... CLC 4, 6, 9, 18, 45
See also CA 1-4R; CANR 6, 29; DLB 2;
DLBY 80; MTCW

Auden, W(ystan) H(ugh)
1907-1973 ..... CLC 1, 2, 3, 4, 6, 9, 11,
14, 43; PC 1
See also CA 9-12R; 45-48; CANR 5;
CDBLB 1914-1945; DLB 10, 20; MTCW;
WLC

Audiberti, Jacques 1900-1965 ...... CLC 38
See also CA 25-28R

Auel, Jean M(arie) 1936-.......... CLC 31
See also AAYA 7; BEST 90:4; CA 103;
CANR 21

Auerbach, Erich 1892-1957 .... TCLC 43
See also CA 118

Augier, Emile 1820-1889 .... NCLC 31

August, John
See De Voto, Bernard (Augustine)

Augustine, St. 354-430........... CMLC 6

Aurelius
See Bourne, Randolph S(illiman)

Austen, Jane
1775-1817 .... NCLC 1, 13, 19, 33
See also CDBLB 1789-1832; DLB 116;
WLC

Auster, Paul 1947- .... CLC 47
See also CA 69-72; CANR 23

Austin, Mary (Hunter)
1868-1934 .... TCLC 25
See also CA 109; DLB 9, 78

Autran Dourado, Waldomiro
See Dourado, (Waldomiro Freitas) Autran

Averroes 1126-1198 .... CMLC 7
See also DLB 115

Avison, Margaret 1918-.......... CLC 2, 4
See also CA 17-20R; DLB 53; MTCW

Ayckbourn, Alan
1939- .... CLC 5, 8, 18, 33, 74
See also CA 21-24R; CANR 31; DLB 13;
MTCW

Aydy, Catherine
See Tennant, Emma (Christina)

Ayme, Marcel (Andre) 1902-1967... CLC 11
See also CA 89-92; CLR 25; DLB 72

Ayrton, Michael 1921-1975......... CLC 7
See also CA 5-8R; 61-64; CANR 9, 21

Azorin...................... CLC 11
See also Martinez Ruiz, Jose

Azuela, Mariano 1873-1952........ TCLC 3
See also CA 104; 131; HW; MTCW

Baastad, Babbis Friis
See Friis-Baastad, Babbis Ellinor

Bab
See Gilbert, W(illiam) S(chwenck)

Babbis, Eleanor
See Friis-Baastad, Babbis Ellinor

Babel, Isaac (Emanuilovich) .... **TCLC 13**
See also Babel, Isaak (Emmanuilovich)

Babel, Isaak (Emmanuilovich)
1894-1941(?) .... **TCLC 2**
See also Babel, Isaac (Emanuilovich)
See also CA 104

Babits, Mihaly 1883-1941 .... **TCLC 14**
See also CA 114

Babur 1483-1530................. **LC 18**

Bacchelli, Riccardo 1891-1985 ..... **CLC 19**
See also CA 29-32R; 117

Bach, Richard (David) 1936- .... **CLC 14**
See also AITN 1; BEST 89:2; CA 9-12R; CANR 18; MTCW; SATA 13

Bachman, Richard
See King, Stephen (Edwin)

Bachmann, Ingeborg 1926-1973..... **CLC 69**
See also CA 93-96; 45-48; DLB 85

Bacon, Francis 1561-1626 .... **LC 18**
See also CDBLB Before 1660

Bacovia, George.................. **TCLC 24**
See also Vasiliu, Gheorghe

Badanes, Jerome 1937-............ **CLC 59**

Bagehot, Walter 1826-1877 ...... **NCLC 10**
See also DLB 55

Bagnold, Enid 1889-1981.......... **CLC 25**
See also CA 5-8R; 103; CANR 5; DLB 13; MAICYA; SATA 1, 25

Bagrjana, Elisaveta
See Belcheva, Elisaveta

Bagryana, Elisaveta
See Belcheva, Elisaveta

Bailey, Paul 1937- .... **CLC 45**
See also CA 21-24R; CANR 16; DLB 14

Baillie, Joanna 1762-1851 .... **NCLC 2**
See also DLB 93

Bainbridge, Beryl (Margaret)
1933- .... **CLC 4, 5, 8, 10, 14, 18, 22, 62**
See also CA 21-24R; CANR 24; DLB 14; MTCW

Baker, Elliott 1922- .... **CLC 8**
See also CA 45-48; CANR 2

Baker, Nicholson 1957- .... **CLC 61**
See also CA 135

Baker, Ray Stannard 1870-1946... **TCLC 47**
See also CA 118

Baker, Russell (Wayne) 1925- ...... **CLC 31**
See also BEST 89:4; CA 57-60; CANR 11; MTCW

Bakshi, Ralph 1938(?)-............ **CLC 26**
See also CA 112; 138

Bakunin, Mikhail (Alexandrovich)
1814-1876 .... **NCLC 25**

Baldwin, James (Arthur)
1924-1987 ..... **CLC 1, 2, 3, 4, 5, 8, 13, 15, 17, 42, 50, 67; DC 1; SSC 10**
See also AAYA 4; BLC 1; BW; CA 1-4R; 124; CABS 1; CANR 3, 24; CDALB 1941-1968; DLB 2, 7, 33; DLBY 87; MTCW; SATA 9, 54; WLC

Ballard, J(ames) G(raham)
1930- .... **CLC 3, 6, 14, 36; SSC 1**
See also AAYA 3; CA 5-8R; CANR 15, 39; DLB 14; MTCW

Balmont, Konstantin (Dmitriyevich)
1867-1943 .... **TCLC 11**
See also CA 109

Balzac, Honore de
1799-1850 .... **NCLC 5, 35; SSC 5**
See also DLB 119; WLC

Bambara, Toni Cade 1939- .... **CLC 19**
See also AAYA 5; BLC 1; BW; CA 29-32R; CANR 24; DLB 38; MTCW

Bamdad, A.
See Shamlu, Ahmad

Banat, D. R.
See Bradbury, Ray (Douglas)

Bancroft, Laura
See Baum, L(yman) Frank

Banim, John 1798-1842 .... **NCLC 13**
See also DLB 116

Banim, Michael 1796-1874 ...... **NCLC 13**

Banks, Iain
See Banks, Iain M(enzies)

Banks, Iain M(enzies) 1954- .... **CLC 34**
See also CA 123; 128

Banks, Lynne Reid .... **CLC 23**
See also Reid Banks, Lynne
See also AAYA 6

Banks, Russell 1940- .... **CLC 37, 72**
See also CA 65-68; CAAS 15; CANR 19

Banville, John 1945- .... **CLC 46**
See also CA 117; 128; DLB 14

Banville, Theodore (Faullain) de
1832-1891 .... **NCLC 9**

Baraka, Amiri
1934- ... **CLC 1, 2, 3, 5, 10, 14, 33; PC 4**
See also Jones, LeRoi
See also BLC 1; BW; CA 21-24R; CABS 3; CANR 27, 38; CDALB 1941-1968; DLB 5, 7, 16, 38; DLBD 8; MTCW

Barbellion, W. N. P................ **TCLC 24**
See also Cummings, Bruce F(rederick)

Barbera, Jack 1945-............... **CLC 44**
See also CA 110

Barbey d'Aurevilly, Jules Amedee
1808-1889 .... **NCLC 1**
See also DLB 119

Barbusse, Henri 1873-1935 .... **TCLC 5**
See also CA 105; DLB 65

Barclay, Bill
See Moorcock, Michael (John)

Barclay, William Ewert
See Moorcock, Michael (John)

Barea, Arturo 1897-1957 .... **TCLC 14**
See also CA 111

Barfoot, Joan 1946- .... **CLC 18**
See also CA 105

Baring, Maurice 1874-1945........ **TCLC 8**
See also CA 105; DLB 34

Barker, Clive 1952- .... **CLC 52**
See also BEST 90:3; CA 121; 129; MTCW

Barker, George Granville
1913-1991 .... **CLC 8, 48**
See also CA 9-12R; 135; CANR 7, 38; DLB 20; MTCW

Barker, Harley Granville
See Granville-Barker, Harley
See also DLB 10

Barker, Howard 1946- .... **CLC 37**
See also CA 102; DLB 13

Barker, Pat 1943-................. **CLC 32**
See also CA 117; 122

Barlow, Joel 1754-1812 .... **NCLC 23**
See also DLB 37

Barnard, Mary (Ethel) 1909-....... **CLC 48**
See also CA 21-22; CAP 2

Barnes, Djuna
1892-1982 ... **CLC 3, 4, 8, 11, 29; SSC 3**
See also CA 9-12R; 107; CANR 16; DLB 4, 9, 45; MTCW

Barnes, Julian 1946-.............. **CLC 42**
See also CA 102; CANR 19

Barnes, Peter 1931- .... **CLC 5, 56**
See also CA 65-68; CAAS 12; CANR 33, 34; DLB 13; MTCW

Baroja (y Nessi), Pio 1872-1956 .... **TCLC 8**
See also CA 104

Baron, David
See Pinter, Harold

Baron Corvo
See Rolfe, Frederick (William Serafino Austin Lewis Mary)

Barondess, Sue K(aufman)
1926-1977 .... **CLC 8**
See also Kaufman, Sue
See also CA 1-4R; 69-72; CANR 1

Baron de Teive
See Pessoa, Fernando (Antonio Nogueira)

Barres, Maurice 1862-1923 .... **TCLC 47**

Barreto, Afonso Henrique de Lima
See Lima Barreto, Afonso Henrique de

Barrett, (Roger) Syd 1946- .... **CLC 35**
See also Pink Floyd

Barrett, William (Christopher)
1913- .... **CLC 27**
See also CA 13-16R; CANR 11

Barrie, J(ames) M(atthew)
1860-1937 .... **TCLC 2**
See also CA 104; 136; CDBLB 1890-1914; CLR 16; DLB 10; MAICYA; YABC 1

Barrington, Michael
See Moorcock, Michael (John)

Barrol, Grady
See Bograd, Larry

Barry, Mike
See Malzberg, Barry N(athaniel)

Barry, Philip 1896-1949.......... **TCLC 11**
See also CA 109; DLB 7

Bart, Andre Schwarz
See Schwarz-Bart, Andre

Barth, John (Simmons)
1930- ...... CLC 1, 2, 3, 5, 7, 9, 10, 14, 27, 51; SSC 10
See also AITN 1, 2; CA 1-4R; CABS 1; CANR 5, 23; DLB 2; MTCW

Barthelme, Donald
1931-1989 ..... CLC 1, 2, 3, 5, 6, 8, 13, 23, 46, 59; SSC 2
See also CA 21-24R; 129; CANR 20; DLB 2; DLBY 80, 89; MTCW; SATA 7, 62

Barthelme, Frederick 1943-........ CLC 36
See also CA 114; 122; DLBY 85

Barthes, Roland (Gerard)
1915-1980 .... CLC 24
See also CA 130; 97-100; MTCW

Barzun, Jacques (Martin) 1907- .... CLC 51
See also CA 61-64; CANR 22

Bashevis, Isaac
See Singer, Isaac Bashevis

Bashkirtseff, Marie 1859-1884 ... NCLC 27

Basho
See Matsuo Basho

Bass, Kingsley B. Jr.
See Bullins, Ed

Bassani, Giorgio 1916-............. CLC 9
See also CA 65-68; CANR 33; MTCW

Bastos, Augusto (Antonio) Roa
See Roa Bastos, Augusto (Antonio)

Bataille, Georges 1897-1962 .... CLC 29
See also CA 101; 89-92

Bates, H(erbert) E(rnest)
1905-1974 .... CLC 46; SSC 10
See also CA 93-96; 45-48; CANR 34; MTCW

Bauchart
See Camus, Albert

Baudelaire, Charles
1821-1867 .... NCLC 6, 29; PC 1
See also WLC

Baudrillard, Jean 1929- .... CLC 60

Baum, L(yman) Frank 1856-1919 ... TCLC 7
See also CA 108; 133; CLR 15; DLB 22; MAICYA; MTCW; SATA 18

Baum, Louis F.
See Baum, L(yman) Frank

Baumbach, Jonathan 1933- .... CLC 6, 23
See also CA 13-16R; CAAS 5; CANR 12; DLBY 80; MTCW

Bausch, Richard (Carl) 1945- ...... CLC 51
See also CA 101; CAAS 14

Baxter, Charles 1947-............. CLC 45
See also CA 57-60

Baxter, James K(eir) 1926-1972 .... CLC 14
See also CA 77-80

Baxter, John
See Hunt, E(verette) Howard Jr.

Bayer, Sylvia
See Glassco, John

Beagle, Peter S(oyer) 1939-......... CLC 7
See also CA 9-12R; CANR 4; DLBY 80; SATA 60

Bean, Normal
See Burroughs, Edgar Rice

Beard, Charles A(ustin)
1874-1948 .... TCLC 15
See also CA 115; DLB 17; SATA 18

Beardsley, Aubrey 1872-1898 ..... NCLC 6

Beattie, Ann
1947- .... CLC 8, 13, 18, 40, 63; SSC 11
See also BEST 90:2; CA 81-84; DLBY 82; MTCW

Beattie, James 1735-1803 .... NCLC 25
See also DLB 109

Beauchamp, Kathleen Mansfield 1888-1923
See Mansfield, Katherine
See also CA 104; 134

Beauvoir, Simone (Lucie Ernestine Marie Bertrand) de
1908-1986 ... CLC 1, 2, 4, 8, 14, 31, 44, 50, 71
See also CA 9-12R; 118; CANR 28; DLB 72; DLBY 86; MTCW; WLC

Becker, Jurek 1937-............ CLC 7, 19
See also CA 85-88; DLB 75

Becker, Walter 1950-.............. CLC 26

Beckett, Samuel (Barclay)
1906-1989 ..... CLC 1, 2, 3, 4, 6, 9, 10, 11, 14, 18, 29, 57, 59
See also CA 5-8R; 130; CANR 33; CDBLB 1945-1960; DLB 13, 15; DLBY 90; MTCW; WLC

Beckford, William 1760-1844 .... NCLC 16
See also DLB 39

Beckman, Gunnel 1910-........... CLC 26
See also CA 33-36R; CANR 15; CLR 25; MAICYA; SAAS 9; SATA 6

Becque, Henri 1837-1899......... NCLC 3

Beddoes, Thomas Lovell
1803-1849 .... NCLC 3
See also DLB 96

Bedford, Donald F.
See Fearing, Kenneth (Flexner)

Beecher, Catharine Esther
1800-1878 .... NCLC 30
See also DLB 1

Beecher, John 1904-1980........... CLC 6
See also AITN 1; CA 5-8R; 105; CANR 8

Beer, Johann 1655-1700............. LC 5

Beer, Patricia 1924-.............. CLC 58
See also CA 61-64; CANR 13; DLB 40

Beerbohm, Henry Maximilian
1872-1956 .... TCLC 1, 24
See also CA 104; DLB 34, 100

Begiebing, Robert J(ohn) 1946-..... CLC 70
See also CA 122

Behan, Brendan
1923-1964 .... CLC 1, 8, 11, 15
See also CA 73-76; CANR 33; CDBLB 1945-1960; DLB 13; MTCW

Behn, Aphra 1640(?)-1689........... LC 1
See also DLB 39, 80; WLC

Behrman, S(amuel) N(athaniel)
1893-1973 .... CLC 40
See also CA 13-16; 45-48; CAP 1; DLB 7, 44

Belasco, David 1853-1931 .... TCLC 3
See also CA 104; DLB 7

Belcheva, Elisaveta 1893- .... CLC 10

Beldone, Phil "Cheech"
See Ellison, Harlan

Beleno
See Azuela, Mariano

Belinski, Vissarion Grigoryevich
1811-1848 .... NCLC 5

Belitt, Ben 1911-................. CLC 22
See also CA 13-16R; CAAS 4; CANR 7; DLB 5

Bell, James Madison 1826-1902 ... TCLC 43
See also BLC 1; BW; CA 122; 124; DLB 50

Bell, Madison (Smartt) 1957- ...... CLC 41
See also CA 111; CANR 28

Bell, Marvin (Hartley) 1937-..... CLC 8, 31
See also CA 21-24R; CAAS 14; DLB 5; MTCW

Bell, W. L. D.
See Mencken, H(enry) L(ouis)

Bellamy, Atwood C.
See Mencken, H(enry) L(ouis)

Bellamy, Edward 1850-1898 ...... NCLC 4
See also DLB 12

Bellin, Edward J.
See Kuttner, Henry

Belloc, (Joseph) Hilaire (Pierre)
1870-1953 .... TCLC 7, 18
See also CA 106; DLB 19, 100; YABC 1

Belloc, Joseph Peter Rene Hilaire
See Belloc, (Joseph) Hilaire (Pierre)

Belloc, Joseph Pierre Hilaire
See Belloc, (Joseph) Hilaire (Pierre)

Belloc, M. A.
See Lowndes, Marie Adelaide (Belloc)

Bellow, Saul
1915- ...... CLC 1, 2, 3, 6, 8, 10, 13, 15, 25, 33, 34, 63
See also AITN 2; BEST 89:3; CA 5-8R; CABS 1; CANR 29; CDALB 1941-1968; DLB 2, 28; DLBD 3; DLBY 82; MTCW; WLC

Belser, Reimond Karel Maria de
1929- .... CLC 14

Bely, Andrey .... TCLC 7
See also Bugayev, Boris Nikolayevich

Benary, Margot
See Benary-Isbert, Margot

Benary-Isbert, Margot 1889-1979 ... CLC 12
See also CA 5-8R; 89-92; CANR 4; CLR 12; MAICYA; SATA 2, 21

Benavente (y Martinez), Jacinto
1866-1954 .... TCLC 3
See also CA 106; 131; HW; MTCW

Benchley, Peter (Bradford)
1940- .... CLC 4, 8
See also AITN 2; CA 17-20R; CANR 12, 35; MTCW; SATA 3

Benchley, Robert (Charles)
1889-1945 .... TCLC 1
See also CA 105; DLB 11

Benedikt, Michael 1935- .... CLC 4, 14
See also CA 13-16R; CANR 7; DLB 5

Benet, Juan 1927-................ CLC 28

Benet, Stephen Vincent
 1898-1943 .... TCLC 7; SSC 10
 See also CA 104; DLB 4, 48, 102; YABC 1

Benet, William Rose 1886-1950 ... TCLC 28
 See also CA 118; DLB 45

Benford, Gregory (Albert) 1941-.... CLC 52
 See also CA 69-72; CANR 12, 24;
 DLBY 82

Bengtsson, Frans (Gunnar)
 1894-1954 .... TCLC 48

Benjamin, Lois
 See Gould, Lois

Benjamin, Walter 1892-1940 ...... TCLC 39

Benn, Gottfried 1886-1956......... TCLC 3
 See also CA 106; DLB 56

Bennett, Alan 1934-............... CLC 45
 See also CA 103; CANR 35; MTCW

Bennett, (Enoch) Arnold
 1867-1931 .... TCLC 5, 20
 See also CA 106; CDBLB 1890-1914;
 DLB 10, 34, 98

Bennett, Elizabeth
 See Mitchell, Margaret (Munnerlyn)

Bennett, George Harold 1930-
 See Bennett, Hal
 See also BW; CA 97-100

Bennett, Hal .... CLC 5
 See also Bennett, George Harold
 See also DLB 33

Bennett, Jay 1912-................ CLC 35
 See also CA 69-72; CANR 11; SAAS 4;
 SATA 27, 41

Bennett, Louise (Simone) 1919-..... CLC 28
 See also BLC 1; DLB 117

Benson, E(dward) F(rederic)
 1867-1940 .... TCLC 27
 See also CA 114

Benson, Jackson J. 1930-.......... CLC 34
 See also CA 25-28R; DLB 111

Benson, Sally 1900-1972 .... CLC 17
 See also CA 19-20; 37-40R; CAP 1;
 SATA 1, 27, 35

Benson, Stella 1892-1933......... TCLC 17
 See also CA 117; DLB 36

Bentham, Jeremy 1748-1832 ..... NCLC 38
 See also DLB 107

Bentley, E(dmund) C(lerihew)
 1875-1956 .... TCLC 12
 See also CA 108; DLB 70

Bentley, Eric (Russell) 1916-...... CLC 24
 See also CA 5-8R; CANR 6

Beranger, Pierre Jean de
 1780-1857 .... NCLC 34

Berger, Colonel
 See Malraux, (Georges-)Andre

Berger, John (Peter) 1926- ...... CLC 2, 19
 See also CA 81-84; DLB 14

Berger, Melvin H. 1927-.......... CLC 12
 See also CA 5-8R; CANR 4; SAAS 2;
 SATA 5

Berger, Thomas (Louis)
 1924- .... CLC 3, 5, 8, 11, 18, 38
 See also CA 1-4R; CANR 5, 28; DLB 2;
 DLBY 80; MTCW

Bergman, (Ernst) Ingmar
 1918- .... CLC 16, 72
 See also CA 81-84; CANR 33

Bergson, Henri 1859-1941........ TCLC 32

Bergstein, Eleanor 1938-........... CLC 4
 See also CA 53-56; CANR 5

Berkoff, Steven 1937-............. CLC 56
 See also CA 104

Bermant, Chaim (Icyk) 1929- ...... CLC 40
 See also CA 57-60; CANR 6, 31

Bernanos, (Paul Louis) Georges
 1888-1948 .... TCLC 3
 See also CA 104; 130; DLB 72

Bernard, April 1956- .... CLC 59
 See also CA 131

Bernhard, Thomas
 1931-1989 .... CLC 3, 32, 61
 See also CA 85-88; 127; CANR 32;
 DLB 85; MTCW

Berrigan, Daniel 1921-............. CLC 4
 See also CA 33-36R; CAAS 1; CANR 11;
 DLB 5

Berrigan, Edmund Joseph Michael Jr.
 1934-1983
 See Berrigan, Ted
 See also CA 61-64; 110; CANR 14

Berrigan, Ted..................... CLC 37
 See also Berrigan, Edmund Joseph Michael
 Jr.
 See also DLB 5

Berry, Charles Edward Anderson 1931-
 See Berry, Chuck
 See also CA 115

Berry, Chuck..................... CLC 17
 See also Berry, Charles Edward Anderson

Berry, Jonas
 See Ashbery, John (Lawrence)

Berry, Wendell (Erdman)
 1934- .... CLC 4, 6, 8, 27, 46
 See also AITN 1; CA 73-76; DLB 5, 6

Berryman, John
 1914-1972 ..... CLC 1, 2, 3, 4, 6, 8, 10,
 13, 25, 62
 See also CA 13-16; 33-36R; CABS 2;
 CANR 35; CAP 1; CDALB 1941-1968;
 DLB 48; MTCW

Bertolucci, Bernardo 1940- .... CLC 16
 See also CA 106

Bertrand, Aloysius 1807-1841 .... NCLC 31

Bertran de Born c. 1140-1215..... CMLC 5

Besant, Annie (Wood) 1847-1933 ... TCLC 9
 See also CA 105

Bessie, Alvah 1904-1985.......... CLC 23
 See also CA 5-8R; 116; CANR 2; DLB 26

Bethlen, T. D.
 See Silverberg, Robert

Beti, Mongo..................... CLC 27
 See also Biyidi, Alexandre
 See also BLC 1

Betjeman, John
 1906-1984 .... CLC 2, 6, 10, 34, 43
 See also CA 9-12R; 112; CANR 33;
 CDBLB 1945-1960; DLB 20; DLBY 84;
 MTCW

Betti, Ugo 1892-1953............. TCLC 5
 See also CA 104

Betts, Doris (Waugh) 1932-.... CLC 3, 6, 28
 See also CA 13-16R; CANR 9; DLBY 82

Bevan, Alistair
 See Roberts, Keith (John Kingston)

Beynon, John
 See Harris, John (Wyndham Parkes Lucas)
 Beynon

Bialik, Chaim Nachman
 1873-1934 .... TCLC 25

Bickerstaff, Isaac
 See Swift, Jonathan

Bidart, Frank 19(?)-.............. CLC 33

Bienek, Horst 1930-............ CLC 7, 11
 See also CA 73-76; DLB 75

Bierce, Ambrose (Gwinett)
 1842-1914(?) ..... TCLC 1, 7, 44; SSC 9
 See also CA 104; CDALB 1865-1917;
 DLB 11, 12, 23, 71, 74; WLC

Billings, Josh
 See Shaw, Henry Wheeler

Billington, Rachel 1942-........... CLC 43
 See also AITN 2; CA 33-36R

Binyon, T(imothy) J(ohn) 1936- .... CLC 34
 See also CA 111; CANR 28

Bioy Casares, Adolfo 1914-.... CLC 4, 8, 13
 See also CA 29-32R; CANR 19; DLB 113;
 HW; MTCW

Bird, C.
 See Ellison, Harlan

Bird, Cordwainer
 See Ellison, Harlan

Bird, Robert Montgomery
 1806-1854 .... NCLC 1

Birney, (Alfred) Earle
 1904- ....CLC 1, 4, 6, 11
 See also CA 1-4R; CANR 5, 20; DLB 88;
 MTCW

Bishop, Elizabeth
 1911-1979 ..... CLC 1, 4, 9, 13, 15, 32;
 PC 3
 See also CA 5-8R; 89-92; CABS 2;
 CANR 26; CDALB 1968-1988; DLB 5;
 MTCW; SATA 24

Bishop, John 1935-................ CLC 10
 See also CA 105

bissett, bill 1939- .... CLC 18
 See also CA 69-72; CANR 15; DLB 53;
 MTCW

Bitov, Andrei (Georgievich) 1937-... CLC 57

Biyidi, Alexandre 1932-
 See Beti, Mongo
 See also BW; CA 114; 124; MTCW

Bjarme, Brynjolf
 See Ibsen, Henrik (Johan)

Bjornson, Bjornstjerne (Martinius)
 1832-1910 .... TCLC 7, 37
 See also CA 104

Black, Robert
See Holdstock, Robert P.

Blackburn, Paul 1926-1971 ...... **CLC 9, 43**
See also CA 81-84; 33-36R; CANR 34; DLB 16; DLBY 81

Black Elk 1863-1950 .... **TCLC 33**

Black Hobart
See Sanders, (James) Ed(ward)

Blacklin, Malcolm
See Chambers, Aidan

Blackmore, R(ichard) D(oddridge)
1825-1900 .... **TCLC 27**
See also CA 120; DLB 18

Blackmur, R(ichard) P(almer)
1904-1965 .... **CLC 2, 24**
See also CA 11-12; 25-28R; CAP 1; DLB 63

Black Tarantula, The
See Acker, Kathy

Blackwood, Algernon (Henry)
1869-1951 .... **TCLC 5**
See also CA 105

Blackwood, Caroline 1931- .... **CLC 6, 9**
See also CA 85-88; CANR 32; DLB 14; MTCW

Blade, Alexander
See Hamilton, Edmond; Silverberg, Robert

Blair, Eric (Arthur) 1903-1950
See Orwell, George
See also CA 104; 132; MTCW; SATA 29

Blais, Marie-Claire
1939- .... **CLC 2, 4, 6, 13, 22**
See also CA 21-24R; CAAS 4; CANR 38; DLB 53; MTCW

Blaise, Clark 1940- .... **CLC 29**
See also AITN 2; CA 53-56; CAAS 3; CANR 5; DLB 53

Blake, Nicholas
See Day Lewis, C(ecil)
See also DLB 77

Blake, William 1757-1827 .... **NCLC 13**
See also CDBLB 1789-1832; DLB 93; MAICYA; SATA 30; WLC

Blasco Ibanez, Vicente
1867-1928 .... **TCLC 12**
See also CA 110; 131; HW; MTCW

Blatty, William Peter 1928- .... **CLC 2**
See also CA 5-8R; CANR 9

Bleeck, Oliver
See Thomas, Ross (Elmore)

Blessing, Lee 1949- .... **CLC 54**

Blish, James (Benjamin)
1921-1975 .... **CLC 14**
See also CA 1-4R; 57-60; CANR 3; DLB 8; MTCW; SATA 66

Bliss, Reginald
See Wells, H(erbert) G(eorge)

Blixen, Karen (Christentze Dinesen)
1885-1962
See Dinesen, Isak
See also CA 25-28; CANR 22; CAP 2; MTCW; SATA 44

Bloch, Robert (Albert) 1917- .... **CLC 33**
See also CA 5-8R; CANR 5; DLB 44; SATA 12

Blok, Alexander (Alexandrovich)
1880-1921 .... **TCLC 5**
See also CA 104

Blom, Jan
See Breytenbach, Breyten

Bloom, Harold 1930- .... **CLC 24**
See also CA 13-16R; CANR 39; DLB 67

Bloomfield, Aurelius
See Bourne, Randolph S(illiman)

Blount, Roy (Alton) Jr. 1941- ...... **CLC 38**
See also CA 53-56; CANR 10, 28; MTCW

Bloy, Leon 1846-1917............ **TCLC 22**
See also CA 121

Blume, Judy (Sussman) 1938- ... **CLC 12, 30**
See also AAYA 3; CA 29-32R; CANR 13, 37; CLR 2, 15; DLB 52; MAICYA; MTCW; SATA 2, 31

Blunden, Edmund (Charles)
1896-1974 .... **CLC 2, 56**
See also CA 17-18; 45-48; CAP 2; DLB 20, 100; MTCW

Bly, Robert (Elwood)
1926- .... **CLC 1, 2, 5, 10, 15, 38**
See also CA 5-8R; DLB 5; MTCW

Bobette
See Simenon, Georges (Jacques Christian)

Boccaccio, Giovanni 1313-1375
See also SSC 10

Bochco, Steven 1943-.............. **CLC 35**
See also CA 124; 138

Bodenheim, Maxwell 1892-1954 ... **TCLC 44**
See also CA 110; DLB 9, 45

Bodker, Cecil 1927- .... **CLC 21**
See also CA 73-76; CANR 13; CLR 23; MAICYA; SATA 14

Boell, Heinrich (Theodor)
1917-1985 ... **CLC 2, 3, 6, 9, 11, 15, 27, 39**
See also Boll, Heinrich (Theodor)
See also CA 21-24R; 116; CANR 24; DLB 69; DLBY 85; MTCW

Bogan, Louise 1897-1970..... **CLC 4, 39, 46**
See also CA 73-76; 25-28R; CANR 33; DLB 45; MTCW

Bogarde, Dirk .... **CLC 19**
See also Van Den Bogarde, Derek Jules Gaspard Ulric Niven
See also DLB 14

Bogosian, Eric 1953- .... **CLC 45**
See also CA 138

Bograd, Larry 1953-.............. **CLC 35**
See also CA 93-96; SATA 33

Boiardo, Matteo Maria 1441-1494 .... **LC 6**

Boileau-Despreaux, Nicolas
1636-1711 .... **LC 3**

Boland, Eavan 1944-........... **CLC 40, 67**
See also DLB 40

Boleslaw, Prus................... **TCLC 48**
See also Glowacki, Aleksander

Boll, Heinrich (Theodor)
1917-1985 ... **CLC 2, 3, 6, 9, 11, 15, 27, 39, 72**
See also Boell, Heinrich (Theodor)
See also DLB 69; DLBY 85; WLC

Bolt, Robert (Oxton) 1924-........ **CLC 14**
See also CA 17-20R; CANR 35; DLB 13; MTCW

Bomkauf
See Kaufman, Bob (Garnell)

Bonaventura................... **NCLC 35**
See also DLB 90

Bond, Edward 1934-....... **CLC 4, 6, 13, 23**
See also CA 25-28R; CANR 38; DLB 13; MTCW

Bonham, Frank 1914-1989......... **CLC 12**
See also AAYA 1; CA 9-12R; CANR 4, 36; MAICYA; SAAS 3; SATA 1, 49, 62

Bonnefoy, Yves 1923-........ **CLC 9, 15, 58**
See also CA 85-88; CANR 33; MTCW

Bontemps, Arna(ud Wendell)
1902-1973 .... **CLC 1, 18**
See also BLC 1; BW; CA 1-4R; 41-44R; CANR 4, 35; CLR 6; DLB 48, 51; MAICYA; MTCW; SATA 2, 24, 44

Booth, Martin 1944-.............. **CLC 13**
See also CA 93-96; CAAS 2

Booth, Philip 1925-................ **CLC 23**
See also CA 5-8R; CANR 5; DLBY 82

Booth, Wayne C(layson) 1921- ..... **CLC 24**
See also CA 1-4R; CAAS 5; CANR 3; DLB 67

Borchert, Wolfgang 1921-1947 ..... **TCLC 5**
See also CA 104; DLB 69

Borges, Jorge Luis
1899-1986 ... **CLC 1, 2, 3, 4, 6, 8, 9, 10, 13, 19, 44, 48; SSC 4**
See also CA 21-24R; CANR 19, 33; DLB 113; DLBY 86; HW; MTCW; WLC

Borowski, Tadeusz 1922-1951...... **TCLC 9**
See also CA 106

Borrow, George (Henry)
1803-1881 .... **NCLC 9**
See also DLB 21, 55

Bosschere, Jean de 1878(?)-1953... **TCLC 19**
See also CA 115

Boswell, James 1740-1795.......... **LC 4**
See also CDBLB 1660-1789; DLB 104; WLC

Bottoms, David 1949-............. **CLC 53**
See also CA 105; CANR 22; DLB 120; DLBY 83

Boucolon, Maryse 1937-
See Conde, Maryse
See also CA 110; CANR 30

Bourget, Paul (Charles Joseph)
1852-1935 .... **TCLC 12**
See also CA 107

Bourjaily, Vance (Nye) 1922- .... **CLC 8, 62**
See also CA 1-4R; CAAS 1; CANR 2; DLB 2

Bourne, Randolph S(illiman)
1886-1918 .... **TCLC 16**
See also CA 117; DLB 63

Bova, Ben(jamin William) 1932-.... **CLC 45**
See also CA 5-8R; CANR 11; CLR 3; DLBY 81; MAICYA; MTCW; SATA 6, 68

Bowen, Elizabeth (Dorothea Cole)
1899-1973 ..... CLC **1, 3, 6, 11, 15, 22;** SSC **3**
See also CA 17-18; 41-44R; CANR 35; CAP 2; CDBLB 1945-1960; DLB 15; MTCW

Bowering, George 1935- .... CLC **15, 47**
See also CA 21-24R; CAAS 16; CANR 10; DLB 53

Bowering, Marilyn R(uthe) 1949- ... CLC **32**
See also CA 101

Bowers, Edgar 1924- .... CLC **9**
See also CA 5-8R; CANR 24; DLB 5

Bowie, David .... CLC **17**
See also Jones, David Robert

Bowles, Jane (Sydney)
1917-1973 .... CLC **3, 68**
See also CA 19-20; 41-44R; CAP 2

Bowles, Paul (Frederick)
1910- .... CLC **1, 2, 19, 53;** SSC **3**
See also CA 1-4R; CAAS 1; CANR 1, 19; DLB 5, 6; MTCW

Box, Edgar
See Vidal, Gore

Boyd, Nancy
See Millay, Edna St. Vincent

Boyd, William 1952- .... CLC **28, 53, 70**
See also CA 114; 120

Boyle, Kay 1902- .. CLC **1, 5, 19, 58;** SSC **5**
See also CA 13-16R; CAAS 1; CANR 29; DLB 4, 9, 48, 86; MTCW

Boyle, Mark
See Kienzle, William X(avier)

Boyle, Patrick 1905-1982 .... CLC **19**
See also CA 127

Boyle, T. Coraghessan 1948- .... CLC **36, 55**
See also BEST 90:4; CA 120; DLBY 86

Brackenridge, Hugh Henry
1748-1816 .... NCLC **7**
See also DLB 11, 37

Bradbury, Edward P.
See Moorcock, Michael (John)

Bradbury, Malcolm (Stanley)
1932- .... CLC **32, 61**
See also CA 1-4R; CANR 1, 33; DLB 14; MTCW

Bradbury, Ray (Douglas)
1920- .... CLC **1, 3, 10, 15, 42**
See also AITN 1, 2; CA 1-4R; CANR 2, 30; CDALB 1968-1988; DLB 2, 8; MTCW; SATA 11, 64; WLC

Bradford, Gamaliel 1863-1932 ..... TCLC **36**
See also DLB 17

Bradley, David (Henry Jr.) 1950- ... CLC **23**
See also BLC 1; BW; CA 104; CANR 26; DLB 33

Bradley, John Ed 1959- .... CLC **55**

Bradley, Marion Zimmer 1930- ..... CLC **30**
See also AAYA 9; CA 57-60; CAAS 10; CANR 7, 31; DLB 8; MTCW

Bradstreet, Anne 1612(?)-1672 .... LC **4**
See also CDALB 1640-1865; DLB 24

Bragg, Melvyn 1939- .... CLC **10**
See also BEST 89:3; CA 57-60; CANR 10; DLB 14

Braine, John (Gerard)
1922-1986 .... CLC **1, 3, 41**
See also CA 1-4R; 120; CANR 1, 33; CDBLB 1945-1960; DLB 15; DLBY 86; MTCW

Brammer, William 1930(?)-1978 .... CLC **31**
See also CA 77-80

Brancati, Vitaliano 1907-1954 ..... TCLC **12**
See also CA 109

Brancato, Robin F(idler) 1936- ..... CLC **35**
See also AAYA 9; CA 69-72; CANR 11; SAAS 9; SATA 23

Brand, Millen 1906-1980 .... CLC **7**
See also CA 21-24R; 97-100

Branden, Barbara .... CLC **44**

Brandes, Georg (Morris Cohen)
1842-1927 .... TCLC **10**
See also CA 105

Brandys, Kazimierz 1916- .... CLC **62**

Branley, Franklyn M(ansfield)
1915- .... CLC **21**
See also CA 33-36R; CANR 14, 39; CLR 13; MAICYA; SATA 4, 68

Brathwaite, Edward (Kamau)
1930- .... CLC **11**
See also BW; CA 25-28R; CANR 11, 26

Brautigan, Richard (Gary)
1935-1984 .... CLC **1, 3, 5, 9, 12, 34, 42**
See also CA 53-56; 113; CANR 34; DLB 2, 5; DLBY 80, 84; MTCW; SATA 56

Braverman, Kate 1950- .... CLC **67**
See also CA 89-92

Brecht, Bertolt
1898-1956 ..... TCLC **1, 6, 13, 35;** DC **3**
See also CA 104; 133; DLB 56; MTCW; WLC

Brecht, Eugen Berthold Friedrich
See Brecht, Bertolt

Bremer, Fredrika 1801-1865 ..... NCLC **11**

Brennan, Christopher John
1870-1932 .... TCLC **17**
See also CA 117

Brennan, Maeve 1917- .... CLC **5**
See also CA 81-84

Brentano, Clemens (Maria)
1778-1842 .... NCLC **1**

Brent of Bin Bin
See Franklin, (Stella Maraia Sarah) Miles

Brenton, Howard 1942- .... CLC **31**
See also CA 69-72; CANR 33; DLB 13; MTCW

Breslin, James 1930-
See Breslin, Jimmy
See also CA 73-76; CANR 31; MTCW

Breslin, Jimmy .... CLC **4, 43**
See also Breslin, James
See also AITN 1

Bresson, Robert 1907- .... CLC **16**
See also CA 110

Breton, Andre 1896-1966 ... CLC **2, 9, 15, 54**
See also CA 19-20; 25-28R; CAP 2; DLB 65; MTCW

Breytenbach, Breyten 1939(?)- .. CLC **23, 37**
See also CA 113; 129

Bridgers, Sue Ellen 1942- .... CLC **26**
See also AAYA 8; CA 65-68; CANR 11, 36; CLR 18; DLB 52; MAICYA; SAAS 1; SATA 22

Bridges, Robert (Seymour)
1844-1930 .... TCLC **1**
See also CA 104; CDBLB 1890-1914; DLB 19, 98

Bridie, James .... TCLC **3**
See also Mavor, Osborne Henry
See also DLB 10

Brin, David 1950- .... CLC **34**
See also CA 102; CANR 24; SATA 65

Brink, Andre (Philippus)
1935- .... CLC **18, 36**
See also CA 104; CANR 39; MTCW

Brinsmead, H(esba) F(ay) 1922- .... CLC **21**
See also CA 21-24R; CANR 10; MAICYA; SAAS 5; SATA 18

Brittain, Vera (Mary)
1893(?)-1970 .... CLC **23**
See also CA 13-16; 25-28R; CAP 1; MTCW

Broch, Hermann 1886-1951 .... TCLC **20**
See also CA 117; DLB 85

Brock, Rose
See Hansen, Joseph

Brodkey, Harold 1930- .... CLC **56**
See also CA 111

Brodsky, Iosif Alexandrovich 1940-
See Brodsky, Joseph
See also AITN 1; CA 41-44R; CANR 37; MTCW

Brodsky, Joseph .... CLC **4, 6, 13, 36, 50**
See also Brodsky, Iosif Alexandrovich

Brodsky, Michael Mark 1948- ..... CLC **19**
See also CA 102; CANR 18

Bromell, Henry 1947- .... CLC **5**
See also CA 53-56; CANR 9

Bromfield, Louis (Brucker)
1896-1956 .... TCLC **11**
See also CA 107; DLB 4, 9, 86

Broner, E(sther) M(asserman)
1930- .... CLC **19**
See also CA 17-20R; CANR 8, 25; DLB 28

Bronk, William 1918- .... CLC **10**
See also CA 89-92; CANR 23

Bronstein, Lev Davidovich
See Trotsky, Leon

Bronte, Anne 1820-1849 .... NCLC **4**
See also DLB 21

Bronte, Charlotte
1816-1855 .... NCLC **3, 8, 33**
See also CDBLB 1832-1890; DLB 21; WLC

Bronte, (Jane) Emily
1818-1848 .... NCLC **16, 35**
See also CDBLB 1832-1890; DLB 21, 32; WLC

Brooke, Frances 1724-1789 .... LC **6**
See also DLB 39, 99

Brooke, Henry 1703(?)-1783 .... LC **1**
See also DLB 39

Brooke, Rupert (Chawner)
1887-1915 .... TCLC **2, 7**
See also CA 104; 132; CDBLB 1914-1945; DLB 19; MTCW; WLC

Brooke-Haven, P.
See Wodehouse, P(elham) G(renville)

Brooke-Rose, Christine 1926- ...... **CLC 40**
See also CA 13-16R; DLB 14

Brookner, Anita 1928- ...... **CLC 32, 34, 51**
See also CA 114; 120; CANR 37; DLBY 87; MTCW

Brooks, Cleanth 1906- .... **CLC 24**
See also CA 17-20R; CANR 33, 35; DLB 63; MTCW

Brooks, George
See Baum, L(yman) Frank

Brooks, Gwendolyn
1917- .... **CLC 1, 2, 4, 5, 15, 49**
See also AITN 1; BLC 1; BW; CA 1-4R; CANR 1, 27; CDALB 1941-1968; CLR 27; DLB 5, 76; MTCW; SATA 6; WLC

Brooks, Mel .... **CLC 12**
See also Kaminsky, Melvin
See also DLB 26

Brooks, Peter 1938- .... **CLC 34**
See also CA 45-48; CANR 1

Brooks, Van Wyck 1886-1963 ...... **CLC 29**
See also CA 1-4R; CANR 6; DLB 45, 63, 103

Brophy, Brigid (Antonia)
1929- .... **CLC 6, 11, 29**
See also CA 5-8R; CAAS 4; CANR 25; DLB 14; MTCW

Brosman, Catharine Savage 1934- .... **CLC 9**
See also CA 61-64; CANR 21

Brother Antoninus
See Everson, William (Oliver)

Broughton, T(homas) Alan 1936- ... **CLC 19**
See also CA 45-48; CANR 2, 23

Broumas, Olga 1949- .... **CLC 10**
See also CA 85-88; CANR 20

Brown, Charles Brockden
1771-1810 .... **NCLC 22**
See also CDALB 1640-1865; DLB 37, 59, 73

Brown, Christy 1932-1981 .... **CLC 63**
See also CA 105; 104; DLB 14

Brown, Claude 1937- .... **CLC 30**
See also AAYA 7; BLC 1; BW; CA 73-76

Brown, Dee (Alexander) 1908- .. **CLC 18, 47**
See also CA 13-16R; CAAS 6; CANR 11; DLBY 80; MTCW; SATA 5

Brown, George
See Wertmueller, Lina

Brown, George Douglas
1869-1902 .... **TCLC 28**

Brown, George Mackay 1921- .... **CLC 5, 48**
See also CA 21-24R; CAAS 6; CANR 12, 37; DLB 14, 27; MTCW; SATA 35

Brown, Moses
See Barrett, William (Christopher)

Brown, Rita Mae 1944- .... **CLC 18, 43**
See also CA 45-48; CANR 2, 11, 35; MTCW

Brown, Roderick (Langmere) Haig-
See Haig-Brown, Roderick (Langmere)

Brown, Rosellen 1939- .... **CLC 32**
See also CA 77-80; CAAS 10; CANR 14

Brown, Sterling Allen
1901-1989 .... **CLC 1, 23, 59**
See also BLC 1; BW; CA 85-88; 127; CANR 26; DLB 48, 51, 63; MTCW

Brown, Will
See Ainsworth, William Harrison

Brown, William Wells
1813-1884 .... **NCLC 2; DC 1**
See also BLC 1; DLB 3, 50

Browne, (Clyde) Jackson 1948(?)- ... **CLC 21**
See also CA 120

Browning, Elizabeth Barrett
1806-1861 .... **NCLC 1, 16**
See also CDBLB 1832-1890; DLB 32; WLC

Browning, Robert
1812-1889 .... **NCLC 19; PC 2**
See also CDBLB 1832-1890; DLB 32; YABC 1

Browning, Tod 1882-1962 .... **CLC 16**
See also CA 117

Bruccoli, Matthew J(oseph) 1931- .. **CLC 34**
See also CA 9-12R; CANR 7; DLB 103

Bruce, Lenny .... **CLC 21**
See also Schneider, Leonard Alfred

Bruin, John
See Brutus, Dennis

Brulls, Christian
See Simenon, Georges (Jacques Christian)

Brunner, John (Kilian Houston)
1934- .... **CLC 8, 10**
See also CA 1-4R; CAAS 8; CANR 2, 37; MTCW

Brutus, Dennis 1924- .... **CLC 43**
See also BLC 1; BW; CA 49-52; CAAS 14; CANR 2, 27; DLB 117

Bryan, C(ourtlandt) D(ixon) B(arnes)
1936- .... **CLC 29**
See also CA 73-76; CANR 13

Bryan, Michael
See Moore, Brian

Bryant, William Cullen
1794-1878 .... **NCLC 6**
See also CDALB 1640-1865; DLB 3, 43, 59

Bryusov, Valery Yakovlevich
1873-1924 .... **TCLC 10**
See also CA 107

Buchan, John 1875-1940 .... **TCLC 41**
See also CA 108; DLB 34, 70; YABC 2

Buchanan, George 1506-1582 .... **LC 4**

Buchheim, Lothar-Guenther 1918- ... **CLC 6**
See also CA 85-88

Buchner, (Karl) Georg
1813-1837 .... **NCLC 26**

Buchwald, Art(hur) 1925- .... **CLC 33**
See also AITN 1; CA 5-8R; CANR 21; MTCW; SATA 10

Buck, Pearl S(ydenstricker)
1892-1973 .... **CLC 7, 11, 18**
See also AITN 1; CA 1-4R; 41-44R; CANR 1, 34; DLB 9, 102; MTCW; SATA 1, 25

Buckler, Ernest 1908-1984 .... **CLC 13**
See also CA 11-12; 114; CAP 1; DLB 68; SATA 47

Buckley, Vincent (Thomas)
1925-1988 .... **CLC 57**
See also CA 101

Buckley, William F(rank) Jr.
1925- .... **CLC 7, 18, 37**
See also AITN 1; CA 1-4R; CANR 1, 24; DLBY 80; MTCW

Buechner, (Carl) Frederick
1926- .... **CLC 2, 4, 6, 9**
See also CA 13-16R; CANR 11, 39; DLBY 80; MTCW

Buell, John (Edward) 1927- .... **CLC 10**
See also CA 1-4R; DLB 53

Buero Vallejo, Antonio 1916- ... **CLC 15, 46**
See also CA 106; CANR 24; HW; MTCW

Bufalino, Gesualdo 1920- .... **CLC 74**

Bugayev, Boris Nikolayevich 1880-1934
See Bely, Andrey
See also CA 104

Bukowski, Charles 1920- .... **CLC 2, 5, 9, 41**
See also CA 17-20R; DLB 5; MTCW

Bulgakov, Mikhail (Afanas'evich)
1891-1940 .... **TCLC 2, 16**
See also CA 105

Bullins, Ed 1935- .... **CLC 1, 5, 7**
See also BLC 1; BW; CA 49-52; CAAS 16; CANR 24; DLB 7, 38; MTCW

Bulwer-Lytton, Edward (George Earle Lytton)
1803-1873 .... **NCLC 1**
See also DLB 21

Bunin, Ivan Alexeyevich
1870-1953 .... **TCLC 6; SSC 5**
See also CA 104

Bunting, Basil 1900-1985 .... **CLC 10, 39, 47**
See also CA 53-56; 115; CANR 7; DLB 20

Bunuel, Luis 1900-1983 .... **CLC 16**
See also CA 101; 110; CANR 32; HW

Bunyan, John 1628-1688 .... **LC 4**
See also CDBLB 1660-1789; DLB 39; WLC

Burford, Eleanor
See Hibbert, Eleanor Burford

Burgess, Anthony
.. **CLC 1, 2, 4, 5, 8, 10, 13, 15, 22, 40, 62**
See also Wilson, John (Anthony) Burgess
See also AITN 1; CDBLB 1960 to Present; DLB 14

Burke, Edmund 1729(?)-1797 .... **LC 7**
See also DLB 104; WLC

Burke, Kenneth (Duva) 1897- .... **CLC 2, 24**
See also CA 5-8R; CANR 39; DLB 45, 63; MTCW

Burke, Leda
See Garnett, David

Burke, Ralph
See Silverberg, Robert

Burney, Fanny 1752-1840 .... **NCLC 12**
See also DLB 39

Burns, Robert 1759-1796 .... **LC 3**
See also CDBLB 1789-1832; DLB 109; WLC

Burns, Tex
See L'Amour, Louis (Dearborn)

Burnshaw, Stanley 1906- ..... CLC 3, 13, 44
See also CA 9-12R; DLB 48

Burr, Anne 1937- .... CLC 6
See also CA 25-28R

Burroughs, Edgar Rice
1875-1950 .... TCLC 2, 32
See also CA 104; 132; DLB 8; MTCW;
SATA 41

Burroughs, William S(eward)
1914- .... CLC 1, 2, 5, 15, 22, 42
See also AITN 2; CA 9-12R; CANR 20;
DLB 2, 8, 16; DLBY 81; MTCW; WLC

Busch, Frederick 1941- ... CLC 7, 10, 18, 47
See also CA 33-36R; CAAS 1; DLB 6

Bush, Ronald 1946- .... CLC 34
See also CA 136

Bustos, F(rancisco)
See Borges, Jorge Luis

Bustos Domecq, H(onorio)
See Bioy Casares, Adolfo; Borges, Jorge
Luis

Bustos Domecq, H(onrio)
See Borges, Jorge Luis

Butler, Octavia E(stelle) 1947- ..... CLC 38
See also BW; CA 73-76; CANR 12, 24, 38;
DLB 33; MTCW

Butler, Samuel 1612-1680 .... LC 16
See also DLB 101

Butler, Samuel 1835-1902 ...... TCLC 1, 33
See also CA 104; CDBLB 1890-1914;
DLB 18, 57; WLC

Butor, Michel (Marie Francois)
1926- .... CLC 1, 3, 8, 11, 15
See also CA 9-12R; CANR 33; DLB 83;
MTCW

Buzo, Alexander (John) 1944- ...... CLC 61
See also CA 97-100; CANR 17, 39

Buzzati, Dino 1906-1972 .... CLC 36
See also CA 33-36R

Byars, Betsy (Cromer) 1928- .... CLC 35
See also CA 33-36R; CANR 18, 36; CLR 1,
16; DLB 52; MAICYA; MTCW; SAAS 1;
SATA 4, 46

Byatt, A(ntonia) S(usan Drabble)
1936- .... CLC 19, 65
See also CA 13-16R; CANR 13, 33;
DLB 14; MTCW

Byrne, David 1952- .... CLC 26
See also CA 127

Byrne, John Keyes 1926- .... CLC 19
See also Leonard, Hugh
See also CA 102

Byron, George Gordon (Noel)
1788-1824 .... NCLC 2, 12
See also CDBLB 1789-1832; DLB 96, 110;
WLC

C.3.3.
See Wilde, Oscar (Fingal O'Flahertie Wills)

Caballero, Fernan 1796-1877 ..... NCLC 10

Cabell, James Branch 1879-1958 ... TCLC 6
See also CA 105; DLB 9, 78

Cable, George Washington
1844-1925 .... TCLC 4; SSC 4
See also CA 104; DLB 12, 74

Cabrera Infante, G(uillermo)
1929- .... CLC 5, 25, 45
See also CA 85-88; CANR 29; DLB 113;
HW; MTCW

Cade, Toni
See Bambara, Toni Cade

Cadmus
See Buchan, John

Caedmon fl. 658-680 .... CMLC 7

Caeiro, Alberto
See Pessoa, Fernando (Antonio Nogueira)

Cage, John (Milton Jr.) 1912- ...... CLC 41
See also CA 13-16R; CANR 9

Cain, G.
See Cabrera Infante, G(uillermo)

Cain, Guillermo
See Cabrera Infante, G(uillermo)

Cain, James M(allahan)
1892-1977 .... CLC 3, 11, 28
See also AITN 1; CA 17-20R; 73-76;
CANR 8, 34; MTCW

Caine, Mark
See Raphael, Frederic (Michael)

Calderon de la Barca, Pedro
1600-1681 .... DC 3

Caldwell, Erskine (Preston)
1903-1987 .... CLC 1, 8, 14, 50, 60
See also AITN 1; CA 1-4R; 121; CAAS 1;
CANR 2, 33; DLB 9, 86; MTCW

Caldwell, (Janet Miriam) Taylor (Holland)
1900-1985 .... CLC 2, 28, 39
See also CA 5-8R; 116; CANR 5

Calhoun, John Caldwell
1782-1850 .... NCLC 15
See also DLB 3

Calisher, Hortense 1911- .... CLC 2, 4, 8, 38
See also CA 1-4R; CANR 1, 22; DLB 2;
MTCW

Callaghan, Morley Edward
1903-1990 .... CLC 3, 14, 41, 65
See also CA 9-12R; 132; CANR 33;
DLB 68; MTCW

Calvino, Italo
1923-1985 .... CLC 5, 8, 11, 22, 33, 39;
SSC 3
See also CA 85-88; 116; CANR 23; MTCW

Cameron, Carey 1952- .... CLC 59
See also CA 135

Cameron, Peter 1959- .... CLC 44
See also CA 125

Campana, Dino 1885-1932 .... TCLC 20
See also CA 117; DLB 114

Campbell, John W(ood Jr.)
1910-1971 .... CLC 32
See also CA 21-22; 29-32R; CANR 34;
CAP 2; DLB 8; MTCW

Campbell, Joseph 1904-1987 .... CLC 69
See also AAYA 3; BEST 89:2; CA 1-4R;
124; CANR 3, 28; MTCW

Campbell, (John) Ramsey 1946- .... CLC 42
See also CA 57-60; CANR 7

Campbell, (Ignatius) Roy (Dunnachie)
1901-1957 .... TCLC 5
See also CA 104; DLB 20

Campbell, Thomas 1777-1844 .... NCLC 19
See also DLB 93

Campbell, Wilfred .... TCLC 9
See also Campbell, William

Campbell, William 1858(?)-1918
See Campbell, Wilfred
See also CA 106; DLB 92

Campos, Alvaro de
See Pessoa, Fernando (Antonio Nogueira)

Camus, Albert
1913-1960 ... CLC 1, 2, 4, 9, 11, 14, 32,
63, 69; DC 2; SSC 9
See also CA 89-92; DLB 72; MTCW; WLC

Canby, Vincent 1924- .... CLC 13
See also CA 81-84

Cancale
See Desnos, Robert

Canetti, Elias 1905- .... CLC 3, 14, 25
See also CA 21-24R; CANR 23; DLB 85;
MTCW

Canin, Ethan 1960- .... CLC 55
See also CA 131; 135

Cannon, Curt
See Hunter, Evan

Cape, Judith
See Page, P(atricia) K(athleen)

Capek, Karel
1890-1938 .... TCLC 6, 37; DC 1
See also CA 104; WLC

Capote, Truman
1924-1984 ..... CLC 1, 3, 8, 13, 19, 34,
38, 58; SSC 2
See also CA 5-8R; 113; CANR 18;
CDALB 1941-1968; DLB 2; DLBY 80,
84; MTCW; WLC

Capra, Frank 1897-1991 .... CLC 16
See also CA 61-64; 135

Caputo, Philip 1941- .... CLC 32
See also CA 73-76

Card, Orson Scott 1951- .... CLC 44, 47, 50
See also CA 102; CANR 27; MTCW

Cardenal (Martinez), Ernesto
1925- .... CLC 31
See also CA 49-52; CANR 2, 32; HW;
MTCW

Carducci, Giosue 1835-1907 .... TCLC 32

Carew, Thomas 1595(?)-1640 .... LC 13

Carey, Ernestine Gilbreth 1908- .... CLC 17
See also CA 5-8R; SATA 2

Carey, Peter 1943- .... CLC 40, 55
See also CA 123; 127; MTCW

Carleton, William 1794-1869 ...... NCLC 3

Carlisle, Henry (Coffin) 1926- ...... CLC 33
See also CA 13-16R; CANR 15

Carlsen, Chris
See Holdstock, Robert P.

Carlson, Ron(ald F.) 1947- .... CLC 54
See also CA 105; CANR 27

Carlyle, Thomas 1795-1881 .... NCLC 22
See also CDBLB 1789-1832; DLB 55

Carman, (William) Bliss
1861-1929 .... TCLC 7
See also CA 104; DLB 92

Carossa, Hans 1878-1956 .... TCLC 48
See also DLB 66

Carpenter, Don(ald Richard)
1931- .... CLC 41
See also CA 45-48; CANR 1

Carpentier (y Valmont), Alejo
1904-1980 .... CLC 8, 11, 38
See also CA 65-68; 97-100; CANR 11;
DLB 113; HW

Carr, Emily 1871-1945 .... TCLC 32
See also DLB 68

Carr, John Dickson 1906-1977 ...... CLC 3
See also CA 49-52; 69-72; CANR 3, 33;
MTCW

Carr, Philippa
See Hibbert, Eleanor Burford

Carr, Virginia Spencer 1929- .... CLC 34
See also CA 61-64; DLB 111

Carrier, Roch 1937- .... CLC 13
See also CA 130; DLB 53

Carroll, James P. 1943(?)- .... CLC 38
See also CA 81-84

Carroll, Jim 1951- .... CLC 35
See also CA 45-48

Carroll, Lewis .... NCLC 2
See also Dodgson, Charles Lutwidge
See also CDBLB 1832-1890; CLR 2, 18;
DLB 18; WLC

Carroll, Paul Vincent 1900-1968 .... CLC 10
See also CA 9-12R; 25-28R; DLB 10

Carruth, Hayden 1921- .... CLC 4, 7, 10, 18
See also CA 9-12R; CANR 4, 38; DLB 5;
MTCW; SATA 47

Carson, Rachel Louise 1907-1964 ... CLC 71
See also CA 77-80; CANR 35; MTCW;
SATA 23

Carter, Angela (Olive)
1940-1991 .... CLC 5, 41
See also CA 53-56; 136; CANR 12, 36;
DLB 14; MTCW; SATA 66; SATO 70

Carter, Nick
See Smith, Martin Cruz

Carver, Raymond
1938-1988 ... CLC 22, 36, 53, 55; SSC 8
See also CA 33-36R; 126; CANR 17, 34;
DLBY 84, 88; MTCW

Cary, (Arthur) Joyce (Lunel)
1888-1957 .... TCLC 1, 29
See also CA 104; CDBLB 1914-1945;
DLB 15, 100

Casanova de Seingalt, Giovanni Jacopo
1725-1798 .... LC 13

Casares, Adolfo Bioy
See Bioy Casares, Adolfo

Casely-Hayford, J(oseph) E(phraim)
1866-1930 .... TCLC 24
See also BLC 1; CA 123

Casey, John (Dudley) 1939- .... CLC 59
See also BEST 90:2; CA 69-72; CANR 23

Casey, Michael 1947- .... CLC 2
See also CA 65-68; DLB 5

Casey, Patrick
See Thurman, Wallace (Henry)

Casey, Warren (Peter) 1935-1988 ... CLC 12
See also CA 101; 127

Casona, Alejandro .... CLC 49
See also Alvarez, Alejandro Rodriguez

Cassavetes, John 1929-1989 .... CLC 20
See also CA 85-88; 127

Cassill, R(onald) V(erlin) 1919- ... CLC 4, 23
See also CA 9-12R; CAAS 1; CANR 7;
DLB 6

Cassity, (Allen) Turner 1929- .... CLC 6, 42
See also CA 17-20R; CAAS 8; CANR 11;
DLB 105

Castaneda, Carlos 1931(?)- .... CLC 12
See also CA 25-28R; CANR 32; HW;
MTCW

Castedo, Elena 1937- .... CLC 65
See also CA 132

Castedo-Ellerman, Elena
See Castedo, Elena

Castellanos, Rosario 1925-1974 ..... CLC 66
See also CA 131; 53-56; DLB 113; HW

Castelvetro, Lodovico 1505-1571 ..... LC 12

Castiglione, Baldassare 1478-1529 ... LC 12

Castle, Robert
See Hamilton, Edmond

Castro, Guillen de 1569-1631 .... LC 19

Castro, Rosalia de 1837-1885 ..... NCLC 3

Cather, Willa
See Cather, Willa Sibert

Cather, Willa Sibert
1873-1947 ...... TCLC 1, 11, 31; SSC 2
See also CA 104; 128; CDALB 1865-1917;
DLB 9, 54, 78; DLBD 1; MTCW;
SATA 30; WLC

Catton, (Charles) Bruce
1899-1978 .... CLC 35
See also AITN 1; CA 5-8R; 81-84;
CANR 7; DLB 17; SATA 2, 24

Cauldwell, Frank
See King, Francis (Henry)

Caunitz, William J. 1933- .... CLC 34
See also BEST 89:3; CA 125; 130

Causley, Charles (Stanley) 1917- ..... CLC 7
See also CA 9-12R; CANR 5, 35; DLB 27;
MTCW; SATA 3, 66

Caute, David 1936- .... CLC 29
See also CA 1-4R; CAAS 4; CANR 1, 33;
DLB 14

Cavafy, C(onstantine) P(eter) ...... TCLC 2, 7
See also Kavafis, Konstantinos Petrou

Cavallo, Evelyn
See Spark, Muriel (Sarah)

Cavanna, Betty .... CLC 12
See also Harrison, Elizabeth Cavanna
See also MAICYA; SAAS 4; SATA 1, 30

Caxton, William 1421(?)-1491(?) ..... LC 17

Cayrol, Jean 1911- .... CLC 11
See also CA 89-92; DLB 83

Cela, Camilo Jose 1916- ...... CLC 4, 13, 59
See also BEST 90:2; CA 21-24R; CAAS 10;
CANR 21, 32; DLBY 89; HW; MTCW

Celan, Paul .... CLC 53
See also Antschel, Paul
See also DLB 69

Celine, Louis-Ferdinand
.... CLC 1, 3, 4, 7, 9, 15, 47
See also Destouches, Louis-Ferdinand
See also DLB 72

Cellini, Benvenuto 1500-1571 .... LC 7

Cendrars, Blaise
See Sauser-Hall, Frederic

Cernuda (y Bidon), Luis
1902-1963 .... CLC 54
See also CA 131; 89-92; HW

Cervantes (Saavedra), Miguel de
1547-1616 .... LC 6
See also WLC

Cesaire, Aime (Fernand) 1913- ... CLC 19, 32
See also BLC 1; BW; CA 65-68; CANR 24;
MTCW

Chabon, Michael 1965(?)- .... CLC 55

Chabrol, Claude 1930- .... CLC 16
See also CA 110

Challans, Mary 1905-1983
See Renault, Mary
See also CA 81-84; 111; SATA 23, 36

Chambers, Aidan 1934- .... CLC 35
See also CA 25-28R; CANR 12, 31;
MAICYA; SAAS 12; SATA 1, 69

Chambers, James 1948-
See Cliff, Jimmy
See also CA 124

Chambers, Jessie
See Lawrence, D(avid) H(erbert Richards)

Chambers, Robert W. 1865-1933 ... TCLC 41

Chandler, Raymond (Thornton)
1888-1959 .... TCLC 1, 7
See also CA 104; 129; CDALB 1929-1941;
DLBD 6; MTCW

Chang, Jung 1952- .... CLC 71

Channing, William Ellery
1780-1842 .... NCLC 17
See also DLB 1, 59

Chaplin, Charles Spencer
1889-1977 .... CLC 16
See also Chaplin, Charlie
See also CA 81-84; 73-76

Chaplin, Charlie
See Chaplin, Charles Spencer
See also DLB 44

Chapman, Graham 1941-1989 ...... CLC 21
See also Monty Python
See also CA 116; 129; CANR 35

Chapman, John Jay 1862-1933 ..... TCLC 7
See also CA 104

Chapman, Walker
See Silverberg, Robert

Chappell, Fred (Davis) 1936- .... CLC 40
See also CA 5-8R; CAAS 4; CANR 8, 33;
DLB 6, 105

Char, Rene(-Emile)
1907-1988 .... CLC 9, 11, 14, 55
See also CA 13-16R; 124; CANR 32;
MTCW

Charby, Jay
See Ellison, Harlan

Chardin, Pierre Teilhard de
See Teilhard de Chardin, (Marie Joseph) Pierre

Charles I 1600-1649 .... **LC 13**

Charyn, Jerome 1937- .... **CLC 5, 8, 18**
See also CA 5-8R; CAAS 1; CANR 7; DLBY 83; MTCW

Chase, Mary (Coyle) 1907-1981 ...... **DC 1**
See also CA 77-80; 105; SATA 17, 29

Chase, Mary Ellen 1887-1973 .... **CLC 2**
See also CA 13-16; 41-44R; CAP 1; SATA 10

Chase, Nicholas
See Hyde, Anthony

Chateaubriand, Francois Rene de
1768-1848 .... **NCLC 3**
See also DLB 119

Chatterje, Sarat Chandra 1876-1936(?)
See Chatterji, Saratchandra
See also CA 109

Chatterji, Bankim Chandra
1838-1894 .... **NCLC 19**

Chatterji, Saratchandra .... **TCLC 13**
See also Chatterje, Sarat Chandra

Chatterton, Thomas 1752-1770 .... **LC 3**
See also DLB 109

Chatwin, (Charles) Bruce
1940-1989 .... **CLC 28, 57, 59**
See also AAYA 4; BEST 90:1; CA 85-88; 127

Chaucer, Daniel
See Ford, Ford Madox

Chaucer, Geoffrey 1340(?)-1400 ..... **LC 17**
See also CDBLB Before 1660

Chaviaras, Strates 1935-
See Haviaras, Stratis
See also CA 105

Chayefsky, Paddy .... **CLC 23**
See also Chayefsky, Sidney
See also DLB 7, 44; DLBY 81

Chayefsky, Sidney 1923-1981
See Chayefsky, Paddy
See also CA 9-12R; 104; CANR 18

Chedid, Andree 1920- .... **CLC 47**

Cheever, John
1912-1982 ..... **CLC 3, 7, 8, 11, 15, 25, 64; SSC 1**
See also CA 5-8R; 106; CABS 1; CANR 5, 27; CDALB 1941-1968; DLB 2, 102; DLBY 80, 82; MTCW; WLC

Cheever, Susan 1943- .... **CLC 18, 48**
See also CA 103; CANR 27; DLBY 82

Chekhonte, Antosha
See Chekhov, Anton (Pavlovich)

Chekhov, Anton (Pavlovich)
1860-1904 ...... **TCLC 3, 10, 31; SSC 2**
See also CA 104; 124; WLC

Chernyshevsky, Nikolay Gavrilovich
1828-1889 .... **NCLC 1**

Cherry, Carolyn Janice 1942-
See Cherryh, C. J.
See also CA 65-68; CANR 10

Cherryh, C. J. .... **CLC 35**
See also Cherry, Carolyn Janice
See also DLBY 80

Chesnutt, Charles W(addell)
1858-1932 .... **TCLC 5, 39; SSC 7**
See also BLC 1; BW; CA 106; 125; DLB 12, 50, 78; MTCW

Chester, Alfred 1929(?)-1971 .... **CLC 49**
See also CA 33-36R

Chesterton, G(ilbert) K(eith)
1874-1936 .... **TCLC 1, 6; SSC 1**
See also CA 104; 132; CDBLB 1914-1945; DLB 10, 19, 34, 70, 98; MTCW; SATA 27

Chiang Pin-chin 1904-1986
See Ding Ling
See also CA 118

Ch'ien Chung-shu 1910- .... **CLC 22**
See also CA 130; MTCW

Child, L. Maria
See Child, Lydia Maria

Child, Lydia Maria 1802-1880 .... **NCLC 6**
See also DLB 1, 74; SATA 67

Child, Mrs.
See Child, Lydia Maria

Child, Philip 1898-1978 .... **CLC 19, 68**
See also CA 13-14; CAP 1; SATA 47

Childress, Alice 1920-.......... **CLC 12, 15**
See also AAYA 8; BLC 1; BW; CA 45-48; CANR 3, 27; CLR 14; DLB 7, 38; MAICYA; MTCW; SATA 7, 48

Chislett, (Margaret) Anne 1943-.... **CLC 34**

Chitty, Thomas Willes 1926- .... **CLC 11**
See also Hinde, Thomas
See also CA 5-8R

Chomette, Rene Lucien 1898-1981 .. **CLC 20**
See also Clair, Rene
See also CA 103

Chopin, Kate .... **TCLC 5, 14; SSC 8**
See also Chopin, Katherine
See also CDALB 1865-1917; DLB 12, 78

Chopin, Katherine 1851-1904
See Chopin, Kate
See also CA 104; 122

Chretien de Troyes
c. 12th cent. - .... **CMLC 10**

Christie
See Ichikawa, Kon

Christie, Agatha (Mary Clarissa)
1890-1976 ...... **CLC 1, 6, 8, 12, 39, 48**
See also AAYA 9; AITN 1, 2; CA 17-20R; 61-64; CANR 10, 37; CDBLB 1914-1945; DLB 13, 77; MTCW; SATA 36

Christie, (Ann) Philippa
See Pearce, Philippa
See also CA 5-8R; CANR 4

Christine de Pizan 1365(?)-1431(?) .... **LC 9**

Chubb, Elmer
See Masters, Edgar Lee

Chulkov, Mikhail Dmitrievich
1743-1792 .... **LC 2**

Churchill, Caryl 1938- .... **CLC 31, 55**
See also CA 102; CANR 22; DLB 13; MTCW

Churchill, Charles 1731-1764......... **LC 3**
See also DLB 109

Chute, Carolyn 1947-............. **CLC 39**
See also CA 123

Ciardi, John (Anthony)
1916-1986 .... **CLC 10, 40, 44**
See also CA 5-8R; 118; CAAS 2; CANR 5, 33; CLR 19; DLB 5; DLBY 86; MAICYA; MTCW; SATA 1, 46, 65

Cicero, Marcus Tullius
106B.C.-43B.C................ **CMLC 3**

Cimino, Michael 1943-............. **CLC 16**
See also CA 105

Cioran, E(mil) M. 1911-........... **CLC 64**
See also CA 25-28R

Cisneros, Sandra 1954-............ **CLC 69**
See also AAYA 9; CA 131; HW

Clair, Rene....................... **CLC 20**
See also Chomette, Rene Lucien

Clampitt, Amy 1920- .... **CLC 32**
See also CA 110; CANR 29; DLB 105

Clancy, Thomas L. Jr. 1947-
See Clancy, Tom
See also CA 125; 131; MTCW

Clancy, Tom...................... **CLC 45**
See also Clancy, Thomas L. Jr.
See also AAYA 9; BEST 89:1, 90:1

Clare, John 1793-1864............ **NCLC 9**
See also DLB 55, 96

Clarin
See Alas (y Urena), Leopoldo (Enrique Garcia)

Clark, (Robert) Brian 1932-........ **CLC 29**
See also CA 41-44R

Clark, Eleanor 1913- .... **CLC 5, 19**
See also CA 9-12R; DLB 6

Clark, J. P.
See Clark, John Pepper
See also DLB 117

Clark, John Pepper 1935- .... **CLC 38**
See also Clark, J. P.
See also BLC 1; BW; CA 65-68; CANR 16

Clark, M. R.
See Clark, Mavis Thorpe

Clark, Mavis Thorpe 1909- .... **CLC 12**
See also CA 57-60; CANR 8, 37; MAICYA; SAAS 5; SATA 8

Clark, Walter Van Tilburg
1909-1971 .... **CLC 28**
See also CA 9-12R; 33-36R; DLB 9; SATA 8

Clarke, Arthur C(harles)
1917- ...... **CLC 1, 4, 13, 18, 35; SSC 3**
See also AAYA 4; CA 1-4R; CANR 2, 28; MAICYA; MTCW; SATA 13, 70

Clarke, Austin C(hesterfield)
1934- .... **CLC 8, 53**
See also BLC 1; BW; CA 25-28R; CAAS 16; CANR 14, 32; DLB 53

Clarke, Austin 1896-1974.......... **CLC 6, 9**
See also CA 29-32; 49-52; CAP 2; DLB 10, 20

Clarke, Gillian 1937- .... **CLC 61**
See also CA 106; DLB 40

Clarke, Marcus (Andrew Hislop)
1846-1881 .... **NCLC 19**

Clarke, Shirley 1925- .... **CLC 16**
.... **CLC 30**
See also Headon, (Nicky) Topper; Jones, Mick; Simonon, Paul; Strummer, Joe

Claudel, Paul (Louis Charles Marie)
1868-1955 .... **TCLC 2, 10**
See also CA 104

Clavell, James (duMaresq)
1925- .... **CLC 6, 25**
See also CA 25-28R; CANR 26; MTCW

Cleaver, (Leroy) Eldridge 1935- .... **CLC 30**
See also BLC 1; BW; CA 21-24R; CANR 16

Cleese, John (Marwood) 1939- ..... **CLC 21**
See also Monty Python
See also CA 112; 116; CANR 35; MTCW

Cleishbotham, Jebediah
See Scott, Walter

Cleland, John 1710-1789 .... **LC 2**
See also DLB 39

Clemens, Samuel Langhorne 1835-1910
See Twain, Mark
See also CA 104; 135; CDALB 1865-1917; DLB 11, 12, 23, 64, 74; MAICYA; YABC 2

Clerihew, E.
See Bentley, E(dmund) C(lerihew)

Clerk, N. W.
See Lewis, C(live) S(taples)

Cliff, Jimmy .... **CLC 21**
See also Chambers, James

Clifton, (Thelma) Lucille
1936- .... **CLC 19, 66**
See also BLC 1; BW; CA 49-52; CANR 2, 24; CLR 5; DLB 5, 41; MAICYA; MTCW; SATA 20, 69

Clinton, Dirk
See Silverberg, Robert

Clough, Arthur Hugh 1819-1861 .. **NCLC 27**
See also DLB 32

Clutha, Janet Paterson Frame 1924-
See Frame, Janet
See also CA 1-4R; CANR 2, 36; MTCW

Clyne, Terence
See Blatty, William Peter

Cobalt, Martin
See Mayne, William (James Carter)

Coburn, D(onald) L(ee) 1938- ...... **CLC 10**
See also CA 89-92

Cocteau, Jean (Maurice Eugene Clement)
1889-1963 .... **CLC 1, 8, 15, 16, 43**
See also CA 25-28; CAP 2; DLB 65; MTCW; WLC

Codrescu, Andrei 1946- .... **CLC 46**
See also CA 33-36R; CANR 13, 34

Coe, Max
See Bourne, Randolph S(illiman)

Coe, Tucker
See Westlake, Donald E(dwin)

Coetzee, J(ohn) M(ichael)
1940- .... **CLC 23, 33, 66**
See also CA 77-80; MTCW

Cohen, Arthur A(llen)
1928-1986 .... **CLC 7, 31**
See also CA 1-4R; 120; CANR 1, 17; DLB 28

Cohen, Leonard (Norman)
1934- .... **CLC 3, 38**
See also CA 21-24R; CANR 14; DLB 53; MTCW

Cohen, Matt 1942- .... **CLC 19**
See also CA 61-64; DLB 53

Cohen-Solal, Annie 19(?)- .... **CLC 50**

Colegate, Isabel 1931- .... **CLC 36**
See also CA 17-20R; CANR 8, 22; DLB 14; MTCW

Coleman, Emmett
See Reed, Ishmael

Coleridge, Samuel Taylor
1772-1834 .... **NCLC 9**
See also CDBLB 1789-1832; DLB 93, 107; WLC

Coleridge, Sara 1802-1852 .... **NCLC 31**

Coles, Don 1928- .... **CLC 46**
See also CA 115; CANR 38

Colette, (Sidonie-Gabrielle)
1873-1954 ...... **TCLC 1, 5, 16; SSC 10**
See also CA 104; 131; DLB 65; MTCW

Collett, (Jacobine) Camilla (Wergeland)
1813-1895 .... **NCLC 22**

Collier, Christopher 1930- .... **CLC 30**
See also CA 33-36R; CANR 13, 33; MAICYA; SATA 16, 70

Collier, James L(incoln) 1928- ..... **CLC 30**
See also CA 9-12R; CANR 4, 33; MAICYA; SATA 8, 70

Collier, Jeremy 1650-1726 .... **LC 6**

Collins, Hunt
See Hunter, Evan

Collins, Linda 1931- .... **CLC 44**
See also CA 125

Collins, (William) Wilkie
1824-1889 .... **NCLC 1, 18**
See also CDBLB 1832-1890; DLB 18, 70

Collins, William 1721-1759 .... **LC 4**
See also DLB 109

Colman, George
See Glassco, John

Colt, Winchester Remington
See Hubbard, L(afayette) Ron(ald)

Colter, Cyrus 1910- .... **CLC 58**
See also BW; CA 65-68; CANR 10; DLB 33

Colton, James
See Hansen, Joseph

Colum, Padraic 1881-1972 .... **CLC 28**
See also CA 73-76; 33-36R; CANR 35; MAICYA; MTCW; SATA 15

Colvin, James
See Moorcock, Michael (John)

Colwin, Laurie 1944- .... **CLC 5, 13, 23**
See also CA 89-92; CANR 20; DLBY 80; MTCW

Comfort, Alex(ander) 1920- .... **CLC 7**
See also CA 1-4R; CANR 1

Comfort, Montgomery
See Campbell, (John) Ramsey

Compton-Burnett, I(vy)
1884(?)-1969 ...... **CLC 1, 3, 10, 15, 34**
See also CA 1-4R; 25-28R; CANR 4; DLB 36; MTCW

Comstock, Anthony 1844-1915 .... **TCLC 13**
See also CA 110

Conan Doyle, Arthur
See Doyle, Arthur Conan

Conde, Maryse .... **CLC 52**
See also Boucolon, Maryse

Condon, Richard (Thomas)
1915- .... **CLC 4, 6, 8, 10, 45**
See also BEST 90:3; CA 1-4R; CAAS 1; CANR 2, 23; MTCW

Congreve, William
1670-1729 .... **LC 5, 21; DC 2**
See also CDBLB 1660-1789; DLB 39, 84; WLC

Connell, Evan S(helby) Jr.
1924- .... **CLC 4, 6, 45**
See also AAYA 7; CA 1-4R; CAAS 2; CANR 2, 39; DLB 2; DLBY 81; MTCW

Connelly, Marc(us Cook)
1890-1980 .... **CLC 7**
See also CA 85-88; 102; CANR 30; DLB 7; DLBY 80; SATA 25

Connor, Ralph .... **TCLC 31**
See also Gordon, Charles William
See also DLB 92

Conrad, Joseph
1857-1924 ...... **TCLC 1, 6, 13, 25, 43; SSC 9**
See also CA 104; 131; CDBLB 1890-1914; DLB 10, 34, 98; MTCW; SATA 27; WLC

Conrad, Robert Arnold
See Hart, Moss

Conroy, Pat 1945- .... **CLC 30, 74**
See also AAYA 8; AITN 1; CA 85-88; CANR 24; DLB 6; MTCW

Constant (de Rebecque), (Henri) Benjamin
1767-1830 .... **NCLC 6**
See also DLB 119

Conybeare, Charles Augustus
See Eliot, T(homas) S(tearns)

Cook, Michael 1933- .... **CLC 58**
See also CA 93-96; DLB 53

Cook, Robin 1940- .... **CLC 14**
See also BEST 90:2; CA 108; 111

Cook, Roy
See Silverberg, Robert

Cooke, Elizabeth 1948- .... **CLC 55**
See also CA 129

Cooke, John Esten 1830-1886 ..... **NCLC 5**
See also DLB 3

Cooke, John Estes
See Baum, L(yman) Frank

Cooke, M. E.
See Creasey, John

Cooke, Margaret
See Creasey, John

Cooney, Ray .... **CLC 62**

Cooper, Henry St. John
See Creasey, John

Cooper, J. California. . . . . **CLC 56**
See also BW; CA 125

Cooper, James Fenimore
1789-1851 . . . . **NCLC 1, 27**
See also CDALB 1640-1865; DLB 3;
SATA 19

Coover, Robert (Lowell)
1932- . . . . **CLC 3, 7, 15, 32, 46**
See also CA 45-48; CANR 3, 37; DLB 2;
DLBY 81; MTCW

Copeland, Stewart (Armstrong)
1952- . . . . **CLC 26**
See also The Police

Coppard, A(lfred) E(dgar)
1878-1957 . . . . **TCLC 5**
See also CA 114; YABC 1

Coppee, Francois 1842-1908 . . . . . . **TCLC 25**

Coppola, Francis Ford 1939- . . . . **CLC 16**
See also CA 77-80; DLB 44

Corcoran, Barbara 1911- . . . . **CLC 17**
See also CA 21-24R; CAAS 2; CANR 11,
28; DLB 52; SATA 3

Cordelier, Maurice
See Giraudoux, (Hippolyte) Jean

Corman, Cid. **CLC 9**
See also Corman, Sidney
See also CAAS 2; DLB 5

Corman, Sidney 1924-
See Corman, Cid
See also CA 85-88

Cormier, Robert (Edmund)
1925- . . . . **CLC 12, 30**
See also AAYA 3; CA 1-4R; CANR 5, 23;
CDALB 1968-1988; CLR 12; DLB 52;
MAICYA; MTCW; SATA 10, 45

Corn, Alfred 1943- . . . . **CLC 33**
See also CA 104; DLB 120; DLBY 80

Cornwell, David (John Moore)
1931- . . . . **CLC 9, 15**
See also le Carre, John
See also CA 5-8R; CANR 13, 33; MTCW

Corrigan, Kevin . . . . **CLC 55**

Corso, (Nunzio) Gregory 1930- . . . **CLC 1, 11**
See also CA 5-8R; DLB 5,16; MTCW

Cortazar, Julio
1914-1984 . . . . . **CLC 2, 3, 5, 10, 13, 15,
33, 34; SSC 7**
See also CA 21-24R; CANR 12, 32;
DLB 113; HW; MTCW

Corwin, Cecil
See Kornbluth, C(yril) M.

Cosic, Dobrica 1921- . . . . **CLC 14**
See also CA 122; 138

Costain, Thomas B(ertram)
1885-1965 . . . . **CLC 30**
See also CA 5-8R; 25-28R; DLB 9

Costantini, Humberto
1924(?)-1987 . . . . **CLC 49**
See also CA 131; 122; HW

Costello, Elvis 1955- . . . . **CLC 21**

Cotter, Joseph S. Sr.
See Cotter, Joseph Seamon Sr.

Cotter, Joseph Seamon Sr.
1861-1949 . . . . **TCLC 28**
See also BLC 1; BW; CA 124; DLB 50

Coulton, James
See Hansen, Joseph

Couperus, Louis (Marie Anne)
1863-1923 . . . . **TCLC 15**
See also CA 115

Court, Wesli
See Turco, Lewis (Putnam)

Courtenay, Bryce 1933- . . . . **CLC 59**
See also CA 138

Courtney, Robert
See Ellison, Harlan

Cousteau, Jacques-Yves 1910- . . . . . . **CLC 30**
See also CA 65-68; CANR 15; MTCW;
SATA 38

Coward, Noel (Peirce)
1899-1973 . . . . **CLC 1, 9, 29, 51**
See also AITN 1; CA 17-18; 41-44R;
CANR 35; CAP 2; CDBLB 1914-1945;
DLB 10; MTCW

Cowley, Malcolm 1898-1989 . . . . **CLC 39**
See also CA 5-8R; 128; CANR 3; DLB 4,
48; DLBY 81, 89; MTCW

Cowper, William 1731-1800 . . . . **NCLC 8**
See also DLB 104, 109

Cox, William Trevor 1928- . . . **CLC 9, 14, 71**
See also Trevor, William
See also CA 9-12R; CANR 4, 37; DLB 14;
MTCW

Cozzens, James Gould
1903-1978 . . . . **CLC 1, 4, 11**
See also CA 9-12R; 81-84; CANR 19;
CDALB 1941-1968; DLB 9; DLBD 2;
DLBY 84; MTCW

Crabbe, George 1754-1832 . . . . **NCLC 26**
See also DLB 93

Craig, A. A.
See Anderson, Poul (William)

Craik, Dinah Maria (Mulock)
1826-1887 . . . . **NCLC 38**
See also DLB 35; MAICYA; SATA 34

Cram, Ralph Adams 1863-1942 . . . . **TCLC 45**

Crane, (Harold) Hart
1899-1932 . . . . **TCLC 2, 5; PC 3**
See also CA 104; 127; CDALB 1917-1929;
DLB 4, 48; MTCW; WLC

Crane, R(onald) S(almon)
1886-1967 . . . . **CLC 27**
See also CA 85-88; DLB 63

Crane, Stephen (Townley)
1871-1900 . . . . . **TCLC 11, 17, 32; SSC 7**
See also CA 109; CDALB 1865-1917;
DLB 12, 54, 78; WLC; YABC 2

Crase, Douglas 1944- . . . . **CLC 58**
See also CA 106

Craven, Margaret 1901-1980 . . . . **CLC 17**
See also CA 103

Crawford, F(rancis) Marion
1854-1909 . . . . **TCLC 10**
See also CA 107; DLB 71

Crawford, Isabella Valancy
1850-1887 . . . . **NCLC 12**
See also DLB 92

Crayon, Geoffrey
See Irving, Washington

Creasey, John 1908-1973 . . . . **CLC 11**
See also CA 5-8R; 41-44R; CANR 8;
DLB 77; MTCW

Crebillon, Claude Prosper Jolyot de (fils)
1707-1777 . . . . **LC 1**

Credo
See Creasey, John

Creeley, Robert (White)
1926- . . . . **CLC 1, 2, 4, 8, 11, 15, 36**
See also CA 1-4R; CAAS 10; CANR 23;
DLB 5, 16; MTCW

Crews, Harry (Eugene)
1935- . . . . **CLC 6, 23, 49**
See also AITN 1; CA 25-28R; CANR 20;
DLB 6; MTCW

Crichton, (John) Michael
1942- . . . . **CLC 2, 6, 54**
See also AITN 2; CA 25-28R; CANR 13;
DLBY 81; MTCW; SATA 9

Crispin, Edmund . . . . **CLC 22**
See also Montgomery, (Robert) Bruce
See also DLB 87

Cristofer, Michael 1945(?)- . . . . **CLC 28**
See also CA 110; DLB 7

Croce, Benedetto 1866-1952 . . . . . . **TCLC 37**
See also CA 120

Crockett, David 1786-1836 . . . . **NCLC 8**
See also DLB 3, 11

Crockett, Davy
See Crockett, David

Croker, John Wilson 1780-1857 . . **NCLC 10**
See also DLB 110

Cronin, A(rchibald) J(oseph)
1896-1981 . . . . **CLC 32**
See also CA 1-4R; 102; CANR 5; SATA 25,
47

Cross, Amanda
See Heilbrun, Carolyn G(old)

Crothers, Rachel 1878(?)-1958 . . . . . **TCLC 19**
See also CA 113; DLB 7

Croves, Hal
See Traven, B.

Crowfield, Christopher
See Stowe, Harriet (Elizabeth) Beecher

Crowley, Aleister. . . . . **TCLC 7**
See also Crowley, Edward Alexander

Crowley, Edward Alexander 1875-1947
See Crowley, Aleister
See also CA 104

Crowley, John 1942- . . . . **CLC 57**
See also CA 61-64; DLBY 82; SATA 65

Crud
See Crumb, R(obert)

Crumarums
See Crumb, R(obert)

Crumb, R(obert) 1943- . . . . **CLC 17**
See also CA 106

Crumbum
See Crumb, R(obert)

Crumski
See Crumb, R(obert)

Crum the Bum
See Crumb, R(obert)

Crunk
See Crumb, R(obert)

Crustt
See Crumb, R(obert)

Cryer, Gretchen (Kiger) 1935- ...... **CLC 21**
See also CA 114; 123

Csath, Geza 1887-1919.......... **TCLC 13**
See also CA 111

Cudlip, David 1933- .... **CLC 34**

Cullen, Countee 1903-1946 ..... **TCLC 4, 37**
See also BLC 1; BW; CA 108; 124;
CDALB 1917-1929; DLB 4, 48, 51;
MTCW; SATA 18

Cum, R.
See Crumb, R(obert)

Cummings, Bruce F(rederick) 1889-1919
See Barbellion, W. N. P.
See also CA 123

Cummings, E(dward) E(stlin)
1894-1962 ..... **CLC 1, 3, 8, 12, 15, 68;**
PC 5
See also CA 73-76; CANR 31;
CDALB 1929-1941; DLB 4, 48; MTCW;
WLC 2

Cunha, Euclides (Rodrigues Pimenta) da
1866-1909 .... **TCLC 24**
See also CA 123

Cunningham, E. V.
See Fast, Howard (Melvin)

Cunningham, J(ames) V(incent)
1911-1985 .... **CLC 3, 31**
See also CA 1-4R; 115; CANR 1; DLB 5

Cunningham, Julia (Woolfolk)
1916- .... **CLC 12**
See also CA 9-12R; CANR 4, 19, 36;
MAICYA; SAAS 2; SATA 1, 26

Cunningham, Michael 1952- .... **CLC 34**
See also CA 136

Cunninghame Graham, R(obert) B(ontine)
1852-1936 .... **TCLC 19**
See also Graham, R(obert) B(ontine)
Cunninghame
See also CA 119; DLB 98

Currie, Ellen 19(?)- .... **CLC 44**

Curtin, Philip
See Lowndes, Marie Adelaide (Belloc)

Curtis, Price
See Ellison, Harlan

Czaczkes, Shmuel Yosef
See Agnon, S(hmuel) Y(osef Halevi)

D. P.
See Wells, H(erbert) G(eorge)

Dabrowska, Maria (Szumska)
1889-1965 .... **CLC 15**
See also CA 106

Dabydeen, David 1955- .... **CLC 34**
See also BW; CA 125

Dacey, Philip 1939- .... **CLC 51**
See also CA 37-40R; CANR 14, 32;
DLB 105

Dagerman, Stig (Halvard)
1923-1954 .... **TCLC 17**
See also CA 117

Dahl, Roald 1916-1990........ **CLC 1, 6, 18**
See also CA 1-4R; 133; CANR 6, 32, 37;
CLR 1, 7; MAICYA; MTCW; SATA 1,
26; SATO 65

Dahlberg, Edward 1900-1977... **CLC 1, 7, 14**
See also CA 9-12R; 69-72; CANR 31;
DLB 48; MTCW

Dale, Colin..................... **TCLC 18**
See also Lawrence, T(homas) E(dward)

Dale, George E.
See Asimov, Isaac

Daly, Elizabeth 1878-1967......... **CLC 52**
See also CA 23-24; 25-28R; CAP 2

Daly, Maureen 1921- .... **CLC 17**
See also AAYA 5; CANR 37; MAICYA;
SAAS 1; SATA 2

Daniels, Brett
See Adler, Renata

Dannay, Frederic 1905-1982 .... **CLC 11**
See also Queen, Ellery
See also CA 1-4R; 107; CANR 1, 39;
MTCW

D'Annunzio, Gabriele
1863-1938 .... **TCLC 6, 40**
See also CA 104

d'Antibes, Germain
See Simenon, Georges (Jacques Christian)

Danvers, Dennis 1947-............ **CLC 70**

Danziger, Paula 1944- .... **CLC 21**
See also AAYA 4; CA 112; 115; CANR 37;
CLR 20; MAICYA; SATA 30, 36, 63

Dario, Ruben..................... **TCLC 4**
See also Sarmiento, Felix Ruben Garcia

Darley, George 1795-1846........ **NCLC 2**
See also DLB 96

Daryush, Elizabeth 1887-1977.... **CLC 6, 19**
See also CA 49-52; CANR 3; DLB 20

Daudet, (Louis Marie) Alphonse
1840-1897 .... **NCLC 1**

Daumal, Rene 1908-1944........ **TCLC 14**
See also CA 114

Davenport, Guy (Mattison Jr.)
1927- .... **CLC 6, 14, 38**
See also CA 33-36R; CANR 23

Davidson, Avram 1923-
See Queen, Ellery
See also CA 101; CANR 26; DLB 8

Davidson, Donald (Grady)
1893-1968 .... **CLC 2, 13, 19**
See also CA 5-8R; 25-28R; CANR 4;
DLB 45

Davidson, Hugh
See Hamilton, Edmond

Davidson, John 1857-1909........ **TCLC 24**
See also CA 118; DLB 19

Davidson, Sara 1943-............. **CLC 9**
See also CA 81-84

Davie, Donald (Alfred)
1922- .... **CLC 5, 8, 10, 31**
See also CA 1-4R; CAAS 3; CANR 1;
DLB 27; MTCW

Davies, Ray(mond Douglas) 1944- .. **CLC 21**
See also CA 116

Davies, Rhys 1903-1978........... **CLC 23**
See also CA 9-12R; 81-84; CANR 4

Davies, (William) Robertson
1913- .... **CLC 2, 7, 13, 25, 42**
See also BEST 89:2; CA 33-36R; CANR 17;
DLB 68; MTCW; WLC

Davies, W(illiam) H(enry)
1871-1940 .... **TCLC 5**
See also CA 104; DLB 19

Davies, Walter C.
See Kornbluth, C(yril) M.

Davis, B. Lynch
See Bioy Casares, Adolfo; Borges, Jorge
Luis

Davis, Gordon
See Hunt, E(verette) Howard Jr.

Davis, Harold Lenoir 1896-1960.... **CLC 49**
See also CA 89-92; DLB 9

Davis, Rebecca (Blaine) Harding
1831-1910 .... **TCLC 6**
See also CA 104; DLB 74

Davis, Richard Harding
1864-1916 .... **TCLC 24**
See also CA 114; DLB 12, 23, 78, 79

Davison, Frank Dalby 1893-1970 ... **CLC 15**
See also CA 116

Davison, Lawrence H.
See Lawrence, D(avid) H(erbert Richards)

Davison, Peter 1928- .... **CLC 28**
See also CA 9-12R; CAAS 4; CANR 3;
DLB 5

Davys, Mary 1674-1732............. **LC 1**
See also DLB 39

Dawson, Fielding 1930- .... **CLC 6**
See also CA 85-88

Day, Clarence (Shepard Jr.)
1874-1935 .... **TCLC 25**
See also CA 108; DLB 11

Day, Thomas 1748-1789............. **LC 1**
See also DLB 39; YABC 1

Day Lewis, C(ecil)
1904-1972 .... **CLC 1, 6, 10**
See also Blake, Nicholas
See also CA 13-16; 33-36R; CANR 34;
CAP 1; DLB 15, 20; MTCW

Dazai, Osamu .... **TCLC 11**
See also Tsushima, Shuji

de Andrade, Carlos Drummond
See Drummond de Andrade, Carlos

Deane, Norman
See Creasey, John

de Beauvoir, Simone (Lucie Ernestine Marie Bertrand)
See Beauvoir, Simone (Lucie Ernestine
Marie Bertrand) de

de Brissac, Malcolm
See Dickinson, Peter (Malcolm)

de Chardin, Pierre Teilhard
See Teilhard de Chardin, (Marie Joseph)
Pierre

Dee, John 1527-1608 .... **LC 20**

Deer, Sandra 1940-............... **CLC 45**

De Ferrari, Gabriella .... **CLC 65**

Defoe, Daniel 1660(?)-1731 .... **LC 1**
See also CDBLB 1660-1789; DLB 39, 95, 101; MAICYA; SATA 22; WLC

de Gourmont, Remy
See Gourmont, Remy de

de Hartog, Jan 1914- .... **CLC 19**
See also CA 1-4R; CANR 1

de Hostos, E. M.
See Hostos (y Bonilla), Eugenio Maria de

de Hostos, Eugenio M.
See Hostos (y Bonilla), Eugenio Maria de

Deighton, Len .... **CLC 4, 7, 22, 46**
See also Deighton, Leonard Cyril
See also AAYA 6; BEST 89:2; CDBLB 1960 to Present; DLB 87

Deighton, Leonard Cyril 1929-
See Deighton, Len
See also CA 9-12R; CANR 19, 33; MTCW

de la Mare, Walter (John)
1873-1956 .... **TCLC 4**
See also CA 110; 137; CDBLB 1914-1945; CLR 23; DLB 19; MAICYA; SATA 16; WLC

Delaney, Franey
See O'Hara, John (Henry)

Delaney, Shelagh 1939- .... **CLC 29**
See also CA 17-20R; CANR 30; CDBLB 1960 to Present; DLB 13; MTCW

Delany, Mary (Granville Pendarves)
1700-1788 .... **LC 12**

Delany, Samuel R(ay Jr.)
1942- .... **CLC 8, 14, 38**
See also BLC 1; BW; CA 81-84; CANR 27; DLB 8, 33; MTCW

Delaporte, Theophile
See Green, Julian (Hartridge)

De La Ramee, (Marie) Louise 1839-1908
See Ouida
See also SATA 20

de la Roche, Mazo 1879-1961 ...... **CLC 14**
See also CA 85-88; CANR 30; DLB 68; SATA 64

Delbanco, Nicholas (Franklin)
1942- .... **CLC 6, 13**
See also CA 17-20R; CAAS 2; CANR 29; DLB 6

del Castillo, Michel 1933- .... **CLC 38**
See also CA 109

Deledda, Grazia (Cosima)
1875(?)-1936 .... **TCLC 23**
See also CA 123

Delibes, Miguel .... **CLC 8, 18**
See also Delibes Setien, Miguel

Delibes Setien, Miguel 1920-
See Delibes, Miguel
See also CA 45-48; CANR 1, 32; HW; MTCW

DeLillo, Don
1936- .... **CLC 8, 10, 13, 27, 39, 54**
See also BEST 89:1; CA 81-84; CANR 21; DLB 6; MTCW

de Lisser, H. G.
See De Lisser, Herbert George
See also DLB 117

De Lisser, Herbert George
1878-1944 .... **TCLC 12**
See also de Lisser, H. G.
See also CA 109

Deloria, Vine (Victor) Jr. 1933- .... **CLC 21**
See also CA 53-56; CANR 5, 20; MTCW; SATA 21

Del Vecchio, John M(ichael)
1947- .... **CLC 29**
See also CA 110; DLBD 9

de Man, Paul (Adolph Michel)
1919-1983 .... **CLC 55**
See also CA 128; 111; DLB 67; MTCW

De Marinis, Rick 1934- .... **CLC 54**
See also CA 57-60; CANR 9, 25

Demby, William 1922- .... **CLC 53**
See also BLC 1; BW; CA 81-84; DLB 33

Demijohn, Thom
See Disch, Thomas M(ichael)

de Montherlant, Henry (Milon)
See Montherlant, Henry (Milon) de

de Natale, Francine
See Malzberg, Barry N(athaniel)

Denby, Edwin (Orr) 1903-1983 ..... **CLC 48**
See also CA 138; 110

Denis, Julio
See Cortazar, Julio

Denmark, Harrison
See Zelazny, Roger (Joseph)

Dennis, John 1658-1734 .... **LC 11**
See also DLB 101

Dennis, Nigel (Forbes) 1912-1989 .... **CLC 8**
See also CA 25-28R; 129; DLB 13, 15; MTCW

De Palma, Brian (Russell) 1940- .... **CLC 20**
See also CA 109

De Quincey, Thomas 1785-1859 ... **NCLC 4**
See also CDBLB 1789-1832; DLB 110

Deren, Eleanora 1908(?)-1961
See Deren, Maya
See also CA 111

Deren, Maya .... **CLC 16**
See also Deren, Eleanora

Derleth, August (William)
1909-1971 .... **CLC 31**
See also CA 1-4R; 29-32R; CANR 4; DLB 9; SATA 5

de Routisie, Albert
See Aragon, Louis

Derrida, Jacques 1930- .... **CLC 24**
See also CA 124; 127

Derry Down Derry
See Lear, Edward

Dersonnes, Jacques
See Simenon, Georges (Jacques Christian)

Desai, Anita 1937- .... **CLC 19, 37**
See also CA 81-84; CANR 33; MTCW; SATA 63

de Saint-Luc, Jean
See Glassco, John

de Saint Roman, Arnaud
See Aragon, Louis

Descartes, Rene 1596-1650 .... **LC 20**

De Sica, Vittorio 1901(?)-1974 ..... **CLC 20**
See also CA 117

Desnos, Robert 1900-1945 .... **TCLC 22**
See also CA 121

Destouches, Louis-Ferdinand
1894-1961 .... **CLC 9, 15**
See also Celine, Louis-Ferdinand
See also CA 85-88; CANR 28; MTCW

Deutsch, Babette 1895-1982 .... **CLC 18**
See also CA 1-4R; 108; CANR 4; DLB 45; SATA 1, 33

Devenant, William 1606-1649 .... **LC 13**

Devkota, Laxmiprasad
1909-1959 .... **TCLC 23**
See also CA 123

De Voto, Bernard (Augustine)
1897-1955 .... **TCLC 29**
See also CA 113; DLB 9

De Vries, Peter
1910- .... **CLC 1, 2, 3, 7, 10, 28, 46**
See also CA 17-20R; DLB 6; DLBY 82; MTCW

Dexter, Pete 1943- .... **CLC 34, 55**
See also BEST 89:2; CA 127; 131; MTCW

Diamano, Silmang
See Senghor, Leopold Sedar

Diamond, Neil 1941- .... **CLC 30**
See also CA 108

di Bassetto, Corno
See Shaw, George Bernard

Dick, Philip K(indred)
1928-1982 .... **CLC 10, 30, 72**
See also CA 49-52; 106; CANR 2, 16; DLB 8; MTCW

Dickens, Charles (John Huffam)
1812-1870 .... **NCLC 3, 8, 18, 26**
See also CDBLB 1832-1890; DLB 21, 55, 70; MAICYA; SATA 15

Dickey, James (Lafayette)
1923- .... **CLC 1, 2, 4, 7, 10, 15, 47**
See also AITN 1, 2; CA 9-12R; CABS 2; CANR 10; CDALB 1968-1988; DLB 5; DLBD 7; DLBY 82; MTCW

Dickey, William 1928- .... **CLC 3, 28**
See also CA 9-12R; CANR 24; DLB 5

Dickinson, Charles 1951- .... **CLC 49**
See also CA 128

Dickinson, Emily (Elizabeth)
1830-1886 .... **NCLC 21; PC 1**
See also CDALB 1865-1917; DLB 1; SATA 29; WLC

Dickinson, Peter (Malcolm)
1927- .... **CLC 12, 35**
See also AAYA 9; CA 41-44R; CANR 31; DLB 87; MAICYA; SATA 5, 62

Dickson, Carr
See Carr, John Dickson

Dickson, Carter
See Carr, John Dickson

Didion, Joan 1934- ..... **CLC 1, 3, 8, 14, 32**
See also AITN 1; CA 5-8R; CANR 14; CDALB 1968-1988; DLB 2; DLBY 81, 86; MTCW

Dietrich, Robert
See Hunt, E(verette) Howard Jr.

Dillard, Annie 1945-............ **CLC 9, 60**
See also AAYA 6; CA 49-52; CANR 3; DLBY 80; MTCW; SATA 10

Dillard, R(ichard) H(enry) W(ilde)
1937-....................... **CLC 5**
See also CA 21-24R; CAAS 7; CANR 10; DLB 5

Dillon, Eilis 1920-.............. **CLC 17**
See also CA 9-12R; CAAS 3; CANR 4, 38; CLR 26; MAICYA; SATA 2

Dimont, Penelope
See Mortimer, Penelope (Ruth)

Dinesen, Isak.......... **CLC 10, 29; SSC 7**
See also Blixen, Karen (Christentze Dinesen)

Ding Ling...................... **CLC 68**
See also Chiang Pin-chin

Disch, Thomas M(ichael) 1940-... **CLC 7, 36**
See also CA 21-24R; CAAS 4; CANR 17, 36; CLR 18; DLB 8; MAICYA; MTCW; SATA 54

Disch, Tom
See Disch, Thomas M(ichael)

d'Isly, Georges
See Simenon, Georges (Jacques Christian)

Disraeli, Benjamin 1804-1881..... **NCLC 2**
See also DLB 21, 55

Ditcum, Steve
See Crumb, R(obert)

Dixon, Paige
See Corcoran, Barbara

Dixon, Stephen 1936-............. **CLC 52**
See also CA 89-92; CANR 17

Doblin, Alfred.................. **TCLC 13**
See also Doeblin, Alfred

Dobrolyubov, Nikolai Alexandrovich
1836-1861................. **NCLC 5**

Dobyns, Stephen 1941-............. **CLC 37**
See also CA 45-48; CANR 2, 18

Doctorow, E(dgar) L(aurence)
1931-..... **CLC 6, 11, 15, 18, 37, 44, 65**
See also AITN 2; BEST 89:3; CA 45-48; CANR 2, 33; CDALB 1968-1988; DLB 2, 28; DLBY 80; MTCW

Dodgson, Charles Lutwidge 1832-1898
See Carroll, Lewis
See also CLR 2; MAICYA; YABC 2

Doeblin, Alfred 1878-1957........ **TCLC 13**
See also Doblin, Alfred
See also CA 110; DLB 66

Doerr, Harriet 1910-.............. **CLC 34**
See also CA 117; 122

Domecq, H(onorio) Bustos
See Bioy Casares, Adolfo; Borges, Jorge Luis

Domini, Rey
See Lorde, Audre (Geraldine)

Dominique
See Proust, (Valentin-Louis-George-Eugene-)Marcel

Don, A
See Stephen, Leslie

Donaldson, Stephen R. 1947-....... **CLC 46**
See also CA 89-92; CANR 13

Donleavy, J(ames) P(atrick)
1926-.............. **CLC 1, 4, 6, 10, 45**
See also AITN 2; CA 9-12R; CANR 24; DLB 6; MTCW

Donne, John 1572-1631....... **LC 10; PC 1**
See also CDBLB Before 1660; DLB 121; WLC

Donnell, David 1939(?)-............ **CLC 34**

Donoso (Yanez), Jose
1924-................ **CLC 4, 8, 11, 32**
See also CA 81-84; CANR 32; DLB 113; HW; MTCW

Donovan, John 1928-1992......... **CLC 35**
See also CA 97-100; 137; CLR 3; MAICYA; SATA 29

Don Roberto
See Cunninghame Graham, R(obert) B(ontine)

Doolittle, Hilda
1886-1961... **CLC 3, 8, 14, 31, 34; PC 5**
See also H. D.
See also CA 97-100; CANR 35; DLB 4, 45; MTCW; WLC

Dorfman, Ariel 1942-............. **CLC 48**
See also CA 124; 130; HW

Dorn, Edward (Merton) 1929-... **CLC 10, 18**
See also CA 93-96; DLB 5

Dorsan, Luc
See Simenon, Georges (Jacques Christian)

Dorsange, Jean
See Simenon, Georges (Jacques Christian)

Dos Passos, John (Roderigo)
1896-1970... **CLC 1, 4, 8, 11, 15, 25, 34**
See also CA 1-4R; 29-32R; CANR 3; CDALB 1929-1941; DLB 4, 9; DLBD 1; MTCW; WLC

Dossage, Jean
See Simenon, Georges (Jacques Christian)

Dostoevsky, Fedor Mikhailovich
1821-1881.... **NCLC 2, 7, 21, 33; SSC 2**
See also WLC

Doughty, Charles M(ontagu)
1843-1926.................. **TCLC 27**
See also CA 115; DLB 19, 57

Douglas, Gavin 1475(?)-1522........ **LC 20**

Douglas, Keith 1920-1944........ **TCLC 40**
See also DLB 27

Douglas, Leonard
See Bradbury, Ray (Douglas)

Douglas, Michael
See Crichton, (John) Michael

Douglass, Frederick 1817(?)-1895.. **NCLC 7**
See also BLC 1; CDALB 1640-1865; DLB 1, 43, 50, 79; SATA 29; WLC

Dourado, (Waldomiro Freitas) Autran
1926-.................... **CLC 23, 60**
See also CA 25-28R; CANR 34

Dourado, Waldomiro Autran
See Dourado, (Waldomiro Freitas) Autran

Dove, Rita (Frances) 1952-........ **CLC 50**
See also BW; CA 109; CANR 27; DLB 120

Dowell, Coleman 1925-1985........ **CLC 60**
See also CA 25-28R; 117; CANR 10

Dowson, Ernest Christopher
1867-1900.................. **TCLC 4**
See also CA 105; DLB 19

Doyle, A. Conan
See Doyle, Arthur Conan

Doyle, Arthur Conan 1859-1930.... **TCLC 7**
See also CA 104; 122; CDBLB 1890-1914; DLB 18, 70; MTCW; SATA 24; WLC

Doyle, Conan
See Doyle, Arthur Conan

Doyle, John
See Graves, Robert (von Ranke)

Doyle, Sir A. Conan
See Doyle, Arthur Conan

Doyle, Sir Arthur Conan
See Doyle, Arthur Conan

Dr. A
See Asimov, Isaac; Silverstein, Alvin

Drabble, Margaret
1939-........ **CLC 2, 3, 5, 8, 10, 22, 53**
See also CA 13-16R; CANR 18, 35; CDBLB 1960 to Present; DLB 14; MTCW; SATA 48

Drapier, M. B.
See Swift, Jonathan

Drayham, James
See Mencken, H(enry) L(ouis)

Drayton, Michael 1563-1631......... **LC 8**

Dreadstone, Carl
See Campbell, (John) Ramsey

Dreiser, Theodore (Herman Albert)
1871-1945............ **TCLC 10, 18, 35**
See also CA 106; 132; CDALB 1865-1917; DLB 9, 102; DLBD 1; MTCW; WLC

Drexler, Rosalyn 1926- .... **CLC 2, 6**
See also CA 81-84

Dreyer, Carl Theodor 1889-1968.... **CLC 16**
See also CA 116

Drieu la Rochelle, Pierre(-Eugene)
1893-1945.................. **TCLC 21**
See also CA 117; DLB 72

Drop Shot
See Cable, George Washington

Droste-Hulshoff, Annette Freiin von
1797-1848.................. **NCLC 3**

Drummond, Walter
See Silverberg, Robert

Drummond, William Henry
1854-1907.................. **TCLC 25**
See also DLB 92

Drummond de Andrade, Carlos
1902-1987.................. **CLC 18**
See also Andrade, Carlos Drummond de
See also CA 132; 123

Drury, Allen (Stuart) 1918-........ **CLC 37**
See also CA 57-60; CANR 18

Dryden, John 1631-1700.... **LC 3, 21; DC 3**
See also CDBLB 1660-1789; DLB 80, 101; WLC

Duberman, Martin 1930-............ **CLC 8**
See also CA 1-4R; CANR 2

Dubie, Norman (Evans) 1945-...... **CLC 36**
See also CA 69-72; CANR 12; DLB 120

Du Bois, W(illiam) E(dward) B(urghardt)
1868-1963 .... **CLC 1, 2, 13, 64**
See also BLC 1; BW; CA 85-88; CANR 34;
CDALB 1865-1917; DLB 47, 50, 91;
MTCW; SATA 42; WLC

Dubus, Andre 1936- .... **CLC 13, 36**
See also CA 21-24R; CANR 17

Duca Minimo
See D'Annunzio, Gabriele

Ducharme, Rejean 1941- .... **CLC 74**
See also DLB 60

Duclos, Charles Pinot 1704-1772 ..... **LC 1**

Dudek, Louis 1918- .... **CLC 11, 19**
See also CA 45-48; CAAS 14; CANR 1;
DLB 88

Duerrenmatt, Friedrich
1921-1990 ...... **CLC 1, 4, 8, 11, 15, 43**
See also Durrenmatt, Friedrich
See also CA 17-20R; CANR 33; DLB 69;
MTCW

Duffy, Bruce (?)- .... **CLC 50**

Duffy, Maureen 1933- .... **CLC 37**
See also CA 25-28R; CANR 33; DLB 14;
MTCW

Dugan, Alan 1923- .... **CLC 2, 6**
See also CA 81-84; DLB 5

du Gard, Roger Martin
See Martin du Gard, Roger

Duhamel, Georges 1884-1966 .... **CLC 8**
See also CA 81-84; 25-28R; CANR 35;
DLB 65; MTCW

Dujardin, Edouard (Emile Louis)
1861-1949 .... **TCLC 13**
See also CA 109

Dumas, Alexandre (Davy de la Pailleterie)
1802-1870 .... **NCLC 11**
See also DLB 119; SATA 18; WLC

Dumas, Alexandre
1824-1895 .... **NCLC 9; DC 1**

Dumas, Claudine
See Malzberg, Barry N(athaniel)

Dumas, Henry L. 1934-1968 ..... **CLC 6, 62**
See also BW; CA 85-88; DLB 41

du Maurier, Daphne
1907-1989 .... **CLC 6, 11, 59**
See also CA 5-8R; 128; CANR 6; MTCW;
SATA 27, 60

Dunbar, Paul Laurence
1872-1906 .... **TCLC 2, 12; PC 5; SSC 8**
See also BLC 1; BW; CA 104; 124;
CDALB 1865-1917; DLB 50, 54, 78;
SATA 34; WLC

Dunbar, William 1460(?)-1530(?) .... **LC 20**

Duncan, Lois 1934- .... **CLC 26**
See also AAYA 4; CA 1-4R; CANR 2, 23,
36; MAICYA; SAAS 2; SATA 1, 36

Duncan, Robert (Edward)
1919-1988 ... **CLC 1, 2, 4, 7, 15, 41, 55;**
PC 2
See also CA 9-12R; 124; CANR 28; DLB 5,
16; MTCW

Dunlap, William 1766-1839 .... **NCLC 2**
See also DLB 30, 37, 59

Dunn, Douglas (Eaglesham)
1942- .... **CLC 6, 40**
See also CA 45-48; CANR 2, 33; DLB 40;
MTCW

Dunn, Katherine (Karen) 1945- ..... **CLC 71**
See also CA 33-36R

Dunn, Stephen 1939- .... **CLC 36**
See also CA 33-36R; CANR 12; DLB 105

Dunne, Finley Peter 1867-1936 .... **TCLC 28**
See also CA 108; DLB 11, 23

Dunne, John Gregory 1932- .... **CLC 28**
See also CA 25-28R; CANR 14; DLBY 80

Dunsany, Edward John Moreton Drax
Plunkett 1878-1957
See Dunsany, Lord; Lord Dunsany
See also CA 104; DLB 10

Dunsany, Lord .... **TCLC 2**
See also Dunsany, Edward John Moreton
Drax Plunkett
See also DLB 77

du Perry, Jean
See Simenon, Georges (Jacques Christian)

Durang, Christopher (Ferdinand)
1949- .... **CLC 27, 38**
See also CA 105

Duras, Marguerite
1914- ...... **CLC 3, 6, 11, 20, 34, 40, 68**
See also CA 25-28R; DLB 83; MTCW

Durban, (Rosa) Pam 1947- .... **CLC 39**
See also CA 123

Durcan, Paul 1944- .... **CLC 43, 70**
See also CA 134

Durrell, Lawrence (George)
1912-1990 .... **CLC 1, 4, 6, 8, 13, 27, 41**
See also CA 9-12R; 132;
CDBLB 1945-1960; DLB 15, 27;
DLBY 90; MTCW

Durrenmatt, Friedrich
.... **CLC 1, 4, 8, 11, 15, 43**
See also Duerrenmatt, Friedrich
See also DLB 69

Dutt, Toru 1856-1877 .... **NCLC 29**

Dwight, Timothy 1752-1817 ...... **NCLC 13**
See also DLB 37

Dworkin, Andrea 1946- .... **CLC 43**
See also CA 77-80; CANR 16, 39; MTCW

Dylan, Bob 1941- .... **CLC 3, 4, 6, 12**
See also CA 41-44R; DLB 16

Eagleton, Terence (Francis) 1943-
See Eagleton, Terry
See also CA 57-60; CANR 7, 23; MTCW

Eagleton, Terry .... **CLC 63**
See also Eagleton, Terence (Francis)

East, Michael
See West, Morris L(anglo)

Eastaway, Edward
See Thomas, (Philip) Edward

Eastlake, William (Derry) 1917- ..... **CLC 8**
See also CA 5-8R; CAAS 1; CANR 5;
DLB 6

Eberhart, Richard (Ghormley)
1904- .... **CLC 3, 11, 19, 56**
See also CA 1-4R; CANR 2;
CDALB 1941-1968; DLB 48; MTCW

Eberstadt, Fernanda 1960- .... **CLC 39**
See also CA 136

Echegaray (y Eizaguirre), Jose (Maria Waldo)
1832-1916 .... **TCLC 4**
See also CA 104; CANR 32; HW; MTCW

Echeverria, (Jose) Esteban (Antonino)
1805-1851 .... **NCLC 18**

Echo
See Proust,
(Valentin-Louis-George-Eugene-)Marcel

Eckert, Allan W. 1931- .... **CLC 17**
See also CA 13-16R; CANR 14; SATA 27,
29

Eckhart, Meister 1260(?)-1328(?) .. **CMLC 9**
See also DLB 115

Eckmar, F. R.
See de Hartog, Jan

Eco, Umberto 1932- .... **CLC 28, 60**
See also BEST 90:1; CA 77-80; CANR 12,
33; MTCW

Eddison, E(ric) R(ucker)
1882-1945 .... **TCLC 15**
See also CA 109

Edel, (Joseph) Leon 1907- ...... **CLC 29, 34**
See also CA 1-4R; CANR 1, 22; DLB 103

Eden, Emily 1797-1869 .... **NCLC 10**

Edgar, David 1948- .... **CLC 42**
See also CA 57-60; CANR 12; DLB 13;
MTCW

Edgerton, Clyde (Carlyle) 1944- .... **CLC 39**
See also CA 118; 134

Edgeworth, Maria 1767-1849 ...... **NCLC 1**
See also DLB 116; SATA 21

Edmonds, Paul
See Kuttner, Henry

Edmonds, Walter D(umaux) 1903- .. **CLC 35**
See also CA 5-8R; CANR 2; DLB 9;
MAICYA; SAAS 4; SATA 1, 27

Edmondson, Wallace
See Ellison, Harlan

Edson, Russell .... **CLC 13**
See also CA 33-36R

Edwards, G(erald) B(asil)
1899-1976 .... **CLC 25**
See also CA 110

Edwards, Gus 1939- .... **CLC 43**
See also CA 108

Edwards, Jonathan 1703-1758 .... **LC 7**
See also DLB 24

Efron, Marina Ivanovna Tsvetaeva
See Tsvetaeva (Efron), Marina (Ivanovna)

Ehle, John (Marsden Jr.) 1925- .... **CLC 27**
See also CA 9-12R

Ehrenbourg, Ilya (Grigoryevich)
See Ehrenburg, Ilya (Grigoryevich)

Ehrenburg, Ilya (Grigoryevich)
1891-1967 .... **CLC 18, 34, 62**
See also CA 102; 25-28R

Ehrenburg, Ilyo (Grigoryevich)
See Ehrenburg, Ilya (Grigoryevich)

Eich, Guenter 1907-1972 .... **CLC 15**
See also CA 111; 93-96; DLB 69

Eichendorff, Joseph Freiherr von
1788-1857 .... NCLC **8**
See also DLB 90

Eigner, Larry...................... CLC **9**
See also Eigner, Laurence (Joel)
See also DLB 5

Eigner, Laurence (Joel) 1927-
See Eigner, Larry
See also CA 9-12R; CANR 6

Eiseley, Loren Corey 1907-1977 ..... CLC **7**
See also AAYA 5; CA 1-4R; 73-76;
CANR 6

Eisenstadt, Jill 1963- .... CLC **50**

Eisner, Simon
See Kornbluth, C(yril) M.

Ekeloef, (Bengt) Gunnar
1907-1968 .... CLC **27**
See also Ekelof, (Bengt) Gunnar
See also CA 123; 25-28R

Ekelof, (Bengt) Gunnar............. CLC **27**
See also Ekeloef, (Bengt) Gunnar

Ekwensi, C. O. D.
See Ekwensi, Cyprian (Odiatu Duaka)

Ekwensi, Cyprian (Odiatu Duaka)
1921- .... CLC **4**
See also BLC 1; BW; CA 29-32R;
CANR 18; DLB 117; MTCW; SATA 66

Elaine....................... TCLC **18**
See also Leverson, Ada

El Crummo
See Crumb, R(obert)

Elia
See Lamb, Charles

Eliade, Mircea 1907-1986 .... CLC **19**
See also CA 65-68; 119; CANR 30; MTCW

Eliot, A. D.
See Jewett, (Theodora) Sarah Orne

Eliot, Alice
See Jewett, (Theodora) Sarah Orne

Eliot, Dan
See Silverberg, Robert

Eliot, George 1819-1880.... NCLC **4, 13, 23**
See also CDBLB 1832-1890; DLB 21, 35,
55; WLC

Eliot, John 1604-1690 .... LC **5**
See also DLB 24

Eliot, T(homas) S(tearns)
1888-1965 .... CLC **1, 2, 3, 6, 9, 10, 13,
15, 24, 34, 41, 55, 57; PC 5**
See also CA 5-8R; 25-28R;
CDALB 1929-1941; DLB 7, 10, 45, 63;
DLBY 88; MTCW; WLC 2

Elizabeth 1866-1941............ TCLC **41**

Elkin, Stanley L(awrence)
1930- .... CLC **4, 6, 9, 14, 27, 51**
See also CA 9-12R; CANR 8; DLB 2, 28;
DLBY 80; MTCW

Elledge, Scott..................... CLC **34**

Elliott, Don
See Silverberg, Robert

Elliott, George P(aul) 1918-1980..... CLC **2**
See also CA 1-4R; 97-100; CANR 2

Elliott, Janice 1931-............. CLC **47**
See also CA 13-16R; CANR 8, 29; DLB 14

Elliott, Sumner Locke 1917-1991 ... CLC **38**
See also CA 5-8R; 134; CANR 2, 21

Elliott, William
See Bradbury, Ray (Douglas)

Ellis, A. E........................ CLC **7**

Ellis, Alice Thomas................. CLC **40**
See also Haycraft, Anna

Ellis, Bret Easton 1964-........ CLC **39, 71**
See also AAYA 2; CA 118; 123

Ellis, (Henry) Havelock
1859-1939 .... TCLC **14**
See also CA 109

Ellis, Landon
See Ellison, Harlan

Ellis, Trey 1962-.................. CLC **55**

Ellison, Harlan 1934-........ CLC **1, 13, 42**
See also CA 5-8R; CANR 5; DLB 8;
MTCW

Ellison, Ralph (Waldo)
1914- .... CLC **1, 3, 11, 54**
See also BLC 1; BW; CA 9-12R; CANR 24;
CDALB 1941-1968; DLB 2, 76; MTCW;
WLC

Ellmann, Lucy (Elizabeth) 1956-.... CLC **61**
See also CA 128

Ellmann, Richard (David)
1918-1987 .... CLC **50**
See also BEST 89:2; CA 1-4R; 122;
CANR 2, 28; DLB 103; DLBY 87;
MTCW

Elman, Richard 1934-............. CLC **19**
See also CA 17-20R; CAAS 3

Elron
See Hubbard, L(afayette) Ron(ald)

Eluard, Paul.................. TCLC **7, 41**
See also Grindel, Eugene

Elyot, Sir Thomas 1490(?)-1546 ..... LC **11**

Elytis, Odysseus 1911-......... CLC **15, 49**
See also CA 102; MTCW

Emecheta, (Florence Onye) Buchi
1944- .... CLC **14, 48**
See also BLC 2; BW; CA 81-84; CANR 27;
DLB 117; MTCW; SATA 66

Emerson, Ralph Waldo
1803-1882 .... NCLC **1, 38**
See also CDALB 1640-1865; DLB 1, 59, 73;
WLC

Eminescu, Mihail 1850-1889 ..... NCLC **33**

Empson, William
1906-1984 .... CLC **3, 8, 19, 33, 34**
See also CA 17-20R; 112; CANR 31;
DLB 20; MTCW

Enchi Fumiko (Ueda) 1905-1986.... CLC **31**
See also CA 129; 121

Ende, Michael (Andreas Helmuth)
1929- .... CLC **31**
See also CA 118; 124; CANR 36; CLR 14;
DLB 75; MAICYA; SATA 42, 61

Endo, Shusaku 1923- ..... CLC **7, 14, 19, 54**
See also CA 29-32R; CANR 21; MTCW

Engel, Marian 1933-1985.......... CLC **36**
See also CA 25-28R; CANR 12; DLB 53

Engelhardt, Frederick
See Hubbard, L(afayette) Ron(ald)

Enright, D(ennis) J(oseph)
1920- .... CLC **4, 8, 31**
See also CA 1-4R; CANR 1; DLB 27;
SATA 25

Enzensberger, Hans Magnus
1929- .... CLC **43**
See also CA 116; 119

Ephron, Nora 1941- .... CLC **17, 31**
See also AITN 2; CA 65-68; CANR 12, 39

Epsilon
See Betjeman, John

Epstein, Daniel Mark 1948- .... CLC **7**
See also CA 49-52; CANR 2

Epstein, Jacob 1956- .... CLC **19**
See also CA 114

Epstein, Joseph 1937-............. CLC **39**
See also CA 112; 119

Epstein, Leslie 1938- .... CLC **27**
See also CA 73-76; CAAS 12; CANR 23

Equiano, Olaudah 1745(?)-1797...... LC **16**
See also BLC 2; DLB 37, 50

Erasmus, Desiderius 1469(?)-1536.... LC **16**

Erdman, Paul E(mil) 1932- .... CLC **25**
See also AITN 1; CA 61-64; CANR 13

Erdrich, Louise 1954-.......... CLC **39, 54**
See also BEST 89:1; CA 114; MTCW

Erenburg, Ilya (Grigoryevich)
See Ehrenburg, Ilya (Grigoryevich)

Erickson, Stephen Michael 1950-
See Erickson, Steve
See also CA 129

Erickson, Steve.................... CLC **64**
See also Erickson, Stephen Michael

Ericson, Walter
See Fast, Howard (Melvin)

Eriksson, Buntel
See Bergman, (Ernst) Ingmar

Eschenbach, Wolfram von
See Wolfram von Eschenbach

Eseki, Bruno
See Mphahlele, Ezekiel

Esenin, Sergei (Alexandrovich)
1895-1925 .... TCLC **4**
See also CA 104

Eshleman, Clayton 1935-........... CLC **7**
See also CA 33-36R; CAAS 6; DLB 5

Espriella, Don Manuel Alvarez
See Southey, Robert

Espriu, Salvador 1913-1985......... CLC **9**
See also CA 115

Esse, James
See Stephens, James

Esterbrook, Tom
See Hubbard, L(afayette) Ron(ald)

Estleman, Loren D. 1952- .... CLC **48**
See also CA 85-88; CANR 27; MTCW

Evans, Mary Ann
See Eliot, George

Evarts, Esther
See Benson, Sally

Everett, Percival
See Everett, Percival L.

Everett, Percival L. 1956- .... **CLC 57**
See also CA 129

Everson, R(onald) G(ilmour)
1903- .... **CLC 27**
See also CA 17-20R; DLB 88

Everson, William (Oliver)
1912- .... **CLC 1, 5, 14**
See also CA 9-12R; CANR 20; DLB 5, 16; MTCW

Evtushenko, Evgenii Aleksandrovich
See Yevtushenko, Yevgeny (Alexandrovich)

Ewart, Gavin (Buchanan)
1916- .... **CLC 13, 46**
See also CA 89-92; CANR 17; DLB 40; MTCW

Ewers, Hanns Heinz 1871-1943 ... **TCLC 12**
See also CA 109

Ewing, Frederick R.
See Sturgeon, Theodore (Hamilton)

Exley, Frederick (Earl) 1929- .... **CLC 6, 11**
See also AITN 2; CA 81-84; 138; DLBY 81

Eynhardt, Guillermo
See Quiroga, Horacio (Sylvestre)

Ezekiel, Nissim 1924- .... **CLC 61**
See also CA 61-64

Ezekiel, Tish O'Dowd 1943- .... **CLC 34**
See also CA 129

Fagen, Donald 1948- .... **CLC 26**

Fainzilberg, Ilya Arnoldovich 1897-1937
See Ilf, Ilya
See also CA 120

Fair, Ronald L. 1932- .... **CLC 18**
See also BW; CA 69-72; CANR 25; DLB 33

Fairbairns, Zoe (Ann) 1948- .... **CLC 32**
See also CA 103; CANR 21

Falco, Gian
See Papini, Giovanni

Falconer, James
See Kirkup, James

Falconer, Kenneth
See Kornbluth, C(yril) M.

Falkland, Samuel
See Heijermans, Herman

Fallaci, Oriana 1930- .... **CLC 11**
See also CA 77-80; CANR 15; MTCW

Faludy, George 1913- .... **CLC 42**
See also CA 21-24R

Faludy, Gyoergy
See Faludy, George

Fanon, Frantz 1925-1961 .... **CLC 74**
See also BLC 2; BW; CA 116; 89-92

Fanshawe, Ann .... **LC 11**

Fante, John (Thomas) 1911-1983 ... **CLC 60**
See also CA 69-72; 109; CANR 23; DLBY 83

Farah, Nuruddin 1945- .... **CLC 53**
See also BLC 2; CA 106

Fargue, Leon-Paul 1876(?)-1947 ... **TCLC 11**
See also CA 109

Farigoule, Louis
See Romains, Jules

Farina, Richard 1936(?)-1966 .... **CLC 9**
See also CA 81-84; 25-28R

Farley, Walter (Lorimer)
1915-1989 .... **CLC 17**
See also CA 17-20R; CANR 8, 29; DLB 22; MAICYA; SATA 2, 43

Farmer, Philip Jose 1918- .... **CLC 1, 19**
See also CA 1-4R; CANR 4, 35; DLB 8; MTCW

Farquhar, George 1677-1707 .... **LC 21**
See also DLB 84

Farrell, J(ames) G(ordon)
1935-1979 .... **CLC 6**
See also CA 73-76; 89-92; CANR 36; DLB 14; MTCW

Farrell, James T(homas)
1904-1979 .... **CLC 1, 4, 8, 11, 66**
See also CA 5-8R; 89-92; CANR 9; DLB 4, 9, 86; DLBD 2; MTCW

Farren, Richard J.
See Betjeman, John

Farren, Richard M.
See Betjeman, John

Fassbinder, Rainer Werner
1946-1982 .... **CLC 20**
See also CA 93-96; 106; CANR 31

Fast, Howard (Melvin) 1914- ...... **CLC 23**
See also CA 1-4R; CANR 1, 33; DLB 9; SATA 7

Faulcon, Robert
See Holdstock, Robert P.

Faulkner, William (Cuthbert)
1897-1962 .... **CLC 1, 3, 6, 8, 9, 11, 14, 18, 28, 52, 68; SSC 1**
See also AAYA 7; CA 81-84; CANR 33; CDALB 1929-1941; DLB 9, 11, 44, 102; DLBD 2; DLBY 86; MTCW; WLC

Fauset, Jessie Redmon
1884(?)-1961 .... **CLC 19, 54**
See also BLC 2; BW; CA 109; DLB 51

Faust, Irvin 1924- .... **CLC 8**
See also CA 33-36R; CANR 28; DLB 2, 28; DLBY 80

Fawkes, Guy
See Benchley, Robert (Charles)

Fearing, Kenneth (Flexner)
1902-1961 .... **CLC 51**
See also CA 93-96; DLB 9

Fecamps, Elise
See Creasey, John

Federman, Raymond 1928- .... **CLC 6, 47**
See also CA 17-20R; CAAS 8; CANR 10; DLBY 80

Federspiel, J(uerg) F. 1931- .... **CLC 42**

Feiffer, Jules (Ralph) 1929- .... **CLC 2, 8, 64**
See also AAYA 3; CA 17-20R; CANR 30; DLB 7, 44; MTCW; SATA 8, 61

Feige, Hermann Albert Otto Maximilian
See Traven, B.

Fei-Kan, Li
See Li Fei-kan

Feinberg, David B. 1956- .... **CLC 59**
See also CA 135

Feinstein, Elaine 1930- .... **CLC 36**
See also CA 69-72; CAAS 1; CANR 31; DLB 14, 40; MTCW

Feldman, Irving (Mordecai) 1928- .... **CLC 7**
See also CA 1-4R; CANR 1

Fellini, Federico 1920- .... **CLC 16**
See also CA 65-68; CANR 33

Felsen, Henry Gregor 1916- .... **CLC 17**
See also CA 1-4R; CANR 1; SAAS 2; SATA 1

Fenton, James Martin 1949- .... **CLC 32**
See also CA 102; DLB 40

Ferber, Edna 1887-1968 .... **CLC 18**
See also AITN 1; CA 5-8R; 25-28R; DLB 9, 28, 86; MTCW; SATA 7

Ferguson, Helen
See Kavan, Anna

Ferguson, Samuel 1810-1886 ..... **NCLC 33**
See also DLB 32

Ferling, Lawrence
See Ferlinghetti, Lawrence (Monsanto)

Ferlinghetti, Lawrence (Monsanto)
1919(?)- .... **CLC 2, 6, 10, 27; PC 1**
See also CA 5-8R; CANR 3; CDALB 1941-1968; DLB 5, 16; MTCW

Fernandez, Vicente Garcia Huidobro
See Huidobro Fernandez, Vicente Garcia

Ferrer, Gabriel (Francisco Victor) Miro
See Miro (Ferrer), Gabriel (Francisco Victor)

Ferrier, Susan (Edmonstone)
1782-1854 .... **NCLC 8**
See also DLB 116

Ferrigno, Robert .... **CLC 65**

Feuchtwanger, Lion 1884-1958 ..... **TCLC 3**
See also CA 104; DLB 66

Feydeau, Georges (Leon Jules Marie)
1862-1921 .... **TCLC 22**
See also CA 113

Ficino, Marsilio 1433-1499 .... **LC 12**

Fiedler, Leslie A(aron)
1917- .... **CLC 4, 13, 24**
See also CA 9-12R; CANR 7; DLB 28, 67; MTCW

Field, Andrew 1938- .... **CLC 44**
See also CA 97-100; CANR 25

Field, Eugene 1850-1895 .... **NCLC 3**
See also DLB 23, 42; MAICYA; SATA 16

Field, Gans T.
See Wellman, Manly Wade

Field, Michael .... **TCLC 43**

Field, Peter
See Hobson, Laura Z(ametkin)

Fielding, Henry 1707-1754 .... **LC 1**
See also CDBLB 1660-1789; DLB 39, 84, 101; WLC

Fielding, Sarah 1710-1768 .... **LC 1**
See also DLB 39

Fierstein, Harvey (Forbes) 1954- ... **CLC 33**
See also CA 123; 129

Figes, Eva 1932- .... **CLC 31**
See also CA 53-56; CANR 4; DLB 14

Finch, Robert (Duer Claydon)
1900- .... **CLC 18**
See also CA 57-60; CANR 9, 24; DLB 88

Findley, Timothy 1930- .... **CLC 27**
See also CA 25-28R; CANR 12; DLB 53

Fink, William
See Mencken, H(enry) L(ouis)

Firbank, Louis 1942-
See Reed, Lou
See also CA 117

Firbank, (Arthur Annesley) Ronald
1886-1926 .... **TCLC 1**
See also CA 104; DLB 36

Fisher, Roy 1930-................ **CLC 25**
See also CA 81-84; CAAS 10; CANR 16; DLB 40

Fisher, Rudolph 1897-1934 .... **TCLC 11**
See also BLC 2; BW; CA 107; 124; DLB 51, 102

Fisher, Vardis (Alvero) 1895-1968.... **CLC 7**
See also CA 5-8R; 25-28R; DLB 9

Fiske, Tarleton
See Bloch, Robert (Albert)

Fitch, Clarke
See Sinclair, Upton (Beall)

Fitch, John IV
See Cormier, Robert (Edmund)

Fitgerald, Penelope 1916- .... **CLC 61**

Fitzgerald, Captain Hugh
See Baum, L(yman) Frank

FitzGerald, Edward 1809-1883 .... **NCLC 9**
See also DLB 32

Fitzgerald, F(rancis) Scott (Key)
1896-1940 .... **TCLC 1, 6, 14, 28; SSC 6**
See also AITN 1; CA 110; 123; CDALB 1917-1929; DLB 4, 9, 86; DLBD 1; DLBY 81; MTCW; WLC

Fitzgerald, Penelope 1916-...... **CLC 19, 51**
See also CA 85-88; CAAS 10; DLB 14

FitzGerald, Robert D(avid)
1902-1987 .... **CLC 19**
See also CA 17-20R

Fitzgerald, Robert (Stuart)
1910-1985 .... **CLC 39**
See also CA 1-4R; 114; CANR 1; DLBY 80

Flanagan, Thomas (James Bonner)
1923- .... **CLC 25, 52**
See also CA 108; DLBY 80; MTCW

Flaubert, Gustave
1821-1880 ..... **NCLC 2, 10, 19; SSC 11**
See also DLB 119; WLC

Flecker, (Herman) James Elroy
1884-1915 .... **TCLC 43**
See also CA 109; DLB 10, 19

Fleming, Ian (Lancaster)
1908-1964 .... **CLC 3, 30**
See also CA 5-8R; CDBLB 1945-1960; DLB 87; MTCW; SATA 9

Fleming, Thomas (James) 1927- .... **CLC 37**
See also CA 5-8R; CANR 10; SATA 8

Fletcher, John Gould 1886-1950... **TCLC 35**
See also CA 107; DLB 4, 45

Fleur, Paul
See Pohl, Frederik

Flying Officer X
See Bates, H(erbert) E(rnest)

Fo, Dario 1926-................. **CLC 32**
See also CA 116; 128; MTCW

Fogarty, Jonathan Titulescu Esq.
See Farrell, James T(homas)

Folke, Will
See Bloch, Robert (Albert)

Follett, Ken(neth Martin) 1949- .... **CLC 18**
See also AAYA 6; BEST 89:4; CA 81-84; CANR 13, 33; DLB 87; DLBY 81; MTCW

Fontane, Theodor 1819-1898..... **NCLC 26**

Foote, Horton 1916-.............. **CLC 51**
See also CA 73-76; CANR 34; DLB 26

Forbes, Esther 1891-1967.......... **CLC 12**
See also CA 13-14; 25-28R; CAP 1; CLR 27; DLB 22; MAICYA; SATA 2

Forche, Carolyn (Louise) 1950-..... **CLC 25**
See also CA 109; 117; DLB 5

Ford, Elbur
See Hibbert, Eleanor Burford

Ford, Ford Madox
1873-1939 .... **TCLC 1, 15, 39**
See also CA 104; 132; CDBLB 1914-1945; DLB 34, 98; MTCW

Ford, John 1895-1973............. **CLC 16**
See also CA 45-48

Ford, Richard 1944-.............. **CLC 46**
See also CA 69-72; CANR 11

Ford, Webster
See Masters, Edgar Lee

Foreman, Richard 1937-.......... **CLC 50**
See also CA 65-68; CANR 32

Forester, C(ecil) S(cott)
1899-1966 .... **CLC 35**
See also CA 73-76; 25-28R; SATA 13

Forez
See Mauriac, Francois (Charles)

Forman, James Douglas 1932-...... **CLC 21**
See also CA 9-12R; CANR 4, 19; MAICYA; SATA 8, 70

Fornes, Maria Irene 1930-...... **CLC 39, 61**
See also CA 25-28R; CANR 28; DLB 7; HW; MTCW

Forrest, Leon 1937- .... **CLC 4**
See also BW; CA 89-92; CAAS 7; CANR 25; DLB 33

Forster, E(dward) M(organ)
1879-1970 .... **CLC 1, 2, 3, 4, 9, 10, 13, 15, 22, 45**
See also AAYA 2; CA 13-14; 25-28R; CAP 1; CDBLB 1914-1945; DLB 34, 98; MTCW; SATA 57; WLC

Forster, John 1812-1876 .... **NCLC 11**

Forsyth, Frederick 1938-...... **CLC 2, 5, 36**
See also BEST 89:4; CA 85-88; CANR 38; DLB 87; MTCW

Forten, Charlotte L.............. **TCLC 16**
See also Grimke, Charlotte L(ottie) Forten
See also BLC 2; DLB 50

Foscolo, Ugo 1778-1827.......... **NCLC 8**

Fosse, Bob..................... **CLC 20**
See also Fosse, Robert Louis

Fosse, Robert Louis 1927-1987
See Fosse, Bob
See also CA 110; 123

Foster, Stephen Collins
1826-1864 .... **NCLC 26**

Foucault, Michel
1926-1984 .... **CLC 31, 34, 69**
See also CA 105; 113; CANR 34; MTCW

Fouque, Friedrich Heinrich Karl) de la Motte
1777-1843 .... **NCLC 2**
See also DLB 90

Fournier, Henri Alban 1886-1914
See Alain-Fournier
See also CA 104

Fournier, Pierre 1916-............ **CLC 11**
See also Gascar, Pierre
See also CA 89-92; CANR 16

Fowles, John
1926- .... **CLC 1, 2, 3, 4, 6, 9, 10, 15, 33**
See also CA 5-8R; CANR 25; CDBLB 1960 to Present; DLB 14; MTCW; SATA 22

Fox, Paula 1923-................ **CLC 2, 8**
See also AAYA 3; CA 73-76; CANR 20, 36; CLR 1; DLB 52; MAICYA; MTCW; SATA 17, 60

Fox, William Price (Jr.) 1926- ..... **CLC 22**
See also CA 17-20R; CANR 11; DLB 2; DLBY 81

Foxe, John 1516(?)-1587 .... **LC 14**

Frame, Janet .... **CLC 2, 3, 6, 22, 66**
See also Clutha, Janet Paterson Frame

France, Anatole................. **TCLC 9**
See also Thibault, Jacques Anatole Francois

Francis, Claude 19(?)- .... **CLC 50**

Francis, Dick 1920- .... **CLC 2, 22, 42**
See also AAYA 5; BEST 89:3; CA 5-8R; CANR 9; CDBLB 1960 to Present; DLB 87; MTCW

Francis, Robert (Churchill)
1901-1987 .... **CLC 15**
See also CA 1-4R; 123; CANR 1

Frank, Anne(lies Marie)
1929-1945 .... **TCLC 17**
See also CA 113; 133; MTCW; SATA 42; WLC

Frank, Elizabeth 1945-............ **CLC 39**
See also CA 121; 126

Franklin, Benjamin
See Hasek, Jaroslav (Matej Frantisek)

Franklin, (Stella Maraia Sarah) Miles
1879-1954 .... **TCLC 7**
See also CA 104

Fraser, Antonia (Pakenham)
1932-..................... **CLC 32**
See also CA 85-88; MTCW; SATA 32

Fraser, George MacDonald 1925-.... **CLC 7**
See also CA 45-48; CANR 2

Fraser, Sylvia 1935-.............. **CLC 64**
See also CA 45-48; CANR 1, 16

Frayn, Michael 1933-...... **CLC 3, 7, 31, 47**
See also CA 5-8R; CANR 30; DLB 13, 14; MTCW

Fraze, Candida (Merrill) 1945-...... **CLC 50**
See also CA 126

Frazer, J(ames) G(eorge)
1854-1941 .... **TCLC 32**
See also CA 118

Frazer, Robert Caine
See Creasey, John

Frazer, Sir James George
See Frazer, J(ames) G(eorge)

Frazier, Ian 1951- .... **CLC 46**
See also CA 130

Frederic, Harold 1856-1898 ...... **NCLC 10**
See also DLB 12, 23

Frederick the Great 1712-1786 ...... **LC 14**

Fredro, Aleksander 1793-1876 ..... **NCLC 8**

Freeling, Nicolas 1927- .... **CLC 38**
See also CA 49-52; CAAS 12; CANR 1, 17; DLB 87

Freeman, Douglas Southall
1886-1953 .... **TCLC 11**
See also CA 109; DLB 17

Freeman, Judith 1946- .... **CLC 55**

Freeman, Mary Eleanor Wilkins
1852-1930 .... **TCLC 9; SSC 1**
See also CA 106; DLB 12, 78

Freeman, R(ichard) Austin
1862-1943 .... **TCLC 21**
See also CA 113; DLB 70

French, Marilyn 1929- ...... **CLC 10, 18, 60**
See also CA 69-72; CANR 3, 31; MTCW

French, Paul
See Asimov, Isaac

Freneau, Philip Morin 1752-1832 .. **NCLC 1**
See also DLB 37, 43

Friedan, Betty (Naomi) 1921- ...... **CLC 74**
See also CA 65-68; CANR 18; MTCW

Friedman, B(ernard) H(arper)
1926- .... **CLC 7**
See also CA 1-4R; CANR 3

Friedman, Bruce Jay 1930- .... **CLC 3, 5, 56**
See also CA 9-12R; CANR 25; DLB 2, 28

Friel, Brian 1929- .... **CLC 5, 42, 59**
See also CA 21-24R; CANR 33; DLB 13; MTCW

Friis-Baastad, Babbis Ellinor
1921-1970 .... **CLC 12**
See also CA 17-20R; 134; SATA 7

Frisch, Max (Rudolf)
1911-1991 ..... **CLC 3, 9, 14, 18, 32, 44**
See also CA 85-88; 134; CANR 32; DLB 69; MTCW

Fromentin, Eugene (Samuel Auguste)
1820-1876 .... **NCLC 10**

Frost, Robert (Lee)
1874-1963 ... **CLC 1, 3, 4, 9, 10, 13, 15, 26, 34, 44; PC 1**
See also CA 89-92; CANR 33; CDALB 1917-1929; DLB 54; DLBD 7; MTCW; SATA 14; WLC

Froy, Herald
See Waterhouse, Keith (Spencer)

Fry, Christopher 1907- .... **CLC 2, 10, 14**
See also CA 17-20R; CANR 9, 30; DLB 13; MTCW; SATA 66

Frye, (Herman) Northrop
1912-1991 .... **CLC 24, 70**
See also CA 5-8R; 133; CANR 8, 37; DLB 67, 68; MTCW

Fuchs, Daniel 1909- .... **CLC 8, 22**
See also CA 81-84; CAAS 5; DLB 9, 26, 28

Fuchs, Daniel 1934- .... **CLC 34**
See also CA 37-40R; CANR 14

Fuentes, Carlos
1928- ...... **CLC 3, 8, 10, 13, 22, 41, 60**
See also AAYA 4; AITN 2; CA 69-72; CANR 10, 32; DLB 113; HW; MTCW; WLC

Fuentes, Gregorio Lopez y
See Lopez y Fuentes, Gregorio

Fugard, (Harold) Athol
1932- .... **CLC 5, 9, 14, 25, 40; DC 3**
See also CA 85-88; CANR 32; MTCW

Fugard, Sheila 1932- .... **CLC 48**
See also CA 125

Fuller, Charles (H. Jr.)
1939- .... **CLC 25; DC 1**
See also BLC 2; BW; CA 108; 112; DLB 38; MTCW

Fuller, John (Leopold) 1937- .... **CLC 62**
See also CA 21-24R; CANR 9; DLB 40

Fuller, Margaret .... **NCLC 5**
See also Ossoli, Sarah Margaret (Fuller marchesa d')

Fuller, Roy (Broadbent)
1912-1991 .... **CLC 4, 28**
See also CA 5-8R; 135; CAAS 10; DLB 15, 20

Fulton, Alice 1952- .... **CLC 52**
See also CA 116

Furphy, Joseph 1843-1912 .... **TCLC 25**

Fussell, Paul 1924- .... **CLC 74**
See also BEST 90:1; CA 17-20R; CANR 8, 21, 35; MTCW

Futabatei, Shimei 1864-1909 ...... **TCLC 44**

Futrelle, Jacques 1875-1912 ...... **TCLC 19**
See also CA 113

G. B. S.
See Shaw, George Bernard

Gaboriau, Emile 1835-1873 ...... **NCLC 14**

Gadda, Carlo Emilio 1893-1973 .... **CLC 11**
See also CA 89-92

Gaddis, William
1922- .... **CLC 1, 3, 6, 8, 10, 19, 43**
See also CA 17-20R; CANR 21; DLB 2; MTCW

Gaines, Ernest J(ames)
1933- .... **CLC 3, 11, 18**
See also AITN 1; BLC 2; BW; CA 9-12R; CANR 6, 24; CDALB 1968-1988; DLB 2, 33; DLBY 80; MTCW

Gaitskill, Mary 1954- .... **CLC 69**
See also CA 128

Galdos, Benito Perez
See Perez Galdos, Benito

Gale, Zona 1874-1938 .... **TCLC 7**
See also CA 105; DLB 9, 78

Galeano, Eduardo (Hughes) 1940- ... **CLC 72**
See also CA 29-32R; CANR 13, 32; HW

Galiano, Juan Valera y Alcala
See Valera y Alcala-Galiano, Juan

Gallagher, Tess 1943- .... **CLC 18, 63**
See also CA 106; DLB 120

Gallant, Mavis
1922- .... **CLC 7, 18, 38; SSC 5**
See also CA 69-72; CANR 29; DLB 53; MTCW

Gallant, Roy A(rthur) 1924- .... **CLC 17**
See also CA 5-8R; CANR 4, 29; MAICYA; SATA 4, 68

Gallico, Paul (William) 1897-1976 ... **CLC 2**
See also AITN 1; CA 5-8R; 69-72; CANR 23; DLB 9; MAICYA; SATA 13

Gallup, Ralph
See Whitemore, Hugh (John)

Galsworthy, John 1867-1933 .... **TCLC 1, 45**
See also CA 104; CDBLB 1890-1914; DLB 10, 34, 98; WLC 2

Galt, John 1779-1839 .... **NCLC 1**
See also DLB 99, 116

Galvin, James 1951- .... **CLC 38**
See also CA 108; CANR 26

Gamboa, Federico 1864-1939 ...... **TCLC 36**

Gann, Ernest Kellogg 1910-1991 .... **CLC 23**
See also AITN 1; CA 1-4R; 136; CANR 1

Garcia Lorca, Federico
1898-1936 ..... **TCLC 1, 7; DC 2; PC 3**
See also CA 104; 131; DLB 108; HW; MTCW; WLC

Garcia Marquez, Gabriel (Jose)
1928- ... **CLC 2, 3, 8, 10, 15, 27, 47, 55; SSC 8**
See also Marquez, Gabriel (Jose) Garcia
See also AAYA 3; BEST 89:1, 90:4; CA 33-36R; CANR 10, 28; DLB 113; HW; MTCW; WLC

Gard, Janice
See Latham, Jean Lee

Gard, Roger Martin du
See Martin du Gard, Roger

Gardam, Jane 1928- .... **CLC 43**
See also CA 49-52; CANR 2, 18, 33; CLR 12; DLB 14; MAICYA; MTCW; SAAS 9; SATA 28, 39

Gardner, Herb .... **CLC 44**

Gardner, John (Champlin) Jr.
1933-1982 .... **CLC 2, 3, 5, 7, 8, 10, 18, 28, 34; SSC 7**
See also AITN 1; CA 65-68; 107; CANR 33; DLB 2; DLBY 82; MTCW; SATA 31, 40

Gardner, John (Edmund) 1926- ..... **CLC 30**
See also CA 103; CANR 15; MTCW

Gardner, Noel
See Kuttner, Henry

Gardons, S. S.
See Snodgrass, William D(e Witt)

Garfield, Leon 1921- .... **CLC 12**
See also AAYA 8; CA 17-20R; CANR 38; CLR 21; MAICYA; SATA 1, 32

Garland, (Hannibal) Hamlin
1860-1940 .... **TCLC 3**
See also CA 104; DLB 12, 71, 78

Garneau, (Hector de) Saint-Denys
1912-1943 .... TCLC 13
See also CA 111; DLB 88

Garner, Alan 1934- .... CLC 17
See also CA 73-76; CANR 15; CLR 20;
MAICYA; MTCW; SATA 18, 69

Garner, Hugh 1913-1979 .... CLC 13
See also CA 69-72; CANR 31; DLB 68

Garnett, David 1892-1981 .... CLC 3
See also CA 5-8R; 103; CANR 17; DLB 34

Garos, Stephanie
See Katz, Steve

Garrett, George (Palmer)
1929- .... CLC 3, 11, 51
See also CA 1-4R; CAAS 5; CANR 1;
DLB 2, 5; DLBY 83

Garrick, David 1717-1779 .... LC 15
See also DLB 84

Garrigue, Jean 1914-1972 .... CLC 2, 8
See also CA 5-8R; 37-40R; CANR 20

Garrison, Frederick
See Sinclair, Upton (Beall)

Garth, Will
See Hamilton, Edmond; Kuttner, Henry

Garvey, Marcus (Moziah Jr.)
1887-1940 .... TCLC 41
See also BLC 2; BW; CA 120; 124

Gary, Romain .... CLC 25
See also Kacew, Romain
See also DLB 83

Gascar, Pierre .... CLC 11
See also Fournier, Pierre

Gascoyne, David (Emery) 1916- .... CLC 45
See also CA 65-68; CANR 10, 28; DLB 20;
MTCW

Gaskell, Elizabeth Cleghorn
1810-1865 .... NCLC 5
See also CDBLB 1832-1890; DLB 21

Gass, William H(oward)
1924- .... CLC 1, 2, 8, 11, 15, 39
See also CA 17-20R; CANR 30; DLB 2;
MTCW

Gasset, Jose Ortega y
See Ortega y Gasset, Jose

Gautier, Theophile 1811-1872 ..... NCLC 1
See also DLB 119

Gawsworth, John
See Bates, H(erbert) E(rnest)

Gaye, Marvin (Penze) 1939-1984 ... CLC 26
See also CA 112

Gebler, Carlo (Ernest) 1954- .... CLC 39
See also CA 119; 133

Gee, Maggie (Mary) 1948- .... CLC 57
See also CA 130

Gee, Maurice (Gough) 1931- .... CLC 29
See also CA 97-100; SATA 46

Gelbart, Larry (Simon) 1923- ... CLC 21, 61
See also CA 73-76

Gelber, Jack 1932- .... CLC 1, 6, 14
See also CA 1-4R; CANR 2; DLB 7

Gellhorn, Martha Ellis 1908- ... CLC 14, 60
See also CA 77-80; DLBY 82

Genet, Jean
1910-1986 ... CLC 1, 2, 5, 10, 14, 44, 46
See also CA 13-16R; CANR 18; DLB 72;
DLBY 86; MTCW

Gent, Peter 1942- .... CLC 29
See also AITN 1; CA 89-92; DLBY 82

George, Jean Craighead 1919- ...... CLC 35
See also AAYA 8; CA 5-8R; CANR 25;
CLR 1; DLB 52; MAICYA; SATA 2, 68

George, Stefan (Anton)
1868-1933 .... TCLC 2, 14
See also CA 104

Georges, Georges Martin
See Simenon, Georges (Jacques Christian)

Gerhardi, William Alexander
See Gerhardie, William Alexander

Gerhardie, William Alexander
1895-1977 .... CLC 5
See also CA 25-28R; 73-76; CANR 18;
DLB 36

Gerstler, Amy 1956- .... CLC 70

Gertler, T. .... CLC 34
See also CA 116; 121

Ghelderode, Michel de
1898-1962 .... CLC 6, 11
See also CA 85-88

Ghiselin, Brewster 1903- .... CLC 23
See also CA 13-16R; CAAS 10; CANR 13

Ghose, Zulfikar 1935- .... CLC 42
See also CA 65-68

Ghosh, Amitav 1956- .... CLC 44

Giacosa, Giuseppe 1847-1906 ...... TCLC 7
See also CA 104

Gibb, Lee
See Waterhouse, Keith (Spencer)

Gibbon, Lewis Grassic .... TCLC 4
See also Mitchell, James Leslie

Gibbons, Kaye 1960- .... CLC 50

Gibran, Kahlil 1883-1931 .... TCLC 1, 9
See also CA 104

Gibson, William (Ford) 1948- ... CLC 39, 63
See also CA 126; 133

Gibson, William 1914- .... CLC 23
See also CA 9-12R; CANR 9; DLB 7;
SATA 66

Gide, Andre (Paul Guillaume)
1869-1951 .... TCLC 5, 12, 36
See also CA 104; 124; DLB 65; MTCW;
WLC

Gifford, Barry (Colby) 1946- .... CLC 34
See also CA 65-68; CANR 9, 30

Gilbert, W(illiam) S(chwenck)
1836-1911 .... TCLC 3
See also CA 104; SATA 36

Gilbreth, Frank B. Jr. 1911- .... CLC 17
See also CA 9-12R; SATA 2

Gilchrist, Ellen 1935- .... CLC 34, 48
See also CA 113; 116; MTCW

Giles, Molly 1942- .... CLC 39
See also CA 126

Gill, Patrick
See Creasey, John

Gilliam, Terry (Vance) 1940- .... CLC 21
See also Monty Python
See also CA 108; 113; CANR 35

Gillian, Jerry
See Gilliam, Terry (Vance)

Gilliatt, Penelope (Ann Douglass)
1932- .... CLC 2, 10, 13, 53
See also AITN 2; CA 13-16R; DLB 14

Gilman, Charlotte (Anna) Perkins (Stetson)
1860-1935 .... TCLC 9, 37
See also CA 106

Gilmour, David 1944- .... CLC 35
See also Pink Floyd
See also CA 138

Gilpin, William 1724-1804 .... NCLC 30

Gilray, J. D.
See Mencken, H(enry) L(ouis)

Gilroy, Frank D(aniel) 1925- .... CLC 2
See also CA 81-84; CANR 32; DLB 7

Ginsberg, Allen
1926- ..... CLC 1, 2, 3, 4, 6, 13, 36, 69;
PC 4
See also AITN 1; CA 1-4R; CANR 2;
CDALB 1941-1968; DLB 5, 16; MTCW;
WLC 3

Ginzburg, Natalia
1916-1991 .... CLC 5, 11, 54, 70
See also CA 85-88; 135; CANR 33; MTCW

Giono, Jean 1895-1970 .... CLC 4, 11
See also CA 45-48; 29-32R; CANR 2, 35;
DLB 72; MTCW

Giovanni, Nikki 1943- ..... CLC 2, 4, 19, 64
See also AITN 1; BLC 2; BW; CA 29-32R;
CAAS 6; CANR 18; CLR 6; DLB 5, 41;
MAICYA; MTCW; SATA 24

Giovene, Andrea 1904- .... CLC 7
See also CA 85-88

Gippius, Zinaida (Nikolayevna) 1869-1945
See Hippius, Zinaida
See also CA 106

Giraudoux, (Hippolyte) Jean
1882-1944 .... TCLC 2, 7
See also CA 104; DLB 65

Gironella, Jose Maria 1917- .... CLC 11
See also CA 101

Gissing, George (Robert)
1857-1903 .... TCLC 3, 24, 47
See also CA 105; DLB 18

Giurlani, Aldo
See Palazzeschi, Aldo

Gladkov, Fyodor (Vasilyevich)
1883-1958 .... TCLC 27

Glanville, Brian (Lester) 1931- ...... CLC 6
See also CA 5-8R; CAAS 9; CANR 3;
DLB 15; SATA 42

Glasgow, Ellen (Anderson Gholson)
1873(?)-1945 .... TCLC 2, 7
See also CA 104; DLB 9, 12

Glassco, John 1909-1981 .... CLC 9
See also CA 13-16R; 102; CANR 15;
DLB 68

Glasscock, Amnesia
See Steinbeck, John (Ernst)

Glasser, Ronald J. 1940(?)- .... CLC 37

Glassman, Joyce
See Johnson, Joyce

Glendinning, Victoria 1937- .... **CLC 50**
See also CA 120; 127

Glissant, Edouard 1928- .... **CLC 10, 68**

Gloag, Julian 1930- .... **CLC 40**
See also AITN 1; CA 65-68; CANR 10

Gluck, Louise 1943- .... **CLC 7, 22, 44**
See also Glueck, Louise
See also CA 33-36R; DLB 5

Glueck, Louise .... **CLC 7, 22**
See also Gluck, Louise
See also DLB 5

Gobineau, Joseph Arthur (Comte) de
1816-1882 .... **NCLC 17**

Godard, Jean-Luc 1930- .... **CLC 20**
See also CA 93-96

Godden, (Margaret) Rumer 1907- ... **CLC 53**
See also AAYA 6; CA 5-8R; CANR 4, 27, 36; CLR 20; MAICYA; SAAS 12; SATA 3, 36

Godoy Alcayaga, Lucila 1889-1957
See Mistral, Gabriela
See also CA 104; 131; HW; MTCW

Godwin, Gail (Kathleen)
1937- .... **CLC 5, 8, 22, 31, 69**
See also CA 29-32R; CANR 15; DLB 6; MTCW

Godwin, William 1756-1836...... **NCLC 14**
See also CDBLB 1789-1832; DLB 39, 104

Goethe, Johann Wolfgang von
1749-1832 .... **NCLC 4, 22, 34; PC 5**
See also DLB 94; WLC 3

Gogarty, Oliver St. John
1878-1957 .... **TCLC 15**
See also CA 109; DLB 15, 19

Gogol, Nikolai (Vasilyevich)
1809-1852 ..... **NCLC 5, 15, 31; DC 1; SSC 4**
See also WLC

Gold, Herbert 1924- .... **CLC 4, 7, 14, 42**
See also CA 9-12R; CANR 17; DLB 2; DLBY 81

Goldbarth, Albert 1948- .... **CLC 5, 38**
See also CA 53-56; CANR 6; DLB 120

Goldberg, Anatol 1910-1982 .... **CLC 34**
See also CA 131; 117

Goldemberg, Isaac 1945- .... **CLC 52**
See also CA 69-72; CAAS 12; CANR 11, 32; HW

Golden Silver
See Storm, Hyemeyohsts

Golding, William (Gerald)
1911- ..... **CLC 1, 2, 3, 8, 10, 17, 27, 58**
See also AAYA 5; CA 5-8R; CANR 13, 33; CDBLB 1945-1960; DLB 15, 100; MTCW; WLC

Goldman, Emma 1869-1940....... **TCLC 13**
See also CA 110

Goldman, William (W.) 1931- .... **CLC 1, 48**
See also CA 9-12R; CANR 29; DLB 44

Goldmann, Lucien 1913-1970 ...... **CLC 24**
See also CA 25-28; CAP 2

Goldoni, Carlo 1707-1793 .... **LC 4**

Goldsberry, Steven 1949-.......... **CLC 34**
See also CA 131

Goldsmith, Oliver 1728(?)-1774....... **LC 2**

Goldsmith, Peter
See Priestley, J(ohn) B(oynton)

Gombrowicz, Witold
1904-1969 .... **CLC 4, 7, 11, 49**
See also CA 19-20; 25-28R; CAP 2

Gomez de la Serna, Ramon
1888-1963 .... **CLC 9**
See also CA 116; HW

Goncharov, Ivan Alexandrovich
1812-1891 .... **NCLC 1**

Goncourt, Edmond (Louis Antoine Huot) de
1822-1896 .... **NCLC 7**

Goncourt, Jules (Alfred Huot) de
1830-1870 .... **NCLC 7**

Gontier, Fernande 19(?)- .... **CLC 50**

Goodman, Paul 1911-1972.... **CLC 1, 2, 4, 7**
See also CA 19-20; 37-40R; CANR 34; CAP 2; MTCW

Gordimer, Nadine
1923- .... **CLC 3, 5, 7, 10, 18, 33, 51, 70**
See also CA 5-8R; CANR 3, 28; MTCW

Gordon, Adam Lindsay
1833-1870 .... **NCLC 21**

Gordon, Caroline
1895-1981 .... **CLC 6, 13, 29**
See also CA 11-12; 103; CANR 36; CAP 1; DLB 4, 9, 102; DLBY 81; MTCW

Gordon, Charles William 1860-1937
See Connor, Ralph
See also CA 109

Gordon, Mary (Catherine)
1949- .... **CLC 13, 22**
See also CA 102; DLB 6; DLBY 81; MTCW

Gordon, Sol 1923-................. **CLC 26**
See also CA 53-56; CANR 4; SATA 11

Gordone, Charles 1925- .... **CLC 1, 4**
See also BW; CA 93-96; DLB 7; MTCW

Gorenko, Anna Andreevna
See Akhmatova, Anna

Gorky, Maxim.................... **TCLC 8**
See also Peshkov, Alexei Maximovich
See also WLC

Goryan, Sirak
See Saroyan, William

Gosse, Edmund (William)
1849-1928 .... **TCLC 28**
See also CA 117; DLB 57

Gotlieb, Phyllis Fay (Bloom)
1926- .... **CLC 18**
See also CA 13-16R; CANR 7; DLB 88

Gottesman, S. D.
See Kornbluth, C(yril) M.; Pohl, Frederik

Gottfried von Strassburg
fl. c. 1210-................. **CMLC 10**

Gottschalk, Laura Riding
See Jackson, Laura (Riding)

Gould, Lois .... **CLC 4, 10**
See also CA 77-80; CANR 29; MTCW

Gourmont, Remy de 1858-1915.... **TCLC 17**
See also CA 109

Govier, Katherine 1948-............ **CLC 51**
See also CA 101; CANR 18

Goyen, (Charles) William
1915-1983 .... **CLC 5, 8, 14, 40**
See also AITN 2; CA 5-8R; 110; CANR 6; DLB 2; DLBY 83

Goytisolo, Juan 1931- .... **CLC 5, 10, 23**
See also CA 85-88; CANR 32; HW; MTCW

Gozzi, (Conte) Carlo 1720-1806 .. **NCLC 23**

Grabbe, Christian Dietrich
1801-1836 .... **NCLC 2**

Grace, Patricia 1937-............. **CLC 56**

Gracian y Morales, Baltasar
1601-1658 .... **LC 15**

Gracq, Julien................... **CLC 11, 48**
See also Poirier, Louis
See also DLB 83

Grade, Chaim 1910-1982 .... **CLC 10**
See also CA 93-96; 107

Graduate of Oxford, A
See Ruskin, John

Graham, John
See Phillips, David Graham

Graham, Jorie 1951-.............. **CLC 48**
See also CA 111; DLB 120

Graham, R(obert) B(ontine) Cunninghame
See Cunninghame Graham, R(obert) B(ontine)
See also DLB 98

Graham, Robert
See Haldeman, Joe (William)

Graham, Tom
See Lewis, (Harry) Sinclair

Graham, W(illiam) S(ydney)
1918-1986 .... **CLC 29**
See also CA 73-76; 118; DLB 20

Graham, Winston (Mawdsley)
1910- .... **CLC 23**
See also CA 49-52; CANR 2, 22; DLB 77

Granville-Barker, Harley
1877-1946 .... **TCLC 2**
See also Barker, Harley Granville
See also CA 104

Grass, Guenter (Wilhelm)
1927- ... **CLC 1, 2, 4, 6, 11, 15, 22, 32, 49**
See also CA 13-16R; CANR 20; DLB 75; MTCW; WLC

Gratton, Thomas
See Hulme, T(homas) E(rnest)

Grau, Shirley Ann 1929- .... **CLC 4, 9**
See also CA 89-92; CANR 22; DLB 2; MTCW

Gravel, Fern
See Hall, James Norman

Graver, Elizabeth 1964-........... **CLC 70**
See also CA 135

Graves, Richard Perceval 1945- .... **CLC 44**
See also CA 65-68; CANR 9, 26

Graves, Robert (von Ranke)
1895-1985 ... **CLC 1, 2, 6, 11, 39, 44, 45**
See also CA 5-8R; 117; CANR 5, 36; CDBLB 1914-1945; DLB 20, 100; DLBY 85; MTCW; SATA 45

Gray, Alasdair (James) 1934- ...... **CLC 41**
See also CA 126; MTCW

Gray, Amlin 1946- .... **CLC 29**
See also CA 138

Gray, Francine du Plessix 1930- .... **CLC 22**
See also BEST 90:3; CA 61-64; CAAS 2;
CANR 11, 33; MTCW

Gray, John (Henry) 1866-1934 .... **TCLC 19**
See also CA 119

Gray, Simon (James Holliday)
1936- .... **CLC 9, 14, 36**
See also AITN 1; CA 21-24R; CAAS 3;
CANR 32; DLB 13; MTCW

Gray, Spalding 1941- .... **CLC 49**
See also CA 128

Gray, Thomas 1716-1771 .... **LC 4; PC 2**
See also CDBLB 1660-1789; DLB 109;
WLC

Grayson, David
See Baker, Ray Stannard

Grayson, Richard (A.) 1951- .... **CLC 38**
See also CA 85-88; CANR 14, 31

Greeley, Andrew M(oran) 1928- .... **CLC 28**
See also CA 5-8R; CAAS 7; CANR 7;
MTCW

Green, Brian
See Card, Orson Scott

Green, Hannah .... **CLC 3**
See also CA 73-76

Green, Hannah
See Greenberg, Joanne (Goldenberg)

Green, Henry .... **CLC 2, 13**
See also Yorke, Henry Vincent
See also DLB 15

Green, Julian (Hartridge)
1900- .... **CLC 3, 11**
See also CA 21-24R; CANR 33; DLB 4, 72;
MTCW

Green, Julien
See Green, Julian (Hartridge)

Green, Paul (Eliot) 1894-1981 ...... **CLC 25**
See also AITN 1; CA 5-8R; 103; CANR 3;
DLB 7, 9; DLBY 81

Greenberg, Ivan 1908-1973
See Rahv, Philip
See also CA 85-88

Greenberg, Joanne (Goldenberg)
1932- .... **CLC 7, 30**
See also CA 5-8R; CANR 14, 32; SATA 25

Greenberg, Richard 1959(?)- .... **CLC 57**
See also CA 138

Greene, Bette 1934- .... **CLC 30**
See also AAYA 7; CA 53-56; CANR 4;
CLR 2; MAICYA; SATA 8

Greene, Gael .... **CLC 8**
See also CA 13-16R; CANR 10

Greene, Graham (Henry)
1904-1991 ... **CLC 1, 3, 6, 9, 14, 18, 27,
37, 70, 72**
See also AITN 2; CA 13-16R; 133;
CANR 35; CDBLB 1945-1960; DLB 13,
15, 77, 100; DLBY 91; MTCW;
SATA 20; WLC

Greer, Richard
See Silverberg, Robert

Greer, Richard
See Silverberg, Robert

Gregor, Arthur 1923- .... **CLC 9**
See also CA 25-28R; CAAS 10; CANR 11;
SATA 36

Gregor, Lee
See Pohl, Frederik

Gregory, Isabella Augusta (Persse)
1852-1932 .... **TCLC 1**
See also CA 104; DLB 10

Gregory, J. Dennis
See Williams, John A(lfred)

Grendon, Stephen
See Derleth, August (William)

Grenville, Kate 1950- .... **CLC 61**
See also CA 118

Grenville, Pelham
See Wodehouse, P(elham) G(renville)

Greve, Felix Paul (Berthold Friedrich)
1879-1948
See Grove, Frederick Philip
See also CA 104

Grey, Zane 1872-1939 .... **TCLC 6**
See also CA 104; 132; DLB 9; MTCW

Grieg, (Johan) Nordahl (Brun)
1902-1943 .... **TCLC 10**
See also CA 107

Grieve, C(hristopher) M(urray)
1892-1978 .... **CLC 11, 19**
See also MacDiarmid, Hugh
See also CA 5-8R; 85-88; CANR 33;
MTCW

Griffin, Gerald 1803-1840 .... **NCLC 7**

Griffin, John Howard 1920-1980 .... **CLC 68**
See also AITN 1; CA 1-4R; 101; CANR 2

Griffin, Peter .... **CLC 39**

Griffiths, Trevor 1935- .... **CLC 13, 52**
See also CA 97-100; DLB 13

Grigson, Geoffrey (Edward Harvey)
1905-1985 .... **CLC 7, 39**
See also CA 25-28R; 118; CANR 20, 33;
DLB 27; MTCW

Grillparzer, Franz 1791-1872 ...... **NCLC 1**

Grimble, Reverend Charles James
See Eliot, T(homas) S(tearns)

Grimke, Charlotte L(ottie) Forten
1837(?)-1914
See Forten, Charlotte L.
See also BW; CA 117; 124

Grimm, Jacob Ludwig Karl
1785-1863 .... **NCLC 3**
See also DLB 90; MAICYA; SATA 22

Grimm, Wilhelm Karl 1786-1859 .. **NCLC 3**
See also DLB 90; MAICYA; SATA 22

**Grimmelshausen, Johann Jakob Christoffel
von** 1621-1676 .... **LC 6**

Grindel, Eugene 1895-1952
See Eluard, Paul
See also CA 104

Grossman, David .... **CLC 67**
See also CA 138

Grossman, Vasily (Semenovich)
1905-1964 .... **CLC 41**
See also CA 124; 130; MTCW

Grove, Frederick Philip .... **TCLC 4**
See also Greve, Felix Paul (Berthold
Friedrich)
See also DLB 92

Grubb
See Crumb, R(obert)

Grumbach, Doris (Isaac)
1918- .... **CLC 13, 22, 64**
See also CA 5-8R; CAAS 2; CANR 9

Grundtvig, Nicolai Frederik Severin
1783-1872 .... **NCLC 1**

Grunge
See Crumb, R(obert)

Grunwald, Lisa 1959- .... **CLC 44**
See also CA 120

Guare, John 1938- .... **CLC 8, 14, 29, 67**
See also CA 73-76; CANR 21; DLB 7;
MTCW

Gudjonsson, Halldor Kiljan 1902-
See Laxness, Halldor
See also CA 103

Guenter, Erich
See Eich, Guenter

Guest, Barbara 1920- .... **CLC 34**
See also CA 25-28R; CANR 11; DLB 5

Guest, Judith (Ann) 1936- .... **CLC 8, 30**
See also AAYA 7; CA 77-80; CANR 15;
MTCW

Guild, Nicholas M. 1944- .... **CLC 33**
See also CA 93-96

Guillemin, Jacques
See Sartre, Jean-Paul

Guillen, Jorge 1893-1984 .... **CLC 11**
See also CA 89-92; 112; DLB 108; HW

Guillen (y Batista), Nicolas (Cristobal)
1902-1989 .... **CLC 48**
See also BLC 2; BW; CA 116; 125; 129;
HW

Guillevic, (Eugene) 1907- .... **CLC 33**
See also CA 93-96

Guillois
See Desnos, Robert

Guiney, Louise Imogen
1861-1920 .... **TCLC 41**
See also DLB 54

Guiraldes, Ricardo (Guillermo)
1886-1927 .... **TCLC 39**
See also CA 131; HW; MTCW

Gunn, Bill .... **CLC 5**
See also Gunn, William Harrison
See also DLB 38

Gunn, Thom(son William)
1929- .... **CLC 3, 6, 18, 32**
See also CA 17-20R; CANR 9, 33;
CDBLB 1960 to Present; DLB 27;
MTCW

Gunn, William Harrison 1934(?)-1989
See Gunn, Bill
See also AITN 1; BW; CA 13-16R; 128;
CANR 12, 25

Gunnars, Kristjana 1948- .... **CLC 69**
See also CA 113; DLB 60

Gurganus, Allan 1947- .... **CLC 70**
See also BEST 90:1; CA 135

Gurney, A(lbert) R(amsdell) Jr.
1930- .... **CLC 32, 50, 54**
See also CA 77-80; CANR 32

Gurney, Ivor (Bertie) 1890-1937 ... **TCLC 33**

Gurney, Peter
See Gurney, A(lbert) R(amsdell) Jr.

Gustafson, Ralph (Barker) 1909- .... **CLC 36**
See also CA 21-24R; CANR 8; DLB 88

Gut, Gom
See Simenon, Georges (Jacques Christian)

Guthrie, A(lfred) B(ertram) Jr.
1901-1991 .... **CLC 23**
See also CA 57-60; 134; CANR 24; DLB 6;
SATA 62; SATO 67

Guthrie, Isobel
See Grieve, C(hristopher) M(urray)

Guthrie, Woodrow Wilson 1912-1967
See Guthrie, Woody
See also CA 113; 93-96

Guthrie, Woody .... **CLC 35**
See also Guthrie, Woodrow Wilson

Guy, Rosa (Cuthbert) 1928- .... **CLC 26**
See also AAYA 4; BW; CA 17-20R;
CANR 14, 34; CLR 13; DLB 33;
MAICYA; SATA 14, 62

Gwendolyn
See Bennett, (Enoch) Arnold

H. D. .... **CLC 3, 8, 14, 31, 34; PC 5**
See also Doolittle, Hilda

Haavikko, Paavo Juhani
1931- .... **CLC 18, 34**
See also CA 106

Habbema, Koos
See Heijermans, Herman

Hacker, Marilyn 1942- .... **CLC 5, 9, 23, 72**
See also CA 77-80; DLB 120

Haggard, H(enry) Rider
1856-1925 .... **TCLC 11**
See also CA 108; DLB 70; SATA 16

Haig, Fenil
See Ford, Ford Madox

Haig-Brown, Roderick (Langmere)
1908-1976 .... **CLC 21**
See also CA 5-8R; 69-72; CANR 4, 38;
DLB 88; MAICYA; SATA 12

Hailey, Arthur 1920- .... **CLC 5**
See also AITN 2; BEST 90:3; CA 1-4R;
CANR 2, 36; DLB 88; DLBY 82; MTCW

Hailey, Elizabeth Forsythe 1938- ... **CLC 40**
See also CA 93-96; CAAS 1; CANR 15

Haines, John (Meade) 1924- .... **CLC 58**
See also CA 17-20R; CANR 13, 34; DLB 5

Haldeman, Joe (William) 1943- ..... **CLC 61**
See also CA 53-56; CANR 6; DLB 8

Haley, Alex(ander Murray Palmer)
1921-1992 .... **CLC 8, 12**
See also BLC 2; BW; CA 77-80; 136;
DLB 38; MTCW

Haliburton, Thomas Chandler
1796-1865 .... **NCLC 15**
See also DLB 11, 99

Hall, Donald (Andrew Jr.)
1928- .... **CLC 1, 13, 37, 59**
See also CA 5-8R; CAAS 7; CANR 2;
DLB 5; SATA 23

Hall, Frederic Sauser
See Sauser-Hall, Frederic

Hall, James
See Kuttner, Henry

Hall, James Norman 1887-1951 ... **TCLC 23**
See also CA 123; SATA 21

Hall, (Marguerite) Radclyffe
1886(?)-1943 .... **TCLC 12**
See also CA 110

Hall, Rodney 1935- .... **CLC 51**
See also CA 109

Halliday, Michael
See Creasey, John

Halpern, Daniel 1945- .... **CLC 14**
See also CA 33-36R

Hamburger, Michael (Peter Leopold)
1924- .... **CLC 5, 14**
See also CA 5-8R; CAAS 4; CANR 2;
DLB 27

Hamill, Pete 1935- .... **CLC 10**
See also CA 25-28R; CANR 18

Hamilton, Clive
See Lewis, C(live) S(taples)

Hamilton, Edmond 1904-1977 .... **CLC 1**
See also CA 1-4R; CANR 3; DLB 8

Hamilton, Eugene (Jacob) Lee
See Lee-Hamilton, Eugene (Jacob)

Hamilton, Franklin
See Silverberg, Robert

Hamilton, Gail
See Corcoran, Barbara

Hamilton, Mollie
See Kaye, M(ary) M(argaret)

Hamilton, (Anthony Walter) Patrick
1904-1962 .... **CLC 51**
See also CA 113; DLB 10

Hamilton, Virginia 1936- .... **CLC 26**
See also AAYA 2; BW; CA 25-28R;
CANR 20, 37; CLR 1, 11; DLB 33, 52;
MAICYA; MTCW; SATA 4, 56

Hammett, (Samuel) Dashiell
1894-1961 .... **CLC 3, 5, 10, 19, 47**
See also AITN 1; CA 81-84;
CDALB 1929-1941; DLBD 6; MTCW

Hammon, Jupiter 1711(?)-1800(?) .. **NCLC 5**
See also BLC 2; DLB 31, 50

Hammond, Keith
See Kuttner, Henry

Hamner, Earl (Henry) Jr. 1923- .... **CLC 12**
See also AITN 2; CA 73-76; DLB 6

Hampton, Christopher (James)
1946- .... **CLC 4**
See also CA 25-28R; DLB 13; MTCW

Hamsun, Knut .... **TCLC 2, 14**
See also Pedersen, Knut

Handke, Peter 1942- .. **CLC 5, 8, 10, 15, 38**
See also CA 77-80; CANR 33; DLB 85;
MTCW

Hanley, James 1901-1985 ... **CLC 3, 5, 8, 13**
See also CA 73-76; 117; CANR 36; MTCW

Hannah, Barry 1942- .... **CLC 23, 38**
See also CA 108; 110; DLB 6; MTCW

Hannon, Ezra
See Hunter, Evan

Hansberry, Lorraine (Vivian)
1930-1965 .... **CLC 17, 62; DC 2**
See also BLC 2; BW; CA 109; 25-28R;
CABS 3; CDALB 1941-1968; DLB 7, 38;
MTCW

Hansen, Joseph 1923- .... **CLC 38**
See also CA 29-32R; CANR 16

Hansen, Martin A. 1909-1955 ..... **TCLC 32**

Hanson, Kenneth O(stlin) 1922- .... **CLC 13**
See also CA 53-56; CANR 7

Hardwick, Elizabeth 1916- .... **CLC 13**
See also CA 5-8R; CANR 3, 32; DLB 6;
MTCW

Hardy, Thomas
1840-1928 ..... **TCLC 4, 10, 18, 32, 48;**
SSC 2
See also CA 104; 123; CDBLB 1890-1914;
DLB 18, 19; MTCW; WLC

Hare, David 1947- .... **CLC 29, 58**
See also CA 97-100; CANR 39; DLB 13;
MTCW

Harford, Henry
See Hudson, W(illiam) H(enry)

Hargrave, Leonie
See Disch, Thomas M(ichael)

Harlan, Louis R(udolph) 1922- ..... **CLC 34**
See also CA 21-24R; CANR 25

Harling, Robert 1951(?)- .... **CLC 53**

Harmon, William (Ruth) 1938- ..... **CLC 38**
See also CA 33-36R; CANR 14, 32, 35;
SATA 65

Harper, F. E. W.
See Harper, Frances Ellen Watkins

Harper, Frances E. W.
See Harper, Frances Ellen Watkins

Harper, Frances E. Watkins
See Harper, Frances Ellen Watkins

Harper, Frances Ellen
See Harper, Frances Ellen Watkins

Harper, Frances Ellen Watkins
1825-1911 .... **TCLC 14**
See also BLC 2; BW; CA 111; 125; DLB 50

Harper, Michael S(teven) 1938- .. **CLC 7, 22**
See also BW; CA 33-36R; CANR 24;
DLB 41

Harper, Mrs. F. E. W.
See Harper, Frances Ellen Watkins

Harris, Christie (Lucy) Irwin
1907- .... **CLC 12**
See also CA 5-8R; CANR 6; DLB 88;
MAICYA; SAAS 10; SATA 6

Harris, Frank 1856(?)-1931 .... **TCLC 24**
See also CA 109

Harris, George Washington
1814-1869 .... **NCLC 23**
See also DLB 3, 11

Harris, Joel Chandler 1848-1908 ... **TCLC 2**
See also CA 104; 137; DLB 11, 23, 42, 78,
91; MAICYA; YABC 1

Harris, John (Wyndham Parkes Lucas)
Beynon 1903-1969 .... **CLC 19**
See also CA 102; 89-92

Harris, MacDonald
See Heiney, Donald (William)

Harris, Mark 1922- .... **CLC 19**
See also CA 5-8R; CAAS 3; CANR 2;
DLB 2; DLBY 80

Harris, (Theodore) Wilson 1921- .... **CLC 25**
See also BW; CA 65-68; CAAS 16;
CANR 11, 27; DLB 117; MTCW

Harrison, Elizabeth Cavanna 1909-
See Cavanna, Betty
See also CA 9-12R; CANR 6, 27

Harrison, Harry (Max) 1925- ...... **CLC 42**
See also CA 1-4R; CANR 5, 21; DLB 8;
SATA 4

Harrison, James (Thomas) 1937-
See Harrison, Jim
See also CA 13-16R; CANR 8

Harrison, Jim .... **CLC 6, 14, 33, 66**
See also Harrison, James (Thomas)
See also DLBY 82

Harrison, Kathryn 1961- .... **CLC 70**

Harrison, Tony 1937- .... **CLC 43**
See also CA 65-68; DLB 40; MTCW

Harriss, Will(ard Irvin) 1922- ...... **CLC 34**
See also CA 111

Harson, Sley
See Ellison, Harlan

Hart, Ellis
See Ellison, Harlan

Hart, Josephine 1942(?)- .... **CLC 70**
See also CA 138

Hart, Moss 1904-1961 .... **CLC 66**
See also CA 109; 89-92; DLB 7

Harte, (Francis) Bret(t)
1836(?)-1902 .... **TCLC 1, 25; SSC 8**
See also CA 104; CDALB 1865-1917;
DLB 12, 64, 74, 79; SATA 26; WLC

Hartley, L(eslie) P(oles)
1895-1972 .... **CLC 2, 22**
See also CA 45-48; 37-40R; CANR 33;
DLB 15; MTCW

Hartman, Geoffrey H. 1929- .... **CLC 27**
See also CA 117; 125; DLB 67

Haruf, Kent 19(?)- .... **CLC 34**

Harwood, Ronald 1934- .... **CLC 32**
See also CA 1-4R; CANR 4; DLB 13

Hasek, Jaroslav (Matej Frantisek)
1883-1923 .... **TCLC 4**
See also CA 104; 129; MTCW

Hass, Robert 1941- .... **CLC 18, 39**
See also CA 111; CANR 30; DLB 105

Hastings, Hudson
See Kuttner, Henry

Hastings, Selina .... **CLC 44**

Hatteras, Amelia
See Mencken, H(enry) L(ouis)

Hatteras, Owen
See Mencken, H(enry) L(ouis)

Hatteras, Owen .... **TCLC 18**
See also Nathan, George Jean

Hauptmann, Gerhart (Johann Robert)
1862-1946 .... **TCLC 4**
See also CA 104; DLB 66, 118

Havel, Vaclav 1936- .... **CLC 25, 58, 65**
See also CA 104; CANR 36; MTCW

Haviaras, Stratis .... **CLC 33**
See also Chaviaras, Strates

Hawes, Stephen 1475(?)-1523(?) ..... **LC 17**

Hawkes, John (Clendennin Burne Jr.)
1925- ...... **CLC 1, 2, 3, 4, 7, 9, 14, 15, 27, 49**
See also CA 1-4R; CANR 2; DLB 2, 7;
DLBY 80; MTCW

Hawking, S. W.
See Hawking, Stephen W(illiam)

Hawking, Stephen W(illiam)
1942- .... **CLC 63**
See also BEST 89:1; CA 126; 129

Hawthorne, Julian 1846-1934 ..... **TCLC 25**

Hawthorne, Nathaniel
1804-1864 ... **NCLC 2, 10, 17, 23; SSC 3**
See also CDALB 1640-1865; DLB 1, 74;
WLC; YABC 2

Hayaseca y Eizaguirre, Jorge
See Echegaray (y Eizaguirre), Jose (Maria
Waldo)

Hayashi Fumiko 1904-1951 .... **TCLC 27**

Haycraft, Anna
See Ellis, Alice Thomas
See also CA 122

Hayden, Robert E(arl)
1913-1980 .... **CLC 5, 9, 14, 37**
See also BLC 2; BW; CA 69-72; 97-100;
CABS 2; CANR 24; CDALB 1941-1968;
DLB 5, 76; MTCW; SATA 19, 26

Hayford, J(oseph) E(phraim) Casely
See Casely-Hayford, J(oseph) E(phraim)

Hayman, Ronald 1932- .... **CLC 44**
See also CA 25-28R; CANR 18

Haywood, Eliza (Fowler)
1693(?)-1756 .... **LC 1**

Hazlitt, William 1778-1830 ...... **NCLC 29**
See also DLB 110

Hazzard, Shirley 1931- .... **CLC 18**
See also CA 9-12R; CANR 4; DLBY 82;
MTCW

Head, Bessie 1937-1986 .... **CLC 25, 67**
See also BLC 2; BW; CA 29-32R; 119;
CANR 25; DLB 117; MTCW

Headon, (Nicky) Topper 1956(?)- ... **CLC 30**
See also The Clash

Heaney, Seamus (Justin)
1939- .... **CLC 5, 7, 14, 25, 37, 74**
See also CA 85-88; CANR 25;
CDBLB 1960 to Present; DLB 40;
MTCW

Hearn, (Patricio) Lafcadio (Tessima Carlos)
1850-1904 .... **TCLC 9**
See also CA 105; DLB 12, 78

Hearne, Vicki 1946- .... **CLC 56**

Hearon, Shelby 1931- .... **CLC 63**
See also AITN 2; CA 25-28R; CANR 18

Heat-Moon, William Least .... **CLC 29**
See also Trogdon, William (Lewis)
See also AAYA 9

Hebert, Anne 1916- .... **CLC 4, 13, 29**
See also CA 85-88; DLB 68; MTCW

Hecht, Anthony (Evan)
1923- .... **CLC 8, 13, 19**
See also CA 9-12R; CANR 6; DLB 5

Hecht, Ben 1894-1964 .... **CLC 8**
See also CA 85-88; DLB 7, 9, 25, 26, 28, 86

Hedayat, Sadeq 1903-1951 .... **TCLC 21**
See also CA 120

Heidegger, Martin 1889-1976 ...... **CLC 24**
See also CA 81-84; 65-68; CANR 34;
MTCW

Heidenstam, (Carl Gustaf) Verner von
1859-1940 .... **TCLC 5**
See also CA 104

Heifner, Jack 1946- .... **CLC 11**
See also CA 105

Heijermans, Herman 1864-1924 ... **TCLC 24**
See also CA 123

Heilbrun, Carolyn G(old) 1926- ..... **CLC 25**
See also CA 45-48; CANR 1, 28

Heine, Heinrich 1797-1856 .... **NCLC 4**
See also DLB 90

Heinemann, Larry (Curtiss) 1944- .. **CLC 50**
See also CA 110; CANR 31; DLBD 9

Heiney, Donald (William) 1921- ..... **CLC 9**
See also CA 1-4R; CANR 3

Heinlein, Robert A(nson)
1907-1988 ...... **CLC 1, 3, 8, 14, 26, 55**
See also CA 1-4R; 125; CANR 1, 20;
DLB 8; MAICYA; MTCW; SATA 9, 56, 69

Helforth, John
See Doolittle, Hilda

Hellenhofferu, Vojtech Kapristian z
See Hasek, Jaroslav (Matej Frantisek)

Heller, Joseph
1923- .... **CLC 1, 3, 5, 8, 11, 36, 63**
See also AITN 1; CA 5-8R; CABS 1;
CANR 8; DLB 2, 28; DLBY 80; MTCW;
WLC

Hellman, Lillian (Florence)
1906-1984 ..... **CLC 2, 4, 8, 14, 18, 34, 44, 52; DC 1**
See also AITN 1, 2; CA 13-16R; 112;
CANR 33; DLB 7; DLBY 84; MTCW

Helprin, Mark 1947- ..... **CLC 7, 10, 22, 32**
See also CA 81-84; DLBY 85; MTCW

Helyar, Jane Penelope Josephine 1933-
See Poole, Josephine
See also CA 21-24R; CANR 10, 26

Hemans, Felicia 1793-1835 ...... **NCLC 29**
See also DLB 96

Hemingway, Ernest (Miller)
1899-1961 ... **CLC 1, 3, 6, 8, 10, 13, 19, 30, 34, 39, 41, 44, 50, 61; SSC 1**
See also CA 77-80;
CDALB 1917-1929; DLB 4, 9, 102;
DLBD 1; DLBY 81, 87; MTCW; WLC

Hempel, Amy 1951- .... **CLC 39**
See also CA 118; 137

Henderson, F. C.
See Mencken, H(enry) L(ouis)

Henderson, Sylvia
See Ashton-Warner, Sylvia (Constance)

Henley, Beth .... **CLC 23**
See also Henley, Elizabeth Becker
See also CABS 3; DLBY 86

Henley, Elizabeth Becker 1952-
See Henley, Beth
See also CA 107; CANR 32; MTCW

Henley, William Ernest
1849-1903 .... **TCLC 8**
See also CA 105; DLB 19

Hennissart, Martha
See Lathen, Emma
See also CA 85-88

Henry, O. .... **TCLC 1, 19; SSC 5**
See also Porter, William Sydney
See also WLC

Henryson, Robert 1430(?)-1506(?).... **LC 20**

Henry VIII 1491-1547 .... **LC 10**

Henschke, Alfred
See Klabund

Hentoff, Nat(han Irving) 1925- ..... **CLC 26**
See also AAYA 4; CA 1-4R; CAAS 6;
CANR 5, 25; CLR 1; MAICYA;
SATA 27, 42, 69

Heppenstall, (John) Rayner
1911-1981 .... **CLC 10**
See also CA 1-4R; 103; CANR 29

Herbert, Frank (Patrick)
1920-1986 .... **CLC 12, 23, 35, 44**
See also CA 53-56; 118; CANR 5; DLB 8;
MTCW; SATA 9, 37, 47

Herbert, George 1593-1633 .... **PC 4**
See also CDBLB Before 1660

Herbert, Zbigniew 1924- .... **CLC 9, 43**
See also CA 89-92; CANR 36; MTCW

Herbst, Josephine (Frey)
1897-1969 .... **CLC 34**
See also CA 5-8R; 25-28R; DLB 9

Hergesheimer, Joseph
1880-1954 .... **TCLC 11**
See also CA 109; DLB 102, 9

Herlihy, James Leo 1927- .... **CLC 6**
See also CA 1-4R; CANR 2

Hermogenes fl. c. 175- .... **CMLC 6**

Hernandez, Jose 1834-1886 ...... **NCLC 17**

Herrick, Robert 1591-1674 .... **LC 13**

Herriot, James .... **CLC 12**
See also Wight, James Alfred
See also AAYA 1

Herrmann, Dorothy 1941- .... **CLC 44**
See also CA 107

Herrmann, Taffy
See Herrmann, Dorothy

Hersey, John (Richard)
1914- .... **CLC 1, 2, 7, 9, 40**
See also CA 17-20R; CANR 33; DLB 6;
MTCW; SATA 25

Herzen, Aleksandr Ivanovich
1812-1870 .... **NCLC 10**

Herzl, Theodor 1860-1904 .... **TCLC 36**

Herzog, Werner 1942- .... **CLC 16**
See also CA 89-92

Hesiod c. 8th cent. B.C.- .... **CMLC 5**

Hesse, Hermann
1877-1962 ... **CLC 1, 2, 3, 6, 11, 17, 25, 69; SSC 9**
See also CA 17-18; CAP 2; DLB 66;
MTCW; SATA 50; WLC

Hewes, Cady
See De Voto, Bernard (Augustine)

Heyen, William 1940- .... **CLC 13, 18**
See also CA 33-36R; CAAS 9; DLB 5

Heyerdahl, Thor 1914- .... **CLC 26**
See also CA 5-8R; CANR 5, 22; MTCW;
SATA 2, 52

Heym, Georg (Theodor Franz Arthur)
1887-1912 .... **TCLC 9**
See also CA 106

Heym, Stefan 1913- .... **CLC 41**
See also CA 9-12R; CANR 4; DLB 69

Heyse, Paul (Johann Ludwig von)
1830-1914 .... **TCLC 8**
See also CA 104

Hibbert, Eleanor Burford 1906- ..... **CLC 7**
See also BEST 90:4; CA 17-20R; CANR 9, 28; SATA 2

Higgins, George V(incent)
1939- .... **CLC 4, 7, 10, 18**
See also CA 77-80; CAAS 5; CANR 17;
DLB 2; DLBY 81; MTCW

Higginson, Thomas Wentworth
1823-1911 .... **TCLC 36**
See also DLB 1, 64

Highet, Helen
See MacInnes, Helen (Clark)

Highsmith, (Mary) Patricia
1921- .... **CLC 2, 4, 14, 42**
See also CA 1-4R; CANR 1, 20; MTCW

Highwater, Jamake (Mamake)
1942(?)- .... **CLC 12**
See also AAYA 7; CA 65-68; CAAS 7;
CANR 10, 34; CLR 17; DLB 52;
DLBY 85; MAICYA; SATA 30, 32, 69

Hijuelos, Oscar 1951- .... **CLC 65**
See also BEST 90:1; CA 123; HW

Hikmet, Nazim 1902-1963 .... **CLC 40**
See also CA 93-96

Hildesheimer, Wolfgang
1916-1991 .... **CLC 49**
See also CA 101; 135; DLB 69

Hill, Geoffrey (William)
1932- .... **CLC 5, 8, 18, 45**
See also CA 81-84; CANR 21;
CDBLB 1960 to Present; DLB 40;
MTCW

Hill, George Roy 1921- .... **CLC 26**
See also CA 110; 122

Hill, Susan (Elizabeth) 1942- .... **CLC 4**
See also CA 33-36R; CANR 29; DLB 14;
MTCW

Hillerman, Tony 1925- .... **CLC 62**
See also AAYA 6; BEST 89:1; CA 29-32R;
CANR 21; SATA 6

Hilliard, Noel (Harvey) 1929- ...... **CLC 15**
See also CA 9-12R; CANR 7

Hillis, Rick 1956- .... **CLC 66**
See also CA 134

Hilton, James 1900-1954 .... **TCLC 21**
See also CA 108; DLB 34, 77; SATA 34

Himes, Chester (Bomar)
1909-1984 .... **CLC 2, 4, 7, 18, 58**
See also BLC 2; BW; CA 25-28R; 114;
CANR 22; DLB 2, 76; MTCW

Hinde, Thomas .... **CLC 6, 11**
See also Chitty, Thomas Willes

Hindin, Nathan
See Bloch, Robert (Albert)

Hine, (William) Daryl 1936- .... **CLC 15**
See also CA 1-4R; CAAS 15; CANR 1, 20;
DLB 60

Hinkson, Katharine Tynan
See Tynan, Katharine

Hinton, S(usan) E(loise) 1950- ..... **CLC 30**
See also AAYA 2; CA 81-84; CANR 32;
CLR 3, 23; MAICYA; MTCW;
SATA 19, 58

Hippius, Zinaida .... **TCLC 9**
See also Gippius, Zinaida (Nikolayevna)

Hiraoka, Kimitake 1925-1970
See Mishima, Yukio
See also CA 97-100; 29-32R; MTCW

Hirsch, Edward 1950- .... **CLC 31, 50**
See also CA 104; CANR 20; DLB 120

Hitchcock, Alfred (Joseph)
1899-1980 .... **CLC 16**
See also CA 97-100; SATA 24, 27

Hoagland, Edward 1932- .... **CLC 28**
See also CA 1-4R; CANR 2, 31; DLB 6;
SATA 51

Hoban, Russell (Conwell) 1925- ... **CLC 7, 25**
See also CA 5-8R; CANR 23, 37; CLR 3;
DLB 52; MAICYA; MTCW; SATA 1, 40

Hobbs, Perry
See Blackmur, R(ichard) P(almer)

Hobson, Laura Z(ametkin)
1900-1986 .... **CLC 7, 25**
See also CA 17-20R; 118; DLB 28;
SATA 52

Hochhuth, Rolf 1931- .... **CLC 4, 11, 18**
See also CA 5-8R; CANR 33; MTCW

Hochman, Sandra 1936- .... **CLC 3, 8**
See also CA 5-8R; DLB 5

Hochwaelder, Fritz 1911-1986...... **CLC 36**
See also Hochwalder, Fritz
See also CA 29-32R; 120; MTCW

Hochwalder, Fritz .... **CLC 36**
See also Hochwaelder, Fritz

Hocking, Mary (Eunice) 1921- ..... **CLC 13**
See also CA 101; CANR 18

Hodgins, Jack 1938- .... **CLC 23**
See also CA 93-96; DLB 60

Hodgson, William Hope
1877(?)-1918 .... **TCLC 13**
See also CA 111; DLB 70

Hoffman, Alice 1952- .... **CLC 51**
See also CA 77-80; CANR 34; MTCW

Hoffman, Daniel (Gerard)
1923- .... **CLC 6, 13, 23**
See also CA 1-4R; CANR 4; DLB 5

Hoffman, Stanley 1944- .... **CLC 5**
See also CA 77-80

Hoffman, William M(oses) 1939- ... **CLC 40**
See also CA 57-60; CANR 11

Hoffmann, E(rnst) T(heodor) A(madeus)
1776-1822 .... **NCLC 2**
See also DLB 90; SATA 27

Hofmann, Gert 1931- .... **CLC 54**
See also CA 128

Hofmannsthal, Hugo von
1874-1929 .... **TCLC 11**
See also CA 106; DLB 81, 118

Hogarth, Charles
See Creasey, John

Hogg, James 1770-1835 .... **NCLC 4**
See also DLB 93, 116

Holbach, Paul Henri Thiry Baron
1723-1789 .... **LC 14**

Holberg, Ludvig 1684-1754 .... **LC 6**

Holden, Ursula 1921- .... **CLC 18**
See also CA 101; CAAS 8; CANR 22

Holderlin, (Johann Christian) Friedrich
1770-1843 .... **NCLC 16; PC 4**

Holdstock, Robert
See Holdstock, Robert P.

Holdstock, Robert P. 1948- .... **CLC 39**
See also CA 131

Holland, Isabelle 1920- .... **CLC 21**
See also CA 21-24R; CANR 10, 25;
MAICYA; SATA 8, 70

Holland, Marcus
See Caldwell, (Janet Miriam) Taylor
(Holland)

Hollander, John 1929- ...... **CLC 2, 5, 8, 14**
See also CA 1-4R; CANR 1; DLB 5;
SATA 13

Hollander, Paul
See Silverberg, Robert

Holleran, Andrew 1943(?)- .... **CLC 38**

Hollinghurst, Alan 1954- .... **CLC 55**
See also CA 114

Hollis, Jim
See Summers, Hollis (Spurgeon Jr.)

Holmes, John
See Souster, (Holmes) Raymond

Holmes, John Clellon 1926-1988.... **CLC 56**
See also CA 9-12R; 125; CANR 4; DLB 16

Holmes, Oliver Wendell
1809-1894 .... **NCLC 14**
See also CDALB 1640-1865; DLB 1;
SATA 34

Holmes, Raymond
See Souster, (Holmes) Raymond

Holt, Victoria
See Hibbert, Eleanor Burford

Holub, Miroslav 1923- .... **CLC 4**
See also CA 21-24R; CANR 10

Homer c. 8th cent. B.C.- .... **CMLC 1**

Honig, Edwin 1919- .... **CLC 33**
See also CA 5-8R; CAAS 8; CANR 4;
DLB 5

Hood, Hugh (John Blagdon)
1928- .... **CLC 15, 28**
See also CA 49-52; CANR 1, 33; DLB 53

Hood, Thomas 1799-1845........ **NCLC 16**
See also DLB 96

Hooker, (Peter) Jeremy 1941- ...... **CLC 43**
See also CA 77-80; CANR 22; DLB 40

Hope, A(lec) D(erwent) 1907- .... **CLC 3, 51**
See also CA 21-24R; CANR 33; MTCW

Hope, Brian
See Creasey, John

Hope, Christopher (David Tully)
1944- .... **CLC 52**
See also CA 106; SATA 62

Hopkins, Gerard Manley
1844-1889 .... **NCLC 17**
See also CDBLB 1890-1914; DLB 35, 57;
WLC

Hopkins, John (Richard) 1931- ...... **CLC 4**
See also CA 85-88

Hopkins, Pauline Elizabeth
1859-1930 .... **TCLC 28**
See also BLC 2; DLB 50

Horatio
See Proust,
(Valentin-Louis-George-Eugene-)Marcel

Horgan, Paul 1903- .... **CLC 9, 53**
See also CA 13-16R; CANR 9, 35;
DLB 102; DLBY 85; MTCW; SATA 13

Horn, Peter
See Kuttner, Henry

Horovitz, Israel 1939- .... **CLC 56**
See also CA 33-36R; DLB 7

Horvath, Odon von
See Horvath, Oedoen von
See also DLB 85

Horvath, Oedoen von 1901-1938... **TCLC 45**
See also Horvath, Odon von
See also CA 118

Horwitz, Julius 1920-1986......... **CLC 14**
See also CA 9-12R; 119; CANR 12

Hospital, Janette Turner 1942-..... **CLC 42**
See also CA 108

Hostos, E. M. de
See Hostos (y Bonilla), Eugenio Maria de

Hostos, Eugenio M. de
See Hostos (y Bonilla), Eugenio Maria de

Hostos, Eugenio Maria
See Hostos (y Bonilla), Eugenio Maria de

Hostos (y Bonilla), Eugenio Maria de
1839-1903 .... **TCLC 24**
See also CA 123; 131; HW

Houdini
See Lovecraft, H(oward) P(hillips)

Hougan, Carolyn 19(?)- .... **CLC 34**

Household, Geoffrey (Edward West)
1900-1988 .... **CLC 11**
See also CA 77-80; 126; DLB 87; SATA 14,
59

Housman, A(lfred) E(dward)
1859-1936 .... **TCLC 1, 10; PC 2**
See also CA 104; 125; DLB 19; MTCW

Housman, Laurence 1865-1959 ..... **TCLC 7**
See also CA 106; DLB 10; SATA 25

Howard, Elizabeth Jane 1923- ... **CLC 7, 29**
See also CA 5-8R; CANR 8

Howard, Maureen 1930- ..... **CLC 5, 14, 46**
See also CA 53-56; CANR 31; DLBY 83;
MTCW

Howard, Richard 1929- ...... **CLC 7, 10, 47**
See also AITN 1; CA 85-88; CANR 25;
DLB 5

Howard, Robert Ervin 1906-1936... **TCLC 8**
See also CA 105

Howard, Warren F.
See Pohl, Frederik

Howe, Fanny 1940- .... **CLC 47**
See also CA 117; SATA 52

Howe, Julia Ward 1819-1910 ..... **TCLC 21**
See also CA 117; DLB 1

Howe, Susan 1937-............... **CLC 72**
See also DLB 120

Howe, Tina 1937-................. **CLC 48**
See also CA 109

Howell, James 1594(?)-1666 .... **LC 13**

Howells, W. D.
See Howells, William Dean

Howells, William D.
See Howells, William Dean

Howells, William Dean
1837-1920 .... **TCLC 41, 7, 17**
See also CA 104; 134; CDALB 1865-1917;
DLB 12, 64, 74, 79

Howes, Barbara 1914- .... **CLC 15**
See also CA 9-12R; CAAS 3; SATA 5

Hrabal, Bohumil 1914-......... **CLC 13, 67**
See also CA 106; CAAS 12

Hsun, Lu .... **TCLC 3**
See also Shu-Jen, Chou

Hubbard, L(afayette) Ron(ald)
1911-1986 .... **CLC 43**
See also CA 77-80; 118; CANR 22

Huch, Ricarda (Octavia)
1864-1947 .... **TCLC 13**
See also CA 111; DLB 66

Huddle, David 1942- .... **CLC 49**
See also CA 57-60

Hudson, Jeffery
See Crichton, (John) Michael

Hudson, W(illiam) H(enry)
1841-1922 .... **TCLC 29**
See also CA 115; DLB 98; SATA 35

Hueffer, Ford Madox
See Ford, Ford Madox

Hughart, Barry .... **CLC 39**
See also CA 137

Hughes, Colin
See Creasey, John

Hughes, David (John) 1930- .... **CLC 48**
See also CA 116; 129; DLB 14

Hughes, (James) Langston
1902-1967 .... **CLC 1, 5, 10, 15, 35, 44;
DC 3; PC 1; SSC 6**
See also BLC 2; BW; CA 1-4R; 25-28R;
CANR 1, 34; CDALB 1929-1941;
CLR 17; DLB 4, 7, 48, 51, 86; MAICYA;
MTCW; SATA 4, 33; WLC

Hughes, Richard (Arthur Warren)
1900-1976 .... CLC 1, 11
See also CA 5-8R; 65-68; CANR 4;
DLB 15; MTCW; SATA 8, 25

Hughes, Ted 1930- ...... CLC 2, 4, 9, 14, 37
See also CA 1-4R; CANR 1, 33; CLR 3;
DLB 40; MAICYA; MTCW; SATA 27, 49

Hugo, Richard F(ranklin)
1923-1982 .... CLC 6, 18, 32
See also CA 49-52; 108; CANR 3; DLB 5

Hugo, Victor (Marie)
1802-1885 .... NCLC 3, 10, 21
See also DLB 119; SATA 47; WLC

Huidobro, Vicente
See Huidobro Fernandez, Vicente Garcia

Huidobro Fernandez, Vicente Garcia
1893-1948 .... TCLC 31
See also CA 131; HW

Hulme, Keri 1947- .... CLC 39
See also CA 125

Hulme, T(homas) E(rnest)
1883-1917 .... TCLC 21
See also CA 117; DLB 19

Hume, David 1711-1776.............. LC 7
See also DLB 104

Humphrey, William 1924- .... CLC 45
See also CA 77-80; DLB 6

Humphreys, Emyr Owen 1919-..... CLC 47
See also CA 5-8R; CANR 3, 24; DLB 15

Humphreys, Josephine 1945-.... CLC 34, 57
See also CA 121; 127

Hungerford, Pixie
See Brinsmead, H(esba) F(ay)

Hunt, E(verette) Howard Jr. 1918-... CLC 3
See also AITN 1; CA 45-48; CANR 2

Hunt, Kyle
See Creasey, John

Hunt, (James Henry) Leigh
1784-1859 .... NCLC 1

Hunt, Marsha 1946-.............. CLC 70

Hunter, E. Waldo
See Sturgeon, Theodore (Hamilton)

Hunter, Evan 1926- .... CLC 11, 31
See also CA 5-8R; CANR 5, 38; DLBY 82;
MTCW; SATA 25

Hunter, Kristin (Eggleston) 1931-... CLC 35
See also AITN 1; BW; CA 13-16R;
CANR 13; CLR 3; DLB 33; MAICYA;
SAAS 10; SATA 12

Hunter, Mollie 1922- .... CLC 21
See also McIlwraith, Maureen Mollie
Hunter
See also CANR 37; CLR 25; MAICYA;
SAAS 7; SATA 54

Hunter, Robert (?)-1734.............. LC 7

Hurston, Zora Neale
1903-1960 .... CLC 7, 30, 61; SSC 4
See also BLC 2; BW; CA 85-88; DLB 51, 86; MTCW

Huston, John (Marcellus)
1906-1987 .... CLC 20
See also CA 73-76; 123; CANR 34; DLB 26

Hutten, Ulrich von 1488-1523....... LC 16

Huxley, Aldous (Leonard)
1894-1963 .. CLC 1, 3, 4, 5, 8, 11, 18, 35
See also CA 85-88; CDBLB 1914-1945;
DLB 36, 100; MTCW; SATA 63; WLC

Huysmans, Charles Marie Georges
1848-1907
See Huysmans, Joris-Karl
See also CA 104

Huysmans, Joris-Karl............. TCLC 7
See also Huysmans, Charles Marie Georges

Hwang, David Henry 1957-........ CLC 55
See also CA 127; 132

Hyde, Anthony 1946-............. CLC 42
See also CA 136

Hyde, Margaret O(ldroyd) 1917-... CLC 21
See also CA 1-4R; CANR 1, 36; CLR 23;
MAICYA; SAAS 8; SATA 1, 42

Hynes, James 1956(?)-............ CLC 65

Ian, Janis 1951- .... CLC 21
See also CA 105

Ibanez, Vicente Blasco
See Blasco Ibanez, Vicente

Ibarguengoitia, Jorge 1928-1983.... CLC 37
See also CA 124; 113; HW

Ibsen, Henrik (Johan)
1828-1906 ..... TCLC 2, 8, 16, 37; DC 2
See also CA 104; WLC

Ibuse Masuji 1898-.............. CLC 22
See also CA 127

Ichikawa, Kon 1915-.............. CLC 20
See also CA 121

Idle, Eric 1943-.................. CLC 21
See also Monty Python
See also CA 116; CANR 35

Ignatow, David 1914-...... CLC 4, 7, 14, 40
See also CA 9-12R; CAAS 3; CANR 31;
DLB 5

Ihimaera, Witi 1944- .... CLC 46
See also CA 77-80

Ilf, Ilya....................... TCLC 21
See also Fainzilberg, Ilya Arnoldovich

Immermann, Karl (Lebrecht)
1796-1840 .... NCLC 4

Inclan, Ramon (Maria) del Valle
See Valle-Inclan, Ramon (Maria) del

Infante, G(uillermo) Cabrera
See Cabrera Infante, G(uillermo)

Ingalls, Rachel (Holmes) 1940-..... CLC 42
See also CA 123; 127

Ingamells, Rex 1913-1955 .... TCLC 35

Inge, William Motter
1913-1973 .... CLC 1, 8, 19
See also CA 9-12R; CDALB 1941-1968;
DLB 7; MTCW

Ingram, Willis J.
See Harris, Mark

Innaurato, Albert (F.) 1948(?)- .. CLC 21, 60
See also CA 115; 122

Innes, Michael
See Stewart, J(ohn) I(nnes) M(ackintosh)

Ionesco, Eugene
1912- .... CLC 1, 4, 6, 9, 11, 15, 41
See also CA 9-12R; MTCW; SATA 7; WLC

Iqbal, Muhammad 1873-1938 ..... TCLC 28

Irland, David
See Green, Julian (Hartridge)

Iron, Ralph
See Schreiner, Olive (Emilie Albertina)

Irving, John (Winslow)
1942- .... CLC 13, 23, 38
See also AAYA 8; BEST 89:3; CA 25-28R;
CANR 28; DLB 6; DLBY 82; MTCW

Irving, Washington
1783-1859 .... NCLC 2, 19; SSC 2
See also CDALB 1640-1865; DLB 3, 11, 30,
59, 73, 74; WLC; YABC 2

Irwin, P. K.
See Page, P(atricia) K(athleen)

Isaacs, Susan 1943- .... CLC 32
See also BEST 89:1; CA 89-92; CANR 20;
MTCW

Isherwood, Christopher (William Bradshaw)
1904-1986 .... CLC 1, 9, 11, 14, 44
See also CA 13-16R; 117; CANR 35;
DLB 15; DLBY 86; MTCW

Ishiguro, Kazuo 1954- ...... CLC 27, 56, 59
See also BEST 90:2; CA 120; MTCW

Ishikawa Takuboku
1886(?)-1912 .... TCLC 15
See also CA 113

Iskander, Fazil 1929- .... CLC 47
See also CA 102

Ivan IV 1530-1584 .... LC 17

Ivanov, Vyacheslav Ivanovich
1866-1949 .... TCLC 33
See also CA 122

Ivask, Ivar Vidrik 1927- .... CLC 14
See also CA 37-40R; CANR 24

Jackson, Daniel
See Wingrove, David (John)

Jackson, Jesse 1908-1983 .... CLC 12
See also BW; CA 25-28R; 109; CANR 27;
CLR 28; MAICYA; SATA 2, 29, 48

Jackson, Laura (Riding) 1901-1991 .. CLC 7
See also Riding, Laura
See also CA 65-68; 135; CANR 28; DLB 48

Jackson, Sam
See Trumbo, Dalton

Jackson, Sara
See Wingrove, David (John)

Jackson, Shirley
1919-1965 .... CLC 11, 60; SSC 9
See also AAYA 9; CA 1-4R; 25-28R;
CANR 4; CDALB 1941-1968; DLB 6;
SATA 2; WLC

Jacob, (Cyprien-)Max 1876-1944 ... TCLC 6
See also CA 104

Jacobs, Jim 1942-................. CLC 12
See also CA 97-100

Jacobs, W(illiam) W(ymark)
1863-1943 .... TCLC 22
See also CA 121

Jacobsen, Jens Peter 1847-1885 .. NCLC 34

Jacobsen, Josephine 1908-......... CLC 48
See also CA 33-36R; CANR 23

Jacobson, Dan 1929- .... CLC 4, 14
See also CA 1-4R; CANR 2, 25; DLB 14;
MTCW

Jacqueline
See Carpentier (y Valmont), Alejo

Jagger, Mick 1944-............... CLC 17

Jakes, John (William) 1932- .... CLC 29
See also BEST 89:4; CA 57-60; CANR 10;
DLBY 83; MTCW; SATA 62

James, Andrew
See Kirkup, James

James, C(yril) L(ionel) R(obert)
 1901-1989 .... CLC 33
See also BW; CA 117; 125; 128; MTCW

James, Daniel (Lewis) 1911-1988
See Santiago, Danny
See also CA 125

James, Dynely
See Mayne, William (James Carter)

James, Henry
 1843-1916 ..... TCLC 2, 11, 24, 40, 47;
                                   SSC 8
See also CA 104; 132; CDALB 1865-1917;
DLB 12, 71, 74; MTCW; WLC

James, Montague (Rhodes)
 1862-1936 .... TCLC 6
See also CA 104

James, P. D. .... CLC 18, 46
See also White, Phyllis Dorothy James
See also BEST 90:2; CDBLB 1960 to
Present; DLB 87

James, Philip
See Moorcock, Michael (John)

James, William 1842-1910..... TCLC 15, 32
See also CA 109

James I 1394-1437 .... LC 20

Jami, Nur al-Din 'Abd al-Rahman
 1414-1492 .... LC 9

Jandl, Ernst 1925- .... CLC 34

Janowitz, Tama 1957- .... CLC 43
See also CA 106

Jarrell, Randall
 1914-1965 .... CLC 1, 2, 6, 9, 13, 49
See also CA 5-8R; 25-28R; CABS 2;
CANR 6, 34; CDALB 1941-1968; CLR 6;
DLB 48, 52; MAICYA; MTCW; SATA 7

Jarry, Alfred 1873-1907........ TCLC 2, 14
See also CA 104

Jarvis, E. K.
See Bloch, Robert (Albert); Ellison, Harlan;
Silverberg, Robert

Jeake, Samuel Jr.
See Aiken, Conrad (Potter)

Jean Paul 1763-1825 .... NCLC 7

Jeffers, (John) Robinson
 1887-1962 .... CLC 2, 3, 11, 15, 54
See also CA 85-88; CANR 35;
CDALB 1917-1929; DLB 45; MTCW;
WLC

Jefferson, Janet
See Mencken, H(enry) L(ouis)

Jefferson, Thomas 1743-1826 .... NCLC 11
See also CDALB 1640-1865; DLB 31

Jeffrey, Francis 1773-1850....... NCLC 33
See also DLB 107

Jelakowitch, Ivan
See Heijermans, Herman

Jellicoe, (Patricia) Ann 1927- ...... CLC 27
See also CA 85-88; DLB 13

Jen, Gish .... CLC 70
See also Jen, Lillian

Jen, Lillian 1956(?)-
See Jen, Gish
See also CA 135

Jenkins, (John) Robin 1912- .... CLC 52
See also CA 1-4R; CANR 1; DLB 14

Jennings, Elizabeth (Joan)
 1926- .... CLC 5, 14
See also CA 61-64; CAAS 5; CANR 8, 39;
DLB 27; MTCW; SATA 66

Jennings, Waylon 1937-........... CLC 21

Jensen, Johannes V. 1873-1950.... TCLC 41

Jensen, Laura (Linnea) 1948- ...... CLC 37
See also CA 103

Jerome, Jerome K(lapka)
 1859-1927 .... TCLC 23
See also CA 119; DLB 10, 34

Jerrold, Douglas William
 1803-1857 .... NCLC 2

Jewett, (Theodora) Sarah Orne
 1849-1909 .... TCLC 1, 22; SSC 6
See also CA 108; 127; DLB 12, 74;
SATA 15

Jewsbury, Geraldine (Endsor)
 1812-1880 .... NCLC 22
See also DLB 21

Jhabvala, Ruth Prawer
 1927- .... CLC 4, 8, 29
See also CA 1-4R; CANR 2, 29; MTCW

Jiles, Paulette 1943-........... CLC 13, 58
See also CA 101

Jimenez (Mantecon), Juan Ramon
 1881-1958 .... TCLC 4
See also CA 104; 131; HW; MTCW

Jimenez, Ramon
See Jimenez (Mantecon), Juan Ramon

Jimenez Mantecon, Juan
See Jimenez (Mantecon), Juan Ramon

Joel, Billy .... CLC 26
See also Joel, William Martin

Joel, William Martin 1949-
See Joel, Billy
See also CA 108

John of the Cross, St. 1542-1591 .... LC 18

Johnson, B(ryan) S(tanley William)
 1933-1973 .... CLC 6, 9
See also CA 9-12R; 53-56; CANR 9;
DLB 14, 40

Johnson, Charles (Richard)
 1948- .... CLC 7, 51, 65
See also BLC 2; BW; CA 116; DLB 33

Johnson, Denis 1949- .... CLC 52
See also CA 117; 121; DLB 120

Johnson, Diane (Lain)
 1934- .... CLC 5, 13, 48
See also CA 41-44R; CANR 17; DLBY 80;
MTCW

Johnson, Eyvind (Olof Verner)
 1900-1976 .... CLC 14
See also CA 73-76; 69-72; CANR 34

Johnson, J. R.
See James, C(yril) L(ionel) R(obert)

Johnson, James Weldon
 1871-1938 .... TCLC 3, 19
See also BLC 2; BW; CA 104; 125;
CDALB 1917-1929; DLB 51; MTCW;
SATA 31

Johnson, Joyce 1935-............. CLC 58
See also CA 125; 129

Johnson, Lionel (Pigot)
 1867-1902 .... TCLC 19
See also CA 117; DLB 19

Johnson, Mel
See Malzberg, Barry N(athaniel)

Johnson, Pamela Hansford
 1912-1981 .... CLC 1, 7, 27
See also CA 1-4R; 104; CANR 2, 28;
DLB 15; MTCW

Johnson, Samuel 1709-1784........ LC 15
See also CDBLB 1660-1789; DLB 39, 95,
104; WLC

Johnson, Uwe
 1934-1984 .... CLC 5, 10, 15, 40
See also CA 1-4R; 112; CANR 1, 39;
DLB 75; MTCW

Johnston, George (Benson) 1913-... CLC 51
See also CA 1-4R; CANR 5, 20; DLB 88

Johnston, Jennifer 1930-........... CLC 7
See also CA 85-88; DLB 14

Jolley, (Monica) Elizabeth 1923- ... CLC 46
See also CA 127; CAAS 13

Jones, Arthur Llewellyn 1863-1947
See Machen, Arthur
See also CA 104

Jones, D(ouglas) G(ordon) 1929-.... CLC 10
See also CA 29-32R; CANR 13; DLB 53

Jones, David (Michael)
 1895-1974 .... CLC 2, 4, 7, 13, 42
See also CA 9-12R; 53-56; CANR 28;
CDBLB 1945-1960; DLB 20, 100; MTCW

Jones, David Robert 1947-
See Bowie, David
See also CA 103

Jones, Diana Wynne 1934- .... CLC 26
See also CA 49-52; CANR 4, 26; CLR 23;
MAICYA; SAAS 7; SATA 9, 70

Jones, Gayl 1949-................ CLC 6, 9
See also BLC 2; BW; CA 77-80; CANR 27;
DLB 33; MTCW

Jones, James 1921-1977.... CLC 1, 3, 10, 39
See also AITN 1, 2; CA 1-4R; 69-72;
CANR 6; DLB 2; MTCW

Jones, John J.
See Lovecraft, H(oward) P(hillips)

Jones, LeRoi .... CLC 1, 2, 3, 5, 10, 14
See also Baraka, Amiri

Jones, Louis B. .... CLC 65

Jones, Madison (Percy Jr.) 1925-.... CLC 4
See also CA 13-16R; CAAS 11; CANR 7

Jones, Mervyn 1922- .... CLC 10, 52
See also CA 45-48; CAAS 5; CANR 1;
MTCW

Jones, Mick 1956(?)- .... CLC 30
See also The Clash

Jones, Nettie (Pearl) 1941- .... CLC 34
See also CA 137

Jones, Preston 1936-1979 .... CLC 10
See also CA 73-76; 89-92; DLB 7

Jones, Robert F(rancis) 1934- .... CLC 7
See also CA 49-52; CANR 2

Jones, Rod 1953- .... CLC 50
See also CA 128

Jones, Terence Graham Parry
1942- .... CLC 21
See also Jones, Terry; Monty Python
See also CA 112; 116; CANR 35; SATA 51

Jones, Terry
See Jones, Terence Graham Parry
See also SATA 67

Jong, Erica 1942- .... CLC 4, 6, 8, 18
See also AITN 1; BEST 90:2; CA 73-76;
CANR 26; DLB 2, 5, 28; MTCW

Jonson, Ben(jamin) 1572(?)-1637...... LC 6
See also CDBLB Before 1660; DLB 62, 121;
WLC

Jordan, June 1936-.......... CLC 5, 11, 23
See also AAYA 2; BW; CA 33-36R;
CANR 25; CLR 10; DLB 38; MAICYA;
MTCW; SATA 4

Jordan, Pat(rick M.) 1941- .... CLC 37
See also CA 33-36R

Jorgensen, Ivar
See Ellison, Harlan

Jorgenson, Ivar
See Silverberg, Robert

Josipovici, Gabriel 1940-........ CLC 6, 43
See also CA 37-40R; CAAS 8; DLB 14

Joubert, Joseph 1754-1824 .... NCLC 9

Jouve, Pierre Jean 1887-1976...... CLC 47
See also CA 65-68

Joyce, James (Augustine Aloysius)
1882-1941 .... TCLC 3, 8, 16, 35; SSC 3
See also CA 104; 126; CDBLB 1914-1945;
DLB 10, 19, 36; MTCW; WLC

Jozsef, Attila 1905-1937.......... TCLC 22
See also CA 116

Juana Ines de la Cruz 1651(?)-1695 ... LC 5

Judd, Cyril
See Kornbluth, C(yril) M.; Pohl, Frederik

Julian of Norwich 1342(?)-1416(?) .... LC 6

Just, Ward (Swift) 1935- .... CLC 4, 27
See also CA 25-28R; CANR 32

Justice, Donald (Rodney) 1925- ... CLC 6, 19
See also CA 5-8R; CANR 26; DLBY 83

Juvenal c. 55-c. 127 .... CMLC 8

Juvenis
See Bourne, Randolph S(illiman)

Kacew, Romain 1914-1980
See Gary, Romain
See also CA 108; 102

Kadare, Ismail 1936- .... CLC 52

Kadohata, Cynthia. .... CLC 59

Kafka, Franz
1883-1924 ...... TCLC 2, 6, 13, 29, 47;
SSC 5
See also CA 105; 126; DLB 81; MTCW;
WLC

Kahn, Roger 1927- .... CLC 30
See also CA 25-28R; SATA 37

Kain, Saul
See Sassoon, Siegfried (Lorraine)

Kaiser, Georg 1878-1945 .... TCLC 9
See also CA 106

Kaletski, Alexander 1946- .... CLC 39
See also CA 118

Kalidasa fl. c. 400- .... CMLC 9

Kallman, Chester (Simon)
1921-1975 .... CLC 2
See also CA 45-48; 53-56; CANR 3

Kaminsky, Melvin 1926-
See Brooks, Mel
See also CA 65-68; CANR 16

Kaminsky, Stuart M(elvin) 1934- ... CLC 59
See also CA 73-76; CANR 29

Kane, Paul
See Simon, Paul

Kane, Wilson
See Bloch, Robert (Albert)

Kanin, Garson 1912-.............. CLC 22
See also AITN 1; CA 5-8R; CANR 7;
DLB 7

Kaniuk, Yoram 1930-............. CLC 19
See also CA 134

Kant, Immanuel 1724-1804 ...... NCLC 27
See also DLB 94

Kantor, MacKinlay 1904-1977 ...... CLC 7
See also CA 61-64; 73-76; DLB 9, 102

Kaplan, David Michael 1946- ...... CLC 50

Kaplan, James 1951- .... CLC 59
See also CA 135

Karageorge, Michael
See Anderson, Poul (William)

Karamzin, Nikolai Mikhailovich
1766-1826 .... NCLC 3

Karapanou, Margarita 1946-....... CLC 13
See also CA 101

Karinthy, Frigyes 1887-1938...... TCLC 47

Karl, Frederick R(obert) 1927- ..... CLC 34
See also CA 5-8R; CANR 3

Kastel, Warren
See Silverberg, Robert

Kataev, Evgeny Petrovich 1903-1942
See Petrov, Evgeny
See also CA 120

Kataphusin
See Ruskin, John

Katz, Steve 1935-................ CLC 47
See also CA 25-28R; CAAS 14; CANR 12;
DLBY 83

Kauffman, Janet 1945-............ CLC 42
See also CA 117; DLBY 86

Kaufman, Bob (Garnell)
1925-1986 .... CLC 49
See also BW; CA 41-44R; 118; CANR 22;
DLB 16, 41

Kaufman, George S. 1889-1961..... CLC 38
See also CA 108; 93-96; DLB 7

Kaufman, Sue .... CLC 3, 8
See also Barondess, Sue K(aufman)

Kavafis, Konstantinos Petrou 1863-1933
See Cavafy, C(onstantine) P(eter)
See also CA 104

Kavan, Anna 1901-1968......... CLC 5, 13
See also CA 5-8R; CANR 6; MTCW

Kavanagh, Dan
See Barnes, Julian

Kavanagh, Patrick (Joseph)
1904-1967 .... CLC 22
See also CA 123; 25-28R; DLB 15, 20;
MTCW

Kawabata, Yasunari
1899-1972 .... CLC 2, 5, 9, 18
See also CA 93-96; 33-36R

Kaye, M(ary) M(argaret) 1909-..... CLC 28
See also CA 89-92; CANR 24; MTCW;
SATA 62

Kaye, Mollie
See Kaye, M(ary) M(argaret)

Kaye-Smith, Sheila 1887-1956..... TCLC 20
See also CA 118; DLB 36

Kaymor, Patrice Maguilene
See Senghor, Leopold Sedar

Kazan, Elia 1909-........... CLC 6, 16, 63
See also CA 21-24R; CANR 32

Kazantzakis, Nikos
1883(?)-1957 .... TCLC 2, 5, 33
See also CA 105; 132; MTCW

Kazin, Alfred 1915- .... CLC 34, 38
See also CA 1-4R; CAAS 7; CANR 1;
DLB 67

Keane, Mary Nesta (Skrine) 1904-
See Keane, Molly
See also CA 108; 114

Keane, Molly..................... CLC 31
See also Keane, Mary Nesta (Skrine)

Keates, Jonathan 19(?)- .... CLC 34

Keaton, Buster 1895-1966 .... CLC 20

Keats, John 1795-1821...... NCLC 8; PC 1
See also CDBLB 1789-1832; DLB 96, 110;
WLC

Keene, Donald 1922- .... CLC 34
See also CA 1-4R; CANR 5

Keillor, Garrison.................. CLC 40
See also Keillor, Gary (Edward)
See also AAYA 2; BEST 89:3; DLBY 87;
SATA 58

Keillor, Gary (Edward) 1942-
See Keillor, Garrison
See also CA 111; 117; CANR 36; MTCW

Keith, Michael
See Hubbard, L(afayette) Ron(ald)

Kell, Joseph
See Wilson, John (Anthony) Burgess

Keller, Gottfried 1819-1890....... NCLC 2

Kellerman, Jonathan 1949- .... CLC 44
See also BEST 90:1; CA 106; CANR 29

Kelley, William Melvin 1937-...... CLC 22
See also BW; CA 77-80; CANR 27; DLB 33

Kellogg, Marjorie 1922- .... CLC 2
 See also CA 81-84

Kellow, Kathleen
 See Hibbert, Eleanor Burford

Kelly, M(ilton) T(erry) 1947- .... CLC 55
 See also CA 97-100; CANR 19

Kelman, James 1946- .... CLC 58

Kemal, Yashar 1923- .... CLC 14, 29
 See also CA 89-92

Kemble, Fanny 1809-1893 .... NCLC 18
 See also DLB 32

Kemelman, Harry 1908- .... CLC 2
 See also AITN 1; CA 9-12R; CANR 6;
 DLB 28

Kempe, Margery 1373(?)-1440(?) ..... LC 6

Kempis, Thomas a 1380-1471 .... LC 11

Kendall, Henry 1839-1882 .... NCLC 12

Keneally, Thomas (Michael)
 1935- ...... CLC 5, 8, 10, 14, 19, 27, 43
 See also CA 85-88; CANR 10; MTCW

Kennedy, Adrienne (Lita) 1931- .... CLC 66
 See also BLC 2; BW; CA 103; CABS 3;
 CANR 26; DLB 38

Kennedy, John Pendleton
 1795-1870 .... NCLC 2
 See also DLB 3

Kennedy, Joseph Charles 1929- ...... CLC 8
 See also Kennedy, X. J.
 See also CA 1-4R; CANR 4, 30; SATA 14

Kennedy, William 1928- ... CLC 6, 28, 34, 53
 See also AAYA 1; CA 85-88; CANR 14,
 31; DLBY 85; MTCW; SATA 57

Kennedy, X. J. .... CLC 42
 See also Kennedy, Joseph Charles
 See also CAAS 9; CLR 27; DLB 5

Kent, Kelvin
 See Kuttner, Henry

Kenton, Maxwell
 See Southern, Terry

Kenyon, Robert O.
 See Kuttner, Henry

Kerouac, Jack ..... CLC 1, 2, 3, 5, 14, 29, 61
 See also Kerouac, Jean-Louis Lebris de
 See also CDALB 1941-1968; DLB 2, 16;
 DLBD 3

Kerouac, Jean-Louis Lebris de 1922-1969
 See Kerouac, Jack
 See also AITN 1; CA 5-8R; 25-28R;
 CANR 26; MTCW; WLC

Kerr, Jean 1923- .... CLC 22
 See also CA 5-8R; CANR 7

Kerr, M. E. .... CLC 12, 35
 See also Meaker, Marijane (Agnes)
 See also AAYA 2; SAAS 1

Kerr, Robert .... CLC 55

Kerrigan, (Thomas) Anthony
 1918- .... CLC 4, 6
 See also CA 49-52; CAAS 11; CANR 4

Kerry, Lois
 See Duncan, Lois

Kesey, Ken (Elton)
 1935- .... CLC 1, 3, 6, 11, 46, 64
 See also CA 1-4R; CANR 22, 38;
 CDALB 1968-1988; DLB 2, 16; MTCW;
 SATA 66; WLC

Kesselring, Joseph (Otto)
 1902-1967 .... CLC 45

Kessler, Jascha (Frederick) 1929- .... CLC 4
 See also CA 17-20R; CANR 8

Kettelkamp, Larry (Dale) 1933- .... CLC 12
 See also CA 29-32R; CANR 16; SAAS 3;
 SATA 2

Kherdian, David 1931- .... CLC 6, 9
 See also CA 21-24R; CAAS 2; CANR 39;
 CLR 24; MAICYA; SATA 16

Khlebnikov, Velimir .... TCLC 20
 See also Khlebnikov, Viktor Vladimirovich

Khlebnikov, Viktor Vladimirovich 1885-1922
 See Khlebnikov, Velimir
 See also CA 117

Khodasevich, Vladislav (Felitsianovich)
 1886-1939 .... TCLC 15
 See also CA 115

Kielland, Alexander Lange
 1849-1906 .... TCLC 5
 See also CA 104

Kiely, Benedict 1919- .... CLC 23, 43
 See also CA 1-4R; CANR 2; DLB 15

Kienzle, William X(avier) 1928- .... CLC 25
 See also CA 93-96; CAAS 1; CANR 9, 31;
 MTCW

Kierkegaard, Soeren 1813-1855 ... NCLC 34

Kierkegaard, Soren 1813-1855 .... NCLC 34

Killens, John Oliver 1916-1987 ..... CLC 10
 See also BW; CA 77-80; 123; CAAS 2;
 CANR 26; DLB 33

Killigrew, Anne 1660-1685 .... LC 4

Kim
 See Simenon, Georges (Jacques Christian)

Kincaid, Jamaica 1949- .... CLC 43, 68
 See also BLC 2; BW; CA 125

King, Francis (Henry) 1923- ..... CLC 8, 53
 See also CA 1-4R; CANR 1, 33; DLB 15;
 MTCW

King, Stephen (Edwin)
 1947- .... CLC 12, 26, 37, 61
 See also AAYA 1; BEST 90:1; CA 61-64;
 CANR 1, 30; DLBY 80; MTCW;
 SATA 9, 55

King, Steve
 See King, Stephen (Edwin)

Kingman, Lee .... CLC 17
 See also Natti, (Mary) Lee
 See also SAAS 3; SATA 1, 67

Kingsley, Charles 1819-1875 ..... NCLC 35
 See also DLB 21, 32; YABC 2

Kingsley, Sidney 1906- .... CLC 44
 See also CA 85-88; DLB 7

Kingsolver, Barbara 1955- .... CLC 55
 See also CA 129; 134

Kingston, Maxine (Ting Ting) Hong
 1940- .... CLC 12, 19, 58
 See also AAYA 8; CA 69-72; CANR 13,
 38; DLBY 80; MTCW; SATA 53

Kinnell, Galway
 1927- .... CLC 1, 2, 3, 5, 13, 29
 See also CA 9-12R; CANR 10, 34; DLB 5;
 DLBY 87; MTCW

Kinsella, Thomas 1928- .... CLC 4, 19
 See also CA 17-20R; CANR 15; DLB 27;
 MTCW

Kinsella, W(illiam) P(atrick)
 1935- .... CLC 27, 43
 See also AAYA 7; CA 97-100; CAAS 7;
 CANR 21, 35; MTCW

Kipling, (Joseph) Rudyard
 1865-1936 .... TCLC 8, 17; PC 3; SSC 5
 See also CA 105; 120; CANR 33;
 CDBLB 1890-1914; DLB 19, 34;
 MAICYA; MTCW; WLC; YABC 2

Kirkup, James 1918- .... CLC 1
 See also CA 1-4R; CAAS 4; CANR 2;
 DLB 27; SATA 12

Kirkwood, James 1930(?)-1989 ...... CLC 9
 See also AITN 2; CA 1-4R; 128; CANR 6

Kis, Danilo 1935-1989 .... CLC 57
 See also CA 109; 118; 129; MTCW

Kivi, Aleksis 1834-1872 .... NCLC 30

Kizer, Carolyn (Ashley) 1925- ... CLC 15, 39
 See also CA 65-68; CAAS 5; CANR 24;
 DLB 5

Klabund 1890-1928 .... TCLC 44
 See also DLB 66

Klappert, Peter 1942- .... CLC 57
 See also CA 33-36R; DLB 5

Klein, A(braham) M(oses)
 1909-1972 .... CLC 19
 See also CA 101; 37-40R; DLB 68

Klein, Norma 1938-1989 .... CLC 30
 See also AAYA 2; CA 41-44R; 128;
 CANR 15, 37; CLR 2, 19; MAICYA;
 SAAS 1; SATA 7, 57

Klein, T(heodore) E(ibon) D(onald)
 1947- .... CLC 34
 See also CA 119

Kleist, Heinrich von 1777-1811 .... NCLC 2
 See also DLB 90

Klima, Ivan 1931- .... CLC 56
 See also CA 25-28R; CANR 17

Klimentov, Andrei Platonovich 1899-1951
 See Platonov, Andrei
 See also CA 108

Klinger, Friedrich Maximilian von
 1752-1831 .... NCLC 1
 See also DLB 94

Klopstock, Friedrich Gottlieb
 1724-1803 .... NCLC 11
 See also DLB 97

Knebel, Fletcher 1911- .... CLC 14
 See also AITN 1; CA 1-4R; CAAS 3;
 CANR 1, 36; SATA 36

Knickerbocker, Diedrich
 See Irving, Washington

Knight, Etheridge 1931-1991 .... CLC 40
 See also BLC 2; BW; CA 21-24R; 133;
 CANR 23; DLB 41

Knight, Sarah Kemble 1666-1727 ..... LC 7
 See also DLB 24

Knowles, John 1926- ...... **CLC 1, 4, 10, 26**
See also CA 17-20R; CDALB 1968-1988;
DLB 6; MTCW; SATA 8

Knox, Calvin M.
See Silverberg, Robert

Knye, Cassandra
See Disch, Thomas M(ichael)

Koch, C(hristopher) J(ohn) 1932- ... **CLC 42**
See also CA 127

Koch, Christopher
See Koch, C(hristopher) J(ohn)

Koch, Kenneth 1925- .... **CLC 5, 8, 44**
See also CA 1-4R; CANR 6, 36; DLB 5;
SATA 65

Kochanowski, Jan 1530-1584....... **LC 10**

Kock, Charles Paul de
1794-1871 .... **NCLC 16**

Koda Shigeyuki 1867-1947
See Rohan, Koda
See also CA 121

Koestler, Arthur
1905-1983 .... **CLC 1, 3, 6, 8, 15, 33**
See also CA 1-4R; 109; CANR 1, 33;
CDBLB 1945-1960; DLBY 83; MTCW

Kohout, Pavel 1928-.............. **CLC 13**
See also CA 45-48; CANR 3

Koizumi, Yakumo
See Hearn, (Patricio) Lafcadio (Tessima Carlos)

Kolmar, Gertrud 1894-1943....... **TCLC 40**

Konrad, George
See Konrad, Gyoergy

Konrad, Gyoergy 1933- .... **CLC 4, 10**
See also CA 85-88

Konwicki, Tadeusz 1926-..... **CLC 8, 28, 54**
See also CA 101; CAAS 9; CANR 39;
MTCW

Kopit, Arthur (Lee) 1937- .... **CLC 1, 18, 33**
See also AITN 1; CA 81-84; CABS 3;
DLB 7; MTCW

Kops, Bernard 1926-............... **CLC 4**
See also CA 5-8R; DLB 13

Kornbluth, C(yril) M. 1923-1958.... **TCLC 8**
See also CA 105; DLB 8

Korolenko, V. G.
See Korolenko, Vladimir Galaktionovich

Korolenko, Vladimir
See Korolenko, Vladimir Galaktionovich

Korolenko, Vladimir G.
See Korolenko, Vladimir Galaktionovich

Korolenko, Vladimir Galaktionovich
1853-1921 .... **TCLC 22**
See also CA 121

Kosinski, Jerzy (Nikodem)
1933-1991 ... **CLC 1, 2, 3, 6, 10, 15, 53, 70**
See also CA 17-20R; 134; CANR 9; DLB 2;
DLBY 82; MTCW

Kostelanetz, Richard (Cory) 1940-.. **CLC 28**
See also CA 13-16R; CAAS 8; CANR 38

Kostrowitzki, Wilhelm Apollinaris de
1880-1918
See Apollinaire, Guillaume
See also CA 104

Kotlowitz, Robert 1924-............ **CLC 4**
See also CA 33-36R; CANR 36

Kotzebue, August (Friedrich Ferdinand) von
1761-1819 .... **NCLC 25**
See also DLB 94

Kotzwinkle, William 1938- ... **CLC 5, 14, 35**
See also CA 45-48; CANR 3; CLR 6;
MAICYA; SATA 24, 70

Kozol, Jonathan 1936-............. **CLC 17**
See also CA 61-64; CANR 16

Kozoll, Michael 1940(?)- .... **CLC 35**

Kramer, Kathryn 19(?)- .... **CLC 34**

Kramer, Larry 1935- .... **CLC 42**
See also CA 124; 126

Krasicki, Ignacy 1735-1801....... **NCLC 8**

Krasinski, Zygmunt 1812-1859 .... **NCLC 4**

Kraus, Karl 1874-1936........... **TCLC 5**
See also CA 104; DLB 118

Kreve (Mickevicius), Vincas
1882-1954 .... **TCLC 27**

Kristofferson, Kris 1936- .... **CLC 26**
See also CA 104

Krizanc, John 1956-............... **CLC 57**

Krleza, Miroslav 1893-1981......... **CLC 8**
See also CA 97-100; 105

Kroetsch, Robert 1927- .... **CLC 5, 23, 57**
See also CA 17-20R; CANR 8, 38; DLB 53;
MTCW

Kroetz, Franz
See Kroetz, Franz Xaver

Kroetz, Franz Xaver 1946- .... **CLC 41**
See also CA 130

Kropotkin, Peter (Alekseevich)
1842-1921 .... **TCLC 36**
See also CA 119

Krotkov, Yuri 1917-.............. **CLC 19**
See also CA 102

Krumb
See Crumb, R(obert)

Krumgold, Joseph (Quincy)
1908-1980 .... **CLC 12**
See also CA 9-12R; 101; CANR 7;
MAICYA; SATA 1, 23, 48

Krumwitz
See Crumb, R(obert)

Krutch, Joseph Wood 1893-1970.... **CLC 24**
See also CA 1-4R; 25-28R; CANR 4;
DLB 63

Krutzch, Gus
See Eliot, T(homas) S(tearns)

Krylov, Ivan Andreevich
1768(?)-1844 .... **NCLC 1**

Kubin, Alfred 1877-1959 .... **TCLC 23**
See also CA 112; DLB 81

Kubrick, Stanley 1928-............. **CLC 16**
See also CA 81-84; CANR 33; DLB 26

Kumin, Maxine (Winokur)
1925- .... **CLC 5, 13, 28**
See also AITN 2; CA 1-4R; CAAS 8;
CANR 1, 21; DLB 5; MTCW; SATA 12

Kundera, Milan
1929- .... **CLC 4, 9, 19, 32, 68**
See also AAYA 2; CA 85-88; CANR 19;
MTCW

Kunitz, Stanley (Jasspon)
1905- .... **CLC 6, 11, 14**
See also CA 41-44R; CANR 26; DLB 48;
MTCW

Kunze, Reiner 1933-.............. **CLC 10**
See also CA 93-96; DLB 75

Kuprin, Aleksandr Ivanovich
1870-1938 .... **TCLC 5**
See also CA 104

Kureishi, Hanif 1954-............. **CLC 64**

Kurosawa, Akira 1910-............ **CLC 16**
See also CA 101

Kuttner, Henry 1915-1958........ **TCLC 10**
See also CA 107; DLB 8

Kuzma, Greg 1944-................ **CLC 7**
See also CA 33-36R

Kuzmin, Mikhail 1872(?)-1936 .... **TCLC 40**

Kyd, Thomas 1558-1594............. **DC 3**
See also DLB 62

Kyprianos, Iossif
See Samarakis, Antonis

La Bruyere, Jean de 1645-1696...... **LC 17**

Laclos, Pierre Ambroise Francois Choderlos de 1741-1803 .... **NCLC 4**

La Colere, Francois
See Aragon, Louis

Lacolere, Francois
See Aragon, Louis

La Deshabilleuse
See Simenon, Georges (Jacques Christian)

Lady Gregory
See Gregory, Isabella Augusta (Persse)

Lady of Quality, A
See Bagnold, Enid

La Fayette, Marie (Madelaine Pioche de la Vergne Comtes 1634-1693....... **LC 2**

Lafayette, Rene
See Hubbard, L(afayette) Ron(ald)

Laforgue, Jules 1860-1887........ **NCLC 5**

Lagerkvist, Paer (Fabian)
1891-1974 .... **CLC 7, 10, 13, 54**
See also CA 85-88; 49-52; MTCW

Lagerkvist, Par
See Lagerkvist, Paer (Fabian)

Lagerloef, Selma (Ottiliana Lovisa)
1858-1940 .... **TCLC 4, 36**
See also Lagerlof, Selma (Ottiliana Lovisa)
See also CA 108; CLR 7; SATA 15

Lagerlof, Selma (Ottiliana Lovisa)
See Lagerloef, Selma (Ottiliana Lovisa)
See also CLR 7; SATA 15

La Guma, (Justin) Alex(ander)
1925-1985 .... **CLC 19**
See also BW; CA 49-52; 118; CANR 25;
DLB 117; MTCW

Laidlaw, A. K.
See Grieve, C(hristopher) M(urray)

Lainez, Manuel Mujica
See Mujica Lainez, Manuel
See also HW

Lamartine, Alphonse (Marie Louis Prat) de
1790-1869 .... NCLC 11

Lamb, Charles 1775-1834........ NCLC 10
See also CDBLB 1789-1832; DLB 93, 107; SATA 17; WLC

Lamb, Lady Caroline 1785-1828.. NCLC 38
See also DLB 116

Lamming, George (William)
1927- .... CLC 2, 4, 66
See also BLC 2; BW; CA 85-88; CANR 26; MTCW

L'Amour, Louis (Dearborn)
1908-1988 .... CLC 25, 55
See also AITN 2; BEST 89:2; CA 1-4R; 125; CANR 3, 25; DLBY 80; MTCW

Lampedusa, Giuseppe (Tomasi) di ... TCLC 13
See also Tomasi di Lampedusa, Giuseppe

Lampman, Archibald 1861-1899 .. NCLC 25
See also DLB 92

Lancaster, Bruce 1896-1963........ CLC 36
See also CA 9-10; CAP 1; SATA 9

Landau, Mark Alexandrovich
See Aldanov, Mark (Alexandrovich)

Landau-Aldanov, Mark Alexandrovich
See Aldanov, Mark (Alexandrovich)

Landis, John 1950-................ CLC 26
See also CA 112; 122

Landolfi, Tommaso 1908-1979... CLC 11, 49
See also CA 127; 117

Landon, Letitia Elizabeth
1802-1838 .... NCLC 15
See also DLB 96

Landor, Walter Savage
1775-1864 .... NCLC 14
See also DLB 93, 107

Landwirth, Heinz 1927-
See Lind, Jakov
See also CA 9-12R; CANR 7

Lane, Patrick 1939-.............. CLC 25
See also CA 97-100; DLB 53

Lang, Andrew 1844-1912........ TCLC 16
See also CA 114; 137; DLB 98; MAICYA; SATA 16

Lang, Fritz 1890-1976 .... CLC 20
See also CA 77-80; 69-72; CANR 30

Lange, John
See Crichton, (John) Michael

Langer, Elinor 1939- .... CLC 34
See also CA 121

Langland, William 1330(?)-1400(?) ... LC 19

Langstaff, Launcelot
See Irving, Washington

Lanier, Sidney 1842-1881 .... NCLC 6
See also DLB 64; MAICYA; SATA 18

Lanyer, Aemilia 1569-1645 .... LC 10

Lao Tzu .... CMLC 7

Lapine, James (Elliot) 1949- .... CLC 39
See also CA 123; 130

Larbaud, Valery (Nicolas)
1881-1957 .... TCLC 9
See also CA 106

Lardner, Ring
See Lardner, Ring(gold) W(ilmer)

Lardner, Ring W. Jr.
See Lardner, Ring(gold) W(ilmer)

Lardner, Ring(gold) W(ilmer)
1885-1933 .... TCLC 2, 14
See also CA 104; 131; CDALB 1917-1929; DLB 11, 25, 86; MTCW

Laredo, Betty
See Codrescu, Andrei

Larkin, Maia
See Wojciechowska, Maia (Teresa)

Larkin, Philip (Arthur)
1922-1985 ... CLC 3, 5, 8, 9, 13, 18, 33, 39, 64
See also CA 5-8R; 117; CANR 24; CDBLB 1960 to Present; DLB 27; MTCW

Larra (y Sanchez de Castro), Mariano Jose de
1809-1837 .... NCLC 17

Larsen, Eric 1941- .... CLC 55
See also CA 132

Larsen, Nella 1891-1964 .... CLC 37
See also BLC 2; BW; CA 125; DLB 51

Larson, Charles R(aymond) 1938-... CLC 31
See also CA 53-56; CANR 4

Latham, Jean Lee 1902-........... CLC 12
See also AITN 1; CA 5-8R; CANR 7; MAICYA; SATA 2, 68

Latham, Mavis
See Clark, Mavis Thorpe

Lathen, Emma................... CLC 2
See also Hennissart, Martha; Latsis, Mary J(ane)

Lathrop, Francis
See Leiber, Fritz (Reuter Jr.)

Latsis, Mary J(ane)
See Lathen, Emma
See also CA 85-88

Lattimore, Richmond (Alexander)
1906-1984 .... CLC 3
See also CA 1-4R; 112; CANR 1

Laughlin, James 1914-........... CLC 49
See also CA 21-24R; CANR 9; DLB 48

Laurence, (Jean) Margaret (Wemyss)
1926-1987 .. CLC 3, 6, 13, 50, 62; SSC 7
See also CA 5-8R; 121; CANR 33; DLB 53; MTCW; SATA 50

Laurent, Antoine 1952- .... CLC 50

Lauscher, Hermann
See Hesse, Hermann

Lautreamont, Comte de
1846-1870 .... NCLC 12

Laverty, Donald
See Blish, James (Benjamin)

Lavin, Mary 1912- ...... CLC 4, 18; SSC 4
See also CA 9-12R; CANR 33; DLB 15; MTCW

Lavond, Paul Dennis
See Kornbluth, C(yril) M.; Pohl, Frederik

Lawler, Raymond Evenor 1922- .... CLC 58
See also CA 103

Lawrence, D(avid) H(erbert Richards)
1885-1930 ...... TCLC 2, 9, 16, 33, 48; SSC 4
See also CA 104; 121; CDBLB 1914-1945; DLB 10, 19, 36, 98; MTCW; WLC

Lawrence, T(homas) E(dward)
1888-1935 .... TCLC 18
See also Dale, Colin
See also CA 115

Lawrence Of Arabia
See Lawrence, T(homas) E(dward)

Lawson, Henry (Archibald Hertzberg)
1867-1922 .... TCLC 27
See also CA 120

Laxness, Halldor................ CLC 25
See also Gudjonsson, Halldor Kiljan

Layamon fl. c. 1200-............ CMLC 10

Laye, Camara 1928-1980 .... CLC 4, 38
See also BLC 2; BW; CA 85-88; 97-100; CANR 25; MTCW

Layton, Irving (Peter) 1912- ...... CLC 2, 15
See also CA 1-4R; CANR 2, 33; DLB 88; MTCW

Lazarus, Emma 1849-1887........ NCLC 8

Lazarus, Felix
See Cable, George Washington

Lea, Joan
See Neufeld, John (Arthur)

Leacock, Stephen (Butler)
1869-1944 .... TCLC 2
See also CA 104; DLB 92

Lear, Edward 1812-1888 .... NCLC 3
See also CLR 1; DLB 32; MAICYA; SATA 18

Lear, Norman (Milton) 1922- ...... CLC 12
See also CA 73-76

Leavis, F(rank) R(aymond)
1895-1978 .... CLC 24
See also CA 21-24R; 77-80; MTCW

Leavitt, David 1961-.............. CLC 34
See also CA 116; 122

Lebowitz, Fran(ces Ann)
1951(?)- .... CLC 11, 36
See also CA 81-84; CANR 14; MTCW

le Carre, John .... CLC 3, 5, 9, 15, 28
See also Cornwell, David (John Moore)
See also BEST 89:4; CDBLB 1960 to Present; DLB 87

Le Clezio, J(ean) M(arie) G(ustave)
1940- .... CLC 31
See also CA 116; 128; DLB 83

Leconte de Lisle, Charles-Marie-Rene
1818-1894 .... NCLC 29

Le Coq, Monsieur
See Simenon, Georges (Jacques Christian)

Leduc, Violette 1907-1972......... CLC 22
See also CA 13-14; 33-36R; CAP 1

Ledwidge, Francis 1887(?)-1917 ... TCLC 23
See also CA 123; DLB 20

Lee, Andrea 1953- .... CLC 36
See also BLC 2; BW; CA 125

Lee, Andrew
See Auchincloss, Louis (Stanton)

Lee, Don L. .... CLC 2
See also Madhubuti, Haki R.

Lee, George W(ashington)
1894-1976 .... CLC 52
See also BLC 2; BW; CA 125; DLB 51

Lee, (Nelle) Harper 1926- ...... CLC 12, 60
See also CA 13-16R; CDALB 1941-1968;
DLB 6; MTCW; SATA 11; WLC

Lee, Julian
See Latham, Jean Lee

Lee, Lawrence 1903- .... CLC 34
See also CA 25-28R

Lee, Manfred B(ennington)
1905-1971 .... CLC 11
See also Queen, Ellery
See also CA 1-4R; 29-32R; CANR 2

Lee, Stan 1922- .... CLC 17
See also AAYA 5; CA 108; 111

Lee, Tanith 1947- .... CLC 46
See also CA 37-40R; SATA 8

Lee, Vernon .... TCLC 5
See also Paget, Violet
See also DLB 57

Lee, William
See Burroughs, William S(eward)

Lee, Willy
See Burroughs, William S(eward)

Lee-Hamilton, Eugene (Jacob)
1845-1907 .... TCLC 22
See also CA 117

Leet, Judith 1935- .... CLC 11

Le Fanu, Joseph Sheridan
1814-1873 .... NCLC 9
See also DLB 21, 70

Leffland, Ella 1931- .... CLC 19
See also CA 29-32R; CANR 35; DLBY 84;
SATA 65

Leger, (Marie-Rene) Alexis Saint-Leger
1887-1975 .... CLC 11
See also Perse, St.-John
See also CA 13-16R; 61-64; MTCW

Leger, Saintleger
See Leger, (Marie-Rene) Alexis Saint-Leger

Le Guin, Ursula K(roeber)
1929- .... CLC 8, 13, 22, 45, 71
See also AAYA 9; AITN 1; CA 21-24R;
CANR 9, 32; CDALB 1968-1988; CLR 3,
28; DLB 8, 52; MAICYA; MTCW;
SATA 4, 52

Lehmann, Rosamond (Nina)
1901-1990 .... CLC 5
See also CA 77-80; 131; CANR 8; DLB 15

Leiber, Fritz (Reuter Jr.) 1910- .... CLC 25
See also CA 45-48; CANR 2; DLB 8;
MTCW; SATA 45

Leimbach, Martha 1963-
See Leimbach, Marti
See also CA 130

Leimbach, Marti .... CLC 65
See also Leimbach, Martha

Leino, Eino .... TCLC 24
See also Loennbohm, Armas Eino Leopold

Leiris, Michel (Julien) 1901-1990 ... CLC 61
See also CA 119; 128; 132

Leithauser, Brad 1953- .... CLC 27
See also CA 107; CANR 27; DLB 120

Lelchuk, Alan 1938- .... CLC 5
See also CA 45-48; CANR 1

Lem, Stanislaw 1921- .... CLC 8, 15, 40
See also CA 105; CAAS 1; CANR 32;
MTCW

Lemann, Nancy 1956- .... CLC 39
See also CA 118; 136

Lemonnier, (Antoine Louis) Camille
1844-1913 .... TCLC 22
See also CA 121

Lenau, Nikolaus 1802-1850 ...... NCLC 16

L'Engle, Madeleine (Camp Franklin)
1918- .... CLC 12
See also AAYA 1; AITN 2; CA 1-4R;
CANR 3, 21, 39; CLR 1, 14; DLB 52;
MAICYA; MTCW; SATA 1, 27

Lengyel, Jozsef 1896-1975.......... CLC 7
See also CA 85-88; 57-60

Lennon, John (Ono)
1940-1980 .... CLC 12, 35
See also CA 102

Lennox, Charlotte Ramsay
1729(?)-1804 .... NCLC 23
See also DLB 39

Lentricchia, Frank (Jr.) 1940- ..... CLC 34
See also CA 25-28R; CANR 19

Lenz, Siegfried 1926- .... CLC 27
See also CA 89-92; DLB 75

Leonard, Elmore (John Jr.)
1925- .... CLC 28, 34, 71
See also AITN 1; BEST 89:1, 90:4;
CA 81-84; CANR 12, 28; MTCW

Leonard, Hugh
See Byrne, John Keyes
See also DLB 13

**Leopardi, (Conte) Giacomo (Talegardo
Francesco di Sales Save**
1798-1837 .... NCLC 22

Le Reveler
See Artaud, Antonin

Lerman, Eleanor 1952- .... CLC 9
See also CA 85-88

Lerman, Rhoda 1936- .... CLC 56
See also CA 49-52

Lermontov, Mikhail Yuryevich
1814-1841 .... NCLC 5

Leroux, Gaston 1868-1927........ TCLC 25
See also CA 108; 136; SATA 65

Lesage, Alain-Rene 1668-1747....... LC 2

Leskov, Nikolai (Semyonovich)
1831-1895 .... NCLC 25

Lessing, Doris (May)
1919- .... CLC 1, 2, 3, 6, 10, 15, 22, 40;
SSC 6
See also CA 9-12R; CAAS 14; CANR 33;
CDBLB 1960 to Present; DLB 15;
DLBY 85; MTCW

Lessing, Gotthold Ephraim
1729-1781 .... LC 8
See also DLB 97

Lester, Richard 1932- .... CLC 20

Lever, Charles (James)
1806-1872 .... NCLC 23
See also DLB 21

Leverson, Ada 1865(?)-1936(?) .... TCLC 18
See also Elaine
See also CA 117

Levertov, Denise
1923- ...... CLC 1, 2, 3, 5, 8, 15, 28, 66
See also CA 1-4R; CANR 3, 29; DLB 5;
MTCW

Levi, Peter (Chad Tigar) 1931- ..... CLC 41
See also CA 5-8R; CANR 34; DLB 40

Levi, Primo 1919-1987......... CLC 37, 50
See also CA 13-16R; 122; CANR 12, 33;
MTCW

Levin, Ira 1929- .... CLC 3, 6
See also CA 21-24R; CANR 17; MTCW;
SATA 66

Levin, Meyer 1905-1981 .... CLC 7
See also AITN 1; CA 9-12R; 104;
CANR 15; DLB 9, 28; DLBY 81;
SATA 21, 27

Levine, Norman 1924- .... CLC 54
See also CA 73-76; CANR 14; DLB 88

Levine, Philip 1928-.. CLC 2, 4, 5, 9, 14, 33
See also CA 9-12R; CANR 9, 37; DLB 5

Levinson, Deirdre 1931- .... CLC 49
See also CA 73-76

Levi-Strauss, Claude 1908- .... CLC 38
See also CA 1-4R; CANR 6, 32; MTCW

Levitin, Sonia (Wolff) 1934- .... CLC 17
See also CA 29-32R; CANR 14, 32;
MAICYA; SAAS 2; SATA 4, 68

Levon, O. U.
See Kesey, Ken (Elton)

Lewes, George Henry
1817-1878 .... NCLC 25
See also DLB 55

Lewis, Alun 1915-1944............ TCLC 3
See also CA 104; DLB 20

Lewis, C. Day
See Day Lewis, C(ecil)

Lewis, C(live) S(taples)
1898-1963 .... CLC 1, 3, 6, 14, 27
See also AAYA 3; CA 81-84; CANR 33;
CDBLB 1945-1960; CLR 3, 27; DLB 15,
100; MAICYA; MTCW; SATA 13; WLC

Lewis, Janet 1899- .... CLC 41
See also Winters, Janet Lewis
See also CA 9-12R; CANR 29; CAP 1;
DLBY 87

Lewis, Matthew Gregory
1775-1818 .... NCLC 11
See also DLB 39

Lewis, (Harry) Sinclair
1885-1951 .... TCLC 4, 13, 23, 39
See also CA 104; 133; CDALB 1917-1929;
DLB 9, 102; DLBD 1; MTCW; WLC

Lewis, (Percy) Wyndham
1884(?)-1957 .... TCLC 2, 9
See also CA 104; DLB 15

Lewisohn, Ludwig 1883-1955...... TCLC 19
See also CA 107; DLB 4, 9, 28, 102

Lezama Lima, Jose 1910-1976 ... **CLC 4, 10**
See also CA 77-80; DLB 113; HW

L'Heureux, John (Clarke) 1934- .... **CLC 52**
See also CA 13-16R; CANR 23

Liddell, C. H.
See Kuttner, Henry

Lie, Jonas (Lauritz Idemil)
1833-1908(?) .... **TCLC 5**
See also CA 115

Lieber, Joel 1937-1971............. **CLC 6**
See also CA 73-76; 29-32R

Lieber, Stanley Martin
See Lee, Stan

Lieberman, Laurence (James)
1935- .... **CLC 4, 36**
See also CA 17-20R; CANR 8, 36

Lieksman, Anders
See Haavikko, Paavo Juhani

Li Fei-kan 1904- .... **CLC 18**
See also CA 105

Lifton, Robert Jay 1926- .... **CLC 67**
See also CA 17-20R; CANR 27; SATA 66

Lightfoot, Gordon 1938- .... **CLC 26**
See also CA 109

Ligotti, Thomas 1953- .... **CLC 44**
See also CA 123

Liliencron, (Friedrich Adolf Axel) Detlev von
1844-1909 .... **TCLC 18**
See also CA 117

Lima, Jose Lezama
See Lezama Lima, Jose

Lima Barreto, Afonso Henrique de
1881-1922 .... **TCLC 23**
See also CA 117

Limonov, Eduard.................. **CLC 67**

Lin, Frank
See Atherton, Gertrude (Franklin Horn)

Lincoln, Abraham 1809-1865..... **NCLC 18**

Lind, Jakov .... **CLC 1, 2, 4, 27**
See also Landwirth, Heinz
See also CAAS 4

Lindsay, David 1878-1945 .... **TCLC 15**
See also CA 113

Lindsay, (Nicholas) Vachel
1879-1931 .... **TCLC 17**
See also CA 114; 135; CDALB 1865-1917;
DLB 54; SATA 40; WLC

Linke-Poot
See Doeblin, Alfred

Linney, Romulus 1930- .... **CLC 51**
See also CA 1-4R

Li Po 701-763 .... **CMLC 2**

Lipsius, Justus 1547-1606 .... **LC 16**

Lipsyte, Robert (Michael) 1938- .... **CLC 21**
See also AAYA 7; CA 17-20R; CANR 8;
CLR 23; MAICYA; SATA 5, 68

Lish, Gordon (Jay) 1934- .... **CLC 45**
See also CA 113; 117

Lispector, Clarice 1925-1977....... **CLC 43**
See also CA 116; DLB 113

Littell, Robert 1935(?)- .... **CLC 42**
See also CA 109; 112

Littlewit, Humphrey Gent.
See Lovecraft, H(oward) P(hillips)

Litwos
See Sienkiewicz, Henryk (Adam Alexander Pius)

Liu E 1857-1909................ **TCLC 15**
See also CA 115

Lively, Penelope (Margaret)
1933- .... **CLC 32, 50**
See also CA 41-44R; CANR 29; CLR 7;
DLB 14; MAICYA; MTCW; SATA 7, 60

Livesay, Dorothy (Kathleen)
1909- .... **CLC 4, 15**
See also AITN 2; CA 25-28R; CAAS 8;
CANR 36; DLB 68; MTCW

Lizardi, Jose Joaquin Fernandez de
1776-1827 .... **NCLC 30**

Llewellyn, Richard .... **CLC 7**
See also Llewellyn Lloyd, Richard Dafydd Vivian
See also DLB 15

Llewellyn Lloyd, Richard Dafydd Vivian
1906-1983
See Llewellyn, Richard
See also CA 53-56; 111; CANR 7;
SATA 11, 37

Llosa, (Jorge) Mario (Pedro) Vargas
See Vargas Llosa, (Jorge) Mario (Pedro)

Lloyd Webber, Andrew 1948-
See Webber, Andrew Lloyd
See also AAYA 1; CA 116; SATA 56

Locke, Alain (Le Roy)
1886-1954 .... **TCLC 43**
See also BW; CA 106; 124; DLB 51

Locke, John 1632-1704 .... **LC 7**
See also DLB 101

Locke-Elliott, Sumner
See Elliott, Sumner Locke

Lockhart, John Gibson
1794-1854 .... **NCLC 6**
See also DLB 110, 116

Lodge, David (John) 1935- .... **CLC 36**
See also BEST 90:1; CA 17-20R; CANR 19;
DLB 14; MTCW

Loennbohm, Armas Eino Leopold 1878-1926
See Leino, Eino
See also CA 123

Loewinsohn, Ron(ald William)
1937- .... **CLC 52**
See also CA 25-28R

Logan, Jake
See Smith, Martin Cruz

Logan, John (Burton) 1923-1987..... **CLC 5**
See also CA 77-80; 124; DLB 5

Lo Kuan-chung 1330(?)-1400(?)...... **LC 12**

Lombard, Nap
See Johnson, Pamela Hansford

London, Jack........ **TCLC 9, 15, 39; SSC 4**
See also London, John Griffith
See also AITN 2; CDALB 1865-1917;
DLB 8, 12, 78; SATA 18; WLC

London, John Griffith 1876-1916
See London, Jack
See also CA 110; 119; MAICYA; MTCW

Long, Emmett
See Leonard, Elmore (John Jr.)

Longbaugh, Harry
See Goldman, William (W.)

Longfellow, Henry Wadsworth
1807-1882 .... **NCLC 2**
See also CDALB 1640-1865; DLB 1, 59;
SATA 19

Longley, Michael 1939- .... **CLC 29**
See also CA 102; DLB 40

Longus fl. c. 2nd cent. - .... **CMLC 7**

Longway, A. Hugh
See Lang, Andrew

Lopate, Phillip 1943- .... **CLC 29**
See also CA 97-100; DLBY 80

Lopez Portillo (y Pacheco), Jose
1920- .... **CLC 46**
See also CA 129; HW

Lopez y Fuentes, Gregorio
1897(?)-1966 .... **CLC 32**
See also CA 131; HW

Lorca, Federico Garcia
See Garcia Lorca, Federico

Lord, Bette Bao 1938- .... **CLC 23**
See also BEST 90:3; CA 107; SATA 58

Lord Auch
See Bataille, Georges

Lord Byron
See Byron, George Gordon (Noel)

Lord Dunsany .... **TCLC 2**
See also Dunsany, Edward John Moreton
Drax Plunkett

Lorde, Audre (Geraldine)
1934- .... **CLC 18, 71**
See also BLC 2; BW; CA 25-28R;
CANR 16, 26; DLB 41; MTCW

Lord Jeffrey
See Jeffrey, Francis

Lorenzo, Heberto Padilla
See Padilla (Lorenzo), Heberto

Loris
See Hofmannsthal, Hugo von

Loti, Pierre .... **TCLC 11**
See also Viaud, (Louis Marie) Julien

Louie, David Wong 1954- .... **CLC 70**

Louis, Father M.
See Merton, Thomas

Lovecraft, H(oward) P(hillips)
1890-1937 .... **TCLC 4, 22; SSC 3**
See also CA 104; 133; MTCW

Lovelace, Earl 1935-.............. **CLC 51**
See also CA 77-80; MTCW

Lowell, Amy 1874-1925 .... **TCLC 1, 8**
See also CA 104; DLB 54

Lowell, James Russell 1819-1891 .. **NCLC 2**
See also CDALB 1640-1865; DLB 1, 11, 64, 79

Lowell, Robert (Traill Spence Jr.)
1917-1977 ... **CLC 1, 2, 3, 4, 5, 8, 9, 11, 15, 37; PC 3**
See also CA 9-12R; 73-76; CABS 2;
CANR 26; DLB 5; MTCW; WLC

429

Lowndes, Marie Adelaide (Belloc)
1868-1947 .... **TCLC 12**
See also CA 107; DLB 70

Lowry, (Clarence) Malcolm
1909-1957 .... **TCLC 6, 40**
See also CA 105; 131; CDBLB 1945-1960;
DLB 15; MTCW

Lowry, Mina Gertrude 1882-1966
See Loy, Mina
See also CA 113

Loxsmith, John
See Brunner, John (Kilian Houston)

Loy, Mina .... **CLC 28**
See also Lowry, Mina Gertrude
See also DLB 4, 54

Loyson-Bridet
See Schwob, (Mayer Andre) Marcel

Lucas, Craig 1951- .... **CLC 64**
See also CA 137

Lucas, George 1944- .... **CLC 16**
See also AAYA 1; CA 77-80; CANR 30;
SATA 56

Lucas, Hans
See Godard, Jean-Luc

Lucas, Victoria
See Plath, Sylvia

Ludlam, Charles 1943-1987 ..... **CLC 46, 50**
See also CA 85-88; 122

Ludlum, Robert 1927- .... **CLC 22, 43**
See also BEST 89:1, 90:3; CA 33-36R;
CANR 25; DLBY 82; MTCW

Ludwig, Ken .... **CLC 60**

Ludwig, Otto 1813-1865.......... **NCLC 4**

Lugones, Leopoldo 1874-1938 ..... **TCLC 15**
See also CA 116; 131; HW

Lu Hsun 1881-1936 .... **TCLC 3**

Lukacs, George .... **CLC 24**
See also Lukacs, Gyorgy (Szegeny von)

Lukacs, Gyorgy (Szegeny von) 1885-1971
See Lukacs, George
See also CA 101; 29-32R

Luke, Peter (Ambrose Cyprian)
1919- .... **CLC 38**
See also CA 81-84; DLB 13

Lunar, Dennis
See Mungo, Raymond

Lurie, Alison 1926- .... **CLC 4, 5, 18, 39**
See also CA 1-4R; CANR 2, 17; DLB 2;
MTCW; SATA 46

Lustig, Arnost 1926- .... **CLC 56**
See also AAYA 3; CA 69-72; SATA 56

Luther, Martin 1483-1546 .... **LC 9**

Luzi, Mario 1914- .... **CLC 13**
See also CA 61-64; CANR 9

Lynch, B. Suarez
See Bioy Casares, Adolfo; Borges, Jorge
Luis

Lynch, David (K.) 1946- .... **CLC 66**
See also CA 124; 129

Lynch, James
See Andreyev, Leonid (Nikolaevich)

Lynch Davis, B.
See Bioy Casares, Adolfo; Borges, Jorge
Luis

Lyndsay, SirDavid 1490-1555 .... **LC 20**

Lynn, Kenneth S(chuyler) 1923- .... **CLC 50**
See also CA 1-4R; CANR 3, 27

Lynx
See West, Rebecca

Lyons, Marcus
See Blish, James (Benjamin)

Lyre, Pinchbeck
See Sassoon, Siegfried (Lorraine)

Lytle, Andrew (Nelson) 1902- ...... **CLC 22**
See also CA 9-12R; DLB 6

Lyttelton, George 1709-1773 .... **LC 10**

Maas, Peter 1929- .... **CLC 29**
See also CA 93-96

Macaulay, Rose 1881-1958 ..... **TCLC 7, 44**
See also CA 104; DLB 36

MacBeth, George (Mann)
1932-1992 .... **CLC 2, 5, 9**
See also CA 25-28R; 136; DLB 40; MTCW;
SATA 4; SATO 70

MacCaig, Norman (Alexander)
1910- .... **CLC 36**
See also CA 9-12R; CANR 3, 34; DLB 27

MacCarthy, (Sir Charles Otto) Desmond
1877-1952 .... **TCLC 36**

MacDiarmid, Hugh ..... **CLC 2, 4, 11, 19, 63**
See also Grieve, C(hristopher) M(urray)
See also CDBLB 1945-1960; DLB 20

MacDonald, Anson
See Heinlein, Robert A(nson)

Macdonald, Cynthia 1928- ...... **CLC 13, 19**
See also CA 49-52; CANR 4; DLB 105

MacDonald, George 1824-1905 ..... **TCLC 9**
See also CA 106; 137; DLB 18; MAICYA;
SATA 33

Macdonald, John
See Millar, Kenneth

MacDonald, John D(ann)
1916-1986 .... **CLC 3, 27, 44**
See also CA 1-4R; 121; CANR 1, 19;
DLB 8; DLBY 86; MTCW

Macdonald, John Ross
See Millar, Kenneth

Macdonald, Ross ..... **CLC 1, 2, 3, 14, 34, 41**
See also Millar, Kenneth
See also DLBD 6

MacDougal, John
See Blish, James (Benjamin)

MacEwen, Gwendolyn (Margaret)
1941-1987 .... **CLC 13, 55**
See also CA 9-12R; 124; CANR 7, 22;
DLB 53; SATA 50, 55

Machado (y Ruiz), Antonio
1875-1939 .... **TCLC 3**
See also CA 104; DLB 108

Machado de Assis, Joaquim Maria
1839-1908 .... **TCLC 10**
See also BLC 2; CA 107

Machen, Arthur .... **TCLC 4**
See also Jones, Arthur Llewellyn
See also DLB 36

Machiavelli, Niccolo 1469-1527 ...... **LC 8**

MacInnes, Colin 1914-1976 ...... **CLC 4, 23**
See also CA 69-72; 65-68; CANR 21;
DLB 14; MTCW

MacInnes, Helen (Clark)
1907-1985 .... **CLC 27, 39**
See also CA 1-4R; 117; CANR 1, 28;
DLB 87; MTCW; SATA 22, 44

Mackenzie, Compton (Edward Montague)
1883-1972 .... **CLC 18**
See also CA 21-22; 37-40R; CAP 2;
DLB 34, 100

Mackintosh, Elizabeth 1896(?)-1952
See Tey, Josephine
See also CA 110

MacLaren, James
See Grieve, C(hristopher) M(urray)

Mac Laverty, Bernard 1942- .... **CLC 31**
See also CA 116; 118

MacLean, Alistair (Stuart)
1922-1987 .... **CLC 3, 13, 50, 63**
See also CA 57-60; 121; CANR 28; MTCW;
SATA 23, 50

MacLeish, Archibald
1892-1982 .... **CLC 3, 8, 14, 68**
See also CA 9-12R; 106; CANR 33; DLB 4,
7, 45; DLBY 82; MTCW

MacLennan, (John) Hugh
1907- .... **CLC 2, 14**
See also CA 5-8R; CANR 33; DLB 68;
MTCW

MacLeod, Alistair 1936- .... **CLC 56**
See also CA 123; DLB 60

MacNeice, (Frederick) Louis
1907-1963 .... **CLC 1, 4, 10, 53**
See also CA 85-88; DLB 10, 20; MTCW

MacNeill, Dand
See Fraser, George MacDonald

Macpherson, (Jean) Jay 1931- ...... **CLC 14**
See also CA 5-8R; DLB 53

MacShane, Frank 1927- .... **CLC 39**
See also CA 9-12R; CANR 3, 33; DLB 111

Macumber, Mari
See Sandoz, Mari(e Susette)

Madach, Imre 1823-1864 .... **NCLC 19**

Madden, (Jerry) David 1933- .... **CLC 5, 15**
See also CA 1-4R; CAAS 3; CANR 4;
DLB 6; MTCW

Maddern, Al(an)
See Ellison, Harlan

Madhubuti, Haki R. 1942- .... **CLC 6; PC 5**
See also Lee, Don L.
See also BLC 2; BW; CA 73-76; CANR 24;
DLB 5, 41; DLBD 8

Madow, Pauline (Reichberg) .... **CLC 1**
See also CA 9-12R

Maepenn, Hugh
See Kuttner, Henry

Maepenn, K. H.
See Kuttner, Henry

Maeterlinck, Maurice 1862-1949 ... **TCLC 3**
See also CA 104; 136; SATA 66

Maginn, William 1794-1842 .... **NCLC 8**
See also DLB 110

Mahapatra, Jayanta 1928- .... **CLC 33**
See also CA 73-76; CAAS 9; CANR 15, 33

Mahfouz, Naguib (Abdel Aziz Al-Sabilgi)
1911(?)-
See Mahfuz, Najib
See also BEST 89:2; CA 128; MTCW

Mahfuz, Najib .... **CLC 52, 55**
See also Mahfouz, Naguib (Abdel Aziz Al-Sabilgi)
See also DLBY 88

Mahon, Derek 1941- .... **CLC 27**
See also CA 113; 128; DLB 40

Mailer, Norman
1923- ...... **CLC 1, 2, 3, 4, 5, 8, 11, 14,
28, 39, 74**
See also AITN 2; CA 9-12R; CABS 1;
CANR 28; CDALB 1968-1988; DLB 2,
16, 28; DLBD 3; DLBY 80, 83; MTCW

Maillet, Antonine 1929- .... **CLC 54**
See also CA 115; 120; DLB 60

Mais, Roger 1905-1955 .... **TCLC 8**
See also BW; CA 105; 124; MTCW

Maitland, Sara (Louise) 1950- ..... **CLC 49**
See also CA 69-72; CANR 13

Major, Clarence 1936- .... **CLC 3, 19, 48**
See also BLC 2; BW; CA 21-24R; CAAS 6;
CANR 13, 25; DLB 33

Major, Kevin (Gerald) 1949- .... **CLC 26**
See also CA 97-100; CANR 21, 38;
CLR 11; DLB 60; MAICYA; SATA 32

Maki, James
See Ozu, Yasujiro

Malabaila, Damiano
See Levi, Primo

Malamud, Bernard
1914-1986 ..... **CLC 1, 2, 3, 5, 8, 9, 11,
18, 27, 44**
See also CA 5-8R; 118; CABS 1; CANR 28;
CDALB 1941-1968; DLB 2, 28;
DLBY 80, 86; MTCW; WLC

Malcolm, Dan
See Silverberg, Robert

Malherbe, Francois de 1555-1628 ..... **LC 5**

Mallarme, Stephane
1842-1898 .... **NCLC 4; PC 4**

Mallet-Joris, Francoise 1930- ...... **CLC 11**
See also CA 65-68; CANR 17; DLB 83

Malley, Ern
See McAuley, James Phillip

Mallowan, Agatha Christie
See Christie, Agatha (Mary Clarissa)

Maloff, Saul 1922- .... **CLC 5**
See also CA 33-36R

Malone, Louis
See MacNeice, (Frederick) Louis

Malone, Michael (Christopher)
1942- .... **CLC 43**
See also CA 77-80; CANR 14, 32

Malory, (Sir) Thomas
1410(?)-1471(?) .... **LC 11**
See also CDBLB Before 1660; SATA 33, 59

Malouf, (George Joseph) David
1934- .... **CLC 28**
See also CA 124

Malraux, (Georges-)Andre
1901-1976 ...... **CLC 1, 4, 9, 13, 15, 57**
See also CA 21-22; 69-72; CANR 34;
CAP 2; DLB 72; MTCW

Malzberg, Barry N(athaniel) 1939- ... **CLC 7**
See also CA 61-64; CAAS 4; CANR 16;
DLB 8

Mamet, David (Alan)
1947- .... **CLC 9, 15, 34, 46**
See also AAYA 3; CA 81-84; CABS 3;
CANR 15; DLB 7; MTCW

Mamoulian, Rouben (Zachary)
1897-1987 .... **CLC 16**
See also CA 25-28R; 124

Mandelstam, Osip (Emilievich)
1891(?)-1938(?) .... **TCLC 2, 6**
See also CA 104

Mander, (Mary) Jane 1877-1949 ... **TCLC 31**

Mandiargues, Andre Pieyre de ...... **CLC 41**
See also Pieyre de Mandiargues, Andre
See also DLB 83

Mandrake, Ethel Belle
See Thurman, Wallace (Henry)

Mangan, James Clarence
1803-1849 .... **NCLC 27**

Maniere, J.-E.
See Giraudoux, (Hippolyte) Jean

Manley, (Mary) Delariviere
1672(?)-1724 .... **LC 1**
See also DLB 39, 80

Mann, Abel
See Creasey, John

Mann, (Luiz) Heinrich 1871-1950 ... **TCLC 9**
See also CA 106; DLB 66

Mann, (Paul) Thomas
1875-1955 ... **TCLC 2, 8, 14, 21, 35, 44;
SSC 5**
See also CA 104; 128; DLB 66; MTCW;
WLC

Manning, Frederic 1887(?)-1935 ... **TCLC 25**
See also CA 124

Manning, Olivia 1915-1980 ...... **CLC 5, 19**
See also CA 5-8R; 101; CANR 29; MTCW

Mano, D. Keith 1942- .... **CLC 2, 10**
See also CA 25-28R; CAAS 6; CANR 26;
DLB 6

Mansfield, Katherine ... **TCLC 2, 8, 39; SSC 9**
See also Beauchamp, Kathleen Mansfield
See also WLC

Manso, Peter 1940- .... **CLC 39**
See also CA 29-32R

Mantecon, Juan Jimenez
See Jimenez (Mantecon), Juan Ramon

Manton, Peter
See Creasey, John

Man Without a Spleen, A
See Chekhov, Anton (Pavlovich)

Manzoni, Alessandro 1785-1873 .. **NCLC 29**

Mapu, Abraham (ben Jekutiel)
1808-1867 .... **NCLC 18**

Mara, Sally
See Queneau, Raymond

Marat, Jean Paul 1743-1793 .... **LC 10**

Marcel, Gabriel Honore
1889-1973 .... **CLC 15**
See also CA 102; 45-48; MTCW

Marchbanks, Samuel
See Davies, (William) Robertson

Marchi, Giacomo
See Bassani, Giorgio

Marie de France c. 12th cent. - .... **CMLC 8**

Marie de l'Incarnation 1599-1672 .... **LC 10**

Mariner, Scott
See Pohl, Frederik

Marinetti, Filippo Tommaso
1876-1944 .... **TCLC 10**
See also CA 107; DLB 114

Marivaux, Pierre Carlet de Chamblain de
1688-1763 .... **LC 4**

Markandaya, Kamala .... **CLC 8, 38**
See also Taylor, Kamala (Purnaiya)

Markfield, Wallace 1926- .... **CLC 8**
See also CA 69-72; CAAS 3; DLB 2, 28

Markham, Edwin 1852-1940 ...... **TCLC 47**
See also DLB 54

Markham, Robert
See Amis, Kingsley (William)

Marks, J
See Highwater, Jamake (Mamake)

Marks-Highwater, J
See Highwater, Jamake (Mamake)

Markson, David M(errill) 1927- .... **CLC 67**
See also CA 49-52; CANR 1

Marley, Bob. .... **CLC 17**
See also Marley, Robert Nesta

Marley, Robert Nesta 1945-1981
See Marley, Bob
See also CA 107; 103

Marlowe, Christopher 1564-1593 ..... **DC 1**
See also CDBLB Before 1660; DLB 62;
WLC

Marmontel, Jean-Francois
1723-1799 .... **LC 2**

Marquand, John P(hillips)
1893-1960 .... **CLC 2, 10**
See also CA 85-88; DLB 9, 102

Marquez, Gabriel (Jose) Garcia. ..... **CLC 68**
See also Garcia Marquez, Gabriel (Jose)

Marquis, Don(ald Robert Perry)
1878-1937 .... **TCLC 7**
See also CA 104; DLB 11, 25

Marric, J. J.
See Creasey, John

Marrow, Bernard
See Moore, Brian

Marryat, Frederick 1792-1848 .... **NCLC 3**
See also DLB 21

Marsden, James
See Creasey, John

Marsh, (Edith) Ngaio
1899-1982 .... **CLC 7, 53**
See also CA 9-12R; CANR 6; DLB 77;
MTCW

Marshall, Garry 1934- .... **CLC 17**
See also AAYA 3; CA 111; SATA 60

Marshall, Paule 1929- .. CLC **27, 72; SSC 3**
See also BLC 3; BW; CA 77-80; CANR 25; DLB 33; MTCW

Marsten, Richard
See Hunter, Evan

Martha, Henry
See Harris, Mark

Martin, Ken
See Hubbard, L(afayette) Ron(ald)

Martin, Richard
See Creasey, John

Martin, Steve 1945- .... CLC **30**
See also CA 97-100; CANR 30; MTCW

Martin, Webber
See Silverberg, Robert

Martin du Gard, Roger
1881-1958 .... TCLC **24**
See also CA 118; DLB 65

Martineau, Harriet 1802-1876.... NCLC **26**
See also DLB 21, 55; YABC 2

Martines, Julia
See O'Faolain, Julia

Martinez, Jacinto Benavente y
See Benavente (y Martinez), Jacinto

Martinez Ruiz, Jose 1873-1967
See Azorin; Ruiz, Jose Martinez
See also CA 93-96; HW

Martinez Sierra, Gregorio
1881-1947 .... TCLC **6**
See also CA 115

Martinez Sierra, Maria (de la O'LeJarraga)
1874-1974 .... TCLC **6**
See also CA 115

Martinsen, Martin
See Follett, Ken(neth Martin)

Martinson, Harry (Edmund)
1904-1978 .... CLC **14**
See also CA 77-80; CANR 34

Marut, Ret
See Traven, B.

Marut, Robert
See Traven, B.

Marvell, Andrew 1621-1678......... LC **4**
See also CDBLB 1660-1789; WLC

Marx, Karl (Heinrich)
1818-1883 .... NCLC **17**

Masaoka Shiki.................... TCLC **18**
See also Masaoka Tsunenori

Masaoka Tsunenori 1867-1902
See Masaoka Shiki
See also CA 117

Masefield, John (Edward)
1878-1967 .... CLC **11, 47**
See also CA 19-20; 25-28R; CANR 33; CAP 2; CDBLB 1890-1914; DLB 10; MTCW; SATA 19

Maso, Carole 19(?)- .... CLC **44**

Mason, Bobbie Ann
1940- .... CLC **28, 43; SSC 4**
See also AAYA 5; CA 53-56; CANR 11, 31; DLBY 87; MTCW

Mason, Ernst
See Pohl, Frederik

Mason, Lee W.
See Malzberg, Barry N(athaniel)

Mason, Nick 1945-............... CLC **35**
See also Pink Floyd

Mason, Tally
See Derleth, August (William)

Mass, William
See Gibson, William

Masters, Edgar Lee
1868-1950 .... TCLC **2, 25; PC 1**
See also CA 104; 133; CDALB 1865-1917; DLB 54; MTCW

Masters, Hilary 1928- .... CLC **48**
See also CA 25-28R; CANR 13

Mastrosimone, William 19(?)- ...... CLC **36**

Mathe, Albert
See Camus, Albert

Matheson, Richard Burton 1926- ... CLC **37**
See also CA 97-100; DLB 8, 44

Mathews, Harry 1930-.......... CLC **6, 52**
See also CA 21-24R; CAAS 6; CANR 18

Mathias, Roland (Glyn) 1915-...... CLC **45**
See also CA 97-100; CANR 19; DLB 27

Matsuo Basho 1644-1694............ PC **3**

Mattheson, Rodney
See Creasey, John

Matthews, Greg 1949- .... CLC **45**
See also CA 135

Matthews, William 1942-.......... CLC **40**
See also CA 29-32R; CANR 12; DLB 5

Matthias, John (Edward) 1941-...... CLC **9**
See also CA 33-36R

Matthiessen, Peter
1927- .... CLC **5, 7, 11, 32, 64**
See also AAYA 6; BEST 90:4; CA 9-12R; CANR 21; DLB 6; MTCW; SATA 27

Maturin, Charles Robert
1780(?)-1824 .... NCLC **6**

Matute (Ausejo), Ana Maria
1925- .... CLC **11**
See also CA 89-92; MTCW

Maugham, W. S.
See Maugham, W(illiam) Somerset

Maugham, W(illiam) Somerset
1874-1965 .... CLC **1, 11, 15, 67; SSC 8**
See also CA 5-8R; 25-28R; CDBLB 1914-1945; DLB 10, 36, 77, 100; MTCW; SATA 54; WLC

Maugham, William Somerset
See Maugham, W(illiam) Somerset

Maupassant, (Henri Rene Albert) Guy de
1850-1893 .... NCLC **1; SSC 1**
See also WLC

Maurhut, Richard
See Traven, B.

Mauriac, Claude 1914-............. CLC **9**
See also CA 89-92; DLB 83

Mauriac, Francois (Charles)
1885-1970 .... CLC **4, 9, 56**
See also CA 25-28; CAP 2; DLB 65; MTCW

Mavor, Osborne Henry 1888-1951
See Bridie, James
See also CA 104

Maxwell, William (Keepers Jr.)
1908- .... CLC **19**
See also CA 93-96; DLBY 80

May, Elaine 1932- .... CLC **16**
See also CA 124; DLB 44

Mayakovski, Vladimir (Vladimirovich)
1893-1930 .... TCLC **4, 18**
See also CA 104

Mayhew, Henry 1812-1887 ...... NCLC **31**
See also DLB 18, 55

Maynard, Joyce 1953-............. CLC **23**
See also CA 111; 129

Mayne, William (James Carter)
1928- .... CLC **12**
See also CA 9-12R; CANR 37; CLR 25; MAICYA; SAAS 11; SATA 6, 68

Mayo, Jim
See L'Amour, Louis (Dearborn)

Maysles, Albert 1926- .... CLC **16**
See also CA 29-32R

Maysles, David 1932-.............. CLC **16**

Mazer, Norma Fox 1931- .... CLC **26**
See also AAYA 5; CA 69-72; CANR 12, 32; CLR 23; MAICYA; SAAS 1; SATA 24, 67

Mazzini, Guiseppe 1805-1872 .... NCLC **34**

Mazzini, Guiseppe 1805-1872 .... NCLC **34**

McAuley, James Phillip
1917-1976 .... CLC **45**
See also CA 97-100

McBain, Ed
See Hunter, Evan

McBrien, William Augustine
1930- .... CLC **44**
See also CA 107

McCaffrey, Anne (Inez) 1926-...... CLC **17**
See also AAYA 6; AITN 2; BEST 89:2; CA 25-28R; CANR 15, 35; DLB 8; MAICYA; MTCW; SAAS 11; SATA 8, 70

McCann, Arthur
See Campbell, John W(ood Jr.)

McCann, Edson
See Pohl, Frederik

McCarthy, Cormac 1933-........ CLC **4, 57**
See also CA 13-16R; CANR 10; DLB 6

McCarthy, Mary (Therese)
1912-1989 ... CLC **1, 3, 5, 14, 24, 39, 59**
See also CA 5-8R; 129; CANR 16; DLB 2; DLBY 81; MTCW

McCartney, (James) Paul
1942- .... CLC **12, 35**

McCauley, Stephen 19(?)- .... CLC **50**

McClure, Michael (Thomas)
1932- .... CLC **6, 10**
See also CA 21-24R; CANR 17; DLB 16

McCorkle, Jill (Collins) 1958-...... CLC **51**
See also CA 121; DLBY 87

McCourt, James 1941-............. CLC **5**
See also CA 57-60

McCoy, Horace (Stanley)
1897-1955 .... TCLC **28**
See also CA 108; DLB 9

McCrae, John 1872-1918 .... **TCLC 12**
See also CA 109; DLB 92

McCreigh, James
See Pohl, Frederik

McCullers, (Lula) Carson (Smith)
1917-1967 .. **CLC 1, 4, 10, 12, 48; SSC 9**
See also CA 5-8R; 25-28R; CABS 1, 3;
CANR 18; CDALB 1941-1968; DLB 2, 7;
MTCW; SATA 27; WLC

McCulloch, John Tyler
See Burroughs, Edgar Rice

McCullough, Colleen 1938(?)- ...... **CLC 27**
See also CA 81-84; CANR 17; MTCW

McElroy, Joseph 1930- .... **CLC 5, 47**
See also CA 17-20R

McEwan, Ian (Russell) 1948- ... **CLC 13, 66**
See also BEST 90:4; CA 61-64; CANR 14;
DLB 14; MTCW

McFadden, David 1940- .... **CLC 48**
See also CA 104; DLB 60

McFarland, Dennis 1950- .... **CLC 65**

McGahern, John 1934- .... **CLC 5, 9, 48**
See also CA 17-20R; CANR 29; DLB 14;
MTCW

McGinley, Patrick (Anthony)
1937- .... **CLC 41**
See also CA 120; 127

McGinley, Phyllis 1905-1978 ...... **CLC 14**
See also CA 9-12R; 77-80; CANR 19;
DLB 11, 48; SATA 2, 24, 44

McGinniss, Joe 1942- .... **CLC 32**
See also AITN 2; BEST 89:2; CA 25-28R;
CANR 26

McGivern, Maureen Daly
See Daly, Maureen

McGrath, Patrick 1950- .... **CLC 55**
See also CA 136

McGrath, Thomas (Matthew)
1916-1990 .... **CLC 28, 59**
See also CA 9-12R; 132; CANR 6, 33;
MTCW; SATA 41; SATO 66

McGuane, Thomas (Francis III)
1939- .... **CLC 3, 7, 18, 45**
See also AITN 2; CA 49-52; CANR 5, 24;
DLB 2; DLBY 80; MTCW

McGuckian, Medbh 1950- .... **CLC 48**
See also DLB 40

McHale, Tom 1942(?)-1982 .... **CLC 3, 5**
See also AITN 1; CA 77-80; 106

McIlvanney, William 1936- .... **CLC 42**
See also CA 25-28R; DLB 14

McIlwraith, Maureen Mollie Hunter
See Hunter, Mollie
See also SATA 2

McInerney, Jay 1955- .... **CLC 34**
See also CA 116; 123

McIntyre, Vonda N(eel) 1948- ..... **CLC 18**
See also CA 81-84; CANR 17, 34; MTCW

McKay, Claude .... **TCLC 7, 41; PC 2**
See also McKay, Festus Claudius
See also BLC 3; DLB 4, 45, 51, 117

McKay, Festus Claudius 1889-1948
See McKay, Claude
See also BW; CA 104; 124; MTCW; WLC

McKuen, Rod 1933- .... **CLC 1, 3**
See also AITN 1; CA 41-44R

McLoughlin, R. B.
See Mencken, H(enry) L(ouis)

McLuhan, (Herbert) Marshall
1911-1980 .... **CLC 37**
See also CA 9-12R; 102; CANR 12, 34;
DLB 88; MTCW

McMillan, Terry 1951- .... **CLC 50, 61**

McMurtry, Larry (Jeff)
1936- .... **CLC 2, 3, 7, 11, 27, 44**
See also AITN 2; BEST 89:2; CA 5-8R;
CANR 19; CDALB 1968-1988; DLB 2;
DLBY 80, 87; MTCW

McNally, Terrence 1939- ...... **CLC 4, 7, 41**
See also CA 45-48; CANR 2; DLB 7

McNamer, Deirdre 1950- .... **CLC 70**

McNeile, Herman Cyril 1888-1937
See Sapper
See also DLB 77

McPhee, John (Angus) 1931- ...... **CLC 36**
See also BEST 90:1; CA 65-68; CANR 20;
MTCW

McPherson, James Alan 1943- ..... **CLC 19**
See also BW; CA 25-28R; CANR 24;
DLB 38; MTCW

McPherson, William (Alexander)
1933- .... **CLC 34**
See also CA 69-72; CANR 28

McSweeney, Kerry .... **CLC 34**

Mead, Margaret 1901-1978 .... **CLC 37**
See also AITN 1; CA 1-4R; 81-84;
CANR 4; MTCW; SATA 20

Meaker, Marijane (Agnes) 1927-
See Kerr, M. E.
See also CA 107; CANR 37; MAICYA;
MTCW; SATA 20, 61

Medoff, Mark (Howard) 1940- ... **CLC 6, 23**
See also AITN 1; CA 53-56; CANR 5;
DLB 7

Meged, Aharon
See Megged, Aharon

Meged, Aron
See Megged, Aharon

Megged, Aharon 1920- .... **CLC 9**
See also CA 49-52; CAAS 13; CANR 1

Mehta, Ved (Parkash) 1934- .... **CLC 37**
See also CA 1-4R; CANR 2, 23; MTCW

Melanter
See Blackmore, R(ichard) D(oddridge)

Melikow, Loris
See Hofmannsthal, Hugo von

Melmoth, Sebastian
See Wilde, Oscar (Fingal O'Flahertie Wills)

Meltzer, Milton 1915- .... **CLC 26**
See also AAYA 8; CA 13-16R; CANR 38;
CLR 13; DLB 61; MAICYA; SAAS 1;
SATA 1, 50

Melville, Herman
1819-1891 ...... **NCLC 3, 12, 29; SSC 1**
See also CDALB 1640-1865; DLB 3, 74;
SATA 59; WLC

Menander
c. 342B.C.-c. 292B.C. ... **CMLC 9; DC 3**

Menander c. 342B.C.-c. 292B.C. ... **CMLC 9**

Mencken, H(enry) L(ouis)
1880-1956 .... **TCLC 13**
See also CA 105; 125; CDALB 1917-1929;
DLB 11, 29, 63; MTCW

Mercer, David 1928-1980 .... **CLC 5**
See also CA 9-12R; 102; CANR 23;
DLB 13; MTCW

Merchant, Paul
See Ellison, Harlan

Meredith, George 1828-1909 ... **TCLC 17, 43**
See also CA 117; CDBLB 1832-1890;
DLB 18, 35, 57

Meredith, William (Morris)
1919- .... **CLC 4, 13, 22, 55**
See also CA 9-12R; CAAS 14; CANR 6;
DLB 5

Merezhkovsky, Dmitry Sergeyevich
1865-1941 .... **TCLC 29**

Merimee, Prosper
1803-1870 .... **NCLC 6; SSC 7**
See also DLB 119

Merkin, Daphne 1954- .... **CLC 44**
See also CA 123

Merlin, Arthur
See Blish, James (Benjamin)

Merrill, James (Ingram)
1926- .... **CLC 2, 3, 6, 8, 13, 18, 34**
See also CA 13-16R; CANR 10; DLB 5;
DLBY 85; MTCW

Merriman, Alex
See Silverberg, Robert

Merritt, E. B.
See Waddington, Miriam

Merton, Thomas
1915-1968 .... **CLC 1, 3, 11, 34**
See also CA 5-8R; 25-28R; CANR 22;
DLB 48; DLBY 81; MTCW

Merwin, W(illiam) S(tanley)
1927- ...... **CLC 1, 2, 3, 5, 8, 13, 18, 45**
See also CA 13-16R; CANR 15; DLB 5;
MTCW

Metcalf, John 1938- .... **CLC 37**
See also CA 113; DLB 60

Metcalf, Suzanne
See Baum, L(yman) Frank

Mew, Charlotte (Mary)
1870-1928 .... **TCLC 8**
See also CA 105; DLB 19

Mewshaw, Michael 1943- .... **CLC 9**
See also CA 53-56; CANR 7; DLBY 80

Meyer, June
See Jordan, June

Meyer-Meyrink, Gustav 1868-1932
See Meyrink, Gustav
See also CA 117

Meyers, Jeffrey 1939- .... **CLC 39**
See also CA 73-76; DLB 111

Meynell, Alice (Christina Gertrude Thompson)
1847-1922 .... **TCLC 6**
See also CA 104; DLB 19, 98

Meyrink, Gustav .... **TCLC 21**
See also Meyer-Meyrink, Gustav
See also DLB 81

Michaels, Leonard 1933- .... **CLC 6, 25**
See also CA 61-64; CANR 21; MTCW

Michaux, Henri 1899-1984 ...... **CLC 8, 19**
See also CA 85-88; 114

Michelangelo 1475-1564. .... **LC 12**

Michelet, Jules 1798-1874 .... **NCLC 31**

Michener, James A(lbert)
1907(?)- .... **CLC 1, 5, 11, 29, 60**
See also AITN 1; BEST 90:1; CA 5-8R;
CANR 21; DLB 6; MTCW

Mickiewicz, Adam 1798-1855 ..... **NCLC 3**

Middleton, Christopher 1926- ...... **CLC 13**
See also CA 13-16R; CANR 29; DLB 40

Middleton, Stanley 1919- .... **CLC 7, 38**
See also CA 25-28R; CANR 21; DLB 14

Migueis, Jose Rodrigues 1901- ..... **CLC 10**

Mikszath, Kalman 1847-1910 ..... **TCLC 31**

Miles, Josephine
1911-1985 .... **CLC 1, 2, 14, 34, 39**
See also CA 1-4R; 116; CANR 2; DLB 48

Militant
See Sandburg, Carl (August)

Mill, John Stuart 1806-1873 ..... **NCLC 11**
See also CDBLB 1832-1890; DLB 55

Millar, Kenneth 1915-1983 .... **CLC 14**
See also Macdonald, Ross
See also CA 9-12R; 110; CANR 16; DLB 2;
DLBD 6; DLBY 83; MTCW

Millay, E. Vincent
See Millay, Edna St. Vincent

Millay, Edna St. Vincent
1892-1950 .... **TCLC 4**
See also CA 104; 130; CDALB 1917-1929;
DLB 45; MTCW

Miller, Arthur
1915- ...... **CLC 1, 2, 6, 10, 15, 26, 47;**
DC 1
See also AITN 1; CA 1-4R; CABS 3;
CANR 2, 30; CDALB 1941-1968; DLB 7;
MTCW; WLC

Miller, Henry (Valentine)
1891-1980 .... **CLC 1, 2, 4, 9, 14, 43**
See also CA 9-12R; 97-100; CANR 33;
CDALB 1929-1941; DLB 4, 9; DLBY 80;
MTCW; WLC

Miller, Jason 1939(?)- .... **CLC 2**
See also AITN 1; CA 73-76; DLB 7

Miller, Sue 19(?)- .... **CLC 44**
See also BEST 90:3

Miller, Walter M(ichael Jr.)
1923- .... **CLC 4, 30**
See also CA 85-88; DLB 8

Millett, Kate 1934- .... **CLC 67**
See also AITN 1; CA 73-76; CANR 32;
MTCW

Millhauser, Steven 1943- .... **CLC 21, 54**
See also CA 110; 111; DLB 2

Millin, Sarah Gertrude 1889-1968 .. **CLC 49**
See also CA 102; 93-96

Milne, A(lan) A(lexander)
1882-1956 .... **TCLC 6**
See also CA 104; 133; CLR 1, 26; DLB 10,
77, 100; MAICYA; MTCW; YABC 1

Milner, Ron(ald) 1938- .... **CLC 56**
See also AITN 1; BLC 3; BW; CA 73-76;
CANR 24; DLB 38; MTCW

Milosz, Czeslaw
1911- .... **CLC 5, 11, 22, 31, 56**
See also CA 81-84; CANR 23; MTCW

Milton, John 1608-1674 .... **LC 9**
See also CDBLB 1660-1789; WLC

Minehaha, Cornelius
See Wedekind, (Benjamin) Frank(lin)

Miner, Valerie 1947- .... **CLC 40**
See also CA 97-100

Minimo, Duca
See D'Annunzio, Gabriele

Minot, Susan 1956- .... **CLC 44**
See also CA 134

Minus, Ed 1938- .... **CLC 39**

Miranda, Javier
See Bioy Casares, Adolfo

Miro (Ferrer), Gabriel (Francisco Victor)
1879-1930 .... **TCLC 5**
See also CA 104

Mishima, Yukio
.... **CLC 2, 4, 6, 9, 27; DC 1; SSC 4**
See also Hiraoka, Kimitake

Mistral, Gabriela. .... **TCLC 2**
See also Godoy Alcayaga, Lucila

Mistry, Rohinton 1952- .... **CLC 71**

Mitchell, Clyde
See Ellison, Harlan; Silverberg, Robert

Mitchell, James Leslie 1901-1935
See Gibbon, Lewis Grassic
See also CA 104; DLB 15

Mitchell, Joni 1943- .... **CLC 12**
See also CA 112

Mitchell, Margaret (Munnerlyn)
1900-1949 .... **TCLC 11**
See also CA 109; 125; DLB 9; MTCW

Mitchell, Peggy
See Mitchell, Margaret (Munnerlyn)

Mitchell, S(ilas) Weir 1829-1914 .. **TCLC 36**

Mitchell, W(illiam) O(rmond)
1914- .... **CLC 25**
See also CA 77-80; CANR 15; DLB 88

Mitford, Mary Russell 1787-1855.. **NCLC 4**
See also DLB 110, 116

Mitford, Nancy 1904-1973 .... **CLC 44**
See also CA 9-12R

Miyamoto, Yuriko 1899-1951 ..... **TCLC 37**

Mo, Timothy (Peter) 1950(?)- ...... **CLC 46**
See also CA 117; MTCW

Modarressi, Taghi (M.) 1931- ...... **CLC 44**
See also CA 121; 134

Modiano, Patrick (Jean) 1945- ..... **CLC 18**
See also CA 85-88; CANR 17; DLB 83

Moerck, Paal
See Roelvaag, O(le) E(dvart)

Mofolo, Thomas (Mokopu)
1875(?)-1948 .... **TCLC 22**
See also BLC 3; CA 121

Mohr, Nicholasa 1935- .... **CLC 12**
See also AAYA 8; CA 49-52; CANR 1, 32;
CLR 22; HW; SAAS 8; SATA 8

Mojtabai, A(nn) G(race)
1938- .... **CLC 5, 9, 15, 29**
See also CA 85-88

Moliere 1622-1673 .... **LC 10**
See also WLC

Molin, Charles
See Mayne, William (James Carter)

Molnar, Ferenc 1878-1952 .... **TCLC 20**
See also CA 109

Momaday, N(avarre) Scott
1934- .... **CLC 2, 19**
See also CA 25-28R; CANR 14, 34;
MTCW; SATA 30, 48

Monroe, Harriet 1860-1936 .... **TCLC 12**
See also CA 109; DLB 54, 91

Monroe, Lyle
See Heinlein, Robert A(nson)

Montagu, Elizabeth 1917- .... **NCLC 7**
See also CA 9-12R

Montagu, Mary (Pierrepont) Wortley
1689-1762 .... **LC 9**
See also DLB 95, 101

Montague, John (Patrick)
1929- .... **CLC 13, 46**
See also CA 9-12R; CANR 9; DLB 40;
MTCW

Montaigne, Michel (Eyquem) de
1533-1592 .... **LC 8**
See also WLC

Montale, Eugenio 1896-1981 ... **CLC 7, 9, 18**
See also CA 17-20R; 104; CANR 30;
DLB 114; MTCW

Montesquieu, Charles-Louis de Secondat
1689-1755 .... **LC 7**

Montgomery, (Robert) Bruce 1921-1978
See Crispin, Edmund
See also CA 104

Montgomery, Marion H. Jr. 1925-... **CLC 7**
See also AITN 1; CA 1-4R; CANR 3;
DLB 6

Montgomery, Max
See Davenport, Guy (Mattison Jr.)

Montherlant, Henry (Milon) de
1896-1972 .... **CLC 8, 19**
See also CA 85-88; 37-40R; DLB 72;
MTCW

Python .... **CLC 21**
See also Chapman, Graham; Cleese, John
(Marwood); Gilliam, Terry (Vance); Idle,
Eric; Jones, Terence Graham Parry; Palin,
Michael (Edward)
See also AAYA 7

Moodie, Susanna (Strickland)
1803-1885 .... **NCLC 14**
See also DLB 99

Mooney, Edward 1951- .... **CLC 25**
See also CA 130

Mooney, Ted
See Mooney, Edward

Moorcock, Michael (John)
1939- .... **CLC 5, 27, 58**
See also CA 45-48; CAAS 5; CANR 2, 17,
38; DLB 14; MTCW

Moore, Brian
1921- .... **CLC 1, 3, 5, 7, 8, 19, 32**
See also CA 1-4R; CANR 1, 25; MTCW

Moore, Edward
See Muir, Edwin

Moore, George Augustus
1852-1933 .... **TCLC 7**
See also CA 104; DLB 10, 18, 57

Moore, Lorrie .... **CLC 39, 45, 68**
See also Moore, Marie Lorena

Moore, Marianne (Craig)
1887-1972 ... **CLC 1, 2, 4, 8, 10, 13, 19, 47; PC 4**
See also CA 1-4R; 33-36R; CANR 3; CDALB 1929-1941; DLB 45; DLBD 7; MTCW; SATA 20

Moore, Marie Lorena 1957-
See Moore, Lorrie
See also CA 116; CANR 39

Moore, Thomas 1779-1852 .... **NCLC 6**
See also DLB 96

Morand, Paul 1888-1976 .... **CLC 41**
See also CA 69-72; DLB 65

Morante, Elsa 1918-1985 .... **CLC 8, 47**
See also CA 85-88; 117; CANR 35; MTCW

Moravia, Alberto .... **CLC 2, 7, 11, 27, 46**
See also Pincherle, Alberto

More, Hannah 1745-1833 .... **NCLC 27**
See also DLB 107, 109, 116

More, Henry 1614-1687 .... **LC 9**

More, Sir Thomas 1478-1535 .... **LC 10**

Moreas, Jean .... **TCLC 18**
See also Papadiamantopoulos, Johannes

Morgan, Berry 1919- .... **CLC 6**
See also CA 49-52; DLB 6

Morgan, Claire
See Highsmith, (Mary) Patricia

Morgan, Edwin (George) 1920- ..... **CLC 31**
See also CA 5-8R; CANR 3; DLB 27

Morgan, (George) Frederick
1922- .... **CLC 23**
See also CA 17-20R; CANR 21

Morgan, Harriet
See Mencken, H(enry) L(ouis)

Morgan, Jane
See Cooper, James Fenimore

Morgan, Janet 1945- .... **CLC 39**
See also CA 65-68

Morgan, Lady 1776(?)-1859 ...... **NCLC 29**
See also DLB 116

Morgan, Robin 1941- .... **CLC 2**
See also CA 69-72; CANR 29; MTCW

Morgan, Scott
See Kuttner, Henry

Morgan, Seth 1949(?)-1990 .... **CLC 65**
See also CA 132

Morgenstern, Christian
1871-1914 .... **TCLC 8**
See also CA 105

Morgenstern, S.
See Goldman, William (W.)

Moricz, Zsigmond 1879-1942 ..... **TCLC 33**

Morike, Eduard (Friedrich)
1804-1875 .... **NCLC 10**

Mori Ogai .... **TCLC 14**
See also Mori Rintaro

Mori Rintaro 1862-1922
See Mori Ogai
See also CA 110

Moritz, Karl Philipp 1756-1793 ...... **LC 2**
See also DLB 94

Morren, Theophil
See Hofmannsthal, Hugo von

Morris, Julian
See West, Morris L(anglo)

Morris, Steveland Judkins 1950(?)-
See Wonder, Stevie
See also CA 111

Morris, William 1834-1896 .... **NCLC 4**
See also CDBLB 1832-1890; DLB 18, 35, 57

Morris, Wright 1910- ... **CLC 1, 3, 7, 18, 37**
See also CA 9-12R; CANR 21; DLB 2; DLBY 81; MTCW

Morrison, Chloe Anthony Wofford
See Morrison, Toni

Morrison, James Douglas 1943-1971
See Morrison, Jim
See also CA 73-76

Morrison, Jim .... **CLC 17**
See also Morrison, James Douglas

Morrison, Toni 1931- ..... **CLC 4, 10, 22, 55**
See also AAYA 1; BLC 3; BW; CA 29-32R; CANR 27; CDALB 1968-1988; DLB 6, 33; DLBY 81; MTCW; SATA 57

Morrison, Van 1945- .... **CLC 21**
See also CA 116

Mortimer, John (Clifford)
1923- .... **CLC 28, 43**
See also CA 13-16R; CANR 21; CDBLB 1960 to Present; DLB 13; MTCW

Mortimer, Penelope (Ruth) 1918- .... **CLC 5**
See also CA 57-60

Morton, Anthony
See Creasey, John

Mosher, Howard Frank .... **CLC 62**

Mosley, Nicholas 1923- .... **CLC 43, 70**
See also CA 69-72; DLB 14

Moss, Howard
1922-1987 .... **CLC 7, 14, 45, 50**
See also CA 1-4R; 123; CANR 1; DLB 5

Motion, Andrew 1952- .... **CLC 47**
See also DLB 40

Motley, Willard (Francis)
1912-1965 .... **CLC 18**
See also BW; CA 117; 106; DLB 76

Mott, Michael (Charles Alston)
1930- .... **CLC 15, 34**
See also CA 5-8R; CAAS 7; CANR 7, 29

Mowat, Farley (McGill) 1921- ..... **CLC 26**
See also AAYA 1; CA 1-4R; CANR 4, 24; CLR 20; DLB 68; MAICYA; MTCW; SATA 3, 55

Moyers, Bill 1934- .... **CLC 74**
See also AITN 2; CA 61-64; CANR 31

Mphahlele, Es'kia
See Mphahlele, Ezekiel

Mphahlele, Ezekiel 1919- .... **CLC 25**
See also BLC 3; BW; CA 81-84; CANR 26

Mqhayi, S(amuel) E(dward) K(rune Loliwe)
1875-1945 .... **TCLC 25**
See also BLC 3

Mr. Martin
See Burroughs, William S(eward)

Mrozek, Slawomir 1930- .... **CLC 3, 13**
See also CA 13-16R; CAAS 10; CANR 29; MTCW

Mrs. Belloc-Lowndes
See Lowndes, Marie Adelaide (Belloc)

Mtwa, Percy (?)- .... **CLC 47**

Mueller, Lisel 1924- .... **CLC 13, 51**
See also CA 93-96; DLB 105

Muir, Edwin 1887-1959 .... **TCLC 2**
See also CA 104; DLB 20, 100

Muir, John 1838-1914 .... **TCLC 28**

Mujica Lainez, Manuel
1910-1984 .... **CLC 31**
See also Lainez, Manuel Mujica
See also CA 81-84; 112; CANR 32; HW

Mukherjee, Bharati 1940- .... **CLC 53**
See also BEST 89:2; CA 107; DLB 60; MTCW

Muldoon, Paul 1951- .... **CLC 32, 72**
See also CA 113; 129; DLB 40

Mulisch, Harry 1927- .... **CLC 42**
See also CA 9-12R; CANR 6, 26

Mull, Martin 1943- .... **CLC 17**
See also CA 105

Mulock, Dinah Maria
See Craik, Dinah Maria (Mulock)

Munford, Robert 1737(?)-1783 .... **LC 5**
See also DLB 31

Mungo, Raymond 1946- .... **CLC 72**
See also CA 49-52; CANR 2

Munro, Alice
1931- .... **CLC 6, 10, 19, 50; SSC 3**
See also AITN 2; CA 33-36R; CANR 33; DLB 53; MTCW; SATA 29

Munro, H(ector) H(ugh) 1870-1916
See Saki
See also CA 104; 130; CDBLB 1890-1914; DLB 34; MTCW; WLC

Murasaki, Lady .... **CMLC 1**

Murdoch, (Jean) Iris
1919- ...... **CLC 1, 2, 3, 4, 6, 8, 11, 15, 22, 31, 51**
See also CA 13-16R; CANR 8; CDBLB 1960 to Present; DLB 14; MTCW

Murphy, Richard 1927- .... **CLC 41**
See also CA 29-32R; DLB 40

Murphy, Sylvia 1937- .... **CLC 34**
See also CA 121

Murphy, Thomas (Bernard) 1935- ... **CLC 51**
See also CA 101

Murray, Les(lie) A(llan) 1938- ..... **CLC 40**
See also CA 21-24R; CANR 11, 27

Murry, J. Middleton
See Murry, John Middleton

Murry, John Middleton
1889-1957 .... TCLC **16**
See also CA 118

Musgrave, Susan 1951- .... CLC **13, 54**
See also CA 69-72

Musil, Robert (Edler von)
1880-1942 .... TCLC **12**
See also CA 109; DLB 81

Musset, (Louis Charles) Alfred de
1810-1857 .... NCLC **7**

My Brother's Brother
See Chekhov, Anton (Pavlovich)

Myers, Walter Dean 1937- .... CLC **35**
See also AAYA 4; BLC 3; BW; CA 33-36R; CANR 20; CLR 4, 16; DLB 33; MAICYA; SAAS 2; SATA 27, 41, 70, 71

Myers, Walter M.
See Myers, Walter Dean

Myles, Symon
See Follett, Ken(neth Martin)

Nabokov, Vladimir (Vladimirovich)
1899-1977 .... CLC **1, 2, 3, 6, 8, 11, 15, 23, 44, 46, 64; SSC 11**
See also CA 5-8R; 69-72; CANR 20; CDALB 1941-1968; DLB 2; DLBD 3; DLBY 80, 91; MTCW; WLC

Nagy, Laszlo 1925-1978............ CLC **7**
See also CA 129; 112

Naipaul, Shiva(dhar Srinivasa)
1945-1985 .... CLC **32, 39**
See also CA 110; 112; 116; CANR 33; DLBY 85; MTCW

Naipaul, V(idiadhar) S(urajprasad)
1932- .... CLC **4, 7, 9, 13, 18, 37**
See also CA 1-4R; CANR 1, 33; CDBLB 1960 to Present; DLBY 85; MTCW

Nakos, Lilika 1899(?)- .... CLC **29**

Narayan, R(asipuram) K(rishnaswami)
1906- .... CLC **7, 28, 47**
See also CA 81-84; CANR 33; MTCW; SATA 62

Nash, (Frediric) Ogden 1902-1971 .. CLC **23**
See also CA 13-14; 29-32R; CANR 34; CAP 1; DLB 11; MAICYA; MTCW; SATA 2, 46

Nathan, Daniel
See Dannay, Frederic

Nathan, George Jean 1882-1958 ... TCLC **18**
See also Hatteras, Owen
See also CA 114

Natsume, Kinnosuke 1867-1916
See Natsume, Soseki
See also CA 104

Natsume, Soseki .... TCLC **2, 10**
See also Natsume, Kinnosuke

Natti, (Mary) Lee 1919-
See Kingman, Lee
See also CA 5-8R; CANR 2

Naylor, Gloria 1950- .... CLC **28, 52**
See also AAYA 6; BLC 3; BW; CA 107; CANR 27; MTCW

Neihardt, John Gneisenau
1881-1973 .... CLC **32**
See also CA 13-14; CAP 1; DLB 9, 54

Nekrasov, Nikolai Alekseevich
1821-1878 .... NCLC **11**

Nelligan, Emile 1879-1941........ TCLC **14**
See also CA 114; DLB 92

Nelson, Willie 1933-.............. CLC **17**
See also CA 107

Nemerov, Howard (Stanley)
1920-1991 ....CLC **2, 6, 9, 36**
See also CA 1-4R; 134; CABS 2; CANR 1, 27; DLB 6; DLBY 83; MTCW

Neruda, Pablo
1904-1973 .... CLC **1, 2, 5, 7, 9, 28, 62; PC 4**
See also CA 19-20; 45-48; CAP 2; HW; MTCW; WLC

Nerval, Gerard de 1808-1855...... NCLC **1**

Nervo, (Jose) Amado (Ruiz de)
1870-1919 .... TCLC **11**
See also CA 109; 131; HW

Nessi, Pio Baroja y
See Baroja (y Nessi), Pio

Neufeld, John (Arthur) 1938- ...... CLC **17**
See also CA 25-28R; CANR 11, 37; MAICYA; SAAS 3; SATA 6

Neville, Emily Cheney 1919- ...... CLC **12**
See also CA 5-8R; CANR 3, 37; MAICYA; SAAS 2; SATA 1

Newbound, Bernard Slade 1930-
See Slade, Bernard
See also CA 81-84

Newby, P(ercy) H(oward)
1918- .... CLC **2, 13**
See also CA 5-8R; CANR 32; DLB 15; MTCW

Newlove, Donald 1928- .... CLC **6**
See also CA 29-32R; CANR 25

Newlove, John (Herbert) 1938-..... CLC **14**
See also CA 21-24R; CANR 9, 25

Newman, Charles 1938- .... CLC **2, 8**
See also CA 21-24R

Newman, Edwin (Harold) 1919- .... CLC **14**
See also AITN 1; CA 69-72; CANR 5

Newman, John Henry
1801-1890 .... NCLC **38**
See also DLB 18, 32, 55

Newton, Suzanne 1936- .... CLC **35**
See also CA 41-44R; CANR 14; SATA 5

Nexo, Martin Andersen
1869-1954 .... TCLC **43**

Nezval, Vitezslav 1900-1958 ...... TCLC **44**
See also CA 123

Ngema, Mbongeni 1955- .... CLC **57**

Ngugi, James T(hiong'o)........ CLC **3, 7, 13**
See also Ngugi wa Thiong'o

Ngugi wa Thiong'o 1938-.......... CLC **36**
See also Ngugi, James T(hiong'o)
See also BLC 3; BW; CA 81-84; CANR 27; MTCW

Nichol, B(arrie) P(hillip)
1944-1988 .... CLC **18**
See also CA 53-56; DLB 53; SATA 66

Nichols, John (Treadwell) 1940-.... CLC **38**
See also CA 9-12R; CAAS 2; CANR 6; DLBY 82

Nichols, Peter (Richard)
1927- .... CLC **5, 36, 65**
See also CA 104; CANR 33; DLB 13; MTCW

Nicolas, F. R. E.
See Freeling, Nicolas

Niedecker, Lorine 1903-1970.... CLC **10, 42**
See also CA 25-28; CAP 2; DLB 48

Nietzsche, Friedrich (Wilhelm)
1844-1900 .... TCLC **10, 18**
See also CA 107; 121

Nievo, Ippolito 1831-1861 .... NCLC **22**

Nightingale, Anne Redmon 1943-
See Redmon, Anne
See also CA 103

Nik.T.O.
See Annensky, Innokenty Fyodorovich

Nin, Anais
1903-1977 ..... CLC **1, 4, 8, 11, 14, 60; SSC 10**
See also AITN 2; CA 13-16R; 69-72; CANR 22; DLB 2, 4; MTCW

Nissenson, Hugh 1933-........... CLC **4, 9**
See also CA 17-20R; CANR 27; DLB 28

Niven, Larry .... CLC **8**
See also Niven, Laurence Van Cott
See also DLB 8

Niven, Laurence Van Cott 1938-
See Niven, Larry
See also CA 21-24R; CAAS 12; CANR 14; MTCW

Nixon, Agnes Eckhardt 1927- ...... CLC **21**
See also CA 110

Nizan, Paul 1905-1940............ TCLC **40**
See also DLB 72

Nkosi, Lewis 1936-................ CLC **45**
See also BLC 3; BW; CA 65-68; CANR 27

Nodier, (Jean) Charles (Emmanuel)
1780-1844 .... NCLC **19**
See also DLB 119

Nolan, Christopher 1965-.......... CLC **58**
See also CA 111

Norden, Charles
See Durrell, Lawrence (George)

Nordhoff, Charles (Bernard)
1887-1947 .... TCLC **23**
See also CA 108; DLB 9; SATA 23

Norman, Marsha 1947- .... CLC **28**
See also CA 105; CABS 3; DLBY 84

Norris, Benjamin Franklin Jr.
1870-1902 .... TCLC **24**
See also Norris, Frank
See also CA 110

Norris, Frank
See Norris, Benjamin Franklin Jr.
See also CDALB 1865-1917; DLB 12, 71

Norris, Leslie 1921- .... CLC **14**
See also CA 11-12; CANR 14; CAP 1; DLB 27

North, Andrew
See Norton, Andre

North, Captain George
See Stevenson, Robert Louis (Balfour)

North, Milou
See Erdrich, Louise

Northrup, B. A.
See Hubbard, L(afayette) Ron(ald)

North Staffs
See Hulme, T(homas) E(rnest)

Norton, Alice Mary
See Norton, Andre
See also MAICYA; SATA 1, 43

Norton, Andre 1912- .... **CLC 12**
See also Norton, Alice Mary
See also CA 1-4R; CANR 2, 31; DLB 8, 52; MTCW

Norway, Nevil Shute 1899-1960
See Shute, Nevil
See also CA 102; 93-96

Norwid, Cyprian Kamil
1821-1883 .... **NCLC 17**

Nosille, Nabrah
See Ellison, Harlan

Nossack, Hans Erich 1901-1978 ..... **CLC 6**
See also CA 93-96; 85-88; DLB 69

Nosu, Chuji
See Ozu, Yasujiro

Nova, Craig 1945-............. **CLC 7, 31**
See also CA 45-48; CANR 2

Novak, Joseph
See Kosinski, Jerzy (Nikodem)

Novalis 1772-1801 .... **NCLC 13**
See also DLB 90

Nowlan, Alden (Albert) 1933-1983 .. **CLC 15**
See also CA 9-12R; CANR 5; DLB 53

Noyes, Alfred 1880-1958 .... **TCLC 7**
See also CA 104; DLB 20

Nunn, Kem 19(?)- .... **CLC 34**

Nye, Robert 1939- .... **CLC 13, 42**
See also CA 33-36R; CANR 29; DLB 14; MTCW; SATA 6

Nyro, Laura 1947- .... **CLC 17**

Oates, Joyce Carol
1938- ..... **CLC 1, 2, 3, 6, 9, 11, 15, 19, 33, 52; SSC 6**
See also AITN 1; BEST 89:2; CA 5-8R; CANR 25; CDALB 1968-1988; DLB 2, 5; DLBY 81; MTCW; WLC

O'Brien, E. G.
See Clarke, Arthur C(harles)

O'Brien, Edna
1936- ... **CLC 3, 5, 8, 13, 36, 65; SSC 10**
See also CA 1-4R; CANR 6; CDBLB 1960 to Present; DLB 14; MTCW

O'Brien, Fitz-James 1828-1862... **NCLC 21**
See also DLB 74

O'Brien, Flann........ **CLC 1, 4, 5, 7, 10, 47**
See also O Nuallain, Brian

O'Brien, Richard 1942- .... **CLC 17**
See also CA 124

O'Brien, Tim 1946-........... **CLC 7, 19, 40**
See also CA 85-88; DLBD 9; DLBY 80

Obstfelder, Sigbjoern 1866-1900... **TCLC 23**
See also CA 123

O'Casey, Sean
1880-1964 .... **CLC 1, 5, 9, 11, 15**
See also CA 89-92; CDBLB 1914-1945; DLB 10; MTCW

O'Cathasaigh, Sean
See O'Casey, Sean

Ochs, Phil 1940-1976............. **CLC 17**
See also CA 65-68

O'Connor, Edwin (Greene)
1918-1968 .... **CLC 14**
See also CA 93-96; 25-28R

O'Connor, (Mary) Flannery
1925-1964 ... **CLC 1, 2, 3, 6, 10, 13, 15, 21, 66; SSC 1**
See also AAYA 7; CA 1-4R; CANR 3; CDALB 1941-1968; DLB 2; DLBY 80; MTCW; WLC

O'Connor, Frank.......... **CLC 23; SSC 5**
See also O'Donovan, Michael John

O'Dell, Scott 1898-1989........... **CLC 30**
See also AAYA 3; CA 61-64; 129; CANR 12, 30; CLR 1, 16; DLB 52; MAICYA; SATA 12, 60

Odets, Clifford 1906-1963 .... **CLC 2, 28**
See also CA 85-88; DLB 7, 26; MTCW

O'Donnell, K. M.
See Malzberg, Barry N(athaniel)

O'Donnell, Lawrence
See Kuttner, Henry

O'Donovan, Michael John
1903-1966 .... **CLC 14**
See also O'Connor, Frank
See also CA 93-96

Oe, Kenzaburo 1935- .... **CLC 10, 36**
See also CA 97-100; CANR 36; MTCW

O'Faolain, Julia 1932-........ **CLC 6, 19, 47**
See also CA 81-84; CAAS 2; CANR 12; DLB 14; MTCW

O'Faolain, Sean
1900-1991 .... **CLC 1, 7, 14, 32, 70**
See also CA 61-64; 134; CANR 12; DLB 15; MTCW

O'Flaherty, Liam
1896-1984 .... **CLC 5, 34; SSC 6**
See also CA 101; 113; CANR 35; DLB 36; DLBY 84

Ogilvy, Gavin
See Barrie, J(ames) M(atthew)

O'Grady, Standish James
1846-1928 .... **TCLC 5**
See also CA 104

O'Grady, Timothy 1951- .... **CLC 59**
See also CA 138

O'Hara, Frank 1926-1966 ..... **CLC 2, 5, 13**
See also CA 9-12R; 25-28R; CANR 33; DLB 5, 16; MTCW

O'Hara, John (Henry)
1905-1970 .... **CLC 1, 2, 3, 6, 11, 42**
See also CA 5-8R; 25-28R; CANR 31; CDALB 1929-1941; DLB 9, 86; DLBD 2; MTCW

O Hehir, Diana 1922- .... **CLC 41**
See also CA 93-96

Okigbo, Christopher (Ifenayichukwu)
1932-1967 .... **CLC 25**
See also BLC 3; BW; CA 77-80; MTCW

Olds, Sharon 1942-............. **CLC 32, 39**
See also CA 101; CANR 18; DLB 120

Oldstyle, Jonathan
See Irving, Washington

Olesha, Yuri (Karlovich)
1899-1960 .... **CLC 8**
See also CA 85-88

Oliphant, Margaret (Oliphant Wilson)
1828-1897 .... **NCLC 11**
See also DLB 18

Oliver, Mary 1935-............. **CLC 19, 34**
See also CA 21-24R; CANR 9; DLB 5

Olivier, Laurence (Kerr)
1907-1989 .... **CLC 20**
See also CA 111; 129

Olsen, Tillie 1913- ..... **CLC 4, 13; SSC 11**
See also CA 1-4R; CANR 1; DLB 28; DLBY 80; MTCW

Olson, Charles (John)
1910-1970 ..... **CLC 1, 2, 5, 6, 9, 11, 29**
See also CA 13-16; 25-28R; CABS 2; CANR 35; CAP 1; DLB 5, 16; MTCW

Olson, Toby 1937- .... **CLC 28**
See also CA 65-68; CANR 9, 31

Olyesha, Yuri
See Olesha, Yuri (Karlovich)

Ondaatje, Michael 1943- .... **CLC 14, 29, 51**
See also CA 77-80; DLB 60

Oneal, Elizabeth 1934-
See Oneal, Zibby
See also CA 106; CANR 28; MAICYA; SATA 30

Oneal, Zibby .... **CLC 30**
See also Oneal, Elizabeth
See also AAYA 5; CLR 13

O'Neill, Eugene (Gladstone)
1888-1953 .... **TCLC 1, 6, 27**
See also AITN 1; CA 110; 132; CDALB 1929-1941; DLB 7; MTCW; WLC

Onetti, Juan Carlos 1909- .... **CLC 7, 10**
See also CA 85-88; CANR 32; DLB 113; HW; MTCW

O Nuallain, Brian 1911-1966
See O'Brien, Flann
See also CA 21-22; 25-28R; CAP 2

Oppen, George 1908-1984 .... **CLC 7, 13, 34**
See also CA 13-16R; 113; CANR 8; DLB 5

Oppenheim, E(dward) Phillips
1866-1946 .... **TCLC 45**
See also CA 111; DLB 70

Orlovitz, Gil 1918-1973 .... **CLC 22**
See also CA 77-80; 45-48; DLB 2, 5

Ortega y Gasset, Jose 1883-1955 ... **TCLC 9**
See also CA 106; 130; HW; MTCW

Ortiz, Simon J(oseph) 1941- .... **CLC 45**
See also CA 134; DLB 120

Orton, Joe .... **CLC 4, 13, 43; DC 3**
See also Orton, John Kingsley
See also CDBLB 1960 to Present; DLB 13

Orton, John Kingsley 1933-1967
  See Orton, Joe
  See also CA 85-88; CANR 35; MTCW

Orwell, George .... **TCLC 2, 6, 15, 31**
  See also Blair, Eric (Arthur)
  See also CDBLB 1945-1960; DLB 15, 98; WLC

Osborne, David
  See Silverberg, Robert

Osborne, George
  See Silverberg, Robert

Osborne, John (James)
  1929- .... **CLC 1, 2, 5, 11, 45**
  See also CA 13-16R; CANR 21;
  CDBLB 1945-1960; DLB 13; MTCW; WLC

Osborne, Lawrence 1958- .... **CLC 50**

Oshima, Nagisa 1932- .... **CLC 20**
  See also CA 116; 121

Oskison, John M(ilton)
  1874-1947 .... **TCLC 35**

Ossoli, Sarah Margaret (Fuller marchesa d')
  1810-1850
  See Fuller, Margaret
  See also SATA 25

Ostrovsky, Alexander
  1823-1886 .... **NCLC 30**

Otero, Blas de 1916- .... **CLC 11**
  See also CA 89-92

Otto, Whitney 1955- .... **CLC 70**

Ouida .... **TCLC 43**
  See also De La Ramee, (Marie) Louise
  See also DLB 18

Ousmane, Sembene 1923- .... **CLC 66**
  See also BLC 3; BW; CA 117; 125; MTCW

Ovid 43B.C.-18th cent. (?)... **CMLC 7; PC 2**

Owen, Wilfred 1893-1918 ...... **TCLC 5, 27**
  See also CA 104; CDBLB 1914-1945;
  DLB 20; WLC

Owens, Rochelle 1936-............. **CLC 8**
  See also CA 17-20R; CAAS 2; CANR 39

Oz, Amos 1939- ... **CLC 5, 8, 11, 27, 33, 54**
  See also CA 53-56; CANR 27; MTCW

Ozick, Cynthia 1928-...... **CLC 3, 7, 28, 62**
  See also BEST 90:1; CA 17-20R; CANR 23;
  DLB 28; DLBY 82; MTCW

Ozu, Yasujiro 1903-1963 .... **CLC 16**
  See also CA 112

Pacheco, C.
  See Pessoa, Fernando (Antonio Nogueira)

Pa Chin
  See Li Fei-kan

Pack, Robert 1929-................ **CLC 13**
  See also CA 1-4R; CANR 3; DLB 5

Padgett, Lewis
  See Kuttner, Henry

Padilla (Lorenzo), Heberto 1932-... **CLC 38**
  See also AITN 1; CA 123; 131; HW

Page, Jimmy 1944-................ **CLC 12**

Page, Louise 1955-................ **CLC 40**

Page, P(atricia) K(athleen)
  1916- .... **CLC 7, 18**
  See also CA 53-56; CANR 4, 22; DLB 68; MTCW

Paget, Violet 1856-1935
  See Lee, Vernon
  See also CA 104

Paget-Lowe, Henry
  See Lovecraft, H(oward) P(hillips)

Paglia, Camille 1947-............. **CLC 68**

Pakenham, Antonia
  See Fraser, Antonia (Pakenham)

Palamas, Kostes 1859-1943 .... **TCLC 5**
  See also CA 105

Palazzeschi, Aldo 1885-1974....... **CLC 11**
  See also CA 89-92; 53-56; DLB 114

Paley, Grace 1922-.... **CLC 4, 6, 37; SSC 8**
  See also CA 25-28R; CANR 13; DLB 28; MTCW

Palin, Michael (Edward) 1943-..... **CLC 21**
  See also Monty Python
  See also CA 107; CANR 35; SATA 67

Palliser, Charles 1947-............ **CLC 65**
  See also CA 136

Palma, Ricardo 1833-1919........ **TCLC 29**

Pancake, Breece Dexter 1952-1979
  See Pancake, Breece D'J
  See also CA 123; 109

Pancake, Breece D'J.............. **CLC 29**
  See also Pancake, Breece Dexter

Papadiamantis, Alexandros
  1851-1911 .... **TCLC 29**

Papadiamantopoulos, Johannes 1856-1910
  See Moreas, Jean
  See also CA 117

Papini, Giovanni 1881-1956....... **TCLC 22**
  See also CA 121

Paracelsus 1493-1541.............. **LC 14**

Parasol, Peter
  See Stevens, Wallace

Parfenie, Maria
  See Codrescu, Andrei

Parini, Jay (Lee) 1948- .... **CLC 54**
  See also CA 97-100; CAAS 16; CANR 32

Park, Jordan
  See Kornbluth, C(yril) M.; Pohl, Frederik

Parker, Bert
  See Ellison, Harlan

Parker, Dorothy (Rothschild)
  1893-1967 .... **CLC 15, 68; SSC 2**
  See also CA 19-20; 25-28R; CAP 2;
  DLB 11, 45, 86; MTCW

Parker, Robert B(rown) 1932-...... **CLC 27**
  See also BEST 89:4; CA 49-52; CANR 1, 26; MTCW

Parkes, Lucas
  See Harris, John (Wyndham Parkes Lucas) Beynon

Parkin, Frank 1940-............... **CLC 43**

Parkman, Francis Jr. 1823-1893.. **NCLC 12**
  See also DLB 1, 30

Parks, Gordon (Alexander Buchanan)
  1912- .... **CLC 1, 16**
  See also AITN 2; BLC 3; BW; CA 41-44R;
  CANR 26; DLB 33; SATA 8

Parnell, Thomas 1679-1718 .... **LC 3**
  See also DLB 94

Parra, Nicanor 1914-.............. **CLC 2**
  See also CA 85-88; CANR 32; HW; MTCW

Parson Lot
  See Kingsley, Charles

Partridge, Anthony
  See Oppenheim, E(dward) Phillips

Pascoli, Giovanni 1855-1912 ...... **TCLC 45**

Pasolini, Pier Paolo
  1922-1975 .... **CLC 20, 37**
  See also CA 93-96; 61-64; MTCW

Pasquini
  See Silone, Ignazio

Pastan, Linda (Olenik) 1932- ...... **CLC 27**
  See also CA 61-64; CANR 18; DLB 5

Pasternak, Boris (Leonidovich)
  1890-1960 .... **CLC 7, 10, 18, 63**
  See also CA 127; 116; MTCW; WLC

Patchen, Kenneth 1911-1972... **CLC 1, 2, 18**
  See also CA 1-4R; 33-36R; CANR 3, 35;
  DLB 16, 48; MTCW

Pater, Walter (Horatio)
  1839-1894 .... **NCLC 7**
  See also CDBLB 1832-1890; DLB 57

Paterson, A(ndrew) B(arton)
  1864-1941 .... **TCLC 32**

Paterson, Katherine (Womeldorf)
  1932- .... **CLC 12, 30**
  See also AAYA 1; CA 21-24R; CANR 28;
  CLR 7; DLB 52; MAICYA; MTCW;
  SATA 13, 53

Patmore, Coventry Kersey Dighton
  1823-1896 .... **NCLC 9**
  See also DLB 35, 98

Paton, Alan (Stewart)
  1903-1988 .... **CLC 4, 10, 25, 55**
  See also CA 13-16; 125; CANR 22; CAP 1;
  MTCW; SATA 11, 56; WLC

Paton Walsh, Gillian 1939-
  See Walsh, Jill Paton
  See also CANR 38; MAICYA; SAAS 3; SATA 4

Paulding, James Kirke 1778-1860.. **NCLC 2**
  See also DLB 3, 59, 74

Paulin, Thomas Neilson 1949-
  See Paulin, Tom
  See also CA 123; 128

Paulin, Tom .... **CLC 37**
  See also Paulin, Thomas Neilson
  See also DLB 40

Paustovsky, Konstantin (Georgievich)
  1892-1968 .... **CLC 40**
  See also CA 93-96; 25-28R

Pavese, Cesare 1908-1950 .... **TCLC 3**
  See also CA 104

Pavic, Milorad 1929-.............. **CLC 60**
  See also CA 136

Payne, Alan
  See Jakes, John (William)

Paz, Gil
See Lugones, Leopoldo

Paz, Octavio
1914- ...... **CLC 3, 4, 6, 10, 19, 51, 65; PC 1**
See also CA 73-76; CANR 32; DLBY 90; HW; MTCW; WLC

Peacock, Molly 1947- .... **CLC 60**
See also CA 103; DLB 120

Peacock, Thomas Love
1785-1866 .... **NCLC 22**
See also DLB 96, 116

Peake, Mervyn 1911-1968....... **CLC 7, 54**
See also CA 5-8R; 25-28R; CANR 3; DLB 15; MTCW; SATA 23

Pearce, Philippa .... **CLC 21**
See also Christie, (Ann) Philippa
See also CLR 9; MAICYA; SATA 1, 67

Pearl, Eric
See Elman, Richard

Pearson, T(homas) R(eid) 1956- .... **CLC 39**
See also CA 120; 130

Peck, John 1941- .... **CLC 3**
See also CA 49-52; CANR 3

Peck, Richard (Wayne) 1934- ...... **CLC 21**
See also AAYA 1; CA 85-88; CANR 19, 38; MAICYA; SAAS 2; SATA 18, 55

Peck, Robert Newton 1928-........ **CLC 17**
See also AAYA 3; CA 81-84; CANR 31; MAICYA; SAAS 1; SATA 21, 62

Peckinpah, (David) Sam(uel)
1925-1984 .... **CLC 20**
See also CA 109; 114

Pedersen, Knut 1859-1952
See Hamsun, Knut
See also CA 104; 119; MTCW

Peeslake, Gaffer
See Durrell, Lawrence (George)

Peguy, Charles Pierre
1873-1914 .... **TCLC 10**
See also CA 107

Pena, Ramon del Valle y
See Valle-Inclan, Ramon (Maria) del

Pendennis, Arthur Esquir
See Thackeray, William Makepeace

Pepys, Samuel 1633-1703........... **LC 11**
See also CDBLB 1660-1789; DLB 101; WLC

Percy, Walker
1916-1990 ... **CLC 2, 3, 6, 8, 14, 18, 47, 65**
See also CA 1-4R; 131; CANR 1, 23; DLB 2; DLBY 80, 90; MTCW

Perec, Georges 1936-1982 .... **CLC 56**
See also DLB 83

Pereda (y Sanchez de Porrua), Jose Maria de
1833-1906 .... **TCLC 16**
See also CA 117

Pereda y Porrua, Jose Maria de
See Pereda (y Sanchez de Porrua), Jose Maria de

Peregoy, George Weems
See Mencken, H(enry) L(ouis)

Perelman, S(idney) J(oseph)
1904-1979 ... **CLC 3, 5, 9, 15, 23, 44, 49**
See also AITN 1, 2; CA 73-76; 89-92; CANR 18; DLB 11, 44; MTCW

Peret, Benjamin 1899-1959 .... **TCLC 20**
See also CA 117

Peretz, Isaac Loeb 1851(?)-1915.... **TCLC 16**
See also CA 109

Peretz, Yitzkhok Leibush
See Peretz, Isaac Loeb

Perez Galdos, Benito 1843-1920 ... **TCLC 27**
See also CA 125; HW

Perrault, Charles 1628-1703 .... **LC 2**
See also MAICYA; SATA 25

Perry, Brighton
See Sherwood, Robert E(mmet)

Perse, St.-John .... **CLC 4, 11, 46**
See also Leger, (Marie-Rene) Alexis Saint-Leger

Perse, Saint-John
See Leger, (Marie-Rene) Alexis Saint-Leger

Peseenz, Tulio F.
See Lopez y Fuentes, Gregorio

Pesetsky, Bette 1932-............. **CLC 28**
See also CA 133

Peshkov, Alexei Maximovich 1868-1936
See Gorky, Maxim
See also CA 105

Pessoa, Fernando (Antonio Nogueira)
1888-1935 .... **TCLC 27**
See also CA 125

Peterkin, Julia Mood 1880-1961.... **CLC 31**
See also CA 102; DLB 9

Peters, Joan K. 1945-.............. **CLC 39**

Peters, Robert L(ouis) 1924-........ **CLC 7**
See also CA 13-16R; CAAS 8; DLB 105

Petofi, Sandor 1823-1849........ **NCLC 21**

Petrakis, Harry Mark 1923-........ **CLC 3**
See also CA 9-12R; CANR 4, 30

Petrov, Evgeny .... **TCLC 21**
See also Kataev, Evgeny Petrovich

Petry, Ann (Lane) 1908- ...... **CLC 1, 7, 18**
See also BW; CA 5-8R; CAAS 6; CANR 4; CLR 12; DLB 76; MAICYA; MTCW; SATA 5

Petursson, Hallgrimur 1614-1674 .... **LC 8**

Philipson, Morris H. 1926- .... **CLC 53**
See also CA 1-4R; CANR 4

Phillips, David Graham
1867-1911 .... **TCLC 44**
See also CA 108; DLB 9, 12

Phillips, Jack
See Sandburg, Carl (August)

Phillips, Jayne Anne 1952- ..... **CLC 15, 33**
See also CA 101; CANR 24; DLBY 80; MTCW

Phillips, Richard
See Dick, Philip K(indred)

Phillips, Robert (Schaeffer) 1938-... **CLC 28**
See also CA 17-20R; CAAS 13; CANR 8; DLB 105

Phillips, Ward
See Lovecraft, H(oward) P(hillips)

Piccolo, Lucio 1901-1969.......... **CLC 13**
See also CA 97-100; DLB 114

Pickthall, Marjorie L(owry) C(hristie)
1883-1922 ....**TCLC 21**
See also CA 107; DLB 92

Pico della Mirandola, Giovanni
1463-1494 .... **LC 15**

Piercy, Marge
1936- .... **CLC 3, 6, 14, 18, 27, 62**
See also CA 21-24R; CAAS 1; CANR 13; DLB 120; MTCW

Piers, Robert
See Anthony, Piers

Pieyre de Mandiargues, Andre 1909-1991
See Mandiargues, Andre Pieyre de
See also CA 103; 136; CANR 22

Pilnyak, Boris .... **TCLC 23**
See also Vogau, Boris Andreyevich

Pincherle, Alberto 1907-1990 ... **CLC 11, 18**
See also Moravia, Alberto
See also CA 25-28R; 132; CANR 33; MTCW

Pineda, Cecile 1942-.............. **CLC 39**
See also CA 118

Pinero, Arthur Wing 1855-1934 ... **TCLC 32**
See also CA 110; DLB 10

Pinero, Miguel (Antonio Gomez)
1946-1988 .... **CLC 4, 55**
See also CA 61-64; 125; CANR 29; HW

Pinget, Robert 1919- .... **CLC 7, 13, 37**
See also CA 85-88; DLB 83

Floyd .... **CLC 35**
See also Barrett, (Roger) Syd; Gilmour, David; Mason, Nick; Waters, Roger; Wright, Rick

Pinkney, Edward 1802-1828 ..... **NCLC 31**

Pinkwater, Daniel Manus 1941- .... **CLC 35**
See also Pinkwater, Manus
See also AAYA 1; CA 29-32R; CANR 12, 38; CLR 4; MAICYA; SAAS 3; SATA 46

Pinkwater, Manus
See Pinkwater, Daniel Manus
See also SATA 8

Pinsky, Robert 1940- .... **CLC 9, 19, 38**
See also CA 29-32R; CAAS 4; DLBY 82

Pinta, Harold
See Pinter, Harold

Pinter, Harold
1930- ..... **CLC 1, 3, 6, 9, 11, 15, 27, 58**
See also CA 5-8R; CANR 33; CDBLB 1960 to Present; DLB 13; MTCW; WLC

Pirandello, Luigi 1867-1936..... **TCLC 4, 29**
See also CA 104; WLC

Pirsig, Robert M(aynard) 1928- ... **CLC 4, 6**
See also CA 53-56; MTCW; SATA 39

Pisarev, Dmitry Ivanovich
1840-1868 .... **NCLC 25**

Pix, Mary (Griffith) 1666-1709....... **LC 8**
See also DLB 80

Plaidy, Jean
See Hibbert, Eleanor Burford

Plant, Robert 1948- .... **CLC 12**

Plante, David (Robert)
1940- . . . . CLC 7, 23, 38
See also CA 37-40R; CANR 12, 36;
DLBY 83; MTCW

Plath, Sylvia
1932-1963 . . . . CLC 1, 2, 3, 5, 9, 11, 14,
17, 50, 51, 62; PC 1
See also CA 19-20; CANR 34; CAP 2;
CDALB 1941-1968; DLB 5, 6; MTCW;
WLC

Plato 428(?)B.C.-348(?)B.C. . . . . CMLC 8

Platonov, Andrei . . . . TCLC 14
See also Klimentov, Andrei Platonovich

Platt, Kin 1911- . . . . CLC 26
See also CA 17-20R; CANR 11; SATA 21

Plick et Plock
See Simenon, Georges (Jacques Christian)

Plimpton, George (Ames) 1927- . . . . . CLC 36
See also AITN 1; CA 21-24R; CANR 32;
MTCW; SATA 10

Plomer, William Charles Franklin
1903-1973 . . . . CLC 4, 8
See also CA 21-22; CANR 34; CAP 2;
DLB 20; MTCW; SATA 24

Plowman, Piers
See Kavanagh, Patrick (Joseph)

Plum, J.
See Wodehouse, P(elham) G(renville)

Plumly, Stanley (Ross) 1939- . . . . . . CLC 33
See also CA 108; 110; DLB 5

Poe, Edgar Allan
1809-1849 . . . NCLC 1, 16; PC 1; SSC 1
See also CDALB 1640-1865; DLB 3, 59, 73,
74; SATA 23; WLC

Poet of Titchfield Street, The
See Pound, Ezra (Weston Loomis)

Pohl, Frederik 1919- . . . . CLC 18
See also CA 61-64; CAAS 1; CANR 11, 37;
DLB 8; MTCW; SATA 24

Poirier, Louis 1910-
See Gracq, Julien
See also CA 122; 126

Poitier, Sidney 1927- . . . . CLC 26
See also BW; CA 117

Polanski, Roman 1933- . . . . CLC 16
See also CA 77-80

Poliakoff, Stephen 1952- . . . . CLC 38
See also CA 106; DLB 13

. . . . CLC 26
See also Copeland, Stewart (Armstrong);
Summers, Andrew James; Sumner,
Gordon Matthew

Pollitt, Katha 1949- . . . . CLC 28
See also CA 120; 122; MTCW

Pollock, Sharon 1936- . . . . CLC 50
See also DLB 60

Pomerance, Bernard 1940- . . . . CLC 13
See also CA 101

Ponge, Francis (Jean Gaston Alfred)
1899-1988 . . . . CLC 6, 18
See also CA 85-88; 126

Pontoppidan, Henrik 1857-1943 . . . TCLC 29

Poole, Josephine . . . . CLC 17
See also Helyar, Jane Penelope Josephine
See also SAAS 2; SATA 5

Popa, Vasko 1922- . . . . CLC 19
See also CA 112

Pope, Alexander 1688-1744 . . . . LC 3
See also CDBLB 1660-1789; DLB 95, 101;
WLC

Porter, Connie 1960- . . . . CLC 70

Porter, Gene(va Grace) Stratton
1863(?)-1924 . . . . TCLC 21
See also CA 112

Porter, Katherine Anne
1890-1980 . . . . . CLC 1, 3, 7, 10, 13, 15,
27; SSC 4
See also AITN 2; CA 1-4R; 101; CANR 1;
DLB 4, 9, 102; DLBY 80; MTCW;
SATA 23, 39

Porter, Peter (Neville Frederick)
1929- . . . . CLC 5, 13, 33
See also CA 85-88; DLB 40

Porter, William Sydney 1862-1910
See Henry, O.
See also CA 104; 131; CDALB 1865-1917;
DLB 12, 78, 79; MTCW; YABC 2

Portillo (y Pacheco), Jose Lopez
See Lopez Portillo (y Pacheco), Jose

Post, Melville Davisson
1869-1930 . . . . TCLC 39
See also CA 110

Potok, Chaim 1929- . . . . CLC 2, 7, 14, 26
See also AITN 1, 2; CA 17-20R; CANR 19,
35; DLB 28; MTCW; SATA 33

Potter, Beatrice
See Webb, (Martha) Beatrice (Potter)
See also MAICYA

Potter, Dennis (Christopher George)
1935- . . . . CLC 58
See also CA 107; CANR 33; MTCW

Pound, Ezra (Weston Loomis)
1885-1972 . . . . . CLC 1, 2, 3, 4, 5, 7, 10,
13, 18, 34, 48, 50; PC 4
See also CA 5-8R; 37-40R;
CDALB 1917-1929; DLB 4, 45, 63;
MTCW; WLC

Povod, Reinaldo 1959- . . . . CLC 44
See also CA 136

Powell, Anthony (Dymoke)
1905- . . . . CLC 1, 3, 7, 9, 10, 31
See also CA 1-4R; CANR 1, 32;
CDBLB 1945-1960; DLB 15; MTCW

Powell, Dawn 1897-1965 . . . . CLC 66
See also CA 5-8R

Powell, Padgett 1952- . . . . CLC 34
See also CA 126

Powers, J(ames) F(arl)
1917- . . . . CLC 1, 4, 8, 57; SSC 4
See also CA 1-4R; CANR 2; MTCW

Powers, John J(ames) 1945-
See Powers, John R.
See also CA 69-72

Powers, John R. . . . . CLC 66
See also Powers, John J(ames)

Pownall, David 1938- . . . . CLC 10
See also CA 89-92; DLB 14

Powys, John Cowper
1872-1963 . . . . CLC 7, 9, 15, 46
See also CA 85-88; DLB 15; MTCW

Powys, T(heodore) F(rancis)
1875-1953 . . . . TCLC 9
See also CA 106; DLB 36

Prager, Emily 1952- . . . . CLC 56

Pratt, Edwin John 1883-1964 . . . . . . CLC 19
See also CA 93-96; DLB 92

Premchand . . . . TCLC 21
See also Srivastava, Dhanpat Rai

Preussler, Otfried 1923- . . . . CLC 17
See also CA 77-80; SATA 24

Prevert, Jacques (Henri Marie)
1900-1977 . . . . CLC 15
See also CA 77-80; 69-72; CANR 29;
MTCW; SATA 30

Prevost, Abbe (Antoine Francois)
1697-1763 . . . . LC 1

Price, (Edward) Reynolds
1933- . . . . CLC 3, 6, 13, 43, 50, 63
See also CA 1-4R; CANR 1, 37; DLB 2

Price, Richard 1949- . . . . CLC 6, 12
See also CA 49-52; CANR 3; DLBY 81

Prichard, Katharine Susannah
1883-1969 . . . . CLC 46
See also CA 11-12; CANR 33; CAP 1;
MTCW; SATA 66

Priestley, J(ohn) B(oynton)
1894-1984 . . . . CLC 2, 5, 9, 34
See also CA 9-12R; 113; CANR 33;
CDBLB 1914-1945; DLB 10, 34, 77, 100;
DLBY 84; MTCW

Prince, F(rank) T(empleton) 1912- . . CLC 22
See also CA 101; DLB 20

Prince 1958(?)- . . . . CLC 35

Prince Kropotkin
See Kropotkin, Peter (Alekseevich)

Prior, Matthew 1664-1721 . . . . LC 4
See also DLB 95

Pritchard, William H(arrison)
1932- . . . . CLC 34
See also CA 65-68; CANR 23; DLB 111

Pritchett, V(ictor) S(awdon)
1900- . . . . CLC 5, 13, 15, 41
See also CA 61-64; CANR 31; DLB 15;
MTCW

Private 19022
See Manning, Frederic

Probst, Mark 1925- . . . . CLC 59
See also CA 130

Prokosch, Frederic 1908-1989 . . . . CLC 4, 48
See also CA 73-76; 128; DLB 48

Prophet, The
See Dreiser, Theodore (Herman Albert)

Prose, Francine 1947- . . . . CLC 45
See also CA 109; 112

Proudhon
See Cunha, Euclides (Rodrigues Pimenta) da

Proust,
(Valentin-Louis-George-Eugene-)Marcel
1871-1922 . . . . TCLC 7, 13, 33
See also CA 104; 120; DLB 65; MTCW;
WLC

Prowler, Harley
See Masters, Edgar Lee

Pryor, Richard (Franklin Lenox Thomas)
1940- .... CLC 26
See also CA 122

Przybyszewski, Stanislaw
1868-1927 .... TCLC 36
See also DLB 66

Pteleon
See Grieve, C(hristopher) M(urray)

Puckett, Lute
See Masters, Edgar Lee

Puig, Manuel
1932-1990 .... CLC 3, 5, 10, 28, 65
See also CA 45-48; CANR 2, 32; DLB 113; HW; MTCW

Purdy, A(lfred) W(ellington)
1918- .... CLC 3, 6, 14, 50
See also Purdy, Al
See also CA 81-84

Purdy, Al
See Purdy, A(lfred) W(ellington)
See also DLB 88

Purdy, James (Amos)
1923- .... CLC 2, 4, 10, 28, 52
See also CA 33-36R; CAAS 1; CANR 19; DLB 2; MTCW

Pure, Simon
See Swinnerton, Frank Arthur

Pushkin, Alexander (Sergeyevich)
1799-1837 .... NCLC 3, 27
See also SATA 61; WLC

P'u Sung-ling 1640-1715 .... LC 3

Putnam, Arthur Lee
See Alger, Horatio Jr.

Puzo, Mario 1920- .... CLC 1, 2, 6, 36
See also CA 65-68; CANR 4; DLB 6; MTCW

Pym, Barbara (Mary Crampton)
1913-1980 .... CLC 13, 19, 37
See also CA 13-14; 97-100; CANR 13, 34; CAP 1; DLB 14; DLBY 87; MTCW

Pynchon, Thomas (Ruggles Jr.)
1937- .. CLC 2, 3, 6, 9, 11, 18, 33, 62, 72
See also BEST 90:2; CA 17-20R; CANR 22; DLB 2; MTCW; WLC

Qian Zhongshu
See Ch'ien Chung-shu

Qroll
See Dagerman, Stig (Halvard)

Quarrington, Paul (Lewis) 1953- .... CLC 65
See also CA 129

Quasimodo, Salvatore 1901-1968 ... CLC 10
See also CA 13-16; 25-28R; CAP 1; DLB 114; MTCW

Queen, Ellery .... CLC 3, 11
See also Dannay, Frederic; Davidson, Avram; Lee, Manfred B(ennington); Sturgeon, Theodore (Hamilton); Vance, John Holbrook

Queen, Ellery Jr.
See Dannay, Frederic; Lee, Manfred B(ennington)

Queneau, Raymond
1903-1976 .... CLC 2, 5, 10, 42
See also CA 77-80; 69-72; CANR 32; DLB 72; MTCW

Quin, Ann (Marie) 1936-1973 .... CLC 6
See also CA 9-12R; 45-48; DLB 14

Quinn, Martin
See Smith, Martin Cruz

Quinn, Simon
See Smith, Martin Cruz

Quiroga, Horacio (Sylvestre)
1878-1937 .... TCLC 20
See also CA 117; 131; HW; MTCW

Quoirez, Francoise 1935- .... CLC 9
See also Sagan, Francoise
See also CA 49-52; CANR 6, 39; MTCW

Raabe, Wilhelm 1831-1910 .... TCLC 45

Rabe, David (William) 1940- ... CLC 4, 8, 33
See also CA 85-88; CABS 3; DLB 7

Rabelais, Francois 1483-1553 .... LC 5
See also WLC

Rabinovitch, Sholem 1859-1916
See Aleichem, Sholom
See also CA 104

Radcliffe, Ann (Ward) 1764-1823 .. NCLC 6
See also DLB 39

Radiguet, Raymond 1903-1923 .... TCLC 29
See also DLB 65

Radnoti, Miklos 1909-1944 .... TCLC 16
See also CA 118

Rado, James 1939- .... CLC 17
See also CA 105

Radvanyi, Netty 1900-1983
See Seghers, Anna
See also CA 85-88; 110

Raeburn, John (Hay) 1941- .... CLC 34
See also CA 57-60

Ragni, Gerome 1942-1991 .... CLC 17
See also CA 105; 134

Rahv, Philip .... CLC 24
See also Greenberg, Ivan

Raine, Craig 1944- .... CLC 32
See also CA 108; CANR 29; DLB 40

Raine, Kathleen (Jessie) 1908- ... CLC 7, 45
See also CA 85-88; DLB 20; MTCW

Rainis, Janis 1865-1929 .... TCLC 29

Rakosi, Carl .... CLC 47
See also Rawley, Callman
See also CAAS 5

Raleigh, Richard
See Lovecraft, H(oward) P(hillips)

Rallentando, H. P.
See Sayers, Dorothy L(eigh)

Ramal, Walter
See de la Mare, Walter (John)

Ramon, Juan
See Jimenez (Mantecon), Juan Ramon

Ramos, Graciliano 1892-1953 ..... TCLC 32

Rampersad, Arnold 1941- .... CLC 44
See also CA 127; 133; DLB 111

Rampling, Anne
See Rice, Anne

Ramuz, Charles-Ferdinand
1878-1947 .... TCLC 33

Rand, Ayn 1905-1982 .... CLC 3, 30, 44
See also CA 13-16R; 105; CANR 27; MTCW; WLC

Randall, Dudley (Felker) 1914- ...... CLC 1
See also BLC 3; BW; CA 25-28R; CANR 23; DLB 41

Randall, Robert
See Silverberg, Robert

Ranger, Ken
See Creasey, John

Ransom, John Crowe
1888-1974 .... CLC 2, 4, 5, 11, 24
See also CA 5-8R; 49-52; CANR 6, 34; DLB 45, 63; MTCW

Rao, Raja 1909- .... CLC 25, 56
See also CA 73-76; MTCW

Raphael, Frederic (Michael)
1931- .... CLC 2, 14
See also CA 1-4R; CANR 1; DLB 14

Ratcliffe, James P.
See Mencken, H(enry) L(ouis)

Rathbone, Julian 1935- .... CLC 41
See also CA 101; CANR 34

Rattigan, Terence (Mervyn)
1911-1977 .... CLC 7
See also CA 85-88; 73-76; CDBLB 1945-1960; DLB 13; MTCW

Ratushinskaya, Irina 1954- .... CLC 54
See also CA 129

Raven, Simon (Arthur Noel)
1927- .... CLC 14
See also CA 81-84

Rawley, Callman 1903-
See Rakosi, Carl
See also CA 21-24R; CANR 12, 32

Rawlings, Marjorie Kinnan
1896-1953 .... TCLC 4
See also CA 104; 137; DLB 9, 22, 102; MAICYA; YABC 1

Ray, Satyajit 1921- .... CLC 16
See also CA 114; 137

Read, Herbert Edward 1893-1968 .... CLC 4
See also CA 85-88; 25-28R; DLB 20

Read, Piers Paul 1941- ...... CLC 4, 10, 25
See also CA 21-24R; CANR 38; DLB 14; SATA 21

Reade, Charles 1814-1884 .... NCLC 2
See also DLB 21

Reade, Hamish
See Gray, Simon (James Holliday)

Reading, Peter 1946- .... CLC 47
See also CA 103; DLB 40

Reaney, James 1926- .... CLC 13
See also CA 41-44R; CAAS 15; DLB 68; SATA 43

Rebreanu, Liviu 1885-1944 .... TCLC 28

Rechy, John (Francisco)
1934- .... CLC 1, 7, 14, 18
See also CA 5-8R; CAAS 4; CANR 6, 32; DLBY 82; HW

Redcam, Tom 1870-1933 .... TCLC 25

Reddin, Keith .... CLC 67

Redgrove, Peter (William)
1932- .... CLC **6, 41**
See also CA 1-4R; CANR 3, 39; DLB 40

Redmon, Anne .... CLC **22**
See also Nightingale, Anne Redmon
See also DLBY 86

Reed, Eliot
See Ambler, Eric

Reed, Ishmael
1938- .... CLC **2, 3, 5, 6, 13, 32, 60**
See also BLC 3; BW; CA 21-24R;
CANR 25; DLB 2, 5, 33; DLBD 8;
MTCW

Reed, John (Silas) 1887-1920 ...... TCLC **9**
See also CA 106

Reed, Lou....................... CLC **21**
See also Firbank, Louis

Reeve, Clara 1729-1807 .... NCLC **19**
See also DLB 39

Reid, Christopher 1949-........... CLC **33**
See also DLB 40

Reid, Desmond
See Moorcock, Michael (John)

Reid Banks, Lynne 1929-
See Banks, Lynne Reid
See also CA 1-4R; CANR 6, 22, 38;
CLR 24; MAICYA; SATA 22

Reilly, William K.
See Creasey, John

Reiner, Max
See Caldwell, (Janet Miriam) Taylor (Holland)

Reis, Ricardo
See Pessoa, Fernando (Antonio Nogueira)

Remarque, Erich Maria
1898-1970 .... CLC **21**
See also CA 77-80; 29-32R; DLB 56;
MTCW

Remizov, A.
See Remizov, Aleksei (Mikhailovich)

Remizov, A. M.
See Remizov, Aleksei (Mikhailovich)

Remizov, Aleksei (Mikhailovich)
1877-1957 .... TCLC **27**
See also CA 125; 133

Renan, Joseph Ernest
1823-1892 .... NCLC **26**

Renard, Jules 1864-1910 .... TCLC **17**
See also CA 117

Renault, Mary............... CLC **3, 11, 17**
See also Challans, Mary
See also DLBY 83

Rendell, Ruth (Barbara) 1930-.. CLC **28, 48**
See also Vine, Barbara
See also CA 109; CANR 32; DLB 87;
MTCW

Renoir, Jean 1894-1979 .... CLC **20**
See also CA 129; 85-88

Resnais, Alain 1922-.............. CLC **16**

Reverdy, Pierre 1889-1960 .... CLC **53**
See also CA 97-100; 89-92

Rexroth, Kenneth
1905-1982 ...... CLC **1, 2, 6, 11, 22, 49**
See also CA 5-8R; 107; CANR 14, 34;
CDALB 1941-1968; DLB 16, 48;
DLBY 82; MTCW

Reyes, Alfonso 1889-1959 .... TCLC **33**
See also CA 131; HW

Reyes y Basoalto, Ricardo Eliecer Neftali
See Neruda, Pablo

Reymont, Wladyslaw (Stanislaw)
1868(?)-1925 .... TCLC **5**
See also CA 104

Reynolds, Jonathan 1942-........ CLC **6, 38**
See also CA 65-68; CANR 28

Reynolds, Joshua 1723-1792 .... LC **15**
See also DLB 104

Reynolds, Michael Shane 1937- .... CLC **44**
See also CA 65-68; CANR 9

Reznikoff, Charles 1894-1976 .... CLC **9**
See also CA 33-36; 61-64; CAP 2; DLB 28, 45

Rezzori (d'Arezzo), Gregor von
1914- .... CLC **25**
See also CA 122; 136

Rhine, Richard
See Silverstein, Alvin

Rhys, Jean
1890(?)-1979 .... CLC **2, 4, 6, 14, 19, 51**
See also CA 25-28R; 85-88; CANR 35;
CDBLB 1945-1960; DLB 36, 117; MTCW

Ribeiro, Darcy 1922-............. CLC **34**
See also CA 33-36R

Ribeiro, Joao Ubaldo (Osorio Pimentel)
1941- .... CLC **10, 67**
See also CA 81-84

Ribman, Ronald (Burt) 1932- .... CLC **7**
See also CA 21-24R

Ricci, Nino 1959-................. CLC **70**
See also CA 137

Rice, Anne 1941- .... CLC **41**
See also AAYA 9; BEST 89:2; CA 65-68;
CANR 12, 36

Rice, Elmer (Leopold)
1892-1967 .... CLC **7, 49**
See also CA 21-22; 25-28R; CAP 2; DLB 4, 7; MTCW

Rice, Tim 1944- .... CLC **21**
See also CA 103

Rich, Adrienne (Cecile)
1929- ..... CLC **3, 6, 7, 11, 18, 36; PC 5**
See also CA 9-12R; CANR 20; DLB 5, 67;
MTCW

Rich, Barbara
See Graves, Robert (von Ranke)

Rich, Robert
See Trumbo, Dalton

Richards, David Adams 1950-...... CLC **59**
See also CA 93-96; DLB 53

Richards, I(vor) A(rmstrong)
1893-1979 .... CLC **14, 24**
See also CA 41-44R; 89-92; CANR 34;
DLB 27

Richardson, Anne
See Roiphe, Anne Richardson

Richardson, Dorothy Miller
1873-1957 .... TCLC **3**
See also CA 104; DLB 36

Richardson, Ethel Florence (Lindesay)
1870-1946
See Richardson, Henry Handel
See also CA 105

Richardson, Henry Handel.......... TCLC **4**
See also Richardson, Ethel Florence (Lindesay)

Richardson, Samuel 1689-1761 .... LC **1**
See also CDBLB 1660-1789; DLB 39; WLC

Richler, Mordecai
1931- .... CLC **3, 5, 9, 13, 18, 46, 70**
See also AITN 1; CA 65-68; CANR 31;
CLR 17; DLB 53; MAICYA; MTCW;
SATA 27, 44

Richter, Conrad (Michael)
1890-1968 .... CLC **30**
See also CA 5-8R; 25-28R; CANR 23;
DLB 9; MTCW; SATA 3

Riddell, J. H. 1832-1906 .... TCLC **40**

Riding, Laura.................. CLC **3, 7**
See also Jackson, Laura (Riding)

Riefenstahl, Berta Helene Amalia 1902-
See Riefenstahl, Leni
See also CA 108

Riefenstahl, Leni.................. CLC **16**
See also Riefenstahl, Berta Helene Amalia

Riffe, Ernest
See Bergman, (Ernst) Ingmar

Riley, Tex
See Creasey, John

Rilke, Rainer Maria
1875-1926 .... TCLC **1, 6, 19; PC 2**
See also CA 104; 132; DLB 81; MTCW

Rimbaud, (Jean Nicolas) Arthur
1854-1891 .... NCLC **4, 35; PC 3**
See also WLC

Ringmaster, The
See Mencken, H(enry) L(ouis)

Ringwood, Gwen(dolyn Margaret) Pharis
1910-1984 .... CLC **48**
See also CA 112; DLB 88

Rio, Michel 19(?)-................. CLC **43**

Ritsos, Giannes
See Ritsos, Yannis

Ritsos, Yannis 1909-1990..... CLC **6, 13, 31**
See also CA 77-80; 133; CANR 39; MTCW

Ritter, Erika 1948(?)-............. CLC **52**

Rivera, Jose Eustasio 1889-1928... TCLC **35**
See also HW

Rivers, Conrad Kent 1933-1968...... CLC **1**
See also BW; CA 85-88; DLB 41

Rivers, Elfrida
See Bradley, Marion Zimmer

Riverside, John
See Heinlein, Robert A(nson)

Rizal, Jose 1861-1896............ NCLC **27**

Roa Bastos, Augusto (Antonio)
1917- .... CLC **45**
See also CA 131; DLB 113; HW

Robbe-Grillet, Alain
1922-...... CLC 1, 2, 4, 6, 8, 10, 14, 43
See also CA 9-12R; CANR 33; DLB 83;
MTCW

Robbins, Harold 1916-............. CLC 5
See also CA 73-76; CANR 26; MTCW

Robbins, Thomas Eugene 1936-
See Robbins, Tom
See also CA 81-84; CANR 29; MTCW

Robbins, Tom................ CLC 9, 32, 64
See also Robbins, Thomas Eugene
See also BEST 90:3; DLBY 80

Robbins, Trina 1938-............. CLC 21
See also CA 128

Roberts, Charles G(eorge) D(ouglas)
1860-1943 .... TCLC 8
See also CA 105; DLB 92; SATA 29

Roberts, Kate 1891-1985 .... CLC 15
See also CA 107; 116

Roberts, Keith (John Kingston)
1935-........................ CLC 14
See also CA 25-28R

Roberts, Kenneth (Lewis)
1885-1957 .... TCLC 23
See also CA 109; DLB 9

Roberts, Michele (B.) 1949-........ CLC 48
See also CA 115

Robertson, Ellis
See Ellison, Harlan; Silverberg, Robert

Robertson, Thomas William
1829-1871 .... NCLC 35

Robinson, Edwin Arlington
1869-1935 .... TCLC 5; PC 1
See also CA 104; 133; CDALB 1865-1917;
DLB 54; MTCW

Robinson, Henry Crabb
1775-1867 .... NCLC 15
See also DLB 107

Robinson, Jill 1936-................ CLC 10
See also CA 102

Robinson, Kim Stanley 1952-....... CLC 34
See also CA 126

Robinson, Lloyd
See Silverberg, Robert

Robinson, Marilynne 1944-......... CLC 25
See also CA 116

Robinson, Smokey.................. CLC 21
See also Robinson, William Jr.

Robinson, William Jr. 1940-
See Robinson, Smokey
See also CA 116

Robison, Mary 1949-.............. CLC 42
See also CA 113; 116

Roddenberry, Eugene Wesley 1921-1991
See Roddenberry, Gene
See also CA 110; 135; CANR 37; SATA 45

Roddenberry, Gene .... CLC 17
See also Roddenberry, Eugene Wesley
See also AAYA 5; SATO 69

Rodgers, Mary 1931-.............. CLC 12
See also CA 49-52; CANR 8; CLR 20;
MAICYA; SATA 8

Rodgers, W(illiam) R(obert)
1909-1969 .... CLC 7
See also CA 85-88; DLB 20

Rodman, Eric
See Silverberg, Robert

Rodman, Howard 1920(?)-1985..... CLC 65
See also CA 118

Rodman, Maia
See Wojciechowska, Maia (Teresa)

Rodriguez, Claudio 1934-.......... CLC 10

Roelvaag, O(le) E(dvart)
1876-1931 .... TCLC 17
See also CA 117; DLB 9

Roethke, Theodore (Huebner)
1908-1963 ...... CLC 1, 3, 8, 11, 19, 46
See also CA 81-84; CABS 2;
CDALB 1941-1968; DLB 5; MTCW

Rogers, Thomas Hunton 1927-..... CLC 57
See also CA 89-92

Rogers, Will(iam Penn Adair)
1879-1935 .... TCLC 8
See also CA 105; DLB 11

Rogin, Gilbert 1929-.............. CLC 18
See also CA 65-68; CANR 15

Rohan, Koda .... TCLC 22
See also Koda Shigeyuki

Rohmer, Eric..................... CLC 16
See also Scherer, Jean-Marie Maurice

Rohmer, Sax .... TCLC 28
See also Ward, Arthur Henry Sarsfield
See also DLB 70

Roiphe, Anne Richardson 1935- ... CLC 3, 9
See also CA 89-92; DLBY 80

Rolfe, Frederick (William Serafino Austin Lewis Mary) 1860-1913...... TCLC 12
See also CA 107; DLB 34

Rolland, Romain 1866-1944....... TCLC 23
See also CA 118; DLB 65

Rolvaag, O(le) E(dvart)
See Roelvaag, O(le) E(dvart)

Romain Arnaud, Saint
See Aragon, Louis

Romains, Jules 1885-1972.......... CLC 7
See also CA 85-88; CANR 34; DLB 65;
MTCW

Romero, Jose Ruben 1890-1952 ... TCLC 14
See also CA 114; 131; HW

Ronsard, Pierre de 1524-1585........ LC 6

Rooke, Leon 1934-............. CLC 25, 34
See also CA 25-28R; CANR 23

Roper, William 1498-1578......... LC 10

Roquelaure, A. N.
See Rice, Anne

Rosa, Joao Guimaraes 1908-1967... CLC 23
See also CA 89-92; DLB 113

Rosen, Richard (Dean) 1949-....... CLC 39
See also CA 77-80

Rosenberg, Isaac 1890-1918....... TCLC 12
See also CA 107; DLB 20

Rosenblatt, Joe .... CLC 15
See also Rosenblatt, Joseph

Rosenblatt, Joseph 1933-
See Rosenblatt, Joe
See also CA 89-92

Rosenfeld, Samuel 1896-1963
See Tzara, Tristan
See also CA 89-92

Rosenthal, M(acha) L(ouis) 1917-... CLC 28
See also CA 1-4R; CAAS 6; CANR 4;
DLB 5; SATA 59

Ross, Barnaby
See Dannay, Frederic

Ross, Bernard L.
See Follett, Ken(neth Martin)

Ross, J. H.
See Lawrence, T(homas) E(dward)

Ross, (James) Sinclair 1908-....... CLC 13
See also CA 73-76; DLB 88

Rossetti, Christina (Georgina)
1830-1894 .... NCLC 2
See also DLB 35; MAICYA; SATA 20;
WLC

Rossetti, Dante Gabriel
1828-1882 .... NCLC 4
See also CDBLB 1832-1890; DLB 35; WLC

Rossner, Judith (Perelman)
1935-........................ CLC 6, 9, 29
See also AITN 2; BEST 90:3; CA 17-20R;
CANR 18; DLB 6; MTCW

Rostand, Edmond (Eugene Alexis)
1868-1918 .... TCLC 6, 37
See also CA 104; 126; MTCW

Roth, Henry 1906-............ CLC 2, 6, 11
See also CA 11-12; CANR 38; CAP 1;
DLB 28; MTCW

Roth, Joseph 1894-1939.......... TCLC 33
See also DLB 85

Roth, Philip (Milton)
1933-...... CLC 1, 2, 3, 4, 6, 9, 15, 22,
31, 47, 66
See also BEST 90:3; CA 1-4R; CANR 1, 22,
36; CDALB 1968-1988; DLB 2, 28;
DLBY 82; MTCW; WLC

Rothenberg, Jerome 1931-....... CLC 6, 57
See also CA 45-48; CANR 1; DLB 5

Roumain, Jacques (Jean Baptiste)
1907-1944 .... TCLC 19
See also BLC 3; BW; CA 117; 125

Rourke, Constance (Mayfield)
1885-1941 .... TCLC 12
See also CA 107; YABC 1

Rousseau, Jean-Baptiste 1671-1741 ... LC 9

Rousseau, Jean-Jacques 1712-1778... LC 14
See also WLC

Roussel, Raymond 1877-1933 ..... TCLC 20
See also CA 117

Rovit, Earl (Herbert) 1927-......... CLC 7
See also CA 5-8R; CANR 12

Rowe, Nicholas 1674-1718........... LC 8
See also DLB 84

Rowley, Ames Dorrance
See Lovecraft, H(oward) P(hillips)

Rowson, Susanna Haswell
1762(?)-1824 .... NCLC 5
See also DLB 37

Roy, Gabrielle 1909-1983....... **CLC 10, 14**
See also CA 53-56; 110; CANR 5; DLB 68; MTCW

Rozewicz, Tadeusz 1921-........ **CLC 9, 23**
See also CA 108; CANR 36; MTCW

Ruark, Gibbons 1941-.............. **CLC 3**
See also CA 33-36R; CANR 14, 31; DLB 120

Rubens, Bernice (Ruth) 1923-... **CLC 19, 31**
See also CA 25-28R; CANR 33; DLB 14; MTCW

Rudkin, (James) David 1936-...... **CLC 14**
See also CA 89-92; DLB 13

Rudnik, Raphael 1933-.............. **CLC 7**
See also CA 29-32R

Ruffian, M.
See Hasek, Jaroslav (Matej Frantisek)

Ruiz, Jose Martinez................ **CLC 11**
See also Martinez Ruiz, Jose

Rukeyser, Muriel
1913-1980............. **CLC 6, 10, 15, 27**
See also CA 5-8R; 93-96; CANR 26; DLB 48; MTCW; SATA 22

Rule, Jane (Vance) 1931-............ **CLC 27**
See also CA 25-28R; CANR 12; DLB 60

Rulfo, Juan 1918-1986.............. **CLC 8**
See also CA 85-88; 118; CANR 26; DLB 113; HW; MTCW

Runyon, (Alfred) Damon
1884(?)-1946................ **TCLC 10**
See also CA 107; DLB 11, 86

Rush, Norman 1933-............... **CLC 44**
See also CA 121; 126

Rushdie, (Ahmed) Salman
1947-.................. **CLC 23, 31, 55**
See also BEST 89:3; CA 108; 111; CANR 33; MTCW

Rushforth, Peter (Scott) 1945-...... **CLC 19**
See also CA 101

Ruskin, John 1819-1900........... **TCLC 20**
See also CA 114; 129; CDBLB 1832-1890; DLB 55; SATA 24

Russ, Joanna 1937-................ **CLC 15**
See also CA 25-28R; CANR 11, 31; DLB 8; MTCW

Russell, George William 1867-1935
See A. E.
See also CA 104; CDBLB 1890-1914

Russell, (Henry) Ken(neth Alfred)
1927-........................ **CLC 16**
See also CA 105

Russell, Willy 1947-................. **CLC 60**
Rutherford, Mark................. **TCLC 25**
See also White, William Hale
See also DLB 18

Ruyslinck, Ward
See Belser, Reimond Karel Maria de

Ryan, Cornelius (John) 1920-1974 ... **CLC 7**
See also CA 69-72; 53-56; CANR 38

Ryan, Michael 1946-.............. **CLC 65**
See also CA 49-52; DLBY 82

Rybakov, Anatoli (Naumovich)
1911-..................... **CLC 23, 53**
See also CA 126; 135

Ryder, Jonathan
See Ludlum, Robert

Ryga, George 1932-1987.......... **CLC 14**
See also CA 101; 124; DLB 60

S. S.
See Sassoon, Siegfried (Lorraine)

Saba, Umberto 1883-1957........ **TCLC 33**
See also DLB 114

Sabatini, Rafael 1875-1950........ **TCLC 47**

Sabato, Ernesto (R.) 1911-...... **CLC 10, 23**
See also CA 97-100; CANR 32; HW; MTCW

Sacastru, Martin
See Bioy Casares, Adolfo

Sacher-Masoch, Leopold von
1836(?)-1895 .... **NCLC 31**

Sachs, Marilyn (Stickle) 1927-..... **CLC 35**
See also AAYA 2; CA 17-20R; CANR 13; CLR 2; MAICYA; SAAS 2; SATA 3, 68

Sachs, Nelly 1891-1970............ **CLC 14**
See also CA 17-18; 25-28R; CAP 2

Sackler, Howard (Oliver)
1929-1982..................... **CLC 14**
See also CA 61-64; 108; CANR 30; DLB 7

Sacks, Oliver (Wolf) 1933-......... **CLC 67**
See also CA 53-56; CANR 28; MTCW

Sade, Donatien Alphonse Francois Comte
1740-1814 .... **NCLC 3**

Sadoff, Ira 1945-.................. **CLC 9**
See also CA 53-56; CANR 5, 21; DLB 120

Saetone
See Camus, Albert

Safire, William 1929-............... **CLC 10**
See also CA 17-20R; CANR 31

Sagan, Carl (Edward) 1934-........ **CLC 30**
See also AAYA 2; CA 25-28R; CANR 11, 36; MTCW; SATA 58

Sagan, Francoise........ **CLC 3, 6, 9, 17, 36**
See also Quoirez, Francoise
See also DLB 83

Sahgal, Nayantara (Pandit) 1927-... **CLC 41**
See also CA 9-12R; CANR 11

Saint, H(arry) F. 1941- .... **CLC 50**
See also CA 127

St. Aubin de Teran, Lisa 1953-
See Teran, Lisa St. Aubin de
See also CA 118; 126

Sainte-Beuve, Charles Augustin
1804-1869 .... **NCLC 5**

Saint-Exupery, Antoine (Jean Baptiste Marie Roger) de 1900-1944 .... **TCLC 2**
See also CA 108; 132; CLR 10; DLB 72; MAICYA; MTCW; SATA 20; WLC

St. John, David
See Hunt, E(verette) Howard Jr.

Saint-John Perse
See Leger, (Marie-Rene) Alexis Saint-Leger

Saintsbury, George (Edward Bateman)
1845-1933 .... **TCLC 31**
See also DLB 57

Sait Faik .... **TCLC 23**
See also Abasiyanik, Sait Faik

Saki .... **TCLC 3**
See also Munro, H(ector) H(ugh)

Salama, Hannu 1936-............. **CLC 18**

Salamanca, J(ack) R(ichard)
1922-..................... **CLC 4, 15**
See also CA 25-28R

Sale, J. Kirkpatrick
See Sale, Kirkpatrick

Sale, Kirkpatrick 1937-............ **CLC 68**
See also CA 13-16R; CANR 10

Salinas (y Serrano), Pedro
1891(?)-1951 .... **TCLC 17**
See also CA 117

Salinger, J(erome) D(avid)
1919- .... **CLC 1, 3, 8, 12, 55, 56; SSC 2**
See also AAYA 2; CA 5-8R; CANR 39; CDALB 1941-1968; CLR 18; DLB 2, 102; MAICYA; MTCW; SATA 67; WLC

Salisbury, John
See Caute, David

Salter, James 1925-......... **CLC 7, 52, 59**
See also CA 73-76

Saltus, Edgar (Everton)
1855-1921................... **TCLC 8**
See also CA 105

Saltykov, Mikhail Evgrafovich
1826-1889 .... **NCLC 16**

Samarakis, Antonis 1919-.......... **CLC 5**
See also CA 25-28R; CAAS 16; CANR 36

Sanchez, Florencio 1875-1910..... **TCLC 37**
See also HW

Sanchez, Luis Rafael 1936-........ **CLC 23**
See also CA 128; HW

Sanchez, Sonia 1934-............... **CLC 5**
See also BLC 3; BW; CA 33-36R; CANR 24; CLR 18; DLB 41; DLBD 8; MAICYA; MTCW; SATA 22

Sand, George 1804-1876.......... **NCLC 2**
See also DLB 119; WLC

Sandburg, Carl (August)
1878-1967 ... **CLC 1, 4, 10, 15, 35; PC 2**
See also CA 5-8R; 25-28R; CANR 35; CDALB 1865-1917; DLB 17, 54; MAICYA; MTCW; SATA 8; WLC

Sandburg, Charles
See Sandburg, Carl (August)

Sandburg, Charles A.
See Sandburg, Carl (August)

Sanders, (James) Ed(ward) 1939- ... **CLC 53**
See also CA 13-16R; CANR 13; DLB 16

Sanders, Lawrence 1920-.......... **CLC 41**
See also BEST 89:4; CA 81-84; CANR 33; MTCW

Sanders, Noah
See Blount, Roy (Alton) Jr.

Sanders, Winston P.
See Anderson, Poul (William)

Sandoz, Mari(e Susette)
1896-1966 .... **CLC 28**
See also CA 1-4R; 25-28R; CANR 17; DLB 9; MTCW; SATA 5

Saner, Reg(inald Anthony) 1931- .... **CLC 9**
See also CA 65-68

Sannazaro, Jacopo 1456(?)-1530...... **LC 8**

Sansom, William 1912-1976....... CLC 2, 6
See also CA 5-8R; 65-68; MTCW

Santayana, George 1863-1952..... TCLC 40
See also CA 115; DLB 54, 71

Santiago, Danny .... CLC 33
See also James, Daniel (Lewis)

Santmyer, Helen Hooven
1895-1986 .... CLC 33
See also CA 1-4R; 118; CANR 15, 33;
DLBY 84; MTCW

Santos, Bienvenido N(uqui) 1911-... CLC 22
See also CA 101; CANR 19

Sapper .... TCLC 44
See also McNeile, Herman Cyril

Sappho fl. 6th cent. B.C.-.... CMLC 3; PC 5

Sarduy, Severo 1937-.............. CLC 6
See also CA 89-92; DLB 113; HW

Sargeson, Frank 1903-1982........ CLC 31
See also CA 25-28R; 106; CANR 38

Sarmiento, Felix Ruben Garcia 1867-1916
See Dario, Ruben
See also CA 104

Saroyan, William
1908-1981 ..... CLC 1, 8, 10, 29, 34, 56
See also CA 5-8R; 103; CANR 30; DLB 7,
9, 86; DLBY 81; MTCW; SATA 23, 24;
WLC

Sarraute, Nathalie
1900- .... CLC 1, 2, 4, 8, 10, 31
See also CA 9-12R; CANR 23; DLB 83;
MTCW

Sarton, (Eleanor) May
1912- .... CLC 4, 14, 49
See also CA 1-4R; CANR 1, 34; DLB 48;
DLBY 81; MTCW; SATA 36

Sartre, Jean-Paul
1905-1980 ... CLC 1, 4, 7, 9, 13, 18, 24,
44, 50, 52; DC 3
See also CA 9-12R; 97-100; CANR 21;
DLB 72; MTCW; WLC

Sassoon, Siegfried (Lorraine)
1886-1967 .... CLC 36
See also CA 104; 25-28R; CANR 36;
DLB 20; MTCW

Satterfield, Charles
See Pohl, Frederik

Saul, John (W. III) 1942- .... CLC 46
See also BEST 90:4; CA 81-84; CANR 16

Saunders, Caleb
See Heinlein, Robert A(nson)

Saura (Atares), Carlos 1932-....... CLC 20
See also CA 114; 131; HW

Sauser-Hall, Frederic 1887-1961.... CLC 18
See also CA 102; 93-96; CANR 36; MTCW

Savage, Catharine
See Brosman, Catharine Savage

Savage, Thomas 1915- .... CLC 40
See also CA 126; 132; CAAS 15

Savan, Glenn .... CLC 50

Saven, Glenn 19(?)- .... CLC 50

Sayers, Dorothy L(eigh)
1893-1957 .... TCLC 2, 15
See also CA 104; 119; CDBLB 1914-1945;
DLB 10, 36, 77, 100; MTCW

Sayers, Valerie 1952-............. CLC 50
See also CA 134

Sayles, John Thomas 1950-... CLC 7, 10, 14
See also CA 57-60; DLB 44

Scammell, Michael .... CLC 34

Scannell, Vernon 1922- .... CLC 49
See also CA 5-8R; CANR 8, 24; DLB 27;
SATA 59

Scarlett, Susan
See Streatfeild, (Mary) Noel

Schaeffer, Susan Fromberg
1941- .... CLC 6, 11, 22
See also CA 49-52; CANR 18; DLB 28;
MTCW; SATA 22

Schary, Jill
See Robinson, Jill

Schell, Jonathan 1943-............ CLC 35
See also CA 73-76; CANR 12

Schelling, Friedrich Wilhelm Joseph von
1775-1854 .... NCLC 30
See also DLB 90

Scherer, Jean-Marie Maurice 1920-
See Rohmer, Eric
See also CA 110

Schevill, James (Erwin) 1920-....... CLC 7
See also CA 5-8R; CAAS 12

Schisgal, Murray (Joseph) 1926-..... CLC 6
See also CA 21-24R

Schlee, Ann 1934-................. CLC 35
See also CA 101; CANR 29; SATA 36, 44

Schlegel, August Wilhelm von
1767-1845 .... NCLC 15

Schlegel, Johann Elias (von)
1719(?)-1749 .... LC 5

Schmidt, Arno (Otto) 1914-1979.... CLC 56
See also CA 128; 109; DLB 69

Schmitz, Aron Hector 1861-1928
See Svevo, Italo
See also CA 104; 122; MTCW

Schnackenberg, Gjertrud 1953-..... CLC 40
See also CA 116; DLB 120

Schneider, Leonard Alfred 1925-1966
See Bruce, Lenny
See also CA 89-92

Schnitzler, Arthur 1862-1931 ...... TCLC 4
See also CA 104; DLB 81, 118

Schor, Sandra (M.) 1932(?)-1990 ... CLC 65
See also CA 132

Schorer, Mark 1908-1977 .... CLC 9
See also CA 5-8R; 73-76; CANR 7;
DLB 103

Schrader, Paul Joseph 1946-....... CLC 26
See also CA 37-40R; DLB 44

Schreiner, Olive (Emilie Albertina)
1855-1920 .... TCLC 9
See also CA 105; DLB 18

Schulberg, Budd (Wilson)
1914- .... CLC 7, 48
See also CA 25-28R; CANR 19; DLB 6, 26,
28; DLBY 81

Schulz, Bruno 1892-1942......... TCLC 5
See also CA 115; 123

Schulz, Charles M(onroe) 1922-.... CLC 12
See also CA 9-12R; CANR 6; SATA 10

Schuyler, James Marcus
1923-1991 .... CLC 5, 23
See also CA 101; 134; DLB 5

Schwartz, Delmore (David)
1913-1966 .... CLC 2, 4, 10, 45
See also CA 17-18; 25-28R; CANR 35;
CAP 2; DLB 28, 48; MTCW

Schwartz, Ernst
See Ozu, Yasujiro

Schwartz, John Burnham 1965- .... CLC 59
See also CA 132

Schwartz, Lynne Sharon 1939-..... CLC 31
See also CA 103

Schwartz, Muriel A.
See Eliot, T(homas) S(tearns)

Schwarz-Bart, Andre 1928-........ CLC 2, 4
See also CA 89-92

Schwarz-Bart, Simone 1938-........ CLC 7
See also CA 97-100

Schwob, (Mayer Andre) Marcel
1867-1905 .... TCLC 20
See also CA 117

Sciascia, Leonardo
1921-1989 .... CLC 8, 9, 41
See also CA 85-88; 130; CANR 35; MTCW

Scoppettone, Sandra 1936-........ CLC 26
See also CA 5-8R; SATA 9

Scorsese, Martin 1942- .... CLC 20
See also CA 110; 114

Scotland, Jay
See Jakes, John (William)

Scott, Duncan Campbell
1862-1947 .... TCLC 6
See also CA 104; DLB 92

Scott, Evelyn 1893-1963........... CLC 43
See also CA 104; 112; DLB 9, 48

Scott, F(rancis) R(eginald)
1899-1985 .... CLC 22
See also CA 101; 114; DLB 88

Scott, Frank
See Scott, F(rancis) R(eginald)

Scott, Joanna 1960- .... CLC 50
See also CA 126

Scott, Paul (Mark) 1920-1978.... CLC 9, 60
See also CA 81-84; 77-80; CANR 33;
DLB 14; MTCW

Scott, Walter 1771-1832......... NCLC 15
See also CDBLB 1789-1832; DLB 93, 107,
116; WLC; YABC 2

Scribe, (Augustin) Eugene
1791-1861 .... NCLC 16

Scrum, R.
See Crumb, R(obert)

Scudery, Madeleine de 1607-1701..... LC 2

Scum
See Crumb, R(obert)

Scumbag, Little Bobby
See Crumb, R(obert)

Seabrook, John
See Hubbard, L(afayette) Ron(ald)

Sealy, I. Allan 1951- .... CLC 55

Search, Alexander
See Pessoa, Fernando (Antonio Nogueira)

Sebastian, Lee
See Silverberg, Robert

Sebastian Owl
See Thompson, Hunter S(tockton)

Sebestyen, Ouida 1924- .... **CLC 30**
See also AAYA 8; CA 107; CLR 17; MAICYA; SAAS 10; SATA 39

Sedges, John
See Buck, Pearl S(ydenstricker)

Sedgwick, Catharine Maria
1789-1867 .... **NCLC 19**
See also DLB 1, 74

Seelye, John 1931- .... **CLC 7**

Seferiades, Giorgos Stylianou 1900-1971
See Seferis, George
See also CA 5-8R; 33-36R; CANR 5, 36; MTCW

Seferis, George .... **CLC 5, 11**
See also Seferiades, Giorgos Stylianou

Segal, Erich (Wolf) 1937- .... **CLC 3, 10**
See also BEST 89:1; CA 25-28R; CANR 20, 36; DLBY 86; MTCW

Seger, Bob 1945- .... **CLC 35**

Seghers, Anna .... **CLC 7**
See also Radvanyi, Netty
See also DLB 69

Seidel, Frederick (Lewis) 1936- ..... **CLC 18**
See also CA 13-16R; CANR 8; DLBY 84

Seifert, Jaroslav 1901-1986 ..... **CLC 34, 44**
See also CA 127; MTCW

Sei Shonagon c. 966-1017(?) ...... **CMLC 6**

Selby, Hubert Jr. 1928- ...... **CLC 1, 2, 4, 8**
See also CA 13-16R; CANR 33; DLB 2

Selzer, Richard 1928- .... **CLC 74**
See also CA 65-68; CANR 14

Sembene, Ousmane
See Ousmane, Sembene

Senancour, Etienne Pivert de
1770-1846 .... **NCLC 16**
See also DLB 119

Sender, Ramon (Jose) 1902-1982 .... **CLC 8**
See also CA 5-8R; 105; CANR 8; HW; MTCW

Seneca, Lucius Annaeus
4B.C.-65.................. **CMLC 6**

Senghor, Leopold Sedar 1906- ...... **CLC 54**
See also BLC 3; BW; CA 116; 125; MTCW

Serling, (Edward) Rod(man)
1924-1975 .... **CLC 30**
See also AITN 1; CA 65-68; 57-60; DLB 26

Serna, Ramon Gomez de la
See Gomez de la Serna, Ramon

Serpieres
See Guillevic, (Eugene)

Service, Robert
See Service, Robert W(illiam)
See also DLB 92

Service, Robert W(illiam)
1874(?)-1958 .... **TCLC 15**
See also Service, Robert
See also CA 115; SATA 20; WLC

Seth, Vikram 1952-............... **CLC 43**
See also CA 121; 127; DLB 120

Seton, Cynthia Propper
1926-1982 .... **CLC 27**
See also CA 5-8R; 108; CANR 7

Seton, Ernest (Evan) Thompson
1860-1946 .... **TCLC 31**
See also CA 109; DLB 92; SATA 18

Seton-Thompson, Ernest
See Seton, Ernest (Evan) Thompson

Settle, Mary Lee 1918- .... **CLC 19, 61**
See also CA 89-92; CAAS 1; DLB 6

Seuphor, Michel
See Arp, Jean

Sevigne, Marie (de Rabutin-Chantal) Marquise de 1626-1696 .... **LC 11**

Sexton, Anne (Harvey)
1928-1974 ... **CLC 2, 4, 6, 8, 10, 15, 53; PC 2**
See also CA 1-4R; 53-56; CABS 2; CANR 3, 36; CDALB 1941-1968; DLB 5; MTCW; SATA 10; WLC

Shaara, Michael (Joseph Jr.)
1929-1988 .... **CLC 15**
See also AITN 1; CA 102; DLBY 83

Shackleton, C. C.
See Aldiss, Brian W(ilson)

Shacochis, Bob .... **CLC 39**
See also Shacochis, Robert G.

Shacochis, Robert G. 1951-
See Shacochis, Bob
See also CA 119; 124

Shaffer, Anthony (Joshua) 1926-.... **CLC 19**
See also CA 110; 116; DLB 13

Shaffer, Peter (Levin)
1926- .... **CLC 5, 14, 18, 37, 60**
See also CA 25-28R; CANR 25; CDBLB 1960 to Present; DLB 13; MTCW

Shakey, Bernard
See Young, Neil

Shalamov, Varlam (Tikhonovich)
1907(?)-1982 .... **CLC 18**
See also CA 129; 105

Shamlu, Ahmad 1925- .... **CLC 10**

Shammas, Anton 1951-............ **CLC 55**

Shange, Ntozake
1948- .... **CLC 8, 25, 38, 74; DC 3**
See also AAYA 9; BLC 3; BW; CA 85-88; CABS 3; CANR 27; DLB 38; MTCW

Shapcott, Thomas William 1935- ... **CLC 38**
See also CA 69-72

Shapiro, Karl (Jay) 1913- .. **CLC 4, 8, 15, 53**
See also CA 1-4R; CAAS 6; CANR 1, 36; DLB 48; MTCW

Sharp, William 1855-1905 .... **TCLC 39**

Sharpe, Thomas Ridley 1928-
See Sharpe, Tom
See also CA 114; 122

Sharpe, Tom..................... **CLC 36**
See also Sharpe, Thomas Ridley
See also DLB 14

Shaw, Bernard.................... **TCLC 45**
See also Shaw, George Bernard

Shaw, G. Bernard
See Shaw, George Bernard

Shaw, George Bernard
1856-1950 .... **TCLC 3, 9, 21**
See also Shaw, Bernard
See also CA 104; 128; CDBLB 1914-1945; DLB 10, 57; MTCW; WLC

Shaw, Henry Wheeler
1818-1885 .... **NCLC 15**
See also DLB 11

Shaw, Irwin 1913-1984....... **CLC 7, 23, 34**
See also AITN 1; CA 13-16R; 112; CANR 21; CDALB 1941-1968; DLB 6, 102; DLBY 84; MTCW

Shaw, Robert 1927-1978 .... **CLC 5**
See also AITN 1; CA 1-4R; 81-84; CANR 4; DLB 13, 14

Shaw, T. E.
See Lawrence, T(homas) E(dward)

Shawn, Wallace 1943- .... **CLC 41**
See also CA 112

Sheed, Wilfrid (John Joseph)
1930- .... **CLC 2, 4, 10, 53**
See also CA 65-68; CANR 30; DLB 6; MTCW

Sheldon, Alice Hastings Bradley
1915(?)-1987
See Tiptree, James Jr.
See also CA 108; 122; CANR 34; MTCW

Sheldon, John
See Bloch, Robert (Albert)

Shelley, Mary Wollstonecraft (Godwin)
1797-1851 .... **NCLC 14**
See also CDBLB 1789-1832; DLB 110, 116; SATA 29; WLC

Shelley, Percy Bysshe
1792-1822 .... **NCLC 18**
See also CDBLB 1789-1832; DLB 96, 110; WLC

Shepard, Jim 1956-................ **CLC 36**
See also CA 137

Shepard, Lucius 19(?)-............. **CLC 34**
See also CA 128

Shepard, Sam
1943- .... **CLC 4, 6, 17, 34, 41, 44**
See also AAYA 1; CA 69-72; CABS 3; CANR 22; DLB 7; MTCW

Shepherd, Michael
See Ludlum, Robert

Sherburne, Zoa (Morin) 1912-...... **CLC 30**
See also CA 1-4R; CANR 3, 37; MAICYA; SATA 3

Sheridan, Frances 1724-1766........ **LC 7**
See also DLB 39, 84

Sheridan, Richard Brinsley
1751-1816 .... **NCLC 5; DC 1**
See also CDBLB 1660-1789; DLB 89; WLC

Sherman, Jonathan Marc.......... **CLC 55**

Sherman, Martin 1941(?)- .... **CLC 19**
See also CA 116; 123

Sherwin, Judith Johnson 1936-... **CLC 7, 15**
See also CA 25-28R; CANR 34

Sherwood, Robert E(mmet)
1896-1955 .... **TCLC 3**
See also CA 104; DLB 7, 26

Shiel, M(atthew) P(hipps)
1865-1947 .... **TCLC 8**
See also CA 106

Shiga, Naoya 1883-1971 .... **CLC 33**
See also CA 101; 33-36R

Shimazaki Haruki 1872-1943
See Shimazaki Toson
See also CA 105; 134

Shimazaki Toson .... **TCLC 5**
See also Shimazaki Haruki

Sholokhov, Mikhail (Aleksandrovich)
1905-1984 .... **CLC 7, 15**
See also CA 101; 112; MTCW; SATA 36

Shone, Patric
See Hanley, James

Shreve, Susan Richards 1939- ...... **CLC 23**
See also CA 49-52; CAAS 5; CANR 5, 38;
MAICYA; SATA 41, 46

Shue, Larry 1946-1985 .... **CLC 52**
See also CA 117

Shu-Jen, Chou 1881-1936
See Hsun, Lu
See also CA 104

Shulman, Alix Kates 1932- ...... **CLC 2, 10**
See also CA 29-32R; SATA 7

Shuster, Joe 1914- .... **CLC 21**

Shute, Nevil .... **CLC 30**
See also Norway, Nevil Shute

Shuttle, Penelope (Diane) 1947- ..... **CLC 7**
See also CA 93-96; CANR 39; DLB 14, 40

Sidney, Mary 1561-1621 .... **LC 19**

Sidney, Sir Philip 1554-1586 .... **LC 19**
See also CDBLB Before 1660

Siegel, Jerome 1914- .... **CLC 21**
See also CA 116

Siegel, Jerry
See Siegel, Jerome

Sienkiewicz, Henryk (Adam Alexander Pius)
1846-1916 .... **TCLC 3**
See also CA 104; 134

Sierra, Gregorio Martinez
See Martinez Sierra, Gregorio

Sierra, Maria (de la O'LeJarraga) Martinez
See Martinez Sierra, Maria (de la O'LeJarraga)

Sigal, Clancy 1926- .... **CLC 7**
See also CA 1-4R

Sigourney, Lydia Howard (Huntley)
1791-1865 .... **NCLC 21**
See also DLB 1, 42, 73

Siguenza y Gongora, Carlos de
1645-1700 .... **LC 8**

Sigurjonsson, Johann 1880-1919 ... **TCLC 27**

Sikelianos, Angelos 1884-1951 .... **TCLC 39**

Silkin, Jon 1930- .... **CLC 2, 6, 43**
See also CA 5-8R; CAAS 5; DLB 27

Silko, Leslie Marmon 1948- .... **CLC 23, 74**
See also CA 115; 122

Sillanpaa, Frans Eemil 1888-1964 ... **CLC 19**
See also CA 129; 93-96; MTCW

Sillitoe, Alan
1928- .... **CLC 1, 3, 6, 10, 19, 57**
See also AITN 1; CA 9-12R; CAAS 2;
CANR 8, 26; CDBLB 1960 to Present;
DLB 14; MTCW; SATA 61

Silone, Ignazio 1900-1978 .... **CLC 4**
See also CA 25-28; 81-84; CANR 34;
CAP 2; MTCW

Silver, Joan Micklin 1935- .... **CLC 20**
See also CA 114; 121

Silverberg, Robert 1935- .... **CLC 7**
See also CA 1-4R; CAAS 3; CANR 1, 20,
36; DLB 8; MAICYA; MTCW; SATA 13

Silverstein, Alvin 1933- .... **CLC 17**
See also CA 49-52; CANR 2; CLR 25;
MAICYA; SATA 8, 69

Silverstein, Virginia B(arbara Opshelor)
1937- .... **CLC 17**
See also CA 49-52; CANR 2; CLR 25;
MAICYA; SATA 8, 69

Sim, Georges
See Simenon, Georges (Jacques Christian)

Simak, Clifford D(onald)
1904-1988 .... **CLC 1, 55**
See also CA 1-4R; 125; CANR 1, 35;
DLB 8; MTCW; SATA 56

Simenon, Georges (Jacques Christian)
1903-1989 .... **CLC 1, 2, 3, 8, 18, 47**
See also CA 85-88; 129; CANR 35;
DLB 72; DLBY 89; MTCW

Simic, Charles 1938- ... **CLC 6, 9, 22, 49, 68**
See also CA 29-32R; CAAS 4; CANR 12,
33; DLB 105

Simmons, Charles (Paul) 1924- ..... **CLC 57**
See also CA 89-92

Simmons, Dan .... **CLC 44**
See also CA 138

Simmons, James (Stewart Alexander)
1933- .... **CLC 43**
See also CA 105; DLB 40

Simms, William Gilmore
1806-1870 .... **NCLC 3**
See also DLB 3, 30, 59, 73

Simon, Carly 1945- .... **CLC 26**
See also CA 105

Simon, Claude 1913- .... **CLC 4, 9, 15, 39**
See also CA 89-92; CANR 33; DLB 83;
MTCW

Simon, (Marvin) Neil
1927- .... **CLC 6, 11, 31, 39, 70**
See also AITN 1; CA 21-24R; CANR 26;
DLB 7; MTCW

Simon, Paul 1942(?)- .... **CLC 17**
See also CA 116

Simonon, Paul 1956(?)- .... **CLC 30**
See also The Clash

Simpson, Harriette
See Arnow, Harriette (Louisa) Simpson

Simpson, Louis (Aston Marantz)
1923- .... **CLC 4, 7, 9, 32**
See also CA 1-4R; CAAS 4; CANR 1;
DLB 5; MTCW

Simpson, Mona (Elizabeth) 1957- ... **CLC 44**
See also CA 122; 135

Simpson, N(orman) F(rederick)
1919- .... **CLC 29**
See also CA 13-16R; DLB 13

Sinclair, Andrew (Annandale)
1935- .... **CLC 2, 14**
See also CA 9-12R; CAAS 5; CANR 14, 38;
DLB 14; MTCW

Sinclair, Emil
See Hesse, Hermann

Sinclair, Mary Amelia St. Clair 1865(?)-1946
See Sinclair, May
See also CA 104

Sinclair, May .... **TCLC 3, 11**
See also Sinclair, Mary Amelia St. Clair
See also DLB 36

Sinclair, Upton (Beall)
1878-1968 .... **CLC 1, 11, 15, 63**
See also CA 5-8R; 25-28R; CANR 7;
CDALB 1929-1941; DLB 9; MTCW;
SATA 9; WLC

Singer, Isaac
See Singer, Isaac Bashevis

Singer, Isaac Bashevis
1904-1991 ... **CLC 1, 3, 6, 9, 11, 15, 23, 38, 69; SSC 3**
See also AITN 1, 2; CA 1-4R; 134;
CANR 1, 39; CDALB 1941-1968; CLR 1;
DLB 6, 28, 52; DLBY 91; MAICYA;
MTCW; SATA 3, 27; SATO 68; WLC

Singer, Israel Joshua 1893-1944 ... **TCLC 33**

Singh, Khushwant 1915- .... **CLC 11**
See also CA 9-12R; CAAS 9; CANR 6

Sinjohn, John
See Galsworthy, John

Sinyavsky, Andrei (Donatevich)
1925- .... **CLC 8**
See also CA 85-88

Sirin, V.
See Nabokov, Vladimir (Vladimirovich)

Sissman, L(ouis) E(dward)
1928-1976 .... **CLC 9, 18**
See also CA 21-24R; 65-68; CANR 13;
DLB 5

Sisson, C(harles) H(ubert) 1914- ..... **CLC 8**
See also CA 1-4R; CAAS 3; CANR 3;
DLB 27

Sitwell, Dame Edith
1887-1964 .... **CLC 2, 9, 67; PC 3**
See also CA 9-12R; CANR 35;
CDBLB 1945-1960; DLB 20; MTCW

Sjoewall, Maj 1935- .... **CLC 7**
See also CA 65-68

Sjowall, Maj
See Sjoewall, Maj

Skelton, Robin 1925- .... **CLC 13**
See also AITN 2; CA 5-8R; CAAS 5;
CANR 28; DLB 27, 53

Skolimowski, Jerzy 1938- .... **CLC 20**
See also CA 128

Skram, Amalie (Bertha)
1847-1905 .... **TCLC 25**

Skvorecky, Josef (Vaclav)
1924- .... **CLC 15, 39, 69**
See also CA 61-64; CAAS 1; CANR 10, 34;
MTCW

Slade, Bernard .... CLC 11, 46
  See also Newbound, Bernard Slade
  See also CAAS 9; DLB 53

Slaughter, Carolyn 1946- .... CLC 56
  See also CA 85-88

Slaughter, Frank G(ill) 1908- ...... CLC 29
  See also AITN 2; CA 5-8R; CANR 5

Slavitt, David R. 1935- .... CLC 5, 14
  See also CA 21-24R; CAAS 3; DLB 5, 6

Slesinger, Tess 1905-1945 .... TCLC 10
  See also CA 107; DLB 102

Slessor, Kenneth 1901-1971 .... CLC 14
  See also CA 102; 89-92

Slowacki, Juliusz 1809-1849 ..... NCLC 15

Smart, Christopher 1722-1771 .... LC 3
  See also DLB 109

Smart, Elizabeth 1913-1986 .... CLC 54
  See also CA 81-84; 118; DLB 88

Smiley, Jane (Graves) 1949- ...... CLC 53
  See also CA 104; CANR 30

Smith, A(rthur) J(ames) M(arshall)
  1902-1980 .... CLC 15
  See also CA 1-4R; 102; CANR 4; DLB 88

Smith, Betty (Wehner) 1896-1972 ... CLC 19
  See also CA 5-8R; 33-36R; DLBY 82;
  SATA 6

Smith, Charlotte (Turner)
  1749-1806 .... NCLC 23
  See also DLB 39, 109

Smith, Clark Ashton 1893-1961 .... CLC 43

Smith, Dave .... CLC 22, 42
  See also Smith, David (Jeddie)
  See also CAAS 7; DLB 5

Smith, David (Jeddie) 1942-
  See Smith, Dave
  See also CA 49-52; CANR 1

Smith, Florence Margaret
  1902-1971 .... CLC 8
  See also Smith, Stevie
  See also CA 17-18; 29-32R; CANR 35;
  CAP 2; MTCW

Smith, Iain Crichton 1928- .... CLC 64
  See also CA 21-24R; DLB 40

Smith, John 1580(?)-1631 .... LC 9

Smith, Johnston
  See Crane, Stephen (Townley)

Smith, Lee 1944- .... CLC 25
  See also CA 114; 119; DLBY 83

Smith, Martin
  See Smith, Martin Cruz

Smith, Martin Cruz 1942- .... CLC 25
  See also BEST 89:4; CA 85-88; CANR 6, 23

Smith, Mary-Ann Tirone 1944- ..... CLC 39
  See also CA 118; 136

Smith, Patti 1946- .... CLC 12
  See also CA 93-96

Smith, Pauline (Urmson)
  1882-1959 .... TCLC 25

Smith, Rosamond
  See Oates, Joyce Carol

Smith, Sheila Kaye
  See Kaye-Smith, Sheila

Smith, Stevie .... CLC 3, 8, 25, 44
  See also Smith, Florence Margaret
  See also DLB 20

Smith, Wilbur A(ddison) 1933- ..... CLC 33
  See also CA 13-16R; CANR 7; MTCW

Smith, William Jay 1918- .... CLC 6
  See also CA 5-8R; DLB 5; MAICYA;
  SATA 2, 68

Smith, Woodrow Wilson
  See Kuttner, Henry

Smolenskin, Peretz 1842-1885 .... NCLC 30

Smollett, Tobias (George) 1721-1771 .. LC 2
  See also CDBLB 1660-1789; DLB 39, 104

Snodgrass, William D(e Witt)
  1926- .... CLC 2, 6, 10, 18, 68
  See also CA 1-4R; CANR 6, 36; DLB 5;
  MTCW

Snow, C(harles) P(ercy)
  1905-1980 .... CLC 1, 4, 6, 9, 13, 19
  See also CA 5-8R; 101; CANR 28;
  CDBLB 1945-1960; DLB 15, 77; MTCW

Snow, Frances Compton
  See Adams, Henry (Brooks)

Snyder, Gary (Sherman)
  1930- .... CLC 1, 2, 5, 9, 32
  See also CA 17-20R; CANR 30; DLB 5, 16

Snyder, Zilpha Keatley 1927- ...... CLC 17
  See also CA 9-12R; CANR 38; MAICYA;
  SAAS 2; SATA 1, 28

Soares, Bernardo
  See Pessoa, Fernando (Antonio Nogueira)

Sobh, A.
  See Shamlu, Ahmad

Sobol, Joshua. .... CLC 60

Soderberg, Hjalmar 1869-1941 .... TCLC 39

Sodergran, Edith (Irene)
  See Soedergran, Edith (Irene)

Soedergran, Edith (Irene)
  1892-1923 .... TCLC 31

Softly, Edgar
  See Lovecraft, H(oward) P(hillips)

Softly, Edward
  See Lovecraft, H(oward) P(hillips)

Sokolov, Raymond 1941- .... CLC 7
  See also CA 85-88

Solo, Jay
  See Ellison, Harlan

Sologub, Fyodor .... TCLC 9
  See also Teternikov, Fyodor Kuzmich

Solomons, Ikey Esquir
  See Thackeray, William Makepeace

Solomos, Dionysios 1798-1857 ... NCLC 15

Solwoska, Mara
  See French, Marilyn

Solzhenitsyn, Aleksandr I(sayevich)
  1918- ... CLC 1, 2, 4, 7, 9, 10, 18, 26, 34
  See also AITN 1; CA 69-72; MTCW; WLC

Somers, Jane
  See Lessing, Doris (May)

Sommer, Scott 1951- .... CLC 25
  See also CA 106

Sondheim, Stephen (Joshua)
  1930- .... CLC 30, 39
  See also CA 103

Sontag, Susan 1933- ... CLC 1, 2, 10, 13, 31
  See also CA 17-20R; CANR 25; DLB 2, 67;
  MTCW

Sophocles
  496(?)B.C.-406(?)B.C. .... CMLC 2; DC 1

Sorel, Julia
  See Drexler, Rosalyn

Sorrentino, Gilbert
  1929- .... CLC 3, 7, 14, 22, 40
  See also CA 77-80; CANR 14, 33; DLB 5;
  DLBY 80

Soto, Gary 1952- .... CLC 32
  See also CA 119; 125; DLB 82; HW

Soupault, Philippe 1897-1990 ...... CLC 68
  See also CA 116; 131

Souster, (Holmes) Raymond
  1921- .... CLC 5, 14
  See also CA 13-16R; CAAS 14; CANR 13,
  29; DLB 88; SATA 63

Southern, Terry 1926- .... CLC 7
  See also CA 1-4R; CANR 1; DLB 2

Southey, Robert 1774-1843 .... NCLC 8
  See also DLB 93, 107; SATA 54

Southworth, Emma Dorothy Eliza Nevitte
  1819-1899 .... NCLC 26

Souza, Ernest
  See Scott, Evelyn

Soyinka, Wole
  1934- .... CLC 3, 5, 14, 36, 44; DC 2
  See also BLC 3; BW; CA 13-16R;
  CANR 27, 39; MTCW; WLC

Spackman, W(illiam) M(ode)
  1905-1990 .... CLC 46
  See also CA 81-84; 132

Spacks, Barry 1931- .... CLC 14
  See also CA 29-32R; CANR 33; DLB 105

Spanidou, Irini 1946- .... CLC 44

Spark, Muriel (Sarah)
  1918- .... CLC 2, 3, 5, 8, 13, 18, 40;
  SSC 10
  See also CA 5-8R; CANR 12, 36;
  CDBLB 1945-1960; DLB 15; MTCW

Spaulding, Douglas
  See Bradbury, Ray (Douglas)

Spaulding, Leonard
  See Bradbury, Ray (Douglas)

Spence, J. A. D.
  See Eliot, T(homas) S(tearns)

Spencer, Elizabeth 1921- .... CLC 22
  See also CA 13-16R; CANR 32; DLB 6;
  MTCW; SATA 14

Spencer, Leonard G.
  See Silverberg, Robert

Spencer, Scott 1945- .... CLC 30
  See also CA 113; DLBY 86

Spender, Stephen (Harold)
  1909- .... CLC 1, 2, 5, 10, 41
  See also CA 9-12R; CANR 31;
  CDBLB 1945-1960; DLB 20; MTCW

Spengler, Oswald (Arnold Gottfried)
1880-1936 .... **TCLC 25**
See also CA 118

Spenser, Edmund 1552(?)-1599 .... **LC 5**
See also CDBLB Before 1660; WLC

Spicer, Jack 1925-1965 ...... **CLC 8, 18, 72**
See also CA 85-88; DLB 5, 16

Spielberg, Peter 1929- .... **CLC 6**
See also CA 5-8R; CANR 4; DLBY 81

Spielberg, Steven 1947- .... **CLC 20**
See also AAYA 8; CA 77-80; CANR 32;
SATA 32

Spillane, Frank Morrison 1918-
See Spillane, Mickey
See also CA 25-28R; CANR 28; MTCW;
SATA 66

Spillane, Mickey .... **CLC 3, 13**
See also Spillane, Frank Morrison

Spinoza, Benedictus de 1632-1677 .... **LC 9**

Spinrad, Norman (Richard) 1940-... **CLC 46**
See also CA 37-40R; CANR 20; DLB 8

Spitteler, Carl (Friedrich Georg)
1845-1924 .... **TCLC 12**
See also CA 109

Spivack, Kathleen (Romola Drucker)
1938- .... **CLC 6**
See also CA 49-52

Spoto, Donald 1941-................ **CLC 39**
See also CA 65-68; CANR 11

Springsteen, Bruce (F.) 1949- ...... **CLC 17**
See also CA 111

Spurling, Hilary 1940-............. **CLC 34**
See also CA 104; CANR 25

Squires, Radcliffe 1917-........... **CLC 51**
See also CA 1-4R; CANR 6, 21

Srivastava, Dhanpat Rai 1880(?)-1936
See Premchand
See also CA 118

Stacy, Donald
See Pohl, Frederik

Stael, Germaine de
See Stael-Holstein, Anne Louise Germaine
Necker Baronn
See also DLB 119

Stael-Holstein, Anne Louise Germaine Necker
Baronn 1766-1817 .... **NCLC 3**
See also Stael, Germaine de

Stafford, Jean 1915-1979... **CLC 4, 7, 19, 68**
See also CA 1-4R; 85-88; CANR 3; DLB 2;
MTCW; SATA 22

Stafford, William (Edgar)
1914- .... **CLC 4, 7, 29**
See also CA 5-8R; CAAS 3; CANR 5, 22;
DLB 5

Staines, Trevor
See Brunner, John (Kilian Houston)

Stairs, Gordon
See Austin, Mary (Hunter)

Stannard, Martin................. **CLC 44**

Stanton, Maura 1946- .... **CLC 9**
See also CA 89-92; CANR 15; DLB 120

Stanton, Schuyler
See Baum, L(yman) Frank

Stapledon, (William) Olaf
1886-1950 .... **TCLC 22**
See also CA 111; DLB 15

Starbuck, George (Edwin) 1931-.... **CLC 53**
See also CA 21-24R; CANR 23

Stark, Richard
See Westlake, Donald E(dwin)

Staunton, Schuyler
See Baum, L(yman) Frank

Stead, Christina (Ellen)
1902-1983 .... **CLC 2, 5, 8, 32**
See also CA 13-16R; 109; CANR 33;
MTCW

Stead, William Thomas
1849-1912 .... **TCLC 48**

Steele, Richard 1672-1729 .... **LC 18**
See also CDBLB 1660-1789; DLB 84, 101

Steele, Timothy (Reid) 1948-........ **CLC 45**
See also CA 93-96; CANR 16; DLB 120

Steffens, (Joseph) Lincoln
1866-1936 .... **TCLC 20**
See also CA 117

Stegner, Wallace (Earle) 1909-... **CLC 9, 49**
See also AITN 1; BEST 90:3; CA 1-4R;
CAAS 9; CANR 1, 21; DLB 9; MTCW

Stein, Gertrude
1874-1946 .... **TCLC 1, 6, 28, 48**
See also CA 104; 132; CDALB 1917-1929;
DLB 4, 54, 86; MTCW; WLC

Steinbeck, John (Ernst)
1902-1968 ..... **CLC 1, 5, 9, 13, 21, 34,
45; SSC 11**
See also CA 1-4R; 25-28R; CANR 1, 35;
CDALB 1929-1941; DLB 7, 9; DLBD 2;
MTCW; SATA 9; WLC

Steinem, Gloria 1934-............... **CLC 63**
See also CA 53-56; CANR 28; MTCW

Steiner, George 1929-............... **CLC 24**
See also CA 73-76; CANR 31; DLB 67;
MTCW; SATA 62

Steiner, Rudolf 1861-1925 .... **TCLC 13**
See also CA 107

Stendhal 1783-1842............. **NCLC 23**
See also DLB 119; WLC

Stephen, Leslie 1832-1904 .... **TCLC 23**
See also CA 123; DLB 57

Stephen, Sir Leslie
See Stephen, Leslie

Stephen, Virginia
See Woolf, (Adeline) Virginia

Stephens, James 1882(?)-1950...... **TCLC 4**
See also CA 104; DLB 19

Stephens, Reed
See Donaldson, Stephen R.

Steptoe, Lydia
See Barnes, Djuna

Sterchi, Beat 1949-................ **CLC 65**

Sterling, Brett
See Bradbury, Ray (Douglas); Hamilton,
Edmond

Sterling, Bruce 1954-............. **CLC 72**
See also CA 119

Sterling, George 1869-1926 .... **TCLC 20**
See also CA 117; DLB 54

Stern, Gerald 1925- .... **CLC 40**
See also CA 81-84; CANR 28; DLB 105

Stern, Richard (Gustave) 1928-... **CLC 4, 39**
See also CA 1-4R; CANR 1, 25; DLBY 87

Sternberg, Josef von 1894-1969..... **CLC 20**
See also CA 81-84

Sterne, Laurence 1713-1768.......... **LC 2**
See also CDBLB 1660-1789; DLB 39; WLC

Sternheim, (William Adolf) Carl
1878-1942 .... **TCLC 8**
See also CA 105; DLB 56, 118

Stevens, Mark 1951- .... **CLC 34**
See also CA 122

Stevens, Wallace
1879-1955 .... **TCLC 3, 12, 45**
See also CA 104; 124; CDALB 1929-1941;
DLB 54; MTCW; WLC

Stevenson, Anne (Katharine)
1933- .... **CLC 7, 33**
See also CA 17-20R; CAAS 9; CANR 9, 33;
DLB 40; MTCW

Stevenson, Robert Louis (Balfour)
1850-1894 .... **NCLC 5, 14; SSC 11**
See also CDBLB 1890-1914; CLR 10, 11;
DLB 18, 57; MAICYA; WLC; YABC 2

Stewart, J(ohn) I(nnes) M(ackintosh)
1906-..................... **CLC 7, 14, 32**
See also CA 85-88; CAAS 3; MTCW

Stewart, Mary (Florence Elinor)
1916- .... **CLC 7, 35**
See also CA 1-4R; CANR 1; SATA 12

Stewart, Mary Rainbow
See Stewart, Mary (Florence Elinor)

Still, James 1906-................ **CLC 49**
See also CA 65-68; CANR 10, 26; DLB 9;
SATA 29

Sting
See Sumner, Gordon Matthew

Stirling, Arthur
See Sinclair, Upton (Beall)

Stitt, Milan 1941-................ **CLC 29**
See also CA 69-72

Stockton, Francis Richard 1834-1902
See Stockton, Frank R.
See also CA 108; 137; MAICYA; SATA 44

Stockton, Frank R................ **TCLC 47**
See also Stockton, Francis Richard
See also DLB 42, 74; SATA 32

Stoddard, Charles
See Kuttner, Henry

Stoker, Abraham 1847-1912
See Stoker, Bram
See also CA 105; SATA 29

Stoker, Bram .... **TCLC 8**
See also Stoker, Abraham
See also CDBLB 1890-1914; DLB 36, 70;
WLC

Stolz, Mary (Slattery) 1920- .... **CLC 12**
See also AAYA 8; AITN 1; CA 5-8R;
CANR 13; MAICYA; SAAS 3;
SATA 10, 70, 71

Stone, Irving 1903-1989............ **CLC 7**
See also AITN 1; CA 1-4R; 129; CAAS 3;
CANR 1, 23; MTCW; SATA 3; SATO 64

Stone, Robert (Anthony)
1937- .... CLC 5, 23, 42
See also CA 85-88; CANR 23; MTCW

Stone, Zachary
See Follett, Ken(neth Martin)

Stoppard, Tom
1937- ... CLC 1, 3, 4, 5, 8, 15, 29, 34, 63
See also CA 81-84; CANR 39;
CDBLB 1960 to Present; DLB 13;
DLBY 85; MTCW; WLC

Storey, David (Malcolm)
1933- .... CLC 2, 4, 5, 8
See also CA 81-84; CANR 36; DLB 13, 14; MTCW

Storm, Hyemeyohsts 1935- .... CLC 3
See also CA 81-84

Storm, (Hans) Theodor (Woldsen)
1817-1888 .... NCLC 1

Storni, Alfonsina 1892-1938 .... TCLC 5
See also CA 104; 131; HW

Stout, Rex (Todhunter) 1886-1975 ... CLC 3
See also AITN 2; CA 61-64

Stow, (Julian) Randolph 1935- .. CLC 23, 48
See also CA 13-16R; CANR 33; MTCW

Stowe, Harriet (Elizabeth) Beecher
1811-1896 .... NCLC 3
See also CDALB 1865-1917; DLB 1, 12, 42, 74; MAICYA; WLC; YABC 1

Strachey, (Giles) Lytton
1880-1932 .... TCLC 12
See also CA 110

Strand, Mark 1934- ...... CLC 6, 18, 41, 71
See also CA 21-24R; DLB 5; SATA 41

Straub, Peter (Francis) 1943- ...... CLC 28
See also BEST 89:1; CA 85-88; CANR 28; DLBY 84; MTCW

Strauss, Botho 1944- .... CLC 22

Streatfeild, (Mary) Noel
1895(?)-1986 .... CLC 21
See also CA 81-84; 120; CANR 31; CLR 17; MAICYA; SATA 20, 48

Stribling, T(homas) S(igismund)
1881-1965 .... CLC 23
See also CA 107; DLB 9

Strindberg, (Johan) August
1849-1912 .... TCLC 1, 8, 21, 47
See also CA 104; 135; WLC

Stringer, Arthur 1874-1950 .... TCLC 37
See also DLB 92

Stringer, David
See Roberts, Keith (John Kingston)

Strugatskii, Arkadii (Natanovich)
1925-1991 .... CLC 27
See also CA 106; 135

Strugatskii, Boris (Natanovich)
1933- .... CLC 27
See also CA 106

Strummer, Joe 1953(?)- .... CLC 30
See also The Clash

Stuart, Don A.
See Campbell, John W(ood Jr.)

Stuart, Ian
See MacLean, Alistair (Stuart)

Stuart, Jesse (Hilton)
1906-1984 .... CLC 1, 8, 11, 14, 34
See also CA 5-8R; 112; CANR 31; DLB 9, 48, 102; DLBY 84; SATA 2, 36

Sturgeon, Theodore (Hamilton)
1918-1985 .... CLC 22, 39
See also Queen, Ellery
See also CA 81-84; 116; CANR 32; DLB 8; DLBY 85; MTCW

Sturges, Preston 1898-1959 .... TCLC 48
See also CA 114; DLB 26

Styron, William
1925- .... CLC 1, 3, 5, 11, 15, 60
See also BEST 90:4; CA 5-8R; CANR 6, 33; CDALB 1968-1988; DLB 2; DLBY 80; MTCW

Suarez Lynch, B.
See Borges, Jorge Luis

Suarez Lynch, B.
See Bioy Casares, Adolfo; Borges, Jorge Luis

Su Chien 1884-1918
See Su Man-shu
See also CA 123

Sudermann, Hermann 1857-1928 .. TCLC 15
See also CA 107; DLB 118

Sue, Eugene 1804-1857 .... NCLC 1
See also DLB 119

Sueskind, Patrick 1949- .... CLC 44

Sukenick, Ronald 1932- ..... CLC 3, 4, 6, 48
See also CA 25-28R; CAAS 8; CANR 32; DLBY 81

Suknaski, Andrew 1942- .... CLC 19
See also CA 101; DLB 53

Sullivan, Vernon
See Vian, Boris

Sully Prudhomme 1839-1907 ...... TCLC 31

Su Man-shu .... TCLC 24
See also Su Chien

Summerforest, Ivy B.
See Kirkup, James

Summers, Andrew James 1942- ..... CLC 26
See also The Police

Summers, Andy
See Summers, Andrew James

Summers, Hollis (Spurgeon Jr.)
1916- .... CLC 10
See also CA 5-8R; CANR 3; DLB 6

Summers, (Alphonsus Joseph-Mary Augustus)
Montague 1880-1948 .... TCLC 16
See also CA 118

Sumner, Gordon Matthew 1951- .... CLC 26
See also The Police

Surtees, Robert Smith
1803-1864 .... NCLC 14
See also DLB 21

Susann, Jacqueline 1921-1974 .... CLC 3
See also AITN 1; CA 65-68; 53-56; MTCW

Suskind, Patrick
See Sueskind, Patrick

Sutcliff, Rosemary 1920- .... CLC 26
See also CA 5-8R; CANR 37; CLR 1; MAICYA; SATA 6, 44

Sutro, Alfred 1863-1933 .... TCLC 6
See also CA 105; DLB 10

Sutton, Henry
See Slavitt, David R.

Svevo, Italo .... TCLC 2, 35
See also Schmitz, Aron Hector

Swados, Elizabeth 1951- .... CLC 12
See also CA 97-100

Swados, Harvey 1920-1972 .... CLC 5
See also CA 5-8R; 37-40R; CANR 6; DLB 2

Swan, Gladys 1934- .... CLC 69
See also CA 101; CANR 17, 39

Swarthout, Glendon (Fred) 1918- ... CLC 35
See also CA 1-4R; CANR 1; SATA 26

Sweet, Sarah C.
See Jewett, (Theodora) Sarah Orne

Swenson, May 1919-1989 ..... CLC 4, 14, 61
See also CA 5-8R; 130; CANR 36; DLB 5; MTCW; SATA 15

Swift, Augustus
See Lovecraft, H(oward) P(hillips)

Swift, Graham 1949- .... CLC 41
See also CA 117; 122

Swift, Jonathan 1667-1745........... LC 1
See also CDBLB 1660-1789; DLB 39, 95, 101; SATA 19; WLC

Swinburne, Algernon Charles
1837-1909 .... TCLC 8, 36
See also CA 105; CDBLB 1832-1890; DLB 35, 57; WLC

Swinfen, Ann .... CLC 34

Swinnerton, Frank Arthur
1884-1982 .... CLC 31
See also CA 108; DLB 34

Swithen, John
See King, Stephen (Edwin)

Sylvia
See Ashton-Warner, Sylvia (Constance)

Symmes, Robert Edward
See Duncan, Robert (Edward)

Symonds, John Addington
1840-1893 .... NCLC 34
See also DLB 57

Symons, Arthur 1865-1945 .... TCLC 11
See also CA 107; DLB 19, 57

Symons, Julian (Gustave)
1912- .... CLC 2, 14, 32
See also CA 49-52; CAAS 3; CANR 3, 33; DLB 87; MTCW

Synge, (Edmund) J(ohn) M(illington)
1871-1909 .... TCLC 6, 37; DC 2
See also CA 104; CDBLB 1890-1914; DLB 10, 19

Syruc, J.
See Milosz, Czeslaw

Szirtes, George 1948- .... CLC 46
See also CA 109; CANR 27

Tabori, George 1914- .... CLC 19
See also CA 49-52; CANR 4

Tagore, Rabindranath 1861-1941 .... TCLC 3
See also CA 104; 120; MTCW

Taine, Hippolyte Adolphe
1828-1893 .... NCLC 15

Talese, Gay 1932- .... CLC 37
  See also AITN 1; CA 1-4R; CANR 9;
  MTCW

Tallent, Elizabeth (Ann) 1954- ..... CLC 45
  See also CA 117

Tally, Ted 1952- .... CLC 42
  See also CA 120; 124

Tamayo y Baus, Manuel
  1829-1898 .... NCLC 1

Tammsaare, A(nton) H(ansen)
  1878-1940 .... TCLC 27

Tan, Amy 1952- .... CLC 59
  See also AAYA 9; BEST 89:3; CA 136

Tandem, Felix
  See Spitteler, Carl (Friedrich Georg)

Tanizaki, Jun'ichiro
  1886-1965 .... CLC 8, 14, 28
  See also CA 93-96; 25-28R

Tanner, William
  See Amis, Kingsley (William)

Tao Lao
  See Storni, Alfonsina

Tarassoff, Lev
  See Troyat, Henri

Tarbell, Ida M(inerva)
  1857-1944 .... TCLC 40
  See also CA 122; DLB 47

Tarkington, (Newton) Booth
  1869-1946 .... TCLC 9
  See also CA 110; DLB 9, 102; SATA 17

Tasso, Torquato 1544-1595 .... LC 5

Tate, (John Orley) Allen
  1899-1979 .... CLC 2, 4, 6, 9, 11, 14, 24
  See also CA 5-8R; 85-88; CANR 32;
  DLB 4, 45, 63; MTCW

Tate, Ellalice
  See Hibbert, Eleanor Burford

Tate, James (Vincent) 1943- ... CLC 2, 6, 25
  See also CA 21-24R; CANR 29; DLB 5

Tavel, Ronald 1940- .... CLC 6
  See also CA 21-24R; CANR 33

Taylor, Cecil Philip 1929-1981 ..... CLC 27
  See also CA 25-28R; 105

Taylor, Edward 1642(?)-1729 .... LC 11
  See also DLB 24

Taylor, Eleanor Ross 1920- .... CLC 5
  See also CA 81-84

Taylor, Elizabeth 1912-1975 ... CLC 2, 4, 29
  See also CA 13-16R; CANR 9; MTCW;
  SATA 13

Taylor, Henry (Splawn) 1942- ...... CLC 44
  See also CA 33-36R; CAAS 7; CANR 31;
  DLB 5

Taylor, Kamala (Purnaiya) 1924-
  See Markandaya, Kamala
  See also CA 77-80

Taylor, Mildred D. .... CLC 21
  See also BW; CA 85-88; CANR 25; CLR 9;
  DLB 52; MAICYA; SAAS 5; SATA 15,
  70

Taylor, Peter (Hillsman)
  1917- ..... CLC 1, 4, 18, 37, 44, 50, 71;
                                      SSC 10
  See also CA 13-16R; CANR 9; DLBY 81;
  MTCW

Taylor, Robert Lewis 1912- .... CLC 14
  See also CA 1-4R; CANR 3; SATA 10

Tchekhov, Anton
  See Chekhov, Anton (Pavlovich)

Teasdale, Sara 1884-1933 .... TCLC 4
  See also CA 104; DLB 45; SATA 32

Tegner, Esaias 1782-1846 .... NCLC 2

Teilhard de Chardin, (Marie Joseph) Pierre
  1881-1955 .... TCLC 9
  See also CA 105

Temple, Ann
  See Mortimer, Penelope (Ruth)

Tennant, Emma (Christina)
  1937- .... CLC 13, 52
  See also CA 65-68; CAAS 9; CANR 10, 38;
  DLB 14

Tenneshaw, S. M.
  See Silverberg, Robert

Tennyson, Alfred 1809-1892 ..... NCLC 30
  See also CDBLB 1832-1890; DLB 32; WLC

Teran, Lisa St. Aubin de .... CLC 36
  See also St. Aubin de Teran, Lisa

Teresa de Jesus, St. 1515-1582 ..... LC 18

Terkel, Louis 1912-
  See Terkel, Studs
  See also CA 57-60; CANR 18; MTCW

Terkel, Studs .... CLC 38
  See also Terkel, Louis
  See also AITN 1

Terry, C. V.
  See Slaughter, Frank G(ill)

Terry, Megan 1932- .... CLC 19
  See also CA 77-80; CABS 3; DLB 7

Tertz, Abram
  See Sinyavsky, Andrei (Donatevich)

Tesich, Steve 1943(?)- .... CLC 40, 69
  See also CA 105; DLBY 83

Teternikov, Fyodor Kuzmich 1863-1927
  See Sologub, Fyodor
  See also CA 104

Tevis, Walter 1928-1984 .... CLC 42
  See also CA 113

Tey, Josephine .... TCLC 14
  See also Mackintosh, Elizabeth
  See also DLB 77

Thackeray, William Makepeace
  1811-1863 .... NCLC 5, 14, 22
  See also CDBLB 1832-1890; DLB 21, 55;
  SATA 23; WLC

Thakura, Ravindranatha
  See Tagore, Rabindranath

Tharoor, Shashi 1956- .... CLC 70

Thelwell, Michael Miles 1939- ..... CLC 22
  See also CA 101

Theobald, Lewis Jr.
  See Lovecraft, H(oward) P(hillips)

The Prophet
  See Dreiser, Theodore (Herman Albert)

Theroux, Alexander (Louis)
  1939- .... CLC 2, 25
  See also CA 85-88; CANR 20

Theroux, Paul (Edward)
  1941- .... CLC 5, 8, 11, 15, 28, 46
  See also BEST 89:4; CA 33-36R; CANR 20;
  DLB 2; MTCW; SATA 44

Thesen, Sharon 1946- .... CLC 56

Thevenin, Denis
  See Duhamel, Georges

Thibault, Jacques Anatole Francois
  1844-1924
  See France, Anatole
  See also CA 106; 127; MTCW

Thiele, Colin (Milton) 1920- .... CLC 17
  See also CA 29-32R; CANR 12, 28;
  CLR 27; MAICYA; SAAS 2; SATA 14

Thomas, Audrey (Callahan)
  1935- .... CLC 7, 13, 37
  See also AITN 2; CA 21-24R; CANR 36;
  DLB 60; MTCW

Thomas, D(onald) M(ichael)
  1935- .... CLC 13, 22, 31
  See also CA 61-64; CAAS 11; CANR 17;
  CDBLB 1960 to Present; DLB 40;
  MTCW

Thomas, Dylan (Marlais)
  1914-1953 .... TCLC 1, 8, 45; PC 2;
                                       SSC 3
  See also CA 104; 120; CDBLB 1945-1960;
  DLB 13, 20; MTCW; SATA 60; WLC

Thomas, (Philip) Edward
  1878-1917 .... TCLC 10
  See also CA 106; DLB 19

Thomas, Joyce Carol 1938- .... CLC 35
  See also BW; CA 113; 116; CLR 19;
  DLB 33; MAICYA; MTCW; SAAS 7;
  SATA 40

Thomas, Lewis 1913- .... CLC 35
  See also CA 85-88; CANR 38; MTCW

Thomas, Paul
  See Mann, (Paul) Thomas

Thomas, Piri 1928- .... CLC 17
  See also CA 73-76; HW

Thomas, R(onald) S(tuart)
  1913- .... CLC 6, 13, 48
  See also CA 89-92; CAAS 4; CANR 30;
  CDBLB 1960 to Present; DLB 27;
  MTCW

Thomas, Ross (Elmore) 1926- ...... CLC 39
  See also CA 33-36R; CANR 22

Thompson, Francis Clegg
  See Mencken, H(enry) L(ouis)

Thompson, Francis Joseph
  1859-1907 .... TCLC 4
  See also CA 104; CDBLB 1890-1914;
  DLB 19

Thompson, Hunter S(tockton)
  1939- .... CLC 9, 17, 40
  See also BEST 89:1; CA 17-20R; CANR 23;
  MTCW

Thompson, Jim 1906-1976 .... CLC 69

Thompson, Judith .... CLC 39

Thomson, James 1700-1748 .... LC 16

Thomson, James 1834-1882 ...... NCLC 18

Thoreau, Henry David
1817-1862 .... **NCLC 7, 21**
See also CDALB 1640-1865; DLB 1; WLC

Thornton, Hall
See Silverberg, Robert

Thurber, James (Grover)
1894-1961 .... **CLC 5, 11, 25; SSC 1**
See also CA 73-76; CANR 17, 39;
CDALB 1929-1941; DLB 4, 11, 22, 102;
MAICYA; MTCW; SATA 13

Thurman, Wallace (Henry)
1902-1934 .... **TCLC 6**
See also BLC 3; BW; CA 104; 124; DLB 51

Ticheburn, Cheviot
See Ainsworth, William Harrison

Tieck, (Johann) Ludwig
1773-1853 .... **NCLC 5**
See also DLB 90

Tiger, Derry
See Ellison, Harlan

Tilghman, Christopher 1948(?)- ..... **CLC 65**

Tillinghast, Richard (Williford)
1940- .... **CLC 29**
See also CA 29-32R; CANR 26

Timrod, Henry 1828-1867 .... **NCLC 25**
See also DLB 3

Tindall, Gillian 1938- .... **CLC 7**
See also CA 21-24R; CANR 11

Tiptree, James Jr. .... **CLC 48, 50**
See also Sheldon, Alice Hastings Bradley
See also DLB 8

Titmarsh, Michael Angelo
See Thackeray, William Makepeace

Tocqueville, Alexis (Charles Henri Maurice Clerel Comte) 1805-1859 ..... **NCLC 7**

Tolkien, J(ohn) R(onald) R(euel)
1892-1973 .... **CLC 1, 2, 3, 8, 12, 38**
See also AITN 1; CA 17-18; 45-48;
CANR 36; CAP 2; CDBLB 1914-1945;
DLB 15; MAICYA; MTCW; SATA 2,
24, 32; WLC

Toller, Ernst 1893-1939 .... **TCLC 10**
See also CA 107

Tolson, M. B.
See Tolson, Melvin B(eaunorus)

Tolson, Melvin B(eaunorus)
1898(?)-1966 .... **CLC 36**
See also BLC 3; BW; CA 124; 89-92;
DLB 48, 76

Tolstoi, Aleksei Nikolaevich
See Tolstoy, Alexey Nikolaevich

Tolstoy, Alexey Nikolaevich
1882-1945 .... **TCLC 18**
See also CA 107

Tolstoy, Count Leo
See Tolstoy, Leo (Nikolaevich)

Tolstoy, Leo (Nikolaevich)
1828-1910 ..... **TCLC 4, 11, 17, 28, 44; SSC 9**
See also CA 104; 123; SATA 26; WLC

Tomasi di Lampedusa, Giuseppe 1896-1957
See Lampedusa, Giuseppe (Tomasi) di
See also CA 111

Tomlin, Lily .... **CLC 17**
See also Tomlin, Mary Jean

Tomlin, Mary Jean 1939(?)-
See Tomlin, Lily
See also CA 117

Tomlinson, (Alfred) Charles
1927- .... **CLC 2, 4, 6, 13, 45**
See also CA 5-8R; CANR 33; DLB 40

Tonson, Jacob
See Bennett, (Enoch) Arnold

Toole, John Kennedy
1937-1969 .... **CLC 19, 64**
See also CA 104; DLBY 81

Toomer, Jean
1894-1967 ..... **CLC 1, 4, 13, 22; SSC 1**
See also BLC 3; BW; CA 85-88;
CDALB 1917-1929; DLB 45, 51; MTCW

Torley, Luke
See Blish, James (Benjamin)

Tornimparte, Alessandra
See Ginzburg, Natalia

Torre, Raoul della
See Mencken, H(enry) L(ouis)

Torrey, E(dwin) Fuller 1937- .... **CLC 34**
See also CA 119

Torsvan, Ben Traven
See Traven, B.

Torsvan, Benno Traven
See Traven, B.

Torsvan, Berick Traven
See Traven, B.

Torsvan, Berwick Traven
See Traven, B.

Torsvan, Bruno Traven
See Traven, B.

Torsvan, Traven
See Traven, B.

Tournier, Michel (Edouard)
1924- .... **CLC 6, 23, 36**
See also CA 49-52; CANR 3, 36; DLB 83;
MTCW; SATA 23

Tournimparte, Alessandra
See Ginzburg, Natalia

Towers, Ivar
See Kornbluth, C(yril) M.

Townsend, Sue 1946- .... **CLC 61**
See also CA 119; 127; MTCW; SATA 48, 55

Townshend, Peter (Dennis Blandford)
1945- .... **CLC 17, 42**
See also CA 107

Tozzi, Federigo 1883-1920 .... **TCLC 31**

Traill, Catharine Parr
1802-1899 .... **NCLC 31**
See also DLB 99

Trakl, Georg 1887-1914 .... **TCLC 5**
See also CA 104

Transtroemer, Tomas (Goesta)
1931- .... **CLC 52, 65**
See also CA 117; 129

Transtromer, Tomas Gosta
See Transtroemer, Tomas (Goesta)

Traven, B. (?)-1969 .... **CLC 8, 11**
See also CA 19-20; 25-28R; CAP 2; DLB 9, 56; MTCW

Treitel, Jonathan 1959- .... **CLC 70**

Tremain, Rose 1943-.............. **CLC 42**
See also CA 97-100; DLB 14

Tremblay, Michel 1942-........... **CLC 29**
See also CA 116; 128; DLB 60; MTCW

Trevanian (a pseudonym) 1930(?)-... **CLC 29**
See also CA 108

Trevor, Glen
See Hilton, James

Trevor, William
1928- .... **CLC 7, 9, 14, 25, 71**
See also Cox, William Trevor
See also DLB 14

Trifonov, Yuri (Valentinovich)
1925-1981 .... **CLC 45**
See also CA 126; 103; MTCW

Trilling, Lionel 1905-1975 .... **CLC 9, 11, 24**
See also CA 9-12R; 61-64; CANR 10;
DLB 28, 63; MTCW

Trimball, W. H.
See Mencken, H(enry) L(ouis)

Tristan
See Gomez de la Serna, Ramon

Tristram
See Housman, A(lfred) E(dward)

Trogdon, William (Lewis) 1939-
See Heat-Moon, William Least
See also CA 115; 119

Trollope, Anthony 1815-1882 .. **NCLC 6, 33**
See also CDBLB 1832-1890; DLB 21, 57;
SATA 22; WLC

Trollope, Frances 1779-1863 ..... **NCLC 30**
See also DLB 21

Trotsky, Leon 1879-1940......... **TCLC 22**
See also CA 118

Trotter (Cockburn), Catharine
1679-1749 .... **LC 8**
See also DLB 84

Trout, Kilgore
See Farmer, Philip Jose

Trow, George W. S. 1943- .... **CLC 52**
See also CA 126

Troyat, Henri 1911-.............. **CLC 23**
See also CA 45-48; CANR 2, 33; MTCW

Trudeau, G(arretson) B(eekman) 1948-
See Trudeau, Garry B.
See also CA 81-84; CANR 31; SATA 35

Trudeau, Garry B.................. **CLC 12**
See also Trudeau, G(arretson) B(eekman)
See also AITN 2

Truffaut, Francois 1932-1984....... **CLC 20**
See also CA 81-84; 113; CANR 34

Trumbo, Dalton 1905-1976 .... **CLC 19**
See also CA 21-24R; 69-72; CANR 10;
DLB 26

Trumbull, John 1750-1831....... **NCLC 30**
See also DLB 31

Trundlett, Helen B.
See Eliot, T(homas) S(tearns)

Tryon, Thomas 1926-1991 .... **CLC 3, 11**
See also AITN 1; CA 29-32R; 135;
CANR 32; MTCW

Tryon, Tom
See Tryon, Thomas

Ts'ao Hsueh-ch'in 1715(?)-1763....... **LC 1**

Tsushima, Shuji 1909-1948
See Dazai, Osamu
See also CA 107

Tsvetaeva (Efron), Marina (Ivanovna)
1892-1941 .... TCLC **7, 35**
See also CA 104; 128; MTCW

Tuck, Lily 1938- .... CLC **70**

Tunis, John R(oberts) 1889-1975 ... CLC **12**
See also CA 61-64; DLB 22; MAICYA;
SATA 30, 37

Tuohy, Frank .... CLC **37**
See also Tuohy, John Francis
See also DLB 14

Tuohy, John Francis 1925-
See Tuohy, Frank
See also CA 5-8R; CANR 3

Turco, Lewis (Putnam) 1934- ... CLC **11, 63**
See also CA 13-16R; CANR 24; DLBY 84

Turgenev, Ivan
1818-1883 .... NCLC **21**; SSC **7**
See also WLC

Turner, Frederick 1943- .... CLC **48**
See also CA 73-76; CAAS 10; CANR 12,
30; DLB 40

Tusan, Stan 1936- .... CLC **22**
See also CA 105

Tutuola, Amos 1920- .... CLC **5, 14, 29**
See also BLC 3; BW; CA 9-12R; CANR 27;
MTCW

Twain, Mark
.... TCLC **6, 12, 19, 36, 48**; SSC **6**
See also Clemens, Samuel Langhorne
See also DLB 11, 12, 23, 64, 74; WLC

Tyler, Anne
1941- .... CLC **7, 11, 18, 28, 44, 59**
See also BEST 89:1; CA 9-12R; CANR 11,
33; DLB 6; DLBY 82; MTCW; SATA 7

Tyler, Royall 1757-1826 .... NCLC **3**
See also DLB 37

Tynan, Katharine 1861-1931 .... TCLC **3**
See also CA 104

Tytell, John 1939- .... CLC **50**
See also CA 29-32R

Tyutchev, Fyodor 1803-1873 ..... NCLC **34**

Tzara, Tristan .... CLC **47**
See also Rosenfeld, Samuel

Uhry, Alfred 1936- .... CLC **55**
See also CA 127; 133

Ulf, Haerved
See Strindberg, (Johan) August

Ulf, Harved
See Strindberg, (Johan) August

Unamuno (y Jugo), Miguel de
1864-1936 .... TCLC **2, 9**; SSC **11**
See also CA 104; 131; DLB 108; HW;
MTCW

Undercliffe, Errol
See Campbell, (John) Ramsey

Underwood, Miles
See Glassco, John

Undset, Sigrid 1882-1949 .... TCLC **3**
See also CA 104; 129; MTCW; WLC

Ungaretti, Giuseppe
1888-1970 .... CLC **7, 11, 15**
See also CA 19-20; 25-28R; CAP 2;
DLB 114

Unger, Douglas 1952- .... CLC **34**
See also CA 130

Updike, John (Hoyer)
1932- ...... CLC **1, 2, 3, 5, 7, 9, 13, 15,
23, 34, 43, 70**
See also CA 1-4R; CABS 1; CANR 4, 33;
CDALB 1968-1988; DLB 2, 5; DLBD 3;
DLBY 80, 82; MTCW; WLC

Upshaw, Margaret Mitchell
See Mitchell, Margaret (Munnerlyn)

Upton, Mark
See Sanders, Lawrence

Urdang, Constance (Henriette)
1922- .... CLC **47**
See also CA 21-24R; CANR 9, 24

Uris, Leon (Marcus) 1924- .... CLC **7, 32**
See also AITN 1, 2; BEST 89:2; CA 1-4R;
CANR 1; MTCW; SATA 49

Urmuz
See Codrescu, Andrei

Ustinov, Peter (Alexander) 1921- .... CLC **1**
See also AITN 1; CA 13-16R; CANR 25;
DLB 13

V
See Chekhov, Anton (Pavlovich)

Vaculik, Ludvik 1926- .... CLC **7**
See also CA 53-56

Valenzuela, Luisa 1938- .... CLC **31**
See also CA 101; CANR 32; DLB 113; HW

Valera y Alcala-Galiano, Juan
1824-1905 .... TCLC **10**
See also CA 106

Valery, (Ambroise) Paul (Toussaint Jules)
1871-1945 .... TCLC **4, 15**
See also CA 104; 122; MTCW

Valle-Inclan, Ramon (Maria) del
1866-1936 .... TCLC **5**
See also CA 106

Vallejo, Antonio Buero
See Buero Vallejo, Antonio

Vallejo, Cesar (Abraham)
1892-1938 .... TCLC **3**
See also CA 105; HW

Valle Y Pena, Ramon del
See Valle-Inclan, Ramon (Maria) del

Van Ash, Cay 1918- .... CLC **34**

Vanbrugh, Sir John 1664-1726 ...... LC **21**
See also DLB 80

Van Campen, Karl
See Campbell, John W(ood Jr.)

Vance, Gerald
See Silverberg, Robert

Vance, Jack .... CLC **35**
See also Vance, John Holbrook
See also DLB 8

Vance, John Holbrook 1916-
See Queen, Ellery; Vance, Jack
See also CA 29-32R; CANR 17; MTCW

**Van Den Bogarde, Derek Jules Gaspard Ulric
Niven** 1921-
See Bogarde, Dirk
See also CA 77-80

Vandenburgh, Jane .... CLC **59**

Vanderhaeghe, Guy 1951- .... CLC **41**
See also CA 113

van der Post, Laurens (Jan) 1906- ... CLC **5**
See also CA 5-8R; CANR 35

van de Wetering, Janwillem 1931- .. CLC **47**
See also CA 49-52; CANR 4

Van Dine, S. S. .... TCLC **23**
See also Wright, Willard Huntington

Van Doren, Carl (Clinton)
1885-1950 .... TCLC **18**
See also CA 111

Van Doren, Mark 1894-1972 ..... CLC **6, 10**
See also CA 1-4R; 37-40R; CANR 3;
DLB 45; MTCW

Van Druten, John (William)
1901-1957 .... TCLC **2**
See also CA 104; DLB 10

Van Duyn, Mona (Jane)
1921- .... CLC **3, 7, 63**
See also CA 9-12R; CANR 7, 38; DLB 5

Van Dyne, Edith
See Baum, L(yman) Frank

van Itallie, Jean-Claude 1936- .... CLC **3**
See also CA 45-48; CAAS 2; CANR 1;
DLB 7

van Ostaijen, Paul 1896-1928 ..... TCLC **33**

Van Peebles, Melvin 1932- ...... CLC **2, 20**
See also BW; CA 85-88; CANR 27

Vansittart, Peter 1920- .... CLC **42**
See also CA 1-4R; CANR 3

Van Vechten, Carl 1880-1964 ...... CLC **33**
See also CA 89-92; DLB 4, 9, 51

Van Vogt, A(lfred) E(lton) 1912- ..... CLC **1**
See also CA 21-24R; CANR 28; DLB 8;
SATA 14

Vara, Madeleine
See Jackson, Laura (Riding)

Varda, Agnes 1928- .... CLC **16**
See also CA 116; 122

Vargas Llosa, (Jorge) Mario (Pedro)
1936- .... CLC **3, 6, 9, 10, 15, 31, 42**
See also CA 73-76; CANR 18, 32; HW;
MTCW

Vasiliu, Gheorghe 1881-1957
See Bacovia, George
See also CA 123

Vassa, Gustavus
See Equiano, Olaudah

Vassilikos, Vassilis 1933- .... CLC **4, 8**
See also CA 81-84

Vaughn, Stephanie .... CLC **62**

Vazov, Ivan (Minchov)
1850-1921 .... TCLC **25**
See also CA 121

Veblen, Thorstein (Bunde)
1857-1929 .... TCLC **31**
See also CA 115

Venison, Alfred
See Pound, Ezra (Weston Loomis)

Verdi, Marie de
See Mencken, H(enry) L(ouis)

Verdu, Matilde
See Cela, Camilo Jose

Verga, Giovanni (Carmelo)
1840-1922 .... TCLC 3
See also CA 104; 123

Vergil 70B.C.-19B.C. .... CMLC 9

Verhaeren, Emile (Adolphe Gustave)
1855-1916 .... TCLC 12
See also CA 109

Verlaine, Paul (Marie)
1844-1896 .... NCLC 2; PC 2

Verne, Jules (Gabriel) 1828-1905 ... TCLC 6
See also CA 110; 131; MAICYA; SATA 21

Very, Jones 1813-1880 .... NCLC 9
See also DLB 1

Vesaas, Tarjei 1897-1970.......... CLC 48
See also CA 29-32R

Vialis, Gaston
See Simenon, Georges (Jacques Christian)

Vian, Boris 1920-1959 .... TCLC 9
See also CA 106; DLB 72

Viaud, (Louis Marie) Julien 1850-1923
See Loti, Pierre
See also CA 107

Vicar, Henry
See Felsen, Henry Gregor

Vicker, Angus
See Felsen, Henry Gregor

Vidal, Gore
1925- ..... CLC 2, 4, 6, 8, 10, 22, 33, 72
See also AITN 1; BEST 90:2; CA 5-8R; CANR 13; DLB 6; MTCW

Viereck, Peter (Robert Edwin)
1916- .... CLC 4
See also CA 1-4R; CANR 1; DLB 5

Vigny, Alfred (Victor) de
1797-1863 .... NCLC 7
See also DLB 119

Vilakazi, Benedict Wallet
1906-1947 .... TCLC 37

Villiers de l'Isle Adam, Jean Marie Mathias Philippe Auguste Comte
1838-1889 .... NCLC 3

Vincent, Gabrielle............. CLC 13
See also CA 126; CLR 13; MAICYA; SATA 61

Vinci, Leonardo da 1452-1519....... LC 12

Vine, Barbara .... CLC 50
See also Rendell, Ruth (Barbara)
See also BEST 90:4

Vinge, Joan D(ennison) 1948- ...... CLC 30
See also CA 93-96; SATA 36

Violis, G.
See Simenon, Georges (Jacques Christian)

Visconti, Luchino 1906-1976....... CLC 16
See also CA 81-84; 65-68; CANR 39

Vittorini, Elio 1908-1966...... CLC 6, 9, 14
See also CA 133; 25-28R

Vizinczey, Stephen 1933-.......... CLC 40
See also CA 128

Vliet, R(ussell) G(ordon)
1929-1984 .... CLC 22
See also CA 37-40R; 112; CANR 18

Vogau, Boris Andreyevich 1894-1937(?)
See Pilnyak, Boris
See also CA 123

Voigt, Cynthia 1942- .... CLC 30
See also AAYA 3; CA 106; CANR 18, 37; CLR 13; MAICYA; SATA 33, 48

Voigt, Ellen Bryant 1943- .... CLC 54
See also CA 69-72; CANR 11, 29; DLB 120

Voinovich, Vladimir (Nikolaevich)
1932- .... CLC 10, 49
See also CA 81-84; CAAS 12; CANR 33; MTCW

Voltaire 1694-1778 .... LC 14
See also WLC

von Daeniken, Erich 1935- .... CLC 30
See also von Daniken, Erich
See also AITN 1; CA 37-40R; CANR 17

von Daniken, Erich............... CLC 30
See also von Daeniken, Erich

von Heidenstam, (Carl Gustaf) Verner
See Heidenstam, (Carl Gustaf) Verner von

von Heyse, Paul (Johann Ludwig)
See Heyse, Paul (Johann Ludwig von)

von Hofmannsthal, Hugo
See Hofmannsthal, Hugo von

von Horvath, Odon
See Horvath, Oedoen von

von Horvath, Oedoen
See Horvath, Oedoen von

von Liliencron, (Friedrich Adolf Axel) Detlev
See Liliencron, (Friedrich Adolf Axel) Detlev von

Vonnegut, Kurt Jr.
1922- ...... CLC 1, 2, 3, 4, 5, 8, 12, 22, 40, 60; SSC 8
See also AAYA 6; AITN 1; BEST 90:4; CA 1-4R; CANR 1, 25; CDALB 1968-1988; DLB 2, 8; DLBD 3; DLBY 80; MTCW; WLC

Von Rachen, Kurt
See Hubbard, L(afayette) Ron(ald)

von Rezzori (d'Arezzo), Gregor
See Rezzori (d'Arezzo), Gregor von

von Sternberg, Josef
See Sternberg, Josef von

Vorster, Gordon 1924-............ CLC 34
See also CA 133

Vosce, Trudie
See Ozick, Cynthia

Voznesensky, Andrei (Andreievich)
1933-.................... CLC 1, 15, 57
See also CA 89-92; CANR 37; MTCW

Waddington, Miriam 1917- .... CLC 28
See also CA 21-24R; CANR 12, 30; DLB 68

Wagman, Fredrica 1937- .... CLC 7
See also CA 97-100

Wagner, Richard 1813-1883........ NCLC 9

Wagner-Martin, Linda 1936-....... CLC 50

Wagoner, David (Russell)
1926- .... CLC 3, 5, 15
See also CA 1-4R; CAAS 3; CANR 2; DLB 5; SATA 14

Wah, Fred(erick James) 1939-...... CLC 44
See also CA 107; DLB 60

Wahloo, Per 1926-1975 .... CLC 7
See also CA 61-64

Wahloo, Peter
See Wahloo, Per

Wain, John (Barrington)
1925- .... CLC 2, 11, 15, 46
See also CA 5-8R; CAAS 4; CANR 23; CDBLB 1960 to Present; DLB 15, 27; MTCW

Wajda, Andrzej 1926-............. CLC 16
See also CA 102

Wakefield, Dan 1932-.............. CLC 7
See also CA 21-24R; CAAS 7

Wakoski, Diane
1937- .... CLC 2, 4, 7, 9, 11, 40
See also CA 13-16R; CAAS 1; CANR 9; DLB 5

Wakoski-Sherbell, Diane
See Wakoski, Diane

Walcott, Derek (Alton)
1930- .... CLC 2, 4, 9, 14, 25, 42, 67
See also BLC 3; BW; CA 89-92; CANR 26; DLB 117; DLBY 81; MTCW

Waldman, Anne 1945- .... CLC 7
See also CA 37-40R; CANR 34; DLB 16

Waldo, E. Hunter
See Sturgeon, Theodore (Hamilton)

Waldo, Edward Hamilton
See Sturgeon, Theodore (Hamilton)

Walker, Alice (Malsenior)
1944- ...... CLC 5, 6, 9, 19, 27, 46, 58; SSC 5
See also AAYA 3; BEST 89:4; BLC 3; BW; CA 37-40R; CANR 9, 27; CDALB 1968-1988; DLB 6, 33; MTCW; SATA 31

Walker, David Harry 1911-1992.... CLC 14
See also CA 1-4R; 137; CANR 1; SATA 8; SATO 71

Walker, Edward Joseph 1934-
See Walker, Ted
See also CA 21-24R; CANR 12, 28

Walker, George F. 1947- .... CLC 44, 61
See also CA 103; CANR 21; DLB 60

Walker, Joseph A. 1935- .... CLC 19
See also BW; CA 89-92; CANR 26; DLB 38

Walker, Margaret (Abigail)
1915- .... CLC 1, 6
See also BLC 3; BW; CA 73-76; CANR 26; DLB 76; MTCW

Walker, Ted.................... CLC 13
See also Walker, Edward Joseph
See also DLB 40

Wallace, David Foster 1962-....... CLC 50
See also CA 132

Wallace, Dexter
See Masters, Edgar Lee

Wallace, Irving 1916-1990 .... CLC 7, 13
See also AITN 1; CA 1-4R; 132; CAAS 1;
CANR 1, 27; MTCW

Wallant, Edward Lewis
1926-1962 .... CLC 5, 10
See also CA 1-4R; CANR 22; DLB 2, 28;
MTCW

Walpole, Horace 1717-1797 .... LC 2
See also DLB 39, 104

Walpole, Hugh (Seymour)
1884-1941 .... TCLC 5
See also CA 104; DLB 34

Walser, Martin 1927- .... CLC 27
See also CA 57-60; CANR 8; DLB 75

Walser, Robert 1878-1956 .... TCLC 18
See also CA 118; DLB 66

Walsh, Jill Paton................ CLC 35
See also Paton Walsh, Gillian
See also CLR 2; SAAS 3

Walter, Villiam Christian
See Andersen, Hans Christian

Wambaugh, Joseph (Aloysius Jr.)
1937- .... CLC 3, 18
See also AITN 1; BEST 89:3; CA 33-36R;
DLB 6; DLBY 83; MTCW

Ward, Arthur Henry Sarsfield 1883-1959
See Rohmer, Sax
See also CA 108

Ward, Douglas Turner 1930- .... CLC 19
See also BW; CA 81-84; CANR 27; DLB 7,
38

Warhol, Andy 1928(?)-1987 .... CLC 20
See also BEST 89:4; CA 89-92; 121;
CANR 34

Warner, Francis (Robert le Plastrier)
1937- .... CLC 14
See also CA 53-56; CANR 11

Warner, Marina 1946- .... CLC 59
See also CA 65-68; CANR 21

Warner, Rex (Ernest) 1905-1986.... CLC 45
See also CA 89-92; 119; DLB 15

Warner, Susan (Bogert)
1819-1885 .... NCLC 31
See also DLB 3, 42

Warner, Sylvia (Constance) Ashton
See Ashton-Warner, Sylvia (Constance)

Warner, Sylvia Townsend
1893-1978 .... CLC 7, 19
See also CA 61-64; 77-80; CANR 16;
DLB 34; MTCW

Warren, Mercy Otis 1728-1814... NCLC 13
See also DLB 31

Warren, Robert Penn
1905-1989 ... CLC 1, 4, 6, 8, 10, 13, 18,
39, 53, 59; SSC 4
See also AITN 1; CA 13-16R; 129;
CANR 10; CDALB 1968-1988; DLB 2,
48; DLBY 80, 89; MTCW; SATA 46, 63;
WLC

Warshofsky, Isaac
See Singer, Isaac Bashevis

Warton, Thomas 1728-1790 .... LC 15
See also DLB 104, 109

Waruk, Kona
See Harris, (Theodore) Wilson

Warung, Price 1855-1911.......... TCLC 45

Warwick, Jarvis
See Garner, Hugh

Washington, Alex
See Harris, Mark

Washington, Booker T(aliaferro)
1856-1915 .... TCLC 10
See also BLC 3; BW; CA 114; 125;
SATA 28

Wassermann, (Karl) Jakob
1873-1934 .... TCLC 6
See also CA 104; DLB 66

Wasserstein, Wendy 1950- ...... CLC 32, 59
See also CA 121; 129; CABS 3

Waterhouse, Keith (Spencer)
1929- .... CLC 47
See also CA 5-8R; CANR 38; DLB 13, 15;
MTCW

Waters, Roger 1944- .... CLC 35
See also Pink Floyd

Watkins, Frances Ellen
See Harper, Frances Ellen Watkins

Watkins, Gerrold
See Malzberg, Barry N(athaniel)

Watkins, Paul 1964- .... CLC 55
See also CA 132

Watkins, Vernon Phillips
1906-1967 .... CLC 43
See also CA 9-10; 25-28R; CAP 1; DLB 20

Watson, Irving S.
See Mencken, H(enry) L(ouis)

Watson, John H.
See Farmer, Philip Jose

Watson, Richard F.
See Silverberg, Robert

Waugh, Auberon (Alexander) 1939- .. CLC 7
See also CA 45-48; CANR 6, 22; DLB 14

Waugh, Evelyn (Arthur St. John)
1903-1966 ... CLC 1, 3, 8, 13, 19, 27, 44
See also CA 85-88; 25-28R; CANR 22;
CDBLB 1914-1945; DLB 15; MTCW;
WLC

Waugh, Harriet 1944- .... CLC 6
See also CA 85-88; CANR 22

Ways, C. R.
See Blount, Roy (Alton) Jr.

Waystaff, Simon
See Swift, Jonathan

Webb, (Martha) Beatrice (Potter)
1858-1943 .... TCLC 22
See also Potter, Beatrice
See also CA 117

Webb, Charles (Richard) 1939- ..... CLC 7
See also CA 25-28R

Webb, James H(enry) Jr. 1946- .... CLC 22
See also CA 81-84

Webb, Mary (Gladys Meredith)
1881-1927 .... TCLC 24
See also CA 123; DLB 34

Webb, Mrs. Sidney
See Webb, (Martha) Beatrice (Potter)

Webb, Phyllis 1927- .... CLC 18
See also CA 104; CANR 23; DLB 53

Webb, Sidney (James)
1859-1947 .... TCLC 22
See also CA 117

Webber, Andrew Lloyd............. CLC 21
See also Lloyd Webber, Andrew

Weber, Lenora Mattingly
1895-1971 .... CLC 12
See also CA 19-20; 29-32R; CAP 1;
SATA 2, 26

Webster, John 1579(?)-1634(?) .... DC 2
See also CDBLB Before 1660; DLB 58;
WLC

Webster, Noah 1758-1843 .... NCLC 30

Wedekind, (Benjamin) Frank(lin)
1864-1918 .... TCLC 7
See also CA 104; DLB 118

Weidman, Jerome 1913- .... CLC 7
See also AITN 2; CA 1-4R; CANR 1;
DLB 28

Weil, Simone (Adolphine)
1909-1943 .... TCLC 23
See also CA 117

Weinstein, Nathan
See West, Nathanael

Weinstein, Nathan von Wallenstein
See West, Nathanael

Weir, Peter (Lindsay) 1944- .... CLC 20
See also CA 113; 123

Weiss, Peter (Ulrich)
1916-1982 .... CLC 3, 15, 51
See also CA 45-48; 106; CANR 3; DLB 69

Weiss, Theodore (Russell)
1916- .... CLC 3, 8, 14
See also CA 9-12R; CAAS 2; DLB 5

Welch, (Maurice) Denton
1915-1948 .... TCLC 22
See also CA 121

Welch, James 1940- .... CLC 6, 14, 52
See also CA 85-88

Weldon, Fay
1933(?)- .... CLC 6, 9, 11, 19, 36, 59
See also CA 21-24R; CANR 16;
CDBLB 1960 to Present; DLB 14;
MTCW

Wellek, Rene 1903- .... CLC 28
See also CA 5-8R; CAAS 7; CANR 8;
DLB 63

Weller, Michael 1942- .... CLC 10, 53
See also CA 85-88

Weller, Paul 1958- .... CLC 26

Wellershoff, Dieter 1925-.......... CLC 46
See also CA 89-92; CANR 16, 37

Welles, (George) Orson
1915-1985 .... CLC 20
See also CA 93-96; 117

Wellman, Mac 1945- .... CLC 65

Wellman, Manly Wade 1903-1986 .. CLC 49
See also CA 1-4R; 118; CANR 6, 16;
SATA 6, 47

Wells, Carolyn 1869(?)-1942 ...... TCLC 35
See also CA 113; DLB 11

455

Wells, H(erbert) G(eorge)
1866-1946 . . . . . . TCLC 6, 12, 19; SSC 6
See also CA 110; 121; CDBLB 1914-1945;
DLB 34, 70; MTCW; SATA 20; WLC

Wells, Rosemary 1943- . . . . CLC 12
See also CA 85-88; CLR 16; MAICYA;
SAAS 1; SATA 18, 69

Welty, Eudora
1909- . . . . CLC 1, 2, 5, 14, 22, 33; SSC 1
See also CA 9-12R; CABS 1; CANR 32;
CDALB 1941-1968; DLB 2, 102;
DLBY 87; MTCW; WLC

Wen I-to 1899-1946 . . . . TCLC 28

Wentworth, Robert
See Hamilton, Edmond

Werfel, Franz (V.) 1890-1945 . . . . . . TCLC 8
See also CA 104; DLB 81

Wergeland, Henrik Arnold
1808-1845 . . . . NCLC 5

Wersba, Barbara 1932- . . . . CLC 30
See also AAYA 2; CA 29-32R; CANR 16,
38; CLR 3; DLB 52; MAICYA; SAAS 2;
SATA 1, 58

Wertmueller, Lina 1928- . . . . CLC 16
See also CA 97-100; CANR 39

Wescott, Glenway 1901-1987 . . . . CLC 13
See also CA 13-16R; 121; CANR 23;
DLB 4, 9, 102

Wesker, Arnold 1932- . . . . CLC 3, 5, 42
See also CA 1-4R; CAAS 7; CANR 1, 33;
CDBLB 1960 to Present; DLB 13;
MTCW

Wesley, Richard (Errol) 1945- . . . . CLC 7
See also BW; CA 57-60; DLB 38

Wessel, Johan Herman 1742-1785 . . . . LC 7

West, Anthony (Panther)
1914-1987 . . . . CLC 50
See also CA 45-48; 124; CANR 3, 19;
DLB 15

West, C. P.
See Wodehouse, P(elham) G(renville)

West, (Mary) Jessamyn
1902-1984 . . . . CLC 7, 17
See also CA 9-12R; 112; CANR 27; DLB 6;
DLBY 84; MTCW; SATA 37

West, Morris L(anglo) 1916- . . . . . CLC 6, 33
See also CA 5-8R; CANR 24; MTCW

West, Nathanael
1903-1940 . . . . TCLC 1, 14, 44
See also CA 104; 125; CDALB 1929-1941;
DLB 4, 9, 28; MTCW

West, Paul 1930- . . . . CLC 7, 14
See also CA 13-16R; CAAS 7; CANR 22;
DLB 14

West, Rebecca 1892-1983 . . CLC 7, 9, 31, 50
See also CA 5-8R; 109; CANR 19; DLB 36;
DLBY 83; MTCW

Westall, Robert (Atkinson) 1929- . . . CLC 17
See also CA 69-72; CANR 18; CLR 13;
MAICYA; SAAS 2; SATA 23, 69

Westlake, Donald E(dwin)
1933- . . . . CLC 7, 33
See also CA 17-20R; CAAS 13; CANR 16

Westmacott, Mary
See Christie, Agatha (Mary Clarissa)

Weston, Allen
See Norton, Andre

Wetcheek, J. L.
See Feuchtwanger, Lion

Wetering, Janwillem van de
See van de Wetering, Janwillem

Wetherell, Elizabeth
See Warner, Susan (Bogert)

Whalen, Philip 1923- . . . . CLC 6, 29
See also CA 9-12R; CANR 5, 39; DLB 16

Wharton, Edith (Newbold Jones)
1862-1937 . . . . TCLC 3, 9, 27; SSC 6
See also CA 104; 132; CDALB 1865-1917;
DLB 4, 9, 12, 78; MTCW; WLC

Wharton, James
See Mencken, H(enry) L(ouis)

Wharton, William (a pseudonym)
. . . . CLC 18, 37
See also CA 93-96; DLBY 80

Wheatley (Peters), Phillis
1754(?)-1784 . . . . LC 3; PC 3
See also BLC 3; CDALB 1640-1865;
DLB 31, 50; WLC

Wheelock, John Hall 1886-1978 . . . . CLC 14
See also CA 13-16R; 77-80; CANR 14;
DLB 45

White, E(lwyn) B(rooks)
1899-1985 . . . . CLC 10, 34, 39
See also AITN 2; CA 13-16R; 116;
CANR 16, 37; CLR 1, 21; DLB 11, 22;
MAICYA; MTCW; SATA 2, 29, 44

White, Edmund (Valentine III)
1940- . . . . CLC 27
See also AAYA 7; CA 45-48; CANR 3, 19,
36; MTCW

White, Patrick (Victor Martindale)
1912-1990 . . CLC 3, 4, 5, 7, 9, 18, 65, 69
See also CA 81-84; 132; MTCW

White, Phyllis Dorothy James 1920-
See James, P. D.
See also CA 21-24R; CANR 17; MTCW

White, T(erence) H(anbury)
1906-1964 . . . . CLC 30
See also CA 73-76; CANR 37; MAICYA;
SATA 12

White, Terence de Vere 1912- . . . . . . CLC 49
See also CA 49-52; CANR 3

White, Walter
See White, Walter F(rancis)
See also BLC 3

White, Walter F(rancis)
1893-1955 . . . . TCLC 15
See also White, Walter
See also CA 115; 124; DLB 51

White, William Hale 1831-1913
See Rutherford, Mark
See also CA 121

Whitehead, E(dward) A(nthony)
1933- . . . . CLC 5
See also CA 65-68

Whitemore, Hugh (John) 1936- . . . . . CLC 37
See also CA 132

Whitman, Sarah Helen (Power)
1803-1878 . . . . NCLC 19
See also DLB 1

Whitman, Walt(er)
1819-1892 . . . . NCLC 4, 31; PC 3
See also CDALB 1640-1865; DLB 3, 64;
SATA 20; WLC

Whitney, Phyllis A(yame) 1903- . . . . CLC 42
See also AITN 2; BEST 90:3; CA 1-4R;
CANR 3, 25, 38; MAICYA; SATA 1, 30

Whittemore, (Edward) Reed (Jr.)
1919- . . . . CLC 4
See also CA 9-12R; CAAS 8; CANR 4;
DLB 5

Whittier, John Greenleaf
1807-1892 . . . . NCLC 8
See also CDALB 1640-1865; DLB 1

Whittlebot, Hernia
See Coward, Noel (Peirce)

Wicker, Thomas Grey 1926-
See Wicker, Tom
See also CA 65-68; CANR 21

Wicker, Tom . . . . CLC 7
See also Wicker, Thomas Grey

Wideman, John Edgar
1941- . . . . CLC 5, 34, 36, 67
See also BLC 3; BW; CA 85-88; CANR 14;
DLB 33

Wiebe, Rudy (H.) 1934- . . . . . . CLC 6, 11, 14
See also CA 37-40R; DLB 60

Wieland, Christoph Martin
1733-1813 . . . . NCLC 17
See also DLB 97

Wieners, John 1934- . . . . CLC 7
See also CA 13-16R; DLB 16

Wiesel, Elie(zer) 1928- . . . . . CLC 3, 5, 11, 37
See also AAYA 7; AITN 1; CA 5-8R;
CAAS 4; CANR 8; DLB 83; DLBY 87;
MTCW; SATA 56

Wiggins, Marianne 1947- . . . . CLC 57
See also BEST 89:3; CA 130

Wight, James Alfred 1916-
See Herriot, James
See also CA 77-80; SATA 44, 55

Wilbur, Richard (Purdy)
1921- . . . . CLC 3, 6, 9, 14, 53
See also CA 1-4R; CABS 2; CANR 2, 29;
DLB 5; MTCW; SATA 9

Wild, Peter 1940- . . . . CLC 14
See also CA 37-40R; DLB 5

Wilde, Oscar (Fingal O'Flahertie Wills)
1854(?)-1900 . . . . TCLC 1, 8, 23, 41;
SSC 11
See also CA 104; 119; CDBLB 1890-1914;
DLB 10, 19, 34, 57; SATA 24; WLC

Wilder, Billy . . . . CLC 20
See also Wilder, Samuel
See also DLB 26

Wilder, Samuel 1906-
See Wilder, Billy
See also CA 89-92

Wilder, Thornton (Niven)
1897-1975 . . . . . CLC 1, 5, 6, 10, 15, 35;
DC 1
See also AITN 2; CA 13-16R; 61-64;
DLB 4, 7, 9; MTCW; WLC

Wiley, Richard 1944- . . . . CLC 44
See also CA 121; 129

Wilhelm, Kate .... CLC 7
See also Wilhelm, Katie Gertrude
See also CAAS 5; DLB 8

Wilhelm, Katie Gertrude 1928-
See Wilhelm, Kate
See also CA 37-40R; CANR 17, 36; MTCW

Wilkins, Mary
See Freeman, Mary Eleanor Wilkins

Willard, Nancy 1936- .... CLC 7, 37
See also CA 89-92; CANR 10, 39; CLR 5;
DLB 5, 52; MAICYA; MTCW;
SATA 30, 37, 71

Williams, C(harles) K(enneth)
1936- .... CLC 33, 56
See also CA 37-40R; DLB 5

Williams, Charles
See Collier, James L(incoln)

Williams, Charles (Walter Stansby)
1886-1945 .... TCLC 1, 11
See also CA 104; DLB 100

Williams, (George) Emlyn
1905-1987 .... CLC 15
See also CA 104; 123; CANR 36; DLB 10,
77; MTCW

Williams, Hugo 1942- .... CLC 42
See also CA 17-20R; DLB 40

Williams, J. Walker
See Wodehouse, P(elham) G(renville)

Williams, John A(lfred) 1925- .... CLC 5, 13
See also BLC 3; BW; CA 53-56; CAAS 3;
CANR 6, 26; DLB 2, 33

Williams, Jonathan (Chamberlain)
1929- .... CLC 13
See also CA 9-12R; CAAS 12; CANR 8;
DLB 5

Williams, Joy 1944- .... CLC 31
See also CA 41-44R; CANR 22

Williams, Norman 1952- .... CLC 39
See also CA 118

Williams, Tennessee
1911-1983 .... CLC 1, 2, 5, 7, 8, 11, 15,
19, 30, 39, 45, 71
See also AITN 1, 2; CA 5-8R; 108;
CABS 3; CANR 31; CDALB 1941-1968;
DLB 7; DLBD 4; DLBY 83; MTCW;
WLC

Williams, Thomas (Alonzo)
1926-1990 .... CLC 14
See also CA 1-4R; 132; CANR 2

Williams, William C.
See Williams, William Carlos

Williams, William Carlos
1883-1963 ... CLC 1, 2, 5, 9, 13, 22, 42,
67
See also CA 89-92; CANR 34;
CDALB 1917-1929; DLB 4, 16, 54, 86;
MTCW

Williamson, David Keith 1942- ..... CLC 56
See also CA 103

Williamson, Jack .... CLC 29
See also Williamson, John Stewart
See also CAAS 8; DLB 8

Williamson, John Stewart 1908-
See Williamson, Jack
See also CA 17-20R; CANR 23

Willie, Frederick
See Lovecraft, H(oward) P(hillips)

Willingham, Calder (Baynard Jr.)
1922- .... CLC 5, 51
See also CA 5-8R; CANR 3; DLB 2, 44;
MTCW

Willis, Charles
See Clarke, Arthur C(harles)

Willy
See Colette, (Sidonie-Gabrielle)

Willy, Colette
See Colette, (Sidonie-Gabrielle)

Wilson, A(ndrew) N(orman) 1950- ... CLC 33
See also CA 112; 122; DLB 14

Wilson, Angus (Frank Johnstone)
1913-1991 .... CLC 2, 3, 5, 25, 34
See also CA 5-8R; 134; CANR 21; DLB 15;
MTCW

Wilson, August
1945- .... CLC 39, 50, 63; DC 2
See also BLC 3; BW; CA 115; 122; MTCW

Wilson, Brian 1942- .... CLC 12

Wilson, Colin 1931- .... CLC 3, 14
See also CA 1-4R; CAAS 5; CANR 1, 22,
33; DLB 14; MTCW

Wilson, Dirk
See Pohl, Frederik

Wilson, Edmund
1895-1972 .... CLC 1, 2, 3, 8, 24
See also CA 1-4R; 37-40R; CANR 1;
DLB 63; MTCW

Wilson, Ethel Davis (Bryant)
1888(?)-1980 .... CLC 13
See also CA 102; DLB 68; MTCW

Wilson, John (Anthony) Burgess
1917- .... CLC 8, 10, 13
See also Burgess, Anthony
See also CA 1-4R; CANR 2; MTCW

Wilson, John 1785-1854 .... NCLC 5

Wilson, Lanford 1937- .... CLC 7, 14, 36
See also CA 17-20R; CABS 3; DLB 7

Wilson, Robert M. 1944- .... CLC 7, 9
See also CA 49-52; CANR 2; MTCW

Wilson, Robert McLiam 1964- ..... CLC 59
See also CA 132

Wilson, Sloan 1920- .... CLC 32
See also CA 1-4R; CANR 1

Wilson, Snoo 1948- .... CLC 33
See also CA 69-72

Wilson, William S(mith) 1932- ..... CLC 49
See also CA 81-84

Winchilsea, Anne (Kingsmill) Finch Counte
1661-1720 .... LC 3

Windham, Basil
See Wodehouse, P(elham) G(renville)

Wingrove, David (John) 1954- ...... CLC 68
See also CA 133

Winters, Janet Lewis .... CLC 41
See also Lewis, Janet
See also DLBY 87

Winters, (Arthur) Yvor
1900-1968 .... CLC 4, 8, 32
See also CA 11-12; 25-28R; CAP 1;
DLB 48; MTCW

Winterson, Jeanette 1959- .... CLC 64
See also CA 136

Wiseman, Frederick 1930- .... CLC 20

Wister, Owen 1860-1938 .... TCLC 21
See also CA 108; DLB 9, 78; SATA 62

Witkacy
See Witkiewicz, Stanislaw Ignacy

Witkiewicz, Stanislaw Ignacy
1885-1939 .... TCLC 8
See also CA 105

Wittig, Monique 1935(?)- .... CLC 22
See also CA 116; 135; DLB 83

Wittlin, Jozef 1896-1976 .... CLC 25
See also CA 49-52; 65-68; CANR 3

Wodehouse, P(elham) G(renville)
1881-1975 ... CLC 1, 2, 5, 10, 22; SSC 2
See also AITN 2; CA 45-48; 57-60;
CANR 3, 33; CDBLB 1914-1945;
DLB 34; MTCW; SATA 22

Woiwode, L.
See Woiwode, Larry (Alfred)

Woiwode, Larry (Alfred) 1941- ... CLC 6, 10
See also CA 73-76; CANR 16; DLB 6

Wojciechowska, Maia (Teresa)
1927- .... CLC 26
See also AAYA 8; CA 9-12R; CANR 4;
CLR 1; MAICYA; SAAS 1; SATA 1, 28

Wolf, Christa 1929- .... CLC 14, 29, 58
See also CA 85-88; DLB 75; MTCW

Wolfe, Gene (Rodman) 1931- .... CLC 25
See also CA 57-60; CAAS 9; CANR 6, 32;
DLB 8

Wolfe, George C. 1954- .... CLC 49

Wolfe, Thomas (Clayton)
1900-1938 .... TCLC 4, 13, 29
See also CA 104; 132; CDALB 1929-1941;
DLB 9, 102; DLBD 2; DLBY 85;
MTCW; WLC

Wolfe, Thomas Kennerly Jr. 1930-
See Wolfe, Tom
See also CA 13-16R; CANR 9, 33; MTCW

Wolfe, Tom .... CLC 1, 2, 9, 15, 35, 51
See also Wolfe, Thomas Kennerly Jr.
See also AAYA 8; AITN 2; BEST 89:1

Wolff, Geoffrey (Ansell) 1937- ..... CLC 41
See also CA 29-32R; CANR 29

Wolff, Sonia
See Levitin, Sonia (Wolff)

Wolff, Tobias (Jonathan Ansell)
1945- .... CLC 39, 64
See also BEST 90:2; CA 114; 117

Wolfram von Eschenbach
c. 1170-c. 1220 .... CMLC 5

Wolitzer, Hilma 1930- .... CLC 17
See also CA 65-68; CANR 18; SATA 31

Wollstonecraft, Mary 1759-1797...... LC 5
See also CDBLB 1789-1832; DLB 39, 104

Wonder, Stevie .... CLC 12
See also Morris, Steveland Judkins

Wong, Jade Snow 1922- .... CLC 17
See also CA 109

Woodcott, Keith
See Brunner, John (Kilian Houston)

Woodruff, Robert W.
See Mencken, H(enry) L(ouis)

Woolf, (Adeline) Virginia
1882-1941 .... **TCLC 1, 5, 20, 43; SSC 7**
See also CA 104; 130; CDBLB 1914-1945;
DLB 36, 100; MTCW; WLC

Woollcott, Alexander (Humphreys)
1887-1943 .... **TCLC 5**
See also CA 105; DLB 29

Wordsworth, Dorothy
1771-1855 .... **NCLC 25**
See also DLB 107

Wordsworth, William
1770-1850 .... **NCLC 12, 38; PC 4**
See also CDBLB 1789-1832; DLB 93, 107;
WLC

Wouk, Herman 1915- .... **CLC 1, 9, 38**
See also CA 5-8R; CANR 6, 33; DLBY 82;
MTCW

Wright, Charles (Penzel Jr.)
1935- .... **CLC 6, 13, 28**
See also CA 29-32R; CAAS 7; CANR 23,
36; DLBY 82; MTCW

Wright, Charles Stevenson 1932- ... **CLC 49**
See also BLC 3; BW; CA 9-12R; CANR 26;
DLB 33

Wright, Jack R.
See Harris, Mark

Wright, James (Arlington)
1927-1980 .... **CLC 3, 5, 10, 28**
See also AITN 2; CA 49-52; 97-100;
CANR 4, 34; DLB 5; MTCW

Wright, Judith (Arandell)
1915- .... **CLC 11, 53**
See also CA 13-16R; CANR 31; MTCW;
SATA 14

Wright, L(aurali) R. .... **CLC 44**
See also CA 138

Wright, Richard B(ruce) 1937- ...... **CLC 6**
See also CA 85-88; DLB 53

Wright, Richard (Nathaniel)
1908-1960 ... **CLC 1, 3, 4, 9, 14, 21, 48,
74; SSC 2**
See also AAYA 5; BLC 3; BW; CA 108;
CDALB 1929-1941; DLB 76, 102;
DLBD 2; MTCW; WLC

Wright, Rick 1945- .... **CLC 35**
See also Pink Floyd

Wright, Rowland
See Wells, Carolyn

Wright, Stephen 1946- .... **CLC 33**

Wright, Willard Huntington 1888-1939
See Van Dine, S. S.
See also CA 115

Wright, William 1930- .... **CLC 44**
See also CA 53-56; CANR 7, 23

Wu Ch'eng-en 1500(?)-1582(?) .... **LC 7**

Wu Ching-tzu 1701-1754 .... **LC 2**

Wurlitzer, Rudolph 1938(?)- ... **CLC 2, 4, 15**
See also CA 85-88

Wycherley, William 1641-1715 .... **LC 8, 21**
See also CDBLB 1660-1789; DLB 80

Wylie, Elinor (Morton Hoyt)
1885-1928 .... **TCLC 8**
See also CA 105; DLB 9, 45

Wylie, Philip (Gordon) 1902-1971... **CLC 43**
See also CA 21-22; 33-36R; CAP 2; DLB 9

Wyndham, John
See Harris, John (Wyndham Parkes Lucas)
Beynon

Wyss, Johann David Von
1743-1818 .... **NCLC 10**
See also MAICYA; SATA 27, 29

Yakumo Koizumi
See Hearn, (Patricio) Lafcadio (Tessima
Carlos)

Yanez, Jose Donoso
See Donoso (Yanez), Jose

Yanovsky, Basile S.
See Yanovsky, V(assily) S(emenovich)

Yanovsky, V(assily) S(emenovich)
1906-1989 .... **CLC 2, 18**
See also CA 97-100; 129

Yates, Richard 1926- .... **CLC 7, 8, 23**
See also CA 5-8R; CANR 10; DLB 2;
DLBY 81

Yeats, W. B.
See Yeats, William Butler

Yeats, William Butler
1865-1939 .... **TCLC 1, 11, 18, 31**
See also CA 104; 127; CDBLB 1890-1914;
DLB 10, 19, 98; MTCW; WLC

Yehoshua, Abraham B. 1936- ... **CLC 13, 31**
See also CA 33-36R

Yep, Laurence Michael 1948- ...... **CLC 35**
See also AAYA 5; CA 49-52; CANR 1;
CLR 3, 17; DLB 52; MAICYA; SATA 7,
69

Yerby, Frank G(arvin)
1916-1991 .... **CLC 1, 7, 22**
See also BLC 3; BW; CA 9-12R; 136;
CANR 16; DLB 76; MTCW

Yesenin, Sergei Alexandrovich
See Esenin, Sergei (Alexandrovich)

Yevtushenko, Yevgeny (Alexandrovich)
1933- .... **CLC 1, 3, 13, 26, 51**
See also CA 81-84; CANR 33; MTCW

Yezierska, Anzia 1885(?)-1970 ..... **CLC 46**
See also CA 126; 89-92; DLB 28; MTCW

Yglesias, Helen 1915- .... **CLC 7, 22**
See also CA 37-40R; CANR 15; MTCW

Yokomitsu Riichi 1898-1947 ...... **TCLC 47**

Yonge, Charlotte (Mary)
1823-1901 .... **TCLC 48**
See also CA 109; DLB 18; SATA 17

York, Jeremy
See Creasey, John

York, Simon
See Heinlein, Robert A(nson)

Yorke, Henry Vincent 1905-1974 ... **CLC 13**
See also Green, Henry
See also CA 85-88; 49-52

Young, Al(bert James) 1939- .... **CLC 19**
See also BLC 3; BW; CA 29-32R;
CANR 26; DLB 33

Young, Andrew (John) 1885-1971.... **CLC 5**
See also CA 5-8R; CANR 7, 29

Young, Collier
See Bloch, Robert (Albert)

Young, Edward 1683-1765 .... **LC 3**
See also DLB 95

Young, Neil 1945- .... **CLC 17**
See also CA 110

Yourcenar, Marguerite
1903-1987 .... **CLC 19, 38, 50**
See also CA 69-72; CANR 23; DLB 72;
DLBY 88; MTCW

Yurick, Sol 1925- .... **CLC 6**
See also CA 13-16R; CANR 25

Zamiatin, Yevgenii
See Zamyatin, Evgeny Ivanovich

Zamyatin, Evgeny Ivanovich
1884-1937 .... **TCLC 8, 37**
See also CA 105

Zangwill, Israel 1864-1926. .... **TCLC 16**
See also CA 109; DLB 10

Zappa, Francis Vincent Jr. 1940-
See Zappa, Frank
See also CA 108

Zappa, Frank .... **CLC 17**
See also Zappa, Francis Vincent Jr.

Zaturenska, Marya 1902-1982.... **CLC 6, 11**
See also CA 13-16R; 105; CANR 22

Zelazny, Roger (Joseph) 1937- ..... **CLC 21**
See also AAYA 7; CA 21-24R; CANR 26;
DLB 8; MTCW; SATA 39, 57

Zhdanov, Andrei A(lexandrovich)
1896-1948 .... **TCLC 18**
See also CA 117

Zhukovsky, Vasily 1783-1852 .... **NCLC 35**

Ziegenhagen, Eric .... **CLC 55**

Zimmer, Jill Schary
See Robinson, Jill

Zimmerman, Robert
See Dylan, Bob

Zindel, Paul 1936- .... **CLC 6, 26**
See also AAYA 2; CA 73-76; CANR 31;
CLR 3; DLB 7, 52; MAICYA; MTCW;
SATA 16, 58

Zinov'Ev, A. A.
See Zinoviev, Alexander (Aleksandrovich)

Zinoviev, Alexander (Aleksandrovich)
1922- .... **CLC 19**
See also CA 116; 133; CAAS 10

Zoilus
See Lovecraft, H(oward) P(hillips)

Zola, Emile (Edouard Charles Antoine)
1840-1902 .... **TCLC 1, 6, 21, 41**
See also CA 104; 138; WLC

Zoline, Pamela 1941- .... **CLC 62**

Zorrilla y Moral, Jose 1817-1893.. **NCLC 6**

Zoshchenko, Mikhail (Mikhailovich)
1895-1958 .... **TCLC 15**
See also CA 115

Zuckmayer, Carl 1896-1977. .... **CLC 18**
See also CA 69-72; DLB 56

Zuk, Georges
See Skelton, Robin

Zukofsky, Louis
1904-1978 .... **CLC 1, 2, 4, 7, 11, 18**
See also CA 9-12R; 77-80; CANR 39;
DLB 5; MTCW

Zweig, Paul 1935-1984......... **CLC 34, 42**
  See also CA 85-88; 113
Zweig, Stefan 1881-1942......... **TCLC 17**
  See also CA 112; DLB 81, 118

Literary Criticism Series
Cumulative Topic Index

This index lists all topic entries in the Gale Literary Criticism Series *Contemporary Literary Criticism, Literature Criticism from 1400 to 1800, Nineteenth-Century Literature Criticism,* and *Twentieth-Century Literary Criticism.*

Age of Johnson LC 15: 1-87
  Johnson's London, 3-15
  aesthetics of neoclassicism, 15-36
  "age of prose and reason," 36-45
  clubmen and bluestockings, 45-56
  printing technology, 56-62
  periodicals: "a map of busy life," 62-74
  transition, 74-86

American Civil War in Literature
NCLC 32: 1-109
  overviews, 2-20
  regional perspectives, 20-54
  fiction popular during the war, 54-79
  the historical novel, 79-108

American Frontier in Literature
NCLC 28: 1-103
  definitions, 2-12
  development, 12-17
  nonfiction writing about the frontier, 17-30
  frontier fiction, 30-45
  frontier protagonists, 45-66
  portrayals of Native Americans, 66-86
  feminist readings, 86-98
  twentieth-century reaction against frontier literature, 98-100

American Popular Song, Golden Age of TCLC 42: 1-49
  background and major figures, 2-34
  the lyrics of popular songs, 34-47

American Western Literature TCLC 46: 1-100
  definition and development of American Western literature, 2-7
  characteristics of the Western novel, 8-23
  Westerns as history and fiction, 23-34
  critical reception of American Western literature, 34-41
  the Western hero, 41-73
  women in Western fiction, 73-91
  later Western fiction, 91-99

Arthurian Literature CMLC 10: 1-127
  historical context and literary beginnings, 2-27
  development of the legend through Malory, 27-64
  development of the legend from Malory to the Victorian Age, 65-81
  themes and motifs, 81-95
  principal characters, 95-125

Arthurian Revival NCLC 36: 1-77
  overviews, 2-12
  Tennyson and his influence, 12-43
  other leading figures, 43-73
  the Arthurian legend in the visual arts, 73-6

Beat Generation, Literature of the TCLC 42: 50-102
  overviews, 51-9
  the Beat generation as a social phenomenon, 59-62
  development, 62-5
  Beat literature, 66-96
  influence, 97-100

***Bildungsroman* in Nineteenth-Century Literature** NCLC 20: 92-168
  surveys, 93-113
  in Germany, 113-40
  in England, 140-56
  female *Bildungsroman,* 156-67

Bloomsbury Group TCLC 34: 1-73
  history and major figures, 2-13
  definitions, 13-17
  influences, 17-27
  thought, 27-40
  prose, 40-52
  and literary criticism, 52-4
  political ideals, 54-61
  response to, 61-71

Bly, Robert, *Iron John: A Book about Men* and Men's Work CLC 70:414-62

The Book of J CLC 65: 289-311

Businessman in American Literature
TCLC 26: 1-48
  portrayal of the businessman, 1-32
  themes and techniques in business fiction, 32-47

Celtic Twilight
  See **Irish Literary Renaissance**

Civic Critics, Russian NCLC 20: 402-46
  principal figures and background, 402-09
  and Russian Nihilism, 410-16
  aesthetic and critical views, 416-45

Columbus, Christopher, Books on the Quincentennial of His Arrival in the New World CLC 70: 329-60

Czechoslovakian Literature of the Twentieth Century TCLC 42: 103-96
  through World War II, 104-35
  de-Stalinization, The Prague Spring, and contemporary literature, 135-72
  Slovak literature, 172-85
  Czech science fiction, 185-93

Dadaism TCLC 46: 101-71
  background and major figures, 102-16
  definitions, 116-26
  manifestos and commentary by Dadaists, 126-40
  theater and film, 140-58
  nature and characteristics of Dadaist writing, 158-70

Darwinism and Literature NCLC 32: 110-206
  background, 110-31
  direct responses to Darwin, 131-71
  collateral effects of Darwinism, 171-205

de Man, Paul, Wartime Journalism of CLC 55: 382-424

Detective Fiction, Nineteenth-Century
NCLC 36: 78-148
 origins of the genre, 79-100
 history of nineteenth-century
   detective fiction, 101-33
 significance of nineteenth-century
   detective fiction, 133-46

Detective Fiction, Twentieth-Century
TCLC 38: 1-96
 genesis and history of the detective
   story, 3-22
 defining detective fiction, 22-32
 evolution and varieties, 32-77
 the appeal of detective fiction, 77-90

Eliot, T. S., Centenary of Birth CLC
55: 345-75

English Caroline Literature LC 13:
221-307
 background, 222-41
 evolution and varieties, 241-62
 the Cavalier mode, 262-75
 court and society, 275-91
 politics and religion, 291-306

**English Decadent Literature of the
1890s** NCLC 28: 104-200
 fin de siècle: the Decadent period,
   105-19
 definitions, 120-37
 major figures: "the tragic
   generation," 137-50
 French literature and English
   literary Decadence, 150-57
 themes, 157-61
 poetry, 161-82
 periodicals, 182-96

English Essay, Rise of the
LC 18: 238-308
 definitions and origins, 239-54
 influences on the essay, 254-69
 historical background, 269-78
 the essay in the seventeenth century,
   279-93
 the essay in the eighteenth century,
   293-307

English Romantic Poetry NCLC 28:
201-327
 overviews and reputation, 202-37
 major subjects and themes, 237-67
 forms of Romantic poetry, 267-78
 politics, society, and Romantic
   poetry, 278-99
 philosophy, religion, and Romantic
   poetry, 299-324

European Romanticism NCLC 36:
149-284
 definitions, 149-77
 origins of the movement, 177-82
 Romantic theory, 182-200
 themes and techniques, 200-23
 Romanticism in Germany, 223-39
 Romanticism in France, 240-61
 Romanticism in Italy, 261-64
 Romanticism in Spain, 264-68
 impact and legacy, 268-82

Existentialism and Literature TCLC
42: 197-268
 overviews and definitions, 198-209
 history and influences, 209-19
 Existentialism critiqued and
   defended, 220-35
 philosophical and religious
   perspectives, 235-41
 Existentialist fiction and drama, 241-67

Feminist Criticism in 1990 CLC 65:
312-60

Fifteenth-Century English Literature
LC 17: 248-334
 background, 249-72
 poetry, 272-315
 drama, 315-23
 prose, 323-33

Film and Literature TCLC 38: 97-226
 overviews, 97-119
 film and theater, 119-34
 film and the novel, 134-45
 the art of the screenplay, 145-66
 genre literature/genre film, 167-79
 the writer and the film industry,
   179-90
 authors on film adaptations of their
   works, 190-200
 fiction into film: comparative essays
   200-23

French Enlightenment LC 14: 81-145
 the question of definition, 82-9
 Le siècle des lumières, 89-94
 women and the salons, 94-105
 censorship, 105-15
 the philosophy of reason, 115-31
 influence and legacy, 131-44

Futurism, Italian TCLC 42: 269-354
 principles and formative influences,
   271-79
 manifestos, 279-88
 literature, 288-303
 theater, 303-19
 art, 320-30
 music, 330-36
 architecture, 336-39
 and politics, 339-46
 reputation and significance, 346-51

Gaelic Revival
 See **Irish Literary Renaissance**

**Gates, Henry Louis, Jr., and African-
American Literary Criticism** CLC 65:
361-405

German Exile Literature TCLC 30:
1-58
 the writer and the Nazi state, 1-10
 definition of, 10-14
 life in exile, 14-32
 surveys, 32-50
 Austrian literature in exile, 50-2
 German publishing in the United
   States, 52-7

German Expressionism TCLC 34: 74-160
 history and major figures, 76-85
 aesthetic theories, 85-109
 drama, 109-26
 poetry, 126-38
 film, 138-42
 painting, 142-47
 music, 147-53
 and politics, 153-58

***Glasnost* and Contemporary Soviet
Literature** CLC 59: 355-97

Gothic Novel NCLC 28: 328-402
 development and major works, 328-34
 definitions, 334-50
 themes and techniques, 350-78
 in America, 378-85
 in Scotland, 385-91
 influence and legacy, 391-400

Harlem Renaissance TCLC 26: 49-125
 principal issues and figures, 50-67
 the literature and its audience, 67-74
 theme and technique in poetry,
   fiction, and drama, 74-115
 and American society, 115-21
 achievement and influence, 121-22

**Havel, Václav, Playwright and
President** CLC 65: 406-63

Holocaust, Literature of the TCLC
42: 355-450

historical overview, 357-61
critical overview, 361-70
diaries and memoirs, 370-95
novels and short stories, 395-425
poetry, 425-41
drama, 441-48

Hungarian Literature of the Twentieth Century TCLC 26: 126-88
surveys of, 126-47
Nyugat and early twentieth-century literature, 147-56
mid-century literature, 156-68
and politics, 168-78
since the 1956 revolt, 178-87

Italian Futurism
See **Futurism, Italian**

Italian Humanism LC 12: 205-77
origins and early development, 206-18
revival of classical letters, 218-23
humanism and other philosophies, 224-39
humanisms and humanists, 239-46
the plastic arts, 246-57
achievement and significance, 258-76

Irish Literary Renaissance TCLC 46: 172-287
overview, 173-83
development and major figures, 184-202
influence of Irish folklore and mythology, 202-22
Irish poetry, 222-34
Irish drama and the Abbey Theatre, 234-56
Irish fiction, 256-86

Muckraking Movement in American Journalism TCLC 34: 161-242
development, principles, and major figures, 162-70
publications, 170-79
social and political ideas, 179-86
targets, 186-208
fiction, 208-19
decline, 219-29
impact and accomplishments, 229-40

Multiculturalism in Literature and Education CLC 70: 361-413

Natural School, Russian NCLC 24: 205-40
history and characteristics, 205-25
contemporary criticism, 225-40

Naturalism NCLC 36: 285-382
definitions and theories, 286-305
critical debates on Naturalism, 305-16
Naturalism in theater, 316-32
European Naturalism, 332-61
American Naturalism, 361-72
the legacy of Naturalism, 372-81

New Criticism TCLC 34: 243-318
development and ideas, 244-70
debate and defense, 270-99
influence and legacy, 299-315

Newgate Novel NCLC 24: 166-204
development of Newgate literature, 166-73
Newgate Calendar, 173-77
Newgate fiction, 177-95
Newgate drama, 195-204

New York Intellectuals and *Partisan Review* TCLC 30: 117-98
development and major figures, 118-28
influence of Judaism, 128-39
Partisan Review, 139-57
literary philosophy and practice, 157-75
political philosophy, 175-87
achievement and significance, 187-97

Nigerian Literature of the Twentieth Century TCLC 30: 199-265
surveys of, 199-227
English language and African life, 227-45
politics and the Nigerian writer, 245-54
Nigerian writers and society, 255-62

Northern Humanism LC 16: 281-356
background, 282-305
precursor of the Reformation, 305-14
the Brethren of the Common Life, the Devotio Moderna, and education, 314-40
the impact of printing, 340-56

Nuclear Literature: Writings and Criticism in the Nuclear Age TCLC 46: 288-390
overviews, 290-301
fiction, 301-35
poetry, 335-38
nuclear war in Russo-Japanese literature, 338-55
nuclear war and women writers, 355-67
the nuclear referent and literary criticism, 367-88

Opium and the Nineteenth-Century Literary Imagination NCLC 20: 250-301
original sources, 250-62
historical background, 262-71
and literary society, 271-79
and literary creativity, 279-300

Periodicals, Nineteenth-Century British NCLC 24: 100-65
overviews, 100-30
in the Romantic Age, 130-41
in the Victorian era, 142-54
and the reviewer, 154-64

Pre-Raphaelite Movement NCLC 20: 302-401
overview, 302-04
genesis, 304-12
Germ and *Oxford and Cambridge Magazine,* 312-20
Robert Buchanan and the "Fleshly School of Poetry," 320-31
satires and parodies, 331-34
surveys, 334-51
aesthetics, 351-75
sister arts of poetry and painting, 375-94
influence, 394-99

Psychoanalysis and Literature TCLC 38: 227-338
overviews, 227-46
Freud on literature, 246-51
psychoanalytic views of the literary process, 251-61
psychoanalytic theories of response to literature, 261-88
psychoanalysis and literary criticism, 288-312
psychoanalysis as literature/literature as psychoanalysis, 313-34

Robin Hood, Legend of LC 19: 205-58
origins and development of the Robin Hood legend, 206-20
representations of Robin Hood, 220-44
Robin Hood as hero, 244-56

Rushdie, Salman, *Satanic Verses* Controversy CLC 55: 214-63; 59: 404-56

Russian Nihilism NCLC 28: 403-47
definitions and overviews, 404-17
women and Nihilism, 417-27
literature as reform: the Civic Critics, 427-33
Nihilism and the Russian novel: Turgenev and Dostoevsky, 433-47

Russian Thaw TCLC 26: 189-247
  literary history of the period, 190-206
  theoretical debate of socialist realism, 206-11
  Novy Mir, 211-17
  Literary Moscow, 217-24
  Pasternak, *Zhivago,* and the Nobel Prize, 224-27
  poetry of liberation, 228-31
  Brodsky trial and the end of the Thaw, 231-36
  achievement and influence, 236-46

Salinger, J. D., Controversy Surrounding *In Search of J. D. Salinger* CLC 55: 325-44

Science Fiction, Nineteenth-Century NCLC 24: 241-306
  background, 242-50
  definitions of the genre, 251-56
  representative works and writers, 256-75
  themes and conventions, 276-305

Scottish Chaucerians LC 20: 363-412

Sherlock Holmes Centenary TCLC 26: 248-310
  Doyle's life and the composition of the Holmes stories, 248-59
  life and character of Holmes, 259-78
  method, 278-79
  Holmes and the Victorian world, 279-92
  Sherlockian scholarship, 292-301
  Doyle and the development of the detective story, 301-07
  Holmes's continuing popularity, 307-09

Slave Narratives, American NCLC 20: 1-91
  background, 2-9
  overviews, 9-24
  contemporary responses, 24-7
  language, theme, and technique, 27-70
  historical authenticity, 70-5
  antecedents, 75-83
  role in development of Black American literature, 83-8

Spanish Civil War Literature TCLC 26: 311-85
  topics in, 312-33
  British and American literature, 333-59
  French literature, 359-62
  Spanish literature, 362-73
  German literature, 373-75
  political idealism and war literature, 375-83

Spasmodic School of Poetry NCLC 24: 307-52
  history and major figures, 307-21
  the Spasmodics on poetry, 321-27
  Firmilian and critical disfavor, 327-39
  theme and technique, 339-47
  influence, 347-51

Steinbeck, John, Fiftieth Anniversary of *The Grapes of Wrath* CLC 59: 311-54

Supernatural Fiction in the Nineteenth Century NCLC 32: 207-87
  major figures and influences, 208-35
  the Victorian ghost story, 236-54
  the influence of science and occultism, 254-66
  supernatural fiction and society, 266-86

Supernatural Fiction, Modern TCLC 30: 59-116
  evolution and varieties, 60-74
  "decline" of the ghost story, 74-86
  as a literary genre, 86-92
  technique, 92-101
  nature and appeal, 101-15

Surrealism TCLC 30: 334-406
  history and formative influences, 335-43
  manifestos, 343-54
  philosophic, aesthetic, and political principles, 354-75
  poetry, 375-81
  novel, 381-86
  drama, 386-92
  film, 392-98
  painting and sculpture, 398-403
  achievement, 403-05

Symbolism, Russian TCLC 30: 266-333
  doctrines and major figures, 267-92
  theories, 293-98
  and French Symbolism, 298-310
  themes in poetry, 310-14
  theater, 314-20
  and the fine arts, 320-32

Symbolist Movement, French NCLC 20: 169-249
  background and characteristics, 170-86
  principles, 186-91
  attacked and defended, 191-97
  influences and predecessors, 197-211
  and Decadence, 211-16
  theater, 216-26
  prose, 226-33
  decline and influence, 233-47

Theater of the Absurd TCLC 38: 339-415
  "The Theater of the Absurd," 340-47
  major plays and playwrights, 347-58
  and the concept of the absurd, 358-86
  theatrical techniques, 386-94
  predecessors of, 394-402
  influence of, 402-13

Tin Pan Alley
  See **American Popular Song, Golden Age of**

Transcendentalism, American NCLC 24: 1-99
  overviews, 3-23
  contemporary documents, 23-41
  theological aspects of, 42-52
  and social issues, 52-74
  literature of, 74-96

Travel Writing in the Twentieth Century TCLC 30: 407-56
  conventions and traditions, 407-27
  and fiction writing, 427-43
  comparative essays on travel writers, 443-54

***Ulysses* and the Process of Textual Reconstruction** TCLC 26: 386-416
  evaluations of the new *Ulysses,* 386-94
  editorial principles and procedures, 394-401
  theoretical issues, 401-16

Utopian Literature, Nineteenth-Century NCLC 24: 353-473
  definitions, 354-74
  overviews, 374-88
  theory, 388-408
  communities, 409-26
  fiction, 426-53
  women and fiction, 454-71

Vampire in Literature TCLC 46: 391-454
  origins and evolution, 392-412
  social and psychological perspectives, 413-44
  vampire fiction and science fiction, 445-53

Victorian Novel NCLC 32: 288-454
  development and major characteristics, 290-310
  themes and techniques, 310-58
  social criticism in the Victorian novel, 359-97

urban and rural life in the Victorian novel, 397-406
women in the Victorian novel, 406-25
Mudie's Circulating Library, 425-34
the late-Victorian novel, 434-51

World War I Literature TCLC 34: 392-486
overview, 393-403
English, 403-27
German, 427-50
American, 450-66
French, 466-74
and modern history, 474-82

Yellow Journalism NCLC 36: 383-456
overviews, 384-96
major figures, 396-413
the role of reporters, 413-28
the Spanish-American War, 428-48
Yellow Journalism and society, 448-54

Young Playwrights Festival
1988—CLC 55: 376-81
1989—CLC 59: 398-403
1990—CLC 65: 444-48

TCLC Cumulative Nationality Index

AMERICAN
Adams, Henry **4**
Agee, James **1, 19**
Anderson, Maxwell **2**
Anderson, Sherwood **1, 10, 24**
Atherton, Gertrude **2**
Austin, Mary **25**
Baker, Ray Stannard **47**
Barry, Philip **11**
Baum, L. Frank **7**
Beard, Charles A. **15**
Belasco, David **3**
Bell, James Madison **43**
Benchley, Robert **1**
Benét, Stephen Vincent **7**
Benét, William Rose **28**
Bierce, Ambrose **1, 7, 44**
Black Elk **33**
Bodenheim, Maxwell **44**
Bourne, Randolph S. **16**
Bradford, Gamaliel **36**
Bromfield, Louis **11**
Burroughs, Edgar Rice **2, 32**
Cabell, James Branch **6**
Cable, George Washington **4**
Cather, Willa **1, 11, 31**
Chambers, Robert W. **41**
Chandler, Raymond **1, 7**
Chapman, John Jay **7**
Chesnutt, Charles Waddell **5, 39**
Chopin, Kate **5, 14**
Comstock, Anthony **13**
Cotter, Joseph Seamon, Sr. **28**
Cram, Ralph Adams **45**
Crane, Hart **2, 5**
Crane, Stephen **11, 17, 32**
Crawford, F. Marion **10**
Crothers, Rachel **19**
Cullen, Countee **4, 37**

Davis, Rebecca Harding **6**
Davis, Richard Harding **24**
Day, Clarence **25**
DeVoto, Bernard **29**
Dreiser, Theodore **10, 18, 35**
Dunbar, Paul Laurence **2, 12**
Dunne, Finley Peter **28**
Fisher, Rudolph **11**
Fitzgerald, F. Scott **1, 6, 14, 28**
Flecker, James Elroy **43**
Fletcher, John Gould **35**
Forten, Charlotte L. **16**
Freeman, Douglas Southall **11**
Freeman, Mary Wilkins **9**
Futrelle, Jacques **19**
Gale, Zona **7**
Garland, Hamlin **3**
Gilman, Charlotte Perkins **9, 37**
Glasgow, Ellen **2, 7**
Goldman, Emma **13**
Grey, Zane **6**
Guiney, Louise Imogen **41**
Hall, James Norman **23**
Harper, Frances Ellen Watkins **14**
Harris, Joel Chandler **2**
Harte, Bret **1, 25**
Hawthorne, Julian **25**
Hearn, Lafcadio **9**
Henry, O. **1, 19**
Hergesheimer, Joseph **11**
Higginson, Thomas Wentworth **36**
Hopkins, Pauline Elizabeth **28**
Howard, Robert E. **8**
Howe, Julia Ward **21**
Howells, William Dean **7, 17, 41**
James, Henry **2, 11, 24, 40, 47**
James, William **15, 32**
Jewett, Sarah Orne **1, 22**
Johnson, James Weldon **3, 19**

Kornbluth, C. M. **8**
Kuttner, Henry **10**
Lardner, Ring **2, 14**
Lewis, Sinclair **4, 13, 23, 39**
Lewisohn, Ludwig **19**
Lindsay, Vachel **17**
Locke, Alain **43**
London, Jack **9, 15, 39**
Lovecraft, H. P. **4, 22**
Lowell, Amy **1, 8**
Markham, Edwin **47**
Marquis, Don **7**
Masters, Edgar Lee **2, 25**
McCoy, Horace **28**
McKay, Claude **7, 41**
Mencken, H. L. **13**
Millay, Edna St. Vincent **4**
Mitchell, Margaret **11**
Mitchell, S. Weir **36**
Monroe, Harriet **12**
Muir, John **28**
Nathan, George Jean **18**
Nordhoff, Charles **23**
Norris, Frank **24**
O'Neill, Eugene **1, 6, 27**
Oskison, John M. **35**
Phillips, David Graham **44**
Porter, Gene Stratton **21**
Post, Melville **39**
Rawlings, Marjorie Kinnan **4**
Reed, John **9**
Roberts, Kenneth **23**
Robinson, Edwin Arlington **5**
Rogers, Will **8**
Rölvaag, O. E. **17**
Rourke, Constance **12**
Runyon, Damon **10**
Saltus, Edgar **8**
Santayana, George **40**

Sherwood, Robert E. 3
Slesinger, Tess 10
Steffens, Lincoln 20
Stein, Gertrude 1, 6, 28, 48
Sterling, George 20
Stevens, Wallace 3, 12, 45
Stockton, Frank R. 47
Sturges, Preston 48
Tarbell, Ida 40
Tarkington, Booth 9
Teasdale, Sara 4
Thurman, Wallace 6
Twain, Mark 6, 12, 19, 36, 48
Van Dine, S. S. 23
Van Doren, Carl 18
Veblen, Thorstein 31
Washington, Booker T. 10
Wells, Carolyn 35
West, Nathanael 1, 14, 44
Wharton, Edith 3, 9, 27
White, Walter 15
Wister, Owen 21
Wolfe, Thomas 4, 13, 29
Woollcott, Alexander 5
Wylie, Elinor 8

ARGENTINE
Arlt, Roberto 29
Güiraldes, Ricardo 39
Lugones, Leopoldo 15
Storni, Alfonsina 5

AUSTRALIAN
Brennan, Christopher John 17
Franklin, Miles 7
Furphy, Joseph 25
Ingamells, Rex 35
Lawson, Henry 27
Paterson, A. B. 32
Richardson, Henry Handel 4
Warung, Price 45

AUSTRIAN
Broch, Hermann 20
Hofmannsthal, Hugo von 11
Kafka, Franz 2, 6, 13, 29, 47
Kraus, Karl 5
Kubin, Alfred 23
Meyrink, Gustav 21
Musil, Robert 12
Roth, Joseph 33
Schnitzler, Arthur 4
Steiner, Rudolf 13
Trakl, Georg 5
Werfel, Franz 8
Zweig, Stefan 17

BELGIAN
Bosschère, Jean de 19
Lemonnier, Camille 22
Maeterlinck, Maurice 3
Van Ostaijen, Paul 33
Verhaeren, Émile 12

BRAZILIAN
Andrade, Mário de 43
Cunha, Euclides da 24
Lima Barreto 23
Machado de Assis, Joaquim Maria 10
Ramos, Graciliano 32

BULGARIAN
Vazov, Ivan 25

CANADIAN
Campbell, Wilfred 9
Carman, Bliss 7
Carr, Emily 32
Connor, Ralph 31
Drummond, William Henry 25
Garneau, Hector Saint-Denys 13
Grove, Frederick Philip 4
Leacock, Stephen 2
McCrae, John 12
Nelligan, Emile 14
Pickthall, Marjorie 21
Roberts, Charles G. D. 8
Scott, Duncan Campbell 6
Service, Robert W. 15
Seton, Ernest Thompson 31
Stringer, Arthur 37

CHILEAN
Huidobro, Vicente 31
Mistral, Gabriela 2

CHINESE
Liu E 15
Lu Hsün 3
Su Man-shu 24
Wen I-to 28

COLOMBIAN
Rivera, Jose Eustasio 35

CZECHOSLOVAKIAN
Čapek, Karel 6, 37
Czechoslovakian Literature of the Twentieth Century 42
Hašek, Jaroslav 4
Nezval, Vítězslav 44

DANISH
Brandes, Georg 10
Hansen, Martin A. 32
Jensen, Johannes V. 41
Nexo, Martin Andersen 43
Pontopiddan, Henrik 29

DUTCH
Couperus, Louis 15
Frank, Anne 17
Heijermans, Herman 24

ENGLISH
Barbellion, W. N. P. 24
Baring, Maurice 8
Beerbohm, Max 1, 24
Belloc, Hilaire 7, 18
Bennett, Arnold 5, 20
Benson, E. F. 27
Benson, Stella 17
Bentley, E. C. 12
Besant, Annie 9
Blackmore, R. D. 27
Blackwood, Algernon 5
Bridges, Robert 1
Brooke, Rupert 2, 7
Butler, Samuel 1, 33
Chesterton, G. K. 1, 6
Conrad, Joseph 1, 6, 13, 25, 43
Coppard, A. E. 5
Crowley, Aleister 7
De la Mare, Walter 4
Doughty, Charles 27
Douglas, Keith 40
Dowson, Ernest 4
Doyle, Arthur Conan 7, 26
Eddison, E. R. 15
Elizabeth 41
Ellis, Havelock 14
Field, Michael 43
Firbank, Ronald 1
Ford, Ford Madox 1, 15, 39
Freeman, R. Austin 21
Galsworthy, John 1, 45
Gilbert, W. S. 3
Gissing, George 3, 24, 47
Gosse, Edmund 28
Granville-Barker, Harley 2
Gray, John 19
Gurney, Ivor 33
Haggard, H. Rider 11
Hall, Radclyffe 12
Hardy, Thomas 4, 10, 18, 32, 48
Henley, William Ernest 8
Hilton, James 21
Hodgson, William Hope 13
Housman, A. E. 1, 10
Housman, Laurence 7
Hudson, W. H. 29
Hulme, T. E. 21
Jacobs, W. W. 22
James, M. R. 6
Jerome, Jerome K. 23
Johnson, Lionel 19
Kaye-Smith, Sheila 20
Kipling, Rudyard 8, 17
Lawrence, D. H. 2, 9, 16, 33, 48
Lawrence, T. E. 18
Lee, Vernon 5
Lee-Hamilton, Eugene 22
Leverson, Ada 18
Lewis, Wyndham 2, 9
Lindsay, David 15
Lowndes, Marie Belloc 12
Lowry, Malcolm 6, 40
Macaulay, Rose 7, 44
MacCarthy, Desmond 36
Manning, Frederic 25
Meredith, George 17, 43
Mew, Charlotte 8
Meynell, Alice 6
Milne, A. A. 6
Murry, John Middleton 16
Noyes, Alfred 7
Oppenheim, E. Phillips 45
Orwell, George 2, 6, 15, 31
Ouida 43
Owen, Wilfred 5, 27
Pinero, Arthur Wing 32
Powys, T. F. 9
Richardson, Dorothy 3
Rohmer, Sax 28
Rolfe, Frederick 12
Rosenberg, Isaac 12
Ruskin, John 20
Rutherford, Mark 25
Sabatini, Rafael 47
Saintsbury, George 31
Saki 3
Sapper 44
Sayers, Dorothy L. 2, 15
Shiel, M. P. 8
Sinclair, May 3, 11

Stapledon, Olaf 22
Stead, William Thomas 48
Stephen, Leslie 23
Strachey, Lytton 12
Summers, Montague 16
Sutro, Alfred 6
Swinburne, Algernon Charles 8, 36
Symons, Arthur 11
Thomas, Edward 10
Thompson, Francis 4
Van Druten, John 2
Walpole, Hugh 5
Warung, Price 45
Webb, Beatrice 22
Webb, Mary 24
Webb, Sidney 22
Welch, Denton 22
Wells, H. G. 6, 12, 19
Williams, Charles 1, 11
Woolf, Virginia 1, 5, 20, 43
Yonge, Charlotte (Mary) 48
Zangwill, Israel 16

ESTONIAN
Tammsaare, A. H. 27

FINNISH
Leino, Eino 24
Södergran, Edith 31

FRENCH
Alain 41
Alain-Fournier 6
Apollinaire, Guillaume 3, 8
Artaud, Antonin 3, 36
Barbusse, Henri 5
Barrès, Maurice 47
Bergson, Henri 32
Bernanos, Georges 3
Bloy, Léon 22
Bourget, Paul 12
Claudel, Paul 2, 10
Colette 1, 5, 16
Coppée, François 25
Daumal, René 14
Desnos, Robert 22
Drieu La Rochelle, Pierre 21
Dujardin, Edouard 13
Eluard, Paul 7, 41
Fargue, Léon-Paul 11
Feydeau, Georges 22
France, Anatole 9
Gide, André 5, 12, 36
Giraudoux, Jean 2, 7
Gourmont, Remy de 17
Huysmans, Joris-Karl 7
Jacob, Max 6
Jarry, Alfred 2, 14
Larbaud, Valéry 9
Leroux, Gaston 25
Loti, Pierre 11
Martin du Gard, Roger 24
Moréas, Jean 18
Nizan, Paul 40
Péguy, Charles 10
Péret, Benjamin 20
Proust, Marcel 7, 13, 33
Radiguet, Raymond 29
Renard, Jules 17
Rolland, Romain 23
Rostand, Edmond 6, 37
Roussel, Raymond 20

Saint-Exupéry, Antoine de 2
Schwob, Marcel 20
Sully Prudhomme 31
Teilhard de Chardin, Pierre 9
Valéry, Paul 4, 15
Verne, Jules 6
Vian, Boris 9
Weil, Simone 23
Zola, Emile 1, 6, 21, 41

GERMAN
Auerbach, Erich 43
Benjamin, Walter 39
Benn, Gottfried 3
Borchert, Wolfgang 5
Brecht, Bertolt 1, 6, 13, 35
Carossa, Hans 48
Döblin, Alfred 13
Ewers, Hanns Heinz 12
Feuchtwanger, Lion 3
George, Stefan 2, 14
Hauptmann, Gerhart 4
Heym, Georg 9
Heyse, Paul 8
Huch, Ricarda 13
Kaiser, Georg 9
Klabund 44
Kolmar, Gertrud 40
Liliencron, Detlev von 18
Mann, Heinrich 9
Mann, Thomas 2, 8, 14, 21, 35, 44
Morgenstern, Christian 8
Nietzsche, Friedrich 10, 18
Raabe, Wilhelm 45
Rilke, Rainer Maria 1, 6, 19
Spengler, Oswald 25
Sternheim, Carl 8
Sudermann, Hermann 15
Toller, Ernst 10
Wassermann, Jakob 6
Wedekind, Frank 7

GHANIAN
Casely-Hayford, J. E. 24

GREEK
Cavafy, C. P. 2, 7
Kazantzakis, Nikos 2, 5, 33
Palamas, Kostes 5
Papadiamantis, Alexandros 29
Sikelianos, Angelos 39

HAITIAN
Roumain, Jacques 19

HUNGARIAN
Ady, Endre 11
Babits, Mihály 14
Csáth, Géza 13
Herzl, Theodor 36
Horváth, Ödön von 45
Hungarian Literature of the Twentieth Century 26
József, Attila 22
Karinthy, Frigyes 47
Mikszáth, Kálmán 31
Molnár, Ferenc 20
Móricz, Zsigmond 33
Radnóti, Miklós 16

ICELANDIC
Sigurjónsson, Jóhann 27

INDIAN
Chatterji, Saratchandra 13
Iqbal, Muhammad 28
Premchand 21
Tagore, Rabindranath 3

INDONESIAN
Anwar, Chairil 22

IRANIAN
Hedayat, Sadeq 21

IRISH
A. E. 3, 10
Cary, Joyce 1, 29
Dunsany, Lord 2
Gogarty, Oliver St. John 15
Gregory, Lady 1
Harris, Frank 24
Joyce, James 3, 8, 16, 26, 35
Ledwidge, Francis 23
Moore, George 7
O'Grady, Standish 5
Riddell, Mrs. J. H. 40
Shaw, Bernard 3, 9, 21, 45
Stephens, James 4
Stoker, Bram 8
Synge, J. M. 6, 37
Tynan, Katharine 3
Wilde, Oscar 1, 8, 23, 41
Yeats, William Butler 1, 11, 18, 31

ITALIAN
Betti, Ugo 5
Brancati, Vitaliano 12
Campana, Dino 20
Carducci, Giosuè 32
Croce, Benedetto 37
D'Annunzio, Gabriele 6, 40
Deledda, Grazia 23
Giacosa, Giuseppe 7
Lampedusa, Giuseppe Tomasi di 13
Marinetti, F. T. 10
Papini, Giovanni 22
Pascoli, Giovanni 45
Pavese, Cesare 3
Pirandello, Luigi 4, 29
Saba, Umberto 33
Svevo, Italo 2, 35
Tozzi, Federigo 31
Verga, Giovanni 3

JAMAICAN
De Lisser, H. G. 12
Garvey, Marcus 41
Mais, Roger 8
Redcam, Tom 25

JAPANESE
Akutagawa Ryūnosuke 16
Dazai Osamu 11
Futabatei Shimei 44
Hayashi Fumiko 27
Ishikawa Takuboku 15
Masaoka Shiki 18
Miyamoto Yuriko 37
Mori Ōgai 14
Natsume, Sōseki 2, 10
Rohan, Kōda 22
Shimazaki, Tōson 5
Yokomitsu Riichi 47

LATVIAN
Rainis, Janis 29

LEBANESE
Gibran, Kahlil 1, 9

LESOTHAN
Mofolo, Thomas 22

LITHUANIAN
Krévé, Vincas 27

MEXICAN
Azuela, Mariano 3
Gamboa, Frederico 36
Nervo, Amado 11
Reyes, Alfonso 33
Romero, José Rubén 14

NATIVE AMERICAN
See American

NEPALI
Devkota, Laxmiprasad 23

NEW ZEALAND
Mander, Jane 31
Mansfield, Katherine 2, 8, 39

NICARAGUAN
Darío, Rubén 4

NIGERIAN
Nigerian Literature of the Twentieth Century 30

NORWEGIAN
Bjørnson, Bjørnstjerne 7, 37
Grieg, Nordhal 10
Hamsun, Knut 2, 14
Ibsen, Henrik 2, 8, 16, 37
Kielland, Alexander 5
Lie, Jonas 5
Obstfelder, Sigbjørn 23
Skram, Amalie 25
Undset, Sigrid 3

PAKISTANI
Iqbal, Muhammad 28

PERUVIAN
Palma, Ricardo 29
Vallejo, César 3

POLISH
Asch, Sholem 3
Borowski, Tadeusz 9
Peretz, Isaac Leib 16
Prus, Bolesław 48
Przybyszewski, Stanisław 36
Reymont, Władysław Stanisław 5
Schulz, Bruno 5
Sienkiewitz, Henryk 3
Singer, Israel Joshua 33
Witkiewicz, Stanisław Ignacy 8

PORTUGUESE
Pessoa, Fernando 27

PUERTO RICAN
Hostos, Eugenio María de 24

RUMANIAN
Bacovia, George 24
Rebreanu, Liviu 28

RUSSIAN
Aldanov, Mark 23
Andreyev, Leonid 3
Annensky, Innokenty 14
Artsybashev, Mikhail 31
Babel, Isaak 2, 13
Balmont, Konstantin Dmitriyevich 11
Bely, Andrey 7
Blok, Aleksandr 5
Bryusov, Valery 10
Bulgakov, Mikhail 2, 16
Bunin, Ivan 6
Chekhov, Anton 3, 10, 31
Esenin, Sergei 4
Gladkov, Fyodor 27
Gorky, Maxim 8
Hippius, Zinaida 9
Ilf, Ilya 21
Ivanov, Vyacheslav 33
Khlebnikov, Velimir 20
Khodasevich, Vladislav 15
Korolenko, Vladimir 22
Kropotkin, Peter 36
Kuprin, Aleksandr 5
Kuzmin, Mikhail 40
Mandelstam, Osip 2, 6
Mayakovsky, Vladimir 4, 18
Merezhkovsky, Dmitri 29
Petrov, Evgeny 21
Pilnyak, Boris 23
Platonov, Andrei 14
Remizov, Alexey 27
Sologub, Fyodor 9
Tolstoy, Alexey Nikolayevich 18
Tolstoy, Leo 4, 11, 17, 28, 44
Trotsky, Leon 22
Tsvetaeva, Marina 7, 35
Zamyatin, Yevgeny Ivanovich 8, 37
Zhdanov, Andrei 18
Zoshchenko, Mikhail 15

SCOTTISH
Barrie, J. M. 2
Bridie, James 3
Brown, George Douglas 28
Buchan, John 41
Davidson, John 24
Frazer, James 32
Gibbon, Lewis Grassic 4
Graham, R. B. Cunninghame 19
Lang, Andrew 16
MacDonald, George 9
Muir, Edwin 2
Sharp. William 39
Tey, Josephine 14

SOUTH AFRICAN
Campbell, Roy 5
Mqhayi, S. E. K. 25
Schreiner, Olive 9
Smith, Pauline 25
Vilakazi, Benedict Wallet 37

SPANISH
Alas, Leopoldo 29
Barea, Arturo 14
Baroja, Pío 8
Benavente, Jacinto 3
Blasco Ibáñez, Vicente 12
Echegaray, José 4
García Lorca, Federico 1, 7
Jiménez, Juan Ramón 4
Machado, Antonio 3
Martínez Sierra, Gregorio 6
Miró, Gabriel 5
Ortega y Gasset, José 9
Pereda, José María de 16
Pérez, Galdós, Benito 27
Salinas, Pedro 17
Unamuno, Miguel de 2, 9
Valera, Juan 10
Valle-Inclán, Ramón del 5

SWEDISH
Bengtsson, Frans (Gunnar) 48
Dagerman, Stig 17
Heidenstam, Verner von 5
Lagerlöf, Selma 4, 36
Soderberg, Hjalmar 39
Strindberg, August 1, 8, 21, 47

SWISS
Ramuz, Charles-Ferdinand 33
Spitteler, Carl 12
Walser, Robert 18

TURKISH
Sait Faik 23

UKRAINIAN
Bialik, Chaim Nachman 25
Sholom Aleichem 1, 35

URUGUAYAN
Quiroga, Horacio 20
Sánchez, Florencio 37

WELSH
Davies, W. H. 5
Lewis, Alun 3
Machen, Arthur 4
Thomas, Dylan 1, 8, 45

TCLC Title Index to Volume 48

Aaron's Rod (Lawrence) **2**:346-47, 350, 358, 371; **9**:215-16; **16**:323; **33**:188; **48**:117, 121, 126
Abbey Church; or, Self-control and Self-conceit (Yonge)
 See *Abbeychurch*
Abbeychurch (*Abbey Church; or, Self-control and Self-conceit*) (Yonge) **48**:366, 373, 387
"Ada" (Stein) **1**:428; **48**:256-57, 260-63
"The Adventure of Stasio" (Prus)
 See "Przygoda Stasia"
The Adventures of Huckleberry Finn (*Huckleberry Finn*) (Twain) **6**:454-57, 459-61, 463, 465-70, 473-76, 478, 480, 482-85; **12**:427-29, 431, 434-37, 439-45, 448, 451, 454; **19**:351-58, 360-69, 372-76, 378-82, 384-88, 391; **36**:352, 354-55, 358-59, 361, 363, 366, 369, 372, 375, 379, 381-84, 386-87, 392; **48**:334, 336, 339, 341-47, 349, 351-52, 356, 359, 361
The Adventures of Tom Sawyer (*Tom Sawyer*) (Twain) **6**:455-56, 460-61, 463-66, 468-70, 473-76, 480, 483-84; **12**:427, 431-32, 437-38, 440, 451-53; **19**:351-58, 361-63, 366-67, 369, 371-72, 407, 409, 411; **36**:354-55, 358, 384, 394, 401, 404, 409; **48**:330, 334-35, 339, 357
"Die Ahnfrau" (Carossa) **48**:24
"All Sunday" (Stein) **48**:235
Alphabets and Birthdays (Stein) **48**:235
The American Claimant (Twain) **6**:461-62; **12**:432, 447-48; **48**:351
"Anielka" (Prus) **48**:182
"Antek" (Prus) **48**:157, 161
Apocalypse (Lawrence) **2**:358, 368, 372; **48**:101, 121, 134-35, 139, 147, 149
"Art and the Individual" (Lawrence) **48**:140-41
"Arthur A. Grammar" (Stein) **48**:255

"As a Wife Has a Cow: A Love Story" (Stein) **48**:237
"Attacks" (Stein) **48**:234
The Autobiography of Alice B. Toklas (Stein) **1**:430-31, 434, 442; **6**:404-06, 410, 412, 415; **28**:313-14, 318, 320, 324, 326, 333-34, 342; **48**:209, 214, 218-22, 236, 240, 245-49, 251-52, 255-56, 258, 260-61, 263
"Ball Gown" (Prus)
 See "Sukienka balowa"
"The Barrel-Organ" (Prus)
 See "Katarynka"
"Bavarian Gentians" (Lawrence) **2**:367-68; **48**:121-22
The Beautiful Blond from Bashful Bend (Sturges) **48**:275, 283, 291, 294, 309
Bee Time Vine (Stein) **48**:234-35
"Before a Bookshelf" (Bengtsson) **48**:13
Before the Flowers of Friendship Faded Friendship Faded (Stein) **48**:253, 255
The Big Pond (Sturges) **48**:283, 294, 311
Boyhood and Youth (Carmack)
 See *Verwandlungen einer Jugend*
By the Century's Deathbed (Hardy) **48**:60
By the Earth's Corpse (Hardy) **48**:60
The Caged Lion (Yonge) **48**:376
Capital Capitals (Stein) **48**:264
Captain Stormfield's Visit to Heaven (Twain) **48**:356
Les Carnets de Major Thompson (*The French They Are a Funny Race*) (Sturges) **48**:283, 291, 309
The Castle Builders; or, The Deferred Confirmation (Yonge) **48**:366, 378, 384
The Chaplet of Pearls; or, The White and Black Ribaumont: A Romance of French History, 1572 (Yonge) **48**:376
Child of Manhattan (Sturges) **48**:283, 285, 311, 316

A Childhood (Carossa)
 See *Eine Kindheit*
The Children (Prus)
 See *Dzieci*
Christmas in July (Sturges) **48**:270-72, 274, 276, 283, 287-89, 301, 303, 309-10, 319, 321-22
The Clasped Skeletons (Hardy) **48**:59
The Clever Woman of the Family (Yonge) **48**:372, 374, 382, 388
"Cold Climate" (Stein) **48**:254
College Swing (Sturges) **48**:312
"Composition as Explanation" (Stein) **48**:242, 253
Composition as Explanation (Stein) **1**:432; **6**:403, 406; **28**:307, 324, 326, 338; **48**:243
A Connecticut Yankee in King Arthur's Court (Twain) **6**:455, 457, 460, 471, 473-74, 477, 480-82; **12**:429, 431-33, 435-36, 446, 448-49; **19**:379, 387; **36**:350-420; **48**:335-37, 339-40, 344, 354-56
A Cup of Coffee (Sturges) **48**:311, 317
"The Curious Republic of Goudour" (Twain) **48**:356
The Daisy Chain; or, Aspirations (Yonge) **48**:365-67, 371, 373, 375-81, 383-85, 388
"The Darkling Thrush" (Hardy) **10**:234; **48**:60
"Der alte Brunnen" (Carossa) **48**:21
"Der alte Taschenspieler" (Carossa) **48**:24
Der Arzt Gion (*Doctor Gion*) (Carossa) **48**:19-20, 22, 27-8, 30
Der Tag des jungen Arztes (Carossa) **48**:30-2, 34
Desperate Remedies (Hardy) **4**:147, 157-58, 160; **10**:215, 217, 225; **18**:100; **48**:71
Diamond Jim (Sturges) **48**:286, 291, 294-95, 311, 316, 321

471

Doctor Faustus Lights the Lights (Stein) 1:435-37; **48**:232, 264
Doctor Gion (Carossa)
See *Der Arzt Gion*
Doktor Bürger (Carossa)
See *Die Schicksale Doktor Bürgers*
The Doll (Prus)
See *Lalka*
The Dove in the Eagle's Nest (Yonge) **48**:376
Down Went McGinty (Sturges)
See *The Great McGinty*
Dr. Bürger (Carossa)
See *Die Schicksale Doktor Bürgers*
The Dynasts: A Drama of the Napoleonic Wars (Hardy) 4:157-58, 163-64, 167, 170-72, 174; **10**:217, 229; **32**:280-82, 307; **48**:59-60
Dynevor Terrace; or, The Clue of Life (Yonge) **48**:364-66, 374-75, 388
Dzieci (*The Children*) (Prus) **48**:166, 168, 180
Easy Living (Sturges) **48**:286-88, 290-91, 294, 301, 309, 312, 321
"An Elegant Escape" (Stein) **48**:234
"An Elucidation" (Stein) **48**:242
The Emancipated Women (Prus)
See *Emancypantki*
The Emancipationists (Prus)
See *Emancypantki*
Emancypantki (*The Emancipated Women*; *The Emancipationists*) (Prus) **48**:159-60, 163-64, 169, 175, 179
The Escaped Cock (Lawrence)
See *The Man Who Died*
Etruscan Places (Lawrence) **2**:368; **48**:121, 149
Everybody's Autobiography (Stein) 1:429-30; **6**:412; **28**:313-14, 326; **48**:211, 213-14, 216, 218, 220, 222, 240
"The Facts Concerning the Recent Carnival of Crime in Connecticut" ("A Recent Carnival of Crime in Connecticut") (Twain) **6**:462; **19**:386, 393; **36**:403-04; **48**:352
Far from the Madding Crowd (Hardy) 4:147-49, 153, 155-56, 158, 160, 168, 175, 177; **10**:217, 226, 229; **18**:87, 92, 111; **32**:268, 274; **48**:40, 51-3, 71, 73, 79, 84
Faraon (*The Pharao*; *The Pharaoh and the Priests*; *Pharoah*) (Prus) **48**:159-60, 164-66, 169-71, 179
Fast and Loose (Sturges) **48**:283, 311
Fernhurst (Stein) **28**:339-40; **48**:264
The First Lady Chatterley (Lawrence) **9**:228; **48**:110-12, 119, 138, 146-47, 149
"Die Flucht" (Carossa) **48**:25
"The Flying Fish" (Lawrence) **2**:359; **48**:121
Folk som sjöng och andra essayer (Bengtsson) **48**:12
Four Saints in Three Acts (Stein) 1:429-30, 432-33; **6**:411-12; **28**:313, 333; **48**:208-10, 230-33, 248, 264
"The Fox" (Lawrence) **2**:362-63; **9**:216; **48**:117
The French They Are a Funny Race (Sturges)
See *Les Carnets de Major Thompson*
Führung und Geleit (*Guidance and Companionship*) (Carossa) **48**:20-1, 27
Geheimnisse des reifen Lebens (Carossa) **48**:20-3, 27-8, 30
"Gehemnisse" (Carossa) **48**:21, 25
"The Gentle Lena" (Stein) **6**:408; **28**:334; **48**:225-27

The Geographical History of America; or, The Relation of Human Nature to the Human Mind (Stein) 1:433-35, 437, 441; **28**:316, 327-28, 330-32, 334-35, 339-40; **48**:212-17, 236, 248
Geography and Plays (Stein) 1:428; **6**:403, 406; **28**:313; **48**:216, 251
Gesammelte Gedichte (Carossa) **48**:25
"Gesang Zur Sonne" (Carossa) **48**:21
Geschichte einer Jugend (Carossa) **48**:34
The Gilded Age (Twain) **6**:457, 462, 467, 476; **12**:430, 432, 437; **19**:355, 359; **36**:358, 407, 409; **48**:335
"The Good Anna" (Stein) **6**:408; **28**:334; **48**:225-26
The Good Fairy (Sturges) **48**:285, 294, 311
"A Grammarian" (Stein) **48**:233
"Grandma's Jewelbox" (Prus)
See "Szkatulka babki"
The Great McGinty (*Down Went McGinty*; *The Vagrant*) (Sturges) **48**:272-74, 276-77, 282-83, 287-88, 291, 301, 303-04, 309, 311, 313, 317, 319-22
The Great Moment (*Triumph over Pain*) (Sturges) **48**:273, 276, 283-85, 291-92, 295-96, 301, 303, 309, 313, 315-17
Guidance and Companionship (Carossa)
See *Führung und Geleit*
The Guinea Pig (Sturges) **48**:310, 317
Hail the Conquering Hero (Sturges) **48**:269, 272-73, 275-77, 279, 283, 289, 291-92, 294-95, 301-09, 314, 316, 319-23
Heartsease; or, The Clue of Life (Yonge) **48**:374-75, 388
"Heimliche Landschaft" ("Secret Landscape") (Carossa) **48**:21, 24
The Heir of Redclffe (Yonge) **48**:364-65, 371, 374, 376-81, 383-88
Hopes and Fears; or, Scenes from the life of a Spinster (Yonge) **48**:365-67, 372, 381-82, 387-88
Hotel Haywire (Sturges) **48**:286, 291, 312
"How I Became an Author" (Bengtsson) **48**:12
How to Write (Stein) 1:427, 435, 441; **6**:415; **28**:330, 340; **48**:250, 253, 255
Huckleberry Finn (Twain)
See *The Adventures of Huckleberry Finn*
If I Were King (Sturges) **48**:285, 291, 295, 312, 316
Imitation of Life (Sturges) **48**:286, 294
In the Saxon Park (Prus) **48**:156
"In This Way, Kissing" (Stein) **48**:235
The Innocents Abroad; or, The New Pilgrim's Progress (Twain) **6**:453-59, 475; **12**:424, 426, 430-31, 436-37; **19**:358, 363; **36**:352, 355, 358, 361, 371-72, 379, 382; **48**:330-32, 334
Das Jahr der Schönen Täuschungen (*Year of Sweet Illusions*) (Carossa) **48**:28-30, 34
"Jean Cocteau" (Stein) **6**:403; **48**:254-55
John Thomas and Lady Jane (Lawrence) **9**:228; **48**:124, 127-29, 135, 139, 147
Jude the Obscure (Hardy) 4:150, 153-54, 159-60, 165, 172, 176-77; **10**:217-23, 227-31; **18**:117; **32**:270, 274-81, 309-10; **48**:40, 46, 63-5, 67, 69, 71, 79
"Kamizelka" ("The Waistcoat") (Prus) **48**:161, 172, 176
Kangaroo (Lawrence) **2**:371; **9**:217; **33**:184, 202, 205; **48**:102, 117

Karl den XII:s levnad (*The Life of Charles XII, King of Sweden 1697-1781*; *The Sword Does Not Jest: The Heroic Life of King Charles XII of Sweden*) (Bengtsson) **48**:2, 5-6, 8-12
"Katarynka" ("The Barrel-Organ"; "Organ-Grinder") (Prus) **48**:156, 161, 176
Eine Kindheit (*A Childhood*) (Carossa) **48**:16-20, 27, 29-30, 34
Kings of England: A History for Young Children (Yonge) **48**:369
Kroniki tugodniowe (*Weekly Chronicles*) (Prus) **48**:176
Lady Chatterley's Lover (Lawrence) **2**:345-46, 348, 350-51, 353-54, 356, 364-67, 370-72; **9**:217-19, 227-29; **16**:284-85, 312; **33**:188, 193-96, 203, 206-07; **48**:90-150
The Lady Eve (Sturges) **48**:270, 274, 281, 283, 287-88, 290-92, 294-96, 301, 303-04, 309, 312-13, 316, 318-19, 321
De låghåriga merovingerna och andra essayer (Bengtsson) **48**:6, 12
Lalka (*The Doll*; *Puppet*) (Prus) **48**:157-59, 162-64, 167-75, 177-81
A Laodicean; or, The Castle of the De Stancys (Hardy) 4:149, 159; **10**:217, 227; **18**:100; **48**:38
Lectures in America (Stein) 1:441; **6**:415; **28**:315; **48**:212, 214, 216, 233, 236, 252, 255
"A Legend of Old Egypt" (Prus)
See "Z legend dawnego Egiptu"
Legendem om Babel (Bengtsson) **48**:5, 12
Letters from Julia (Stead) **48**:193
The Life and Death of the Mayor of Casterbridge: A Story of a Man of Character (Hardy)
See *The Mayor of Casterbridge: The Life and Death of a Man of Character*
Life of Bishop Patteson (*Life of John Coleridge Patteson, Missionary Bishop of the Melanesian Islands*) (Yonge) **48**:377
The Life of Charles XII, King of Sweden 1697-1781 (Bengtsson)
See *Karl den XII:s levnad*
Life of John Coleridge Patteson, Missionary Bishop of the Melanesian Islands (Yonge)
See *Life of Bishop Patteson*
Life on the Mississippi (Twain) **6**:455, 458, 468, 473-74; **12**:429-30; **19**:353, 355, 358-59, 363, 377-78, 382-83, 386; **36**:355, 366, 369, 371, 373, 384, 409; **48**:336-37
"Lipschitz" (Stein) **48**:254
Litteratörer och militärer (Bengtsson) **48**:6, 12
The Little Duke; or, Richard the Fearless (Yonge) **48**:376-77
"Lokator poddasza" ("A Tenant in a Garret") (Prus) **48**:176
A Long Gay Book (Stein) 1:428; **28**:313, 315, 328, 331-32, 338; **48**:264
"The Long-haired Merovingians" (Bengtsson) **48**:4
The Long Ships (Bengtsson)
See *Röde Orm, sjöfarare i västerled*
The Long Ships: A Saga of the Viking Age (Bengtsson)
See *Röde Orm, hemma i österled*
Look! We Have Come Through! (Lawrence) **2**:367; **9**:213; **16**:310; **33**:181; **48**:121
Love Before Breakfast (Sturges) **48**:312
Lucy Church, Amiably (Stein) 1:430; **28**:315, 322, 324, 332-33; **48**:237
Mad Wednesday (Sturges)
See *The Sin of Harold Diddlebock*

"Das Mädchen von Dobrowlany" (Carossa) 48:24
The Maiden Tribute of Modern Babylon (Stead) 48:186, 189-91, 193-96, 198, 200
The Making of Americans: Being a History of a Family's Progress (*The Making of Americans: The Hersland Family*) (Stein) 1:427-31, 433-34, 438, 440. 442; 6:404, 406-07, 409-11, 414-15; 28:312-13, 315, 318-20, 327-28, 331-33, 335-36, 338-41; 48:211, 233, 242, 246, 248, 253, 264
The Making of Americans: The Hersland Family (Stein)
See *The Making of Americans: Being a History of a Family's Progress*
"Making Pictures" (Lawrence) 48:122
The Man Who Died (*The Escaped Cock*) (Lawrence) 2:356-57, 360, 367, 371-72; 16:284, 322; 33:206; 48:121, 125
Many, Many Women (Stein) 1:428; 48:264
The Mayor of Casterbridge (Hardy)
See *The Mayor of Casterbridge: The Life and Death of a Man of Character*
The Mayor of Casterbridge: The Life and Death of a Man of Character (*The Life and Death of the Mayor of Casterbridge: A Story of a Man of Character*, *The Mayor of Casterbridge*) (Hardy) 4:149, 153, 157, 159, 174-75, 177; 10:217, 220-21, 227; 18:100, 102; 32:265-327; 48:38, 40, 59, 63-4, 67, 69
A Meeting with Despair (Hardy) 48:60
"Melanctha" (Stein) 1:427, 430, 433, 437, 440; 6:405, 408, 410, 413; 28:306, 311-12, 324, 336; 48:225-29, 245, 253, 255, 263
"Michałko" (Prus) 48:162, 172, 177
"Middle Age Phrases for a Historical Study" (Twain) 48:357
The Miracle of Morgan's Creek (Sturges) 48:268, 272, 275-76, 279, 283, 285, 288, 291-92, 295, 301-09, 313-14, 316, 321, 323
"Miss Furr and Miss Skeene" (Stein) 48:252-53, 255
"A Mistake" (Prus)
See "Omyłka"
"Morality and the Novel" (Lawrence) 48:132
The Most General Ideals of Life (Prus)
See *Najogólniejsze ideały zyciowe*
The Moth-Signal (Hardy) 48:60
The Mother of Us All (Stein) 28:341; 48:231-32, 248, 257
Mrs. Reynolds (Stein) 28:332, 334-36; 48:249, 264
"My Closet Companions" (Bengtsson) 48:13
My Father: The Rev. William Stead (Stead) 48:199
The Mysterious Stranger (Twain) 6:460, 466, 486; 12:432, 434, 436-37, 442, 449; 19:387; 36:361, 363-64, 378, 392, 399, 411; 48:344
"Mysterium der Liebe" (Carossa) 48:25
Najogólniejsze ideały zyciowe (*The Most General Ideals of Life*) (Prus) 48:166
Narration (Stein) 1:427; 48:214, 221
"Die Nebel" (Carossa) 48:24
Never Say Die (Sturges) 48:312
Next Time We Love (Sturges) 48:286, 294, 312
A Novel of Thank You (Stein) 28:332-33; 48:264
"Omyłka" ("A Mistake") (Prus) 48:181-84
"Organ-Grinder" (Prus)
See "Katarynka"
"Orta or the One Dancing" (Stein) 48:235

The Outpost (Prus)
See *Placówka*
A Pair of Blue Eyes (Hardy) 4:148-49, 156, 158-59; 10:217, 225, 227; 18:92; 32:268; 48:38, 71, 74
The Palm Beach Story (Sturges) 48:270-71, 275, 280, 283, 287-88, 290-92, 294-96, 299, 301, 303, 304-05, 309, 316, 318, 324
Pansies (Lawrence) 2:372; 48:112
Paris France (Stein) 1:433, 442; 28:313; 48:250-51, 253-55
"Patriarchal Poetry" (Stein) 28:340; 48:238, 248-49
Personal Recollections of Joan of Arc (Twain) 6:455, 457, 460, 466, 471-72, 486; 12:431-32, 436, 438; 48:342-43
The Pharao (Prus)
See *Faraon*
The Pharaoh and the Priests (Prus)
See *Faraon*
Pharoah (Prus)
See *Faraon*
Phoenix (Lawrence) 48:112, 121, 132, 140, 147
Phoenix II (Lawrence) 48:136, 141, 146
"A Piece of Coffee" (Stein) 48:252
The Pillars of the House; or, Under Wode, Under Rode (Yonge) 48:375-78
"Pink Melon Joy" (Stein) 48:254
Placówka (*The Outpost*) (Prus) 48:157, 162, 166-67, 172-73, 177, 181
A Play (Stein) 48:264
The Plumed Serpent (Lawrence) 2:346, 355-57, 359, 371; 33:216; 48:102, 104, 110, 115-17, 120-22, 125, 131, 133
"Poetry and Grammar" (Stein) 28:322-23, 330; 48:236
"Poetry of the Present" (Lawrence) 48:140
Port of Seven Seas (Sturges) 48:285, 291, 312
"A Portrait of Carl Van Vechten" (Stein) 48:210
Portrait of Mabel Dodge at the Villa Curonia (Stein) 28:306; 48:241
Portraits and Prayers (Stein) 48:209, 249, 254
"Portraits and Repitition" (Stein) 48:249
The Power and the Glory (Sturges) 48:273-74, 276, 283-85, 290-96, 311, 316, 320-21
The Prince and the Pauper (Twain) 6:455, 457, 462, 466, 471, 476, 480; 12:431, 436; 36:352, 369, 379-80, 402,409; 48:327-37, 339-52, 355-61
The Profitable Reading of Fiction (Hardy) 48:51
"A Propos of *Lady Chatterley's Lover*" (Lawrence) 48:55, 102, 108, 112, 122, 130, 132, 149
"Przygoda Stasia" ("The Adventure of Stasio"; "Stasio's Adventure") (Prus) 48:156, 162, 182
Pudd'nhead Wilson (Twain)
See *The Tragedy of Pudd'nhead Wilson*
Puppet (Prus)
See *Lalka*
Q.E.D. (Stein)
See *Things As They Are*
The Rainbow (Lawrence) 48:121, 125, 130, 132, 134, 142
Recapture (Sturges) 48:310, 316-17
"A Recent Carnival of Crime in Connecticut" (Twain)
See "The Facts Concerning the Recent Carnival of Crime in Connecticut"

Red Orm (Bengtsson)
See *Röde Orm, sjöfarare i västerled*
Remember the Night (Sturges) 48:286, 291, 295, 312, 316
A Reputed Changeling; or, Three Seventh Years Two Centuries Ago (Yonge) 48:377
The Return of the Native (Carossa) 48:37
The Return of the Native (Hardy) 4:147-49, 153-55, 158, 162-63, 166, 174-75; 10:216, 226-28; 18:92, 97, 100, 102, 111, 116; 32:274-75, 277, 280-81, 288, 300, 306, 312, 317, 323; 48:36-89
Returning Wave (Prus) 48:157
"The Risen Lord" (Lawrence) 48:121
Röde Orm, hemma i österled (*The Long Ships: A Saga of the Viking Age*) (Bengtsson) 48:5-7, 9-10, 12
Röde Orm, sjöfarare i västerled (*The Long Ships*; *Red Orm*) (Bengtsson) 48:3-5, 12-13
The Roman Gravemounds (Hardy) 48:59
Roughing It (Twain) 6:455, 457-58, 471, 476; 12:426, 430, 435, 437, 452; 36:355, 358, 371, 379; 48:344, 358
A Roumanian Diary (Carossa)
See *Tagebuch im Kriege*
"Sacred Emily" (Stein) 48:237
St. Mawr (Lawrence) 2:356-57, 361-63, 373-74; 9:219; 33:203; 48:121, 125, 142
Sällskap för en eremit (Bengtsson) 48:6, 12
Satan's Invisible World Displayed; or, Despairing of Democracy: A Study of Greater New York (Stead) 48:188
Scenes and Characters; or, Eighteen Months at Beechcroft (Yonge) 48:375
Die Schicksale Doktor Bürgers (*Doktor Bürger*; *Dr. Bürger*) (Carossa) 48:20, 22, 27-9
"Secret Landscape" (Carossa)
See "Heimliche Landschaft"
Selected Writings of Gertrude Stein (Stein) 48:249, 251
Shall I Slay My Brother Boer? (Stead) 48:194
"The Ship of Death" (Lawrence) 48:121
Silversködarna (Bengtsson) 48:6, 12
The Sin of Harold Diddlebock (*Mad Wednesday*) (Sturges) 48:282-283, 285, 289, 291, 309, 313
1601; or, Conversation as It Was by the Fireside in the Time of the Tudors (Twain) 6:476; 12:436; 48:349, 357, 360
Sketches New and Old (Borg) 48:349
"Some Rambling Notes of an Idle Excursion" (Twain) 48:349
Sons and Lovers (Lawrence) 2:343-44, 346, 348, 354-56, 359-60; 9:212, 216, 222-27; 16:274-326; 33:179, 200-01, 204, 209, 224, 226-27; 48:100-01, 116, 121, 123, 141
Stanzas in Meditation (Stein) 1:441-42; 48:219, 249, 255
"Stasio's Adventure" (Prus)
See "Przygoda Stasia"
Strictly Dishonorable (Sturges) 48:283-84, 290, 310-12, 316-17
Study of Thomas Hardy (Lawrence) 16:302, 305; 48:117
"Sukienka balowa" ("Ball Gown") (Prus) 48:176
Sullivan's Travel (Sturges) 48:270-75, 279, 283-85, 287-88, 290-91, 294-303, 309, 313, 315-17, 319-20, 322-23
"Sun" (Lawrence) 2:356-57; 48:121, 140
"Surgery for the Novel - or a Bomb" (Lawrence) 48:147

The Sword Does Not Jest: The Heroic Life of King Charles XII of Sweden (Bengtsson)
See *Karl den XII:s levnad*
"Szkatulka babki" ("Grandma's Jewelbox") (Prus) **48**:181
Tagebuch im Kriege (*A Roumanian Diary*) (Carossa) **48**:15-16, 19-20, 22, 27-9
Tärningkast (Bengtsson) **48**:5, 12
"A Tenant in a Garret" (Prus)
See "Lokator poddasza"
Tender Buttons: Objects, Food, Rooms (Stein) **1**:428, 430-31, 434-37, 441-42; **6**:404-06, 410-11, 413, 415-16; **28**:306, 311, 313, 315, 318, 320, 322, 325, 328-32, 336-42; **48**:211, 213, 216, 236-39, 247-49, 252, 254-55, 264
Tess of the D'Urbervilles: A Pure Woman Faithfully Presented (Hardy) **4**:152-53, 159-61, 170-71, 174, 176-77; **10**:215-17, 220, 225, 227-29; **18**:79-81, 84-9, 94-100, 102-04, 108, 110-11, 114, 116, 120-24; **32**:270, 275-76, 278-81, 287-89, 309-10, 321; **48**:40, 46, 49, 56, 59, 73-4, 79
They Just Had to Get Married (Sturges) **48**:311
Things As They Are (*Q.E.D.*) (Stein) **1**:433; **6**:410, 412-13; **28**:319-20, 327, 330, 338; **48**:226-28, 242, 264
Thirty Day Princess (Sturges) **48**:285, 311
"This Is the Dress, Aider" (Stein) **48**:239
The Three Brides (Yonge) **48**:372, 374-75, 378
Three Lives (Stein) **1**:426-28, 430, 433-34, 440-41; **6**:404-05, 407-10, 412, 414-15; **28**:306, 309, 311-12, 318-20, 322, 324, 328, 331, 334, 336-39; **48**:211, 220, 224-27, 230, 240-42, 246-48, 250, 252, 257, 261, 264
Tom Sawyer (Twain)
See *The Adventures of Tom Sawyer*
Tom Sawyer Abroad (Twain) **6**:474, 477, 486; **12**:432, 439; **19**:414; **48**:346
Tom Sawyer Detective (Twain) **6**:477; **12**:432; **48**:335, 344, 349, 351, 356, 359, 361
The Tragedy of Pudd'nhead Wilson (*Pudd'nhead Wilson*) (Twain) **6**:455-56, 461-62, 465, 474-75, 477; **12**:432, 439-40, 449-51; **19**:364, 372; **36**:361, 363, 373, 386; **48**:344
A Tramp Abroad (Twain) **6**:455, 458, 460, 476; **12**:426, 431; **36**:369-70; **48**:330, 332, 342, 350, 357, 360
"A Transatlantic Interview, 1946" (Stein) **48**:224-25, 241, 252
The Trial: More Links of the Daisy Chain (Yonge) **48**:372, 376-77, 383, 388
Triumph over Pain (Sturges)
See *The Great Moment*
A True Story and the Recent Carnival of Crime (Twain) **48**:360
"Two" (Stein) **48**:235
The Two Guardians; or, Home in this World (Yonge) **48**:366, 378
The Two Sides of the Shield (Yonge) **48**:389
"Und wie manche Nacht" (Carossa) **48**:21
Unfaithfully Yours (Sturges) **48**:275, 283, 287-88, 291-92, 297, 309, 311, 317-18
Ungleiche Welten (Carossa) **48**:33-4
Unkown to History: A Story of the Captivity of Mary of Scotland (Yonge) **48**:377
Useful Knowledge (Stein) **6**:403; **28**:312-13; **48**:214
The Vagrant (Sturges)
See *The Great McGinty*

Verwandlungen einer Jugend (*Boyhood and Youth*) (Carossa) **48**:16, 20, 25, 30
"The Virgin and the Gipsy" (Lawrence) **2**:364, 371; **48**:102, 118, 121
"Von Lust zu Lust" (Carossa) **48**:25
"A Waist" (Stein) **48**:254
"The Waistcoat" (Prus)
See "Kamizelka"
"Wald im Winter" (Carossa) **48**:21
A Walk to an Ant Hill, and other Essays (Bengtsson) **48**:4, 13
Wars I Have Seen (Stein) **1**:430-31; **6**:412; **28**:313-14, 329, 335, **48**:249
We Live Again (Sturges) **48**:285, 311
Weekly Chronicles (Prus)
See *Kroniki tugodniowe*
The Well of Romance (Sturges) **48**:310, 316-17
What Are Masterpieces (Stein) **48**:217
"What Are Masterpieces and Why Are There So Few of Them" (Stein) **28**:316, 330; **48**:218, 236
What Happened (Stein) **6**:411; **48**:248, 264
What Is Man? (Twain) **6**:460, 466, 469, 472, 477, 485; **12**:432, 434, 436-37; **36**:367, 411; **48**:351
The White Peacock (Lawrence) **2**:343, 358-60; **9**:211, 222-23, 226; **16**:277, 283, 285, 287, 302; **33**:184; **48**:117, 119
"The Woman Who Rode Away" (Lawrence) **48**:121, 125
Women in Love (Lawrence) **2**:344, 348, 350, 357-61, 366, 368-69, 371-75; **9**:214, 216, 221-22, 226-27, 230; **16**:291, 295, 300, 313; **33**:176-231; **48**:100-02, 113, 115-17, 123, 125-26, 130-32, 134, 136, 142
The Woodlanders (Hardy) **4**:149, 153; **10**:217, 227-28, 230, 233; **18**:90, 100; **32**:274, 280-81; **48**:71
The Yale Edition of the Unpublished Works of Gertrude Stein (Stein)
See *The Yale Gertrude Stein*
The Yale Gertrude Stein (*The Yale Edition of the Unpublished Works of Gertrude Stein*) (Stein) **48**:245, 248
Year of Sweet Illusions (Carossa)
See *Das Jahr der Schönen Täuschungen*
The Young Stepmother; or, A Chronicle of Mistakes (Yonge) **48**:374
"Z legend dawnego Egiptu" ("A Legend of Old Egypt") (Prus) **48**:161